AN INTRODUCTION TO
LITERATURE

6th Edition

AN INTRODUCTION TO
LITERATURE

FICTION / POETRY / DRAMA

Edited by

Sylvan Barnet, Tufts University
Morton Berman, Boston University
William Burto, University of Lowell

LITTLE, BROWN AND COMPANY
Boston   Toronto

Library of Congress Catalog Card No. 76-14252

ISBN 0-316-081671

10   9   8   7

MV

Published simultaneously in Canada
by Little, Brown & Company (Canada) Limited

Printed in the United States of America

Acknowledgments

W. H. Auden. "Musée des Beaux Arts" and "The Unknown Citizen" from *Collected Shorter Poems 1927–1957*, by W. H. Auden. Copyright 1940 and renewed 1968 by W. H. Auden. Reprinted by permission of Random House, Inc., and Faber and Faber Ltd.

Toni Cade Bambara. "The Lesson" from *Gorilla, My Love* by Toni Cade Bambara. Copyright © 1972 by Toni Cade Bambara. Reprinted by permission of Random House, Inc.

Louise Bogan. "Women" from *The Blue Estuaries* by Louise Bogan. Copyright © 1923, 1929, 1930, 1931, 1933, 1934, 1935, 1936, 1937, 1938, 1941, 1949, 1951, 1952, 1954 by Louise Bogan. Reprinted with the permission of Farrar, Straus & Giroux, Inc.

Ray Bradbury. "August 2026: There Will Come Soft Rains" by Ray Bradbury. Copyright 1950 by Ray Bradbury. Reprinted by permission of Harold Matson Co., Inc.

Richard Brautigan. "Romeo and Juliet" and "Memoirs of Jesse James" excerpted from *Rommel Drives on Deep into Egypt* by Richard Brautigan. Copyright © 1970 by Richard Brautigan. Reprinted with the permission of Delacorte Press/Seymour Lawrence.

Gwendolyn Brooks. "We Real Cool: The Pool Players. Seven at the Golden Shovel" from *The World of Gwendolyn Brooks* (1971) by Gwendolyn Brooks. Copyright © 1959 by Gwendolyn Brooks. Reprinted by permission of Harper & Row, Publishers, Inc.

Anton Chekhov. "Gooseberries" from *The Portable Chekhov* edited by Avrahm Yarmolinsky. Copyright 1947, © 1975 by The Viking Press, Inc. Reprinted by permission of Viking Penguin, Inc.

Lucille Clifton. "in the inner city" from *Good Times* by Lucille Clifton. Copyright © 1969 by Lucille Clifton. Reprinted by permission of Random House, Inc.

Robert Coover. "The Brother" from the book *Pricksongs & Descants* by Robert Coover. Copyright © 1969 by Robert Coover. Reprinted by permission of the publishers, E. P. Dutton & Co., Inc.

E. E. Cummings. "next to of course god america i," copyright, 1926, by Horace Liveright; copyright, 1954, by E. E. Cummings, and "anyone lived in a pretty how town," copyright, 1940, by E. E. Cummings; copyright, 1968, by

Marion Morehouse Cummings, reprinted from *Complete Poems 1913–1962* by E. E. Cummings by permission of Harcourt Brace Jovanovich, Inc.

Walter de la Mare. "The Listeners" from *The Complete Poems of Walter de la Mare 1970*. Reprinted by permission of The Literary Trustees of Walter de la Mare, and The Society of Authors as their representatives.

Emily Dickinson. "Because I could not stop for Death," "A narrow Fellow in the Grass," "The Soul selects her own Society," and "I heard a Fly buzz — when I died" reprinted by permission of the publishers and the Trustees of Amherst College from *The Poems of Emily Dickinson*, edited by Thomas H. Johnson, Cambridge, Mass.: The Belknap Press of Harvard University Press, © 1951, 1955 by the President and Fellows of Harvard College.

Bob Dylan. "Mister Tambourine Man." © 1964 Warner Bros. Inc. All rights reserved. Used by permission.

T. S. Eliot. "The Love Song of J. Alfred Prufrock" and "Journey of the Magi" from *Collected Poems 1909–1962* by T. S. Eliot. Copyright, 1936, by Harcourt Brace Jovanovich, Inc.; copyright, 1963, 1964, by T. S. Eliot. Reprinted by permission of Harcourt Brace Jovanovich, Inc., and Faber and Faber Ltd.

William Faulkner. "The Bear," copyright 1942 and renewed 1970 by Estelle Faulkner and Jill Faulkner Summers. An expanded version of this story appears in *Go Down, Moses* by William Faulkner. "A Rose for Emily" from *Collected Stories of William Faulkner*. Copyright 1930 and renewed 1958 by William Faulkner. These stories reprinted by permission of Random House, Inc.

Lawrence Ferlinghetti. "Constantly risking absurdity" from *A Coney Island of the Mind* by Lawrence Ferlinghetti. Copyright © 1958 by Lawrence Ferlinghetti. Reprinted by permission of New Directions Publishing Corporation.

F. Scott Fitzgerald. "Babylon Revisited" (copyright 1931 The Curtis Publishing Company) is reprinted by permission of Charles Scribner's Sons from *Taps at Reveille* by F. Scott Fitzgerald.

Robert Frost. "Stopping by Woods on a Snowy Evening," "The Pasture," "Design," "Desert Places," and "Acquainted with the Night" from *The Poetry of Robert Frost* edited by Edward Connery Lathem. Copyright 1923, 1928, 1939, © 1967, 1969 by Holt, Rinehart and Winston. Copyright 1936, 1951, © 1956 by Robert Frost. Copyright © 1964 by Lesley Frost Ballantine. Reprinted by permission of Holt, Rinehart and Winston, Publishers.

Allen Ginsberg. "A Supermarket in California" from *Howl and Other Poems* by Allen Ginsberg. Copyright © 1956, 1959 by Allen Ginsberg. Reprinted by permission of City Lights Books.

Donald Hall. "My Son, My Executioner" from *The Alligator Bride* by Donald Hall. Copyright © 1969 by Donald Hall. Reprinted by permission of Curtis Brown, Ltd.

Thomas Hardy. "Ah, Are You Digging on My Grave?" from *Collected Poems of Thomas Hardy*. Copyright 1925 by Macmillan Publishing Co., Inc. Reprinted by permission of Macmillan Publishing Co., Inc. (New York); the Trustees of the Hardy Estate; Macmillan London & Basingstoke; and The Macmillan Company of Canada Limited.

Anthony Hecht. "The Dover Bitch" from *The Hard Hours* by Anthony Hecht. Copyright © 1960 by Anthony E. Hecht. Appeared originally in *Transatlantic Review*. Reprinted by permission of Atheneum Publishers.

Ernest Hemingway. "The Short Happy Life of Francis Macomber" (copyright 1936 Ernest Hemingway; renewal copyright © 1964 Mary Hemingway) from *The Short Stories of Ernest Hemingway*. Reprinted with the permission of Charles Scribner's Sons.

Gerald Manley Hopkins. "Spring and Fall: To a Young Child" and "God's Grandeur" from *The Poems of Gerard Manley Hopkins*, 4th ed., edited by W. H. Gardner and N. H. Mackenzie, published by arrangement with the Society of Jesus (London: Oxford University Press, 1967).

A. E. Housman. "To an Athlete Dying Young" (#19) and "On Wenlock Edge" (#31) from "A Shropshire Lad" — Authorized Edition — from *The Collected Poems of A. E. Housman*. Copyright 1939, 1940, © 1965 by Holt, Rinehart and Winston. Copyright © 1967, 1968 by Robert E. Symons. Reprinted by permission of Holt, Rinehart and Winston, Publishers; The Society of Authors as the literary representative of the Estate of A. E. Housman; and Jonathan Cape Ltd., publishers of A. E. Housman's *Collected Poems*.

Langston Hughes. "Evenin' Air Blues" from *Shakespeare in Harlem* by Langston Hughes. Copyright © 1942 by Langston Hughes. Renewed. Reprinted by permission of Harold Ober Associates Incorporated.

Ted Hughes. "Hawk Roosting" from *Lupercal* (1960) by Ted Hughes. Copyright © 1959 by Ted Hughes. Reprinted by permission of Harper & Row, Publishers, Inc., and Faber and Faber Ltd.

Eugene Ionesco. *The Gap* by Eugene Ionesco, translated by Rosette Lamont. Reprinted from *The Massachusetts Review*, © 1969 The Massachusetts Review, Inc.

Shirley Jackson. "The Lottery" from *The Lottery* by Shirley Jackson. Copyright 1948, 1949 by Shirley Jackson, copyright renewed 1976 by Laurence Hyman, Barry Hyman, Mrs. Sarah Webster, and Mrs. Joanne Schnurer. "The Lottery" originally appeared in *The New Yorker*. Reprinted with the permission of Farrar, Straus & Giroux, Inc.

Randall Jarrell. "The Death of the Ball Turret Gunner" from *The Complete Poems* by Randall Jarrell. Copyright 1945 by Randall Jarrell, copyright renewed 1973 by Mary von Schrader Jarrell. Reprinted with the permission of Farrar, Straus & Giroux, Inc. "In Montecito" from *The Lost World* by Randall Jarrell. Copyright © 1963, 1965 Randall Jarrell. Originally appeared in *The New Yorker*. Reprinted with permission of Macmillan Publishing Co., Inc.

James Joyce. "Araby" from *Dubliners* by James Joyce. Copyright © 1967 by the Estate of James Joyce. All rights reserved. Reprinted by permission of Viking Penguin, Inc.

Franz Kafka. "The Metamorphosis" from *The Penal Colony* by Franz Kafka, translated by Willa and Edwin Muir. Copyright © 1948, 1976 by Schocken Books Inc. Reprinted by permission of Schocken Books Inc.

X. J. Kennedy. "In a Prominent Bar in Secaucus One Day" from *Nude Descending a Staircase* by X. J. Kennedy. Copyright © 1961 by X. J. Kennedy. "Nothing in Heaven Functions as It Ought" from *Growing into Love* by X.J. Kennedy. Copyright © 1962 by The Yeoman Committee for an Oberlin Quarterly. These poems reprinted by permission of Doubleday & Company, Inc.

D. H. Lawrence. "The Horse-Dealer's Daughter" from *The Complete Short Stories of D. H. Lawrence*, Vol. II. Copyright ©1961 by Angelo Ravagli and C. M. Weekley, Executors of the Estate of Frieda Lawrence Ravagli. "Snake" from *The Complete Poems of D. H. Lawrence*, Vol. I, edited by Vivian de Sola Pinto and F. Warren Roberts. Copyright ©1964, 1971 by Angelo Ravagli and C. M. Weekley, Executors of the Estate of Frieda Lawrence Ravagli. These selections reprinted by permission of Viking Penguin, Inc.

Don L. Lee. "But He Was Cool or: he even stopped for green lights" from

Don't Cry Scream, copyright © 1969 by Don L. Lee. Reprinted by permission of Broadside Press.

John Lennon and Paul McCartney. "Eleanor Rigby" copyright © 1966 Northern Songs Limited. All rights reserved. Used by permission.

Doris Lessing. "A Man and Two Women" from *A Man and Two Women* by Doris Lessing. Copyright © 1958, 1962, 1963 by Doris Lessing. Reprinted by permission of Simon & Schuster, Inc., and John Cushman Associates, Inc.

Denise Levertov. "The Mutes" from *The Sorrow Dance* by Denise Levertov. Copyright © 1966 by Denise Levertov. Reprinted by permission of New Directions Publishing Corporation.

Robert Lowell. "Skunk Hour" from *Life Studies* by Robert Lowell. Copyright © 1956, 1959 by Robert Lowell. Reprinted with the permission of Farrar, Straus & Giroux, Inc.

Archibald MacLeish. "You, Andrew Marvell" and "Ars Poetica" from *Collected Poems* by Archibald MacLeish. Copyright 1962 by Archibald MacLeish. Reprinted by permission of Houghton Mifflin Company.

Arthur Miller. *Death of a Salesman* by Arthur Miller. Copyright 1949 by Arthur Miller. Reprinted by permission of The Viking Press, Inc.

Marianne Moore. "Silence" and "Poetry" from *Collected Poems* by Marianne Moore. Copyright 1935 by Marianne Moore, renewed 1963 by Marianne Moore and T. S. Eliot. Reprinted with permission of Macmillan Publishing Co., Inc.

Joyce Carol Oates. "Where Are You Going, Where Have You Been?" from *The Wheel of Love* by Joyce Carol Oates. Copyright © 1970, 1969, 1968, 1967, 1966, 1965, by Joyce Carol Oates. Reprinted by permission of the publisher, Vanguard Press, Inc.

Flannery O'Connor. "A Good Man Is Hard to Find" from *A Good Man Is Hard to Find and Other Stories* by Flannery O'Connor. Copyright, 1953, by Flannery O'Connor. Reprinted by permission of Harcourt Brace Jovanovich, Inc.

Frank O'Connor. "Guests of the Nation" from *More Stories by Frank O'Connor*. Published 1954 by Alfred A. Knopf, Inc. Reprinted by permission of Alfred A. Knopf, Inc., and A. D. Peters & Company Ltd.

Frank O'Hara. "Ave Maria" from *Lunch Poems* by Frank O'Hara. Copyright © 1964 by Frank O'Hara. Reprinted by permission of City Lights Books.

Dorothy Parker. "Indian Summer" from *The Portable Dorothy Parker*. Copyright 1926, 1954 by Dorothy Parker. Reprinted by permission of Viking Penguin, Inc.

Petronius. "The Widow of Ephesus" from *The Satyricon of Petronius Arbiter*, translated by William Arrowsmith. Copyright © 1959 by The University of Michigan Press. Reprinted by permission.

Sylvia Plath. "Metaphors" from *The Colossus* published by Faber and Faber, and also from *Crossing the Water* (1975) published by Harper & Row. Copyright © 1960 by Sylvia Plath, 1967 by Ted Hughes. Reprinted by permission of Harper & Row, Publishers, Inc., and Olwyn Hughes. "Medallion" from *The Colossus and Other Poems* by Sylvia Plath. Copyright © 1960, 1962 by Sylvia Plath, 1967 by Ted Hughes. Reprinted by permission of Alfred A. Knopf, Inc., and Olwyn Hughes. "Daddy" from *Ariel* (1966) by Sylvia Plath. Copyright © 1963 by Ted Hughes. Reprinted by permission of Harper & Row, Publishers, Inc., and Olwyn Hughes.

Katherine Anne Porter. "The Jilting of Granny Weatherall" from *Flowering Judas and Other Stories* by Katherine Anne Porter. Copyright, 1930, 1958, by Katherine Anne Porter. Reprinted by permission of Harcourt Brace Jovanovich, Inc.

Ezra Pound. "The River-Merchant's Wife: A Letter" from *Personae* by Ezra Pound. Copyright 1926 by Ezra Pound. Reprinted by permission of New Directions Publishing Corporation. "An Immorality" from *Lustra* by Ezra Pound. Copyright 1917 by Ezra Pound. Reprinted by permission of New Directions Publishing Corporation, for the Trustees of the Ezra Pound Literary Property Trust.

John Crowe Ransom. "Piazza Piece," copyright 1927 by Alfred A. Knopf, Inc., and renewed 1955 by John Crowe Ransom, and "Bells for John Whiteside's Daughter," copyright 1924 by Alfred A. Knopf, Inc., and renewed 1952 by John Crowe Ransom, from *Selected Poems*, Third Edition, Revised and Enlarged, by John Crowe Ransom. Reprinted by permission of Alfred A. Knopf, Inc.

Adrienne Rich. "The Roofwalker," "Aunt Jennifer's Tigers," and "Living in Sin" from *Poems, Selected and New, 1950–1974*, by Adrienne Rich. Copyright © 1975, 1973, 1971, 1969, 1966 by W. W. Norton & Company, Inc. Copyright © 1967, 1963, 1962, 1961, 1960, 1959, 1958, 1957, 1956, 1955, 1954, 1953, 1952, 1951 by Adrienne Rich. Reprinted by permission of W. W. Norton & Company, Inc.

Edwin Arlington Robinson. "Richard Cory" is reprinted by permission of Charles Scribner's Sons from *The Children of the Night* by Edwin Arlington Robinson. "Mr. Flood's Party" from *Collected Poems* by Edwin Arlington Robinson. Copyright 1921 by Edwin Arlington Robinson, renewed 1949 by Ruth Nivison. Reprinted with permission of Macmillan Publishing Co., Inc.

Theodore Roethke. "My Papa's Waltz," copyright 1942 by Hearst Magazines, Inc., and "Elegy for Jane," copyright 1950 by Theodore Roethke, from *The Collected Poems of Theodore Roethke*. Reprinted by permission of Doubleday & Company, Inc.

Anne Sexton. "Cinderella" from *Transformations* by Anne Sexton. Copyright © 1971 by Anne Sexton. Reprinted by permission of Houghton Mifflin Company.

William Shakespeare. From *The Tragedy of Othello* by William Shakespeare, edited by Alvin Kernan. Copyright © 1963 by Alvin Kernan. Copyright © 1963 by Sylvan Barnet. Reprinted by arrangement with The New American Library, Inc., New York, N.Y.

Bernard Shaw. *Pygmalion* by Bernard Shaw. Copyright 1913, 1914, 1916, 1930, 1941, 1944, George Bernard Shaw, copyright 1957 The Public Trustee as Executor of the Estate of George Bernard Shaw. Reprinted by permission of Dodd, Mead & Company, Inc., and The Society of Authors for the Estate of George Bernard Shaw.

Gary Snyder. "Hay for the Horses" reprinted by permission of Gary Snyder.

Sophocles. *Antigonê*, An English Version by Dudley Fitts and Robert Fitzgerald, copyright, 1939, by Harcourt Brace Jovanovich, Inc.; copyright, 1967, by Dudley Fitts and Robert Fitzgerald. Reprinted by permission of Harcourt Brace Jovanovich, Inc. *Oedipus Rex*, An English Version by Dudley Fitts and Robert Fitzgerald, copyright, 1949, by Harcourt Brace Jovanovich, Inc., and reprinted with their permission. *Caution:* All rights, including professional, amateur, motion picture, recitation, lecturing, public reading, radio broadcasting, and television, are strictly reserved. Inquiries on all rights should be addressed to Harcourt Brace Jovanovich, Inc., 757 Third Avenue, New York, N.Y. 10017.

George Starbuck. "Fable for Blackboard" from *Bone Thoughts* by George Starbuck. Copyright © 1960 by George Starbuck. Reprinted by permission of Yale University Press.

renewed 1934 by William Butler Yeats. "Leda and the Swan" and "Sailing to Byzantium" from *Collected Poems* by William Butler Yeats. Copyright 1928 by Macmillan Publishing Co., Inc., 1956 by Georgie Yeats. These poems reprinted by permission of Macmillan Publishing Co., Inc., A. P. Watt & Son, The Macmillan Company of London & Basingstoke, Mr. M. B. Yeats, and Miss Anne Yeats.

Preface

"A big book," said Callimachus, "is a big misfortune." He might have added that a big book is heavy. Aware that many instructors have found needlessly bulky most of the textbooks designed for introductory courses in literature, the editors and publisher of *An Introduction to Literature* have produced a book that is smaller than most books intended for such courses. They have kept in mind Dr. Johnson's maxim: "Books that you may . . . hold readily in your hand are the most useful after all."

The relative brevity of this volume has been achieved partly by assuming that much of what is included here will please the instructor and therefore need not be reinforced by numerous alternative selections, and partly by refusing to allow the editorial apparatus to usurp the province of the classroom. Both of these points deserve further comment.

We have offered much material that can be called "classical," both to keep the bulk down and because we believe that students ought for the most part to read first-rate material. There is something wrong with a book that includes a dozen stories of the last year or two and nothing by Hawthorne. We include some very recent work, and almost half of the selections are from the last few decades, but we have tried not to neglect such classic writers as Hawthorne, Faulkner, Kakfa, Shakespeare, and Yeats. Classic works, of course, are not the same things as chestnuts. The former, Maurice Beebe has explained, "are in a sense the freshest of stories simply because they obviously may be seen in many different lights and even yet have not given up all their secrets. The chestnuts are those stories that — like 'Haircut,' 'The Necklace,' and 'The Furnished Room' — give up all their secrets on an initial reading and hence require as little classroom discussion as they have evoked published criticism. I see no objection to a text made up primarily of classics."

The editorial material is brief and yet fairly complete. The paradox is easily explained: this book does not try to do what only the teacher can do. The proper place for a detailed discussion of the multiple meanings in a word or line is, we believe, the classroom. Textbook analyses that for pages drag the student through a short poem or story rarely accomplish much. The object of an anthology of literature is to allow the student to read and to think and perhaps to write down his responses, but it is doubtful if a long exegesis stimulates a student. We have tried in our editorial apparatus to give succinct definitions of the terms commonly used in talking about literature, and to *begin* (but by no means to finish) a critical reading of literatuare. About half of the selections in the book are briefly discussed or have questions appended; the other half are unsullied. We have kept in mind Frost's remark: "You don't chew a poem — macerate a poem — for an evening's pleasure, for a Roman holiday. You touch it. You are aware that a good deal of it is missed."

USING THE BOOK

Probably most instructors teach fiction, then poetry, and then drama — the order followed here. But the three sections can be taught in any sequence, because each is relatively independent; for example, symbolism is discussed in each of the three sections, and although the three discussions have a cumulative effect, any of the three can be used first. This flexibility runs throughout the book; we hope that instructors will not feel that the first chapter must be taught first. Indeed, the first chapter — a survey of some theories of literature — can be used effectively midway or even at the end. There is a similar flexibility within the three chief sections of the book: one can teach everything straight through a section, or skip one's way through a section, or bring in wherever one wishes the stories and poems that conclude the sections. One might jump from Aesop's fable to Kafka's "Metamorphosis" midway in the section. If the instructor wishes to skip a good many poems, he can run through the first eight chapters in the poetry section in a few meetings; if, on the other hand, he wishes to examine closely most or all of the poems in these chapters, he can spend as much as half a semester with them.

Although comparatively brief, *An Introduction to Literature* contains ample material for a one-semester course; supplemented by a few paperback books, it can provide a core volume for a full-year course. We have not tried to predict what paperback novels might be added, but we have included "Observations on the Novel," an attempt to distinguish the novel from other prose fiction. We have tried to make our apparatus sufficiently broad so that it can serve as an aid to whatever additional books are read. The introduction to tragedy is not an introduction to *Antigone* or to *Othello* but an introduction to *tragedy;* because it examines definitions of tragedy by a Jacobean dramatist, a Soviet critic, and an American dramatist, and discusses such terms as *hamartia, hybris,* and *catharsis,* it will be helpful in thinking about all tragedies, from Greek to contemporary American. We have also included "Some Observations on Film," in which we discuss the relation of film to literature.

The material on versification is reprinted with a few abridgements from our *Dictionary of Literary, Dramatic, and Cinematic Terms.* Some of the ideas in the section of drama were earlier contributed, in slightly different form, to Newman P. Birk and Genevieve B. Birk, *Understanding and Using English.*

In response to many requests, we have added to this edition an appendix called "Writing Essays about Literature." This section — distilling material on fiction, poetry, drama, and film from Sylvan Barnet's *A Short Guide to Writing about Literature,* Third Edition (1975) — includes not only information about manuscript form, a sample explication, and a sample analysis, but also detailed suggestions that may help students to choose a topic and get their responses down on paper.

If this new edition has been strengthened and enhanced, it is primarily because of the encouraging comments from users of the earlier editions. Among the new selections are stories by Robert Coover, Shirley Jackson, Doris Lessing, Alice Walker, and Edith Wharton, and poems by Louise Bogan, Ted Hughes, Denise Levertov, Andrew Marvell, Edward Arlington Robinson, and Adrienne Rich. Also new to this edition is a long poem, Whitman's "Out of the Cradle Endlessly Rocking." The drama section in particular has been enlarged and now includes *Pygmalion* and *Death of a Salesman.*

Finally, after this elaborate explanation of what has been done, we wish to thank people who helped us do it: Jane Aaron, Linda Bamber, David Cavitch, Charles Christensen, Robert Cyr, Doris Holmes Eyges, Arthur Friedman, David Giele, Nancy Grayson, Margaret Guindon, X. J. Kennedy, Bernard McCabe, Patricia Meier, Geoffrey Movius, Ronald E. Pepin, William Roberts, Warren R. Stone, Marcia Stubbs, Ruth Sullivan, Jeff Titon, Helen Vendler, Charles L. Walker, Ann Chalmers Watts, and Margaret Zusky.

Our thanks also to the following users of the 5th edition who gave us advice on how and where to make improvements: Lee Adnepos, Marcia J. Anderson, Deborah L. Asher, John F. Barnier, Anthony J. Bialas, Thomas Boghosian, Colin E. Bourn, Cheryl Ann Brehm, Earl F. Briden, Pamela L. Bridgmon, Edward T. Byrnes, Michael Carroll, Mollie S. Chaffin, John Chedester, Larry Conrad, Kathy Cowan, Wallace Coyle, Lois M. Cundiff, David Curtis, C. Spurgeon Didier, Leta DiSalvo, Kathleen Deopken, Estella Easterly, David R. Eastwood, Allison Ensor, Hazel Flock, Cole N. Foster, Norma Gaskey, Karen N. Gleeman, Arline Golden, John R. Griffin, Ann Hardy, James Hausman, James J. Haydock, Steven Hind, Eileen M. Hoag, Ranella Holley, Robert T. Howling, Mary Loubris Jones, Janice Nyman Keefe, Dorothea Kehler, Lorraine Keilstrup, Joseph Knight, Bea Knodel, Joy A. Labishak, Linda Ringer Leff, Maureen E. Lippert, Elizabeth Lowe, Bruce MacBeth, Alice R. McFarland, Michael G. McGunnigle, Robin C. Mitchell, Patricia Moots, Louis E. Murphy, Thomas P. Murphy, Mark Reynolds, Alec Ross, Hilary Ross, Phyliss Roth, Patricia Ruemping, Margery Rutbell, Ann Stone Schorr, Raoda I. Sherwood, C. K. Sigler, D. M. Smith, Margaret Smyser, Leland Thiel, William Ward, Leslie A. Wardenaar, Theodore A. Wiebe, Addie Williams, Nancy T. Zuercher.

S. B.

M. B.

W. B.

Contents

POETRY

The Voice of the Satirist.

11   Figurative Language: Simile, Metaphor, Personification, Apostrophe   394

Simile.

Metaphor.

Personification. Apostrophe.

12   Figurative Language: Imagery and Symbolism   411

DRAMA

17   Some Elements of Drama   531

18   Tragedy   552

A Note on Greek Tragedy.

19   Comedy   591

AN INTRODUCTION TO
LITERATURE

1 Some Theories
of Literature

WHAT IS LITERATURE?

Although literature is sometimes defined as anything written, this definition is both too broad and too narrow. Although it is true that anyone can ask the Department of Agriculture for "literature" about canning artichokes, surely we can distinguish between literature in the sense of any writing, and literature in the sense of verbal works of art. And to say that literature must be written or printed is too narrow, because it excludes such oral literature as ballads that are sung and stories that are recited.

We can begin by saying that literature is (to quote Robert Frost) a "performance in words." It has in it an element of entertaining display, and surely we expect literature to be in some sense entertaining, or to afford pleasure. That literature is an adult game, a sort of make-believe, is suggested in some of the words we apply to pieces of literature — "fiction," "story," "tale," "play."

Now, what is it that makes literature pleasant? Without attempting a complete answer, perhaps we can say that a literary work seizes our interest and more or less — at least for a moment — makes the rest of the world fade or vanish. If the writer has done his job well, our attention is focused on the work, and we are at least partially detached from our usual surroundings. Consider, as an analogy, our reaction when we suddenly get a whiff of new-mown hay. We are walking along a road, either fretting about a dozen things or engaged in a pleasant vague reverie, when suddenly we smell the hay. At once we are caught up, keenly interested in this experience, intensely aware of this one thing, a thing that seems complete and satisfying in itself. For the moment we forget about the time of day, the dust of the road, the heat of the sun, and we find in this thing which is complete, whole, independent, something that catches us up and delights us. A work of art has this power to catch us up momentarily, and to delight us.

But it may well be objected that *Hamlet* is surely more than a load of hay. Art, it is commonly said, offers truth as well as pleasure. Such a view is at least superficially plausible, but when we begin to think about it, we encounter problems. What "truth" is there in *Hamlet*? The characters in the play are fictional, so we cannot say that Shakespeare is giving us a true picture of Danish history. There is a ghost in the play, but many people today have serious doubts about the existence of ghosts. Perhaps we will seize on certain lines, such as "Neither a borrower nor a lender be," but even this much-quoted line can hardly be defended as an unquestioned truth: there are surely times when it is good to borrow or to lend. Let us leave *Hamlet* (though not with the implication that the concept of truth is irrelevant to it), and glance at a short poem, "Heart's-ease," by Walter Savage Landor (1775–1864):

> There is a flower I wish to wear,
>> But not until first worn by you —
> Heart's-ease — of all earth's flowers most rare;
>> Bring it; and bring enough for two.

Is it true that the flower called heart's-ease is the earth's rarest flower? If we want to know about flowers, hadn't we better listen to botanists than to poets? Poets may occasionally stumble on scientific truths, but aren't scientists more likely to give us scientific truths? Isn't it apparent that whatever value Landor's poem has is not in its botany?

These are big problems, and they have not yet been solved to general satisfaction. Not only literary critics but creative writers themselves have held numerous theories about the nature of literature. A glance at an anthology of criticism reveals a confusing diversity. In *Writers at Work*, a paperback collection (edited by Malcolm Cowley) of interviews with contemporary novelists, one finds a writer who holds that the artist presents experience and is a teacher incidentally, and a writer who holds that the artist is essentially (to use Frank O'Connor's own words) "a reformer." We may as well face the fact that there is a diversity of theories; nothing is gained by pretending that everyone knows or agrees what literature is or does. But most theories of literature can, without much distortion, be put into one of three pigeon-holes — which can be called "imitative," "expressive," and "affective" — and these are what we want to talk about first. Good literature deserves to be talked about as well as read and enjoyed, and such discussion may help sharpen a reader's perceptions.

THE IMITATIVE THEORY

The imitative theory holds that art is an imitation of something. In his *Poetics*, Aristotle (384–322 B.C.) says that a tragedy is an imitation of an action that is serious and complete. Because imitation now has pejorative associations, it is well to think of Aristotle's *mimesis* as not only "imitation" but also "re-creation" or "re-presentation." In an artistic imitation, Aristotle holds, a form is presented in a substance not natural to it. Thus, Michelangelo imitated Moses in stone; Cézanne imitated Mont Sainte Victoire in pigment on canvas; Shakespeare imitated Caesar in an actor's words and gestures. Music, too, Aristotle holds, is imitative; Tchaikovsky imitates Napoleon's defeat in Russia in the "1812 Overture." Aristotle would have approved of Thomas De Quincey's remark that although no one whistled at Waterloo, one might whistle Waterloo. The imitative instinct, of course, is not the artist's private possession. A small boy says to another, "You be the cop and I'll be the robber and you say 'Halt' and I'll run away." This natural tendency to imitate is combined, Aristotle says, with a tendency toward rhythm or pattern, and the result can be a work of art. In its simplest form the imitative theory appeals to the naive: "How lifelike that wax apple is!" "How like a Frenchman that actor looks!" But more sophisticated people may ask: "What is so pleasing about a wax apple or a fake Frenchman? There are plenty of real apples and real Frenchmen for us to look at." Aristotle's theory includes such a close copy of nature as a wax apple, but it goes further. He says that art is superior to history because although history must stick to the facts, art refines nature, showing, one might say, not what happened but what should have happened in a world free from accident. The artist is a sort of greenhouse keeper, producing not the rose that grows wild, cankered, and stunted, but the rose that has fulfilled all its potential, the rose that is more a rose than any wild rose. The artist, in short, does not imitate servilely; he re-creates reality and presents it to us in a fashion in which we see its essence more clearly.

It is only half-true, then, to say that Aristotle's imitator is a maker of an imitation. (This idea of the artist as a maker, by the way, survives dimly in the word "playwright" — "wright" being a maker, as in "shipwright," and having nothing to do with "write.") Because the artist's imitation is more than a copy of what is apparent to every eye, his imitation is in some measure a creation. It is imaginative and interpretive; it reflects a special view of reality. Thomas Mann, attributing such an inspired sort of imitating to Anton Chekhov, comments on the boy Chekhov's propensity for mimicking the dentist, the policeman, and other acquaintances: "What makes its appearance here is the primitive origin of all art, the inclination to ape, the jester's desire and talent to entertain; . . . it was to ally itself [in Chekhov's maturity] with spiritual principles, to undergo moral ennoblement, and to rise from merely amusing trifles to soul-searching achievements." Presumably, then, the reader of a work written by a Chekhov will learn something.

The imitative theory often includes the notion that art gives us not only pleasure but also knowledge, insight into the nature of reality. If you say that we enjoy wax apples simply because we enjoy seeing exhibitions of man's skill at imitation, you are not introducing the criterion of knowledge. If, however, you say that by looking at the imitation we come to know something about reality, you are saying that art furnishes knowledge, and that its value depends partly on its truth. This problem of truth does not arise in all the arts: no one asks the Taj Mahal to be true. But many people want their literature to be true — to be an illuminating reflection of reality. The danger, of course, is that the reader may turn literature into a message: he hunts for detachable tags ("Frailty, thy name is woman," "To thine own self be true"), or he reduces the whole work to a neat moral. He begins to neglect artistry and to give A's to those works whose messages (as he conceives them) seem right to him. But what does anyone really learn from a work of literature? Do we learn from *Julius Caesar* not to be a tyrant? Or not to assassinate a tyrant? Or the difficulty of assassinating a tyrant and getting away with it? Surely we knew all this before. Perhaps the answer to the question, "Does literature give knowledge?" is that we do not learn from literature how to act in a particular situation (we'll never get the chance to be Roman tyrants), but we do learn something about life in general. After seeing a play, we feel that we have achieved at least a momentary understanding of some of the facts of life. The happenings in the book or on the stage not only resemble things in real life, but also clarify real life, making us say: "Yes, people are like that, but I hadn't noticed it before." James Baldwin has said that in *Julius Caesar* he discovered the tension between idealism and blind passion, or, to put it another way, the guilt that is part of a hero's "desperate singlemindedness." When we read a piece of literature, we may have known intellectually that this or that is so, but now what earlier had been a lifeless platitude is a vital part of our being. We may not translate this vivified knowledge into any specific action, but we may nevertheless feel that we have acquired new insight and that our lives will be in some degree changed. James Joyce expressed such a view when he complained to a publisher who refused to issue his book of stories, *Dubliners:*

> It is not my fault that the odor of ashpits and old weeds and offal hangs round my stories. I seriously believe that you will retard the course of civilization in Ireland by preventing the Irish people from having one good look at themselves in my nicely polished looking-glass.

THE EXPRESSIVE THEORY

The second theory, usually called the expressive theory, can be treated more briefly. It holds that the artist is not essentially an imitator but one who expresses his feelings. D. H. Lawrence said, "One sheds one's sicknesses in books, repeats and presents again one's emotions to be master of them." Here is a powerful expression of feeling, thinly disguised as a statement about the ancient Israelites:

> When Israel was in Egypt's land,
> > Let my people go!
> Oppressed so hard they could not stand,
> > Let my people go!
> *Chorus:* Go down, Moses,
> > 'Way down in Egypt's land;
> > Tell old Pharaoh,
> > Let my people go!

One understands easily enough what Frederick Douglass, a fugitive slave, meant when he said that songs can relieve an aching heart, and that he often sang to drown his sorrow. Two quotations from William Wordsworth may be useful. "Poetry," he said, "is the spontaneous overflow of powerful feelings"; the poet's job is "to treat of things not as they *are* . . . but as they *seem* to exist to the *senses*, and the *passions*." (This is by no means a complete summary of Wordsworth's theories, but it is enough to illustrate the gist of expressive theories.) The artist's vision, the theory holds, is more inward than outward; the work of art is not an imitation of the external world but an expression of the internal world, the embodiment of an emotion. This theory sometimes holds that "truth" has nothing to do with literature; Landor's "Heart's-ease," it might be said, expresses his feelings, and his feelings cannot be true or false. They simply exist. But sometimes an expressive theory insists that a work is true if it is sincere. We do not ordinarily say that laughter or tears are true or false, but if we discover that the laughter or tears are hypocritical rather than sincere, we call them false. Since, however, the reader of a piece of literature cannot know if the author was sincere when he wrote it, the criterion of sincerity is valueless. We cannot say that *Julius Caesar* is sincere; perhaps Shakespeare wrote it merely to make money. We cannot even say that his sonnets reflect his true feelings; though Wordsworth said that in them Shakespeare "unlocked his heart," how can we be sure? Furthermore, writing that is indubitably sincere is not necessarily good writing. Aldous Huxley is surely correct in his observation that "a bad book is as much labor to write as a good one; it comes as sincerely from the author's soul." Moreover, what value does expressive writing have? One can reply it is valuable for the writer: "If I don't write to empty my mind," Byron said, "I go mad." But if this relief from pressure is its only value, the written piece might just as well be left lying on the writer's desk. Most expressions of emotions, after all, are valueless to everyone but the person expressing them. Our laughter, mumblings, and cries of despair are all very expressive, and afford us a relief, but who would call them works of art that are of value to other people? Not all expressions of emotion, clearly, are works of art, and conversely, if a work of art is an expression of emotion, it must be a very special kind of expression.

Advocates of the expressive theory, however, have yet another argument, this one stronger: by showing us how he sees and feels something, the writer may pluck the blinders from our eyes and melt the ice around our heart. He may jolt us out of our usual rut, and widen the area of our sensibilities. Wordsworth's view of daffodils may force upon us the awareness that our own views are narrow. An awareness of how other people feel is, after all, a way of expanding and enriching one's own personality.

THE AFFECTIVE THEORY

Finally, there is the affective theory of art, which holds that a work of art ought to arouse a particular emotion, or affect (to use the psychologist's term), in the perceiver. This theory is often closely related to the expressive theory: the artist allegedly expresses his emotion, embodying it in a work of art, and this work evokes in the perceiver a similar or identical emotion. Presumably by describing certain things in a certain way the writer can evoke the proper response. The most famous presentation of this theory is Tolstoi's *What Is Art?*, a sentence of which is here quoted:

Art is a human activity consisting in this, that one man consciously, by means of certain external signs, hands on to others feelings he has lived through, and that others are infected by these feelings, and also experience them.

Here is another statement of the theory, this one by Alexander Pope:

Let me for once presume to instruct the times,
To know the poet from the man of rhymes:
'Tis he, who gives my breast a thousand pains,
Can make me feel each passion that he feigns;
Enrage, compose, with more than magic art,
With pity and with terror tear my heart;
And snatch me o'er the earth or through the air,
To Thebes, to Athens, when he will, and where.

(It is worth mentioning, incidentally, that although Pope's lines say that poetry arouses passions in the reader or hearer, they themselves, like most of Pope's writing, do not arouse fierce passions, but rather arouse interest and attention.) Affective theories hold that the stimulation of certain emotions is, for some reason, good: we need an occasional release (a good cry), or we need to have our emotions organized into a pleasant pattern (as the fretful child needs his mother's smile, to induce in him good spirits). That some readers seek emotional stimulus from books is beyond doubt. Often the reader who asks the rental librarian to recommend a good novel is asking for a book that will allow the reader fully to identify with the central character, experiencing bursts of love, sorrow, and so forth. But a good work of art neither invites this identification nor triggers stereotyped emotions. How many people have felt totally at one with Hamlet, Macbeth, Brutus?

Usually the affective theory insists that the aim is not to induce a temporary emotional state, but to induce an emotional state that will lead to action. Such a theory might hold that the artist should stimulate in people an awareness of the horror of war so that they will go out and do something about stopping wars. Tolstoi, who held such a view, regarded the evocation of emotion not as an end but as a means:

The task of art is enormous. Through the influence of real art, aided by science, guided by religion, that peaceful co-operation of man which is now maintained by external means — by our lawcourts, police, charitable institutions, factory inspection, and so forth — should be obtained by man's free and joyous activity. Art should cause violence to be set aside.

Pope, too, holds that the aim of art is to reform those whom it touches:

> To wake the soul by tender strokes of art,
> To raise the genius, and to mend the heart;
> To make mankind, in conscious virtue bold,
> Live o'er each scene, and be what they behold:
> For this the Tragic Muse first trod the stage,
> Commanding tears to stream through ev'ry age;
> Tyrants no more their savage nature kept,
> And foes to virtue wondered how they wept.

Jean Pierre Gorin, close associate of film director Jean-Luc Godard, put the matter quite simply when asked "What is the function of cinema?" "Cinema is part of the ideological struggle. And a revolutionary film is on the side of revolution." Ezekiel Mphahlele, an exiled South African black writer, has said that the best poetry is a "memorable" expression of "revolutionary passion and ideas," and Imamu Amiri Baraka (LeRoi Jones) has said that revolutionary writing must "transform reality." But against the view that a good work of art prompts us to action, one can put Robert Frost's deceptively simple question: "How soon?"

SOME TENTATIVE CONCLUSIONS

This chapter opened with the query, "What is literature?" and it has not yet given a satisfactory answer. Nor will it. No one has come up with a satisfactory answer so far. Textbooks and theoretical treatises are filled with neat definitions, but no definition has yet withstood all criticism. It would be nice to say that literature evokes emotion, but so does a good deal of nonliterature (for example, a documentary account of the bombing of Hiroshima), and, as we suggest above, perhaps much literature evokes "attention" rather than "emotion." It would be nice to say that literature is essentially fictional, but is a poem on, say, the power of God fictional? Is such a poem fictional to the believer who composes it or to the believer who reads it? Moreover, it can be argued that although works of art are superficially fictional, they are essentially true. It would be nice to say that in literature there is complexity and unity, but these are characteristics of a telephone book as well as of *Julius Caesar*. And so it goes, definition after definition failing when applied to specific works that we know are works of art.

The brief sketch of critical theories in the preceding pages, however, may help a reader toward a tentative definition. Surely we can agree that a piece of literature is a performance in words; it strongly holds our attention, seeming complete in itself; it is not primarily regarded as a source of factual information; it offers a unique delight or satisfaction. To these, most people would add that literature offers some sort of truth, though not the sort of truth found in factual propositions such as $E=mc^2$. Finally, most people would say that it has a beneficial effect on the perceiver. Tolstoi and Pope may be claiming too much for the arts, but is it absurd to believe that they can play a role in civilizing man? Music has beneficial effects on animals: cows are said to give more milk when music is played in barns, race horses are soothed by music at the starting-gate at Aqueduct, and wolves reduce their howling when they hear classical music. Is there nothing in the following lines from *The Merchant of Venice?*

> *Jessica.* I am never merry when I hear sweet music.
> *Lorenzo.* The reason is your spirits are attentive;
> For do but note a wild and wanton herd,
> Or race of youthful and unhandled colts,
> Fetching mad bounds, bellowing and neighing loud,
> Which is the hot condition of their blood —
> If they but hear perchance a trumpet sound,
> Or any air of music touch their ears,
> You shall perceive them make a mutual stand,
> Their savage eyes turned to a modest gaze
> By the sweet power of music. Therefore the poet
> Did feign that Orpheus drew trees, stones, and floods,
> Since nought so stockish, hard, and full of rage,
> But music for the time doth change his nature.
> The man that hath no music in himself,
> Nor is not moved with concord of sweet sounds,
> Is fit for treasons, stratagems, and spoils.

Is it not possible that works of art give us an insight into reality (as the imitative theory usually holds), that they broaden our awareness of the possibilities of experience (as the expressive theory usually holds), and that they valuably affect our nervous system (as the affective theory usually holds)? This is not to say that every work of art does all these things, but only that all of these theories may have something to contribute to a deeper and more conscious awareness of what is valuable in the works we read. If we look back into our experiences, can we not find moments that seem to verify aspects of each theory? This book will offer further experiences; as the reader encounters them, he is invited to test these theories.

FICTION

Stories and Meanings

Narrative Point of View

Allegory and Symbolism

Style

A Collection of Short Fiction

Observations on the Novel

2 Stories and Meanings

People tell stories for many reasons, including the sheer egotistical delight of talking, but probably most of the best storytelling proceeds from one of two more commendable desires: a desire to entertain, or a desire to instruct. Among the most famous of the stories designed to instruct are the parables that Jesus told. (*Parable* comes from the Greek word meaning "to throw beside," that is, "to compare," and we are to compare these little stories with our own behavior.) Here is one of them, addressed to a man who asked Jesus what is meant by "neighbor" in the command to love one's neighbor as one's self.

Luke 10 : 30–37

Parable of the Good Samaritan

And Jesus answering said, "A certain man went down from Jerusalem to Jericho, and fell among thieves, which stripped him of his raiment, and wounded him, and departed, leaving him half dead. And by chance there came down a certain priest that way: and when he saw him, he passed by on the other side. And likewise a Levite, when he was at the place, came and looked on him, and passed by on the other side. But a certain Samaritan, as he journeyed, came where he was: and when he saw him, he had compassion on him, and went to him, and bound up his wounds, pouring in oil and wine, and set him on his own beast, and brought him to an inn, and took care of him. And on the morrow when he departed, he took out two pence, and gave them to the host, and said unto him. 'Take care of him; and whatsoever thou spendest more, when I come again, I will repay thee.' Which now of these three, thinkest thou, was neighbor unto him that fell among the thieves?"

And he said, "He that shewed mercy on him."

Then said Jesus unto him, "Go, and do thou likewise."

The narrative proper concludes before the question at the end of the first paragraph, and then the theme, or point, or message — for the story is about something more than an imagined encounter between a wounded man and three passers-by — is made explicit in a few additional lines. We say that the story is told for the sake of the point; we can also say that it is told for our sake, because we are implicitly invited to see ourselves in the story, and to live our lives in accordance with it. This simple but powerful story, with its memorable characters — though nameless and briefly sketched — makes us feel the point in our hearts.

Even older than Jesus' parables are the fables attributed to Aesop, some of which go back to the seventh century before Christ. These stories also teach lessons by telling brief incidents from which homely morals may easily be drawn, even though the stories are utterly fanciful. Among famous examples are the stories of the hare and the tortoise, the boy who cried "Wolf," the ant and the grasshopper, and a good many others that stick in the mind because of the sharply contrasted characters in sharply imagined situations. The fables just mentioned take only four or five sentences apiece, but, brief as they are, Aesop told some briefer ones. Here is the briefest of all:

> A vixen sneered at a lioness because she never bore more than one cub.
> "Only one," the lioness replied, "but a lion."

Just that: a situation with a conflict (the mere confrontation of a fox and a lion brings together the ignoble and the noble) and a resolution (*something* must come out of such a confrontation). There is no setting (we are not told that "one day in June a vixen, walking down a road, met a lioness"), but none is needed here. What there is — however briefly set forth — is characterization. The fox's baseness is effectively communicated through the verb "sneered" and through her taunt, and the lioness's nobility is even more effectively communicated through the brevity and the decisiveness of her reply. This reply at first seems to agree with the fox ("Only one") and then, after a suspenseful delay provided by the words "the lioness replied," the reply is tersely and powerfully completed ("but a lion"), placing the matter firmly in a new light. Granted that the story is not much of a story, still, it is finely told, and more potent — more memorable, more lively, we might even say more real, despite its talking animals — than the mere moral, "Small-minded people confuse quantity with quality."

Here is a much later short tale, from nineteenth-century Japan. It is said to be true, but whether it really occurred or not is scarcely of any importance. It is the story, not the history, that counts.

> Tanzan and Ekido were once traveling together down a muddy road. A heavy rain was still falling.
> Coming around a bend, they met a lovely girl in a silk kimono and sash, unable to cross the intersection.
> "Come on, girl," said Tanzan at once. Lifting her in his arms, he carried her over the mud.
> Ekido did not speak again until that night when they reached a lodging temple. Then he no longer could restrain himself. "We monks don't go near females," he told Tanzan, "especially not young and lovely ones. It is dangerous. Why did you do that?"
> "I left the girl there," said Tanzan. "Are you still carrying her?"

A superb story. The opening paragraph, though simple and matter-of-fact, holds our attention: we sense that something interesting is going to happen during this journey along a muddy road on a rainy day. Perhaps we even sense, somehow, by virtue of the references to the mud and the rain, that the journey itself rather than the travelers' destination will be the heart of the story: getting there will be more than half the fun. And then, after the introduction of the two characters and the setting, we quickly get the complicating factor, the encounter with the girl. Still there is apparently no conflict, though in "Ekido did not speak again until that night" we sense an unspoken conflict, an action (or, in this case, an inaction) that must be explained, an imbalance that must be righted before we are finished. At last Ekido, no longer able to contain his thoughts, lets his indignation burst out: "We monks don't go near females . . . , especially not young and lovely ones. It is dangerous. Why did you do that?" His statement and his question reveal not only his moral principles but also his insecurity and the anger that grows from it. And now, when the conflict is out in the open, comes the brief reply that reveals Tanzan's very different character as clearly as the outburst revealed Ekido's. This reply — though we could not have predicted it — strikes us as exactly right, bringing the story to a perfect end, i.e., to a point (like the ends of Christ's parable and Aesop's fable) at which there is no more to be said.

Let us look at another short piece, though this one, from the *Satyricon*, a witty, cynical book attributed to Petronius, director-in-chief of Nero's entertainments, is considerably longer than the stories we have just read, and it is aimed more at entertaining than at teaching.

Petronius (1st Century A.D.)

The Widow of Ephesus

Translated by William Arrowsmith

"Once upon a time there was a certain married woman in the city of Ephesus whose fidelity to her husband was so famous that the women from all the neighboring towns and villages used to troop into Ephesus merely to stare at this prodigy. It happened, however, that her husband one day died. Finding the normal custom of following the cortege with hair unbound and beating her breast in public quite inadequate to express her grief, the lady insisted on following the corpse right into the tomb, an underground vault of the Greek type, and there set herself to guard the body, weeping and wailing night and day. Although in her extremes of grief she was clearly courting death from starvation, her parents were utterly unable to persuade her to leave, and even the magistrates, after one last supreme attempt, were rebuffed and driven away. In short, all Ephesus had gone into mourning for this extraordinary woman, all the more since the lady was now passing her fifth consecutive day without once tasting food. Beside the failing woman sat her devoted maid, sharing her mistress' grief and relighting the lamp whenever it flickered out. The whole city could speak, in fact, of nothing else: here at last, all classes alike agreed, was the one true example of conjugal fidelity and love.

"In the meantime, however, the governor of the province gave orders that several thieves should be crucified in a spot close by the vault where the lady was mourning her dead husband's corpse. So, on the following night, the soldier who had been assigned to keep watch on the crosses so that nobody could remove the thieves' bodies for burial suddenly noticed a light blazing among the tombs and heard the sounds of groaning. And prompted by a natural human curiosity to know who or what was making those sounds, he descended into the vault.

"But at the sight of a strikingly beautiful woman, he stopped short in terror, thinking he must be seeing some ghostly apparition out of hell. Then, observing the corpse and seeing the tears on the lady's face and the scratches her fingernails had gashed in her cheeks, he realized what it was: a widow, in inconsolable grief. Promptly fetching his little supper back down to the tomb, he implored the lady not to persist in her sorrow or break her heart with useless mourning. All men alike, he reminded her, have the same end; the same resting place awaits us all. He used, in short, all those platitudes we use to comfort the suffering and bring them back to life. His consolations, being unwelcome, only exasperated the widow more; more violently than ever she beat her breast, and tearing out her hair by the roots, scattered it over the dead man's body. Undismayed, the soldier repeated his arguments and pressed her to take some food, until the little maid, quite overcome by the smell of the wine, succumbed and stretched out her hand to her tempter. Then, restored by the food and wine, she began herself to assail her mistress' obstinate refusal.

" 'How will it help you,' she asked the lady, 'if you faint from hunger? Why should you bury yourself alive, and go down to death before the Fates have called you? What does Vergil say? —

Do you suppose the shades and ashes of the dead are by such sorrow touched?

No, begin your life afresh. Shake off these woman's scruples; enjoy the light while you can. Look at that corpse of your poor husband: doesn't it tell you more eloquently than any words that you should live?'

"None of us, of course, really dislikes being told that we must eat, that life is to be lived. And the lady was no exception. Weakened by her long days of fasting, her resistance crumbled at last, and she ate the food the soldier offered her as hungrily as the little maid had eaten earlier.

"Well, you know what temptations are normally aroused in a man on a full stomach. So the soldier, mustering all those blandishments by means of which he had persuaded the lady to live, now laid determined siege to her virtue. And chaste though she was, the lady found him singularly attractive and his arguments persuasive. As for the maid, she did all she could to help the soldier's cause, repeating like a refrain the appropriate line of Vergil:

If love is pleasing, lady, yield yourself to love.

To make the matter short, the lady's body soon gave up the struggle; she yielded and our happy warrior enjoyed a total triumph on both counts. That very night their marriage was consummated, and they slept together the second and the third night too, carefully shutting the door of the tomb so that any passing friends or strangers would have thought the lady of famous chastity had at last expired over her dead husband's body.

"As you can perhaps imagine, our soldier was a very happy man, utterly delighted with his lady's ample beauty and that special charm that a secret love confers. Every night, as soon as the sun had set, he bought what few provisions his slender pay permitted and smuggled them down to the tomb. One night, however, the parents of one of the crucified thieves, noticing that the watch was being badly kept, took advantage of our hero's absence to remove their son's body and bury it. The next morning, of course, the soldier was horror-struck to discover one of the bodies missing from its cross, and ran to tell his mistress of the horrible punishment which awaited him for neglecting his duty. In the circumstances, he told her, he would not wait to be tried and sentenced, but would punish himself then and there with his own sword. All he asked of her was that she make room for another corpse and allow the same gloomy tomb to enclose husband and lover together.

"Our lady's heart, however, was no less tender than pure. 'God forbid,' she cried, 'that I should have to see at one and the same time the dead bodies of the only two men I have ever loved. No, better far, I say, to hang the dead than kill the living.' With these words, she gave orders that her husband's body should be taken from its bier and strung up on the empty cross. The soldier followed this good advice, and the next morning the whole city wondered by what miracle the dead man had climbed up on the cross."

Petronius tells us that the sailors who heard this tale greeted it "with great guffaws," surely the appropriate response. It is an amusing story, largely because it is well-told. Let us look at it as a piece of craftsmanship. The happenings, as they are selected and arranged by the author, are the **plot**; the participants are the **characters**; the meaning or point is the **theme**.

The traditional plot has this structure:

1. **Exposition** (setting forth of the beginning)
2. **Conflict** (a complication that moves to a climax)
3. **Dénouement** (literally, "unknotting," the outcome of the conflict; the resolution)

Petronius's exposition is in the opening paragraph, which sets forth a situation that seems to be stable (the lady is resolved to die). We do not ask why she was so virtuous or of what her husband died; we simply accept the exposition, and wait for something to disturb the situation it describes. The second paragraph begins the conflict by introducing a complication (a soldier goes to the tomb). It is important that the conflict is not so much the lady against the soldier as it is the lady against her own ideals. This conflict or complication (literally, folding or weaving together) is momentarily resolved when the lady exchanges widowhood for a new marriage, but the resolution gives rise to another complication, the disappearance of the thief's body. At this point the conflict is at its height, for the soldier's life is at stake. (Although at the start the widow's life was in danger, the tension was slight because she was doing what she wished; now that the lovers wish to live, the tension is greatest.) This moment of greatest tension is called the **climax**; it is here dissipated by an action of the lady, whose love for the soldier is as great as was her grief for her husband. Her suggestion to substitute her husband's corpse for the missing one unties the knot or the weaving begun with the complication. The soldier's acceptance of her suggestion, and the townsmen's bewilderment, constitute the dénouement. We have moved, then, from a situation that seemed static (the widow's grief), through a complication that became acute, into a new situation that is stable. The lady may later leave the soldier for another man, but such happenings do not concern us; we feel that we have seen a unified action — something with a beginning, a middle, and an end.*

The things that happen are in large measure caused by the characters, who act believably. Although in Petronius's tale it is a coincidence that a thief has been crucified near the tomb containing the grieving wife, all the subsequent happenings arise from **character** (the personality of each of the characters): the soldier visits the tomb "prompted by a natural human curiosity," and, after he has consoled the widow and has eaten, he undergoes the

> temptations [that] are normally aroused in a man on a full stomach. So the soldier, mustering all those blandishments by means of which he had persuaded the lady to live, now laid determined siege to her virtue. And chaste though she was, the lady found him singularly attractive and his arguments persuasive.

* Though we have defined "plot" as the author's selection and arrangement of happenings, some critics define "plot" as the happenings in their chronological order. The term is further discussed on pages 533–535.

Similarly, there is **motivation** (a basis in character) for the disappearance of the thief's corpse; the fact that the soldier had been
stationed to guard it gives us clear indication that the thief's family
will bury it if given the chance. The soldier's fear and despair are
similarly plausible, and, finally, so too is the lady's ingenious suggestion that saves the soldier, for her love for him is now as deep as it
had been for her husband. The crucifixion of her husband's corpse,
then, like the soldier's visit and the lady's change of heart, is motivated; we feel it is plausible in the light of the characters involved.
And our interest in the tale is not only an interest in occurrences, but
also an interest in the people who engender the occurrences.

In some stories, of course, we are chiefly interested in plot (the
arrangement of happenings or doings), in others we are chiefly interested in character (the personalities of the doers), but on the whole
the two are so intertwined that interest in one involves interest in the
other. Happenings occur (people cross paths), and personalities respond to them, engendering further happenings. As Henry James
rhetorically asked, "What is character but the determination of incident? What is incident but the illustration of character?" Commonly,
as a good story proceeds and we become increasingly familiar with
the characters, we get intimations of what they may do in the future.
We may not know precisely how they will act, but we have a fairly
good idea, and when in fact we see their subsequent actions, we
usually recognize the appropriateness. Sometimes there are hints of
what is to come, and because of this **foreshadowing** we are not
shocked by what happens, but rather we experience suspense as we
wait for the expected to come about. Coleridge had Shakespeare's
use of foreshadowing in mind when he praised him for giving us not
surprise but expectation and then the satisfaction of perfect knowledge. E. M. Forster, in *Aspects of the Novel*, has a shrewd comment
on the importance of both fulfilling expectation and offering a slight
surprise: "Shock, followed by the feeling, 'Oh, that's all right,' is a
sign that all is well with the plot: characters, to be real, ought to run
smoothly, but a plot ought to cause surprise."

Finally, a few words about **theme**. Usually, a story is about something, it has a meaning, a point — a theme. The narrator of "The
Widow of Ephesus" prefaced the tale by declaring that "no woman
was so chaste or faithful that she couldn't be seduced," and his story
was told in order to make this statement meaningful. A vulgar fellow,
he interprets his story rather cheaply, even indecently. But the reader
can more accurately restate the theme, giving it greater significance
and making it more acceptable: life and love are too strong to be
buried alive. A word of caution, however, is needed here: a story is
not simply an illustration of a theme. A story has a variety of details

that modify any abstract statement; in Petronius's story the lady was "weakened by her long days of fasting," and the soldier was "singularly attractive." Such details, not present in the narrator's own statement of his "theme," are important modifications of the theme. To state the theme either as the narrator stated it or as we have restated it is to falsify the story, for Petronius's story is about a particular widow's encounter with a particular soldier, under particular circumstances. And what lives in our memory is not an abstract statement — and certainly not a thesis, i.e., a proposition offered and argued. What lives is an image that by every word in the story has convinced us that it is a representation, if not of "reality," at least of an aspect of reality. Still, the artist was guided by a theme in his choice of details; of many possible details he chose to present only a few. The musical sense of the word "theme" can help us to understand what a theme in literature is: "a melody constituting the basis of variation, development, or the like." The variations and the development cannot be random but must have a basis. What is it, Robert Frost asks, that prevents the writer from kicking himself "from one chance suggestion to another in all directions as of a hot afternoon in the life of a grasshopper?" Frost's answer: "Theme alone can steady us down."

We can, then, talk about the theme — what the story adds up to — as long as we do not think a statement of the theme is equivalent to or a substitute for the whole story. As Flannery O'Connor says: "Some people have the notion that you can read the story and then climb out of it into the meaning, but for the fiction writer himself the whole story is the meaning." A theme, Miss O'Connor says, is not like a string tying a sack of chicken feed, to be pulled out so that the feed can be got at. "A story is a way to say something that can't be said any other way." (On theme, see also pages 1047-48.)

Questions

1. Most of the story is narrated, rather than dramatized through dialogue. Is the use of dialogue haphazard or is it in the right place?

2. What does the presence of the maid contribute to the story?

3. We are told that the lady decides to surrender the corpse because she is "no less tender than pure." Does the narrator mean exactly what he says? Explain.

4. The lady's virtue is set forth at some length; the desecration of the corpse is set forth very briefly. Why is this disparity effective?

5. The last sentence of the story is characteristic of the prevailing tone in which the story is told. How would you describe that tone, and how does it affect the theme?

Below are three additional short pieces: the first is another of Jesus' parables; the second (a Russian story) and the third (an American story) were written in the late nineteenth century.

Luke 15

Parable of the Prodigal Son

And he said, "A certain man had two sons: and the younger of them said to his father, 'Father, give me the portion of goods that falleth to me.' And he divided unto them his living. And not many days after, the younger son gathered all together, and took his journey into a far country, and there wasted his substance with riotous living. And when he had spent all, there arose a mighty famine in that land, and he began to be in want. And he went and joined himself to a citizen of that country, and he sent him into his fields to feed swine. And he would fain have filled his belly with the husks that the swine did eat: and no man gave unto him. And when he came to himself, he said, 'How many hired servants of my father's have bread enough and to spare, and I perish with hunger? I will arise and go to my father, and will say unto him, "Father, I have sinned against heaven, and before thee. And am no more worthy to be called thy son: make me as one of thy hired servants."' And he arose, and came to his father. But when he was yet a great way off, his father saw him, and had compassion, and ran, and fell on his neck, and kissed him. And the son said unto him, 'Father, I have sinned against heaven, and in thy sight, and am no more worthy to be called thy son.' But the father said to his servants, 'Bring forth the best robe, and put it on him, and put a ring on his hand, and shoes on his feet. And bring hither the fatted calf, and kill it, and let us eat, and be merry. For this my son was dead, and is alive again; he was lost, and is found.' And they began to be merry. Now his elder son was in the field, and as he came and drew nigh to the house, he heard music and dancing. And he called one of the servants, and asked what these things meant. And he said unto him, 'Thy brother is come, and thy father hath killed the fatted calf, because he hath received him safe and sound.' And he was angry, and would not go in: therefore came his father out, and entreated him. And he answering said to his father, 'Lo, these many years do I serve thee, neither transgressed I at any time thy commandment, and yet thou never gavest me a kid, that I might make merry with my friends:

but as soon as this thy son was come, which hath devoured thy living with harlots, thou hast killed for him the fatted calf.' And he said unto him, 'Son, thou art ever with me, and all that I have is thine. It was meet that we should make merry, and be glad: for this thy brother was dead, and is alive again: and was lost, and is found.' "

Leo Tolstoi (1828–1910)

The Three Hermits

An Old Legend Current in the Vólga District

Translated by Aylmer Maude

"And in praying use not vain repetitions as the Gentiles do: for they think that they shall be heard for their much speaking. Be not therefore like unto them: for your Father knoweth what things ye have need of, before ye ask Him."

Matt. vi. 7, 8.

A Bishop was sailing from Archangel to the Solovétsk Monastery, and on the same vessel were a number of pilgrims on their way to visit the shrines at that place. The voyage was a smooth one. The wind favourable and the weather fair. The pilgrims lay on deck, eating, or sat in groups talking to one another. The Bishop, too, came on deck, and as he was pacing up and down he noticed a group of men standing near the prow and listening to a fisherman, who was pointing to the sea and telling them something. The Bishop stopped, and looked in the direction in which the man was pointing. He could see nothing, however, but the sea glistening in the sunshine. He drew nearer to listen, but when the man saw him, he took off his cap and was silent. The rest of the people also took off their caps and bowed.

"Do not let me disturb you, friends," said the Bishop. "I came to hear what this good man was saying."

"The fisherman was telling us about the hermits," replied one, a tradesman, rather bolder than the rest.

"What hermits?" asked the Bishop, going to the side of the vessel and seating himself on a box. "Tell me about them. I should like to hear. What were you pointing at?"

"Why, that little island you can just see over there," answered the man, pointing to a spot ahead and a little to the right. "That is the island where the hermits live for the salvation of their souls."

"Where is the island?" asked the Bishop. "I see nothing."

"There, in the distance, if you will please look along my hand. Do you see that little cloud? Below it, and a bit to the left, there is just a faint streak. That is the island."

The Bishop looked carefully, but his unaccustomed eyes could make out nothing but the water shimmering in the sun.

"I cannot see it," he said. "But who are the hermits that live there?"

"They are holy men," answered the fisherman. "I had long heard tell of them, but never chanced to see them myself till the year before last."

And the fisherman related how once, when he was out fishing, he had been stranded at night upon that island, not knowing where he was. In the morning, as he wandered about the island, he came across an earth hut, and met an old man standing near it. Presently two others came out, and after having fed him and dried his things, they helped him mend his boat.

"And what are they like?" asked the Bishop.

"One is a small man and his back is bent. He wears a priest's cassock and is very old; he must be more than a hundred, I should say. He is so old that the white of his beard is taking a greenish tinge, but he is always smiling, and his face is as bright as an angel's from heaven. The second is taller, but he also is very old. He wears a tattered peasant coat. His beard is broad, and of a yellowish grey colour. He is a strong man. Before I had time to help him, he turned my boat over as if it were only a pail. He too is kindly and cheerful. The third is tall, and has a beard as white as snow and reaching to his knees. He is stern, with overhanging eyebrows; and he wears nothing but a piece of matting tied round his waist."

"And did they speak to you?" asked the Bishop.

"For the most part they did everything in silence, and spoke but little even to one another. One of them would just give a glance, and the others would understand him. I asked the tallest whether they had lived there long. He frowned, and muttered something as if he were angry; but the oldest one took his hand and smiled, and then the tall one was quiet. The oldest one only said:'Have mercy upon us,' and smiled."

While the fisherman was talking, the ship had drawn nearer to the island.

"There, now you can see it plainly, if your Lordship will please to look," said the tradesman, pointing with his hand.

The Bishop looked, and now he really saw a dark streak — which was the island. Having looked at it a while, he left the prow of the vessel, and going to the stern, asked the helmsman:

"What island is that?"

"That one," replied the man, "has no name. There are many such in this sea."

"Is it true that there are hermits who live there for the salvation of their souls?"

"So it is said, your Lordship, but I don't know if it's true. Fishermen say they have seen them; but of course they may only be spinning yarns."

"I should like to land on the island and see these men," said the Bishop. "How could I manage it?"

"The ship cannot get close to the island," replied the helmsman, "but you might be rowed there in a boat. You had better speak to the captain."

The captain was sent for and came.

"I should like to see these hermits," said the Bishop. "Could I not be rowed ashore?"

The captain tried to dissuade him.

"Of course it could be done," said he, "but we should lose much time. And if I might venture to say so to your Lordship, the old men are not worth your pains. I have heard say that they are foolish old fellows, who understand nothing, and never speak a word, any more than the fish in the sea."

"I wish to see them," said the Bishop, "and I will pay you for your trouble and loss of time. Please let me have a boat."

There was no help for it; so the order was given. The sailors trimmed the sails, the steersman put up the helm, and the ship's course was set for the island. A chair was placed at the prow for the Bishop, and he sat there, looking ahead. The passengers all collected at the prow, and gazed at the island. Those who had the sharpest eyes could presently make out the rocks on it, and then a mud hut was seen. At last one man saw the hermits themselves. The captain brought a telescope and, after looking through it, handed it to the Bishop.

"It's right enough. There are three men standing on the shore. There, a little to the right of that big rock."

The Bishop took the telescope, got it into position, and he saw the three men: a tall one, a shorter one, and one very small and bent, standing on the shore and holding each other by the hand.

The captain turned to the Bishop.

"The vessel can get no nearer in than this, your Lordship. If you wish to go ashore, we must ask you to go in the boat, while we anchor here."

The cable was quickly let out; the anchor cast, and the sails furled. There was a jerk, and the vessel shook. Then, a boat having been lowered, the oarsmen jumped in, and the Bishop descended the ladder and took his seat. The men pulled at their oars and the boat moved rapidly towards the island. When they came within a stone's throw, they saw three old men: a tall one with only a piece of matting tied round his waist, a shorter one in a tattered peasant coat, and a very old one bent with age and wearing an old cassock — all three standing hand in hand.

The oarsmen pulled in to the shore, and held on with the boathook while the Bishop got out.

The old men bowed to him, and he gave them his blessing, at which they bowed still lower. Then the Bishop began to speak to them.

"I have heard," he said, "that you, godly men, live here saving your own souls and praying to our Lord Christ for your fellow men. I, an unworthy servant of Christ, am called, by God's mercy, to keep and teach His flock. I wished to see you, servants of God, and to do what I can to teach you, also."

The old men looked at each other smiling, but remained silent.

"Tell me," said the Bishop, "what you are doing to save your souls, and how you serve God on this island."

The second hermit sighed, and looked at the oldest, the very ancient one. The latter smiled, and said:

"We do not know how to serve God. We only serve and support ourselves, servant of God."

"But how do you pray to God?" asked the Bishop.

"We pray in this way," replied the hermit. "Three are ye, three are we, have mercy upon us."

And when the old man said this, all three raised their eyes to heaven, and repeated:

"Three are ye, three are we, have mercy upon us!"

The Bishop smiled.

"You have evidently heard something about the Holy Trinity," said he. "But you do not pray aright. You have won my affection, godly men. I see you wish to please the Lord, but you do not know how to serve Him. That is not the way to pray; but listen to me, and I will teach you. I will teach you, not a way of my own, but the way in which God in the Holy Scriptures has commanded all men to pray to Him."

And the Bishop began explaining to the hermits how God had

revealed Himself to men; telling them of God the Father, and God the Son, and God the Holy Ghost.

"God the Son came down on earth," said he, "to save men, and this is how He taught us all to pray. Listen, and repeat after me: 'Our Father.' "

And the first old man repeated after him, "Our Father," and the second said, "Our Father," and the third said, "Our Father."

"Which art in heaven," continued the Bishop.

The first hermit repeated, "Which art in heaven," but the second blundered over the words, and the tall hermit could not say them properly. His hair had grown over his mouth so that he could not speak plainly. The very old hermit, having no teeth, also mumbled indistinctly.

The Bishop repeated the words again, and the old men repeated them after him. The Bishop sat down on a stone, and the old men stood before him, watching his mouth, and repeating the words as he uttered them. And all day long the Bishop laboured, saying a word twenty, thirty, a hundred times over, and the old men repeated it after him. They blundered, and he corrected them, and made them begin again.

The Bishop did not leave off till he had taught them the whole of the Lord's Prayer so that they could not only repeat it after him, but could say it by themselves. The middle one was the first to know it, and to repeat the whole of it alone. The Bishop made him say it again and again, and at last the others could say it too.

It was getting dark and the moon was appearing over the water, before the Bishop rose to return to the vessel. When he took leave of the old men they all bowed down to the ground before him. He raised them, and kissed each of them, telling them to pray as he had taught them. Then he got into the boat and returned to the ship.

And as he sat in the boat and was rowed to the ship he could hear the three voices of the hermits loudly repeating the Lord's Prayer. As the boat drew near the vessel their voices could no longer be heard, but they could still be seen in the moonlight, standing as he had left them on the shore, the shortest in the middle, the tallest on the right, the middle one on the left. As soon as the Bishop had reached the vessel and got on board, the anchor was weighed and the sails unfurled. The wind filled them and the ship sailed away, and the Bishop took a seat in the stern and watched the island they had left. For a time he could still see the hermits, but presently they disappeared from sight, though the island was still visible. At last it too vanished, and only the sea was to be seen, rippling in the moonlight.

The pilgrims lay down to sleep, and all was quiet on deck. The Bishop did not wish to sleep, but sat alone at the stern, gazing at the sea where the island was no longer visible, and thinking of the good old men. He thought how pleased they had been to learn the Lord's Prayer; and he thanked God for having sent him to teach and help such godly men.

So the Bishop sat, thinking, and gazing at the sea where the island had disappeared. And the moonlight flickered before his eyes, sparkling, now here, now there, upon the waves. Suddenly he saw something white and shining, on the bright path which the moon cast across the sea. Was it a seagull, or the little gleaming sail of some small boat? The Bishop fixed his eyes on it, wondering.

"It must be a boat sailing after us," thought he, "but it is overtaking us very rapidly. It was far, far away a minute ago, but now it is much nearer. It cannot be a boat, for I can see no sail; but whatever it may be, it is following us and catching up."

And he could not make out what it was. Not a boat, nor a bird, nor a fish! It was too large for a man, and besides a man could not be out there in the midst of the sea. The Bishop rose, and said to the helmsman:

"Look there, what is that, my friend? What is it?" the Bishop repeated, though he could now see plainly what it was — the three hermits running upon the water, all gleaming white, their grey beards shining, and approaching the ship as quickly as though it were not moving.

The steersman looked, and let go the helm in terror.

"Oh Lord! The hermits are running after us on the water as though it were dry land!"

The passengers, hearing him, jumped up and crowded to the stern. They saw the hermits coming along hand in hand, and the two outer ones beckoning the ship to stop. All three were gliding along upon the water without moving their feet. Before the ship could be stopped, the hermits had reached it, and raising their heads, all three as with one voice, began to say:

"We have forgotten your teaching, servant of God. As long as we kept repeating it we remembered, but when we stopped saying it for a time, a word dropped out, and now it has all gone to pieces. We can remember nothing of it. Teach us again."

The Bishop crossed himself, and leaning over the ship's side, said:

"Your own prayer will reach the Lord, men of God. It is not for me to teach you. Pray for us sinners."

And the Bishop bowed low before the old men; and they turned and went back across the sea. And a light shone until daybreak on the spot where they were lost to sight.

Kate Chopin (1851–1904)

The Story of an Hour

Knowing that Mrs. Mallard was afflicted with a heart trouble, great care was taken to break to her as gently as possible the news of her husband's death.

It was her sister Josephine who told her, in broken sentences, veiled hints that revealed in half concealing. Her husband's friend Richards was there, too, near her. It was he who had been in the newspaper office when intelligence of the railroad disaster was received, with Brently Mallard's name leading the list of "killed." He had only taken the time to assure himself of its truth by a second telegram, and had hastened to forestall any less careful, less tender friend in bearing the sad message.

She did not hear the story as many women have heard the same, with a paralyzed inability to accept its significance. She wept at once, with sudden, wild abandonment, in her sister's arms. When the storm of grief had spent itself she went away to her room alone. She would have no one follow her.

There stood, facing the open window, a comfortable, roomy armchair. Into this she sank, pressed down by a physical exhaustion that haunted her body and seemed to reach into her soul.

She could see in the open square before her house the tops of trees that were all aquiver with the new spring life. The delicious breath of rain was in the air. In the street below a peddler was crying his wares. The notes of a distant song which some one was singing reached her faintly, and countless sparrows were twittering in the eaves.

There were patches of blue sky showing here and there through the clouds that had met and piled above the other in the west facing her window.

She sat with her head thrown back upon the cushion of the chair quite motionless, except when a sob came up into her throat and shook her, as a child who has cried itself to sleep continues to sob in its dreams.

She was young, with a fair, calm face, whose lines bespoke repression and even a certain strength. But now there was a dull stare in her eyes, whose gaze was fixed away off yonder on one of those patches of blue sky. It was not a glance of reflection, but rather indicated a suspension of intelligent thought.

There was something coming to her and she was waiting for it, fearfully. What was it? She did not know; it was too subtle and elusive to name. But she felt it, creeping out of the sky, reaching toward her through the sounds, the scents, the color that filled the air.

Now her bosom rose and fell tumultuously. She was beginning to recognize this thing that was approaching to possess her, and she was striving to beat it back with her will — as powerless as her two white slender hands would have been.

When she abandoned herself a little whispered word escaped her slightly parted lips. She said it over and over under her breath: "Free, free, free!" The vacant stare and the look of terror that had followed it went from her eyes. They stayed keen and bright. Her pulses beat fast, and the coursing blood warmed and relaxed every inch of her body.

She did not stop to ask if it were not a monstrous joy that held her. A clear and exalted perception enabled her to dismiss the suggestion as trivial.

She knew that she would weep again when she saw the kind, tender hands folded in death; the face that had never looked save with love upon her, fixed and gray and dead. But she saw beyond that bitter moment a long procession of years to come that would belong to her absolutely. And she opened and spread her arms out to them in welcome.

There would be no one to live for during those coming years; she would live for herself. There would be no powerful will bending her in that blind persistence with which men and women believe they have a right to impose a private will upon a fellow-creature. A kind intention or a cruel intention made the act seem no less a crime as she looked upon it in that brief moment of illumination.

And yet she had loved him — sometimes. Often she had not. What did it matter! What could love, the unsolved mystery, count for in face of this possession of self-assertion which she suddenly recognized as the strongest impulse of her being

"Free! Body and soul free!" she kept whispering.

Josephine was kneeling before the closed door with her lips to the keyhole, imploring for admission. "Louise, open the door! I beg; open the door — you will make yourself ill. What are you doing, Louise? For heaven's sake open the door."

"Go away. I am not making myself ill." No; she was drinking in a very elixir of life through that open window.

Her fancy was running riot along those days ahead of her. Spring days, and summer days, and all sorts of days that would be her own. She breathed a quick prayer that life might be long. It was only yesterday she had thought with a shudder that life might be long.

She arose at length and opened the door to her sister's importunities. There was a feverish triumph in her eyes, and she carried herself unwittingly like a goddess of Victory. She clasped her sister's waist, and together they descended the stairs. Richards stood waiting for them at the bottom.

Some one was opening the front door with a latchkey. It was Brently Mallard who entered, a little travel-stained, composedly carrying his grip-sack and umbrella. He had been far from the scene of accident, and did not even know there had been one. He stood amazed at Josephine's piercing cry; at Richards' quick motion to screen him from the view of his wife.

But Richards was too late.

When the doctors came they said she had died of heart disease — of joy that kills.

Questions

1. Is Mrs. Mallard's grief sincere?
2. In the first half of the story, how does Chopin help to prepare for Mrs. Mallard's words, "Free, free, free"?
3. How accurate is the doctors' final diagnosis?

3 Narrative Point of View

Every story is told by someone. "The Widow of Ephesus" was written by Petronius, but it is told by one Eumolpus, who makes no claim to have witnessed the happening. It might, however, have been told by the lady, or by an outraged moralist. An author must choose a point of view (or several points of view) from which he will narrate his story. His choice is perhaps analogous to the poet's choice of free verse, blank verse, or rhyme, and the choice will contribute to the total effect that the story will have. Eumolpus, the teller of "The Widow of Ephesus," recounts the tale with very little intrusion of himself, but just before the end he analyzes the lady's feelings: "Our lady's heart, however, was no less tender than pure." Now, this wry, inexact, seemingly ingenuous appraisal of her character is largely what gives the story its effect; if the story had been told by a moralist or by the lady herself or by the soldier, it would have been a different story.

Narrative points of view can be divided into two sorts: **participant** (or **first person**) and **nonparticipant** (or **third person**). Each of these two divisions can be subdivided:

    I. Participant (first person)
        A. Narrator as a major character
        B. Narrator as a minor character
    II. Nonparticipant (third person)
        A. Omniscient
        B. Selective omniscient
        C. Objective

PARTICIPANT POINTS OF VIEW

In the story by Frank O'Connor at the end of this chapter the narrator is a major character. He, and not O'Connor, tells the story, and the story is chiefly about him; hence one can say that O'Connor uses a first person (or participant) point of view. O'Connor has invented an Irishman who has fought against the English, and this narrator tells of the impact a happening had on him: "And anything that happened to me afterwards, I never felt the same about again." But sometimes a first-person narrator is telling a story that focuses on someone other than himself; he is a minor character, a peripheral witness, for example, to a story about Jones, and we get the story of Jones filtered through, say, the eyes of Jones's friend or brother or cat. One special kind of first-person narrator (whether major or minor) is the **innocent eye:** the narrator is naive (usually a child, an idiot, or a not-too-bright adult), telling what he sees and feels; the contrast between what he perceives and what the reader understands produces an ironic effect. Such a story, in which the reader understands more than the teller himself does, is Ring Lardner's "Haircut," a story told by a garrulous barber who does not perceive that the "accident" he is describing is in fact a murder.

NONPARTICIPANT POINTS OF VIEW

In a nonparticipant (third-person) point of view, the teller of the tale does not introduce himself as a character. He has receded from the story. If the point of view is **omniscient,** the narrator relates what he wishes about the thoughts as well as the deeds of his characters. When he chooses, the omniscient teller enters the mind of any or all of his characters; whereas the first-person narrator can only say, "I was angry," or "Jones seemed angry to me," the omniscient narrator can say, "Jones was inwardly angry but gave no sign; Smith continued chatting, but he sensed Jones's anger." Furthermore, a distinction can be made between **neutral omniscience** (the narrator recounts deeds and thoughts, but does not judge) and **editorial omniscience** (the narrator not only recounts but judges). The narrator in Hawthorne's "Young Goodman Brown" knows what goes on in the mind of Brown, and he comments approvingly or disapprovingly: "With this excellent resolve for the future, Goodman Brown felt himself justified in making more haste on his present evil purpose." Because a short story can scarcely hope to develop effectively a picture of several minds, an author may prefer to limit his omniscience to the minds of only a few of his characters, or even to one of his characters; that is, he may use **selective omniscience** as his point of view. Selective omniscience provides a focus, especially if it is limited to a single character. When thus limited, the author hovers over the shoulder of one of his characters, seeing him from outside and from inside, and seeing other characters from the outside and from the impact they make upon the mind of this selected receptor. In "Young Goodman Brown" the reader sees things mostly as they make their impact upon the protagonist's mind:

> He could have well-nigh sworn that the shape of his own dead father beckoned him to advance, looking downward from a smoke wreath, while a woman with dim features of despair, threw out her hand to warn him back. Was it his mother? But he had no power to retreat one step, nor to resist, even in thought, when the minister and good old Deacon Gookin seized his arms and led him to the blazing rock.

When selective omniscience attempts to record mental activity ranging from consciousness to unconsciousness, it is sometimes labeled the **stream-of-consciousness** point of view. The following example is from Katherine Anne Porter's "The Jilting of Granny Weatherall":

> Her eyelids wavered and let in streamers of blue-gray light like tissue paper over her eyes. She must get up and pull the shades down or she'd never sleep. She was in bed again and the shades were not down. How could that happen? Better turn over, hide from the light, sleeping in the light gave you nightmares. "Mother, how do you feel now?" and a stinging wetness on her forehead. But I don't like having my face washed in cold water!

In an effort to reproduce the unending activity of the mind, some authors who use the stream-of-consciousness point of view dispense with conventional syntax, punctuation, and logical transitions. The last forty-six pages in James Joyce's *Ulysses* are an unpunctuated flow of one character's thoughts.

Finally, sometimes a third-person narrator does not enter even a single mind, but records only what crosses a dispassionate eye and ear. Such a point of view is **objective** (sometimes called **the camera** or **fly-on-the-wall**). The absence of editorializing and of dissection of the mind often produces the effect of a play; we see and hear the characters in action. Much of Hemingway's "The Short Happy Life of Francis Macomber" is objective, consisting of bits of dialogue that make the story look like a play:

> "Good morning," she said. "Are we going after that lion?"
> "As soon as you deal with your breakfast," Wilson said. "How are you feeling?"

"Marvellous," she said. "I'm very excited."
"I'll just go and see that everything is ready." Wilson went off. As he
left the lion roared again.

But the word "objective" is almost a misnomer, for to describe happenings is — by one's choice of words — to comment on them too,
however unobtrusively. How objective is the point of view if a man is
described as "fat" instead of "stout" or "stout" instead of "heavy" or
"heavy" instead of "two hundred and fifty pounds in weight"? The
objective point of view, even though it expressly enters no mind,
often is a camouflaged version of the selective omniscient point of
view. When Joyce writes, "Maria was a very, very small person indeed but she had a very long nose and a very long chin," he is not
giving us her thought but he is (by his sentence structure and his
repetition of "very") giving us the quality of her rather simple mind;
the description is given in Maria's language though the line gives the
impression of being objectively set down.

THE POINT OF A POINT OF VIEW

Generalizations about the effect of a point of view are risky, but
two have already been made: that the innocent eye can achieve an
ironic effect otherwise unattainable, and that an objective point of
view is dramatic. Three other generalizations are often made: that a
first-person point of view lends a sense of immediacy or reality, that
an omniscient point of view suggests human littleness, and that the
point of view must be consistent. To take the first of these: it is true
that when Poe begins a story "The thousand injuries of Fortunato I
had borne as I best could, but when he ventured upon insult, I vowed
revenge," we feel that the author has gripped us by the lapels; but, on
the other hand, we know that we are only reading a piece of fiction,
and we do not really believe in the existence of the "I" or of Fortunato; and furthermore, when we pick up a story that begins with *any*
point of view we agree (by picking up the book) to pretend to believe
the fictions we are being told. That is, all fiction — whether in the
first person or not — is known to be literally false but is read with the
pretense that it is true. The writer must hold our attention, and make
us feel that his fiction is meaningful, but the use of the first-person
pronoun does not of itself confer reality. The second generalization,
that an omniscient point of view can make puppets of its characters, is
equally misleading; this point of view can also reveal in them a depth
and complexity quite foreign to the idea of human littleness. The
third generalization, that the narrator's point of view must be consis-

tent lest the illusion of reality be shattered, has been much preached
by the followers of Henry James. But E. M. Forster has suggested, in
Aspects of the Novel, that what is important is not consistency but
"the power of the writer to bounce the reader into accepting what he
says." Forster notes that in *Bleak House* Dickens uses in Chapter I
an omniscient point of view, in Chapter II a selective omniscient
point of view, and in Chapter III a first-person point of view. "Logically," Forster says, "*Bleak House* is all to pieces, but Dickens
bounces us, so that we do not mind the shiftings of the view-point."

Perhaps the only sound generalizations possible are that (1) because point of view is one of the things that give form to a story, a
good author chooses the point (or points) of view that he feels best for
his particular story, and (2) the use of any other point of view would
turn the story into a different story.

Frank O'Connor (1903–1966)

Guests of the Nation

I

At dusk the big Englishman, Belcher, would shift his long legs out
of the ashes and say "Well, chums, what about it?" and Noble or me
would say "All right, chum" (for we had picked up some of their
curious expressions), and the little Englishman, Hawkins, would
light the lamp and bring out the cards. Sometimes Jeremiah Donovan
would come up and supervise the game and get excited over Hawkins's cards, which he always played badly, and shout at him as if he
was one of our own "Ah, you divil, you, why didn't you play the
tray?"

But ordinarily Jeremiah was a sober and contented poor devil like
the big Englishman, Belcher, and was looked up to only because he
was a fair hand at documents, though he was slow enough even with
them. He wore a small cloth hat and big gaiters over his long pants,
and you seldom saw him with his hands out of his pockets. He reddened when you talked to him, tilting from toe to heel and back, and
looking down all the time at his big farmer's feet. Noble and me used
to make fun of his broad accent, because we were from the town.

I couldn't at the time see the point of me and Noble guarding
Belcher and Hawkins at all, for it was my belief that you could have
planted that pair down anywhere from this to Claregalway and they'd

have taken root there like a native weed. I never in my short experience seen two men to take to the country as they did.

They were handed on to us by the Second Battalion when the search for them became too hot, and Noble and myself, being young, took over with a natural feeling of responsibility, but Hawkins made us look like fools when he showed that he knew the country better than we did.

"You're the bloke they calls Bonaparte," he says to me. "Mary Brigid O'Connell told me to ask you what you done with the pair of her brother's socks you borrowed."

For it seemed, as they explained it, that the Second used to have little evenings, and some of the girls of the neighborhood turned in, and, seeing they were such decent chaps, our fellows couldn't leave the two Englishmen out of them. Hawkins learned to dance "The Walls of Limerick," "The Siege of Ennis," and "The Waves of Tory" as well as any of them, though, naturally, we couldn't return the compliment, because our lads at that time did not dance foreign dances on principle.

So whatever privileges Belcher and Hawkins had with the Second they just naturally took with us, and after the first day or two we gave up all pretense of keeping a close eye on them. Not that they could have got far, for they had accents you could cut with a knife and wore khaki tunics and overcoats with civilian pants and boots. But it's my belief that they never had any idea of escaping and were quite content to be where they were.

It was a treat to see how Belcher got off with the old woman of the house where we were staying. She was a great warrant to scold, and cranky even with us, but before ever she had a chance of giving our guests, as I may call them, a lick of her tongue, Belcher had made her his friend for life. She was breaking sticks, and Belcher, who hadn't been more than ten minutes in the house, jumped up from his seat and went over to her.

"Allow me, madam," he says, smiling his queer little smile, "please allow me"; and he takes the bloody hatchet. She was struck too paralytic to speak, and after that, Belcher would be at her heels, carrying a bucket, a basket, or a load of turf, as the case might be. As Noble said, he got into looking before she leapt, and hot water, or any little thing she wanted, Belcher would have it ready for her. For such a huge man (and though I am five foot ten myself I had to look up at him) he had an uncommon shortness — or should I say lack? — of speech. It took us some time to get used to him, walking in and out, like a ghost, without a word. Especially because Hawkins talked enough for a platoon, it was strange to hear big Belcher with his toes in the ashes come out with a solitary "Excuse me, chum," or "That's

right, chum." His one and only passion was cards, and I will say for
him that he was a good cardplayer. He could have fleeced myself and
Noble, but whatever we lost to him Hawkins lost to us, and Hawkins
played with the money Belcher gave him.

Hawkins lost to us because he had too much old gab, and we
probably lost to Belcher for the same reason. Hawkins and Noble
would spit at one another about religion into the early hours of the
morning, and Hawkins worried the soul out of Noble, whose brother
was a priest, with a string of questions that would puzzle a cardinal.
To make it worse, even in treating of holy subjects, Hawkins had a
deplorable tongue. I never in all my career met a man who could mix
such a variety of cursing and bad language into an argument. He was
a terrible man, and a fright to argue. He never did a stroke of work,
and when he had no one else to talk to, he got stuck in the old woman.

He met his match in her, for one day when he tried to get her to
complain profanely of the drought, she gave him a great come-down
by blaming it entirely on Jupiter Pluvius (a deity neither Hawkins
nor I had ever heard of, though Noble said that among the pagans it
was believed that he had something to do with the rain). Another day
he was swearing at the capitalists for starting the German war when
the old lady laid down her iron, puckered up her little crab's mouth,
and said: "Mr. Hawkins, you can say what you like about the war, and
think you'll deceive me because I'm only a simple poor country-
woman, but I know what started the war. It was the Italian Count that
stole the heathen divinity out of the temple in Japan. Believe me, Mr.
Hawkins, nothing but sorrow and want can follow the people that
disturb the hidden powers."

A queer old girl, all right.

II

We had our tea one evening, and Hawkins lit the lamp and we all
sat into cards. Jeremiah Donovan came in too, and sat down and
watched us for a while, and it suddenly struck me that he had no great
love for the two Englishmen. It came as a great surprise to me, because I hadn't noticed anything about him before.

Late in the evening a really terrible argument blew up between
Hawkins and Noble, about capitalists and priests and love of your
country.

"The capitalists," says Hawkins with an angry gulp, "pays the
priests to tell you about the next world so as you won't notice what
the bastards are up to in this."

"Nonsense, man!" says Noble, losing his temper. "Before ever a
capitalist was thought of, people believed in the next world."

Hawkins stood up as though he was preaching a sermon.

"Oh, they did, did they?" he says with a sneer. "They believed all the things you believe, isn't that what you mean? And you believe that God created Adam, and Adam created Shem, and Shem created Jehoshaphat. You believe all that silly old fairytale about Eve and Eden and the apple. Well, listen to me, chum. If you're entitled to hold a silly belief like that, I'm entitled to hold my silly belief — which is that the first thing your God created was a bleeding capitalist, with morality and Rolls-Royce complete. Am I right, chum?" he says to Belcher.

"You're right, chum," says Belcher with his amused smile, and got up from the table to stretch his long legs into the fire and stroke his moustache. So, seeing that Jeremiah Donovan was going, and that there was no knowing when the argument about religion would be over, I went out with him. We strolled down to the village together, and then he stopped and started blushing and mumbling and saying I ought to be behind, keeping guard on the prisoners. I didn't like the tone he took with me, and anyway I was bored with life in the cottage, so I replied by asking him what the hell we wanted guarding them at all for. I told him I'd talked it over with Noble, and that we'd both rather be out with a fighting column.

"What use are those fellows to us?" says I.

He looked at me in surprise and said: "I thought you knew we were keeping them as hostages."

"Hostages?" I said.

"The enemy have prisoners belonging to us," he says, "and now they're talking of shooting them. If they shoot our prisoners, we'll shoot theirs."

"Shoot them?" I said.

"What else did you think we were keeping them for?" he says.

"Wasn't it very unforeseen of you not to warn Noble and myself of that in the beginning?" I said.

"How was it?" says he. "You might have known it."

"We couldn't know it, Jeremiah Donovan," says I. "How could we when they were on our hands so long?"

"The enemy have our prisoners as long and longer," says he.

"That's not the same thing at all," says I.

"What difference is there?" says he.

I couldn't tell him, because I knew he wouldn't understand. If it was only an old dog that was going to the vet's, you'd try and not get too fond of him, but Jeremiah Donovan wasn't a man that would ever be in danger of that.

"And when is this thing going to be decided?" says I.

"We might hear tonight," he says. "Or tomorrow or the next day at latest. So if it's only hanging round here that's a trouble to you, you'll be free soon enough."

It wasn't the hanging round that was a trouble to me at all by this time. I had worse things to worry about. When I got back to the cottage the argument was still on. Hawkins was holding forth in his best style, maintaining that there was no next world, and Noble was maintaining that there was; but I could see that Hawkins had had the best of it.

"Do you know what, chum?" he was saying with a saucy smile. "I think you're just as big a bleeding unbeliever as I am. You say you believe in the next world, and you know just as much about the next world as I do, which is sweet damn-all. What's heaven? You don't know. Where's heaven? You don't know. You know sweet damn-all! I ask you again, do they wear wings?"

"Very well, then," says Noble, "they do. Is that enough for you? They do wear wings."

"Where do they get them, then? Who makes them? Have they a factory for wings? Have they a sort of store where you hands in your chit and takes your bleeding wings?"

"You're an impossible man to argue with," says Noble. "Now, listen to me — " And they were off again.

It was long after midnight when we locked up and went to bed. As I blew out the candle I told Noble what Jeremiah Donovan was after telling me. Noble took it very quietly. When we'd been in bed about an hour he asked me did I think we ought to tell the Englishmen. I didn't think we should, because it was more than likely that the English wouldn't shoot our men, and even if they did, the brigade officers, who were always up and down with the Second Battalion and knew the Englishmen well, wouldn't be likely to want them plugged. "I think so too," says Noble. "It would be great cruelty to put the wind up them now."

"It was very unforeseen of Jeremiah Donovan anyhow," says I.

It was next morning that we found it so hard to face Belcher and Hawkins. We went about the house all day scarcely saying a word. Belcher didn't seem to notice; he was stretched into the ashes as usual, with his usual look of waiting in quietness for something unforeseen to happen, but Hawkins noticed and put it down to Noble's being beaten in the argument of the night before.

"Why can't you take a discussion in the proper spirit?" he says severely. "You and your Adam and Eve! I'm a Communist, that's what I am. Communist or anarchist, it all comes to much the same thing." And for hours he went round the house, muttering when the fit took him. "Adam and Eve! Adam and Eve! Nothing better to do with their time than picking bleeding apples!"

III

I don't know how we got through that day, but I was very glad when it was over, the tea things were cleared away, and Belcher said in his peaceable way: "Well, chums, what about it?" We sat round the table and Hawkins took out the cards, and just then I heard Jeremiah Donovan's footstep on the path and a dark presentiment crossed my mind. I rose from the table and caught him before he reached the door.

"What do you want?" I asked.

"I want those two soldier friends of yours," he says, getting red.

"Is that the way, Jeremiah Donovan?" I asked.

"That's the way. There were four of our lads shot this morning, one of them a boy of sixteen."

"That's bad," I said.

At that moment Noble followed me out, and the three of us walked down the path together, talking in whispers. Feeney, the local intelligence officer, was standing by the gate.

"What are you going to do about it?" I asked Jeremiah Donovan.

"I want you and Noble to get them out; tell them they're being shifted again; that'll be the quietest way."

"Leave me out of that," says Noble under his breath.

Jeremiah Donovan looks at him hard.

"All right," he says. "You and Feeney get a few tools from the shed and dig a hole by the far end of the bog. Bonaparte and myself will be after you. Don't let anyone see you with the tools. I wouldn't like it to go beyond ourselves."

We saw Feeney and Noble go round to the shed and went in ourselves. I left Jeremiah Donovan to do the explanations. He told them that he had orders to send them back to the Second Battalion. Hawkins let out a mouthful of curses, and you could see that though Belcher didn't say anything, he was a bit upset too. The old woman was for having them stay in spite of us, and she didn't stop advising them until Jeremiah Donovan lost his temper and turned on her. He had a nasty temper, I noticed. It was pitch-dark in the cottage by this time, but no one thought of lighting the lamp, and in the darkness the two Englishmen fetched their topcoats and said good-bye to the old woman.

"Just as a man makes a home of a bleeding place, some bastard at headquarters thinks you're too cushy and shunts you off," says Hawkins, shaking her hand.

"A thousand thanks, madam," says Belcher. "A thousand thanks for everything" — as though he'd made it up.

We went round to the back of the house and down towards the

bog. it was only then that Jeremiah Donovan told them. He was shaking with excitement.

"There were four of our fellows shot in Cork this morning and now you're to be shot as a reprisal."

"What are you talking about?" snaps Hawkins. "It's bad enough being mucked about as we are without having to put up with your funny jokes."

"It isn't a joke," says Donovan. "I'm sorry, Hawkins, but it's true," and begins on the usual rigmarole about duty and how unpleasant it is.

I never noticed that people who talk a lot about duty find it much of a trouble to them.

"Oh, cut it out!" says Hawkins.

"Ask Bonaparte," says Donovan, seeing that Hawkins isn't taking him seriously. "Isn't it true, Bonaparte?"

"It is," I say, and Hawkins stops.

"Ah, for Christ's sake, chum."

"I mean it, chum," I say.

"You don't sound as if you meant it."

"If he doesn't mean it, I do," says Donovan, working himself up.

"What have you against me, Jeremiah Donovan?"

"I never said I had anything against you. But why did your people take out four of our prisoners and shoot them in cold blood?"

He took Hawkins by the arm and dragged him on, but it was impossible to make him understand that we were in earnest. I had the Smith and Wesson in my pocket and I kept fingering it and wondering what I'd do if they put up a fight for it or ran, and wishing to God they'd do one or the other. I knew if they did run for it, that I'd never fire on them. Hawkins wanted to know was Noble in it, and when we said yes, he asked us why Noble wanted to plug him. Why did any of us want to plug him? What had he done to us? Weren't we all chums? Didn't we understand him and didn't he understand us? Did we imagine for an instant that he'd shoot us for all the so-and-so officers in the so-and-so British Army?

By this time we'd reached the bog, and I was so sick I couldn't even answer him. We walked along the edge of it in the darkness, and every now and then Hawkins would call a halt and begin all over again, as if he was wound up, about our being chums, and I knew that nothing but the sight of the grave would convince him that we had to do it. And all the time I was hoping that something would happen; that they'd run for it or that Noble would take over the responsibility from me. I had the feeling that it was worse on Noble than on me.

IV

At last we saw the lantern in the distance and made towards it. Noble was carrying it, and Feeney was standing somewhere in the darkness behind him, and the picture of them so still and silent in the bogland brought it home to me that we were in earnest, and banished the last bit of hope I had.

Belcher, on recognizing Noble, said: "Hallo, chum," in his quiet way, but Hawkins flew at him at once, and the argument began all over again, only this time Noble had nothing to say for himself and stood with his head down, holding the lantern between his legs.

It was Jeremiah Donovan who did the answering. For the twentieth time, as though it was haunting his mind, Hawkins asked if anybody thought he'd shoot Noble.

"Yes, you would," says Jeremiah Donovan.

"No, I wouldn't, damn you!"

"You would, because you'd know you'd be shot for not doing it."

"I wouldn't, not if I was to be shot twenty times over. I wouldn't shoot a pal. And Belcher wouldn't — isn't that right, Belcher?"

"That's right, chum," Belcher said, but more by way of answering the question than of joining in the argument. Belcher sounded as though whatever unforeseen thing he'd always been waiting for had come at last.

"Anyway, who says Noble would be shot if I wasn't? What do you think I'd do if I was in his place, out in the middle of a blasted bog?"

"What would you do?" asks Donovan.

"I'd go with him wherever he was going, of course. Share my last bob with him and stick by him through thick and thin. No one can ever say of me that I let down a pal."

"We had enough of this," says Jeremiah Donovan, cocking his revolver. "Is there any message you want to send?"

"No, there isn't."

"Do you want to say your prayers?"

Hawkins came out with a cold-blooded remark that even shocked me and turned on Noble again.

"Listen to me, Noble," he says. "You and me are chums. You can't come over to my side, so I'll come over to your side. That show you I mean what I say? Give me a rifle and I'll go along with you and the other lads."

Nobody answered him. We knew that was no way out.

"Hear what I'm saying?" he says. "I'm through with it. I'm a deserter or anything else you like. I don't believe in your stuff, but it's no worse then mine. That satisfy you?"

Noble raised his head, but Donovan began to speak and he lowered it again without replying.

"For the last time, have you any messages to send?" says Donovan in a cold, excited sort of voice.

"Shut up, Donovan! You don't understand me, but these lads do. They're not the sort to make a pal and kill a pal. They're not the tools of any capitalist."

I alone of the crowd saw Donovan raise his Webley to the back of Hawkins's neck, and as he did so I shut my eyes and tried to pray. Hawkins had begun to say something else when Donovan fired, and as I opened my eyes at the bang, I saw Hawkins stagger at the knees and lie out flat at Noble's feet, slowly and as quiet as a kid falling asleep, with the lantern-light on his lean legs and bright farmer's boots. We all stood very still, watching him settle out in the last agony.

Then Belcher took out a handkerchief and began to tie it about his own eyes (in our excitement we'd forgotten to do the same for Hawkins), and, seeing it wasn't big enough, turned and asked for the loan of mine. I gave it to him and he knotted the two together and pointed with his foot at Hawkins.

"He's not quite dead," he says. "Better give him another."

Sure enough, Hawkins's left knee is beginning to rise. I bend down and put my gun to his head; then, recollecting myself, I get up again. Belcher understands what's in my mind.

"Give him his first," he says. "I don't mind. Poor bastard, we don't know what's happening to him now."

I knelt and fired. By this time I didn't seem to know what I was doing. Belcher, who was fumbling a bit awkwardly with the handkerchiefs, came out with a laugh as he heard the shot. It was the first time I heard him laugh and it sent a shudder down my back; it sounded so unnatural.

"Poor bugger!" he said quietly. "And last night he was so curious about it all. It's very queer, chums, I always think. Now he knows as much about it as they'll ever let him know, and last night he was all in the dark."

Donovan helped him to tie the handkerchiefs about his eyes. "Thanks, chum," he said. Donovan asked if there were any messages he wanted sent.

"No, chum," he says. "Not for me. If any of you would like to write to Hawkins's mother, you'll find a letter from her in his pocket. He and his mother were great chums. But my missus left me eight years ago. Went away with another fellow and took the kid with her. I like the feeling of a home, as you may have noticed, but I couldn't start again after that."

It was an extraordinary thing, but in those few minutes Belcher said more than in all the weeks before. It was just as if the sound of the shot had started a flood of talk in him and he could go on the whole night like that, quite happily, talking about himself. We stood round like fools now that he couldn't see us any longer. Donovan looked at Noble, and Noble shook his head. Then Donovan raised his Webley, and at that moment Belcher gives his queer laugh again. He may have thought we were talking about him, or perhaps he noticed the same thing I'd noticed and couldn't understand it.

"Excuse me, chums," he says. "I feel I'm talking the hell of a lot, and so silly, about my being so handy about a house and things like that. But this thing came on me suddenly. You'll forgive me, I'm sure."

"You don't want to say a prayer?" asked Donovan.

"No, chum," he says. "I don't think it would help. I'm ready, and you boys want to get it over."

"You understand that we're only doing our duty?" says Donovan.

Belcher's head was raised like a blind man's, so that you could only see his chin and the tip of his nose in the lantern-light.

"I never could make out what duty was myself," he said. "I think you're all good lads, if that's what you mean. I'm not complaining."

Noble, just as if he couldn't bear any more of it, raised his fist at Donovan, and in a flash Donovan raised his gun and fired. The big man went over like a sack of meal, and this time there was no need of a second shot.

I don't remember much about the burying, but that it was worse than all the rest because we had to carry them to the grave. It was all mad lonely with nothing but a patch of lantern-light between ourselves and the dark, and birds hooting and screeching all round, disturbed by the guns. Noble went through Hawkins's belongings to find the letter from his mother, and then joined his hands together. He did the same with Belcher. Then, when we'd filled in the grave, we separated from Jeremiah Donovan and Feeney and took our tools back to the shed. All the way we didn't speak a word. The kitchen was dark and cold as we'd left it, and the old woman was sitting over the hearth, saying her beads. We walked past her into the room, and Noble struck a match to light the lamp. She rose quietly and came to the doorway with all her cantankerousness gone.

"What did ye do with them?" she asked in a whisper, and Noble started so that the match went out in his hand.

"What's that?" he asked without turning round.

"I heard ye," she said.

"What did you hear?" asked Noble.

"I heard ye. Do ye think I didn't hear ye, putting the spade back in the houseen?"

Noble struck another match and this time the lamp lit for him. "Was that what ye did to them?" she asked.

Then, by God, in the very doorway, she fell on her knees and began praying, and after looking at her for a minute or two Noble did the same by the fireplace. I pushed my way out past her and left them at it. I stood at the door, watching the stars and listening to the shrieking of the birds dying out over the bogs. It is so strange what you feel at times like that you can't describe it. Noble says he saw everything ten times the size, as though there were nothing in the whole world but that little patch of bog with the two Englishmen stiffening into it, but with me it was as if the patch of bog where the Englishmen were was a million miles away, and even Noble and the old woman, mumbling behind me, and the birds and the bloody stars were all far away, and I was somehow very small and very lost and lonely like a child astray in the snow. And anything that happened to me afterwards, I never felt the same about again.

Questions

1. Although the narrator, Noble, and Donovan are all patriotic Irishmen, Donovan's attitude toward the English prisoners is quite different from that of the other two. How does that difference in attitude help point up the story's theme?

2. How does the constant bickering between Noble and Hawkins help to prepare us for the conclusion of the story? How does it contribute to the theme?

3. When he hears he is about to be shot, Hawkins, to save his life, volunteers to join the Irish cause. Is his turnabout simply evidence of his cowardice and hypocrisy? Explain.

4. Throughout most of the story Belcher is shy and speaks little; just before his execution, however, he suddenly becomes loquacious. Is he trying to stall for time? Would it have been more in character for Belcher to have remained stoically taciturn to the end, or do the narrator's remarks about Belcher's change make it plausible?

5. Does the old woman's presence in the story merely furnish local color or picturesqueness? If so, is it necessary or desirable? Or does her presence further contribute to the story's meaning? If so, how?

6. The following is the last paragraph of an earlier version:

So then, by God, she fell on her two knees by the door, and began telling her beads, and after a minute or two Noble went on his knees by the fireplace, so I pushed my way past her, and stood at the door, watching the stars and listening to the damned shrieking of the birds. It is so strange what you feel at such moments, and not to be written afterwards. Noble says he felt he seen everything ten times as big, perceiving nothing around him but the little patch of black bog with the two Englishmen stiffening into it; but with me it was the other way, as though the patch of bog where the two Englishmen were was a thousand miles away from me, and even Noble mumbling just behind me and the old woman and the birds and the bloody stars were all far away, and I was somehow very small and very lonely. And anything that ever happened me after I never felt the same about again.

Which is the more effective conclusion? Why?

7. How does the point of view help to emphasize the narrator's development from innocence to awareness? If the story had been told in the third person, how would it have affected the story's impact?

4 Allegory and Symbolism

In Chapter 2 we looked at some fables and parables, short fictions that were evidently meant to teach us: the characters clearly stood for principles of behavior, and the fictions as a whole evidently taught us lessons. Closely related to these forms is the **allegory**, which presents items that are understood to have equivalents: Bunyan's allegory, *The Pilgrim's Progress*, tells of a man named Christian, who, on the road to the Celestial City, encounters, among others, Giant Despair, Mr. Worldly Wiseman, and Faithful. What these are equivalent to is clear from their names, and it is clear that Christian's journey stands for the trials of a soul in this world.

Modern short stories rarely have either the parable's explicit moral or the allegory's clear system of equivalents, but they nevertheless can be said to be about something. As Robert Frost once said, "There is no story written that has any value at all, however straightforward it looks and free from doubleness, double entendre, and duplicity and double play, that you'd value at all if it didn't have intimations of something more than itself." Such a detailed, realistic story as "Guests of the Nation" may be a very good picture of Irish military life, but it also implies or suggests things not limited to this subject. This is not to say that after reading the story we discard the richly detailed narrative in favor of some abstraction that it implies — we do not throw away the narrative and cling to the implication. Frost went on to say, "The anecdote, the parable, the surface meaning has got to be good and got to be sufficient in itself." We feel that the narrative is meaningful. "Guests of the Nation" presents abundant precise details, and these details somehow add up to give the stories a generality or universality. The numerous details are so inter-related that they are a revelation of what is otherwise inexpressible.

In "Guests of the Nation" the narrative forces into the edges of our minds thoughts of the inhumanity of officialdom, the power of hatred, the average man's impotence, the power of friendship, and the enor-mous aftereffect a deed can have. These thoughts are sharply con-trolled by the details of the story, and they do not separate them-selves from the details. But the thoughts are there, though we scarcely think of them; in the story they are just under the surface. Quite properly we take small notice of the substratum and concentrate on the surface details. But in other stories — such as parables and alle-gories — the details are so presented that we are forced to look from them to their implied equivalents. Between these two extremes, writ-ing that is almost all surface and writing that is almost all implication, are stories in which we strongly feel both the surface happenings and their implication. In *Place in Fiction*, Eudora Welty uses an image of a china lamp that unlit showed London and lit showed the Great Fire of London to explain literature that presents an interesting surface texture filled with rich significance. Though she is talking about the novel, her words apply equally to the short story, as a reading of her story, "Livvie" (page 70), will show. Like a painted porcelain lamp which, when illuminated, reveals an inner picture shining through the outer, the physical details in a work are illuminated from within by the author's imaginative vision. The outer painting, the literal details, presents "a continuous, shapely, pleasing, and finished sur-face to the eye," but this surface is not the whole: "The lamp alight is the combination of internal and external, glowing at the imagination as one; and so is the good novel. . . . The good novel should be steadily alight, revealing."

The unified picture, the details and what they suggest by virtue of the inner illumination with which the artist endows them, constitutes the symbolic level of a piece of literature. Here is Ishmael, in *Moby Dick*, perceiving the symbolic meaning of Father Mapple's ascent into the pulpit:

> I was not prepared to see Father Mapple after gaining the height, slowly turn round, and stooping over the pulpit, deliberately drag up the ladder step by step, till the whole was deposited within, leaving him impregnable in his little Quebec.
>
> I pondered some time without fully comprehending the reason for this. Father Mapple enjoyed such a wide reputation for sincerity and sanctity, that I could not suspect him of courting notoriety by any mere tricks of the stage. No, thought I, there must be some sober reason for this thing; furthermore, it must symbolize something unseen. Can it be,

then, that by that act of physical isolation, he signifies his spiritual
withdrawal from the time, from all outward worldly ties and connections? Yes, for replenished with the meat and wine of the world, to the
faithful man of God, this pulpit, I see, is a self-containing stronghold —
a lofty Ehrenbreitstein, with a perennial well of water within the walls.

Ishmael's interpretation strikes the reader as well-stated and convincing, but many symbolic interpretations of literature (especially of
Moby Dick) are neither. An ingenious reader may overcomplicate or
overemphasize the symbolism of a work, or he may distort it by
omitting some of the details and by unduly focusing on others. In
many works the details glow, but the glow is so gentle and subtle that
even to talk about them is to overstate them and to understate other
equally important aspects of the work.

Yet if it is false to overstate the significance of a detail, it is also
false to understate a significant detail. For example, the let's-have-no-
nonsense literal reader who holds that Faulkner's "The Bear" (which
appears later in this chapter) is only an adventure story about a bear
hunt impoverishes the story by neglecting the rich symbolic meaning
just as much as the symbol-hunter impoverishes O'Connor's "Guests
of the Nation" by slighting the literal meaning. Faulkner's insistence
on the bear's magnificence (the beast is compared to King Priam, to a
locomotive, to an immortal creature) compels the reader to attend to
its symbolic meaning, as does his insistence that not until "the three
lifeless mechanicals" (the watch, the compass, and the stick) are surrendered can the bear be fully seen. Near the end of the story Faulkner underlines the symbolic quality by having the boy's father explain that Keats's "Ode on a Grecian Urn" is not (as the son says) only
"about a girl"; the talk about a girl, the father goes on, is a vehicle by
which Keats communicates an insight about truth. "He had to talk
about something. . . . He was talking about truth." Faulkner, too, had
to talk about something in order to communicate his insight, so he
chose as a meaningful vehicle a bear hunt.

There has been a tendency, for about a century and a half now, to
call **allegoric** those works whose images have precise equivalents
that can be paraphrased with some accuracy, and to call **symbolic**
those works whose images cast long shadows, give off multiple suggestions that do not allow for easy substitutions. This view might turn
Father Mapple's gesture into an allegory and *Moby Dick* (which Melville called an allegory) into a symbolic work. D. H. Lawrence's
pronouncement can serve as an example of modern usage:

You can't give a great symbol a "meaning," any more than you can give
a cat a "meaning." Symbols are organic units of consciousness with a

life of their own, and you can never explain them away, because their value is dynamic, emotional, belonging to the sense-consciousness of the body and soul, and not simply mental. An allegorical image has a *meaning*. Mr. Facing-both-ways has a meaning. But I defy you to lay your finger on the full meaning of Janus, who is a symbol.

Whether or not we like the modern distinction between allegory and symbol (much that today is called symbolic was in the Middle Ages called allegorical), the distinction seems here to stay. But we should recall that every piece of art — including allegory as well as writing that might be called "realistic" — is, in Robert Frost's words, "a symbol small or great of the way the will has to pitch into commitments deeper and deeper to a rounded conclusion."

A NOTE ON SETTING

The **setting** of a story — not only the physical locale but also the time of day or year or century — may or may not be symbolic. Sometimes the setting is lightly sketched, presented only because the story had to take place somewhere and at some time. Often, however, the setting is more important, giving us the feel of the people who move through it. But if scenery is drawn in detail, yet adds up to nothing, we share the impatience Robert Louis Stevenson expressed in a letter: " 'Roland approached the house; it had green doors and window blinds; and there was a scraper on the upper step.' To hell with Roland and the scraper." Yes, of course; but if the green doors and the scraper were to tell us something about the tenant, they could be important. And it might even be that the green doors and the scraper were so important that the story would be more or less about them. As the novelist Elizabeth Bowen has said, "Nothing can happen nowhere. The locale of the happening always colors the happening, and often, to a degree, shapes it." A rocky New England farm may be an analogue to the farmer who cultivates it, and the story may be as much about the farm as about the farmer. An obvious example is the setting in Thomas Hardy's *The Return of the Native.* Oppressive Egdon Heath is so much a part of the novel that it almost takes on the role of a major character and, in large part, it is made responsible for the tragic fate of the novel's characters.

Though the wilderness in "The Bear" is described in little detail, it is not mere background but an important part of what the story is about. Take, for example, the following passage:

On the second day he even found the gutted log where he had first seen the crooked print. It was almost completely crumbled now, healing with unbelievable speed, a passionate and almost visible relinquishment, back into the earth from which the tree had grown.

This is not just local color: it is also one of the ways by which Faulkner talks about the importance of contact with nature; it helps us
understand what is involved when (a page or two later) the boy

> . . . stood for a moment, alien and small in the green and topless soli
> tude. . . . He hung the watch and compass carefully on a bush and
> leaned the stick beside them and relinquished completely to it.

It is no accident that "relinquish" appears in both passages; like the
gutted log, the boy derives his vitality by merging himself with the
wilderness. What the wilderness stands for is something that can be
grasped only by reading the story.

William Faulkner (1897–1962)

The Bear

He was ten. But it had already begun, long before that day when at
last he wrote his age in two figures and he saw for the first time the
camp where his father and Major de Spain and old General Compson
and the others spent two weeks each November and two weeks again
each June. He had already inherited then, without ever having seen
it, the tremendous bear with one trap-ruined foot which, in an area
almost a hundred miles deep, had earned itself a name, a definite
designation like a living man.

He had listened to it for years: the long legend of corncribs rifled,
of shotes and grown pigs and even calves carried bodily into the
woods and devoured, of traps and deadfalls overthrown and dogs
mangled and slain, and shotgun and even rifle charges delivered at
point-blank range and with no more effect than so many peas blown
through a tube by a boy — a corridor of wreckage and destruction
beginning back before he was born, through which sped, not fast but
rather with the ruthless and irresistible deliberation of a locomotive,
the shaggy tremendous shape.

It ran in his knowledge before he ever saw it. It loomed and towered in his dreams before he even saw the unaxed woods where it left
its crooked print, shaggy, huge, red-eyed, not malevolent but just

big — too big for the dogs which tried to bay it, for the horses which tried to ride it down, for the men and the bullets they fired into it, too big for the very country which was its constricting scope. He seemed to see it entire with a child's complete divination before he ever laid eyes on either — the doomed wilderness whose edges were being constantly and punily gnawed at by men with axes and plows who feared it because it was wilderness, men myriad and nameless even to one another in the land where the old bear had earned a name, through which ran not even a mortal animal but an anachronism, indomitable and invincible, out of an old dead time, a phantom, epitome and apotheosis of the old wild life at which the puny humans swarmed and hacked in a fury of abhorrence and fear, like pygmies about the ankles of a drowsing elephant: the old bear solitary, indomitable and alone, widowered, childless, and absolved of mortality — old Priam reft of his old wife and having outlived all his sons.

Until he was ten, each November he would watch the wagon containing the dogs and the bedding and food and guns and his father and Tennie's Jim, the Negro, and Sam Fathers, the Indian, son of a slave woman and a Chickasaw chief, depart on the road to town, to Jefferson, where Major de Spain and the others would join them. To the boy, at seven, eight, and nine, they were not going into the Big Bottom to hunt bear and deer, but to keep yearly rendezvous with the bear which they did not even intend to kill. Two weeks later they would return, with no trophy, no head and skin. He had not expected it. He had not even been afraid it would be in the wagon. He believed that even after he was ten and his father would let him go too, for those two weeks in November, he would merely make another one, along with his father and Major de Spain and General Compson and the others, the dogs which feared to bay at it and the rifles and shotguns which failed even to bleed it, in the yearly pageant of the old bear's furious immortality.

Then he heard the dogs. It was in the second week of his first time in the camp. He stood with Sam Fathers against a big oak beside the faint crossing where they had stood each dawn for nine days now, hearing the dogs. He had heard them once before, one morning last week — a murmur, sourceless, echoing through the wet woods, swelling presently into separate voices which he could recognize and call by name. He had raised and cocked the gun as Sam told him and stood motionless again while the uproar, the invisible course, swept up and past and faded; it seemed to him that he could actually see the deer, the buck, blond, smoke-colored, elongated with speed, fleeing, vanishing, the woods, the gray solitude, still ringing even when the cries of the dogs had died away.

"Now let the hammers down," Sam said.

"You knew they were not coming here too," he said.

"Yes," Sam said. "I want you to learn how to do when you didn't shoot. It's after the chance for the bear or the deer has done already come and gone that men and dogs get killed."

"Anyway," he said, "it was just a deer."

Then on the tenth morning he heard the dogs again. And he readied the too-long, too-heavy gun as Sam had taught him, before Sam even spoke. But this time it was no deer, no ringing chorus of dogs running strong on a free scent, but a moiling yapping an octave too high, with something more than indecision and even abjectness in it, not even moving very fast, taking a long time to pass completely out of hearing, leaving then somewhere in the air that echo, thin, slightly hysterical, abject, almost grieving, with no sense of a fleeting, unseen, smoke-colored, grass-eating shape ahead of it, and Sam, who had taught him first of all to cock the gun and take position where he could see everywhere and then never move again, had himself moved up beside him; he could hear Sam breathing at his shoulder, and he could see the arched curve of the old man's inhaling nostrils.

"Hah," Sam said. "Not even running. Walking."

"Old Ben!" the boy said. "But up here!" he cried. "Way up here!"

"He do it every year," Sam said. "Once. Maybe to see who in camp this time, if he can shoot or not. Whether we got the dog yet that can bay and hold him. He'll take them to the river, then he'll send them back home. We may as well go back too; see how they look when they come back to camp."

When they reached the camp the hounds were already there, ten of them crouching back under the kitchen, the boy and Sam squatting to peer back into the obscurity where they had huddled, quiet, the eyes luminous, glowing at them and vanishing, and no sound, only that effluvium of something more than dog, stronger than dog and not just animal, just beast, because still there had been nothing in front of that abject and almost painful yapping save the solitude, the wilderness, so that when the eleventh hound came in at noon and with all the others watching — even old Uncle Ash, who called himself first a cook — Sam daubed the tattered ear and the raked shoulder with turpentine and axle grease, to the boy it was still no living creature, but the wilderness which, leaning for the moment down, had patted lightly once the hound's temerity.

"Just like a man," Sam said. "Just like folks. Put off as long as she could having to be brave, knowing all the time that sooner or later she would have to be brave to keep on living with herself, and knowing all the time beforehand what was going to happen to her when she done it."

That afternoon, himself on the one-eyed wagon mule which did not mind the smell of blood nor, as they told him, of bear, and with Sam on the other one, they rode for more than three hours through the rapid, shortening winter day. They followed no path, no trail even that he could see; almost at once they were in a country which he had never seen before. Then he knew why Sam had made him ride the mule which would not spook. The sound one stopped short and tried to whirl and bolt even as Sam got down, blowing its breath, jerking and wrenching at the rein, while Sam held it, coaxing it forward with his voice, since he could not risk tying it, drawing it forward while the boy got down from the marred one.

Then, standing beside Sam in the gloom of the dying afternoon, he looked down at the rotted over-turned log, gutted and scored with claw marks and, in the wet earth beside it, the print of the enormous warped two-toed foot. He knew now what he had smelled when he peered under the kitchen where the dogs huddled. He realized for the first time that the bear which had run in his listening and loomed in his dreams since before he could remember to the contrary, and which, therefore, must have existed in the listening and dreams of his father and Major de Spain and even old General Compson, too, before they began to remember in their turn, was a mortal animal, and that if they had departed for the camp each November without any actual hope of bringing its trophy back, it was not because it could not be slain, but because so far they had had no actual hope to.

"Tomorrow," he said.

"We'll try tomorrow," Sam said. "We ain't got the dog yet."

"We've got eleven. They ran him this morning."

"It won't need but one," Sam said. "He ain't here. Maybe he ain't nowhere. The only other way will be for him to run by accident over somebody that has a gun."

"That wouldn't be me," the boy said. "It will be Walter or Major or — "

"It might," Sam said. "You watch close in the morning. Because he's smart. That's how come he has lived this long. If he gets hemmed up and has to pick out somebody to run over, he will pick out you."

"How?" the boy said. "How will he know — " He ceased. "You mean he already knows me, that I ain't never been here before, ain't had time to find out yet whether I — " He ceased again, looking at Sam, the old man whose face revealed nothing until it smiled. He said humbly, not even amazed. "It was me he was watching. I don't reckon he did need to come but once."

The next morning they left the camp three hours before daylight. They rode this time because it was too far to walk, even the dogs in the wagon; again the first gray light found him in a place which he had never seen before, where Sam had placed him and told him to stay and then departed. With the gun which was too big for him, which did not even belong to him, but to Major de Spain, and which he had fired only once — at a stump on the first day, to learn the recoil and how to reload it — he stood against a gum tree beside a little bayou whose black still water crept without movement out of a canebrake and crossed a small clearing and into cane again, where, invisible, a bird — the big woodpecker called Lord-to-God by Negroes — clattered at a dead limb.

It was a stand like any other, dissimilar only in incidentals to the one where he had stood each morning for ten days; a territory new to him, yet no less familiar than that other one which, after almost two weeks, he had come to believe he knew a little — the same solitude, the same loneliness through which human beings had merely passed without altering it, leaving no mark, no scar, which looked exactly as it must have looked when the first ancestor of Sam Fathers' Chickasaw predecessors crept into it and looked about, club or stone ax or bone arrow drawn and poised; different only because, squatting at the edge of the kitchen, he smelled the hounds huddled and cringing beneath it and saw the raked ear and shoulder of the one who, Sam said, had had to be brave once in order to live with herself, and saw yesterday in the earth beside the gutted log the print of the living foot.

He heard no dogs at all. He never did hear them. He only heard the drumming of the woodpecker stop short off and knew that the bear was looking at him. He never saw it. He did not know whether it was in front of him or behind him. He did not move, holding the useless gun, which he had not even had warning to cock and which even now he did not cock, tasting in his saliva that taint as of brass which he knew now because he had smelled it when he peered under the kitchen at the huddled dogs.

Then it was gone. As abruptly as it had ceased, the woodpecker's dry, monotonous clatter set up again, and after a while he even believed he could hear the dogs — a murmur, scarce a sound even, which he had probably been hearing for some time before he even remarked it, drifting into hearing and then out again, dying away. They came nowhere near him. If it was a bear they ran, it was another bear. It was Sam himself who came out of the cane and crossed the bayou, followed by the injured bitch of yesterday. She was almost at heel, like a bird dog, making no sound. She came and crouched against his leg, trembling, staring off into the cane.

"I didn't see him," he said. "I didn't, Sam!"

"I know it," Sam said. "He done the looking. You didn't hear him neither, did you?"

"No," the boy said. "I — "

"He's smart," Sam said. "Too smart." He looked down at the hound, trembling faintly and steadily against the boy's knee. From the raked shoulder a few drops of fresh blood oozed and clung. "Too big. We ain't got the dog yet. But maybe someday. Maybe not next time. But someday."

So I must see him, he thought. *I must look at him.* Otherwise, it seemed to him that it would go on like this forever, as it had gone on with his father and Major de Spain, who was older than his father, and even with old General Compson, who had been old enough to be a brigade commander in 1865. Otherwise, it would go on so forever, next time and next time, after and after and after. It seemed to him that he could never see the two of them, himself and the bear, shadowy in the limbo from which time emerged, becoming time; the old bear absolved of mortality and himself partaking, sharing a little of it, enough of it. And he knew now what he had smelled in the huddled dogs and tasted in his saliva. He recognized fear. *So I will have to see him,* he thought, without dread or even hope. *I will have to look at him.*

It was in June of the next year. He was eleven. They were in camp again, celebrating Major de Spain's and General Compson's birthdays. Although the one had been born in September and the other in the depth of winter and in another decade, they had met for two weeks to fish and shoot squirrels and turkey and run coons and wildcats with the dogs at night. That is, he and Boon Hoggenbeck and the Negroes fished and shot squirrels and ran the coons and cats, because the proved hunters, not only Major de Spain and old General Compson, who spent those two weeks sitting in a rocking chair before a tremendous iron pot of Brunswick stew, stirring and tasting, with old Ash to quarrel with about how he was making it and Tennie's Jim to pour whiskey from the demijohn into the tin dipper from which he drank it, but even the boy's father and Walter Ewell, who were still young enough, scorned such, other than shooting the wild gobblers with pistols for wagers on their marksmanship.

Or, that is, his father and the others believed he was hunting squirrels. Until the third day, he thought that Sam Fathers believed that too. Each morning he would leave the camp right after breakfast. He had his own gun now, a Christmas present. He went back to the tree beside the bayou where he had stood that morning. Using the compass which old General Compson had given him, he ranged from that point; he was teaching himself to be a better-than-fair woodsman without knowing he was doing it. On the second day he even found the gutted log where he had first seen the crooked print. It was almost completely crumbled now, healing with unbelievable speed, a passionate and almost visible relinquishment, back into the earth from which the tree had grown.

He ranged the summer woods now, green with gloom; if anything, actually dimmer than in November's gray dissolution, where, even at noon, the sun fell only in intermittent dappling upon the earth, which never completely dried out and which crawled with snakes — moccasins and water snakes and rattlers, themselves the color of the dappling gloom, so that he would not always see them until they moved, returning later and later, first day, second day, passing in the twilight of the third evening the little log pen enclosing the log stable where Sam was putting up the horses for the night.

"You ain't looked right yet," Sam said.

He stopped. For a moment he didn't answer. Then he said peacefully, in a peaceful rushing burst as when a boy's miniature dam in a little brook gives way, "All right. But how? I went to the bayou. I even found that log again. I — "

"I reckon that was all right. Likely he's been watching you. You never saw his foot?"

"I," the boy said — "I didn't — I never thought — "

"It's the gun," Sam said. He stood beside the fence motionless — the old man, the Indian, in the battered faded overalls and the five-cent straw hat which in the Negro's race had been the badge of his enslavement and was now the regalia of his freedom. The camp — the clearing, the house, the barn and its tiny lot with which Major de Spain in his turn had scratched punily and evanescently at the wilderness — faded in the dusk, back into the immemorial darkness of the woods. *The gun*, the boy thought. *The gun.*

"Be scared," Sam said. "You can't help that. But don't be afraid. Ain't nothing in the woods going to hurt you unless you corner it, or it smells that you are afraid. A bear or a deer, too, has got to be scared of a coward the same as a brave man has got to be."

The gun, the boy thought.

"You will have to choose," Sam said.

He left the camp before daylight, long before Uncle Ash would wake in his quilts on the kitchen floor and start the fire for breakfast. He had only the compass and a stick for snakes. He could go almost a mile before he would begin to need the compass. He sat on a log, the invisible compass in his invisible hand, while the secret night sounds, fallen still at his movements, scurried again and then ceased for good, and the owls ceased and gave over to the waking of day birds, and he could see the compass. Then he went fast yet still quietly; he was becoming better and better as a woodsman, still without having yet realized it.

He jumped a doe and a fawn at sunrise, walked them out of the bed, close enough to see them — the crash of undergrowth, the white scut, the fawn scudding behind her faster than he had believed it could run. He was hunting right, upwind, as Sam had taught him; not that it mattered now. He had left the gun; of his own will and relinquishment he had accepted not a gambit, not a choice, but a condition in which not only the bear's heretofore inviolable anonymity but all the old rules and balances of hunter and hunted had been abrogated. He would not even be afraid, not even in the moment when the fear would take him completely — blood, skin, bowels, bones, memory from the long time before it became his memory — all save that thin, clear, immortal lucidity which alone differed him from this bear and from all the other bear and deer he would ever kill in the humility and pride of his skill and endurance, to which Sam had spoken when he leaned in the twilight on the lot fence yesterday.

By noon he was far beyond the little bayou, farther into the new and alien country than he had ever been. He was traveling now not only by the compass but by the old, heavy, biscuit-thick silver watch which had belonged to his grandfather. When he stopped at last, it was for the first time since he had risen from the log at dawn when he could see the compass. It was far enough. He had left the camp nine hours ago; nine hours from now, dark would have already been an hour old. But he didn't think that. He thought, *All right. Yes. But what?* and stood for a moment, alien and small in the green and topless solitude, answering his own question before it had formed and ceased. It was the watch, the compass, the stick — the three lifeless mechanicals with which for nine hours he had fended the wilderness off; he hung the watch and compass carefully on a bush and leaned the stick beside them and relinquished completely to it.

He had not been going very fast for the last two or three hours. He went no faster now, since distance would not matter even if he could have gone fast. And he was trying to keep a bearing on the tree where he had left the compass, trying to complete a circle which would bring him back to it or at least intersect itself, since direction would not matter now either. But the tree was not here, and he did as Sam had schooled him — made the next circle in the opposite direction, so that the two patterns would bisect somewhere, but crossing no print of his own feet, finding the tree at last, but in the wrong place — no bush, no compass, no watch — and the tree not even the tree, because there was a down log beside it and he did what Sam Fathers had told him was the next thing and the last.

As he sat down on the log he saw the crooked print — the warped,

tremendous, two-toed indentation which, even as he watched it,
filled with water. As he looked up, the wilderness coalesced, solidified — the glade, the tree he sought, the bush, the watch and the
compass glinting where the ray of sunshine touched them. Then he
saw the bear. It did not emerge, appear; it was just there, immobile,
solid, fixed in the hot dappling of the green and windless noon, not as
big as he had dreamed it, but as big as he had expected it, bigger,
dimensionless, against the dappled obscurity, looking at him where
he sat quietly on the log and looked back at it.

Then it moved. It made no sound. It did not hurry. It crossed the
glade, walking for an instant into the full glare of the sun; when it
reached the other side it stopped again and looked back at him across
one shoulder while his quiet breathing inhaled and exhaled three
times.

Then it was gone. It didn't walk into the woods, the undergrowth.
It faded, sank back into the wilderness as he had watched a fish, a
huge old bass, sink and vanish into the dark depths of its pool without
even any movement of its fins.

He thought, *It will be next fall*. But it was not next fall, nor the
next nor the next. He was fourteen then. He had killed his buck, and
Sam Fathers had marked his face with the hot blood, and in the next
year he killed a bear. But even before that accolade he had become as
competent in the woods as many grown men with the same experience; by his fourteenth year he was better woodsman than most
grown men with more. There was no territory within thirty miles of
the camp that he did not know — bayou, ridge, brake, landmark, tree
and path. He could have led anyone to any point in it without devia-
tion, and brought them out again. He knew the game trails that even
Sam Fathers did not know; in his thirteenth year he found a buck's
bedding place, and unbeknown to his father he borrowed Walter
Ewell's rifle and lay in wait at dawn and killed the buck when it
walked back to the bed, as Sam had told him how the old Chickasaw
fathers did.

But not the old bear, although by now he knew its footprints better
than he did his own, and not only the crooked one. He could see any
one of three sound ones and distinguish it from any other, and not
only by its size. There were other bears within these thirty miles
which left tracks almost as large, but this was more than that. If Sam
Fathers had been his mentor and the back-yard rabbits and squirrels
at home his kindergarten, then the wilderness the old bear ran was
his college, the old male bear itself, so long unwifed and childless as
to have become its own ungendered progenitor, was his alma mater.
But he never saw it.

He could find the crooked print now almost whenever he liked, fifteen or ten or five miles, or sometimes nearer the camp than that. Twice while on stand during the three years he heard the dogs strike its trail by accident; on the second time they jumped it seemingly, the voices high, abject, almost human in hysteria, as on that first morning two years ago. But not the bear itself. He would remember that noon three years ago, the glade, himself and the bear fixed during that moment in the windless and dappled blaze, and it would seem to him that it had never happened, that he had dreamed that too. But it had happened. They had looked at each other, they had emerged from the wilderness old as earth, synchronized to the instant by something more than the blood that moved the flesh and bones which bore them, and touched, pledged something, affirmed, something more lasting than the frail web of bones and flesh which any accident could obliterate.

Then he saw it again. Because of the very fact that he thought of nothing else, he had forgotten to look for it. He was still hunting with Walter Ewell's rifle. He saw it cross the end of a long blow-down, a corridor where a tornado had swept, rushing through rather than over the tangle of trunks and branches as a locomotive would have, faster than he had ever believed it could move, almost as fast as a deer even, because a deer would have spent most of that time in the air, faster than he could bring the rifle sights up with it. And now he knew what had been wrong during all the three years. He sat on a log, shaking and trembling as if he had never seen the woods before nor anything that ran them, wondering with incredulous amazement how he could have forgotten the very thing which Sam Fathers had told him and which the bear itself had proved the next day and had now returned after three years to reaffirm.

And now he knew what Sam Fathers had meant about the right dog, a dog in which size would mean less than nothing. So when he returned alone in April — school was out then, so that the sons of farmers could help with the land's planting, and at last his father had granted him permission, on his promise to be back in four days — he had the dog. It was his own, a mongrel of the sort called by Negroes a fyce, a ratter, itself not much bigger than a rat and possessing that bravery which had long since stopped being courage and had become foolhardiness.

It did not take four days. Alone again, he found the trail on the first morning. It was not a stalk; it was an ambush. He timed the meeting almost as if it were an appointment with a human being. Himself holding the fyce muffled in a feed sack and Sam Fathers with two of the hounds on a piece of a plowline rope, they lay down wind of the trail at dawn of the second morning. They were so close that the bear turned without even running, as if in surprised amazement at the shrill and frantic uproar of the released fyce, turning at bay against the trunk of a tree, on its hind feet; it seemed to the boy that it would never stop rising, taller and taller, and even the two hounds seemed to take a desperate and despairing courage from the fyce, following it as it went in.

Then he realized that the fyce was actually not going to stop. He flung, threw the gun away, and ran; when he overtook and grasped the frantically pin-wheeling little dog, it seemed to him that he was directly under the bear.

He could smell it, strong and hot and rank. Sprawling, he looked up to where it loomed and towered over him like a cloudburst and colored like a thunderclap, quite familiar, peacefully and even lucidly familiar, until he remembered: This was the way he had used to dream about it. Then it was gone. He didn't see it go. He knelt, holding the frantic fyce with both hands, hearing the abashed wailing of the hounds drawing farther and farther away, until Sam came up. He carried the gun. He laid it down quietly beside the boy and stood looking down at him.

"You've done seed him twice now with a gun in your hands," he said. "This time you couldn't have missed him."

The boy rose. He still held the fyce. Even in his arms and clear of the ground, it yapped frantically, straining and surging after the fading uproar of the two hounds like a tangle of wire springs. He was panting a little but he was neither shaking nor trembling now.

"Neither could you!" he said. "You had the gun! Neither did you!"

"And you didn't shoot," his father said. "How close were you?"

"I don't know, sir," he said. "There was a big wood tick inside his right hind leg. I saw that. But I didn't have the gun then."

"But you didn't shoot when you had the gun," his father said. "Why?"

But he didn't answer, and his father didn't wait for him to, rising and crossing the room, across the pelt of the bear which the boy had killed two years ago and the larger one which his father had killed before he was born, to the bookcase beneath the mounted head of the boy's first buck. It was the room which his father called the office, from which all the plantation business was transacted; in it for the fourteen years of his life he had heard the best of all talking. Major de Spain would be there and sometimes old General Compson, and Walter Ewell and Boon Hoggenbeck and Sam Fathers and Tennie's Jim, too, were hunters, knew the woods and what ran them.

He would hear it, not talking himself but listening — the wilderness, the big woods, bigger and older than any recorded document of

white man fatuous enough to believe he had bought any fragment of
it or Indian ruthless enough to pretend that any fragment of it had
been his to convey. It was of the men, not white nor black nor red, but
men, hunters with the will and hardihood to endure and the humility
and skill to survive, and the dogs and the bear and deer juxtaposed
and reliefed against it, ordered and compelled by and within the
wilderness in the ancient and unremitting contest by the ancient and
immitigable rules which voided all regrets and brooked no quarter,
the voices quiet and weighty and deliberate for retrospection and
recollection and exact remembering, while he squatted in the blazing
firelight as Tennie's Jim squatted, who stirred only to put more wood
on the fire and to pass the bottle from one glass to another. Because
the bottle was always present, so that after a while it seemed to him
that those fierce instants of heart and brain and courage and wiliness
and speed were concentrated and distilled into that brown liquor
which not women, not boys and children, but only hunters drank,
drinking not of the blood they had spilled but some condensation of
the wild immortal spirit, drinking it moderately, humbly even, not
with the pagan's base hope of acquiring the virtues of cunning and
strength and speed, but in salute to them.

His father returned with the book and sat down again and opened
it. "Listen," he said. He read the five stanzas aloud, his voice quiet
and deliberate in the room where there was no fire now because it
was already spring. Then he looked up. The boy watched him. "All
right," his father said. "Listen." He read again, but only the second
stanza this time, to the end of it, the last two lines, and closed the
book and put it on the table beside him. "She cannot fade, though
thou has not thy bliss, forever wilt thou love, and she be fair," he said.

"He's talking about a girl," the boy said.

"He had to talk about something," his father said. Then he said,
"He was talking about truth. Truth doesn't change. Truth is one
thing. It covers all things which touch the heart — honor and pride
and pity and justice and courage and love. Do you see now?"

He didn't know. Somehow it was simpler than that. There was an
old bear, fierce and ruthless, not merely just to stay alive, but with the
fierce pride of liberty and freedom, proud enough of the liberty and
freedom to see it threatened without fear or even alarm; nay, who at
times even seemed deliberately to put that freedom and liberty in
jeopardy in order to savor them, to remind his old strong bones and
flesh to keep supple and quick to defend and preserve them. There
was an old man, son of a Negro slave and an Indian king, inheritor on
the one side of the long chronicle of a people who had learned humility through suffering, and pride through the endurance which survived the suffering and injustice, and on the other side, the chronicle

of a people even longer in the land than the first, yet who no longer existed in the land at all save in the solitary brotherhood of an old Negro's alien blood and the wild and invincible spirit of an old bear. There was a boy who wished to learn humility and pride in order to become skillful and worthy in the woods, who suddenly found himself becoming so skillful so rapidly that he feared he would never become worthy because he had not learned humility and pride, although he had tried to, until one day and as suddenly he discovered that an old man who could not have defined either had led him, as though by the hand, to that point where an old bear and a little mongrel of a dog showed him that, by possessing one thing other, he would possess them both.

And a little dog, nameless and mongrel and many-fathered, grown, yet weighing less than six pounds, saying as if to itself, "I can't be dangerous, because there's nothing much smaller than I am; I can't be fierce, because they would call it just a noise; I can't be humble, because I'm already too close to the ground to genuflect; I can't be proud, because I wouldn't be near enough to it for anyone to know who was casting the shadow, and I don't even know that I'm not going to heaven, because they have already decided that I don't possess an immortal soul. So all I can be is brave. But it's all right. I can be that, even if they still call it just noise."

That was all. It was simple, much simpler than somebody talking in a book about youth and a girl he would never need to grieve over, because he could never approach any nearer her and would never have to get any farther away. He had heard about a bear, and finally got big enough to trail it, and he trailed it four years and at last met it with a gun in his hands and he didn't shoot. Because a little dog — But he could have shot long before the little dog covered the twenty yards to where the bear waited, and Sam Fathers could have shot at any time during that interminable minute while Old Ben stood on his hind feet over them. He stopped. His father was watching him gravely across the spring-rife twilight of the room; when he spoke, his words were as quiet as the twilight, too, not loud, because they did not need to be because they would last. "Courage, and honor, and pride," his father said, "and pity, and love of justice and of liberty. They all touch the heart, and what the heart holds to becomes truth, as far as we know the truth. Do you see now?"

Sam, and Old Ben, and Nip, he thought. And himself too. He had been all right too. His father had said so. "Yes, sir," he said.

Several of Faulkner's comments on "The Bear," made during interviews at the University of Virginia (printed in *Faulkner in the*

University, ed. F. L. Gwynn and J. W. Blotner, 1959), though not necessarily definitive, are suggestive:

> One symbol was the bear represented the vanishing wilderness. The little dog that wasn't scared of the bear represented the indomitable spirit of man. I'll have to dig back and get up some more of those symbols, because I have learned around an even dozen that I put into that story without knowing it. But there are two pretty good ones that you can hold to.

Asked the significance of the fyce, Faulkner said that it is

> . . . the antithesis of the bear. The bear represented the obsolete primitive. The fyce represents the creature who has coped with environment and is still on top of it, you might say. That he has — instead of sticking to his breeding and becoming a decadent degenerate creature, he has mixed himself up with the good stock where he picked and chose. And he's quite smart, he's quite brave. All's against him is his size. But I never knew a fyce yet that realized that he wasn't big as anything else he ever saw, even a bear.

Asked to explain what the "one thing" was that would enable the boy to learn "humility and pride," Faulkner replied: "Courage, it was. A little dog that never saw a bear bigger than he was."

Questions

1. In the opening three paragraphs of the story, the pronoun "it" usually refers to Old Ben. But does "it" always have the same referent in this opening section of the story? How might the "it" be said to function ambiguously and thus prepare the reader for the symbolism in the story? How does the fact that the boy is nameless throughout the story add to the symbolic meaning?

2. Compare the characterizations of the bear in the second and third paragraphs. How do they affect our attitude toward the bear? Does the fact that it is given a name and does the name itself affect our attitude toward Old Ben?

3. What is the distinction Sam Fathers makes between being "scared" and being "afraid"? Aren't the words synonymous, or is there, in the context, some crucial difference? If so, what might it be?

4. The boy relinquishes the three lifeless mechanicals before he is permitted to see the bear. Why? Is Faulkner making some social comment about modern man that goes beyond the limits of a bear hunt? How is the following letter, written by Faulkner to *The New York Times* (December 26, 1954), relevant to "The Bear"?

> This is about the Italian airliner which undershot the runway and crashed at Idlewild after failing three times to hold the instrument glide-path which would have brought it down to the runway.

It is written on the idea (postulate, if you like) that the instrument or instruments — altimeter-cum-drift-indicator — failed or had failed, was already out of order or incorrect before the moment when the pilot committed irrevocably the aircraft to it.

It is written in grief. Not just for the sorrow of the bereaved ones of those who died in the crash, and for the airline, the public carrier which, in selling the tickets, promised or anyway implied security for the trip, but for the crew, the pilot himself, who will be blamed for the crash and whose record and memory will be tarnished by it; who, along with his unaware passengers, was victim not even of the failed instruments but victim of that mystical, unquestioning, almost religious awe and veneration in which our culture has trained us to hold gadgets — any gadget, if it is only complex enough and cryptic enough and costs enough.

I imagine that even after the first failure to hold the glide-path, certainly after the second one, his instinct — the seat of his pants, call it what you will — after that many hours in the air, told him that something was wrong. And his seniority as a four-engine over-water captain probably told him where the trouble was. But he dared not accept that knowledge and (this presumes that even after the second failure he still had enough fuel left to reach a field which he could see) act on it.

Possibly at some time during the four attempts to land, very likely at some one of the final rapid seconds before he had irrevocably committed the aircraft — that compounding of mass and weight by velocity — to the ground, his co-pilot (or flight engineer or whoever else might have been in the cockpit at the time) probably said to him: "Look. We're wrong. Get the flaps and gear up and let's get to hell out of here." But he dared not. He dared not so flout and affront, even with his own life too at stake, our cultural postulate of the infallibility of machines, instruments, gadgets — a Power more ruthless even than the old Hebrew concept of its God, since ours is not even jealous and vengeful, caring nothing about individuals.

He dared not commit that sacrilege. If he had, nothing would have remained to him save to open the cockpit hatch and (a Roman) cast himself onto the turning blades of one of the inboard air-screws. I grieve for him, for that moment's victims. We all had better grieve for all people beneath a culture which holds any mechanical superior to any man simply because the one, being mechanical, is infallible, while the other, being nothing but man, is not just subject to failure but doomed to it.

5. On page 63 the hunters pass around a bottle. What is symbolized by this action?

6. Why doesn't the boy kill the bear?

7. A careful reading of Keats "Ode on a Grecian Urn" (pages 373–374) may illuminate the father's comments to his son. What is the particular relevance of the second stanza?

5 Style

In the preface to *The Nigger of the "Narcissus"* Joseph Conrad wrote:

> My task which I am trying to achieve is, by the power of the written word, to make you hear, to make you feel — it is, before all, to make you see. That — and no more, and it is everything.

Most writers set themselves Conrad's task, attempting to make us "see" by their choice and arrangement of words into sentences. These sentences constitute the writer's style, and they are an important part of his meaning, just as a speaker's style — in addition to choice of sentences, his pace, tone of voice, gestures — helps communicate his meaning. What is good **style**? Jonathan Swift defined it as "proper words in proper places." But what are the proper words and the proper places? Shall the writer heap up details, or shall he be highly selective? Shall he be explicit, or shall he understate, and allow the reader to leap to the meaning himself? Shall he use abundant dialogue, thereby letting us hear his characters, or shall he use abundant summaries, thereby keeping his characters at a distance from us? Shall he use short sentences or long ones? If long, shall they be constructed to suggest forethought and self-assurance, or improvisation and uncertainty? Contrast, for example, these two long sentences, chosen, for the sake of clarity, from expository prose rather than from fiction. The first is by Samuel Johnson:

> To search his plays for vigorous sallies and sententious elegances, or to fix the dates of any little pieces which he wrote by chance or by solicitation, were labor too tedious and minute.

The second is by John Donne:

> We study health, and we deliberate upon our meats and drink and air and exercises, and we hew and we polish every stone that goes to the building; and so our health is a long and regular work.

Johnson, by placing his finite verb near the end, indicates that his sentence has been formed before it is uttered; in contrast, Donne, by placing his finite verb near the beginning, and by adding modifications and parenthetical thoughts in clauses linked by semicolons and such a simple coordinate as "and," suggests a writer in the process of thinking.

What style shall a writer use?

Put this way, it is clear that there is no simple answer; anything can be right or wrong, depending on what effect is sought. James Joyce, in *A Portrait of the Artist as a Young Man*, uses a variety of styles, and each of them is right, beginning with a childlike style in describing the protagonist's infancy, moving to a luxuriant style in describing his adolescence, and concluding with a sparer style in describing his preparations for self-exile. Here are three passages from the novel — the opening sentence, a sentence from the middle, and the closing sentence:

> Once upon a time and a very good time it was there was a moocow coming down along the road and this moocow that was down along the road met a nicens little boy named baby tuckoo. . . .

> Only at times, in the pauses of his desire, when the luxury that was wasting him gave room to a softer languor, the image of Mercedes traversed the background of his memory.

> April 27. Old father, old artificer, stand me now and ever in good stead.

The following are the first two sentences in the opening paragraph of Eudora Welty's "Livvie":

> Solomon carried Livvie twenty-one miles away from her home when he married her. He carried her away up on the Old Natchez Trace into the deep country to live in his house.

These sentences can easily be transposed and combined into:

> When Solomon married Livvie, he carried her away up on the Old Natchez Trace into the deep country to live in his house, twenty-one miles away.

The words are the same, but everything is changed. By failing to repeat the structure of subject-verb ("Solomon carried." "He carried"), the suggestion of Livvie's own voice is lost. Though the lines, as Miss Welty wrote them, are not spoken by Livvie, they carry within them a suggestion of her simplicity. Take the first two sentences of the second paragraph:

> It was a nice house, inside and outside both. In the first place, it had three rooms.

These can be combined into:

> The three-room house was nice, inside and out.

Again, the innocence of Livvie's voice is missing. In these lines, Miss Welty is not communicating information only about Livvie's house; she is also giving us an image of Livvie's mind, and the paraphrase does not.

A more subtle example may be useful. When Miss Welty first published "Livvie," the third sentence of the opening paragraph was simply:

> She was sixteen then.

But in the revision, printed in this book, the sentence runs:

> She was sixteen — an only girl, then.

Of course the revision has an additional piece of information, but what is important for our present purpose is the difference in style. "She was sixteen then" is a quite ordinary sentence, such as any of us might write. But "She was sixteen — an only girl, then" presents us with a special mind. It almost seems to suggest that Livvie is no longer an only girl, yet this point is never made. What the revision adds is a hint of Livvie's slightly wistful, disjointed view of the past. Ordinarily the sentence might run, "She was sixteen then, an only girl"; by being placed at the end of the sentence, after some material that it does not logically follow, "then" is somewhat unexpected, rather like the last step down to the cellar. The slight jolt we feel in "then" both reveals Livvie's special way of thinking and gives the past an emphasis lacking in the original "She was sixteen then" and lacking in "She was sixteen then, an only girl."

These comments do not come near to revealing the special power of Miss Welty's sentences, but perhaps they have made clear that in good writing words cannot be rearranged without change in meaning. "I began to speak of style," Isaac Babel writes in one of his stories, "of the army of words, of the army in which all kinds of weapons may come into play. No iron can stab the heart with such force as a period put just at the right place."

A NOTE ON TONE

A speaker's tone of voice conveys part of his meaning: "Good Lord" can be a pious invocation; it can also be a blasphemous expletive, and the tone, quite as well as the context, can tell us which it is. **Tone** in a story is commonly defined as the author's voice (in distinction from the voices of his characters); it is, let us say, the author's attitude as the reader infers it. His characters may speak angrily, but the reader may rightly detect that the author's tone is gentle and compassionate. His characters may speak gaily and wittily, but the reader may rightly detect that the author's tone is scornful. When we talk about the author's sympathies and antipathies, his cynicism or his solemnity or his flippancy, we are talking about his tone. And it is through his pervasive style that his tone is heard.*

Eudora Welty (b. 1909)

Livvie

Solomon carried Livvie twenty-one miles away from her home when he married her. He carried her away up on the Old Natchez Trace into the deep country to live in his house. She was sixteen — an only girl, then. Once people said he thought nobody would ever come along there. He told her himself that it had been a long time, and a day she did not know about, since that road was a traveled road with *people* coming and going. He was good to her, but he kept her in the house. She had not thought that she could not get back. Where she came from, people said an old man did not want anybody in the world to ever find his wife, for fear they would steal her back from him. Solomon asked her before he took her, "Would she be

---

* Although Chapter 10, "The Speaking Tone of Voice," draws its illustrative material from poems, the points it makes are relevant here. The reader may find it useful to consult the first half-dozen pages of that chapter now.

happy?" — very dignified, for he was a colored man that owned his
land and had it written down in the courthouse; and she said, "Yes,
sir," since he was an old man and she was young and just listened and
answered. He asked her, if she was choosing winter, would she pine
for spring, and she said, "No indeed." Whatever she said, always, was
because he was an old man . . . while nine years went by. All the time,
he got old, and he got so old he gave out. At least he slept the whole
day in bed, and she was young still.

It was a nice house, inside and outside both. In the first place, it
had three rooms. The front room was papered in holly paper, with
green palmettos from the swamp spaced at careful intervals over the
walls. There was fresh newspaper cut with fancy borders on the
mantelshelf, on which were propped photographs of old or very
young men printed in faint yellow — Solomon's people. Solomon
had a houseful of furniture. There was a double settee, a tall scrolled
rocker and an organ in the front room, all around a three-legged table
with a pink marble top, on which was set a lamp with three gold feet,
besides a jelly glass with pretty hen feathers in it. Behind the front
room, the other room had the bright iron bed with the polished knobs
like a throne, in which Solomon slept all day. There were snow-white
curtains of wiry lace at the window, and a lace bedspread belonged
on the bed. But what old Solomon slept sound under was a big
feather-stitched piece-quilt in the pattern "Trip Around the World,"
which had twenty-one different colors, four hundred and forty
pieces, and a thousand yards of thread, and that was what Solomon's
mother made in her life and old age. There was a table holding the
Bible, and a trunk with a key. On the wall were two calendars, and a
diploma from somewhere in Solomon's family, and under that Livvie's one possession was nailed, a picture of the little white baby of
the family she worked for, back in Natchez before she was married.
Going through that room and on to the kitchen, there was a big wood
stove and a big round table always with a wet top and with the knives
and forks in one jelly glass and the spoons in another, and a cut-glass
vinegar bottle between, and going out from those, many shallow
dishes of pickled peaches, fig preserves, watermelon pickles and
blackberry jam always sitting there. The churn sat in the sun, the
doors of the safe were always both shut, and there were four baited
mouse-traps in the kitchen, one in every corner.

The outside of Solomon's house looked nice. It was not painted,
but across the porch was an even balance. On each side there was one
easy chair with high springs, looking out, and a fern basket hanging
over it from the ceiling, and a dishpan of zinnia seedlings growing at
its foot on the floor. By the door was a plow-wheel, just a pretty iron
circle, nailed up on one wall and a square mirror on the other, a

turquoise-blue comb stuck up in the frame, with the wash stand beneath it. On the door was a wooden knob with a pearl in the end, and Solomon's black hat hung on that, if he was in the house.

Out front was a clean dirt yard with every vestige of grass patiently uprooted and the ground scarred in deep whorls from the strike of Livvie's broom. Rose bushes with tiny blood-red roses blooming every month grew in threes on either side of the steps. On one side was a peach tree, on the other a pomegranate. Then coming around up the path from the deep cut of the Natchez Trace below was a line of bare crape-myrtle trees with every branch of them ending in a colored bottle, green or blue. There was no word that fell from Solomon's lips to say what they were for, but Livvie knew that there could be a spell put in trees, and she was familiar from the time she was born with the way bottle trees kept evil spirits from coming into the house — by luring them inside the colored bottles, where they cannot get out again. Solomon had made the bottle trees with his own hands over the nine years, in labor amounting to about a tree a year, and without a sign that he had any uneasiness in his heart, for he took as much pride in his precautions against spirits coming in the house as he took in the house, and sometimes in the sun the bottle trees looked prettier than the house did.

It was a nice house. It was in a place where the days would go by and surprise anyone that they were over. The lamplight and the firelight would shine out the door after dark, over the still and breathing country, lighting the roses and the bottle trees, and all was quiet there.

But there was nobody, nobody at all, not even a white person. And if there had been anybody, Solomon would not have let Livvie look at them, just as he would not let her look at a field hand, or a field hand look at her. There was no house near, except for the cabins of the tenants that were forbidden to her, and there was no house as far as she had been, stealing away down the still, deep Trace. She felt as if she waded a river when she went, for the dead leaves on the ground reached as high as her knees, and when she was all scratched and bleeding she said it was not like a road that went anywhere. One day, climbing up the high bank, she had found a graveyard without a church; with ribbon-grass growing about the foot of an angel (she had climbed up because she thought she saw angel wings), and in the sun, trees shining like burning flames through the great caterpillar nets which enclosed them. Scarey thistles stood looking like the prophets in the Bible in Solomon's house. Indian paint brushes grew over her head, and the mourning dove made the only sound in the world. Oh for a stirring of the leaves, and a breaking of the nets! But not by a ghost, prayed Livvie, jumping down the bank. After Solomon took to his bed, she never went out, except one more time.

Livvie knew she made a nice girl to wait on anybody. She fixed things to eat on a tray like a surprise. She could keep from singing when she ironed, and to sit by a bed and fan away the flies, she could be so still she could not hear herself breathe. She could clean up the house and never drop a thing, and wash the dishes without a sound, and she would step outside to churn, for churning sounded too sad to her, like sobbing, and if it made her home-sick and not Solomon, she did not think of that.

But Solomon scarcely opened his eyes to see her, and scarcely tasted his food. He was not sick or paralyzed or in any pain that he mentioned, but he was surely wearing out in the body, and no matter what nice hot thing Livvie would bring him to taste, he would only look at it now, as if he were past seeing how he could add anything more to himself. Before she could beg him, he would go fast asleep. She could not surprise him any more, if he would not taste, and she was afraid that he was never in the world going to taste another thing she brought him — and so how could he last?

But one morning it was breakfast time and she cooked his eggs and grits, carried them in on a tray, and called his name. He was sound asleep. He lay in a dignified way with his watch beside him, on his back in the middle of the bed. One hand drew the quilt up high, though it was the first day of spring. Through the white lace curtains a little puffy wind was blowing as if it came from round cheeks. All night the frogs had sung out in the swamp, like a commotion in the room, and he had not stirred, though she lay wide awake and saying "Shh, frogs!" for fear he would mind them.

He looked as if he would like to sleep a little longer, and so she put back the tray and waited a little. When she tiptoed and stayed so quiet, she surrounded herself with a little reverie, and sometimes it seemed to her when she was so stealthy that the quiet she kept was for a sleeping baby, and that she had a baby and was its mother. When she stood at Solomon's bed and looked down at him, she would be thinking, "He sleeps so well," and she would hate to wake him up. And in some other way, too, she was afraid to wake him up because even in his sleep he seemed to be such a strict man.

Of course, nailed to the wall over the bed — only she would forget who it was — there was a picture of him when he was young. Then he had a fan of hair over his forehead like a king's crown. Now his hair lay down on his head, the spring had gone out of it. Solomon had a lightish face, with eyebrows scattered but rugged, the way privet grows, strong eyes, with second sight, a strict mouth, and a little gold smile. This was the way he looked in his clothes, but in bed in the daytime he looked like a different and smaller man, even when he was wide awake, and holding the Bible. He looked like somebody kin to himself. And then sometimes when he lay in sleep and she stood fannng the flies away, and the light came in, his face was like new, so smooth and clear that it was like a glass of jelly held to the window, and she could almost look through his forehead and see what he thought.

She fanned him and at length he opened his eyes and spoke her name, but he would not taste the nice eggs she had kept warm under a pan.

Back in the kitchen she ate heartily, his breakfast and hers, and looked out the open door at what went on. The whole day, and the whole night before, she had felt the stir of spring close to her. It was as present in the house as a young man would be. The moon was in the last quarter and outside they were turning the sod and planting peas and beans. Up and down the red fields, over which smoke from the brush-burning hung showing like a little skirt of sky, a white horse and a white mule pulled the plow. At intervals hoarse shouts came through the air and roused her as if she dozed neglectfully in the shade, and they were telling her, "Jump up!" She could see how over each ribbon of field were moving men and girls, on foot and mounted on mules, with hats set on their heads and bright with tall hoes and forks as if they carried streamers on them and were going to some place on a journey — and how as if at a signal now and then they would all start at once shouting, hollering, cajoling, calling and answering back, running, being leaped on and breaking away, flinging to earth with a shout and lying motionless in the trance of twelve o'clock. The old women came out of the cabins and brought them food they had ready for them, and then all worked together, spread evenly out. The little children came too, like a bouncing stream overflowing the fields, and set upon the men, the women, the dogs, the rushing birds, and the wave-like rows of earth, their little voices almost too high to be heard. In the middle distance like some white-and-gold towers were the haystacks, with black cows coming around to eat their edges. High above everything, the wheel of fields, house, and cabins, and the deep road surrounding like a moat to keep them in, was the turning sky, blue with long, far-flung white mare's-tail clouds, serene and still as high flames. And sound asleep while all this went around him that was his, Solomon was like a little still spot in the middle.

Even in the house the earth was sweet to breathe. Solomon had never let Livvie go any farther than the chicken house and the well. But what if she would walk now into the heart of the fields and take a hoe and work until she fell stretched out and drenched with her efforts, like other girls, and laid her cheek against the laid-open earth, and shamed the old man with her humbleness and delight? To shame him! A cruel wish could come in uninvited and so fast while she looked out the back door. She washed the dishes and scrubbed the table. She could hear the cries of the little lambs. Her mother, that she had not seen since her wedding day, had said one time, "I rather a man be anything, than a woman be mean."

So all morning she kept tasting the chicken broth on the stove, and when it was right she poured off a nice cupful. She carried it in to Solomon, and there he lay having a dream. Now what did he dream about? For she saw him sigh gently as if not to disturb some whole thing he held round in his mind, like a fresh egg. So even an old man dreamed about something pretty. Did he dream of her, while his eyes were shut and sunken, and his small hand with the wedding ring curled close in sleep around the quilt? He might be dreaming of what time it was, for even through his sleep he kept track of it like a clock, and knew how much of it went by, and waked up knowing where the hands were even before he consulted the silver watch that he never let go. He would sleep with the watch in his palm, and even holding it to his cheek like a child that loves a plaything. Or he might dream of journeys and travels on a steamboat to Natchez. Yet she thought he dreamed of her; but even while she scrutinized him, the rods of the foot of the bed seemed to rise up like a rail fence between them, and she could see that people never could be sure of anything as long as one of them was asleep and the other awake. To look at him dreaming of her when he might be going to die frightened her a little, as if he might carry her with him that way, and she wanted to run out of the room. She took hold of the bed and held on, and Solomon opened his eyes and called her name, but he did not want anything. He would not taste the good broth.

Just a little after that, as she was taking up the ashes in the front room for the last time in the year, she heard a sound. It was somebody coming. She pulled the curtains together and looked through the slit.

Coming up the path under the bottle trees was a white lady. At first she looked young, but then she looked old. Marvelous to see, a little car stood steaming like a kettle out in the field-track — it had come without a road.

Livvie stood listening to the long, repeated knockings at the door, and after a while she opened it just a little. The lady came in through the crack, though she was more than middle-sized and wore a big hat.

"My name is Miss Baby Marie," she said.

Livvie gazed respectfully at the lady and at the little suitcase she was holding close to her by the handle until the proper moment. The lady's eyes were running over the room, from palmetto to palmetto, but she was saying, "I live at home . . . out from Natchez . . . and get out and show these pretty cosmetic things to the white people and the colored people both . . . all around . . . years and years. . . . Both shades of powder and rouge. . . . It's the kind of work a girl can do and not go clear 'way from home. . . ." And the harder she looked, the more she talked. Suddenly she turned up her nose and said, "It is not Christian or sanitary to put feathers in a vase," and then she took a gold key out of the front of her dress and began unlocking the locks on her suitcase. Her face drew the light, the way it was covered with intense white and red, with a little patty-cake of white between the wrinkles by her upper lip. Little red tassels of hair bobbed under the rusty wires of her picture-hat, as with an air of triumph and secrecy she now drew open her little suitcase and brought out bottle after bottle and jar after jar, which she put down on the table, the mantelpiece, the settee, and the organ.

"Did you ever see so many cosmetics in your life?" cried Miss Baby Marie.

"No'm," Livvie tried to say, but the cat had her tongue.

"Have you ever applied cosmetics?" asked Miss Baby Marie next.

"No'm," Livvie tried to say.

"Then look!" she said, and pulling out the last thing of all, "Try this!" she said. And in her hand was unclenched a golden lipstick which popped open like magic. A fragrance came out of it like incense, and Livvie cried out suddenly, "Chinaberry flowers!"

Her hand took the lipstick, and in an instant she was carried away in the air through the spring, and looking down with a half-drowsy smile from a purple cloud she saw from above a chinaberry tree, dark and smooth and neatly leaved, neat as a guinea hen in the dooryard, and there was her home that she had left. On one side of the tree was her mama holding up her heavy apron, and she could see it was loaded with ripe figs, and on the other side was her papa holding a fish-pole over the pond, and she could see it transparently, the little clear fishes swimming up to the brim.

"Oh, no, not chinaberry flowers — secret ingredients," said Miss Baby Marie. "My cosmetics have secret ingredients — not chinaberry flowers."

"It's purple," Livvie breathed, and Miss Baby Marie said, "Use it freely. Rub it on."

Livvie tiptoed out to the wash stand on the front porch and before the mirror put the paint on her mouth. In the wavery surface her face danced before her like a flame. Miss Baby Marie followed her out, took a look at what she had done, and said, "That's it."

Livvie tried to say "Thank you" without moving her parted lips where the paint lay so new.

By now Miss Baby Marie stood behind Livvie and looked in the mirror over her shoulder, twisting up the tassels of her hair. "The lipstick I can let you have for only two dollars," she said, close to her neck.

"Lady, but I don't have no money, never did have," said Livvie.

"Oh, but you don't pay the first time. I make another trip, that's the way I do. I come back again — later."

"Oh," said Livvie, pretending she understood everything so as to please the lady.

"But if you don't take it now, this may be the last time I'll call at your house," said Miss Baby Marie sharply. "It's far away from anywhere, I'll tell you that. You don't live close to anywhere."

"Yes'm. My husband, he keep the *money*," said Livvie, trembling. "He is strict as he can be. He don't know *you* walk in here — Miss Baby Marie!"

"Where is he?"

"Right now, he in yonder sound asleep, an old man. I wouldn't ever ask him for anything."

Miss Baby Marie took back the lipstick and packed it up. She gathered up the jars for both black and white and got them all inside the suitcase, with the same little fuss of triumph with which she had brought them out. She started away.

"Goodbye," she said, making herself look grand from the back, but at the last minute she turned around in the door. Her old hat wobbled as she whispered, "Let me see your husband."

Livvie obediently went on tiptoe and opened the door to the other room. Miss Baby Marie came behind her and rose on her toes and looked in.

"My, what a little tiny old, old man!" she whispered, clasping her hands and shaking her head over them. "What a beautiful quilt! What a tiny old, old man!"

"He can sleep like that all day," whispered Livvie proudly.

They looked at him awhile so fast asleep, and then all at once they looked at each other. Somehow that was as if they had a secret, for he had never stirred. Livvie then politely, but all at once, closed the door.

"Well! I'd certainly like to leave you with a lipstick!" said Miss Baby Marie vivaciously. She smiled in the door.

"Lady, but I told you I don't have no money, and never did have."

"And never will?" In the air and all around, like a bright halo around the white lady's nodding head, it was a true spring day.

"Would you take eggs, lady?" asked Livvie softly.

"No, I have plenty of eggs — plenty," said Miss Baby Marie.

"I still don't have no money," said Livvie, and Miss Baby Marie took her suitcase and went on somewhere else. Livvie stood watching her go, and all the time she felt her heart beating in her left side. She touched the place with her hand. It seemed as if her heart beat and her whole face flamed from the pulsing color of her lips. She went to sit by Solomon and when he opened his eyes he could not see a change in her. "He's fixin' to die," she said inside. That was the secret. That was when she went out of the house for a little breath of air.

She went down the path and down the Natchez Trace a way, and she did not know how far she had gone, but it was not far, when she saw a sight. It was a man, looking like a vision — she standing on one side of the Old Natchez Trace and he standing on the other.

As soon as this man caught sight of her, he began to look himself over. Starting at the bottom with his pointed shoes, he began to look up, lifting his peg-top pants the higher to see fully his bright socks. His coat long and wide and leaf-green he opened like doors to see his high-up tawny pants and his pants he smoothed downward from the points of his collar, and he wore a luminous baby-pink satin shirt. At the end, he reached gently above his wide platter-shaped round hat, the color of a plum, and one finger touched at the feather, emerald green, blowing in the spring winds.

No matter how she looked, she could never look so fine as he did, and she was not sorry for that, she was pleased.

He took three jumps, one down and two up, and was by her side.

"My name is Cash," he said.

He had a guinea pig in his pocket. They began to walk along. She stared on and on at him, as if he were doing some daring spectacular thing, instead of just walking beside her. It was not simply the city way he was dressed that made her look at him and see hope in its insolence looking back. It was not only the way he moved along kicking the flowers as if he could break through everything in the way and destroy anything in the world, that made her eyes grow bright. It might be, if he had not appeared the way he did appear that day she would never have looked so closely at him, but the time people come makes a difference.

They walked through the still leaves of the Natchez Trace, the light and the shade falling through trees about them, the white irises shining like candles on the banks and the new ferns shining like green stars up in the oak branches. They came out at Solomon's house, bottle trees and all. Livvie stopped and hung her head.

Cash began whistling a little tune. She did not know what it was, but she had heard it before from a distance, and she had a revelation. Cash was a field hand. He was a transformed field hand. Cash belonged to Solomon. But he had stepped out of his overalls into this. There in front of Solomon's house he laughed. He had a round head, a round face, all of him was young, and he flung his head up, rolled it against the mare's-tail sky in his round hat, and he could laugh just to see Solomon's house sitting there. Livvie looked at it, and there was Solomon's black hat hanging on the peg on the front door, the blackest thing in the world.

"I been to Natchez," Cash said, wagging his head around against the sky. "*I* taken a trip, *I* ready for Easter!"

How was it possible to look so fine before the harvest? Cash must have stolen the money, stolen it from Solomon. He stood in the path and lifted his spread hand high and brought it down again and again in his laughter. He kicked up his heels. A little chill went through her. It was as if Cash was bringing that strong hand down to beat a drum or to rain blows upon a man, such an abandon and menace were in his laugh. Frowning, she went closer to him and his swinging arm drew her in at once and the fright was crushed from her body, as a little match-flame might be smothered out by what it lighted. She gathered the folds of his coat behind him and fastened her red lips to his mouth, and she was dazzled by herself then, the way he had been dazzled at himself to begin with.

In that instant she felt something that could not be told — that Solomon's death was at hand, that he was the same to her as if he were dead now. She cried out, and uttering little cries turned and ran for the house.

At once Cash was coming, following after, he was running behind her. He came close, and half-way up the path he laughed and passed her. He even picked up a stone and sailed it into the bottle trees. She put her hands over her head, and sounds clattered through the bottle trees like cries of outrage. Cash stamped and plunged zigzag up the front steps and in at the door.

When she got there, he had stuck his hands in his pockets and was turning slowly about in the front room. The little guinea pig peeped out. Around Cash, the pinned-up palmettos looked as if a lazy green monkey had walked up and down and around the walls leaving green prints of his hands and feet.

She got through the room and his hands were still in his pockets, and she fell upon the closed door to the other room and pushed it open. She ran to Solomon's bed, calling "Solomon! Solomon!" The little shape of the old man never moved at all, wrapped under the quilt as if it were winter still.

"Solomon!" She pulled the quilt away, but there was another one

under that, and she fell on her knees beside him. He made no sound
except a sigh, and then she could hear in the silence the light springy
steps of Cash walking and walking in the front room, and the ticking
of Solomon's silver watch, which came from the bed. Old Solomon
was far away in his sleep, his face looked small, relentless, and devout, as if he were walking somewhere where she could imagine the
snow falling.

Then there was a noise like a hoof pawing the floor, and the door
gave a creak, and Cash appeared beside her. When she looked up,
Cash's face was so black it was bright, and so bright and bare of pity
that it looked sweet to her. She stood up and held up her head. Cash
was so powerful that his presence gave her strength even when she
did not need any.

Under their eyes Solomon slept. People's faces tell of things and
places not known to the one who looks at them while they sleep, and
while Solomon slept under the eyes of Livvie and Cash his face told
them like a mythical story that all his life he had built, little scrap by
little scrap, respect. A beetle could not have been more laborious or
more ingenious in the task of its destiny. When Solomon was young,
as he was in his picture overhead, it was the infinite thing with him,
and he could see no end to the respect he would contrive and keep in
a house. He had built a lonely house, the way he would make a cage,
but it grew to be the same with him as a great monumental pyramid
and sometimes in his absorption of getting it erected he was like the
builder-slaves of Egypt who forgot or never knew the origin and
meaning of the thing to which they gave all the strength of their
bodies and used up all their days. Livvie and Cash could see that as a
man might rest from a life-labor he lay in his bed, and they could hear
how, wrapped in his quilt, he sighed to himself comfortably in sleep,
while in his dreams he might have been an ant, a beetle, a bird, an
Egyptian, assembling and carrying on his back and building with his
hands, or he might have been an old man of India or a swaddled
baby, about to smile and brush all away.

Then without warning old Solomon's eyes flew wide open under
the hedgelike brows. He was wide awake.

And instantly Cash raised his quick arm. A radiant sweat stood on
his temples. But he did not bring his arm down — it stayed in the air,
as if something might have taken hold.

It was not Livvie — she did not move. As if something said
"Wait," she stood waiting. Even while her eyes burned under motionless lids, her lips parted in a stiff grimace, and with her arms stiff at
her sides she stood above the prone old man and the panting young
one, erect and apart.

Movement when it came came in Solomon's face. It was an old and strict face, a frail face, but behind it, like a covered light, came an animation that could play hide and seek, that would dart and escape, had always escaped. The mystery flickered in him, and invited from his eyes. It was that very mystery that Cash with his quick arm would have to strike, and that Livvie could not weep for. But Cash only stood holding his arm in the air, when the gentlest flick of his great strength, almost a puff of his breath, would have been enough, if he had known how to give it, to send the old man over the obstruction that kept him away from death.

If it could not be that the tiny illumination in the fragile and ancient face caused a crisis, a mystery in the room that would not permit a blow to fall, at least it was certain that Cash, throbbing in his Easter clothes, felt a pang of shame that the vigor of a man would come to such an end that he could not be struck without warning. He took down his hand and stepped back behind Livvie, like a round-eyed schoolboy on whose unsuspecting head the dunce cap has been set.

"Young ones can't wait," said Solomon.

Livvie shuddered violently, and then in a gush of tears she stooped for a glass of water and handed it to him, but he did not see her.

"So here come the young man Livvie wait for. Was no prevention. No prevention. Now I lay eyes on young man and it come to be somebody I know all the time, and been knowing since he were born in a cotton patch, and watched grow up year to year, Cash McCord, growed to size, growed up to come in my house in the end — ragged and barefoot."

Solomon gave a cough of distaste. Then he shut his eyes vigorously, and his lips began to move like a chanter's.

"When Livvie married, her husband were already somebody. He had paid great cost for his land. He spread sycamore leaves over the ground from wagon to door, day he brought her home, so her foot would not have to touch ground. He carried her through his door. Then he growed old and could not lift her, and she were still young."

Livvie's sobs followed his words like a soft melody repeating each thing as he stated it. His lips moved for a little without sound, or she cried too fervently, and unheard he might have been telling his whole life, and then he said, "God forgive Solomon for sins great and small. God forgive Solomon for carrying away too young girl for wife and keeping her away from her people and from all the young people would clamor for her back."

Then he lifted up his right hand toward Livvie where she stood by the bed and offered her his silver watch. He dangled it before her eyes, and she hushed crying; her tears stopped. For a moment the watch could be heard ticking as it always did, precisely in his proud hand. She lifted it away. Then he took hold of the quilt; then he was dead.

Livvie left Solomon dead and went out of the room. Stealthily, nearly without noise, Cash went beside her. He was like a shadow, but his shiny shoes moved over the floor in spangles, and the green downy feather shone like a light in his hat. As they reached the front room, he seized her deftly as a long black cat and dragged her hanging by the waist round and round him, while he turned in a circle, his face bent down to hers. The first moment, she kept one arm and its hand stiff and still, the one that held Solomon's watch. Then the fingers softly let go, all of her was limp, and the watch fell somewhere on the floor. It ticked away in the still room, and all at once there began outside the full song of a bird.

They moved around and around the room and into the brightness of the open door, then he stopped and shook her once. She rested in silence in his trembling arms, unprotesting as a bird on a nest. Outside the redbirds were flying and criss-crossing, the sun was in all the bottles on the prisoned trees, and the young peach was shining in the middle of them with the bursting light of spring.

Questions

1. Of another of her stories, Eudora Welty wrote:

> Above all I had no wish to sound mystical, but did expect to sound mysterious now and then, if I could: this was a circumstantial realistic story in which the reality *was* mystery.

"Livvie," too, can be described as a "realistic story in which the reality *was* mystery." Which details in the story serve to make it both "realistic" and mysterious? Why does the story take place shortly before Easter? Why are Cash's clothes "luminous" and green and brown, and why is he described as "looking like a vision" (page 78)?

2. To a large extent the story is one of contrast, both explicit and implicit. What are some of the contrasting elements, and how do they reflect or illuminate the story's theme? Compare and contrast the four characters. Are any of their names significant? How?

3. Does Miss Welty say explicitly that Livvie is confined? Does Livvie feel confined? Do we feel that Livvie is confined? Explain.

4. Though there is a basic conflict between young Livvie and old Solomon, how does Miss Welty avoid a simple "good-bad" dichotomy?

5. Is the appearance of Miss Baby Marie an intrusion? Is she introduced merely for comic relief? Explain.

6. How are the bottle trees and Solomon's watch significant?

7. Compare the tone of "Livvie" with the tone of another story with a somewhat similar theme, "The Widow of Ephesus." How would you characterize the tone of each of the stories? How does it, in each case, help to illuminate the theme?

8. In the last two paragraphs of the story, which sentences most reflect Livvie's thought? Which sentences least reflect Livvie's thought? Explain.

6 A Collection of Short Fiction

The stories of Ruth, Samson, and Joseph in the Old Testament and the parables of Jesus in the New Testament are sufficient evidence that brief narratives existed in ancient times. The short tales in Boccaccio's *Decameron* and Chaucer's *Canterbury Tales* (the latter an amazing variety of narrative poems ranging from bawdy stories to legends of saints) are medieval examples of the ancient form. But, speaking generally, short narratives before the nineteenth century were either didactic pieces, with the narrative existing for the sake of a moral point, or they were "curious and striking" tales (to use Maugham's words for his favorite kind of story) recounted in order to entertain. The contemporary short story is rather different from both of these genres, which can be called the **parable** and the **anecdote**. Like the parable, the contemporary short story has a point, a meaning; but unlike the parable, it has a richness of surface as well as depth, so that it is interesting whether or not the reader goes on to ponder "the meaning." The short story, like the anecdote, relates a happening, but whereas the happening in the anecdote is curious and the center of interest, the happening in the contemporary story often is less interesting in itself than as a manifestation of a character's state of mind. A good short story usually has a psychological interest that an anecdote lacks.

The anecdotal story is what "story" means for most unsophisticated readers. It is an interesting happening or series of happenings, usually with a somewhat surprising ending. The anecdotal story, however, though sometimes excellently written, is quite different from most of the contemporary short stories in this book. The anecdote is good entertainment, and good entertainment should not be lightly dismissed. But it has two elements within it that prevent it (unless it is something in addition to an anecdote) from taking high place among the world's literature. First, it cannot be reread with increasing or even continued pleasure. Even when it is well told, once we know the happening we may lose patience with the telling. Second, effective anecdotes are often highly implausible. Now, implausible anecdotes alleged to be true have a special impact by virtue of their alleged truth: they make us say to ourselves, "Truth is stranger than fiction." But the invented anecdote lacks this power; its unlikely coincidence, its unconvincing ironic situation, its surprise ending, are both untrue and unbelieveable. It is entertaining but it is usually not especially meaningful.

The modern short story is not an anecdote and is not an abbreviated novel. If it were the latter, *Reader's Digest* condensations of novels would be short stories. But they aren't; they are only eviscerated novels. The novelist usually covers a long period of time, presenting not only a few individuals but also something of a society. He often tells of the development of several many-sided figures. In contrast, the short-story writer, having only a few pages, usually focuses on a single figure in a single episode, revealing his character rather than recording his development. Whereas the novel is narrative, the contemporary short story often seems less narrative than lyric or dramatic: in the short story we have a sense of a present mood or personality revealed, rather than the sense of a history reported. The revelation in a story is presented through incidents, of course, but the interest commonly resides in the character revealed through the incidents, rather than in the incidents themselves. Little "happens," in the sense that there is little rushing from place to place. What does "happen" is usually a mental reaction to an experience, and the mental reaction, rather than the external experience, is the heart of the story. In older narratives the plot usually involves a conflict that is resolved, bringing about a change in the protagonist's condition; in contemporary stories the plot usually is designed to reveal a protagonist's state of mind. This de-emphasis of overt actions results in an affinity with the lyric and the drama.

The de-emphasis on narrative in the contemporary short story is not an invention of the twentieth-century mind. It goes back at least to three important American writers of the early nineteenth century — Washington Irving, Nathaniel Hawthorne, and Edgar Allan Poe. In 1824 Irving wrote:

> I fancy much of what I value myself upon in writing, escapes the observation of the great mass of my readers: who are intent more upon the

story than the way in which it is told. For my part I consider a story
merely as a frame on which to stretch my materials. It is the play of
thought, and sentiments and language; the weaving in of characters,
lightly yet expressively delineated; the familiar and faithful exhibition
of scenes in common life; and the half-concealed vein of humor that is
often playing through the whole — these are among what I aim at, and
upon which I felicitate myself in proportion as I think I succeed.

Hawthorne and Poe may seem stranger than Irving as forebears of the
contemporary short story: both are known for their fantastic narratives (and, in addition, Poe is known as the inventor of the detective story, a genre in which there is strong interest in curious happenings). But because Hawthorne's fantastic narratives are, as he
said, highly allegorical, the reader's interest is pushed beyond the
narrative to the moral significance. Poe's "arabesques," as he called
his fanciful tales (in distinction from his detective tales of "ratiocina-
tion"), are aimed at revealing and arousing unusual mental states.
The weird happenings and personages are symbolic representations
of the mind or soul. In "The Fall of the House of Usher" the twins
Roderick and Madeline probably represent complementary parts of a
single personality, just as the house described in the poem within
this story represents a person: the "banners yellow" are hair, the
"two luminous windows" are eyes, the "fair palace door" of "pearl
and ruby" is a mouth, and so on. But, it must be noted, in both
Hawthorne and Poe we usually get what is commonly called the **tale**
rather than the **short story**: we get short prose fiction dealing with the
strange rather than the usual. (This distinction between the wondrous and the ordinary is discussed at some length in "Observations
on the Novel," page 339.)

A paragraph from Poe's review (1842) of Hawthorne's *Twice-Told
Tales*, though more useful in revealing Poe's theory of fiction than
Hawthorne's, illuminates something of the kinship between the contemporary short story and the best short fictions of the earlier nineteenth century. In the review Poe has been explaining that because
"unity of effect or impression" is essential, a tale (Poe doubtless uses
"tale" to mean short fiction in general, rather than the special type
just discussed) which can be read at a single sitting has an advantage
over the novel.

> A skillful artist has constructed a tale. He has not fashioned his thoughts
> to accommodate his incidents, but having deliberately conceived a cer-
> tain single effect to be wrought, he then invents such incidents, he then
> combines such events, and discusses them in such tone as may best
> serve him in establishing this preconceived effect. If his very first sen-
> tence tends not to the outbringing of this effect, then in his very first

step has he committed a blunder. In the whole composition there should be no word written of which the tendency, direct or indirect, is not to the one pre-established design. And by such means, with such care and skill a picture is at length painted which leaves in the mind of him who contemplates it with a kindred art, a sense of the fullest satisfaction. The idea of the tale, its thesis, has been presented unblemished, because undisturbed — an end absolutely demanded, yet, in the novel, altogether unattainable.

Nothing that has been said here should be construed as suggesting that contemporary short stories are necessarily better than older short narratives. The object of these comments has not been to evaluate, but to call attention to the characteristics dominating most good contemporary brief fiction. Furthermore, it should not be thought that contemporary fiction is all of a piece; the preceding stories have already demonstrated its variety. The following are also varied; if the reader does not like one he need not despair; he need only (in Chaucer's words) "turne over the leef and chese another tale."

Nathaniel Hawthorne (1804–1864)

Young Goodman Brown

Young Goodman Brown came forth at sunset into the street at Salem village; but put his head back, after crossing the threshold, to exchange a parting kiss with his young wife. And Faith, as the wife was aptly named, thrust her own pretty head into the street, letting the wind play with the pink ribbons of her cap while she called to Goodman Brown.

"Dearest heart," whispered she, softly and rather sadly, when her lips were close to his ear, "prithee put off your journey until sunrise and sleep in your own bed to-night. A lone woman is troubled with such dreams and such thoughts that she's afeared of herself sometimes. Pray tarry with me this night, dear husband, of all nights in the year."

"My love and my Faith," replied young Goodman Brown, "of all nights in the year, this one night must I tarry away from thee. My journey, as thou callest it, forth and back again, must needs be done 'twixt now and sunrise. What, my sweet, pretty wife, dost thou doubt me already, and we but three months married?"

"Then God bless you!" said Faith, with the pink ribbons; "and may you find all well when you come back."

"Amen!" cried Goodman Brown. "Say thy prayers, dear Faith, and go to bed at dusk, and no harm will come to thee."

So they parted; and the young man pursued his way until, being about to turn the corner by the meeting-house, he looked back and saw the head of Faith still peeping after him with a melancholy air, in spite of her pink ribbons.

"Poor little Faith!" thought he, for his heart smote him. "What a wretch am I to leave her on such an errand! She talks of dreams, too. Methought as she spoke there was trouble in her face, as if a dream had warned her what work is to be done to-night. But no, no; 'twould kill her to think it. Well, she's a blessed angel on earth; and after this one night I'll cling to her skirts and follow her to heaven."

With this excellent resolve for the future, Goodman Brown felt himself justified in making more haste on his present evil purpose. He had taken a dreary road, darkened by all the gloomiest trees of the forest, which barely stood aside to let the narrow path creep through, and closed immediately behind. It was all as lonely as could be; and there is this peculiarity in such a solitude, that the traveller knows not who may be concealed by the innumerable trunks and the thick boughs overhead; so that with lonely footsteps he may yet be passing through an unseen multitude.

"There may be a devilish Indian behind every tree," said Goodman Brown to himself; and he glanced fearfully behind him as he added, "What if the devil himself should be at my very elbow!"

His head being turned back, he passed a crook of the road, and, looking forward again, beheld the figure of a man, in grave and decent attire, seated at the foot of an old tree. He arose at Goodman Brown's approach and walked onward side by side with him.

"You are late, Goodman Brown," said he. "The clock of the Old South was striking as I came through Boston, and that is full fifteen minutes agone."

"Faith kept me back a while," replied the young man, with a tremor in his voice, caused by the sudden appearance of his companion, though not wholly unexpected.

It was now deep dusk in the forest, and deepest in that part of it where these two were journeying. As nearly as could be discerned, the second traveller was about fifty years old, apparently in the same rank of life as Goodman Brown, and bearing a considerable resemblance to him, though perhaps more in expression than features. Still they might have been taken for father and son. And yet, though the elder person was as simply clad as the younger, and as simple in manner too, he had an indescribable air of one who knew the world, and who would not have felt abashed at the governor's dinner table or in King William's court, were it possible that his affairs should call him thither. But the only thing about him that could be fixed upon as remarkable was his staff, which bore the likeness of a great black snake, so curiously wrought that it might almost be seen to twist and wriggle itself like a living serpent. This, of course, must have been an ocular deception, assisted by the uncertain light.

"Come, Goodman Brown," cried his fellow-traveller, "this is a dull pace for the beginning of a journey. Take my staff, if you are so soon weary."

"Friend," said the other, exchanging his slow pace for a full stop, "having kept covenant by meeting thee here, it is my purpose now to return whence I came. I have scruples touching the matter thou wot'st of."

"Sayest thou so?" replied he of the serpent, smiling apart. "Let us walk on, nevertheless, reasoning as we go; and if I convince thee not thou shalt turn back. We are but a little way in the forest yet."

"Too far! too far!" exclaimed the goodman, unconsciously resuming his walk. "My father never went into the woods on such an errand, nor his father before him. We have been a race of honest men and good Christians since the days of the martyrs; and shall I be the first of the name of Brown that ever took this path and kept — "

"Such company, thou wouldst say," observed the elder person, interpreting his pause. "Well said, Goodman Brown! I have been as well acquainted with your family as with ever a one among the Puritans; and that's no trifle to say. I helped your grandfather, the constable, when he lashed the Quaker woman so smartly through the streets of Salem; and it was I that brought your father a pitch-pine knot, kindled at my own hearth, to set fire to an Indian village, in King Philip's war. They were my good friends, both; and many a pleasant walk have we had along this path, and returned merrily after midnight. I would fain be friends with you for their sake."

"If it be as thou sayest," replied Goodman Brown, "I marvel they never spoke of these matters; or, verily, I marvel not, seeing that the least rumor of the sort would have driven them from New England. We are a people of prayer, and good works to boot, and abide no such wickedness."

"Wickedness or not," said the traveller with the twisted staff, "I have a very general acquaintance here in New England. The deacons of many a church have drunk the communion wine with me; the selectmen of divers towns make me their chairman; and a majority of the Great and General Court are firm supporters of my interest. The governor and I, too — But these are state secrets."

"Can this be so?" cried Goodman Brown, with a stare of amazement at his undisturbed companion. "Howbeit, I have nothing to do with the governor and council; they have their own ways, and are no rule for a simple husbandman like me. But, were I to go on with thee, how should I meet the eye of that good old man, or minister, at Salem village? Oh, his voice would make me tremble both Sabbath day and lecture day."

Thus far the elder traveller had listened with due gravity; but now burst into a fit of irrepressible mirth, shaking himself so violently that his snake-like staff actually seemed to wriggle in sympathy.

"Ha! ha! ha!" shouted he again and again; then composing himself, "Well, go on, Goodman Brown, go on; but, prithee, don't kill me with laughing."

"Well, then, to end the matter at once," said Goodman Brown, considerably nettled, "there is my wife, Faith. It would break her dear little heart; and I'd rather break my own."

"Nay, if that be the case," answered the other, "e'en go thy ways, Goodman Brown. I would not for twenty old women like the one hobbling before us that Faith should come to any harm."

As he spoke he pointed his staff at a female figure on the path, in whom Goodman Brown recognized a very pious and exemplary dame, who had taught him his catechism in youth, and was still his moral and spiritual adviser, jointly with the minister and Deacon Gookin.

"A marvel, truly, that Goody Cloyse should be so far in the wilderness at nightfall," said he. "But with your leave, friend, I shall take a cut through the woods until we have left this Christian woman behind. Being a stranger to you, she might ask whom I was consorting with and whither I was going."

"Be it so," said his fellow-traveller. "Betake you the woods, and let me keep the path."

Accordingly the young man turned aside, but took care to watch his companion, who advanced softly along the road until he had come within a staff's length of the old dame. She, meanwhile, was making the best of her way, with singular speed for so aged a woman, and mumbling some indistinct words — a prayer, doubtless — as she went. The traveller put forth his staff and touched her withered neck with what seemed the serpent's tail.

"The devil!" screamed the pious old lady.

"Then Goody Cloyse knows her old friend?" observed the traveller, confronting her and leaning on his writhing stick.

"Ah, forsooth, and is it your worship indeed?" cried the good dame. "Yea, truly is it, and in the very image of my old gossip, Goodman Brown, the grandfather of the silly fellow that now is. But — would your worship believe it? — my broomstick hath strangely disappeared, stolen, as I suspect, by that unhanged witch, Goody Cory, and that, too, when I was all anointed with the juice of smallage, and cinquefoil, and wolf's bane — "

"Mingled with fine wheat and the fat of a new-born babe," said the shape of old Goodman Brown.

"Ah, your worship knows the recipe," cried the old lady, cackling aloud. "So, as I was saying, being all ready for the meeting, and no horse to ride on, I made up my mind to foot it; for they tell me there is a nice young man to be taken into communion to-night. But now your good worship will lend me your arm, and we shall be there in a twinkling."

"That can hardly be," answered her friend. "I may not spare you my arm, Goody Cloyse; but here is my staff, if you will."

So saying, he threw it down at her feet, where, perhaps, it assumed life, being one of the rods which its owner had formerly lent to the Egyptian magi. Of this fact, however, Goodman Brown could not take cognizance. He had cast up his eyes in astonishment, and, looking down again, beheld neither Goody Cloyse nor the serpentine staff, but his fellow-traveller alone, who waited for him as calmly as if nothing had happened.

"That old woman taught me my catechism," said the young man; and there was a world of meaning in this simple comment.

They continued to walk onward, while the elder traveller exhorted his companion to make good speed and persevere in the path, discoursing so aptly that his arguments seemed rather to spring up in the bosom of his auditor than to be suggested by himself. As they went, he plucked a branch of maple to serve for a walking stick, and began to strip it of the twigs and little boughs, which were wet with evening dew. The moment his fingers touched them they became strangely withered and dried up as with a week's sunshine. Thus the pair proceeded, at a good free pace, until suddenly, in a gloomy hollow of the road, Goodman Brown sat himself down on the stump of a tree and refused to go any farther.

"Friend," said he, stubbornly, "my mind is made up. Not another step will I budge on this errand. What if a wretched old woman do choose to go to the devil when I thought she was going to heaven: is that any reason why I should quit my dear Faith and go after her?"

"You will think better of this by and by," said his acquaintance, composedly. "Sit here and rest yourself a while; and when you feel like moving again, there is my staff to help you along."

Without more words, he threw his companion the maple stick, and was as speedily out of sight as if he had vanished into the deepening gloom. The young man sat a few moments by the roadside, applauding himself greatly, and thinking with how clear a conscience he should meet the minister in his morning walk, nor shrink from the eye of good old Deacon Gookin. And what calm sleep would be his that very night, which was to have been spent so wickedly, but so purely and sweetly now, in the arms of Faith! Amidst these pleasant and praiseworthy meditations, Goodman Brown heard the tramp of horses along the road, and deemed it advisable to conceal himself within the verge of the forest, conscious of the guilty purpose that had brought him thither, though now so happily turned from it.

On came the hoof tramps and the voices of the riders, two grave old voices, conversing soberly as they drew near. These mingled sounds appeared to pass along the road, within a few yards of the young man's hiding-place; but, owing doubtless to the depth of the gloom at that particular spot, neither the travellers nor their steeds were visible. Though their figures brushed the small boughs by the wayside, it could not be seen that they intercepted, even for a moment, the faint gleam from the strip of bright sky athwart which they must have passed. Goodman Brown alternately crouched and stood on tiptoe, pulling aside the branches and thrusting forth his head as far as he durst without discerning so much as a shadow. It vexed him the more, because he could have sworn, were such a thing possible, that he recognized the voices of the minister and Deacon Gookin, jogging along quietly, as they were wont to do, when bound to some ordination or ecclesiastical council. While yet within hearing, one of the riders stopped to pluck a switch.

"Of the two, reverend sir," said the voice like the deacon's, "I had rather miss an ordination dinner than to-night's meeting. They tell me that some of our community are to be here from Falmouth and beyond, and others from Connecticut and Rhode Island, besides several of the Indian powwows, who, after their fashion, know almost as much deviltry as the best of us. Moreover, there is a goodly young woman to be taken into communion."

"Mighty well, Deacon Gookin!" replied the solemn old tones of the minister. "Spur up, or we shall be late. Nothing can be done, you know, until I get on the ground."

The hoofs clattered again; and the voices, talking so strangely in the empty air, passed on through the forest, where no church had ever been gathered or solitary Christian prayed. Whither, then, could these holy men be journeying so deep into the heathen wilderness? Young Goodman Brown caught hold of a tree for support, being ready to sink down on the ground, faint and overburdened with the heavy sickness of his heart. He looked up to the sky, doubting whether there really was a heaven above him. Yet there was the blue arch, and the stars brightening in it.

"With heaven above and Faith below, I will yet stand firm against the devil!" cried Goodman Brown.

While he still gazed upward into the deep arch of the firmament and had lifted his hands to pray, a cloud, though no wind was stirring, hurried across the zenith and hid the brightening stars. The blue sky was still visible, except directly overhead, where this black mass of cloud was sweeping swiftly northward. Aloft in the air, as if from the depths of the cloud, came a confused and doubtful sound of voices. Once the listener fancied that he could distinguish the accents of townspeople of his own, men and women, both pious and ungodly, many of whom he had met at the communion table, and had seen others rioting at the tavern. The next moment, so indistinct were the sounds, he doubted whether he had heard aught but the murmur of the old forest, whispering without a wind. Then came a stronger swell of those familiar tones, heard daily in the sunshine at Salem village, but never until now from a cloud of night. There was one voice, of a young woman, uttering lamentations, yet with an uncertain sorrow, and entreating for some favor, which, perhaps, it would grieve her to obtain; and all the unseen multitude, both saints and sinners, seemed to encourage her onward.

"Faith!" shouted Goodman Brown, in a voice of agony and desperation; and the echoes of the forest mocked him, crying, "Faith! Faith!" as if bewildered wretches were seeking her all through the wilderness.

The cry of grief, rage, and terror was yet piercing the night, when the unhappy husband held his breath for a response. There was a scream, drowned immediately in a louder murmur of voices, fading into far-off laughter, as the dark cloud swept away, leaving the clear and silent sky above Goodman Brown. But something fluttered lightly down through the air and caught on the branch of a tree. The young man seized it, and beheld a pink ribbon.

"My Faith is gone!" cried he, after one stupefied moment. "There is no good on earth; and sin is but a name. Come, devil; for to thee is this world given."

And, maddened with despair, so that he laughed loud and long, did Goodman Brown grasp his staff and set forth again, at such a rate that he seemed to fly along the forest path rather than to walk or run. The road grew wilder and drearier and more faintly traced, and vanished at length, leaving him in the heart of the dark wilderness, still rushing onward with the instinct that guides mortal man to evil. The whole forest was peopled with frightful sounds — the creaking of the trees, the howling of wild beasts, and the yell of Indians; while sometimes the wind tolled like a distant church bell, and sometimes gave a broad roar around the traveller, as if all Nature were laughing him to scorn. But he was himself the chief horror of the scene, and shrank not from its other horrors. "Ha! ha! ha!" roared Goodman Brown when the wind laughed at him. "Let us hear which will laugh loudest. Think not to frighten me with your deviltry. Come witch, come wizard, come Indian powwow, come devil himself, and here comes Goodman Brown. You may as well fear him as he fear you."

In truth, all through the haunted forest there could be nothing more frightful than the figure of Goodman Brown. On he flew among the black pines, brandishing his staff with frenzied gestures, now giving vent to an inspiration of horrid blasphemy, and now shouting forth such laughter as set all the echoes of the forest laughing like demons around him. The fiend in his own shape is less hideous than when he rages in the breast of man. Thus sped the demoniac on his course, until, quivering among the trees, he saw a red light before him, as when the felled trunks and branches of a clearing have been set on fire, and throw up their lurid blaze against the sky, at the hour of midnight. He paused, in a lull of the tempest that had driven him onward, and heard the swell of what seemed a hymn, rolling solemnly from a distance with the weight of many voices. He knew the tune; it was a familiar one in the choir of the village meeting-house. The verse died heavily away, and was lengthened by a chorus, not of human voices, but of all the sounds of the benighted wilderness pealing in awful harmony together. Goodman Brown cried out, and his cry was lost to his own ear by its unison with the cry of the desert.

In the interval of silence he stole forward until the light glared full upon his eyes. At one extremity of an open space, hemmed in by the dark wall of the forest, arose a rock, bearing some rude, natural resemblance either to an altar or a pulpit, and surrounded by four blazing pines, their tops aflame, their stems untouched, like candles at an evening meeting. The mass of foliage that had overgrown the summit of the rock was all on fire, blazing high into the night and fitfully illuminating the whole field. Each pendent twig and leafy festoon was in a blaze. As the red light arose and fell, a numerous congregation alternately shone forth, then disappeared in shadow, and again grew, as it were, out of the darkness, peopling the heart of the solitary woods at once.

"A grave and dark-clad company," quoth Goodman Brown.

In truth they were such. Among them, quivering to and fro between gloom and splendor, appeared faces that would be seen next day at the council board of the province, and others which, Sabbath after Sabbath, looked devoutly heavenward, and benignantly over the crowded pews, from the holiest pulpits in the land. Some affirm that the lady of the governor was there. At least there were high dames well known to her, and wives of honored husbands, and widows, a great multitude, and ancient maidens, all of excellent repute, and fair young girls, who trembled lest their mothers should espy them. Either the sudden gleams of light flashing over the obscure field bedazzled Goodman Brown, or he recognized a score of the church members of Salem village famous for their especial sanctity. Good old Deacon Gookin had arrived, and waited at the skirts of that venerable saint, his revered pastor. But, irreverently consorting with these grave, reputable, and pious people, these elders of the church, these chaste dames and dewy virgins, there were men of dissolute lives and women of spotted fame, wretches given over to all mean and filthy vice, and suspected even of horrid crimes. It was strange to see that the good shrank not from the wicked, nor were the sinners abashed by the saints. Scattered also among their pale-faced enemies were the Indian priests, or powwows, who had often scared their native forest with more hideous incantations than any known to English witchcraft.

"But where is Faith?" thought Goodman Brown; and, as hope came into his heart, he trembled.

Another verse of the hymn arose, a slow and mournful strain, such as the pious love, but joined to words which expressed all that our nature can conceive of sin, and darkly hinted at far more. Unfathomable to mere mortals is the lore of fiends. Verse after verse was sung; and still the chorus of the desert swelled between like the deepest tone of a mighty organ; and with the final peal of that dreadful anthem there came a sound, as if the roaring wind, the rushing streams, the howling beasts, and every other voice of the unconcerted wilderness were mingling and according with the voice of guilty man in homage to the prince of all. The four blazing pines threw up a loftier flame, and obscurely discovered shapes and visages of horror on the smoke wreaths above the impious assembly. At the same moment the fire on the rock shot redly forth and formed a glowing arch above its base, where now appeared a figure. With reverence be it spoken, the figure bore no slight similitude, both in garb and manner, to some grave divine of the New England churches.

"Bring forth the converts!" cried a voice that echoed through the field and rolled into the forest.

At the word, Goodman Brown stepped forth from the shadow of the trees and approached the congregation, with whom he felt a loathful brotherhood by the sympathy of all that was wicked in his heart. He could have well-nigh sworn that the shape of his own dead father beckoned him to advance, looking downward from a smoke wreath, while a woman, with dim features of despair, threw out her hand to warn him back. Was it his mother? But he had no power to retreat one step, nor to resist, even in thought, when the minister and good old Deacon Gookin seized his arms and led him to the blazing rock. Thither came also the slender form of a veiled female, led between Goody Cloyse, that pious teacher of the catechism, and Martha Carrier, who had received the devil's promise to be queen of hell. A rampant hag was she. And there stood the proselytes beneath the canopy of fire.

"Welcome, my children" said the dark figure, "to the communion of your race. Ye have found thus young your nature and your destiny. My children, look behind you!"

They turned; and flashing forth, as it were, in a sheet of flame, the fiend worshippers were seen; the smile of welcome gleamed darkly on every visage.

"There," resumed the sable form, "are all whom ye have reverenced from youth. Ye deemed them holier than yourselves, and shrank from your own sin, contrasting it with their lives of righteousness and prayerful aspirations heavenward. Yet here are they all in my worshipping assembly. This night it shall be granted you to know their secret deeds: how hoary-bearded elders of the church have whispered wanton words to the young maids of their households; how many a woman, eager for widows' weeds, has given her husband a drink at bedtime and let him sleep his last sleep in her bosom; how beardless youths have made haste to inherit their fathers' wealth; and how fair damsels — blush not, sweet ones — have dug little graves in the garden, and bidden me, the sole guest, to an infant's funeral. By the sympathy of your human hearts for sin ye shall scent out all the places — whether in church, bed-chamber, street, field, or forest — where crime has been committed, and shall exult to behold the whole earth one stain of guilt, one mighty blood spot. Far more than this. It shall be yours to penetrate, in every bosom, the deep mystery of sin, the fountain of all wicked arts, and which inexhaustibly supplies more evil impulses than human power — than my power at its utmost — can make manifest in deeds. And now, my children, look upon each other."

They did so; and, by the blaze of the hell-kindled torches, the wretched man beheld his Faith, and the wife her husband, trembling before that unhallowed altar.

"Lo, there ye stand, my children," said the figure, in a deep and solemn tone, almost sad with its despairing awfulness, as if his once angelic nature could yet mourn for our miserable race. "Depending upon one another's hearts, ye had still hoped that virtue were not all a dream. Now are ye undeceived. Evil is the nature of mankind. Evil must be your only happiness. Welcome again, my children, to the communion of your race."

"Welcome," repeated the fiend worshippers, in one cry of despair and triumph.

And there they stood, the only pair, as it seemed, who were yet hesitating on the verge of wickedness in this dark world. A basin was hollowed, naturally, in the rock. Did it contain water, reddened by the lurid light! or was it blood? or, perchance, a liquid flame? Herein did the shape of evil dip his hand and prepare to lay the mark of baptism upon their foreheads, that they might be partakers of the mystery of sin, more conscious of the secret guilt of others, both in deed and thought, than they could now be of their own. The husband cast one look at his pale wife, and Faith at him. What polluted wretches would the next glance show them to each other, shuddering alike at what they disclosed and what they saw!

"Faith! Faith!" cried the husband, "look up to heaven, and resist the wicked one."

Whether Faith obeyed he knew not. Hardly had he spoken when he found himself amid calm night and solitude, listening to a roar of the wind which died heavily away through the forest. He staggered against the rock, and felt it chill and damp; while a hanging twig, that had been all on fire, besprinkled his cheek with the coldest dew.

The next morning young Goodman Brown came slowly into the street of Salem village, staring around him like a bewildered man. The good old minister was taking a walk along the graveyard to get an appetite for breakfast and meditate his sermon, and bestowed a blessing, as he passed, on Goodman Brown. He shrank from the venerable saint as if to avoid an anathema. Old Deacon Gookin was at domestic worship, and the holy words of his prayer were heard through the open window. "What God doth the wizard pray to?" quoth Goodman Brown. Goody Cloyse, that excellent old Christian, stood in the early sunshine at her own lattice, catechizing a little girl who had brought her a pint of morning's milk. Goodman Brown snatched away the child as from the grasp of the fiend himself. Turning the corner by the meeting-house, he spied the head of Faith, with the pink ribbons, gazing anxiously forth, and bursting into such joy at sight of him that she skipped along the street and almost kissed her husband before the whole village. But Goodman Brown looked sternly and sadly into her face, and passed on without a greeting.

Had Goodman Brown fallen asleep in the forest and only dreamed a wild dream of a witch-meeting?

Be it so if you will; but, alas! it was a dream of evil omen for young Goodman Brown. A stern, a sad, a darkly meditative, a distrustful, if not a desperate man did he become from the night of that fearful dream. On the Sabbath day, when the congregation were singing a holy psalm, he could not listen because an anthem of sin rushed loudly upon his ear and drowned all the blessed strain. When the minister spoke from the pulpit with power and fervid eloquence, and, with his hand on the open Bible, of the sacred truths of our religion, and of saint-like lives and triumphant deaths, and of future bliss or misery unutterable, then did Goodman Brown turn pale, dreading lest the roof should thunder down upon the gray blasphemer and his hearers. Often, awaking suddenly at midnight, he shrank from the bosom of Faith; and at morning or eventide, when the family knelt down at prayer, he scowled and muttered to himself, and gazed sternly at his wife, and turned away. And when he had lived long, and was borne to his grave a hoary corpse, followed by Faith, an aged woman, and children and grandchildren, a goodly procession, besides neighbors not a few, they carved no hopeful verse upon his tombstone, for his dying hour was gloom.

Edgar Allan Poe (1809–1849)

The Cask of Amontillado

The thousand injuries of Fortunato I had borne as I best could, but when he ventured upon insult, I vowed revenge. You, who so well know the nature of my soul, will not suppose, however, that I gave utterance to a threat. *At length* I would be avenged; this was a point definitely settled — but the very definitiveness with which it was resolved precluded the idea of risk. I must not only punish, but punish with impunity. A wrong is unredressed when retribution overtakes its redresser. It is equally unredressed when the avenger fails to make himself felt as such to him who has done the wrong.

It must be understood that neither by word nor deed had I given Fortunato cause to doubt my good will. I continued, as was my wont, to smile in his face, and he did not perceive that my smile *now* was at the thought of his immolation.

He had a weak point — this Fortunato — although in other regards he was a man to be respected and even feared. He prided himself on his connoisseurship in wine. Few Italians have the true virtuoso spirit. For the most part their enthusiasm is adopted to suit the time and opportunity to practice imposture upon the British and Austrian *millionaires.* In painting and gemmary Fortunato, like his countrymen, was a quack, but in the matter of old wines he was sincere. In this respect I did not differ from him materially; — I was skillful in the Italian vintages myself, and bought largely whenever I could.

It was about dusk, one evening during the supreme madness of the carnival season, that I encountered my friend. He accosted me with excessive warmth, for he had been drinking much. The man wore motley. He had on a tight-fitting parti-striped dress, and his head was surmounted by the conical cap and bells. I was so pleased to see him, that I thought I should never have done wringing his hand.

I said to him — "My dear Fortunato, you are luckily met. How remarkably well you are looking to-day! But I have received a pipe° of what passes for Amontillado, and I have my doubts."

"How?" said he, "Amontillado? A pipe? Impossible! And in the middle of the carnival?"

"I have my doubts," I replied; "and I was silly enough to pay the full Amontillado price without consulting you in the matter. You were not to be found, and I was fearful of losing a bargain."

"Amontillado!"

"I have my doubts."

"Amontillado!"

"And I must satisfy them."

"Amontillado!"

"As you are engaged, I am on my way to Luchesi. If any one has a critical turn, it is he. He will tell me — "

"Luchesi cannot tell Amontillado from Sherry."

"And yet some fools will have it that his taste is a match for your own."

"Come, let us go."

"Whither?"

"To your vaults."

"My friend, no; I will not impose upon your good nature. I perceive you have an engagement. Luchesi — "

"I have no engagement; come."

"My friend, no. It is not the engagement, but the severe cold with which I perceive you are afflicted. The vaults are insufferably damp. They are encrusted with nitre."

"Let us go, nevertheless. The cold is merely nothing. Amontillado! You have been imposed upon; and as for Luchesi, he cannot distinguish Sherry from Amontillado."

Thus speaking, Fortunato possessed himself of my arm. Putting on

pipe wine cask

a mask of black silk, and drawing a *roquelaure*° closely about my person, I suffered him to hurry me to my palazzo.

There were no attendants at home; they had absconded to make merry in honor of the time. I had told them that I should not return until the morning, and had given them explicit orders not to stir from the house. These orders were sufficient, I well knew, to insure their immediate disappearance, one and all, as soon as my back was turned.

I took from their sconces two flambeaux, and giving one to Fortunato, bowed him through several suites of rooms to the archway that led into the vaults. I passed down a long and winding staircase, requesting him to be cautious as he followed. We came at length to the foot of the descent, and stood together on the damp ground of the catacombs of the Montresors.

The gait of my friend was unsteady, and the bells upon his cap jingled as he strode.

"The pipe," said he.

"It is farther on," said I; "but observe the white web-work which gleams from these cavern walls."

He turned towards me, and looked into my eyes with two filmy orbs that distilled the rheum of intoxication.

"Nitre?" he asked, at length.

"Nitre," I replied. "How long have you had that cough?"

"Ugh! ugh! ugh! — ugh! ugh! ugh! — ugh! ugh! ugh! — ugh! ugh! ugh! — ugh! ugh! ugh!"

My poor friend found it impossible to reply for many minutes.

"It is nothing," he said, at last.

"Come," I said, with decision, "we will go back; your health is precious. You are rich, respected, admired, beloved; you are happy, as once I was. You are a man to be missed. For me it is no matter. We will go back; you will be ill, and I cannot be responsible. Besides, there is Luchesi — "

"Enough," he said; "the cough is a mere nothing: it will not kill me. I shall not die of a cough."

"True — true," I replied; "and, indeed, I had no intention of alarming you unnecessarily — but you should use all proper caution. A draught of this Medoc will defend us from the damps."

Here I knocked off the neck of a bottle which I drew from a long row of its fellows that lay upon the mould.

"Drink," I said, presenting him the wine.

He raised it to his lips with a leer. He paused and nodded to me familiarly, while his bells jingled.

roquelaure   short cloak

"I drink," he said, "to the buried that repose around us."

"And I to your long life."

He again took my arm, and we proceeded.

"These vaults," he said, "are extensive."

"The Montresors," I replied, "were a great and numerous family."

"I forget your arms."

"A huge human foot d'or, in a field azure; the foot crushes a serpent rampant whose fangs are imbedded in the heel."

"And the motto?"

"*Nemo me impune lacessit.*"°

"Good!" he said.

The wine sparkled in his eyes and the bells jingled. My own fancy grew warm with the Medoc. We had passed through walls of piled bones, with casks and puncheons intermingling, into the inmost recesses of the catacombs. I paused again, and this time I made bold to seize Fortunato by an arm above the elbow.

"The nitre!" I said; "see, it increases. It hangs like moss upon the vaults. We are below the river's bed. The drops of moisture trickle among the bones. Come, we will go back ere it is too late. Your cough — "

"It is nothing," he said; "let us go on. But first, another draught of the Medoc."

I broke and reached him a flagon of De Grâve. He emptied it at a breath. His eyes flashed with a fierce light. He laughed and threw the bottle upwards with a gesticulation I did not understand.

I looked at him in surprise. He repeated the movement — a grotesque one.

"You do not comprehend?" he said.

"Not I," I replied.

"Then you are not of the brotherhood."

"How?"

"You are not of the masons."

"Yes, yes," I said, "yes, yes."

"You? Impossible! A mason?"

"A mason," I replied.

"A sign," he said.

"It is this," I answered, producing a trowel from beneath the folds of my *roquelaure*.

"You jest," he exclaimed, recoiling a few paces. "But let us proceed to the Amontillado."

"Be it so," I said, replacing the tool beneath the cloak, and again

Nemo me impune lacessit.   No one dare attack me with impunity (the motto of Scotland)

offering him my arm. He leaned upon it heavily. We continued our route in search of the Amontillado. We passed through a range of low arches, descended, passed on, and descending again, arrived at a deep crypt, in which the foulness of the air caused our flambeaux rather to glow than flame.

At the most remote end of the crypt there appeared another less spacious. Its walls had been lined with human remains piled to the vault overhead, in the fashion of the great catacombs of Paris. Three sides of this interior crypt were still ornamented in this manner. From the fourth the bones had been thrown down, and lay promiscuously upon the earth, forming at one point a mound of some size. Within the wall thus exposed by the displacing of the bones, we perceived a still interior recess, in depth about four feet, in width three, in height six or seven. It seemed to have been constructed for no especial use within itself, but formed merely the interval between two of the colossal supports of the roof of the catacombs, and was backed by one of their circumscribing walls of solid granite.

It was in vain that Fortunato, uplifting his dull torch, endeavored to pry into the depths of the recess. Its termination the feeble light did not enable us to see.

"Proceed," I said; "herein is the Amontillado. As for Luchesi — "

"He is an ignoramus," interrupted my friend, as he stepped unsteadily forward, while I followed immediately at his heels. In an instant he had reached the extremity of the niche, and finding his progress arrested by the rock, stood stupidly bewildered. A moment more and I had fettered him to the granite. In its surface were two iron staples, distant from each other about two feet, horizontally. From one of these depended a short chain, from the other a padlock. Throwing the links about his waist, it was but the work of a few seconds to secure it. He was too much astounded to resist. Withdrawing the key I stepped back from the recess.

"Pass your hand," I said, "over the wall; you cannot help feeling the nitre. Indeed it is *very* damp. Once more let me *implore* you to return. No? Then I must positively leave you. But I must first render you all the little attentions in my power."

"The Amontillado!" ejaculated my friend, not yet recovered from his astonishment.

"True," I replied; "the Amontillado."

As I said these words I busied myself among the pile of bones of which I have before spoken. Throwing them aside, I soon uncovered a quantity of building-stone and mortar. With these materials and with the aid of my trowel, I began vigorously to wall up the entrance of the niche.

I had scarcely laid the first tier of the masonry when I discovered that the intoxication of Fortunato had in a great measure worn off. The earliest indication I had of this was a low moaning cry from the depth of the recess. It was *not* the cry of a drunken man. There was then a long and obstinate silence. I laid the second tier, and the third, and the fourth; and then I heard the furious vibrations of the chain. The noise lasted for several minutes, during which, that I might hearken to it with the more satisfaction, I ceased my labors and sat down upon the bones. When at last the clanking subsided, I resumed the trowel, and finished without interruption the fifth, the sixth, and the seventh tier. The wall was now nearly upon a level with my breast. I again paused, and holding the flambeaux over the mason-work, threw a few feeble rays upon the figure within.

A succession of loud and shrill screams, bursting suddenly from the throat of the chained form, seemed to thrust me violently back. For a brief moment I hesitated — I trembled. Unsheathing my rapier, I began to grope with it about the recess; but the thought of an instant reassured me. I placed my hand upon the solid fabric of the catacombs, and felt satisfied. I reapproached the wall. I replied to the yells of him who clamored. I re-echoed — I aided — I surpassed them in volume and in strength. I did this, and the clamorer grew still.

It was now midnight, and my task was drawing to a close. I had completed the eighth, the ninth, and the tenth tier. I had finished a portion of the last and the eleventh; there remained but a single stone to be fitted and plastered in. I struggled with its weight; I placed it partially in its destined position. But now there came from out the niche a low laugh that erected the hairs upon my head. It was succeeded by a sad voice, which I had difficulty in recognizing as that of the noble Fortunato. The voice said —

"Ha! ha! ha! — he! he! he! — a very good joke indeed — an excellent jest. We will have many a rich laugh about it at the palazzo — he! he! he! — over our wine — he! he! he!"

"The Amontillado!" I said.

"He! he! he! — he! he! he! — yes, the Amontillado. But is it not getting late? Will not they be awaiting us at the palazzo, the Lady Fortunato and the rest? Let us be gone."

"Yes," I said, "let us be gone."

"For the love of God, Montresor!"

"Yes," I said, "for the love of God!"

But to these words I hearkened in vain for a reply. I grew impatient. I called aloud;

"Fortunato!"

No answer. I called again;

"Fortunato!"

No answer still, I thrust a torch through the remaining aperture and let it fall within. There came forth in return only a jingling of the bells. My heart grew sick — on account of the dampness of the catacombs. I hastened to make an end of my labor. I forced the last stone into its position; I plastered it up. Against the new masonry I re-erected the old rampart of bones. For the half of a century no mortal has disturbed them. *In pace requiescat!*°

Anton Chekhov (1860–1904)

Gooseberries

Translated by Avrahm Yarmolinsky

The sky had been overcast since early morning; it was a still day, not hot, but tedious, as it usually is when the weather is gray and dull, when clouds have been hanging over the fields for a long time, and you wait for the rain that does not come. Ivan Ivanych, a veterinary, and Burkin, a high school teacher, were already tired with walking, and the plain seemed endless to them. Far ahead were the scarcely visible windmills of the village of Mironositzkoe; to the right lay a range of hills that disappeared in the distance beyond the village, and both of them knew that over there were the river, and fields, green willows, homesteads, and if you stood on one of the hills, you could see from there another vast plain, telegraph poles, and a train that from afar looked like a caterpillar crawling, and in clear weather you could even see the town. Now, when it was still and when nature seemed mild and pensive, Ivan Ivanych and Burkin were filled with love for this plain, and both of them thought what a beautiful land it was.

"Last time when we were in Elder Prokofy's barn," said Burkin, "you were going to tell me a story."

"Yes; I wanted to tell you about my brother."

Ivan Ivanych heaved a slow sigh and lit his pipe before beginning his story, but just then it began to rain. And five minutes later there was a downpour, and it was hard to tell when it would be over. The two men halted, at a loss; the dogs, already wet, stood with their tails between their legs and looked at them feelingly.

In pace requiescat!   May he rest in peace!

"We must find shelter somewhere," said Burkin. "Let's go to Alyohin's; it's quite near."

"Let's."

They turned aside and walked across a mown meadow, now going straight ahead, now bearing to the right, until they reached the road. Soon poplars came into view, a garden, then the red roofs of barns; the river gleamed, and the view opened on a broad expanse of water with a mill and a white bathing-cabin. That was Sofyino, Alyohin's place.

The mill was going, drowning out the sound of the rain; the dam was shaking. Wet horses stood near the carts, their heads drooping, and men were walking about, their heads covered with sacks. It was damp, muddy, dreary; and the water looked cold and unkind. Ivan Ivanych and Burkin felt cold and messy and uncomfortable through and through; their feet were heavy with mud and when, having crossed the dam, they climbed up to the barns, they were silent as though they were cross with each other.

The noise of a winnowing-machine came from one of the barns, the door was open, and clouds of dust were pouring from within. On the threshold stood Alyohin himself, a man of forty, tall and rotund, with long hair, looking more like a professor or an artist than a gentleman farmer. He was wearing a white blouse, badly in need of washing, that was belted with a rope, and drawers, and his high boots were plastered with mud and straw. His eyes and nose were black with dust. He recognized Ivan Ivanych and Burkin and was apparently very glad to see them.

"Please go up to the house, gentlemen," he said, smiling; "I'll be there directly, in a moment."

It was a large structure of two stories. Alyohin lived downstairs in what was formerly the stewards' quarters: two rooms that had arched ceilings and small windows; the furniture was plain, and the place smelled of rye bread, cheap vodka, and harness. He went into the showy rooms upstairs only rarely, when he had guests. Once in the house, the two visitors were met by a chambermaid, a young woman so beautiful that both of them stood still at the same moment and glanced at each other.

"You can't imagine how glad I am to see you, gentlemen," said Alyohin, joining them in the hall. "What a surprise! Pelageya," he said, turning to the chambermaid, "give the guests a change of clothes. And, come to think of it, I will change, too. But I must go and bathe first, I don't think I've had a wash since spring. Don't you want to go into the bathing-cabin? In the meanwhile things will be got ready here."

The beautiful Pelageya, with her soft, delicate air, brought them bath towels and soap, and Alyohin went to the bathing-cabin with his guests.

"Yes, it's a long time since I've bathed," he said, as he undressed. "I've an excellent bathing-cabin, as you see — it was put up by my father — but somehow I never find time to use it." He sat down on the steps and lathered his long hair and neck, and the water around him turned brown.

"I say — " observed Ivan Ivanych significantly, looking at his head.

"I haven't had a good wash for a long time," repeated Alyohin, embarrassed, and soaped himself once more; the water about him turned dark-blue, the color of ink.

Ivan Ivanych came out of the cabin, plunged into the water with a splash and swam in the rain, thrusting his arms out wide; he raised waves on which white lilies swayed. He swam out to the middle of the river and dived and a minute later came up in another spot and swam on and kept diving, trying to touch bottom. "By God!" he kept repeating delightedly, "by God!" He swam to the mill, spoke to the peasants there, and turned back and in the middle of the river lay floating, exposing his face to the rain. Burkin and Alyohin were already dressed and ready to leave, but he kept on swimming and diving. "By God!" he kept exclaiming. "Lord, have mercy on me."

"You've had enough!" Burkin shouted to him.

They returned to the house. And only when the lamp was lit in the big drawing room upstairs, and the two guests, in silk dressing-gowns and warm slippers, were lounging in armchairs, and Alyohin himself, washed and combed, wearing a new jacket, was walking about the room, evidently savoring the warmth, the cleanliness, the dry clothes and light footwear, and when pretty Pelageya, stepping noiselessly across the carpet and smiling softly, brought in a tray with tea and jam, only then did Ivan Ivanych begin his story, and it was as though not only Burkin and Alyohin were listening, but also the ladies, old and young, and the military men who looked down upon them, calmly and severely, from their gold frames.

"We are two brothers," he began, "I, Ivan Ivanych, and my brother, Nikolay Ivanych, who is two years my junior. I went in for a learned profession and became a veterinary; Nikolay at nineteen began to clerk in a provincial branch of the Treasury. Our father was a *kantonist*, but he rose to be an officer and so a nobleman, a rank that he bequeathed to us together with a small estate. After his death there was a lawsuit and we lost the estate to creditors, but be that as it may, we spent our childhood in the country. Just like peasant children we passed days and nights in the fields and the woods, herded horses, stripped bast from the trees, fished, and so on. And, you know, whoever even once in his life has caught a perch or seen thrushes migrate in the autumn, when on clear, cool days they sweep in flocks over the village, will never really be a townsman and to the day of his death will have a longing for the open. My brother was unhappy in the government office. Years passed, but he went on warming the same seat, scratching away at the same papers, and thinking of one and the same thing: how to get away to the country. And little by little this vague longing turned into a definite desire, into a dream of buying a little property somewhere on the banks of a river or a lake.

"He was a kind and gentle soul and I loved him, but I never sympathized with his desire to shut himself up for the rest of his life on a little property of his own. It is a common saying that a man needs only six feet of earth. But six feet is what a corpse needs, not a man. It is also asserted that if our educated class is drawn to the land and seeks to settle on farms, that's a good thing. But these farms amount to the same six feet of earth. To retire from the city, from the struggle, from the hubbub, to go off and hide on one's own farm — that's not life, it is selfishness, sloth, it is a kind of monasticism, but monasticism without works. Man needs not six feet of earth, not a farm, but the whole globe, all of Nature, where unhindered he can display all the capacities and peculiarities of his free spirit.

"My brother Nikolay, sitting in his office, dreamed of eating his own *shchi*, which would fill the whole farmyard with a delicious aroma, of picnicking on the green grass, of sleeping in the sun, of sitting for hours on the seat by the gate gazing at field and forest. Books on agriculture and the farming items in almanacs were his joy, the delight of his soul. He liked newspapers too, but the only things he read in them were advertisements of land for sale, so many acres of tillable land and pasture, with house, garden, river, mill, and mill-pond. And he pictured to himself garden paths, flowers, fruit, bird-houses with starlings in them, crucians in the pond, and all that sort of thing, you know. These imaginary pictures varied with the advertisements he came upon, but somehow gooseberry bushes figured in every one of them. He could not picture to himself a single country-house, a single rustic nook, without gooseberries.

" 'Country life has its advantages,' he used to say. 'You sit on the veranda having tea, and your ducks swim in the pond, and everything smells delicious and — the gooseberries are ripening.'

"He would draw a plan of his estate and invariably it would contain the following features: a) the master's house; b) servants' quarters; c) kitchen-garden; d) a gooseberry patch. He lived meagerly: he deprived himself of food and drink; he dressed God knows how, like a beggar, but he kept on saving and salting money away in the bank. He was terribly stingy. It was painful for me to see it, and I used to give him small sums and send him something on holidays, but he would put that away too. Once a man is possessed by an idea, there is no doing anything with him.

"Years passed. He was transferred to another province, he was already past forty, yet he was still reading newspaper advertisements and saving up money. Then I heard that he was married. Still for the sake of buying a property with a gooseberry patch he married an elderly, homely widow, without a trace of affection for her, but simply because she had money. After marrying her, he went on living parsimoniously, keeping her half-starved, and he put her money in the bank in his own name. She had previously been the wife of a postmaster, who had got her used to pies and cordials. This second husband did not even give her enough black bread. She began to sicken, and some three years later gave up the ghost. And, of course, it never for a moment occurred to my brother that he was to blame for her death. Money, like vodka, can do queer things to a man. Once in our town a merchant lay on his deathbed; before he died, he ordered a plateful of honey and he ate up all his money and lottery tickets with the honey, so that no one should get it. One day when I was inspecting a drove of cattle at a railway station, a cattle dealer fell under a locomotive and it sliced off his leg. We carried him in to the infirmary, the blood was gushing from the wound — a terrible business, but he kept begging us to find his leg and was very anxious about it: he had twenty rubles in the boot that was on that leg, and he was afraid they would be lost."

"That's a tune from another opera," said Burkin.

Ivan Ivanych paused a moment and then continued:

"After his wife's death, my brother began to look around for a property. Of course, you may scout about for five years and in the end make a mistake, and buy something quite different from what you have been dreaming of. Through an agent my brother bought a mortgaged estate of three hundred acres with a house, servants' quarters, a park, but with no orchard, no gooseberry patch, no duck-pond. There was a stream, but the water in it was the color of coffee, for on one of its banks there was a brickyard and on the other a glue factory. But my brother was not at all disconcerted: he ordered a score of gooseberry bushes, planted them, and settled down to the life of a country gentleman.

"Last year I paid him a visit. I thought I would go and see how things were with him. In his letter to me my brother called his estate 'Chumbaroklov Waste, or Himalaiskoe' (our surname was Chimsha-Himalaisky). I reached the place in the afternoon. It was hot. Everywhere there were ditches, fences, hedges, rows of fir trees, and I was at a loss as to how to get to the yard and where to leave my horse. I made my way to the house and was met by a fat dog with reddish hair that looked like a pig. It wanted to bark, but was too lazy. The cook, a fat, barelegged woman, who also looked like a pig, came out of the kitchen and said that the master was resting after dinner. I went in to see my brother, and found him sitting up in bed, with a quilt over his knees. He had grown older, stouter, flabby; his cheeks, his nose, his lips jutted out: it looked as though he might grunt into the quilt at any moment.

"We embraced and dropped tears of joy and also of sadness at the thought that the two of us had once been young, but were now gray and nearing death. He got dressed and took me out to show me his estate.

" 'Well, how are you getting on here?' I asked.

" 'Oh, all right, thank God. I am doing very well.'

"He was no longer the poor, timid clerk he used to be but a real landowner, a gentleman. He had already grown used to his new manner of living and developed a taste for it. He ate a great deal, steamed himself in the bathhouse, was growing stout, was already having a lawsuit with the village commune and the two factories and was very much offended when the peasants failed to address him as 'Your Honor.' And he concerned himself with his soul's welfare too in a substantial, upper-class manner, and performed good deeds not simply, but pompously. And what good works! He dosed the peasants with bicarbonate and castor oil for all their ailments and on his name day he had a thanksgiving service celebrated in the center of the village, and then treated the villagers to a gallon of vodka, which he thought was the thing to do. Oh, those horrible gallons of vodka! One day a fat landowner hauls the peasants up before the rural police officer for trespassing, and the next, to mark a feast day, treats them to a gallon of vodka, and they drink and shout 'Hurrah' and when they are drunk bow down at his feet. A higher standard of living, over-eating and idleness develop the most insolent self-conceit in a Russian. Nikolay Ivanych, who when he was a petty official was afraid to have opinions of his own even if he kept them to himself, now uttered nothing but incontrovertible truths and did so in the tone of a minister of state: 'Education is necessary, but the masses are not ready for it; corporal punishment is generally harmful, but in some cases it is useful and nothing else will serve.'

" 'I know the common people, and I know how to deal with them,' he would say. 'They love me. I only have to raise my little finger, and they will do anything I want.'

"And all this, mark you, would be said with a smile that bespoke kindness and intelligence. Twenty times over he repeated: 'We, of the gentry,' 'I, as a member of the gentry.' Apparently he no longer remembered that our grandfather had been a peasant and our father just a private. Even our surname, 'Chimsha-Himalaisky,' which in reality is grotesque, seemed to him sonorous, distinguished, and delightful.

"But I am concerned now not with him, but with me. I want to tell you about the change that took place in me during the few hours that I spent on his estate. In the evening when we were having tea, the cook served a plateful of gooseberries. They were not bought, they were his own gooseberries, the first ones picked since the bushes were planted. My brother gave a laugh and for a minute looked at the gooseberries in silence, with tears in his eyes — he could not speak for excitement. Then he put one berry in his mouth, glanced at me with a triumph of a child who has at last been given a toy he was longing for and said: 'How tasty!' And he ate the gooseberries greedily, and kept repeating: 'Ah, how delicious! Do taste them!'

"They were hard and sour, but as Pushkin has it,

The falsehood that exalts we cherish more
Than meaner truths that are a thousand strong.

I saw a happy man, one whose cherished dream had so obviously come true, who had attained his goal in life, who had got what he wanted, who was satisfied with his lot and with himself. For some reason an element of sadness had always mingled with my thoughts of human happiness, and now at the sight of a happy man I was assailed by an oppressive feeling bordering on despair. It weighed on me particularly at night. A bed was made up for me in a room next to my brother's bedroom, and I could hear that he was wakeful, and that he would get up again and again, go to the plate of gooseberries and eat one after another. I said to myself: how many contented, happy people there really are! What an overwhelming force they are! Look at life: the insolence and idleness of the strong, the ignorance and brutishness of the weak, horrible poverty everywhere, overcrowding, degeneration, drunkenness, hypocrisy, lying — Yet in all the houses and on all the streets there is peace and quiet; of the fifty thousand people who live in our town there is not one who would cry out, who would vent his indignation aloud. We see the people who go to market, eat by day, sleep by night, who babble nonsense, marry, grow old, good-naturedly drag their dead to the cemetery, but we do not see or hear those who suffer, and what is terrible in life goes on somewhere behind the scenes. Everything is peaceful and quiet and only mute statistics protest: so many people gone out of their minds, so many gallons of vodka drunk, so many children dead from malnutrition — And such a state of things is evidently necessary; obviously the happy man is at ease only because the unhappy ones bear their burdens in silence, and if there were not this silence, happiness would be impossible. It is a general hypnosis. Behind the door of every contented, happy man there ought to be someone standing with a little hammer and continually reminding him with a knock that there are unhappy people, that however happy he may be, life will sooner or later show him its claws, and trouble will come to him — illness, poverty, losses, and then no one will see or hear him, just as now he neither sees nor hears others. But there is no man with a hammer. The happy man lives at his ease, faintly fluttered by small daily cares, like an aspen in the wind — and all is well."

"That night I came to understand that I too had been contented and happy," Ivan Ivanych continued, getting up. "I too over the dinner table or out hunting would hold forth on how to live, what to believe, the right way to govern the people. I too would say that learning was the enemy of darkness, that education was necessary but that for the common people the three R's were sufficient for the time being. Freedom is a boon, I used to say, it is as essential as air, but we must wait awhile. Yes, that's what I used to say, and now I ask: Why must we wait?" said Ivan Ivanych, looking wrathfully at Burkin. "Why must we wait, I ask you? For what reason? I am told that nothing can be done all at once, that every idea is realized gradually, in its own time. But who is it that says so? Where is the proof that it is just? You cite the natural order of things, the law governing all phenomena, but is there law, is there order in the fact that I, a living, thinking man, stand beside a ditch and wait for it to close up of itself or fill up with silt, when I could jump over it or throw a bridge across it? And again, why must we wait? Wait, until we have no strength to live, and yet we have to live and are eager to live!

"I left my brother's place early in the morning, and ever since then it has become intolerable for me to stay in town. I am oppressed by the peace and the quiet, I am afraid to look at the windows, for there is nothing that pains me more than the spectacle of a happy family sitting at table having tea. I am an old man now and unfit for combat, I am not even capable of hating. I can only grieve inwardly, get irritated, worked up, and at night my head is ablaze with the rush of ideas and I cannot sleep. Oh, if I were young!"

Ivan Ivanych paced up and down the room excitedly and repeated, "If I were young!"

He suddenly walked up to Alyohin and began to press now one of his hands, now the other.

"Pavel Konstantinych," he said imploringly, "don't quiet down, don't let yourself be lulled to sleep! As long as you are young, strong, alert, do not cease to do good! There is no happiness and there should be none, and if life has a meaning and a purpose, that meaning and purpose is not our happiness but something greater and more rational. Do good!"

All this Ivan Ivanych said with a pitiful, imploring smile, as though he were asking a personal favor.

Afterwards all three of them sat in armchairs in different corners of the drawing room and were silent. Ivan Ivanych's story satisfied neither Burkin nor Alyohin. With the ladies and generals looking down from the golden frames, seeming alive in the dim light, it was tedious to listen to the story of the poor devil of a clerk who ate gooseberries. One felt like talking about elegant people, about women. And the fact that they were sitting in a drawing room where everything — the chandelier under its cover, the armchairs, the carpets underfoot — testified that the very people who were now looking down from the frames had once moved about here, sat and had tea, and the fact that lovely Pelageya was noiselessly moving about — that was better than any story.

Alyohin was very sleepy; he had gotten up early, before three o'clock in the morning, to get some work done, and now he could hardly keep his eyes open, but he was afraid his visitors might tell an interesting story in his absence, and he would not leave. He did not trouble to ask himself if what Ivan Ivanych had just said was intelligent or right. The guests were not talking about groats, or hay, or tar, but about something that had no direct bearing on his life, and he was glad of it and wanted them to go on.

"However, it's bedtime," said Burkin, rising. "Allow me to wish you good night."

Aloyohin took leave of his guests and went downstairs to his own quarters, while they remained upstairs. They were installed for the night in a big room in which stood two old wooden beds decorated with carvings and in the corner was an ivory crucifix. The wide cool beds which had been made by the lovely Pelageya gave off a pleasant smell of clean linen.

Ivan Ivanych undressed silently and got into bed.

"Lord forgive us sinners!" he murmured, and drew the bedclothes over his head.

His pipe, which lay on the table, smelled strongly of burnt tobacco, and Burkin, who could not sleep for a long time, kept wondering where the unpleasant odor came from.

The rain beat against the window panes all night.

Edith Wharton (1862–1937)

Roman Fever

I

From the table at which they had been lunching two American ladies of ripe but well-cared-for middle age moved across the lofty terrace of the Roman restaurant and, leaning on its parapet, looked first at each other, and then down on the outspread glories of the Palatine and the Forum, with the same expression of vague but benevolent approval.

As they leaned there a girlish voice echoed up gaily from the stairs leading to the court below. "Well, come along, then," it cried, not to them but to an invisible companion, "and let's leave the young things to their knitting"; and a voice as fresh laughed back: "Oh, look here, Babs, not actually *knitting* — " "Well, I mean figuratively," rejoined the first. "After all, we haven't left our poor parents much else to do . . . " and at that point the turn of the stairs engulfed the dialogue.

The two ladies looked at each other again, this time with a tinge of smiling embarrassment, and the smaller and paler one shook her head and colored slightly.

"Barbara!" she murmured, sending an unheard rebuke after the mocking voice in the stairway.

The other lady, who was fuller, and higher in color, with a small determined nose supported by vigorous black eyebrows, gave a good-humored laugh. "That's what our daughters think of us!"

Her companion replied by a deprecating gesture. "Not of us individually. We must remember that. It's just the collective modern idea of Mothers. And you see — " Half guiltily she drew from her handsomely mounted black hand-bag a twist of crimson silk run through by two fine knitting needles. "One never knows," she murmured. "The new system has certainly given us a good deal of time to kill; and sometimes I get tired just looking — even at this." Her gesture was now addressed to the stupendous scene at their feet.

The dark lady laughed again, and they both relapsed upon the view, contemplating it in silence, with a sort of diffused serenity which might have been borrowed from the spring effulgence of the Roman skies. The luncheon-hour was long past, and the two had their end of the vast terrace to themselves. At this opposite extremity a few groups, detained by a lingering look at the outspread city, were gathering up guide-books and fumbling for tips. The last of them scattered, and the two ladies were alone on the air-washed height.

"Well, I don't see why we shouldn't just stay here," said Mrs. Slade, the lady of the high color and energetic brows. Two derelict basket-chairs stood near, and she pushed them into the angle of the parapet, and settled herself in one, her gaze upon the Palatine. "After all, it's still the most beautiful view in the world."

"It always will be, to me," assented her friend Mrs. Ansley, with so slight a stress on the "me" that Mrs. Slade, though she noticed it, wondered if it were not merely accidental, like the random under-linings of old-fashioned letter-writers.

"Grace Ansley was always old-fashioned," she thought; and added aloud, with a retrospective smile: "It's a view we've both been famil-iar with for a good many years. When we first met here we were younger than our girls are now. You remember?"

"Oh, yes, I remember," murmured Mrs. Ansley, with the same undefinable stress. — "There's that head-waiter wondering," she in-terpolated. She was evidently far less sure than her companion of herself and of her rights in the world.

"I'll cure him of wondering," said Mrs. Slade, stretching her hand toward a bag as discreetly opulent-looking as Mrs. Ansley's. Signing to the head-waiter, she explained that she and her friend were old lovers of Rome, and would like to spend the end of the afternoon looking down on the view — that is, if it did not disturb the service? The head-waiter, bowing over her gratuity, assured her that the ladies were most welcome, and would be still more so if they would condescend to remain for dinner. A full moon night, they would remember. . . .

Mrs. Slade's black brows drew together, as though references to the moon were out-of-place and even unwelcome. But she smiled away her frown as the head-waiter retreated. "Well, why not? We might do worse. There's no knowing, I suppose, when the girls will be back. Do you even know back from *where*? I don't!"

Mrs. Ansley again colored slightly. "I think those young Italian aviators we met at the Embassy invited them to fly to Tarquinia for tea. I suppose they'll want to wait and fly back by moonlight."

"Moonlight — moonlight! What a part it still plays. Do you sup-pose they're as sentimental as we were?"

"I've come to the conclusion that I don't in the least know what they are," said Mrs. Ansley. "And perhaps we didn't know much more about each other."

"No; perhaps we didn't."

Her friend gave her a shy glance. "I never should have supposed you were sentimental, Alida."

"Well, perhaps I wasn't." Mrs. Slade drew her lids together in retrospect; and for a few moments the two ladies, who had been intimate since childhood, reflected how little they knew each other. Each one, of course, had a label ready to attach to the other's name; Mrs. Delphin Slade, for instance, would have told herself, or any one who asked her, that Mrs. Horace Ansley, twenty-five years ago, had been exquisitely lovely — no, you wouldn't believe it, would you? . . . though, of course, still charming, distinguished . . . Well, as a girl she had been exquisite; far more beautiful than her daughter Barbara, though certainly Babs, according to the new standards at any rate, was more effective — had more edge, as they say. Funny where she got it, with those two nullities as parents. Yes; Horace Ansley was — well, just the duplicate of his wife. Museum specimens of old New York. Good-looking, irreproachable, exemplary. Mrs. Slade and Mrs. Ansley had lived opposite each other — actually as well as figuratively — for years. When the drawing-room curtains in No. 20 East 73rd Street were renewed, No. 23, across the way, was always aware of it. And of all the movings, buyings, travels, anniversaries, illnesses — the tame chronicle of an estimable pair. Little of it escaped Mrs. Slade. But she had grown bored with it by the time her husband made his big *coup* in Wall Street, and when they bought in upper Park Avenue had already begun to think: "I'd rather live opposite a speak-easy for a change; at least one might see it raided." The idea of seeing Grace raided was so amusing that (before the move) she launched it at a woman's lunch. It made a hit, and went the rounds — she sometimes wondered if it had crossed the street, and reached Mrs. Ansley. She hoped not, but didn't much mind. Those were the days when respectability was at a discount, and it did the irreproachable no harm to laugh at them a little.

A few years later, and not many months apart, both ladies lost their husbands. There was an appropriate exchange of wreaths and condolences, and a brief renewal of intimacy in the half-shadow of their mourning; and now, after another interval, they had run across each other in Rome, at the same hotel, each of them the modest appendage of a salient daughter. The similarity of their lot had again drawn them together, lending itself to mild jokes, and the mutual confession that, if in old days it must have been tiring to "keep up" with daughters, it was now, at times, a little dull not to.

No doubt, Mrs. Slade reflected, she felt her unemployment more than poor Grace ever would. It was a big drop from being the wife of Delphin Slade to being his widow. She had always regarded herself (with a certain conjugal pride) as his equal in social gifts, as contributing her full share to the making of the exceptional couple they were: but the difference after his death was irremediable. As the wife of the famous corporation lawyer, always with an international case or two on hand, every day brought its exciting and unexpected obligation: the impromptu entertaining of eminent colleagues from abroad, the hurried dashes on legal business to London, Paris or Rome, where the entertaining was so handsomely reciprocated; the amusement of hearing in her wake: "What, that handsome woman with the good clothes and eyes is Mrs. Slade — *the* Slade's wife? Really? Generally the wives of celebrities are such frumps."

Yes; being *the* Slade's widow was a dullish business after that. In living up to such a husband all her faculties had been engaged; now she had only her daughter to live up to, for the son who seemed to have inherited his father's gifts had died suddenly in boyhood. She had fought through that agony because her husband was there, to be helped and to help; now, after the father's death, the thought of the boy had become unbearable. There was nothing left but to mother her daughter; and dear Jenny was such a perfect daughter that she needed no excessive mothering. "Now with Babs Ansley I don't know that I *should* be so quiet," Mrs. Slade sometimes half-enviously reflected; but Jenny, who was younger than her brilliant friend, was that rare accident, an extremely pretty girl who somehow made youth and prettiness seem as safe as their absence. It was all perplexing — and to Mrs. Slade a little boring. She wished that Jenny would fall in love — with the wrong man, even; that she might have to be watched, out-maneuvered, rescued. And instead, it was Jenny who watched her mother, kept her out of draughts, made sure that she had taken her tonic . . .

Mrs. Ansley was much less articulate than her friend, and her mental portrait of Mrs. Slade was slighter, and drawn with fainter touches, "Alida Slade's awfully brilliant; but not as brilliant as she thinks," would have summed it up; though she would have added, for the enlightenment of strangers, that Mrs. Slade had been an extremely dashing girl; much more so than her daughter, who was pretty, of course, and clever in a way, but had none of her mother's — well, "vividness," some one had once called it. Mrs. Ansley would take up current words like this, and cite them in quotation marks, as unheard-of audacities. No; Jenny was not like her mother. Sometimes Mrs. Ansley thought Alida Slade was disappointed; on the whole she had had a sad life. Full of failures and mistakes; Mrs. Ansley had always been rather sorry for her . . .

So these two ladies visualized each other, each through the wrong end of her little telescope.

II

For a long time they continued to sit side by side without speaking. It seemed as though, to both, there was a relief in laying down their somewhat futile activities in the presence of the vast Memento

Mori which faced them. Mrs. Slade sat quite still, her eyes fixed on
the golden slope of the Palace of the Cæsars, and after a while Mrs.
Ansley ceased to fidget with her bag, and she too sank into meditation. Like many intimate friends, the two ladies had never before
had occasion to be silent together, and Mrs. Ansley was slightly embarrassed by what seemed, after so many years, a new stage in their
intimacy, and one with which she did not yet know how to deal.

Suddenly the air was full of that deep clangor of bells which peri-
odically covers Rome with a roof of silver. Mrs. Slade glanced at her
wrist-watch. "Five o'clock already," she said, as though surprised.

Mrs. Ansley suggested interrogatively: "There's bridge at the Embassy at five." For a long time Mrs. Slade did not answer. She appeared to be lost in contemplation, and Mrs. Ansley thought the
remark had escaped her. But after a while she said, as if speaking out
of a dream: "Bridge, did you say? Not unless you want to . . . But I
don't think I will, you know."

"Oh, no," Mrs. Ansley hastened to assure her. "I don't care to at
all. It's so lovely here; and so full of old memories, as you say." She
settled herself in her chair, and almost furtively drew forth her knitting. Mrs. Slade took sideway note of this activity, but her own beautifully cared-for hands remained motionless on her knee.

"I was just thinking," she said slowly, "what different things
Rome stands for to each generation of travellers. To our grandmothers, Roman fever; to our mothers, sentimental dangers — how
we used to be guarded! — to our daughters, no more dangers than the
middle of Main Street. They don't know it — but how much they're
missing!"

The long golden light was beginning to pale, and Mrs. Ansley
lifted her knitting a little closer to her eyes. "Yes; how we were
guarded!"

"I always used to think," Mrs. Slade continued, "that our mothers
had a much more difficult job than our grandmothers. When Roman
fever stalked the streets it must have been comparatively easy to
gather in the girls at the danger hour; but when you and I were
young, with such beauty calling us, and the spice of disobedience
thrown in, and no worse risk than catching cold during the cool hour
after sunset, the mothers used to be put to it to keep us in — didn't
they?"

She turned again toward Mrs. Ansley, but the latter had reached a
delicate point in her knitting. "One, two, three — slip two; yes, they
must have been," she assented, without looking up.

Mrs. Slade's eyes rested on her with a deepened attention. "She
can knit — in the face of *this!* How like her . . ."

Mrs. Slade leaned back, brooding, her eyes ranging from the ruins
which faced her to the long green hollow of the Forum, the fading

glow of the church fronts beyond it, and the outlying immensity of the Colosseum. Suddenly she thought: "It's all very well to say that our girls have done away with sentiment and moonlight. But if Babs Ansley isn't out to catch that young aviator — the one who's a Marchese — then I don't know anything. And Jenny has no chance beside her. I know that too. I wonder if that's why Grace Ansley likes the two girls to go everywhere together? My poor Jenny as a foil — !" Mrs. Slade gave a hardly audible laugh, and at the sound Mrs. Ansley dropped her knitting.

"Yes — ?"

"I — oh, nothing. I was only thinking how your Babs carries everything before her. That Campolieri boy is one of the best matches in Rome. Don't look so innocent, my dear — you know he is. And I was wondering, ever so respectfully, you understand . . . wondering how two such exemplary characters as you and Horace had managed to produce anything quite so dynamic." Mrs. Slade laughed again, with a touch of asperity.

Mrs. Ansley's hands lay inert across her needles. She looked straight out at the great accumulated wreckage of passion and splendor at her feet. But her small profile was almost expressionless. At length she said: "I think you overrate Babs, my dear."

Mrs. Slade's tone grew easier. "No; I don't. I appreciate her. And perhaps envy you. Oh, my girl's perfect; if I were a chronic invalid I'd — well, I think I'd rather be in Jenny's hands. There must be times . . . but there! I always wanted a brilliant daughter . . . and never quite understood why I got an angel instead."

Mrs. Ansley echoed her laugh in a faint murmur. "Babs is an angel too."

"Of course — of course! But she's got rainbow wings. Well, they're wandering by the sea with their young men; and here we sit . . . and it all brings back the past a little too acutely."

Mrs. Ansley had resumed her knitting. One might almost have imagined (if one had known her less well, Mrs. Slade reflected) that, for her also, too many memories rose from the lengthening shadows of those august ruins. But no; she was simply absorbed in her work. What was there for her to worry about? She knew that Babs would almost certainly come back engaged to the extremely eligible Campolieri. "And she'll sell the New York house, and settle down near them in Rome, and never be in their way . . . she's much too tactful. But she'll have an excellent cook, and just the right people in for bridge and cocktails . . . and a perfectly peaceful old age among her grandchildren."

Mrs. Slade broke off this prophetic flight with a recoil of self-disgust. There was no one of whom she had less right to think unkindly than of Grace Ansley. Would she never cure herself of envying her? Perhaps she had begun too long ago.

She stood up and leaned against the parapet, filling her troubled eyes with the tranquillizing magic of the hour. But instead of tranquillizing her the sight seemed to increase her exasperation. Her gaze turned toward the Colosseum. Already its golden flank was drowned in purple shadow, and above it the sky curved crystal clear, without light or color. It was the moment when afternoon and evening hang balanced in mid-heaven.

Mrs. Slade turned back and laid her hand on her friend's arm. The gesture was so abrupt that Mrs. Ansley looked up, startled.

"The sun's set. You're not afraid, my dear?"

"Afraid — ?"

"Of Roman fever or pneumonia? I remember how ill you were that winter. As a girl you had a very delicate throat, hadn't you?"

"Oh, we're all right up here. Down below, in the Forum, it does get deathly cold, all of a sudden . . . but not here."

"Ah, of course you know because you had to be so careful." Mrs. Slade turned back to the parapet. She thought: "I must make one more effort not to hate her." Aloud she said: "Whenever I look at the Forum from up here, I remember that story about a great-aunt of yours, wasn't she? A dreadfully wicked great-aunt?"

"Oh, yes; Great-aunt Harriet. The one who was supposed to have sent her young sister out to the Forum after sunset to gather a night-blooming flower for her album. All our great-aunts and grandmothers used to have albums of dried flowers."

Mrs. Slade nodded. "But she really sent her because they were in love with the same man — "

"Well, that was the family tradition. They said Aunt Harriet confessed it years afterward. At any rate, the poor little sister caught the fever and died. Mother used to frighten us with the story when we were children."

"And you frightened *me* with it, that winter when you and I were here as girls. The winter I was engaged to Delphin."

Mrs. Ansley gave a faint laugh. "Oh, did I? Really frightened you? I don't believe you're easily frightened."

"Not often; but I was then. I was easily frightened because I was too happy. I wonder if you know what that means?"

"I — yes . . . " Mrs. Ansley faltered.

"Well, I suppose that was why the story of your wicked aunt made such an impression on me. And I thought: 'There's no more Roman fever, but the Forum is deathly cold after sunset — especially after a hot day. And the Colosseum's even colder and damper'."

"The Colosseum — ?"

"Yes. It wasn't easy to get in, after the gates were locked for the night. Far from easy. Still, in those days it could be managed; it was managed, often. Lovers met there who couldn't meet elsewhere. You knew that?"

"I — I daresay. I don't remember."

"You don't remember? You don't remember going to visit some ruins or other one evening, just after dark, and catching a bad chill? You were supposed to have gone to see the moon rise. People always said that expedition was what caused your illness."

There was a moment's silence; then Mrs. Ansley rejoined: "Did they? It was all so long ago."

"Yes. And you got well again — so it didn't matter. But I suppose it struck your friends — the reason given for your illness, I mean — because everybody knew you were so prudent on account of your throat, and your mother took such care of you . . . You *had* been out late sightseeing, hadn't you, that night?"

"Perhaps I had. The most prudent girls aren't always prudent. What made you think of it now?"

Mrs. Slade seemed to have no answer ready. But after a moment she broke out: "Because I simply can't bear it any longer — !"

Mrs. Ansley lifted her head quickly. Her eyes were wide and very pale. "Can't bear what?"

"Why — your not knowing that I've always known why you went."

"Why I went — ?"

"Yes. You think I'm bluffing, don't you? Well, you went to meet the man I was engaged to — and I can repeat every word of the letter that took you there."

While Mrs. Slade spoke Mrs. Ansley had risen unsteadily to her feet. Her bag, her knitting and gloves, slid in a panic-stricken heap to the ground. She looked at Mrs. Slade as though she were looking at a ghost.

"No, no — don't," she faltered out.

"Why not? Listen, if you don't believe me. 'My one darling, things can't go on like this. I must see you alone. Come to the Colosseum immediately after dark tomorrow. There will be somebody to let you in. No one whom you need fear will suspect' — but perhaps you've forgotten what the letter said?"

Mrs. Ansley met the challenge with an unexpected composure. Steadying herself against the chair she looked at her friend, and replied: "No, I know it by heart too."

"And the signature? 'Only *your* D.S.' Was that it? I'm right, am I? That was the letter that took you out that evening after dark?"

Mrs. Ansley was still looking at her. It seemed to Mrs. Slade that a slow struggle was going on behind the voluntarily controlled mask of her small quiet face. "I shouldn't have thought she had herself so well in hand," Mrs. Slade reflected, almost resentfully. But at this moment Mrs. Ansley spoke. "I don't know how you knew. I burnt that letter at once."

"Yes; you would, naturally — you're so prudent!" The sneer was open now. "And if you burnt the letter you're wondering how on earth I know what was in it. That's it, isn't it?"

Mrs. Slade waited, but Mrs. Ansley did not speak.

"Well, my dear, I know what was in that letter because I wrote it!"

"You wrote it?"

"Yes."

The two women stood for a minute staring at each other in the last golden light. Then Mrs. Ansley dropped back into her chair. "Oh," she murmured, and covered her face with her hands.

Mrs. Slade waited nervously for another word or movement. None came, and at length she broke out: "I horrify you."

Mrs. Ansley's hands dropped to her knee. The face they uncovered was streaked with tears. "I wasn't thinking of you. I was thinking — it was the only letter I ever had from him!"

"And I wrote it. Yes; I wrote it! But I was the girl he was engaged to. Did you happen to remember that?"

Mrs. Ansley's head dropped again. "I'm not trying to excuse myself . . . I remembered . . ."

"And still you went?"

"Still I went."

Mrs. Slade stood looking down on the small bowed figure at her side. The flame of her wrath had already sunk, and she wondered why she had ever thought there would be any satisfaction in inflicting so purposeless a wound on her friend. But she had to justify herself.

"You do understand? I found out — and I hated you, hated you. I knew you were in love with Delphin — and I was afraid; afraid of you, of your quiet ways, your sweetness . . . your . . . well, I wanted you out of the way, that's all. Just for a few weeks; just till I was sure of him. So in a blind fury I wrote that letter . . . I don't know why I'm telling you now."

"I suppose," said Mrs. Ansley slowly, "it's because you've always gone on hating me."

"Perhaps. Or because I wanted to get the whole thing off my mind." She paused. "I'm glad you destroyed the letter. Of course I never thought you'd die."

Mrs. Ansley relapsed into silence, and Mrs. Slade, leaning above her, was conscious of a strange sense of isolation, of being cut off from the warm current of human communion. "You think me a monster!"

"I don't know . . . It was the only letter I had, and you say he didn't write it?"

"Ah, how you care for him still!"

"I cared for that memory," said Mrs. Ansley.

Mrs. Slade continued to look down on her. She seemed physically reduced by the blow — as if, when she got up, the wind might scatter her like a puff of dust. Mrs. Slade's jealousy suddenly leapt up again at the sight. All these years the woman had been living on that letter. How she must have loved him, to treasure the mere memory of its ashes! The letter of the man her friend was engaged to. Wasn't it she who was the monster?

"You tried your best to get him away from me, didn't you? But you failed; and I kept him. That's all."

"Yes. That's all."

"I wish now I hadn't told you. I'd no idea you'd feel about it as you do; I thought you'd be amused. It all happened so long ago, as you say; and you must do me the justice to remember that I had no reason to think you'd ever taken it seriously. How could I, when you were married to Horace Ansley two months afterward? As soon as you could get out of bed your mother rushed you off to Florence and married you. People were rather surprised — they wondered at its being done so quickly; but I thought I knew. I had an idea you did it out of *pique* — to be able to say you'd got ahead of Delphin and me. Girls have such silly reasons for doing the most serious things. And your marrying so soon convinced me that you'd never really cared."

"Yes, I suppose it would," Mrs. Ansley assented.

The clear heaven overhead was emptied of all its gold. Dusk spread over it, abruptly darkening the Seven Hills. Here and there lights began to twinkle through the foliage at their feet. Steps were coming and going on the deserted terrace — waiters looking out of the doorway at the head of the stairs, then reappearing with trays and napkins and flasks of wine. Tables were moved, chairs straightened. A feeble string of electric lights flickered out. Some vases of faded flowers were carried away, and brought back replenished. A stout lady in a dust-coat suddenly appeared, asking in broken Italian if any one had seen the elastic band which held together her tattered Baedeker. She poked with her stick under the table at which she had lunched, the waiters assisting.

The corner where Mrs. Slade and Mrs. Ansley sat was still shadowy and deserted. For a long time neither of them spoke. At length Mrs. Slade began again: "I suppose I did it as a sort of joke — "

"A joke?"

"Well, girls are ferocious sometimes, you know. Girls in love especially. And I remember laughing to myself all that evening at the idea that you were waiting around there in the dark, dodging out of sight, listening for every sound, trying to get in — . Of course I was upset when I heard you were so ill afterward."

Mrs. Ansley had not moved for a long time. But now she turned slowly toward her companion. "But I didn't wait. He'd arranged everything. He was there. We were let in at once," she said.

Mrs. Slade sprang up from her leaning position. "Delphin there? They let you in? — Ah, now you're lying!" she burst out with violence.

Mrs. Ansley's voice grew clearer, and full of surprise. "But of course he was there. Naturally he came — "

"Came?" How did he know he'd find you there? You must be raving!"

Mrs. Ansley hesitated, as though reflecting. "But I answered the letter! I told him I'd be there. So he came."

Mrs. Slade flung her hands up to her face. "Oh, God — you answered! I never thought of your answering . . . "

"It's odd you never thought of it, if you wrote the letter."

"Yes. I was blind with rage."

Mrs. Ansley rose, and drew her fur scarf about her. "It is cold here. We'd better go . . . I'm sorry for you," she said, as she clasped the fur about her throat.

The unexpected words sent a pang through Mrs. Slade. "Yes; we'd better go." She gathered up her bag and cloak. "I don't know why you should be sorry for me," she muttered.

Mrs. Ansley stood looking away from her toward the dusky secret mass of the Colosseum. "Well — because I didn't have to wait that night."

Mrs. Slade gave an unquiet laugh. "Yes; I was beaten there. But I oughtn't to begrudge it to you, I suppose. At the end of all these years. After all, I had everything; I had him for twenty-five years. And you had nothing but that one letter that he didn't write."

Mrs. Ansley was again silent. At length she turned toward the door of the terrace. She took a step, and turned back, facing her companion.

"I had Barbara," she said, and began to move ahead of Mrs. Slade toward the stairway.

James Joyce (1882–1941)

Araby

North Richmond Street, being blind, was a quiet street except at
the hour when the Christian Brothers' School set the boys free. An
uninhabited house of two storeys stood at the blind end, detached
from its neighbours in a square ground. The other houses of the
street, conscious of decent lives within them, gazed at one another
with brown imperturbable faces.

The former tenant of our house, a priest, had died in the back
drawing-room. Air, musty from having been long enclosed, hung in
all the rooms, and the waste room behind the kitchen was littered
with old useless papers. Among these I found a few paper-covered
books, the pages of which were curled and damp: *The Abbot*, by
Walter Scott, *The Devout Communicant* and *The Memoirs of Vidocq*.
I liked the last best because its leaves were yellow. The wild garden
behind the house contained a central apple-tree and a few straggling
bushes under one of which I found the late tenant's rusty bicycle-
pump. He had been a very charitable priest; in his will he had left all
his money to institutions and the furniture of his house to his sister.

When the short days of winter came dusk fell before we had well
eaten our dinners. When we met in the street the houses had grown
sombre. The space of sky above us was the colour of ever-changing
violet and towards it the lamps of the street lifted their feeble lan-
terns. The cold air stung us and we played till our bodies glowed.
Our shouts echoed in the silent street. The career of our play brought
us through the dark muddy lanes behind the houses where we ran
the gantlet of the rough tribes from the cottages, to the back doors of
the dark dripping gardens where odours arose from the ashpits, to the
dark odorous stables where a coachman smoothed and combed the
horse or shook music from the buckled harness. When we returned to
the street light from the kitchen windows had filled the areas. If my
uncle was seen turning the corner we hid in the shadow until we had
seen him safely housed. Or if Mangan's sister came out on the doorstep to call her brother in to his tea we watched her from our shadow
peer up and down the street. We waited to see whether she would
remain or go in and, if she remained, we left our shadow and walked
up to Mangan's steps resignedly. She was waiting for us, her figure
defined by the light from the half-opened door. Her brother always
teased her before he obeyed and I stood by the railings looking at
her. Her dress swung as she moved her body and the soft rope of her
hair tossed from side to side.

Every morning I lay on the floor in the front parlour watching her door. The blind was pulled down to within an inch of the sash so that I could not be seen. When she came out on the doorstep my heart leaped. I ran to the hall, seized my books and followed her. I kept her brown figure always in my eye and, when we came near the point at which our ways diverged, I quickened my pace and passed her. This happened morning after morning. I had never spoken to her, except for a few casual words, and yet her name was like a summons to all my foolish blood.

Her image accompanied me even in places the most hostile to romance. On Saturday evenings when my aunt went marketing I had to go to carry some of the parcels. We walked through the flaring streets, jostled by drunken men and bargaining women, amid the curses of labourers, the shrill litanies of shop-boys who stood on guard by the barrels of pigs' cheeks, the nasal chanting of street-singers, who sang a *come-all-you* about O'Donovan Rossa, or a ballad about the troubles in our native land. These noises converged in a single sensation of life for me: I imagined that I bore my chalice safely through a throng of foes. Her name sprang to my lips at moments in strange prayers and praises which I myself did not understand. My eyes were often full of tears (I could not tell why) and at times a flood from my heart seemed to pour itself out into my bosom. I thought little of the future. I did not know whether I would ever speak to her or not or, if I spoke to her, how I could tell her of my confused adoration. But my body was like a harp and her words and gestures were like fingers running upon the wires.

One evening I went into the back drawing-room in which the priest had died. It was a dark rainy evening and there was no sound in the house. Through one of the broken panes I heard the rain impinge upon the earth, the fine incessant needles of water playing in the sodden beds. Some distant lamp or lighted window gleamed below me. I was thankful that I could see so little. All my senses seemed to desire to veil themselves and, feeling that I was about to slip from them, I pressed the palms of my hands together until they trembled, murmuring: *O love! O love!* many times.

At last she spoke to me. When she addressed the first words to me I was so confused that I did not know what to answer. She asked me was I going to *Araby*. I forget whether I answered yes or no. It would be a splendid bazaar, she said; she would love to go.

— And why can't you? I asked.

While she spoke she turned a silver bracelet round and round her wrist. She could not go, she said, because there would be a retreat that week in her convent. Her brother and two other boys were fighting for their caps and I was alone at the railings. She held one of the spikes, bowing her head towards me. The light from the lamp opposite our door caught the white curve of her neck, lit up her hair that rested there and, falling, lit up the hand upon the railing. It fell over one side of her dress and caught the white border of a petticoat, just visible as she stood at ease.

— It's well for you, she said.

— If I go, I said, I will bring you something.

What innumerable follies laid waste my waking and sleeping thoughts after that evening! I wished to annihilate the tedious intervening days. I chafed against the work of school. At night in my bedroom and by day in the classroom her image came between me and the page I strove to read. The syllables of the word *Araby* were called to me through the silence in which my soul luxuriated and cast an Eastern enchantment over me. I asked for leave to go to the bazaar on Saturday night. My aunt was surprised and hoped it was not some Freemason affair. I answered few questions in class, I watched my master's face pass from amiability to sternness; he hoped I was not beginning to idle. I could not call my wandering thoughts together. I had hardly any patience with the serious work of life which, now that it stood between me and my desire, seemed to me child's play, ugly monotonous child's play.

On Saturday morning I reminded my uncle that I wished to go to the bazaar in the evening. He was fussing at the hallstand, looking for the hat-brush, and answered me curtly:

— Yes, boy, I know.

As he was in the hall I could not go into the front parlour and lie at the window. I left the house in bad humour and walked slowly towards the school. The air was pitilessly raw and already my heart misgave me.

When I came home to dinner my uncle had not yet been home. Still it was early. I sat staring at the clock for some time and, when its ticking began to irritate me, I left the room. I mounted the staircase and gained the upper part of the house. The high cold empty gloomy rooms liberated me and I went from room to room singing. From the front window I saw my companions playing below in the street. Their cries reached me weakened and indistinct and, leaning my forehead against the cool glass, I looked over at the dark house where she lived. I may have stood there for an hour, seeing nothing but the brown-clad figure cast by my imagination, touched discreetly by the lamplight at the curved neck, at the hand upon the railings and at the border below the dress.

When I came downstairs again I found Mrs Mercer sitting at the fire. She was an old garrulous woman, a pawnbroker's widow, who collected used stamps for some pious purpose. I had to endure the gossip of the tea-table. The meal was prolonged beyond an hour and still my uncle did not come. Mrs Mercer stood up to go: she was sorry she couldn't wait any longer, but it was after eight o'clock and she did not like to be out late, as the night air was bad for her. When she had gone I began to walk up and down the room, clenching my fists. My aunt said:

— I'm afraid you may put off your bazaar for this night of Our Lord.

At nine o'clock I heard my uncle's latchkey in the halldoor. I heard him talking to himself and heard the hallstand rocking when it had received the weight of his overcoat. I could interpret these signs. When he was midway through his dinner I asked him to give me the money to go to the bazaar. He had forgotten.

— The people are in bed and after their first sleep now, he said.

I did not smile. My aunt said to him energetically:

— Can't you give him the money and let him go? You've kept him late enough as it is.

My uncle said he was very sorry he had forgotten. He said he believed in the old saying: *All work and no play makes Jack a dull boy.* He asked me where I was going and, when I had told him a second time he asked me did I know *The Arab's Farewell to his Steed.* When I left the kitchen he was about to recite the opening lines of the piece to my aunt.

I held a florin tightly in my hand as I strode down Buckingham Street towards the station. The sight of the streets thronged with buyers and glaring with gas recalled to me the purpose of my journey. I took my seat in a third-class carriage of a deserted train. After an intolerable delay the train moved out of the station slowly. It crept onward among ruinous houses and over the twinkling river. At Westland Row Station a crowd of people pressed to the carriage doors; but the porters moved them back, saying that it was a special train for the bazaar. I remained alone in the bare carriage. In a few minutes the train drew up beside an improvised wooden platform. I passed out on to the road and saw by the lighted dial of a clock that it was ten minutes to ten. In front of me was a large building which displayed the magical name.

I could not find any sixpenny entrance and, fearing that the bazaar would be closed, I passed in quickly through a turnstile, handing a shilling to a weary-looking man. I found myself in a big hall girdled at half its height by a gallery. Nearly all the stalls were closed and the greater part of the hall was in darkness. I recognised a silence like that which pervades a church after a service. I walked into the centre of the bazaar timidly. A few people were gathered about the stalls which were still open. Before a curtain, over which the words *Café*

Chantant were written in coloured lamps, two men were counting money on a salver. I listened to the fall of the coins.

Remembering with difficulty why I had come I went over to one of the stalls and examined porcelain vases and flowered tea-sets. At the door of the stall a young lady was talking and laughing with two young gentlemen. I remarked their English accents and listened vaguely to their conversation.

— O, I never said such a thing!

— O, but you did!

— O, but I didn't!

— Didn't she say that?

— Yes. I heard her.

— O, there's a . . . fib!

Observing me the young lady came over and asked me did I wish to buy anything. The tone of her voice was not encouraging; she seemed to have spoken to me out of a sense of duty. I looked humbly at the great jars that stood like eastern guards at either side of the dark entrance to the stall and murmured:

— No, thank you.

The young lady changed the position of one of the vases and went back to the two young men. They began to talk of the same subject. Once or twice the young lady glanced at me over her shoulder.

I lingered before her stall, though I knew my stay was useless, to make my interest in her wares seem the more real. Then I turned away slowly and walked down the middle of the bazaar. I allowed the two pennies to fall against the sixpence in my pocket. I heard a voice call from one end of the gallery that the light was out. The upper part of the hall was now completely dark.

Gazing up into the darkness I saw myself as a creature driven and derided by vanity; and my eyes burned with anguish and anger.

Franz Kafka (1883–1924)

The Metamorphosis

Translated by Willa and Edwin Muir

I

As Gregor Samsa awoke one morning from uneasy dreams he found himself transformed in his bed into a gigantic insect. He was lying on his hard, as it were armor-plated, back and when he lifted his head a little he could see his dome-like brown belly divided into stiff arched segments on top of which the bed quilt could hardly keep in position and was about to slide off completely. His numerous legs, which were pitifully thin compared to the rest of his bulk, waved helplessly before his eyes.

What has happened to me? he thought. It was no dream. His room, a regular human bedroom, only rather too small, lay quiet between the four familiar walls. Above the table on which a collection of cloth samples was unpacked and spread out — Samsa was a commercial traveler — hung the picture which he had recently cut out of an illustrated magazine and put into a pretty gilt frame. It showed a lady, with a fur cap on and a fur stole, sitting upright and holding out to the spectator a huge fur muff into which the whole of her forearm had vanished!

Gregor's eyes turned next to the window, and the overcast sky — one could hear rain drops beating on the window gutter — made him quite melancholy. What about sleeping a little longer and forgetting all this nonsense, he thought, but it could not be done, for he was accustomed to sleep on his right side and in his present condition he could not turn himself over. However violently he forced himself towards his right side he always rolled on to his back again. He tried it at least a hundred times, shutting his eyes to keep from seeing his struggling legs, and only desisted when he began to feel in his side a faint dull ache he had never experienced before.

Oh God, he thought, what an exhausting job I've picked on! Traveling about day in, day out. It's much more irritating work than doing the actual business in the office, and on top of that there's the trouble of constant traveling, of worrying about train connections, the bed and irregular meals, casual acquaintances that are always new and never become intimate friends. The devil take it all! He felt a slight itching up on his belly; slowly pushed himself on his back nearer to the top of the bed so that he could lift his head more easily; identified the itching place which was surrounded by many small white spots the nature of which he could not understand and made to touch it with a leg, but drew the leg back immediately, for the contact made a cold shiver run through him.

He slid down again into his former position. This getting up early, he thought, makes one quite stupid. A man needs his sleep. Other commercials live like harem women. For instance, when I come back to the hotel of a morning to write up the orders I've got, these others are only sitting down to breakfast. Let me just try that with my chief; I'd be sacked on the spot. Anyhow, that might be quite a good thing for me, who can tell? If I didn't have to hold my hand because of my parents I'd have given notice long ago, I'd have gone to the chief and told him exactly what I think of him. That would knock him endways from his desk! It's a queer way of doing, too, this sitting on high at a desk and talking down to employees, especially when they have to come quite near because the chief is hard of hearing. Well, there's still hope; once I've saved enough money to pay back my parents' debts to him — that should take another five or six years — I'll do it without fail. I'll cut myself completely loose then. For the moment, though, I'd better get up, since my train goes at five.

He looked at the alarm clock ticking on the chest. Heavenly Father! he thought. It was half-past six o'clock and the hands were quietly moving on, it was even past the half-hour, it was getting on toward a quarter to seven. Had the alarm clock not gone off? From the bed one could see that it had been properly set for four o'clock; of course it must have gone off. Yes, but was it possible to sleep quietly through that ear-splitting noise? Well, he had not slept quietly, yet apparently all the more soundly for that. But what was he to do now? The next train went at seven o'clock; to catch that he would need to hurry like mad and his samples weren't even packed up, and he himself wasn't feeling particularly fresh and active. And even if he did catch the train he wouldn't avoid a row with the chief, since the firm's porter would have been waiting for the five o'clock train and would have long since reported his failure to turn up. The porter was a creature of the chief's, spineless and stupid. Well, supposing he were to say he was sick? But that would be most unpleasant and would look suspicious, since during his five years' employment he had not been ill once. The chief himself would be sure to come with the sick-insurance doctor, would reproach his parents with their son's laziness and would cut all excuses short by referring to the insurance doctor, who of course regarded all mankind as perfectly healthy malingerers. And would he be so far wrong on this occasion? Gregor really felt quite well, apart from a drowsiness that was utterly superfluous after such a long sleep, and he was even unusually hungry.

As all this was running through his mind at top speed without his being able to decide to leave his bed — the alarm clock had just struck a quarter to seven — there came a cautious tap at the door behind the head of his bed. "Gregor," said a voice — it was his mother's — "it's a quarter to seven. Hadn't you a train to catch?" That gentle voice! Gregor had a shock as he heard his own voice answering hers, unmistakably his own voice, it was true, but with a persistent horrible twittering squeak behind it like an undertone, that left the words in their clear shape only for the first moment and then rose up reverberating round them to destroy their sense, so that one could not be sure one had heard them rightly. Gregor wanted to answer at length and explain everything, but in the circumstances he confined himself to saying: "Yes, yes, thank you, Mother, I'm getting up now." The wooden door between them must have kept the change in his voice from being noticeable outside, for his mother contented herself with this statement and shuffled away. Yet this brief exchange of words had made the other members of the family aware that Gregor was still in the house, as they had not expected, and at one of the side doors his father was already knocking, gently, yet with his fist. "Gregor, Gregor," he called, "what's the matter with you?" And after a little while he called again in a deeper voice: "Gregor! Gregor!" At the other side door his sister was saying in a low, plaintive tone: "Gregor? Aren't you well? Are you needing anything?" He answered them both at once: "I'm just ready," and did his best to make his voice sound as normal as possible by enunciating the words very clearly and leaving long pauses between them. So his father went back to this breakfast, but his sister whispered: "Gregor, open the door, do." However, he was not thinking of opening the door, and felt thankful for the prudent habit he had acquired in traveling of locking all doors during the night, even at home.

His immediate intention was to get up quietly without being disturbed, to put on his clothes and above all eat his breakfast, and only then to consider what else was to be done, since in bed, he was well aware, his meditations would come to no sensible conclusion. He remembered that often enough in bed he had felt small aches and pains, probably caused by awkward postures, which had proved purely imaginary once he got up, and he looked forward eagerly to seeing this morning's delusions gradually fall away. That the change in his voice was nothing but the precursor of a severe chill, a standing ailment of commercial travelers, he had not the least possible doubt.

To get rid of the quilt was quite easy; he had only to inflate himself a little and it fell off by itself. But the next move was difficult, especially because he was so uncommonly broad. He would have needed arms and hands to hoist himself up; instead he had only the numerous little legs which never stopped waving in all directions and which he could not control in the least. When he tried to bend one of them it was the first to stretch itself straight; and did he succeed at last in making it do what he wanted, all the other legs meanwhile waved the more wildly in a high degree of unpleasant agitation. "But what's the use of lying idle in bed," said Gregor to himself.

He thought that he might get out of bed with the lower part of his body first, but this lower part, which he had not yet seen and of which he could form no clear conception, proved too difficult to move; it shifted so slowly; and when finally, almost wild with annoyance, he gathered his forces together and thrust out recklessly, he had miscalculated the direction and bumped heavily against the lower end of the bed, and the stinging pain he felt informed him that precisely this lower part of his body was at the moment probably the most sensitive.

So he tried to get the top part of himself out first, and cautiously moved his head towards the edge of the bed. That proved easy enough, and despite its breadth and mass the bulk of his body at last slowly followed the movement of his head. Still, when he finally got his head free over the edge of the bed he felt too scared to go on advancing, for after all if he let himself fall in this way it would take a miracle to keep his head from being injured. And at all costs he must not lose consciousness now, precisely now; he would rather stay in bed.

But when after a repetition of the same efforts he lay in his former position again, sighing, and watched his little legs struggling against each other more wildly than ever, if that were possible, and saw no way of bringing any order into this arbitrary confusion, he told himself again that it was impossible to stay in bed and that the most sensible course was to risk everything for the smallest hope of getting away from it. At the same time he did not forget meanwhile to remind himself that cool reflection, the coolest possible, was much better than desperate resolves. In such moments he focused his eyes as sharply as possible on the window, but, unfortunately, the prospect of the morning fog, which muffled even the other side of the narrow street, brought him little encouragement and comfort. "Seven o'clock already," he said to himself when the alarm clock chimed again, "seven o'clock already and still such a thick fog." And for a little while he lay quiet, breathing lightly, as if perhaps expecting such complete repose to restore all things to their real and normal condition.

But then he said to himself: "Before it strikes a quarter past seven I must be quite out of this bed, without fail. Anyhow, by that time someone will have come from the office to ask for me, since it opens before seven." And he set himself to rocking his whole body at once in a regular rhythm, with the idea of swinging it out of the bed. If he tipped himself out in that way he could keep his head from injury by lifting it at an acute angle when he fell. His back seemed to be hard and was not likely to suffer from a fall on the carpet. His biggest worry was the loud crash he would not be able to help making, which would probably cause anxiety, if not terror, behind all the doors. Still, he must take the risk.

When he was already half out of the bed — the new method was more a game than an effort, for he needed only to hitch himself across by rocking to and fro — it struck him how simple it would be if he

could get help. Two strong people — he thought of his father and the
servant girl — would be amply sufficient; they would only have to
thrust their arms under his convex back, lever him out of the bed,
bend down with their burden and then be patient enough to let him
turn himself right over on to the floor, where it was to be hoped his
legs would then find their proper function. Well, ignoring the fact
that the doors were all locked, ought he really to call for help? In
spite of his misery he could not suppress a smile at the very idea of it.

He had got so far that he could barely keep his equilibrium when
he rocked himself strongly, and he would have to nerve himself very
soon for the final decision since in five minutes' time it would be a
quarter past seven — when the front door bell rang. "That's someone
from the office," he said to himself, and grew almost rigid, while his
little legs only jigged about all the faster. For a moment everything
stayed quiet. "They're not going to open the door," said Gregor to
himself, catching at some kind of irrational hope. But then of course
the servant girl went as usual to the door with her heavy tread and
opened it. Gregor needed only to hear the first good morning of the
visitor to know immediately who it was — the chief clerk himself.
What a fate, to be condemned to work for a firm where the smallest
omission at once gave rise to the gravest suspicion! Were all employees in a body nothing but scoundrels, was there not among them
one single loyal devoted man who, had he wasted only an hour or so
of the firm's time in a morning, was so tormented by conscience as to
be driven out of his mind and actually incapable of leaving his bed?
Wouldn't it really have been sufficient to send an apprentice to inquire — if any inquiry were necessary at all — did the chief clerk
himself have to come and thus indicate to the entire family, an innocent family, that this suspicious circumstance could be investigated
by no one less versed in affairs than himself? And more through the
agitation caused by these reflections than through any act of will
Gregor swung himself out of bed with all his strength. There was a
loud thump, but it was not really a crash. His fall was broken to some
extent by the carpet, his back, too, was less stiff than he thought, and
so there was merely a dull thud, not so very startling. Only he had not
lifted his head carefully enough and had hit it; he turned it and
rubbed it on the carpet in pain and irritation.

"That was something falling down in there," said the chief clerk in
the next room to the left. Gregor tried to suppose to himself that
something like what had happened to him today might some day
happen to the chief clerk; one really could not deny that it was possible. But as if in brusque reply to this supposition the chief clerk
took a couple of firm steps in the next-door room and his patent
leather boots creaked. From the right-hand room his sister was whis-

pering to inform him of the situation: "Gregor, the chief clerk's here." "I know," muttered Gregor to himself; but he didn't dare to make his voice loud enough for his sister to hear it.

"Gregor," said his father now from the left-hand room, "the chief clerk has come and wants to know why you didn't catch the early train. We don't know what to say to him. Besides, he wants to talk to you in person. So open the door, please. He will be good enough to excuse the untidiness of your room." "Good morning, Mr. Samsa," the chief clerk was calling amiably meanwhile. "He's not well," said his mother to the visitor, while his father was still speaking through the door, "he's not well, sir, believe me. What else would make him miss a train! The boy thinks about nothing but his work. It makes me almost cross the way he never goes out in the evenings; he's been here the last eight days and has stayed at home every single evening. He just sits there quietly at the table reading a newspaper or looking through railway timetables. The only amusement he gets is doing fretwork. For instance, he spent two or three evenings cutting out a little picture frame; you would be surprised to see how pretty it is; it's hanging in his room; you'll see it in a minute when Gregor opens the door. I must say I'm glad you've come, sir; we should never have got him to unlock the door by ourselves; he's so obstinate; and I'm sure he's unwell, though he wouldn't have it to be so this morning." "I'm just coming," said Gregor slowly and carefully, not moving an inch for fear of losing one word of the conversation. "I can't think of any other explanation, madam," said the chief clerk, "I hope it's nothing serious. Although on the other hand I must say that we men of business — fortunately or unfortunately — very often simply have to ignore any slight indisposition, since business must be attended to." "Well, can the chief clerk come in now?" asked Gregor's father impatiently, again knocking on the door. "No," said Gregor. In the left-hand room a painful silence followed this refusal, in the right-hand room his sister began to sob.

Why didn't his sister join the others? She was probably newly out of bed and hadn't even begun to put on her clothes yet. Well, why was she crying? Because he wouldn't get up and let the chief clerk in, because he was in danger of losing his job, and because the chief would begin dunning his parents again for the old debts? Surely these were things one didn't need to worry about for the present. Gregor was still at home and not in the least thinking of deserting the family. At the moment, true, he was lying on the carpet and no one who knew the condition he was in could seriously expect him to admit the chief clerk. But for such a small discourtesy, which could plausibly be explained away somehow later on, Gregor could hardly be dismissed on the spot. And it seemed to Gregor that it would be much more sensible to leave him in peace for the present than to trouble him with tears and entreaties. Still, of course, their uncertainty bewildered them all and excused their behavior.

"Mr. Samsa," the chief clerk called now in a louder voice, "what's the matter with you? Here you are, barricading yourself in your room, giving only 'yes' and 'no' for answers, causing your parents a lot of unnecessary trouble and neglecting — I mention this only in passing — neglecting your business duties in an incredible fashion. I am speaking here in the name of your parents and of your chief, and I beg you quite seriously to give me an immediate and precise explanation. You amaze me, you amaze me. I thought you were a quiet, dependable person, and now all at once you seem bent on making a disgraceful exhibition of yourself. The chief did hint to me early this morning a possible explanation for your disappearance — with reference to the cash payments that were entrusted to you recently — but I almost pledged my solemn word of honor that this could not be so. But now that I see how incredibly obstinate you are, I no longer have the slightest desire to take your part at all. And your position in the firm is not so unassailable. I came with the intention of telling you all this in private, but since you are wasting my time so needlessly I don't see why your parents shouldn't hear it too. For some time past your work has been most unsatisfactory; this is not the season of the year for a business boom, of course, we admit that, but a season of the year for doing no business at all, that does not exist, Mr. Samsa, must not exist."

"But, sir," cried Gregor, beside himself and in his agitation forgetting everything else, "I'm just going to open the door this very minute. A slight illness, an attack of giddiness, has kept me from getting up. I'm still lying in bed. But I feel all right again. I'm getting out of bed now. Just give me a moment or two longer! I'm not quite so well as I thought. But I'm all right, really. How a thing like that can suddenly strike one down! Only last night I was quite well, my parents can tell you, or rather I did have a slight presentiment. I must have showed some sign of it. Why didn't I report it at the office! But one always thinks that an indisposition can be got over without staying in the house. Oh sir, do spare my parents! All that you're reproaching me with now has no foundation; no one has ever said a word to me about it. Perhaps you haven't looked at the last orders I sent in. Anyhow, I can still catch the eight o'clock train, I'm much the better for my few hours' rest. Don't let me detain you here, sir; I'll be attending to business very soon, and do be good enough to tell the chief so and to make my excuses to him!"

And while all this was tumbling out pell-mell and Gregor hardly knew what he was saying, he had reached the chest quite easily, perhaps because of the practice he had had in bed, and was now trying to lever himself upright by means of it. He meant actually to open the door, actually to show himself and speak to the chief clerk; he was eager to find out what the others, after all their insistence, would say at the sight of him. If they were horrified then the responsibility was no longer his and he could stay quiet. But if they took it calmly, then he had no reason either to be upset, and could really get to the station for the eight o'clock train if he hurried. At first he slipped down a few times from the polished surface of the chest, but at length with a last heave he stood upright; he paid no more attention to the pains in the lower part of his body, however they smarted. Then he let himself fall against the back of a nearby chair, and clung with his little legs to the edges of it. That brought him into control of himself again and he stopped speaking, for now he could listen to what the chief clerk was saying.

"Did you understand a word of it?" the chief clerk was asking; "surely he can't be trying to make fools of us?" "Oh dear," cried his mother, in tears, "perhaps he's terribly ill and we're tormenting him. Grete! Grete!" she called out then. "Yes Mother?" called his sister from the other side. They were calling to each other across Gregor's room. "You must go this minute for the doctor. Gregor is ill. Go for the doctor, quick. Did you hear how he was speaking?" "That was no human voice," said the chief clerk in a voice noticeably low beside the shrillness of the mother's. "Anna! Anna!" his father was calling through the hall to the kitchen, clapping his hands, "get a locksmith at once!" And the two girls were already running through the hall with a swish of skirts — how could his sister have got dressed so quickly? — and were tearing the front door open. There was no sound of its closing again; they had evidently left it open, as one does in houses where some great misfortune has happened.

But Gregor was now much calmer. The words he uttered were no longer understandable, apparently, although they seemed clear enough to him, even clearer than before, perhaps because his ear had grown accustomed to the sound of them. Yet at any rate people now believed that something was wrong with him, and were ready to help him. The positive certainty with which these first measures had been taken comforted him. He felt himself drawn once more into the human circle and hoped for great and remarkable results from both the doctor and the locksmith, without really distinguishing precisely between them. To make his voice as clear as possible for the decisive conversation that was now imminent he coughed a little, as quietly as he could, of course, since this noise too might not sound like a human cough for all he was able to judge. In the next room meanwhile there was complete silence. Perhaps his parents were sitting at the table with the chief clerk, whispering, perhaps they were all leaning against the door and listening.

Slowly Gregor pushed the chair towards the door, then let go of it, caught hold of the door for support — the soles at the end of his little legs were somewhat sticky — and rested against it for a moment after his efforts. Then he set himself to turning the key in the lock with his mouth. It seemed, unhappily, that he hadn't really any teeth — what could he grip the key with? — but on the other hand his jaws were certainly very strong; with their help he did manage to set the key in motion, heedless of the fact that he was undoubtedly damaging them somewhere, since a brown fluid issued from his mouth, flowed over the key and dripped on the floor. "Just listen to that," said the chief clerk next door; "he's turning the key." That was a great encouragement to Gregor; but they should all have shouted encouragement to him, his father and mother too: "Go on, Gregor," they should have called out, "keep going, hold on to that key!" And in the belief that they were all following his efforts intently, he clenched his jaws recklessly on the key with all the force at his command. As the turning of the key progressed he circled round the lock, holding on now only with his mouth, pushing on the key, as required, or pulling it down again with all the weight of his body. The louder click of the finally yielding lock literally quickened Gregor. With a deep breath of relief he said to himself: "So I didn't need the locksmith," and laid his head on the handle to open the door wide.

Since he had to pull the door towards him, he was still invisible when it was really wide open. He had to edge himself slowly round the near half of the double door, and to do it very carefully if he was not to fall plump upon his back just on the threshold. He was still carrying out this difficult manoeuvre, with no time to observe anything else, when he heard the chief clerk utter a loud "Oh!" — it sounded like a gust of wind — and now he could see the man, standing as he was nearest to the door, clapping one hand before his open mouth and slowly backing away as if driven by some invisible steady pressure. His mother — in spite of the chief clerk's being there her hair was still undone and sticking up in all directions — first clasped her hands and looked at his father, then took two steps towards Gregor and fell on the floor among her outspread skirts, her face quite hidden on her breast. His father knotted his fist with a fierce expression on his face as if he meant to knock Gregor back into his room, then looked uncertainly round the living room, covered his eyes with his hands and wept till his great chest heaved.

Gregor did not go now into the living room, but leaned against the inside of the firmly shut wing of the door, so that only half his body was visible and his head above it bending sideways to look at the others. The light had meanwhile strengthened; on the other side of the street one could see clearly a section of the endlessly long, dark gray building opposite — it was a hospital — abruptly punctuated by its row of regular windows; the rain was still falling, but only in large singly discernible and literally singly splashing drops. The breakfast dishes were set out on the table lavishly, for breakfast was the most important meal of the day to Gregor's father, who lingered it out for hours over various newspapers. Right opposite Gregor on the wall hung a photograph of himself on military service, as a lieutenant, hand on sword, a carefree smile on his face, inviting one to respect his uniform and military bearing. The door leading to the hall was open, and one could see that the front door stood open too, showing the landing beyond and the beginning of the stairs going down.

"Well," said Gregor, knowing perfectly that he was the only one who had retained any composure, "I'll put my clothes on at once, pack up my samples and start off. Will you only let me go? You see, sir, I'm not obstinate, and I'm willing to work; traveling is a hard life, but I couldn't live without it. Where are you going, sir? To the office? Yes? Will you give a true account of all this? One can be temporarily incapacitated, but that's just the moment for remembering former services and bearing in mind that later on, when the incapacity has been got over, one will certainly work with all the more industry and concentration. I'm loyally bound to serve the chief, you know that very well. Besides, I have to provide for my parents and my sister. I'm in great difficulties, but I'll get out of them again. Don't make things any worse for me than they are. Stand up for me in the firm. Travelers are not popular there, I know. People think they earn sacks of money and just have a good time. A prejudice there's no particular reason for revising. But you, sir, have a more comprehensive view of affairs than the rest of the staff, yes, let me tell you in confidence, a more comprehensive view than the chief himself, who, being the owner, lets his judgment easily be swayed against one of his employees. And you know very well that the traveler, who is never seen in the office almost the whole year round, can so easily fall a victim to gossip and ill luck and unfounded complaints, which he mostly knows nothing about, except when he comes back exhausted from his rounds, and only then suffers in person from their evil consequences, which he can no longer trace back to the original causes. Sir, sir, don't go away without a word to me to show that you think me in the right at least to some extent!"

But at Gregor's very first words the chief clerk had already backed away and only stared at him with parted lips over one twitching shoulder. And while Gregor was speaking he did not stand still one moment but stole away towards the door, without taking his eyes off

Gregor, yet only an inch at a time, as if obeying some secret injunc-
tion to leave the room. He was already at the hall, and the sudden-
ness with which he took his last step out of the living room would
have made one believe he had burned the sole of his foot. Once in
the hall he stretched his right arm before him towards the staircase,
as if some supernatural power were waiting there to deliver him.

Gregor perceived that the chief clerk must on no account be allowed to go away in this frame of mind if his position in the firm were
not to be endangered to the utmost. His parents did not understand
this so well; they had convinced themselves in the course of years
that Gregor was settled for life in this firm, and besides they were so
occupied with their immediate troubles that all foresight had forsaken them. Yet Gregor had this foresight. The chief clerk must be
detained, soothed, persuaded and finally won over; the whole future
of Gregor and his family depended on it! If only his sister had been
there! She was intelligent; she had begun to cry while Gregor was
still lying quietly on his back. And no doubt the chief clerk, so partial
to ladies, would have been guided by her; she would have shut the
door of the flat and in the hall talked him out of his horror. But she
was not there, and Gregor would have to handle the situation himself. And without remembering that he was still unaware what
powers of movement he possessed, without even remembering that
his words in all possibility, indeed in all likelihood, would again be
unintelligible, he let go the wing of the door, pushed himself through
the opening, started to walk towards the chief clerk, who was already
ridiculously clinging with both hands to the railing on the landing;
but immediately, as he was feeling for a support, he fell down with a
little cry upon all his numerous legs. Hardly was he down when he
experienced for the first time this morning a sense of physical comfort; his legs had firm ground under them; they were completely
obedient, as he noted with joy; they even strove to carry him forward
in whatever direction he chose; and he was inclined to believe that a
final relief from all his sufferings was at hand. But in the same moment as he found himself on the floor, rocking with suppressed eagerness to move, not far from his mother, indeed just in front of her, she,
who had seemed so completely crushed, sprang all at once to her
feet, her arms and fingers outspread, cried: "Help, for God's sake,
help!" bent her head down as if to see Gregor better, yet on the
contrary kept backing senselessly away; had quite forgotten that the
laden table stood behind her; sat upon it hastily, as if in absence of
mind, when she bumped into it; and seemed altogether unaware that
the big coffee pot beside her was upset and pouring coffee in a flood
over the carpet.

"Mother, Mother," said Gregor in a low voice, and looked up at her. The chief clerk, for the moment, had quite slipped from his mind; instead, he could not resist snapping his jaws together at the sight of the streaming coffee. That made his mother scream again, she fled from the table and fell into the arms of his father, who hastened to catch her. But Gregor had now no time to spare for his parents; the chief clerk was already on the stairs; with his chin on the banisters he was taking one last backward look. Gregor made a spring, to be as sure as possible of overtaking him; the chief clerk must have divined his intention, for he leaped down several steps and vanished; he was still yelling "Ugh!" and it echoed through the whole staircase.

Unfortunately, the flight of the chief clerk seemed completely to upset Gregor's father, who had remained relatively calm until now, for instead of running after the man himself, or at least not hindering Gregor in his pursuit, he seized in his right hand the walking stick which the chief clerk had left behind on a chair, together with a hat and greatcoat, snatched in his left hand a large newspaper from the table and began stamping his feet and flourishing the stick and the newspaper to drive Gregor back into his room. No entreaty of Gregor's availed, indeed no entreaty was even understood; however humbly he bent his head his father only stamped on the floor the more loudly. Behind his father his mother had torn open a window, despite the cold weather, and was leaning far out of it with her face in her hands. A strong draught set in from the street to the staircase, the window curtain blew in, the newspapers on the table fluttered, stray pages whisked over the floor. Pitilessly Gregor's father drove him back, hissing and crying "Shoo!" like a savage. But Gregor was quite unpracticed in walking backwards, it really was a slow business. If he only had a chance to turn round he could get back to his room at once, but he was afraid of exasperating his father by the slowness of such a rotation and at any moment the stick in his father's hand might hit him a fatal blow on the back or on the head. In the end, however, nothing else was left for him to do since to his horror he observed that in moving backwards he could not even control the direction he took; and so, keeping an anxious eye on his father all the time over his shoulder, he began to turn round as quickly as he could, which was in reality very slowly. Perhaps his father noted his good intentions, for he did not interfere except every now and then to help him in the manoeuvre from a distance with the point of the stick. If only he would have stopped making that unbearable hissing noise! It made Gregor quite lose his head. He had turned almost completely round when the hissing noise so distracted him that he even turned a little the wrong way again. But when at last his head was fortunately right in front of the doorway, it appeared that his body was too broad simply to get through the opening. His father, of course, in his present mood was far from thinking of such a thing as opening the other half of the door, to let Gregor have enough space. He had merely the fixed idea of driving Gregor back into his room as quickly as possible. He would never have suffered Gregor to make the circumstantial preparations for standing up on end and perhaps slipping his way through the door. Maybe he was now making more noise than ever to urge Gregor forward, as if no obstacle impeded him; to Gregor, anyhow, the noise in his rear sounded no longer like the voice of one single father; this was really no joke, and Gregor thrust himself — come what might — into the doorway. One side of his body rose up, he was tilted at an angle in the doorway, his flank was quite bruised, horrid blotches stained the white door, soon he was stuck fast and, left to himself, could not have moved at all, his legs on one side fluttered trembling in the air, those on the other were crushed painfully to the floor — when from behind his father gave him a strong push which was literally a deliverance and he flew far into the room, bleeding freely. The door was slammed behind him with the stick, and then at last there was silence.

II

Not until it was twilight did Gregor awake out of a deep sleep, more like a swoon than a sleep. He would certainly have waked up of his own accord not much later, for he felt himself sufficiently rested and well-slept, but it seemed to him as if a fleeting step and a cautious shutting of the door leading into the hall had aroused him. The electric lights in the street cast a pale sheen here and there on the ceiling and the upper surfaces of the furniture, but down below, where he lay, it was dark. Slowly, awkwardly trying out his feelers, which he now first learned to appreciate, he pushed his way to the door to see what had been happening there. His left side felt like one single long, unpleasantly tense scar, and he had actually to limp on his two rows of legs. One little leg, moreover, had been severely damaged in the course of that morning's events — it was almost a miracle that only one had been damaged — and trailed uselessly behind him.

He had reached the door before he discovered what had really drawn him to it: the smell of food. For there stood a basin filled with fresh milk in which floated little sops of white bread. He could almost have laughed with joy, since he was now still hungrier than in the morning, and he dipped his head almost over the eyes straight into the milk. But soon in disappointment he withdrew it again; not only did he find it difficult to feed because of his tender left side — and he could only feed with the palpitating collaboration of his whole body — he did not like the milk either, although milk had been his favorite drink and that was certainly why his sister had set it there for him, indeed it was almost with repulsion that he turned away from the basin and crawled back to the middle of the room.

He could see through the crack of the door that the gas was turned on in the living room, but while usually at this time his father made a habit of reading the afternoon newspaper in a loud voice to his mother and occasionally to his sister as well, not a sound was now to be heard. Well, perhaps his father had recently given up this habit of reading aloud, which his sister had mentioned so often in converstion and in her letters. But there was the same silence all around, although the flat was certainly not empty of occupants. "What a quiet life our family has been leading," said Gregor to himself, and as he sat there motionless staring into the darkness he felt great pride in the fact that he had been able to provide such a life for his parents and sister in such a fine flat. But what if all the quiet, the comfort, the contentment were now to end in horror? To keep himself from being lost in such thoughts Gregor took refuge in movement and crawled up and down the room.

Once during the long evening one of the side doors was opened a little and quickly shut again, later the other side door too; someone had apparently wanted to come in and then thought better of it. Gregor now stationed himself immediately before the living room door, determined to persuade any hesitating visitor to come in or at least to discover who it might be; but the door was not opened again and he waited in vain. In the early morning, when the doors were locked, they had all wanted to come in, now that he had opened one door and the other had apparently been opened during the day, no one came in and even the keys were on the other side of the doors.

It was late at night before the gas went out in the living room, and Gregor could easily tell that his parents and his sister had all stayed awake until then, for he could clearly hear the three of them stealing away on tiptoe. No one was likely to visit him, not until the morning, that was certain; so he had plenty of time to meditate at his leisure on how he was to arrange his life afresh. But the lofty, empty room in which he had to lie flat on the floor filled him with an apprehension he could not account for, since it had been his very own room for the past five years — and with a half-unconscious action, not without a slight feeling of shame, he scuttled under the sofa, where he felt comfortable at once, although his back was a little cramped and he could not lift his head up, and his only regret was that his body was too broad to get the whole of it under the sofa.

He stayed there all night, spending the time partly in a light slumber, from which his hunger kept waking him up with a start, and partly in worrying and sketching vague hopes, which all led to the same conclusion, that he must lie low for the present and, by exercising patience and the utmost consideration, help the family to bear the inconvenience he was bound to cause them in his present condition.

Very early in the morning, it was still almost night, Gregor had the chance to test the strength of his new resolutions, for his sister, nearly fully dressed, opened the door from the hall and peered in. She did not see him at once, yet when she caught sight of him under the sofa — well, he had to be somewhere, he couldn't have flown away, could he? — she was so startled that without being able to help it she slammed the door shut again. But as if regretting her behavior she opened the door again immediately and came in on tiptoe, as if she were visiting an invalid or even a stranger. Gregor had pushed his head forward to the very edge of the sofa and watched her. Would she notice that he had left the milk standing, and not for lack of hunger, and would she bring in some other kind of food more to his taste? If she did not do it of her own accord, he would rather starve than draw her attention to the fact, although he felt a wild impulse to dart out from under the sofa, throw himself at her feet and beg her for something to eat. But his sister at once noticed, with surprise, that the basin was still full, except for a little milk that had been spilt all around it, she lifted it immediately, not with her bare hands, true, but with a cloth and carried it away. Gregor was wildly curious to know what she would bring instead, and made various speculations about it. Yet what she actually did next, in the goodness of her heart, he could never have guessed at. To find out what he liked she brought him a whole selection of food, all set out on an old newspaper. There were old, half-decayed vegetables, bones from last night's supper covered with a white sauce that had thickened; some raisins and almonds; a piece of cheese that Gregor would have called uneatable two days ago; a dry roll of bread, a buttered roll, and a roll both buttered and salted. Besides all that, she set down again the same basin, into which she had poured some water, and which was apparently to be reserved for his exclusive use. And with fine tact, knowing that Gregor would not eat in her presence, she withdrew quickly and even turned the key, to let him understand that he could take his ease as much as he liked. Gregor's legs all whizzed towards the food. His wounds must have healed completely, moreover, for he felt no disability, which amazed him and made him reflect how more than a month ago he had cut one finger a little with a knife and had still suffered pain from the wound only the day before yesterday. Am I less sensitive now? he thought, and sucked greedily at the cheese, which above all the other edibles attracted him at once and strongly. One after another and with tears of satisfaction in his eyes he quickly devoured the cheese, the vegetables and the sauce; the fresh food, on the other hand, had no charms for him, he could not even stand the smell of it and actually dragged away to some little distance the things he could eat. He had long finished his meal and was only lying lazily on the same spot when his sister turned the key slowly as a sign for him to retreat. That roused him at once, although he was nearly asleep, and he hurried under the sofa again. But it took considerable self-control for him to stay under the sofa, even for the short time his sister was in the room, since the large meal had swollen his body somewhat and he was so cramped he could hardly breathe. Slight attacks of breathlessness afflicted him and his eyes were starting a little out of his head as he watched his unsuspecting sister sweeping together with a broom not only the remains of what he had eaten but even the things he had not touched, as if these were now of no use to anyone, and hastily shoveling it all into a bucket, which she covered with a wooden lid and carried away. Hardly had she turned her back when Gregor came from under the sofa and stretched and puffed himself out.

In this manner Gregor was fed, once in the early morning while his parents and the servant girl were still asleep, and a second time after they had all had their midday dinner, for then his parents took a short nap and the servant girl could be sent out on some errand or other by his sister. Not that they would have wanted him to starve, of course, but perhaps they could not have borne to know more about his feeding than from hearsay, perhaps too his sister wanted to spare them such little anxieties wherever possible, since they had quite enough to bear as it was.

Under what pretext the doctor and the locksmith had been got rid of on that first morning Gregor could not discover, for since what he said was not understood by the others it never struck any of them, not even his sister, that he could understand what they said, and so whenever his sister came into his room he had to content himself with hearing her utter only a sigh now and then and an occasional appeal to the saints. Later on, when she had got a little used to the situation — of course she could never get completely used to it — she sometimes threw out a remark which was kindly meant or could be so interpreted. "Well, he liked his dinner today," she would say when Gregor had made a good clearance of his food; and when he had not eaten, which gradually happened more and more often, she would say almost sadly: "Everything's been left standing again."

But although Gregor could get no news directly, he overheard a lot from the neighboring rooms, and as soon as voices were audible, he would run to the door of the room concerned and press his whole body against it. In the first few days especially there was no conversation that did not refer to him somehow, even if only indirectly. For two whole days there were family consultations at every mealtime about what should be done; but also between meals the same subject was discussed, for there were always at least two members of the family at home, since no one wanted to be alone in the flat and to leave it quite empty was unthinkable. And on the very first of these days the household cook — it was not quite clear what and how much she knew of the situation — went down on her knees to his mother and begged leave to go, and when she departed, a quarter of an hour later, gave thanks for her dismissal with tears in her eyes as if for the greatest benefit that could have been conferred on her, and without any prompting swore a solemn oath that she would never say a single word to anyone about what had happened.

Now Gregor's sister had to cook too, helping her mother; true, the cooking did not amount to much, for they ate scarcely anything. Gregor was always hearing one of the family vainly urging another to eat and getting no answer but: "Thanks, I've had all I want," or something similar. Perhaps they drank nothing either. Time and again his sister kept asking his father if he wouldn't like some beer and offered kindly to go and fetch it herself, and when he made no answer suggested that she could ask the concierge to fetch it, so that he need feel no sense of obligation, but then a round "No" came from his father and no more was said about it.

In the course of that very first day Gregor's father explained the family's financial position and prospects to both his mother and his sister. Now and then he rose from the table to get some voucher or memorandum out of the small safe he had rescued from the collapse of his business five years earlier. One could hear him opening the complicated lock and rustling papers out and shutting it again. This statement made by his father was the first cheerful information Gregor had heard since his imprisonment. He had been of the opinion that nothing at all was left over from his father's business, at least his father had never said anything to the contrary, and of course he had not asked him directly. At that time Gregor's sole desire was to do his utmost to help the family to forget as soon as possible the catastrophe which had overwhelmed the business and thrown them all into a state of complete despair. And so he had set to work with unusual ardor and almost overnight has become a commercial traveler instead of a little clerk, with of course much greater chances of earning money, and his success was immediately translated into good round coin which he could lay on the table for his amazed and happy family. These had been fine times, and they had never recurred, at least not with the same sense of glory, although later on Gregor had earned so much money that he was able to meet the expenses of the whole household and did so. They had simply got used to it, both the family and Gregor; the money was gratefully accepted and gladly given, but there was no special uprush of warm feeling. With his sister alone had he remained intimate, and it was a secret plan of his that she, who loved music, unlike himself, and could play movingly on the violin, should be sent next year to study at the Conservatorium, despite the great expense that would entail, which must be made up in some other way. During his brief visits home the Conservatorium was often mentioned in the talks he had with his sister, but always merely as a beautiful dream which could never come true, and his parents discouraged even these innocent references to it; yet Gregor had made up his mind firmly about it and meant to announce the fact with due solemnity on Christmas Day.

Such were the thoughts, completely futile in his present condition, that went through his head as he stood clinging upright to the door and listening. Sometimes out of sheer weariness he had to give up listening and let his head fall negligently against the door, but he always had to pull himself together again at once, for even the slight sound his head made was audible next door and brought all conversation to a stop. "What can he be doing now?" his father would say after a while, obviously turning towards the door, and only then would the interrupted conversation gradually be set going again.

Gregor was now informed as amply as he could wish — for his father tended to repeat himself in his explanations, partly because it was a long time since he had handled such matters and partly because his mother could not always grasp things at once — that a certain amount of investments, a very small amount it was true, had survived the wreck of their fortunes and had even increased a little because the dividends had not been touched meanwhile. And besides that, the money Gregor brought home every month — he had kept only a few dollars for himself — had never been quite used up and now amounted to a small capital sum. Behind the door Gregor nodded his head eagerly, rejoiced at this evidence of unexpected thrift and foresight. True, he could really have paid off some more of his father's debts to the chief with his extra money, and so brought much nearer the day on which he could quit his job, but doubtless it was better the way his father had arranged it.

Yet this capital was by no means sufficient to let the family live on the interest of it; for one year, perhaps, or at the most two, they could live on the principal, that was all. It was simply a sum that ought not to be touched and should be kept for a rainy day; money for living expenses would have to be earned. Now his father was still hale enough but an old man, and he had done no work for the past five years and could not be expected to do much; during these five years, the first years of leisure in his laborious though unsuccessful life, he had grown rather fat and become sluggish. And Gregor's old mother, how was she to earn a living with her asthma, which troubled her even when whe walked through the flat and kept her lying on a sofa every other day panting for breath beside an open window? And was his sister to earn her bread, she who was still a child of seventeen and whose life hitherto had been so pleasant, consisting as it did in dressing herself nicely, sleeping long, helping in the housekeeping, going out to a few modest entertainments and above all playing the violin? At first whenever the need for earning money was mentioned Gregor let go his hold on the door and threw himself down on the cool leather sofa beside it, he felt so hot with shame and grief.

Often he just lay there the long nights through without sleeping at all, scrabbling for hours on the leather. Or he nerved himself to the great effort of pushing an armchair to the window, then crawled up over the window sill and, braced against the chair, leaned against the window panes, obviously in some recollection of the sense of freedom that looking out of a window always used to give him. For in reality day by day things that were even a little way off were growing dimmer to his sight; the hospital across the street, which he used to execrate for being all too often before his eyes, was now quite beyond his range of vision, and if he had not known that he lived in Charlotte Street, a quiet street but still a city street, he might have believed that his window gave on a desert waste where gray sky and gray land blended indistinguishably into each other. His quick-witted sister only needed to observe twice that the armchair stood by the window; after that whenever she had tidied the room she always pushed the chair back to the same place at the window and even left the inner casements open.

If he could have spoken to her and thanked her for all she had to do for him, he could have borne her ministrations better; as it was, they oppressed him. She certainly tried to make as light as possible of whatever was disagreeable in her task, and as time went on she succeeded, of course, more and more, but time brought more enlightenment to Gregor too. The very way she came in distressed him. Hardly was she in the room when she rushed to the window, without even taking time to shut the door, careful as she was usually to shield the sight of Gregor's room from the others, and as if she were almost suffocating tore the casements open with hasty fingers, standing then in the open draught for a while even in the bitterest cold and drawing deep breaths. This noisy scurry of hers upset Gregor twice a day; he would crouch trembling under the sofa all the time, knowing quite well that she would certainly have spared him such a disturbance had she found it at all possible to stay in his presence without opening the window.

On one occasion, about a month after Gregor's metamorphosis, when there was surely no reason for her to be still startled at his appearance, she came a little earlier than usual and found him gazing out of the window, quite motionless, and thus well placed to look like a bogey. Gregor would not have been surprised had she not come in at all, for she could not immediately open the window while he was there, but not only did she retreat, she jumped back as if in alarm and banged the door shut; a stranger might well have thought that he had been lying in wait for her there meaning to bite her. Of course he hid himself under the sofa at once, but he had to wait until midday before she came again, and she seemed more ill at ease than usual. This made him realize how repulsive the sight of him still was to her, and that it was bound to go on being repulsive, and what an effort it must cost her not to run away even from the sight of the small portion of his body that stuck out from under the sofa. In order to spare her that, therefore, one day he carried a sheet on his back to the sofa — it cost him four hours' labor — and arranged it there in such a way as to hide him completely, so that even if she were to bend down she could not see him. Had she considered the sheet unnecessary, she would certainly have stripped it off the sofa again, for it was clear enough that this curtaining and confining of himself was not likely to conduce Gregor's comfort, but she left it where it was, and Gregor even fancied that he caught a thankful glance from her eye when he lifted the sheet carefully a very little with his head to see how she was taking the new arrangement.

For the first fortnight his parents could not bring themselves to the point of entering his room, and he often heard them expressing their appreciation of his sister's activities, whereas formerly they had frequently scolded her for being as they thought a somewhat useless daughter. But now, both of them often waited outside the door, his father and his mother, while his sister tidied his room, and as soon as she came out she had to tell them exactly how things were in the room, what Gregor had eaten, how he had conducted himself this time and whether there was not perhaps some slight improvement in his condition. His mother, moreover, began relatively soon to want to visit him, but his father and sister dissuaded her at first with arguments which Gregor listened to very attentively and altogether approved. Later, however, she had to be held back by main force, and when she cried out: "Do let me in to Gregor, he is my unfortunate son! Can't you understand that I must go to him?" Gregor thought that it might be well to have her come in, not every day, of course, but perhaps once a week; she understood things, after all, much better than his sister, who was only a child despite the efforts she was making and had perhaps taken on so difficult a task merely out of childish thoughtlessness.

Gregor's desire to see his mother was soon fulfilled. During the daytime he did not want to show himself at the window, out of consideration for his parents, but he could not crawl very far around the few square yards of floor space he had, nor could he bear lying quietly at rest all during the night, while he was fast losing any interest he had ever taken in food, so that for mere recreation he had formed the habit of crawling crisscross over the walls and ceiling. He especially enjoyed hanging suspended from the ceiling; it was much better than lying on the floor. One could breathe more freely; one's body swung and rocked lightly; and in the almost blissful absorption induced by this suspension it could happen to his own surprise that he let go and fell plump on the floor. Yet he now had his body much better under control than formerly, and even such a big fall did him no harm. His sister at once remarked the new distraction Gregor had found for himself — he left traces behind him of the sticky stuff on his soles wherever he crawled — and she got the idea in her head of giving him as wide a field as possible to crawl in and of removing the pieces of furniture that hindered him, above all the chest of drawers and the writing desk. But that was more than she could manage all by herself; she did not dare ask her father to help her; and as for the servant girl, a young creature of sixteen who had had the courage to stay on after the cook's departure, she could not be asked to help, for she had begged as an especial favor that she might keep the kitchen door locked and open it only on a definite summons; so there was nothing left but to apply to her mother at an hour when her father was out. And the old lady did come, with exclamations of joyful eagerness, which, however, died away at the door of Gregor's room. Gregor's sister, of course, went in first, to see that everything was in order before letting his mother enter. In great haste Gregor pulled the sheet lower and tucked it more in folds so that it really looked as if it had been thrown accidentally over the sofa. And this time he did not peer out from under it; he renounced the pleasure of seeing his mother on this occasion and was only glad that she had come at all. "Come in, he's out of sight," said his sister, obviously leading her mother in by the hand. Gregor could now hear the two women struggling to shift the heavy old chest from its place, and his sister claiming the greater part of the labor for herself, without listening to the admonitions of her mother who feared she might overstrain herself. It took a long time. After at least a quarter of an hour's tugging his mother objected that the chest had better be left where it was, for in the first place it was too heavy and could never be got out before his father came home, and standing in the middle of the room like that it would only hamper Gregor's movements, while in the second place it was not at all certain that removing the furniture would be doing a service to Gregor. She was inclined to think to the contrary; the sight of the naked walls made her own heart heavy, and why shouldn't Gregor have the same feeling, considering that he had been used to his furniture for so long and might feel forlorn without it. "And doesn't it look," she concluded in a low voice — in fact she had been almost whispering all the time as if to avoid letting Gregor, whose exact whereabouts she did not know, hear even the tones of her voice, for she was convinced that he could not understand her words — "doesn't it look as if we were showing him, by taking away his furniture, that we have given up hope of his ever getting better and are just leaving him coldly to himself? I think it would be best to keep his room exactly as it has always been, so that when he comes back to us he will find everything unchanged and be able all the more easily to forget what has happened in between."

On hearing these words from his mother Gregor realized that the lack of all direct human speech for the past two months together with the monotony of family life must have confused his mind, otherwise he could not account for the fact that he had quite earnestly looked forward to having his room emptied of furnishing. Did he really want his warm room, so comfortably fitted with old family furniture, to be turned into a naked den in which he would certainly be able to crawl unhampered in all directions but at the price of shedding simultaneously all recollection of his human background? He had indeed been so near the brink of forgetfulness that only the voice of his mother, which he had not heard for so long, had drawn him back from it. Nothing should be taken out of his room; everything must stay as it was; he could not dispense with the good influence of the furniture on his state of mind; and even if the furniture did hamper him in his senseless crawling round and round, that was no drawback but a great advantage.

Unfortunately his sister was of the contrary opinion; she had grown accustomed, and not without reason, to consider herself an expert in Gregor's affairs as against her parents, and so her mother's advice was now enough to make her determined on the removal not only of the chest and the writing desk, which had been her first intention, but of all the furniture except the indispensable sofa. This determination was not, of course, merely the outcome of childish recalcitrance and of the self-confidence she had recently developed so unexpectedly and at such cost; she had in fact perceived that Gregor needed a lot of space to crawl about in, while on the other hand he never used the furniture at all, so far as could be seen. Another factor might have been also the enthusiastic temperament of an adolescent girl, which seeks to indulge itself on every opportunity and which now tempted Grete to exaggerate the horror of her brother's circumstances in order that she might do all the more for him. In a room where Gregor lorded it all alone over empty walls no one save herself was likely ever to set foot.

And so she was not to be moved from her resolve by her mother who seemed moreover to be ill at ease in Gregor's room and therefore unsure of herself, was soon reduced to silence and helped her daughter as best she could to push the chest outside. Now, Gregor could do without the chest, if need be, but the writing desk he must retain. As soon as the two women had got the chest out of his room, groaning as they pushed it, Gregor stuck his head out from under the sofa to see how he might intervene as kindly and cautiously as possible. But as bad luck would have it, his mother was the first to return, leaving Grete clasping the chest in the room next door where she was trying to shift it all by herself, without of course moving it from the spot. His mother however was not accustomed to the sight of him, it might sicken her and so in alarm Gregor backed quickly to the other end of the sofa, yet could not prevent the sheet from swaying a little in front. That was enough to put her on the alert. She paused, stood still for a moment and then went back to Grete.

Although Gregor kept reassuring himself that nothing out of the way was happening, but only a few bits of furniture were being changed round, he soon had to admit that all this trotting to and fro of the two women, their little ejaculations and the scraping of furniture along the floor affected him like a vast disturbance coming from all sides at once, and however much he tucked in his head and legs and cowered to the very floor he was bound to confess that he would not be able to stand it for long. They were clearing his room out; taking away everything he loved; the chest in which he kept his fret saw and other tools was already dragged off; they were now loosening the writing desk which had almost sunk into the floor, the desk at which he had done all his homework when he was at the commercial academy, at the grammar school before that, and, yes, even at the primary school — he had no more time to waste in weighing the good intentions of the two women, whose existence he had by now almost forgotten, for they were so exhausted that they were laboring in silence and nothing could be heard but the heavy scuffling of their feet.

And so he rushed out — the women were just leaning against the writing desk in the next room to give themselves a breather — and four times changed his direction, since he really did not know what to rescue first, then on the wall opposite, which was already otherwise cleared, he was struck by the picture of the lady muffled in so much fur and quickly crawled up to it and pressed himself to the glass, which was a good surface to hold on to and comforted his hot belly. This picture at least, which was entirely hidden beneath him, was going to be removed by nobody. He turned his head towards the door of the living room so as to observe the women when they came back.

They had not allowed themselves much of a rest and were already coming; Grete had twined her arm round her mother and was almost supporting her. "Well, what shall we take now?" said Grete, looking round. Her eyes met Gregor's from the wall. She kept her composure, presumably because of her mother, bent her head down to her mother, to keep her from looking up, and said, although in a fluttering, unpremeditated voice: "Come, hadn't we better go back to the living room for a moment?" Her intentions were clear enough to Gregor, she wanted to bestow her mother in safety and then chase him down from the wall. Well, just let her try it! He clung to his picture and would not give it up. He would rather fly in Grete's face.

But Grete's words had succeeded in disquieting her mother, who took a step to one side, caught sight of the huge brown mass on the flowered wallpaper, and before she was really conscious that what she saw was Gregor screamed in a loud, hoarse voice: "Oh God, oh God!" fell with outspread arms over the sofa as if giving up and did not move. "Gregor!" cried his sister, shaking her fist and glaring at him. This was the first time she had directly addressed him since his metamorphosis. She ran into the next room for some aromatic essence with which to rouse her mother from her fainting fit. Gregor wanted to help too — there was still time to rescue the picture — but he was stuck fast to the glass and had to tear himself loose; he then ran after his sister into the next room as if he could advise her, as he used to do; but then had to stand helplessly behind her; she meanwhile searched among various small bottles and when she turned round started in alarm at the sight of him; one bottle fell on the floor and broke; a splinter of glass cut Gregor's face and some kind of corrosive medicine splashed him; without pausing a moment longer Grete gathered up all the bottles she could carry and ran to her mother with them; she banged the door shut with her foot. Gregor was now cut off from his mother, who was perhaps nearly dying because of him; he dared not open the door for fear of frightening away his sister, who had to stay with her mother; there was nothing he could do but wait; and harassed by self-reproach and worry he began now to crawl to and fro, over everything, walls, furniture and ceiling, and finally in his despair, when the whole room seemed to be reeling round him, fell down on to the middle of the big table.

A little while elapsed, Gregor was still lying there feebly and all around was quiet, perhaps that was a good omen. Then the doorbell rang. The servant girl was of course locked in her kitchen, and Grete would have to open the door. It was his father. "What's been happening?" were his first words; Grete's face must have told him everything. Grete answered in a muffled voice, apparently hiding her head on his breast: "Mother has been fainting, but she's better now. Gregor's broken loose." "Just what I expected," said his father, "just what I've been telling you, but you women would never listen." It was clear to Gregor that his father had taken the worst interpretation of Grete's all too brief statement and was assuming that Gregor had been guilty of some violent act. Therefore Gregor must now try to propitiate his father, since he had neither time nor means for an explanation. And so he fled to the door of his own room and crouched against it, to let his father see as soon as he came in from the hall that his son had the good intention of getting back into his room immediately and that it was not necessary to drive him there, but that if only the door were opened he would disappear at once.

Yet his father was not in the mood to perceive such fine distinctions. "Ah!" he cried as soon as he appeared, in a tone which sounded at once angry and exultant. Gregor drew his head back from the door and lifted it to look at his father. Truly, this was not the father he had imagined to himself; admittedly he had been too absorbed of late in his new recreation of crawling over the ceiling to take the same interest as before in what was happening elsewhere in the flat, and he ought really to be prepared for some changes. And yet, and yet, could that be his father? The man who used to lie wearily sunk in bed whenever Gregor set out on a business journey; who welcomed him back of an evening lying in a long chair in a dressing gown; who could not really rise to his feet but only lifted his arms in greeting, and on the rare occasions when he did go out with his family, on one or two Sundays a year and on high holidays, walked between Gregor and his mother, who were slow walkers anyhow, even more slowly than they did, muffled in his old greatcoat, shuffling laboriously forward with the help of his crook-handled stick which he set down most cautiously at every step and, whenever he wanted to say anything, nearly always came to a full stop and gathered his escort around him? Now he was standing there in fine shape; dressed in a smart blue uniform with gold buttons, such as bank messengers wear; his strong double chin bulged over the stiff high collar of his jacket; from under his bushy eyebrows his black eyes darted fresh and penetrating glances; his one-time tangled white hair had been combed flat on either side of a shining and carefully exact parting. He pitched his cap, which bore a gold monogram, probably the badge of some bank, in a wide sweep across the whole room on to a sofa and with the tail-ends of his jacket thrown back, his hands in his trouser pockets, advanced with a grim visage towards Gregor. Likely enough he did not himself know what he meant to do; at any rate he lifted his feet uncommonly high, and Gregor was dumbfounded at the enormous size of his shoe soles. But Gregor could not risk standing up to him, aware as he had been from the very first day of his new life that his father believed only the severest measures suitable for dealing with him. And so he ran before his father, stopping when he stopped and scuttling forward again when his father made any kind of move. In this way they circled the room several times without anything decisive happening, indeed the whole operation did not even look like a pursuit because it was carried out so slowly. And so Gregor did not leave the floor, for he feared that his father might take as a piece of peculiar wickedness any excursion of his over the walls or the ceiling. All the same, he could not stay this course much longer, for while his father took one step he had to carry out a whole series of movements. He was already beginning to feel breathless, just as in his former life his lungs had not been very dependable. As he was staggering along, trying to concentrate his energy on running, hardly keeping his eyes open; in his dazed state never even thinking of any other escape than simply going forward; and having almost forgotten that the walls were free to him, which in this room were well provided with finely carved pieces of furniture full of knobs and crevices — suddenly something lightly flung landed close behind him and rolled before him. It was an apple; a second apple followed immediately; Gregor came to a stop in alarm; there was no point in running on, for his father was determined to bombard him. He had filled his pockets with fruit from the dish on the sideboard and was now shying apple after apple, without taking particularly good aim for the moment. The small red apples rolled about the floor as if magnetized and cannoned into each other. An apple thrown without much force grazed Gregor's back and glanced off harmlessly. But another following immediately landed right on his back and sank in; Gregor wanted to drag himself forward, as if this startling, incredible pain could be left behind him; but he felt as if nailed to the spot and flattened himself out in a complete derangement of all his senses. With his last conscious look he saw the door of his room being torn open and his mother rushing out ahead of his screaming sister, in her underbodice, for her daughter had loosened her clothing to let her breathe more freely and recover from her swoon, he saw his mother rushing towards his father, leaving one after another behind her on the floor her loosened petticoats, stumbling over her petticoats straight to his father and embracing him, in

complete union with him — but here Gregor's sight began to fail —
with her hands clasped round his father's neck as she begged for her
son's life.

III

The serious injury done to Gregor, which disabled him for more
than a month — the apple went on sticking in his body as a visible
reminder, since no one ventured to remove it — seemed to have
made even his father recollect that Gregor was a member of the
family, despite his present unfortunate and repulsive shape, and
ought not to be treated as an enemy, that, on the contrary, family duty
required the suppression of disgust and the exercise of patience,
nothing but patience.
And although his injury had impaired, probably for ever, his
power of movement, and for the time being it took him long, long
minutes to creep across his room like an old invalid — there was no
question now of crawling up the wall — yet in his own opinion he
was sufficiently compensated for this worsening of his condition by
the fact that towards evening the living-room door, which he used to
watch intently for an hour or two beforehand, was always thrown
open, so that lying in the darkness of his room, invisible to the family,
he could see them all at the lamp-lit table and listen to their talk, by
general consent as it were, very different from his earlier eaves-
dropping.
True, their intercourse lacked the lively character of former times,
which he had always called to mind with a certain wistfulness in the
small hotel bedrooms where he had been wont to throw himself
down, tired out, on damp bedding. They were now mostly very silent. Soon after supper his father would fall asleep in his armchair;
his mother and sister would admonish each other to be silent; his
mother, bending low over the lamp, stitched at fine sewing for an
underwear firm; his sister, who had taken a job as a salesgirl, was
learning shorthand and French in the evenings on the chance of
bettering herself. Sometimes his father woke up, and as if quite unaware that he had been sleeping said to his mother: "What a lot of
sewing you're doing today!" and at once fell asleep again, while the
two women exchanged a tired smile.
With a kind of mulishness his father persisted in keeping his uniform on even in the house; his dressing gown hung uselessly on its
peg and he slept fully dressed where he sat, as if he were ready for
service at any moment and even here only at the beck and call of his
superior. As a result, his uniform, which was not brand-new to start
with, began to look dirty, despite all the loving care of the mother and

sister to keep it clean, and Gregor often spent whole evenings gazing at the many greasy spots on the garment, gleaming with gold buttons always in a high state of polish, in which the old man sat sleeping in extreme discomfort and yet quite peacefully.

As soon as the clock struck ten his mother tried to rouse his father with gentle words and to persuade him after that to get into bed, for sitting there he could not have a proper sleep and that was what he needed most, since he had to go to duty at six. But with the mulishness that had obsessed him since he became a bank messenger he always insisted on staying longer at the table, although he regularly fell asleep again and in the end only with the greatest trouble could be got out of his armchair and into his bed. However insistently Gregor's mother and sister kept urging him with gentle reminders, he would go on slowly shaking his head for a quarter of an hour, keeping his eyes shut, and refuse to get to his feet. The mother plucked at his sleeve, whispering endearments in his ear, the sister left her lessons to come to her mother's help, but Gregor's father was not to be caught. He would only sink down deeper in his chair. Not until the two women hoisted him up by the armpits did he open his eyes and look at them both, one after the other, usually with the remark: "This is a life. This is the peace and quiet of my old age." And leaning on the two of them he would heave himself up, with difficulty, as if he were a great burden to himself, suffer them to lead him as far as the door and then wave them off and go on alone, while the mother abandoned her needlework and the sister her pen in order to run after him and help him farther.

Who could find time, in this overworked and tired-out family, to bother about Gregor more than was absolutely needful? The household was reduced more and more; the servant girl was turned off; a gigantic bony charwoman with white hair flying round her head came in morning and evening to do the rough work; everything else was done by Gregor's mother, as well as great piles of sewing. Even various family ornaments, which his mother and sister used to wear with pride at parties and celebrations, had to be sold, as Gregor discovered of an evening from hearing them all discuss the prices obtained. But what they lamented most was the fact that they could not leave the flat which was much too big for their present circumstances, because they could not think of any way to shift Gregor. Yet Gregor saw well enough that consideration for him was not the main difficulty preventing the removal, for they could have easily shifted him in some suitable box with a few air holes in it; what really kept them from moving into another flat was rather their own complete hopelessness and the belief that they had been singled out for a misfortune such as had never happened to any of their relations or acquaintances. They fulfilled to the uttermost all that the world demands of poor people, the father fetched breakfast for the small clerks in the bank, the mother devoted her energy to making underwear for strangers, the sister trotted to and fro behind the counter at the behest of customers, but more than this they had not the strength to do. And the wound in Gregor's back began to nag at him afresh when his mother and sister, after getting his father into bed, came back again, left their work lying, drew close to each other and sat cheek by cheek; when his mother, pointing towards his room, said: "Shut that door now, Grete," and he was left again in darkness, while next door the women mingled their tears or perhaps sat dry-eyed staring at the table.

Gregor hardly slept at all by night or by day. He was often haunted by the idea that next time the door opened he would take the family's affairs in hand again just as he used to do; once more, after this long interval, there appeared in his thoughts the figures of the chief and the chief clerk, the commercial travelers and the apprentices, the porter who was so dull-witted, two or three friends in other firms, a chambermaid in one of the rural hotels, a sweet and fleeting memory, a cashier in a milliner's shop, whom he had wooed earnestly but too slowly — they all appeared, together with strangers or people he had quite forgotten, but instead of helping him and his family they were one and all unapproachable and he was glad when they vanished. At other times he would not be in the mood to bother about his family, he was only filled with rage at the way they were neglecting him, and although he had no clear idea of what he might care to eat he would make plans for getting into the larder to take the food that was after all his due, even if he were not hungry. His sister no longer took thought to bring him what might especially please him, but in the morning and at noon before she went to business hurriedly pushed into his room with her foot any food that was available, and in the evening cleared it out again with one sweep of the broom, heedless of whether it had been merely tasted, or — as most frequently happened — left untouched. The cleaning of his room, which she now did always in the evenings, could not have been more hastily done. Streaks of dirt stretched along the walls, here and there lay balls of dust and filth. At first Gregor used to station himself in some particularly filthy corner when his sister arrived, in order to reproach her with it, so to speak. But he could have sat there for weeks without getting her to make any improvements; she could see the dirt as well as he did, but she had simply made up her mind to leave it alone. And yet, with a touchiness that was new to her, which seemed anyhow to have infected the whole family, she jealously guarded her claim to be the sole caretaker of Gregor's room. His mother once subjected his room to a thorough cleaning, which was achieved only by means of several buckets of water — all this dampness of course upset Gregor too and he lay widespread, sulky and motionless on the sofa — but she was well punished for it. Hardly had his sister noticed the changed aspect of his room that evening than she rushed in high dudgeon into the living room and, despite the imploringly raised hands of her mother, burst into a storm of weeping, while her parents — her father had of course been startled out of his chair — looked on at first in helpless amazement; then they too began to go into action; the father reproached the mother on his right for not having left the cleaning of Gregor's room to his sister; shrieked at the sister on his left that never again was she to be allowed to clean Gregor's room; while the mother tried to pull the father into his bedroom, since he was beyond himself with agitation; the sister, shaken with sobs, then beat upon the table with her small fists; and Gregor hissed loudly with rage because not one of them thought of shutting the door to spare him such a spectacle and so much noise.

Still, even if the sister, exhausted by her daily work, had grown tired of looking after Gregor as she did formerly, there was no need for his mother's intervention or for Gregor's being neglected at all. The charwoman was there. This old widow, whose strong bony frame had enabled her to survive the worst a long life could offer, by no means recoiled from Gregor. Without being in the least curious she had once by chance opened the door of his room and at the sight of Gregor, who, taken by surprise, began to rush to and fro although no one was chasing him, merely stood there with her arms folded. From that time she never failed to open his door a little for a moment, morning and evening, to have a look at him. At first she even used to call him to her, with words which apparently she took to be friendly, such as: "Come along, then, you old dung beetle!" or "Look at the old dung beetle, then!" To such allocutions Gregor made no answer, but stayed motionless where he was, as if the door had never been opened. Instead of being allowed to disturb him so senselessly whenever the whim took her, she should rather have been ordered to clean out his room daily, that charwoman! Once, early in the morning — heavy rain was lashing on the windowpanes, perhaps a sign that spring was on the way — Gregor was so exasperated when she began addressing him again that he ran for her, as if to attack her, although slowly and feebly enough. But the charwomam instead of showing fright merely lifted high a chair that happened to be beside the door, and as she stood there with her mouth wide open it was clear that she meant to shut it only when she brought the chair down on Gregor's back. "So you're not coming any nearer?" she asked, as Gregor turned away again, and quietly put the chair back into the corner.

Gregor was now eating hardly anything. Only when he happened to pass the food laid out for him did he take a bit of something in his mouth as a pastime, kept it there for an hour at a time and usually spat it out again. At first he thought it was chagrin over the state of his room that prevented him from eating, yet he soon got used to the various changes in his room. It had become a habit in the family to push into his room things there was no room for elsewhere, and there were plenty of these now, since one of the rooms had been let to three lodgers. These serious gentlemen — all three of them with full beards, as Gregor once observed through a crack in the door — had a passion for order, not only in their own room but, since they were now members of the household, in all its arrangements, especially in the kitchen. Superfluous, not to say dirty, objects they could not bear. Besides, they had brought with them most of the furnishings they needed. For this reason many things could be dispensed with that it was no use trying to sell but that should not be thrown away either. All of them found their way into Gregor's room. The ash can likewise and the kitchen garbage can. Anything that was not needed for the moment was simply flung into Gregor's room by the charwoman, who did everything in a hurry; fortunately Gregor usually saw only the object, whatever it was, and the hand that held it. Perhaps she intended to take the things away again as time and opportunity offered, or to collect them until she could throw them all out in a heap, but in fact they just lay wherever she happened to throw them, except when Gregor pushed his way through the junk heap and shifted it somewhat, at first out of necessity, because he had not room enough to crawl, but later with increasing enjoyment, although after such excursions, being sad and weary to death, he would lie motionless for hours. And since the lodgers often ate their supper at home in the common living room, the living-room door stayed shut many an evening, yet Gregor reconciled himself quite easily to the shutting of the door, for often enough on evenings when it was opened he had disregarded it entirely and lain in the darkest corner of his room, quite unnoticed by the family. But on one occasion the charwoman left the door open a little and it stayed ajar even when the lodgers came in for supper and the lamp was lit. They set themselves at the top end of the table where formerly Gregor and his father and mother had eaten their meals, unfolded their napkins and took knife and fork in hand. At once his mother appeared in the doorway with a dish of meat and close behind her his sister with a dish of potatoes piled high. The food steamed with a thick vapor. The lodgers bent over the food set before them as if to scrutinize it before eating, in fact the man in the middle, who seemed to pass for an authority with the other two, cut a piece of meat as it lay on the dish, obviously to discover if it were tender or should be sent back to the kitchen. He showed satisfaction, and Gregor's mother and sister, who had been watching anxiously, breathed freely and began to smile. The family itself took its meals in the kitchen. None the less, Gregor's father came into the living room before going into the kitchen and with one prolonged bow, cap in hand, made a round of the table. The lodgers all stood up and murmured something in their beards. When they were alone again they ate their food in almost complete silence. It seemed remarkable to Gregor that among the various noises coming from the table he could always distinguish the sound of their masticating teeth, as if this were a sign to Gregor that one needed teeth in order to eat, and that with toothless jaws even of the finest make one could do nothing. "I'm hungry enough," said Gregor sadly to himself, "but not for that kind of food. How these lodgers are stuffing themselves, and here am I dying of starvation!"

On that very evening — during the whole of his time there Gregor could not remember ever having heard the violin — the sound of violin-playing came from the kitchen. The lodgers had already finished their supper, the one in the middle had brought out a newspaper and given the other two a page apiece, and now they were leaning back at ease reading and smoking. When the violin began to play they pricked up their ears, got to their feet, and went on tiptoe to the hall door where they stood huddled together. Their movements must have been heard in the kitchen, for Gregor's father called out: "Is the violin-playing disturbing you gentlemen? It can be stopped at once." "On the contrary," said the middle lodger, "could not Fräulein Samsa come and play in this room, beside us, where it is much more convenient and comfortable?" "Oh certainly," cried Gregor's father, as if he were the violin-player. The lodgers came back into the living room and waited. Presently Gregor's father arrived with the music stand, his mother carrying the music and his sister with the violin. His sister quietly made everything ready to start playing; his parents, who had never let rooms before and so had an exaggerated idea of the courtesy due to lodgers, did not venture to sit down on their own chairs; his father leaned against the door, the right hand thrust between two buttons of his livery coat, which was formally buttoned up; but his mother was offered a chair by one of the lodgers and, since she left the chair just where he had happened to put it, sat down in a corner to one side.

Gregor's sister began to play; the father and mother, from either side, intently watched the movements of her hands. Gregor, attracted by the playing, ventured to move forward a little until his head was actually inside the living room. He felt hardly any surprise at his growing lack of consideration for the others; there had been a time when he prided himself on being considerate. And yet just on this occasion he had more reason than ever to hide himself, since owing to the amount of dust which lay thick in his room and rose into the air at the slightest movement, he too was covered with dust; fluff and hair and remnants of food trailed with him, caught on his back and along his sides; his indifference to everything was much too great for him to turn on his back and scrape himself clean on the carpet, as once he had done several times a day. And in spite of his condition, no shame deterred him from advancing a little over the spotless floor of the living room.

To be sure, no one was aware of him. The family was entirely absorbed in the violin-playing; the lodgers, however, who first of all had stationed themselves, hands in pockets, much too close behind the music stand so that they could all have read the music, which must have bothered his sister, had soon retreated to the window, half-whispering with downbent heads, and stayed there while his father turned an anxious eye on them. Indeed, they were making it more than obvious that they had been disappointed in their expectation of hearing good or enjoyable violin-playing, that they had had more than enough of the performance and only out of courtesy suffered a continued disturbance of their peace. From the way they all kept blowing the smoke of their cigars high in the air through nose and mouth one could divine their irritation. And yet Gregor's sister was playing so beautifully. Her face leaned sideways, intently and sadly her eyes followed the notes of music. Gregor crawled a little farther forward and lowered his head to the ground so that it might be possible for his eyes to meet hers. Was he an animal, that music had such an effect upon him? He felt as if the way were opening before him to the unknown nourishment he craved. He was determined to push forward till he reached his sister, to pull at her skirt and so let her know that she was to come into his room with her violin, for no one here appreciated her playing as he would appreciate it. He would never let her out of his room, at least, not so long as he lived; his frightful appearance would become, for the first time, useful to him; he would watch all the doors of his room at once and spit at intruders; but his sister should need no constraint, she should stay with him of her own free will; she should sit beside him on the sofa, bend down her ear to him and hear him confide that he had had the firm intention of sending her to the Conservatorium, and that, but for his mishap, last Christmas — surely Christmas was long past? — he would have announced it to everybody without allowing a single objection. After this confession his sister would be so touched that she would burst

into tears, and Gregor would then raise himself to her shoulder and
kiss her on the neck, which, now that she went to business, she kept
free of any ribbon or collar.

"Mr. Samsa!" cried the middle lodger, to Gregor's father, and
pointed, without wasting any more words, at Gregor, now working
himself slowly forwards. The violin fell silent, the middle lodger first
smiled to his friends with a shake of the head and then looked at
Gregor again. Instead of driving Gregor out, his father seemed to
think it more needful to begin by soothing down the lodgers, although they were not at all agitated and apparently found Gregor
more entertaining than the violin-playing. He hurried towards them
and, spreading out his arms, tried to urge them back into their own
room and at the same time to block their view of Gregor. They now
began to be really a little angry, one could not tell whether because of
the old man's behavior or because it had just dawned on them that all
unwittingly they had such a neighbor as Gregor next door. They
demanded explanations of his father, they waved their arms like him,
tugged uneasily at their beards, and only with reluctance backed
towards their room. Meanwhile Gregor's sister, who stood there as if
lost when her playing was so abruptly broken off, came to life again,
pulled herself together all at once after standing for a while holding
violin and bow in nervelessly hanging hands and staring at her
music, pushed her violin into the lap of her mother, who was still
sitting in her chair fighting asthmatically for breath, and ran into the
lodgers' room to which they were now being shepherded by her
father rather more quickly than before. One could see the pillows and
blankets on the beds flying under her accustomed fingers and being
laid in order. Before the lodgers had actually reached their room she
had finished making the beds and slipped out.

The old man seemed once more to be so possessed by his mulish
self-assertiveness that he was forgetting all the respect he should
show to his lodgers. He kept driving them on and driving them on
until in the very door of the bedroom the middle lodger stamped his
foot loudly on the floor and so brought him to a halt. "I beg to announce," said the lodger, lifting one hand and looking also at Gregor's mother and sister, "that because of the disgusting conditions
prevailing in this household and family" — here he spat on the floor
with emphatic brevity — "I give you notice on the spot. Naturally I
won't pay you a penny for the days I have lived here, on the contrary
I shall consider bringing an action for damages against you, based on
claims — believe me — that will be easily susceptible of proof." He
ceased and stared straight in front of him, as if he expected something. In fact his two friends at once rushed into the breach with

these words: "And we too give notice on the spot." On that he seized the door-handle and shut the door with a slam.

Gregor's father, groping with his hands, staggered forward and fell into his chair; it looked as if he were stretching himself there for his ordinary evening nap, but the marked jerkings of his head, which was as if uncontrollable, showed that he was far from asleep. Gregor had simply stayed quietly all the time on the spot where the lodgers had espied him. Disappointment at the failure of his plan, perhaps also the weakness arising from extreme hunger, made it impossible for him to move. He feared, with a fair degree of certainty, that at any moment the general tension would discharge itself in a combined attack upon him, and he lay waiting. He did not react even to the noise made by the violin as it fell off his mother's lap from under her trembling fingers and gave out a resonant note.

"My dear parents," said his sister, slapping her hand on the table by way of introduction, "things can't go on like this. Perhaps you don't realize that, but I do. I won't utter my brother's name in the presence of this creature, and so all I say is: we must try to get rid of it. We've tried to look after it and to put up with it as far as is humanly possible, and I don't think anyone could reproach us in the slightest."

"She is more than right," said Gregor's father to himself. His mother, who was still choking for lack of breath, began to cough hollowly into her hand with a wild look in her eyes.

His sister rushed over to her and held her forehead. His father's thoughts seemed to have lost their vagueness at Grete's words, he sat more upright, fingering his service cap that lay among the plates still lying on the table from the lodgers' supper, and from time to time looked at the still form of Gregor.

"We must try to get rid of it," his sister now said explicitly to her father, since her mother was coughing too much to hear a word, "it will be the death of both of you, I can see that coming. When one has to work as hard as we do, all of us, one can't stand this continual torment at home on top of it. At least I can't stand it any longer." And she burst into such a passion of sobbing that her tears dropped on her mother's face, where she wiped them off mechanically.

"My dear," said the old man sympathetically, and with evident understanding, "but what can we do?"

Gregor's sister merely shrugged her shoulders to indicate the feeling of helplessness that had now overmastered her during her weeping fit, in contrast to her former confidence.

"If he could understand us," said her father, half questioningly; Grete, still sobbing, vehemently waved a hand to show how unthinkable that was.

"If he could understand us," repeated the old man, shutting his eyes to consider his daughter's conviction that understanding was impossible, "then perhaps we might come to some agreement with him. But as it is —"

"He must go," cried Gregor's sister, "that's the only solution, Father. You must just try to get rid of the idea that this is Gregor. The fact that we've believed it for so long is the root of all our trouble. But how can it be Gregor? If this were Gregor, he would have realized long ago that human beings can't live with such a creature, and he'd have gone away on his own accord. Then we wouldn't have any brother, but we'd be able to go on living and keep his memory in honor. As it is, this creature persecutes us, drives away our lodgers, obviously wants the whole apartment to himself and would have us all sleep in the gutter. Just look, Father," she shrieked all at once, "he's at it again!" And in an access of panic that was quite incomprehensible to Gregor she even quitted her mother, literally thrusting the chair from her as if she would rather sacrifice her mother than stay so near to Gregor, and rushed behind her father, who also rose up, being simply upset by her agitation, and half-spread his arms out as if to protect her.

Yet Gregor had not the slightest intention of frightening anyone, far less his sister. He had only begun to turn round in order to crawl back to his room, but it was certainly a startling operation to watch, since because of his disabled condition he could not execute the difficult turning movements except by lifting his head and then bracing it against the floor over and over again. He paused and looked round. His good intentions seemed to have been recognized; the alarm had only been momentary. Now they were all watching him in melancholy silence. His mother lay in her chair, her legs stiffly outstretched and pressed together, her eyes almost closing for sheer weariness; his father and his sister were sitting beside each other, his sister's arm around the old man's neck.

Perhaps I can go on turning round now, thought Gregor, and began his labors again. He could not stop himself from panting with the effort, and had to pause now and then to take breath. Nor did anyone harass him, he was left entirely to himself. When he had completed the turn-round he began at once to crawl straight back. He was amazed at the distance separating him from his room and could not understand how in his weak state he had managed to accomplish the same journey so recently, almost without remarking it. Intent on crawling as fast as possible, he barely noticed that not a single word, not an ejaculation from his family, interfered with his progress. Only when he was already in the doorway did he turn his head round, now completely, for his neck muscles were getting stiff, but enough to see that nothing had changed behind him except that his sister had risen to her feet. His last glance fell on his mother, who was not quite overcome by sleep.

Hardly was he well inside his room when the door was hastily pushed shut, bolted and locked. The sudden noise in his rear startled him so much that his little legs gave beneath him. It was his sister who had shown such haste. She had been standing ready waiting and had made a light spring forward. Gregor had not even heard her coming, and she cried "At last!" to her parents as she turned the key in the lock.

"And what now?" said Gregor to himself, looking round in the darkness. Soon he made the discovery that he was now unable to stir a limb. This did not surprise him, rather it seemed unnatural that he should ever actually have been able to move on these feeble little legs. Otherwise he felt relatively comfortable. True, his whole body was aching, but it seemed that the pain was gradually growing less and would finally pass away. The rotting apple in his back and the inflamed area around it, all covered with soft dust, already hardly troubled him. He thought of his family with tenderness and love. The decision that he must disappear was one that he held to even more strongly than his sister, if that were possible. In this state of vacant and peaceful meditation he remained until the tower clock struck three in the morning. The first broadening of light in the world outside the window entered his consciousness once more. Then his head sank to the floor of its own accord and from his nostrils came the last faint flicker of his breath.

When the charwoman arrived early in the morning — what between her strength and her impatience she slammed all the doors so loudly, never mind how often she had been begged not to do so, that no one in the whole apartment could enjoy any quiet sleep after her arrival — she noticed nothing unusual as she took her customary peep into Gregor's room. She thought he was lying motionless on purpose, pretending to be in the sulks; she credited him with every kind of intelligence. Since she happened to have the long-handled broom in her hand she tried to tickle him up with it from the doorway. When that too produced no reaction she felt provoked and poked at him a little harder, and only when she had pushed him along the floor without meeting any resistance was her attention aroused. It did not take her long to establish the truth of the matter, and her eyes widened, she let out a whistle, yet did not waste much time over it but tore open the door of the Samsas' bedroom and yelled into the darkness at the top of her voice: "Just look at this, it's dead; it's lying here dead and done for!"

Mr. and Mrs. Samsa started up in their double bed and before they

realized the nature of the charwoman's announcement had some difficulty in overcoming the shock of it. But then they got out of bed
quickly, one on either side, Mr. Samsa throwing a blanket over his
shoulders, Mrs. Samsa in nothing but her nightgown; in this array
they entered Gregor's room. Meanwhile the door of the living room
opened, too, where Grete had been sleeping since the advent of the
lodgers; she was completely dressed as if she had not been to bed,
which seemed to be confirmed also by the paleness of her face.
"Dead?" said Mrs. Samsa, looking questioningly at the charwoman,
although she could have investigated for herself, and the fact was
obvious enough without investigation. "I should say so," said the
charwoman, proving her words by pushing Gregor's corpse a long
way to one side with her broomstick. Mrs. Samsa made a movement
as if to stop her, but checked it. "Well," said Mr. Samsa, "now thanks
be to God." He crossed himself, and the three women followed his
example. Grete, whose eyes never left the corpse, said: "Just see how
thin he was. It's such a long time since he's eaten anything. The food
came out again just as it went in." Indeed, Gregor's body was completely flat and dry, as could only now be seen when it was no longer
supported by the legs and nothing prevented one from looking
closely at it.

"Come in beside us, Grete, for a little while," said Mrs. Samsa
with a tremulous smile, and Grete, not without looking back at the
corpse, followed her parents into their bedroom. The charwoman
shut the door and opened the window wide. Although it was so early
in the morning a certain softness was perceptible in the fresh air.
After all, it was already the end of March.

The three lodgers emerged from their room and were surprised to
see no breakfast; they had been forgotten. "Where's our breakfast?"
said the middle lodger peevishly to the charwoman. But she put her
finger to her lips and hastily, without a word, indicated by gestures
that they should go into Gregor's room. They did so and stood, their
hands in the pockets of their somewhat shabby coats, around Gregor's corpse in the room where it was now fully light.

At that the door of the Samsas' bedroom opened and Mr. Samsa
appeared in his uniform, his wife on one arm, his daughter on the
other. They all looked a little as if they had been crying; from time to
time Grete hid her face on her father's arm.

"Leave my house at once!" said Mr. Samsa, and pointed to the
door without disengaging himself from the women. "What do you
mean by that?" said the middle lodger, taken somewhat aback, with
a feeble smile. The two others put their hands behind them and kept
rubbing them together, as if in gleeful expectation of a fine set-to in
which they were bound to come off the winners. "I mean just what I

say," answered Mr. Samsa, and advanced in a straight line with his
two companions towards the lodger. He stood his ground at first
quietly, looking at the floor as if his thoughts were taking a new
pattern in his head. "Then let us go, by all means," he said and
looked up at Mr. Samsa as if in a sudden access of humility he were
expecting some renewed sanction for this decision. Mr. Samsa
merely nodded briefly once or twice with meaning eyes. Upon that
the lodger really did go with long strides into the hall, his two friends
had been listening and had quite stopped rubbing their hands for
some moments and now went scuttling after him as if afraid that Mr.
Samsa might get into the hall before them and cut them off from their
leader. In the hall they all three took their hats from the rack, their
sticks from the umbrella stand, bowed in silence and quitted the
apartment. With a suspiciousness which proved quite unfounded Mr.
Samsa and the two women followed them out to the landing; leaning
over the banister they watched the three figures slowly but surely
going down the long stairs, vanishing from sight at a certain turn of
the staircase on every floor and coming into view again after a
moment or so; the more they dwindled, the more the Samsa family's
interest in them dwindled, and when a butcher's boy met them and
passed them on the stairs coming up proudly with a tray on his head,
Mr. Samsa and the two women soon left the landing and as if a
burden had been lifted from them went back into their apartment.

They decided to spend this day in resting and going for a stroll;
they had not only deserved such a respite from work, but absolutely
needed it. And so they sat down at the table and wrote three notes of
excuse, Mr. Samsa to his board of management, Mrs. Samsa to her
employer and Grete to the head of her firm. While they were writing,
the charwoman came in to say that she was going now, since her
morning's work was finished. At first they only nodded without looking up, but as she kept hovering there they eyed her irritably.
"Well?" said Mr. Samsa. The charwoman stood grinning in the
doorway as if she had good news to impart to the family but meant not
to say a word unless properly questioned. The small ostrich feather
standing upright on her hat, which had annoyed Mr. Samsa ever
since she was engaged, was waving gaily in all directions. "Well,
what is it then?" asked Mrs. Samsa, who obtained more respect from
the charwoman than the others. "Oh," said the charwoman, giggling
so amiably that she could not at once continue, "just this, you don't
need to bother about how to get rid of the thing next door. It's been
seen to already." Mrs. Samsa and Grete bent over their letters again,
as if preoccupied; Mr. Samsa, who perceived that she was eager to
begin describing it all in detail, stopped her with a decisive hand.
But since she was not allowed to tell her story, she remembered the

great hurry she was in, being obviously deeply huffed: "Bye, every-body," she said, whirling off violently, and departed with a frightful slamming of doors.

"She'll be given notice tonight," said Mr. Samsa, but neither from his wife nor his daughter did he get any answer, for the charwoman seemed to have shattered again the composure they had barely achieved. They rose, went to the window and stayed there, clasping each other tight. Mr. Samsa turned in his chair to look at them and quietly observed them for a little. Then he called out: "Come along, now, do. Let bygones be bygones. And you might have some consideration for me." The two of them complied at once, hastened to him, caressed him and quickly finished their letters.

Then they all three left the apartment together, which was more than they had done for months, and went by tram into the open country outside the town. The tram, in which they were the only passengers, was filled with warm sunshine. Leaning comfortably back in their seats they canvassed their prospects for the future, and it appeared on closer inspection that these were not at all bad, for the jobs they had got, which so far they had never really discussed with each other, were all three admirable and likely to lead to better things later on. The greatest immediate improvement in their condition would of course arise from moving to another house; they wanted to take a smaller and cheaper but also better situated and more easily run apartment than the one they had, which Gregor had selected. While they were thus conversing, it struck both Mr. and Mrs. Samsa, almost at the same moment, as they became aware of their daughter's increasing vivacity, that in spite of all the sorrow of recent times, which had made her cheeks pale, she had bloomed into a pretty girl with a good figure. They grew quieter and half unconsciously exchanged glances of complete agreement, having come to the conclusion that it would soon be time to find a good husband for her. And it was like a confirmation of their new dreams and excellent intentions that at the end of their journey their daughter sprang to her feet first and stretched her young body.

D. H. Lawrence (1885–1930)

The Horse Dealer's Daughter

"Well, Mabel, and what are you going to do with yourself?" asked Joe, with foolish flippancy. He felt quite safe himself. Without listening for an answer, he turned aside, worked a grain of tobacco to the tip of his tongue and spat it out. He did not care about anything, since he felt safe himself.

The three brothers and the sister sat round the desolate breakfast table, attempting some sort of desultory consultation. The morning's post had given the final tap to the family fortune, and all was over. The dreary dining room itself, with its heavy mahogany furniture, looked as if it were waiting to be done away with.

But the consultation amounted to nothing. There was a strange air of ineffectuality about the three men, as they sprawled at table, smoking and reflecting vaguely on their own condition. The girl was alone, a rather short, sullen-looking young woman of twenty-seven. She did not share the same life as her brothers. She would have been good-looking, save for the impassive fixity of her face, "bull-dog," as her brothers called it.

There was a confused tramping of horses' feet outside. The three men all sprawled round in their chairs to watch. Beyond the dark holly bushes that separated the strip of lawn from the highroad, they could see a cavalcade of shire horses swinging out of their own yard, being taken for exercise. This was the last time. These were the last horses that would go through their hands. The young men watched with critical, callous look. They were all frightened at the collapse of their lives, and the sense of disaster in which they were involved left them no inner freedom.

Yet they were three fine, well-set fellows enough. Joe, the eldest, was a man of thirty-three, broad and handsome in a hot, flushed way. His face was red, he twisted his black moustache over a thick finger, his eyes were shallow and restless. He had a sensual way of uncovering his teeth when he laughed, and his bearing was stupid. Now he watched the horses with a glazed look of helplessness in his eyes, a certain stupor of downfall.

The great draught-horses swung past. They were tied head to tail, four of them, and they heaved along to where a lane branched off from the highroad, planting their great hoofs floutingly in the fine black mud, swinging their great rounded haunches sumptuously, and trotting a few sudden steps as they were led into the lane, round the corner. Every movement showed a massive, slumbrous strength, and a stupidity which held them in subjection. The groom at the head looked back, jerking the leading rope. And the cavalcade moved out of sight up the lane, the tail of the last horse, bobbed up tight and stiff, held out taut from the swinging great haunches as they rocked behind the hedges in a motion-like sleep.

Joe watched with glazed hopeless eyes. The horses were almost like his own body to him. He felt he was done for now. Luckily he was engaged to a woman as old as himself, and therefore her father, who was steward of a neighboring estate, would provide him with a job. He would marry and go into harness. His life was over, he would be a subject animal now.

He turned uneasily aside, the retreating steps of the horses echoing in his ears. Then, with foolish restlessness, he reached for the scraps of bacon rind from the plates, and making a faint whistling sound, flung them to the terrier that lay against the fender. He watched the dog swallow them, and waited till the creature looked into his eyes. Then a faint grin came on his face, and in a high, foolish voice he said:

"You won't get much more bacon, shall you, you little bitch?"

The dog faintly and dismally wagged its tail, then lowered its haunches, circled round, and lay down again.

There was another helpless silence at the table. Joe sprawled uneasily in his seat, not willing to go till the family conclave was dissolved. Fred Henry, the second brother, was erect, clean-limbed, alert. He had watched the passing of the horses with more sang-froid. If he was an animal, like Joe, he was an animal which controls, not one which is controlled. He was master of any horse, and he carried himself with a well-tempered air of mastery. But he was not master of the situations of life. He pushed his coarse brown moustache upwards, off his lip, and glanced irritably at his sister, who sat impassive and inscrutable.

"You'll go and stop with Lucy for a bit, shan't you?" he asked. The girl did not answer.

"I don't see what else you can do," persisted Fred Henry.

"Go as a skivvy," Joe interpolated laconically.

The girl did not move a muscle.

"If I was her, I should go in for training for a nurse," said Malcolm, the youngest of them all. He was the baby of the family, a young man of twenty-two, with a fresh, jaunty *museau.*

But Mabel did not take any notice of him. They had talked at her and round her for so many years, that she hardly heard them at all.

The marble clock on the mantelpiece softly chimed the half-hour, the dog rose uneasily from the hearthrug and looked at the party at the breakfast table. But still they sat on in ineffectual conclave.

"Oh, all right," said Joe suddenly, apropos of nothing. "I'll get a move on."

He pushed back his chair, straddled his knees with a downward jerk, to get them free, in horsey fashion, and went to the fire. Still he did not go out of the room; he was curious to know what the others would do or say. He began to charge his pipe, looking down at the dog and saying, in a high, affected voice:

"Going wi' me? Going wi' me are ter? Tha'rt goin' further tha that counts on just now, dost hear?"

The dog faintly wagged its tail, the man stuck out his jaw and covered his pipe with his hands, and puffed intently, losing himself in the tobacco, looking down all the while at the dog with an absent brown eye. The dog looked at him in mournful distrust. Joe stood with his knees stuck out, in real horsey fashion.

"Have you had a letter from Lucy?" Fred Henry asked of his sister.

"Last week," came the neutral reply.

"And what does she say?"

There was no answer.

"Does she *ask* you to go and stop there?" persisted Fred Henry.

"She says I can if I like."

"Well, then, you'd better. Tell her you'll come on Monday."

This was received in silence.

"That's what you'll do then, is it?" said Fred Henry, in some exasperation.

But she made no answer. There was a silence of futility and irritation in the room. Malcolm grinned fatuously.

"You'll have to make up your mind between now and next Wednesday," said Joe loudly, "or else find yourself lodgings on the curbstone."

The face of the young woman darkened, but she sat on immutable.

"Here's Jack Fergusson!" exclaimed Malcolm, who was looking aimlessly out of the window.

"Where?" exclaimed Joe, loudly.

"Just gone past."

"Coming in?"

Malcolm craned his neck to see the gate.

"Yes," he said.

There was a silence. Mabel sat on like one condemned, at the head of the table. Then a whistle was heard from the kitchen. The dog got up and barked sharply. Joe opened the door and shouted:

"Come on."

After a moment a young man entered. He was muffled up in overcoat and a purple woolen scarf, and his tweed cap, which he did not remove, was pulled down on his head. He was of medium height, his face was rather long and pale, his eyes looked tired.

"Hello, Jack! Well, Jack!" exclaimed Malcolm and Joe. Fred Henry merely said, "Jack."

"What's doing?" asked the newcomer, evidently addressing Fred Henry.

"Same. We've got to be out by Wednesday. Got a cold?"

"I have — got it bad, too."

"Why don't you stop in?"

"*Me* stop in? When I can't stand on my legs, perhaps I shall have a chance." The young man spoke huskily. He had a slight Scotch accent.

"It's a knock-out, isn't it," said Joe, boisterously, "if a doctor goes round croaking with a cold. Looks bad for the patients, doesn't it?" The young doctor looked at him slowly.

"Anything the matter with *you*, then?" he asked sarcastically.

"Not as I know of. Damn your eyes, I hope not. Why?"

"I thought you were very concerned about the patients, wondered if you might be one yourself."

"Damn it, no, I've never been patient to no flaming doctor, and hope I never shall be," returned Joe.

At this point Mabel rose from the table, and they all seemed to become aware of her existence. She began putting the dishes together. The young doctor looked at her, but did not address her. He had not greeted her. She went out of the room with the tray, her face impassive and unchanged.

"When are you off then, all of you?" asked the doctor.

"I'm catching the eleven-forty," replied Malcolm. "Are you goin' down wi' th' trap, Joe?"

"Yes, I've told you I'm going down wi' th' trap, haven't I?"

"We'd better be getting her in then. So long, Jack, if I don't see you before I go," said Malcolm, shaking hands.

He went out, followed by Joe, who seemed to have his tail between his legs.

"Well, this is the devil's own," exclaimed the doctor, when he was left alone with Fred Henry. "Going before Wednesday, are you?"

"That's the orders," replied the other.

"Where, to Northampton?"

"That's it."

"The devil!" exclaimed Fergusson, with quiet chagrin.

And there was silence between the two.

"All settled up, are you?" asked Fergusson.

"About."

There was another pause.

"Well, I shall miss yer, Freddy, boy," said the young doctor.

"And I shall miss thee, Jack," returned the other.

"Miss you like hell," mused the doctor.

Fred Henry turned aside. There was nothing to say. Mabel came in again, to finish clearing the table.

"What are *you* going to do, then, Miss Pervin?" asked Fergusson. Going to your sister's, are you?"

Mabel looked at him with her steady, dangerous eyes, that always made him uncomfortabe, unsettling his superficial ease.

"No," she said.

"Well, what in the name of fortune *are* you going to do? Say what you mean to do," cried Fred Henry, with futile intensity.

But she only averted her head, and continued her work. She folded the white table-cloth, and put on the chenille cloth.

"The sulkiest bitch that ever trod!" muttered her brother.

But she finished her task with perfectly impassive face, the young doctor watching her interestedly all the while. Then she went out.

Fred Henry stared after her, clenching his lips, his blue eyes fixing in sharp antagonism, as he made a grimace of sour exasperation.

"You could bray her into bits, and that's all you'd get out of her," he said in a small, narrowed tone.

The doctor smiled faintly.

"What's she *going* to do, then?" he asked.

"Strike me if *I* know!" returned the other.

There was a pause. Then the doctor stirred.

"I'll be seeing you to-night, shall I?" he said to his friend.

"Ay — where's it to be? Are we going over to Jessdale?"

"I don't know. I've got such a cold on me. I'll come round to the Moon and Stars, anyway."

"Let Lizzie and May miss their night for once, eh?"

"That's it — if I feel as I do now."

"All's one — "

The two young men went through the passage and down to the back door together. The house was large, but it was servantless now, and desolate. At the back was a small bricked house-yard, and beyond that a big square, graveled fine and red, and having stables on two sides. Sloping, dank, winter-dark fields stretched away on the open sides.

But the stables were empty. Joseph Pervin, the father of the family, had been a man of no education, who had become a fairly large horse dealer. The stables had been full of horses, there was a great turmoil and come-and-go of horses and of dealers and grooms. Then the kitchen was full of servants. But of late things had declined. The old man had married a second time, to retrieve his fortunes. Now he was dead and everything was gone to the dogs, there was nothing but debt and threatening.

For months, Mabel had been servantless in the big house, keeping the home together in penury for her ineffectual brothers. She had kept house for ten years. But previously it was with unstinted means. Then, however brutal and coarse everything was, the sense of money had kept her proud, confident. The men might be foul-mouthed, the women in the kitchen might have bad reputations, her brothers might have illegitimate children. But so long as there was money, the girl felt herself established, and brutally proud, reserved.

No company came to the house, save dealers and coarse men. Mabel had no associates of her own sex, after her sister went away. But she did not mind. She went regularly to church, she attended to her father. And she lived in the memory of her mother, who had died when she was fourteen, and whom she had loved. She had loved her father, too, in a different way, depending upon him, and feeling secure in him, until at the age of fifty-four he married again. And then she had set hard against him. Now he had died and left them all hopelessly in debt.

She had suffered badly during the period of poverty. Nothing, however, could shake the curious sullen, animal pride that dominated each member of the family. Now, for Mabel, the end had come. Still she would not cast about her. She would follow her own way just the same. She would always hold the keys of her own situation. Mindless and persistent, she endured from day to day. Why should she think? Why should she answer anybody? It was enough that this was the end, and there was no way out. She need not pass any more darkly along the main street of the small town, avoiding every eye. She need not demean herself any more, going into the shops and buying the cheapest food. This was at an end. She thought of nobody, not even of herself. Mindless and persistent, she seemed in a sort of ecstasy to be coming nearer to her fulfillment, her own glorification, approaching her dead mother, who was glorified.

In the afternoon she took a little bag, with shears and sponge and a small scrubbing brush, and went out. It was a gray, wintry day, with saddened, dark green fields and an atmosphere blackened by the smoke of foundries not far off. She went quickly, darkly along the causeway, heeding nobody, through the town to the churchyard.

There she always felt secure, as if no one could see her, although as a matter of fact she was exposed to the stare of every one who passed along under the churchyard wall. Nevertheless, once under the shadow of the great looming church, among the graves, she felt immune from the world, reserved within the thick churchyard wall as in another country.

Carefully she clipped the grass from the grave, and arranged the pinky white, small chrysanthemums in the tin cross. When this was done, she took an empty jar from a neighboring grave, brought water, and carefully, most scrupulously sponged the marble headstone and the coping-stone.

It gave her sincere satisfaction to do this. She felt in immediate contact with the world of her mother. She took minute pains, went through the park in a state bordering on pure happiness, as if in performing this task she came into a subtle, intimate connection with her mother. For the life she followed here in the world was far less real than the world of death she inherited from her mother.

The doctor's house was just by the church. Fergusson, being a mere hired assistant, was slave to the countryside. As he hurried now to attend to the outpatients in the surgery, glancing across the graveyard with his quick eyes, he saw the girl at her task at the grave. She seemed so intent and remote, it was like looking into another world. Some mystical element was touched in him. He slowed down as he walked, watching her as if spellbound.

She lifted her eyes, feeling him looking. Their eyes met. And each looked away again at once, each feeling, in some way, found out by the other. He lifted his cap and passed on down the road. There remained distinct in his consciousness, like a vision, the memory of her face, lifted from the tombstone in the churchyard, and looking at him with slow, large, portentous eyes. It *was* portentous, her face. It seemed to mesmerize him. There was a heavy power in her eyes which laid hold of his whole being, as if he had drunk some powerful drug. He had been feeling weak and done before. Now the life came back into him, he felt delivered from his own fretted, daily self.

He finished his duties at the surgery as quickly as might be, hastily filling up the bottle of the waiting people with cheap drugs. Then, in perpetual haste, he set off again to visit several cases in another part of his round, before teatime. At all times he preferred to walk if he could, but particularly when he was not well. He fancied the motion restored him.

The afternoon was falling. It was gray, deadened, and wintry, with a slow, moist, heavy coldness sinking in and deadening all the faculties. But why should he think or notice? He hastily climbed the hill and turned across the dark green fields, following the black cindertrack. In the distance, across a shallow dip in the country, the small town was clustered like smouldering ash, a tower, a spire, a heap of low, raw, extinct houses. And on the nearest fringe of the town, sloping into the dip, was Oldmeadow, the Pervins' house. He could see the stables and the outbuildings distinctly, as they lay towards him on the slope. Well, he would not go there many more times! Another resource would be lost to him, another place gone: the only company he cared for in the alien, ugly little town he was losing. Nothing but work, drudgery, constant hastening from dwelling to dwelling among the colliers and the iron-workers. It wore him out, but at the same time he had a craving for it. It was a stimulant to him to be in the homes of the working people, moving as it were through the innermost body of their life. His nerves were excited and gratified. He could come so near, into the very lives of the rough, inarticulate, powerfully emotional men and women. He grumbled, he said he hated the hellish hole. But as a matter of fact it excited him, the contact with the rough, strongly-feeling people was a stimulant applied direct to his nerves.

Below Oldmeadow, in the green, shallow, soddened hollow of fields, lay a square, deep pond. Roving across the landscape, the doctor's quick eye detected a figure in black passing through the gate of the field, down towards the pond. He looked again. It would be Mabel Pervin. His mind suddenly became alive and attentive.

Why was she going down there? He pulled up on the path on the slope above, and stood staring. He could just make sure of the small black figure moving in the hollow of the failing day. He seemed to see her in the midst of such obscurity, that he was like a clairvoyant, seeing rather with the mind's eye than with ordinary sight. Yet he could see her positively enough, while he kept his eye attentive. He felt, if he looked away from her, in the thick, ugly falling dusk, he would lose her altogether.

He followed her minutely as she moved, direct and intent, like something transmitted rather than stirring in voluntary activity, straight down the field towards the pond. There she stood on the bank for a moment. She never raised her head. Then she waded slowly into the water.

He stood motionless as the small black figure walked slowly and deliberately towards the center of the pond, very slowly, gradually moving deeper into the motionless water, and still moving forward as the water got up to her breast. Then he could see her no more in the dusk of the dead afternoon.

"There!" he exclaimed. "Would you believe it?"

And he hastened straight down, running over the wet, soddened fields, pushing through the hedges, down into the depression of callous wintry obscurity. It took him several minutes to come to the pond. He stood on the bank, breathing heavily. He could see nothing. His eyes seemed to penetrate the dead water. Yes, perhaps that was the dark shadow of her black clothing beneath the surface of the water.

He slowly ventured into the pond. The bottom was deep, soft clay, he sank in, and the water clasped dead cold round his legs. As he stirred he could smell the cold, rotten clay that fouled up into the water. It was objectionable in his lungs. Still, repelled and yet not heeding, he moved deeper into the pond. The cold water rose over his thighs, over his loins, upon his abdomen. The lower part of his body was all sunk in the hideous cold element. And the bottom was so deeply soft and uncertain he was afraid of pitching with his mouth underneath. He could not swim, and was afraid.

He crouched a little, spreading his hands under the water and moving them round, trying to feel for her. The dead cold pond swayed upon his chest. He moved again, a little deeper, and again, with his hands underneath, he felt all around under the water. And he touched her clothing. But it evaded his fingers. He made a desperate effort to grasp it.

And so doing he lost his balance and went under, horribly, suffocating in the foul earthy water, struggling madly for a few moments. At last, after what seemed an eternity, he got his footing, rose again into the air and looked around. He gasped, and knew he was in the world. Then he looked at the water. She had risen near him. He grasped her clothing, and drawing her nearer, turned to take his way to land again.

He went very slowly, carefully, absorbed in the slow progress. He rose higher, climbing out of the pond. The water was now only about his legs; he was thankful, full of relief to be out of the clutches of the pond. He lifted her and staggered on to the bank, out of the horror of wet, gray clay.

He laid her down on the bank. She was quite unconscious and running with water. He made the water come from her mouth, he worked to restore her. He did not have to work very long before he could feel the breathing begin again in her; she was breathing naturally. He worked a little longer. He could feel her live beneath his hands; she was coming back. He wiped her face, wrapped her in his overcoat, looked round into the dim, dark gray world, then lifted her and staggered down the bank and across the fields.

It seemed an unthinkably long way, and his burden so heavy he felt he would never get to the house. But at last he was in the stableyard, and then in the house-yard. He opened the door and went into the house. In the kitchen he laid her down on the hearthrug, and called. The house was empty. But the fire was burning in the grate.

Then again he kneeled to attend to her. She was breathing regularly, her eyes were wide open and as if conscious, but there seemed something missing in her look. She was conscious in herself, but unconscious of her surroundings.

He ran upstairs, took blankets from a bed, and put them before the fire to warm. Then he removed her saturated, earthy-smelling clothing, rubbed her dry with a towel, and wrapped her naked in the blankets. Then he went into the dining-room, to look for spirits. There was a little whisky. He drank a gulp himself, and put some into her mouth.

The effect was instantaneous. She looked full into his face, as if she had been seeing him for some time, and yet had only just become conscious of him.

"Dr. Fergusson?" she said.

"What?" he answered.

He was divesting himself of his coat, intending to find some dry clothing upstairs. He could not bear the smell of the dead, clayey water, and he was mortally afraid of his own health.

"What did I do?" she asked.

"Walked into the pond," he replied. He had begun to shudder like one sick, and could hardly attend to her. Her eyes remained full on him, he seemed to be going dark in his mind, looking back at her helplessly. The shuddering became quieter in him, his life came back in him, dark and unknowing, but strong again.

"Was I out of my mind?" she asked, while her eyes were fixed on him all the time.

"Maybe, for the moment," he replied. He felt quiet, because his strength came back. The strange fretful strain had left him.

"Am I out of my mind now?" she asked.

"Are you?" he reflected a moment. "No," he answered truthfully, "I don't see that you are." He turned his face aside. He was afraid now, because he felt dazed, and felt dimly that her power was stronger than his, in this issue. And she continued to look at him fixedly all the time. "Can you tell me where I shall find some dry things to put on?" he asked.

"Did you dive into the pond for me?" she asked.

"No," he answered. "I walked in. But I went in overhead as well."

There was silence for a moment. He hesitated. He very much wanted to go upstairs to get into dry clothing. But there was another desire in him. And she seemed to hold him. His will seemed to have gone to sleep, and left him, standing there slack before her. But he felt warm inside himself. He did not shudder at all, though his clothes were sodden on him.

"Why did you?" she asked.

"Because I didn't want you to do such a foolish thing," he said.

"It wasn't foolish," she said, still gazing at him as she lay on the floor, with a sofa cushion under her head. "It was the right thing to do. *I* knew best, then."

"I'll go and shift these wet things," he said. But still he had not the power to move out of her presence, until she sent him. It was as if she had the life of his body in her hands, and he could not extricate himself. Or perhaps he did not want to.

Suddenly she sat up. Then she became aware of her own immediate condition. She felt the blankets about her, she knew her own limbs. For a moment it seemed as if her reason were going. She looked round, with wild eye, as if seeking something. He stood still with fear. She saw her clothing lying scattered.

"Who undressed me?" she asked, her eyes resting full and inevitable on his face.

"I did," he replied, "to bring you round."

For some moments she sat and gazed at him awfully, her lips parted.

"Do you love me, then?" she asked.

He only stood and stared at her, fascinated. His soul seemed to melt.

She shuffled forward on her knees, and put her arms round him, round his legs, as he stood there, pressing her breasts against his knees and thighs, clutching him with strange, convulsive certainty, pressing his thighs against her, drawing him to her face, her throat, as she looked up at him with flaring, humble eyes of transfiguration, triumphant in first possession.

"You love me," she murmured, in strange transport, yearning and triumphant and confident. "You love me. I know you love me, I know."

And she was passionately kissing his knees, through the wet clothing, passionately and indiscriminately kissing his knees, his legs, as if unaware of everything.

He looked down at the tangled wet hair, the wild, bare, animal shoulders. He was amazed, bewildered, and afraid. He had never thought of loving her. He had never wanted to love her. When he rescued her and restored her, he was a doctor, and she was a patient. He had had no single personal thought of her. Nay, this introduction of the personal element was very distasteful to him, a violation of his professional honor. It was horrible to have her there embracing his knees. It was horrible. He revolted from it, violently. And yet — and yet — he had not the power to break away.

She looked at him again, with the same supplication of powerful love, and that same transcendent, frightening light of triumph. In view of the delicate flame which seemed to come from her face like a light, he was powerless. And yet he had never intended to love her. He had never intended. And something stubborn in him could not give way.

"You love me," she repeated, in a murmur of deep, rhapsodic assurance. "You love me."

Her hands were drawing him, drawing him down to her. He was afraid, even a little horrified. For he had, really, no intention of loving her. Yet her hands were drawing him towards her. He put out his hand quickly to steady himself, and grasped her bare shoulder. A flame seemed to burn the hand that grasped her soft shoulder. He had no intention of loving her: his whole will was against his yielding. It was horrible. And yet wonderful was the touch of her shoulders, beautiful the shining of her face. Was she perhaps mad? He had a horror of yielding to her. Yet something in him ached also.

He had been staring away at the door, away from her. But his hand remained on her shoulder. She had gone suddenly very still. He looked down at her. Her eyes were now wide with fear, with doubt, the light was dying from her face, a shadow of terrible grayness was returning. He could not bear the touch of her eyes' question upon him, and the look of death behind the question.

With an inward groan he gave way, and let his heart yield towards her. A sudden gentle smile came on his face. And her eyes, which never left his face, slowly, slowly filled with tears. He watched the strange water rise in her eyes, like some slow fountain coming up. And his heart seemed to burn and melt away in his breast.

He could not bear to look at her any more. He dropped on his knees and caught her head with his arms and pressed her face against his throat. She was very still. His heart, which seemed to have broken, was burning with a kind of agony in his breast. And he felt her slow, hot tears wetting his throat. But he could not move.

He felt the hot tears wet his neck and the hollows of his neck, and he remained motionless, suspended through one of man's eternities. Only now it had become indispensable to him to have her face pressed close to him; he could never let her go again. He could never let her head go away from the close clutch of his arm. He wanted to remain like that for ever, with his heart hurting him in a pain that was also life to him. Without knowing, he was looking down on her damp, soft brown hair.

Then, as it were suddenly, he smelt the horrid stagnant smell of that water. And at the same moment she drew away from him and looked at him. Her eyes were wistful and unfathomable. He was afraid of them, and he fell to kissing her, not knowing what he was doing. He wanted her eyes not to have that terrible, wistful, unfathomable look.

When she turned her face to him again, a faint delicate flush was glowing, and there was again dawning that terrible shining of joy in her eyes, which really terrified him, and yet which he now wanted to see, because he feared the look of doubt still more.

"You love me?" she said, rather faltering.

"Yes." The word cost him a painful effort. Not because it wasn't true. But because it was too newly true, the *saying* seemed to tear open again his newly torn heart. And he hardly wanted it to be true, even now.

She lifted her face to him, and he bent forward and kissed her on the mouth, gently, with the one kiss that is an eternal pledge. And as he kissed her his heart strained again in his breast. He never intended to love her. But now it was over. He had crossed over the gulf to her, and all that he had left behind had shriveled and become void.

After the kiss, her eyes again slowly filled with tears. She sat still, away from him, with her face drooped aside, and her hands folded in her lap. The tears fell very slowly. There was complete silence. He too sat there motionless and silent on the hearthrug. The strange pain of his heart that was broken seemed to consume him. That he should love her? That this was love! That he should be ripped open in this way! Him, a doctor! How they would all jeer if they knew! It was agony to him to think they might know.

In the curious naked pain of the thought he looked again to her. She was sitting there drooped into a muse. He saw a tear fall, and his heart flared hot. He saw for the first time that one of her shoulders was quite uncovered, one arm bare, he could see one of her small breasts; dimly, because it had become almost dark in the room.

"Why are you crying?" he asked, in an altered voice.

She looked up at him, and behind her tears the consciousness of her situation for the first time brought a dark look of shame to her eyes.

"I'm not crying, really," she said, watching him half frightened.

He reached his hand, and softly closed it on her bare arm.

"I love you! I love you!" he said in a soft, low vibrating voice, unlike himself.

She shrank, and dropped her head. The soft, penetrating grip of his hand on her arm distressed her. She looked up at him.

"I want to go," she said. "I want to go and get you some dry things."

"Why?" he said. "I'm all right."

"But I want to go," she said. "And I want you to change your things."

He released her arm, and she wrapped herself in the blanket, looking at him rather frightened. And still she did not rise.

"Kiss me," she said wistfully.

He kissed her, but briefly, half in anger.

Then, after a second, she rose nervously, all mixed up in the blanket. He watched her in her confusion, as she tried to extricate herself and wrap herself up so that she could walk. He watched her relentlessly, as she knew. And as she went, the blanket trailing, and as he saw a glimpse of her feet and her white leg, he tried to remember her as she was when he had wrapped her in the blanket. But then he didn't want to remember, because she had been nothing to him then, and his nature revolted from remembering her as she was when she was nothing to him.

A tumbling, muffled noise from within the dark house startled him. Then he heard her voice: — "There are clothes." He rose and went to the foot of the stairs, and gathered up the garments she had thrown down. Then he came back to the fire, to rub himself down and dress. He grinned at his own appearance when he had finished.

The fire was sinking, so he put on coal. The house was now quite dark, save for the light of a street-lamp that shone in faintly from beyond the holly trees. He lit the gas with matches he found on the mantelpiece. Then he emptied the pockets of his own clothes, and threw all his wet things in a heap into the scullery. After which he gathered up her sodden clothes, gently, and put them in a separate heap on the copper-top in the scullery.

It was six o'clock on the clock. His own watch had stopped. He ought to go back to the surgery. He waited, and still she did not come down. So he went to the foot of the stairs and called:

"I shall have to go."

Almost immediately he heard her coming down. She had on her best dress of black voile, and her hair was tidy, but still damp. She looked at him — and in spite of herself, smiled.

"I don't like you in those clothes," she said.

"Do I look a sight?" he answered.

They were shy of one another.

"I'll make you some tea," she said.

"No, I must go."

"Must you?" And she looked at him again with the wide, strained, doubtful eyes. And again, from the pain of his breast, he knew how he loved her. He went and bent to kiss her, gently, passionately, with his heart's painful kiss.

"And my hair smells so horrible," she murmured in distraction. "And I'm so awful, I'm so awful! Oh, no, I'm too awful." And she broke into bitter, heart-broken sobbing. "You can't want to love me, I'm horrible."

"Don't be silly, don't be silly," he said, trying to comfort her, kissing her, holding her in his arms. "I want you, I want to marry you, we're going to be married, quickly, quickly — tomorrow if I can."

But she only sobbed terribly, and cried:

"I feel awful. I feel awful. I feel I'm horrible to you."

"No, I want you, I want you," was all he answered, blindly, with that terrible intonation which frightened her almost more than her horror lest he should *not* want her.

Katherine Anne Porter (b. 1890)

The Jilting of Granny Weatherall

She flicked her wrist neatly out of Doctor Harry's pudgy careful fingers and pulled the sheet up to her chin. The brat ought to be in knee breeches. Doctoring around the country with spectacles on his nose! "Get along now, take your schoolbooks and go. There's nothing wrong with me."

Doctor Harry spread a warm paw like a cushion on her forehead where the forked green vein danced and made her eyelids twitch. "Now, now, be a good girl, and we'll have you up in no time."

"That's no way to speak to a woman nearly eighty years old just because she's down. I'd have you respect your elders, young man."

"Well, Missy, excuse me." Doctor Harry patted her cheek. "But I've got to warn you, haven't I? You're a marvel, but you must be careful or you're going to be good and sorry."

"Don't tell me what I'm going to be. I'm on my feet now, morally speaking. It's Cornelia. I had to go to bed to get rid of her."

Her bones felt loose, and floated around in her skin, and Doctor Harry floated like a balloon around the foot of the bed. He floated and pulled down his waistcoat and swung his glasses on a cord. "Well, stay where you are, it certainly can't hurt you."

"Get along and doctor your sick," said Granny Weatherall. "Leave a well woman alone. I'll call for you when I want you.... Where were you forty years ago when I pulled through milk-leg and double pneumonia? You weren't even born. Don't let Cornelia lead you on," she shouted, because Doctor Harry appeared to float up to the ceiling and out. "I pay my own bills, and I don't throw my money away on nonsense!"

She meant to wave good-by, but it was too much trouble. Her eyes closed of themselves, it was like a dark curtain drawn around the bed. The pillow rose and floated under her, pleasant as a hammock in a light wind. She listened to the leaves rustling outside the window. No, somebody was swishing newspapers: no, Cornelia and Doctor Harry were whispering together. She leaped broad awake, thinking they whispered in her ear.

"She was never like this, *never* like this!" "Well, what can we expect?" "Yes, eighty years old...."

Well, and what if she was? She still had ears. It was like Cornelia to whisper around doors. She always kept things secret in such a public way. She was always being tactful and kind. Cornelia was dutiful; that was the trouble with her. Dutiful and good: "So good

and dutiful," said Granny, "and I'd like to spank her." She saw herself spanking Cornelia and making a fine job of it.

"What'd you say, Mother?"

Granny felt her face tying up in hard knots.

"Can't a body think, I'd like to know?"

"I thought you might want something."

"I do. I want a lot of things. First off, go away and don't whisper."

She lay and drowsed, hoping in her sleep that the children would
keep out and let her rest a minute. It had been a long day. Not that
she was tired. It was always pleasant to snatch a minute now and
then. There was always so much to be done, let me see: tomorrow.

Tomorrow was far away and there was nothing to trouble about.
Things were finished somehow when the time came; thank God
there was always a little margin over for peace: then a person could
spread out the plan of life and tuck in the edges orderly. It was good
to have everything clean and folded away, with the hair brushes and
tonic bottles sitting straight on the white embroidered linen: the day
started without fuss and the pantry shelves laid out with rows of jelly
glasses and brown jugs and white stone-china jars with blue whirl-
igigs and words painted on them: coffee, tea, sugar, ginger, cinna-
mon, allspice: and the bronze clock with the lion on top nicely dusted
off. The dust that lion could collect in twenty-four hours! The box in
the attic with all those letters tied up, well, she'd have to go through
that tomorrow. All those letters — George's letters and John's letters
and her letters to them both — lying around for the children to find
afterwards made her uneasy. Yes, that would be tomorrow's business.
No use to let them know how silly she had been once.

While she was rummaging around she found death in her mind
and it felt clammy and unfamiliar. She had spent so much time preparing for death there was no need for bringing it up again. Let it take
care of itself now. When she was sixty she had felt very old, finished,
and went around making farewell trips to see her children and grandchildren, with a secret in her mind: This is the very last of your
mother, children! Then she made her will and came down with a
long fever. That was all just a notion like a lot of other things, but it
was lucky too, for she had once for all got over the idea of dying for a
long time. Now she couldn't be worried. She hoped she had better
sense now. Her father had lived to be one hundred and two years old
and had drunk a noggin of strong hot toddy on his last birthday. He
told the reporters it was his daily habit, and he owed his long life to
that. He had made quite a scandal and was very pleased about it. She
believed she'd just plague Cornelia a little.

"Cornelia! Cornelia!" No footsteps, but a sudden hand on her
cheek. "Bless you, where have you been?"

"Here, Mother."

"Well, Cornelia, I want a noggin of hot toddy."

"Are you cold, darling?"

"I'm chilly, Cornelia. Lying in bed stops the circulation. I must have told you that a thousand times."

Well, she could just hear Cornelia telling her husband that Mother was getting a little childish and they'd have to humor her. The thing that most annoyed her was that Cornelia thought she was deaf, dumb, and blind. Little hasty glances and tiny gestures tossed around her and over her head saying, "Don't cross her, let her have her way, she's eighty years old," and she sitting there as if she lived in a thin glass cage. Sometimes Granny almost made up her mind to pack up and move back to her own house where nobody could remind her every minute that she was old. Wait, wait, Cornelia, till your own children whisper behind your back!

In her day she had kept a better house and had got more work done. She wasn't too old yet for Lydia to be driving eighty miles for advice when one of the children jumped the track, and Jimmy still dropped in and talked things over: "Now, Mammy, you've a good business head, I want to know what you think of this? . . ." Old. Cornelia couldn't change the furniture around without asking. Little things, little things! They had been so sweet when they were little. Granny wished the old days were back again with the children young and everything to be done over. It had been a hard pull, but not too much for her. When she thought of all the food she had cooked, and all the clothes she had cut and sewed, and all the gardens she had made — well, the children showed it. There they were, made out of her, and they couldn't get away from that. Sometimes she wanted to see John again and point to them and say, Well, I didn't do so badly, did I? But that would have to wait. That was for tomorrow. She used to think of him as a man, but now all the children were older than their father, and he would be a child beside her if she saw him now. It seemed strange and there was something wrong in the idea. Why, he couldn't possibly recognize her. She had fenced in a hundred acres once, digging the post holes herself and clamping the wires with just a negro boy to help. That changed a woman. John would be looking for a young woman with the peaked Spanish comb in her hair and the painted fan. Digging post holes changed a woman. Riding country roads in the winter when women had their babies was another thing: sitting up nights with sick horses and sick negroes and sick children and hardly ever losing one. John, I hardly ever lost one of them! John would see that in a minute, that would be something he could understand, she wouldn't have to explain anything!

It made her feel like rolling up her sleeves and putting the whole place to rights again. No matter if Cornelia was determined to be everywhere at once, there were a great many things left undone on this place. She would start tomorrow and do them. It was good to be strong enough for everything, even if all you made melted and changed and slipped under your hands, so that by the time you finished you almost forgot what you were working for. What was it I set out to do? she asked herself intently, but she could not remember. A fog rose over the valley, she saw it marching across the creek swallowing the trees and moving up the hill like an army of ghosts. Soon it would be at the near edge of the orchard, and then it was time to go in and light the lamps. Come in, children, don't stay out in the night air.

Lighting the lamps had been beautiful. The children huddled up to her and breathed like little calves waiting at the bars in the twilight. Their eyes followed the match and watched the flame rise and settle in a blue curve, then they moved away from her. The lamp was lit, they didn't have to be scared and hang on to mother any more. Never, never, never more. God, for all my life I thank Thee. Without Thee, my God, I could never have done it. Hail, Mary, full of grace.

I want you to pick all the fruit this year and see that nothing is wasted. There's always someone who can use it. Don't let good things rot for want of using. You waste life when you waste good food. Don't let things get lost. It's bitter to lose things. Now, don't let me get to thinking, not when I am tired and taking a little nap before supper. . . .

The pillow rose about her shoulders and pressed against her heart and the memory was being squeezed out of it: oh, push down the pillow, somebody: it would smother her if she tried to hold it. Such a fresh breeze blowing and such a green day with no threats in it. But he had not come, just the same. What does a woman do when she has put on the white veil and set out the white cake for a man and he doesn't come? She tried to remember. No, I swear he never harmed me but in that. He never harmed me but in that . . . and what if he did? There was the day, the day, but a whirl of dark smoke rose and covered it, crept up and over into the bright field where everything was planted so carefully in orderly rows. That was hell, she knew hell when she saw it. For sixty years she had prayed against remembering him and against losing her soul in the deep pit of hell, and now the two things were mingled in one and the thought of him was a smoky cloud from hell that moved and crept in her head when she had just got rid of Doctor Harry and was trying to rest a minute. Wounded vanity, Ellen, said a sharp voice in the top of her mind. Don't let your wounded vanity get the upper hand of you. Plenty of girls get jilted. You were jilted, weren't you? Then stand up to it. Her eyelids wavered and let in streamers of blue-gray light like tissue paper over her eyes. She must get up and pull the shades down or she'd never sleep. She was in bed again and the shades were not down. How could that happen? Better turn over, hide from the light, sleeping in the light gave you nightmares. "Mother, how do you feel now?" and a stinging wetness on her forehead. But I don't like having my face washed in cold water!

Hapsy? George? Lydia? Jimmy? No, Cornelia, and her features were swollen and full of little puddles. "They're coming, darling, they'll all be here soon." Go wash your face, child, you look funny.

Instead of obeying, Cornelia knelt down and put her head on the pillow. She seemed to be talking but there was no sound. "Well, are you tongue-tied? Whose birthday is it? Are you going to give a party?"

Cornelia's mouth moved urgently in strange shapes. "Don't do that, you bother me, daughter."

"Oh, no, Mother. Oh, no...."

Nonsense. It was strange about children. They disputed your every word. "No what, Cornelia?"

"Here's Doctor Harry."

"I won't see that boy again. He just left five minutes ago."

"That was this morning, Mother. It's night now. Here's the nurse."

"This is Doctor Harry, Mrs. Weatherall. I never saw you look so young and happy!"

"Ah, I'll never be young again — but I'd be happy if they'd let me lie in peace and get rested."

She thought she spoke up loudly, but no one answered. A warm weight on her forehead, a warm bracelet on her wrist, and a breeze went on whispering, trying to tell her something. A shuffle of leaves in the everlasting hand of God. He blew on them and they danced and rattled. "Mother, don't mind, we're going to give you a little hypodermic." "Look here, daughter, how do ants get in this bed? I saw sugar ants yesterday." Did you send for Hapsy too?

It was Hapsy she really wanted. She had to go a long way back through a great many rooms to find Hapsy standing with a baby on her arm. She seemed to herself to be Hapsy also, and the baby on Hapsy's arm was Hapsy and himself and herself, all at once, and there was no surprise in the meeting. Then Hapsy melted from within and turned flimsy as gray gauze and the baby was a gauzy shadow, and Hapsy came up close and said, "I thought you'd never come," and looked at her very searchingly and said, "You haven't changed a bit!" They leaned forward to kiss, when Cornelia began whispering from a long way off, "Oh, is there anything you want to tell me? Is there anything I can do for you?"

Yes, she had changed her mind after sixty years and she would like to see George. I want you to find George. Find him and be sure to tell him I forgot him. I want him to know I had my husband just the same and my children and my house like any other woman. A good house too and a good husband that I loved and fine children out of him. Better than I hoped for even. Tell him I was given back everything he took away and more. Oh, no, oh, God, no, there was something else besides the house and the man and the children. Oh, surely they were not all? What was it? Something not given back. . . . Her breath crowded down under her ribs and grew into a monstrous frightening shape with cutting edges; it bored up into her head, and the agony was unbelievable: Yes, John, get the doctor now, no more talk, my time has come.

When this one was born it should be the last. The last. It should have been born first, for it was the one she had truly wanted. Everything came in good time. Nothing left out, left over. She was strong, in three days she would be as well as ever. Better. A woman needed milk in her to have her full health.

"Mother, do you hear me?"

"I've been telling you — "

"Mother, Father Connolly's here."

"I went to Holy Communion only last week. Tell him I'm not so sinful as all that."

"Father just wants to speak to you."

He could speak as much as he pleased. It was like him to drop in and inquire about her soul as if it were a teething baby, and then stay on for a cup of tea and a round of cards and gossip. He always had a funny story of some sort, usually about an Irishman who made his little mistakes and confessed them, and the point lay in some absurd thing he would blurt out in the confessional showing his struggles between native piety and original sin. Granny felt easy about her soul. Cornelia, where are your manners? Give Father Connolly a chair. She had her secret comfortable understanding with a few favorite saints who cleared a straight road to God for her. All as surely signed and sealed as the papers for the new Forty Acres. Forever . . . heirs and assigns forever. Since the day the wedding cake was not cut, but thrown out and wasted. The whole bottom dropped out of the world, and there she was blind and sweating with nothing under her feet and the walls falling away. His hand had caught her under the breast, she had not fallen, there was the freshly polished floor with the green rug on it, just as before. He had cursed like a sailor's parrot and said, "I'll kill him for you." Don't lay a hand on him, for my sake leave something to God. "Now, Ellen, you must believe what I tell you. . . . "

So there was nothing, nothing to worry about any more, except sometimes in the night one of the children screamed in a nightmare, and they both hustled out shaking and hunting for the matches and calling, "There, wait a minute, here we are!" John, get the doctor now, Hapsy's time has come. But there was Hapsy standing by the bed in a white cap. "Cornelia, tell Hapsy to take off her cap. I can't see her plain."

Her eyes opened very wide and the room stood out like a picture she had seen somewhere. Dark colors with the shadows rising towards the ceiling in long angles. The tall black dresser gleamed with nothing on it but John's picture, enlarged from a little one, with John's eyes very black when they should have been blue. You never saw him, so how do you know how he looked? But the man insisted the copy was perfect, it was very rich and handsome. For a picture, yes, but it's not my husband. The table by the bed had a linen cover and a candle and a crucifix. The light was blue from Cornelia's silk lampshades. No sort of light at all, just frippery. You had to live forty years with kerosene lamps to appreciate honest electricity. She felt very strong and she saw Doctor Harry with a rosy nimbus around him.

"You look like a saint, Doctor Harry, and I vow that's as near as you'll ever come to it."

"She's saying something."

"I heard you, Cornelia. What's all this carrying on?"

"Father Connolly's saying — "

Cornelia's voice staggered and bumped like a cart in a bad road. it rounded corners and turned back again and arrived nowhere. Granny stepped up in the cart very lightly and reached for the reins, but a man sat beside her and she knew him by his hands, driving the cart. She did not look in his face, for she knew without seeing, but looked instead down the road where the trees leaned over and bowed to each other and a thousand birds were singing a Mass. She felt like singing too, but she put her hand in the bosom of her dress and pulled out a rosary, and Father Connolly murmured Latin in a very solemn voice and tickled her feet. My God, will you stop that nonsense? I'm a married woman. What if he did run away and leave me to face the priest by myself? I found another a whole world better. I wouldn't have exchanged my husband for anybody except St. Michael himself, and you may tell him that for me with a thank you in the bargain.

Light flashed on her closed eyelids, and a deep roaring shook her. Cornelia, is that lightning? I hear thunder. There's going to be a storm. Close all the windows. Call the children in. . . . "Mother, here we are, all of us." "Is that you, Hapsy?" "Oh, no, I'm Lydia. We drove as fast as we could." Their faces drifted above her, drifted away. The rosary fell out of her hands and Lydia put it back. Jimmy tried to help, their hands fumbled together, and Granny closed two fingers around Jimmy's thumb. Beads wouldn't do, it must be something alive. She was so amazed her thoughts ran round and round. So, my dear Lord, this is my death and I wasn't even thinking about it. My children have come to see me die. But I can't, it's not time. Oh, I always hated surprises. I wanted to give Cornelia the amethyst set — Cornelia, you're to have the amethyst set, but Hapsy's to wear it when she wants, and, Doctor Harry, do shut up. Nobody sent for you. Oh, my dear Lord, do wait a minute. I meant to do something about the Forty Acres, Jimmy doesn't need it and Lydia will later on, with that worthless husband of hers. I meant to finish the altar cloth and send six bottles of wine to Sister Borgia for her dyspepsia. I want to send six bottles of wine to Sister Borgia, Father Connolly, now don't let me forget.

Cornelia's voice made short turns and tilted over and crashed. "Oh, Mother, oh, Mother, oh, Mother...."

"I'm not going, Cornelia. I'm taken by surprise. I can't go."

You'll see Hapsy again. What about her? "I thought you'd never come." Granny made a long journey outward, looking for Hapsy. What if I don't find her? What then? Her heart sank down and down, there was no bottom to death, she couldn't come to the end of it. The blue light from Cornelia's lampshade drew into a tiny point in the center of her brain, it flickered and winked like an eye, quietly it fluttered and dwindled. Granny lay curled down within herself, amazed and watchful, staring at the point of light that was herself; her body was now only a deeper mass of shadow in an endless darkness and this darkness would curl around the light and swallow it up. God, give a sign!

For the second time there was no sign. Again no bridegroom and the priest in the house. She could not remember any other sorrow because this grief wiped them all away. Oh, no, there's nothing more cruel than this — I'll never forgive it. She stretched herself with a deep breath and blew out the light.

James Thurber (1894–1961)

The Secret Life of Walter Mitty

"We're going through!" The Commander's voice was like thin ice breaking. He wore his full-dress uniform, with the heavily braided white cap pulled down rakishly over one cold gray eye. "We can't make it, sir. It's spoiling for a hurricane, if you ask me." "I'm not asking you, Lieutenant Berg," said the Commander. "Throw on the power lights! Rev her up to 8500! We're going through!" The pounding of the cylinders increased; ta-pocketa-pocketa-pocketa-*pocketa-pocketa*. The Commander stared at the ice forming on the pilot window. He walked over and twisted a row of complicated dials. "Switch on No. 8 auxiliary!" he shouted. "Switch on No. 8 auxiliary!" repeated Lieutenant Berg. "Full strength in No. 3 turret!" shouted the Commander, "Full strength in No. 3 turret!" The crew, bending to their various tasks in the huge, hurtling eight-engined Navy hydroplane, looked at each other and grinned. "The Old Man'll get us through," they said to one another. "The Old Man ain't afraid of Hell!" . . .

"Not so fast! You're driving too fast!" said Mrs. Mitty. "What are you driving so fast for?"

"Hmm?" said Walter Mitty. He looked at his wife, in the seat beside him, with shocked astonishment. She seemed grossly unfamiliar, like a strange woman who had yelled at him in a crowd. "You were up to fifty-five," she said, "You know I don't like to go more than forty. You were up to fifty-five." Walter Mitty drove on toward Waterbury in silence, the roaring of the SN202 through the worst storm in twenty years of Navy flying fading in the remote, intimate airways of his mind. "You're tensed up again," said Mrs. Mitty. "It's one of your days. I wish you'd let Dr. Renshaw look you over."

Walter Mitty stopped the car in front of the building where his wife went to have her hair done. "Remember to get those overshoes while I'm having my hair done," she said, "I don't need overshoes," said Mitty. She put her mirror back into her bag. "We've been all through that," she said, getting out of the car. "You're not a young man any longer." He raced the engine a little. "Why don't you wear your gloves? Have you lost your gloves?" Walter Mitty reached in a pocket and brought out the gloves. He put them on, but after she had turned and gone into the building and he had driven on to a red light, he took them off again. "Pick it up, brother," snapped a cop as the light changed, and Mitty hastily pulled on his gloves and lurched ahead. He drove around the streets aimlessly for a time, and then he drove past the hospital on his way to the parking lot.

. . . "It's the millionaire banker, Wellington McMillan," said the pretty nurse. "Yes?" said Walter Mitty, removing his gloves slowly. "Who has the case?" "Dr. Renshaw and Dr. Benbow, but there are two specialists here, Dr. Remington from New York and Dr. Pritchard-Mitford from London. He flew over." A door opened down a

long, cool corridor and Dr. Renshaw came out. He looked distraught
and haggard. "Hello, Mitty," he said. "We're having the devil's own
time with McMillan, the millionaire banker and close personal friend
of Roosevelt. Obstreosis of the ductal tract. Tertiary. Wish you'd take
a look at him." "Glad to," said Mitty.

In the operating room there were whispered introductions: "Dr.
Remington, Dr. Mitty. Dr. Pritchard-Mitford, Dr. Mitty." "I've read
your book on streptothricosis," said Pritchard-Mitford, shaking
hands. "A brilliant performance, sir." "Thank you," said Walter
Mitty. "Didn't know you were in the States, Mitty," grumbled Remington. "Coals to Newcastle, bringing Mitford and me up here for a
tertiary." "You are very kind," said Mitty. A huge, complicated machine, connected to the operating table, with many tubes and wires,
began at this moment to go pocketa-pocketa-pocketa. "The new an-
aesthetizer is giving away!" shouted an intern. "There is no one in
the East who knows how to fix it!" "Quiet, man!" said Mitty, in a low,
cool voice. He sprang to the machine, which was now going pocketa-
pocketa-queep-pocketa-queep. He began fingering delicately a row
of glistening dials. "Give me a fountain pen!" he snapped. Someone
handed him a fountain pen. He pulled a faulty piston out of the
machine and inserted the pen in its place. "That will hold for ten
minutes," he said. "Get on with the operation." A nurse hurried over
and whispered to Renshaw, and Mitty saw the man turn pale. "Co-
reopsis has set in," said Renshaw nervously. "If you would take over,
Mitty?" Mitty looked at him and at the craven figure of Benbow, who
drank, and at the grave, uncertain faces of the two great specialists.
"If you wish," he said. They slipped a white gown on him; he
adjusted a mask and drew on thin gloves; nurses handed him
shining . . .

"Back it up, Mac! Look out for that Buick!" Walter Mitty jammed
on the brakes. "Wrong lane, Mac," said the parking-lot attendant,
looking at Mitty closely. "Gee. Yeh," muttered Mitty. He began cautiously to back out of the lane marked Exit Only. Leave her sit
there," said the attendant. "I'll put her away." Mitty got out of the
car. "Hey, better leave the key." "Oh," said Mitty, handing the man
the ignition key. The attendant vaulted into the car, backed it up with
insolent skill, and put it where it belonged.

They're so damn cocky, thought Walter Mitty, walking along Main
Street; they think they know everything. Once he had tried to take
his chains off, outside New Milford, and he had got them wound
around the axles. A man had had to come out in a wrecking car and
unwind them, a young, grinning garage man. Since then Mrs. Mitty
always made him drive to a garage to have the chains taken off. The
next time, he thought, I'll wear my right arm in a sling; they won't

grin at me then. I'll have my right arm in a sling and they'll see I couldn't possibly take the chains off myself. He kicked at the slush on the sidewalk. "Overshoes," he said to himself, and he began looking for a shoe store.

When he came out into the street again, with the overshoes in a box under his arm, Walter Mitty began to wonder what the other thing was his wife had told him to get. She had told him, twice before they set out from their house for Waterbury. In a way he hated these weekly trips to town — he was always getting something wrong. Kleenex, he thought, Squibb's, razor blades? No. Toothpaste, toothbrush, bicarbonate, carborundum, initiative and referendum? He gave it up. But she would remember it. "Where's the what's-its-name? She would ask. "Don't tell me you forgot the what's-its-name." A newsboy went by shouting something about the Waterbury trial.

. . . "Perhaps this will refresh your memory." The District Attorney suddenly thrust a heavy automatic at the quiet figure on the witness stand. "Have you ever seen this before?" Walter Mitty took the gun and examined it expertly. "This is my Webley-Vickers 50.80," he said calmly. An excited buzz ran around the courtroom. The judge rapped for order. "You are a crack shot with any sort of firearms, I believe?" said the District Attorney, insinuatingly. "Objection!" shouted Mitty's attorney. "We have shown that the defendant could not have fired the shot. We have shown that he wore his right arm in a sling on the night of the fourteenth of July." Walter Mitty raised his hand briefly and the bickering attorneys were stilled. "With any known make of gun," he said evenly, "I could have killed Gregory Fitzhurst at three hundred feet *with my left hand.*" Pandemonium broke loose in the courtroom. A woman's scream rose above the bedlam and suddenly a lovely, dark-haired girl was in Walter Mitty's arms. The District Attorney struck at her savagely. Without rising from his chair, Mitty let the man have it on the point of the chin. "You miserable cur!" . . .

"Puppy biscuit," said Walter Mitty. He stopped walking and the buildings of Waterbury rose up out of the misty courtroom and surrounded him again. A woman who was passing laughed. "He said 'Puppy biscuit,' " she said to her companion. "That man said 'Puppy biscuit' to himself." Walter Mitty hurried on. He went into an A. & P., not the first one he came to but a smaller one farther up the street. "I want some biscuit for small, young dogs," he said to the clerk. "Any special brand, sir?" The greatest pistol shot in the world thought a moment. "It says 'Puppies Bark for It' on the box," said Walter Mitty.

His wife would be through at the hairdresser's in fifteen minutes, Mitty saw in looking at his watch, unless they had trouble drying it; sometimes they had trouble drying it. She didn't like to get to the hotel first; she would want him to be there waiting for her as usual. He found a big leather chair in the lobby, facing a window, and he put the overshoes and the puppy biscuit on the floor beside it. He picked up an old copy of *Liberty* and sank down into the chair. "Can Germany Conquer the World through the Air?" Walter Mitty looked at the pictures of bombing planes and of ruined streets.

. . . "The cannonading has got the wind up in young Raleigh, sir," said the sergeant. Captain Mitty looked up at him through tousled hair. "Get him to bed," he said wearily, "with the others. I'll fly alone." "But you can't, sir," said the sergeant anxiously. "It takes two men to handle that bomber and the Archies are pounding hell out of the air. Von Richtman's circus is between here and Saulier." "Somebody's got to get that ammunition dump," said Mitty. "I'm going over. Spot of brandy?" He poured a drink for the sergeant and one for himself. War thundered and whined around the dugout and battered at the door. There was a rending of wood and splinters flew through the room. "A bit of a near thing," said Captain Mitty carelessly. "The box barrage is closing in," said the sergeant. "We only live once, sergeant," said Mitty, with his faint, fleeting smile. "Or do we?" He poured another brandy and tossed it off. "I never see a man could hold his brandy like you, sir," said the sergeant. "Begging your pardon, sir." Captain Mitty stood up and strapped on his huge Webley-Vickers automatic. "It's forty kilometers through hell, sir," said the sergeant. Mitty finished one last brandy. "After all," he said softly, "what isn't?" The pounding of the cannon increased; there was the rat-tat-tatting of machine guns, and from somewhere came the menacing pocketa-pocketa-pocketa of the new flame-throwers. Walter Mitty walked to the door of the dugout humming *Auprès de Ma Blonde.* He turned and waved to the sergeant. "Cheerio!" he said. . . .

Something struck his shoulder. "I've been looking all over this hotel for you," said Mrs. Mitty. "Why do you have to hide in this old chair?" How did you expect me to find you?" "Things close in," said Walter Mitty vaguely. "What?" Mrs. Mitty said. "Did you get the what's-its-name? The puppy biscuit? What's in that box?" "Overshoes," said Mitty. "Couldn't you have put them on in the store?" "I was thinking," said Walter Mitty. "Does it ever occur to you that I am sometimes thinking?" She looked at him. "I'm going to take your temperature when I get you home," she said.

They went out through the revolving doors that made a faintly derisive whistling sound when you pushed them. It was two blocks to the parking lot. At the drugstore on the corner she said. "Wait here for me. I forgot something. I won't be a minute. She was more than a minute. Walter Mitty lighted a cigarette. It began to rain, rain with sleet in it. He stood up against the wall of the drugstore, smoking. . . . He put his shoulders back and his heels together. "To hell with the handkerchief," said Walter Mitty scornfully. He took one last drag on his cigarette and snapped it away. Then, with that faint, fleeting smile playing about his lips, he faced the firing squad; erect and motionless, proud and disdainful, Walter Mitty the Undefeated, inscrutable to the last.

F. Scott Fitzgerald (1896–1940)

Babylon Revisited

I

"And where's Mr. Campbell?" Charlie asked.

"Gone to Switzerland. Mr. Campbell's a pretty sick man, Mr. Wales."

"I'm sorry to hear that. And George Hardt?" Charlie inquired.

"Back in America, gone to work."

"And where is the Snow Bird?"°

"He was in here last week. Anyway, his friend, Mr. Schaeffer, is in Paris."

Two familiar names from the long list of a year and a half ago. Charlie scribbled an address in his notebook and tore out the page.

"If you see Mr. Schaeffer, give him this," he said. "It's my brother-in-law's address. I haven't settled on a hotel yet."

He was not really disappointed to find Paris was so empty. But the stillness in the Ritz bar was strange and portentous. It was not an American bar any more — he felt polite in it, and not as if he owned it. It had gone back into France. He felt the stillness from the moment he got out of the taxi and saw the doorman, usually in a frenzy of activity at this hour, gossiping with a *chasseur*° by the servants' entrance.

Passing through the corridor, he heard only a single, bored voice in the once-clamorous women's room. When he turned into the bar he travelled the twenty feet of green carpet with his eyes fixed straight ahead by old habit; and then, with his foot firmly on the rail, he turned and surveyed the room, encountering only a single pair of

Snow Bird   an addict or seller of cocaine or heroin
chasseur   porter

eyes that fluttered up from a newspaper in the corner. Charlie asked for the head barman Paul, who in the latter days of the bull market had come to work in his own custom-built car — disembarking, however, with due nicety at the nearest corner. But Paul was at his country house today and Alix giving him information.

"No, no more," Charlie said, "I'm going slow these days."

Alix congratulated him: "You were going pretty strong a couple of years ago."

"I'll stick to it all right," Charlie assured him. "I've stuck to it for over a year and a half now."

"How do you find conditions in America?"

"I haven't been to America for months. I'm in business in Prague, representing a couple of concerns there. They don't know about me down there."

Alix smiled.

"Remember the night of George Hardt's bachelor dinner here?" said Charlie. "By the way, what's become of Claude Fessenden?"

Alix lowered his voice confidentially: "He's in Paris, but he doesn't come here any more. Paul doesn't allow it. He ran up a bill of thirty thousand francs, charging all his drinks and his lunches, and usually his dinner, for more than a year. And when Paul finally told him he had to pay, he gave him a bad check."

Alix shook his head sadly.

"I don't understand it, such a dandy fellow. Now he's all bloated up — " He made a plump apple of his hands.

Charlie watched a group of strident queens installing themselves in a corner.

"Nothing affects them," he thought. "Stocks rise and fall, people loaf or work, but they go on forever." The place oppressed him. He called for the dice and shook with Alix for the drink.

"Here for long, Mr. Wales?"

"I'm here for four or five days to see my little girl."

"Oh-h! You have a little girl?"

Outside, the fire-red, gas-blue, ghost-green signs shone smokily through the tranquil rain. It was late afternoon and the streets were in movement; the *bistros* gleamed. At the corner of the Boulevard des Capucines he took a taxi. The Place de la Concorde moved by in pink majesty; they crossed the logical Seine, and Charlie felt the sudden provincial quality of the Left Bank.

Charlie directed his taxi to the Avenue de l'Opéra, which was out of his way. But he wanted to see the blue hour spread over the magnificent façade, and imagine that the cab horns, playing endlessly the first few bars of *Le Plus que Lent*, were the trumpets of the Second Empire. They were closing the iron grill in front of Brentano's Bookstore, and people were already at dinner behind the trim little bourgeois hedge of Duval's. He had never eaten at a really cheap restaurant in Paris. Five-course dinner, four francs fifty, eighteen cents, wine included. For some odd reason he wished that he had.

As they rolled on to the Left Bank and he felt its sudden provincialism, he thought, "I spoiled this city for myself. I didn't realize it, but the days came along one after another, and then two years were gone, and everything was gone, and I was gone."

He was thirty-five, and good to look at. The Irish mobility of his face was sobered by a deep wrinkle between his eyes. As he rang his brother-in-law's bell in the Rue Palatine, the wrinkle deepened till it pulled down his brows; he felt a cramping sensation in his belly. From behind the maid who opened the door darted a lovely little girl of nine who shrieked "Daddy!" and flew up, struggling like a fish, into his arms. She pulled his head around by one ear and set her cheek against his.

"My old pie," he said.

"Oh, daddy, daddy, daddy, daddy, dads, dads, dads!"

She drew him into the salon, where the family waited, a boy and a girl his daughter's age, his sister-in-law and her husband. He greeted Marion with his voice pitched carefully to avoid either feigned enthusiasm or dislike, but her response was more frankly tepid, though she minimized her expression of unalterable distrust by directing her regard toward his child. The two men clasped hands in a friendly way and Lincoln Peters rested his for a moment on Charlie's shoulder.

The room was warm and comfortably American. The three children moved intimately about, playing through the yellow oblongs that led to other rooms; the cheer of six o'clock spoke in the eager smacks of the fire and the sounds of French activity in the kitchen. But Charlie did not relax; his heart sat up rigidly in his body and he drew confidence from his daughter, who from time to time came close to him, holding in her arms the doll he had brought.

"Really extremely well," he declared in answer to Lincoln's question. "There's a lot of business there that isn't moving at all, but we're doing even better than ever. In fact, damn well. I'm bringing my sister over from America next month to keep house for me. My income last year was bigger than it was when I had money. You see, the Czechs —"

His boasting was for a specific purpose; but after a moment, seeing a faint restiveness in Lincoln's eye, he changed the subject:

"Those are fine children of yours, well brought up, good manners."

"We think Honoria's a great little girl too."

Marion Peters came back from the kitchen. She was a tall woman with worried eyes, who had once possessed a fresh American loveliness. Charlie had never been sensitive to it and was always surprised when people spoke of how pretty she had been. From the first there had been an instinctive antipathy between them.

"Well, how do you find Honoria?" she asked.

"Wonderful. I was astonished how much she's grown in ten months. All the children are looking well."

"We haven't had a doctor for a year. How do you like being back in Paris?"

"It seems very funny to see so few Americans around."

"I'm delighted," Marion said vehemently. "Now at least you can go into a store without their assuming you're a millionaire. We've suffered like everybody, but on the whole it's a good deal pleasanter."

"But it was nice while it lasted," Charlie said. "We were a sort of royalty, almost infallible, with a sort of magic around us. In the bar this afternoon" — he stumbled, seeing his mistake — "there wasn't a man I knew."

She looked at him keenly. "I should think you'd have had enough of bars."

"I only stayed a minute. I take one drink every afternoon, and no more."

"Don't you want a cocktail before dinner?" Lincoln asked.

"I take only one drink every afternoon, and I've had that."

"I hope you keep to it," said Marion.

Her dislike was evident in the coldness with which she spoke, but Charlie only smiled; he had larger plans. Her very aggressiveness gave him an advantage, and he knew enough to wait. He wanted them to initiate the discussion of what they knew had brought him to Paris.

At dinner he couldn't decide whether Honoria was most like him or her mother. Fortunate if she didn't combine the traits of both that had brought them to disaster. A great wave of protectiveness went over him. He thought he knew what to do for her. He believed in character; he wanted to jump back a whole generation and trust in character again as the eternally valuable element. Everything else wore out.

He left soon after dinner, but not to go home. He was curious to see Paris by night with clearer and more judicious eyes than those of other days. He bought a *strapontin*° for the Casino and watched Josephine Baker go through her chocolate arabesques.

strapontin   inexpensive jump seat

After an hour he left and strolled toward Montmartre, up the Rue Pigalle into the Place Blanche. The rain had stopped and there were a few people in evening clothes disembarking from taxis in front of cabarets, and *cocottes*° prowling singly or in pairs, and many Negroes. He passed a lighted door from which issued music, and stopped with the sense of familiarity; it was Bricktop's, where he had parted with so many hours and so much money. A few doors farther on he found another ancient rendezvous and incautiously put his head inside. Immediately an eager orchestra burst into sound, a pair of professional dancers leaped to their feet and a maître d'hôtel swooped toward him, crying, "Crowd just arriving, sir!" But he withdrew quickly.

"You have to be damn drunk," he thought.

Zelli's was closed, the bleak and sinister cheap hotels surrounding it were dark; up in the Rue Blanche there was more light and a local, colloquial French crowd. The Poet's Cave had disappeared, but the two great mouths of the Café of Heaven and the Café of Hell still yawned — even devoured, as he watched, the meagre contents of a tourist bus — a German, a Japanese, and an American couple who glanced at him with frightened eyes.

So much for the effort and ingenuity of Montmartre. All the catering to vice and waste was on an utterly childish scale, and he suddenly realized the meaning of the word "dissipate" — to dissipate into thin air; to make nothing out of something. In the little hours of the night every move from place to place was an enormous human jump, an increase of paying for the privilege of slower and slower motion.

He remembered thousand-franc notes given to an orchestra for playing a single number, hundred-franc notes tossed to a doorman for calling a cab.

But it hadn't been given for nothing.

It had been given, even the most wildly squandered sum, as an offering to destiny that he might not remember the things most worth remembering, the things that now he would always remember — his child taken from his control, his wife escaped to a grave in Vermont.

In the glare of a *brasserie*° a woman spoke to him. He bought her some eggs and coffee, and then, eluding her encouraging stare, gave her a twenty-franc note and took a taxi to his hotel.

---

cocottes prostitutes
brasserie restaurant

II

He woke upon a fine fall day — football weather. The depression of yesterday was gone and he liked the people on the streets. At noon he sat opposite Honoria at Le Grand Vatel, the only restaurant he could think of not reminiscent of champagne dinners and long luncheons that began at two and ended in a blurred and vague twilight.

"Now, how about vegetables? Oughtn't you to have some vegetables?"

"Well, yes."

"Here's *épinards* and *chou-fleur* and carrots and *haricots*."°

"I'd like *chou-fleur*."

"Wouldn't you like to have two vegetables?"

"I usually only have one at lunch."

The waiter was pretending to be inordinately fond of children. *"Qu'elle est mignonne la petite! Elle parle exactement comme une française."*°

"How about dessert? Shall we wait and see?"

The waiter disappeared. Honoria looked at her father expectantly.

"What are we going to do?"

"First, we're going to that toy store in the Rue Saint-Honoré and buy you anything you like. And then we're going to the vaudeville at the Empire."

She hesitated. "I like it about the vaudeville, but not the toy store."

"Why not?"

"Well, you brought me this doll." She had it with her. "And I've got lots of things. And we're nor rich any more, are we?"

"We never were. But today you are to have anything you want."

"All right," she agreed resignedly.

When there had been her mother and a French nurse he had been inclined to be strict; now he extended himself, reached out for a new tolerance; he must be both parents to her and not shut any of her out of communication.

"I want to get to know you," he said gravely. "First let me introduce myself. My name is Charles J. Wales, of Prague."

"Oh, daddy!" her voice cracked with laughter.

"And who are you, please?" he persisted, and she accepted a rôle immediately: "Honoria Wales, Rue Palatine, Paris."

"Married or single?"

---

epinards . . . chou-fleur . . . haricots   spinach, cauliflower, beans
"Qu'elle . . . une française."   "How charming she is, the little one. She speaks just like a French girl."

"No, not married. Single."

He indicated the doll. "But I see you have a child, madame."

Unwilling to disinherit it, she took it to her heart and thought quickly: "Yes, I've been married, but I'm not married now. My husband is dead."

He went on quickly, "And the child's name?"

"Simone. That's after my best friend at school."

"I'm very pleased that you're doing so well at school."

"I'm third this month," she boasted. "Elsie" — that was her cousin — "is only about eighteenth, and Richard is about at the bottom."

"You like Richard and Elsie, don't you?"

"Oh, yes. I like Richard quite well and I like her all right."

Cautiously and casually he asked: "And Aunt Marion and Uncle Lincoln — which do you like best?"

"Oh, Uncle Lincoln, I guess."

He was increasingly aware of her presence. As they came in, a murmur of ". . . adorable" followed them, and now the people at the next table bent all their silences upon her, staring as if she were something no more conscious than a flower.

"Why don't I live with you?" she asked suddenly. "Because mamma's dead?"

"You must stay here and learn more French. It would have been hard for daddy to take care of you so well."

"I don't really need much taking care of any more. I do everything for myself."

Going out of the restaurant, a man and a woman unexpectedly hailed him.

"Well, the old Wales!"

"Hello there, Lorraine. . . . Dunc."

Sudden ghosts out of the past: Duncan Schaeffer, a friend from college. Lorraine Quarrles, a lovely, pale blonde of thirty; one of a crowd who had helped them make months into days in the lavish times of three years ago.

"My husband couldn't come this year," she said, in answer to his question. "We're poor as hell. So he gave me two hundred a month and told me I could do my worst on that. . . . This your little girl?"

"What about coming back and sitting down?" Duncan asked.

"Can't do it." He was glad for an excuse. As always, he felt Lorraine's passionate, provocative attraction, but his own rhythm was different now.

"Well, how about dinner?" she asked.

"I'm not free. Give me your address and let me call you."

"Charlie, I believe you're sober," she said judicially. "I honestly believe he's sober, Dunc. Pinch him and see if he's sober."

Charlie indicated Honoria with his head. They both laughed.

"What's your address?" said Duncan sceptically.

He hesitated, unwilling to give the name of his hotel.

"I'm not settled yet. I'd better call you. We're going to see the vaudeville at the Empire."

"There! That's what I want to do," Lorraine said. "I want to see some clowns and acrobats and jugglers. That's just what we'll do, Dunc."

"We've got to do an errand first," said Charlie. "Perhaps we'll see you there."

"All right, you snob. . . . Goodbye, beautiful little girl."

"Good-bye."

Honoria bobbed politely.

Somehow, an unwelcome encounter. They liked him because he was functioning, because he was serious; they wanted to see him, because he was stronger than they were now, because they wanted to draw a certain sustenance from his strength.

At the Empire, Honoria proudly refused to sit upon her father's folded coat. She was already an individual with a code of her own, and Charlie was more and more absorbed by the desire of putting a little of himself into her before she crystallized utterly. It was hopeless to try to know her in so short a time.

Between the acts they came upon Duncan and Lorraine in the lobby where the band was playing.

"Have a drink?"

"All right, but not up at the bar. We'll take a table."

"The perfect father."

Listening abstractedly to Lorraine, Charlie watched Honoria's eyes leave their table, and he followed them wistfully about the room, wondering what they saw. He met her glance and she smiled.

"I like that lemonade," she said.

What had she said? What had he expected? Going home in a taxi afterward, he pulled her over until her head rested against his chest.

"Darling, do you ever think about your mother?"

"Yes, sometimes," she answered vaguely.

"I don't want you to forget her. Have you got a picture of her?"

"Yes, I think so. Anyhow, Aunt Marion has. Why don't you want me to forget her?"

"She loved you very much."

"I loved her too."

They were silent for a moment.

"Daddy, I want to come and live with you," she said suddenly.

His heart leaped; he had wanted it to come like this.

"Aren't you perfectly happy?"

"Yes, but I love you better than anybody else. And you love me better than anybody, don't you, now that mummy's dead?"

"Of course I do. But you won't always like me best, honey. You'll grow up and meet somebody your own age and go marry him and forget you ever had a daddy."

"Yes, that's true," she agreed tranquilly.

He didn't go in. He was coming back at nine o'clock and he wanted to keep himself fresh and new for the thing he must say then.

"When you're safe inside, just show yourself in that window."

"All right. Good-bye, dads, dads, dads, dads."

He waited in the dark street until she appeared, all warm and glowing, in the window above and kissed her fingers out into the night.

III

They were waiting. Marion sat behind the coffee service in a dignified black dinner dress that just faintly suggested mourning. Lincoln was walking up and down with the animation of one who had already been talking. They were as anxious as he was to get into the question. He opened it almost immediately:

"I suppose you know what I want to see you about — why I really came to Paris."

Marion played with the black stars on her necklace and frowned.

"I'm awfully anxious to have a home," he continued. "And I'm awfully anxious to have Honoria in it. I appreciate your taking in Honoria for her mother's sake, but things have changed now" — he hesitated and then continued more forcibly — "changed radically with me, and I want to ask you to reconsider the matter. It would be silly for me to deny that about three years ago I was acting badly — "

Marion looked up at him with hard eyes.

" — but all that's over. As I told you, I haven't had more than a drink a day for over a year, and I take that drink deliberately, so that the idea of alcohol won't get too big in my imagination. You see the idea?"

"No," said Marion succinctly.

"It's a sort of stunt I set myself. It keeps the matter in proportion."

"I get you," said Lincoln. "You don't want to admit it's got any attraction for you."

"Something like that. Sometimes I forget and don't take it. But I try to take it. Anyhow, I couldn't afford to drink in my position. The people I represent are more than satisfied with what I've done, and I'm bringing my sister over from Burlington to keep house for me, and I want awfully to have Honoria too. You know that even when her mother and I weren't getting along well we never let anything that happened touch Honoria. I know she's fond of me and I know I'm able to take care of her and — well, there you are. How do you feel about it?"

He knew that now he would have to take a beating. It would last an hour or two hours, and it would be difficult, but if he modulated his inevitable resentment to the chastened attitude of the reformed sinner, he might win his point in the end.

Keep your temper, he told himself. You don't want to be justified. You want Honoria.

Lincoln spoke first: "We've been talking it over ever since we got your letter last month. We're happy to have Honoria here. She's a dear little thing, and we're glad to be able to help her, but of course that isn't the question — "

Marion interrupted suddenly. "How long are you going to stay sober, Charlie?" she asked.

"Permanently, I hope."

"How can anybody count on that?"

"You know I never did drink heavily until I gave up business and came over here with nothing to do. Then Helen and I began to run around with — "

"Please leave Helen out of it. I can't bear to hear you talk about her like that."

He stared at her grimly; he had never been certain how fond of each other the sisters were in life.

"My drinking only lasted about a year and a half — from the time we came over until I — collapsed."

"It was time enough."

"It was time enough," he agreed.

"My duty is entirely to Helen," she said. "I try to think what she would have wanted me to do. Frankly, from the night you did that terrible thing you haven't really existed for me. I can't help that. She was my sister."

"Yes."

"When she was dying she asked me to look out for Honoria. If you hadn't been in a sanitarium then, it might have helped matters."

He had no answer.

"I'll never in my life be able to forget the morning when Helen knocked at my door, soaked to the skin and shivering, and said you'd locked her out."

Charlie gripped the sides of the chair. This was more difficult than he expected; he wanted to launch out into a long expostulation and explanation, but he only said: "The night I locked her out — " and she interrupted, "I don't feel up to going over that again."

After a moment's silence Lincoln said: "We're getting off the subject. You want Marion to set aside her legal guardianship and give you Honoria. I think the main point for her is whether she has confidence in you or not."

"I don't blame Marion," Charlie said slowly, "but I think she can have entire confidence in me. I had a good record up to three years ago. Of course, it's within human possibilities I might go wrong any time. But if we wait much longer I'll lose Honoria's childhood and my chance for a home." He shook his head, "I'll simply lose her, don't you see?"

"Yes, I see," said Lincoln.

"Why didn't you think of all this before?" Marion asked.

"I suppose I did, from time to time, but Helen and I were getting along badly. When I consented to the guardianship, I was flat on my back in a sanitarium and the market had cleaned me out. I knew I'd acted badly, and I thought if it would bring any peace to Helen, I'd agree to anything. But now it's different. I'm functioning, I'm behaving damn well, so far as — "

"Please don't swear at me," Marion said.

He looked at her, startled. With each remark the force of her dislike became more and more apparent. She had built up all her fear of life into one wall and faced it toward him. This trivial reproof was possibly the result of some trouble with the cook several hours before. Charlie became increasingly alarmed at leaving Honoria in this atmosphere of hostility against himself; sooner or later it would come out, in a word here, a shake of the head there, and some of that distrust would be irrevocably implanted in Honoria. But he pulled his temper down out of his face and shut it up inside him; he had won a point, for Lincoln realized the absurdity of Marion's remark and asked her lightly since when she had objected to the word "damn."

"Another thing," Charlie said: "I'm able to give her certain advantages now. I'm going to take a French governess to Prague with me. I've got a lease on a new apartment — "

He stopped, realizing that he was blundering. They couldn't be expected to accept with equanimity the fact that his income was again twice as large as their own.

"I suppose you can give her more luxuries than we can," said Marion. "When you were throwing away money we were living along watching every ten francs. . . . I suppose you'll start doing it again."

"Oh, no," he said. "I've learned. I worked hard for ten years, you know — until I got lucky in the market, like so many people. Terribly lucky. It didn't seem any use working any more, so I quit. It won't happen again."

There was a long silence. All of them felt their nerves straining, and for the first time in a year Charlie wanted a drink. He was sure now that Lincoln Peters wanted him to have his child.

Marion shuddered suddenly; part of her saw that Charlie's feet were planted on the earth now, and her own maternal feeling recognized the naturalness of his desire; but she had lived for a long time with a prejudice — a prejudice founded on a curious disbelief in her sister's happiness, and which, in the shock of one terrible night, had turned to hatred for him. It had all happened at a point in her life where the discouragement of ill health and adverse circumstances made it necessary for her to believe in tangible villainy and a tangible villain.

"I can't help what I think!" she cried out suddenly. "How much you were responsible for Helen's death, I don't know. It's something you'll have to square with your own conscience."

An electric current of agony surged through him; for a moment he was almost on his feet, an unuttered sound echoing in his throat. He hung on to himself for a moment, another moment.

"Hold on there," said Lincoln uncomfortably. "I never thought you were responsible for that."

"Helen died of heart trouble," Charlie said dully.

"Yes, heart trouble." Marion spoke as if the phrase had another meaning for her.

Then, in the flatness that followed her outburst, she saw him plainly and she knew he had somehow arrived at control over the situation. Glancing at her husband, she found no help from him, and as abruptly as if it were a matter of no importance, she threw up the sponge.

"Do what you like!" she cried, springing up from her chair. "She's your child. I'm not the person to stand in your way. I think if it were my child I'd rather see her — " She managed to check herself. "You two decide it. I can't stand this. I'm sick. I'm going to bed."

She hurried from the room; after a moment Lincoln said:

"This has been a hard day for her. You know how strongly she feels — " His voice was almost apologetic: "When a woman gets an idea in her head."

"Of course."

"It's going to be all right. I think she sees now that you — can provide for the child, and so we can't very well stand in your way or Honoria's way."

"Thank you, Lincoln."

"I'd better go along and see how she is."

"I'm going."

He was still trembling when he reached the street, but a walk down the Rue Bonaparte to the *quais* set him up, and as he crossed the Seine, fresh and new by the *quai* lamps, he felt exultant. But back in his room he couldn't sleep. The image of Helen haunted him. Helen whom he had loved so until they had senselessly begun to abuse each other's love, tear it into shreds. On that terrible February night that Marion remembered so vividly, a slow quarrel had gone on for hours. There was a scene at the Florida, and then he attempted to take her home, and then she kissed young Webb at a table; after that there was what she had hysterically said. When he arrived home alone he turned the key in the lock in wild anger. How could he know she would arrive an hour later alone, that there would be a snowstorm in which she wandered about in slippers, too confused to find a taxi? Then the aftermath, her escaping pneumonia by a miracle, and all the attendant horror. They were "reconciled," but that was the beginning of the end, and Marion, who had seen with her own eyes and who imagined it to be one of many scenes from her sister's martyrdom, never forgot.

Going over it again brought Helen nearer, and in the white, soft light that steals upon half sleep near morning he found himself talking to her again. She said that he was perfectly right about Honoria and that she wanted Honoria to be with him. She said she was glad he was being good and doing better. She said a lot of other things — very friendly things — but she was in a swing in a white dress, and swinging faster and faster all the time, so that at the end he could not hear clearly all that she said.

IV

He woke up feeling happy. The door of the world was open again. He made plans, vistas, futures for Honoria and himself, but suddenly he grew sad, remembering all the plans he and Helen had made. She had not planned to die. The present was the thing — work to do and someone to love. But not to love too much, for he knew the injury that a father can do to a daughter or a mother to a son by attaching them too closely: afterward, out in the world, the child would seek in the marriage partner the same blind tenderness and, failing probably to find it, turn against love and life.

It was another bright, crisp day. He called Lincoln Peters at the bank where he worked and asked if he could count on taking Honoria when he left for Prague. Lincoln agreed that there was no reason for delay. One thing — the legal guardianship. Marion wanted to retain that a while longer. She was upset by the whole matter, and it would oil things if she felt that the situation was still in her control for another year. Charlie agreed, wanting only the tangible, visible child.

Then the question of a governess. Charlie sat in a gloomy agency and talked to a cross Bernaise and to a buxom Breton peasant, neither of whom he could have endured. There were others whom he would see tomorrow.

He lunched with Lincoln Peters at Griffons, trying to keep down his exultation.

"There's nothing quite like your own child," Lincoln said. "But you understand how Marion feels too."

"She's forgotten how hard I worked for seven years there," Charlie said. "She just remembers one night."

"There's another thing." Lincoln hesitated. "While you and Helen were tearing around Europe throwing money away, we were just getting along. I didn't touch any of the prosperity because I never got ahead enough to carry anything but my insurance. I think Marion felt there was some kind of injustice in it — you not even working toward the end, and getting richer and richer."

"It went just as quick as it came," said Charlie.

"Yes, a lot of it stayed in the hands of *chasseurs* and saxophone players and maîtres d'hôtel — well, the big party's over now. I just said that to explain Marion's feelings about those crazy years. If you drop in about six o'clock tonight before Marion's too tired, we'll settle the details on the spot."

Back at his hotel, Charlie found a *pneumatique*° that had been redirected from the Ritz bar where Charlie had left his address for the purpose of finding a certain man.

Dear Charlie: You were so strange when we saw you the other day that I wondered if I did something to offend you. If so, I'm not conscious of it. In fact, I have thought about you too much for the last year, and it's always been in the back of my mind that I might see you if I came over here. We *did* have such good times that crazy spring, like the night you and I stole the butcher's tricycle, and the time we tried to call on the president and you had the old derby rim and the wire cane. Everybody seems so old lately, but I don't feel old a bit. Couldn't we get together some time today for old time's sake? I've got a vile hang-over for the moment, but will be feeling better this afternoon and will look for you about five in the sweatshop at the Ritz.
Always devotedly,
Lorraine

pneumatique   express letter transmitted in Paris by pneumatic tube

His first feeling was one of awe that he had actually, in his mature years, stolen a tricycle and pedalled Lorraine all over the Étoile between the small hours and dawn. In retrospect it was a nightmare. Locking out Helen didn't fit in with any other act of his life, but the tricycle incident did — it was one of many. How many weeks or months of dissipation to arrive at that condition of utter irresponsibility?

He tried to picture how Lorraine had appeared to him then — very attractive; Helen was unhappy about it, though she said nothing. Yesterday, in the restaurant, Lorraine had seemed trite, blurred, worn away. He emphatically did not want to see her, and he was glad Alix had not given away his hotel address. It was a relief to think, instead, of Honoria, to think of Sundays spent with her and of saying good morning to her and of knowing she was there in his house at night, drawing her breath in the darkness.

At five he took a taxi and bought presents for all the Peters — a piquant cloth doll, a box of Roman soldiers, flowers for Marion, big linen handkerchiefs for Lincoln.

He saw, when he arrived in the apartment, that Marion had accepted the inevitable. She greeted him now as though he were a recalcitrant member of the family, rather than a menacing outsider. Honoria had been told she was going; Charlie was glad to see that her tact made her conceal her excessive happiness. Only on his lap did she whisper her delight and the question "When?" before she slipped away with the other children.

He and Marion were alone for a minute in the room, and on an impulse he spoke out boldly:

"Family quarrels are bitter things. They don't go according to any rules. They're not like aches or wounds; they're more like splits in the skin that won't heal because there's not enough material. I wish you and I could be on better terms."

"Some things are hard to forget," she answered. "It's a question of confidence." There was no answer to this and presently she asked, "When do you propose to take her?"

"As soon as I can get a governess. I hoped the day after tomorrow."

"That's impossible. I've got to get her things in shape. Not before Saturday."

He yielded. Coming back into the room, Lincoln offered him a drink.

"I'll take my daily whisky," he said.

It was warm here, it was a home, people together by a fire. The children felt very safe and important; the mother and father were serious, watchful. They had things to do for the children more important than his visit here. A spoonful of medicine was, after all, more important than the strained relations between Marion and himself. They were not dull people, but they were very much in the grip of life and circumstances. He wondered if he couldn't do something to get Lincoln out of his rut at the bank.

A long peal at the door-bell; the *bonne à tout faire°* passed through and went down the corridor. The door opened upon another long ring, and then voices, and the three in the salon looked up expectantly; Richard moved to bring the corridor within his range of vision, and Marion rose. Then the maid came back along the corridor, closely followed by the voices, which developed under the light into Duncan Schaeffer and Lorraine Quarrles.

They were gay, they were hilarious, they were roaring with laughter. For a moment Charlie was astounded; unable to understand how they ferreted out the Peters' address.

"Ah-h-h!" Duncan wagged his finger roguishly at Charlie. "Ah-h-h!".

They both slid down under another cascade of laughter. Anxious and at a loss, Charlie shook hands with them quickly and presented them to Lincoln and Marion. Marion nodded, scarcely speaking. She had drawn back a step toward the fire; her little girl beside her, and Marion put an arm about her shoulder.

With growing annoyance at the intrusion, Charlie waited for them to explain themselves. After some concentration Duncan said:

"We came to invite you out to dinner. Lorraine and I insist that all this shishi, cagy business 'bout your address got to stop."

Charlie came closer to them, as if to force them backward down the corridor.

"Sorry, but I can't. Tell me where you'll be and I'll phone you in half an hour."

This made no impression. Lorraine sat down suddenly on the side of a chair, and focussing her eyes on Richard, cried. "Oh, what a nice little boy! Come here, little boy." Richard glanced at his mother, but did not move. With a perceptible shrug of her shoulders, Lorraine turned back to Charlie:

"Come and dine. Sure your cousins won' mine. See you so sel'om. Or solemn."

"I can't," said Charlie sharply. "You two have dinner and I'll phone you."

Her voice became suddenly unpleasant. "All right, we'll go. But I remember once when you hammered on my door at four A.M. I was enough of a good sport to give you a drink. Come on, Dunc."

bonne à toute faire   maid-of-all-work

Still in slow motion, with blurred, angry faces, with uncertain feet, they retired along the corridor.

"Good night," Charlie said.

"Good night!" responded Lorraine emphatically.

When he went back into the salon Marion had not moved, only now her son was standing in the circle of her other arm. Lincoln was still swinging Honoria back and forth like a pendulum from side to side.

"What an outrage!" Charlie broke out. "What an absolute outrage!"

Neither of them answered. Charlie dropped into an armchair, picked up his drink, set it down again and said:

"People I haven't seen for two years having the colossal nerve — "

He broke off. Marion had made the sound "Oh!" in one swift, furious breath, turned her body from him with a jerk and left the room.

Lincoln set down Honoria carefully.

"You children go in and start your soup," he said, and when they obeyed, he said to Charlie:

"Marion's not well and she can't stand shocks. That kind of people make her really physically sick."

"I didn't tell them to come here. They wormed your name out of somebody. They deliberately — "

"Well, it's too bad. It doesn't help matters. Excuse me a minute."

Left alone, Charlie sat tense in his chair. In the next room he could hear the children eating, talking in monosyllables, already oblivious to the scene between their elders. He heard a murmur of conversation from a farther room and then the ticking bell of a telephone receiver picked up, and in a panic he moved to the other side of the room and out of earshot.

In a minute Lincoln came back. "Look here, Charlie. I think we'd better call off dinner for tonight. Marion's in bad shape."

"Is she angry with me?"

"Sort of," he said, almost roughly. "She's not strong and — "

"You mean she's changed her mind about Honoria?"

"She's pretty bitter right now. I don't know. You phone me at the bank tomorrow."

"I wish you'd explain to her I never dreamed these people would come here. I'm just as sore as you are."

"I couldn't explain anything to her now."

Charlie got up. He took his coat and hat and started down the corridor. Then he opened the door of the dining room and said in a strange voice, "Good night, children."

Honoria rose and ran around the table to hug him.

"Good night, sweetheart," he said vaguely, and then trying to make his voice more tender, trying to conciliate something. "Good night, dear children."

V

Charlie went directly to the Ritz bar with the furious idea of finding Lorraine and Duncan, but they were not there, and he realized that in any case there was nothing he could do. He had not touched his drink at the Peters', and now he ordered a whisky-and-soda. Paul came over to say hello.

"It's a great change," he said sadly. "We do about half the business we did. So many fellows I hear about back in the States lost everything, maybe not in the first crash, but then in the second. Your friend George Hardt lost every cent, I hear. Are you back in the States?"

"No, I'm in business in Prague."

"I heard that you lost a lot in the crash."

"I did," and he added grimly, "but I lost everything I wanted in the boom."

"Selling short."

"Something like that."

Again the memory of those days swept over him like a nightmare — the people they had met traveling; then people who couldn't add a row of figures or speak a coherent sentence. The little man Helen had consented to dance with at the ship's party, who had insulted her ten feet from the table; the women and girls carried screaming with drink or drugs out of public places —

— The men who locked their wives out in the snow, because the snow of twenty-nine wasn't real snow. If you didn't want it to be snow, you just paid some money.

He went to the phone and called the Peters' apartment; Lincoln answered.

"I called up because this thing is on my mind. Has Marion said anything definite?"

"Marion's sick," Lincoln answered abruptly. "I know this thing isn't altogether your fault, but I can't have her go to pieces about it. I'm afraid we'll have to let it slide for six months; I can't take the chance of working her up to this state again."

"I see."

"I'm sorry, Charlie."

He went back to his table. His whisky glass was empty, but he shook his head when Alix looked at it questioningly. There wasn't much he could do now except send Honoria some things; he would send her a lot of things tomorrow. He thought rather angrily that this was just money — he had given so many people money. . . .

"No, no more," he said to another waiter. "What do I owe you?"

He would come back some day; they couldn't make him pay forever. But he wanted his child, and nothing was much good now, beside that fact. He wasn't young any more, with a lot of nice thoughts and dreams to have by himself. He was absolutely sure Helen wouldn't have wanted him to be so alone.

William Faulkner (1897–1962)

A Rose for Emily

I

When Miss Emily Grierson died, our whole town went to her funeral: the men through a sort of respectful affection for a fallen monument, the women mostly out of curiosity to see the inside of her house, which no one save an old manservant — a combined gardener and cook — had seen in at least ten years.

It was a big, squarish frame house that had once been white, decorated with cupolas and spires and scrolled balconies in the heavily lightsome style of the seventies, set on what had once been our most select street. But garages and cotton gins had encroached and obliterated even the august names of that neighborhood; only Miss Emily's house was left, lifting its stubborn and coquettish decay above the cotton wagons and the gasoline pumps — an eyesore among eyesores. And now Miss Emily had gone to join the representatives of those august names where they lay in the cedar-bemused cemetery among the ranked and anonymous graves of Union and Confederate soldiers who fell at the battle of Jefferson.

Alive, Miss Emily had been a tradition, a duty, and a care; a sort of hereditary obligation upon the town, dating from that day in 1894 when Colonel Sartoris, the mayor — he who fathered the edict that no Negro woman should appear on the streets without an apron — remitted her taxes, the dispensation dating from the death of her father on into perpetuity. Not that Miss Emily would have accepted charity. Colonel Sartoris invented an involved tale to the effect that Miss Emily's father had loaned money to the town, which the town, as a matter of business, preferred this way of repaying. Only a man of Colonel Sartoris' generation and thought could have invented it, and only a woman could have believed it.

When the next generation, with its more modern ideas, became mayors and aldermen, this arrangement created some little dissatisfaction. On the first of the year they mailed her a tax notice. February came, and there was no reply. They wrote her a formal letter, asking her to call at the sheriff's office at her convenience. A week later the mayor wrote her himself, offering to call or to send his car for her, and received in reply a note on paper of an archaic shape, in a thin, flowing calligraphy in faded ink, to the effect that she no longer went out at all. The tax notice was also enclosed, without comment.

They called a special meeting of the Board of Aldermen. A deputation waited upon her, knocked at the door through which no visitor had passed since she ceased giving china-painting lessons eight or ten years earlier. They were admitted by the old Negro into a dim hall from which a staircase mounted into still more shadow. It smelled of dust and disuse — a close, dank smell. The Negro led them into the parlor. It was furnished in heavy, leather-covered furniture. When the Negro opened the blinds of one window, a faint dust rose sluggishly about their thighs, spinning with slow motes in the single sunray. On a tarnished gilt easel before the fireplace stood a crayon portrait of Miss Emily's father.

They rose when she entered — a small, fat woman in black, with a thin gold chain descending to her waist and vanishing into her belt, leaning on an ebony cane with a tarnished gold head. Her skeleton was small and spare; perhaps that was why what would have been merely plumpness in another was obesity in her. She looked bloated, like a body long submerged in motionless water, and of that pallid hue. Her eyes, lost in the fatty ridges of her face, looked like two small pieces of coal pressed into a lump of dough as they moved from one face to another while the visitors stated their errand.

She did not ask them to sit. She just stood in the door and listened quietly until the spokesman came to a stumbling halt. Then they could hear the invisible watch ticking at the end of the gold chain.

Her voice was dry and cold. "I have no taxes in Jefferson. Colonel Sartoris explained it to me. Perhaps one of you can gain access to the city records and satisfy yourselves."

"But we have. We are the city authorities, Miss Emily. Didn't you get a notice from the sheriff, signed by him?"

"I received a paper, yes," Miss Emily said. "Perhaps he considers himself the sheriff. . . . I have no taxes in Jefferson."

"But there is nothing on the books to show that, you see. We must go by the —"

"See Colonel Sartoris. I have no taxes in Jefferson."

"But, Miss Emily —"

"See Colonel Sartoris." (Colonel Sartoris had been dead almost ten years.) "I have no taxes in Jefferson. Tobe!" The Negro appeared. "Show these gentlemen out."

II

So she vanquished them, horse and foot, just as she had vanquished their fathers thirty years before about the smell. That was two years after her father's death and a short time after her sweetheart — the one we believed would marry her — had deserted her. After her father's death she went out very little; after her sweetheart went away, people hardly saw her at all. A few of the ladies had the temerity to call, but were not received, and the only sign of life about the place was the Negro man — a young man then — going in and out with a market basket.

"Just as if a man — any man — could keep a kitchen properly," the ladies said; so they were not surprised when the smell developed. It was another link between the gross, teeming world and the high and mighty Griersons.

A neighbor, a woman, complained to the mayor, Judge Stevens, eighty years old.

"But what will you have me do about it, madam?" he said.

"Why, send her word to stop it," the woman said. "Isn't there a law?"

"I'm sure that won't be necessary," Judge Stevens said. "It's probably just a snake or a rat that nigger of hers killed in the yard. I'll speak to him about it."

The next day he received two more complaints, one from a man who came in diffident deprecation. "We really must do something about it, Judge. I'd be the last one in the world to bother Miss Emily, but we've got to do something." That night the Board of Aldermen met — three gray-beards and one younger man, a member of the rising generation.

"It's simple enough," he said. "Send her word to have her place cleaned up. Give her a certain time to do it in, and if she don't . . ."

"Dammit, sir," Judge Stevens said, "will you accuse a lady to her face of smelling bad?"

So the next night, after midnight, four men crossed Miss Emily's lawn and slunk about the house like burglars, sniffing along the base of the brickwork and at the cellar openings while one of them performed a regular sowing motion with his hand out of a sack slung from his shoulder. They broke open the cellar door and sprinkled lime there, and in all the out-buildings. As they recrossed the lawn, a window that had been dark was lighted and Miss Emily sat in it, the light behind her, and her upright torso motionless as that of an idol. They crept quietly across the lawn and into the shadow of the locusts that lined the street. After a week or two the smell went away.

That was when people had begun to feel really sorry for her. People in our town remembering how old lady Wyatt, her great-aunt, had gone completely crazy at last, believed that the Griersons held themselves a little too high for what they really were. None of the young men were quite good enough for Miss Emily and such. We had long thought of them as a tableau; Miss Emily a slender figure in white in the background, her father a spraddled silhouette in the foreground, his back to her and clutching a horsewhip, the two of them framed by the back-flung front door. So when she got to be thirty and was still single, we were not pleased exactly, but vindicated; even with insanity in the family she wouldn't have turned down all of her chances if they had really materialized.

When her father died, it got about that the house was all that was left to her; and in a way, people were glad. At last they could pity Miss Emily. Being left alone, and a pauper, she had become humanized. Now she too would know the old thrill and the old despair of a penny more or less.

The day after his death all the ladies prepared to call at the house and offer, condolence and aid, as is our custom. Miss Emily met them at the door, dressed as usual and with no trace of grief on her face. She told them that her father was not dead. She did that for three days, with the ministers calling on her, and the doctors, trying to persuade her to let them dispose of the body. Just as they were about to resort to law and force, she broke down, and they buried her father quickly.

We did not say she was crazy then. We believed she had to do that. We remembered all the young men her father had driven away, and we knew that with nothing left, she would have to cling to that which had robbed her, as people will.

III

She was sick for a long time. When we saw her again, her hair was cut short, making her look like a girl, with a vague resemblance to those angels in colored church windows — sort of tragic and serene.

The town had just let the contracts for paving the sidewalks, and in the summer after her father's death they began to work. The construction company came with niggers and mules and machinery, and a foreman named Homer Barron, a Yankee — a big, dark, ready man, with a big voice and eyes lighter than his face. The little boys would follow in groups to hear him cuss the niggers, and the niggers singing in time to the rise and fall of picks. Pretty soon he knew everybody in town. Whenever you heard a lot of laughing anywhere about the square, Homer Barron would be in the center of the group. Presently we began to see him and Miss Emily on Sunday afternoons driving in the yellow-wheeled buggy and the matched team of bays from the livery stable.

At first we were glad that Miss Emily would have an interest, because the ladies all said, "Of course a Grierson would not think seriously of a Northerner, a day laborer." But there were still others, older people, who said that even grief could not cause a real lady to forget *noblesse oblige* — without calling it *noblesse oblige*. They just said, "Poor Emily. Her kinsfolk should come to her." She had some kin in Alabama; but years ago her father had fallen out with them over the estate of old lady Wyatt, the crazy woman, and there was no communication between the two families. They had not even been represented at the funeral.

And as soon as the old people said, "Poor Emily," the whispering began. "Do you suppose it's really so?" they said to one another. "Of course it is. What else could . . ." This behind their hands; rustling of craned silk and satin behind jalousies closed upon the sun of Sunday afternoon as the thin, swift clop-clop-clop of the matched team passed: "Poor Emily."

She carried her head high enough — even when we believed that she was fallen. It was as if she demanded more than ever the recognition of her dignity as the last Grierson; as if it had wanted that touch of earthiness to reaffirm her imperviousness. Like when she bought the rat poison, the arsenic. That was over a year after they had begun to say "Poor Emily," and while the two female cousins were visiting her.

"I want some poison," she said to the druggist. She was over thirty then, still a slight woman, though thinner than usual, with cold, haughty black eyes in a face the flesh of which was strained across the temples and about the eyesockets as you imagine a lighthouse-keeper's face ought to look. "I want some poison," she said.

"Yes, Miss Emily. What kind? For rats and such? I'd recom —"

"I want the best you have. I don't care what kind."

The druggist named several. "They'll kill anything up to an elephant. But what you want is —"

"Arsenic," Miss Emily said. "Is that a good one?"

"Is . . . arsenic? Yes ma'am. But what you want —"

"I want arsenic."

The druggist looked down at her. She looked back at him, erect, her face like a strained flag. "Why, of course," the druggist said. "If that's what you want. But the law requires you to tell what you are going to use it for."

Miss Emily just stared at him, her head tilted back in order to look him eye for eye, until he looked away and went and got the arsenic and wrapped it up. The Negro delivery boy brought her the package; the druggist didn't come back. When she opened the package at home there was written on the box, under the skull and bones: "For rats."

IV

So the next day we all said, "She will kill herself"; and we said it would be the best thing. When she had first begun to be seen with Homer Barron, we had said, "She will marry him." Then we said, "She will persuade him yet," because Homer himself had re-marked — he liked men, and it was known that he drank with the younger men in the Elk's Club — that he was not a marrying man. Later we said, "Poor Emily," behind the jalousies as they passed on Sunday afternoon in the glittering buggy, Miss Emily with her head high and Homer Barron with his hat cocked and a cigar in his teeth, reins and whip in a yellow glove.

Then some of the ladies began to say that it was a disgrace to the town and a bad example to the young people. The men did not want to interfere, but at last the ladies forced the Baptist minister — Miss Emily's people were Episcopal — to call upon her. He would never divulge what happened during that interview, but he refused to go back again. The next Sunday they again drove about the streets, and the following day the minister's wife wrote to Miss Emily's relations in Alabama.

So she had blood-kin under her roof again and we sat back to watch developments. At first nothing happened. Then we were sure that they were to be married. We learned that Miss Emily had been to the jeweler's and ordered a man's toilet set in silver, with the letters H.B. on each piece. Two days later we learned that she had bought a complete outfit of men's clothing, including a nightshirt, and we said, "They are married." We were really glad. We were glad because the two female cousins were even more Grierson than Miss Emily had ever been.

So we were surprised when Homer Barron — the streets had been finished some time since — was gone. We were a little disappointed that there was not a public blowing-off, but we believed that he had gone on to prepare for Miss Emily's coming, or to give a chance to get rid of the cousins. (By that time it was a cabal, and we were all Miss

Emily's allies to help circumvent the cousins.) Sure enough, after another week they departed. And, as we had expected all along, within three days Homer Barron was back in town. A neighbor saw the Negro man admit him at the kitchen door at dusk one evening.

And that was the last we saw of Homer Barron. And of Miss Emily for some time. The Negro man went in and out with the market basket, but the front door remained closed. Now and then we would see her at a window for a moment, as the men did that night when they sprinkled the lime, but for almost six months she did not appear on the streets. Then we knew that this was to be expected too; as if that quality of her father which had thwarted her woman's life so many times had been too virulent and too furious to die.

When we next saw Miss Emily, she had grown fat and her hair was turning gray. During the next few years it grew grayer and grayer until it attained an even pepper-and-salt iron-gray, when it ceased turning. Up to the day of her death at seventy-four it was still that vigorous iron-gray, like the hair of an active man.

From that time on her front door remained closed, save for a period of six or seven years, when she was about forty, during which she gave lessons in china-painting. She fitted up a studio in one of the downstairs rooms, where the daughters and granddaughters of Colonel Sartoris' contemporaries were sent to her with the same regularity and in the same spirit that they were sent on Sundays with a twenty-five cent piece for the collection plate. Meanwhile her taxes had been remitted.

Then the newer generation became the backbone and the spirit of the town, and the painting pupils grew up and fell away and did not send their children to her with boxes of color and tedious brushes and pictures cut from the ladies' magazines. The front door closed upon the last one and remained closed for good. When the town got free postal delivery Miss Emily alone refused to let them fasten the metal numbers above her door and attach a mailbox to it. She would not listen to them.

Daily, monthly, yearly we watched the Negro grow grayer and more stooped, going in and out with the market basket. Each December we sent her a tax notice, which would be returned by the post office a week later, unclaimed. Now and then we would see her in one of the downstairs windows — she had evidently shut up the top floor of the house — like the carven torso of an idol in a niche, looking or not looking at us, we could never tell which. Thus she passed from generation to generation — dear, inescapable, impervious, tranquil, and perverse.

And so she died. Fell ill in the house filled with dust and shadows, with only a doddering Negro man to wait on her. We did not even know she was sick; we had long since given up trying to get any information from the Negro. He talked to no one, probably not even to her, for his voice had grown harsh and rusty, as if from disuse.

She died in one of the downstairs rooms, in a heavy walnut bed with a curtain, her gray head propped on a pillow yellow and moldy with age and lack of sunlight.

V

The Negro met the first of the ladies at the front door and let them in, with their hushed, sibilant voices and their quick, curious glances, and then he disappeared. He walked right through the house and out the back and was not seen again.

The two female cousins came at once. They held the funeral on the second day, with the town coming to look at Miss Emily beneath a mass of bought flowers, with the crayon face of her father musing profoundly above the bier and the ladies sibilant and macabre; and the very old men — some in their brushed Confederate uniforms — on the porch and the lawn, talking of Miss Emily as if she had been a contemporary of theirs, believing that they had danced with her and courted her perhaps, confusing time with its mathematical progression, as the old do, to whom all the past is not a diminishing road, but, instead, a huge meadow which no winter ever quite touches, divided from them now by the narrow bottleneck of the most recent decade of years.

Already we knew that there was one room in that region above stairs which no one had seen in forty years, and which would have to be forced. They waited until Miss Emily was decently in the ground before they opened it.

The violence of breaking down the door seemed to fill this room with pervading dust. A thin, acrid pall as of the tomb seemed to lie everywhere upon this room decked and furnished as for a bridal: upon the valance curtains of faded rose color, upon the rose-shaded lights, upon the dressing table, upon the delicate array of crystal and the man's toilet things backed with tarnished silver, silver so tarnished that the monogram was obscured. Among them lay a collar and tie, as if they had just been removed, which, lifted, left upon the surface a pale crescent in the dust. Upon a chair hung the suit, carefully folded; beneath it the two mute shoes and the discarded socks.

The man himself lay in the bed.

For a long while we just stood there, looking down at the profound and fleshless grin. The body had apparently once lain in the attitude of an embrace, but now the long sleep that outlasts love, that conquers even the grimace of love, had cuckolded him. What was left of him, rotted beneath what was left of the nightshirt, had become inextricable from the bed in which he lay; and upon him and upon the pillow beside him lay that even coating of the patient and biding dust.

Then we noticed that in the second pillow was the indentation of a head. One of us lifted something from it, and leaning forward, that faint and invisible dust dry and acrid in the nostrils, we saw a long strand of iron-gray hair.

Ernest Hemingway (1899–1961)

The Short Happy Life of Francis Macomber

It was now lunchtime and they were all sitting under the double green fly of the dining tent pretending that nothing had happened.

"Will you have lime juice or lemon squash?" Macomber asked.

"I'll have a gimlet," Robert Wilson told him.

"I'll have a gimlet too. I need something," Macomber's wife said.

"I suppose it's the thing to do," Macomber agreed. "Tell him to make three gimlets."

The mess boy had started them already, lifting the bottles out of the canvas cooling bags that sweated wet in the wind that blew through the trees that shaded the tents.

"What had I ought to give them?" Macomber asked.

"A quid would be plenty," Wilson told him. "You don't want to spoil them."

"Will the headman distribute it?"

"Absolutely."

Francis Macomber had, half an hour before, been carried to his tent from the edge of the camp in triumph on the arms and shoulders of the cook, the personal boys, the skinner and the porters. The gun-bearers had taken no part in the demonstration. When the native boys put him down at the door of his tent, he had shaken all their hands, received their congratulations, and then gone into the tent and sat on the bed until his wife came in. She did not speak to him when she came in and he left the tent at once to wash his face and hands in the portable wash basin outside and go over to the dining tent to sit in a comfortable canvas chair in the breeze and the shade.

"You've got your lion," Robert Wilson said to him, "and a damned fine one too."

Mrs. Macomber looked at Wilson quickly. She was an extremely handsome and well-kept woman of the beauty and social position which had, five years before, commanded five thousand dollars as the price of endorsing, with photographs, a beauty product which she had never used. She had been married to Francis Macomber for eleven years.

"He is a good lion, isn't he?" Macomber said. His wife looked at him now. She looked at both these men as though she had never seen them before.

One, Wilson, the white hunter, she knew she had never truly seen before. He was about middle height with sandy hair, a stubby mustache, a very red face and extremely cold blue eyes with faint white wrinkles at the corners that grooved merrily when he smiled. He smiled at her now and she looked away from his face at the way his shoulders sloped in the loose tunic he wore with the four big cartridges held in loops where the left breast pocket should have been, at his big brown hands, his old slacks, his very dirty boots and back to his red face again. She noticed where the baked red of his face stopped in a white line that marked the circle left by his Stetson hat that hung now from one of the pegs of the tent pole.

"Well, here's to the lion," Robert Wilson said. He smiled at her again and, not smiling, she looked curiously at her husband.

Francis Macomber was very tall, very well built if you did not mind that length of bone, dark, his hair cropped like an oarsman, rather thin-lipped, and was considered handsome. He was dressed in the same sort of safari clothes that Wilson wore except that his were new, he was thirty-five years old, kept himself very fit, was good at court games, had a number of big-game fishing records, and had just shown himself, very publicly, to be a coward.

"Here's to the lion," he said. "I can't ever thank you for what you did."

Margaret, his wife, looked away from him and back to Wilson.

"Let's not talk about the lion," she said.

Wilson looked over at her without smiling and now she smiled at him.

"It's been a very strange day," she said. "Hadn't you ought to put your hat on even under the canvas at noon? You told me that, you know."

"Might put it on," said Wilson.

"You know you have a very red face, Mr. Wilson," she told him and smiled again.

"Drink," said Wilson.

"I don't think so," she said. "Francis drinks a great deal, but his face is never red."

"It's red today," Macomber tried a joke.

"No," said Margaret. "It's mine that's red today. But Mr. Wilson's is always red."

"Must be racial," said Wilson. "I say, you wouldn't like to drop my beauty as a topic, would you?"

"I've just started on it."

"Let's chuck it," said Wilson.

"Conversation is going to be so difficult," Margaret said.

"Don't be silly, Margot," her husband said.

"No difficulty," Wilson said. "Got a damn fine lion."

Margot looked at them both and they both saw that she was going to cry. Wilson had seen it coming for a long time and he dreaded it. Macomber was past dreading it.

"I wish it hadn't happened. Oh, I wish it hadn't happened," she said and started for her tent. She made no noise of crying but they could see that her shoulders were shaking under the rose-colored, sun-proofed shirt she wore.

"Women upset," said Wilson to the tall man. "Amounts to nothing. Strain on the nerves and one thing'n another."

"No," said Macomber. "I suppose that I rate that for the rest of my life now."

"Nonsense. Let's have a spot of the giant killer," said Wilson. "Forget the whole thing. Nothing to it anyway."

"We might try," said Macomber. "I won't forget what you did for me though."

"Nothing," said Wilson. "All nonsense."

So they sat there in the shade where the camp was pitched under some wide-topped acacia trees with a boulder-strewn cliff behind them, and a stretch of grass that ran to the bank of a boulder-filled stream in front with forest beyond it, and drank their just-cool lime drinks and avoided one another's eyes while the boys set the table for lunch. Wilson could tell that the boys all knew about it now and when he saw Macomber's personal boy looking curiously at his master while he was putting dishes on the table he snapped at him in Swahili. The boy turned away with his face blank.

"What were you telling him?" Macomber asked.

"Nothing. Told him to look alive or I'd see he got about fifteen of the best."

"What's that? Lashes?"

"It's quite illegal," Wilson said. "You're supposed to fine them."

"Do you still have them whipped?"

"Oh, yes. They could raise a row if they chose to complain. But they don't. They prefer it to the fines."

"How strange!" said Macomber.

"Not strange, really," Wilson said. "Which would you rather do? Take a good birching or lose your pay?"

Then he felt embarrassed at asking it and before Macomber could answer he went on, "We all take a beating every day, you know, one way or another."

This was no better. "Good God," he thought. "I am a diplomat, aren't I?"

"Yes, we take a beating," said Macomber, still not looking at him. "I'm awfully sorry about that lion business. It doesn't have to go any further, does it? I mean no one will hear about it, will they?"

"You mean will I tell it at the Mathaiga Club?" Wilson looked at him now coldly. He had not expected this. So he's a bloody four-letter man as well as a bloody coward, he thought. I rather liked him too until today. But how is one to know about an American?

"No," said Wilson. "I'm a professional hunter. We never talk about our clients. You can be quite easy on that. It's supposed to be bad form to ask us not to talk though."

He had decided now that to break would be much easier. He would eat, then, by himself and could read a book with his meals. They would eat by themselves. He would see them through the safari on a very formal basis — what was it the French called it? Distinguished consideration — and it would be a damn sight easier than having to go through this emotional trash. He'd insult him and make a good clean break. Then he could read a book with his meals and he'd still be drinking their whisky. That was the phrase for it when a safari went bad. You ran into another white hunter and you asked, "How is everything going?" and he answered, "Oh, I'm still drinking their whisky," and you knew everything had gone to pot.

"I'm sorry," Macomber said and looked at him with his American face that would stay adolescent until it became middle-aged, and Wilson noted his crew-cropped hair, fine eyes only faintly shifty, good nose, thin lips and handsome jaw. "I'm sorry I didn't realize that. There are lots of things I don't know."

So what could he do, Wilson thought. He was all ready to break it off quickly and neatly and here the beggar was apologizing after he had just insulted him. He made one more attempt. "Don't worry about me talking," he said. "I have a living to make. You know in Africa no woman ever misses her lion and no white man ever bolts."

"I bolted like a rabbit," Macomber said.

Now what in hell were you going to do about a man who talked like that, Wilson wondered.

Wilson looked at Macomber with his flat, blue, machine-gunner's eyes and the other smiled back at him. He had a pleasant smile if you did not notice how his eyes showed when he was hurt.

"Maybe I can fix it up on buffalo," he said. "We're after them next, aren't we?"

"In the morning if you like," Wilson told him. Perhaps he had been wrong. This was certainly the way to take it. You most certainly could not tell a damned thing about an American. He was all for Macomber again. If you could forget the morning. But, of course, you couldn't. The morning had been about as bad as they come.

"Here comes the Memsahib," he said. She was walking over from her tent looking refreshed and cheerful and quite lovely. She had a very perfect oval face, so perfect that you expected her to be stupid. But she wasn't stupid, Wilson thought, no, not stupid.

"How is the beautiful red-faced Mr. Wilson? Are you feeling better, Francis, my pearl?"

"Oh, much," said Macomber.

"I've dropped the whole thing," she said, sitting down at the table. "What importance is there to whether Francis is any good at killing lions? That's not his trade. That's Mr. Wilson's trade. Mr. Wilson is really very impressive killing anything. You do kill anything, don't you?"

"Oh, anything," said Wilson. "Simply anything." They are, he thought, the hardest in the world; the hardest, the cruelest, the most predatory and the most attractive and their men have softened or gone to pieces nervously as they have hardened. Or is it that they pick men they can handle? They can't know that much at the age they marry, he thought. He was grateful that he had gone through his education on American women before now because this was a very attractive one.

"We're going after buff in the morning," he told her.

"I'm coming," she said.

"No, you're not."

"Oh, yes, I am. Mayn't I, Francis?"

"Why not stay in camp?"

"Not for anything," she said. "I wouldn't miss something like today for anything."

When she left, Wilson was thinking, when she went off to cry, she seemed a hell of a fine woman. She seemed to understand, to realize, to be hurt for him and for herself and to know how things really stood. She is away for twenty minutes and now she is back, simply enamelled in that American female cruelty. They are the damnedest women. Really the damnedest.

"We'll put on another show for you tomorrow," Francis Macomber said.

"You're not coming," Wilson said.

"You're very mistaken," she told him. "And I want *so* to see you perform again. You were lovely this morning. That is if blowing things' heads off is lovely."

"Here's the lunch," said Wilson. "You're very merry, aren't you?"

"Why not? I didn't come here to be dull."

"Well, it hasn't been dull," Wilson said. He could see the boulders in the river and the high bank beyond with the trees and he remembered the morning.

"Oh, no," she said. "It's been charming. And tomorrow. You don't know how I look forward to tomorrow."

"That's eland he's offering you," Wilson said.

"They're the big cowy things that jump like hares, aren't they?"

"I suppose that describes them," Wilson said.

"It's very good meat," Macomber said.

"Did you shoot it, Francis?" she asked.

"Yes."

"They're not dangerous, are they?"

"Only if they fall on you," Wilson told her.

"I'm so glad."

"Why not let up on the bitchery just a little, Margot," Macomber said, cutting the eland steak and putting some mashed potato, gravy and carrot on the down-turned fork that tined through the piece of meat.

"I suppose I could," she said, "since you put it so prettily."

"Tonight we'll have champagne for the lion," Wilson said. "It's a bit too hot at noon."

"Oh, the lion," Margot said. "I'd forgotten the lion!"

So, Robert Wilson thought to himself, she *is* giving him a ride, isn't she? Or do you suppose that's her idea of putting up a good show? How should a woman act when she discovers her husband is a bloody coward? She's damn cruel but they're all cruel. They govern, of course, and to govern one has to be cruel sometimes. Still, I've seen enough of their damn terrorism.

"Have some more eland," he said to her politely.

That afternoon, late, Wilson and Macomber went out in the motor car with the native driver and the two gun-bearers. Mrs. Macomber stayed in the camp. It was too hot to go out, she said, and she was going with them in the early morning. As they drove off Wilson saw her standing under the big tree, looking pretty rather than beautiful in her faintly rosy khaki, her dark hair drawn back off her forehead and gathered in a knot low on her neck, her face as fresh, he thought, as though she were in England. She waved to them as the car went off through the swale of high grass and curved around through the trees into the small hills of orchard bush.

In the orchard bush they found a herd of impala, and leaving the car they stalked one old ram with long, wide-spread horns and Macomber killed it with a very creditable shot that knocked the buck down at a good two hundred yards and sent the herd off bounding wildly and leaping over one another's backs in long, leg-drawn-up leaps as unbelievable and as floating as those one makes sometimes in dreams.

"That was a good shot," Wilson said. "They're a small target."

"Is it a worth-while head?" Macomber asked.

"It's excellent," Wilson told him. "You shoot like that and you'll have no trouble."

"Do you think we'll find buffalo tomorrow?"

"There's a good chance of it. They feed out early in the morning and with luck we may catch them in the open."

"I'd like to clear away that lion business," Macomber said. "It's not very pleasant to have your wife see you do something like that."

I should think it would be even more unpleasant to do it, Wilson thought, wife or no wife, or to talk about it having done it. But he said, "I wouldn't think about that any more. Any one could be upset by his first lion. That's all over."

But that night after dinner and a whisky and soda by the fire before going to bed, as Francis Macomber lay on his cot with the mosquito bar over him and listened to the night noises it was not all over. It was neither all over nor was it beginning. It was there exactly as it happened with some parts of it indelibly emphasized and he was miserably ashamed at it. But more than shame he felt cold, hollow fear in him. The fear was still there like a cold slimy hollow in all the emptiness where once his confidence had been and it made him feel sick. It was still there with him now.

It had started the night before when he had wakened and heard the lion roaring somewhere up along the river. It was a deep sound and at the end there were sort of coughing grunts that made him seem just outside the tent, and when Francis Macomber woke in the night to hear it he was afraid. He could hear his wife breathing quietly, asleep. There was no one to tell he was afraid, nor to be afraid with him, and, lying alone, he did not know the Somali proverb that says a brave man is always frightened three times by a lion; when he first sees his track, when he first hears him roar and when he first confronts him. Then while they were eating breakfast by lantern light out in the dining tent, before the sun was up, the lion roared again and Francis thought he was just at the edge of camp.

"Sounds like an old-timer," Robert Wilson said, looking up from his kippers and coffee. "Listen to him cough."

"Is he very close?"

"A mile or so up the stream."

"Will we see him?"

"We'll have a look."

"Does his roaring carry that far? It sounds as though he were right in camp."

"Carries a hell of a long way," said Robert Wilson. "It's strange the way it carries. Hope he's a shootable cat. The boys said there was a very big one about here."

"If I get a shot, where should I hit him," Macomber asked, "to stop him?"

"In the shoulders," Wilson said. "In the neck if you can make it. Shoot for bone. Break him down."

"I hope I can place it properly," Macomber said.

"You shoot very well," Wilson told him. "Take your time. Make sure of him. The first one is the one that counts."

"What range will it be?"

"Can't tell. Lion has something to say about that. Won't shoot unless it's close enough so you can make sure."

"At under a hundred yards?" Macomber asked.

Wilson looked at him quickly.

"Hundred's about right. Might have to take him a bit under. Shouldn't chance a shot at much over that. A hundred's a decent range. You can hit him wherever you want at that. Here comes the Memsahib."

"Good morning," she said. "Are we going after that lion?"

"As soon as you deal with your breakfast," Wilson said. "How are you feeling?"

"Marvellous," she said. "I'm very excited."

"I'll just go and see that everything is ready," Wilson went off. As he left the lion roared again.

"Noisy beggar," Wilson said. "We'll put a stop to that."

"What's the matter, Francis?" his wife asked him.

"Nothing," Macomber said.

"Yes, there is," she said. "What are you upset about?"

"Nothing," he said.

"Tell me," she looked at him. "Don't you feel well?"

"It's that damned roaring," he said. "It's been going on all night, you know."

"Why didn't you wake me," she said. "I'd love to have heard it."

"I've got to kill the damned thing," Macomber said, miserably.

"Well, that's what you're out here for, isn't it?"

"Yes. But I'm nervous. Hearing the thing roar gets on my nerves."

"Well then, as Wilson said, kill him and stop his roaring."

"Yes, darling," said Francis Macomber. "It sounds easy, doesn't it?"

"You're not afraid, are you?"

"Of course not. But I'm nervous from hearing him roar all night."

"You'll kill him marvellously," she said. "I know you will. I'm awfully anxious to see it."

"Finish your breakfast and we'll be starting."

"It's not light yet," she said. "This is a ridiculous hour."

Just then the lion roared in a deep-chested moaning, suddenly guttural, ascending vibration that seemed to shake the air and ended in a sigh and a heavy, deep-chested grunt.

"He sounds almost here," Macomber's wife said.

"My God," said Macomber. "I hate that damned noise."

"It's very impressive."

"Impressive. It's frightful."

Robert Wilson came up then carrying his short, ugly, shockingly big-bored .505 Gibbs and grinning.

"Come on," he said. "Your gun-bearer has your Springfield and the big gun. Everything's in the car. Have you solids?"

"Yes."

"I'm ready," Mrs. Macomber said.

"Must make him stop that racket," Wilson said. "You get in front. The Memsahib can sit back here with me."

They climbed into the motor car and, in the gray first daylight, moved off up the river through the trees. Macomber opened the breech of his rifle and saw he had metal-cased bullets, shut the bolt and put the rifle on safety. He saw his hand was trembling. He felt in his pocket for more cartridges and moved his fingers over the cartridges in the loops of his tunic front. He turned back to where Wilson sat in the rear seat of the doorless, bow-bodied motor car beside his wife, them both grinning with excitement, and Wilson leaned forward and whispered,

"See the birds dropping. Means the old boy has left his kill."

On the far bank of the stream Macomber could see, above the trees, vultures circling and plummeting down.

"Chances are he'll come to drink along here," Wilson whispered. "Before he goes to lay up. Keep an eye out."

They were driving slowly along the high bank of the stream which here cut deeply to its boulder-filled bed, and they wound in and out through big trees as they drove. Macomber was watching the opposite bank when he felt Wilson take hold of his arm. The car stopped.

"There he is," he heard the whisper. "Ahead and to the right. Get out and take him. He's a marvellous lion."

Macomber saw the lion now. He was standing almost broadside, his great head up and turned toward them. The early morning breeze that blew toward them was just stirring his dark mane, and the lion looked huge, silhouetted on the rise of bank in the gray morning light, his shoulders heavy, his barrel of a body bulking smoothly.

"How far is he?" asked Macomber, raising his rifle.

"About seventy-five. Get out and take him."

"Why not shoot from where I am?"

"You don't shoot them from cars," he heard Wilson saying in his ear. "Get out. He's not going to stay there all day."

Macomber stepped out of the curved opening at the side of the front seat, onto the step and down onto the ground. The lion still stood looking majestically and coolly toward this object that his eyes only showed in silhouette, bulking like some super-rhino. There was no man smell carried toward him and he watched the object, moving his great head a little from side to side. Then watching the object, not afraid, but hesitating before going down the bank to drink with such a thing opposite him, he saw the man figure detach itself from it and he turned his heavy head and swung away toward the cover of the trees as he heard a cracking crash and felt the slam of a .30–06 220-grain solid bullet that bit his flank and ripped in sudden hot scalding nausea through his stomach. He trotted, heavy, big-footed, swinging wounded full-bellied, through the trees toward the tall grass and cover, and the crash came again to go past him ripping the air apart. Then it crashed again and he felt the blow as it hit his lower ribs and ripped on through, blood sudden hot and frothy in his mouth, and he galloped toward the high grass where he could crouch and not be seen and make them bring the crashing thing close enough so he could make a rush and get the man that held it.

Macomber had not thought how the lion felt as he got out of the car. He only knew his hands were shaking and as he walked away from the car it was almost impossible for him to make his legs move. They were stiff in the thighs, but he could feel the muscles fluttering. He raised the rifle, sighted on the junction of the lion's head and shoulders and pulled the trigger. Nothing happened though he pulled until he thought his finger would break. Then he knew he had the safety on and as he lowered the rifle to move the safety over he moved another frozen pace forward, and the lion seeing his silhouette now clear of the silhouette of the car, turned and started off at a trot, and, as Macomber fired, he heard a whunk that meant that the bullet was home; but the lion kept on going. Macomber shot again and every one saw the bullet throw a spout of dirt beyond the trotting lion. He shot again, remembering to lower his aim, and they all heard the bullet hit, and the lion went into a gallop and was in the tall grass before he had the bolt pushed forward.

Macomber stood there feeling sick at his stomach, his hands that held the Springfield still cocked, shaking, and his wife and Robert

Wilson were standing by him. Beside him too were the two gunbear-
ers chattering in Wakamba.

"I hit him," Macomber said. "I hit him twice."

"You gut-shot him and you hit him somewhere forward," Wilson
said without enthusiasm. The gun-bearers looked very grave. They
were silent now.

"You may have killed him," Wilson went on. "We'll have to wait a
while before we go in to find out."

"What do you mean?"

"Let him get sick before we follow him up."

"Oh," said Macomber.

"He's a hell of a fine lion," Wilson said cheerfully. "He's gotten
into a bad place though."

"Why is it bad?"

"Can't see him until you're on him."

"Oh," said Macomber.

"Come on," said Wilson. "The Memsahib can stay here in the car.
We'll go to have a look at the blood spoor."

"Stay here, Margot," Macomber said to his wife. His mouth was
very dry and it was hard for him to talk.

"Why?" she asked.

"Wilson says to."

"We're going to have a look," Wilson said. "You stay here. You can
see even better from here."

"All right."

Wilson spoke in Swahili to the driver. He nodded and said, "Yes,
Bwana."

Then they went down the steep bank and across the stream, climbing over and around the boulders and up the other bank, pulling up
by some projecting roots, and along it until they found where the lion
had been trotting when Macomber first shot. There was dark blood
on the short grass that the gun-bearers pointed out with grass stems,
and that ran away behind the river bank trees.

"What do we do?" asked Macomber.

"Not much choice," said Wilson. "We can't bring the car over.
Bank's too steep. We'll let him stiffen up a bit and then you and I'll go
in and have a look for him."

"Can't we set the grass on fire?" Macomber asked.

"Too green."

"Can't we send beaters?"

Wilson looked at him appraisingly. "Of course we can," he said.
"But it's just a touch murderous. You see we know the lion's
wounded. You can drive an unwounded lion — he'll move on ahead
of a noise — but a wounded lion's going to charge. You can't see him

until you're right on him. He'll make himself perfectly flat in cover you wouldn't think would hide a hare. You can't very well send boys in there to that sort of a show. Somebody's bound to get mauled."

"What about the gun-bearers?"

"Oh, they'll go with us. It's their *shauri*. You see, they signed on for it. They don't look too happy though, do they?"

"I don't want to go in there," said Macomber. It was out before he knew he'd said it.

"Neither do I, said Wilson very cheerily. "Really no choice though." Then, as an afterthought, he glanced at Macomber and saw suddenly how he was trembling and the pitiful look on his face.

"You don't have to go in, of course," he said. "That's what I'm hired for, you know. That's why I'm so expensive."

"You mean you'd go in by yourself? Why not leave him there?"

Robert Wilson, whose entire occupation had been with the lion and the problem he presented, and who had not been thinking about Macomber except to note that he was rather windy, suddenly felt as though he had opened the wrong door in a hotel and seen something shameful.

"What do you mean?"

"Why not just leave him?"

"You mean pretend to ourselves he hasn't been hit?"

"No. Just drop it."

"It isn't done."

"Why not?"

"For one thing, he's certain to be suffering. For another, some one else might run onto him."

"I see."

"But you don't have to have anything to do with it."

"I'd like to," Macomber said. "I'm just scared, you know."

"I'll go ahead when we go in," Wilson said, "with Kongoni tracking. You keep behind me and a little to one side. Chances are we'll hear him growl. If we see him we'll both shoot. Don't worry about anything. I'll keep you backed up. As a matter of fact, you know, perhaps you'd better not go. It might be much better. Why don't you go over and join the Memsahib while I just get it over with?"

"No, I want to go."

"All right," said Wilson. "But don't go in if you don't want to. This is my *shauri* now, you know."

"I want to go," said Macomber.

They sat under a tree and smoked.

"Want to go back and speak to the Memsahib while we're waiting?" Wilson asked.

"No."

"I'll just step back and tell her to be patient."

"Good," said Macomber. He sat there, sweating under his arms, his mouth dry, his stomach hollow feeling, wanting to find courage to tell Wilson to go on and finish off the lion without him. He could not know that Wilson was furious because he had not noticed the state he was in earlier and sent him back to his wife. While he sat there Wilson came up. "I have your big gun," he said. "Take it. We've given him time, I think. Come on."

Macomber took the big gun and Wilson said:

"Keep behind me and about five yards to the right and do exactly as I tell you." Then he spoke in Swahili to the two gun-bearers who looked the picture of gloom.

"Let's go," he said.

"Could I have a drink of water?" Macomber asked. Wilson spoke to the older gun-bearer, who wore a canteen on his belt, and the man unbuckled it, unscrewed the top and handed it to Macomber, who took it noticing how heavy it seemed and how hairy and shoddy the felt covering was in his hand. He raised it to drink and looked ahead at the high grass with the flat-topped trees behind it. A breeze was blowing toward them and the grass rippled gently in the wind. He looked at the gun-bearer and he could see the gun-bearer was suffering too with fear.

Thirty-five yards into the grass the big lion lay flattened out along the ground. His ears were back and his only movement was a slight twitching up and down of his long, black-tufted tail. He had turned at bay as soon as he had reached this cover and he was sick with the wound through his full belly, and weakening with the wound through his lungs that brought a thin foamy red to his mouth each time he breathed. His flanks were wet and hot and flies were on the little openings the solid bullets had made in his tawny hide, and his big yellow eyes, narrowed with hate, looked straight ahead, only blinking when the pain came as he breathed, and his claws dug in the softbaked earth. All of him, pain, sickness, hatred and all of his remaining strength, was tightening into an absolute concentration for a rush. He could hear the men talking and he waited, gathering all of himself into this preparation for a charge as soon as the men would come into the grass. As he heard their voices his tail stiffened to twitch up and down, and, as they came into the edge of the grass, he made a coughing grunt and charged.

Kongoni, the old gun-bearer, in the lead watching the blood spoor, Wilson watching the grass for any movement, his big gun ready, the second gun-bearer looking ahead and listening, Macomber close to Wilson, his rifle cocked, they had just moved into the grass when Macomber heard the blood-choked coughing grunt, and saw the swishing rush in the grass. The next thing he knew he was running; running wildly, in panic in the open, running toward the stream. He heard the *ca-ra-wong!* of Wilson's big rifle, and again in a second crashing *carawong!* and turning saw the lion, horrible-looking now, with half his head seeming to be gone, crawling toward Wilson in the edge of the tall grass while the red-faced man worked the bolt on the short ugly rifle and aimed carefully as another blasting *carawong!* came from the muzzle, and the crawling, heavy, yellow bulk of the lion stiffened and the huge, mutilated head slid forward and Macomber, standing by himself in the clearing where he had run, holding a loaded rifle, while two black men and a white man looked back at him in contempt, knew the lion was dead. He came toward Wilson, his tallness all seeming a naked reproach, and Wilson looked at him and said:

"Want to take pictures?"

"No," he said.

That was all any one had said until they reached the motor car. Then Wilson had said:

"Hell of a fine lion. Boys will skin him out. We might as well stay here in the shade."

Macomber's wife had not looked at him nor he at her and he had sat by her in the back seat with Wilson sitting in the front seat. Once he had reached over and taken his wife's hand without looking at her and she had removed her hand from his. Looking across the stream to where the gun-bearers were skinning out the lion he could see that she had been able to see the whole thing. While they sat there his wife had reached forward and put her hand on Wilson's shoulder. He turned and she had leaned forward over the low seat and kissed him on the mouth.

"Oh, I say," said Wilson, going redder than his natural baked color.

"Mr. Robert Wilson," she said. "The beautiful red-faced Mr. Robert Wilson."

Then she sat down beside Macomber again and looked away across the stream to where the lion lay, with uplifted, white-muscled, tendon-marked naked forearms, and white bloating belly, as the black men fleshed away the skin. Finally the gun-bearers brought the skin over, wet and heavy, and climbed in behind with it, rolling it up before they got in, and the motor car started. No one had said anything more until they were back in camp.

That was the story of the lion. Macomber did not know how the lion had felt before he started his rush, nor during it when the unbelievable smash of the .505 with a muzzle velocity of two tons had hit him in the mouth, nor what kept him coming after that, when the second ripping crash had smashed his hind quarters and he had come crawling on toward the crashing, blasting thing that had destroyed him. Wilson knew something about it and only expressed it by saying, "Damned fine lion," but Macomber did not know how Wilson felt about things either. He did not know how his wife felt except that she was through with him.

His wife had been through with him before but it never lasted. He was very wealthy, and would be much wealthier, and he knew she would not leave him ever now. That was one of the few things that he really knew. He knew about that, about motor cycles — that was earliest — about motor cars, about duck-shooting, about fishing, trout, salmon and big-sea, about sex in books, many books, too many books, about all court games, about dogs, not much about horses, about hanging on to his money, about most of the other things his world dealt in, and about his wife not leaving him. His wife had been a great beauty and she was still a great beauty in Africa, but she was not a great enough beauty any more at home to be able to leave him and better herself and she knew it and he knew it. She had missed the chance to leave him and he knew it. If he had been better with women she would probably have started to worry about him getting another new, beautiful wife; but she knew too much about him to worry about him either. Also, he had always had a great tolerance which seemed the nicest thing about him if it were not the most sinister.

All in all they were known as a comparatively happily married couple, one of those whose disruption is often rumored but never occurs, and as the society columnist put it, they were adding more than a spice of *adventure* to their much envied and ever-enduring *Romance* by a *Safari* in what was known as *Darkest Africa* until the Martin Johnsons lighted it on so many silver screens where they were pursuing *Old Simba* the lion, the buffalo, *Tembo* the elephant and as well collecting specimens for the Museum of Natural History. This same columnist had reported them *on the verge* at least three times in the past and they had been. But they always made it up. They had a sound basis of union. Margot was too beautiful for Macomber to divorce her and Macomber had too much money for Margot ever to leave him.

It was now about three o'clock in the morning and Francis Macomber, who had been asleep a little while after he had stopped thinking about the lion, wakened and then slept again, woke suddenly, frightened in a dream of the bloody-headed lion standing over him, and listening while his heart pounded, he realized that his wife was not in the other cot in the tent. He lay awake with that knowledge for two hours.

At the end of that time his wife came into the tent, lifted her mosquito bar and crawled cozily into bed.

"Where have you been?" Macomber asked in the darkness.

"Hello," she said. "Are you awake?"

"Where have you been?"

"I just went out to get a breath of air."

"You did, like hell."

"What do you want me to say, darling?"

"Where have you been?"

"Out to get a breath of air."

"That's a new name for it. You *are* a bitch."

"Well, you're a coward."

"All right," he said. "What of it?"

"Nothing as far as I'm concerned. But please let's not talk, darling, because I'm very sleepy."

"You think that I'll take anything."

"I know you will, sweet."

"Well, I won't."

"Please, darling, let's not talk. I'm so very sleepy."

"There wasn't going to be any of that. You promised there wouldn't be."

"Well, there is now," she said sweetly.

"You said if we made this trip that there would be none of that. You promised."

"Yes, darling. That's the way I meant it to be. But the trip was spoiled yesterday. We don't have to talk about it, do we?"

"You don't wait long when you have an advantage, do you?"

"Please let's not talk. I'm so sleepy, darling."

"I'm going to talk."

"Don't mind me then, because I'm going to sleep." And she did.

At breakfast they were all three at the table before daylight and Francis Macomber found that, of all the many men that he had hated, he hated Robert Wilson the most.

"Sleep well?" Wilson asked in his throaty voice, filling a pipe.

"Did you?"

"Topping," the white hunter told him.

You bastard, thought Macomber, you insolent bastard.

So she woke him when she came in, Wilson thought, looking at them both with his flat, cold eyes. Well, why doesn't he keep his wife where she belongs? What does he think I am, a bloody plaster saint? Let him keep her where she belongs. It's his own fault.

"Do you think we'll find buffalo?" Margot asked, pushing away a dish of apricots.

"Chance of it," Wilson said and smiled at her. "Why don't you stay in camp?"

"Not for anything," she told him.

"Why not order her to stay in camp?" Wilson said to Macomber.

"You order her," said Macomber coldly.

"Let's not have any ordering, nor," turning to Macomber, "any silliness, Francis," Margot said quite pleasantly.

"Are you ready to start?" Macomber asked.

"Any time," Wilson told him. "Do you want the Memsahib to go?"

"Does it make any difference whether I do or not?"

The hell with it, thought Robert Wilson. The utter complete hell with it. So this is what it's going to be like. Well, this is what it's going to be like, then.

"Makes no difference," he said.

"You're sure you wouldn't like to stay in camp with her yourself and let me go out and hunt the buffalo?" Macomber asked.

"Can't do that," said Wilson. "Wouldn't talk rot if I were you."

"I'm not talking rot. I'm disgusted."

"Bad word, disgusted."

"Francis, will you please try to speak sensibly?" his wife said.

"I speak too damned sensibly," Macomber said. "Did you ever eat such filthy food?"

"Something wrong with the food?" asked Wilson quietly.

"No more than with everything else."

"I'd pull yourself together, laddybuck," Wilson said very quietly. "There's a boy waits at table that understands a little English."

"The hell with him."

Wilson stood up and puffing on his pipe strolled away, speaking a few words in Swahili to one of the gun-bearers who was standing waiting for him. Macomber and his wife sat on at the table. He was staring at his coffee cup.

"If you make a scene I'll leave you, darling," Margot said quietly.

"No, you won't."

"You can try it and see."

"You won't leave me."

"No," she said. "I won't leave you and you'll behave yourself."

"Behave myself? That's a way to talk. Behave myself."

"Yes. Behave yourself."

"Why don't *you* try behaving?"

"I've tried it so long. So very long."

"I hate that red-faced swine," Macomber said. "I loathe the sight of him."

"He's really *very* nice."

"Oh, *shut up*," Macomber almost shouted. Just then the car came up and stopped in front of the dining tent and the driver and the two gun-bearers got out. Wilson walked over and looked at the husband and wife sitting there at the table.

"Going shooting?" he asked.

"Yes," said Macomber, standing up. "Yes."

"Better bring a woolly. It will be cool in the car," Wilson said.

"I'll get my leather jacket," Margot said.

"The boy has it," Wilson told her. He climbed into the front with the driver and Francis Macomber and his wife sat, not speaking, in the back seat.

Hope the silly beggar doesn't take a notion to blow the back of my head off, Wilson thought to himself. Women *are* a nuisance on safari.

The car was grinding down to cross the river at a pebbly ford in the gray daylight and then climbed, angling up the steep bank, where Wilson had ordered a way shovelled out the day before so they could reach the park-like wooded rolling country on the far side.

It was a good morning, Wilson thought. There was a heavy dew and as the wheels went through the grass and low bushes he could smell the odor of the crushed fronds. It was an odor like verbena and he liked this early morning smell of the dew, the crushed bracken and the look of the tree trunks showing black through the early morning mist, as the car made its way through the untracked, parklike country. He had put the two in the back seat out of his mind now and was thinking about buffalo. The buffalo that he was after stayed in the day-time in a thick swamp where it was impossible to get a shot, but in the night they fed out into an open stretch of country and if he could come between them and their swamp with the car, Macomber would have a good chance at them in the open. He did not want to hunt buff with Macomber in thick cover. He did not want to hunt buff or anything else with Macomber at all, but he was a professional hunter and he had hunted with some rare ones in his time. If they got buff today there would only be rhino to come and the poor man would have gone through his dangerous game and things might pick up. He'd have nothing more to do with the woman and Macomber would get over that too. He must have gone through plenty of that before by the look of things. Poor beggar. He must have a way of getting over it. Well, it was the poor sod's own bloody fault.

He, Robert Wilson, carried a double size cot on safari to accommodate any windfalls he might receive. He had hunted for a certain clientele, the international, fast, sporting set, where the women did not feel they were getting their money's worth unless they had shared that cot with the white hunter. He despised them when he was away from them although he liked some of them well enough at the time, but he made his living by them; and their standards were his standards as long as they were hiring him.

They were his standards in all except the shooting. He had his own standards about the killing and they could live up to them or get some one else to hunt them. He knew, too, that they all respected him for this. This Macomber was an odd one though. Damned if he wasn't. Now the wife. Well, the wife. Yes, the wife. Hm, the wife. Well he'd dropped all that. He looked around at them. Macomber sat grim and furious. Margot smiled at him. She looked younger today, more innocent and fresher and not so professionally beautiful. What's in her heart God knows, Wilson thought. She hadn't talked much last night. At that it was a pleasure to see her.

The motor car climbed up a slight rise and went on through the trees and then out into a grassy prairie-like opening and kept in the shelter of the trees along the edge, the driver going slowly and Wilson looking carefully out across the prairie and all along its far side. He stopped the car and studied the opening with his field glasses. Then he motioned to the driver to go on and the car moved slowly along, the driver avoiding wart-hog holes and driving around the mud castles ants had built. Then, looking across the opening, Wilson suddenly turned and said,

"By God, there they are!"

And looking where he pointed, while the car jumped forward and Wilson spoke in rapid Swahili to the driver, Macomber saw three huge, black animals looking almost cylindrical in their long heaviness, like big black tank cars, moving at a gallop across the far edge of the open prairie. They moved at a stiff-necked, stiff-bodied gallop and he could see the upswept wide black horns on their heads as they galloped heads out; the heads not moving.

"They're three old bulls," Wilson said. "We'll cut them off before they get to the swamp."

The car was going a wild forty-five miles an hour across the open and as Macomber watched, the buffalo got bigger and bigger until he could see the gray, hairless, scabby look of one huge bull and how his neck was a part of his shoulders and the shiny black of his horns as he galloped a little behind the others that were strung out in that steady plunging gait; and then the car swaying as though it had just jumped a road, they drew up close and he could see the plunging hugeness of the bull, and the dust in his sparsely haired hide, the wide boss of horn and his outstretched wide-nostrilled muzzle, and he was raising his rifle when Wilson shouted, "Not from the car, you fool!" and he had no fear, only hatred of Wilson, while the brakes clamped on and the car skidded, plowing sideways to an almost stop and Wilson was out on one side and he on the other, stumbling as his feet hit the still speeding-by of the earth, and then he was shooting at the bull as he moved away, hearing the bullets whunk into him, emptying his rifle at him as he moved steadily away, finally remembering to get his shots forward into the shoulder, and as he fumbled to re-load, he saw the bull was down. Down on his knees, his big head tossing, and seeing the other two still galloping he shot at the leader and hit him. He shot again and missed and he heard the *carawonging* roar as Wilson shot and saw the leading bull slide forward onto his nose.

"Get that other," Wilson said. "Now you're shooting!"

But the other bull was moving steadily at the same gallop and he missed, throwing a spout of dirt, and Wilson missed and the dust rose in a cloud and Wilson shouted, "Come on. He's too far!" and grabbed his arm and they were in the car again, Macomber and Wilson hanging on the sides and rocketing swayingly over the uneven ground, drawing up on the steady, plunging, heavy-necked, straight-moving gallop of the bull.

They were behind him and Macomber was filling his rifle, dropping shells onto the ground, jamming it, clearing the jam, then they were almost up with the bull when Wilson yelled "Stop," and the car skidded so that it almost swung over and Macomber fell forward onto his feet, slammed his bolt forward and fired as far forward as he could aim into the galloping, rounded black back, aimed and shot again, then again, then again, and the bullets, all of them hitting, had no effect on the buffalo that he could see. Then Wilson shot, the roar deafening him, and he could see the bull stagger. Macomber shot again, aiming carefully, and down he came, onto his knees.

"All right," Wilson said. "Nice work. That's the three."

Macomber felt a drunken elation.

"How many times did you shoot?" he asked.

"Just three," Wilson said. "You killed the first bull. The biggest one. I helped you finish the other two. Afraid they might have got into cover. You had them killed. I was just mopping up a little. You shot damn well."

"Let's go to the car," said Macomber. "I want a drink."

"Got to finish off that buff first," Wilson told him. The buffalo was on his knees and he jerked his head furiously and bellowed in pig-eyed, roaring rage as they came toward him.

"Watch he doesn't get up," Wilson said. Then, "Get a little broadside and take him in the neck just behind the ear."

Macomber aimed carefully at the center of the huge, jerking, rage-driven neck and shot. At the shot the head dropped forward.

"That does, it," said Wilson. "Got the spine. They're a hell of a looking thing, aren't they?"

"Let's get the drink," said Macomber. In his life he had never felt so good.

In the car Macomber's wife sat very white faced. "You were marvellous, darling," she said to Macomber. "What a ride."

"Was it rough?" Wilson asked.

"It was frightful. I've never been more frightened in my life."

"Let's all have a drink," Macomber said.

"By all means," said Wilson. "Give it to the Memsahib." She drank the neat whisky from the flask and shuddered a little when she swallowed. She handed the flask to Macomber who handed it to Wilson.

"It was frightfully exciting," she said. "It's given me a dreadful headache. I didn't know you were allowed to shoot them from cars though."

"No one shot from cars," said Wilson coldly.

"I mean chase them from cars."

"Wouldn't ordinarily," Wilson said. "Seemed sporting enough to me though while we were doing it. Taking more chance driving that way across the plain full of holes and one thing and another than hunting on foot. Buffalo could have charged us each time we shot if he liked. Gave him every chance. Wouldn't mention it to any one though. It's illegal if that's what you mean."

"It seemed very unfair to me," Margot said, "chasing those big helpless things in a motor car."

"Did it?" said Wilson.

"What would happen if they heard about it in Nairobi?"

"I'd lose my license for one thing. Other unpleasantnesses," Wilson said, taking a drink from the flask. "I'd be out of business."

"Really?"

"Yes, really."

"Well," said Macomber, and he smiled for the first time all day. "Now she has something on you."

"You have such a pretty way of putting things, Francis," Margot Macomber said. Wilson looked at them both. If a four-letter man marries a five-letter woman, he was thinking, what number of letters would their children be? What he said was, "We lost a gun-bearer. Did you notice it?"

"My God, no," Macomber said.

"Here he comes," Wilson said. "He's all right. He must have fallen off when we left the first bull."

Approaching them was the middle-aged gun-bearer, limping along in his knitted cap, khaki tunic, shorts and rubber sandals, gloomy-faced and disgusted looking. As he came up he called out to Wilson in Swahili and they all saw the change in the white hunter's face.

"What does he say?" asked Margot.

"He says the first bull got up and went into the bush," Wilson said with no expression in his voice.

"Oh," said Macomber blankly.

"Then it's going to be just like the lion," said Margot, full of anticipation.

"It's not going to be a damned bit like the lion," Wilson told her. "Did you want another drink, Macomber?"

"Thanks, yes," Macomber said. He expected the feeling he had had about the lion to come back but it did not. For the first time in his life he really felt wholly without fear. Instead of fear he had a feeling of definite elation.

"We'll go and have a look at the second bull," Wilson said. "I'll tell the driver to put the car in the shade."

"What are you going to do?" asked Margaret Macomber.

"Take a look at the buff," Wilson said.

"I'll come."

"Come along."

The three of them walked over to where the second buffalo bulked blackly in the open, head forward on the grass, the massive horns swung wide.

"He's a very good head," Wilson said. "That's close to a fifty-inch spread." Macomber was looking at him with delight.

"He's hateful looking," said Margot. "Can't we go into the shade?"

"Of course," Wilson said. "Look," he said to Macomber, and pointed. "See that patch of bush?"

"Yes."

"That's where the first bull went in. The gun-bearer said when he fell off the bull was down. He was watching us helling along and the other two buff galloping. When he looked up there was the bull up and looking at him. Gun-bearer ran like hell and the bull went off slowly into that bush."

"Can we go in after him now?" asked Macomber eagerly.

Wilson looked at him appraisingly. Damned if this isn't a strange one, he thought. Yesterday he's scared sick and today he's a ruddy fire eater.

"No, we'll give him a while."

"Let's please go into the shade," Margot said. Her face was white and she looked ill.

They made their way to the car where it stood under a single, wide-spreading tree and all climbed in.

"Chances are he's dead in there," Wilson remarked. "After a little we'll have a look."

Macomber felt a wild unreasonable happiness that he had never known before.

"By God, that was a chase," he said. "I've never felt any such feeling. Wasn't it marvellous, Margot?"

"I hated it."

"Why?"

"I hated it," she said bitterly. "I loathed it."

"You know I don't think I'd ever be afraid of anything again," Macomber said to Wilson. "Something happened in me after we first saw the buff and started after him. Like a dam bursting. It was pure excitement."

"Cleans out your liver," said Wilson. "Damn funny things happen to people."

Macomber's face was shining. "You know something did happen to me," he said. "I feel absolutely different."

His wife said nothing and eyed him strangely. She was sitting far back in the seat and Macomber was sitting forward talking to Wilson who turned sideways talking over the back of the front seat.

"You know, I'd like to try another lion," Macomber said, "I'm really not afraid of them now. After all, what can they do to you?"

"That's it," said Wilson. "Worst one can do is kill you. How does it go? Shakespeare. Damned good. See if I can remember. Oh, damned good. Used to quote it to myself at one time. Let's see. 'By my troth, I care not; a man can die but once; we owe God a death and let it go which way it will he that dies this year is quit for the next.' Damned fine, eh?"

He was very embarrassed, having brought out this thing he had lived by, but he had seen men come of age before and it always moved him. It was not a matter of their twenty-first birthday.

It had taken a strange chance of hunting, a sudden precipitation into action without opportunity for worrying beforehand, to bring this about with Macomber, but regardless of how it had happened it had most certainly happened. Look at the beggar now, Wilson thought. It's that some of them stay little boys so long, Wilson thought. Sometimes all their lives. Their figures stay boyish when they're fifty. The great American boy-men. Damned strange people. But he liked this Macomber now. Damned strange fellow. Probably meant the end of cuckoldry too. Well, that would be a damned good thing. Damned good thing. Beggar had probably been afraid all his life. Don't know what started it. But over now. Hadn't had time to be afraid with the buff. That and being angry too. Motor car too. Motor cars made it familiar. Be a damn fire eater now. He'd seen it in the war work the same way. More of a change than any loss of virginity. Fear gone like an operation. Something else grew in its place. Main thing a man had. Made him into a man. Women knew it too. No bloody fear.

From the far corner of the seat Margaret Macomber looked at the two of them. There was no change in Wilson. She saw Wilson as she had seen him the day before when she had first realized what his great talent was. But she saw the change in Francis Macomber now.

"Do you have that feeling of happiness about what's going to happen?" Macomber asked, still exploring his new wealth.

"You're not supposed to mention it," Wilson said, looking in the other's face. "Much more fashionable to say you're scared. Mind you, you'll be scared too, plenty of times."

"But you *have* a feeling of happiness about action to come?"

"Yes," said Wilson. "There's that. Doesn't do to talk too much about all this. Talk the whole thing away. No pleasure in anything if you mouth it up too much."

"You're both talking rot," said Margot. "Just because you've chased some helpless animals in a motor car you talk like heroes."

"Sorry," said Wilson. "I have been gassing too much." She's worried about it already, he thought.

"If you don't know what we're talking about why not keep out of it?" Macomber asked his wife.

"You've gotten awfully brave, awfully suddenly," his wife said contemptuously, but her contempt was not secure. She was very afraid of something.

Macomber laughed, a very natural hearty laugh. "You know I *have*," he said. "I really have."

"Isn't it sort of late?" Margot said bitterly. Because she had done the best she could for many years back and the way they were together now was no one person's fault.

"Not for me," said Macomber.

Margot said nothing but sat back in the corner of the seat.

"Do you think we've given him time enough?" Macomber asked Wilson cheerfully.

"We might have a look," Wilson said. "Have you any solids left?"

"The gun-bearer has some."

Wilson called in Swahili and the older gun-bearer, who was skinning out one of the heads, straightened up, pulled a box of solids out of his pocket and brought them over to Macomber, who filled his magazine and put the remaining shells in his pocket.

"You might as well shoot the Springfield," Wilson said. "You're used to it. We'll leave the Mannlicher in the car with the Memsahib. Your gun-bearer can carry your heavy gun. I've this damned cannon. Now let me tell you about them."

He had saved this until the last because he did not want to worry

Macomber. "When a buff comes he comes with his head high and thrust straight out. The boss of the horns covers any sort of a brain shot. The only shot is straight into the nose. The only other shot is into his chest or, if you're to one side, into the neck or the shoulders. After they've been hit once they take a hell of a lot of killing. Don't try anything fancy. Take the easiest shot there is. They've finished skinning out that head now. Should we get started?"

He called to the gun-bearers, who came up wiping their hands, and the older one got into the back.

"I'll only take Kongoni," Wilson said. "The other can watch to keep the birds away."

As the car moved slowly across the open space toward the island of brushy trees that ran in a tongue of foliage along a dry water course that cut the open swale, Macomber felt his heart pounding and his mouth was dry again, but it was excitement, not fear.

"Here's where he went in," Wilson said. Then to the gun-bearer in Swahili, "Take the blood spoor."

The car was parallel to the patch of bush. Macomber, Wilson and the gunbearer got down. Macomber, looking back, saw his wife, with the rifle by her side, looking at him. He waved to her and she did not wave back.

The brush was very thick ahead and the ground was dry. The middle-aged gun-bearer was sweating heavily and Wilson had his hat down over his eyes and his red neck showed just ahead of Macomber. Suddenly the gun-bearer said something in Swahili to Wilson and ran forward.

"He's dead in there," Wilson said. "Good work," and he turned to grip Macomber's hand and as they shook hands, grinning at each other, the gun-bearer shouted wildly and they saw him coming out of the bush sideways, fast as a crab, and the bull coming, nose out, mouth tight closed, blood dripping, massive head straight out, coming in a charge, his little pig eyes bloodshot as he looked at them. Wilson, who was ahead, was kneeling shooting, and Macomber, as he fired, unhearing his shot in the roaring of Wilson's gun, saw fragments like slate burst from the huge boss of the horns, and the head jerked, he shot again at the wide nostrils and saw the horns jolt again and fragments fly, and he did not see Wilson now and, aiming carefully, shot again with the buffalo's huge bulk almost on him and his rifle almost level with the oncoming head, nose cut, and he could see the little wicked eyes and the head started to lower and he felt a sudden white-hot, blinding flash explode inside his head and that was all he ever felt.

Wilson had ducked to one side to get in a shoulder shot. Macomber had stood solid and shot for the nose, shooting a touch high each time and hitting the heavy horns, splintering and chipping them like hitting a slate roof, and Mrs. Macomber, in the car, had shot at the buffalo with the 6.5 Mannlicher as it seemed about to gore Macomber and had hit her husband about two inches up and a little to one side of the base of his skull.

Francis Macomber lay now face down, not two yards from where the buffalo lay on his side and his wife knelt over him with Wilson beside her.

"I wouldn't turn him over," Wilson said.

The woman was crying hysterically.

"I'd get back in the car," Wilson said. "Where's the rifle?"

She shook her head, her face contorted. The gun-bearer picked up the rifle.

"Leave it as it is," said Wilson. Then, "Go get Abdulla so that he may witness the manner of the accident."

He knelt down, took a handkerchief from his pocket, and spread it over Francis Macomber's crew-cropped head where it lay. The blood sank into the dry, loose earth.

Wilson stood up and saw the buffalo on his side, his legs out, his thinly-haired belly crawling with ticks. "Hell of a good bull," his brain registered automatically. "A good fifty inches, or better. Better." He called to the driver and told him to spread a blanket over the body and stay by it. Then he walked over to the motor car where the woman sat crying in the corner.

"That was a pretty thing to do," he said in a toneless voice. "He *would* have left you too."

"Stop it," she said.

"Of course it's an accident," he said. "I know that."

"Stop it," she said.

"Don't worry," he said. "There will be a certain amount of unpleasantness but I will have some photographs taken that will be very useful at the inquest. There's the testimony of the gun-bearers and the driver too. You're perfectly all right."

"Stop it," she said.

"There's a hell of a lot to be done," he said. "And I'll have to send a truck off to the lake to wireless for a plane to take the three of us into Nairobi. Why didn't you poison him? That's what they do in England."

"Stop it. Stop it. Stop it," the woman cried.

Wilson looked at her with his flat blue eyes.

"I'm through now," he said. "I was a little angry. I'd begun to like your husband."

"Oh, please stop it," she said. "Please, please stop it."

"That's better," Wilson said. "Please is much better. Now I'll stop."

Shirley Jackson (1919–1965)

The Lottery

The morning of June 27th was clear and sunny, with the fresh warmth of a full-summer day; the flowers were blossoming profusely and the grass was richly green. The people of the village began to gather in the square, between the post office and the bank, around ten o'clock; in some towns there were so many people that the lottery took two days and had to be started on June 26th, but in this village, where there were only about three hundred people, the whole lottery took less than two hours, so it could begin at ten o'clock in the morning and still be through in time to allow the villagers to get home for noon dinner.

The children assembled first, of course. School was recently over for the summer, and the feeling of liberty sat uneasily on most of them; they tended to gather together quietly for a while before they broke into boisterous play, and their talk was still of the classroom and the teacher, of books and reprimands. Bobby Martin had already stuffed his pockets full of stones, and the other boys soon followed his example, selecting the smoothest and roundest stones; Bobby and Harry Jones and Dickie Delacroix — the villagers pronounced this name "Dellacroy" — eventually made a great pile of stones in one corner of the square and guarded it against the raids of the other boys. The girls stood aside, talking among themselves, looking over their shoulders at the boys, and the very small children rolled in the dust or clung to the hands of their older brothers or sisters.

Soon the men began to gather, surveying their own children, speaking of planting and rain, tractors and taxes. They stood together, away from the pile of stones in the corner, and their jokes were quiet and they smiled rather than laughed. The women, wearing faded house dresses and sweaters, came shortly after their menfolk. They greeted one another and exchanged bits of gossip as they went to join their husbands. Soon the women, standing by their husbands, began to call to their children, and the children came reluctantly, having to be called four or five times. Bobby Martin ducked under his mother's grasping hand and ran, laughing, back to the pile of stones. His father spoke up sharply, and Bobby came quickly and took his place between his father and his oldest brother.

The lottery was conducted — as were the square dances, the teenage club, the Halloween program — by Mr. Summers, who had time and energy to devote to civic activities. He was a round-faced, jovial man and he ran the coal business, and people were sorry for him, because he had no children and his wife was a scold. When he arrived in the square, carrying the black wooden box, there was a murmur of conversation among the villagers and he waved and called, "Little late today, folks." The postmaster, Mr. Graves, followed him, carrying a three-legged stool, and the stool was put in the center of the square and Mr. Summers set the black box down on it. The villagers kept their distance, leaving a space between themselves and the stool, and when Mr. Summers said, "Some of you fellows want to give me a hand?" there was a hesitation before two men, Mr. Martin and his oldest son, Baxter, came forward to hold the box steady on the stool while Mr. Summers stirred up the papers inside it.

The original paraphernalia for the lottery had been lost long ago, and the black box now resting on the stool had been put into use even before Old Man Warner, the oldest man in town, was born. Mr. Summers spoke frequently to the villagers about making a new box, but no one liked to upset even as much tradition as was represented by the black box. There was a story that the present box had been made with some pieces of the box that had preceded it, the one that had been constructed when the first people settled down to make a village here. Every year, after the lottery, Mr. Summers began talking again about a new box, but every year the subject was allowed to fade off without anything's being done. The black box grew shabbier each year; by now it was no longer completely black but splintered badly along one side to show the original wood color, and in some places faded or stained.

Mr. Martin and his oldest son, Baxter, held the black box securely on the stool until Mr. Summers had stirred the papers thoroughly with his hand. Because so much of the ritual had been forgotten or discarded, Mr. Summers had been successful in having slips of paper substituted for the chips of wood that had been used for generations. Chips of wood, Mr. Summers had argued, had been all very well when the village was tiny, but now that the population was more than three hundred and likely to keep on growing, it was necessary to use something that would fit more easily into the black box. The night before the lottery, Mr. Summers and Mr. Graves made up the slips of paper and put them in the box, and it was then taken to the safe of Mr. Summers' coal company and locked up until Mr. Summers was ready to take it to the square next morning. The rest of the year, the box was put away, sometimes one place, sometimes another; it had spent one year in Mr. Graves's barn and another year underfoot in the post office, and sometimes it was set on a shelf in the Martin grocery and left there.

There was a great deal of fussing to be done before Mr. Summers declared the lottery open. There were lists to make up — of heads of families, heads of households in each family, members of each household in each family. There was the proper swearing-in of Mr. Summers by the postmaster, as the official of the lottery; at one time, some people remembered, there had been a recital of some sort, performed by the official of the lottery, a perfunctory, tuneless chant that had been rattled off duly each year; some people believed that the official of the lottery used to stand just so when he said or sang it, others believed that he was supposed to walk among the people, but years and years ago this part of the ritual had been allowed to lapse. There had been, also, a ritual salute, which the official of the lottery had had to use in addressing each person who came up to draw from the box, but this also had changed with time, until now it was felt necessary only for the official to speak to each person approaching. Mr. Summers was very good at all this; in his clean white shirt and blue jeans, with one hand resting carelessly on the black box, he seemed very proper and important as he talked interminably to Mr. Graves and the Martins.

Just as Mr. Summers finally left off talking and turned to the assembled villagers, Mrs. Hutchinson came hurriedly along the path to the square, her sweater thrown over her shoulders, and slid into place in the back of the crowd. "Clean forgot what day it was," she said to Mrs. Delacroix, who stood next to her, and they both laughed softly. "Thought my old man was out back stacking wood," Mrs. Hutchinson went on, "and then I looked out the window and the kids were gone, and then I remembered it was the twenty-seventh and came a-running." She dried her hands on her apron, and Mrs. Delacroix said, "You're in time, though. They're still talking away up there."

Mrs. Hutchinson craned her neck to see through the crowd and found her husband and children standing near the front. She tapped Mrs. Delacroix on the arm as a farewell and began to make her way through the crowd. The people separated good-humoredly to let her through; two or three people said, in voices just loud enough to be heard across the crowd, "Here comes your Missus, Hutchinson," and "Bill, she made it after all." Mrs. Hutchinson reached her husband, and Mr. Summers, who had been waiting, said cheerfully, "Thought we were going to have to get on without you, Tessie." Mrs. Hutchinson said, grinning. "Wouldn't have me leave m'dishes in the sink, now would you, Joe?," and soft laughter ran through the crowd as the people stirred back into position after Mrs. Hutchinson's arrival.

"Well, now," Mr. Summers said soberly, "guess we better get started, get this over with, so's we can go back to work. Anybody ain't here?"

"Dunbar," several people said. "Dunbar, Dunbar."

Mr. Summers consulted his list. "Clyde Dunbar," he said. "That's right. He's broke his leg, hasn't he? Who's drawing for him?"

"Me, I guess," a woman said, and Mr. Summers turned to look at her. "Wife draws for her husband," Mr. Summers said. "Don't you have a grown boy to do it for you, Janey?" Although Mr. Summers and everyone else in the village knew the answer perfectly well, it was the business of the official of the lottery to ask such questions formally. Mr. Summers waited with an expression of polite interest while Mrs. Dunbar answered.

"Horace's not but sixteen yet," Mrs. Dunbar said regretfully. "Guess I gotta fill in for the old man this year."

"Right," Mr. Summers said. He made a note on the list he was holding. Then he asked, "Watson boy drawing this year?"

A tall boy in the crowd raised his hand. "Here," he said. "I'm drawing for m'mother and me." He blinked his eyes nervously and ducked his head as several voices in the crowd said things like "Good fellow, Jack," and "Glad to see your mother's got a man to do it."

"Well," Mr. Summers said, "guess that's everyone. Old Man Warner make it?"

"Here," a voice said, and Mr. Summers nodded.

A sudden hush fell on the crowd as Mr. Summers cleared his throat and looked at the list. "All ready?" he called. "Now, I'll read the names — heads of families first — and the men come up and take a paper out of the box. Keep the paper folded in your hand without looking at it until everyone has had a turn. Everything clear?"

The people had done it so many times that they only half listened to the directions, most of them were quiet, wetting their lips, not looking around. Then Mr. Summers raised one hand high and said, "Adams." A man disengaged himself from the crowd and came forward. "Hi, Steve," Mr. Summers said, and Mr. Adams said, "Hi, Joe." They grinned at one another humorlessly and nervously. Then Mr. Adams reached into the black box and took out a folded paper. He held it firmly by one corner as he turned and went hastily back to his place in the crowd, where he stood a little apart from his family, not looking down at his hand.

"Allen," Mr. Summers said. "Anderson. . . . Bentham."

"Seems like there's no time at all between lotteries any more," Mrs. Delacroix said to Mrs. Graves in the back row. "Seems like we got through with the last one only last week."

"Time sure goes fast," Mrs. Graves said.

"Clark. . . . Delacroix."

"There goes my old man," Mrs. Delacroix said. She held her breath while her husband went forward.

"Dunbar," Mr. Summers said, and Mrs. Dunbar went steadily to the box while one of the women said, "Go on, Janey," and another said, "There she goes."

"We're next," Mrs. Graves said. She watched while Mr. Graves came around from the side of the box, greeted Mr. Summers gravely, and selected a slip of paper from the box. By now, all through the crowd there were men holding the small folded papers in their large hands, turning them over and over nervously. Mrs. Dunbar and her two sons stood together, Mrs. Dunbar holding the slip of paper.

"Harburt.... Hutchinson."

"Get up there, Bill," Mrs. Hutchinson said, and the people near her laughed.

"Jones."

"They do say," Mr. Adams said to Old Man Warner, who stood next to him, "that over in the north village they're talking of giving up the lottery."

Old Man Warner snorted, "Pack of crazy fools," he said. "Listening to the young folks, nothing's good enough for *them*. Next thing you know, they'll be wanting to go back to living in caves, nobody work any more, live *that* way for a while. Used to be a saying about 'Lottery in June, corn be heavy soon.' First thing you know, we'd all be eating stewed chickweed and acorns. There's *always* been a lottery," he added petulantly. "Bad enough to see young Joe Summers up there joking with everybody."

"Some places have already quit lotteries," Mrs. Adams said.

"Nothing but trouble in *that*," Old Man Warner said stoutly. "Pack of young fools."

"Martin." And Bobby Martin watched his father go forward. "Overdyke.... Percy."

"I wish they'd hurry," Mrs. Dunbar said to her older son. "I wish they'd hurry."

"They're almost through," her son said.

"You get ready to run tell Dad," Mrs. Dunbar said.

Mr. Summers called his own name and then stepped forward precisely and selected a slip from the box. Then he called, "Warner."

"Seventy-seventh year I been in the lottery," Old Man Warner said as he went through the crowd. "Seventy-seventh time."

"Watson." The tall boy came awkwardly through the crowd. Someone said, "Don't be nervous, Jack," and Mr. Summers said, "Take your time, son."

"Zanini."

After that, there was a long pause, a breathless pause, until Mr. Summers, holding his slip of paper in the air, said, "All right, fellows." For a minute, no one moved, and then all the slips of paper were opened. Suddenly, all women began to speak at once, saying, "Who is it?," "Who's got it?," "Is it the Dunbars?," "Is it the Watsons?" Then the voices began to say, "It's Hutchinson. It's Bill." "Bill Hutchinson's got it."

"Go tell your father," Mrs. Dunbar said to her older son.

People began to look around to see the Hutchinsons. Bill Hutchinson was standing quiet, staring down at the paper in his hand. Suddenly, Tessie Hutchinson shouted to Mr. Summers, "You didn't give him time enough to take any paper he wanted. I saw you. It wasn't fair!"

"Be a good sport, Tessie," Mrs. Delacroix called, and Mrs. Graves said, "All of us took the same chance."

"Shut up, Tessie," Bill Hutchinson said.

"Well, everyone," Mr. Summers said, "that was done pretty fast, and now we've got to be hurrying a little more to get done in time." He consulted his next list. "Bill," he said, "you draw for the Hutchinson family. You got any other households in the Hutchinsons?"

"There's Don and Eva," Mrs. Hutchinson yelled. "Make *them* take their chance!"

"Daughters draw with their husbands' families, Tessie," Mr. Summers said gently. "You know that as well as anyone else."

"It wasn't fair," Tessie said.

"I guess not, Joe," Bill Hutchinson said regretfully. "My daughter draws with her husband's family, that's only fair. And I've got no other family except the kids."

"Then, as far as drawing for families is concerned, it's you," Mr. Summers said in explanation, "and as far as drawing for households is concerned, that's you, too. Right?"

"Right," Bill Hutchinson said.

"How many kids, Bill?" Mr. Summers asked formally.

"Three," Bill Hutchinson said. "There's Bill, Jr., and Nancy, and little Dave. And Tessie and me."

"All right, then," Mr. Summers said. "Harry, you got their tickets back?"

Mr. Graves nodded and held up the slips of paper. "Put them in the box, then," Mr. Summers directed. "Take Bill's and put it in."

"I think we ought to start over," Mrs. Hutchinson said, as quietly as she could. "I tell you it wasn't *fair*. You didn't give him time enough to choose. *Every*body saw that."

Mr. Graves had selected the five slips and put them in the box, and he dropped all the papers but those onto the ground, where the breeze caught them and lifted them off.

"Listen, everybody," Mrs. Hutchinson was saying to the people around her.

"Ready, Bill?" Mr. Summers asked, and Bill Hutchinson, with one quick glance around at his wife and children, nodded.

"Remember," Mr. Summers said, "take the slips and keep them folded until each person has taken one. Harry, you help little Dave." Mr. Graves took the hand of the little boy, who came willingly with him up to the box. "Take a paper out of the box, Davy," Mr. Summers said. Davy put his hand into the box and laughed. "Take just *one* paper," Mr. Summers said. "Harry, you hold it for him." Mr. Graves took the child's hand and removed the folded paper from the tight fist and held it while little Dave stood next to him and looked up at him wonderingly.

"Nancy next," Mr. Summers said. Nancy was twelve, and her school friends breathed heavily as she went forward, switching her skirt, and took a slip daintily from the box. "Bill, Jr.," Mr. Summers said, and Billy, his face red and his feet over-large, nearly knocked the box over as he got a paper out. "Tessie," Mr. Summers said. She hesitated for a minute, looking around defiantly, and then set her lips and went up to the box. She snatched a paper out and held it behind her.

"Bill," Mr. Summers said, and Bill Hutchinson reached into the box and felt around, bringing his hand out at last with the slip of paper in it.

The crowd was quiet. A girl whispered, "I hope it's not Nancy," and the sound of the whisper reached the edges of the crowd.

"It's not the way it used to be," Old Man Warner said clearly. "People ain't the way they used to be."

"All right," Mr. Summers said. "Open the papers. Harry, you open little Dave's."

Mr. Graves opened the slip of paper and there was a general sigh through the crowd as he held it up and everyone could see that it was blank. Nancy and Bill, Jr., opened theirs at the same time, and both beamed and laughed, turning around to the crowd and holding their slips of papers above their heads.

"Tessie," Mr. Summers said. There was a pause, and then Mr. Summers looked at Bill Hutchinson, and Bill unfolded his paper and showed it. It was blank.

"It's Tessie," Mr. Summers said, and his voice was hushed. "Show us her paper, Bill."

Bill Hutchinson went over to his wife and forced the slip of paper out of her hand. It had a black spot on it, the black spot Mr. Summers had made the night before with the heavy pencil in the coal-company office. Bill Hutchinson held it up, and there was a stir in the crowd.

"All right, folks," Mr. Summers said, "Let's finish quickly."

Although the villagers had forgotten the ritual and lost the original black box, they still remembered to use stones. The pile of stones the boys had made earlier was ready; there were stones on the ground with the blowing scraps of paper that had come out of the box. Mrs. Delacroix selected a stone so large she had to pick it up with both hands and turned to Mrs. Dunbar. "Come on," she said. "Hurry up."

Mrs. Dunbar had small stones in both hands, and she said, gasping for breath, "I can't run at all. You'll have to go ahead and I'll catch up with you."

The children had stones already, and someone gave little Davy Hutchinson a few pebbles.

Tessie Hutchinson was in the center of a cleared space by now, and she held her hands out desperately as the villagers moved in on her. "It isn't fair," she said. A stone hit her on the side of the head.

Old Man Warner was saying, "Come on, come on, everyone." Steve Adams was in the front of the crowd of villagers, with Mrs. Graves beside him.

"It isn't fair, it isn't right," Mrs. Hutchinson screamed, and then they were upon her.

Doris Lessing (b. 1919)

A Man and Two Women

Stella's friends the Bradfords had taken a cheap cottage in Essex for the summer, and she was going down to visit them. She wanted to see them, but there was no doubt there was something of a letdown (and for them too) in the English cottage. Last summer Stella had been wandering with her husband around Italy; had seen the English couple at a café table, and found them sympathetic. They all liked each other, and the four went about for some weeks, sharing meals, hotels, trips. Back in London the friendship had not, as might have been expected, fallen off. Then Stella's husband departed abroad, as he often did, and Stella saw Jack and Dorothy by herself. There were a great many people she might have seen but it was the Bradfords she saw most often, two or three times a week, at their flat or hers. They were at ease with each other. Why were they? Well, for one thing they were all artists — in different ways. Stella designed wallpapers and materials; she had a name for it.

The Bradfords were real artists. He painted, she drew. They had lived mostly out of England in cheap places around the Mediterranean. Both from the North of England, they had met at art school, married at twenty, had taken flight from England, then returned to it, needing it, then off again: and so on, for years, in the rhythm of so many of their kind, needing, hating, loving England. There had been seasons of real poverty, while they lived on *pasta* or bread or rice, and wine and fruit and sunshine, in Majorca, southern Spain, Italy, North Africa.

A French critic had seen Jack's work, and suddenly he was successful. His show in Paris, then one in London, made money; and now he charged in the hundreds where a year or so ago he charged ten or twenty guineas. This had deepened his contempt for the values of the markets. For a while Stella thought that this was the bond between the Bradfords and herself. They were so very much, as she was, of the new generation of artists (and poets and playwrights and novelists) who had one thing in common, a cool derision about the racket. They were so very unlike (they felt) the older generation with their societies and their lunches and their salons and their cliques: their atmosphere of connivance with the snobberies of success. Stella, too, had been successful by a fluke. Not that she did not consider herself talented; it was that others as talented were unfêted, and unbought. When she was with the Bradfords and other fellow spirits, they would talk about the racket, using each other as yardsticks or fellow consciences about how much to give in, what to give, how to use without being used, how to enjoy without becoming dependent on enjoyment.

Of course Dorothy Bradford was not able to talk in quite the same way, since she had not yet been "discovered"; she had not "broken through." A few people with discrimination bought her unusual delicate drawings, which had a strength that was hard to understand unless one knew Dorothy herself. But she was not at all, as Jack was, a great success. There was a strain here, in the marriage, nothing much; it was kept in check by their scorn for their arbitrary rewards of "the racket." But it was there, nevertheless.

Stella's husband had said: "Well, I can understand that, it's like me and you — you're creative, whatever that may mean, I'm just a bloody TV journalist." There was no bitterness in this. He was a good journalist, and besides he sometimes got the chance to make a good small film. All the same, there was that between him and Stella, just as there was between Jack and his wife.

After a time Stella saw something else in her kinship with the couple. It was that the Bradfords had a close bond, bred of having spent so many years together in foreign places, dependent on each other because of their poverty. It had been a real love marriage, one could see it by looking at them. It was now. And Stella's marriage was a real marriage. She understood she enjoyed being with the Bradfords because the two couples were equal in this. Both marriages were those of strong, passionate, talented individuals; they shared a battling quality that strengthened them, not weakened them.

The reason why it had taken Stella so long to understand this was that the Bradfords had made her think about her own marriage, which she was beginning to take for granted, sometimes even found exhausting. She had understood, through them, how lucky she was in her husband; how lucky they all were. No marital miseries; nothing of (what they saw so often in friends) one partner in a marriage victim to the other, resenting the other; no claiming of outsiders as sympathizers or allies in an unequal battle.

There had been a plan for these four people to go off again to Italy or Spain, but then Stella's husband departed, and Dorothy got pregnant. So there was the cottage in Essex instead, a bad second choice, but better, they all felt, to deal with a new baby on home ground, at least for the first year. Stella, telephoned by Jack (on Dorothy's particular insistence, he said), offered and received commiserations on its being only Essex and not Majorca or Italy. She also received sympathy because her husband had been expected back this weekend, but had wired to say he wouldn't be back for another month, probably — there was trouble in Venezuela. Stella wasn't really forlorn; she didn't mind living alone, since she was always supported by knowing her man would be back. Besides, if she herself were offered the chance of a month's "trouble" in Venezuela, she wouldn't hesitate, so it wasn't unfair . . . fairness characterized their relationship. All the same, it was nice that she could drop down (or up) to the Bradfords, people with whom she could always be herself, neither more nor less.

She left London at midday by train, armed with food unobtainable in Essex: salamis, cheeses, spices, wine. The sun shone, but it wasn't particularly warm. She hoped there would be heating in the cottage, July or not.

The train was empty. The little station seemed stranded in a green nowhere. She got out, cumbered by bags full of food. A porter and a stationmaster examined, then came to succour her. She was a tallish, fair woman, rather ample; her soft hair, drawn back escaped in tendrils, and she had great helpless-looking blue eyes. She wore a dress made in one of the materials she had designed. Enormous green leaves laid hands all over her body, and fluttered about her knees. She stood smiling, accustomed to men running to wait on her, enjoying them enjoying her. She walked with them to the barrier where

Jack waited, appreciating the scene. He was a smallish man, compact, dark. He wore a blue-green summer shirt, and smoked a pipe and smiled, watching. The two men delivered her into the hands of the third, and departed, whistling, to their duties.

Jack and Stella kissed, then pressed their cheeks together.

"Food," he said, "food," relieving her of the parcels.

"What's it like here, shopping?"

"Vegetables all right, I suppose."

Jack was still Northern in this: he seemed brusque, to strangers; he wasn't shy, he simply hadn't been brought up to enjoy words. Now he put his arm briefly around Stella's waist, and said: "Marvellous, Stell, marvellous." They walked on, pleased with each other. Stella had with Jack, her husband had with Dorothy, these moments, when they said to each other wordlessly: If I were not married to my husband, if you were not married to your wife, how delightful it would be to be married to you. These moments were not the least of the pleasures of this four-sided friendship.

"Are you liking it down here?"

"It's what we bargained for."

There was more than his usual shortness in this, and she glanced at him to find him frowning. They were walking to the car, parked under a tree.

"How's the baby?"

"Little bleeder never sleeps, he's wearing us out, but he's fine."

The baby was six weeks old. Having the baby was a definite achievement: getting it safely conceived and born had taken a couple of years. Dorothy, like most independent women, had had divided thoughts about a baby. Besides, she was over thirty and complained she was set in her ways. All this — the difficulties, Dorothy's hesitations — had added up to an atmosphere which Dorothy herself described as "like wondering if some damned horse is going to take the fence." Dorothy would talk, while she was pregnant, in a soft staccato voice: "Perhaps I don't really want a baby at all? Perhaps I'm not fitted to be a mother? Perhaps . . . and if so . . . and how . . . ?"

She said: "Until recently Jack and I were always with people who took it for granted that getting pregnant was a disaster, and now suddenly all the people we know have young children and baby-sitters and . . . perhaps . . . if . . ."

Jack said: "You'll feel better when it's born."

Once Stella had heard him say, after one of Dorothy's long troubled dialogues with herself: "Now that's enough, that's enough, Dorothy." He had silenced her, taking the responsibility.

They reached the car, got in. It was a second-hand job recently bought. "They" (being the press, the enemy generally) "wait for us" (being artists or writers who have made money) "to buy flashy cars." They had discussed it, decided that *not* to buy an expensive car if they felt like it would be allowing themselves to be bullied; but bought a second-hand one after all. Jack wasn't going to give *them* so much satisfaction, apparently.

"Actually we could have walked," he said, as they shot down a narrow lane, "but with these groceries, it's just as well."

"If the baby's giving you a tough time, there can't be much time for cooking." Dorothy was a wonderful cook. But now again there was something in the air as he said: "Food's definitely not too good just now. You can cook supper, Stell, we could do with a good feed."

Now Dorothy hated anyone in her kitchen, except, for certain specified jobs, her husband; and this was surprising.

"The truth is, Dorothy's worn out," he went on, and now Stella understood he was warning her.

"Well, it is tiring," said Stella soothingly.

"You were like that?"

Like that was saying a good deal more than just worn out, or tired, and Stella understood that Jack was really uneasy. She said, plaintively humorous: "You two always expect me to remember things that happened a hundred years ago. Let me think. . . ."

She had been married when she was eighteen, got pregnant at once. Her husband had left her. Soon she had married Philip, who also had a small child from a former marriage. These two children, her daughter, seventeen, his son, twenty, had grown up together.

She remembered herself at nineteen, alone, with a small baby. "Well, I was alone," she said. "That makes a difference. I remember I was exhausted. Yes, I was definitely irritable and unreasonable."

"Yes," said Jack, with a brief reluctant look at her.

"All right, don't worry," she said, replying aloud as she often did to things that Jack had not said aloud.

"Good," he said.

Stella thought of how she had seen Dorothy, in the hospital room, with the new baby. She had sat up in bed, in a pretty bed jacket, the baby beside her in a basket. He was restless. Jack stood between basket and bed, one large hand on his son's stomach. "Now, you just shut up, little bleeder," he had said, as he grumbled. Then he had picked him up, as if he'd been doing it always, held him against his shoulder, and, as Dorothy held her arms out, had put the baby into them. "Want your mother, then? Don't blame you."

That scene, the ease of it, the way the two parents were together, had, for Stella, made nonsense of all the months of Dorothy's self-questioning. As for Dorothy, she had said, parodying the expected words but meaning them: "He's the most beautiful baby ever born. I can't imagine why I didn't have him before."

"There's the cottage," said Jack. Ahead of them was a small labourer's cottage, among full green trees, surrounded by green grass. It was painted white, had four sparkling windows. Next to it a long shed or structure that turned out to be a greenhouse.

"The man grew tomatoes," said Jack. "Fine studio now."

The car came to rest under another tree.

"Can I just drop in to the studio?"

"Help yourself." Stella walked into the long, glass-roofed shed. In London Jack and Dorothy shared a studio. They had shared huts, sheds, any suitable building, all around the Mediterranean. They always worked side by side. Dorothy's end was tidy, exquisite, Jack's lumbered with great canvases, and he worked in a clutter. Now Stella looked to see if this friendly arrangement continued, but as Jack came in behind her he said: "Dorothy's not set herself up yet. I miss her, I can tell you."

The greenhouse was still partly one: trestles with plants stood along the ends. It was lush and warm.

"As hot as hell when the sun's really going, it makes up. And Dorothy brings Paul in sometimes, so he can get used to a decent climate young."

Dorothy came in, at the far end, without the baby. She had recovered her figure. She was a small dark woman, with neat, delicate limbs. Her face was white, with scarlet rather irregular lips, and black glossy brows, a little crooked. So while she was not pretty, she was lively and dramatic-looking. She and Stella had their moments together, when they got pleasure from contrasting their differences, one woman so big and soft and blond, the other so dark and vivacious.

Dorothy came forward through shafts of sunlight, stopped, and said: "Stella, I'm glad you've come." Then forward again, to a few steps off, where she stood looking at them. "You two look good together," she said, frowning. There was something heavy and over-emphasized about both statements, and Stella said: "I was wondering what Jack had been up to."

"Very good, I think," said Dorothy, coming to look at the new canvas on the easel. It was of sunlit rocks, brown and smooth, with blue sky, blue water, and people swimming in spangles of light. When Jack was in the South he painted pictures that his wife described as "dirt and grime and misery"— which was how they both described their joint childhood background. When he was in England he painted scenes like these.

"Like it? It's good, isn't it?" said Dorothy.

"Very much," said Stella. She always took pleasure from the contrast between Jack's outward self — the small, self-contained little man who could have vanished in a moment into a crowd of factory workers in, perhaps Manchester, and the sensuous bright pictures like these.

"And you?" asked Stella.

"Having a baby's killed everything creative in me — quite different from being pregnant," said Dorothy, but not complaining of it. She had worked like a demon while she was pregnant.

"Have a heart," said Jack, "he's only just got himself born."

"Well, I don't care," said Dorothy. "That's the funny thing, I *don't* care." She said this flat, indifferent. She seemed to be looking at them both again from a small troubled distance. "You two look good together," she said, and again there was the small jar.

"Well, how about some tea?" said Jack, and Dorothy said at once: "I made it when I heard the car. I thought better inside, it's not really hot in the sun." She led the way out of the greenhouse, her white linen dress dissolving in lozenges of yellow light from the glass panes above, so that Stella was reminded of the white limbs of Jack's swimmers disintegrating under sunlight in his new picture. The work of these two people was always reminding one of each other, or each other's work, and in all kinds of ways: they were so much married, so close.

The time it took to cross the space of rough grass to the door of the little house was enough to show Dorothy was right: it was really chilly in the sun. Inside two electric heaters made up for it. There had been two little rooms downstairs, but they had been knocked into one fine low-ceilinged room, stone-floored, whitewashed. A tea table, covered with a purple checked cloth, stood waiting near a window where flowering bushes and trees showed through clean panes. Charming. They adjusted the heaters and arranged themselves so they could admire the English countryside through glass. Stella looked for the baby; Dorothy said: "In the pram at the back." Then she asked: "Did yours cry a lot?"

Stella laughed and said again: "I'll try to remember."

"We expect you to guide and direct, with all your experience," said Jack.

"As far as I can remember, she was a little demon for about three months, for no reason I could see, then suddenly she became civilized."

"Roll on the three months," said Jack.

"Six weeks to go," said Dorothy, handling teacups in a languid indifferent manner Stella found new in her.

"Finding it tough going?"

"I've never felt better in my life," said Dorothy at once, as if being accused.

"You look fine."

She looked a bit tired, nothing much; Stella couldn't see what reason there was for Jack to warn her. Unless he meant the languor, a look of self-absorption? Her vivacity, a friendly aggressiveness that was the expression of her lively intelligence, was dimmed. She sat leaning back in a deep armchair, letting Jack manage things, smiling vaguely.

"I'll bring him in in a minute," she remarked, listening to the silence from the sunlit garden at the back.

"Leave him," said Jack. "He's quiet seldom enough. Relax, woman, and have a cigarette."

He lit a cigarette for her, and she took it in the same vague way, and sat breathing out smoke, her eyes half closed.

"Have you heard from Philip?" she asked, not from politeness, but with sudden insistence.

"Of course she has, she got a wire," said Jack.

"I want to know how she feels," said Dorothy. "How do you feel, Stell?" She was listening for the baby all the time.

"Feel about what?"

"About his not coming back."

"But he is coming back, it's only a month," said Stella, and heard, with surprise, that her voice sounded edgy.

"You see?" said Dorothy to Jack, meaning the words, not the edge on them.

At this evidence that she and Philip had been discussed, Stella felt, first, pleasure: because it was pleasurable to be understood by two such good friends, then she felt discomfort, remembering Jack's warning.

"See what?" she asked Dorothy, smiling.

"That's enough now," said Jack to his wife in a flash of stubborn anger, which continued the conversation that had taken place.

Dorothy took direction from her husband, and kept quiet a moment, then seemed impelled to continue: "I've been thinking it must be nice, having your husband go off, then come back. Do you realise Jack and I haven't been separated since we married? That's over ten years. Don't you think there's something awful in two grown people stuck together all the time like Siamese twins?" This ended in a wail of genuine appeal to Stella.

"No, I think it's marvellous."

"But you don't mind being alone so much?"

"It's not so much, it's two or three months in a year. Well of course I mind. But I enjoy being alone, really. But I'd enjoy it too if we were together all the time. I envy you two." Stella was surprised to find her eyes wet with self-pity because she had to be without her husband another month.

"And what does he think?" demanded Dorothy. "What does Philip think?"

Stella said: "Well, I think he likes getting away from time to time — yes. He likes intimacy, he enjoys it, but it doesn't come as easily to him as it does to me." She had never said this before because she had never thought about it. She was annoyed with herself that she had had to wait for Dorothy to prompt her. Yet she knew that getting annoyed was what she must not do, with the state Dorothy was in, whatever it was. She glanced at Jack for guidance, but he was determinedly busy on his pipe.

"Well, I'm like Philip," announced Dorothy. "Yes, I'd love it if Jack went off sometimes. I think I'm being stifled being shut up with Jack day and night, year in year out."

"Thanks," said Jack, short but good-humoured.

"No, but I mean it. There's something humiliating about two adult people never for one second out of each other's sight."

"Well," said Jack, "when Paul's a bit bigger, you buzz off for a month or so and you'll appreciate me when you get back."

"It's not that I don't appreciate you, it's not that at all," said Dorothy, insistent, almost strident, apparently fevered with restlessness. Her languor had quite gone, and her limbs jerked and moved. And now the baby, as if he had been prompted by his father's mentioning him, let out a cry. Jack got up, forestalling his wife, saying: "I'll get him."

Dorothy sat, listening for her husband's movements with the baby, until he came back, which he did, supporting the infant sprawled against his shoulder with a competent hand. He sat down, let his son slide onto his chest, and said: "There now, you shut up and leave us in peace a bit longer." The baby was looking up into his face with the astonished expression of the newly born, and Dorothy sat smiling at both of them. Stella understood that her restlessness, her repeated curtailed movements, meant that she longed — more, needed — to have the child in her arms, have its body against hers. And Jack seemed to feel this, because Stella could have sworn it was not a conscious decision that made him rise and slide the infant into his wife's arms. Her flesh, her needs, had spoken direct to him without words, and he had risen at once to give her what she wanted. This silent instinctive conversation between husband and wife made Stella miss her own husband violently, and with resentment against fate that kept them apart so often. She ached for Philip.

Meanwhile Dorothy, now the baby was sprawled softly against

her chest, the small feet in her hand, seemed to have lapsed into good humour. And Stella, watching, remembered something she really had forgotten: the close, fierce physical tie between herself and her daughter when she had been a tiny baby. She saw this bond in the way Dorothy stroked the small head that trembled on its neck as the baby looked up into his mother's face. Why, she remembered it was like being in love, having a new baby. All kinds of forgotten or unused instincts woke in Stella. She lit a cigarette, took herself in hand; set herself to enjoy the other woman's love affair with her baby instead of envying her.

The sun, dropping into the trees, struck the windowpanes; and there was a dazzle and a flashing of yellow and white light into the room, particularly over Dorothy in her white dress and the baby. Again Stella was reminded of Jack's picture of the white-limbed swimmers in sun-dissolving water. Dorothy shielded the baby's eyes with her hand and remarked dreamily: "This is better than any man, isn't it, Stell? Isn't it better than any man?"

"Well — no," said Stella laughing. "No, not for long."

"If you say so, you should know . . . but I can't imagine ever . . . tell me, Stell, does your Philip have affairs when he's away?"

"For God's sake!" said Jack, angry. But he checked himself.

"Yes, I am sure he does."

"Do you mind?" asked Dorothy, loving the baby's feet with her enclosing palm.

And now Stella was forced to remember, to think about having minded, minding, coming to terms, and the ways in which she now did not mind.

"I don't think about it," she said.

"Well, I don't think I'd mind," said Dorothy.

"Thanks for letting me know," said Jack, short despite himself. Then he made himself laugh.

"And you, do you have affairs while Philip's away?"

"Sometimes. Not really."

"Do you know, Jack was unfaithful to me this week," remarked Dorothy, smiling at the baby.

"That's *enough*," said Jack, really angry.

"No it isn't enough, it isn't. Because what's awful is, I don't care."

"Well why should you care, in the circumstances?" Jack turned to Stella. "There's a silly bitch Lady Edith lives across that field. She got all excited, real live artists living down her lane. Well Dorothy was lucky, she had an excuse in the baby, but I had to go to her silly party. Booze flowing in rivers, and the most incredible people — you know. If you read about them in a novel you'd never believe . . . but I can't remember much after about twelve."

"Do you know what happened?" said Dorothy. "I was feeding the baby, it was terribly early. Jack sat straight up in bed and said: 'Jesus, Dorothy, I've just remembered, I screwed that silly bitch Lady Edith on her brocade sofa.' "

Stella laughed. Jack let out a snort of laughter. Dorothy laughed, an unscrupulous chuckle of appreciation. Then she said seriously: "But that's the point, Stella — the thing is, I don't care a tuppenny damn."

"But why should you?" asked Stella.

"But it's the first time he ever has, and surely I should have minded?"

Don't you be too sure of that," said Jack, energetically puffing his pipe. "Don't be too sure." But it was only for form's sake, and Dorothy knew it, and said: "Surely I should have cared, Stell?"

"No. You'd have cared if you and Jack weren't so marvellous together. Just as I'd care if Philip and I weren't. . . ." Tears came running down her face. She let them. These were her good friends; and besides, instinct told her tears weren't a bad thing, with Dorothy in this mood. She said, sniffing: "When Philip gets home, we always have a flaming bloody row in the first day or two, about something unimportant, but what it's really about, and we know it, is that I'm jealous of any affair he's had and vice versa. Then we go to bed and make up." She wept, bitterly, thinking of this happiness, postponed for a month, to be succeeded by the delightful battle of their day to day living.

"Oh Stella," said Jack. "Stell . . ." He got up, fished out a handkerchief, dabbed her eyes for her. "There, love, he'll be back soon."

"Yes, I know. It's just that you two are so good together and whenever I'm with you I miss Philip."

"Well, I suppose we're good together?" said Dorothy, sounding surprised. Jack, bending over Stella with his back to his wife, made a warning grimace, then stood up and turned, commanding the situation. "It's nearly six. You'd better feed Paul. Stella's going to cook supper."

"Is she? How nice," said Dorothy. "There's everything in the kitchen, Stella. How lovely to be looked after."

"I'll show you our mansion," said Jack.

Upstairs were two small white rooms. One was the bedroom, with their things and the baby's in it. The other was an overflow room, jammed with stuff. Jack picked up a large leather folder off the spare bed and said: "Look at these, Stell." He stood at the window, back to her, his thumb at work in his pipe bowl, looking into the garden. Stella sat on the bed, opened the folder and at once exclaimed: "When did she do these?"

"The last three months she was pregnant. Never seen anything like it, she just turned them out one after the other."

There were a couple of hundred pencil drawings, all of two bodies in every kind of balance, tension, relationship. The two bodies were Jack's and Dorothy's, mostly unclothed, but not all. The drawings startled, not only because they marked a real jump forward in Dorothy's achievement, but because of their bold sensuousness. They were a kind of chant, or exaltation about the marriage. The instinctive closeness, the harmony of Jack and Dorothy, visible in every movement they made towards or away from each other, visible even when they were not together, was celebrated here with a frank, calm triumph.

"Some of them are pretty strong," said Jack, the Northern working-class boy reviving in him for a moment's puritanism.

But Stella laughed, because the prudishness masked pride: some of the drawings were indecent.

In the last few of the series the woman's body was swollen in pregnancy. They showed her trust in her husband, whose body, commanding hers, stood or lay in positions of strength and confidence. In the very last Dorothy stood turned away from her husband, her two hands supporting her big belly, and Jack's hands were protective on her shoulders.

"They are marvellous," said Stella.

"They are, aren't they."

Stella looked, laughing, and with love, towards Jack; for she saw that his showing her the drawings was not only pride in his wife's talent; but that he was using this way of telling Stella not to take Dorothy's mood too seriously. And to cheer himself up. She said, impulsively: "Well that's all right then, isn't it?"

"What? Oh yes, I see what you mean, yes, I think it's all right."

"Do you know what?" said Stella, lowering her voice. "I think Dorothy's guilty because she feels unfaithful to you."

"What?"

"No, I mean, with the baby, and that's what it's all about."

He turned to face her, troubled, then slowly smiling. There was the same rich unscrupulous quality of appreciation in that smile as there had been in Dorothy's laugh over her husband and Lady Edith. "You think so?" They laughed together, irrepressibly and loudly.

"What's the joke?" shouted Dorothy.

"I'm laughing because your drawings are so good," shouted Stella.

"Yes, they are, aren't they?" But Dorothy's voice changed to flat incredulity: "The trouble is, I can't imagine how I ever did them, I can't imagine ever being able to do it again."

"Downstairs," said Jack to Stella, and they went down to find

Dorothy nursing the baby. He nursed with his whole being, all of him in movement. He was wrestling with the breast, thumping Dorothy's plump pretty breast with his fists. Jack stood looking down at the two of them, grinning. Dorothy reminded Stella of a cat, half closing her yellow eyes to stare over her kittens at work on her side, while she stretched out a paw where claws sheathed and unsheathed themselves, making a small rip-rip-rip on the carpet she lay on.

"You're a savage creature," said Stella, laughing.

Dorothy raised her small vivid face and smiled. "Yes, I am," she said, and looked at the two of them calm, and from a distance, over the head of her energetic baby.

Stella cooked supper in a stone kitchen, with a heater brought by Jack to make it tolerable. She used the good food she had brought with her, taking trouble. It took some time, then the three ate slowly over a big wooden table. The baby was not asleep. He grumbled for some minutes on a cushion on the floor, then his father held him briefly, before passing him over, as he had done earlier, in response to his mother's need to have him close.

"I'm supposed to let him cry," remarked Dorothy. "But why should he? If he were an Arab or an African baby he'd be plastered to my back."

"And very nice too," said Jack. "I think they come out too soon into the light of day, they should just stay inside for about eighteen months, much better all around."

"Have a heart," said Dorothy and Stella together, and they all laughed; but Dorothy added, quite serious: "Yes, I've been thinking so too."

This good nature lasted through the long meal. The light went cool and thin outside; and inside they let the summer dusk deepen, without lamps.

"I've got to go quite soon," said Stella, with regret.

"Oh, no, you've got to stay!" said Dorothy, strident. It was sudden, the return of the woman who made Jack and Dorothy tense themselves to take strain.

"We all thought Philip was coming. The children will be back tomorrow night, they've been on holiday."

"Then stay till tomorrow, I *want* you," said Dorothy, petulant.

"But I can't," said Stella.

"I never thought I'd want another woman around, cooking in my kitchen, looking after me, but I do," said Dorothy, apparently about to cry.

"Well, love, you'll have to put up with me," said Jack.

"Would you mind, Stell?"

"Mind *what?*" asked Stella, cautious.

"Do you find Jack attractive?"

"Very."

"Well I know you do. Jack, do you find Stella attractive?"

"Try me," said Jack, grinning; but at the same time signalling warnings to Stella.

"Well, then!" said Dorothy.

"A *ménage à trois?*" asked Stella laughing. "And how about my Philip? Where does he fit in?"

"Well, if it comes to that, I wouldn't mind Philip myself," said Dorothy, knitting her sharp black brows and frowning.

"I don't blame you," said Stella, thinking of her handsome husband.

"Just for a month, till he comes back," said Dorothy. "I tell you what, we'll abandon this silly cottage, we must have been mad to stick ourselves away in England in the first place. The three of us'll just pack up and go off to Spain or Italy with the baby."

"And what else?" enquired Jack, good-natured at all costs, using his pipe as a safety valve.

"Yes, I've decided I approve of polygamy," announced Dorothy. She had opened her dress and the baby was nursing again, quietly this time, relaxed against her. She stroked his head, softly, softly, while her voice rose and insisted at the other two people: "I never understood it before, but I do now. I'll be the senior wife, and you two can look after me."

"Any other plans?" enquired Jack, angry now. "You just drop in from time to time to watch Stella and me have a go, is that it? Or are you going to tell us when we can go off and do it, give us your gracious permission?"

"Oh I don't care what you do, that's the point," said Dorothy, sighing, sounding forlorn, however.

Jack and Stella, careful not to look at each other, sat waiting.

"I read something in the newspaper yesterday, it struck me," said Dorothy, conversational. "A man and two women living together — here, in England. They are both his wives, they consider themselves his wives. The senior wife has a baby, and the younger wife sleeps with him — well, that's what it looked like, reading between the lines."

"You'd better stop reading between lines," said Jack. "It's not doing you any good."

"No, I'd like it," insisted Dorothy. "I think our marriages are silly. Africans and people like that, they know better, they've got some sense."

"I can just see you if I did make love to Stella," said Jack.

"Yes!" said Stella, with a short laugh which, against her will, was resentful.

"But I wouldn't mind," said Dorothy, and burst into tears.

"Now, Dorothy, that's enough," said Jack. He got up, took the baby, whose sucking was mechanical now, and said: "Now listen, you're going right upstairs and you're going to sleep. This little stinker's full as a tick, he'll be asleep for hours, that's my bet."

"I don't feel sleepy," said Dorothy, sobbing.

"I'll give you a sleeping pill, then."

Then started a search for sleeping pills. None to be found.

"That's just like us," wailed Dorothy, "we don't even have a sleeping pill in the place. . . . Stella, I wish you'd stay, I really do. Why can't you?"

"Stella's going in just a minute, I'm taking her to the station," said Jack. He poured some Scotch into a glass, handed it to his wife and said: "Now drink that, love, and let's have an end of it. I'm getting fed-up." He sounded fed-up.

Dorothy obediently drank the Scotch, got unsteadily from her chair and went slowly upstairs. "Don't let him cry," she demanded, as she disappeared.

"Oh you silly bitch," he shouted after her. "When have I let him cry? Here, you hold on a minute," he said to Stella, handing her the baby. He ran upstairs.

Stella held the baby. This was almost for the first time, since she sensed how much another woman's holding her child made Dorothy's fierce new possessiveness uneasy. She looked down at the small, sleepy, red face and said softly: "Well, you're causing a lot of trouble, aren't you?"

Jack shouted from upstairs: "Come up a minute, Stell." She went up, with the baby. Dorothy was tucked up in bed, drowsy from the Scotch, the bedside light turned away from her. She looked at the baby, but Jack took it from Stella.

"Jack says I'm a silly bitch," said Dorothy, apologetic, to Stella.

"Well, never mind, you'll feel different soon."

"I suppose so, if you say so. All right, I *am* going to sleep," said Dorothy, in a stubborn, sad little voice. She turned over, away from them. In the last flare of her hysteria she said: "Why don't you two walk to the station together? It's a lovely night."

"We're going to," said Jack, "don't worry."

She let out a weak giggle, but did not turn. Jack carefully deposited the now sleeping baby in the bed, about a foot from Dorothy. Who suddenly wriggled over until her small, defiant white back was in contact with the blanketed bundle that was her son.

Jack raised his eyebrows at Stella: but Stella was looking at mother and baby, the nerves of her memory filling her with sweet warmth. What right had this woman, who was in possession of such delight, to torment her husband, to torment her friend, as she had been doing — what right had she to rely on their decency as she did?

Surprised by these thoughts, she walked away downstairs, and stood at the door into the garden, her eyes shut, holding herself rigid against tears.

She felt a warmth on her bare arm — Jack's hand. She opened her eyes to see him bending towards her, concerned.

"It'd serve Dorothy right if I did drag you off into the bushes. . . ."

"Wouldn't have to drag me," she said; and while the words had the measure of facetiousness the situation demanded, she felt his seriousness envelop them both in danger.

The warmth of his hand slid across her back, and she turned towards him under its pressure. They stood together, cheeks touching, scents of skin and hair mixing with the smells of warmed grass and leaves.

She thought: What is going to happen now will blow Dorothy and Jack and that baby sky-high; it's the end of my marriage; I'm going to blow everything to bits. There was almost uncontrollable pleasure in it.

She saw Dorothy, Jack, the baby, her husband, the two half-grown children, all dispersed, all spinning downwards through the sky like bits of debris after an explosion.

Jack's mouth was moving along her cheek towards her mouth, dissolving her whole self in delight. She saw, against closed lids, the bundled baby upstairs, and pulled back from the situation, exclaiming energetically: "Damn Dorothy, damn her, damn her, I'd like to kill her. . . ."

And he, exploding into reaction, said in a low furious rage: "Damn you both! I'd like to wring both your bloody necks. . . ."

Their faces were at a foot's distance from each other, their eyes staring hostility. She thought that if she had not had the vision of the helpless baby they would now be in each other's arms — generating tenderness and desire like a couple of dynamos, she said to herself, trembling with dry anger.

"I'm going to miss my train if I don't go," she said.

"I'll get your coat," he said, and went in, leaving her defenceless against the emptiness of the garden.

When he came out, he slid the coat around her without touching her, and said: "Come on, I'll take you by car." He walked away in front of her to the car, and she followed meekly over rough lawn. It really was a lovely night.

Ray Bradbury (b. 1920)

August 2026: There Will Come Soft Rains

In the living room the voice-clock sang, *Tick-tock, seven o'clock, time to get up, time to get up, seven o'clock!* as if it were afraid that nobody would. The morning house lay empty. The clock ticked on, repeating and repeating its sounds into the emptiness. *Seven-nine, breakfast time, seven-nine!*

In the kitchen the breakfast stove gave a hissing sigh and ejected from its warm interior eight pieces of perfectly browned toast, eight eggs sunnyside up, sixteen slices of bacon, two coffees, and two cool glasses of milk.

"Today is August 4, 2026," said a second voice from the kitchen ceiling, "in the city of Allendale, California." It repeated the date three times for memory's sake. "Today is Mr. Featherstone's birthday. Today is the anniversary of Tilita's marriage. Insurance is payable, as are the water, gas, and light bills."

Somewhere in the walls, relays clicked, memory tapes glided under electric eyes.

Eight-one, tick-tock, eight-one o'clock, off to school, off to work, run, run, eight-one! But no doors slammed, no carpets took the soft tread of rubber heels. It was raining outside. The weather box on the front door sang quietly: "Rain, rain, go away; rubbers, raincoats for today . . ." And the rain tapped on the empty house, echoing.

Outside, the garage chimed and lifted its door to reveal the waiting car. After a long wait the door swung down again.

At eight-thirty the eggs were shriveled and the toast was like stone. An aluminum wedge scraped them into the sink, where hot water whirled them down a metal throat which digested and flushed them away to the distant sea. The dirty dishes were dropped into a hot washer and emerged twinkling dry.

Nine-fifteen, sang the clock, *time to clean.*

Out of warrens in the wall, tiny robot mice darted. The rooms were acrawl with the small cleaning animals, all rubber and metal. They thudded against chairs, whirling their mustached runners, kneading the rug nap, sucking gently at hidden dust. Then, like mysterious invaders, they popped into their burrows. Their pink electric eyes faded. The house was clean.

Ten o'clock. The sun came out from behind the rain. The house stood alone in a city of rubble and ashes. This was the one house left standing. At night the ruined city gave off a radioactive glow which could be seen for miles.

Ten-fifteen. The garden sprinklers whirled up in golden founts, filling the soft morning air with scatterings of brightness. The water pelted windowpanes, running down the charred west side where the house had been burned evenly free of its white paint. The entire west face of the house was black, save for five places. Here the silhouette in paint of a man mowing a lawn. Here, as in a photograph, a woman bent to pick flowers. Still farther over, their images burned on wood in one titanic instant, a small boy, hands flung into the air; higher up, the image of a thrown ball, and opposite him a girl, hands raised to catch a ball which never came down.

The five spots of paint — the man, the woman, the children, the ball — remained. The rest was a thin charcoaled layer.

The gentle sprinkler rain filled the garden with falling light.

Until this day, how well the house had kept its peace. How carefully it had inquired, "Who goes there? What's the password?" and, getting no answer from lonely foxes and whining cats, it had shut up its windows and drawn shades in an oldmaidenly preoccupation with self-protection which bordered on a mechanical paranoia.

It quivered at each sound, the house did. If a sparrow brushed a window, the shade snapped up. The bird, startled, flew off! No, not even a bird must touch the house!

The house was an altar with ten thousand attendants, big, small, servicing, attending, in choirs. But the gods had gone away, and the ritual of the religion continued senselessly, uselessly.

Twelve noon.

A dog whined, shivering, on the front porch.

The front door recognized the dog voice and opened. The dog, once huge and fleshy, but now gone to bone and covered with sores, moved in and through the house, tracking mud. Behind it whirred angry mice, angry at having to pick up mud, angry at inconvenience.

For not a leaf fragment blew under the door but what the wall panels flipped open and the copper scrap rats flashed swiftly out. The offending dust, hair, or paper, seized in miniature steel jaws, was raced back to the burrows. There, down tubes which fed into the cellar, it was dropped into the sighing vent of an incinerator which sat like evil Baal in a dark corner.

The dog ran upstairs, hysterically yelping to each door, at last realizing, as the house realized, that only silence was here.

It sniffed the air and scratched the kitchen door. Behind the door, the stove was making pancakes which filled the house with a rich baked odor and the scent of maple syrup.

The dog frothed at the mouth, lying at the door, sniffing, its eyes turned to fire. It ran wildly in circles, biting at its tail, spun in a frenzy, and died. It lay in the parlor for an hour.

Two o'clock, sang a voice.

Delicately sensing decay at last, the regiments of mice hummed out as softly as blown gray leaves in an electrical wind.

Two-fifteen.

The dog was gone.

In the cellar, the incinerator glowed suddenly and a whirl of sparks leaped up the chimney.

Two thirty-five.

Bridge tables sprouted from patio walls. Playing cards fluttered onto pads in a shower of pips. Martinis manifested on an oaken bench with egg-salad sandwiches. Music played.

But the tables were silent and the cards untouched.

At four o'clock the tables folded like great butterflies back through the paneled walls.

Four-thirty.

The nursery walls glowed.

Animals took shape: yellow giraffes, blue lions, pink antelopes, lilac panthers cavorting in crystal substance. The walls were glass. They looked out upon color and fantasy. Hidden films clocked through well-oiled sprockets, and the walls lived. The nursery floor was woven to resemble a crisp, cereal meadow. Over this ran aluminum roaches and iron crickets, and in the hot still air butterflies of delicate red tissue wavered among the sharp aroma of animal spoors! There was the sound like a great matted yellow hive of bees within a dark bellows, the lazy bumble of a purring lion. And there was the patter of okapi feet and the murmur of a fresh jungle rain, like other hoofs, falling upon the summer-starched grass. Now the walls dissolved into distances of parched weed, mile on mile, and warm endless sky. The animals drew away into thorn brakes and water holes.

It was the children's hour.

Five o'clock. The bath filled with clear hot water.

Six, seven, eight o'clock. The dinner dishes manipulated like magic tricks, and in the study a *click.* In the metal stand opposite the hearth where a fire now blazed up warmly, a cigar popped out, half an inch of soft gray ash on it, smoking, waiting.

Nine o'clock. The beds warmed their hidden circuits, for nights were cool here.

Nine-five. A voice spoke from the study ceiling:

"Mrs. McClellan, which poem would you like this evening?"

The house was silent.

The voice said at last, "Since you express no preference, I shall select a poem at random." Quiet music rose to back the voice. "Sara Teasdale. As I recall, your favorite. . . .

"There will come soft rains and the smell of the ground,
And swallows circling with their shimmering sound;

And frogs in the pools singing at night,
And wild plum trees in tremulous white;

Robins will wear their feathery fire,
Whistling their whims on a low fence-wire;

And not one will know of the war, not one
Will care at last when it is done.

Not one would mind, neither bird nor tree,
If mankind perished utterly;

And Spring herself, when she woke at dawn
Would scarcely know that we were gone."

The fire burned on the stone hearth and the cigar fell away into a mound of quiet ash on its tray. The empty chairs faced each other between the silent walls, and the music played.

At ten o'clock the house began to die.

The wind blew. A falling tree bough crashed through the kitchen window. Cleaning solvent, bottled, shattered over the stove. The room was ablaze in an instant!

"Fire!" screamed a voice. The house lights flashed, water pumps shot water from the ceilings. But the solvent spread on the linoleum, licking, eating, under the kitchen door, while the voices took it up in chorus: "Fire, fire, fire!"

The house tried to save itself. Doors sprang tightly shut, but the windows were broken by the heat and the wind blew and sucked upon the fire.

The house gave ground as the fire in ten billion angry sparks moved with flaming ease from room to room and then up the stairs. While scurrying water rats squeaked from the walls, pistoled their water, and ran for more. And the wall sprays let down showers of mechanical rain.

But too late. Somewhere, sighing, a pump shrugged to a stop. The quenching rain ceased. The reserve water supply which had filled baths and washed dishes for many quiet days was gone.

The fire crackled up the stairs. It fed upon Picassos and Matisses in the upper halls, like delicacies, baking off the oily flesh, tenderly crisping the canvases into black shavings.

Now the fire lay in beds, stood in windows, changed the colors of drapes!

And then, reinforcements.

From attic trapdoors, blind robot faces peered down with faucet mouths gushing green chemical.

The fire backed off, as even an elephant must at the sight of a dead snake. Now there were twenty snakes whipping over the floor, killing the fire with a clear cold venom of green froth.

But the fire was clever. It had sent flames outside the house, up through the attic to the pumps there. An explosion! The attic brain which directed the pumps was shattered into bronze shrapnel on the beams.

The fire rushed back into every closet and felt of the clothes hung there.

The house shuddered, oak bone on bone, its bared skeleton cringing from the heat, its wire, its nerves revealed as if a surgeon had torn the skin off to let the red veins and capillaries quiver in the scalded air. Help, help! Fire! Run, run! Heat snapped mirrors like the brittle winter ice. And the voices wailed Fire, fire, run, run, like a tragic nursery rhyme, a dozen voices, high, low, like children dying in a forest, alone, alone. And the voices fading as the wires popped their sheathings like hot chestnuts. One, two, three, four, five voices died.

In the nursery the jungle burned. Blue lions roared, purple giraffes bounded off. The panthers ran in circles, changing color, and ten million animals, running before the fire, vanished off toward a distant steaming river. . . .

Ten more voices died. In the last instant under the fire avalanche, other choruses, oblivious, could be heard announcing the time, playing music, cutting the lawn by remote-control mower, or setting an umbrella frantically out and in the slamming and opening front door, a thousand things happening, like a clock shop when each clock strikes the hour insanely before or after the other, a scene of maniac confusion, yet unity; singing, screaming, a few last cleaning mice darting bravely out to carry the horrid ashes away! and one voice, with sublime disregard for the situation, read poetry aloud in the fiery study, until all the film spools burned, until all the wires withered and the circuits cracked.

The fire burst the house and let it slam flat down, puffing out skirts of spark and smoke.

In the kitchen, an instant before the rain of fire and timber, the stove could be seen making breakfasts at a psychopathic rate, ten dozen eggs, six loaves of toast, twenty dozen bacon strips, which, eaten by fire, started the stove working again, hysterically hissing!

The crash. The attic smashing into kitchen and parlor. The parlor into cellar, cellar into sub-cellar. Deep freeze, armchair, film tapes, circuits, beds, and all like skeletons thrown in a cluttered mound deep under.

Smoke and silence. A great quantity of smoke.

Dawn showed faintly in the east. Among the ruins, one wall stood alone. Within the wall, a last voice said, over and over again and again, even as the sun rose to shine upon the heaped rubble and steam:

"Today is August 5, 2026, today is August 5, 2026, today is . . ."

Kurt Vonnegut, Jr. (b. 1922)

Who Am I This Time?

The North Crawford Mask and Wig Club, an amateur theatrical society I belong to, voted to do Tennessee Williams's *A Streetcar Named Desire* for the spring play. Doris Sawyer, who always directs, said she couldn't direct this time because her mother was so sick. And she said the club ought to develop some other directors anyway, because she couldn't live forever, even though she'd made it safely to seventy-four.

So I got stuck with the directing job, even though the only thing I'd ever directed before was the installation of combination aluminum storm windows and screens I'd sold. That's what I am, a salesman of storm windows and doors, and here and there a bathtub enclosure. As far as acting goes, the highest rank I ever held on stage was either butler or policeman, whichever's higher.

I made a lot of conditions before I took the directing job, and the biggest one was that Harry Nash, the only real actor the club has, had to take the Marlon Brando part in the play. To give you an idea of how versatile Harry is, inside of one year he was Captain Queeg in *The Caine Mutiny Court Martial*, then Abe Lincoln in *Abe Lincoln in Illinois* and then the young architect in *The Moon Is Blue*. The year after that, Harry Nash was Henry the Eighth in *Anne of the Thousand Days* and Doc in *Come Back Little Sheba*, and I was after him for Marlon Brando in *A Streetcar Named Desire*. Harry wasn't at the meeting to say whether he'd take the part or not. He never came to meetings. He was too shy. He didn't stay away from meetings because he had something else to do. He wasn't married, didn't go out with women — didn't have any close men friends either. He stayed away from all kinds of gatherings because he never could think of anything to say or do without a script.

So I had to go down to Miller's Hardware Store, where Harry was a clerk, the next day and ask him if he'd take the part. I stopped off at the telephone company to complain about a bill I'd gotten for a call to Honolulu, I'd never called Honolulu in my life.

And there was this beautiful girl I'd never seen before behind the counter at the phone company, and she explained that the company had put in an automatic billing machine and that the machine didn't have all the bugs out of it yet. It made mistakes. "Not only did I not call Honolulu," I told her, "I don't think anybody in North Crawford ever has or will."

So she took the charge off the bill, and I asked her if she was from around North Crawford. She said no. She said she just came with the new billing machine to teach local girls how to take care of it. After that, she said, she would go with some other machine to someplace else. "Well," I said, "as long as people have to come along with the machines, I guess we're all right."

"What?" she said.

"When machines start delivering themselves," I said, "I guess that's when the people better start really worrying."

"Oh," she said. She didn't seem very interested in that subject, and I wondered if she was interested in anything. She seemed kind of numb, almost a machine herself, an automatic phone-company politeness machine.

"How long will you be in town here?" I asked her.

"I stay in each town eight weeks, sir," she said. She had pretty blue eyes, but there sure wasn't much hope or curiosity in them. She told me she had been going from town to town like that for two years, always a stranger.

And I got it in my head that she might make a good Stella for the play. Stella was the wife of the Marlon Brando character, the wife of the character I wanted Harry Nash to play. So I told her where and when we were going to hold tryouts, and said the club would be very happy if she'd come.

She looked surprised, and she warmed up a little. "You know," she said, "that's the first time anybody ever asked me to participate in any community thing."

"Well," I said, "there isn't any other way to get to know a lot of nice people faster than to be in a play with 'em."

She said her name was Helene Shaw. She said she might just surprise me — and herself. She said she just might come.

You would think that North Crawford would be fed up with Harry Nash in plays after all the plays he'd been in. But the fact was that

North Crawford probably could have gone on enjoying Harry forever, because he was never Harry on stage. When the maroon curtain went up on the stage in the gymnasium of the Consolidated Junior-Senior High School, Harry, body and soul, was exactly what the script and the director told him to be.

Somebody said one time that Harry ought to go to a psychiatrist so he could be something important and colorful in real life, too — so he could get married anyway, and maybe get a better job than just clerking in Miller's Hardware Store for fifty dollars a week. But I don't know what a psychiatrist could have turned up about him that the town didn't already know. The trouble with Harry was he'd been left on the doorstep of the Unitarian Church when he was a baby, and he never did find out who his parents were.

When I told him there in Miller's that I'd been appointed director, that I wanted him in my play, he said what he always said to anybody who asked him to be in a play — and it was kind of sad, if you think about it.

"Who am I this time?" he said.

So I held the tryouts where they're always held — in the meeting room on the second floor of the North Crawford Public Library. Doris Sawyer, the woman who usually directs, came to give me the benefit of all her experience. The two of us sat in state upstairs, while the people who wanted parts waited below. We called them upstairs one by one.

Harry Nash came to the tryouts, even though it was a waste of time. I guess he wanted to get that little bit more acting in.

For Harry's pleasure, and our pleasure, too, we had him read from the scene where he beats up his wife. It was a play in itself, the way Harry did it, and Tennessee Williams hadn't written it all either. Tennessee Williams didn't write the part, for instance, where Harry, who weights about one hundred forty-five, who's about five feet eight inches tall, added fifty pounds to his weight and four inches to his height by just picking up a playbook. He had a short little double-breasted bellows-back grade-school graduation suit coat on and a dinky little red tie with a horsehead on it. He took off the coat and tie, opened his collar, then turned his back to Doris and me, getting up steam for the part. There was a great big rip in the back of his shirt, and it looked like a fairly new shirt too. He'd ripped it on purpose, so he could be that much more like Marlon Brando, right from the first.

When he faced us again, he was huge and handsome and conceited and cruel. Doris read the part of Stella, the wife, and Harry bullied that old, old lady into believing that she was a sweet, pregnant girl married to a sexy gorilla who was going to beat her brains out. She had me believing it too. And I read the lines of Blanche, her sister in the play, and darned if Harry didn't scare me into feeling like a drunk and faded Southern belle.

And then, while Doris and I were getting over our emotional experiences, like people coming out from under ether, Harry put down the playbook, put on his coat and tie, and turned into the pale hardware-store clerk again.

"Was — was that all right?" he said, and he seemed pretty sure he wouldn't get the part.

"Well," I said, "for a first reading, that wasn't too bad."

"Is there a chance I'll get the part?" he said. I don't know why he always had to pretend there was some doubt about his getting a part, but he did.

"I think we can safely say we're leaning powerfully in your direction," I told him.

He was very pleased. "Thanks! Thanks a lot!" he said, and he shook my hand.

"Is there a pretty new girl downstairs?" I said, meaning Helene Shaw.

"I didn't notice," said Harry.

It turned out that Helene Shaw *had* come for the tryouts, and Doris and I had our hearts broken. We thought the North Crawford Mask and Wig Club was finally going to put a really good-looking, really young girl on stage, instead of one of the beat-up forty-year-old women we generally have to palm off as girls.

But Helene Shaw couldn't act for sour apples. No matter what we gave her to read, she was the same girl with the same smile for anybody who had a complaint about his phone bill.

Doris tried to coach her some, to make her understand that Stella in the play was a very passionate girl who loved a gorilla because she needed a gorilla. But Helene just read the lines the same way again. I don't think a volcano could have stirred her up enough to say, "Oo."

"Dear," said Doris, "I'm going to ask you a personal question."

"All right," said Helene.

"Have you ever been in love?" said Doris. "The reason I ask," she said, "remembering some old love might help you put more warmth in your acting."

Helene frowned and thought hard. "Well," she said, "I travel a lot, you know. And practically all the men in the different companies I visit are married and I never stay anyplace long enough to know many people who aren't."

"What about school?" said Doris. "What about puppy love and all the other kinds of love in school?"

So Helene thought hard about that, and then she said, "Even in school I was always moving around a lot. My father was a construction worker, following jobs around, so I was always saying hello or good-by to someplace, without anything in between."

"Um," said Doris.

"Would movie stars count?" said Helene. "I don't mean in real life. I never knew any. I just mean up on the screen."

Doris looked at me and rolled her eyes. "I guess that's love of a kind," she said.

And then Helene got a little enthusiastic. "I used to sit through movies over and over again," she said, "and pretend I was married to whoever the man movie star was. They were the only people who came with us. No matter where we moved, movie stars were there."

"Uh huh," said Doris.

"Well, thank you, Miss Shaw," I said. "You go downstairs and wait with the rest. We'll let you know."

So we tried to find another Stella. And there just wasn't one, not one woman in the club with the dew still on her. "All we've got are Blanches," I said, meaning all we had were faded women who could play the part of Blanche, Stella's faded sister. "That's life, I guess — twenty Blanches to one Stella."

"And when you find a Stella," said Doris, "it turns out she doesn't know what love is."

Doris and I decided there was one last thing we could try. We could get Harry Nash to play a scene along with Helene. "He just might make her bubble the least little bit," I said.

"That girl hasn't got a bubble in her," said Doris.

So we called down the stairs for Helene to come back on up, and we told somebody to go find Harry. Harry never sat with the rest of the people at tryouts — or at rehearsals either. The minute he didn't have a part to play, he'd disappear into some hiding place where he could hear people call him, but where he couldn't be seen. At tryouts in the library he generally hid in the reference room, passing the time looking at flags of different countries in the front of the dictionary.

Helene came back upstairs, and we were very sorry and surprised to see that she'd been crying.

"Oh, dear," said Doris. "Oh, my — now what on earth's the trouble, dear?"

"I was terrible, wasn't I?" said Helene, hanging her head.

Doris said the only thing anybody can say in an amateur theatrical society when somebody cries. She said, "Why, no dear — you were marvelous."

"No, I wasn't," said Helene. "I'm a walking icebox, and I know it."

"Nobody could look at you and say that," said Doris.

"When they get to know me, they can say it," said Helene. "When people get to know me, that's what they *do* say." Her tears got worse. "I don't want to be the way I am," she said. "I just can't help it, living the way I've lived all my life. The only experiences I've had have been in crazy dreams of movie stars. When I meet somebody nice in real life, I feel as though I were in some kind of big bottle, as though I couldn't touch that person, no matter how hard I tried." And Helene pushed on air as though it were a big bottle all around her.

"You ask me if I've ever been in love," she said to Doris. "No — but I want to be. I know what this play's about. I know what Stella's supposed to feel and why she feels it. I — I — I —" she said, and her tears wouldn't let her go on.

"You what, dear?" said Doris gently.

"I — " said Helene, and she pushed on the imaginary bottle again. "I just don't know how to begin," she said.

There was heavy clumping on the library stairs. It sounded like a deep-sea diver coming upstairs in his lead shoes. It was Harry Nash, turning himself into Marlon Brando. In he came, practically dragging his knuckles on the floor. And he was so much in character that the sight of a weeping woman made him sneer.

"Harry," I said, "I'd like you to meet Helene Shaw. Helene — this is Harry Nash. If you get the part of Stella, he'll be your husband in the play." Harry didn't offer to shake hands. He put his hands in his pockets, and he hunched over, and he looked her up and down, gave her looks that left her naked. Her tears stopped right then and there.

"I wonder if you two would play the fight scene," I said, "and then the reunion scene right after it."

"Sure," said Harry, his eyes still on her. Those eyes burned up clothes faster than she could put them on. "Sure," he said, "if Stell's game."

"What?" said Helene. She'd turned the color of cranberry juice.

"Stell — Stella," said Harry. "That's you. Stell's my wife."

I handed the two of them playbooks. Harry snatched his from me without a word of thanks. Helene's hands weren't working very well, and I had to kind of mold them around the book.

"I'll want something I can throw," said Harry.

"What?" I said.

"There's one place where I throw a radio out a window," said Harry. "What can I throw?"

So I said an iron paperweight was the radio, and I opened the window wide. Helene Shaw looked scared to death.

"Where you want us to start?" said Harry, and he rolled his shoulders like a prizefighter warming up.

"Start a few lines back from where you throw the radio out the window," I said.

"O.K., O.K.," said Harry, warming up, warming up. He scanned the stage directions. "Let's see," he said, "after I throw the radio, she runs off stage, and I chase her, and I sock her one."

"Right," I said.

"O.K., baby," Harry said to Helene, his eyelids drooping. What was about to happen was wilder than the chariot race in *Ben Hur*. "On your mark," said Harry. "Get ready, baby. Go!"

When the scene was over, Helene Shaw was as hot as a hod carrier, as limp as an eel. She sat down with her mouth open and her head hanging to one side. She wasn't in any bottle any more. There wasn't any bottle to hold her up and keep her safe and clean. The bottle was gone.

"Do I get the part or don't I?" Harry snarled at me.

"You'll do," I said.

"You said a mouthful!" he said. "I'll be going now. . . . See you around, Stella," he said to Helene, and he left. He slammed the door behind him.

"Helene?" I said. "Miss Shaw?"

"Me?" she said.

"The part of Stella is yours," I said. "You were great!"

"I was?" she said.

"I had no idea you had that much fire in you, dear," Doris said to her.

"Fire?" said Helene. She didn't know if she was afoot or on horseback.

"Skyrockets! Pinwheels! Roman candles!" said Doris.

"Me," said Helene. And that was all she said. She looked as though she were going to sit in the chair with her mouth open forever.

"Stella," I said.

"Huh?" she said.

"You have my permission to go."

So we started having rehearsals four nights a week on the stage of the Consolidated School. And Harry and Helene set such a pace that everybody in the production was half crazy with excitement and exhaustion before we'd rehearsed four times. Usually a director has to beg people to learn their lines, but I had no such trouble. Harry and Helene were working so well together that everybody else in the cast regarded it as a duty and an honor and a pleasure to support them.

I was certainly lucky — or thought I was. Things were going so well, so hot and heavy, so early in the game that I had to say to Harry and Helene after one love scene, "Hold a little something back for the actual performance, would you please? You'll burn yourselves out."

I said that at the fourth or fifth rehearsal, and Lydia Miller, who was playing Blanche, the faded sister, was sitting next to me in the audience. In real life, she's the wife of Verne Miller. Verne owns Miller's Hardware Store. Verne was Harry's boss.

"Lydia," I said to her, "have we got a play or have we got a play?"

"Yes," she said, "you've got a play, all right." She made it sound as though I'd committed some kind of crime, done something just terrible. "You should be very proud of yourself."

"What do you mean by that?" I said.

Before Lydia could answer, Harry yelled at me from the stage, asked if I was through with him, asked if he could go home. I told him he could and, still Marlon Brando, he left, kicking furniture out of his way and slamming doors. Helene was left all alone on the stage, sitting on a couch with the same gaga look she'd had after the tryouts. That girl was drained.

I turned to Lydia again and I said, "Well — until now, I thought I had every reason to be happy and proud. Is there something going on I don't know about?"

"Do you know that girl's in love with Harry?" said Lydia.

"In the play?" I said.

"What play?" said Lydia. "There isn't any play going on now, and look at her up there." She gave a sad cackle. "You aren't directing this play."

"Who is?" I said.

"Mother Nature at her worst," said Lydia. "And think what it's going to do to that girl when she discovers what Harry really is." She corrected herself. "What Harry really isn't," she said.

I didn't do anything about it, because I didn't figure it was any of my business. I heard Lydia try to do something about it, but she didn't get very far.

"You know," Lydia said to Helene one night, "I once played Ann Rutledge, and Harry was Abraham Lincoln."

Helene clapped her hands. "That must have been heaven!" she said.

"It was, in a way," said Lydia. "Sometimes I'd get so worked up, I'd love Harry the way I'd love Abraham Lincoln. I'd have to come back to earth and remind myself that he wasn't ever going to free the slaves, that he was just a clerk in my husband's hardware store."

"He's the most marvelous man I ever met," said Helene.

"Of course, one thing you have to get set for, when you're in a play with Harry," said Lydia, "is what happens after the last performance."

"What are you talking about?" said Helene.

"Once the show's over," said Lydia, "whatever you thought Harry was just evaporates into thin air."

"I don't believe it," said Helene.

"I admit it's hard to believe," said Lydia.

Then Helen got a little sore. "Anyway, why tell me about it?" she said. "Even if it is true, what do I care?"

"I — I don't know," said Lydia, backing away. "I — I just thought you might find it interesting."

"Well, I don't," said Helene.

And Lydia slunk away, feeling about as frowzy and unloved as she was supposed to feel in the play. After that nobody said anything more to Helene to warn her about Harry, not even when word got around that she'd told the telephone company that she didn't want to be moved around anymore, that she wanted to stay in North Crawford.

So the time finally came to put on the play. We ran it for three nights — Thursday, Friday, and Saturday — and we murdered those audiences. They believed every word that was said on stage, and when the maroon curtain came down they were ready to go to the nut house along with Blanche, the faded sister.

On Thursday night the other girls at the telephone company sent Helene a dozen red roses. When Helene and Harry were taking a curtain call together, I passed the roses over the footlights to her. She came forward for them, took one rose from the bouquet to give to Harry. But when she turned to give Harry the rose in front of everybody, Harry was gone. The curtain came down on that extra little scene — that girl offering a rose to nothing and nobody.

I went backstage, and I found her still holding that one rose. She'd put the rest of the bouquet aside. There were tears in her eyes. "What did I do wrong?" she said to me. "Did I insult him some way?"

"No," I said. "He always does that after a performance. The minute it's over, he clears out as fast as he can."

"And tomorrow he'll disappear again?"

"Without even taking off his makeup."

"And Saturday?" she said. "He'll stay for the cast party on Saturday, won't he?"

"Harry never goes to parties," I said. "When the curtain comes down on Saturday, that's the last anybody will see of him till he goes to work on Monday."

"How sad," she said.

Helene's performance on Friday night wasn't nearly so good as Thursday's. She seemed to be thinking about other things. She watched Harry take off after curtain call. She didn't say a word.

On Saturday she put on the best performance yet. Ordinarily it was Harry who set the pace. But on Saturday Harry had to work to keep up with Helene. When the curtain came down on the final curtain call, Harry wanted to get away, but he couldn't. Helene wouldn't let go of his hand. The rest of the cast and the stage crew and a lot of well-wishers from the audience were all standing around Harry and Helene, and Harry was trying to get his hand back.

"Well," he said, "I've got to go."

"Where?" she said.

"Oh," he said, "home."

"Won't you please take me to the cast party?" she said.

He got very red. "I'm afraid I'm not much on parties," he said. All the Marlon Brando in him was gone. He was tongue-tied, he was scared, he was shy — he was everything Harry was famous for being between plays.

"All right," she said. "I'll let you go — if you promise me one thing."

"What's that?" he said, and I thought he would jump out a window if she let go of him then.

"I want you to promise to stay here until I get you your present," she said.

"Present?" he said, getting even more panicky.

"Promise?" she said.

He promised. It was the only way he could get his hand back. And he stood there miserably while Helene went down to the ladies' dressing room for the present. While he waited, a lot of people congratulated him on being such a fine actor. But congratulations never made him happy. He just wanted to get away.

Helene came back with the present. It turned out to be a little blue book with a big red ribbon for a place marker. It was a copy of *Romeo and Juliet*. Harry was very embarrassed. It was all he could do to say "Thank you."

"The marker marks my favorite scene," said Helene.

"Um," said Harry.

"Don't you want to see what my favorite scene is?" she said.

So Harry had to open the book to the red ribbon.

Helene got close to him, and read a line of Juliet's. " 'How cam'st thou hither, tell me, and wherefore?' " she read. " 'The orchard walls are high and hard to climb, and the place death, considering who thou art, if any of my kinsmen find thee here.' " She pointed to the next line. "Now, look what Romeo says," she said.

"Um," said Harry.

"Read what Romeo says," said Helene.

Harry cleared his throat. He didn't want to read the line, but he had to. " 'With love's light wings did I o'erperch these walls,' " he read out loud in his everyday voice. But then a change came over him. " 'For stony limits cannot hold love out,' " he read, and he straightened up, and eight years dropped away from him, and he was brave and gay. " 'And what love can do, that dares love attempt,' " he read, " 'therefore thy kinsmen are no let to me.' "

" 'If they do see thee they will murther thee,' " said Helene, and she started him walking toward the wings.

" 'Alack!' " said Harry, " 'there lies more peril in thine eye than twenty of their swords.' " Helene led him toward the backstage exit.

" 'Look thou but sweet,' " said Harry, " 'and I am proof against their enmity.' "

" 'I would not for the world they saw thee here,' " said Helene, and that was the last we heard. The two of them were out the door and gone.

They never did show up at the cast party. One week later they were married.

They seem very happy, although they're kind of strange from time to time, depending on which play they're reading to each other at the time.

I dropped into the phone company office the other day, on account of the billing machine was making dumb mistakes again. I asked her what plays she and Harry'd been reading lately.

"In the past week," she said, "I've been married to Othello, been loved by Faust and been kidnaped by Paris. Wouldn't you say I was the luckiest girl in town?"

I said I thought so, and I told her most of the women in town thought so too.

"They had their chance," she said.

"Most of 'em couldn't stand the excitement," I said. And I told her I'd been asked to direct another play. I asked if she and Harry would be available for the cast. She gave me a big smile and said, "Who are we this time?"

Flannery O'Connor (1925–1964)

A Good Man Is Hard to Find

The grandmother didn't want to go to Florida. She wanted to visit some of her connections in east Tennessee and she was seizing at every chance to change Bailey's mind. Bailey was the son she lived with, her only boy. He was sitting on the edge of his chair at the table, bent over the orange sports section of the *Journal*. "Now look here, Bailey," she said, "see here, read this," and she stood with one hand on her thin hip and the other rattling the newspaper at his bald head. "Here this fellow that calls himself The Misfit is aloose from the Federal Pen and headed toward Florida and you read here what it says he did to these people. Just you read it. I wouldn't take my children in any direction with a criminal like that aloose in it. I couldn't answer to my conscience if I did."

Bailey didn't look up from his reading so she wheeled around then and faced the children's mother, a young woman in slacks, whose face was as broad and innocent as a cabbage and was tied round with a green head-kerchief that had two points on the top like rabbit's ears. She was sitting on the sofa, feeding the baby his apricots out of a jar. "The children have been to Florida before," the old lady said. "You all ought to take them somewhere else for a change so they would see different parts of the world and be broad. They never have been to east Tennessee."

The children's mother didn't seem to hear her but the eight-year-old boy, John Wesley, a stocky child with glasses, said, "If you don't want to go to Florida, why dontcha stay at home?" He and the little girl, June Star, were reading the funny papers on the floor.

"She wouldn't stay at home to be queen for a day," June Star said without raising her yellow head.

"Yes and what would you do if this fellow, The Misfit, caught you?" the grandmother asked.

"I'd smack his face," John Wesley said.

"She wouldn't stay at home for a million bucks," June Star said. "Afraid she'd miss something. She has to go everywhere we go."

"All right, Miss," the grandmother said. "Just remember that the next time you want me to curl your hair."

June Star said her hair was naturally curly.

The next morning the grandmother was the first one in the car, ready to go. She had her big black valise that looked like the head of a hippopotamus in one corner, and underneath it she was hiding a basket with Pitty Sing, the cat, in it. She didn't intend for the cat to be left alone in the house for three days because he would miss her too much and she was afraid he might brush against one of the gas burners and accidentally asphyxiate himself. Her son, Bailey, didn't like to arrive at a motel with a cat.

She sat in the middle of the back seat with John Wesley and June Star on either side of her. Bailey and the children's mother and the baby sat in the front and they left Atlanta at eight forty-five with the mileage on the car at 55890. The grandmother wrote this down because she thought it would be interesting to say how many miles they had been when they got back. It took them twenty minutes to reach the outskirts of the city.

The old lady settled herself comfortably, removing her white cotton gloves and putting them up with her purse on the shelf in front of the back window. The children's mother still had on slacks and still had her head tied up in a green kerchief, but the grandmother had on a navy blue straw sailor hat with a bunch of white violets on the brim and a navy blue dress with a small white dot in the print. Her collar and cuffs were white organdy trimmed with lace and at her neckline she had pinned a purple spray of cloth violets containing a sachet. In case of an accident, anyone seeing her dead on the highway would know at once that she was a lady.

She said she thought it was going to be a good day for driving, neither too hot nor too cold, and she cautioned Bailey that the speed limit was fifty-five miles an hour and that the patrolmen hid themselves behind billboards and small clumps of trees and sped out after you before you had a chance to slow down. She pointed out interesting details of the scenery: Stone Mountain; the blue granite that in some places came up to both sides of the highway; the brilliant red clay banks slightly streaked with purple; and the various crops that made rows of green lace-work on the ground. The trees were full of silver-white sunlight and the meanest of them sparkled. The children were reading comic magazines and their mother had gone back to sleep.

"Let's go through Georgia fast so we won't have to look at it much," John Wesley said.

"If I were a little boy," said the grandmother, "I wouldn't talk about my native state that way. Tennessee has the mountains and Georgia has the hills."

"Tennessee is just a hillbilly dumping ground," John Wesley said, "and Georgia is a lousy state too."

"You said it," June Star said.

"In my time," said the grandmother, folding her thin veined fingers, "children were more respectful of their native states and their parents and everything else. People did right then. Oh look at the cute little pickaninny!" she said and pointed to a Negro child standing in the door of a shack. "Wouldn't that make a picture, now?" she asked and they all turned and looked at the little Negro out of the back window. He waved.

"He didn't have any britches on," June Star said.

"He probably didn't have any," the grandmother explained. "Little niggers in the country don't have things like we do. If I could paint, I'd paint that picture," she said.

The children exchanged comic books.

The grandmother offered to hold the baby and the children's mother passed him over the front seat to her. She set him on her knee and bounced him and told him about the things they were passing. She rolled her eyes and screwed up her mouth and stuck her leathery thin face into his smooth bland one. Occasionally he gave her a faraway smile. They passed a large cotton field with five or six graves fenced in the middle of it, like a small island. "Look at the graveyard!" the grandmother said, pointing it out. "That was the old family burying ground. That belonged to the plantation."

"Where's the plantation?" John Wesley asked.

"Gone With the Wind," said the grandmother. "Ha. Ha."

When the children finished all the comic books they had brought, they opened the lunch and ate it. The grandmother ate a peanut butter sandwich and an olive and would not let the children throw the box and the paper napkins out the window. When there was nothing else to do they played a game by choosing a cloud and making the other two guess what shape it suggested. John Wesley took one the shape of a cow and June Star guessed a cow and John Wesley said, no, an automobile, and June Star said he didn't play fair, and they began to slap each other over the grandmother.

The grandmother said she would tell them a story if they would keep quiet. When she told a story, she rolled her eyes and waved her head and was very dramatic. She said once when she was a maiden lady she had been courted by a Mr. Edgar Atkins Teagarden from Jasper, Georgia. She said he was a very good-looking man and a gentleman and that he brought her a watermelon every Saturday afternoon with his initials cut in it, E. A. T. Well, one Saturday, she said, Mr. Teagarden brought the watermelon and there was nobody at home and he left it on the front porch and returned in his buggy to Jasper, but she never got the watermelon, she said, because a nigger boy ate it when he saw the initials, E. A. T.! This story tickled John Wesley's funny bone and he giggled and giggled but June Star didn't think it was any good. She said she wouldn't marry a man that just brought her a watermelon on Saturday. The grandmother said she would have done well to marry Mr. Teagarden because he was a gentleman and had bought Coca-Cola stock when it first came out and that he had died only a few years ago, a very wealthy man.

They stopped at The Tower for barbecued sandwiches. The Tower was a part stucco and part wood filling station and dance hall set in a clearing outside of Timothy. A fat man named Red Sammy Butts ran it and there were signs stuck here and there on the building and for miles up and down the highway saying, TRY RED SAMMY'S FAMOUS BARBECUE. NONE LIKE FAMOUS RED SAMMY'S! RED SAM! THE

FAT BOY WITH THE HAPPY LAUGH. A VETERAN! RED SAMMY'S YOUR MAN!

Red Sammy was lying on the bare ground outside The Tower with his head under a truck while a gray monkey about a foot high, chained to a small chinaberry tree, chattered nearby. The monkey sprang back into the tree and got on the highest limb as soon as he saw the children jump out of the car and run toward him.

Inside, The Tower was a long dark room with a counter at one end and tables at the other and dancing space in the middle. They all sat down at a broad table next to the nickelodeon and Red Sam's wife, a tall burnt-brown woman with hair and eyes lighter than her skin, came and took their order. The children's mother put a dime in the machine and played "The Tennessee Waltz," and the grandmother said that tune always made her want to dance. She asked Bailey if he would like to dance but he only glared at her. He didn't have a naturally sunny disposition like she did and trips made him nervous. The grandmother's brown eyes were very bright. She swayed her head from side to side and pretended she was dancing in her chair. June Star said play something she could tap to so the children's mother put in another dime and played a fast number and June Star stepped out onto the dance floor and did her tap routine.

"Ain't she cute?" Red Sam's wife said, leaning over the counter. "Would you like to come be my little girl?"

"No I certainly wouldn't," June Star said. "I wouldn't live in a broken-down place like this for a million bucks!" and she ran back to the table.

"Ain't she cute?" the woman repeated, stretching her mouth politely.

"Aren't you ashamed?" hissed the grandmother.

Red Sam came in and told his wife to quit lounging on the counter and hurry with these people's order. His khaki trousers reached just to his hip bones and his stomach hung over them like a sack of meal swaying under his shirt. He came over and sat down at a table nearby and let out a combination sigh and yodel. "You can't win," he said. "You can't win," and he wiped his sweating red face off with a gray handkerchief. "These days you don't know who to trust," he said. "Ain't that the truth?"

"People are certainly not nice like they used to be," said the grandmother.

"Two fellers come in here last week," Red Sammy said, "driving a Chrysler. It was a old beat-up car but it was a good one and these boys looked all right to me. Said they worked at the mill and you know I let them fellers charge the gas they bought? Now why did I do that?"

"Because you're a good man!" the grandmother said at once.

"Yes'm, I suppose so," Red Sam said as if he were struck with the answer.

His wife brought the orders, carrying the five plates all at once without a tray, two in each hand and one balanced on her arm. "It isn't a soul in this green world of God's that you can trust," she said. "And I don't count anybody out of that, not nobody," she repeated, looking at Red Sammy.

"Did you read about that criminal, The Misfit, that's escaped?" asked the grandmother.

"I wouldn't be a bit surprised if he didn't attact this place right here," said the woman. "If he hears about it being here, I wouldn't be none surprised to see him. If he hears it's two cent in the cash register, I wouldn't be a tall surprised if he ... "

"That'll do," Red Sam said. "Go bring these people their Co'Colas," and the woman went off to get the rest of the order.

"A good man is hard to find," Red Sammy said. "Everything is getting terrible. I remember the day you could go off and leave your screen door unlatched. Not no more."

He and the grandmother discussed better times. The old lady said that in her opinion Europe was entirely to blame for the way things were now. She said the way Europe acted you would think we were made of money and Red Sam said it was no use talking about it, she was exactly right. The children ran outside into the white sunlight and looked at the monkey in the lacy chinaberry tree. He was busy catching fleas on himself and biting each one carefully between his teeth as if it were a delicacy.

They drove off again into the hot afternoon. The grandmother took cat naps and woke up every few minutes with her own snoring. Outside of Toombsboro she woke up and recalled an old plantation that she had visited in his neighborhood once when she was a young lady. She said the house had six white columns across the front and that there was an avenue of oaks leading up to it and two little wooden trellis arbors on either side in front where you sat down with your suitor after a stroll in the garden. She recalled exactly which road to turn off to get to it. She knew that Bailey would not be willing to lose any time looking at an old house, but the more she talked about it, the more she wanted to see it once again and find out if the little twin arbors were still standing. "There was a secret panel in this house," she said craftily, not telling the truth but wishing that she were, "and the story went that all the family silver was hidden in it when Sherman came through but it was never found ... "

"Hey!" John Wesley said. "Let's go see it! We'll find it! We'll poke all the woodwork and find it! Who lives there? Where do you turn off at? Hey Pop, can't we turn off there!"

"We never have seen a house with a secret panel!" June Star shrieked. "Let's go to the house with the secret panel! Hey, Pop, can't we go see the house with the secret panel!"

"It's not far from here, I know," the grandmother said. "It wouldn't take over twenty minutes."

Bailey was looking straight ahead. His jaw was as rigid as a horseshoe. "No," he said.

The children began to yell and scream that they wanted to see the house with the secret panel. John Wesley kicked the back of the front seat and June Star hung over her mother's shoulder and whined desperately into her ear that they never had any fun even on their vacation, and that they could never do what THEY wanted to do. The baby began to scream and John Wesley kicked the back of the seat so hard that his father could feel the blows in his kidney.

"All right!" he shouted, and drew the car to a stop at the side of the road. "Will you all shut up? Will you all just shut up for one second? If you don't shut up, we won't go anywhere."

"It would be very educational for them," the grandmother murmured.

"All right," Bailey said, "but get this: this is the only time we're going to stop for anything like this. This is the one and only time."

"The dirt road that you have to turn down is about a mile back," the grandmother directed. "I marked it when we passed."

"A dirt road," Bailey groaned.

After they had turned around and were headed toward the dirt road, the grandmother recalled other points about the house, the beautiful glass over the front doorway and the candle-lamp in the hall. John Wesley said that the secret panel was probably in the fireplace.

"You can't go inside this house," Bailey said. "You don't know who lives there."

"While you all talk to the people in front, I'll run around behind and get in a window," John Wesley suggested.

"We'll all stay in the car," his mother said.

They turned onto the dirt road and the car raced roughly along in a swirl of pink dust. The grandmother recalled the times when there were no paved roads and thirty miles was a day's journey. The dirt road was hilly and there were sudden washes in it and sharp curves on dangerous embankments. All at once they would be on a hill, looking down over the blue tops of trees for miles around, then the next minute, they would be in a red depression with the dust-coated trees looking down on them.

"This place had better turn up in a minute," Bailey said, "or I'm going to turn around."

The road looked as if no one had traveled on it in months.

"It's not much farther," the grandmother said and just as she said it, a horrible thought came to her. The thought was so embarrassing that she turned red in the face and her eyes dilated and her feet jumped up, upsetting her valise in the corner. The instant the valise moved, the newspaper top she had over the basket under it rose with a snarl and Pitty Sing, the cat, sprang onto Bailey's shoulder.

The children were thrown to the floor and their mother, clutching the baby, was thrown out the door onto the ground, the old lady was thrown into the front seat. The car turned over once and landed right-side up in a gulch on the side of the road. Bailey remained in the driver's seat with the cat — gray-striped with a broad white face and an orange nose — clinging to his neck like a caterpillar.

As soon as the children saw they could move their arms and legs, they scrambled out of the car, shouting, "We've had an ACCIDENT!" The grandmother was curled up under the dashboard, hoping she was injured so that Bailey's wrath would not come down on her all at once. The horrible thought she had had before the accident was that the house she had remembered so vividly was not in Georgia but in Tennessee.

Bailey removed the cat from his neck with both hands and flung it out the window against the side of a pine tree. Then he got out of the car and started looking for the children's mother. She was sitting against the side of the red gutted ditch, holding the screaming baby, but she only had a cut down her face and a broken shoulder. "We've had an ACCIDENT!" the children screamed in a frenzy of delight.

"But nobody's killed," June Star said with disappointment as the grandmother limped out of the car, her hat still pinned to her head but the broken front brim standing up at a jaunty angle and the violet spray hanging off the side. They all sat down in the ditch, except the children, to recover from the shock. They were all shaking.

"Maybe a car will come along," said the children's mother hoarsely.

"I believe I have injured an organ," said the grandmother, pressing her side, but no one answered her. Bailey's teeth were clattering. He had on a yellow sport shirt with bright blue parrots designed in it and his face was as yellow as the shirt. The grandmother decided that she would not mention that the house was in Tennessee.

The road was about ten feet above and they could see only the tops of the trees on the other side of it. Behind the ditch they were setting in there were more woods, tall and dark and deep. In a few minutes they saw a car some distance away on top of a hill, coming slowly as if the occupants were watching them. The grandmother stood up and waved both arms dramatically to attract their attention. The car continued to come on slowly, disappeared around a bend and appeared again, moving even slower, on top of the hill they had gone over. It was a big black battered hearselike automobile. There were three men in it.

It came to a stop just over them and for some minutes, the driver looked down with a steady expressionless gaze to where they were sitting, and didn't speak. Then he turned his head and muttered something to the other two and they got out. One was a fat boy in black trousers and a red sweat shirt with a silver stallion embossed on the front of it. He moved around on the right side of them and stood staring, his mouth partly open in a kind of loose grin. The other had on khaki pants and a blue striped coat and a gray hat pulled down very low, hiding most of his face. He came around slowly on the left side. Neither spoke.

The driver got out of the car and stood by the side of it, looking down at them. He was an older man than the other two. His hair was just beginning to gray and he wore silver-rimmed spectacles that gave him a scholarly look. He had a long creased face and didn't have on any shirt or undershirt. He had on blue jeans that were too tight for him and was holding a black hat and a gun. The two boys also had guns.

"We've had an ACCIDENT!" the children screamed.

The grandmother had the peculiar feeling that the bespectacled man was someone she knew. His face was as familiar to her as if she had known him all her life but she could not recall who he was. He moved away from the car and began to come down the embankment, placing his feet carefully so that he wouldn't slip. He had on tan and white shoes and no socks, and his ankles were red and thin. "Good afternoon," he said. "I see you all had you a little spill."

"We turned over twice!" said the grandmother.

"Oncet," he corrected. "We seen it happen. Try their car and see will it run, Hiram," he said quietly to the boy with the gray hat.

"What you got that gun for?" John Wesley asked. "Watcha gonna do with that gun?"

"Lady," the man said to the children's mother, "would you mind calling them children to set down by you? Children make me nervous. I want all you all to sit down right together there were you're at."

"What are you telling us what to do for?" June Star asked.

Behind them the line of woods gaped like a dark open mouth. "Come here," said their mother.

"Look here now," Bailey began suddenly, "we're in a predicament! We're in . . ."

The grandmother shrieked. She scrambled to her feet and stood staring. "You're The Misfit!" she said. "I recognized you at once."

"Yes'm," the man said, smiling slightly as if he were pleased in spite of himself to be known, "but it would have been better for all of you, lady, if you hadn't of recognized me."

Bailey turned his head sharply and said something to his mother that shocked even the children. The old lady began to cry and The Misfit reddened.

"Lady," he said, "don't you get upset. Sometimes a man says things he don't mean. I don't reckon he meant to talk to you that-away."

"You wouldn't shoot a lady, would you?" the grandmother said and removed a clean handkerchief from her cuff and began to slap at her eyes with it.

The Misfit pointed the toe of his shoe into the ground and made a little hole and then covered it up again. "I would hate to have to," he said.

"Listen," the grandmother almost screamed, "I know you're a good man. You don't look a bit like you have common blood. I know you must come from nice people!"

"Yes ma'm," he said, "finest people in the world." When he smiled he showed a row of strong white teeth. "God never made a finer woman than my mother and my daddy's heart was pure gold," he said. The boy with the red sweat shirt had come around behind them and was standing with his gun at his hip. The Misfit squatted down on the ground. "Watch them children, Bobby Lee," he said. "You know they make me nervous." He looked at the six of them huddled together in front of him and he seemed to be embarrassed as if he couldn't think of anything to say. "Ain't a cloud in the sky," he remarked, looking up at it. "Don't see no sun but don't see no cloud neither."

"Yes, it's a beautiful day," said the grandmother. "Listen," she said, "you shouldn't call yourself The Misfit because I know you're a good man at heart. I can just look at you and tell."

"Hush!" Bailey yelled. "Hush! Everybody shut up and let me handle this!" He was squatting in the position of a runner about to sprint forward but he didn't move.

"I pre-chate that, lady," The Misfit said an drew a little circle in the ground with the butt of his gun.

"It'll take a half a hour to fix this here car," Hiram called, looking over the raised hood of it.

"Well, first you and Bobby Lee get him and that little boy to step over yonder with you," The Misfit said, pointing to Bailey and John Wesley. "The boys want to ask you something," he said to Bailey. "Would you mind stepping back in them woods there with them?"

"Listen," Bailey began, "we're in a terrible predicament. Nobody realizes what this is," and his voice cracked. His eyes were as blue and intense as the parrots in his shirt and he remained perfectly still.

The grandmother reached up to adjust her hat brim as if she were going to the woods with him but it came off in her hand. She stood staring at it and after a second she let it fall on the ground. Hiram pulled Bailey up by the arm as if he were assisting an old man. John Wesley caught hold of his father's hand and Bobby Lee followed. They went off toward the woods and just as they reached the dark edge, Bailey turned and supporting himself against a gray naked pine trunk, he shouted, "I'll be back in a minute, Mamma, wait on me!"

"Come back this instant!" his mother shrilled but they all disappeared into the woods.

"Bailey Boy!" the grandmother called in a tragic voice but she found she was looking at The Misfit squatting on the ground in front of her. "I just know you're a good man," she said desperately. "You're not a bit common!"

"Nome, I ain't a good man," The Misfit said after a second as if he had considered her statement carefully, "but I ain't the worst in the world neither. My daddy said I was different breed of dog from my brothers and sisters. 'You know,' Daddy said, 'it's some that can live their whole life out without asking about it and it's others has to know why it is, and this boy is one of the latters. He's going to be into everything!'" He put on his black hat and looked up suddenly and then away deep into the woods as if he were embarrassed again. "I'm sorry I don't have on a shirt before you ladies," he said, hunching his shoulders slightly. "We buried our clothes that we had on when we escaped and we're just making do until we can get better. We borrowed these from some folks we met," he explained.

"That's perfectly all right," the grandmother said. "Maybe Bailey has an extra shirt in his suitcase."

"I'll look and see terrectly," The Misfit said.

"Where are they taking him?" the children's mother screamed.

"Daddy was a card himself," The Misfit said. "You couldn't put anything over on him. He never got in trouble with the Authorities though. Just had the knack of handling them."

"You could be honest too if you'd only try," said the grandmother. "Think how wonderful it would be to settle down and live a comfortable life and not have to think about somebody chasing you all the time."

The Misfit kept scratching in the ground with the butt of his gun as if he were thinking about it. "Yes'm, somebody is always after you," he murmured.

The grandmother noticed how thin his shoulder blades were just behind his hat because she was standing up looking down on him. "Do you ever pray?" she asked.

He shook his head. All she saw was the black hat wiggle between shoulder blades. "Nome," she said.

There was a pistol shot from the woods, followed closely by another. Then silence. The old lady's head jerked around. She could hear the wind move through the tree tops like a long satisfied insuck of breath. "Bailey Boy!" she called.

"I was a gospel singer for a while," The Misfit said. "I been most everything. Been in the arm service, both land and sea, at home and abroad, been twict married, been an undertaker, been with the railroads, plowed Mother Earth, been in a tornado, seen a man burnt alive oncet," and he looked up at the children's mother and the little girl who were sitting close together, their faces white and their eyes glassy; "I even seen a woman flogged," he said.

"Pray, pray," the grandmother began, "pray, pray . . . "

"I never was a bad boy that I remember of," The Misfit said in an almost dreamy voice, "but somewheres along the line I done something wrong and got sent to the penitentiary. I was buried alive," and he looked up and held her attention to him by a steady stare.

"That's when you should have started to pray," she said. "What did you do to get sent to the penitentiary that first time?"

"Turn to the right, it was a wall," The Misfit said, looking up again at the cloudless sky. "Turn to the left, it was a wall. Look up it was a ceiling, look down it was a floor. I forgot what I done, lady. I set there and set there, trying to remember what it was I done and I ain't recalled it to this day. Oncet in a while, I would think it was coming to me, but it never come."

"Maybe they put you in by mistake," the old lady said vaguely.

"Nome," he said. "It wasn't no mistake. They had the papers on me."

"You must have stolen something," she said.

The Misfit sneered slightly. "Nobody had nothing I wanted," he said. "It was a head-doctor at the penitentiary said what I had done was kill my daddy but I know that for a lie. My daddy died in nineteen ought nineteen of the epidemic flu and I never had a thing to do with it. He was buried in the Mount Hopewell Baptist churchyard and you can go there and see for yourself."

"If you would pray," the old lady said, "Jesus would help you."

"That's right," The Misfit said.

"Well then, why don't you pray?" she asked trembling with delight suddenly.

"I don't want no hep," he said. "I'm doing all right by myself."

Bobby Lee and Hiram came ambling back from the woods. Bobby Lee was dragging a yellow shirt with bright blue parrots in it.

"Throw me that shirt, Bobby Lee," The Misfit said. The shirt came flying at him and landed on his shoulder and he put it on. The grandmother couldn't name what the shirt reminded her of. "No, lady," The Misfit said while he was buttoning it up. "I found out the crime don't matter. You can do one thing or you can do another, kill a man or take a tire off his car, because sooner or later you're going to forget what it was you done and just be punished for it."

The children's mother had begun to make heaving noises as if she couldn't get her breath. "Lady," he asked, "would you and that little girl like to step off yonder with Bobby Lee and Hiram and join your husband?"

"Yes, thank you," the mother said faintly. Her left arm dangled helplessly and she was holding the baby, who had gone to sleep, in the other. "Hep that lady up, Hiram," The Misfit said as she struggled to climb out of the ditch, "and Bobby Lee, you hold onto that little girl's hand."

"I don't want to hold hands with him" June Star said. "He reminds me of a pig."

The fat boy blushed and laughed and caught her by the arm and pulled her off into the woods after Hiram and her mother.

Alone with The Misfit, the grandmother found that she had lost her voice. There was not a cloud in the sky nor any sun. There was nothing around her but woods. She wanted to tell him that he must pray. She opened and closed her mouth several times before anything came out. Finally she found herself saying, "Jesus, Jesus," meaning Jesus will help you, but the way she was saying it, it sounded as if she might be cursing.

"Yes'm," The Misfit said as if he agreed. "Jesus thown everything off balance. It was the same case with Him as with me except He hadn't committed any crime and they could prove I had committed one because they had the papers on me. Of course," he said, "they never shown me my papers. That's why I sign myself now. I said long ago, you get you a signature and sign everything you do and keep a copy of it. Then you'll know what you done and you can hold up the crime to the punishment and see do they match and in the end you'll have something to prove you ain't been treated right. I call myself The Misfit," he said, "because I can't make what all I done wrong fit what all I gone through in punishment."

There was a piercing scream from the woods, followed closely by a pistol report. "Does it seem right to you, lady, that one is punished a heap and another ain't punished at all?"

"Jesus!" the old lady cried. "You've got good blood! I know you wouldn't shoot a lady! I know you come from nice people! Pray! Jesus, you ought not to shoot a lady. I'll give you all the money I've got!"

"Lady," The Misfit said, looking beyond her far into the woods, "there never was a body that give the undertaker a tip."

There were two more pistol reports and the grandmother raised her head like a parched old turkey hen crying for water and called, "Bailey Boy, Bailey Boy!" as if her heart would break.

"Jesus was the only One that ever raised the dead." The Misfit continued "and He shouldn't have done it. He thrown everything off balance. If He did what He said, then it's nothing for you to do but thow away everything and follow Him, and if He didn't, then it's nothing for you to do but enjoy the few minutes you got left the best way you can — by killing somebody or burning down his house or doing some other meanness to him. No pleasure but meanness," he said and his voice had become almost a snarl.

"Maybe He didn't raise the dead," the old lady mumbled, not knowing what she was saying and feeling so dizzy that she sank down in the ditch with her legs twisted under her.

"I wasn't there so I can't say He didn't," The Misfit said. "I wisht I had of been there," he said, hitting the ground with his fist. "It ain't right I wasn't there because if I had of been there I would of known. Listen lady," he said in a high voice, "if I had of been there I would of known and I wouldn't be like I am now." His voice seemed about to crack and the grandmother's head cleared for an instant. She saw the man's face twisted close to her own as if he were going to cry and she murmured, "Why you're one of my babies. You're one of my own children!" She reached out and touched him on the shoulder. The Misfit sprang back as if a snake had bitten him and shot her three times through the chest. Then he put his gun down on the ground and took off his glasses and began to clean them.

Hiram and Bobby Lee returned from the woods and stood over the ditch, looking down at the grandmother who half sat and half lay in a puddle of blood with her legs crossed under her like a child's and her face smiling up at the cloudless sky.

Without his glasses, The Misfit's eyes were red-rimmed and pale and defenseless-looking. "Take her off and thow her where you thown the others," he said, picking up the cat that was rubbing itself against his leg.

"She was a talker, wasn't she?" Bobby Lee said, sliding down the ditch with a yodel.

"She would of been a good woman," The Misfit said, "if it had been somebody there to shoot her every minute of her life."

"Some fun!" Bobby Lee said.

"Shut up, Bobby Lee," The Misfit said. "It's no real pleasure in life."

John Updike (b. 1932)

A & P

In walks these three girls in nothing but bathing suits. I'm in the third checkout slot, with my back to the door, so I don't see them until they're over by the bread. The one that caught my eye first was the one in the plaid green two-piece. She was a chunky kid, with a good tan and a sweet broad soft-looking can with those two crescents of white just under it, where the sun never seems to hit, at the top of the backs of her legs. I stood there with my hand on a box of HiHo crackers trying to remember if I rang it up or not. I ring it up again and the customer starts giving me hell. She's one of these cash-regis-ter-watchers, a witch about fifty with rouge on her cheekbones and no eyebrows, and I know it made her day to trip me up. She'd been watching cash registers for fifty years and probably never seen a mistake before.

By the time I got her feathers smoothed and her goodies into a bag — she gives me a little snort in passing, if she'd been born at the right time they would have burned her over in Salem — by the time I get her on her way the girls had circled around the bread and were coming back, without a pushcart, back my way along the counters, in the aisle between the checkouts and the Special bins. They didn't even have shoes on. There was this chunky one, with the two-piece — it was bright green and the seams on the bra were still sharp and her belly was still pretty pale so I guessed she just got it (the suit) — there was this one, with one of those chubby berry-faces, the lips all bunched together under her nose, this one, and a tall one, with black hair that hadn't quite frizzed right, and one of these sun-burns right across under the eyes, and a chin that was too long — you know, the kind of girl other girls think is very "striking" and "attrac-tive" but never quite makes it, as they very well know, which is why they like her so much — and then the third one, that wasn't quite so tall. She was the queen. She kind of led them, the other two peeking around and making their shoulders round. She didn't look around, not this queen, she just walked straight on slowly, on these long white prima-donna legs. She came down a little hard on her heels, as if she didn't walk in her bare feet that much, putting down her heels and then letting the weight move along to her toes as if she was testing the floor with every step, putting a little deliberate extra action into it. You never know for sure how girls' minds work (do you really think it's a mind in there or just a little buzz like a bee in a glass jar?) but you got the idea she had talked the other two into coming in here with her, and now she was showing them how to do it, walk slow and hold yourself straight.

She had on a kind of dirty-pink — beige maybe, I don't know — bathing suit with a little nubble all over it and, what got me, the straps were down. They were off her shoulders looped loose around the cool tops of her arms, and I guess as a result the suit had slipped a little on her, so all around the top of the cloth there was this shining rim. If it hadn't been there you wouldn't have known there could have been anything whiter than those shoulders. With the straps pushed off, there was nothing between the top of the suit and the top of her head except just *her,* this clean bare plane of the top of her chest down from the shoulder bones like a dented sheet of metal tilted in the light. I mean, it was more than pretty.

She had sort of oaky hair that the sun and salt had bleached, done up in a bun that was unravelling, and a kind of prim face. Walking into the A & P with your straps down, I suppose it's the only kind of face you *can* have. She held her head so high her neck, coming up out of those white shoulders, looked kind of stretched, but I didn't mind. The longer her neck was, the more of her there was.

She must have felt in the corner of her eye me and over my shoulder Stokesie in the second slot watching, but she didn't tip. Not this queen. She kept her eyes moving across the racks, and stopped, and turned so slow it made my stomach rub the inside of my apron, and buzzed to the other two, who kind of huddled against her for relief, and then they all three of them went up the cat and dog food breakfast cereal-macaroni-rice-raisins-seasonings-spreads-spaghetti-soft drinks-crackers-and-cookies aisle. From the third slot I look straight up this aisle to the meat counter, and I watched them all the way. The fat one with the tan sort of fumbled with the cookies, but on second thought she put the package back. The sheep pushing their carts down the aisle — the girls were walking against the usual traffic (not that we have one-way signs or anything) — were pretty hilarious. You could see them, when Queenie's white shoulders dawned on them, kind of jerk, or hop, or hiccup, but their eyes snapped back to their own baskets and on they pushed. I bet you could set off dynamite in an A & P and the people would by and large keep reaching and checking oatmeal off their lists and muttering "Let me see, there was a third thing, began with A, asparagus, no, ah, yes, applesauce!"

or whatever it is they do mutter. But there was no doubt, this jiggled them. A few houseslaves in pin curlers even look around after pushing their carts past to make sure what they had seen was correct.

You know, it's one thing to have a girl in a bathing suit down on the beach, where what with the glare nobody can look at each other much anyway, and another thing in the cool of the A & P, under the fluorescent lights, against all those stacked packages, with her feet paddling along naked over our checker-board green-and-cream rubber-tile floor.

"Oh Daddy," Stokesie said beside me. "I feel so faint."

"Darling," I said. "Hold me tight." Stokesie's married, with two babies chalked up on his fuselage already, but as far as I can tell that's the only difference. He's twenty-two, and I was nineteen this April.

"Is it done?" he asks, the responsible married man finding his voice. I forgot to say he thinks he's going to be manager some sunny day, maybe in 1990 when it's called the Great Alexandrov and Petrooshki Tea Company or something.

What he meant was, our town is five miles from a beach, with a big summer colony out on the Point, but we're right in the middle of town, and the women generally put on a shirt or shorts or something before they get out of the car into the street. And anyway these are usually women with six children and varicose veins mapping their legs and nobody, including them, could care less. As I say, we're right in the middle of town, and if you stand at our front doors you can see two banks and the Congregational church and the newspaper store and three real estate offices and about twenty-seven old free-loaders tearing up Central Street because the sewer broke again. It's not as if we're on the Cape; we're north of Boston and there's people in this town haven't seen the ocean for twenty years.

The girls had reached the meat counter and were asking McMahon something. He pointed, they pointed, and they shuffled out of sight behind a pyramid of Diet Delight peaches. All that was left for us to see was old McMahon patting his mouth and looking after them sizing up their joints. Poor kids, I began to feel sorry for them, they couldn't help it.

Now here comes the sad part of the story, at least my family says it's sad, but I don't think it's so sad myself. The store's pretty empty, it being Thursday afternoon, so there was nothing much to do except lean on the register and wait for the girls to show up again. The whole store was like a pinball machine and I didn't know which tunnel they'd come out of. After a while they come around out of the far aisle, around the light bulbs, records at discount of the Caribbean Six or Tony Martin Sings or some such gunk you wonder they waste the wax on, sixpacks of candy bars, and plastic toys done up in cellophane that fall apart when a kid looks at them anyway. Around they come, Queenie still leading the way, and holding a little gray jar in her hand. Slots Three through Seven are unmanned and I could see her wondering between Stokes and me, but Stokesie with his usual luck draws an old party in baggy gray pants who stumbles up with four giant cans of pineapple juice (what do these bums *do* with all that pineapple juice? I've often asked myself) so the girls come to me. Queenie puts down the jar and I take it into my fingers icy cold. Kingfish Fancy Herring Snacks in Pure Sour Cream: 49¢. Now her hands are empty, not a ring or a bracelet, bare as God made them, and I wonder where the money's coming from. Still with that prim look she lifts a folded dollar bill out of the hollow at the center of her nubbled pink top. The jar went heavy in my hand. Really, I thought that was so cute.

Then everybody's luck begins to run out. Lengel comes in from haggling with a truck full of cabbages on the lot and is about to scuttle into the door marked MANAGER behind which he hides all day when the girls touch his eye. Lengel's pretty dreary, teaches Sunday school and the rest, but he doesn't miss that much. He comes over and says, "Girls, this isn't the beach."

Queenie blushes, though maybe it's just a brush of sunburn I was noticing for the first time, now that she was so close. "My mother asked me to pick up a jar of herring snacks." Her voice kind of startled me, the way voices do when you see the people first, coming out so flat and dumb yet kind of tony, too, the way it ticked over "pick up" and "snacks." All of a sudden I slid right down her voice into her living room. Her father and the other men were standing around in ice-cream coats and bow ties and the women were in sandals picking up herring snacks on toothpicks off a big glass plate and they were all holding drinks the color of water with olives and sprigs of mint in them. When my parents have somebody over they get lemonade and if it's a real racy affair Schlitz in tall glasses with "They'll Do It Every Time" cartoons stencilled on.

"That's all right," Lengel said. "But this isn't the beach." His repeating this struck me as funny, as if it had just occurred to him, and he had been thinking all these years the A & P was a great big dune and he was the head lifeguard. He didn't like my smiling — as I say he doesn't miss much — but he concentrates on giving the girls that sad Sunday-school-superintendent stare.

Queenie's blush is no sunburn now, and the plump one in plaid, that I liked better from the back — a really sweet can — pipes up, "We weren't doing any shopping. We just came in for the one thing."

"That makes no difference," Lengel tells her, and I could see from the way his eyes went that he hadn't noticed she was wearing a two-

piece before. "We want you decently dressed when you come in
here."

"We *are* decent," Queenie says suddenly, her lower lip pushing,
getting sore now that she remembers her place, a place from which
the crowd that runs the A & P must look pretty crummy. Fancy
Herring Snacks flashed in her very blue eyes.

"Girls, I don't want to argue with you. After this come in here with
your shoulders covered. It's our policy." He turns his back. That's
policy for you. Policy is what the kingpins want. What the others
want is juvenile delinquency.

All this while, the customers had been showing up with their carts
but, you know, sheep, seeing a scene, they had all bunched up on
Stokesie, who shook open a paper bag as gently as peeling a peach,
not wanting to miss a word. I could feel in the silence everybody
getting nervous, most of all Lengel, who asks me, "Sammy, have you
rung up this purchase?"

I thought and said "No" but it wasn't about that I was thinking. I
go through the punches, 4, 9, GROC, TOT — it's more complicated
than you think, and after you do it often enough, it begins to make a
little song, that you hear words to, in my case "Hello (*bing*) there, you
(*gung*) hap-py *pee*-pul (*splat*)!" — the *splat* being the drawer flying
out. I uncrease the bill, tenderly as you may imagine, it just having
come from between the two smoothest scoops of vanilla I had ever
known were there, and pass a half and a penny into her narrow pink
palm, and nestle the herrings in a bag and twist its neck and hand it
over, all the time thinking.

The girls, and who'd blame them, are in a hurry to get out, so I say
"I quit" to Lengel quick enough for them to hear, hoping they'll stop
and watch me, their unsuspected hero. They keep right on going, into
the electric eye; the door flies open and they flicker across the lot to
their car, Queenie and Plaid and Big Tall Goony-Goony (not that as
raw material she was so bad), leaving me with Lengel and a kink in
his eyebrow.

"Did you say something, Sammy?"

"I said I quit."

"I thought you did."

"You didn't have to embarrass them."

"It was they who were embarrassing us."

I started to say something that came out "Fiddle-de-doo." It's a
saying of my grandmother's, and I know she would have been
pleased.

"I don't think you know what you're saying," Lengel said.

"I know you don't," I said. "But I do." I pull the bow at the back of
my apron and start shrugging it off my shoulders. A couple customers

that had been heading for my slot begin to knock against each other, like scared pigs in a chute.

Lengel sighs and begins to look very patient and old and gray. He's been a friend of my parents for years. "Sammy, you don't want to do this to your Mom and Dad," he tells me. It's true, I don't. But it seems to me that once you begin a gesture it's fatal not to go through with it. I fold the apron, "Sammy" stitched in red on the pocket, and put it on the counter, and drop the bow tie on top of it. The bow tie is theirs, if you've ever wondered. "You'll feel this for the rest of your life," Lengel says, and I know that's true, too, but remembering how he made that pretty girl blush makes me so scrunchy inside I punch the No Sale tab and the machine whirs "pee-pul" and the drawer splats out. One advantage to this scene taking place in summer, I can follow this up with a clean exit, there's no fumbling around getting your coat and galoshes, I just saunter into the electric eye in my white shirt that my mother ironed the night before, and the door heaves itself open, and outside the sunshine is skating around on the asphalt.

I look around for my girls, but they're gone, of course. There wasn't anybody but some young married screaming with her children about some candy they didn't get by the door of a powder-blue Falcon station wagon. Looking back in the big windows, over the bags of peat moss and aluminum lawn furniture stacked on the pavement, I could see Lengel in my place in the slot, checking the sheep through. His face was dark gray and his back stiff, as if he'd just had an injection of iron, and my stomach kind of fell as I felt how hard the world was going to be to me hereafter.

Robert Coover (b.1932)

The Brother

right there right there in the middle of the damn field he says he wants to put that thing together him and his buggy ideas and so me I says "how the hell you gonna get it down to the water?" but he just focuses me out sweepin the blue his eyes rollin like they do when he gets het on some new lunatic notion and he says not to worry none about that just would I help him for God's sake and because he don't know how he can get it down in time otherwise and though you'd have to be loonier than him to say yes I says I will of course I always would crazy as my brother is I've done little else since I was born and

my wife she says "I can't figure it out I can't see why you always have
to be babyin that old fool he ain't never done nothin for you God
knows and you got enough to do here fields need plowin it's a bad
enough year already my God and now that red eyed brother of yours
wingin around like a damn cloud and not knowin what in the world
he's doin buildin a damn boat in the country my God what next?
you're a damn fool I tell you" but packs me some sandwiches just the
same and some sandwiches for my brother Lord knows *his* wife don't
have no truck with him no more says he can go starve for all she cares
she's fed up every since the time he made her sit out on a hillside for
three whole days rain and everything because he said she'd see God
and she didn't see nothin and in fact she like to die from hunger
nothin but berries and his boys too they ain't so bright neither but at
least they come to help him out with his damn boat so it ain't just the
two of us thank God for *that* and it ain't no goddamn fishin boat he
wants to put up neither in fact it's the biggest damn thing I ever
heard of and for weeks *weeks* I'm tellin you we ain't doin nothin but
cutting down pine trees and haulin them out of his field which is
really pretty high up a hill and my God *that's* work lemme tell you
and my wife she sighs and says I am really crazy r-e-a-l-l-y crazy and
her four months with a child and tryin to do my work and hers too and
still when I come home from haulin timbers around all day she's got
enough left to rub my shoulders and the small of my back and fix a hot
meal her long black hair pulled to a knot behind her head and hangin
marvelously down her back her eyes gentle but very tired my God
and I says to my brother I says "look I got a lotta work to do buddy
you'll have to finish this idiot thing yourself I wanna help you all I
can you know that but" and he looks off and he says "it don't matter
none your work" and I says "the hell it don't how you think me and
my wife we're gonna eat I mean where do you think this food comes
from you been puttin away man? you can't eat this goddamn boat out
here ready to rot in that bastard sun" and he just sighs long and says
"no it just don't matter" and he sits him down on a rock kinda tired
like and stares off and looks like he might even for God's sake cry and
so I go back to bringin wood up to him and he's already started on the
keel and frame God knows how *he* ever found out to build a damn
boat lost in *his* fog where he is Lord he was twenty when I was born
and the first thing I remember was havin to lead him around so he
didn't get kicked by a damn mule him who couldn't never do nothin
in a normal way just a huge oversize fuzzyface boy so anyway I take
to gettin up a few hours earlier ever day to do my farmin my wife apt
to lose the baby if she should keep pullin around like she was doin
then I go to work on the boat until sundown and on and on the days
hot and dry and my wife keepin good food in me or else I'd of

dropped sure and no matter what I say to try and get out of it my
brother he says "you come and help now the rest don't matter" and
we just keep hammerin away and my God the damn thing is big
enough for a hundred people and at least I think at *least* it's a place to
live and not too bad at that at least it's good for somethin but my wife
she just sighs and says no good will come of it and runs her hands
through my hair but she don't ask me to stop helpin no more because
she knows it won't do no good and she's kinda turned into herself
now these days and gettin herself all ready and still we keep workin
on that damn thing that damn boat and the days pass and my brother
he says we gotta work harder we ain't got much time and from time to
time he gets a coupla neighbors to come over and give a hand them
sucked in by the size and the novelty of the thing makin jokes some
but they don't stay around more than a day or two and they go away
shakin their heads and swearin under their breath and disgusted they
got weaseled into the thing in the first place and me I only get half
my place planted and see to my stock as much as I can my wife she
takes more care of them than I can but at least we won't starve say
if we just get some rain and finally we get the damn thing done all
finished by God and we cover it in and out with pitch and put a kinda
fancy roof on it and I come home on that last day and I ain't never
goin back ain't *never* gonna let him talk me into nothin again and I'm
all smellin of tar and my wife she cries and cries and I says to her not
to worry no more I'll be home all the time and me I'm cryin a little
too though she don't notice just thinkin how she's had it so lonely
and hard and all and for one whole day I just sleep the whole damn
day and the rest of the week I work around the farm and one day I get
an idea and I go over to my brother's place and get some pieces of
wood left over and whaddaya know? they are all livin on that damn
boat there in the middle of nowhere him and his boys and some
women and my brother's wife she's there too but she's madder than
hell and carpin at him to get outa that damn boat and come home and
he says she's got just one more day and then he's gonna drug her on
the boat but he don't say it like a threat or nothin more like a fact a
plain fact tomorrow he's gonna drug her on the boat well I ain't one to
get mixed up in domestic quarrels God knows so I grab up the wood
and beat it back to my farm and that evenin I make a little cradle a
kinda fancy one with little animal figures cut in it and polished down
and after supper I give it to my wife as a surprise and she cries and
cries and holds me tight and says don't never go away again and stay
close by her and all and I feel so damn good and warm about it all and
glad the boat thing is over and we get out a little wine and we decide
the baby's name is gonna be either Nathaniel or Anna and so we
drink an extra cup to Nathaniel's health and we laugh and we sigh

and drink one to Anna and my wife she gently fingers the little animal figures and says they're beautiful and really they ain't I ain't much good at that sorta thing but I know what she means and then she says "where did you get the wood?" and I says "it's left over from the boat" and she don't say nothin for a moment and then she says "you been over there again today?" and I says "yes just to get the wood" and she says "what's he doin now he's got the boat done?" and I says "funny thing they're all living in the damn thing all except the old lady she's over there hollerin at him how he's gettin senile and where does he think he's sailin to and how if he ain't afraid of runnin into a octypuss on the way he oughta get back home and him sayin she's a nut there ain't no water and her sayin that's what *she's* been tellin *him* for six months" and my wife she laughs and it's the happiest laugh I've heard from her in half a year and I laugh and we both have another cup of wine and my wife she says "so he's just livin on that big thing all by hisself?" and I says "no he's got his boys on there and some young women who are maybe wives of the boys or somethin I don't know I ain't never seen them before and all kindsa damn animals and birds and things I ain't never seen the likes" and my wife she says "animals? what animals?" and I says "oh all kinds I don't know a whole damn menagerie all clutterin and stinkin up the boat *God* what a mess" and my wife laughs again and she's a little silly with the wine and she says "I bet he ain't got no pigs" and "oh yes I seen them" I says and we laugh thinkin about pigs rootin around in that big tub and she says "I bet he ain't got no jackdaws" and I says "yes I seen a couple of them too or mostly I heard them you couldn't hardly hear nothin else" and we laugh again thinkin about them crows and his old lady and the pigs and all and my wife she says "*I* know what he ain't got I bet he ain't got no lice" and we both laugh like crazy and when I can I says "oh yes he does less he's took a bath" and we both laugh till we're cryin and we finish off the wine and my wife says "look now I *know* what he ain't got he ain't got no termites" and I says "you're right I don't recollect no termites maybe we oughta make him a present" and my wife she holds me close quiet all of a sudden and says "he's really movin Nathaniel's really movin" and she puts my hand down on her round belly and the little fella is kickin up a terrific storm and I says kinda anxious "does it hurt? do you think that — ?" and "no" she says "it's good" she says and so I says with my hand on her belly "here's to you Nathaniel" and we drain what's left in the bottom of our cups and the next day we wake up in each other's arms and its' rainin and *thank God* we say and since it's rainin real good we stay inside and do things around the place and we're happy because the rain has come just in time and in the evenin things smell green and fresh and delicious and it's still

rainin a little but not too hard so I decide to take a walk and I wander
over by my brother's place thinkin I'll ask him if he'd like to take on
some pet termites to go with his collection and there by God is his
wife on the boat and I don't know if he drug her on or if she just
finally come by herself but she ain't saying nothin which is damn
unusual and the boys they ain't sayin nothing neither and my brother
he ain't sayin nothing they're just all standin up there on top and gazin
off and I holler up at them "nice rain ain't it?" and my brother he
looks down at me standin there in the rain and still he don't say
nothin but he raises his hand kinda funny like and then puts it back
on the rail and I decide not to say nothin about the termites and it's
startin to rain a little harder again so I turn away and go back home
and I tell my wife about what happened and my wife she just laughs
and says "they're *all* crazy he's finally got them *all* crazy" and she's
cooked me up a special pastry with fresh meat and so we forget about
them but by God the next day the rain's still comin down harder than
ever and water's beginnin to stand around in places and after a week
of rain I can see the crops is pretty well ruined and I'm havin trouble
keepin my stock fed and my wife she's cryin and talkin about our bad
luck that we might as well of built a damn boat as plant all them crops
and still we don't figure things out I mean it just don't come to our
minds not even when the rain keeps spillin down like a ocean
dumped upsidedown and now water is beginnin to stand around in
big pools really big ones and water up to the ankles around the house
and leakin in and pretty soon the whole damn house is gettin fulla
water and I keep sayin maybe we oughta go use my brother's boat till
this blows over but my wife she says "never" and then she starts in
cryin again so finally I says to her I says "we can't be so proud I'll go
ask him" and so I set out in the storm and I can hardly see where I'm
goin and I slip up to my neck in places and finally I get to where the
boat is and I holler up and my brother he comes out and he looks
down at where I am and he don't say nothin that bastard he just looks
at me and I shout up at him I says "hey is it all right for me and my
wife to come over until this thing blows over?" and still he don't say
a damn word he just raises his hand in that same sillyass way and I
holler "hey you stupid sonuvabitch I'm soakin wet goddamn it and
my house is fulla water and my wife she's about to have a kid and
she's apt to get sick all wet and cold to the bone and all I'm askin
you — " and right then right while I'm still talkin he turns around and
he goes back in the boat and I can't hardly believe it me his brother
but he don't come back out and I push up under the boat and I beat
on it with my fists and scream at him and call him every name I can
think up and I shout for his boys and for his wife and for anybody inside and nobody comes out "GOD*damn* YOU" I cry out at the top of my

lungs and half sobbin and sick and then feelin too beat out to do anythin more I turn around and head back for home but the rain is thunderin down like mad now and it places I gotta swim and I can't make it no further and I recollect a hill nearby and I head for it and when I get to it I climb up on top of it and it feels good to be on land again even if it is soggy and greasy and I vomit and retch there awhile and move further up and the next thing I know I'm wakin up the rain still in my face and the water halfway up the hill toward me and I look out and I can see my brother's boat is floatin and I wave at it but I don't see nobody wave back and then I quick look out towards my own place and all I can see is the top of it and of a sudden I'm scared scared about my wife and I go tearin for the house swimmin most all the way and cryin and shoutin and the rain still comin down like crazy and so now well now I'm back here on the hill again what little there is left of it and I'm figurin maybe I got a day left if the rain keeps comin and it don't show no signs of stoppin and I can't see my brother's boat no more gone just water how *how* did he know? that bastard and yet I gotta hand it to him it's not hard to see who's crazy around here I can't see my house no more I just left my wife inside where I found her I couldn't hardly stand to look at her the way she was

Joyce Carol Oates (b. 1938)

Where Are You Going, Where Have You Been?

To Bob Dylan

Her name was Connie. She was fifteen and she had a quick nervous giggling habit of craning her neck to glance into mirrors or checking other people's faces to make sure her own was all right. Her mother, who noticed everything and knew everything and who hadn't much reason any longer to look at her own face, always scolded Connie about it. "Stop gawking at yourself, who are you? You think you're so pretty?" she would say. Connie would raise her eyebrows at these familiar complaints and look right through her mother, into a shadowy vision of herself as she was right at that moment: she knew she was pretty and that was everything. Her mother had been pretty once too, if you could believe those old snapshots in the album, but now her looks were gone and that was why she was always after Connie.

"Why don't you keep your room clean like your sister? How've you got your hair fixed — what the hell stinks? Hair spray? You don't see your sister using that junk."

Her sister June was twenty-four and still lived at home. She was a secretary in the high school Connie attended, and if that wasn't bad enough — with her in the same building — she was so plain and chunky and steady that Connie had to hear her praised all the time by her mother and her mother's sisters. June did this, June did that, she saved money and helped clean the house and cooked and Connie couldn't do a thing, her mind was all filled with trashy daydreams. Their father was away at work most of the time and when he came home he wanted supper and he read the newpaper at supper and after supper he went to bed. He didn't bother talking much to them, but around his bent head Connie's mother kept picking at her until Connie wished her mother were dead and she herself were dead and it were all over. "She makes me want to throw up sometimes," she complained to her friends. she had a high, breathless, amused voice which made everything she said sound a little forced, whether it was sincere or not.

There was one good thing: June went places with girlfriends of hers, girls who were just as plain and steady as she, and so when Connie wanted to do that her mother had no objections. The father of Connie's best girlfriend drove the girls the three miles to town and left them off at a shopping plaza, so that they could walk through the stores or go to a movie, and when he came to pick them up again at eleven he never bothered to ask what they had done.

They must have been familiar sights, walking around that shopping plaza in their shorts and flat ballerina slippers that always scuffed the sidewalk, with charm bracelets jingling on their thin wrists; they would lean together to whisper and laugh secretly if someone passed by who amused or interested them. Connie had long dark blond hair that drew anyone's eye to it, and she wore part of it pulled up on her head and puffed out and the rest of it she let fall down her back. She wore a pullover jersey blouse that looked one way when she was at home and another way when she was away from home. Everything about her had two sides to it, one for home and one for anywhere that was not home: her walk that could be childlike and bobbing, or languid enough to make anyone think she was hearing music in her head, her mouth which was pale and smirking most of the time, but bright and pink on these evenings out, her laugh which was cynical and drawling at home — "Ha, ha, very funny" — but high-pitched and nervous anywhere else, like the jingling of the charms on her bracelet.

Sometimes they did go shopping or to a movie, but sometimes

they went across the highway, ducking fast across the busy road, to a drive-in restaurant where older kids hung out. The restaurant was shaped like a big bottle, though squatter than a real bottle, and on its cap was a revolving figure of a grinning boy who held a hamburger aloft. One night in midsummer they ran across, breathless with daring, and right away someone leaned out a car window and invited them over, but it was just a boy from high school they didn't like. It made them feel good to be able to ignore him. They went up through the maze of parked and cruising cars to the bright-lit, fly-infested restaurant, their faces pleased and expectant as if they were entering a sacred building that loomed out of the night to give them what haven and what blessing they yearned for. They sat at the counter and crossed their legs at the ankles, their thin shoulders rigid with excitement, and listened to the music that made everything so good: the music was always in the background like music at a church service, it was something to depend upon.

A boy named Eddie came in to talk with them. He sat backward on his stool, turning himself jerkily around in semicircles and then stopping and turning again, and after awhile he asked Connie if she would like something to eat. She said she did and so she tapped her friend's arm on her way out — her friend pulled her face up into a brave droll look — and Connie said she would meet her at eleven, across the way. "I just hate to leave her like that," Connie said earnestly, but the boy said that she wouldn't be alone for long. So they went out to his car and on the way Connie couldn't help but let her eyes wander over the windshields and faces all around her, her face gleaming with a joy that had nothing to do with Eddie or even this place; it might have been the music. She drew her shoulders up and sucked in her breath with the pure pleasure of being alive, and just at that moment she happened to glance at a face just a few feet from hers. It was a boy with shaggy black hair, in a convertible jalopy painted gold. He stared at her and then his lips widened into a grin. Connie slit her eyes at him and turned away, but she couldn't help glancing back and there he was still watching her. He wagged a finger and laughed and said, "Gonna get you, baby," and Connie turned away again without Eddie noticing anything.

She spent three hours with him, at the restaurant where they ate hamburgers and drank Cokes in wax cups that were always sweating, and then down an alley a mile or so away, and when he left her off at five to eleven only the movie house was still open at the plaza. Her girlfriend was there, talking with a boy. When Connie came up the two girls smiled at each other and Connie said, "How was the movie?" and the girl said, "*You* should know." They rode off with the girl's father, sleepy and pleased, and Connie couldn't help but look at the darkened shopping plaza with its big empty parking lot and its signs that were faded and ghostly now, and over at the drive-in restaurant where cars were still circling tirelessly. She couldn't hear the music at this distance.

Next morning June asked her how the movie was and Connie said, "So-so."

She and that girl and occasionally another girl went out several times a week that way, and the rest of the time Connie spent around the house — it was summer vacation — getting in her mother's way and thinking, dreaming, about the boys she met. But all the boys fell back and dissolved into a single face that was not even a face, but an idea, a feeling, mixed up with the urgent insistent pounding of the music and the humid night air of July. Connie's mother kept dragging her back to the daylight by finding things for her to do or saying, suddenly, "What's this about the Pettinger girl?"

And Connie would say nervously, "Oh, her. That dope." She always drew thick clear lines between herself and such girls, and her mother was simple and kindly enough to believe her. Her mother was so simple, Connie thought, that it was maybe cruel to fool her so much. Her mother went scuffling around the house in old bedroom slippers and complained over the telephone to one sister about the other, then the other called up and the two of them complained about the third one. If June's name was mentioned her mother's tone was approving, and if Connie's name was mentioned it was disapproving. This did not really mean she disliked Connie and actually Connie thought that her mother preferred her to June because she was prettier, but the two of them kept up a pretense of exasperation, a sense that they were tugging and struggling over something of little value to either of them. Sometimes, over coffee, they were almost friends, but something would come up — some vexation that was like a fly buzzing suddenly around their heads — and their faces went hard with contempt.

One Sunday Connie got up at eleven — none of them bothered with church — and washed her hair so that it could dry all day long, in the sun. Her parents and sisters were going to a barbecue at an aunt's house and Connie said no, she wasn't interested, rolling her eyes to let her mother know just what she thought of it. "Stay home alone then," her mother said sharply. Connie sat out back in a lawn chair and watched them drive away, her father quiet and bald, hunched around so that he could back the car out, her mother with a look that was still angry and not at all softened through the windshield, and in the back seat poor old June all dressed up as if she didn't know what a barbecue was, with all the running yelling kids and the flies. Connie sat with her eyes closed in the sun, dreaming and dazed with the warmth about her as if this were a kind of love, the caresses of love, and her mind slipped over onto thoughts of the boy she had been with the night before and how nice he had been, how sweet it always was, not the way someone like June would suppose but sweet, gentle, the way it was in movies and promised in songs; and when she opened her eyes she hardly knew where she was, the back yard ran off into weeds and a fence line of trees and behind it the sky was perfectly blue and still. The asbestos "ranch house" that was now three years old startled her — it looked small. She shook her head as if to get awake.

It was too hot. She went inside the house and turned on the radio to drown out the quiet. She sat on the edge of her bed, barefoot, and listened for an hour and a half to a program called XYZ Sunday Jamboree, record after record of hard, fast, shrieking songs she sang along with, interspersed by exclamations from "Bobby King": "An' look here you girls at Napoleon's — Son and Charley want you to pay real close attention to this song coming up!"

And Connie paid close attention herself, bathed in a glow of slow-pulsed joy that seemed to rise mysteriously out of the music itself and lay languidly about the airless little room, breathed in and breathed out with each gentle rise and fall of her chest.

After a while she heard a car coming up the drive. She sat up at once, startled, because it couldn't be her father so soon. The gravel kept crunching all the way in from the road — the driveway was long — and Connie ran to the window. It was a car she didn't know. It was an open jalopy, painted a bright gold that caught the sunlight opaquely. Her heart began to pound and her fingers snatched at her hair, checking it, and she whispered "Christ, Christ," wondering how bad she looked. The car came to a stop at the side door and the horn sounded four short taps as if this were a signal Connie knew.

She went into the kitchen and approached the door slowly, then hung out the screen door, her bare toes curling down off the step. There were two boys in the car and now she recognized the driver: he had shaggy, shabby black hair that looked crazy as a wig and he was grinning at her.

"I ain't late, am I?" he said.

"Who the hell do you think you are?" Connie said.

"Toldja I'd be out, didn't I?"

"I don't even know who you are."

She spoke sullenly, careful to show no interest or pleasure, and he spoke in a fast bright monotone. Connie looked past him to the other boy, taking her time. He had fair brown hair, with a lock that fell onto his forehead. His sideburns gave him a fierce, embarrassed look, but so far he hadn't even bothered to glance at her. Both boys wore sunglasses. The driver's glasses were metallic and mirrored everything in miniature.

"You wanta come for a ride!" he said.

Connie smirked and let her hair fall loose over one shoulder.

"Don'tcha like my car? New paint job," he said. "Hey."

"What?"

"You're cute."

She pretended to fidget, chasing flies away from the door.

"Don'tcha believe me, or what?" he said.

"Look, I don't even know who you are," Connie said in disgust.

"Hey, Ellie's got a radio, see. Mine's broke down." He lifted his friend's arm and showed her the little transistor the boy was holding, and now Connie began to hear the music. It was the same program that was playing inside the house.

"Bobby King?" she said.

"I listen to him all the time. I think he's great."

"He's kind of great," Connie said reluctantly.

"Listen, that guy's *great*. He knows where the action is."

Connie blushed a little, because the glasses made it impossible for her to see just what this boy was looking at. She couldn't decide if she liked him or if he was just a jerk, and so she dawdled in the doorway and wouldn't come down or go back inside. She said, "What's all that stuff painted on your car?"

"Can'tcha read it?" He opened the door very carefully, as if he was afraid it might fall off. He slid out just as carefully, planting his feet firmly on the ground, the tiny metallic world in his glasses slowing down like gelatine hardening and in the midst of it Connie's bright green blouse. "This here is my name, to begin with," he said. ARNOLD FRIEND was written in tarlike black letters on the side, with a drawing of a round grinning face that reminded Connie of a pumpkin, except it wore sunglasses. "I wanta introduce myself, I'm Arnold Friend and that's my real name and I'm gonna be your friend, honey, and inside the car's Ellie Oscar, he's kinda shy." Ellie brought his transistor radio up to his shoulder and balanced it there. "Now these numbers are a secret code, honey," Arnold Friend explained. He read off the numbers 33, 19, 17 and raised his eyebrows at her to see what she thought of that, but she didn't think much of it. The left rear fender had been smashed and around it was written, on the gleaming gold background: DONE BY CRAZY WOMAN DRIVER. Connie had to laugh at that. Arnold Friend was pleased at her laughter and looked up at her. "Around the other side's a lot more — you wanta come and see them?"

"No."

"Why not?"

"Why should I?"

"Don'tcha wanta see what's on the car? Don'tcha wanta go for a ride?"

"I don't know."

"Why not?"

"I got things to do."

"Like what?"

"Things."

He laughed as if she had said something funny. He slapped his thighs. He was standing in a strange way, leaning back against the car as if he were balancing himself. He wasn't tall, only an inch or so taller than she would be if she came down to him. Connie liked the way he was dressed, which was the way all of them dressed: tight faded jeans stuffed into black, scuffed boots, a belt that pulled his waist in and showed how lean he was, and a white pullover shirt that was a little soiled and showed the hard small muscles of his arms and shoulders. He looked as if he probably did hard work, lifting and carrying things. Even his neck looked muscular. And his face was a familiar face, somehow: the jaw and chin and cheeks slightly darkened, because he hadn't shaved for a day or two, and the nose long and hawklike, sniffing as if she were a treat he was going to gobble up and it was all a joke.

"Connie, you ain't telling the truth. This is your day set aside for a ride with me and you know it," he said, still laughing. The way he straightened and recovered from his fit of laughing showed that it had been all fake.

"How do you know what my name is?" she said suspiciously.

"It's Connie."

"Maybe and maybe not."

"I know my Connie," he said, wagging his finger. Now she remembered him even better, back at the restaurant, and her cheeks warmed at the thought of how she sucked in her breath just at the moment she passed him — how she must have looked at him. And he had remembered her. "Ellie and I come out here especially for you," he said. "Ellie can sit in back. How about it?"

"Where?"

"Where what?"

"Where're we going?"

He looked at her. He took off the sunglasses and she saw how pale the skin around his eyes was, like holes that were not in shadow but instead in light. His eyes were like chips of broken glass that catch the light in an amiable way. He smiled. It was as if the idea of going for a ride somewhere, to some place, was a new idea to him.

"Just for a ride, Connie sweetheart."

"I never said my name was Connie," she said.

"But I know what it is. I know your name and all about you, lots of things," Arnold Friend said. He had not moved yet but stood still leaning back against the side of his jalopy. "I took a special interest in you, such a pretty girl, and found out all about you like I know your parents and sister are gone somewheres and I know where and how long they're going to be gone, and I know who you were with last night, and your best girlfriend's name is Betty. Right?"

He spoke in a simple lilting voice, exactly as if he were reciting the words to a song. His smile assured her that everything was fine. In the car Ellie turned up the volume on his radio and did not bother to look around at them.

"Ellie can sit in the back seat," Arnold Friend said. He indicated his friend with a casual jerk of his chin, as if Ellie did not count and she should not bother with him.

"How'd you find out all that stuff?" Connie said.

"Listen: Betty Schultz and Tony Fitch and Jimmy Pettinger and Nancy Pettinger," he said, in a chant. "Raymond Stanley and Bob Hutter — "

"Do you know all those kids?"

"I know everybody."

"Look, you're kidding. You're not from around here."

"Sure."

"But — how come we never saw you before?"

"Sure you saw me before," he said. He looked down at his boots, as if he were a little offended. "You just don't remember."

"I guess I'd remember you," Connie said.

"Yeah?" He looked up at this, beaming. He was pleased. He began to mark time with the music from Ellie's radio, tapping his fists lightly together. Connie looked away from his smile to the car, which was painted so bright it almost hurt her eyes to look at it. She looked at that name. ARNOLD FRIEND. And up at the front fender was an expression that was familiar — MAN THE FLYING SAUCERS. It was an expression kids had used the year before, but didn't use this year. She looked at it for a while as if the words meant something to her that she did not yet know.

"What're you thinking about? Huh?" Arnold Friend demanded. "Not worried about your hair blowing around in the car, are you?"

"No."

"Think I maybe can't drive good?"

"How do I know?"

"You're a hard girl to handle. How come?" he said. "Don't you know I'm your friend? Didn't you see me put my sign in the air when you walked by?"

"What sign?"

"My sign." And he drew an X in the air, leaning out toward her. They were maybe ten feet apart. After his hand fell back to his side the X was still in the air, almost visible. Connie let the screen door close and stood perfectly still inside it, listening to the music from her radio and the boy's blend together. She stared at Arnold Friend. He stood there so stiffly relaxed, pretending to be relaxed, with one hand idly on the door handle as if he were keeping himself up that way and had no intention of ever moving again. She recognized most things about him, the tight jeans that showed his thighs and buttocks and the greasy leather boots and the tight shirt, and even that slippery friendly smile of his, that sleepy dreamy smile that all the boys used to get across ideas they didn't want to put into words. She recognized all this and also the singsong way he talked, slightly mocking, kidding, but serious and a little melancholy, and she recognized the way he tapped one fist against the other in homage of the perpetual music behind him. But all these things did not come together.

She said suddenly, "Hey, how old are you?"

His smile faded. She could see then that he wasn't a kid, he was much older — thirty, maybe more. At this knowledge her heart began to pound faster.

"That's a crazy thing to ask. Can'tcha see I'm your own age?"

"Like hell you are."

"Or maybe a coupla years older, I'm eighteen."

"Eighteen?" she said doubtfully.

He grinned to reassure her and lines appeared at the corners of his mouth. His teeth were big and white. He grinned so broadly his eyes became slits and she saw how thick the lashes were, thick and black as if painted with a black tarlike material. Then he seemed to become embarrassed, abruptly, and looked over his shoulder at Ellie. "*Him*, he's crazy," he said. "Ain't he a riot, he's a nut, a real character." Ellie was still listening to the music. His sunglasses told nothing about what he was thinking. He wore a bright orange shirt unbuttoned halfway to show his chest, which was a pale, bluish chest and not muscular like Arnold Friend's, His shirt collar was turned up all around and the very tips of the collar pointed out past his chin as if they were protecting him. He was pressing the transistor radio up against his ear and sat there in a kind of daze, right in the sun.

"He's kinda strange," Connie said.

"Hey, she says you're kinda strange! Kinda strange!" Arnold Friend cried. He pounded on the car to get Ellie's attention. Ellie turned for the first time and Connie saw with shock that he wasn't a kid either — he had a fair, hairless face, cheeks reddened slightly as if the veins grew too close to the surface of his skin, the face of a forty-year-old baby. Connie felt a wave of dizziness rise in her at this sight and she stared at him as if waiting for something to change the shock of the moment, make it all right again. Ellie's lips kept shaping words, mumbling along with the words blasting in his ear.

"Maybe you two better go away," Connie said faintly.

"What? How come?" Arnold Friend cried. "We come out here to take you for a ride. It's Sunday." He had the voice of the man on the radio now. It was the same voice, Connie thought. "Don'tcha know it's Sunday all day and honey, no matter who you were with last night today you're with Arnold Friend and don't you forget it! — Maybe you better step out here," he said, and this last was in a different voice. It was a little flatter, as if the heat was finally getting to him.

"No. I got things to do."

"Hey."

"You two better leave."

"We ain't leaving until you come with us."

"Like hell I am — "

"Connie, don't fool around with me. I mean, I mean, don't fool *around*," he said, shaking his head. He laughed incredulously. He placed his sunglasses on top of his head, carefully, as if he were indeed wearing a wig, and brought the stems down behind his ears. Connie stared at him, another wave of dizziness and fear rising in her so that for a moment he wasn't even in focus but was just a blur, standing there against his gold car, and she had the idea that he had driven up the driveway all right but had come from nowhere before that and belonged nowhere and that everything about him and even about the music that was so familiar to her was only half real.

"If my father comes and sees you — "

"He ain't coming. He's at a barbecue."

"How do you know that?"

"Aunt Tillie's. Right now they're — uh — they're drinking. Sitting around," he said vaguely, squinting as if he were staring all the way to town and over to Aunt Tillie's back yard. Then the vision seemed to get clear and he nodded energetically. "Yeah. Sitting around. There's your sister in a blue dress, huh? And high heels, the poor sad bitch — nothing like you, sweetheart! And your mother's helping some fat woman with the corn, they're cleaning the corn — husking the corn — "

"What fat woman?" Connie cried.

"How do I know what fat woman, I don't know every goddam fat woman in the world!" Arnold laughed.

"Oh, that's Mrs. Hornby . . . Who invited her?" Connie said. She felt a little light-headed. Her breath was coming quickly.

"She's too fat. I don't like them fat. I like them the way you are, honey," he said, smiling sleepily at her. They stared at each other for a while, through the screen door. He said softly, "Now what you're going to do is this: you're going to come out that door. You're going to sit up front with me and Ellie's going to sit in the back, the hell with Ellie, right? This isn't Ellie's date. You're my date. I'm your lover, honey."

"What? You're crazy — "

"Yes, I'm your lover. You don't know what that is but you will," he said. "I know that too. I know all about you. But look: it's real nice and you couldn't ask for nobody better than me, or more polite. I always keep my word. I'll tell you how it is, I'm always nice at first, the first time. I'll hold you so tight you won't think you have to try to get away or pretend anything because you'll know you can't. And I'll come inside you where it's all secret and you'll give in to me and you'll love me — "

"Shut up! You're crazy!" Connie said. She backed away from the door. She put her hands against her ears as if she'd heard something terrible, something not meant for her. "People don't talk like that, you're crazy," she muttered. Her heart was almost too big now for her chest and its pumping made sweat break out all over her. She looked out to see Arnold Friend pause and then take a step toward the porch lurching. He almost fell. But, like a clever drunken man, he managed to catch his balance. He wobbled in his high boots and grabbed hold of one of the porch posts.

"Honey?" he said. "You still listening?"

"Get the hell out of here!"

"Be nice, honey. Listen."

"I'm going to call the police — "

He wobbled again and out of the side of his mouth came a fast spat curse, an aside not meant for her to hear. but even this "Christ!" sounded forced. Then he began to smile again. She watched this smile come, awkward as if he were smiling from inside a mask. His whole face was a mask, she thought wildly, tanned down onto his throat but then running out as if he had plastered makeup on his face but had forgotten about his throat.

"Honey — ? Listen, here's how it is. I always tell the truth and I promise you this: I ain't coming in that house after you."

"You better not! I'm going to call the police if you — if you don't — "

"Honey," he said, talking right through her voice, "honey, I'm not coming in there but you are coming out here. You know why?"

She was panting. The kitchen looked like a place she had never seen before, some room she had run inside but which wasn't good enough, wasn't going to help her. The kitchen window had never had a curtain, after three years, and there were dishes in the sink for her to do — probably — and if you ran your hand across the table you'd probably feel something sticky there.

"You listening, honey? Hey?"

" — going to call the police — "

"Soon as you touch the phone I don't need to keep my promise and can come inside. You won't want that."

She rushed forward and tried to lock the door. Her fingers were shaking. "But why lock it," Arnold Friend said gently, talking right into her face. "It's just a screen door. It's just nothing." One of his boots was at a strange angle, as if his foot wasn't in it. It pointed out to the left, bent at the ankle. "I mean, anybody can break through a screen door and glass and wood and iron or anything else if he needs to, anybody at all and specially Arnold Friend. If the place got lit up with a fire honey you'd come runnin' out into my arms, right into my arms an' safe at home — like you knew I was your lover and'd stopped fooling around. I don't mind a nice shy girl but I don't like no fooling around." Part of those words were spoken with a slight rhythmic lilt, and Connie somehow recognized them — the echo of a song from last year, about a girl rushing into her boyfriend's arms and coming home again —

Connie stood barefoot on the linoleum floor, staring at him. "What do you want?" she whispered.

"I want you," he said.

"What?"

"Seen you that night and thought, that's the one, yes sir. I never needed to look any more."

"But my father's coming back. He's coming to get me. I had to wash my hair first — " She spoke in a dry, rapid voice, hardly raising it for him to hear.

"No, your Daddy is not coming and yes, you had to wash your hair and you washed it for me. It's nice and shining and all for me, I thank you, sweetheart," he said, with a mock bow, but again he almost lost his balance. He had to bend and adjust his boots. Evidently his feet did not go all the way down; the boots must have been stuffed with something so that he would seem taller. Connie stared out at him and behind him Ellie in the car, who seemed to be looking off toward Connie's right into nothing. This Ellie said, pulling the words out of the air one after another as if he were just discovering them, "You want me to pull out the phone?"

"Shut your mouth and keep it shut," Arnold Friend said, his face red from bending over or maybe from embarrassment because Connie had seen his boots. "This ain't none of your business."

"What — what are you doing? What do you want?" Connie said. "If I call the police they'll get you, they'll arrest you — "

"Promise was not to come in unless you touch that phone, and I'll keep that promise," he said. He resumed his erect position and tried to force his shoulders back. He sounded like a hero in a movie, declaring something important. He spoke too loudly and it was as if he were speaking to someone behind Connie. "I ain't made plans for coming in that house where I don't belong but just for you to come out to me, the way you should. Don't you know who I am?"

"You're crazy," she whispered. She backed away from the door but did not want to go into another part of the house, as if this would give him permission to come through the door. "What do you . . . You're crazy, you . . . "

"Huh? What're you saying, honey?"

Her eyes darted everywhere in the kitchen. She could not remember what it was, this room.

"This is how it is, honey: you come out and we'll drive away, have a nice ride. But if you don't come out we're gonna wait till your people come home and then they're all going to get it."

"You want that telephone pulled out?" Ellie said. He held the radio away from his ear and grimaced, as if without the radio the air was too much for him.

"I toldja shut up, Ellie," Arnold Friend said, "you're deaf, get a hearing aid, right? Fix yourself up. This little girl's no trouble and's gonna be nice to me, so Ellie keep to yourself, this ain't your date — right? Don't hem in on me. Don't hog. Don't crush. Don't bird dog. Don't trail me," he said in a rapid meaningless voice, as if he were running through all the expressions he'd learned but was no longer sure which one of them was in style, then rushing on to new ones, making them up with his eyes closed, "Don't crawl under my fence, don't squeeze in my chipmunk hole, don't sniff my glue, suck my popsicle, keep your own greasy fingers on yourself!" He shaded his eyes and peered in at Connie, who was backed against the kitchen table. "Don't mind him honey he's just a creep. He's a dope. Right? I'm the boy for you and like I said you come out here nice like a lady and give me your hand, and nobody else gets hurt, I mean, your nice old bald-headed daddy and your mummy and your sister in her high heels. Because listen: why bring them in this?"

"Leave me alone," Connie whispered.

"Hey, you know that old woman down the road, the one with the chickens and stuff — you know her?"

"She's dead!"

"Dead? What? You know her?" Arnold Friend said.

"She's dead — "

"Don't you like her?"

"She's dead — she's — she isn't here any more — "

"But don't you like her, I mean, you got something against her? Some grudge or something?" Then his voice dipped as if he were conscious of a rudeness. He touched the sunglasses perched on top of his head as if to make sure they were still there. "Now you be a good girl."

"What are you going to do?"

"Just two things, or maybe three," Arnold Friend said. "But I promise it won't last long and you'll like me the way you get to like people you're close to. You will. It's all over for you here, so come on out. You don't want your people in any trouble, do you?"

She turned and bumped against a chair or something, hurting her leg, but she ran into the back room and picked up the telephone. Something roared in her ear, a tiny roaring, and she was so sick with fear that she could do nothing but listen to it — the telephone was clammy and very heavy and her fingers groped down to the dial but were too weak to touch it. She began to scream into the phone, into the roaring. She cried out, she cried for her mother, she felt her breath start jerking back and forth in her lungs as if it were something Arnold Friend were stabbing her with again and again with no tenderness. A noisy sorrowful wailing rose all about her and she was locked inside it the way she was locked inside this house.

After a while she could hear again. She was sitting on the floor with her wet back against the wall.

Arnold Friend was saying from the door, "That's a good girl. Put the phone back."

She kicked the phone away from her.

"No, honey. Pick it up. Put it back right."

She picked it up and put it back. The dial tone stopped.

"That's a good girl. Now you come outside."

She was hollow with what had been fear, but what was now just an emptiness. All that screaming had blasted it out of her. She sat, one leg cramped under her, and deep inside her brain was something like a pinpoint of light that kept going and would not let her relax. She thought, I'm not going to see my mother again. She thought, I'm not going to sleep in my bed again. Her bright green blouse was all wet.

Arnold Friend said, in a gentle-loud voice that was like a stage voice, "The place where you came from ain't there any more, and where you had in mind to go is canceled out. This place you are now — inside your daddy's house — is nothing but a cardboard box I can knock down any time. You know that and always did know it. You hear me?"

She thought, I have got to think. I have to know what to do.

"We'll go out to a nice field, out in the country here where it smells so nice and it's sunny," Arnold Friend said. "I'll have my arms tight around you so you won't need to try to get away and I'll show you what love is like, what it does. The hell with this house! It looks solid all right," he said. He ran a fingernail down the screen and the noise did not make Connie shiver, as it would have the day before. "Now put your hand on your heart, honey. Feel that? That feels solid too but we know better, be nice to me, be sweet like you can because what else is there for a girl like you but to be sweet and pretty and give in? — and get away before her people come back?"

She felt her pounding heart. Her hand seemed to enclose it. She thought for the first time in her life that it was nothing that was hers, that belonged to her, but just a pounding, living thing inside this body that wasn't really hers either.

"You don't want them to get hurt," Arnold Friend went on. "Now get up, honey. Get up all by yourself."

She stood.

"Now turn this way. That's right. Come over here to me — Ellie, put that away, didn't I tell you? You dope. You miserable creepy dope," Arnold Friend said. His words were not angry but only part of an incantation. The incantation was kindly. "Now come out through the kitchen to me honey, and let's see a smile, try it, you're a brave sweet little girl and now they're eating corn and hot dogs cooked to bursting over an outdoor fire, and they don't know one thing about you and never did and honey you're better than them because not a one of them would have done this for you."

Connie felt the linoleum under her feet; it was cool. She brushed her hair back out of her eyes. Arnold Friend let go of the post tentatively and opened his arms for her, his elbows pointing in toward each other and his wrists limp, to show that this was an embarrassed embrace and a little mocking, he didn't want to make her self-conscious.

She put out her hand against the screen. She watched herself push the door slowly open as if she were safe back somewhere in the other doorway, watching this body and this head of long hair moving out into the sunlight where Arnold Friend waited.

"My sweet little blue-eyed girl," he said, in a half-sung sigh that had nothing to do with her brown eyes but was taken up just the same by the vast sunlit reaches of the land behind him and on all sides of him, so much land that Connie had never seen before and did not recognize except to know that she was going to it.

Toni Cade Bambara

The Lesson

Back in the days when everyone was old and stupid or young and foolish and me and Sugar were the only ones just right, this lady moved on our block with nappy hair and proper speech and no makeup. And quite naturally we laughed at her, laughed the way we did at the junk man who went about his business like he was some big-time president and his sorry-ass horse his secretary. And we kinda hated her too, hated the way we did the winos who cluttered up our parks and pissed on our handball walls and stank up our hallways and stairs so you couldn't halfway play hide-and-seek without a goddamn gas mask. Miss Moore was her name. The only woman on the block with no first name. And she was black as hell, cept for her feet, which were fish-white and spooky. And she was always planning these boring-ass things for us to do, us being my cousin, mostly, who lived on the block cause we all moved North the same time and to the same apartment then spread out gradual to breathe. And our parents would yank our heads into some kinda shape and crisp up our clothes so we'd be presentable for travel with Miss Moore, who always looked like she was going to church, though she never did. Which is just one of things the grownups talked about when they talked behind her back like a dog. But when she came calling with some sachet she'd sewed up or some gingerbread she'd made or some book, why then they'd all be too embarrassed to turn her down and we'd get handed over all spruced up. She'd been to college and said it was only right that she should take responsibility for the young ones' education, and she not even related by marriage or blood. So they'd go for it. Specially Aunt Gretchen. She was the main gofer in the family. You got some ole dumb shit foolishness you want somebody to go for, you send for Aunt Gretchen. She been screwed into the go-along for so long, it's a blood-deep natural thing with her. Which is how she got saddled with me and Sugar and Junior in the first place while our mothers were in a la-de-da apartment up the block having a good ole time.

So this one day Miss Moore rounds us all up at the mailbox and it's puredee hot and she's knockin herself out about arithmetic. And school suppose to let up in summer I heard, but she don't never let up. And the starch in my pinafore scratching the shit outta me and I'm really hating this nappy-head bitch and her goddamn college degree. I'd much rather go to the pool or to the show where it's cool. So me and Sugar leaning on the mailbox being surly, which is a Miss Moore word. And Flyboy checking out what everybody brought for lunch. And Fat Butt already wasting his peanut-butter-and-jelly sandwich like the pig he is. And Junebug punchin on Q.T.'s arm for potato chips. And Rosie Giraffe shifting from one hip to the other waiting for somebody to step on her foot or ask her if she from Georgia so she can kick ass, preferably Mercedes'. And Miss Moore asking us do we know what money is, like we a bunch of retards. I mean real money, she say, like it's only poker chips or monopoly papers we lay on the grocer. So right away I'm tired of this and say so. And would much rather snatch Sugar and go to the Sunset and terrorize the West Indian kids and take their hair ribbons and their money too. And Miss Moore files that remark away for next week's lesson on brotherhood, I can tell. And finally I say we oughta get to the subway cause it's cooler and besides we might meet some cute boys. Sugar done swiped her mama's lipstick, so we ready.

So we heading down the street and she's boring us silly about what things cost and what our parents make and how much goes for rent and how money ain't divided up right in this country. And then she gets to the part about we all poor and live in the slums, which I don't feature. And I'm ready to speak on that, but she steps out in the street and hails two cabs just like that. Then she hustles half the crew in with her and hands me a five-dollar bill and tells me to calculate 10 percent tip for the driver. And we're off. Me and Sugar and Junebug and Flyboy hangin out the window and hollering to everybody, putting lipstick on each other cause Flyboy a faggot anyway, and making farts with our sweaty armpits. But I'm mostly trying to figure how to spend this money. But they all fascinated with the meter ticking and Junebug starts laying bets as to how much it'll read when Flyboy can't hold his breath no more. Then Sugar lays bets as to how much it'll be when we get there. So I'm stuck. Don't nobody want to go for my plan, which is to jump out at the next light and run off to the first bar-b-que we can find. Then the driver tells us to get the hell out cause we there already. And the meter reads eighty-five cents. And I'm stalling to figure out the tip and Sugar say give him a dime. And I decide he don't need it bad as I do, so later for him. But then he tries to take off with Junebug foot still in the door so we talk about his mama something ferocious. Then we check out that we on Fifth Avenue and everybody dressed up in stockings. One lady in a fur coat, hot as it is. White folks crazy.

"This is the place," Miss Moore say, presenting it to us in the voice she uses at the museum. "Let's look in the windows before we go in."

"Can we steal?" Sugar asks very serious like she's getting the ground rules squared away before she plays. "I beg your pardon," say

Miss Moore, and we fall out. So she leads us around the windows of the toy store and me and Sugar screamin, "This is mine, that's mine, I gotta have that, that was made for me, I was born for that," till Big Butt drowns us out.

"Hey, I'm goin to buy that there."

"That there? You don t even know what it is, stupid."

"I do so," he say punchin on Rosie Giraffe. "It's a microscope."

"Whatcha gonna do with a microscope, fool?"

"Look at things."

"Like what, Ronald?" ask Miss Moore. And Big Butt ain't got the first notion. So here go Miss Moore gabbing about the thousands of bacteria in a drop of water and the somethinorother in a speck of blood and the million and one living things in the air around us is invisible to the naked eye. And what she say that for? Junebug go to town on that "naked" and we rolling. Then Miss Moore ask what it cost. So we all jam into the window smudgin it up and the price tag say $300. So then she ask how long'd take for Big Butt and Junebug to save up their allowances. "Too long," I say. "Yeh," adds Sugar, "outgrown it by that time." And Miss Moore say no, you never outgrow learning instruments. "Why, even medical students and interns and," blah, blah, blah. And we ready to choke Big Butt for bringing it up in the first damn place.

"This here costs four hundred eighty dollars," say Rosie Giraffe. So we pile up all over her to see what she pointin out. My eyes tell me it's a chunk of glass cracked with something heavy, and different-color inks dripped into the splits, then the whole thing put into a oven or something. But for $480 it don't make sense.

"That's a paperweight made of semi-precious stones fused together under tremendous pressure," she explains slowly, with her hands doing the mining and all the factory work.

"So what's a paperweight?" asks Rosie Giraffe.

"To weigh paper with, dumbbell," say Flyboy, the wise man from the East.

"Not exactly," say Miss Moore, which is what she say when you warm or way off too. "It's to weigh paper down so it won't scatter and make your desk untidy." So right away me and Sugar curtsy to each other and then to Mercedes who is more the tidy type.

"We don't keep paper on top of the desk in my class," say Junebug, figuring Miss Moore crazy or lyin one.

"At home, then," she say. "Don't you have a calendar and a pencil case and a blotter and a letter-opener on your desk at home where you do your homework?" And she know damn well what our homes look like cause she nosys around in them every chance she gets.

"I don't even have a desk," say Junebug. "Do we?"

"No. And I don't get no homework neither," says Big Butt.

"And I don't even have a home," say Flyboy like he do at school to keep the white folks off his back and sorry for him. Send this poor kid to camp posters, is his specialty.

"I do," says Mercedes. "I have a box of stationery on my desk and a picture of my cat. My godmother bought the stationery and the desk. There's a big rose on each sheet and the envelopes smell like roses."

"Who wants to know about your smelly-ass stationery," say Rosie Giraffe fore I can get my two cents in.

"It's important to have a work area all your own so that . . ."

"Will you look at this sailboat, please," say Flyboy, cuttin her off and pointin to the thing like it was his. So once again we tumble all over each other to gaze at this magnificent thing in the toy store which is just big enough to maybe sail two kittens across the pond if you strap them to the posts tight. We all start reciting the price tag like we in assembly. "Handcrafted sailboat of fiberglass at one thousand one hundred ninety-five dollars."

"Unbelievable," I hear myself say and am really stunned. I read it again for myself just in case the group recitation put me in a trance. Same thing. For some reason this pisses me off. We look at Miss Moore and she lookin at us, waiting for I dunno what.

"Who'd pay all that when you can buy a sailboat set for a quarter at Pop's, a tube of glue for a dime, and a ball of string for eight cents? It must have a motor and a whole lot else besides," I say. "My sailboat cost me about fifty cents."

"But will it take water?" say Mercedes with her smart ass.

"Took mine to Alley Pond Park once," say Flyboy. "String broke. Lost it. Pity."

"Sailed mine in Central Park and it keeled over and sank. Had to ask my father for another dollar."

"And you got the strap," laugh Big Butt. "The jerk didn't even have a string on it. My old man wailed on his behind."

Little Q.T. was staring hard at the sailboat and you could see he wanted it bad. But he too little and somebody'd just take it from him. So what the hell. "This boat for kids, Miss Moore?"

"Parents silly to buy something like that just to get all broke up," say Rosie Giraffe.

"That much money it should last forever," I figure.

"My father'd buy it for me if I wanted it."

"Your father, my ass," say Rosie Giraffe getting a chance to finally push Mercedes.

"Must be rich people shop here," say Q.T.

"You are a very bright boy," say Flyboy. "What was your first clue?" And he rap him on the head with the back of his knuckles, since Q.T. the only one he could get away with. Though Q.T. liable to come up behind you years later and get his licks in when you half expect it.

"What I want to know is," I says to Miss Moore though I never talk to her, I wouldn't give the bitch that satisfaction, "is how much a real boat costs? I figure a thousand'd get you a yacht any day."

"Why don't you check that out," she says, "and report back to the group?" Which really pains my ass. If you gonna mess up a perfectly good swim day least you could do is have some answers. "Let's go in," she say like she got something up her sleeve. Only she don't lead the way. So me and Sugar turn the corner to where the entrance is, but when we get there I kinda hang back. Not that I'm scared, what's there to be afraid of, just a toy store. But I feel funny, shame. But what I got to be shamed about? Got as much right to go in as anybody. But somehow I can't seem to get hold of the door, so I step away for Sugar to lead. But she hangs back too. And I look at her and she looks at me and this is ridiculous. I mean, damn, I have never ever been shy about doing nothing or going nowhere. But then Mercedes steps up and then Rosie Giraffe and Big Butt crowd in behind and shove, and next thing we all stuffed into the doorway with only Mercedes squeezing past us, smoothing out her jumper and walking right down the aisle. Then the rest of us tumble in like a glued-together jigsaw done all wrong. And people lookin at us. And it's like the time me and Sugar crashed into the Catholic church on a dare. But once we got in there and everything so hushed and holy and the candles and the bowin and the handkerchiefs on all the drooping heads, I just couldn't go through with the plan. Which was for me to run up to the altar and do a tap dance while Sugar played the nose flute and messed around in the holy water. And Sugar kept givin me the elbow. Then later teased me so bad I tied her up in the shower and turned it on and locked her in. And she'd be there till this day if Aunt Gretchen hadn't finally figured I was lyin about the boarder takin a shower.

Same thing in the store. We all walkin on tiptoe and hardly touchin the games and puzzles and things. And I watched Miss Moore who is steady watchin us like she waitin for a sign. Like Mama Drewery watches the sky and sniffs the air and takes note of just how much slant is in the bird formation. Then me and Sugar bump smack into each other, so busy gazing at the toys, 'specially the sailboat. But we don't laugh and go into our fat-lady bump-stomach routine. We just stare at that price tag. Then Sugar run a finger over the whole boat. And I'm jealous and want to hit her. Maybe not her, but I sure want to punch somebody in the mouth.

"Watcha bring us here for, Miss Moore?"

"You sound angry, Sylvia. Are you mad about something?" Givin me one of them grins like she tellin a grown-up joke that never turns out to be funny. And she's lookin very closely at me like maybe she plannin to do my portrait from memory. I'm mad, but I won't give her that satisfaction. So I slouch around the store bein very bored and say, "Let's go."

Me and Sugar at the back of the train watchin the tracks whizzin by large then small then gettin gobbled up in the dark. I'm thinkin about this tricky toy I saw in the store. A clown that somersaults on a bar then does chin-ups just cause you yank lightly at his leg. Cost $35. I could see me askin my mother for a $35 birthday clown. "You wanna who that costs what?" she'd say, cocking her head to the side to get a better view of the hole in my head. Thirty-five dollars could buy new bunk beds for Junior and Gretchen's boy. Thirty-five dollars and the whole household could go visit Granddaddy Nelson in the country. Thirty-five dollars would pay for the rent and the piano bill too. Who are these people that spend that much for performing clowns and $1000 for toy sailboats? What kinda work they do and how they live and how come we ain't in on it? Where we are is who we are, Miss Moore always pointin out. But it don't necessarily have to be that way, she always adds then waits for somebody to say that poor people have to wake up and demand their share of the pie and don't none of us know what kind of pie she talkin about in the first damn place. But she ain't so smart cause I still got her four dollars from the taxi and she sure ain't gettin it. Messin up my day with this shit. Sugar nudges me in my pocket and winks.

Miss Moore lines us up in front of the mailbox where we started from, seem like years ago, and I got a headache for thinkin so hard. And we lean all over each other so we can hold up under the draggy-ass lecture she always finishes us off with at the end before we thank her for borin us to tears. But she just looks at us like she readin tea leaves. Finally she say, "Well, what did you think of F. A. O. Schwarz?"

Rosie Giraffe mumbles, "White folks crazy."

"I'd like to go there again when I get my birthday money," says Mercedes, and we shove her out the pack so she has to lean on the mailbox by herself.

"I'd like a shower. Tiring day," say Flyboy.

Then Sugar surprises me by sayin, "You know, Miss Moore, I don't think all of us here put together eat in a year what that sailboat costs." And Miss Moore lights up like somebody goosed her. "And?" she say, urging Sugar on. Only I'm standin on her foot so she don't continue.

"Imagine for a minute what kind of society it is in which some people can spend on a toy what it would cost to feed a family of six or seven. What do you think?"

"I think," say Sugar pushing me off her feet like she never done before, cause I whip her ass in a minute, "that this is not much of a democracy if you ask me. Equal chance to pursue happiness means an equal crack at the dough, don't it?" Miss Moore is besides herself and I am disgusted with Sugar's treachery. So I stand on her foot one more time to see if she'll shove me. She shuts up, and Miss Moore looks at me, sorrowfully I'm thinkin. And somethin weird is goin on, I can feel it in my chest.

"Anybody else learn anything today?" lookin dead at me. I walk away and Sugar has to run to catch up and don't even seem to notice when I shrug her arm off my shoulder.

"Well, we got four dollars anyway," she says.

"Uh hunh."

"We could go to Hascombs and get half a chocolate layer and then go to the Sunset and still have plenty money for potato chips and ice cream sodas."

"Uh hunh."

"Race you to Hascombs," she say.

We start down the block and she gets ahead which is O.K. by me cause I'm goin to the West End and then over to the Drive to think this day through. She can run if she want to and even run faster. But ain't nobody gonna beat me at nuthin.

Alice Walker (b. 1944)

Everyday Use

for your grandmama

I will wait for her in the yard that Maggie and I made so clean and wavy yesterday afternoon. A yard like this is more comfortable than most people know. It is not just a yard. It is like an extended living room. When the hard clay is swept clean as a floor and the fine sand around the edges lined with tiny, irregular grooves anyone can come and sit and look up into the elm tree and wait for the breezes that never come inside the house.

Maggie will be nervous until after her sister goes: she will stand hopelessly in corners homely and ashamed of the burn scars down her arms and legs, eyeing her sister with a mixture of envy and awe. She thinks her sister has held life always in the palm of one hand, that "no" is a word the world never learned to say to her.

You've no doubt seen those TV shows where the child who has "made it" is confronted, as a surprise, by her own mother and father, tottering in weakly from backstage. (A pleasant surprise, of course: What would they do if parent and child came on the show only to curse out and insult each other?) On TV mother and child embrace and smile into each other's faces. Sometimes the mother and father weep, the child wraps them in her arms and leans across the table to tell how she would not have made it without their help. I have seen these programs.

Sometimes I dream a dream in which Dee and I are suddenly brought together on a TV program of this sort. Out of a dark and soft-seated limousine I am ushered into a bright room filled with many people. There I meet a smiling, gray, sporty man like Johnny Carson who shakes my hand and tells me what a fine girl I have. Then we are on the stage and Dee is embracing me with tears in her eyes. She pins on my dress a large orchid, even though she has told me once that she thinks orchids are tacky flowers.

In real life I am a large, big-boned woman with rough, man-working hands. In the winter I wear flannel nightgowns to bed and overalls during the day. I can kill and clean a hog as mercilessly as a man. My fat keeps me hot in zero weather. I can work outside all day, breaking ice to get water for washing; I can eat pork liver cooked over the open fire minutes after it comes steaming from the hog. One winter I knocked a bull calf straight in the brain between the eyes with a sledge hammer and had the meat hung up to chill before nightfall. But of course all this does not show on television. I am the way my daughter would want me to be: a hundred pounds lighter, my skin like an uncooked barley pancake. My hair glistens in the hot bright lights. Johnny Carson has much to do to keep up with my quick and witty tongue.

But that is a mistake. I know even before I wake up. Who ever knew a Johnson with a quick tongue? Who can even imagine me looking a strange white man in the eye? It seems to me I have talked to them always with one foot raised in flight, with my head turned in whichever way is farthest from them. Dee, though. She would always look anyone in the eye. Hesitation was no part of her nature.

"How do I look, Mama?" Maggie says, showing just enough of her thin body enveloped in pink skirt and red blouse for me to know she's there, almost hidden by the door.

"Come out into the yard," I say.

Have you ever seen a lame animal, perhaps a dog run over by some careless person rich enough to own a car, sidle up to someone who is ignorant enough to be kind to him? That is the way my Maggie walks. She has been like this, chin on chest, eyes on ground, feet in shuffle, ever since the fire that burned the other house to the ground.

Dee is lighter than Maggie, with nicer hair and a fuller figure. She's a woman now, though sometimes I forget. How long ago was it that the other house burned? Ten, twelve years? Sometimes I can still hear the flames and feel Maggie's arms sticking to me, her hair smoking and her dress falling off her in little black papery flakes. Her eyes seemed stretched open, blazed open by the flames reflected in them. And Dee. I see her standing off under the sweet gum tree she used to dig gum out of; a look of concentration on her face as she watched the last dingy gray board of the house fall in toward the red-hot brick chimney. Why don't you do a dance around the ashes? I'd wanted to ask her. She had hated the house that much.

I used to think she hated Maggie, too. But that was before we raised the money, the church and me, to send her to Augusta to school. She used to read to us without pity; forcing words, lies, other folks' habits, whole lives upon us two, sitting trapped and ignorant underneath her voice. She washed us in a river of make-believe, burned us with a lot of knowledge we didn't necessarily need to know. Pressed us to her with the serious way she read, to shove us away at just the moment, like dimwits, we seemed about to understand.

Dee wanted nice things. A yellow organdy dress to wear to her graduation from high school; black pumps to match a green suit she'd made from an old suit somebody gave me. She was determined to stare down any disaster in her efforts. Her eyelids would not flicker for minutes at a time. Often I fought off the temptation to shake her. At sixteen she had a style of her own: and knew what style was.

I never had an education myself. After second grade the school was closed down. Don't ask me why: in 1927 colored asked fewer questions than they do now. Sometimes Maggie reads to me. She stumbles along good-naturedly but can't see well. She knows she is not bright. Like good looks and money, quickness passed her by. She will marry John Thomas (who has mossy teeth in an earnest face) and then I'll be free to sit here and I guess just sing church songs to myself. Although I never was a good singer. Never could carry a tune. I was always better at a man's job. I used to love to milk till I was hoofed in the side in '49. Cows are soothing and slow and don't bother you, unless you try to milk them the wrong way.

I have deliberately turned my back on the house. It is three rooms, just like the one that burned, except the roof is tin; they don't make shingle roofs any more. There are no real windows, just some holes cut in the sides, like the portholes in a ship, but not round and not square, with rawhide holding the shutters up on the outside. This house is in a pasture, too, like the other one. No doubt when Dee sees it she will want to tear it down. She wrote me once that no matter where we "choose" to live, she will manage to come see us. But she will never bring her friends. Maggie and I thought about this and Maggie asked me, "Mama, when did Dee ever *have* any friends?"

She had a few. Furtive boys in pink shirts hanging about on wash-day after school. Nervous girls who never laughed. Impressed with her they worshiped the well-turned phrase, the cute shape, the scalding humor that erupted like bubbles in lye. She read to them.

When she was courting Jimmy T she didn't have much time to pay to us, but turned all her faultfinding power on him. He *flew* to marry a cheap gal from a family of ignorant flashy people. She hardly had time to recompose herself.

When she comes I will meet — but there they are!

Maggie attempts to make a dash for the house, in her shuffling way, but I stay her with my hand. "Come back here," I say. And she stops and tries to dig a well in the sand with her toe.

It is hard to see them clearly through the strong sun. But even the first glimpse of leg out of the car tells me it is Dee. Her feet were always neat-looking, as if God himself had shaped them with a certain style. From the other side of the car comes a short, stocky man. Hair is all over his head a foot long and hanging from his chin like a kinky mule tail. I hear Maggie suck in her breath. "Uhnnnh," is what it sounds like. Like when you see the wriggling end of a snake just in front of your foot on the road. "Uhnnnh."

Dee next. A dress down to the ground, in this hot weather. A dress so loud it hurts my eyes. There are yellows and oranges enough to throw back the light of the sun. I feel my whole face warming from the heat waves it throws out. Earrings, too, gold and hanging down to her shoulders. Bracelets dangling and making noises when she moves her arm up to shake the folds of the dress out of her armpits. The dress is loose and flows, and as she walks closer, I like it. I hear Maggie go "Uhnnnh" again. It is her sister's hair. It stands straight up like the wool on a sheep. It is black as night and around the edges are two long pigtails that rope about like small lizards disappearing behind her ears.

"Wa-su-zo-Tean-o!" she says, coming on in that gliding way the dress makes her move. The short stocky fellow with the hair to his navel is all grinning and he follows up with "Asalamalakim, my mother and sister!" He moves to hug Maggie but she falls back, right up against the back of my chair. I feel her trembling there and when I look up I see the perspiration falling off her chin.

"Don't get up," says Dee. Since I am stout it takes something of a push. You can see me trying to move a second or two before I make it. She turns, showing white heels through her sandals, and goes back to the car. Out she peeks next with a Polaroid. She stoops down quickly and lines up picture after picture of me sitting there in front of the house with Maggie cowering behind me. She never takes a shot without making sure the house is included. When a cow comes nibbling around the edge of the yard she snaps it and me and Maggie *and* the house. Then she puts the Polaroid in the back seat of the car, and comes up and kisses me on the forehead.

Meanwhile Asalamalakim is going through the motions with Maggie's hand. Maggie's hand is as limp as a fish, and probably as cold, despite the sweat, and she keeps trying to pull it back. It looks like Asalamalakim wants to shake hands but wants to do it fancy. Or maybe he don't know how people shake hands. Anyhow, he soon gives up on Maggie.

"Well," I say. "Dee."

"No, Mama," she says. "Not 'Dee,' Wangero Leewanika Kemanjo!"

"What happened to 'Dee'?" I wanted to know.

"She's dead," Wangero said. "I couldn't bear it any longer being named after the people who oppress me."

"You know as well as me you was named after your aunt Dicie," I said. Dicie is my sister. She named Dee. We called her "Big Dee" after Dee was born.

"But who was *she* named after?" asked Wangero.

"I guess after Grandma Dee," I said.

"And who was she named after?" asked Wangero.

"Her mother," I said, and saw Wangero was getting tired. "That's about as far back as I can trace it," I said. Though, in fact, I probably could have carried it back beyond the Civil War through the branches.

"Well," said Asalamalakim, "there you are."

"Uhnnnh," I heard Maggie say.

"There I was not," I said, "before 'Dicie' cropped up in our family, so why should I try to trace it that far back?"

He just stood there grinning, looking down on me like somebody inspecting a Model A car. Every once in a while he and Wangero sent eye signals over my head.

"How do you pronounce this name?" I asked.

"You don't have to call me by it if you don't want to," said Wangero.

"Why shouldn't I?" I asked. "If that's what you want us to call you, we'll call you."

"I know it might sound awkward at first," said Wangero.

"I'll get used to it," I said. "Ream it out again."

Well, soon we got the name out of the way. Asalamalakim had a name twice as long and three times as hard. After I tripped over it two or three times he told me to just call him Hakim-a-barber. I wanted to ask him was he a barber, but I didn't really think he was, so I didn't ask.

"You must belong to those beef-cattle peoples down the road," I said. They said "Asalamalakim" when they met you, too, but they didn't shake hands. Always too busy: feeding the cattle, fixing the fences, putting up salt-lick shelters, throwing down hay. When the white folks poisoned some of the herd the men stayed up all night with rifles in their hands. I walked a mile and a half just to see the sight.

Hakim-a-barber said, "I accept some of their doctrines, but farming and raising cattle is not my style." (They didn't tell me, and I didn't ask, whether Wangero [Dee] had really gone and married him.)

We sat down to eat and right away he said he didn't eat collards and pork was unclean. Wangero, though, went on through the chitlins and corn bread, the greens and everything else. She talked a blue streak over the sweet potatoes. Everything delighted her. Even the fact that we still used the benches her daddy made for the table when we couldn't afford to buy chairs.

"Oh, Mama!" she cried. Then turned to Hakim-a-barber. "I never knew how lovely these benches are. You can feel the rump prints," she said, running her hands underneath her and along the bench. Then she gave a sigh and her hand closed over Grandma Dee's butter dish. "That's it!" she said. "I knew there was something I wanted to ask you if I could have." She jumped up from the table and went over in the corner where the churn stood, the milk in it clabber by now. She looked at the churn and looked at it.

"This churn top is what I need," she said. "Didn't Uncle Buddy whittle it out of a tree you all used to have?"

"Yes," I said.

"Uh huh," she said happily. "And I want the dasher, too."

"Uncle Buddy whittle that, too?" asked the barber.

Dee (Wangero) looked up at me.

"Aunt Dee's first husband whittled the dash," said Maggie so low you almost couldn't hear her. "His name was Henry, but they called him Stash."

"Maggie's brain is like an elephant's," Wangero said, laughing. "I can use the churn top as a centerpiece for the alcove table," she said, sliding a plate over the churn, "and I'll think of something artistic to do with the dasher."

When she finished wrapping the dasher the handle stuck out. I took it for a moment in my hands. You didn't even have to look close to see where hands pushing the dasher up and down to make butter had left a kind of sink in the wood. In fact, there were a lot of small sinks; you could see where thumbs and fingers had sunk into the wood. It was beautiful light yellow wood, from a tree that grew in the yard where Big Dee and Stash had lived.

After dinner Dee (Wangero) went to the trunk at the foot of my bed and started rifling through it. Maggie hung back in the kitchen over the dishpan. Out came Wangero with two quilts. They had been pieced by Grandma Dee and then Big Dee and me had hung them on the quilt frames on the front porch and quilted them. One was in the Lone Star pattern. The other was Walk Around the Mountain. In both of them were scraps of dresses Grandma Dee had worn fifty and more years ago. Bits and pieces of Grandpa Jarrell's Paisley shirts. And one teeny faded blue piece, about the piece of a penny matchbox, that was from Great Grandpa Ezra's uniform that he wore in the Civil War.

"Mama," Wangero said sweet as a bird. "Can I have these old quilts?"

I heard something fall in the kitchen, and a minute later the kitchen door slammed.

"Why don't you take one or two of the others?" I asked. "These old things was just done by me and Big Dee from some tops your grandma pieced before she died."

"No," said Wangero. "I don't want those. They are stitched around the borders by machine."

"That's make them last better," I said.

"That's not the point," said Wangero. "These are all pieces of dresses Grandma used to wear. She did all this stitching by hand. Imagine!" She held the quilts securely in her arms, stroking them.

"Some of the pieces, like those lavender ones, come from old clothes her mother handed down to her," I said, moving up to touch the quilts. Dee (Wangero) moved back just enough so that I couldn't reach the quilts. They already belonged to her.

"Imagine!" she breathed again, clutching them closely to her bosom.

"The truth is," I said, "I promised to give them quilts to Maggie, for when she marries John Thomas."

She gasped like a bee had stung her.

"Maggie can't appreciate these quilts!" she said. "She'd probably be backward enough to put them to everyday use."

"I reckon she would," I said. "God knows I been saving 'em for long enough with nobody using 'em. I hope she will!" I didn't want to bring up how I had offered Dee (Wangero) a quilt when she went away to college. Then she had told me they were old-fashioned, out of style.

"But they're *priceless!*" she was saying now, furiously; for she has a temper. "Maggie would put them on the bed and in five years they'd be in rags. Less than that!"

"She can always make some more," I said. "Maggie knows how to quilt."

Dee (Wangero) looked at me with hatred. "You just will not understand. The point is these quilts, *these* quilts!"

"Well," I said, stumped. "What would *you* do with them?"

"Hang them," she said. As if that was the only thing you *could* do with quilts.

Maggie by now was standing in the door. I could almost hear the sound her feet made as they scraped over each other.

"She can have them, Mama," she said, like somebody used to never winning anything, or having anything reserved for her. "I can 'member Grandma Dee without the quilts."

I looked at her hard. She had filled her bottom lip with checkerberry snuff and it gave her face a kind of dopey, hangdog look. It was Grandma Dee and Big Dee who taught her how to quilt herself. She stood there with her scarred hands hidden in the folds of her skirt. She looked at her sister with something like fear but she wasn't mad at her. This was Maggie's portion. This was the way she knew God to work.

When I looked at her like that something hit me in the top of my head and ran down to the soles of my feet. Just like when I'm in church and the spirit of God touches me and I get happy and shout. I did something I never had done before: hugged Maggie to me, then dragged her on into the room, snatched the quilts out of Miss Wangero's hands and dumped them into Maggie's lap. Maggie just sat there on my bed with her mouth open.

"Take one or two of the others," I said to Dee.

But she turned without a word and went out to Hakim-a-barber.

"You just don't understand," she said, as Maggie and I came out to the car.

"What don't I understand?" I wanted to know.

"Your heritage," she said. And then she turned to Maggie, kissed her, and said, "You ought to try to make something of yourself, too, Maggie. It's really a new day for us. But from the way you and Mama still live you'd never know it."

She put on some sunglasses that hid everything above the tip of her nose and her chin.

Maggie smiled; maybe at the sunglasses. But a real smile, not scared. After we watched the car dust settle I asked Maggie to bring me a dip of snuff. And then the two of us sat there just enjoying, until it was time to go in the house and go to bed.

7 Observations on the Novel

Most of what has been said about short stories (on probability, narrative point of view, style) is relevant to the novel. And just as the short story of the last hundred years or so is rather different from earlier short fiction (see page 84), the novel — though here we must say of the last few hundred years — is different from earlier long fiction.

The ancient epic is at best a distant cousin to the novel, for though a narrative, the epic is in verse, and deals with godlike men and even with gods themselves. One has only to think of the *Odyssey* or the *Iliad* or the *Aeneid* or *Beowulf* or *Paradise Lost* to recall that the epic does not deal with the sort of people one meets in *Tom Jones, David Copperfield, Crime and Punishment, The Return of the Native, The Portrait of a Lady, The Sun Also Rises,* or *The Catcher in the Rye.*

The romance is perhaps a closer relative to the novel. Ancient romances were even in prose. But the hallmark of the romance, whether the romance is by a Greek sophist (Longus's *Daphnis and Chloe*) or by a medieval English poet (Chaucer's "The Knight's Tale") or by an American (Hawthorne's *The House of the Seven Gables*), is a presentation of the remote or the marvelous, rather than the local and the ordinary. The distinction is the same as that between the tale and the short story. "Tale" has the suggestion of a yarn, of unreality or of wondrous reality. (A case can be made for excluding Hawthorne's "Young Goodman Brown" from a collection of short stories on the ground that its remoteness and its allegorical implications mark it as a tale rather than a short story. This is not to say that it is inferior to a story, but only different.) In his preface to *The House of the Seven Gables* Hawthorne himself distinguishes between the romance and the novel:

> The latter form of composition is presumed to aim at a very minute fidelity, not merely to the possible, but to the probable and ordinary course of man's experience. The former — while, as a work of art, it must rigidly subject itself to laws, and while it sins unpardonably so far as it may swerve aside from the truth of the human heart — has fairly a right to present that truth under circumstances, to a great extent, of the writer's own choosing or creation.

In his preface to *The Marble Faun* Hawthorne explains that he chose "Italy as the site of his Romance" because it afforded him "a sort of poetic or fairy precinct, where actualities would not be so terribly insisted upon as they are . . . in America."

"Actualities . . . insisted upon." That, in addition to prose and length, is the hallmark of the novel. The novel is a sort of long newspaper story; the very word "novel" comes from an Italian word meaning a little new thing, and is related to the French word that gives us "news." (It is noteworthy that the French cognate of Hawthorne's "actualities," *actualités*, means "news" or "current events.") It is no accident that many novelists have been newspapermen: Defoe, Dickens, Crane, Dreiser, Joyce, Hemingway, Camus. And this connection with reportage perhaps helps to account for the relatively low esteem in which the novel is occasionally held: to some college students, a course in the novel does not seem quite up to a course in poetry, and people who read novels but not poetry are not likely to claim an interest in "literature."

Though Defoe's *Robinson Crusoe* is set in a far-off place, and thus might easily have been a romance, in Defoe's day it was close to current events, for it is a fictionalized version of events that had recently made news — Alexander Selkirk's life on the island of Juan Fernandez. And the story is not about marvelous happenings, but about a man's struggle for survival in dismal surroundings. Crusoe is not armed with Arthur's Excalibur or with Gawain's supposedly magic girdle, nor does he struggle as does Arthur with a Demon Cat and with a giant of St. Michael's Mount or as does Gawain with a Green Knight who survives decapitation; he has a carpenter's chest of tools and he struggles against commonplace nature. This chest was "much more valuable than a shiploading of gold would have been at that time." The world of romance contains splendid castles and enchanted forests, but Crusoe's world contains not much more than a plot of ground, some animals and vegetables, and Friday. "I fancied I

could make all but the wheel [of a wheelbarrow Crusoe needed], but
that I had no notion of, neither did I know how to go about it; besides,
I had no possible way to make the iron gudgeons for the spindle or
axis of the wheel to run in, so I gave it over." The book, in short,
emphasizes not the strange, but (given the initial situation) the usual,
the common-sensical, the probable. The world of *Robinson Crusoe* is
hardly different from the world we meet in the beginning of almost
any novel:

> We were in study hall when the headmaster walked in, followed by
> a new boy not wearing a school uniform, and by a janitor carrying a
> large desk. Those who were sleeping awoke, and we all stood up as
> though interrupting our work.
>
> Gustave Flaubert, *Madame Bovary*

> My father's family name being Pirrip, and my christian name Philip,
> my infant tongue could make of both names nothing longer or more
> explicit than Pip. So I called myself Pip, and came to be called Pip.
> I give Pirrip as my father's family name, on the authority of his
> tombstone and my sister — Mrs. Joe Gargery, who married the black-
> smith.
>
> Charles Dickens, *Great Expectations*

> In beginning the life story of my hero, Alexey Fyodorovich Karama-
> zov, I find myself in somewhat of a quandary. Namely, although I call
> Alexey Fyodorovich my hero, I myself know that he is by no means a
> great man, and hence I foresee such unavoidable questions as these:
> "What is so remarkable about your Alexey Fyodorovich, that you have
> chosen him as your hero? What has he accomplished? What is he
> known for, and by whom? Why should I, the reader, spend time learn-
> ing the facts of his life?"
>
> Fyodor Dostoyevsky, *The Brothers Karamazov*

> If you really want to hear about it, the first thing you'll probably
> want to know is where I was born, and what my lousy childhood was
> like, and how my parents were occupied and all before they had me,
> and all that David Copperfield kind of crap, but I don't feel like going
> into it, if you want to know the truth.
>
> J. D. Salinger, *The Catcher in the Rye*

> It was June, 1933, one week after Commencement, when Kay
> Leiland Strong, Vassar '33, the first of her class to run around the table
> at the Class Day dinner, was married to Harald Petersen, Reed '27, in
> the chapel of St. George's Church, P.E., Karl F. Reiland, Rector. Out-
> side, on Stuyvesant Square, the trees were in full leaf, and the wedding
> guests arriving by twos and threes in taxis heard the voices of children
> playing round the statue of Peter Stuyvesant in the park.
>
> Mary McCarthy, *The Group*

Sleepy boys in a school room; the brother of the wife of a black-smith named Joe Gargery; a hero who "is by no means a great man"; a boy who in boy's language seems reluctant to talk of his "lousy childhood"; a young woman who ran around the table at the Class Day dinner. In all of these passages, and in the openings of most other novels, we are confronted with current biography, and, indeed, a fair number of important novels — e.g., D. H. Lawrence's *Sons and Lovers*, James Joyce's *Portrait of the Artist as a Young Man*, Jack Kerouac's *On the Road* — are highly autobiographical.* In contrast to these beginnings, look at the beginning of one of Chaucer's great romances:

Whilom,° as olde stories tellen us,	*once*
There was a duc that highte° Theseus;	*was named*
Of Atthenes he was lord and governour,	
And in his tyme swich° a conquerour,	*such*
That gretter was ther noon under the sonne.	

"Whilom." "Olde stories." "Gretter was ther noon under the sonne." We are in a timeless past, in which unusual people dwell. But the novel is almost always set in the present or very recent past (Updike even casts the whole novel in the present tense: "Boys are playing. . . . Rabbit Angstrom . . . stops and watches"), and it deals with ordinary people. It so often deals with ordinary people, and presents them, apparently, in so ordinary a fashion that we sometimes wonder what is the point of it. Although the romance is often "escape" literature, it usually is didactic, holding up to us images of noble and ignoble behavior, revealing the rewards of courage and the power of love. In the preface to *The Marble Faun*, for instance, Hawthorne says he "proposed to himself to merely write a fanciful story, evolving a thoughtful moral, and did not propose attempting a portraiture of Italian manners and character." But portraiture is what the novelist gives us. Intent on revealing the world of real men and women going about their daily work and play, he does not simplify his characters into representatives of vices and virtues as does the

---

* Recently even the veil of fiction has been removed, and a new form, the "nonfiction novel" has developed. The term apparently was coined by Truman Capote to describe *In Cold Blood*, his account of a multiple murder committed in Kansas in 1959. The details are all true, but the book is written with a novelist's sense of irony and of symbolic details; in short, it is history written by a novelist — but this form is not to be confused with the "historical novel," which by its usual emphasis on plot and on the exotic is a kind of romance. Another example of the nonfiction novel: Norman Mailer's *The Armies of the Night*, describing the anti–Vietnam War march of 1967 and subsequent related events, in which Mailer writes of himself in the third person.

romancer who wishes to evolve a thoughtful moral, but gives abundant detail — some of it apparently irrelevant. The innumerable details add up to a long book, although there need not be many physical happenings. The novel tells a story, of course, but the story is not only about what people overtly do but also about what they think (i.e., their mental doings) and about the society in which they are immersed and by which they are in part shaped. In the much-quoted preface to *Pierre and Jean*, Maupassant says:

> The skill of the novelist's plan will not reside in emotional effects, in attractive writing, in a striking beginning or a moving dénouement, but in the artful building up of solid details from which the essential meaning of the work will emerge.

As we read a novel we feel we are seeing not the "higher reality" or the "inner reality" so often mentioned by students of the arts, but the real reality.*

The short story, too, is detailed, but commonly it reveals only a single character at a moment of crisis, whereas the novel commonly traces the development of an individual, a group of people, a world. The novelist, of course, has an attitude toward his world; he is not compiling an almanac but telling an invented story, making a work of art, offering not merely a representation of reality but a response to it, and he therefore selects and shapes his material. One way of selecting and shaping the material is through the chosen point of view: we do not get everything in nineteenth-century England, but only everything that Pip remembers or chooses to set down about his experiences, and what he sets down is colored by his personality. "I remember Mr. Hubble as a tough high-shouldered stooping old man, of a saw-dusty fragrance, with his legs extraordinarily wide apart: so that in my short days I always saw some miles of open country between them when I met him coming up the lane." In any case, the coherence in a novel seems inclusive rather than exclusive. The

---

* It should be mentioned that in the 1950s the *nouveau roman* or "new novel" developed, in reaction to the novels of the sort we have teen talking about. Writers of the new novel (such as Alain Robbe-Grillet, Nathalie Sarraute, and Claude Simon) argue that the traditional novel is utterly false, for it presents characters (whereas people are not psychologically consistent creatures, but a complex series of appearances), plots (whereas plots do not exist in nature), cause and effect (a naive assumption), and it assumes that there is a connection between people and the objects of the world they move in (another naive assumption). The new novel, instead of presenting a story of coherent characters acting in a context, offers a sort of dreamlike series of perceptions; the identities of the perceivers and the chronology are usually unclear, and, of course, the story has no conclusion.

novelist usually conveys the sense that he, as distinct from his characters, is — in the words of Christoper Isherwood's *The Berlin Stories* —"a camera with its shutter open, quite passive, recording not thinking. Recording the man shaving at the windows opposite and the woman in the kimono washing her hair. Some day, all of this will have to developed, carefully fixed, printed."

It is not merely that the novel gives us details. *Gulliver's Travels* has plenty of details about people six inches tall and people sixty feet tall, and about a flying island and rational horses. But these things are recognized as fanciful inventions, though they do turn our mind toward the real world. *Gulliver* is a satire that holds up to us a picture of a fantastic world by which, paradoxically, we come to see the real world a little more clearly. The diminutive stature of the Lilliputians is an amusing and potent metaphor for the littleness of man, the flying island for abstract thinkers who have lost touch with reality, and so on. But the novelist who wants to show us the littleness of man invents not Lilliputians but a world of normal-sized people who do little things and have little thoughts. Voltaire's *Candide* is a second example of a book that is prose fiction but not a novel. There are plenty of details, and even (as in *Gulliver*) references to events that were recent history. But the historical references are like raisins in a cake rather than like yeast; they do not permeate the whole. The details are often heaped up and incongruously juxtaposed to provoke laughter rather than credibility (the Portuguese governor's name is Don Fernando d'Ibarraa y Figueora y Mascarenes y Lampourdos y Souza; the old lady repeatedly reminds us that she has only half of a backside). The world of *Candide* is a world in which the main characters, participating in coincidence after coincidence, survive innumerable disasters — including shipwreck, earthquake, hanging, sword thrusts, and capture by cannibals. It is a world in which things happen at so breakneck a speed (think of the Marx Brothers wrecking all they touch; or think of animated cartoons in which a cat is chasing a mouse, swallows a firecracker, is blown high into the air, and a moment later is chasing the mouse again) that in a sense nothing much *really* happens. It is a world in which a character threatened with "re-killing" can say to Candide, "You can kill me again, if you like, but while I live, you shall never marry my sister." What we have in *Candide* is not a novel but a *conte philosophique*, improbable prose fiction used as a vehicle to convey a philosophic attitude. *Candide* is not a coherent image of reality but a comic rejection of one philosophic view of reality. It is not a novel; it is a fable and a parody.

Having spent so much time saying that the novel is not the epic or romance or fable, we must mention that a work may hover on the borderlines of these forms. Insofar as *Moby Dick* narrates with abundant realistic detail the experiences of a whaler ("This book," Dorothy Parker has said, "taught me more about whales than I ever wanted to know"), it is a novel; but in its evocation of mystery — Queequeg, the prophecies, Ishmael's miraculous rescue from the sea filled with sharks who "glided by as if with padlocks on their mouths"— it is a romance with strong symbolic implications.

The point is that although a reader of a long piece of prose fiction can complain that he did not get what he paid for, he should find out what he did get, rather than damn it for not being what it isn't. Bishop Butler's famous remark is relevant to literary criticism: "Everything is what it is and not another thing."

POETRY

Narrative Poetry

Lyric Poetry

The Speaking Tone of Voice

Figurative Language: Simile, Metaphor, Personification, Apostrophe

Figurative Language: Imagery, Symbolism

Irony and Paradox

Rhythm

Some Principles of Versification

A Collection of Poems

8 Narrative Poetry

European literature begins with Homer's *Iliad* and *Odyssey*, which means that it begins with stories in verse. We are accustomed to thinking of a story as prose in a book, but until a few hundred years ago stories were commonly poetry that was sung or recited. In nonliterate societies people got their stories from storytellers who relied on memory rather than on the written word; the memorized stories were often poems, partly because (in Sir Philip Sidney's words) "verse far exceedeth prose in the knitting up of the memory." Even in literate societies, few people could read or write until the invention of the printing press at the close of the fifteenth century. Although the printing press did not immediately destroy oral verse narratives, as the centuries passed, an increasingly large reading public developed which preferred prose narratives.

Among the great verse narratives are the English and Scottish **popular ballads,** some of the best of which are attributed to the fifteenth century, though they were not recorded until much later. These anonymous stories in song acquired their distinctive flavor by being passed down orally from generation to generation, each singer consciously or unconsciously modifying his inheritance. It is not known who made up the popular ballads; often they were made up partly out of earlier ballads by singers as bold as Kipling's cockney:

> When 'Omer smote 'is blooming lyre,
> He'd 'eard men sing by land an' sea;
> An' what he thought 'e might require,
> 'E went an' took — the same as me!

Most ballad singers probably were composers only by accident; they intended to transmit what they had heard, but their memories were sometimes faulty and their imaginations active. The modifications effected by oral transmission generally give a ballad three noticeable qualities. First, it is impersonal; even if there is an "I" who sings the tale, he is usually characterless. Second, the ballad — like other oral literature such as the nursery rhyme, the counting-out rhyme ("one potato, two potato") — is filled with repetition, sometimes of lines, sometimes of words. Consider, for example, "Go saddle me the black, the black, / Go saddle me the brown," or "O wha is this has done this deid, / This ill deid don to me?" Sometimes, in fact, the story is told by repeating lines with only a few significant variations. This **incremental repetition** (repetition with slight variations advancing the narrative) is the heart of "Edward" (page 356). Furthermore, **stock epithets** are repeated from ballad to ballad: "true love," "milk-white steed," "golden hair." Oddly, these clichés do not bore us but by their impersonality often lend a simplicity that effectively contrasts with the violence of the tale. Third, because the ballads are transmitted orally, residing in the memory rather than on the printed page, weak stanzas have often been dropped, leaving a series of sharp scenes, frequently with dialogue:

> The king sits in Dumferling toune,
>   Drinking the blude-reid wine:
> "O whar will I get guid sailor,
>   To sail this schip of mine?"

Because ballads were sung rather than printed, and because singers made alterations, there is no one version of a ballad that is the "correct" one. The versions printed here have become such favorites that they are almost regarded as definitive, but the reader should consult a collection of ballads (for example, *The Viking Book of Folk Ballads*, ed. Albert B. Friedman [1958]) to get some idea of the wide variety.

Popular ballads have been much imitated by professional poets, especially since the late eighteenth century. Three such **literary ballads** are Keats's "La Belle Dame sans Merci" (page 469), Coleridge's "The Rime of the Ancient Mariner," W. H. Auden's "O what is that sound," and X. J. Kennedy's "In a Prominent Bar in Secaucus One Day" (page 362). In a literary ballad (though not in Kennedy's) the story is often infused with multiple meanings, with insistent symbolic implications. Ambiguity is often found in the popular ballad also, but it is of a rather different sort. Whether it is due to the loss of stanzas or to the creator's unconcern with some elements of the narrative, the ambiguity of the popular ballad commonly lies in the narrative itself rather than in the significance of the narrative.

Finally, a word about some of the most popular professional folk-

singers today. They have aptly been called "folksongers" because unlike illiterate or scarcely literate folksingers — who intend only to
sing the traditional songs in the traditional way for themselves or
their neighbors — these professionals are vocal artists who make commercial and political use (not bad things in themselves) of traditional
folk songs, deliberately adapting old songs and inventing new songs
that only loosely resemble the old ones. These contemporary ballads
tend to be more personal than traditional ballads and they tend to
have a social consciousness that is alien to traditional balladry. Many
of the songs of Pete Seeger and Bob Dylan, for instance, are conspicuous examples of art in the service of morality; they call attention
to injustice and they seek to move the hearers to action. That traditional ballads have assisted in this task is not the least of their value;
the influence of a work of art is never finished, and the old ballads
can rightly claim to share in the lives of their modern descendants.

Anonymous

Sir Patrick Spence

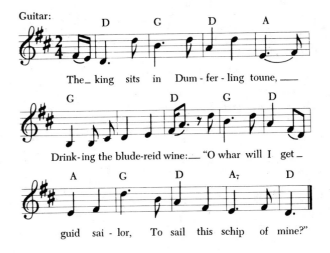

The king sits in Dumferling toune,
    Drinking the blude-reid wine:
"O whar will I get guid sailor,
    To sail this schip of mine?"

4

Up and spak an eldern knicht,
    Sat at the kings richt kne:
"Sir Patrick Spence is the best sailor,
    That sails upon the se."   8

The king has written a braid° letter,   *broad, open*
    And signed it wi' his hand,
And sent it to Sir Patrick Spence,
    Was walking on the sand.   12

The first line that Sir Patrick red,
    A loud lauch° lauched he;   *laugh*
The next line that Sir Patrick red,
    The teir blinded his ee.   16

"O wha is this has done this deid,
    This ill deid don to me,
To send me out this time o' the yeir,
    To sail upon the se?   20

"Mak hast, mak hast, my mirry men all,
    Our guid schip sails the morne:"
"O say na sae, my master deir,
    For I feir a deadlie storme.   24

"Late late yestreen I saw the new moone,
    Wi' the auld moone in hir arme,
And I feir, I feir, my deir master,
    That we will cum to harme."   28

O our Scots nobles wer richt laith°   *loath*
    To weet their cork-heild schoone;°   *cork-heeled shoes*
Bot lang owre° a' the play wer playd,   *ere*
    Thair hats they swam aboone.°   *above* 32

O lang, lang may their ladies sit,
    Wi' thair fans into their hand,
Or eir° they se Sir Patrick Spence   *ere*
    Cum sailing to the land.   36

O lang, lang may the ladies stand,
    Wi' thair gold kems in their hair,
Waiting for their ain deir lords,
    For they'll se thame na mair.   40

Have owre,° have owre to Aberdour,   *half over*
    It's fiftie fadom deip,
And thair lies guid Sir Patrick Spence,
    Wi' the Scots lords at his feit.   44

Questions

1. The shipwreck occurs between lines 29 and 32, but it is not described. Does the omission stimulate the reader to imagine the details of the wreck? Or does it suggest that the poem is not so much about a shipwreck as about kinds of behavior? Explain.

2. Might lines 17–18 warrant the inference that the "eldern knicht" (line 5) is Sir Patrick's enemy?

3. Explain lines 13–16.

4. In place of lines 37–40, another version of this ballad has the following stanza:

> The ladies crack't their fingers white,
>> The maidens tore their hair,
> A' for the sake o' their true loves,
>> For them they ne'er saw mair.

Why is one more effective than the other?

5. In the other version, the stanza that is here the final one (lines 41–44) precedes the stanzas about the ladies (lines 33–40). Which stanza makes a better conclusion? Why?

Anonymous

The Three Ravens

There were three ravens sat on a tree, *Downe a downe, hay*

downe, hay downe There were three ravens sat on a tree, *With a*

---

* Alternate guitar chords transposing the tune into a key easier to play on a guitar are given in parentheses.

downe There were three ravens sat on a tree, They were as blacke as

they might be, With a downe der-rie, der-rie, der-rie, downe, downe.

There were three ravens sat on a tree,
    Downe a downe, hay down, hay downe
There were three ravens sat on a tree,
    With a downe
There were three ravens sat on a tree,
They were as blacke as they might be,   5
    With a downe derrie, derrie, derrie, downe, downe.

The one of them said to his mate,
"Where shall we our breakfast take?"

"Down in yonder greene field,   10
There lies a knight slain under his shield.

"His hounds they lie downe at his feete,
So well they can their master keepe.

"His haukes they flie so eagerly,
There's no fowle dare him come nie."   15

Downe there comes a fallow° doe,*   *brown*
As great with yong as she might goe.

She lift up his bloudy hed,
And kist his wounds that were so red.

She got him up upon her backe,   20
And carried him to earthen lake.°   *pit*

* The "doe" (line 16), often taken as a suggestive description of the knight's beloved, is probably a vestige of the folk belief that an animal may be an enchanted human being.

She buried him before the prime,°	*about nine* A.M.
She was dead herselfe ere even-song time.	

God send every gentleman
Such haukes, such hounds, and such a leman.°   *sweetheart* 25

Questions

1. The hounds and the hawks are loyal followers of the knight, as is the doe. How do the references to the hounds and hawks in some degree prepare us for the doe? Is preparation necessary? Why?

2. Why does the poet include the ravens? Do they confuse a poem on loyalty, or do they provide an effective contrast? Do the ravens help to give a fuller, more realistic picture of life? Explain.

3. Are the final two lines an intrusive comment? Explain.

Anonymous

The Twa Corbies

As I was walking all alane,	
I heard twa corbies° making a mane;°	*two ravens; lament*
The tane° unto the t' other say,	*one*
"Where sall we gang° and dine to-day?"	*shall we go* 4
"In behint yon auld fail dyke,°	*old turf wall*
I wot° there lies a new-slain knight;	*know*
And naebody kens° that he lies there,	*knows*
But his hawk, his hound, and lady fair.	8
"His hound is to the hunting gane,	
His hawk, to fetch the wild-fowl hame,	
His lady's ta'en another mate,	
So we may mak our dinner sweet.	12
"Ye'll sit on his white hause-bane,°	*neck bone*
And I'll pike out his bonny blue een.°	*eyes*
Wi' ae° lock o' his gowden° hair	*with one; golden*
We'll theek° our nest when it grows bare.	*thatch* 16
"Mony a one for him makes mane,	
But nane sall ken whare he is gane;	
O'er his white banes, when they are bare,	
The wind sall blaw for evermair."	20

Questions

1. The story in this poem is implied (in the second and third stanzas) rather than made explicit. What is it? Is it the worse for being implicit? Explain.
2. How do lines 9–10 reinforce or parallel the basic story?
3. Hair is usually "gowden" in ballads. What does this conventional detail tell us about the knight's age? Why is his age significant?
4. What does the fourth stanza (especially lines 15–16) contribute to the poem?
5. Animals can't speak; is the poem therefore an absurdity? Explain.
6. How accurate is the observation that this ballad is a "cynical variation" of "The Three Ravens"?

Anonymous

Edward

"Why dois your brand° sae° drap wi' bluid,   *sword; so*
  Edward, Edward?
Why dois your brand sae drap wi' bluid?
  And why sae sad gang° yee, O?"   *go* 4
"O, I hae killed my hauke sae guid,
  Mither, mither,
O, I hae killed my hauke sae guid,
  And I had nae mair bot hee, O."   8

"Your haukis bluid was nevir sae reid,
  Edward, Edward,
Your haukis bluid was nevir sae reid,
  My deir son I tell thee, O."   12
"O, I hae killed my reid-roan steid,
  Mither, mither,
O, I hae killed my reid-roan steid,
  That erst° was sae fair and frie,° O."   *once; spirited* 16

"Your steid was auld, and ye hae gat mair,
  Edward, Edward,
Your steid was auld, and ye hae gat mair,
  Sum other dule° ye drie,° O."   *grief; suffer* 20
"O, I hae killed my fadir deir,
  Mither, mither,
O, I hae killed my fadir, deir,
  Alas, and wae is mee, O!"   24

"And whatten penance wul ye drie for that,
      Edward, Edward?
And whatten penance wul ye drie for that?
      My deir son, now tell me, O."   28
"Ile set my feit in yonder boat,
      Mither, mither,
Ile set my feit in yonder boat,
      And Ile fare ovir the sea, O."   32

"And what wul ye doe wi' your towirs and your ha',°   *hall*
      Edward, Edward,
And what wul ye doe wi' your towirs and your ha',
      That were sae fair to see, O?"   36
"Ile let thame stand tul they doun fa',°   *fall*
      Mither, mither,
Ile let thame stand tul they doun fa',
      For here nevir mair maun° I bee, O."   *must* 40

"And what wul ye leive to your bairns° and your wife,   *children*
      Edward, Edward?
And what wul ye leive to your bairns and your wife,
      When ye gang ovir the sea, O?"   44
"The warldis° room, late° them beg thrae° life,   *world's; let; through*
      Mither, mither,
The warldis room, late them beg thrae life,
      For thame nevir mair wul I see, O."   48

"And what wul ye leive to your ain mither deir,
      Edward, Edward?
And what wul ye leive to your ain mither deir?
      My deir son, now tell me, O."   52
"The curse of hell frae me sall ye beir,
      Mither, mither,
The curse of hell frae me sall ye beir,
      Sic° counseils ye gave to me, O."   *such* 56

Questions

1. The poem consists of two parts. How does the structure of the first part parallel that of the second?

2. What might have been the mother's motives? Would the story be improved if we knew the motives behind her "counseils"? Explain.

3. Can Edward's statements about his wife and children be explained?

4. What do the refrains ("Edward, Edward" and "Mither, mither") contribute to the poem?

5. Line 21 offers a surprise, but it is topped by the surprise in the final four lines. Can the poem be reread with pleasure once the surprises are known? Explain.

Many ballads, such as the next one, deal with supernatural happenings. "The Demon Lover" exists in many versions, and is often titled "The House Carpenter" or "James Harris," though in the eighteenth-century version printed here the man is unnamed. The gist of the various versions is along these lines: James Harris and Jane Reynolds had exchanged vows of marriage. He was impressed as a sailor, and when three years later he was reported dead, the girl married a carpenter. Four years after the marriage James's spirit visited Jane, assured her he was a shipowner, and enticed her to leave her family. Destruction followed.

Anonymous

The Demon Lover

"O where have you been, my long, long love,
    This long seven years and mair?"
"O I'm come to seek my former vows
    Ye granted me before."

"O hold your tongue of your former vows,
 For they will breed sad strife;
O hold your tongue of your former vows,
 For I am become a wife."   8

He turned him right and round about,
 And the tear blinded his ee:
"I wad never hae trodden on Irish ground,
 If it had not been for thee.   12

"I might hae had a king's daughter,
 Far, far beyond the sea;
I might have had a king's daughter,
 Had it not been for love o thee."   16

"If ye might have had a king's daughter,
 Yer sel ye had to blame;
Ye might have taken the king's daughter,
 For ye kend° that I was nane.   *knew* 20

"If I was to leave my husband dear,
 And my two babes also,
O what have you to take me to,
 If with you I should go?"   24

"I hae seven ships upon the sea —
 The eighth brought me to land —
With four-and-twenty bold mariners,
 And music on every hand."   28

She has taken up her two little babes,
 Kissed them baith cheek and chin:
"O fair ye weel, my ain two babes,
 For I'll never see you again."   32

She set her foot upon the ship,
 No mariners could she behold;
But the sails were o the taffetie,
 And the masts o the beaten gold.   36

They had not sailed a league, a league,
 A league but barely three,
When dismal grew his countenance,
 And drumlie° grew his ee.   *gloomy* 40

They had not sailed a league, a league,
 A league but barely three,
Until she espied his cloven foot,
 And she wept right bitterlie.   44

"O hold your tongue of your weeping," says he,
    "Of your weeping now let me be;
I will show you how the lilies grow
    On the banks of Italy."   48

"O what hills are yon, yon pleasant hills,
    That the sun shines sweetly on?"
"O yon are the hills of heaven," he said,
    Where you will never win."°   *gain, get to*   52

"O whaten mountain is yon," she said,
    "All so dreary wi frost and snow?"
"O yon is the mountain of hell," he cried,
    "Where you and I will go."   56

He strack the tap-mast wi his hand,
    The fore-mast wi his knee,
And he brake that gallant ship in twain,
    And sank her in the sea.   60

Questions

1. What takes place between lines 28 and 29? Between 48 and 49?
2. What is the first hint that supernatural forces are at work?
3. What does the "cloven foot" (line 43) signify? Is the spirit motivated by malice? By love? By both?

John Henry, a black steel-driver from West Virginia, worked on the Chesapeake and Ohio's Big Bend Tunnel around 1870. The steel-driver hammered a drill (held by his assistant, the "shaker") into rocks, so that explosives could then be poured in. In the 1870s mechanical steel drills were introduced, displacing the steel-driver.

Anonymous

John Henry

John Henry was a very small boy,
Sitting on his mammy's knee;
He picked up a hammer and a little piece of steel,
Saying, "A hammer'll be the death of me, O Lord,
A hammer'll be the death of me."   5

John Henry went up on the mountain
And he came down on the side.
The mountain was so tall and John Henry was so small
That he laid down his hammer and he cried, "O Lord,"
He laid down his hammer and he cried.   10

John Henry was a man just six feet in height,
Nearly two feet and a half across the breast.
He'd take a nine-pound hammer and hammer all day long
And never get tired and want to rest, O Lord,
And never get tired and want to rest.   15

John Henry was a steel-driving man, O Lord,
He drove all over the world.
He come to Big Bend Tunnel on the C. & O. Road
Where he beat the steam drill down, O Lord,
Where he beat the steam drill down.   20

John Henry said to the captain,
"Captain, you go to town,
Bring me back a twelve-pound hammer
And I'll beat that steam drill down, O Lord,
And I'll beat that steam drill down."   25

They placed John Henry on the right-hand side,
The steam drill on the left;
He said, "Before I let that steam drill beat me down
I'll die with my hammer in my hand, O Lord,
And send my soul to rest."   30

The white folks all got scared,
Thought Big Bend was a-fallin' in;
John Henry hollered out with a very loud shout,
"It's my hammer a-fallin' in the wind, O Lord,
It's my hammer a-fallin' in the wind."   35

John Henry said to his shaker,
"Shaker, you better pray,
For if I miss that little piece of steel
Tomorrow'll be your buryin' day, O Lord,
Tomorrow'll be your buryin' day."   40

The man that invented that steam drill
He thought he was mighty fine.
John Henry sunk the steel fourteen feet
While the steam drill only made nine, O Lord,
While the steam drill only made nine.   45

John Henry said to his loving little wife,
"I'm sick and want to go to bed.
Fix me a place to lay down, Child;
There's a roarin' in my head, O Lord,
There's a roarin' in my head."   50

Questions

1. How does the first stanza contribute to John Henry's grandeur?
2. Some versions contain an additional stanza at the end:

They took John Henry to the buryin' ground,
And they buried him in the sand;
And every locomotive come roarin' round
Says "There lies a steel-drivin' man,"
Says "There lies a steel-drivin' man."

Is the ending as given in the present text unsatisfactory? Is there any
doubt about John Henry's death?

This poem, a recent imitation of a ballad, can be sung to the tune
of "Sweet Betsy from Pike," a song associated with the Gold Rush.

X. J. Kennedy (b. 1929)

In a Prominent Bar in Secaucus One Day

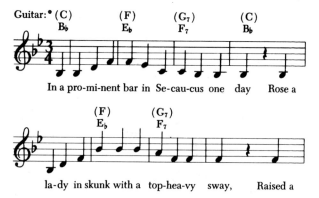

---

* Because the music is written in B♭, a difficult key for the folk guitarist, alternate chords are given in parentheses.

knob-by old fin-ger—all turned from their beer—While with

eyes bright as snow-crust she sang high and clear:

In a prominent bar in Secaucus one day
Rose a lady in skunk with a topheavy sway,
Raised a knobby old finger — all turned from their beer —
While with eyes bright as snowcrust she sang high and clear: 4

"Now who of you'd think from an eyeload of me
That I once was a lady as proud as could be?
Oh I'd never sit down by a tumbledown drunk
If it wasn't, my dears, for the high cost of junk.   8

"All the gents used to swear that the white of my calf
Beat the down of the swan by a length and a half.
In the kerchief of linen I caught to my nose
Ah, there never fell snot, but a little gold rose.   12

"I had seven gold teeth and a toothpick of gold,
My Virginia cheroot was a leaf of it rolled
And I'd light it each time with a thousand in cash —
Why the bums used to fight if I flicked them an ash.   16

"Once the toast of the Biltmore, the belle of the Taft,
I would drink bottle beer at the Drake, never draft,
And dine at the Astor on Salisbury steak
With a clean tablecloth for each bite I did take.   20

"In a car like the Roxy I'd roll to the track,
A steel-guitar trio, a bar in the back,
And the wheels made no noise, they turned over so fast,
Still it took you ten minutes to see me go past.   24

"When the horses bowed down to me that I might choose,
I bet on them all, for I hated to lose.
Now I'm saddled each night for my butter and eggs
And the broken threads race down the backs of my legs.   28

"Let you hold in mind, girls, that your beauty must pass
Like a lovely white clover that rusts with its grass.
Keep your bottoms off barstools and marry you young
Or be left — an old barrel with many a bung.   32

"For when time takes you out for a spin in his car
You'll be hard-pressed to stop him from going too far
And be left by the roadside, for all your good deeds,
Two toadstools for tits and a face full of weeds."   36

All the house raised a cheer, but the man at the bar
Made a phonecall and up pulled a red patrol car
And she blew us a kiss as they copped her away
From that prominent bar in Secaucus, N.J.   40

John Lennon (b. 1940)
Paul McCartney (b. 1942)

Eleanor Rigby

Ah, look at all the lonely people!
Ah, look at all the lonely people!

Eleanor Rigby
Picks up the rice in the church where a wedding has been,
Lives in a dream.   5
Waits at the window
Wearing the face that she keeps in a jar by the door.
Who is it for?

All the lonely people,
Where do they all come from?   10
All the lonely people,
Where do they all belong?

Father McKenzie,
Writing the words of a sermon that no one will hear,
No one comes near.   15

Look at him working,
Darning his socks in the night when there's nobody there.
What does he care?

All the lonely people,
Where do they all come from?   20
All the lonely people,
Where do they all belong?

Ah, look at all the lonely people!
Ah, look at all the lonely people!

Eleanor Rigby   25
Died in the church and was buried along with her name,
Nobody came.
Father McKenzie,
Wiping the dirt from his hands as he walks from the grave,
No one was saved.   30

All the lonely people,
Where do they all come from?
All the lonely people,
Where do they all belong?

Ah, look at all the lonely people!   35
Ah, look at all the lonely people!

Questions

1. This song, of course, is not a traditional ballad, passed on orally
from generation to generation. In what ways does it resemble a traditional ballad? In what ways does it not?

2. Is the poem chiefly about Eleanor Rigby? What is Father
McKenzie doing in the poem?

3. What are the implications (line 7) of "wearing the face that she
keeps in a jar by the door"? Is the sermon (line 14) only a sermon or
are there further implications?

9 Lyric Poetry

The preceding chapter suggested that narrative poetry is far less common than it was before the age of printing. Today when we think of poetry we are less likely to think of the *Aeneid, Paradise Lost,* or the ballads than of lyric poems — pieces that seem to be emotional or reflective soliloquies — such as Wordsworth's "I wandered lonely as a cloud" (page 468). Wordsworth, it is true, narrates a happening (he wandered and came across some daffodils) and describes a scene (the daffodils were "fluttering and dancing in the breeze"). But the poem is about the speaker's emotional response to the flowers he happened upon: when he recalls them his "heart with pleasure fills, / And dances with the daffodils." The recollection of an emotion, which causes a new emotion, is in fact at the root of Wordsworth's theory of poetry. In his Preface to the second edition (1800) of *Lyrical Ballads* he wrote:

> I have said that poetry is the spontaneous overflow of powerful feel-ings: it takes its origin from emotion recollected in tranquillity; the emotion is comtemplated till, by a species of reaction, the tranquillity gradually disappears, and an emotion, kindred to that which was before the subject of contemplation, is gradually produced, and does itself actually exist in the mind. In this mood successful composition gener-ally begins, and in a mood similar to this it is carried on.

Though Wordsworth wrote some narrative and dramatic poetry, he was most often successful with lyric poetry, and this is probably the sort to which his theory chiefly applies. For the Greeks a **lyric** was a song accompanied by a lyre, but by Wordsworth's time it had its present meaning of a poem that, neither narrative (telling a story) nor strictly dramatic (performed by actors), is an emotional or reflective soliloquy. Still, it is rarely very far from a singing voice. James Joyce saw the lyric as the "verbal vesture of an instant of emotion, a rhythmical cry such as ages ago cheered on the man who pulled at the oar." Such lyrics, too, were sung more recently than "ages ago." Here is a song that American slaves sang when rowing heavy loads:

Anonymous

Michael Row the Boat Ashore

Michael row the boat ashore, Hallelujah!
Michael's boat's a freedom boat, Hallelujah!
Sister, help to trim the sail, Hallelujah!
Jordan stream is wide and deep, Hallelujah!
Freedom stands on the other side, Hallelujah!

Why do people sing at work? There are at least three reasons: (1) work done rhythmically goes more efficiently; (2) the songs relieve the boredom of the work; (3) the songs — whether narrative or lyrical — provide something of an outlet for the workers' frustrations.

Speaking roughly, we can say that whereas the narrative is set in the past, telling what happened, the lyric is set in the present, catching a speaker in a moment of expression. But lyric can, of course, glance backward or forward as in this folk song, usually called "Careless Love":

Anonymous

Careless Love

Love, O love, O careless love,
You see what careless love can do.

When I wore my apron low,
Couldn't keep you from my do,°   *door*
    Fare you well, fare you well.
Now I wear my apron high,
Scarce see you passin' by,
    Fare you well, fare you well.

Notice, too, that a lyric, like a narrative, can have a sort of plot: "Michael" moves toward the idea of freedom, and "Careless Love" implies a story of desertion, but, again, the emphasis is on a present state of mind.

Lyrics are sometimes differentiated among themselves. For example, if a lyric is melancholy or mournfully contemplative, especially if it laments a death, it may be called an **elegy** (though before Gray's famous "Elegy" the word often denoted a personal poem written in pairs of lines, on whatever theme). If a lyric is rather long, elaborate, and on a lofty theme such as immortality or a hero's victory, it may be called an **ode.** Greek odes were choral pieces, more or less hymns of praise in elaborate stanzas, but in Rome, Horace (65–8 B.C.) applied the word to quieter pieces, usually in stanzas of four lines, celebrating love, patriotism, or duty. Distinctions among lyrics are often vague, and one man's ode may be another man's elegy. Still, when a writer uses one of these words in his title, he is inviting the reader to recall the tradition in which he is working. Of the poet's link to tradition T. S. Eliot said:

> No poet, no artist of any art, has his complete meaning alone. His significance, his appreciation is the appreciation of his relation to the dead poets and artists. You cannot value him alone; you must set him, for contrast and comparison, among the dead.

Although the lyric is often ostensibly addressed to someone (the "you" in "Careless Love"), the reader usually feels that the speaker is really talking to himself. In "Careless Love," the speaker need not be in the presence of her man; rather, her heart is overflowing (the reader senses) and she pretends to address him. A comment by John Stuart Mill on poetry is especially true of the lyric:

> Eloquence is *heard,* poetry is *over*heard. Eloquence supposes an audience; the peculiarity of poetry appears to us to lie in the poet's utter unconsciousness of a listener. Poetry is feeling confessing itself to itself, in moments of solitude.

This is especially true, of course, in work-songs such as "Michael
Row the Boat Ashore," where there is no audience: the singers sing
for themselves, participating rather than performing. As one prisoner
in Texas said: "They really be singing about the way they feel inside.
Since they can't say it to nobody, they sing a song about it." The
sense of "feeling confessing itself to itself, in moments of solitude,"
or of "singing about the way they feel inside," is strong and clear in
this short cowboy song:

Anonymous

The Colorado Trail

Eyes like the morning star,
Cheeks like a rose,
Laura was a pretty girl,
God Almighty knows.

Weep all ye little rains,
Wail winds wail,
All along, along, along
The Colorado trail.

Here is another anonymous lyric, this one sung by coal miners whose
most constant companions during their long hours below the surface
of the earth were mules that dragged carts of coal:

Anonymous

My Sweetheart's the Mule in the Mines

My sweetheart's the mule in the mines,
I drive her without any lines,
On the bumper I sit,
I chew and I spit,
All over my sweetheart's behind.

One other anonymous poem:

Anonymous

Western Wind

Western wind, when wilt thou blow,
The small rain down can rain?
Christ, if my love were in my arms,
And I in my bed again!

Questions

1. In "Western Wind," what is the tone of the speaker's voice in
the first two lines? Angry? Impatient? Supplicating? Be as precise as
possible. What is the tone in the next two lines?
2. In England the west wind, warmed by the Gulf Stream, rises in
the spring. What associations link the wind and rain of lines 1 and 2
with lines 3 and 4?
3. Ought we to have been told why the lovers are separated?
Explain.

Langston Hughes (1902–1967)

Evenin' Air Blues

Folks, I come up North
Cause they told me de North was fine.
I come up North
Cause they told me de North was fine.
Been up here six months —   5
I'm about to lose my mind.

This mornin' for breakfast
I chawed de mornin' air.
This mornin' for breakfast
Chawed de mornin' air.   10
But this evenin' for supper,
I got evenin' air to spare.

Believe I'll do a little dancin'
Just to drive my blues away —
A little dancin'   15
To drive my blues away,
Cause when I'm dancin'
De blues forgets to stay.

But if you was to ask me
How de blues they come to be,   20
Says if you was to ask me
How de blues they come to be —
You wouldn't need to ask me:
Just look at me and see!

Question

1. In what ways (subject, language) does this poem resemble
blues you may have heard? Does it differ in any ways?

Walt Whitman (1819–1892)

A Noiseless Patient Spider

A noiseless patient spider,
I mark'd where on a little promontory it stood isolated,
Mark'd how to explore the vacant vast surrounding,
It launch'd forth filament, filament, filament, out of itself,
Ever unreeling them, ever tirelessly speeding them.   5

And you O my soul where you stand,
Surrounded, detached, in measureless oceans of space,
Ceaselessly musing, venturing, throwing, seeking the spheres
      to connect them,
Till the bridge you will need be form'd, till the ductile anchor hold,
Till the gossamer thread you fling catch somewhere, O my soul.   10

Questions

1. How are the suggestions in "launch'd" (line 4) and "unreeling"
(line 5) continued in the second stanza?
2. How are the varying lengths of lines 1, 4, and 8 relevant to their
ideas?

3. The second stanza is not a complete sentence. Why? The poem
is unrhymed. What is the effect of the near-rhyme (hold : soul) in the
last two lines?

Robert Frost (1874–1963)

Stopping by Woods on a Snowy Evening

Whose woods these are I think I know.
His house is in the village though;
He will not see me stopping here
To watch his woods fill up with snow.   4

My little horse must think it queer
To stop without a farmhouse near
Between the woods and frozen lake
The darkest evening of the year.   8

He gives his harness bells a shake
To ask if there is some mistake.
The only other sound's the sweep
Of easy wind and downy flake.   12

The woods are lovely, dark and deep.
But I have promises to keep,
And miles to go before I sleep,
And miles to go before I sleep.   16

Questions

1. Line 5 originally read: "The steaming horses think it queer."
Line 7 read: "Between a forest and a lake." Evaluate the changes.

2. The rhyming words in the first stanza can be indicated by *aaba*;
the second stanza picks up the *b* rhyme: *bbcb*. Indicate the rhymes
for the third stanza. For the fourth. Why is it appropriate that the
rhyme scheme differs in the fourth stanza?

3. Hearing that the poem had been interpreted as a "death
poem," Frost said, "I never intended that, but I did have the feeling
it was loaded with ulteriority." What "ulteriority" is implicit? How is
the time of day and year significant? How does the horse's attitude
make a contrast with the man's?

John Keats (1795–1821)

Ode on a Grecian Urn

I

Thou still unravished bride of quietness,
   Thou foster-child of silence and slow time,
Sylvan historian, who canst thus express
   A flowery tale more sweetly than our rhyme:
What leaf-fringed legend haunts about thy shape   5
   Of deities or mortals, or of both,
      In Tempe or the dales of Arcady?
   What men or gods are these? What maidens loth?
What mad pursuit? What struggle to escape?
      What pipes and timbrels? What wild ecstasy?   10

II

Heard melodies are sweet, but those unheard
   Are sweeter; therefore, ye soft pipes, play on;
Not to the sensual° ear, but, more endeared,   *sensuous*
   Pipe to the spirit ditties of no tone:
Fair youth, beneath the trees, thou canst not leave   15
   Thy song, nor ever can those trees be bare;
      Bold Lover, never, never canst thou kiss,
Though winning near the goal — yet, do not grieve;
      She cannot fade, though thou hast not thy bliss,
   For ever wilt thou love, and she be fair!   20

III

Ah, happy, happy boughs! that cannot shed
   Your leaves, nor ever bid the Spring adieu;
And, happy melodist, unwearied,
   For ever piping songs for ever new;
More happy love! more happy, happy love!   25
   For ever warm and still to be enjoyed,
      For ever panting, and for ever young;
All breathing human passion far above,
   That leaves a heart high-sorrowful and cloyed,
      A burning forehead, and a parching tongue.   30

IV

Who are these coming to the sacrifice?
    To what green altar, O mysterious priest,
Lead'st thou that heifer lowing at the skies,
    And all her silken flanks with garlands drest?
What little town by river or sea shore,   35
    Or mountain-built with peaceful citadel,
       Is emptied of this folk, this pious morn?
And, little town, thy streets for evermore
    Will silent be; and not a soul to tell
       Why thou art desolate can e'er return.   40

V

O Attic shape! Fair attitude! with brede°   *design*
    Of marble men and maidens overwrought,
With forest branches and the trodden weed;
    Thou, silent form, dost tease us out of thought
As doth eternity: Cold Pastoral!   45
When old age shall this generation waste,
       Thou shalt remain, in midst of other woe
    Than ours, a friend to man, to whom thou say'st,
"Beauty is truth, truth beauty, — that is all
    Ye know on earth, and all ye need to know."   50

Questions

1. Why "sylvan" historian (line 3)? As the poem continues, what evidence is there that the urn cannot "express" (line 3) a tale so sweetly as the speaker said?

2. What is the meaning of lines 11–14?

3. What might the urn stand for in the first three stanzas? In the third stanza is the speaker caught up in the urn's world or is he sharply aware of his own?

4. Does "tease us out of thought" (line 44) mean "draw us into a realm of imaginative experience superior to that of reason," or "draw us into futile and frustrating questions"? Or both, or neither? What are the suggestions in "Cold Pastoral" (line 45)?

5. Do lines 49–50 perhaps mean that imagination, stimulated by the urn, achieves a realm richer than the daily world? Or perhaps that art, the highest earthly wisdom, suggests there is a realm wherein earthly troubles are resolved?

There is a further problem: although here we have the last two

lines in quotation marks, attributing them to the urn, Keats's own
punctuation is uncertain. Many have held that the last line and a half
are the speaker's reply to the urn's assertion that "Beauty is truth,
truth beauty." The speaker of the poem (one argument goes), aware
of the sorrows and surfeits of life in this world (lines 29–30), rejects
the urn's short-sighted assertion that only beauty exists. To hold this
interpretation, one must say that the speaker's last remark is addressed to the figures on the urn ("Ye" is plural), and one must more
or less ignore "*on* earth" (line 50). Or is the speaker of the last line
and a half — if the speaker is not the urn — turning (as another interpretation holds) to address people in general?

Julia Ward Howe (1819–1910)

Battle Hymn of the Republic

Mine eyes have seen the glory of the coming of the Lord:
He is trampling out the vintage where the grapes of wrath are stored;
He hath loosed the fateful lightning of his terrible swift sword;
    His truth is marching on.   4

Chorus
    Glory! glory! Hallelujah!
    Glory! glory! Hallelujah!
    Glory! glory! Hallelujah!
        His truth is marching on!   8

I have seen him in the watch-fires of a hundred circling camps;
They have builded him an altar in the evening dews and damps;
I can read his righteous sentence by the dim and flaring lamps:
    His day is marching on.   12

I have read a fiery gospel, writ in burnished rows of steel:
"As ye deal with my contemners, so with you my grace shall deal;
Let the Hero, born of woman, crush the serpent with his heel,
    Since God is marching on."   16

He has sounded forth the trumpet that shall never call retreat;
He is sifting out the hearts of men before his judgment-seat;
Oh, be swift, my soul, to answer him! be jubilant, my feet!
    Our God is marching on.   20

In the beauty of the lilies Christ was born across the sea,
With a glory in his bosom that transfigures you and me:
As he died to make men holy, let us die to make men free,
    While God is marching on.   24

Question

1. This poem of the Civil War, written to the tune of "John
Brown's Body," draws some of its militant imagery from the Bible,
especially from Revelation 19 : 11–15. Do the lines on Christ seem
incongruous here?

10 The Speaking Tone of Voice

Everything written is as good as it is dramatic. . . . [A poem is] heard as sung or spoken by a person in a scene — in character, in a setting. By whom, where and when is the question. By the dreamer of a better world out in a storm in Autumn; by a lover under a window at night.

Robert Frost, Preface, *A Way Out*

If we fall into the habit of saying "Whitman says, 'A noiseless patient spider, / I mark'd,' " or "Keats says, 'Heard melodies are sweet, but those unheard are sweeter,' " we neglect the important truth in Frost's comment: a poem is written by an author, but it is spoken by an invented speaker. The author counterfeits the speech of a person in a particular situation. The anonymous author of "Edward" (page 356) invents the speeches of a murderer and his mother; the anonymous author of "Western Wind" (page 370) invents the speech of an unhappy lover who longs for the spring; Robert Frost in "Stopping by Woods" (page 372) invents the speech of a man who, sitting in a horse-drawn sleigh, is surveying woods that are "lovely, dark and deep." Had the setting in Frost's poem been different — say, a snowbound cabin — the speaker of the poem would have said something different.

The speaker's voice, of course, often has the ring of the author's own voice, and to make a distinction between speaker and author may at times seem perverse. Robert Burns, for example, sometimes lets us know that the poem is spoken by "Rob"; he may address his wife by name; beneath the title "To a Mouse" he writes, "On Turning Up Her Nest With the Plow, November, 1785," and beneath the title "To a Mountain Daisy" he writes, "On Turning One Down With the Plow in April, 1786." Still, even in these allegedly autobiographical poems, it may be convenient to distinguish between author and speaker; the speaker is Burns the lover, or Burns the meditative man, or Burns the compassionate man, not simply Robert Burns the poet. Here are two poems by Burns; in the first the lover speaks, in the second we hear a different speaker.

Robert Burns (1759–1796)

Mary Morison

O Mary, at thy window be,
    It is the wished, the trysted hour!
Those smiles and glances let me see,
    That make the miser's treasure poor: 4
How blithely wad I bide the stour,°   *endure the struggle*
    A weary slave frae sun to sun,
Could I the rich reward secure,
    The lovely Mary Morison.   8

Yestreen when to the trembling string
    The dance gaed through the lighted ha',
To thee my fancy took its wing,
    I sat, but neither heard nor saw: 12
Though this was fair, and that was braw,°   *handsome*
    And yon the toast of a' the town,
I sighed, and said amang them a',
    "Ye are na Mary Morison."   16

O Mary, canst thou wreck his peace,
    Wha for thy sake wad gladly die?
Or canst thou break that heart of his,
    Whase only faut is loving thee?   20
If love for love thou wilt na gie,°   *give*
    At least be pity to me shown!
A thought ungentle canna be
    The thought o' Mary Morison.   24

Robert Burns (1759–1796)

John Anderson My Jo

John Anderson my jo,° John,   *sweetheart*
    When we were first acquent,
Your locks were like the raven,
    Your bonnie brow was brent;°   *smooth*   4
But now your brow is beld, John,
    Your locks are like the snaw,
But blessings on your frosty pow,°   *head*
    John Anderson my jo!   8

John Anderson my jo, John,
    We clamb the hill thegither,
And monie a cantie° day, John   *happy*
    We've had wi' ane anither: 12
Now we maun° totter down, John,   *must*
    And hand in hand we'll go,
And sleep thegither at the foot,
    John Anderson my jo!   16

Questions

1. In the first poem, is the speaker addressing Mary Morison?
2. In "Mary Morison," how convincing are the assertions of the
first stanza (that her smiles and glances are more valuable than great
wealth; that he would willingly be a "weary slave" if only he could
win her)? How does the third stanza enlarge our conception of the
speaker's personality? For example, do lines 21–22 introduce an aspect not present earlier? The poem is excellent throughout, but many
readers find the second stanza the best of the three. Do you?
3. In "John Anderson My Jo," the speaker cannot be identified
with Burns, but do we feel that there is in the poem anything of the
particular accent of an old lady? Why?

Although all poems are "dramatic" in Frost's sense of being uttered by a speaker in a situation, and although most short poems are
monologues, the term **dramatic monologue** is reserved for those
poems in which a single character — not the poet — is speaking at a
critical moment to a person or persons whose presence we strongly
feel. The most famous example is Robert Browning's "My Last Duch-

ess," but we can for a moment postpone a reading of that poem while we look at a short poem by Richard Brautigan.

Richard Brautigan (b. 1935)

Romeo and Juliet

If you will die for me
I will die for you

and our graves will
be like two lovers washing
their clothes together
in a laundromat.

If you will bring the soap,
I will bring the bleach.

Questions

1. Who is speaking? To whom? Judging from the first two lines, what is the speaker's emotional state? Do the last two lines, which in their initial words resemble the first two lines, reveal a *different* state, or do they help us to better understand the voice we hear in the first two lines?

Now for one of the most famous of all dramatic monologues:

Robert Browning (1812–1889)

My Last Duchess

FERRARA°   *town in Italy*

That's my last Duchess painted on the wall,
Looking as if she were alive. I call
That piece a wonder, now; Frà Pandolf's° hands   *a fictitious painter*
Worked busily a day, and there she stands.
Will't please you sit and look at her? I said   5

"Frà Pandolf" by design, for never read
Strangers like you that pictured countenance,
The depth and passion of its earnest glance,
But to myself they turned (since none puts by
The curtain I have drawn for you, but I)   10
And seemed as they would ask me, if they durst,
How such a glance came there; so, not the first
Are you to turn and ask thus. Sir, 'twas not
Her husband's presence only, called that spot
Of joy into the Duchess' cheek; perhaps   15
Frà Pandolf chanced to say "Her mantle laps
Over my Lady's wrist too much," or, "Paint
Must never hope to reproduce the faint
Half-flush that dies along her throat." Such stuff
Was courtesy, she thought, and cause enough   20
For calling up that spot of joy. She had
A heart — how shall I say? — too soon made glad,
Too easily impressed; she liked whate'er
She looked on, and her looks went everywhere.
Sir, 'twas all one! My favor at her breast,   25
The dropping of the daylight in the west,
The bough of cherries some officious fool
Broke in the orchard for her, the white mule
She rode with round the terrace — all and each
Would draw from her alike the approving speech,   30
Or blush, at least. She thanked men — good! but thanked
Somehow — I know not how — as if she ranked
My gift of a nine-hundred-years-old name
With anybody's gift. Who'd stoop to blame
This sort of trifling? Even had you skill   35
In speech — (which I have not) — to make your will
Quite clear to such an one, and say, "Just this
Or that in you disgusts me; here you miss,
Or there exceed the mark" — and if she let
Herself be lessoned so, nor plainly set   40
Her wits to yours, forsooth, and made excuse,
— E'en then would be some stooping; and I choose
Never to stoop. Oh, Sir, she smiled, no doubt,
Whene'er I passed her; but who passed without
Much the same smile? This grew; I gave commands;   45
Then all smiles stopped together. There she stands
As if alive. Will't please you rise? We'll meet
The company below, then. I repeat,
The Count your master's known munificence

Is ample warrant that no just pretense   50
Of mine for dowry will be disallowed;
Though his fair daughter's self, as I avowed
At starting, is my object. Nay, we'll go
Together down, Sir. Notice Neptune, though,
Taming a sea-horse, thought a rarity,   55
Which Claus of Innsbruck° cast in bronze for me!   *a fictitious sculptor*

Questions

1. Who is speaking to whom? On what occasion?
2. What words or lines especially convey the speaker's arrogance? What is our attitude toward the speaker? Loathing? Fascination? Respect? Explain.
3. The time and place are Renaissance Italy; how do they affect our attitude toward the duke? What would be the effect if the poem were set in the twentieth century?
4. Why does this poem sound more like talk and less like song than Burns's "John Anderson"?
5. Years after writing this poem, Browning explained that the duke's "commands" (line 45) were "that she should be put to death, or he might have had her shut up in a convent." Should the poem have been more explicit? Does Browning's later uncertainty indicate that the poem is badly thought out? Suppose we did not have Browning's comment on line 45; could the line then mean only that he commanded her to stop smiling and that she obeyed? Explain.
6. Elizabeth Barrett (not yet Mrs. Browning) wrote to Robert Browning that it was not "by the dramatic medium that poets teach most impressively. . . . It is too difficult for the common reader to analyze, and to discern between the vivid and the earnest." She went on, urging him to teach "in the directest and most impressive way, the mask thrown off." What teaching, if any, is in this poem? If there is any teaching here, would it be more impressive if Browning had not used the mask of a Renaissance duke? Explain.

DICTION

From the whole of language, one consciously or unconsciously selects certain words and grammatical constructions; this selection constitutes one's **diction**. It is partly by the diction that we come to know the speaker of a poem. "Amang" and "frae sun to sun" tell us that the speaker of "Mary Morison" is a Scot. In "My Last Duchess" such words as "countenance," "munificence," and "disallowed" — none of which is conceivable in Burns's poem — help us form our impression of the duke. Of course, some words are used in both poems: "I said," "and," "smile[s]," "glance[s]," etc. The fact remains, however, that although a large part of language is shared by all speakers, certain parts of language are used only by certain speakers.

Like some words, some grammatical constructions are used only by certain kinds of speakers. Consider these two passages:

In Adam's fall
We sinned all.
— from *The New England Primer*

Of Man's first disobedience, and the fruit
Of that forbidden tree whose mortal taste
Brought death into the World, and all our woe,
With loss of Eden, till one greater Man
Restore us, and regain the blissful seat,
Sing, Heavenly Muse, that, on the secret top
Of Oreb, or of Sinai, didst inspire
That shepherd who first taught the chosen seed
In the beginning how the heavens and earth
Rose out of Chaos. . . .
— Milton, from *Paradise Lost*

There is an enormous difference in the diction of these two passages. Milton, speaking as an inspired poet who regards his theme as "a great argument," appropriately uses words and grammatical constructions somewhat removed from common life. Hence, while the anonymous author of the primer speaks directly of "Adam's fall," Milton speaks allusively of the fall, calling it "Man's first disobedience." Milton's sentence is nothing that any Englishman ever said in conversation; its genitive beginning, its length (the sentence continues for six lines beyond the quoted passage), and its postponement of the main verb until the sixth line mark it as the utterance of a poet working in the tradition of Latin poetry. The primer's statement, by its choice of words as well as by its brevity, suggests a far less sophisticated speaker.

TONE

A speaker has attitudes toward himself, his subject, and his audience, and (consciously or unconsciously) he chooses his words, pitch, and modulation accordingly; all these add up to his **tone**. In written literature, tone must be detected without the aid of the ear; the reader must understand by the selection and sequence of words the way in which they are meant to be heard (that is, playfully, angrily, confidentially, sarcastically, etc.). The reader must catch what Frost calls "the speaking tone of voice somehow entangled in the words and fastened to the page of the ear of the imagination."* Some examples will clarify what is meant by "the speaking tone of voice." Innumerable poems present a young man urging a young lady to wake up and enjoy the beauty of a spring morning. But such a young man may speak impatiently, or tenderly, or politely, or cozily. In a song from Shakespeare's *Cymbeline* there is the line "My lady sweet, arise"; in Robert Herrick's "Corinna's Going A-Maying," "Get up, sweet slug-a-bed." In "My lady sweet, arise," we detect a somewhat formal tone, as is entirely proper in the context (a minstrel is serenading a princess at the request of a royal wooer). In "Get up, sweet slug-a-bed," we detect, at least in context, a cozy, intimate, playful tone (the speaker is presumably addressing an intimate friend). One might paraphrase either line as "Wake up, lady," but this restatement distorts both lines because it obliterates the distinctions in diction, tone, and speaker.

The following poem was written by Robert Herrick, but the speaker is not the impatient young man who said (in "Corinna") "Get up, sweet slug-a-bed."

Robert Herrick (1591–1674)

To the Virgins, to Make Much of Time

Gather ye rosebuds while ye may,
    Old Time is still a-flying;
And this same flower that smiles today,
    Tomorrow will be dying.   4

The glorious lamp of heaven, the sun,
    The higher he's a-getting,
The sooner will his race be run,
    And nearer he's to setting.   8

* This discussion concentrates on the speaker's tone. But one can also talk of the author's tone, that is, of the author's attitude toward his invented speaker. The speaker's tone might, for example, be angry, but the author's tone (as detected by the reader) might be humorous. For further comment on the author's tone, see page 70.

That age is best which is the first,
    When youth and blood are warmer;
But being spent, the worse, and worst
    Times still succeed the former.   12

Then be not coy, but use your time;
    And while ye may, go marry:
For having lost but once your prime,
    You may for ever tarry.   16

Carpe diem (Latin: "seize the day") is the theme. But if we want to get the full force of the poem, we must understand who is talking to whom. Look, for example, at "Old Time" in line 2. Time is "old," of course, in the sense of having been around a long while, but doesn't "old" in this context suggest also that the speaker regards Time with easy familiarity, almost affection? We visit the old school, and our friend is old George. Time is destructive, yes, and the speaker urges the young maidens to make the most of their spring, but the speaker is neither bitter nor importunate; rather, he seems to be the wise old man, the counselor, the man who has made his peace with time and is giving advice to the young. Time moves rapidly in the poem (the rosebud of line 1 is already a flower in line 3), but the speaker is unhurried; in line 5 he has leisure to explain that the glorious lamp of heaven is the sun.

Ezra Pound (1885–1973)

The River-Merchant's Wife: A Letter

While my hair was still cut straight across my forehead
I played about the front gate, pulling flowers.
You came by on bamboo stilts, playing horse,
You walked about my seat, playing with blue plums.
And we went on living in the village of Chokan: 5
Two small people, without dislike or suspicion.

At fourteen I married My Lord you.
I never laughed, being bashful.
Lowering my head, I looked at the wall.
Called to, a thousand times, I never looked back.   10

At fifteen I stopped scowling,
I desired my dust to be mingled with yours
Forever and forever and forever.
Why should I climb the look out?

At sixteen you departed,   15
You went into far Ku-to-yen, by the river of swirling eddies,
And you have been gone five months.
The monkeys make sorrowful noise overhead.

You dragged your feet when you went out.
By the gate now, the moss is grown, the different mosses,   20
Too deep to clear them away!
The leaves fall early this autumn, in wind.
The paired butterflies are already yellow with August
Over the grass in the West garden;
They hurt me. I grow older.   25
If you are coming down through the narrows of the river Kiang,
Please let me know beforehand,
And I will come out to meet you
            As far as Cho-fu-Sa.

                                        By *Rihaku*

Pound's poem is based on Ernest Fenollosa's prose draft of a translation of an eighth-century Chinese poem by Li Po (called Rihaku in
Japanese). Fenollosa's translation begins:

My hair was at first covering my brows (child's method of wearing hair)
Breaking flowers I was frolicking in front of our gate
When you came riding on bamboo stilts (you — ride on — bamboo
      horse — come)
And going about my seat you played with the blue plums
Together we dwelt in the same Chokan Village
And we too little ones had neither mutual dislike nor suspicion.

Questions

1. Is the writer of the letter nagging her husband to return? Or is
she conveying her love and with admirable concreteness and restraint?

2. Ford Maddox Ford, reviewing the book in which this poem
appeared, said in 1927: "The quality of great poetry is that without

comment as without effort it presents you with images that stir your
emotions; so you are made a better man; you are softened, rendered
more supple of mind, more open to the vicissitudes and necessities of
your fellow men. When you have read 'The River-Merchant's Wife'
you are added to. You are a better man or woman than you were
before." Do you believe it? If so, are we in this case "added to"
because we see a model for behavior? But how, then, would "My
Last Duchess" add to us?

3. The last sentence is the longest, and it immediately follows a
sentence of only three words. What, then, is the effect of the last
sentence?

Gary Snyder (b. 1930)

Hay for the Horses

He had driven half the night
From far down San Joaquin
Through Mariposa, up the
Dangerous mountain roads,
And pulled in at eight a.m.   5
With his big truckload of hay
        behind the barn.
With winch and ropes and hooks
We stacked the bales up clean
To splintery redwood rafters   10
High in the dark, flecks of alfalfa
Whirling through shingle-cracks of light,
Itch of haydust in the
        sweaty shirt and shoes.
At lunchtime under Black oak   15
Out in the hot corral,
    — The old mare nosing lunchpails,
Grasshoppers crackling in the weeds —
"I'm sixty-eight" he said,
"I first bucked hay when I was seventeen.   20
I thought, that day I started,
I sure would hate to do this all my life.
And dammit, that's just what
I've gone and done."

Questions

1. The speaker does not explicitly offer his opinion of the man who "had driven half the night" but do the first two sentences (lines 1–14) communicate at least a hint of an attitude?
2. The old man who speaks lines 19–24 sums up his life. He seems to regard it as wasted, but as we hear his words do we hear bitterness? Self-pity? What is our attitude toward him, and how does it compare with that of the speaker of the poem?

John Crowe Ransom (1888–1974)

Piazza Piece

— I am a gentleman in a dustcoat trying
To make you hear. Your ears are soft and small
And listen to an old man not at all,
They want the young men's whispering and sighing.   4
But see the roses on your trellis dying
And hear the spectral singing of the moon;
For I must have my lovely lady soon,
I am a gentleman in a dustcoat trying.   8

— I am a lady young in beauty waiting
Until my truelove comes, and then we kiss.
But what gray man among the vines is this
Whose words are dry and faint as in a dream?   12
Back from my trellis, Sir, before I scream!
I am a lady young in beauty waiting.

Questions

1. This sonnet (for details, see page 456), like many others, is divided into an octave (the first eight lines) and a sestet (the next six). Who speaks the octave? What words especially characterize him? Characterize the speaker of the sestet.
2. In lines 9–10, she is waiting for her "truelove." Comment on the suggestions in this word. In line 14 she is still "waiting." For whom does she think she is waiting? For whom does the reader know she is waiting? How?

Gerard Manley Hopkins (1844–1889)

Spring and Fall: To a Young Child

Márgarét, áre you gríeving
Over Goldengrove unleaving?
Leáves, líke the things of man, you
With your fresh thoughts care for, can you?
Áh! ás the heart grows older   5
It will come to such sights colder
By and by, nor spare a sigh
Though worlds of wanwood leafmeal lie;
And yet you will weep and know why.
Now no matter, child, the name: 10
Sórrow's spríngs áre the same.
Nor mouth had, no nor mind, expressed
What heart heard of, ghost° guessed: *spirit*
It ís the blight man was born for,
It ís Margaret you mourn for.   15

Questions

1. What is the speaker's age? His tone? What is the relevance of
the title to the speaker and to Margaret? What meanings are in
"Fall"?
2. What is meant by Margaret's "fresh thoughts" (line 4)? Paraphrase lines 3–4 and lines 12–13.
3. "Wanwood" and "leafmeal" are words coined by Hopkins.
What are their suggestions?
4. Why is it not contradictory for the speaker to say that Margaret
weeps for herself (line 15) after saying that she weeps for "Goldengrove unleaving" (line 2)?

Ted Hughes (b. 1930)

Hawk Roosting

I sit in the top of the wood, my eyes closed.
Inaction, no falsifying dream
Between my hooked head and hooked feet:
Or in sleep rehearse perfect kills and eat.   4

The convenience of the high trees!
The air's buoyancy and the sun's ray
Are of advantage to me;
And the earth's face upward for my inspection.   8

My feet are locked upon the rough bark.
It took the whole of Creation
To produce my foot, my each feather:
Now I hold Creation in my foot   12

Or fly up, and revolve it all slowly —
I kill where I please because it is all mine.
There is no sophistry in my body:
My manners are tearing off heads —   16

The allotment of death.
For the one path of my flight is direct
Through the bones of the living.
No arguments assert my right: 20

The sun is behind me.
Nothing has changed since I began.
My eye has permitted no change.
I am going to keep things like this.   24

Questions

1. Many of the sentences are short — only one line long. What is the effect of these short sentences, especially in the last stanza, where each of the four lines is a separate sentence?
2. Hawks cannot speak. Is this poem therefore nonsense?

THE VOICE OF THE SATIRIST

The writer of **satire**, in one way or another, ridicules an aspect or several aspects of human behavior, seeking to arouse in the reader some degree of amused contempt for the object. However urbane in tone, the satirist is always critical. By cleverly holding up foibles or vices for the world's derision, satire (Alexander Pope claimed) "heals with morals what it hurts with wit." The laughter of comedy is an end in itself; the laughter of satire is a weapon against the world: "The intellectual dagger," Frank O'Connor called satire, "opposing the real dagger." Jonathan Swift, of whom O'Connor is speaking, insisted that his satires were not malice but medicine:

His satire points at no defect
But what all mortals may correct. . . .
He spared a hump or crooked nose,
Whose owners set not up for beaux.

But Swift, although he claimed that satire is therapeutic, also saw its futility: "Satire is a sort of glass wherein beholders do generally discover everybody's face but their own."

Sometimes the satirist speaks out directly as defender of public morals, abusively but wittily chopping off heads. Byron, for example, wrote:

Prepare for rhyme — I'll publish, right or wrong:
Fools are my theme, let Satire be my song.

But sometimes the satirist chooses to invent a speaker far removed from himself, just as Browning chose to invent a Renaissance duke. The satirist may, for example, invent a callous brigadier-general or a pompous judge who unconsciously annihilates himself. Consider this satirical poem by E. E. Cummings:

E. E. Cummings (1894–1963)

next to of course god america i

"next to of course god america i
love you land of the pilgrims' and so forth oh
say can you see by the dawn's early my
country 'tis of centuries come and go   4
and are no more what of it we should worry
in every language even deafanddumb
thy sons acclaim your glorious name by gorry
by jingo by gee by gosh by gum   8
why talk of beauty what could be more beauti-
ful than these heroic happy dead
who rushed like lions to the roaring slaughter
they did not stop to think they died instead   12
then shall the voice of liberty be mute?"

He spoke. And drank rapidly a glass of water

Cummings might have written, in the voice of a solid citizen or a
good poet, a direct attack on chauvinistic windbags; instead, he chose
to invent a windbag whose rhetoric punctures itself. Yet the last line
tells that we are really hearing someone who is recounting what the
windbag said; that is, the speaker of all the lines but the last is a sort
of combination of the chauvinist *and* the satiric observer of the chauvinist. (When Cummings himself recited these lines there was mockery in his voice.) Only in the final line of the poem does the author
seem to speak entirely on his own, and even here he adopts a matter-
of-fact pose that is far more potent than **invective** (direct abuse)
would be. Yet the last line is not totally free of explicit hostility. It
might, for example, have run, "He spoke. And poured slowly a glass
of water." Why does this version lack the punch of Cummings's? And
what is implied by the absence of a final period in line 14?

John Updike (b. 1932)

Youth's Progress

*Dick Schneider of Wisconsin . . . was elected "Greek God" for an
interfraternity ball.*

— *Life*

When I was born, my mother taped my ears
So they lay flat. When I had aged ten years,
My teeth were firmly braced and much improved.
Two years went by; my tonsils were removed.   4

At fourteen, I began to comb my hair
A fancy way. Though nothing much was there,
I shaved my upper lip — next year, my chin.
At seventeen, the freckles left my skin.   8

Just turned nineteen, a nicely molded lad,
I said goodbye to Sis and Mother; Dad
Drove me to Wisconsin and set me loose.
At twenty-one, I was elected Zeus.   12

Questions

1. Suppose the first two lines ran thus:

> To keep them flat, my mother taped my ears;
> And then, at last, when I had aged ten years. . . .

How does this revision destroy the special tone of voice in the original two lines? (Notice that in the revision there is a heavy pause at the end of the first line.) Why, in the second line of the revision, is "at last" false to the "tone" or "voice" in the rest of the poem?

2. What is the speaker's attitude toward himself? What is the author's attitude toward the speaker?

Dorothy Parker (1893–1967)

Indian Summer

In youth, it was a way I had
    To do my best to please,
And change, with every passing lad,
    To suit his theories.

But now I know the things I know,
    And do the things I do;
And if you do not like me so,
    To hell, my love, with you!

Questions

1. Perhaps "lad" in the first stanza has a touch of romantic language. But what is the effect of rhyming "please" with "theories"?

2. How do the repetitions in the first two lines of the second stanza affect the tone of the lines? How do they help to prepare for the explosion in the last line?

11 Figurative Language: Simile, Metaphor, Personification, Apostrophe

Hippolyta. 'Tis strange, my Theseus, that these lovers speak of.
Theseus. More strange than true. I never may believe
   These antique fables, nor these fairy toys.
   Lovers and madmen have such seething brains,
   Such shaping fantasies, that apprehend
   More than cool reason ever comprehends.
   The lunatic, the lover, and the poet,
   Are of imagination all compact.
   One sees more devils than vast hell can hold,
   That is the madman. The lover, all as frantic,
   Sees Helen's beauty in a brow of Egypt.
   The poet's eye, in a fine frenzy rolling,
   Doth glance from heaven to earth, from earth to heaven;
   And as imagination bodies forth
   The forms of things unknown, the poet's pen
   Turns them to shapes, and gives to airy nothing
   A local habitation and a name.
   Such tricks hath strong imagination,
   That, if it would but apprehend some joy,

It comprehends the bringer of that joy;
Or in the night, imagining some fear,
How easy is a bush suppos'd a bear!

> —*A Midsummer Night's Dream*, V.i. 1–22

Theseus was neither the first nor the last to suggest that poets, like lunatics and lovers, freely employ their imagination. Terms such as "poetic license" and "poetic justice" imply that poets are free to depict a never-never land. One has only to leaf through any anthology of poetry to encounter numerous statements that are, from a logical point of view, lunacies. Here are a few:

Look like th' innocent flower,
But be the serpent under 't.

> — Shakespeare

Each outcry from the hunted hare
A fiber from the brain does tear.

> — William Blake

Every thread of summer is at last unwoven.

> — Wallace Stevens

On a literal level such assertions are nonsense (so, too, is Theseus's notion that reason is cool). But of course they are not to be taken literally; rather, they employ **figures of speech** — departures from logical usage that are aimed at gaining special effects. Consider the lunacies that Robert Burns heaps up here:

Robert Burns (1759–1796)

A Red, Red Rose

O, my luve is like a red, red rose,
    That's newly sprung in June.
O, my luve is like the melodie,
    That's sweetly played in tune.   4

As fair art thou, my bonnie lass,
    So deep in luve am I,
And I will luve thee still, my dear,
    Till a'° the seas gang° dry.   *all; go* 8

Till a' the seas gang dry, my dear,
    And the rocks melt wi' the sun!
And I will luve thee still, my dear,
    While the sands o' life shall run.   12

And fare thee weel, my only luve,
    And fare thee weel awhile!
And I will come again, my luve,
    Though it were ten thousand mile!   16

To the charge that these lines are lunacies or untruths, at least two replies can be made. First, it might be said that the speaker is not really making assertions about a girl; he is saying he feels a certain way. His words, it can be argued, are not assertions about external reality but expressions of his state of mind, just as a tune one whistles asserts nothing about external reality but expresses the whistler's state of mind. In this view, the nonlogical language of poetry (like groans of pain and exclamations of joy) is an expression of emotion; its further aim, if it has one, is to induce in the hearer an emotion. Second, and more to the point here, it can be said that non-logical language does indeed make assertions about external reality, and even gives the reader an insight into this reality that logical language cannot. The opening comparison in Burns's poem ("my luve is like a red, red rose") brings before our eyes the lady's beauty in a way that the reasonable assertion "She is beautiful" does not. By comparing the woman to a rose, the poet invites us to see the woman through a special sort of lens: she is fragrant; her skin is perhaps like a rose in texture and (in some measure) color; she will not keep her beauty long.

The poet, then, has not only communicated a state of mind but also has discovered, through the lens of his imagination, some things (both in the beloved and in the lover's own feelings) that interest us. His discovery is not world-shaking; it is less important than the discovery of America, or the discovery that the meek are blessed, but it *is* a discovery and it leaves the reader with the feeling, "Yes, that's right. I hadn't quite thought of it that way, but that's right." A poem, Robert Frost said, "assumes direction with the first line laid down, . . . runs a course of lucky events, and ends in a clarification of life — not necessarily a great clarification, such as sects and cults are founded on, but in a momentary stay against confusion." What is clarified? In another paragraph Frost gives an answer: "For me the initial delight is in the surprise of remembering something I didn't know I knew." John Keats made a similar statement: "Poetry . . . should strike the Reader as a wording of his own highest thoughts, and appear almost a Remembrance."

Some figures of speech are, in effect, riddling ways of speech. To call fishermen "farmers of the sea" — a metaphor — is a sort of veiled description of fishermen, bringing out, when it is properly understood, certain aspects of a fisherman's activities. And a riddle, after all, is a veiled description — though intentionally obscure or deceptive — calling attention to characteristics, especially similarities, not usually noticed. ("Riddle," like "read," is from Old English *redan*, "to guess," "to interpret," and thus its solution provides knowledge.) "Two sisters upstairs, often looking but never seeing each other" is (after the riddle is explained) a way of calling attention to the curious fact that the eye, the instrument of vision, never sees its mate.

In the next poem the connection between riddles and metaphors is easily seen:

Sylvia Plath (1932–1963)

Metaphors

I'm a riddle in nine syllables,
An elephant, a ponderous house,
A melon strolling on two tendrils.
O red fruit, ivory, fine timbers!
This loaf's big with its yeasty rising.
Money's new-minted in this fat purse.
I'm a means, a stage, a cow in calf.
I've eaten a bag of green apples,
Boarded the train there's no getting off.

Now for a more difficult riddle:*

Richard Wilbur (b. 1921)

A Riddle

For M.M.

Where far in forest I am laid,
In a place ringed around by stones,
Look for no melancholy shade,
And have no thoughts of buried bones;
For I am bodiless and bright,
And fill this glade with sudden glow;
The leaves are washed in under-light;
Shade lies upon the boughs like snow.

Of course in a figurative comparison, not *all* the qualities of one
item are relevant to the other. A comparison of a beloved woman to a
rose will probably *not* make use of the fact that roses have thorns, or
that they flourish in dirt — although these things too can be relevant
in some poems. A right reading will seize on the relevant properties
and will ignore the irrelevant.

Richard Brautigan (b. 1935)

The Memoirs of Jesse James

I remember all those thousands of hours
that I spent in grade school watching the clock,
waiting for recess or lunch or to go home.
        Waiting: for anything but school.
My teachers could easily have ridden with Jesse James
        for all the time they stole from me.

* For the answer, look under "Wilbur" in the index of this book.

Clearly any romantic associations that Jesse James may have (for instance, generosity to the poor) are irrelevant here.

SIMILE

In a **simile** items from different classes are explicitly compared by a connective such as "like," "as," or "than," or by a verb such as "appears" or "seems." (If the objects compared are from the same class, e.g., "New York is like London," no simile is present.)

Sometimes I feel like a motherless child.
> — Anonymous

It is a beauteous evening, calm and free.
The holy time is quiet as a Nun,
Breathless with adoration.
> — Wordsworth

How sharper than a serpent's tooth it is
To have a thankless child.
> — Shakespeare

Seems he a dove? His feathers are but borrowed.
> — Shakespeare

The following two lines constitute an entire poem:

Robert Herrick (1591–1674)

Her Legs

Fain would I kiss my Julia's dainty leg,
Which is as white and hairless as an egg.

METAPHOR

A **metaphor** asserts the identity, without a connective such as "like" or a verb such as "appears," or terms that are literally incompatible.

She is the rose, the glory of the day.
> — Spenser

O western orb sailing the heaven.
> — Whitman

Notice how in the second example only one of the terms ("orb") is stated; the other ("ship") is implied in "sailing."

Poets not only use similes and metaphors but, naturally, sometimes talk about them:

William Carlos Williams (1883–1963)

A Sort of a Song

Let the snake wait under
his weed
and the writing
be of words, slow and quick, sharp
to strike, quiet to wait,
sleepless.

— through metaphor to reconcile
the people and the stones.
Compose. (No ideas
but in things) Invent!
Saxifrage is my flower that splits
the rocks.

Questions

1. Most people find snakes unpleasant; was it inadvisable of Williams to compare words to snakes? Does the introduction of saxifrage (from Latin *saxum:* rock, and *frangere:* to break), a flower that grows in the crevices of rocks, indicate a tardy attempt to prettify the poem? And what is the relevance of the poet's preference among flowers to a poem on writing and metaphor?

2. What do you think is meant by "through metaphor to reconcile / the people and the stones"?

In the next poem, Keats's excitement on reading Chapman's translation of Homer is communicated first through a metaphor and then through a simile.

John Keats (1795–1821)

On First Looking into Chapman's Homer

Much have I traveled in the realms of gold,
And many goodly states and kingdoms seen;
Round many western islands have I been
Which bards in fealty to Apollo hold.   4
Oft of one wide expanse have I been told
That deep-browed Homer ruled as his demesne;
Yet did I never breathe its pure serene
Til I heard Chapman speak out loud and bold: 8

Then felt I like some watcher of the skies
When a new planet swims into his ken;
Or like stout Cortez when with eagle eyes
He stared at the Pacific — and all his men   12
Looked at each other with a wild surmise —
Silent, upon a peak in Darien.

Questions

1. In line 1, what does "realms of gold" stand for? Chapman was an Elizabethan; how does this fact add relevance to the metaphor in the first line?
2. Does line 9 introduce a totally new idea, or is it somewhat connected to the opening metaphor?

Two types of metaphor deserve special mention. In **metonymy,** something is named that replaces something closely related to it; "City Hall," for example, sometimes is used to stand for municipal authority. In the following passage James Shirley names certain objects, using them to replace social classes to which they are related:

> Scepter and crown must tumble down
> And in the dust be equal made
> With the poor crooked scythe and spade.

In **synecdoche**, the whole is replaced by the part, or the part by the whole. For example, "bread" in "Give us this day our daily bread" replaces the whole class of edibles. Robert Frost was fond of calling himself "a Synecdochist" because he believed that it is the nature of poetry to "have intimations of something more than itself. It almost always comes under the head of synecdoche, a part, a hem of the garment for the whole garment."

PERSONIFICATION

The attribution of human feelings or characteristics to abstractions or to inanimate objects is called **personification.**

> But Time did beckon to the flowers, and they
> By noon most cunningly did steal away.
> — Herbert

Herbert attributes a human gesture to Time and shrewdness to flowers. Of all figures, personification most surely gives to airy nothings to local habitation and a name:

> There's Wrath who has learnt every trick of guerilla warfare,
> The shamming dead, the night-raid, the feinted retreat.
> — Auden

> Hope, thou bold taster of delight.
> — Crashaw

APOSTROPHE

Crashaw's personification, "Hope, thou bold taster of delight," is also an example of the figure called **apostrophe,** an address to a person or thing not literally listening. Wordsworth begins a sonnet by apostrophizing Milton:

> Milton, thou shouldst be living at this hour,

and Shelley begins an ode by apostrophizing a skylark:

> Hail to thee, blithe Spirit!

The following poem is largely built on apostrophe:

Edmund Waller (1606–1687)

Song

Go, lovely rose,
Tell her that wastes her time and me,
    That now she knows,
When I resemble her to thee,
    How sweet and fair she seems to be.   5

Tell her that's young,
And shuns to have her graces spied,
    That hadst thou sprung
In deserts where no men abide,
    Thou must have uncommended died.   10

Small is the worth
Of beauty from the light retired:
    Bid her come forth,
Suffer her self to be desired,
    And not blush so to be admired.   15

Then die, that she
The common fate of all things rare
    May read in thee,
How small a part of time they share,
    That are so wondrous sweet and fair.   20

What conclusions, then, can we draw about **figurative language?** First, figurative language, with its literally incompatible terms, forces the reader to attend to the **connotations** (suggestions, associations) rather than to the **denotations** (dictionary definitions) of one of the terms. Second, although figurative language is said to differ from ordinary discourse, it is found in ordinary discourse as well as in literature. "It rained cats and dogs," "War is hell," "Don't be a pig," and other tired figures comprise part of our daily utterances. But through repeated use, these (and most of the figures we use) have lost whatever impact they once had and are only a shade removed from expressions which, though once figurative, have become literal: the *eye* of a needle, a *branch* office, the *face* of a clock. Third, good figurative language is usually (*a*) concrete, (*b*) condensed, and (*c*) interesting. The concreteness lends precision and vividness; when Keats writes that he felt "like some watcher of the skies / When a new planet swims into his ken," he more sharply characterizes his feelings than if he had said, "I felt excited." His simile isolates for us a precise kind of excitement, and the metaphoric "swims" vividly brings up the oceanic aspect of the sky. The second of these three qualities, condensation, can be seen by attempting to paraphrase some of the figures. A paraphrase will commonly use more words than the original and it will have less impact — as the gradual coming of night usually has less impact on us than a sudden darkening of the sky, or as a prolonged push has less impact than a sudden blow. The third quality, interest, is largely dependent on the previous two: the successful figure often makes us open our eyes wider and take notice. Keats's "deep-browed Homer" arouses our interest in Homer as "thoughtful Homer" or "meditative Homer" does not. Similarly when W. B. Yeats says (page 488):

An aged man is but a paltry thing,
A tattered coat upon a stick, unless
Soul clap its hands and sing, and louder sing
For every tatter in its mortal dress,

the metaphoric identification of an old man with a scarecrow jolts us out of all our usual unthinking attitudes about old men as kind, happy folk content to have passed from youth to senior citizenship.

Finally, two points must be made: first, though figurative language is common in poetry it is not essential; and second, a poem that seems to contain no figures may in fact be one extended figure. Let us take the first point first. The anonymous ballad "Edward" (page 356) contains no figures, yet surely it is a poem and no one would say that the addition of figures would make it a better poem. Here is another poem that employs no figures, the epigraph to Robert Frost's *Collected Poems:*

Robert Frost (1874–1963)

The Pasture ·

I'm going out to clean the pasture spring;
I'll only stop to rake the leaves away
(And wait to watch the water clear, I may):
I shan't be gone long. — You come too.

I'm going out to fetch the little calf
That's standing by the mother. It's so young
It totters when she licks it with her tongue.
I shan't be gone long. — You come too.

Everything here can be taken literally; a man might have said this to someone, and there is not a word in it that is illogical. Yet surely it is a poem. Now for the second point, that an entire poem may be an extended figure. By placing "The Pasture" at the opening of his *Collected Poems,* Frost allows us to read it as a figure; the invitation to accompany the speaker on a trip to the pasture can easily be read as an invitation to accompany the poet on a trip to the poet's world — his poems. But even in isolation the poem as a whole is more than the sum of its parts. The clearing of the water, the calf solicitously tended by its mother and by the speaker, somehow join, and somehow are related to the speaker's solicitous care for the "you" whom he addresses, and we feel that the poem is not only about what the speaker plans to do, but about the loving care that enhances life.

Here is one more poem without any figures of speech:

William Carlos Williams (1883–1963)

The Red Wheelbarrow

so much depends
upon

a red wheel
barrow

glazed with rain
water

beside the white
chickens.

Unlike the two previous poems, the following poems rely heavily on figures of speech.

Alfred, Lord Tennyson (1809–1892)

The Eagle

Fragment

He clasps the crag with crooked hands;
Close to the sun in lonely lands,
Ringed with the azure world, he stands.

The wrinkled sea beneath him crawls:
He watches from his mountain walls,
And like a thunderbolt he falls.

Questions

1. What figure is used in line 1? In line 4? In line 6? Can it be argued that the figures give us a sense of the eagle that is not to be found in a literal description?

2. In line 2 we get overstatement, or hyperbole, for the eagle is not really close to the sun. Suppose instead of "close to the sun" Tennyson had written "Waiting on high"? Would the poem be improved or worsened?

Emily Dickinson (1830–1886)

Because I could not stop for Death

Because I could not stop for Death –
He kindly stopped for me –
The Carriage held but just Ourselves –
And Immortality.   4

We slowly drove – He knew no haste
And I had put away
My labor and my leisure too,
For His Civility –   8

We passed the School, where Children strove
At Recess – in the Ring –
We passed the Fields of Gazing Grain –
We passed the Setting Sun –   12

Or rather – He passed Us –
The Dews drew quivering and chill –
For only Gossamer, my Gown –
My Tippet – only Tulle –   16

We paused before a House that seemed
A Swelling of the Ground –
The Roof was scarcely visible –
The Cornice – in the Ground –   20

Since then – 'tis Centuries – and yet
Feels shorter than the Day
I first surmised the Horses Heads
Were toward Eternity –   24

Questions

1. Characterize death as it appears in lines 1–8.
2. What is the significance of the details and their arrangement in the third stanza? Why "strove" rather than "played" (line 9)? What meanings does "Ring" (line 10) have? Is "Gazing Grain" better than "Golden Grain"?
3. The "House" in the fifth stanza is a sort of riddle. What is the answer? Does this stanza introduce an aspect of death not present — or present only very faintly — in the rest of the poem? Explain.
4. Evaluate this statement about the poem (from Yvor Winters's *In Defense of Reason*): "In so far as it concentrates on the life that is being left behind, it is wholly successful; in so far as it attempts to experience the death to come, it is fraudulent, however exquisitely."

Matthew Arnold (1822–1888)

Dover Beach

The sea is calm to-night.
The tide is full, the moon lies fair
Upon the straits; — on the French coast the light
Gleams and is gone; the cliffs of England stand,
Glimmering and vast, out in the tranquil bay.   5
Come to the window, sweet is the night-air!
Only, from the long line of spray
Where the sea meets the moon-blanch'd land,
Listen! you hear the grating roar
Of pebbles which the waves draw back, and fling,   10
At their return, up the high strand,
Begin, and cease, and then again begin,
With tremulous cadence slow, and bring
The eternal note of sadness in.

Sophocles long ago   15
Heard it on the Ægean, and it brought
Into his mind the turbid ebb and flow
Of human misery; we
Find also in the sound a thought,
Hearing it by this distant northern sea.   20

The Sea of Faith
Was once, too, at the full, and round earth's shore
Lay like the folds of a bright girdle furl'd.
But now I only hear
Its melancholy, long, withdrawing roar,   25
Retreating, to the breath
Of the night-wind, down the vast edges drear
And naked shingles° of the world.   *pebbled beaches*

Ah, love, let us be true
To one another! for the world, which seems   30
To lie before us like a land of dreams,
So various, so beautiful, so new,
Hath really neither joy, nor love, nor light,
Nor certitude, nor peace, nor help for pain;
And we are here as on a darkling plain   35
Swept with confused alarms of struggle and flight,
Where ignorant armies clash by night.

Questions

1. Is there any implication that the "Sea of Faith," now at ebb, will (like the literal sea) again be at the full? Explain.

2. The last section (lines 29–37) makes no use of the sea metaphor, but introduces the "darkling plain." Does this ending seem tacked on? Or is it sufficiently related by references to darkness and to noises? Explain.

3. How do lines 30–33 alter the meaning of the first five lines?

4. In lines 15–28 what do the varying lengths of the lines suggest?

Randall Jarrell (1914–1965)

The Death of the Ball Turret Gunner

From my mother's sleep I fell into the State,
And I hunched in its belly till my wet fur froze.
Six miles from earth, loosed from its dream of life,
I woke to black flak and the nightmare fighters.
When I died they washed me out of the turret with a hose.

Jarrell has furnished an explanatory note: "A ball turret was a plexiglass sphere set into the belly of a B-17 or B-24, and inhabited by two .50 caliber machine-guns and one man, a short small man. When this gunner tracked with his machine-guns a fighter attacking his bomber from below, he revolved with the turret; hunched upside-down in his little sphere, he looked like the fetus in the womb. The fighters which attacked him were armed with cannon firing explosive shells. The hose was a steam hose."

Questions

1. What is implied in the first line? In "I woke to . . . nightmare"? Taking account of the title, is "wet fur" literal or metaphoric or both? Is the simplicity of the last line anticlimactic? How does it continue the metaphor of birth?

2. What effect is gained by having punctuation at the end of every line?

12 Figurative Language: Imagery and Symbolism

When we read "rose" we may more or less call to mind a picture of a rose, or perhaps we are reminded of the odor or texture of a rose. Whatever in a poem appeals to any of our senses (including sensations of heat and pressure as well as of sight, smell, taste, touch, sound) is an **image.** In short, images are the sensory content of a work, whether literal or figurative. Waller's rose (page 403) is an image that happens to be compared in the first stanza to the woman ("I resemble her to thee"); later in the poem this image comes to stand for "all things rare." Yet we never forget that the rose is a rose, and that the poem is chiefly a revelation of the poet's attitude toward his beloved.

When a poet says "My rose" and he is speaking about a rose, we have no figure of speech — though we still have an image. If, however, "My rose" is a shortened form of "My beloved is a rose," some would say that he is using a metaphor, but others would say that because the first term is omitted ("My beloved is"), the rose is a **symbol.** A poem about the transience of a rose might, for example, compel the reader to feel that the transience of female beauty is the larger theme even though it is never explicitly stated. Some symbols are **conventional symbols,** which people have agreed to accept as standing for something other than themselves: a poem about the

411

cross would probably be about Christianity. Similarly, the rose has long been a symbol for love. In Virginia Woolf's novel, *Mrs. Dalloway*, the husband communicates his love by proffering this conventional symbol: "He was holding out flowers — roses, red and white roses. (But he could not bring himself to say he loved her; not in so many words.)" Objects that are not conventional symbols, however, may also give rise to rich, multiple, indefinable associations. (Nonconventional symbolism is evident in Faulkner's "The Bear," page 52, a highly symbolic story in which the wilderness, the bear, the compass, the dog, and other things acquire a significance far beyond anything that tradition has attributed to them.) The following poem uses the traditional symbol of the rose, but uses it in a nontraditional way.

William Blake (1757–1827)

The Sick Rose

O rose, thou art sick!
The invisible worm
That flies in the night,
In the howling storm,

Has found out thy bed
Of crimson joy,
And his dark secret love
Does thy life destroy.

One might perhaps argue that the worm is "invisible" (line 2) merely because it is hidden within the rose, but an "invisible worm / That flies in the night" is more than a long, slender, soft-bodied creeping animal; and a rose that has, or is, a "bed / Of crimson joy" is more than a gardener's rose. Blake's worm and rose suggest things beyond themselves — a stranger, more vibrant world than the world we are usually aware of. One finds oneself half-thinking, for example, that the worm is male, the rose female, and the poem is about the violation of virginity. Or that the poem is about the destruction of beauty: woman's beauty, rooted in joy, is destroyed by a power that feeds on her. But these interpretations are not fully satisfying: the poem presents a worm and a rose, and yet it is not merely about a worm and a rose. These objects resonate, stimulating our thoughts toward something else, but the something else is elusive, whereas it is not elusive in Burns's "A Red, Red Rose" or in Waller's "Go, lovely rose."

A **symbol**, then, is an image so loaded with significance that it is not simply literal, and it does not simply stand for something else; it is both itself *and* something else that it richly suggests, a kind of manifestation of something too complex or too elusive to be otherwise revealed. Blake's poem is about a blighted rose and at the same time about much more. In a symbol, as Thomas Carlyle wrote, "the Infinite is made to blend with the Finite, to stand visible, and as it were, attainable there."* Probably it is not fanciful to say that the American slaves who sang "Joshua fought the battle of Jericho, / And the walls came tumbling down" were singing both about an ancient occurrence *and* about a new embodiment of the ancient, the imminent collapse of slavery in the nineteenth century. Not one or the other, but both: the present partook of the past, and the past partook of the present.

The following "anecdote" has a further meaning — but what is it?

Wallace Stevens (1879–1955)

Anecdote of the Jar

I placed a jar in Tennessee,
And round it was, upon a hill.
It made the slovenly wilderness
Surround that hill.   4

* Isabel C. Hungerland defines a symbol somewhat differently. She says:

> A man may remind me of my father, a kitchen bowl of a certain recipe; neither, according to my proposal, is *ipso facto* a symbol.
>   What is lacking? . . . It is the transference of trains of thought and the accompanying attitude and feelings (which may work mainly in one or in both directions) from one object to another. If I began to think and feel about a man, in certain respects, as I did about my father, and to treat him as I treated my father, then he becomes a father symbol for me. Analogously, in fictional contexts, when we transfer trains of thought and the related attitudes and feelings from one object to another, a symbol is established.
>   — *Poetic Discourse* (Berkeley, Cal., 1958), p. 138

The wilderness rose up to it,
And sprawled around, no longer wild.
The jar was round upon the ground
And tall and of a port in air.   8

It took dominion everywhere.
The jar was gray and bare.
It did not give of bird or bush,
Like nothing else in Tennessee.   12

Stevens, asked for an interpretation of another poem, said (in *The Explicator*, November 1948): "Things that have their origin in the imagination or in the emotions (poems) . . . very often take on a form that is ambiguous or uncertain. It is not possible to attach a single, rational meaning to such things without destroying the imaginative or emotional ambiguity or uncertainty that is inherent in them and that is why poets do not like to explain. That the meanings given by others are sometimes meanings not intended by the poet or that were never present in his mind does not impair them as meanings."

Questions

1. What is the meaning of line 8? Check "port" in a dictionary.
2. Does the poem suggest that the jar organizes slovenly nature, or that the jar impoverishes abundant nature? Or both, or neither? Is the jar a symbol of the imagination, or of the arts, or of man's material progress?

Wallace Stevens (1879–1955)

Thirteen Ways of Looking at a Blackbird

I

Among twenty snowy mountains,
The only moving thing
Was the eye of the blackbird.

II

I was of three minds,
Like a tree   5
In which there are three blackbirds.

III

The blackbird whirled in the autumn winds.
It was a small part of the pantomime.

IV

A man and a woman
Are one.   10
A man and a woman and a blackbird
Are one.

V

I do not know which to prefer,
The beauty of inflections
Or the beauty of innuendos,   15
The blackbird whistling
Or just after.

VI

Icicles filled the long window
With barbaric glass.
The shadow of the blackbird   20
Crossed it, to and fro.
The mood
Traced in the shadow
An indecipherable cause.

VII

O thin men of Haddam,   25
Why do you imagine golden birds?
Do you not see how the blackbird
Walks around the feet
Of the women about you?

VIII

I know noble accents   30
And lucid, inescapable rhythms;
But I know, too,
That the blackbird is involved
In what I know.

IX

When the blackbird flew out of sight,   35
It marked the edge
Of one of many circles.

X

At the sight of blackbirds
Flying in a green light,
Even the bawds of euphony   40
Would cry out sharply.

XI

He rode over Connecticut
In a glass coach.
Once, a fear pierced him,
In that he mistook
The shadow of his equipage   45
For blackbirds.

XII

The river is moving.
The blackbird must be flying.

XIII

It was evening all afternoon.   50
It was snowing
And it was going to snow.
The blackbird sat
In the cedar-limbs.

Questions

1. Stevens once mentioned that he was especially fond of a poem that "wears a deliberately commonplace costume, and yet seems to me to contain something of the essential gaudiness of poetry." Does the statement apply to "Thirteen Ways"?

2. What are the usual associations you have of blackbirds? What qualities do the first two stanzas guide us to attribute to blackbirds?

3. In a letter Stevens says of stanza 7, "In Haddam, Connecticut, men grow thin seeking gold." Does this comment help us to make sense of the stanza, or is the stanza sufficient without it?

4. Who are "the bawds of euphony" (stanza 10)? Is stanza 8 relevant here?

5. Might "He rode over Connecticut / In a glass coach" be interpreted as a description of man insulated from reality by civilization — including "lucid, inescapable rhythms" (stanza 8) and "euphony" (stanza 10)?

6. Is the presence of the blackbird in the last stanza reassuring, or menacing, or what?

7. What do you think of the idea that the blackbird is a way of seeing, or speaking, that is opposed to "lucid, inescapable rhythms"?

D. H. Lawrence (1885–1930)

Snake

A snake came to my water-trough
On a hot, hot day, and I in pajamas for the heat,
To drink there.

In the deep, strange-scented shade of the great dark carob-tree
I came down the steps with my pitcher   5
And must wait, must stand and wait, for there he was at the
    trough before me.

He reached down from a fissure in the earth-wall in the gloom
And trailed his yellow-brown slackness soft-bellied down,
    over the edge of the stone trough
And rested his throat upon the stone bottom,
And where the water had dripped from the tap,
    in a small clearness,   10
He sipped with his straight mouth,
Softly drank through his straight gums, into his slack long body,
Silently.

Someone was before me at my water-trough,
And I, like a second comer, waiting.   15

He lifted his head from his drinking, as cattle do,
And looked at me vaguely, as drinking cattle do,
And flickered his two-forked tongue from his lips,
    and mused a moment,
And stooped and drank a little more,
Being earth-brown, earth-golden from the
    burning bowels of the earth   20
On the day of Sicilian July, with Etna smoking.

The voice of my education said to me
He must be killed,
For in Sicily the black, black snakes are innocent,
    the gold are venomous.

And voices in me said, If you were a man   25
You would take a stick and break him now, and finish him off.

But must I confess how I liked him,
How glad I was he had come like a guest in quiet,
    to drink at my water-trough
And depart peaceful, pacified, and thankless,
Into the burning bowels of this earth?   30

Was it cowardice, that I dared not kill him?
Was it perversity, that I longed to talk to him?
Was it humility, to feel so honored?
I felt so honored.

And yet those voices: 35
If you were not afraid, you would kill him!

And truly I was afraid, I was most afraid,
But even so, honored still more
That he should seek my hospitality
From out the dark door of the secret earth.   40

He drank enough
And lifted his head, dreamily, as one who has drunken,
And flickered his tongue like a forked night on the air, so black,
Seeming to lick his lips,
And looked around like a god, unseeing, into the air,   45
And slowly turned his head,
And slowly, very slowly, as if thrice adream,
Proceeded to draw his slow length curving round
And climb again the broken bank of my wall-face.

And as he put his head into that dreadful hole,   50
And as he slowly drew up, snake-easing his shoulders,
    and entered farther,
A sort of horror, a sort of protest against his withdrawing
    into that horrid black hole,
Deliberately going into the blackness, and slowly
    drawing himself after,
Overcame me now his back was turned.

I looked round, I put down my pitcher,   55
I picked up a clumsy log
And threw it at the water-trough with a clatter.

I think it did not hit him,
But suddenly that part of him that was left behind
    convulsed in undignified haste,
Writhed like lightning, and was gone   60
Into the black hole, the earth-lipped fissure in the wall-front,
At which, in the intense still noon, I stared with fascination.

And immediately I regretted it.
I thought how paltry, how vulgar, what a mean act!
I despised myself and the voices of my accursed
    human education.   65

And I thought of the albatross,
And I wished he would come back, my snake.

For he seemed to me again like a king,
Like a king in exile, uncrowned in the underworld,
Now due to be crowned again.   70

And so, I missed my chance with one of the lords
Of life.
And I have something to expiate:
A pettiness.

Questions

1. In line 6 and later Lawrence calls the snake "he"; in line 14
"someone," thus elevating the snake. What other figures are used to
give the snake dignity? How does Lawrence diminish himself?

2. What is meant by "The voice of my education" (line 22)? It
explicitly speaks in lines 23–26. Where else in the poem do we hear
this voice? What might we call the opposing voice?

When Coleridge published "Kubla Khan" in 1816, he prefaced it with this explanatory note:

> The following fragment is here published at the request of a poet of great and deserved celebrity, and, as far as the author's own opinions are concerned, rather as a psychological curiosity, than on the ground of any supposed *poetic* merits.
>
> In the summer of the year 1797, the author, then in ill health, had retired to a lonely farmhouse between Porlock and Linton, on the Exmoor confines of Somerset and Devonshire. In consequence of a slight indisposition, an anodyne had been prescribed, from the effects of which he fell asleep in his chair at the moment that he was reading the following sentence, or words of the same substance, in *Purchas's Pilgrimage:* "Here the Khan Kubla commanded a palace to be built, and a stately garden thereunto. And thus ten miles of fertile ground were inclosed with a wall." The author continued for about three hours in a profound sleep, at least of the external senses, during which time he has the most vivid confidence that he could not have composed less than from two to three hundred lines; if that indeed can be called composition in which all the images rose up before him as *things*, with a parallel production of the correspondent expressions, without any sensation or consciousness of effort. On awaking he appeared to himself to have a distinct recollection of the whole, and taking his pen, ink, and paper, instantly and eagerly wrote down the lines that are here preserved. At this moment he was unfortunately called out by a person on business from Porlock, and detained by him above an hour, and on his return to his room, found, to his no small surprise and mortification, that though he still retained some vague and dim recollection of the general purport of the vision, yet, with the exception of some eight or ten scattered lines and images, all the rest had passed away like the images on the surface of a stream into which a stone has been cast, but, alas! without the after restoration of the latter!

>   Then all the charm
> Is broken — all that phantom world so fair
> Vanishes, and a thousand circlets spread,
> And each misshape[s] the other. Stay awhile,
> Poor youth! who scarcely dar'st lift up thine eyes —
> The stream will soon renew its smoothness, soon
> The visions will return! And lo, he stays,
> And soon the fragments dim of lovely forms
> Come trembling back, unite, and now once more
> The pool becomes a mirror.

> — Coleridge, from *The Picture; or, the Lover's Resolution*, lines 91–100

Yet from the still surviving recollections in his mind, the author has frequently purposed to finish for himself what had been originally, as it were, given to him. Σαμερον αδιον ασω [today I shall sing more sweetly]: But the tomorrow is yet to come.

Samuel Taylor Coleridge (1772–1834)

Kubla Khan

Or, A Vision in a Dream. A Fragment.

In Xanadu did Kubla Khan
A stately pleasure-dome decree:
Where Alph, the sacred river, ran
Through caverns measureless to man
  Down to a sunless sea.   5
So twice five miles of fertile ground
With walls and towers were girdled round:
And here were gardens bright with sinuous rills,
Where blossomed many an incense-bearing tree;
And here were forests ancient as the hills,   10
Enfolding sunny spots of greenery.

But oh! that deep romantic chasm which slanted
Down the green hill athwart a cedarn cover!
A savage place! as holy and enchanted
As e'er beneath a waning moon was haunted   15
By woman wailing for her demon-lover!
And from this chasm, with ceaseless turmoil seething,
As if this earth in fast thick pants were breathing
A mighty fountain momently was forced;
Amid whose swift half-intermitted burst   20
Huge fragments vaulted like rebounding hail,
Or chaffy grain beneath the thresher's flail:
And 'mid these dancing rocks at once and ever
It flung up momently the sacred river.
Five miles meandering with a mazy motion   25
Through wood and dale the sacred river ran,
Then reached the caverns measureless to man,
And sank in tumult to a lifeless ocean:
And 'mid this tumult Kubla heard from far
Ancestral voices prophesying war!   30
   The shadow of the dome of pleasure
   Floated midway on the waves;
   Where was heard the mingled measure
   From the fountain and the caves.
It was a miracle of rare device,   35
A sunny pleasure-dome with caves of ice!

A damsel with a dulcimer
In a vision once I saw:
It was an Abyssinian maid,
And on her dulcimer she played,   40
Singing of Mount Abora.
Could I revive within me
Her symphony and song,
To such a deep delight 'twould win me,
That with music loud and long,   45
I would build that dome in air,
That sunny dome! those caves of ice!
And all who heard should see them there,
And all should cry, Beware! Beware!
His flashing eyes, his floating hair!   50
Weave a circle round him thrice,
And close your eyes with holy dread,
For he on honey-dew hath fed,
And drunk the milk of Paradise.

Questions

1. Coleridge changed the "palace" of his source into a "dome" (line 2). What are the relevant associations of "dome"?

2. What pairs of contrasts (e.g., underground river, fountain) do you find? What do they contribute to the poem?

3. If Coleridge had not said that the poem is a fragment, might it seem to us to be a complete poem, the first thirty-six lines describing the creative imagination, and the remainder lamenting the loss of poetic power?

Walter de la Mare (1873–1956)

The Listeners

"Is there anybody there?" said the Traveler,
    Knocking on the moonlit door;
And his horse in the silence champed the grasses
    Of the forest's ferny floor.
And a bird flew up out of the turret,   5
    Above the Traveler's head:

And he smote upon the door again a second time;
   "Is there anybody there?" he said.
But no one descended to the Traveler;
   No head from the leaf-fringed sill   10
Leaned over and looked into his gray eyes,
   Where he stood perplexed and still.
But only a host of phantom listeners
   That dwelt in the lone house then
Stood listening in the quiet of the moonlight   15
   To that voice from the world of men:
Stood thronging the faint moonbeams on the dark stair
   That goes down to the empty hall,
Hearkening in an air stirred and shaken
   By the lonely Traveler's call.   20

And he felt in his heart their strangeness,
   Their stillness answering his cry,
While his horse moved, cropping the dark turf,
   'Neath the starred and leafy sky;
For he suddenly smote on the door, even   25
   Louder, and lifted his head: —
"Tell them I came, and no one answered,
   That I kept my word," he said.
Never the least stir made the listeners,
   Though every word he spake   30
Fell echoing through the shadowiness of the still house
   From the one man left awake:
Aye, they heard his foot upon the stirrup,
   And the sound of iron on stone,
And how the silence surged softly backward,   35
   When the plunging hoofs were gone.

Questions

1. Walter de la Mare is reported to have said that the Traveler is a ghost. He is also reported to have said on another occasion that the poem records a class reunion at which he found himself the only one present. Is either of these explanations convincing? Is there anything in the poem to refute the first explanation?

2. Is the poem a narrative of a man who fulfilled a promise, though the ones to whom the promise was made are dead? Is it a narrative of a man who fulfilled a promise in the face of evil forces? Of man's frustrated heroic search for an explanation of the meaning of life? Of man's mysterious separation from the dead? Evaluate each interpretation.

3. Why are the actions of the horse described (lines 3, 23)?

Adrienne Rich (b. 1929)

The Roofwalker

for Denise Levertov

Over the half-finished houses
night comes. The builders
stand on the roof. It is
quiet after the hammers,
the pulleys hang slack.   5
Giants, the roofwalkers,
on a listing deck, the wave
of darkness about to break
on their heads. The sky
is a torn sail where figures   10
pass magnified, shadows
on a burning deck.

I feel like them up there:
exposed, larger than life,
and due to break my neck.   15

Was it worth while to lay —
with infinite exertion —
a roof I can't live under?
— All those blueprints,
closings of gaps,   20
measurings, calculations?
A life I didn't choose
chose me: even
my tools are the wrong ones
for what I have to do.   25
I'm naked, ignorant,
a naked man fleeing
across the roofs
who could with a shade of difference
be sitting in the lamplight   30
against the cream wallpaper
reading — not with indifference —
about a naked man
fleeing across the roofs.

Questions

1. Is "wave / of darkness" (lines 7–8) a tired, worn-out figure, or is it effective in this context?

2. What are the associations in this poem of "a naked man"? And why would a female writer portray herself as a man instead of a woman?

A NOTE ON HAIKU

A **haiku** is a Japanese poem of seventeen syllables, arranged in three lines of five, seven, and five syllables. Japanese poetry is unrhymed, but English versions sometimes rhyme the first and third lines. The subject matter, often connected with the seasons, is usually described objectively and sharply. For example:

Shiki (1867–1902)

River in summer

River in summer:
there is a bridge, but my horse
walks through the water.

Like many haiku, Shiki's poem sets forth a sense of *where*, *what*, and *when*. Concentrating his attention on the phenomena, the poet nevertheless conveys an emotion through the images, stirring the reader's imagination to supply the emotion that completes the experience.

Haiku and Zen Buddhism are closely connected; the poet concentrates on the object for its own sake, but by fully experiencing the object, he achieves (in Zen thinking) an "illumination" or a "realizing of reality," an awareness of the inner spirit of the object he views.

Here is another haiku, which in translation does not preserve the syllabic count:

Basho (1644–1694)

An old pond

An old pond
A frog jumps in —
The sound of the water.

Basho said, "He who creates three to five haiku during a lifetime is a haiku poet. He who attains to ten is a master." You have a lifetime ahead.

13 Irony and Paradox

There is a kind of discourse which, though nonliteral, need not use similes, metaphors, apostrophes, personification, or symbols. A speaker, without using these figures may say things that are not to be taken literally. He may, in short, employ **irony.** In Greek comedy the *eiron* was the sly underdog who, by dissembling inferiority, out-witted his opponent. As Aristotle put it, irony (employed by the *eiron*) is a "pretense tending toward the underside" of truth. Later, Cicero somewhat altered the meaning of the word: he defined it as saying one thing and meaning another (*aliud dicere ac sentias*), and he held that Socrates, who feigned ignorance and let his opponents entrap themselves in their own arguments, was the ironist par excellence. In **verbal irony,** as the term is now used, what is stated is in some degree negated by what is suggested. A classic example is Lady Macbeth's order to get ready for King Duncan's visit: "He that's coming / Must be provided for." The words seem to say that she and Macbeth must busy themselves with household preparations so that the king may be received in appropriate style, but this suggestion of hospitality is undercut by an opposite meaning: preparations must be made for the murder of the king. Two other examples of verbal irony are Melville's comment,

> What like a bullet can undeceive!

and the lover's assertion (in Marvell's "To His Coy Mistress") that

> The grave's a fine and private place,
> But none, I think, do there embrace.

Under Marvell's cautious words we detect a wryness; the **understatement** masks yet reveals a deep-felt awareness of mortality and the barrenness of the grave. The self-mockery in this understatement proclaims modesty, but suggests assurance. The speaker here, like most ironists, is both playful and serious at once. Irony packs a great deal into a few words.*

Overstatement (hyperbole) as well as understatement is ironic when it contains a contradictory suggestion:

> For Brutus is an honorable man;
> So are they all, all honorable men.

Similarly, Alexander Pope damns the proud not with faint praise but with encouragement to be yet more proud:

> Go, wiser thou! and, in thy scale of sense,
> Weigh thy opinion against Providence....
> Snatch from His hand the balance of the rod,
> Re-judge His justice, be the God of God.

The sense of contradiction that is inherent in verbal irony is also inherent in a paradox. **Paradox** has several meanings for philosophers, but we need only be concerned with its meaning of an apparent contradiction. In Gerard Manley Hopkins's "Spring and Fall" (page 389), there is an apparent contradiction in the assertions that Margaret is weeping for the woods (line 2) and for herself (line 15), but the contradiction is not real: both the woods and Margaret are parts of the nature blighted by Adam's sin. Other paradoxes are:

> The child is father of the man;
> — Wordsworth

and (on the soldiers who died to preserve the British Empire):

> The saviors come not home tonight;
> Themselves they could not save;
> — Housman

---

* A word of caution: We have been talking about verbal irony, not **irony of situation**. Like ironic words, ironic situations have in them an element of contrast. A clown whose heart is breaking must make his audience laugh; an author's worst book is his only financial success; a fool solves a problem that vexes the wise.

and:

> One short sleep past, we wake eternally,
> And Death shall be no more; Death, thou shalt die.
>
> — Donne

Donne's lines are a reminder that paradox is not only an instrument of the poet. Christianity embodies several paradoxes: God became man; through the death on the cross, man can obtain eternal life; man does not live fully until he dies.

Some critics have put a high premium on ironic and paradoxical poetry. Briefly, the argument runs that great poetry recognizes the complexity of experience, and that irony and paradox are ways of doing justice to this complexity. I. A. Richards uses "irony" to denote "The bringing in of the opposite, the complementary impulses," and suggests (in *The Principles of Literary Criticism*) that irony in this sense is a characteristic of poetry of "the highest order." It is dubious that all poets must always bring in the opposite, but it is certain that much poetry is ironic and paradoxical.

Percy Bysshe Shelley (1792–1822)

Ozymandias

I met a traveler from an antique land
Who said: Two vast and trunkless legs of stone
Stand in the desert . . . Near them, on the sand,
Half sunk, a shattered visage lies, whose frown,   4
And wrinkled lip, and sneer of cold command,
Tell that its sculptor well those passions read
Which yet survive, stamped on these lifeless things,
The hand that mocked them, and the heart that fed: 8
And on the pedestal these words appear:
"My name is Ozymandias, king of kings:
Look on my works, ye Mighty, and despair!"
Nothing beside remains. Round the decay   12
Of that colossal wreck, boundless and bare
The lone and level sands stretch far away.

Lines 4–8 are somewhat obscure, but the gist is that the passions —
still evident in the "shattered visage" — survive the sculptor's hand
that "mocked" — i.e., (1) copied, (2) derided — them, and the passions also survive the king's heart that had nourished them.

Questions

1. There is, of course, a sort of irony of plot here: Ozymandias
believed that he created enduring works, but his intentions came to
nothing. However, another sort of irony is also present: How are his
words, in a way he did not intend, true?

William Shakespeare (1564–1616)

Sonnet 146

Poor soul, the center of my sinful earth,
My sinful earth these rebel pow'rs that thee array,
Why dost thou pine within and suffer dearth,
Painting thy outward walls so costly gay?   4
Why so large cost,° having so short a lease,   *expense*
Dost thou upon thy fading mansion spend?
Shall worms, inheritors of this excess,
Eat up thy charge? Is this thy body's end?   8
Then, soul, live thou upon thy servant's loss,
And let that pine to aggravate thy store;
Buy terms divine° in selling hours of dross;   *buy ages of immortality*
Within be fed, without be rich no more.   12
  So shalt thou feed on Death, that feeds on men,
  And death once dead, there's no more dying then.

Questions

1. In line 2, "My sinful earth" is doubtless a printer's error.
Among suggested emendations are "Thrall to," "Fooled by," "Rebuke these," "Leagued with," "Feeding." Which do you prefer?
Why?
2. What is the tone of the first two lines? Where in the poem does
the thought take its chief turn? What is the tone of the couplet?
3. What does "array" (line 2) mean?
4. Explain the paradox in lines 13–14.

2. What is the tone of the first two lines? Where in the poem does the thought take its chief turn? What is the tone of the couplet?

3. What does "array" (line 2) mean?

4. Explain the paradox in lines 13–14.

5. In a poem on the relation between the body and the soul, is battle imagery surprising? Commercial imagery (lines 5–12)? What other imagery is in the poem? Is the sonnet a dull preachment? If not, why not?

Donald Hall (b. 1928)

My Son, My Executioner

My son, my executioner,
    I take you in my arms,
Quiet and small and just astir,
    And whom my body warms.   4

Sweet death, small son, our instrument
    Of immortality,
Your cries and hungers document
    Our bodily decay.   8

We twenty-five and twenty-two,
    Who seemed to live forever,
Observe enduring life in you
    And start to die together.   12

Questions

1. In what sense is the son an "executioner"? Why is he called "sweet death"?

2. In what sense does the son embody "enduring life"? Why the "instrument / Of immortality"?

John Crowe Ransom (1888–1974)

Bells for John Whiteside's Daughter

There was such speed in her little body,
And such lightness in her footfall,
It is no wonder her brown study
Astonishes us all.   4

Her wars were bruited in our high window.
We looked among orchard trees and beyond
Where she took arms against her shadow,
Or harried unto the pond   8

The lazy geese, like a snow cloud
Dripping their snow on the green grass,
Tricking and stopping, sleepy and proud,
Who cried in goose, Alas,   12

For the tireless heart within the little
Lady with rod that made them rise
From their noon apple-dreams and scuttle
Goose-fashion under the skies!   16

But now go the bells, and we are ready,
In one house we are sternly stopped
To say we are vexed at her brown study,
Lying so primly propped.   20

Questions

1. What is the literal meaning of "a brown study" in line 3? For
what is it an understatement here? What is meant by "her wars" (line
5)? What are the literal and figurative suggestions of "took arms
against her shadow" in line 7?

2. Why is "tireless heart" (line 13) ironic?

3. In line 17 the speaker says "we are ready." Ready for what?
What word in a later line indicates that he is not "ready"?

Andrew Marvell (1621–1678)

To His Coy Mistress

Had we but world enough, and time,
This coyness, lady, were no crime.
We would sit down, and think which way
To walk, and pass our long love's day.
Thou by the Indian Ganges' side   5
Should'st rubies find: I by the tide
Of Humber would complain.° I would   *write love poems*
Love you ten years before the Flood,
And you should, if you please, refuse
Till the conversion of the Jews.   10
My vegetable° love should grow   *i.e., unconsciously*
Vaster than empires, and more slow.   *growing*
An hundred years should go to praise
Thine eyes, and on thy forehead gaze:
Two hundred to adore each breast: 15
But thirty thousand to the rest.
An age at least to every part,
And the last age should show your heart.
For, lady, you deserve this state,
Nor would I love at lower rate.   20
     But at my back I always hear
Time's winged chariot hurrying near;
And yonder all before us lie
Deserts of vast eternity.
Thy beauty shall no more be found,   25
Nor in thy marble vault shall sound
My echoing song; then worms shall try
That long preserved virginity,
And your quaint honor turn to dust,
And into ashes all my lust.   30
The grave's a fine and private place,
But none, I think, do there embrace.
     Now therefore, while the youthful hue
Sits on thy skin like morning dew,
And while thy willing soul transpires   35
At every pore with instant fires,
Now let us sport us while we may;
And now, like am'rous birds of prey,
Rather at once our time devour,

Than languish in his slow-chapt power,   40
Let us roll all our strength, and all
Our sweetness, up into one ball;
And tear our pleasures with rough strife
Thorough° the iron gates of life.   *through*
Thus, though we cannot make our sun   45
Stand still, yet we will make him run.

Questions

1. Are the assertions in lines 1–20 so inflated that we detect behind them a playfully ironic tone? Explain. Why does the speaker
say, in line 8, that he would love "ten years before the Flood," rather
than merely "since the Flood"?

2. Explain lines 21–24. Why is time behind the speaker, and eternity in front of him? Is this "eternity" the same as the period discussed in lines 1–20? Discuss the change in the speaker's tone after
line 20.

3. Do you agree with the comment on pages 427–428 about the
understatement in lines 31–32? What more can be said about these
lines, in context?

4. Why "am'rous birds of prey" (line 38) rather than the conventional doves? Is the idea of preying continued in the poem?

5. What is meant by "slow-chapt" (line 40)? Consult a dictionary
for various meanings of "chap." In the seventeenth century a cannon-
ball was simply called a "ball." Could lines 42–44 suggest a can-
nonball ripping through a city's fortifications?

6. Is there any verbal irony in lines 33–46? Explain the last two
lines, and characterize the speaker's tone. Are they anticlimactic?

7. The poem is organized in the form of an argument. Trace the
steps.

Andrew Marvell (1621–1678)

The Definition of Love

My Love is of a birth as rare
As 'tis for object strange and high:
It was begotten by Despair
Upon Impossibility.   4

Magnanimous Despair alone
Could show me so divine a thing,
Where feeble Hope could ne'er have flown
But vainly flapped its tinsel wing.   8

And yet I quickly might arrive
Where my extended soul is fixed,
But Fate does iron wedges drive,
And always crowds itself betwixt.   12

For Fate with jealous eye does see
Two perfect loves; nor lets them close:
Their union would her ruin be,
And her tyrannic power depose.   16

And therefore her decrees of steel
Us as the distant poles have placed
(Though Love's whole world on us doth wheel),
Not by themselves to be embraced: 20

Unless the giddy heaven fall,
And earth some new convulsion tear;
And, us to join, the world should all
Be cramped into a planisphere.   24

As lines so loves oblique may well
Themselves in every angle greet:
But ours so truly parallel,
Though infinite, can never meet.   28

Therefore the Love which us doth bind,
But Fate so enviously debars,
Is the conjunction of the mind,
And opposition of the stars.   32

The central paradox in the poem is this: the lovers' spiritual identity keeps them separate. In line 10, *extended* means stretched out
(the speaker imagines that his soul has gone out of his body); *fixed*
means attached. In line 24, *planisphere* (literally a flat sphere) is a
two-dimensional representation of the globe or heavenly sphere.
Conjunction (line 31) refers in astrology to two planets in the same
sign of the zodiac; in astronomy, to two planets in a direct line as
seen from the earth.

Questions

1. Why in line 5 is Despair called "magnanimous"? Paraphrase the paradox of lines 5–6. To what is Hope implicitly compared (lines 7–8)?

2. What is the tone of lines 1–2? Of 9–10? Of 11–12? Why would the union of "two perfect loves" be the "ruin" of Fate (lines 14–15)?

3. What is the tone of the final stanza?

4. Does the poem disparage the physical union of ordinary lovers and celebrate platonic love?

Matthew Prior (1664–1721)

To a Child of Quality* of Five Years
Old the Author Supposed Forty

Lords, knights, and squires, the num'rous band
    That wear the fair Miss Mary's fetters,
Were summoned by her high command,
    To show their passion by their letters.   4

My pen amongst the rest I took,
    Lest those bright eyes that cannot read
Should dart their kindling fires, and look
    The power they have to be obeyed.   8

Nor quality, nor reputation,
    Forbid me yet my flame to tell,
Dear Five-years-old befriends my passion,
    And I may write till she can spell.   12

For while she makes her silkworms beds
    With all the tender things I swear,
Whilst all the house my passion reads,
    In papers° round her baby's hair,   *used for curling hair* 16

She may receive and own° my flame,   *confess*
    For though the strictest prudes should know it,
She'll pass for a most virtuous dame,
    And I for an unhappy poet.   20

* High social position

Then too, alas, when she shall tear
    The lines some younger rival sends,
She'll give me leave to write, I fear,
    And we shall still continue friends.   24

For as our diff'rent ages move,
    'Tis so ordained, would fate but mend it,
That I shall be past making love,
    When she begins to comprehend it.   28

Questions

1. The poem is based on the convention that normally a lover does not publicize his love for the woman. The title makes clear why the speaker can openly declare his love. What does he mean, in the first stanza, when he says that lords, knights, and squires "wear the fair Miss Mary's fetters"? How serious is he?
2. What is especially amusing in the second stanza? In the third?
3. Do we feel that the speaker is a potential child-molester? Why?

John Donne (1572–1631)

The Flea

Mark but this flea, and mark in this
How little that which thou deny'st me is;
It sucked me first, and now sucks thee,
And in this flea our two bloods mingled be;
Thou know'st that this cannot be said   5
A sin, nor shame, nor loss of maidenhead;
    Yet this enjoys before it woo,
    And pampered swells with one blood made of two,
    And this, alas, is more than we would do.

Oh stay, three lives in one flea spare,   10
Where we almost, yea, more than married are.
This flea is you and I, and this
Our marriage bed and marriage temple is;
Though parents grudge, and you, we are met
And cloistered in these living walls of jet.   15

Though use° make you apt to kill me,   custom
Let not to that, self-murder added be,
And sacrilege, three sins in killing three.

Cruel and sudden, has thou since
Purpled thy nail in blood of innocence?   20
Wherein could this flea guilty be,
Except in that drop which it sucked from thee?
Yet thou triumph'st and say'st that thou
Find'st not thyself, nor me the weaker now.
   'Tis true. Then learn how false fears be: 25
   Just so much honor, when thou yield'st to me,
   Will waste, as this flea's death took life from thee.

Questions

1. In the first stanza the speaker argues that because the blood of
the lovers is mixed in the flea, it would be "little," or no consequence, for the woman to give herself sexually to the speaker. What
evidence is there in the poem that he does not really think that a
sexual union is of no importance?

2. What is hyperbolic about line 10? Why does the speaker overstate the matter in the second stanza? How does the overstatement
serve to diminish the subject?

3. What has the lady done between the second and third stanzas?
In line 25 the speaker says that the lady's view is "true." Has he
changed his mind during the course of the poem, or has he been
leading up to this point?

John Donne (1572–1631)

Holy Sonnet XIV

Batter my heart, three-personed God; for you
As yet but knock, breathe, shine, and seek to mend;
That I may rise and stand, o'erthrow me, and bend
Your force, to break, blow, burn, and make me new.   4
I, like an usurped town, to another due,
Labor to admit you, but oh, to no end,
Reason, your viceroy in me, me should defend,
But is captived, and proves weak or untrue.   8

Yet dearly I love you, and would be loved fain,
But am betrothed unto your enemy:
Divorce me, untie, or break that knot again,
Take me to you, imprison me, for I   12
Except you enthrall me, never shall be free,
Nor ever chaste, except you ravish me.

Questions

1. Explain the paradoxes in lines 1, 3, 13, 14. Explain the double meanings of "enthrall" (line 13) and "ravish" (line 14).

2. In lines 1–4 what is God implicitly compared to (considering especially lines 2 and 4)? How does this comparison lead into the comparison that dominates lines 5–8? What words in lines 9–12 are especially related to the earlier lines?

3. What is gained by piling up verbs in lines 2–4?

4. Are sexual references necessarily irreverent in a religious poem? Donne, incidentally, was an Anglican priest.

14 Rhythm

Ezra Pound (1885–1973)

Immorality

Sing we for love and idleness,
Naught else is worth the having.

Though I have been in many a land,
There is naught else in living.

And I would rather have my sweet,
Though rose-leaves die of grieving,

Than do high deeds in Hungary
To pass all men's believing.

A good poem. To begin with, it sings; as Pound has said, "Poetry withers and dries out when it leaves music, or at least imagined music, too far behind it. Poets who are not interested in music are, or become, bad poets." The ballads in a preceding chapter, it must be remembered, are songs, and other poetry too is sung, especially by children. A child reciting a counting-out rhyme, or singing on his way home from school, is enjoying poetry:

> Pease-porridge hot,
>   Pease-porridge cold,
> Pease-porridge in the pot
>   Nine days old.

Nothing very important is being said, but for generations children have enjoyed the music of these lines, and adults, too, have recalled them with pleasure — though few people know what pease-porridge is.

The "music" — the catchiness of certain sounds — should not be underestimated. Here are lines chanted by the witches in *Macbeth:*

> Double, double, toil and trouble;
> Fire burn and cauldron bubble.

This is rather far from words that mean approximately the same thing: "Twice, twice, work and care; / Fire ignite, and pot boil." The difference is more in the sounds than in the instructions. What is lost in the paraphrase is the magic, the incantation, which resides in elaborate repetitions of sounds and stresses.

Rhythm (most simply, in English poetry, stresses at regular intervals) has a power of its own. A highly pronounced rhythm is common in such forms of poetry as charms, college yells, and lullabies; all of them (like the witches' speech) are aimed at inducing a special effect magically. It is not surpising that *carmen*, the Latin word for verse or song, is also the Latin word for charm, and the word from which "charm" is derived.

> Rain, rain, go away;
> Come again another day.

> Block that kick! Block that kick! Block that kick!

> Rock a-bye baby, on the tree top,
> When the wind blows, the cradle will rock.

In much poetry rhythm is only half-heard, but its omnipresence is suggested by the fact that when poetry is printed it is customary to begin each line with a capital letter. Prose (from Latin *prorsus*, "forward," "straight on") keeps running across the paper until the right-hand margin is reached, and then, merely because the paper has given out, the write or printer starts again at the left, with a small letter. But verse (Latin *versus*, "a turning") often ends well short of the righthand margin, and the next line begins at the left — usually with a capital — not because paper has run out but because the rhythmic pattern begins again. Lines of poetry are continually reminding us that they have a pattern.

Before turning to some other highly rhythmic pieces, a word of caution: a mechanical, unvarying rhythm may be good to put the baby to sleep, but it can be deadly to readers who wish to keep awake. A poet varies his rhythm according to his purpose; he ought not to be so regular that he is (in W. H. Auden's words) an "accentual pest." In competent hands, rhythm contributes to meaning; it says something. The rhythm in the lines from *Macbeth*, for example, helps suggest the strong binding power of magic. Again Ezra Pound has a relevant comment: "Rhythm *must* have meaning. It can't be merely a careless dash off, with no grip and no real hold to the words and sense, a tumty tum tumty tum tum ta." Consider this description of Hell from *Paradise Lost* (the heavier stresses are marked by ´):

Rócks, caves, lakes, féns, bógs, déns, and shádes of death.

Milton immediately follows one heavy stress with another (in contrast to the iambic feet — alternating unstressed and stressed syllables — that are the norm in the poem), helping to communicate the "meaning" — the impressive monotony of Hell. As a second example, consider the function of the rhythm in two lines by Alexander Pope:

When Ájax strives some rock's vast wéight to thrów,

The líne too lábors, and the words móve slow.

The heavier stresses (again, marked by ´) do not merely alternate with the lighter ones (marked ˘); rather, the great weight of the rock is suggested by three consecutive stressed words, "rock's vast weight," and the great effort involved in moving it is suggested by another three consecutive stresses, "line too labors," and by yet another three, "words move slow." Note, also, the abundant pauses within the lines. In the first line, unless one's speech is slovenly, one must pause at least slightly after "Ajax," "strives," "rock's," "vast," "weight," and "throw." The grating sounds in "Ajax" and "rock's" do their work, too, and so do the explosive *t*'s. When Pope wishes to suggest lightness, he reverses his procedure and he groups *un*stressed syllables:

Not so, when swift Camilla scours the plain,

Flíes o'er th'unbénding córn, and skims along the máin.

This last line has twelve syllables, and is thus longer than the line about Ajax, but the addition of "along" helps to communicate lightness and swiftness because in this line (it can be argued) neither syllable of "along" is strongly stressed. If "along" is omitted, the line still makes grammatical sense and becomes more "regular," but it also becomes less imitative of lightness.

The very regularity of a line may be meaningful too. Shakespeare begins a sonnet thus:

When I do count the clock that tells the time.

This line about a mechanism runs with appropriate regularity. (It is worth noting, too, that "*c*ount the *c*lock" and "*t*ells the *t*ime" emphasize the regularity by the repetition of sounds and syntax.) But notice what Shakespeare does in the middle of the next line:

And see the brave day sunk in hideous night.

Following are some poems in which the strongly felt pulsations are highly important. In the first of these, notice that many lines begin with a stressed syllable, a relatively unusual practice.

William Shakespeare (1564–1616)

Fear no more the heat o' th' sun*

Guiderius:	Fear no more the heat o' the' sun
	Nor the furious winter's rages;
	Thou thy worldly task hast done,
	Home art gone, and ta'en thy wages;
	Golden lads and girls all must, 5
	As chimney-sweepers, come to dust.

Arviragus:	Fear no more the frown o' th' great,
	Thou art past the tyrant's stroke;
	Care no more to clothe and eat,
	To thee the reed is as the oak: 10
	The scepter, learning, physic,° must *medicine, i.e.,*
	All follow this and come to dust. *the physician*

* These lines, from *Cymbeline* (IV.ii), are spoken by two brothers over the body of their sister, who they think is dead.

Guiderius:	Fear no more the lightning flash,
Arviragus:	Nor the all-dreaded thunder-stone;° *thunderbolt*
Guiderius:	Fear not slander, censure rash; 15
Arviragus:	Thou hast finished joy and moan:
Both:	All lovers young, all lovers must
	Consign to thee° and come to dust. *sign the contract*
	along with you
Guiderius:	No exorciser harm thee!
Arviragus:	Nor no witchcraft charm thee! 20
Guiderius:	Ghost unlaid° forbear thee! *wandering ghost*
Arviragus:	Nothing ill come near thee!
Both:	Quiet consummation have,
	And renowned be thy grave.

Questions

1. Characterize the tone of lines 19–24. How and why does it differ from the tone of the earlier lines?
2. What effect is gained by repeating "Fear no more" in lines 1, 7, 13? Note, too, "Fear not" in line 15. In English poetry it is unusual for a poem to begin many lines with a stressed syllable. How many such lines are in this poem? what is the effect?
3. What are the connotations in "golden" (line 5)?
4. What figure of speech is used in line 11?

George Herbert (1593–1633)

Discipline

Throw away thy rod,
Throw away thy wrath.
O my God,
Take the gentle path.   4

For my heart's desire
Unto thine is bent;
    I aspire
To a full consent.   8

Not a word or look
I affect to own,
    But by book,
And thy book alone.   12

Though I fail, I weep.
Though I halt in pace,
    Yet I creep
To the throne of grace.   16

Then let wrath remove;
Love will do the deed,
    For with love
Stony hearts will bleed.   20

Love is swift of foot,
Love's a man of war,
    And can shoot,
And can hit from far.   24

Who can 'scape his bow?
That which wrought on thee,
    Brought thee low,
Needs must work on me.   28

Throw away thy rod.
Though man frailties hath,
    Thou art God.
Throw away thy wrath.   32

Questions

1. What is the effect of the short third line in each stanza? Is the line prolonged in reading?

2. Is the poem "disciplined"? What do the lengths of the lines and the emphatic rhymes contribute?

3. Explain the paradox (lines 19–28) that love is warlike. What figure of speech is used in lines 21–24? Explain lines 26–27. Would "Love" be a better title than "Discipline"? Why?

4. Compare the tone of the last stanza with that of the first. Would the poem be more effective if the last stanza were identical with the first? Why?

5. The Christian usually petitions God rather than commands Him. Is this poem offensively imperious? Explain.

The next three poems all take dancing as their nominal subject.

William Carlos Williams (1883–1963)

The Dance

In Breughel's great picture, The Kermess,
the dancers go round, they go round and
around, the squeal and the blare and the
tweedle of bagpipes, a bugle and fiddles
tipping their bellies (round as the thick-   5
sided glasses whose wash they impound)
their hips and their bellies off balance
to turn them. Kicking and rolling about
the Fair Grounds, swinging their butts, those
shanks must be sound to bear up under such   10
rollicking measures, prance as they dance
in Breughel's great picture, The Kermess.

Questions

1. Read the poem aloud several times, and decide where the heavy stresses fall. Mark the heavily stressed syllables (´), the lightly stressed ones (`), and the unstressed ones (˘). Are all the lines identical? What effect is thus gained, especially when read aloud? What does the parenthetical statement (lines 5–6) do to the rhythm? Does a final syllable often receive a heavy stress here? Are there noticeable pauses at the ends of the lines? What is the consequence? Are the dancers waltzing?

2. What syllables rhyme or are repeated (e.g., "round" in lines 2 and 5, and "-pound" in line 6; "-ing" in lines 5, 8, 9, 11)? What effect do they have? Does the poem contain much assonance and consonance? Is there any onomatopoeia? (See pages 454–455 for definitions of these terms.)

3. How does the absence at the beginning of each line of the customary capital contribute to the meaning? Why is the last line the same as the first?

William Carlos Williams (1883–1963)

The Artist

Mr. T.
    bareheaded
        in a soiled undershirt
his hair standing out
    on all sides   5
        stood on his toes
heels together
    arms gracefully
        for the moment
curled above his head.   10
    Then he whirled about
        bounded
into the air
    and with an *entrechat*°   *a leap in ballet*
        perfectly achieved   15
completed the figure.
    My mother
        taken by surprise
where she sat
    in her invalid's chair   20
        was left speechless.
Bravo! she cried at last
    and clapped her hands.
        The man's wife
came from the kitchen: 25
    What goes on here? she said.
        But the show was over.

Question

1. Would anything be lost if the poem were printed conventionally, e.g., if the first line were: "Mr. T. bareheaded in a soiled undershirt"?

Theodore Roethke (1908–1963)

My Papa's Waltz

The whiskey on your breath
Could make a small boy dizzy;
But I hung on like death:
Such waltzing was not easy.   4

We romped until the pans
Slid from the kitchen shelf;
My mother's countenance
Could not unfrown itself.   8

The hand that held my wrist
Was battered on one knuckle;
At every step you missed
My right ear scraped a buckle.   12

You beat time on my head
With a palm caked hard by dirt,
Then waltzed me off to bed
Still clinging to your shirt.   16

Questions

1. Is the rhythm more regular than in Williams's "The Dance"?
Do the syntactical pauses vary much from stanza to stanza? Be
specific. Would you say that the rhythm suggests lightness? Why?
2. Does the rhythm parallel, or ironically contrast with, the episode described? Was the dance a graceful waltz? Explain.
3. Is the stress on "Slid" (line 6) expected? Are the stresses in
lines 13–14 functional? Explain.

Dylan Thomas (1914–1953)

Do not go gentle into that good night

Do not go gentle into that good night,
Old age should burn and rave at close of day;
Rage, rage against the dying of the light.

Though wise men at their end know dark is right,
Because their words had forked no lightning they   5
Do not go gentle into that good night.

Good men, the last wave by, crying how bright
Their frail deeds might have danced in a green bay,
Rage, rage against the dying of the light.

Wild men who caught and sang the sun in flight,   10
And learn, too late, they grieved it on its way,
Do not go gentle into that good night.

Grave men, near death, who see with blinding sight
Blind eyes could blaze like meteors and be gay,
Rage, rage against the dying of the light.   15

And you, my father, there on the sad height,
Curse, bless, me now with your fierce tears, I pray.
Do not go gentle into that good night.
Rage, rage against the dying of the light.

This poem is written in an elaborate French form, the **villanelle,**
i.e., five tercets (stanzas of three lines each, the first and third lines
rhyming) and a final quatrain (stanza of four lines, the first, third, and
fourth lines all rhyming with the first and third lines of the tercets,
and the second line rhyming with the middle lines of the tercets).
Moreover, the first line of the poem is the last line of the second and
fourth tercets; the third line of the poem is the last line of the third
and fifth tercets, and these two lines reappear yet again as a pair of
rhyming lines at the end of the poem.

Question

1. The intricate form of the villanelle might seem too fussy for a
serious poem about dying. Is it too fussy? Or does the form here
somehow succeed?

15 Some Principles of Versification

The technical vocabulary of **prosody** (the study of the principles of verse structure, including meter, rhyme and other sound effects, and stanzaic patterns) is large. An understanding of these terms will not turn anyone into a poet, but it will enable one to discuss some aspects of poetry more efficiently. A knowledge of them, like a knowledge of most other technical terms (e.g., "misplaced modifier," "woofer," "automatic transmission") allows for quick and accurate communication. The following are the chief terms of prosody.

Most English poetry has a pattern of **stressed (accented)** sounds, and this pattern is the **meter** (from the Greek word for "measure"). Although in Old English poetry (poetry written in England before the Norman-French Conquest in 1066) a line may have any number of unstressed syllables in addition to four stressed syllables, most poetry written in England since the Conquest not only has a fixed number of stresses in a line but also a fixed number of unstressed syllables before or after each stressed one. (One really ought not to talk of "unstressed" or "unaccented" syllables, since to utter a syllable — however lightly — is to give it some stress. But the fact is that "unstressed" or "unaccented" are parts of the established terminology of versification.)

In a line of poetry the **foot** is the basic unit of measurement. On rare occasions it is a single stressed syllable; but generally a foot consists of two or three syllables, one of which is stressed. (Stress is indicated by ´; lack of stress by ˘.) The repetition of feet, then, produces a pattern of stresses throughout the poem.

Two cautions:

1. A poem will seldom contain only one kind of foot throughout; significant variations usually occur, but one kind of foot is dominant.

2. In reading a poem one pays attention to the sense as well as to the metrical pattern. By paying attention to the sense one often finds that the stress falls on a word that according to the metrical pattern would be unstressed. Or a word that according to the pattern would be stressed may be seen to be unstressed. Furthermore, by reading for sense one finds that not all stresses are equally heavy; some are almost as light as unstressed syllables, and sometimes there is a **hovering stress**, that is, the stress is equally distributed over two adjacent syllables. To repeat: one reads for sense, allowing the syntax to help indicate the stresses.

The most common feet in English poetry are:

iamb (adjective: **iambic**): one unstressed syllable followed by one stressed syllable. The iamb, said to be the most common pattern in English speech, is surely the most common in English poetry. It is called a **rising meter**, the foot rising toward the stress. The following example has five iambic feet:

Ĭ sáw | thĕ ský | dĕscénd | ĭng bláck | ănd whíte.
— Robert Lowell

trochee (**trochaic**): one stressed syllable followed by one unstressed; a **falling meter**, the foot falling away from the stress.

Lét hĕr | líve tŏ | eárn hĕr | dínnĕrs.
— J. M. Synge

anapest (**anapestic**): two unstressed syllables followed by one stressed; a rising meter.

Thĕre arĕ mán | y̆ who sáy | that ă dóg | has his dáy.
— Dylan Thomas

dactyl (**dactylic**): one stressed syllable followed by two unstressed; a falling meter. This trisyllabic foot, like the anapest, is common in light verse, or verse suggesting joy, but its use is not limited to such material. Thomas Hood's sentimental "The Bridge of Sighs" begins:

Táke hĕr ŭp | ténderlў.
— Hood

spondee (spondaic): two stressed syllables; most often used as a substitute for an iamb or trochee; it neither rises nor falls.

Smárt lád, | tŏ slíp | bĕtimés | ăwáy.
— A. E. Housman

Because the **pyrrhic** foot (two unstressed syllables) lacks a stress, it is often not considered a legitimate foot in English.

A metrical line consists of one or more feet and is named for the number of feet in it. The following names are used:

monometer:	one foot	**pentameter:**	five feet
dimeter:	two feet	**hexameter:**	six feet
trimeter:	three feet	**heptameter:**	seven feet
tetrameter:	four feet	**octameter:**	eight feet

A line is scanned for the kind and number of feet in it, and the **scansion** tells you if it is, say, anapestic trimeter (three anapests):

Ăs Ĭ came | tŏ thĕ edgé | ŏf thĕ wóods.
— Frost

Another example, this time iambic pentameter:

Sĭnce bráss, nŏr stóne, nŏr eárth, nŏr boúndlĕss séa.
— Shakespeare

In prosody, as in the rest of life, male chauvinism has left its mark: a line ending with a stress has a **masculine ending** or **strong ending;** a line ending with an unstressed syllable has a **feminine ending** or **weak ending.** The lines above by Synge and Hood have feminine endings; those by Lowell, Thomas, Housman, Frost, and Shakespeare have masculine endings. The **caesura** (usually indicated by the symbol / /) is a slight pause within the line. It need not be indicated by punctuation, and it does not affect the metrical count:

Awake, my St. John ! / / leave all meaner things
To low ambition, / / and the pride of kings.
Let us / / (since Life can little more supply
Than just to look about us / / and to die)

Expatiate free / / o'er all this scene of Man;
A mighty maze! / / but not without a plan;
A wild, / / where weeds and flowers promiscuous shoot;
Or garden, / / tempting with forbidden fruit.

— Pope

The varying position of the caesura helps to give Pope's lines an informality that plays against the formality of the pairs of rhyming lines.

An **end-stopped line** concludes with a distinct syntactical pause, but a **run-on line** has its sense carried over into the next line without syntactical pause. (The running-on of a line is called **enjambment.**) In the following passage, only the first is a run-on line:

Yet if we look more closely we shall find
Most have the seeds of judgment in their mind:
Nature affords at least a glimmering light;
The lines, though touched but faintly, are drawn right.

— Pope

Meter produces **rhythm,** recurrences at equal intervals, but rhythm (from a Greek word meaning "flow") is usually applied to larger units than feet. Often it depends most obviously on pauses. Thus, a poem with run-on lines will have a different rhythm from a poem with end-stopped lines, even though both are in the same meter. And prose, though it is unmetrical, can thus have rhythm, too. In addition to being affected by syntactical pauses, rhythm is affected by pauses due to consonant clusters and the length of words. Polysyllabic words establish a different rhythm from monosyllabic words, even in metrically identical lines. One can say, then, that rhythm is altered by shifts in meter, syntax, and the ease of pronunciation. But even with no such shift, even if a line is repeated verbatim, a reader may sense a change in rhythm. The rhythm of the final line of a poem may well differ from that of the line before, even though in all other respects the lines are identical, as in Frost's "Stopping by Woods" (page 372), which concludes by repeating "And miles to go before I sleep." One may simply sense that this final line ought to be spoken, say, more slowly.

Though rhythm is basic to poetry, **rhyme** is not. Rhyme is the repetition of the identical or similar stressed sound or sounds. It is, presumably, pleasant in itself; it suggests order; and it also may be related to meaning, for it brings two words sharply together, often implying a relationship, as in overworked rhymes "moon" and "June," "love" and "dove." **Perfect** or **exact rhymes** occur when differing consonant sounds are followed by identical stressed vowel sounds, and the following sounds, if any, are identical (foe : toe; meet : fleet; buffer : rougher). Notice that perfect rhyme involves identity of sound, not of spelling. "Fix" and "sticks," like "buffer" and "rougher," are perfect rhymes.

In **half-rhyme** (or **slant rhyme, approximate rhyme, near-rhyme, off-rhyme**) only the final consonant sounds of the rhyming words are identical; the stressed vowel sounds as well as the initial consonant sounds, if any, differ (soul : oil; mirth : forth; trolley : bully). **Eye rhyme** is not really rhyme; it merely looks like rhyme (cough : bough : rough). The final syllables in **masculine rhyme** are stressed and, after their differing initial consonant sounds, are identical in sound (stark : mark; support : retort). In **feminine rhyme** (or **double rhyme**) stressed rhyming syllables are followed by identical untressed syllables (revival : arrival; flatter : batter). **Triple rhyme** is a kind of feminine rhyme in which identical stressed vowel sounds are followed by two identical unstressed syllables (machinery:scenery; tenderly:slenderly). **End rhyme** (or **terminal rhyme**) has the rhyming word at the end of the line. **Internal rhyme** has at least one of the rhyming words within the line (as in Wilde's "Each narrow *cell* in which we *dwell*").

Alliteration is sometimes defined as the repetition of initial sounds ("*All* the *aw*ful *au*guries" or "*B*ring me my *b*ow of *b*urning gold"), sometimes as the prominent repetition of a consonant ("a*f*ter li*f*e's *f*it*f*ul *f*ever"). In **assonance** identical vowel sounds in words in proximity are preceded and followed by differing consonant sounds. Whereas "tide" and "hide" are rhymes, "tide" and "mine" are assonantal. **Consonance** is the repetition of a pattern of identical consonant-sounds and differing vowel-sounds in words in proximity (fail : feel; rough : roof; pitter : patter). Sometimes consonance is more loosely defined merely as the repetition of a consonant (fai*l* : pee*l*). The following poem makes witty use of assonance and consonance:

George Starbuck (b.1931)

Fable for Blackboard

Here is the grackle, people.
Here is the fox, folks.
The grackle sits in the bracken. The fox hopes.

Here are the fronds, friends,
that cover the fox.
The fronds get in a frenzy. The grackle looks.

Here are the ticks, tykes,
that live in the leaves, loves.
The fox is confounded,
and God is above.

Onomatopoeia is said to occur when the sound of a word echoes or suggests the meaning of a word. "Hiss" and "buzz" are onomatopoetic. There is a mistaken tendency to see onomatopoeia everywhere, for example, in "thunder" and "horror." Many words sometimes thought to be onomatopoetic are not clearly imitative of the thing they denote; they merely contain some sounds which — when we know what the word means — seem to have some resemblance to the thing they denote. Tennyson's lines from "Come down, O maid" are usually cited as an example of onomatopoeia:

> The moan of doves in immemorial elms
> And murmuring of innumerable bees.

But John Crowe Ransom has pointed out that if many of the sounds of "murmuring of innumerable bees" are reproduced in a line of different meaning — "murdering of innumerable beeves" — the suggestiveness is lost.

Lines of poetry are commonly arranged in a rhythmical unit called a **stanza** (from an Italian word meaning a "room" or "stopping-place"). Usually all the stanzas in a poem have the same rhyme pattern. A stanza is sometimes called a **verse**, though "verse" may also mean a single line of poetry. (In discussing stanzas, rhymes are indicated by identical letters. Thus, *abab* indicates that the first and third lines rhyme with each other, while the second and fourth lines are linked by a different rhyme. An unrhymed line is denoted by *x*.) The following stanzaic forms are common in English poetry:

couplet: stanza of two lines, usually, but not necessarily, with end rhymes. "Couplet" is also used for a pair of rhyming lines. the **octosyllabic couplet** is iambic or trochaic tetrameter:

> Had we but world enough, and time,
> This coyness, lady, were no crime.
> — Marvell

heroic couplet: a rhyming couplet of iambic pentameter, often "closed," that is, containing a complete thought, with a fairly heavy pause at the end of the first line and a still heavier one at the end of the second. Commonly, there is a parallel or an antithesis within a line, or between the two lines. It is called heroic because in England, especially in the eighteenth century, it was much used for heroic (epic) poems.

> Some foreign writers, some our own despise;
> The ancients only, or the moderns, prize.
>   — Pope

triplet (or **tercet**): a three-line stanza, usually with one rhyme.

> Whenas in silks my Julia goes
> Then, then (methinks) how sweetly flows
> That liquefaction of her clothes.
>   — Herrick

One kind of tercet is **terza rima**, rhyming *aba bcb cdc*, and so forth. Robert Frost's "Acquainted with the Night" (page 1050) is in terza rima.

quatrain: a four-line stanza, rhymed or unrhymed. The **heroic** (or **elegiac**) **quatrain** is iambic pentameter, rhyming *abab*. The **ballad stanza** is a quatrain alternating iambic tetrameter with iambic trimeter lines, usually rhyming *abxb*. Sometimes it is followed by a **refrain,** a line or lines repeated several times.

sonnet: a fourteen-line poem. The rhyme scheme of the **Petrarchan** (or **Italian**) sonnet is organized into an **octave** (the first eight lines) and a **sestet** (the last six). It usually rhymes *abbaabba cdecde*, but the sestet often has variations. In Petrarch's sonnets and in those of many of his imitators, there is a "turn" with the beginning of the ninth line; for example, a generalization in the octave may be illustrated by a particularization in the sestet. The sestet is something of a restatement of the octave, or a comment on it. But, whether from indifference or inability, this nice disposition of parts is not always observed by English writers, and it is dangerous to generalize about the perfection of the Italian structure as a lyric vehicle. Milton in particular had a tendency to run straight on beyond the octave; rather than saying he composed faulty Petrarchan sonnets, scholars say he composed Miltonic sonnets.

The **Shakespearean** (or **English**) sonnet has the fourteen lines of the Petrarchan, but organizes them into three quatrains (four lines each) and a couplet (pair of lines): *abab cdcd efef gg.* The couplet has frequently caused trouble: sometimes it seems a needless appendage, often it seems too snappy a close; less often it seems just right.

Why poets choose to imprison themselves in fourteen tightly rhymed lines is something of a mystery. Tradition has a great deal to do with it: the form, having been handled successfully by major poets, stands as a challenge. In writing a sonnet a poet gains a little of the authority of Petrarch, Shakespeare, Milton, Wordsworth, and other masters who showed that the sonnet is not merely a trick. A second reason perhaps resides in the very tightness of the rhymes, which can help as well as hinder. Many poets have felt, along with Richard Wilbur (in *Mid-Century American Poets,* ed. John Ciardi), that the need for a rhyme has suggested

> . . . arbitrary connections of which the mind may take advantage if it likes. For example, if one has to rhyme with *tide,* a great number of rhyme-words at once come to mind (ride, bide, shied, confide, Akenside, etc.). Most of these, in combination with *tide,* will probably suggest nothing apropos, but one of them may reveal precisely what one wanted to say. If none of them does, *tide* must be dispensed with. Rhyme, austerely used, may be a stimulus to discovery and a stretcher of the attention.

A good deal of English poetry is unrhymed, much of it in **blank verse,** that is, unrhymed iambic pentameter. Introduced into English poetry by Surrey in the middle of the sixteenth century, late in the century it became the standard medium (especially in the hands of Marlowe and Shakespeare) of English drama. In the seventeenth century, Milton used it for *Paradise Lost,* and it has continued to be used in both dramatic and nondramatic literature. For an example see the passage from Shakespeare on page 394. A passage of blank verse that has a rhetorical unity is sometimes called a **verse paragraph.**

The second kind of unrhymed poetry fairly common in English, especially in the twentieth century, is **free verse** (or **vers libre**): rhythmical lines varying in length, adhering to no fixed metrical pattern and usually unrhymed. The pattern is often largely based on repetition and parallel grammatical structure. Whitman's "A Noiseless Patient Spider" (page 371) is an example; Arnold's "Dover Beach" (page 408) is another example, though less typical because it uses rhyme. Thoroughly typical is Whitman's "When I Heard the Learn'd Astronomer":

Walt Whitman (1819–1892)

When I Heard the Learn'd Astronomer

When I heard the learn'd astronomer,
When the proofs, the figures, were ranged in columns before me,
When I was shown the charts and diagrams, to add, divide, and
    measure them,
When I sitting heard the astronomer where he lectured with much
    applause in the lecture-room,
How soon unaccountable I became tired and sick,
Till rising and gliding out I wander'd off by myself,
In the mystical moist night-air, and from time to time,
Look'd up in perfect silence at the stars.

What can be said about the rhythmic structure of this poem?
Rhymes are absent, and the lines vary greatly in the number of syllables, ranging from nine (the first line) to twenty-three (the fourth
line), but when we read the poem we sense a rhythmic structure. The
first four lines obviously hang together, each beginning with "When";
indeed, three of these four lines begin "When I." We may notice, too,
that each of these four lines has more syllables than its predecessor
(the numbers are nine, fourteen, eighteen, and twenty-three); this increase in length, like the initial repetition, is a kind of pattern. But
then, with the fifth line, which speaks of fatigue and surfeit, there is a
shrinkage to fourteen syllables, offering an enormous relief from the
previous swollen line with its twenty-three syllables. The second
half of the poem — the pattern established by "When" in the first four
lines is dropped, and in effect we get a new stanza, also of four
lines — does not relentlessly diminish the number of syllables in
each succeeding line, but it *almost* does so: fourteen, fourteen, thirteen, ten. The second half of the poem thus has a pattern too, and this
pattern is more or less the reverse of the first half of the poem. We
may notice too that the last line (in which the poet, now released from
the oppressive lecture hall, is in communion with nature) is very
close to an iambic pentameter line, i.e., the poem concludes with a
metrical form said to be the most natural in English. The effect of
naturalness or ease in this final line, moreover, is increased by the
absence of repetitions (e.g., not only of "When I," but even of such
syntactic repetitions as "charts and diagrams," "tired and sick," "rising and gliding") that characterize most of the previous lines. But of

course this final effect of naturalness is part of a carefully constructed pattern in which rhythmic structure is part of meaning. Though at first glance free verse may appear unrestrained, as T. S. Eliot (a practitioner) said, "No *vers* is *libre* for the man who wants to do a good job" or for the woman who wants to do a good job.

16 A Collection
of Poems

William Shakespeare (1564–1616)

Sonnet 29

When, in disgrace with Fortune and men's eyes,
I all alone beweep my outcast state,
And trouble deaf heaven with my bootless° cries,   *useless*
And look upon myself and curse my fate,   4
Wishing me like to one more rich in hope,
Featured like him, like him° with friends possessed, *like a second man,*
Desiring this man's art, and that man's scope,   *like a third man*
With what I most enjoy contented least;   8
Yet in these thoughts myself almost despising,
Haply° I think on thee, and then my state,   *perchance*
Like to the lark at break of day arising
From sullen earth, sings hymns at heaven's gate;   12
    For thy sweet love rememb'red such wealth brings,
    That then I scorn to change my state with kings.

William Shakespeare (1564–1616)

Sonnet 73

That time of year thou mayst in me behold
When yellow leaves, or none, or few, do hang
Upon those boughs which shake against the cold,
Bare ruined choirs where late the sweet birds sang.   4
In me thou see'st the twilight of such day
As after sunset fadeth in the west,
Which by-and-by black night doth take away,
Death's second self that seals up all in rest.   8
In me thou see'st the glowing of such fire
That on the ashes of his youth doth lie,
As the deathbed whereon it must expire,
Consumed with that which it was nourished by.   12
    This thou perceiv'st, which makes thy love more strong,
    To love that well which thou must leave ere long.

John Donne (1572–1631)

A Valediction: Forbidding Mourning

As virtuous men pass mildly away;
    And whisper to their souls, to go,
Whilst some of their sad friends do say,
    "The breath goes now," and some say, "No":   4

So let us melt, and make no noise.
    No tear-floods, nor sigh-tempests move.
'Twere profanation of our joys
    To tell the laity our love.   8

Moving of the earth° brings harms and fears,   *an earthquake*
    Men reckon what it did and meant;
But trepidation of the spheres,
    Though greater far, is innocent.*   12

* But the movement of the heavenly spheres (in Ptolemaic astronomy), though far greater, is harmless.

Dull sublunary° lovers' love   *under the moon, i.e., earthly*
　　(Whose soul is sense) cannot admit
Absence, because it doth remove
　　Those things which elemented it.   16

But we, by a love so much refined
　　That our selves know not what it is,
Inter-assuréd of the mind,
　　Care less, eyes, lips, and hands to miss.   20

Our two souls therefore, which are one,
　　Though I must go, endure not yet
A breach, but an expansion,
　　Like gold to airy thinness beat.   24

If they be two, they are two so
　　As stiff twin compasses° are two: *i.e., a carpenter's compass*
Thy soul, the fixed foot, makes no show
　　To move, but doth, if the other do.   28

And though it in the center sit,
　　Yet when the other far doth roam,
It leans, and hearkens after it,
　　And grows erect, as that comes home.   32

Such wilt thou be to me, who must
　　Like the other foot, obliquely run:
Thy firmness makes my circle just,
　　And makes me end where I begun.   36

Robert Herrick (1591–1674)

Corinna's Going A-Maying

Get up, get up, for shame; the blooming morn
Upon her wings presents the god unshorn.*
　　See how Aurora throws her fair
　　Fresh-quilted colors through the air.
　　Get up, sweet slug-a-bed, and see   5
　　The dew bespangling herb and tree.

* Apollo, the sun god, whose uncut locks are rays.

Each flower has wept, and bowed toward the East,
Above an hour since; yet you not dressed,
    Nay! not so much as out of bed?
    When all the birds have matins said   10
    And sung their thankful hymns, 'tis sin,
    Nay, profanation to keep in,
Whenas a thousand virgins on this day
Spring, sooner than the lark, to fetch in May.

Rise! and put on your foliage, and be seen   15
To come forth, like the springtime, fresh and green,
    And sweet as Flora. Take no care
    For jewels for your gown, or hair;
    Fear not, the leaves will strew
    Gems in abundance upon you;   20
Besides, the childhood of the day has kept,
Against ° you come, some orient pearls unwept;   *until*
    Come, and receive them while the light
    Hangs on the dewlocks of the night,
    And Titan° on the eastern hill   *the sun* 25
    Retires himself or else stands still
Till you come forth. Wash, dress, be brief in praying!
Few beads° are best, when once we go a-Maying.   *rosary beads*

Come, my Corinna, come; and, coming, mark
How each field turns a street, each street a park   30
    Made green and trimmed with trees. See how
    Devotion gives each house a bough
    Or branch; each porch, each door, ere this
    An ark, a tabernacle, is,
Made up of white-thorn, neatly interwove;   35
As if here were those cooler shades of love.
    Can such delights be in the street
    And open fields, and we not see't?
    Come, we'll abroad; and let's obey
    The proclamation made for May,   40
And sin no more, as we have done, by staying;
But, my Corinna, come, let's go a-Maying.

There's not a budding boy or girl this day
But is got up, and gone to bring in May.
    A deal of youth, ere this, is come   45
    Back, and with white-thorn laden home.
    Some have despatched their cakes and cream,
    Before that we have left to dream;

And some have wept and wooed and plighted troth,
And chose their priest, ere we can cast off sloth.   50
  Many a green-gown° has been given,   *grass-stained gown*
  Many a kiss, both odd and even;
  Many a glance, too, has been sent
  From out the eye, love's firmament;
Many a jest told of the keys' betraying   55
This night, and locks picked, yet we're not a-Maying.

Come, let us go while we are in our prime,
And take the harmless folly of the time.
  We shall grow old apace, and die
  Before we know our liberty.   60
  Our life is short, and our days run
  As fast away as does the sun;
And, as a vapor or a drop of rain,
Once lost, can ne'er be found again,
  So, when or you or I are made   65
  A fable, song, or fleeting shade,
  All love, all liking, all delight,
  Lies drowned with us in endless night.
Then while time serves, and we are but decaying,
Come, my Corinna, come, let's go a-Maying.   70

John Milton (1608–1674)

When I consider how my light is spent

When I consider how my light is spent
  Ere half my days, in this dark world and wide,
  And that one talent which is death to hide*
  Lodged with me useless, though my soul more bent   4
To serve therewith my Maker, and present
  My true account, lest he returning chide;
  "Doth God exact day-labor, light denied?"
  I fondly° ask; but Patience to prevent°   *foolishly; forestall*   8

---

* There is a pun here, relating Milton's literary talent to Christ's Parable of
the Talents (Matthew 25: 14 ff.), in which a servant is rebuked for not putting
his talent (a unit of money) to use. Note also line 4, where *useless* includes a
pun on *use*, i.e., usury, interest.

That murmur, soon replies, "God doth not need
    Either man's work or his own gifts; who best
    Bear his mild yoke, they serve him best. His state
Is kingly. Thousands at his bidding speed   12
    And post o'er land and ocean without rest:
    They also serve who only stand and wait."

Sir John Suckling (1609–1642)

Song

Why so pale and wan, fond lover?
    Prithee, why so pale?
Will, when looking well can't move her,
    Looking ill prevail?
    Prithee, why so pale?   5

Why so dull and mute, young sinner?
    Prithee, why so mute?
Will, when speaking well can't win her,
    Saying nothing do 't?
    Prithee, why so mute?   10

Quit, quit, for shame; this will not move,
    This cannot take her.
If of herself she will not love,
    Nothing can make her:
    The devil take her!   15

William Blake (1757–1827)

The Lamb

    Little Lamb, who made thee?
    Dost thou know who made thee?
Gave thee life, and bid thee feed
By the stream and o'er the mead;
Gave thee clothing of delight,   5

Softest clothing, wooly, bright;
Gave thee such a tender voice,
Making all the vales rejoice?
     Little Lamb, who made thee?
     Dost thou know who made thee?   10

     Little Lamb, I'll tell thee,
     Little Lamb, I'll tell thee:
He is callèd by thy name,
For he calls himself a Lamb.
He is meek, and he is mild;   15
He became a little child.
I a child, and thou a lamb,
We are callèd by his name.
     Little Lamb, God bless thee!
     Little Lamb, God bless thee!   20

William Blake (1757–1827)

The Tyger

Tyger! Tyger! burning bright
In the forests of the night,
What immortal hand or eye
Could frame thy fearful symmetry?   4

In what distant deeps or skies
Burnt the fire of thine eyes?
On what wings dare he aspire?
What the hand dare seize the fire?   8

And what shoulder, and what art,
Could twist the sinews of thy heart?
And, when thy heart began to beat,
What dread hand? and what dread feet?   12

What the hammer? what the chain?
In what furnace was thy brain?
What the anvil? what dread grasp
Dare its deadly terrors clasp?   16

When the stars threw down their spears,
And watered heaven with their tears,
Did he smile his work to see?
Did he who made the lamb make thee?   20

Tyger! Tyger! burning bright
In the forests of the night,
What immortal hand or eye,
Dare frame thy fearful symmetry?   24

William Blake (1757–1827)

London

I wander through each chartered street,
Near where the chartered Thames does flow,
And mark in every face I meet
Marks of weakness, marks of woe.   4

In every cry of every man,
In every Infant's cry of fear,
In every voice, in every ban,
The mind-forged manacles I hear.   8

How the Chimney-sweeper's cry
Every black'ning Church appalls;
And the hapless Soldier's sigh
Runs in blood down Palace walls.   12

But most through midnight streets I hear
How the youthful Harlot's curse
Blasts the new-born Infant's tear,
And blights with plagues the Marriage hearse.   16

William Wordsworth (1770–1850)

Composed upon Westminster Bridge, September 3, 1802

Earth has not anything to show more fair:
Dull would he be of soul who could pass by
A sight so touching in its majesty:
This city now doth, like a garment, wear   4
The beauty of the morning; silent, bare,
Ships, towers, domes, theaters, and temples lie
Open unto the fields, and to the sky;
All bright and glittering in the smokeless air.   8
Never did sun more beautifully steep
In his first splendor, valley, rock, or hill;
Ne'er saw I, never felt, a calm so deep!
The river glideth at his own sweet will: 12
Dear God! the very houses seem asleep;
And all that mighty heart is lying still!

William Wordsworth (1770–1850)

I Wandered Lonely as a Cloud

I wandered lonely as a cloud
That floats on high o'er vales and hills,
When all at once I saw a crowd,
A host, of golden daffodils,
Beside the lake, beneath the trees,   5
Fluttering and dancing in the breeze.

Continuous as the stars that shine
And twinkle on the milky way,
They stretched in never-ending line
Along the margin of a bay;   10
Ten thousand saw I at a glance,
Tossing their heads in sprightly dance.

The waves beside them danced, but they
Outdid the sparkling waves in glee;
A poet could not but be gay, 15
In such a jocund company;
I gazed — and gazed — but little thought
What wealth the show to me had brought:

For oft, when on my couch I lie
In vacant or in pensive mood, 20
They flash upon that inward eye
Which is the bliss of solitude;
And then my heart with pleasure fills,
And dances with the daffodils.

John Keats (1795–1821)

La Belle Dame sans Merci

O what can ail thee, knight-at-arms,
  Alone and palely loitering?
The sedge has withered from the lake,
  And no birds sing. 4

O what can ail thee, knight-at-arms,
  So haggard and so woe-begone?
The squirrel's granary is full,
  And the harvest's done. 8

I see a lily on thy brow,
  With anguish moist and fever dew,
And on thy cheeks a fading rose
  Fast withereth too. 12

"I met a lady in the meads,
  Full beautiful — a faery's child,
Her hair was long, her foot was light,
  And her eyes were wild. 16

"I made a garland for her head,
  And bracelets too, and fragrant zone;° *belt of flowers*
She looked at me as she did love,
  And made sweet moan. 20

"I set her on my pacing steed,
    And nothing else saw all day long,
For sidelong would she bend and sing
    A faery's song.   24

"She found me roots of relish sweet,
    And honey wild, and manna dew,
And sure in language strange she said
    'I love thee true.'   28

"She took me to her elfin grot,
    And there she wept and sighed full sore,
And there I shut her wild wild eyes
    With kisses four.   32

"And there she lulléd me asleep,
    And there I dreamed — Ah! woe betide!
The latest dream I ever dreamt
    On the cold hill side.   36

"I saw pale kings and princes too,
    Pale warriors, death-pale were they all;
They cried, 'La Belle Dame sans Merci°   *the beautiful pitiless lady*
    Thee hath in thrall!'   40

"I saw their starved lips in the gloam
    With horrid warning gaped wide,
And I awoke, and found me here,
    On the cold hill's side.   44

"And this is why I sojourn here,
    Alone and palely loitering,
Though the sedge is withered from the lake,
    And no birds sing."   48

John Keats (1795–1821)

To Autumn

I

Season of mists and mellow fruitfulness,
    Close bosom-friend of the maturing sun;
Conspiring with him how to load and bless
    With fruit the vines that round the thatch-eaves run;

To bend with apples the mossed cottage-trees,   5
    And fill all fruit with ripeness to the core;
        To swell the gourd, and plump the hazel shells
With a sweet kernel; to set budding more,
    And still more, later flowers for the bees,
    Until they think warm days will never cease,   10
        For summer has o'er-brimmed their clammy cells.

II

Who hath not seen thee oft amid thy store?
    Sometimes whoever seeks abroad may find
Thee sitting careless on a granary floor,
    Thy hair soft-lifted by the winnowing wind;   15
Or on a half-reaped furrow sound asleep,
    Drowsed with the fume of poppies, while thy hook
        Spares the next swath and all its twinéd flowers:
And sometime like a gleaner thou dost keep
    Steady thy laden head across a brook;   20
    Or by a cider-press, with patient look,
        Thou watchest the last oozings hours by hours.

III

Where are the songs of Spring? Ay, where are they?
    Think not of them, thou hast thy music too, —
While barred clouds bloom the soft-dying day,   25
    And touch the stubble-plains with rosy hue;
Then in a wailful choir the small gnats mourn
    Among the river sallows, borne aloft
        Or sinking as the light wind lives or dies;
And full-grown lambs loud bleat from hilly bourn;   30
    Hedge-crickets sing; and now with treble soft
    The red-breast whistles from a garden-croft;
        And gathering swallows twitter in the skies.

Alfred, Lord Tennyson (1809–1892)

Ulysses

It little profits that an idle king,
By this still hearth, among these barren crags,
Matched with an aged wife, I mete and dole
Unequal laws unto a savage race,
That hoard, and sleep, and feed, and know not me.   5
I cannot rest from travel; I will drink
Life to the lees. All times I have enjoyed
Greatly, have suffered greatly, both with those
That loved me, and alone; on shore, and when
Thro' scudding drifts the rainy Hyades   10
Vext the dim sea. I am become a name;
For always roaming with a hungry heart
Much have I seen and known, — cities of men
And manners, climates, councils, governments,
Myself not least, but honored of them all, —   15
And drunk delight of battle with my peers,
Far on the ringing plains of windy Troy.
I am a part of all that I have met;
Yet all experience is an arch wherethro'
Gleams that untravelled world whose margin fades   20
For ever and for ever when I move.
How dull it is to pause, to make an end,
To rust unburnished, not to shine in use!
As tho' to breathe were life! Life piled on life
Were all too little, and of one to me   25
Little remains; but every hour is saved
From that eternal silence, something more,
A bringer of new things; and vile it were
For some three suns to store and hoard myself,
And this gray spirit yearning in desire   30
To follow knowledge like a sinking star,
Beyond the utmost bound of human thought.

    This is my son, mine own Telemachus,
To whom I leave the scepter and the isle, —
Well-loved of me, discerning to fulfill   35
This labor, by slow prudence to make mild
A rugged people, and thro' soft degrees
Subdue them to the useful and the good.
Most blameless is he, centered in the sphere

Of common duties, decent not to fail   40
In offices of tenderness, and pay
Meet adoration to my household gods,
When I am gone. He works his work, I mine.

    There lies the port; the vessel puffs her sail;
There gloom the dark, broad seas. My mariners,   45
Souls that have toiled, and wrought, and thought with me, —
That ever with a frolic welcome took
The thunder and the sunshine, and opposed
Free hearts, free foreheads, — you and I are old;
Old age hath yet his honor and his toil.   50
Death closes all; but something ere the end,
Some work of noble note, may yet be done,
Not unbecoming men that strove with Gods.
The lights begin to twinkle from the rocks;
The long day wanes; the slow moon climbs; the deep   55
Moans round with many voices. Come, my friends.
'Tis not too late to seek a newer world.
Push off, and sitting well in order smite
The sounding furrows; for my purpose holds
To sail beyond the sunset, and the baths   60
Of all the western stars, until I die.
It may be that the gulfs will wash us down;
It may be we shall touch the Happy Isles,
And see the great Achilles, whom we knew.
Tho' much is taken, much abides; and tho'   65
We are not now that strength which in old days
Moved earth and heaven, that which we are, we are.
One equal temper of heroic hearts,
Made weak by time and fate, but strong in will
To strive, to seek, to find, and not to yield.   70

Robert Browning (1812–1889)

Porphyria's Lover

The rain set early in tonight,
    The sullen wind was soon awake,
It tore the elm-tops down for spite,
    And did its worst to vex the lake:
I listened with heart fit to break.   5

When glided in Porphyria; straight
    She shut the cold out and the storm,
And kneeled and made the cheerless grate
    Blaze up, and all the cottage warm;
Which done, she rose, and from her form   10
Withdrew the dripping cloak and shawl,
    And laid her soiled gloves by, untied
Her hat and let the damp hair fall,
    And, last, she sat down by my side
And called me. When no voice replied,   15
She put my arm about her waist,
    And made her smooth white shoulder bare
And all her yellow hair displaced,
    And, stooping, made my cheek lie there,
And spread, o'er all, her yellow hair,   20
Murmuring how she loved me — she
    Too weak, for all her heart's endeavor,
To set its struggling passion free
    From pride, and vainer ties dissever,
And give herself to me forever.   25
But passion sometimes would prevail,
    Nor could tonight's gay feast restrain
A sudden thought of one so pale
    For love of her, and all in vain:
So, she was come through wind and rain.   30
Be sure I looked up at her eyes
    Happy and proud; at last I knew
Porphyria worshipped me; surprise
    Made my heart swell, and still it grew
While I debated what to do.   35
That moment she was mine, mine, fair,
    Perfectly pure and good: I found
A thing to do, and all her hair
    In one long yellow string I wound
Three times her little throat around,   40
And strangled her. No pain felt she;
    I am quite sure she felt no pain.
As a shut bud that holds a bee,
    I warily oped her lids: again
Laughed the blue eyes without a stain.   45
And I untightened next the tress
    About her neck; her cheek once more
Blushed bright beneath my burning kiss:
    I propped her head up as before,

Only, this time my shoulder bore 50
Her head, which droops upon it still:
    The smiling rosy little head,
So glad it has its utmost will,
    That all it scorned at once is fled,
And I, its love, am gained instead! 55
Porphyria's love: she guessed not how
    Her darling one wish would be heard.
And thus we sit together now,
    And all night long we have not stirred,
And yet God has not said a word! 60

Walt Whitman (1819–1892)

Out of the Cradle Endlessly Rocking

Out of the cradle endlessly rocking,
Out of the mocking-bird's throat, the musical shuttle,
Out of the Ninth-month midnight,
Over the sterile sands and the fields beyond, where the child
    leaving his bed wander'd alone, bareheaded, barefoot,
Down from the shower'd halo, 5
Up from the mystic play of shadows twining and twisting
    as if they were alive,
Out from the patches of briers and blackberries,
From the memories of the bird that chanted to me,
From your memories sad brother, from the fitful risings
    and fallings I heard,
From under that yellow half-moon late-risen and swollen
    as if with tears, 10
From those beginning notes of yearning and love there in the mist,
From the thousand responses of my heart never to cease,
From the myriad thence-arous'd words,
From the word stronger and more delicious than any,
From such as now they start the scene revisiting, 15
As a flock, twittering, rising, or overhead passing,
Borne hither, ere all eludes me, hurriedly,
A man, yet by these tears a little boy again,
Throwing myself on the sand, confronting the waves,
I, chanter of pains and joys, uniter of here and hereafter, 20

Taking all hints to use them, but swiftly leaping beyond them,
A reminiscence sing.

Once Paumanok,*
When the lilac-scent was in the air and Fifth-month grass
    was growing,
Up this seashore in some briers,   25
Two feather'd guests from Alabama, two together,
And their nest, and four light-green eggs spotted with brown,
And every day the he-bird to an fro near at hand,
And every day the she-bird crouch'd on her nest, silent,
    with bright eyes,
And every day I, a curious boy, never too close,
    never disturbing them,   30
Cautiously peering, absorbing, translating.

Shine! shine! shine!
Pour down your warmth, great sun!
While we bask, we two together.

Two together!   35
Winds blow south, or winds blow north,
Day come white, or night come black,
Home, or rivers and mountains from home,
Singing all time, minding no time,
While we two keep together.   40

Till of a sudden,
May-be kill'd, unknown to her mate,
One forenoon the she-bird crouch'd not on the nest,
Nor return'd that afternoon, nor the next,
Nor ever appear'd again.   45

And thenceforward all summer in the sound of the sea,
And at night under the full of the moon in calmer weather,
Over the hoarse surging of the sea,
Or flitting from brier to brier by day,
I saw, I heard at intervals the remaining one, the he-bird,   50
The solitary guest from Alabama.

Blow! blow! blow!
Blow up sea-winds along Paumanok's shore;
I wait and I wait till you blow my mate to me.

* Indian name for Long Island

Yes, when the stars glisten'd,   55
All night long on the prong of a moss-scallop'd stake,
Down almost amid the slapping waves,
Sat the lone singer wonderful causing tears.

He call'd on his mate,
He pour'd forth the meaning which I of all men know.   60

Yes my brother I know,
The rest might not, but I have treasur'd every note,
For more than once dimly down to the beach gliding,
Silent, avoiding the moonbeams, blending myself
    with the shadows,
Recalling now the obscure shapes, the echoes, the sounds
    and sights after their sorts,   65
The white arms out in the breakers tirelessly tossing,
I, with bare feet, a child, the wind wafting my hair,
Listen'd long and long.

Listen'd to keep, to sing, now translating the notes,
Following you my brother.   70

Soothe! soothe! soothe!
Close on its wave soothes the wave behind,
And again another behind embracing and lapping, every one close,
But my love soothes not me, not me.

Low hangs the moon, it rose late,   75
It is lagging — O I think it is heavy with love, with love.

O madly the sea pushes upon the land,
With love, with love.

O night! do I not see my love fluttering out among the breakers?
What is that little black thing I see there in the white?   80

Loud! loud! loud!
Loud I call to you, my love!

High and clear I shoot my voice over the waves,
Surely you must know who is here, is here,
You must know who I am, my love.   85

Low-hanging moon!
What is that dusky spot in your brown yellow?
O it is the shape, the shape of my mate!
O moon do not keep her from me any longer.

Land! land! O land!   90
Whichever way I turn, O I think you could give me my
        mate back again if you only would,
For I am almost sure I see her dimly whichever way I look.

O rising stars!
Perhaps the one I want so much will rise, will rise
        with some of you.

O throat! O trembling throat!   95
Sound clearer through the atmosphere!
Pierce the woods, the earth,
Somewhere listening to catch you must be the one I want.

Shake out carols!
Solitary here, the night's carols!   100
Carols of lonesome love! death's carols!
Carols under that lagging, yellow, waning moon!
O under that moon where she droops almost down into the sea!
O reckless despairing carols.

But soft! sink low!   105
Soft! let me just murmur,
And do you wait a moment you husky-nois'd sea,
For somewhere I believe I heard my mate responding to me,
So faint, I must be still, be still to listen,
But not altogether still, for then she might not come
        immediately to me.   110

Hither my love!
Here I am! here!
With this just-sustain'd note I announce myself to you,
This gentle call is for you my love, for you.

Do not be decoy'd elsewhere,   115
That is the whistle of the wind, it is not my voice,
That is the fluttering, the fluttering of the spray,
Those are the shadows of leaves.

O darkness! O in vain!
O I am very sick and sorrowful.   120
O brown halo in the sky near the moon, drooping upon the sea!
O troubled reflection in the sea!
O throat! O throbbing heart!
And I singing uselessly, uselessly all the night.

O past! O happy life! O songs of joy!   125
In the air, in the woods, over fields,
Loved! loved! loved! loved! loved!
But my mate no more, no more with me!
We two together no more.

The aria sinking,   130
All else continuing, the stars shining,
The winds blowing, the notes of the bird continuous echoing,
With angry moans the fierce old mother incessantly moaning,
On the sands of Paumanok's shore gray and rustling,
The yellow half-moon enlarged, sagging down, drooping,
      the face of the sea almost touching.   135
The boy ecstatic, with his bare feet the waves,
      with his hair the atmosphere dallying,
The love in the heart long pent, now loose, now at last
      tumultuously bursting,
The aria's meaning, the ears, the soul, swiftly depositing,
The strange tears down the cheeks coursing,
The colloquy there, the trio, each uttering,   140
The undertone, the savage old mother incessantly crying,
To the boy's soul's questions sullenly timing,
      some drown'd secret hissing,
To the outsetting bard.

Demon* or bird! (said the boy's soul,)
Is it indeed toward your mate you sing? or is it really to me?   145
For I, that was a child, my tongue's use sleeping,
      now I have heard you,
Now in a moment I know what I am for, I awake,
And already a thousand singers, a thousand songs, clearer,
      louder and more sorrowful than yours,
A thousand warbling echoes have started to life within me,
      never to die.

O you singer solitary, singing by yourself, projecting me,   150
O solitary me listening, never more shall I cease perpetuating you,
Never more shall I escape, never more the reverberations,
Never more the cries of unsatisfied love be absent from me,
Never again leave me to be the peaceful child I was before
      what there in the night,

* attendant spirit

By the sea under the yellow and sagging moon,   155
The messenger there arous'd, the fire, the sweet hell within,
The unknown want, the destiny of me.

O give me the clew! (it lurks in the night here somewhere,)
O if I am to have so much, let me have more!

A word then, (for I will conquer it,)   160
The word final, superior to all,
Subtle, sent up — what is it? — I listen;
Are you whispering it, and have been all the time, you sea-waves?
Is that it from your liquid rims and wet sands?

Whereto answering, the sea,   165
Delaying not, hurrying not,
Whisper'd me through the night, and very plainly before daybreak,
Lisp'd to me the low and delicious word death,
And again death, death, death, death,
Hissing melodious, neither like the bird nor like my arous'd
    child's heart,   170
But edging near as privately for me rustling at my feet,
Creeping thence steadily up to my ears and laving me
    softly all over,
Death, death, death, death, death.

Which I do not forget,
But fuse the song of my dusky demon and brother,   175
That he sang to me in the moonlight on Paumanok's gray beach,
With the thousand responsive songs at random,
My own songs awaked from that hour,
And with them the key, the word up from the waves,
The word of the sweetest song and all songs,   180
That strong and delicious word which, creeping to my feet,
(Or like some old crone rocking the cradle, swathed in
    sweet garments, bending aside,)
The sea whisper'd me.

Emily Dickinson (1830–1886)

A narrow Fellow in the Grass

A narrow Fellow in the Grass
Occasionally rides –
You may have met Him – did you not
His notice sudden is –   4

The Grass divides as with a Comb –
A spotted shaft is seen –
And then it closes at your feet
And opens further on –   8

He likes a Boggy Acre
A Floor too cool for Corn –
Yet when a Boy, and Barefoot –
I more than once at Noon   12
Have passed, I thought, a Whip lash
Unbraiding in the Sun
When stopping to secure it
It wrinkled, and was gone –   16

Several of Nature's People
I know, and they know me –
I feel for them a transport
Of cordiality –   20

But never met this Fellow
Attended, or alone
Without a tighter breathing
And Zero at the Bone –   24

Emily Dickinson (1830–1886)

The Soul selects her own Society

The Soul selects her own Society –
Then – shuts the Door –
To her divine Majority –
Present no more –   4

Unmoved – she notes the Chariots – pausing –
At her low Gate –
Unmoved – an Emperor be kneeling
Upon her Mat – 8

I've known her – from an ample nation –
Choose One –
Then – close the Valves of her attention –
Like Stone – 12

Emily Dickinson (1830–1886)

I heard a Fly buzz – when I died

I heard a Fly buzz – when I died –
The Stillness in the Room
Was like the Stillness in the Air –
Between the Heaves of Storm – 4

The Eyes around – had wrung them dry –
And Breaths were gathering firm
For the last Onset – when the King
Be witnessed – in the Room – 8

I willed my Keepsakes – Signed away
What portion of me be
Assignable – and then it was
There interposed a Fly – 12

With Blue – uncertain stumbling Buzz –
Between the light – and me –
And then the Windows failed – and then
I could not see to see – 16

Thomas Hardy (1840–1928)

Ah, Are You Digging on My Grave?

"Ah, are you digging on my grave,
    My loved one? — planting rue?"
— "No: yesterday he went to wed
One of the brightest wealth has bred.
'It cannot hurt her now,' he said,   5
    'That I should not be true.' "

"Then who is digging on my grave?
    My nearest dearest kin?"
— "Ah, no: they sit and think, 'What use!
What good will planting flowers produce?   10
No tendance of her mound can loose
    Her spirit from Death's gin.' "

"But some one digs upon my grave?
    My enemy? — prodding sly?"
— "Nay: When she heard you had passed the Gate   15
That shuts on all flesh soon or late,
She thought you no more worth her hate,
    And cares not where you lie."

"Then, who is digging on my grave?
    Say — since I have not guessed!"   20
— "O it is I, my mistress dear,
Your little dog, who still lives near,
And much I hope my movements here
    Have not disturbed your rest?"

"Ah, yes! *You* dig upon my grave . . .   25
    Why flashed it not on me
That one true heart was left behind!
What feeling do we ever find
To equal among human kind
    A dog's fidelity!"   30

"Mistress, I dug upon your grave
    To bury a bone, in case
I should be hungry near this spot
When passing on my daily trot.
I am sorry, but I quite forgot   35
    It was your resting-place."

Gerard Manley Hopkins (1844–1899)

God's Grandeur

The world is charged with the grandeur of God.
    It will flame out, like shining from shook foil;
    It gathers to a greatness, like the ooze of oil
Crushed. Why do men then now not reck his rod?   4
Generations have trod, have trod, have trod;
    And all is seared with trade; bleared, smeared with toil;
    And wears man's smudge and shares man's smell: the soil
Is bare now, nor can foot feel, being shod.   8

And for all this, nature is never spent;
    There lives the dearest freshness deep down things;
And though the last lights off the black West went
    Oh, morning, at the brown brink eastward, springs —   12
Because the Holy Ghost over the bent
    World broods with warm breast and with ah! bright wings.

A. E. Housman (1859–1936)

Shropshire Lad #19 (To an Athlete Dying Young)

The time you won your town the race
We chaired you through the market-place;
Man and boy stood cheering by,
And home we brought you shoulder-high.   4

Today, the road all runners come,
Shoulder-high we bring you home,
And set you at your threshold down,
Townsman of a stiller town.   8

Smart lad, to slip betimes away
From fields where glory does not stay
And early though the laurel grows
It withers quicker than the rose.   12

Eyes the shady night has shut
Cannot see the record cut,
And silence sounds no worse than cheers
After earth has stopped the ears: 16

Now you will not swell the rout
Of lads that wore their honors out,
Runners whom renown outran
And the name died before the man.   20

So set, before its echoes fade,
The fleet foot on the sill of shade,
And hold to the low lintel° up   *beam over a doorway*
The still-defended challenge-cup.   24

And round that early-laureled head
Will flock to gaze the strengthless dead,
And find unwithered on its curls
The garland briefer than a girl's.   28

A. E. Housman (1859–1936)

Shropshire Lad #31 (On Wenlock Edge)*

On Wenlock Edge the wood's in trouble;
His forest fleece the Wrekin heaves;
The gale, it plies the saplings double,
And thick on Severn snow the leaves.   4

'Twould blow like this through holt and hanger°   *wood and thicket*
When Uricon the city stood:
'Tis the old wind in the old anger,
But then it threshed another wood.   8

* Wenlock Edge is a range of hills southeast of Shrewsbury; the Wrekin (line 2) is an extinct volcano, and the Severn (line 4) a river. Uricon (line 6) or Uriconium, an ancient Roman city also southeast of Shrewsbury, was burned by the Saxons in 584, and only ruins are left.

Then, 'twas before my time, the Roman
At yonder heaving hill would stare:
The blood that warms an English yeoman,
The thoughts that hurt him, they were there.   12

There, like the wind through woods in riot,
Through him the gale of life blew high;
The tree of man was never quiet:
Then 'twas the Roman, now 'tis I.   16

The gale, it plies the saplings double,
It blows so hard, 'twill soon be gone:
To-day the Roman and his trouble
Are ashes under Uricon.   20

William Butler Yeats (1865–1939)

The Lake Isle of Innisfree

I will arise and go now, and go to Innisfree,
And a small cabin build there, of clay and wattles made:
Nine bean-rows will I have there, a hive for the honey-bee
And live alone in the bee-loud glade.   4

And I shall have some peace there, for peace comes dropping slow,
Dropping from the veils of the morning to where the cricket sings;
There midnight's all a glimmer, and noon a purple glow,
And evening full of the linnet's wings.   8

I will arise and go now, for always night and day
I hear lake water lapping with low sounds by the shore;
While I stand on the roadway, or on the pavements gray,
I hear it in the deep heart's core.   12

William Butler Yeats (1865–1939)

Leda and the Swan*

A sudden blow: the great wings beating still
Above the staggering girl, her thighs caressed
By the dark webs, her nape caught in his bill,
He holds her helpless breast upon his breast.   4

How can those terrified vague fingers push
The feathered glory from her loosening thighs?
And how can body, laid in that white rush,
But feel the strange heart beating where it lies?   8

A shudder in the loins engenders there
The broken wall, the burning roof and tower
And Agamemnon dead.
                         Being so caught up,
So mastered by the brute blood of the air,   12
Did she put on his knowledge with his power
Before the indifferent beak could let her drop?

William Butler Yeats (1865–1939)

Sailing to Byzantium

I

That is no country for old men. The young
In one another's arms, birds in the trees
— Those dying generations — at their song,
The salmon-falls, the mackerel-crowded seas,   4

* According to Greek mythology, Zeus fell in love with Leda, disguised himself as a swan, and raped her. Among the offspring of this union were Helen
and Clytemnestra. Paris abducted Helen, causing the Greeks to raze Troy;
Clytemnestra, wife of Agamemnon, murdered her husband on his triumphant
return to Greece.

Fish, flesh, or fowl, commend all summer long
Whatever is begotten, born, and dies.
Caught in that sensual music all neglect
Monuments of unaging intellect.   8

II

An aged man is but a paltry thing,
A tattered coat upon a stick, unless
Soul clap its hands and sing, and louder sing
For every tatter in its mortal dress,   12
Nor is there singing school but studying
Monuments of its own magnificence;
And therefore I have sailed the seas and come
To the holy city of Byzantium.   16

III

O sages standing in God's holy fire
As in the gold mosaic of a wall,
Come from the holy fire, perne° in a gyre,   *whirl down*
And be the singing-masters of my soul.   20
Consume my heart away; sick with desire
And fastened to a dying animal
It knows not what it is; and gather me
Into the artifice of eternity.   24

IV

Once out of nature I shall never take
My bodily form from any natural thing,
But such a form as Grecian goldsmiths make
Of hammered gold and gold enameling   28
To keep a drowsy Emperor awake;
Or set upon a golden bough to sing
To lords and ladies of Byzantium
Of what is past, or passing, or to come.   32

Edwin Arlington Robinson (1869–1935)

Richard Cory

Whenever Richard Cory went down town,
We people on the pavement looked at him:
He was a gentleman from sole to crown,
Clean favored, and imperially slim.   4

And he was always quietly arrayed,
And he was always human when he talked;
But still he fluttered pulses when he said,
"Good-morning," and he glittered when he walked.   8

And he was rich — yes, richer than a king —
And admirably schooled in every grace:
In fine, we thought that he was everything
To make us wish that we were in his place.   12

So on we worked, and waited for the light,
And went without the meat, and cursed the bread;
And Richard Cory, one calm summer night,
Went home and put a bullet through his head.   16

Edwin Arlington Robinson (1869–1935)

Mr. Flood's Party

Old Eben Flood, climbing alone one night
Over the hill between the town below
And the forsaken upland hermitage
That held as much as he should ever know   4
On earth again of home, paused warily.
The road was his with not a native near;
And Eben, having leisure, said aloud;
For no man else in Tilbury Town to hear: 8

"Well, Mr. Flood, we have the harvest moon
Again, and we may not have many more;
The bird is on the wing, the poet says,
And you and I have said it here before.   12
Drink to the bird." He raised up to the light
The jug that he had gone so far to fill,
And answered huskily: "Well, Mr. Flood,
Since you propose it, I believe I will."   16

Alone, as if enduring to the end
A valiant armor of scarred hopes outworn,
He stood there in the middle of the road
Like Roland's ghost winding a silent horn.   20
Below him, in the town among the trees,
Where friends of other days had honored him,
A phantom salutation of the dead
Rang thinly till old Eben's eyes were dim.   24

Then, as a mother lays her sleeping child
Down tenderly, fearing it may awake,
He set the jug down slowly at his feet
With trembling care, knowing that most things break;   28
And only when assured that on firm earth
It stood, as the uncertain lives of men
Assuredly did not, he paced away,
And with his hand extended paused again: 32

"Well, Mr. Flood, we have not met like this
In a long time; and many a change has come
To both of us, I fear, since last it was
We had a drop together. Welcome home!"   36
Convivially returning with himself,
Again he raised the jug up to the light;
And with an acquiescent quaver said:
"Well, Mr. Flood, if you insist, I might.   40

"Only a very little, Mr. Flood —
For auld lang syne. No more, sir; that will do."
So, for the time, apparently it did,
And Eben evidently thought so too;   44
For soon amid the silver loneliness
Of night he lifted up his voice and sang,
Secure, with only two moons listening,
Until the whole harmonious landscape rang —   48

"For auld lang syne." The weary throat gave out,
The last word wavered; and the song being done,
He raised again the jug regretfully
And shook his head, and was again alone.   52
There was not much that was ahead of him,
And there was nothing in the town below —
Where strangers would have shut the many doors
That many friends had opened long ago.   56

Robert Frost (1874–1963)

Design

I found a dimpled spider, fat and white,
On a white heal-all, holding up a moth
Like a white piece of rigid satin cloth —
Assorted characters of death and blight   4
Mixed ready to begin the morning right,
Like the ingredients of a witches' broth —
A snow-drop spider, a flower like froth,
And dead wings carried like a paper kite.   8

What had that flower to do with being white,
The wayside blue and innocent heal-all?
What brought the kindred spider to that height,
Then steered the white moth thither in the night?   12
What but design of darkness to appall? —
If design govern in a thing so small.

Robert Frost (1874–1963)

Desert Places

Snow falling and night falling fast, oh, fast
In a field I looked into going past,
And the ground almost covered smooth in snow,
But a few weeds and stubble showing last.   4

The woods around it have it — it is theirs.
All animals are smothered in their lairs.
I am too absent-spirited to count;
The loneliness includes me unawares.   8

And lonely as it is that loneliness
Will be more lonely ere it will be less —
A blanker whiteness of benighted snow
With no expression, nothing to express.   12

They cannot scare me with their empty spaces
Between stars — on stars where no human race is.
I have it in me so much nearer home
To scare myself with my own desert places.   16

William Carlos Williams (1883–1963)

Spring and All

By the road to the contagious hospital
under the surge of the blue
mottled clouds driven from the
northeast — a cold wind. Beyond, the
waste of broad, muddy fields   5
brown with dried weeds, standing and fallen

patches of standing water
the scattering of tall trees

All along the road the reddish
purplish, forked, upstanding, twiggy   10
stuff of bushes and small trees
with dead, brown leaves under them
leafless vines —

Lifeless in appearance, sluggish
dazed spring approaches —   15

They enter the new world naked,
cold, uncertain of all
save that they enter. All about them
the cold, familiar wind —

Now the grass, tomorrow 20
the stiff curl of wildcarrot leaf
One by one objects are defined —
It quickens: clarity, outline of leaf

But now the stark dignity of
entrance — Still, the profound change 25
has come upon them: rooted, they
grip down and begin to awaken

Marianne Moore (1887–1972)

Poetry*

I, too, dislike it: there are things that are important beyond all
this fiddle.
Reading it, however, with a perfect contempt for it, one
discovers in
it after all, a place for the genuine.
Hands that can grasp, eyes
that can dilate, hair that can rise 5
if it must, these things are important not because a
high-sounding interpretation can be put upon them but because
they are
useful. When they become so derivative as to become
unintelligible,
the same thing may be said for all of us, that we
do not admire what 10
we cannot understand: the bat
holding on upside down or in quest of something to

---

* In a note to this poem, Miss Moore says that the quotation in lines 17–18 is
derived from *The Diaries of Leo Tolstoy;* the quotation in lines 21–22 from
W. B. Yeats's *Ideas of Good and Evil.*
    A comment in *Predilections*, Miss Moore's volume of literary essays, affords
some insight into her style: "My own fondness for the unaccepted rhyme
derives, I think, from an instinctive effort to ensure naturalness. Even elate
and fearsome rightness like Shakespeare's is only preserved from the offense
of being 'poetic' by his well-nested effects of helpless naturalness."

eat, elephants pushing, a wild horse taking a roll, a tireless
                            wolf under
  a tree, the immovable critic twitching his skin like a horse
                      that feels a flea, the base-
  ball fan, the statistician —   15
    nor is it valid
      to discriminate against "business documents and

school-books"; all these phenomena are important. One must
                  make a distinction
  however: when dragged into prominence by half poets, the
                result is not poetry,
  nor till the poets among us can be   20
    "literalists of
    the imagination" — above
      insolence and triviality and can present

for inspection, "imaginary gardens with real toads in them"
                  shall we have
  it. In the meantime, if you demand on the one hand,   25
  the raw material of poetry in
    all its rawness and
    that which is on the other hand
      genuine, you are interested in poetry.

Marianne Moore (1887–1972)

Silence

My father used to say,
"Superior people never make long visits,
have to be shown Longfellow's grave
or the glass flowers at Harvard.
Self-reliant like the cat —   5
that takes its prey to privacy,
the mouse's limp tail hanging like a shoelace from its mouth —
they sometimes enjoy solitude,
and can be robbed of speech
by speech which has delighted them.   10

The deepest feeling always shows itself in silence;
not in silence, but restraint."
Nor was he insincere in saying, "Make my house your inn."
Inns are not residences.

T. S. Eliot (1888–1965)

The Love Song of J. Alfred Prufrock

S'io credesse che mia risposta fosse
A persona che mai tornasse al mondo,
Questa fiamma staria senza piu scosse.
Ma perciocche giammai di questo fondo
Non torno vivo alcun, s' i' odo il vero,
*Senza tema d'infamia ti rispondo.**

Let us go then, you and I,
When the evening is spread out against the sky
Like a patient etherised upon a table;
Let us go, through certain half-deserted streets,
The muttering retreats   5
Of restless nights in one-night cheap hotels
And sawdust restaurants with oyster-shells:
Streets that follow like a tedious argument
Of insidious intent

---

* In Dante's *Inferno* XXVII:61–66, a damned soul who had sought absolution before committing a crime addresses Dante, thinking that his words will never reach the earth: "If I believed that my answer were to a person who could ever return to the world, this flame would no longer quiver. But because no one ever returned from this depth, if what I hear is true, without fear of infamy, I answer you."

 Explanations of allusions in the poem may be helpful. "Works and days" (line 29) is the title of a poem on farm life by Hesiod (eighth century B.C.); "dying fall" (line 52) echoes *Twelfth Night* I.i.4; lines 81–83 allude to John the Baptist (see Matthew 14:1–11); line 92 echoes lines 41–42 of Marvell's "To His Coy Mistress" (see page 433); for "Lazarus" (line 94) see Luke 16 and John 11; lines 112–117 allude to Polonius and perhaps to other figures in *Hamlet;* "full of high sentence" (line 117) comes from Chaucer's description of the Clerk of Oxford in *The Canterbury Tales.*

To lead you to an overwhelming question . . .   10
Oh, do not ask, "What is it?"
Let us go and make our visit.

In the room the women come and go
Talking of Michelangelo.

The yellow fog that rubs its back upon the window-panes,   15
The yellow smoke that rubs its muzzle on the window-panes
Licked its tongue into the corners of the evening,
Lingered upon the pools that stand in drains,
Let fall upon its back the soot that falls from chimneys,
Slipped by the terrace, made a sudden leap,   20
And seeing that it was a soft October night,
Curled once about the house, and fell asleep.

And indeed there will be time
For the yellow smoke that slides along the street,
Rubbing its back upon the window-panes;   25
There will be time, there will be time
To prepare a face to meet the faces that you meet;
There will be time to murder and create,
And time for all the works and days of hands
That lift and drop a question on your plate;   30
Time for you and time for me,
And time yet for a hundred indecisions,
And for a hundred visions and revisions,
Before the taking of a toast and tea.

In the room the women come and go   35
Talking of Michelangelo.

And indeed there will be time
To wonder, "Do I dare?" and, "Do I dare?"
Time to turn back and descend the stair,
With a bald spot in the middle of my hair —   40
[They will say: "How his hair is growing thin!"]
My morning coat, my collar mounting firmly to the chin,
My necktie rich and modest, but asserted by a simple pin —
[They will say: "But how his arms and legs are thin!"]
Do I dare   45
Disturb the universe?
In a minute there is time
For decisions and revisions which a minute will reverse.

For I have known them all already, known them all: —
Have known the evenings, mornings, afternoons,   50
I have measured out my life with coffee spoons;
I know the voices dying with a dying fall
Beneath the music from a farther room.
        So how should I presume?

And I have known the eyes already, known them all —   55
The eyes that fix you in a formulated phrase,
And when I am formulated, sprawling on a pin,
When I am pinned and wriggling on the wall,
Then how should I begin
To spit out all the butt-ends of my days and ways?   60
        And how should I presume?

And I have known the arms already, known them all —
Arms that are braceleted and white and bare
[But in the lamplight, downed with light brown hair!]
Is it perfume from a dress   65
That makes me so digress?
Arms that lie along a table, or wrap about a shawl.
        And should I then presume?
        And how should I begin?

                    .   .   .   .   .

Shall I say, I have gone at dusk through narrow streets   70
And watched the smoke that rises from the pipes
Of lonely men in shirt-sleeves, leaning out of windows? . . .

I should have been a pair of ragged claws
Scuttling across the floors of silent seas.

                    .   .   .   .   .

And the afternoon, the evening, sleeps so peacefully!   75
Smoothed by long fingers,
Asleep . . . tired . . . or it malingers,
Stretched on the floor, here beside you and me.
Should I, after tea and cakes and ices,
Have the strength to force the moment to its crisis?   80
But though I have wept and fasted, wept and prayed,
Though I have seen my head [grown slightly bald]
    brought in upon a platter,

I am no prophet — and here's no great matter;
I have seen the moment of my greatness flicker,
And I have seen the eternal Footman hold my coat, and snicker,   85
And in short, I was afraid.

And would it have been worth it, after all,
After the cups, the marmalade, the tea,
Among the porcelain, among some talk of you and me,
Would it have been worth while,   90
To have bitten off the matter with a smile,
To have squeezed the universe into a ball
To roll it toward some overwhelming question,
To say: "I am Lazarus, come from the dead,
Come back to tell you all, I shall tell you all" —   95
If one, settling a pillow by her head,
        Should say: "That is not what I meant at all.
        That is not it, at all."

And would it have been worth it, after all,
Would it have been worth while,   100
After the sunsets and the dooryards and the sprinkled streets,
After the novels, after the teacups, after the skirts
        that trail along the floor —
And this, and so much more? —
It is impossible to say just what I mean!
But as if a magic lantern threw the nerves in patterns on a screen: 105
Would it have been worth while
If one, settling a pillow or throwing off a shawl,
And turning toward the window, should say:
        "That is not it at all,
        That is not what I meant, at all."   110

No! I am not Prince Hamlet, nor was meant to be;
Am an attendant lord, one that will do
To swell a progress, start a scene or two,
Advise the prince; no doubt, an easy tool,
Deferential, glad to be of use,   115
Politic, cautious, and meticulous;
Full of high sentence, but a bit obtuse;
At times, indeed, almost ridiculous —
Almost, at times, the Fool.

I grow old . . . I grow old . . .   120
I shall wear the bottoms of my trousers rolled.

Shall I part my hair behind? Do I dare to eat a peach?
I shall wear white flannel trousers, and walk upon the beach.
I have heard the mermaids singing, each to each.

I do not think that they will sing to me.   125

I have seen them riding seaward on the waves
Combing the white hair of the waves blown back
When the wind blows the water white and black.

We have lingered in the chambers of the sea
By sea-girls wreathed with seaweed red and brown   130
Till human voices wake us, and we drown.

T. S. Eliot (1888–1965)

Journey of the Magi*

"A cold coming we had of it,
Just the worst time of the year
For a journey, and such a long journey:
The ways deep and the weather sharp,
The very dead of winter."   5
And the camels galled, sore-footed, refractory,
Lying down in the melting snow.
There were times we regretted
The summer palaces on slopes, the terraces,
And the silken girls bringing sherbet.   10
Then the camel men cursing and grumbling
And running away, and wanting their liquor and women,
And the night-fires going out, and the lack of shelters,
And the cities hostile and the towns unfriendly
And the villages dirty and charging high prices: 15

---

* For the Journey of the Magi, see Matthew 2. Lines 1–5 are in quotation
marks because they are adapted from a sermon on the Nativity by Lancelot
Andrewes (1555–1626). For line 24, see Matthew 27 : 38; for line 25, see
Revelation 6: 2 and 19 : 11. Perhaps, too, the white horse that gallops away is
partly derived from G. K. Chesterton's *The Ballad of the White Horse,* in
which the disappearance of the horse represents the disappearance of pagan-
ism at the advent of Christianity. The vine (line 26) is often associated with
Christ; see, for example, John 15. Line 27 may allude to Matthew 27: 3–6, 35.

A hard time we had of it.
At the end we preferred to travel all night,
Sleeping in snatches,
With the voices singing in our ears, saying
That this was all folly.   20

Then at dawn we came down to a temperate valley,
Wet, below the snow line, smelling of vegetation;
With a running stream and a water-mill beating the darkness,
And three trees on the low sky,
And an old white horse galloped away in the meadow.   25
Then we came to a tavern with vine-leaves over the lintel,
Six hands at an open door dicing for pieces of silver,
And feet kicking the empty wine-skins.
But there was no information, and so we continued
And arrived at evening, not a moment too soon   30
Finding the place; it was (you may say) satisfactory.

All this was a long time ago, I remember,
And I would do it again, but set down
This set down
This: were we led all that way for   35
Birth or Death? There was a Birth, certainly,
We had evidence and no doubt. I had seen birth and death,
But had thought they were different; this Birth was
Hard and bitter agony for us, like Death, our death.
We returned to our places, these Kingdoms,   40
But no longer at ease here, in the old dispensation,
With an alien people clutching their gods.
I should be glad of another death.

Archibald MacLeish (b. 1892)

You, Andrew Marvell

And here face down beneath the sun
And here upon earth's noonward height
To feel the always coming on
The always rising of the night   4

To feel creep up the curving east
The earthy chill of dusk and slow
Upon those under lands the vast
And ever climbing shadow grow   8

And strange at Ecbatan the trees
Take leaf by leaf the evening strange
The flooding dark about their knees
The mountains over Persia change   12

And now at Kermanshah the gate
Dark empty and the withered grass
And through the twilight now the late
Few travelers in the westward pass   16

And Baghdad darken and the bridge
Across the silent river gone
And through Arabia the edge
Of evening widen and steal on   20

And deepen on Palmyra's street
The wheel rut in the ruined stone
And Lebanon fade out and Crete
High through the clouds and overblown   24

And over Sicily the air
Still flashing with the landward gulls
And loom and slowly disappear
The sails above the shadowy hulls   28

And Spain go under and the shore
Of Africa the gilded sand
And evening vanish and no more
The low pale light across that land   32

Nor now the long light on the sea:

And here face downward in the sun
To feel how swift how secretly
The shadow of the night comes on . . .   36

Archibald MacLeish (b. 1892)

Ars Poetica

A poem should be palpable and mute
As a globed fruit,

Dumb
As old medallions to the thumb,   4

Silent as the sleeve-worn stone
Of casement ledges where the moss has grown —

A poem should be wordless
As the flight of birds.   8

•

A poem should be motionless in time
As the moon climbs,

Leaving, as the moon releases
Twig by twig the night-entangled trees,   12

Leaving, as the moon behind the winter leaves,
Memory by memory the mind —

A poem should be motionless in time
As the moon climbs.   16

•

A poem should be equal to:
Not true.

For all the history of grief
An empty doorway and a maple leaf.   20

For love
The leaning grasses and two lights above the sea —

A poem should not mean
But be.   24

E. E. Cummings (1894–1963)

anyone lived in a pretty how town

anyone lived in a pretty how town
(with up so floating many bells down)
spring summer autumn winter
he sang his didn't he danced his did.   4

Women and men(both little and small)
cared for anyone not at all
they sowed their isn't they reaped their same
sun moon stars rain   8

children guessed(but only a few
and down they forgot as up they grew
autumn winter spring summer)
that noone loved him more by more   12

when by now and tree by leaf
she laughed his joy she cried his grief
bird by snow and stir by still
anyone's any was all to her   16

someones married their everyones
laughed their cryings and did their dance
(sleep wake hope and then)they
said their nevers they slept their dream   20

stars rain sun moon
(and only the snow can begin to explain
how children are apt to forget to remember
with up so floating many bells down)   24

one day anyone died i guess
(and noone stopped to kiss his face)
busy folk buried them side by side
little by little and was by was   28

all by all and deep by deep
and more by more they dream their sleep
noone and anyone earth by april
wish by spirit and if by yes.   32

Women and men(both dong and ding)
summer autumn winter spring
reaped their sowing and went their came
sun moon stars rain   36

Louise Bogan (1897–1970)

Women

Women have no wilderness in them,
They are provident instead,
Content in the tight hot cell of their hearts
To eat dusty bread.   4

They do not see cattle cropping red winter grass,
They do not hear
Snow water going down under culverts
Shallow and clear.   8

They wait, when they should turn to journeys,
They stiffen, when they should bend.
They use against themselves that benevolence
To which no man is friend.   12

They cannot think of so many crops to a field
Or of clean wood cleft by an axe.
Their love is an eager meaninglessness
Too tense, or too lax.   16

They hear in every whisper that speaks to them
A shout and a cry.
As like as not, when they take life over their door-sills
Thye should let it go by.   20

W. H. Auden (1907–1973)

Musée des Beaux Arts

About suffering they were never wrong,
The Old Masters: how well they understood
Its human position; how it takes place
While someone else is eating or opening a window
    or just walking dully along;
How, when the aged are reverently, passionately waiting   5
For the miraculous birth, there always must be
Children who did not specially want it to happen, skating
On a pond at the edge of the wood:
They never forgot
That even the dreadful martyrdom must run its course   10
Anyhow in a corner, some untidy spot
Where the dogs go on with their doggy life and the torturer's horse
Scratches its innocent behind on a tree.

In Brueghel's *Icarus*, for instance: how everything turns away
Quite leisurely from the disaster; the ploughman may   15
Have heard the splash, the forsaken cry,
But for him it was not an important failure; the sun shone
As it had to on the white legs disappearing into the green
Water; and the expensive delicate ship that must have seen
Something amazing, a boy falling out of the sky,   20
Had somewhere to get to and sailed calmly on.

W. H. Auden (1907–1973)

The Unknown Citizen

*(To JS/07/M/378
This Marble Monument
Is Erected by the State)*

He was found by the Bureau of Statistics to be
One against whom there was no official complaint,
And all the reports on his conduct agree
That, in the modern sense of an old-fashioned word, he was a saint,

For in everything he did he served the Greater Community.   5
Except for the War till the day he retired
He worked in a factory and never got fired,
But satisfied his employers, Fudge Motors Inc.
Yet he wasn't a scab or odd in his views,
For his Union reports that he paid his dues,   10
(Our report on his Union shows it was sound)
And our Social Psychology workers found
That he was popular with his mates and liked a drink.
The Press are convinced that he bought a paper every day
And that his reactions to advertisements were normal
    in every way.   15
Policies taken out in his name prove that he was fully insured,
And his Health-card shows he was once in hospital
    but left it cured.
Both Producers Research and High-Grade Living declare
He was fully sensible to the advantages of the Installment Plan
And had everything necessary to the Modern Man,   20
A phonograph, radio, a car and a frigidaire.
Our researchers into Public Opinion are content
That he held the proper opinions for the time of year;
When there was peace, he was for peace; when there
    was war, he went.
He was married and added five children
    to the population,   25
Which our Eugenist says was the right number
    for a parent of his generation,
And our teachers report that he never interfered
    with their education.
Was he free? Was he happy? The question is absurd:
Had anything been wrong, we should certainly have heard.

Theodore Roethke (1908–1963)

Elegy for Jane

(My student, thrown by a horse)

I remember the neckcurls, limp and damp as tendrils;
And her quick look, a sidelong pickerel smile;
And how, once startled into talk, the light syllables leaped for her,
And she balanced in the delight of her thought,

A wren, happy, tail into the wind,   5
Her song trembling the twigs and small branches.
The shade sang with her;
The leaves, their whispers turned to kissing,
And the mould sang in the bleached valleys under the rose.

Oh, when she was sad, she cast herself down
    into such a pure depth,   10
Even a father could not find her:
Scraping her cheek against straw,
Stirring the clearest water.

My sparrow, you are not here,
Waiting like a fern, making a spiney shadow.   15
The sides of wet stones cannot console me,
Nor the moss, wound with the last light.

If only I could nudge you from this sleep,
My maimed darling, my skittery pigeon.
Over this damp grave I speak the words of my love: 20
I, with no rights in this matter,
Neither father nor lover.

Dylan Thomas (1914–1953)

Fern Hill

Now as I was young and easy under the apple boughs
About the lilting house and happy as the grass was green,
    The night above the dingle starry,
      Time let me hail and climb
    Golden in the heydays of his eyes,   5
And honored among wagons I was prince of the apple towns
And once below a time I lordly had the trees and leaves
    Trail with daisies and barley
  Down the rivers of the windfall light.

And as I was green and carefree, famous among the barns   10
About the happy yard and singing as the farm was home,
    In the sun that is young once only,
      Time let me play and be
    Golden in the mercy of his means,
And green and golden I was huntsman and herdsman, the calves   15

Sang to my horn, the foxes on the hills barked clear and cold,
　　　And the sabbath rang slowly
　　　In the pebbles of the holy streams.

All the sun long it was running, it was lovely, the hay
Fields high as the house, the tunes from the chimneys, it was air   20
　　　And playing, lovely and watery
　　　　And fire green as grass.
　　　And nightly under the simple stars
As I rode to sleep the owls were bearing the farm away,
All the moon long I heard, blessed among stables, the nightjars   25
　　　Flying with the ricks, and the horses
　　　　Flashing into the dark.

And then to awake, and the farm, like a wanderer white
With the dew, come back, the cock on his shoulder: it was all
　　　Shining, it was Adam and maiden,   30
　　　　The sky gathered again
　　　And the sun grew round that very day.
So it must have been after the birth of the simple light
In the first, spinning place, the spellbound horses walking warm
　　　Out of the whinnying green stable   35
　　　　On to the fields of praise.

And honored among foxes and pheasants by the gay house
Under the new made clouds and happy as the heart was long,
　　　In the sun born over and over,
　　　　I ran my heedless ways,   40
　　　My wishes raced through the house high hay
And nothing I cared, at my sky blue trades, that time allows
In all his tuneful turning so few and such morning songs
　　　Before the children green and golden
　　　　Follow him out of grace,   45

Nothing I cared, in the lamb white days, that time would take me
Up to the swallow thronged loft by the shadow of my hand,
　　　In the moon that is always rising,
　　　　Nor that riding to sleep
　　　I should hear him fly with the high fields   50
And wake to the farm forever fled from the childless land.
Oh as I was young and easy in the mercy of his means,
　　　　Time held me green and dying
　　　Though I sang in my chains like the sea.

Randall Jarrell (1914–1965)

In Montecito

In a fashionable suburb of Santa Barbara,
Montecito, there visited me one night at midnight
A scream with breasts. As it hung there in the sweet air
That was always the right temperature, the contractors
Who had undertaken to dismantle it, stripped off   5
The lips, let the air out of the breasts.
                                        People disappear
Even in Montecito. Greenie Taliaferro,
In her white maillot, her good figure almost firm,
Her old pepper-and-salt hair stripped by the hairdresser
To nothing and dyed platinum — Greenie has
      left her Bentley.   10
They have thrown away her electric toothbrush, someone else slips
The key into the lock of her safety-deposit box
At the Crocker-Anglo Bank; her seat at the cricket matches
Is warmed by buttocks less delectable than hers.
Greenie's girdle is empty.
                                A scream hangs there in the night: 15
They strip off the lips, let the air out of the breasts,
And Greenie has gone into the Greater Montecito
That surrounds Montecito like the echo of a scream.

Gwendolyn Brooks (b. 1915)

We Real Cool

The Pool Players.
Seven at the Golden Shovel.

We real cool. We
Left school. We

Lurk late. We
Strike straight. We

Sing sin. We
Thin gin. We

Jazz June. We
Die soon.

Robert Lowell (b. 1917)

Skunk Hour

(For Elizabeth Bishop)

Nautilus Island's hermit
heiress still lives through winter in her Spartan cottage;
her sheep still graze above the sea.
Her son's a bishop. Her farmer
is first selectman in our village;   5
she's in her dotage.

Thirsting for
the hierarchic privacy
of Queen Victoria's century,
she buys up all   10
the eyesores facing her shore,
and lets them fall.

The season's ill —
we've lost our summer millionaire,
who seemed to leap from an L. L. Bean   15
catalogue. His nine-knot yawl
was auctioned off to lobstermen.
A red fox stain covers Blue Hill.

And now our fairy
decorator brightens his shop for fall;   20
his fishnet's filled with orange cork,
orange, his cobbler's bench and awl;
there is no money in his work,
he'd rather marry.

One dark night,   25
my Tudor Ford climbed the hill's skull;
I watched the love-cars. Lights turned down,

they lay together, hull to hull,
where the graveyard shelves on the town. . . .
My mind's not right.   30

A car radio bleats,
"Love, O careless Love. . . ." I hear
my ill-spirit sob in each blood cell,
as if my hand were at its throat. . . .
I myself am hell;   35
nobody's here —

only skunks, that search
in the moonlight for a bite to eat.
They march on their soles up Main Street:
white stripes, moonstruck eyes' red fire   40
under the chalk-dry and spar spire
of the Trinitarian Church.

I stand on top
of our back steps and breathe the rich air —
a mother skunk with her column of kittens swills
      the garbage pail.   45
She jabs her wedge-head in a cup
of sour cream, drops her ostrich tail,
and will not scare.

Lawrence Ferlinghetti (b. 1919)

Constantly risking absurdity

Constantly risking absurdity
                        and death
            whenever he performs
                        above the heads
                              of his audience   5
      the poet like an acrobat
                  climbs on rime
                        to a high wire of his own making
and balancing on eyebeams
                  above a sea of faces   10

                    paces his way
                              to the other side of day
            performing *entrechats*°   *a leap in ballet*
                              and sleight-of-foot tricks
and other high theatrics   15
                              and all without mistaking
                    any thing
                              for what it may not be

For he's the super realist
                              who must perforce perceive   20
                    taut truth
                              before the taking of each stance or step
            in his supposed advance
                              toward that still higher perch
where Beauty stands and waits   25
                              with gravity
                              to start her death-defying leap

            And he
                    a little charleychaplin man
                              who may or may not catch   30
                    her fair eternal form
                              spreadeagled in the empty air
                    of existence

Anthony Hecht (b. 1922)

The Dover Bitch

A Criticism of Life

for Andrews Wanning

So there stood Matthew Arnold and this girl
With the cliffs of England crumbling away behind them,
And he said to her, "Try to be true to me,
And I'll do the same for you, for things are bad
All over, etc., etc."   5

Well now, I knew this girl. It's true she had read
Sophocles in a fairly good translation
And caught that bitter allusion to the sea,
But all the time he was talking she had in mind
The notion of what his whiskers would feel like   10
On the back of her neck. She told me later on
That after a while she got to looking out
At the lights across the channel, and really felt sad,
Thinking of all the wine and enormous beds
And blandishments in French and the perfumes.   15
And then she got really angry. To have been brought
All the way down from London, and then be addressed
As sort of a mournful cosmic last resort
Is really tough on a girl, and she was pretty.
Anyway, she watched him pace the room   20
And finger his watch-chain and seem to sweat a bit,
And then she said one or two unprintable things.
But you mustn't judge her by that. What I mean to say is,
She's really all right. I still see her once in a while
And she always treats me right.
We have a drink   25
And I give her a good time, and perhaps it's a year
Before I see her again, but there she is,
Running to fat, but dependable as they come,
And sometimes I bring her a bottle of *Nuit d'Amour*.

Denise Levertov (b. 1923)

The Mutes

Those groans men use
passing a woman on the street
or on the steps of the subway

to tell her she is a female
and their flesh knows it,   5

are they a sort of tune,
an ugly enough song, sung
by a bird with a slit tongue

but meant for music?

Or are they the muffled roaring   10
of deafmutes trapped in a building that is
slowly filling with smoke?

Perhaps both.

Such men most often
look as if groan were all they could do,   15
yet a woman, in spite of herself,

knows it's a tribute:
if she were lacking all grace
they'd pass her in silence:

so it's not only to say she's   20
a warm hole. It's a word

in grief-language, nothing to do with
primitive, not an ur-language;
language stricken, sickened, cast down

in decrepitude. She wants to   25
throw the tribute away, dis-
gusted, and can't,

it goes on buzzing in her ear,
it changes the pace of her walk,
the torn posters in echoing corridors   30

spell it out, it
quakes and gnashes as the train comes in.
Her pulse sullenly

had picked up speed,
but the cars slow down and   35
jar to a stop while her understanding

keeps on translating:
'Life after life after life goes by

without poetry,
without seemliness   40
without love.'

Allen Ginsberg (b. 1926)

A Supermarket in California

What thoughts I have of you tonight, Walt Whitman, for I walked down the sidestreets under the trees with a headache self-conscious looking at the full moon.

In my hungry fatigue, and shopping for images, I went into the neon fruit supermarket, dreaming of your enumerations!

What peaches and what penumbras! Whole families shopping at night! Aisles full of husbands! Wives in the avocados, babies in the tomatoes! — and you, Garcia Lorca, what were you doing down by the watermelons?

I saw you, Walt Whitman, childless, lonely old grubber, poking among the meats in the refrigerator and eyeing the grocery boys.

I heard you asking questions of each: Who killed the pork chops? What price bananas? Are you my Angel?   5

I wandered in and out of the brilliant stacks of cans following you, and followed in my imagination by the store detective.

We strode down the open corridors together in our solitary fancy tasting artichokes, possessing every frozen delicacy, and never passing the cashier.

Where are we going, Walt Whitman? The doors close in an hour. Which way does your beard point tonight?

(I touch your book and dream of our odyssey in the supermarket and feel absurd.)

Will we walk all night through solitary streets? The trees add shade to shade, lights out in the houses, we'll both be lonely.   10

Will we stroll dreaming of the lost America of love past blue automobiles in driveways, home to our silent cottage?

Ah, dear father, graybeard, lonely old courage-teacher, what America did you have when Charon quit poling his ferry and you got out on a smoking bank and stood watching the boat disappear on the black waters of Lethe?

Frank O'Hara (1926–1966)

Ave Maria

Mothers of America
        let your kids go to the movies!
get them out of the house so they won't know what you're up to
it's true that fresh air is good for the body
                     but what about the soul   5
that grows in darkness, embossed by silvery images
and when you grow old as grow old you must
                     they won't hate you
they won't criticise you they won't know
             they'll be in some glamorous country   10
they first saw on a Saturday afternoon or playing hookey
they may even be grateful to you
            for their first sexual experience
which only cost you a quarter
             and didn't upset the peaceful home   15
they will know where candy bars come from
            and gratuitous bags of popcorn
as gratuitous as leaving the movie before it's over
with a pleasant stranger whose apartment is in the
                Heaven on Earth Bldg   20
near the Williamsburg Bridge
        oh mothers you will have made the little tykes
so happy because if nobody does pick them up in the movies
they won't know the difference
            and if somebody does it'll be sheer gravy   25
and they'll have been truly entertained either way
instead of hanging around the yard
           or up in their room
                  hating you
prematurely since you won't have done anything horribly
    mean yet   30
except keeping them from the darker joys
             it's unforgivable the latter
so don't blame me if you won't take this advice
           and the family breaks up
and your children grow old and blind in front of a TV set
              seeing
movies you wouldn't let them see when they were young

Anne Sexton (1928–1975)

Cinderella

You always read about it:
the plumber with twelve children
who wins the Irish Sweepstakes.
From toilets to riches.
That story.   5

Or the nursemaid,
some luscious sweet from Denmark
who captures the oldest son's heart.
From diapers to Dior.
That story.   10

Or a milkman who serves the wealthy,
eggs, cream, butter, yogurt, milk,
the white truck like an ambulance
who goes into real estate
and makes a pile.   15
From homogenized to martinis at lunch.

Or the charwoman
who is on the bus when it cracks up
and collects enough from the insurance.
From mops to Bonwit Teller.   20
That story.

Once
the wife of a rich man was on her deathbed
and she said to her daughter Cinderella:
Be devout. Be good. Then I will smile   25
down from heaven in the seam of a cloud.
The man took another wife who had
two daughters, pretty enough
but with hearts like blackjacks.
Cinderella was their maid.   30
She slept on the sooty hearth each night
and walked around looking like Al Jolson.
Her father brought presents home from town,
jewels and gowns for the other women
but the twig of a tree for Cinderella.   35

She planted that twig on her mother's grave
and it grew to a tree where a white dove sat.
Whenever she wished for anything the dove
would drop it like an egg upon the ground.
The bird is important, my dears, so heed him.   40

Next came the ball, as you all know.
It was a marriage market.
The prince was looking for a wife.
All but Cinderella were preparing
and gussying up for the big event.   45
Cinderella begged to go too.
Her stepmother threw a dish of lentils
into the cinders and said: Pick them
up in an hour and you shall go.
The white dove brought all his friends;   50
all the warm wings of the fatherland came,
and picked up the lentils in a jiffy.
No, Cinderella, said the stepmother,
you have no clothes and cannot dance.
That's the way with stepmothers.   55

Cinderella went to the tree at the grave
and cried forth like a gospel singer:
Mama! Mama! My turtledove,
send me to the prince's ball!
The bird dropped down a golden dress   60
and delicate little gold slippers.
Rather a large package for a simple bird.
So she went. Which is no surprise.
Her stepmother and sisters didn't
recognize her without her cinder face   65
and the prince took her hand on the spot
and danced with no other the whole day.

As nightfall came she thought she'd better
get home. The prince walked her home
and she disappeared into the pigeon house   70
and although the prince took an axe and broke
it open she was gone. Back to her cinders.
These events repeated themselves for three days.
However on the third day the prince
covered the palace steps with cobbler's wax   75
and Cinderella's gold shoe stuck upon it.

Now he would find whom the shoe fit
and find his strange dancing girl for keeps.

He went to their house and the two sisters
were delighted because they had lovely feet.   80
The eldest went into a room to try the slipper on
but her big toe got in the way so she simply
sliced it off and put on the slipper.
The prince rode away with her until the white dove
told him to look at the blood pouring forth.   85
That is the way with amputations.
They don't just heal up like a wish.
The other sister cut off her heel
but the blood told as blood will.
The prince was getting tired.   90
He began to feel like a shoe salesman.
But he gave it one last try.
This time Cinderella fit into the shoe
like a love letter into its envelope.

At the wedding ceremony   95
the two sisters came to curry favor
and the white dove pecked their eyes out.
Two hollow spots were left
like soup spoons.

Cinderella and the prince   100
lived, they say, happily ever after,
like two dolls in a museum case
never bothered by diapers or dust,
never arguing over the timing of an egg,
never telling the same story twice,   105
never getting a middle-aged spread,
their darling smiles pasted on for eternity.
Regular Bobbsey Twins.
That story.

X. J. Kennedy (b. 1929)

Nothing in Heaven Functions as It Ought*

Nothing in Heaven functions as it ought:
Peter's bifocals, blindly sat on, crack;
His gates lurch wide with the cackle of a cock,
Not turn with a hush of gold as Milton had thought;   4
Gangs of the slaughtered innocents keep huffing
The nimbus off the Venerable Bede
Like that of an old dandelion gone to seed;
And the beatific choir keep breaking up, coughing.   8

But Hell, sleek Hell hath no freewheeling part:
None takes his own sweet time, none quickens pace.
Ask anyone, How come you here, poor heart? —
And he will slot a quarter through his face,   12
You'll hear an instant click, a tear will start
Imprinted with an abstract of his case.

Adrienne Rich (b. 1929)

Aunt Jennifer's Tigers

Aunt Jennifer's tigers stride across a screen,
Bright topaz denizens of a world of green.
They do not fear the men beneath the tree,
They pace in sleek chivalric certainty.   4

Aunt Jennifer's fingers, fluttering through her wool,
Find even the ivory needle hard to pull.
The massive weight of Uncle's wedding-band
Sits heavily upon Aunt Jennifer's hand.   8

---

* Line 4 alludes to Milton's *Paradise Lost,* VII, 205–207: "Heaven opened wide / Her ever-during gates, harmonious sound / On golden hinges moving. . . . " For an account of the slaughter of the innocents, see Matthew 2:16. The Venerable Bede (673–735) was an English theologian and historian.

When Aunt is dead, her terrified hands will lie
Still ringed with ordeals she was mastered by.
The tigers in the panel that she made
Will go on striding, proud and unafraid.   12

Adrienne Rich (b. 1929)

Living in Sin

She had thought the studio would keep itself;
no dust upon the furniture of love.
Half heresy, to wish the taps less vocal,
the panes relieved of grime. A plate of pears,
a piano with a Persian shawl, a cat   5
stalking the picturesque amusing mouse
had risen at his urging.
Not that at five each separate stair would writhe
under the milkman's tramp; that morning light
so coldly would delineate the scraps   10
of last night's cheese and three sepulchral bottles;
that on the kitchen shelf among the saucers
a pair of beetle-eyes would fix her own —
envoy from some black village in the mouldings . . .
Meanwhile, he, with a yawn,   15
sounded a dozen notes upon the keyboard,
declared it out of tune, shrugged at the mirror,
rubbed at his beard, went out for cigarettes;
while she, jeered by the minor demons,
pulled back the sheets and made the bed and found   20
a towel to dust the table-top,
and let the coffee-pot boil over on the stove.
By evening she was back in love again,
though not so wholly but throughout the night
she woke sometimes to feel the daylight coming   25
like a relentless milkman up the stairs.

Sylvia Plath (1932–1963)

Medallion

By the gate with star and moon
Worked into the peeled orange wood
The bronze snake lay in the sun

Inert as a shoelace; dead
But pliable still, his jaw   5
Unhinged and his grin crooked,

Tongue a rose-colored arrow.
Over my hand I hung him.
His little vermilion eye

Ignited with a glassed flame   10
As I turned him in the light;
When I split a rock one time

The garnet bits burned like that.
Dust dulled his back to ochre
The way sun ruins a trout.   15

Yet his belly kept its fire
Going under the chainmail,
The old jewels smoldering there

In each opaque belly-scale:
Sunset looked at through milk glass.   20
And I saw white maggots coil

Thin as pins in the dark bruise
Where his innards bulged as if
He were digesting a mouse.

Knifelike, he was chaste enough,   25
Pure death's-metal. The yardman's
Flung brick perfected his laugh.

Sylvia Plath (1932–1963)

Daddy

You do not do, you do not do
Any more, black shoe
In which I have lived like a foot
For thirty years, poor and white,
Barely daring to breathe or Achoo.   5

Daddy, I have had to kill you.
You died before I had time —
Marble-heavy, a bag full of God,
Ghastly statue with one grey toe
Big as a Frisco seal   10

And a head in the freakish Atlantic
Where it pours bean green over blue
In the waters off beautiful Nauset.
I used to pray to recover you.
Ach, du.   15

In the German tongue, in the Polish town
Scraped flat by the roller
Of wars, wars, wars.
But the name of the town is common.
My Polack friend   20

Says there are a dozen or two.
So I never could tell where you
Put your foot, your root,
I never could talk to you.
The tongue stuck in my jaw.   25

It stuck in a barb wire snare.
Ich, ich, ich, ich,
I could hardly speak.
I thought every German was you.
And the language obscene   30

An engine, an engine
Chuffing me off like a Jew.
A Jew to Dachau, Auschwitz, Belsen.
I began to talk like a Jew.
I think I may well be a Jew.   35

The snows of the Tyrol, the clear beer of Vienna
Are not very pure or true.
With my gypsy ancestress and my weird luck
And my Taroc pack and my Taroc pack
I may be a bit of a Jew.   40

I have always been scared of *you*,
With your Luftwaffe, your gobbledygoo.
And your neat moustache
And your Aryan eye, bright blue,
Panzer-man, panzer-man, O You —   45

Not God but a swastika
So black no sky could squeak through.
Every woman adores a Fascist,
The boot in the face, the brute
Brute heart of a brute like you.   50

You stand at the blackboard, daddy,
In the picture I have of you,
A cleft in your chin instead of your foot
But no less a devil for that, no not
Any less the black man who   55

Bit my pretty red heart in two.
I was ten when they buried you.
At twenty I tried to die
And get back, back, back to you.
I thought even the bones would do.   60

But they pulled me out of the sack,
And they stuck me together with glue,
And then I knew what to do.
I made a model of you,
A man in black with a Meinkampf look   65

And a love of the rack and the screw.
And I said I do, I do.
So daddy, I'm finally through.
The black telephone's off at the root,
The voices just can't worm through.   70

If I've killed one man, I've killed two —
The vampire who said he was you
And drank my blood for a year,
Seven years, if you want to know.
Daddy, you can lie back now.   75

There's a stake in your fat black heart
And the villagers never liked you.
They are dancing and stamping on you.
They always *knew* it was you.
Daddy, daddy, you bastard, I'm through.   80

Lucille Clifton (b. 1936)

in the inner city

in the inner city
or
like we call it
home
we think a lot about uptown   5
and the silent nights
and the houses straight as
dead men
and the pastel lights
and we hang on to our no place   10
happy to be alive
and in the inner city
or
like we call it
home   15

Bob Dylan (b. 1941)

Mister Tambourine Man

Chorus

Hey! Mister Tambourine Man, play a song for me,
I'm not sleepy and there is no place I'm going to.
Hey! Mister Tambourine Man, play a song for me,
In the jingle jangle morning I'll come followin' you.

I

Though I know that evenin's empire has returned into sand,   5
Vanished from my hand,
Left me blindly here to stand but still not sleeping.
My weariness amazes me, I'm branded on my feet,
I have no one to meet
And the ancient empty street's too dead for dreaming.   10
Chorus

II

Take me on a trip upon your magic swirlin' ship,
My senses have been stripped, my hands can't feel to grip,
My toes too numb to step, wait only for my boot heels
To be wanderin'.   15
I'm ready to go anywhere, I'm ready for to fade
Into my own parade, cast your dancing spell my way,
I promise to go under it.
Chorus

III

Though you might hear laughin', spinnin', swingin'
          madly across the sun,   20
It's not aimed at anyone, it's just escapin' on the run
And but for the sky there are no fences facin'.
And if you hear vague traces of skippin' reels of rhyme
To your tambourine in time, it's just a ragged clown behind,
I wouldn't pay it any mind, it's just a shadow you're   25
Seein' that he's chasing.
Chorus

IV

Then take me disappearin' through the smoke rings of my mind,
Down the foggy ruins of time, far past the frozen leaves,
The haunted, frightened trees, out to the windy beach,   30
Far from the twisted reach of crazy sorrow.
Yes, to dance beneath the diamond sky with one hand waving free,
Silhouetted by the sea, circled by the circus sands,
With all memory and fate driven deep beneath the waves,
Let me forget about today until tomorrow.   35
Chorus

Don L. Lee (b. 1942)

But He Was Cool
or: he even stopped for green lights

super-cool
ultrablack
a tan / purple
had a beautiful shade.

he had a double-natural   5
that wd put the sisters to shame.
his dashikis were tailor made
& his beads were imported sea shells
        (from some blk/country i never heard of)
he was triple-hip.   10

his tikis were hand carved
out of ivory
& came express from the motherland.
he would greet u in swahili
& say good-by in yoruba.   15

wooooooooooooo-jim he bes so cool & ill tel li gent
        cool-cool is so cool he was un-cooled by other niggers' cool
        cool-cool ultracool was bop-cool / ice box cool so cool cold cool
        his wine didn't have to be cooled, him was air conditioned cool
        cool-cool / real cool made me cool — now ain't that cool   20
        cool-cool so cool him nick-named refrigerator.

cool-cool so cool
he didn't know,
after detroit, newark, chicago &c.,
we had to hip   25
        cool-cool / super-cool / real cool

        that
to be black
is
to be   30
very-hot.

DRAMA

Some Elements of Drama

Tragedy

Comedy

Six Plays for Further Study

Some Observations on Film

Writing Essays on Literature

17 Some Elements
of Drama

The earlier parts of this book have dealt with narrative, both in prose
and in verse, and with what can roughly be called song or lyric. A
third literary type (to use a traditional system of classification) is
drama, consisting of plays written for the theater.* In a play, the
author has receded from his creation; the words are communicated
by actors who impersonate the characters. Of course both story and
song have their dramatic aspects. In a narrative, the author usually
includes **dialogue** (conversation), in which the characters are heard
directly rather than through the voice of the narrator, and the narrator
himself may be an invented character. Similarly, the author of a lyric
poem invents a speaker and a situation. The distinguishing characteristic of a play, then, is not invented speakers or dialogue, but impersonation by actors.

Below is a brief play, a tenth-century imitation (that is, representation or recreation) of the New Testament narrative of the discovery
that the crucified Christ had arisen from the tomb.† Three priests

* **Drama**, unfortunately, has acquired too many meanings. It can denote (as
above) the whole body of work written for the theater, or a single play, or a
serious but untragic play, or (as in "Life is full of drama") events that contain
conflict, tension, surprise.

† This play, known as *Quem Quaeritis* (Latin: "whom do you seek") is commonly considered the earliest extant European play after the end of the
Roman drama. The few lines were amplified in the following centuries, and
extended dramas of events in the Old and New Testaments gradually developed. Still later, secular subjects were dramatized, but the Biblical plays
survived even into Shakespeare's boyhood.

represent the three Marys who visited the tomb. They go to a place representing the tomb and find an angel (a fourth priest, dressed in white, holding a palm branch) who, by displaying a cloth in which the cross had previously been wrapped, shows that Christ has arisen. The bits of dialogue (based closely on Matthew 28 : 1–7 and Mark 16 : 1–8) had developed in the ninth century, but the tenth-century Latin account by Ethelwold, Bishop of Winchester, gives us the stage directions for the play. What follows is a translation of Ethelwold,* run together with a translation of the play.

Anonymous

Quem Quaeritis

While the third lesson is being chanted, let four brethren vest themselves. Let one of these, vested in an alb, enter as though to take part in the service, and let him approach the sepulcher without attracting attention and sit there quietly with a palm in his hand. While the third respond is chanted, let the remaining three follow, and let them all, vested in copes, bearing in their hands thuribles with incense, and stepping delicately as those who seek something, approach the sepulcher. These things are done in imitation of the angel sitting in the monument, and the women with spices coming to anoint the body of Jesus. When therefore he who sits there beholds the three approach him like folk lost and seeking something, let him begin in a dulcet voice of medium pitch to sing:

Whom do you seek in the sepulcher, O followers of Christ?

And when he has sung it to the end, let the three reply in unison:

Jesus of Nazareth who was crucified, O celestial one!

So he:

He is not here, He has risen as He foretold.
Go, announce that He is risen from the dead.

At the word of this bidding let those three turn to the choir and say:

* The translation is by E. K. Chambers, *The Medieval Stage,* II, 14–15 (Oxford, 1903).

Alleluia! The Lord is risen today,
The strong lion, Christ the Son of God! Unto God give thanks, eia!

This said, let the one, still sitting there and as if recalling them, say the anthem:

Come, and see the place where the Lord was laid,
Alleluia! Alleluia!

And saying this, let him rise, and lift the veil, and show them the place bare of the cross, but only the cloths laid there in which the cross was wrapped:

Go quickly, and tell the disciples that the Lord is risen.
Alleluia! Alleluia!

And when they have seen this, let them set down the thuribles which they bare in that same sepulcher, and take the cloth, and hold it up in the face of the clergy, and as if to demonstrate that the Lord has risen and is no longer wrapped therein, let them sing the anthem:

The Lord is risen from the sepulcher,
Who for us was hanged on the cross, alleluia!

and lay the cloth upon the altar. When the anthem is done, let the prior, sharing in their gladness at the triumph of our King, in that, having vanquished death, He rose again, begin the hymn *Te Deum laudamus*. And this begun, all the bells chime out together.

All the elements of a play are here: an action (i.e., not the gestures but a story, a happening, the movement from doubt to joyful certainty) imitated by impersonators (priests). Notice, too, that the impersonation is aided by scenery ("the place bare of the cross"), properties (the angel's palm branch), costumes (copes and an alb), and gestures ("stepping delicately as those who seek something"). Even sound effects are used: "All the bells chime out together."

Before looking at a longer and more complex play, a few words should be said about **plot.** Although plot is sometimes equated with the gist of the narrative — the story — it is sometimes reserved to denote the writer's arrangement of the happenings in the story. Thus, all plays about the assassination of Julius Caesar have pretty much the same story, but by beginning his play with a scene of workmen enjoying a holiday (and thereby introducing the motif of the fickleness of the mob) Shakespeare's play has a plot different from a play that omits such a scene.

Handbooks on the drama often suggest that a plot (arrangement of happenings) should have a **rising action**, a **climax**, and a **falling action**. This sort of plot can be diagramed as a pyramid, the tension rising through complications or **crises** to a climax, at which point the fate of the **protagonist** (chief character) is firmly established; the climax is the apex, and the tension allegedly slackens as we witness the **dénouement** (unknotting). Shakespeare sometimes used a pyramidal structure, placing his climax neatly in the middle of what seems to us to be the third of five acts.* Roughly the first half of *Julius Caesar* shows Brutus rising, reaching his height in III.i with the death of Caesar; but later in this scene he gives Marc Antony permission to speak at Caesar's funeral and thus he sets in motion his own fall, which occupies the second half of the play. In *Macbeth*, the protagonist attains his height in III.i ("Thou hast it now: King"), but he soon perceives that he is going downhill:

> I am in blood
> Stepped in so far, that, should I wade no more,
> Returning were as tedious as go o'er.

In *Hamlet*, the protagonist proves to his own satisfaction Claudius's guilt (by the play within the play) in III.ii, but almost immediately he begins to worsen his position by failing to kill Claudius when he is an easy target (III.iii) and by contaminating himself with the murder of Polonius (III.iv).

Of course, no law demands such a structure, and a hunt for the pyramid usually causes the hunter to overlook all the crises but the middle one. William Butler Yeats once suggestively diagramed a good plot not as a pyramid but as a line moving diagonally upward, punctuated by several crises. Perhaps it is sufficient to say that a good

---

* An **act** is a main division in a drama or opera. Act divisions probably stem from Roman theory and derive ultimately from the Greek practice of separating episodes in a play by choral interludes, but Greek (and probably Roman) plays were performed without interruption, for the choral interludes were part of the plays themselves. Elizabethan plays, too, may have been performed without breaks; the division of Elizabethan plays into five acts is usually the work of editors rather than of authors. Frequently an act division today (commonly indicated by lowering the curtain and turning up the houselights) denotes change in locale and lapse of time. A **scene** is a smaller unit, either (1) a division with no change of locale or abrupt shift of time, or (2) a division consisting of an actor or group of actors on the stage; according to the second definition, the departure or entrance of an actor changes the composition of the group and thus introduces a new scene. (In an entirely different sense, the scene is the locale where a work is set.)

plot has its moments of tension, but the location of these will vary with the play. They are the product of **conflict,** but not all conflict produces tension; there is conflict but little tension in a ball game when the score is 10–0 and the visiting pitcher comes to bat in the ninth inning with two out and none on base.

Regardless of how a plot is diagramed, the **exposition** is that part that tells the audience what it has to know about the past, the **antecedent action.** When the three Marys say they are seeking Jesus, "who was crucified," they are offering exposition. In later plays, the two gossiping servants who tell each other that after a year away in Paris the young master is coming home tomorrow with a new wife are giving the audience the exposition. The Elizabethans and the Greeks sometimes tossed out all pretense at dialogue, and began with a **prologue,** like the one spoken by the Chorus at the outset of *Romeo and Juliet:*

> Two households, both alike in dignity
>> In fair Verona, where we lay our scene,
> From ancient grudge break to new mutiny,
>> Where civil blood makes civil hands unclean.
> From forth the fatal loins of these two foes
>> A pair of star-crossed lovers take their life. . . .

And in Tennesee Williams's *The Glass Menagerie,* Tom's first speech is a sort of prologue. However, the exposition may also extend far into the play, being given in dribs and drabs. Occasionally the **soliloquy** (speech of a character alone on the stage, revealing his thoughts) or the **aside** (speech in the presence of others but unheard by them) is used to do the job of putting the audience in possession of the essential facts. The soliloquy and the aside, of course, are not limited to exposition; they are used to reveal the private thoughts of characters who, like people in real life, do not always tell others what their inner thoughts are. The soliloquy is especially used for meditation, where we might say the character is interacting not with another character but with himself.

Exposition has been discussed as though it consists simply of informing the audience about events; but exposition can do much more. It can give us an understanding of the characters who themselves are talking about other characters, it can evoke a mood, and it can generate tension. The first scene in *Julius Caesar,* in which the tribunes drive the commoners from the stage, is less important for the details it gives us about Caesar and Pompey than for its picture of a fickle mob, a mob that will later applaud the death of Caesar and then turn and drive the assassins out of Rome. When we summarize the opening act of a play and treat it as "mere exposition" we are probably losing what is in fact dramatic in it.

Because a play is not simply words but words spoken with accompanying gestures by performers who are usually costumed and in a particular setting, it may be argued that to read a play (rather than to see and hear it) is to falsify it. Drama is not literature, some people hold, but theater. However, there are replies: a play can be literature as well as theater, and the reader of a play can perhaps enact in the theater of his mind a more effective play than the one put on by imperfect actors ("The best in this kind are but shadows," Shakespeare's Duke Theseus says) in front of an audience that coughs and whispers. This mental enactment is aided by abundant stage direction in many contemporary plays. In Eugene O'Neill's *Desire Under the Elms,* about four hundred words (describing the set and the gestures of some of the characters) precede the first speech. This speech consists of two words, "God! Purty!" and it is followed by two hundred words of further description. O'Neill informs the reader that the elms over the house have "a sinister maternity," that Eben, twenty-five years old, "finds himself trapped but inwardly unsubdued," that Simeon is thirty-nine, that Peter is thirty-seven, and so forth. (In the theater, not every actor can communicate by his words, gestures, and make-up that he is twenty-five or thirty-nine or thirty-seven.) Bernard Shaw sometimes outdid O'Neill in writing for the reader: many of his plays have enormous prefaces, and some (such as *Candida*) have unactable stage directions: "They embrace. But they do not know the secret in the poet's heart." Furthermore, the author's dialogue rarely reaches the stage intact; in addition to interpreting, directors cut and reshape scenes, so that it is often accurate to say we get Gielgud's or Olivier's rather than Shakespeare's *Hamlet.*

Finally (to reverse our tactics), even if it be granted that a good performance reveals qualities in a play that a reading misses, half a loaf is better than none. You may never get a chance to see Synge's *Riders to the Sea,* but why not experience at least a good part of it in a reading?

John Millington Synge (1871–1909)

Riders to the Sea

List of Characters

Maurya, an old woman
Bartley, her son
Cathleen, her daughter
Nora, a younger daughter
Men and Women

Scene. *An Island off the West of Ireland.*

*Cottage kitchen, with nets, oil-skins, spinning-wheel, some new
boards standing by the wall, etc. Cathleen, a girl of about twenty,
finishes kneading cake, and puts it down in the pot-oven by the
fire; then wipes her hands, and begins to spin at the wheel. Nora,
a young girl, puts her head in at the door.*

Nora (in a low voice). Where is she?
Cathleen. She's lying down, God help her, and may be sleeping, if
she's able.

Nora comes in softly, and takes a bundle from under her shawl.

Cathleen (spinning the wheel rapidly). What is it you have?
Nora. The young priest is after bringing them. It's a shirt and a plain
stocking were got off a drowned man in Donegal.

*Cathleen stops her wheel with a sudden movement, and leans out
to listen.*

Nora. We're to find out if it's Michael's they are, some time herself
will be down looking by the sea.
Cathleen. How would they be Michael's, Nora? How would he go
the length of that way to the far north?
Nora. The young priest says he's known the like of it. "If it's Michael's they are," says he, "you can tell herself he's got a clean
burial by the grace of God, and if they're not his, let no one say a
word about them, for she'll be getting her death," says he, "with
crying and lamenting."

The door which Nora half-closed is blown open by a gust of wind.

Cathleen (looking out anxiously). Did you ask him would he stop Bartley going this day with the horses to the Galway fair?

Nora. "I won't stop him," says he, "but let you not be afraid. Herself does be saying prayers half through the night, and the Almighty God won't leave her destitute," says he, "with no son living."

Cathleen. Is the sea bad by the white rocks, Nora?

Nora. Middling bad, God help us. There's a great roaring in the west, and it's worse it'll be getting when the tide's turned to the wind.

She goes over to the table with the bundle.

Shall I open it now?

Cathleen. Maybe she'd wake up on us, and come in before we'd done. *(Coming to the table.)* It's a long time we'll be, and the two of us crying.

Nora (goes to the inner door and listens). She's moving about on the bed. She'll be coming in a minute.

Cathleen. Give me the ladder, and I'll put them up in the turf-loft, the way she won't know of them at all, and maybe when the tide turns she'll be going down to see would he be floating from the east.

They put the ladder against the gable of the chimney; Cathleen goes up a few steps and hides the bundle in the turf-loft. Maurya comes from the inner room.

Maurya (looking up at Cathleen and speaking querulously). Isn't it turf enough you have for this day and evening?

Cathleen. There's a cake baking at the fire for a short space *(throwing down the turf)* and Bartley will want it when the tide turns if he goes to Connemara.

Nora picks up the turf and puts it round the pot-oven.

Maurya (sitting down on a stool at the fire). He won't go this day with the wind rising from the south and west. He won't go this day, for the young priest will stop him surely.

Nora. He'll not stop him, mother, and I heard Eamon Simon and Stephen Pheety and Colum Shawn saying he would go.

Maurya. Where is he itself?

Nora. He went down to see would there be another boat sailing in the week, and I'm thinking it won't be long till he's here now, for the tide's turning at the green head, and the hooker's° tacking from the east.

hooker sailing boat

Cathleen. I hear some one passing the big stones.

Nora (looking out). He's coming now, and he in a hurry.

Bartley (comes in and looks round the room. Speaking sadly and quietly). Where is the bit of new rope, Cathleen, was bought in Connemara?

Cathleen (coming down). Give it to him, Nora; it's on a nail by the white boards. I hung it up this morning, for the pig with the black feet was eating it.

Nora (giving him a rope). Is that it, Bartley?

Maurya. You'd do right to leave that rope, Bartley, hanging by the boards. *(Bartley takes the rope.)* It will be wanting in this place, I'm telling you, if Michael is washed up to-morrow morning, or the next morning, or any morning in the week, for it's a deep grave we'll make him by the grace of God.

Bartley (beginning to work with the rope). I've no halter the way I can ride down on the mare, and I must go now quickly. This is the one boat going for two weeks or beyond it, and the fair will be a good fair for horses I heard them saying below.

Maurya. It's a hard thing they'll be saying below if the body is washed up and there's no man in it to make the coffin, and I after giving a big price for the finest white boards you'd find in Connemara.

She looks round at the boards.

Bartley. How would it be washed up, and we after looking each day for nine days, and a strong wind blowing a while back from the west and south?

Maurya. If it wasn't found itself, that wind is raising the sea, and there was a star up against the moon, and it rising in the night. If it was a hundred horses, or a thousand horses you had itself, what is the price of a thousand horses against a son where there is one son only?

Bartley (working at the halter, to Cathleen). Let you go down each day, and see the sheep aren't jumping in on the rye, and if the jobber comes you can sell the pig with the black feet if there is a good price going.

Maurya. How would the like of her get a good price for a pig?

Bartley (to Cathleen). If the west wind holds with the last bit of the moon let you and Nora get up weed enough for another cock for the kelp.° It's hard set we'll be from this day with no one in it but one man to work.

kelp   seaweed (used for manure)

Maurya. It's hard set we'll be surely the day you're drownd'd with the rest. What way will I live and the girls with me, and I an old woman looking for the grave?

Bartley lays down the halter, takes off his old coat, and puts on a newer one of the same flannel.

Bartley (to Nora). Is she coming to the pier?

Nora (looking out). She's passing the green head and letting fall her sails.

Bartley (getting his purse and tobacco). I'll have half an hour to go down, and you'll see me coming again in two days, or in three days, or maybe in four days if the wind is bad.

Maurya (turning round to the fire, and putting her shawl over her head). Isn't it a hard and cruel man won't hear a word from an old woman, and she holding him from the sea?

Cathleen. It's the life of a young man to be going on the sea, and who would listen to an old woman with one thing and she saying it over?

Bartley (taking the halter). I must go now quickly. I'll ride down on the red mare, and the gray pony'll run behind me. . . . The blessing of God on you.

He goes out.

Maurya (crying out as he is in the door). He's gone now, God spare us, and we'll not see him again. He's gone now, and when the black night is falling I'll have no son left me in the world.

Cathleen. Why wouldn't you give him your blessing and he looking round in the door? Isn't it sorrow enough is on every one in this house without your sending him out with an unlucky word behind him, and a hard word in his ear?

Maurya takes up the tongs and begins raking the fire aimlessly without looking round.

Nora (turning towards her). You're taking away the turf from the cake.

Cathleen (crying out). The Son of God forgive us, Nora, we're after forgetting his bit of bread.

She comes over to the fire.

Nora. And it's destroyed he'll be going till dark night, and he after eating nothing since the sun went up.

Cathleen (turning the cake out of the oven). It's destroyed he'll be, surely. There's no sense left on any person in a house where an old woman will be talking for ever.

Maurya sways herself on her stool.

Cathleen (cutting off some of the bread and rolling it in a cloth; to Maurya). Let you go down now to the spring well and give him this and he passing. You'll see him then and the dark word will be broken, and you can say "God speed you," the way he'll be easy in his mind.

Maurya (taking the bread). Will I be in it as soon as himself?

Cathleen. If you go now quickly.

Maurya (standing up unsteadily). It's hard set I am to walk.

Cathleen (looking at her anxiously). Give her the stick, Nora, or maybe she'll slip on the big stones.

Nora. What stick?

Cathleen. The stick Michael brought from Connemara.

Maurya (taking a stick Nora gives her). In the big world the old people do be leaving things after them for their sons and children, but in this place it is the young men do be leaving things behind for them that do be old.

She goes out slowly. Nora goes over to the ladder.

Cathleen. Wait, Nora, maybe she'd turn back quickly. She's that sorry, God help her, you wouldn't know the thing she'd do.

Nora. Is she gone around by the bush?

Cathleen (looking out). She's gone now. Throw it down quickly, for the Lord knows when she'll be out of it again.

Nora (getting the bundle from the loft). The young priest said he'd be passing to-morrow, and we might go down and speak to him below if it's Michael's they are surely.

Cathleen (taking the bundle). Did he say what way they were found?

Nora (coming down). "There were two men," says he, "and they rowing round with poteen° before the cocks crowed, and the oar of one of them caught the body, and they passing the black cliffs of the north."

Cathleen (trying to open the bundle). Give me a knife, Nora, the strings perished with the salt water, and there's a black knot on it you wouldn't loosen in a week.

Nora (giving her a knife). I've heard tell it was a long way to Donegal.

poteen illegal whiskey

Cathleen (cutting the string). It is surely. There was a man in here a while ago — the man sold us that knife — and he said if you set off walking from the rock beyond, it would be seven days you'd be in Donegal.

Nora. And what time would a man take, and he floating?

Cathleen opens the bundle and takes out a bit of a stocking. They look at them eagerly.

Cathleen (in a low voice). The Lord spare us, Nora! isn't it a queer hard thing to say if it's his they are surely?

Nora. I'll get his shirt off the hook the way we can put the one flannel on the other. *(She looks through some clothes hanging in the corner.)* It's not with them, Cathleen, and where will it be?

Cathleen. I'm thinking Bartley put it on him in the morning, for his own shirt was heavy with the salt in it. *(Pointing to the corner.)* There's a bit of a sleeve was of the same stuff. Give me that and it will do.

Nora brings it to her and they compare the flannel.

Cathleen. It's the same stuff, Nora; but if it is itself aren't there great rolls of it in the shops of Galway, and isn't it many another man may have a shirt of it as well as Michael himself?

Nora (who has taken up the stocking and counted the stitches, crying out). It's Michael, Cathleen, it's Michael; God spare his soul, and what will herself say when she hears this story, and Bartley on the sea?

Cathleen (taking the stocking). It's a plain stocking.

Nora. It's the second one of the third pair I knitted, and I put up three score stitches, and I dropped four of them.

Cathleen (counts the stitches). It's that number is in it. *(Crying out.)* Ah, Nora, isn't it a bitter thing to think of him floating that way to the far north, and no one to keen° him but the black hags that do be flying on the sea?

Nora (swinging herself round, and throwing out her arms on the clothes). And isn't it a pitiful thing when there is nothing left of a man who was a great rower and fisher, but a bit of an old shirt and a plain stocking?

Cathleen (after an instant). Tell me is herself coming, Nora? I hear a little sound on the path.

Nora (looking out). She is, Cathleen. She's coming up to the door.

Cathleen. Put these things away before she'll come in. Maybe it's

keen lament

easier she'll be after giving her blessing to Bartley, and we won't
let on we've heard anything the time he's on the sea.

Nora (helping Cathleen to close the bundle). We'll put them here in
the corner.

*They put them into a hole in the chimney corner. Cathleen goes
back to the spinning-wheel.*

Nora. Will she see it was crying I was?

Cathleen. Keep your back to the door the way the light'll not be on
you.

*Nora sits down at the chimney corner, with her back to the door.
Maurya comes in very slowly, without looking at the girls, and
goes over to her stool at the other side of the fire. The cloth with
the bread is still in her hand. The girls look at each other, and
Nora points to the bundle of bread.*

Cathleen (after spinning for a moment). You didn't give him his bit
of bread?

Maurya begins to keen softly, without turning round.

Cathleen. Did you see him riding down?

Maurya goes on keening.

Cathleen (a little impatiently). God forgive you; isn't it a better
thing to raise your voice and tell what you seen, than to be making
lamentation for a thing that's done? Did you see Bartley, I'm
saying to you.

Maurya (with a weak voice). My heart's broken from this day.

Cathleen (as before). Did you see Bartley?

Maurya. I seen the fearfulest thing.

Cathleen (leaves her wheel and looks out). God forgive you; he's
riding the mare now over the green head, and the gray pony behind him.

*Maurya (starts, so that her shawl falls back from her head and shows
her white tossed hair. With a frightened voice).* The gray pony
behind him.

Cathleen (coming to the fire). What is it ails you, at all?

Maurya (speaking very slowly). I've seen the fearfulest thing any
person has seen, since the day Bride Dara seen the dead man with
the child in his arms.

Cathleen and Nora. Uah.

They crouch down in front of the old woman at the fire.

Nora. Tell us what it is you seen.

Maurya. I went down to the spring well, and I stood there saying a prayer to myself. Then Bartley came along, and he riding on the red mare with the gray pony behind him. *(She puts up her hands, as if to hide something from her eyes.)* The Son of God spare us, Nora!

Cathleen. What is it you seen?

Maurya. I seen Michael himself.

Cathleen (speaking softly). You did not, mother; it wasn't Michael you seen, for his body is after being found in the far north, and he's got a clean burial by the grace of God.

Maurya (a little defiantly). I'm after seeing him this day, and he riding and galloping. Bartley came first on the red mare; and I tried to say "God speed you," but something choked the words in my throat. He went by quickly; and "the blessing of God on you," says he, and I could say nothing. I looked up then, and I crying, at the gray pony, and there was Michael upon it — with fine clothes on him, and new shoes on his feet.

Cathleen (begins to keen). It's destroyed we are from this day. It's destroyed, surely.

Nora. Didn't the young priest say the Almighty God wouldn't leave her destitute with no son living?

Maurya (in a low voice, but clearly). It's little the like of him knows of the sea. . . . Bartley will be lost now, and let you call in Eamon and make me a good coffin out of the white boards, for I won't live after them. I've had a husband, and a husband's father, and six sons in this house — six fine men, though it was a hard birth I had with every one of them and they coming to the world — and some of them were found and some of them were not found, but they're gone now the lot of them. . . . There were Stephen, and Shawn, were lost in the great wind, and found after in the Bay of Gregory of the Golden Mouth, and carried up the two of them on the one plank, and in by that door.

She pauses for a moment, the girls start as if they heard something through the door that is half open behind them.

Nora (in a whisper). Did you hear that, Cathleen? Did you hear a noise in the north-east?

Cathleen (in a whisper). There's some one after crying out by the seashore.

Maurya (continues without hearing anything). There was Sheamus and his father, and his own father again, were lost in a dark night, and not a stick or sign was seen of them when the sun went up. There was Patch after was drowned out of a curagh° that turned

curagh unstable vessel of tarred canvas on a wood frame; canoe

over. I was sitting here with Bartley, and he a baby, lying on my two knees, and I seen two women, and three women, and four women coming in, and they crossing themselves, and not saying a word. I looked out then, and there were men coming after them, and they holding a thing in the half of a red sail, and water dripping out of it — it was a dry day, Nora — and leaving a track to the door.

She pauses again with her hand stretched out towards the door. It opens softly and old women begin to come in, crossing themselves on the threshold, and kneeling down in front of the stage with red petticoats over their heads.

Maurya (*half in a dream, to Cathleen*). Is it Patch, or Michael, or what is it at all?

Cathleen. Michael is after being found in the far north, and when he is found there how could he be here in this place?

Maurya. There does be a power of young men floating round in the sea, and what way would they know if it was Michael they had, or another man like him, for when a man is nine days in the sea, and the wind blowing, it's hard set his own mother would be to say what man was it.

Cathleen. It's Michael, God spare him, for they're after sending us a bit of his clothes from the far north.

She reaches out and hands Maurya the clothes that belonged to Michael. Maurya stands up slowly and takes them in her hand. Nora looks out.

Nora. They're carrying a thing among them and there's water dripping out of it and leaving a track by the big stones.

Cathleen (*in a whisper to the women who have come in*). Is it Bartley it is?

One of the Women. It is surely, God rest his soul.

Two younger women come in and pull out the table. Then men carry in the body of Bartley, laid on a plank, with a bit of sail over it, and lay it on the table.

Cathleen (*to the women, as they are doing so*). What way was he drowned?

One of the Women. The gray pony knocked him into the sea, and he was washed out where there is a great surf on the white rocks.

Maurya has gone over and knelt down at the head of the table. The women are keening softly and swaying themselves with a slow movement. Cathleen and Nora kneel at the other end of the table. The men kneel near the door.

Maurya *(raising her head and speaking as if she did not see the people around her).* They're all gone now, and there isn't anything more the sea can do to me. . . . I'll have no call now to be up crying and praying when the wind breaks from the south, and you can hear the surf is in the east, and the surf is in the west, making a great stir with the two noises, and they hitting one on the other. I'll have no call now to be going down and getting Holy Water in the dark nights after Samhain,° and I won't care what way the sea is when the other women will be keening. *(To Nora.)* Give me the Holy Water, Nora, there's a small sup still on the dresser.

Nora gives it to her.

Maurya *(drops Michael's clothes across Bartley's feet, and sprinkles the Holy Water over him).* It isn't that I haven't prayed for you, Bartley, to the Almighty God. It isn't that I haven't said prayers in the dark night till you wouldn't know what I'ld be saying; but it's a great rest I'll have now, and it's time surely. It's a great rest I'll have now, and great sleeping in the long nights after Samhain, if it's only a bit of wet flour we do have to eat, and maybe a fish that would be stinking.

She kneels down again, crossing herself, and saying prayers under her breath.

Cathleen *(to an old man).* Maybe yourself and Eamon would make a coffin when the sun rises. We have fine white boards herself bought, God help her, thinking Michael would be found, and I have a new cake you can eat while you'll be working.

The Old Man (looking at the boards). Are there nails with them?

Cathleen. There are not, Colum; we didn't think of the nails.

Another Man. It's a great wonder she wouldn't think of the nails, and all the coffins she's seen made already.

Cathleen. It's getting old she is, and broken.

Maurya stands up again very slowly and spreads out the pieces of Michael's clothes beside the body, sprinkling them with the last of the Holy Water.

Nora *(in a whisper to Cathleen).* She's quiet now and easy; but the day Michael was drowned you could hear her crying out from this to the spring well. It's fonder she was of Michael, and would any one have thought that?

Samhain   November 1, All Saints' Day

Cathleen (slowly and clearly). An old woman will be soon tired with anything she will do, and isn't it nine days herself is after crying and keening, and making great sorrow in the house?

Maurya (puts the empty cup mouth downwards on the table, and lays her hands together on Bartley's feet). They're all together this time, and the end is come. May the Almighty God have mercy on Bartley's soul, and on Michael's soul, and on the souls of Sheamus and Patch, and Stephen and Shawn *(bending her head);* and may He have mercy on my soul, Nora, and on the soul of every one is left living in the world.

She pauses, and the keen rises a little more loudly from the women, then sinks away.

Maurya (continuing). Michael has a clean burial in the far north, by the grace of the Almighty God. Bartley will have a fine coffin out of the white boards, and a deep grave surely. What more can we want than that? No man at all can be living for ever, and we must be satisfied.

She kneels down again and the curtain falls slowly.

Synge first visited the Aran Islands (three rocky places off the west coast of Ireland, inhabited by Gaelic-speaking fishermen) in the summer of 1898. From this visit and subsequent ones he derived the material for *The Aran Islands,* an account of life there, full of observations and bits of folklore he had picked up. In it one can find something of the origins of *Riders to the Sea:* descriptions of bringing horses across the sound, including an account of an old woman who had a vision of her drowned son riding on a horse; a reference to a coffin untimely made out of boards prepared for another person; and a reference to a body that floated ashore some weeks after the man drowned. In writing the play Synge chose among the innumerable things he saw and heard, selecting (as any artist does) from the welter or chaos of experience to put together a unified story. A summary of the play's story would run along these lines: an old woman named Maurya, who has lost her husband and five sons to the sea — one very recently — learns that a drowned man has been found, and almost simultaneously she learns of the death of her sixth son. This summary of the story proceeds chronologically, but the play does not. The play begins with a daughter, Cathleen, kneading a cake, setting it in the oven, and then spinning at a wheel. Another daughter enters and speaks the first line, asking about some third woman, who we later come to understand is Maurya. The next few speeches are about "a shirt and a plain stocking were got off a drowned man in Donegal," and we learn that these remnants may belong to someone named Michael. In another moment we learn that Michael and the woman (still referred to only as "she") are closely related. With the eighth speech yet another important character is named, Bartley, who intends to take horses to the Galway fair. And so we are introduced to the characters, with oblique references, and bit by bit we put together the relationships. The playwright's *arrangement of the story*, rather than a strictly chronological arrangement, is (for many critics) Synge's **plot.**

In a play, **gesture** no less than dialogue is a means of communication. What Cathleen *says* is important, but so too is what she *does*. Her actions, described in the first stage direction, tell us a good deal about the islanders' laborious existence. She finishes one task, kneading the dough, and turns to another, spinning. Synge tells us in another stage direction that during the first few lines she turns the wheel "rapidly," but when Nora mentions the clothing that has been found, "Cathleen stops her wheel with a sudden movement, and leans out to listen." She stops turning the wheel, of course, in order to concentrate on Nora's words, but the abrupt halting of the wheel also is part of the dramatist's way of saying that Michael no longer lives: his thread of life has been spun and untimely cut. A moment later there is another stage direction that has symbolic implications: "The door which Nora half closed is blown open by a gust of wind," suggesting (no less than the abundant talk of the bad weather) the periodic intrusion of powerful natural forces upon the lives of the islanders.

One need not compare *Riders to the Sea* (in which everything is related to everything else) with *The Aran Islands* (in which we have a wonderful grab bag of scarcely related details) to see that the careful arrangement of physical happenings and dialogue gives us more than a slice of life, more than a picture of a certain kind of Irish life. Synge's art extends beyond his plot to his language. The islanders spoke Gaelic, and Synge claimed that his English was close to a translation of their language; but the speeches — as distinct from the words — are Synge's, just as Macbeth's "I am in blood / Stepped in so far, that, should I wade no more, / Returning were as tedious as go o'er" is Shakespeare's creation although the individual words are pretty much the property of any literate American or Englishman. The speeches Synge creates, no less than his plot, belong to the world of art, though the speeches and the events are made up of the materials of Aran life.

Synge chose the peasant idiom because it seemed to him to have beauty and even grandeur, while at the same time it was rooted in people who lived an elemental existence. He saw no need to choose between beauty and truth: beauty without truth led writers of the late nineteenth century (he believed) to highly wrought yet trivial or even meaningless verse, and truth without beauty to dull pictures of man's insignificance. It is partly by making "every speech . . . as fully flavored as a nut or apple" that Synge produced a work that (although it deals with multiple deaths) is not depressing but is, like every work of art, stimulating: "Let you go down each day, and see the sheep aren't jumping in on the rye, and if the jobber comes you can sell the pig with the black feet if there is a good price going." Even the speeches on the inevitable end of man have, while they call attention to man's ignominious remains, richness and dignity: "And isn't it a pitiful thing when there is nothing left of a man who was a great rower and fisher, but a bit of an old shirt and a plain stocking?" Throughout the play this artful use of language communicates a picture of heroism and humbleness that is reassuring as well as grievous, nowhere more so than in Maurya's final speech, which calls attention to the hardness of life and the inevitability of death in such a way as almost to offer a kind of reassurance.

What is *Riders to the Sea* "about"? It is, of course, about people named Maurya, Bartley, and so forth, and it is about the life of Irish islanders — particularly the women — of 1900 and earlier. But clearly it is about something more; it has a theme, a vision.

What is this **theme**? Life proceeds from the sea, and is nourished by the sea, but the sea is also a source of death: "It's the life of a young man to be going on the sea," Cathleen says, suggesting something of man's inevitable struggle against the enormous impersonal forces of nature. "They're all gone now, and there isn't anything more the sea can do to me," Maurya says a little later, suggesting something of man's inevitable defeat in this struggle and yet of man's ability to triumph — in a way — by a clarity of vision. And finally Maurya says, in the last speech of the play: "Michael has a clean burial in the far north, by the grace of the Almighty God. Bartley will have a fine coffin out of the white boards, and a deep grave surely. What more can we want than that? No man at all can be living for ever, and we must be satisfied." Michael has a clean burial — but we know that the loss is grievous. Bartley will have a fine coffin — but the coffin was not meant for him, and we may recall two of Maurya's earlier speeches, when Bartley was alive: "It's hard set we'll be surely the day you're drownd'd with the rest. What way will I live and the girls with me, and I an old woman looking for the grave?" And: "In the big world the old people do be leaving things after them for their sons and children, but in this place it is the young men do be leaving things behind for them that do be old." At the end of the play, the young men are all gone, the last of them "knocked . . . into the sea" by a gray pony, but, paradoxically, Maurya's final speech reveals a majesty she lacked in the early part of the play when, a little better off, she spoke "querulously" and raked the fire "aimlessly." In the most important sense, then, the action of the play is this movement of Maurya's mind, rather than the physical doings of men and women who enter, cut open a bundle, bring in a corpse, and so forth. The word "drama" is from the Greek verb *dran*, to do, to accomplish; in *Riders to the Sea* the thing accomplished is not only the identification of Michael's clothing and the death of Bartley, but the shift in Maurya's mind. Early in the play the priest (Nora says) suggested that Michael may have had "a clean burial by the grace of God"; midway in the play Cathleen says it is "a bitter thing to think of him floating that way to the far north, and no one to keen him but the black hags that do be flying on the sea." Finally, after the death of Bartley, Maurya derives some comfort from the thought that "Bartley will have a fine coffin out of the white boards," and Michael "a clean burial in the far north." But we distinguish between Maurya's view, born out of suffering, and the simple faith of "the young priest" (his youth is insisted on); she has been "hard set," known despair, seen the worst that can happen ("They're all gone now, and there isn't anything more the sea can do to me"), and now from the vantage point of one stripped of all that one has cherished she can utter with dignity the most terrible facts of life.

This is not to say that the play has a message. Synge abhorred didactic drama, and in a preface to another play insisted that "the drama, like the symphony, does not teach or prove anything." It offers us "pleasure and excitement," rather than solutions that inevitably become old-fashioned. The best plays, he said in a characteristically homely figure, "can no more go out of fashion than the blackberries on the hedges."

Questions

1. What is revealed about Maurya's state of mind by her speech (page 538): "He won't go this day with the wind rising from the south and west. He won't go this day, for the young priest will stop him surely." Why is her reference to the need for the rope (page 539) one of the strongest arguments she can propose for Bartley's staying?.

2. Notice the references to the bread (or cake). Why are they in the play? And why the emphasis upon the rope?

3. What is implied by Maurya's vision of Michael "with fine clothes on him, and new shoes on his feet" (page 544)?

4. Trace the foreshadowing of Bartley's death.

5. Nora and Cathleen hear someone calling out by the seashore (page 544). Why doesn't Maurya hear the noise? Why does Synge not have a stage direction calling for a cry?

6. Does the fact that Maurya has forgotten the coffin-nails indicate (as Cathleen says, page 546) that she is "broken"?

7. Evaluate James Joyce's complaint that the catastrophe is brought about by a pony rather than by the sea. It has been suggested that a reply can be made to Joyce: Bartley is knocked into the sea by the gray pony, but this in not an accident, for the ghost of his brother Michael is riding the pony, and Irish ghosts commonly seek to bring the living into the realm of the dead. Is this reply satisfactory, or does it introduce a red herring?

18 Tragedy

Aristotle defined tragedy as a dramatization of a serious happening —
not necessarily one ending with the death of the protagonist — and
his definition remains among the best. But many plays have been
written since Aristotle defined tragedy. When we think of Shakespeare's tragedies we cannot resist narrowing Aristotle's definition
by adding something like "showing a struggle that rends the protagonist's whole being"; and when we think of the "problem plays" of
the last hundred years — the serious treatments of such sociological
problems as alcoholism and race prejudice — we cannot resist
excluding some of them by adding to the definition something about
the need for universal appeal. The question remains: Is there a
single quality present in all works that we call tragedy and absent
from works not called tragedy? If there is, no one has yet pointed it
out to general satisfaction. But this failure does not mean that there is
no such classification as tragedy. We sense that tragedies resemble
each other as members of the same family resemble each other: two
children have the mother's coloring and eyes, a third child has the
mother's coloring but the father's eyes, a fourth child has the
mother's eyes but the father's coloring.

The next few pages will examine three comments on tragedy,
none of which is entirely acceptable, but each of which seems to have
some degree of truth, and each of which can help us detect resemblances and differences among tragedies. The first comment is by
Cyril Tourneur, a tragic dramatist of the early seventeenth century:

> When the bad bleed, then is the tragedy good.

We think of Macbeth ("usurper," "butcher"). Macbeth, of course, is
much more than a usurper and butcher, but it is undeniable that he is

an offender against the moral order. Whatever the merits of Tourneur's statement, however, if we think of *Romeo and Juliet* (to consider only one play), we realize its inadequacy. Tourneur so stresses
the guilt of the protagonist that his suffering becomes mere retribu-
tive justice. But we cannot plausibly say, for example, that Romeo
and Juliet deserved to die because they married without their parents' consent; it is much too simple to call them "bad." Romeo and
Juliet are young, in love, nobler in spirit than their parents. Tourneur's view is probably derived ultimately from an influential passage in Aristotle's *Poetics* in which Aristotle speaks of **hamartia,**
sometimes literally translated as "missing the target," sometimes as
"vice" or "flaw" or "weakness," but perhaps best translated as "mistake." Aristotle seems to imply that the hero is undone because of
some mistake he commits, but this mistake need not be the result of a
moral fault; it may be simply a miscalculation — for example, failure
to foresee the consequences of a deed. Brutus makes a strategic mistake when he lets Marc Antony speak at Caesar's funeral, but we can
hardly call it a vice. Because Aristotle's *hamartia* includes mistakes
of this sort, the common translation "**tragic flaw**" is erroneous. In
many Greek tragedies the hero's *hamartia* is **hybris** (or **hubris**), usually translated as "overweening pride." The hero forgets that he is
fallible, attributes to himself the power and wisdom of the gods, and
is later humbled for his arrogance. But a number of recent scholars
have insisted that this self-assertiveness is not a vice but a virtue, not
a weakness but a strength; if the hero is destroyed for his self-assertion, he is (they hold) nevertheless greater than the people around
him, just as the man who tries to stem a lynch mob is greater than the
mob although he too may be lynched for his virtue. Or a hero may be
undone by a highmindedness that makes him vulnerable. The noble
Othello is ultimately brought to death because the villainous Iago
knows that Othello "thinks men honest that but seem to be so."
     Next, here is a statement more or less the reverse of Tourneur's,
by a Soviet critic, L. I. Timofeev:

> Tragedy in Soviet literature arouses a feeling of pride for the man who
> has accomplished a great deed for the people's happiness; it calls for
> continued struggle against the things which brought about the hero's
> death.

The distortions in Soviet criticism are often amusing: Hamlet is sometimes seen as an incipient Communist, undone by the decadent
aristocracy; or Romeo and Juliet as young people of the future, undone by bourgeois parents. Recent Soviet drama so consistently
shows the triumph of the worker that Western visitors to Russia have

commented on the absence of contemporary tragic plays. Still, there is much in the idea that the tragic hero accomplishes "a great deed" and perhaps we do resent "the things which brought about the hero's death." The stubbornness of the Montagues and Capulets, the fury of the mob that turns against Brutus, the wickedness of Iago in *Othello* — all these would seem in some measure to call for our indignation.

The third comment is by Arthur Miller:

> If it is true to say that in essence the tragic hero is intent upon claiming his whole due as a personality, and if this struggle must be total and without reservation, then it automatically demonstrates the indestructible will of man to achieve his humanity. . . . It is curious, although edifying, that the plays we revere, century after century, are the tragedies. In them, and in them alone, lies the belief — optimistic, if you will — in the perfectibility of man.

There is much in Mr. Miller's suggestions that the tragic hero makes a large and total claim and that the audience often senses triumph rather than despair in tragedies. We often feel that we have witnessed human greatness — that the hero, despite profound suffering, has lived according to his ideals. We may feel that we have achieved new insight into human greatness. But the perfectibility of man? Do we feel that *Julius Caesar* or *Macbeth* or *Othello* have to do with human perfectibility? Don't these plays suggest rather that man, whatever his nobility, has within him the seeds of his own destruction? Without overstressing the guilt of the protagonists, don't we feel that in part the plays dramatize the *im*perfectibility of man? In much tragedy, after all, the destruction comes from within, not from without:

> In tragic life, God wot,
> No villain need be! Passions spin the plot:
> We are betrayed by what is false within.
> — George Meredith

Othello aims at justice when he kills Desdemona, but he performs an act of terrible injustice. What we are talking about is **tragic irony**, the contrast between what is believed to be so and what is so, or between expectations and accomplishments.* Several examples from *Macbeth*

---

* Tragic irony is sometimes called **dramatic irony** or **Sophoclean irony**. The terms are often applied to speeches or actions that the audience understands in a sense fuller than or different from the sense in which the dramatic characters understand them. It is tragically ironic, for example, that the rope that Bartley (in *Riders to the Sea*) uses as a bridle when he goes to sell the horses to help support the family will presumably be used to lower his coffin. Sim-

illustrate something of the range of tragic irony within a single play. In the first act, King Duncan bestows on Macbeth the title of Thane of Cawdor. By his kindness Duncan seals his own doom, for Macbeth, having achieved this rank, will next want to achieve a higher one. In the third act Macbeth, knowing that Banquo will soon be murdered, hypocritically urges Banquo to "fail not our feast." But Macbeth's hollow request is ironically fulfilled: the ghost of Banquo terrorizes Macbeth during the feast. The most pervasive irony of all, of course, is that Macbeth aims at happiness when he kills Duncan and takes the throne, but he wins only sorrow.

Aristotle's discussion of **peripeteia (reversal)** and **anagnorisis (recognition)** may be a way of getting at this sort of irony. He may simply have meant a reversal of fortune (for example, good luck ceases) and a recognition of who is who (for example, the pauper is really the prince), but more likely he meant profounder things. One can say that the reversal in *Macbeth* lies in the sorrow that Macbeth's increased power brings; the recognition comes when he realizes the consequences of his deeds:

> I have lived long enough: my way of life
> Is fall'n into the sere, the yellow leaf;
> And that which should accompany old age,
> As honor, love, obedience, troops of friends,
> I must not look to have; but, in their stead,
> Curses, not loud but deep, mouth-honor, breath
> Which the poor heart would fain deny, and dare not.

That a person's deeds often undo him, that a person aiming at his good can produce his ruin, was not, of course, a discovery of the tragic dramatists. The archetype is the story of Adam and Eve: these two aimed at becoming like God, and as a consequence they brought upon themselves corruption, death, the loss of their earthly paradise. The Bible is filled with stories of tragic irony. A brief quotation from Ecclesiastes (10 : 8–9) can stand as an epitome of these stories:

> He that diggeth a pit shall fall into it; and whoso breaketh an hedge,
> a serpent shall bite him.
> Whoso removeth stones shall be hurt therewith; and he that cleaveth wood shall be endangered thereby.

"He that cleaveth wood shall be endangered thereby." Activity involves danger. To be inactive is, often, to be ignoble, but to be active

---

ilarly, it is ironic that while Maurya is describing how Patch was carried in "in the half of a red sail, and water dripping out of it," Bartley is being carried to her door, "water dripping" from him, on a plank with "a bit of sail."

is necessarily to imperil oneself. Perhaps we can attempt a summary of tragic man: he acts, and he suffers, usually as a consequence of his action. The question is not of his action's being particularly bad (Tourneur's view), or particularly good (Timofeev's view); the action is often both good and bad, a sign of man's courage and also of his arrogance, a sign of man's greatness and also of his limitations.

Finally, a brief consideration of the pleasure of tragedy: Why do we enjoy plays about suffering? Aristotle has some obscure comments on **catharsis (purgation)** that are often interpreted as saying that tragedy arouses in us both pity and fear and then purges us of these emotions. The idea, perhaps, is that just as we can harmlessly discharge our aggressive impulses by witnessing a prize fight or by shouting at an umpire, so we can harmlessly discharge our impulses to pity and to fear by witnessing the dramatization of a man's destruction. The theater in this view is an outlet for emotions that elsewhere would be harmful. But, it must be repeated, Aristotle's comments on catharsis are obscure; perhaps, too, they are wrong. Most later theories on the pleasure of tragedy are footnotes to Aristotle's words on catharsis. Some say that our pleasure is sadistic (we enjoy the sight of suffering); some, that our pleasure is masochistic (we enjoy lacerating ourselves); some, that it lies in sympathy (we enjoy extending pity and benevolence to the wretched); some, that it lies in self-congratulation (we are reminded, when we see suffering, of our own good fortune); some, that we take pleasure in tragedy because the tragic hero acts out our secret desires, and we rejoice in his aggression, expiating our guilt in his suffering; and so on. But this is all rather uncertain psychology, and it mostly neglects the distinction between real suffering and dramatized suffering. In the latter, surely, part of the pleasure is in the contemplation of an esthetic object, an object that is unified and complete. The chaos of real life seems, for a few moments in drama, to be ordered: the protagonist's action, his subsequent suffering, and the total cosmos seem somehow related. Tragedy has no use for the passerby who is killed by a falling brick. The events (the man's walk, the brick's fall) have no meaningful relation. But suppose a man chooses to climb a mountain, and in making the ascent sets in motion an avalanche that destroys him. Here we find (however simple the illustration) something closer to tragedy. We do not say that men should avoid mountains, or that mountain-climbers deserve to die by avalanches. But we feel that the event is unified, as the accidental conjunction of brick and passerby is not. Tragedy thus presents some sort of ordered action; tragic drama itself is orderly. As we see or read it we feel it cannot be otherwise; word begets word, deed begets deed, and every moment is exquisitely appropriate. Whatever the relevance of sadism, masochism, sympathy, and the rest, the pleasure of tragedy surely comes in part from the artistic shaping of the material.

A NOTE ON GREEK TRAGEDY

Little or nothing is known for certain of the origin of Greek tragedy. The most common hypothesis holds that it developed from improvised speeches during choral dances honoring Dionysus, a Greek nature god associated with spring, fertility, and wine. Thespis (who perhaps never existed) is said to have introduced an actor into these choral performances in the sixth century B.C. Aeschylus (525–456 B.C.), Greece's first great writer of tragedies, added the second actor, and Sophocles (496?–406 B.C.) added the third actor and fixed the size of the chorus at fifteen. (Because the chorus leader often functioned as an additional actor, and because the actors sometimes doubled in their parts, a Greek tragedy could have more characters than might at first be thought.)

All of the extant great Greek tragedy is of the fifth century B.C. It was performed at religious festivals in the winter and early spring, in large outdoor amphitheaters built on hillsides. Some of these theaters were enormous; the one at Epidaurus held about fifteen thousand people. The audience sat in tiers, looking down on the **orchestra** (a dancing place), with the acting area behind it and the **skene** (the scene building) yet farther back. The scene building served as dressing room, background (suggesting a palace or temple), and place for occasional entrances and exits. Furthermore, this building helped to provide good acoustics, for speech travels well if there is a solid barrier behind the speaker and a hard, smooth surface in front of him, and if the audience sits in tiers. The wall of the scene building provided the barrier; the orchestra provided the surface in front of the actors; and the seats on the hillside fulfilled the third requirement. Moreover, the acoustics were somewhat improved by slightly elevating the actors above the orchestra, but it is not known exactly when this platform was first constructed in front of the scene building.

A tragedy commonly begins with a **prologos** (prologue), during which the exposition is given. Next comes the **parodos,** the chorus's ode of entrance, sung while the chorus marches into the theater, down the side aisles and onto the orchestra. The **epeisodion** (episode) is the ensuing scene; it is followed by a **stasimon** (choral song, ode). Usually there are four or five **epeisodia,** alternating with **stasima.** Each of these choral odes has a **strophe** (lines presumably sung while the chorus dances in one direction) and an **antistrophe** (lines presumably sung while the chorus retraces its steps). Sometimes a third part, an **epode,** concludes an ode. (In addition to odes that are

stasima, there can be odes within episodes; the fourth episode of
Antigonê contains an ode complete with *epode.*) After the last part of
the last ode comes the **exodos,** the epilogue or final scene.
The actors (all male) wore masks, and seem to have chanted much
of the play. Perhaps the total result of combining speech with music
and dancing was a sort of music-drama roughly akin to opera with
some spoken dialogue, such as Mozart's *Magic Flute.*

Sophocles (496?–406 B.C.)

Antigonê

An English Version by Dudley Fitts and Robert Fitzgerald

List of Characters

Antigonê
Ismenê
Eurydicê
Creon
Haimon
Teiresias
A Sentry
A Messenger
Chorus

Scene. *Before the palace of Creon, King of Thebes. A central
double door, and two lateral doors. A platform extends the length
of the façade, and from this platform three steps lead down into
the "orchestra," or chorus-ground.*

Time. *Dawn of the day after the repulse of the Argive army
from the assault on Thebes.*

PROLOGUE

Antigonê and Ismenê enter from the central door of the palace.

Antigonê. Ismenê, dear sister,
     You would think that we had already suffered enough
     For the curse on Oedipus:°

Prologue. ³ (Oedipus, once King of Thebes, was the father of Antigonê and
Ismenê, and of their brothers Polyneicês and Eteoclês. Oedipus unwittingly

I cannot imagine any grief
That you and I have not gone through. And now —   5
Have they told you of the new decree of our King Creon?
Ismenê. I have heard nothing: I know
That two sisters lost two brothers, a double death
In a single hour; and I know that the Argive army
Fled in the night; but beyond this, nothing.   10
Antigonê. I thought so. And that is why I wanted you
To come out here with me. There is something we must do.
Ismenê. Why do you speak so strangely?
Antigonê. Listen, Ismenê:
Creon buried our brother Eteoclês   15
With military honors, gave him a soldier's funeral,
And it was right that he should; but Polyneicês,
Who fought as bravely and died as miserably, —
They say that Creon has sworn
No one shall bury him, no one mourn for him,   20
But his body must lie in the fields, a sweet treasure
For carrion birds to find as they search for food.
That is what they say, and our good Creon is coming here
To announce it publicly; and the penalty —
Stoning to death in the public square!
                          There it is,   25
And now you can prove what you are:
A true sister, or a traitor to your family.
Ismenê. Antigonê, you are mad! What could I possibly do?
Antigonê. You must decide whether you will help me or not.
Ismenê. I do not understand you. Help you in what?   30
Antigonê. Ismenê, I am going to bury him. Will you come?
Ismenê. Bury him! You have just said the new law forbids it.
Antigonê. He is my brother. And he is your brother, too.
Ismenê. But think of the danger! Think what Creon will do!
Antigonê. Creon is not strong enough to stand in my way.   35
Ismenê. Ah sister!
Oedipus died, everyone hating him
For what his own search brought to light, his eyes
Ripped out by his own hand; and Iocastê died,
His mother and wife at once: she twisted the cords   40

---

killed his father, Laïos, and married his own mother, Iocastê. When he
learned what he had done, he blinded himself and left Thebes. Eteoclês and
Polyneicês quarreled; Polyneicês was driven out but returned to assault
Thebes. In the battle each brother killed the other; Creon became king
and ordered that Polyneicês be left to rot unburied on the battlefield as a
traitor).

That strangled her life; and our two brothers died,
Each killed by the other's sword. And we are left:
But oh, Antigonê,
Think how much more terrible than these
Our own death would be if we should go against Creon   45
And do what he has forbidden! We are only women,
We cannot fight with men, Antigonê!
The law is strong, we must give in to the law
In this thing, and in worse. I beg the Dead
To forgive me, but I am helpless: I must yield   50
To those in authority. And I think it is dangerous business
To be always meddling.

Antigonê.   If that is what you think,
I should not want you, even if you asked to come.
You have made your choice, you can be what you want to be.
But I will bury him; and if I must die,   55
I say that this crime is holy: I shall lie down
With him in death, and I shall be as dear
To him as he to me.
           It is the dead,
Not the living, who make the longest demands:
We die for ever . . .
           You may do as you like,   60
Since apparently the laws of the gods mean nothing to you.

Ismenê. They mean a great deal to me; but I have no strength
To break laws that were made for the public good.

Antigonê. That must be your excuse, I suppose. But as for me,
I will bury the brother I love.

Ismenê.   Antigonê,   65
I am so afraid for you!

Antigonê.   You need not be:
You have yourself to consider, after all.

Ismenê. But no one must hear of this, you must tell no one!
I will keep it a secret, I promise!

Antigonê.   O tell it! Tell everyone!
Think how they'll hate you when it all comes out   70
If they learn that you knew about it all the time!

Ismenê. So fiery! You should be cold with fear.

Antigonê. Perhaps. But I am doing only what I must.

Ismenê. But can you do it? I say that you cannot.

Antigonê. Very well: when my strength gives out,
     I shall do no more.   75

Ismenê. Impossible things should not be tried at all.

Antigonê. Go away, Ismenê:

I shall be hating you soon, and the dead will too,
For your words are hateful. Leave me my foolish plan:
I am not afraid of the danger; if it means death,   80
It will not be the worst of deaths — death without honor.
Ismenê. Go then, if you feel that you must.
You are unwise,
But a loyal friend indeed to those who love you.

Exit into the palace. Antigonê goes off, left. Enter the Chorus.

PÁRODOS

Chorus. Now the long blade of the sun, lying   *Strophe 1*
      Level east to west, touches with glory
      Thebes of the Seven Gates. Open, unlidded
      Eye of golden day! O marching light
      Across the eddy and rush of Dircê's stream,°   5
      Striking the white shields of the enemy
      Thrown headlong backward from the blaze of morning!
Choragos.° Polyneicês their commander
      Roused them with windy phrases,
      He the wild eagle screaming   10
      Insults above our land,
      His wings their shields of snow,
      His crest their marshalled helms.

Chorus. Against our seven gates in a yawning ring   *Antistrophe 1*
      The famished spears came onward in the night;   15
      But before his jaws were sated with our blood,
      Or pinefire took the garland of our towers,
      He was thrown back; and as he turned, great Thebes —
      No tender victim for his noisy power —
      Rose like a dragon behind him, shouting war.   20
Choragos. For God hates utterly
      The bray of bragging tongues;
      And when he beheld their smiling,
      Their swagger of golden helms,
      The frown of his thunder blasted   25
      Their first man from our walls.

Párodos. ⁵ *Dircê's stream* a stream west of Thebes   ⁸ *Choragos* leader of the
Chorus

Chorus. We heard his shout of triumph high in the air   *Strophe 2*
        Turn to a scream; far out in a flaming arc
        He fell with his windy torch, and the earth struck him.
        And others storming in fury no less than his   30
        Found shock of death in the dusty joy of battle.
Choragos. Seven captains at seven gates
        Yielded their clanging arms to the god
        That bends the battle-line and breaks it
        These two only, brothers in blood,   35
        Face to face in matchless rage,
        Mirroring each the other's death,
        Clashed in long combat.

Chorus. But now in the beautiful morning of victory   *Antistrophe 2*
        Let Thebes of the many chariots sing for joy!   40
        With hearts for dancing we'll take leave of war:
        Our temples shall be sweet with hymns of praise,
        And the long nights shall echo with our chorus.

SCENE I

Choragos. But now at last our new King is coming:
        Creon of Thebes, Menoikeus' son.
        In this auspicious dawn of his reign
        What are the new complexities
        That shifting Fate has woven for him?   5
        What is his counsel? Why has he summoned
        The old men to hear him?

        *Enter Creon from the palace, center. He addresses the Chorus
        from the top step.*

Creon. Gentlemen: I have the honor to inform you that our
        Ship of State, which recent storms have threatened to des-
        troy, has come safely to harbor at last, guided by the merciful   10
        wisdom of Heaven. I have summoned you here this morning
        because I know that I can depend upon you: your devotion to
        King Laïos was absolute; you never hesitated in your duty to
        our late ruler Oedipus; and when Oedipus died, your loyalty
        was transferred to his children. Unfortunately, as you know,   15
        his two sons, the princes Eteoclês and Polyneicês, have
        killed each other in battle; and I, as the next in blood, have
        succeeded to the full power of the throne.
            I am aware, of course, that no Ruler can expect complete
        loyalty from his subjects until he has been tested in office.   20

Nevertheless, I say to you at the very outset that I have nothing but contempt for the kind of Governor who is afraid, for whatever reason, to follow the course that he knows is best for the State; and as for the man who sets private friendship above the public welfare, — I have no use for him, either. I 25
call God to witness that if I saw my country headed for ruin, I should not be afraid to speak out plainly; and I need hardly remind you that I would never have any dealings with an enemy of the people. No one values friendship more highly than I; but we must remember that friends made at the risk of 30
wrecking our Ship are not real friends at all.

These are my principles, at any rate, and that is why I have made the following decision concerning the sons of Oedipus: Eteoclês, who died as a man should die, fighting for his country, is to be buried with full military honors, with all the 35
ceremony that is usual when the greatest heroes die; but his brother Polyneicês, who broke his exile to come back with fire and sword against his native city and the shrines of his fathers' gods, whose one idea was to spill the blood of his blood and sell his own people into slavery — Polyneicês, I 40
say, is to have no burial: no man is to touch him or say the least prayer for him; he shall lie on the plain, unburied; and the birds and the scavenging dogs can do with him whatever they like.

This is my command, and you can see the wisdom behind 45
it. As long as I am King, no traitor is going to be honored with the loyal man. But whoever shows by word and deed that he is on the side of the State, — he shall have my respect while he is living and my reverence when he is dead.

Choragos. If that is your will, Creon son of Menoikeus, 50
    You have the right to enforce it: we are yours.
Creon. That is my will. Take care that you do your part.
Choragos. We are old men: let the younger ones carry it out.
Creon. I do not mean that: the sentries have been appointed.
Choragos. Then what is it that you would have us do? 55
Creon. You will give no support to whoever breaks this law.
Choragos. Only a crazy man is in love with death!
Creon. And death it is; yet money talks, and the wisest
    Have sometimes been known to count a few coins too many.

Enter Sentry from left.

Sentry. I'll not say that I'm out of breath from running, King, 60
    because every time I stopped to think about what I have to
    tell you, I felt like going back. And all the time a voice kept

saying, "You fool, don't you know you're walking straight into
trouble?"; and then another voice: "Yes, but if you let somebody else get the news to Creon first, it will be even worse   65
than that for you!" But good sense won out, at least I hope it
was good sense, and here I am with a story that makes no
sense at all; but I'll tell it anyhow, because, as they say,
what's going to happen's going to happen and —
Creon.   Come to the point. What have you to say?   70
Sentry.   I did not do it. I did not see who did it. You must not punish
   me for what someone else has done.
Creon.   A comprehensive defense! More effective, perhaps,
   If I knew its purpose. Come: what is it?
Sentry: A dreadful thing . . . I don't know how to put it —   75
Creon.   Out with it!
Sentry.   Well, then;
   The dead man —
                      Polyneicês —

*Pause. The Sentry is overcome, fumbles for words. Creon waits
impassively.*

                         out there —
                                        someone, —
New dust on the slimy flesh!

Pause. No sign from Creon.

Someone has given it burial that way, and   80
Gone . . .

Long pause. Creon finally speaks with deadly control.

Creon.   And the man who dared do this?
Sentry.   I swear I
   Do not know! You must believe me!
                                        Listen:
   The ground was dry, not a sign of digging, no,
   Not a wheeltrack in the dust, no trace of anyone.   85
   It was when they relieved us this morning: and one of them,
   The corporal, pointed to it.
                            There it was,
   The strangest —
              Look:
   The body, just mounded over with light dust: you see?
   Not buried really, but as if they'd covered it   90

Just enough for the ghost's peace. And no sign
Of dogs or any wild animal that had been there.

And then what a scene there was! Every man of us
Accusing the other: we all proved the other man did it,
We all had proof that we could not have done it.   95
We were ready to take hot iron in our hands,
Walk through fire, swear by all the gods,
It was not I!
I do not know who it was, but it was not I!

*Creon's rage has been mounting steadily, but the Sentry is too
intent upon his story to notice it.*

And then, when this came to nothing, someone said   100
A thing that silenced us and made us stare
Down at the ground: you had to be told the news,
And one of us had to do it! We threw the dice,
And the bad luck fell to me. So here I am,
No happier to be here than you are to have me: 105
Nobody likes the man who brings bad news.
Choragos. I have been wondering, King: can it be that the
       gods have done this?
Creon (furiously). Stop!
Must you doddering wrecks   110
Go out of your heads entirely? "The gods"!
Intolerable!
The gods favor this corpse? Why? How had he served them?
Tried to loot their temples, burn their images,
Yes, and the whole State, and its laws with it!   115
Is it your senile opinion that the gods love to honor bad men?
A pious thought! —
                    No, from the very beginning
There have been those who have whispered together,
Stiff-necked anarchists, putting their heads together,
Scheming against me in alleys. These are the men,   120
And they have bribed my own guard to do this thing.
(Sententiously.) Money!
There's nothing in the world so demoralizing as money.
Down go your cities,
Homes gone, men gone, honest hearts corrupted,   125
Crookedness of all kinds, and all for money!
(To Sentry.)   But you — !
I swear by God and by the throne of God,
The man who has done this thing shall pay for it!

Find that man, bring him here to me, or your death
Will be the least of your problems: I'll string you up   130
Alive, and there will be certain ways to make you
Discover your employer before you die;
And the process may teach you a lesson you seem to have missed:
The dearest profit is sometimes all too dear:
That depends on the source. Do you understand me?   135
A fortune won is often misfortune.
Sentry. King, may I speak?
Creon.   Your very voice distresses me.
Sentry. Are you sure that it is my voice, and not your conscience?
Creon. By God, he wants to analyze me now!
Sentry. It is not what I say, but what has been done, that hurts
    you.   140
Creon. You talk too much.
Sentry.   Maybe; but I've done nothing.
Creon. Sold your soul for some silver: that's all you've done.
Sentry. How dreadful it is when the right judge judges wrong!
Creon. Your figures of speech
    May entertain you now; but unless you bring me the man,   145
You will get little profit from them in the end.

Exit Creon into the palace.

Sentry. "Bring me the man" — !
    I'd like nothing better than bringing him the man!
But bring him or not, you have seen the last of me here.
At any rate, I am safe!   *(Exit Sentry.)* 150

ODE I

Chorus. Numberless are the world's wonders, but none   *Strophe 1*
    More wonderful than man; the stormgray sea
Yields to his prows, the huge crests bear him high;
Earth, holy and inexhaustible, is graven
With shining furrows where his plows have gone   5
Year after year, the timeless labor of stallions.

The lightboned birds and beasts that cling to cover,   *Antistrophe 1*
The lithe fish lighting their reaches of dim water,
All are taken, tamed in the net of his mind;
The lion on the hill, the wild horse windy-maned,   10
Resign to him; and his blunt yoke has broken
The sultry shoulders of the mountain bull.

Words also, and thought as rapid as air, *Strophe* 2
He fashions to his good use; statecraft is his,
And his the skill that deflects the arrows of snow, 15
The spears of winter rain: from every wind
He has made himself secure — from all but one:
In the late wind of death he cannot stand.

O clear intelligence, force beyond all measure! *Antistrophe* 2
O fate of man, working both good and evil! 20
When the laws are kept, how proudly his city stands!
When the laws are broken, what of his city then?
Never may the anárchic man find rest at my hearth,
Never be it said that my thought are his thoughts.

SCENE II

Re-enter Sentry leading Antigonê.

Choragos. What does this mean? Surely this captive woman
Is the Princess, Antigonê. Why should she be taken?
Sentry. Here is the one who did it! We caught her
In the very act of burying him. — Where is Creon?
Choragos. Just coming from the house.

Enter Creon, center.

Creon.
What has happened? 5
Why have you come back so soon?
Sentry (expansively).
O King,
A man should never be too sure of anything:
I would have sworn
That you'd not see me here again: your anger
Frightened me so, and the things you threatened me with; 10
But how could I tell then
That I'd be able to solve the case so soon?
No dice-throwing this time: I was only too glad to come!
Here is this woman. She is the guilty one:
We found her trying to bury him. 15
Take her, then; question her; judge her as you will.
I am through with the whole thing now, and glád óf it.
Creon. But this is Antigonê! Why have you brought her here?
Sentry. She was burying him, I tell you!
Creon (severely). Is this the truth?

Sentry. I saw her with my own eyes. Can I say more? 20
Creon. The details: come, tell me quickly!
Sentry. It was like this:
After those terrible threats of yours, King,
We went back and brushed the dust away from the body.
The flesh was soft by now, and stinking,
So we sat on a hill to windward and kept guard. 25
No napping this time! We kept each other awake.
But nothing happened until the white round sun
Whirled in the center of the round sky over us:
Then, suddenly,
A storm of dust roared up from the earth, and the sky 30
Went out, the plain vanished with all its trees
In the stinging dark. We closed our eyes and endured it.
The whirlwind lasted a long time, but it passed;
And then we looked, and there was Antigonê!
I have seen 35
A mother bird come back to a stripped nest, heard
Her crying bitterly a broken note or two
For the young ones stolen. Just so, when this girl
Found the bare corpse, and all her love's work wasted,
She wept, and cried on heaven to damn the hands 40
That had done this thing.
                          And then she brought more dust
And sprinkled wine three times for her brother's ghost.

We ran and took her at once. She was not afraid,
Not even when we charged her with what she had done.
She denied nothing.
                    And this was a comfort to me, 45
And some uneasiness: for it is a good thing
To escape from death, but it is no great pleasure
To bring death to a friend.
                            Yet I always say
There is nothing so comfortable as your own safe skin!
Creon (slowly, dangerously). And you, Antigonê, 50
You with your head hanging, — do you confess this thing?
Antigonê. I do. I deny nothing.
Creon (to Sentry).
                          You may go.   *Exit Sentry.*
  (To Antigonê.) Tell me, tell me briefly:
Had you heard my proclamation touching this matter?
Antigonê. It was public. Could I help hearing it? 55
Creon. And yet you dared defy the law.

Antigonê. I dared.
It was not God's proclamation. That final Justice
That rules the world below makes no such laws.

Your edict, King, was strong,
But all your strength is weakness itself against 60
The immortal unrecorded laws of God.
They are not merely now: they were, and shall be,
Operative for ever, beyond man utterly.

I knew I must die, even without your decree:
I am only mortal. And if I must die 65
Now, before it is my time to die,
Surely this is no hardship: can anyone
Living, as I live, with evil all about me,
Think Death less than a friend? This death of mine
Is of no importance; but if I had left my brother 70
Lying in death unburied, I should have suffered.
Now I do not.
                    You smile at me. Ah Creon,
Think me a fool, if you like; but it may well be
That a fool convicts me of folly.
Choragos. Like father, like daughter: both headstrong,
        deaf to reason! 75
She has never learned to yield:
Creon.   She has much to learn.
The inflexible heart breaks first, the toughest iron
Cracks first, and the wildest horses bend their necks
At the pull of the smallest curb.
                        Pride? In a slave?
This girl is guilty of a double insolence, 80
Breaking the given laws and boasting of it.
Who is the man here,
She or I, if this crime goes unpunished?
Sister's child, or more than sister's child,
Or closer yet in blood — she and her sister 85
Win bitter death for this!

(To Servants.)   Go, some of you,
Arrest Ismenê. I accuse her equally.
Bring her: you will find her sniffling in the house there.

Her mind's a traitor: crimes kept in the dark
Cry for light, and the guardian brain shudders; 90
But how much worse than this
Is brazen boasting of barefaced anarchy!

Antigonê. Creon, what more do you want than my death?
Creon.   Nothing.
    That gives me everything.
Antigonê.   Then I beg you: kill me.
    This talking is a great weariness: your words   95
    Are distasteful to me, and I am sure that mine
    Seem so to you. And yet they should not seem so:
    I should have praise and honor for what I have done.
    All these men here would praise me
    Were their lips not frozen shut with fear of you.   100
    (Bitterly.) Ah the good fortune of kings,
    Licensed to say and do whatever they please!
Creon. You are alone here in that opinion.
Antigonê. No, they are with me. But they keep
    their tongues in leash.
Creon. Maybe. But you are guilty, and they are not.   105
Antigonê. There is no guilt in reverence for the dead.
Creon. But Eteoclês — was he not your brother too?
Antigonê. My brother too.
Creon.   And you insult his memory?
Antigonê (softly). The dead man would not say that I insult it.
Creon. He would: for you honor a traitor as much as him.   110
Antigonê. His own brother, traitor or not, and equal in blood.
Creon. He made war on his country. Eteoclês defended it.
Antigonê. Nevertheless, there are honors due all the dead.
Creon. But not the same for the wicked as for the just.
Antigonê. Ah Creon, Creon,   115
    Which of us can say what the gods hold wicked?
Creon. An enemy is an enemy, even dead.
Antigonê. It is my nature to join in love, not hate.
Creon (finally losing patience). Go join them then; if you must
        have your love,
    Find it in hell!   120
Choragos. But see, Ismenê comes:

    Enter Ismenê, guarded.

    Those tears are sisterly, the cloud
    That shadows her eyes rains down gentle sorrow.
Creon. You too, Ismenê,
    Snake in my ordered house, sucking my blood   125
    Stealthily — and all the time I never knew
    That these two sisters were aiming at my throne!
                                                        Ismenê,
    Do you confess your share in this crime, or deny it?
    Answer me.

Ismenê. Yes, if she will let me say so. I am guilty.   130
Antigonê (coldly). No, Ismenê. You have no right to say so.
    You would not help me, and I will not have you help me.
Ismenê. But now I know what you meant; and I am here
    To join you, to take my share of punishment.
Antigonê. The dead man and the gods who rule the dead   135
    Know whose act this was. Words are not friends.
Ismenê. Do you refuse me, Antigonê? I want to die with you:
    I too have a duty that I must discharge to the dead.
Antigonê. You shall not lessen my death by sharing it.
Ismenê. What do I care for life when you are dead?   140
Antigonê. Ask Creon. You're always hanging on his opinions.
Ismenê. You are laughing at me. Why, Antigonê?
Antigonê. It's a joyless laughter, Ismenê.
Ismenê.   But can I do nothing?
Antigonê. Yes. Save yourself. I shall not envy you.
    There are those who will praise you; I shall have honor, too.   145
Ismenê. But we are equally guilty!
Antigonê.   No more, Ismenê.
    You are alive, but I belong to Death.
Creon (to the Chorus). Gentlemen, I beg you to observe these
        girls:
    One has just now lost her mind; the other,
    It seems, has never had a mind at all.   150
Ismenê. Grief teaches the steadiest minds to waver, King.
Creon. Yours certainly did, when you assumed guilt
        with the guilty!
Ismenê. But how could I go on living without her?
Creon.   You are.
    She is already dead.
Ismenê.   But your own son's bride!
Creon. There are places enough for him to push his plow.   155
    I want no wicked women for my sons!
Ismenê. O dearest Haimon, how your father wrongs you!
Creon. I've had enough of your childish talk of marriage!
Choragos. Do you really intend to steal this girl from your son?
Creon. No; Death will do that for me.
Choragos.   Then she must die?   160
Creon (ironically). You dazzle me.
                                — But enough of this talk!
    (To Guards.) You, there, take them away and guard them well:
    For they are but women, and even brave men run
    When they see Death coming.

                            Exeunt Ismenê, Antigonê, and Guards.

ODE II

Chorus. Fortunate is the man who has never
       tasted God's vengeance!   *Strophe 1*
Where once the anger of heaven has struck, that house is shaken
For ever: damnation rises behind each child
Like a wave cresting out of the black northeast,
When the long darkness under sea roars up   5
And bursts drumming death upon the windwhipped sand.

I have seen this gathering sorrow from time long
       past   *Antistrophe 1*
Loom upon Oedipus' children: generation from generation
Takes the compulsive rage of the enemy god.
So lately this last flower of Oedipus' line   10
Drank the sunlight! but now a passionate word
And a handful of dust have closed up all its beauty.

    What mortal arrogance   *Strophe 2*
    Transcends the wrath of Zeus?
Sleep cannot lull him nor the effortless long months   15
Of the timeless gods: but he is young for ever,
And his house is the shining day of high Olympos.
    All that is and shall be,
    And all the past, is his.
No pride on earth is free of the curse of heaven.   20

The straying dreams of men   *Antistrophe 2*
    May bring them ghosts of joy:
But as they drowse, the waking embers burn them;
Or they walk with fixed éyes, as blind men walk.
But the ancient wisdom speaks for our own time: 25
    Fate works most for woe
    With Folly's fairest show.
Man's little pleasure is the spring of sorrow.

SCENE III

Choragos. But here is Haimon, King, the last of all your sons.
    Is it grief for Antigonê that brings him here,
    And bitterness at being robbed of his bride?

    Enter Haimon.

Creon. We shall soon see, and no need of diviners.
                                                   — Son,

You have heard my final judgment on that girl: 5
Have you come here hating me, or have you come
With deference and with love, whatever I do?
Haimon. I am your son, father. You are my guide.
You make things clear for me, and I obey you.
No marriage means more to me than your continuing wisdom.   10
Creon. Good. That is the way to behave: subordinate
Everything else, my son, to your father's will.
This is what a man prays for, that he may get
Sons attentive and dutiful in his house,
Each one hating his father's enemies.   15
Honoring his father's friends. But if his sons
Fail him, if they turn out unprofitably,
What has he fathered but trouble for himself
And amusement for the malicious?
                                 So you are right
Not to lose your head over this woman.   20
Your pleasure with her would soon grow cold, Haimon,
And then you'd have a hell cat in bed and elsewhere.
Let her find her husband in Hell!
Of all the people in this city, only she
Has had contempt for my law and broken it.   25

Do you want me to show myself weak before the people?
Or to break my sworn word? No, and I will not.
The woman dies.
I suppose she'll plead "family ties." Well, let her.
If I permit my own family to rebel,   30
How shall I earn the world's obedience?
Show me the man who keeps his house in hand,
He's fit for public authority.
                          I'll have no dealings
With law-breakers, critics of the government:
Whoever is chosen to govern should be obeyed —   35
Must be obeyed, in all things, great and small,
Just and unjust! O Haimon,
The man who knows how to obey, and that man only,
Knows how to give commands when the time comes.
You can depend on him, no matter how fast   40
The spears come: he's a good soldier, he'll stick it out.

Anarchy, anarchy! Show me a greater evil!
This is why cities tumble and the great houses rain down,
This is what scatters armies!

No, no: good lives are made so by discipline.   45
We keep the laws then, and the lawmakers,
And no woman shall seduce us. If we must lose,
Let's lose to a man, at least! Is a woman stronger than we?
Choragos. Unless time has rusted my wits,
What you say, King, is said with point and dignity.   50
Haimon (boyishly earnest). Father:
Reason is God's crowning gift to man, and you are right
To warn me against losing mine. I cannot say —
I hope that I shall never want to say! — that you
Have reasoned badly. Yet there are other men   55
Who can reason, too; and their opinions might be helpful.
You are not in a position to know everything
That people say or do, or what they feel:
Your temper terrifies — everyone
Will tell you only what you like to hear.   60
But I, at any rate, can listen; and I have heard them
Muttering and whispering in the dark about this girl.
They say no woman has ever, so unreasonably,
Died so shameful a death for a generous act:
"She covered her brother's body. Is this indecent?   65
She kept him from dogs and vultures. Is this a crime?
Death? — She should have all the honor that we can give her?"

This is the way they talk out there in the city.

You must believe me:
Nothing is closer to me than your happiness.   70
What could be closer? Must not any son
Value his father's fortune as his father does his?
I beg you, do not be unchangeable:
Do not believe that you alone can be right.
The man who thinks that,   75
The man who maintains that only he has the power
To reason correctly, the gift to speak, the soul —
A man like that, when you know him, turns out empty.

It is not reason never to yield to reason!

In flood time you can see how some trees bend,   80
And because they bend, even their twigs are safe,
While stubborn trees are torn up, roots and all.
And the same thing happens in sailing:
Make your sheet fast, never slacken, — and over you go,
Head over heels and under: and there's your voyage.   85

Forget you are angry! Let yourself be moved!
I know I am young; but please let me say this:
The ideal condition
Would be, I admit, that men should be right by instinct;
But since we are all too likely to go astray,   90
The reasonable thing is to learn from those who can teach.
Choragos. You will do well to listen to him, King,
   If what he says is sensible. And you, Haimon,
   Must listen to your father. — Both speak well.
Créon. You consider it right for a man of my years
         and experience   95
   To go to school to a boy?
Haimon.   It is not right
   If I am wrong. But if I am young, and right,
   What does my age matter?
Creon. You think it right to stand up for an anarchist?
Haimon. Not at all. I pay no respect to criminals.   100
Creon. Then she is not a criminal?
Haimon. The City would deny it, to a man.
Creon. And the City proposes to teach me how to rule?
Haimon. Ah. Who is it that's talking like a boy now?
Creon. My voice is the one voice giving orders in this City!   105
Haimon. It is no City if it takes orders from one voice.
Creon. The State is the King!
Haimon.   Yes, if the State is a desert.

   Pause.

Creon. This boy, it seems, has sold out to a woman.
Haimon. If you are a woman: my concern is only for you.
Creon. So? Your "concern"! In a public brawl with your father!   110
Haimon. How about you, in a public brawl with justice?
Creon. With justice, when all that I do is within my rights?
Haimon. You have no right to trample on God's right.
Creon (completely out of control). Fool, adolescent fool! Taken
         in by a woman!
Haimon. You'll never see me taken in by anything vile.   115
Creon. Every word you say is for her!
Haimon (quietly, darkly).   And for you.
   And for me. And for the gods under the earth.
Creon. You'll never marry her while she lives.
Haimon. Then she must die. — But her death will cause another.
Creon. Another?   120
   Have you lost your senses? Is this an open threat?

Haimon. There is no threat in speaking to emptiness.
Creon. I swear you'll regret this superior tone of yours!
   You are the empty one!
Haimon.   If you were not my father,
   I'd say you were perverse.   125
Creon. You girlstruck fool, don't play at words with me!
Haimon. I am sorry. You prefer silence.
Creon.   Now, by God — !
   I swear, by all the gods in heaven above us,
   You'll watch it, I swear you shall!
   (To the Servants.)   Bring her out!
   Bring the woman out! Let her die before his eyes!   130
   Here, this instant, with her bridegroom beside her!
Haimon. Not here, no; she will not die here, King.
   And you will never see my face again.
   Go on raving as long as you've a friend to endure you. *Exit Haimon.*
Choragos. Gone, gone.   135
   Creon, a young man in a rage is dangerous!
Creon. Let him do, or dream to do, more than a man can.
   He shall not save these girls from death.
Choragos.   These girls?
   You have sentenced them both?
Creon.   No, you are right.
   I will not kill the one whose hands are clean.   140
Choragos. But Antigonê?
Creon (somberly).   I will carry her far away
   Out there in the wilderness, and lock her
   Living in a vault of stone. She shall have food,
   As the custom is, to absolve the State of her death.
   And there let her pray to the gods of hell: 145
   They are her only gods:
   Perhaps they will show her an escape from death,
   Or she may learn,
         though late,
   That piety shown the dead is pity in vain.   *(Exit Creon.)*

ODE III

Chorus. Love, unconquerable   *Strophe*
   Waster of rich men, keeper
   Of warm lights and all-night vigil
   In the soft face of a girl:
   Sea-wanderer, forest-visitor!   5

Even the pure Immortals cannot escape you,
And mortal man, in his one day's dusk,
Trembles before your glory.

Surely you swerve upon ruin   *Antistrophe*
The just man's consenting heart,   10
As here you have made bright anger
Strike between father and son —
And none has conquered but Love!
A girl's glánce wórking the will of heaven:
Pleasure to her alone who mocks us,   15
Merciless Aphroditê.°

SCENE IV

Choragos (as Antigonê enters guarded). But I can no longer
    stand in awe of this,
  Nor, seeing what I see, keep back my tears.
  Here is Antigonê, passing to that chamber
  Where all find sleep at last.

Antigonê. Look upon me, friends, and pity me   *Strophe 1* 5
  Turning back at the night's edge to say
  Good-by to the sun that shines for me no longer;
  Now sleepy Death
  Summons me down to Acheron,° that cold shore:
  There is no bridesong there, nor any music.   10
Chorus. Yet not unpraised, not without a kind of honor,
  You walk at last into the underworld;
  Untouched by sickness, broken by no sword.
  What woman has ever found your way to death?

Antigonê. How often I have heard the story of Niobê,° *Antistrophe 1* 15
  Tantalos' wretched daughter, how the stone
  Clung fast about her, ivy-close: and they say
  The rain falls endlessly
  And sifting soft snow; her tears are never done.
  I feel the loneliness of her death in mine.   20
Chorus. But she was born of heaven, and you
  Are woman, woman-born. If her death is yours,

Ode III. [16] **Aphroditê** goddess of love   Scene IV. [9] **Acheron** a river of the
underworld, which was ruled by Hades   [15] **Niobê** (Niobê boasted of her
numerous children, provoking Leto, the mother of Apollo, to destroy them.
Niobê wept profusely, and finally was turned into a stone on Mount Sipylus,
whose streams are her tears)

A mortal woman's, is this not for you
Glory in our world and in the world beyond?

Antigonê. You laugh at me. Ah, friends, friends,   *Strophe 2*   25
Can you not wait until I am dead? O Thebes,
O men many-charioted, in love with Fortune,
Dear springs of Dircê, sacred Theban grove,
Be witnesses for me, denied all pity,
Unjustly judged! and think a word of love   30
For her whose path turns
Under dark earth, where there are no more tears.

Chorus. You have passed beyond human daring and come at last
Into a place of stone where Justice sits.
I cannot tell   35
What shape of your father's guilt appears in this.

Antigonê. You have touched it at last:
             that bridal bed   *Antistrophe 2*
Unspeakable, horror of son and mother mingling:
Their crime, infection of all our family!
O Oedipus, father and brother!   40
Your marriage strikes from the grave to murder mine.
I have been a stranger here in my own land:
All my life
The blasphemy of my birth has followed me.

Chorus. Reverence is a virtue, but strength   45
Lives in established law: that must prevail.
You have made your choice,
Your death is the doing of your conscious hand.

Antigonê. Then let me go, since all your words are bitter,   *Epode*
And the very light of the sun is cold to me.   50
Lead me to my vigil, where I must have
Neither love nor lamentation; no song, but silence.

   Creon interrupts impatiently.

Creon. If dirges and planned lamentations could put off death,
Men would be singing for ever.
(To the Servants.)   Take her, go!
You know your orders: take her to the vault   55
And leave her alone there. And if she lives or dies,
That's her affair, not ours: our hands are clean.

Antigonê. O tomb, vaulted bride-bed in eternal rock,
Soon I shall be with my own again
Where Persephonê° welcomes the thin ghosts underground: 60

---

⁶⁰ *Persephonê* queen of the underworld

And I shall see my father again, and you, mother,
And dearest Polyneicês —
                              dearest indeed
To me, since it was my hand
That washed him clean and poured the ritual wine:
And my reward is death before my time!   65

And yet, as men's hearts know, I have done no wrong,
I have not sinned before God. Or if I have,
I shall know the truth in death. but if the guilt
Lies upon Creon who judged me, then, I pray,
May his punishment equal my own.
Choragos.   O passionate heart,   70
Unyielding, tormented still by the same winds!
Creon. Her guards shall have good cause to regret their delaying.
Antigonê. Ah! That voice is like the voice of death!
Creon. I can give you no reason to think you are mistaken.
Antigonê. Thebes, and you my fathers' gods,   75
And rulers of Thebes, you see me now, the last
Unhappy daughter of a line of kings,
Your kings, led away to death. You will remember
What things I suffer, and at what men's hands,
Because I would not transgress the laws of heaven.   80
(To the Guards, simply.) Come: let us wait no longer.

                                   Exit Antigonê, left, guarded.

ODE IV

Chorus. All Danaê's beauty was locked away   *Strophe 1*
In a brazen cell where the sunlight could not come:
A small room still as any grave, enclosed her.
Yet she was a princess too,
And Zeus in a rain of gold poured love upon her.   5
O child, child,
No power in wealth or war
Or tough sea-blackened ships
Can prevail against untiring Destiny!

And Dryas' son° also, that furious king,   *Antistrophe 1* 10
Bore the god's prisoning anger for his pride:
Sealed up by Dionysos in deaf stone,
His madness died among echoes.
So at the last he learned what dreadful power

Ode IV. ¹⁰ **Dryas' son** Lycurgus, King of Thrace

His tongue had mocked: 15
For he had profaned the revels,
And fired the wrath of the nine
Implacable Sisters° that love the sound of the flute.

And old men tell a half-remembered tale   *Strophe 2*
Of horror where a dark ledge splits the sea   20
And a double surf beats on the gráy shóres:
How a king's new woman°, sick
With hatred for the queen he had imprisoned,
Ripped out his two sons' eyes with her bloody hands
While grinning Arês° watched the shuttle plunge   25
Four times: gour blind wounds crying for revenge,

Crying, tears and blood mingled. — Piteously born,   *Antistrophe 2*
Those sons whose mother was of heavenly birth!
Her father was the god of the North Wind
And she was cradled by gales,   30
She raced with young colts on the glittering hills
And walked untrammeled in the open light:
But in her marriage deathless Fate found means
To build a tomb like yours for all her joy.

SCENE V

Enter blind Teiresias, led by a boy. The opening speeches of Teiresias should be in singsong contrast to the realistic lines of Creon.

Teiresias. This is the way the blind man comes, Princes, Princes,
    Lock-step, two heads lit by the eyes of one.
Creon. What new thing have you to tell us, old Teiresias?
Teiresias. I have much to tell you: listen to the prophet, Creon.
Creon. I am not aware that I have ever failed to listen.   5
Teiresias. Then you have done wisely, King, and ruled well.
Creon. I admit my debt to you. But what have you to say?
Teiresias. This, Creon: you stand once more on the edge of fate.
Creon. What do you mean? Your words are a kind of dread.
Teiresias. Listen, Creon: 10
    I was sitting in my chair of augury, at the place

---

[18] **Sisters** the Muses   [22] **king's new woman** (Eidothea, second wife of King Phineus, blinded her stepsons. Their mother, Cleopatra, had been imprisoned in a cave. Phineus was the son of a king, and Cleopatra, his first wife, was the daughter of Boreas, the North wind, but this illustrious ancestry could not protect his sons from violence and darkness)   [25] **Arês** god of war

Where the birds gather about me. They were all a-chatter,
As is their habit, when suddenly I heard
A strange note in their jangling, a scream, a
Whirring fury; I knew that they were fighting,   15
Tearing each other, dying
In a whirlwind of wings clashing. And I was afraid.
I began the rites of burnt-offering at the altar,
But Hephaistos° failed me: instead of bright flame,
There was only the sputtering slime of the fat thigh-flesh   20
Melting: the entrails dissolved in gray smoke,
The bare bone burst from the welter. And no blaze!

This was a sign from heaven. My boy described it,
Seeing for me as I see for others.

I tell you, Creon, you yourself have brought   25
This new calamity upon us. Our hearths and altars
Are stained with the corruption of dogs and carrion birds
That glut themselves on the corpse of Oedipus' son.
The gods are deaf when we pray to them, their fire
Recoils from our offering, their birds of omen   30
Have no cry of comfort, for they are gorged
With the thick blood of the dead.
                                   O my son,
These are no trifles! Think: all men make mistakes,
But a good man yields when he knows his course is wrong,
And repairs the evil. The only crime is pride.   35

Give in to the dead man, then: do not fight with a corpse —
What glory is it to kill a man who is dead?
Think, I beg you:
It is for your own good that I speak as I do.
You should be able to yield for your own good.   40
Creon. It seems that prophets have made me their especial province.
All my life long
I have been a kind of butt for the dull arrows
Of doddering fortune-tellers!
                              No, Teiresias:
If your birds — if the great eagles of God himself   45
Should carry him stinking bit by bit to heaven,
I would not yield. I am not afraid of pollution:
No man can defile the gods.
                           Do what you will,
Go into business, make money, speculate

Scene V. 19 *Hephaistos* god of fire

In India gold or that synthetic gold from Sardis,   50
Get rich otherwise than by my consent to bury him.
Teiresias, it is a sorry thing when a wise man
Sells his wisdom, lets out his words for hire!
Teiresias. Ah Creon! Is there no man left in the world —
Creon. To do what? — Come, let's have the aphorism!   55
Teiresias. No man who knows that wisdom outweighs any wealth?
Creon. As surely as bribes are baser than any baseness.
Teiresias. You are sick, Creon! You are deathly sick!
Creon. As you say: it is not my place to challenge a prophet.
Teiresias. Yet you have said my prophecy is for sale.   60
Creon. The generation of prophets has always loved gold.
Teiresias. The generation of kings has always loved brass.
Creon. You forget yourself! You are speaking to your King.
Teiresias. I know it. You are a king because of me.
Creon. You have a certain skill; but you have sold out.   65
Teiresias. King, you will drive me to words that —
Creon.   Say them, say them!
Only remember: I will not pay you for them.
Teiresias. No, you will find them too costly.
Creon.   No doubt. Speak:
Whatever you say, you will not change my will.
Teiresias. Then take this, and take it to heart!   70
The time is not far off when you shall pay back
Corpse for corpse, flesh of your own flesh.
You have thrust the child of this world into living night,
You have kept from the gods below the child that is theirs:
The one in a grave before her death, the other,   75
Dead, denied the grave. This is your crime:
And the Furies and the dark gods of Hell
Are swift with terrible punishment for you.

Do you want to buy me now, Creon?

                                          Not many days,
And your house will be full of men and women weeping,   80
And curses will be hurled at you from far
Cities grieving for sons unburied, left to rot
Before the walls of Thebes.

These are my arrows, Creon: they are all for you.

(To Boy.) But come, child: lead me home.   85
Let him waste his fine anger upon younger men.
Maybe he will learn at last
To control a wiser tongue in a better head.   *(Exit Teiresias.)*

Choragos. The old man has gone, King, but his words
    Remain to plague us. I am old, too,   90
    But I cannot remember that he was ever false.
Creon. That is true. . . . It troubles me.
    Oh it is hard to give in! but it is worse
    To risk everything for stubborn pride.
Choragos. Creon: take my advice.
Creon.   What shall I do?   95
Choragos. Go quickly: free Antigonê from her vault
    And build a tomb for the body of Polyneicês.
Creon. You would have me do this!
Choragos.   Creon, yes!
    And it must be done at once: God moves
    Swiftly to cancel the folly of stubborn men.   100
Creon. It is hard to deny the heart! But I
    Will do it: I will not fight with destiny.
Choragos. You must go yourself, you cannot leave it to others.
Creon. I will go.
             — Bring axes, servants:
    Come with me to the tomb. I buried her, I   105
    Will set her free.
                 Oh quickly!
    My mind misgives —
    The laws of the gods are mighty, and a man must serve them
    To the last day of his life!   *(Exit Creon.)*

PAEAN°

Choragos. God of many names   *Strophe 1*
Chorus.   O Iacchos
                     son
    of Kadmeian Sémelê
              O born of the Thunder!
    Guardian of the West
              Regent
    of Eleusis' plain
              O Prince of maenad Thebes
    and the Dragon Field by rippling Ismenos:°   5

Paean   a hymn (here dedicated to Iacchos, also called Dionysos. His father
was Zeus, his mother was Sémelê, daughter of Kadmos. Iacchos's worshipers
were the Maenads, whose cry was *"Evohé evohé"*)   **5 Ismenós**   a river east of
Thebes (from a dragon's teeth, sown near the river, there sprang men who
became the ancestors of the Theban nobility)

Choragos. God of many names   *Antistrophe 1*
Chorus.   the flame of torches
    flares on our hills
                    the nymphs of Iacchos
    dance at the spring of Castalia:°
    from the vine-close mountain
                        come ah come in ivy:
Evohé evohé! sings through the streets of Thebes   10

Choragos. God of many names   *Strophe 2*
Chorus.   Iacchos of Thebes
    heavenly Child
            of Sémelê bride of the Thunderer!
    The shadow of plague is upon us:
                                come
    with clement feet
                    oh come from Parnasos
    down the long slopes
                    across the lamenting water   15

Choragos. Iô Fire! Chorister of the throbbing stars!   *Antistrophe 2*
    O purest among the voices of the night!
    Thou son of God, blaze for us!
Chorus. Come with choric rapture of circling Maenads
    Who cry *Iô Iacche!*
                    God of many names!   20

EXODOS

Enter Messenger from left.

Messenger. Men of the line of Kadmos,° you who live
    Near Amphion's citadel,°
                    I cannot say
    Of any condition of human life "This is fixed,
    This is clearly good, or bad." Fate raises up,
    And Fate casts down the happy and unhappy alike: 5
    No man can foretell his Fate.
                    Take the case of Creon:

Paean. ⁸*Castalia* a spring on Mount Parnasos Exodos. ¹*Kadmos,* who
sowed the dragon's teeth, was founder of Thebes ²*Amphion's citadel*
Amphion played so sweetly on his lyre that he charmed stones to form a wall
around Thebes)

Creon was happy once, as I count happiness:
Victorious in battle, sole governor of the land,
Fortunate father of children nobly born.
And now it has all gone from him! Who can say   10
That a man is still alive when his life's joy fails?
He is a walking dead man. Grant him rich,
Let him live like a king in his great house:
If his pleasure is gone, I would not give
So much as the shadow of smoke for all he owns.   15
Choragos.   Your words hint at sorrow: what is your news for us?
Messenger.   They are dead. The living are guilty of their death.
Choragos.   Who is guilty? Who is dead? Speak!
Messenger.   Haimon.
      Haimon is dead; and the hand that killed him
      Is his own hand.
Choragos.   His father's? or his own?   20
Messenger.   His own, driven mad by the murder his father had
      done.
Choragos.   Teiresias, Teiresias, how clearly you saw it all!
Messenger.   This is my news: you must draw what conclusions
      you can from it.
Choragos.   But look: Eurydicê, our Queen:
      Has she overheard us?   25

      Enter Eurydicê from the palace, center.

Eurydicê.   I have heard something, friends:
      As I was unlocking the gate of Pallas'° shrine,
      For I needed her help today, I heard a voice
      Telling of some new sorrow. And I fainted
      There at the temple with all my maidens about me.   30
      But speak again: whatever it is, I can bear it:
      Grief and I are no strangers.
Messenger.   Dearest Lady,
      I will tell you plainly all that I have seen.
      I shall not try to comfort you: what is the use,
      Since comfort could lie only in what is not true?   35
      The truth is always best.
                              I went with Creon
      To the outer plain where Polyneicês was lying,
      No friend to pity him, his body shredded by dogs.
      We made our prayers in that place to Hecatê
      And Pluto,° that they would be merciful. And we bathed   40

---

²⁷ *Pallas,* Pallas Athene, goddess of wisdom   ⁴⁰ *Hecatê* / *And Pluto* Hecatê
and Pluto (also known at Hades) were deities of the underworld

The corpse with holy water, and we brought
Fresh-broken branches to burn what was left of it,
And upon the urn we heaped up a towering barrow
Of the earth of his own land.
                              When we were done, we ran
To the vault where Antigonê lay on her couch of stone.   45
One of the servants had gone ahead,
And while he was yet far off he heard a voice
Grieving within the chamber, and he came back
And told Creon. And as the King went closer,
The air was full of wailing, the words lost,   50
And he begged us to make all haste. "Am I a prophet?"
He said, weeping, "And must I walk this road,
The saddest of all that I have gone before?
My son's voice calls me on. Oh quickly, quickly!
Look through the crevice there, and tell me   55
If it is Haimon, or some deception of the gods!"

We obeyed; and in the cavern's farthest corner
We saw her lying:
She had made a noose of her fine linen veil
And hanged herself. Haimon lay beside her,   60
His arms about her waist, lamenting her,
His love lost under ground, crying out
That his father had stolen her away from him.

When Creon saw him the tears rushed to his eyes
And he called to him: "What have you done, child?
    Speak to me.   65
What are you thinking that makes your eyes so strange?
O my son, my son, I come to you on my knees!"
But Haimon spat in his face. He said not a word,
Staring —
            And suddenly drew his sword
And lunged. Creon shrank back, the blade missed; and the boy,   70
Desperate against himself, drove it half its length
Into his own side, and fell. And as he died
He gathered Antigonê close in his arms again,
Choking, his blood bright red on her white cheek.
And now he lies dead with the dead, and she is his   75
At last, his bride in the house of the dead.

                              Exit Eurydicê into the palace.

Choragos. She has left us without a word. What can this mean?
Messenger. It troubles me, too; yet she knows what is best,

Her grief is too great for public lamentation,
And doubtless she has gone to her chamber to weep   80
For her dead son, leading her maidens in his dirge.

Pause.

Choragos. It may be so: but I fear this deep silence.
Messenger. I will see what she is doing. I will go in.

Exit Messenger into the palace.
Enter Creon with attendants, bearing Haimon's body.

Choragos. But here is the King himself: oh look at him,
Bearing his own damnation in his arms.   85
Creon. Nothing you say can touch me any more.
My own blind heart has brought me
From darkness to final darkness. Here you see
The father murdering, the murdered son —
And all my civic wisdom!   90

Haimon my son, so young, so young to die,
I was the fool, not you; and you died for me.
Choragos. That is the truth; but you were late in learning it.
Creon. This truth is hard to bear. Surely a god
Has crushed me beneath the hugest weight of heaven,   95
And driven me headlong a barbaric way
To trample out the thing I held most dear.

The pains that men will take to come to pain!

Enter Messenger from the palace.

Messenger. The burden you carry in your hands is heavy,
But it is not all: you will find more in your house.   100
Creon. What burden worse than this shall I find there?
Messenger. The Queen is dead.
Creon. O port of death, deaf world,
Is there no pity for me? And you, Angel of evil,
I was dead, and your words are death again.   105
Is it true, boy? Can it be true?
Is my wife dead? Has death bred death?
Messenger. You can see for yourself.

*The doors are opened and the body of Eurydicê is
disclosed within.*

Creon. Oh pity!
All true, all true, and more than I can bear!   110
O my wife, my son!

Messenger.   She stood before the altar, and her heart
   Welcomed the knife her own hand guided,
   And a great cry burst from her lips for Megareus° dead,
   And for Haimon dead, her sons; and her last breath   115
   Was a curse for their father, the murderer of her sons.
   And she fell, and the dark flowed in through her closing eyes.
Creon.   O God, I am sick with fear.
   Are there no swords here? Has no one a blow for me?
Messenger.   Her curse is upon you for the deaths of both.   120
Creon.   It is right that it should be. I alone am guilty.
   I know it, and I say it. Lead me in,
   Quickly, friends.
   I have neither life nor substance. Lead me in.
Choragos.   You are right, if there can be right in so much wrong.   125
   The briefest way is best in a world of sorrow.
Creon.   Let it come,
   Let death come quickly, and be kind to me.
   I would not ever see the sun again.
Choragos.   All that will come when it will; but we, meanwhile,   130
   Have much to do. Leave the future to itself.
Creon.   All my heart was in that prayer!
Choragos.   Then do not pray any more: the sky is deaf.
Creon.   Lead me away. I have been rash and foolish.
   I have killed my son and my wife.   135
   I look for comfort; my comfort lies here dead.
   Whatever my hands have touched has come to nothing.
   Fate has brought all my pride to a thought of dust.

*As Creon is being led into the house, the Choragos advances and
speaks directly to the audience.*

Choragos.   There is no happiness where there is no wisdom;
   No wisdom but in submission to the gods.   140
   Big words are always punished,
   And proud men in old age learn to be wise.

Questions

   1. Although Sophocles called his play *Antigonê*, many critics say
that Creon is the real tragic hero, pointing out that Antigonê is absent
from the last third of the play. Evaluate this view.
   2. In some Greek tragedies, fate plays a great role in bringing
about the downfall of the tragic hero. Though there are references to

---

114 **Megareus** Megareus, brother of Haimon, had died in the assault on
Thebes

the curse on the House of Oedipus in *Antigonê*, do we feel that Antigonê goes to her death as a result of the workings of fate? Do we feel that fate is responsible for Creon's fall? Is the Messenger right to introduce the notion of "fate" (*Exodos*, line 4)? Or are both Antigonê and Creon the creators of their own tragedy?

3. Are the words *hamartia* and *hybris* (pages 553) relevant to Antigonê? To Creon?

4. Why does Creon, contrary to the Chorus's advice (Scene V, lines 96–97), bury the body of Polyneicês before he releases Antigonê? Does his action show a zeal for piety as short-sighted as his earlier zeal for law? Is his action plausible, in view of the facts that Teiresias has dwelt on the wrong done to Polyneicês, and that Antigonê has ritual food to sustain her? Or are we not to worry about Creon's motive?

5. A "foil" is a character who, by contrast, sets off or helps define another character. To what extent is Ismenê a foil to Antigonê? Is she entirely without courage?

6. What function does Eurydicê serve? How deeply do we feel about her fate?

7. Some readers have been bothered by a passage, omitted from the present version, that follows line 65 in Scene IV. It runs (in Paul Roche's translation) thus:

> No husband dead and gone,
> No children lisping "mother" ever could
> Have forced me to withstand the city to its face.
> On what principles do I assert so much?
> Just this:
> A husband dead, another can be found;
> A child, replaced; but once a brother's lost
> (Mother and father dead and buried too)
> No other brother can be born or grows again.
> That's my principle, which Creon stigmatized
> As criminal — my principle for honoring
> You my dearest brother.

Goethe, for example, says (in *Conversations of Goethe with Eckermann*):

> There is a passage in *Antigonê* which I always look upon as a blemish and I would give a great deal for an apt philologist to prove that it is interpolated and spurious. after the heroine has explained the noble motives for her action, and displayed the elevated purity of her soul, she at last, when she is led to death, brings forward a motive that is quite unworthy and almost borders upon the comic. . . . This passage, . . . in my opinion, when placed in the mouth of a heroine going to her death, disturbs the tragic tone and appears to me very far-fetched — to savor too much of dialetical calculation.

On the other hand H. D. F. Kitto has justified the passage thus (in *Form and Meaning in Drama*):

> Antigonê is neither a philosopher nor a *dévote*, but a passionate impulsive girl, and we need not expect consistency from one such, when for doing what to her was her manifest duty she is about to be buried alive, without a gleam of understanding from anybody. She thought she was obeying a divine law — as of course she was; now the gods seem to have deserted her — as they have, for they do not work miracles. Therefore nothing is left to her but her deep instinct that she had to do it, and it is neither surprising nor undramatic that she should now find what reason she can for asserting that in this special case she had no choice.

Evaluate these views.

19 Comedy

Though etymology is not always helpful (after all, is it really illuminating to say that "tragedy" may come from a Greek word meaning "goat song"?), the etymology of "comedy" helps to reveal comedy's fundamental nature. **Comedy** (Greek: *komoidia*) is a revel-song; ancient Greek comedies are descended from fertility rituals, and they dramatize the joy of renewal, the joy of triumphing over obstacles, the joy of being (in a sense) reborn. The movement of tragedy, speaking roughly, is from prosperity to disaster; the movement of comedy is from some sort of minor disaster to prosperity.

To say, however, that comedy dramatizes the triumph over obstacles is to describe it as though it were melodrama, a play in which, after hairbreadth adventures, good prevails over evil, often in the form of the hero's unlikely last-minute rescue of the fair Belinda from the clutches of the villain. What distinguishes comedy from melodrama is the pervasive high spirits of comedy. The joyous ending in comedy — usually a marriage — is in the spirit of what has gone before; the entire play, not only the end, is a celebration of fecundity.

The threats in the world of comedy are not taken very seriously; the parental tyranny that helps make *Romeo and Juliet* and *Antigonê* tragedies is, in comedy, laughable throughout. Parents may fret, fume, and lock doors, but in doing so they make themselves ridiculous, for love will find a way. Villains may threaten, but the audience never takes the the threats seriously.

In the first act of *As You Like It*, Rosalind, at the mercy of a cruel uncle who has driven her father from his own dukedom, says: "O, how full of briers is this working-day world." The immediate reply is, "They are but burrs, cousin, thrown upon thee in holiday foolery." And this spirit of holiday foolery dominates the whole play and culminates in marriage, the symbol of life renewing itself. The banished duke lives zestfully in the green woods, plentifully supplied with meat and song; when Rosalind herself is banished to the woods, she disguises herself and has a good time teasing her lover. In the last act things work out — as from the start we knew they would. Whereas *Antigonê* concludes with Creon looking at the corpses of his wife, son, and intended daughter-in-law, *As You Like It* concludes with four marriages, the repentance of the wicked duke, and the return of the rightful duke to his dukedom.

These exiles, marrriages, and renewals of society are most improbable, but they do not therefore weaken the comedy. The stuff of comedy is, in part, improbability. In *A Midsummer Night's Dream* Puck speaks for the spectator when he says:

> And those things do best please me
> That befall preposterously.

In tragedy, probability is important; in comedy, the improbable is often desirable, for at least three reasons. First, comedy seeks to include as much as possible, to reveal the rich abundance of life. The four marriages (and the reunion of the duke with his people, and the union of the usurper with a better way of life) in *As You Like It* do not weaken the play but strengthen it; the motto of comedy (and the implication in the weddings with which it usually concludes) is the more the merrier. Second, the improbable is the surprising; surprise often evokes laughter, and laughter surely has a central place in comedy. Third, by getting his characters into improbable situations, the dramatist can show off the absurdity of their behavior — a point that needs amplification.

Comedy often shows the absurdity of man's ideals. The miser, the puritan, the health-faddist, and so on, are men of ideals, but their ideals are suffocating. The miser, for example, treats everything in terms of money; his ideal causes him to renounce much of the abundance and joy of life. He is in love, but is unwilling to support a wife; or he has a headache, but he will not be so extravagant as to take an aspirin tablet. If a thief accosts him with "Your money or your life," he will prefer to give up his life — and that is what in fact he has been doing all the while. Now, by putting this miser in a series of improbable situations, the dramatist can continue to demonstrate entertainingly the miser's absurdity.*

* A character who is dominated by a single trait — avarice, jealousy, timidity, etc. — is sometimes called a **humor character.** Medieval and Renaissance psychology held that a man's personality depended on the mixture of four liquids (humors): blood (Latin: *sanguis*), choler, phlegm, and bile. An overabundance

The comic protagonist's tenacious hold on his ideals is not very far from the tragic protagonist's desperate hold on his. In general, however, tragedy suggests the nobility of ideals; the tragic hero's ideals undo him, and they may be ideals about which we have serious reservations, but still we admire him for them and recognize them as part of his nobility. Romeo and Juliet will not put off their love for each other; Antigonê will not yield to Creon, and Creon holds almost impossibly long to his stern position. But the comic protagonist who is always trying to keep his hands clean is funny; we laugh at his refusal to touch dirt with the rest of us, his refusal to enjoy the abundance life has to offer. The comic protagonist who is always talking about his beloved is funny; we laugh at his failure to see that the world is filled with women more attractive than the one who obsesses him. In short, the ideals for which the tragic protagonist loses the world seem important to us and gain, in large measure, our sympathy; but the ideals for which the comic protagonist loses the world seem trivial compared with the rich variety that life has to offer, and we laugh at their absurdity. The tragic figure makes a claim on our sympathy. The absurd comic figure continually sets up obstacles to our sympathetic interest; we feel detached from him, superior to him, and amused by him. Something along these lines is behind William Butler Yeats's insistence that character is always present in comedy but not in tragedy. Though Yeats is eccentric in his notion that individual character is obliterated in tragedy, he interestingly gets at one of the important elements in comedy:

> When the tragic reverie is at its height . . . (we do not say,) "How well that man is realized. I should know him were I to meet him in the street," for it is always ourselves that we see upon the (tragic) stage. . . . Tragedy must always be a drowning and breaking of the dikes that separate man from man, and . . . it is upon these dikes comedy keeps house.

One additional comparison between tragedy and comedy is in order. Although the happenings in tragedy seem inevitable, they seem also to have occurred partly because of the pressure of time. In the short time, things had to turn out this way, we feel; but if there

---

of one fluid produced a dominant trait, and even today "sanguine," "choleric," "phlegmatic," and "bilious" describe personalities.

Not all comedy, of course, depends on humor characters placed in situations that exhibit their absurdity. **High comedy** is largely verbal, depending on witty language; **farce**, at the other extreme, is dependent on inherently ludicrous situations, e.g., a hobo is mistaken for a millionaire. Situation comedy, then, may use humor characters, but it need not do so.

had only been more time. . . . In *Romeo and Juliet* Friar Laurence writes a letter to Romeo, explaining that Juliet will take a potion that will put her in a temporary, death-like trance, but the letter is delayed. Romeo mistakenly hears that Juliet is dead, and he kills himself. A few moments after his suicide Juliet revives. Had Friar Laurence's message arrived on schedule, or had Romeo not been so quick to commit suicide, no great harm would have been done. But throughout the play one feels oppressed by time. Romeo early anticipates an "untimely death"; when the lovers first swear their allegiance, Juliet fears that things are moving too quickly:

> Although I joy in thee,
> I have no joy of this contract tonight:
> It is too rash, too unadvised, too sudden;
> Too like the lightning, which doth cease to be
> Ere one can say it lightens.

In *Antigonê*, after condemning his niece to death, Creon changes his mind, but before he releases her he performs the ritual of burying Polyneicês. When he then turns to save Antigonê, it is too late. A little more time and all might have been well, but as it is there are three corpses at the end of the play, and Creon is left — now with years at his disposal — to lament his isolation. In comedy, however, there is usually a sense of leisure. Things are difficult now, but they will work themselves out. Sooner or later people will realize that the strange goings-on are due to the existence of identical twins. Sooner or later the stubborn parents will realize that they cannot further stand in the way of the young lovers, and all will be well. In the world of comedy, one is always safe in relying on time. Viola, in *Twelfth Night,* is an ingenious young lady, but even she cannot solve all the problems. She knows, however, that things have a way of working themselves out all right:

> O Time! thou must untangle this, not I;
> It is too hard a knot for me to untie!

Most comic plays can roughly be sorted into one of two types, depending on who is the protagonist: satiric comedies and romantic comedies. In **satiric comedy** attention is centered on a protagonist who during much of the play interferes with the happy outcome. The jealous spouse, the demanding parent, the decrepit wooer, goes through his paces, revealing again and again his absurdity. The writer of this sort of comedy often justifies himself by claiming to reform society: misers and other antisocial members of the audience will see their image on the stage and reform themselves when they leave the theater. But it is hard to believe that this theory is rooted in fact. Jonathan Swift (as we mentioned earlier) was probably right when he said, "Satire is a sort of glass wherein beholders do generally discover everybody's face but their own."

Near the conclusion of a satiric comedy, the obstructing characters are dismissed, often perfunctorily, when the lost letter turns up, allowing for a happy ending — commonly the marriage of the colorless young lovers who have moved in the background. And so all-encompassing are the festivities at the end that even the obstructionists are invited to join in the wedding feast. (If they cannot be invited to join, they are kept off the stage, as is Shylock at the end of *The Merchant of Venice*.) The overall movement, then, is from conflict to social harmony, joy, and abundance. Such an ending might be called romantic, but because the bulk of the play has been satiric, the term romantic comedy is reserved for another sort.

Whereas satiric comedy is critical, holding a mirror up to the folly of the real world so that it may reform itself closer to the ideal, **romantic comedy** presents the ideal world, a golden world, a world in which if there are any difficulties they are not briers but "burrs . . . thrown upon thee in holiday foolery." It is the world of most of Shakespeare's comedies, a world of Illyria, of the Forest of Arden, of Belmont. The protagonists are young lovers who dominate this world; the course of their love is not smooth, but the outcome is never in doubt and the course is the more fun for being a little bumpy. Portia teases Bassanio, Lysander and Demetrius sometimes pursue the wrong girls, but they are all pleasant people. Of course, there are villains and lions, but the villains are great bunglers, and the lions are rather like the lion that Snug impersonates in *A Midsummer Night's Dream*. Bernard Shaw's *Pygmalion* (1912) combines romance and satire. Curiously, although the comedy is subtitled "A Romance," the romantic aspect may be less evident than the satiric because of Shaw's insistence that Liza Doolittle and Henry Higgins do *not* marry. An ancient tale told of how the sculptor Pygmalion, dissatisfied with all women, created a marble statue of an ideal woman, fell in love with it, and by his love so moved the goddess Aphrodite that she gave the statue life. Pygmalion married his creation, but Shaw rejects this ending, insisting that in his play there is enough romance in turning a poor, almost inarticulate flower girl into a woman who speaks as elegantly as a duchess. The play is thus a version of the Cinderella tale, but without the marriage to the prince: a seemingly nondescript girl is turned into royalty, or at least into someone who can be passed off as royalty. Moreover, this beautifully dressed doll with beautiful speech turns into an energetic, resourceful, independent woman. The public, however, has wanted more romance than Shaw gave it: the film version of *Pygmalion* ends with the implication that Liza and Higgins will marry, and Lerner and Loewe's musical version, *My Fair Lady*, makes the implication of marriage unmistakable.

Bernard Shaw (1856–1950)

Pygmalion

List of Characters

Clara Eynsford-Hill
Mrs Eynsford-Hill
A Bystander
Freddy Eynsford-Hill
Eliza Doolittle
Colonel Pickering
Henry Higgins
A Sarcastic Bystander
Mrs Pearce
Alfred Doolittle
Mrs Higgins
Parlormaid

Period — The Present

Act I   *The Portico of St Paul's, Covent Garden. 11.15 p.m.*

Act II   *Professor Higgins's Phonetic Laboratory, Wimpole Street. Next day. 11 a.m.*

Act III   *The Drawing Room in Mrs Higgins's Flat on Chelsea Embankment. Several Months Later. At-Home Day*

Act IV   *The Same as Act 2. Several Months Later. Midnight.*

Act V   *The Same as Act 3. The Following Morning.*

Note for Technicians A complete representation of the play as printed for the first time in this edition is technically possible only on the cinema screen or on stages furnished with exceptionally elaborate machinery. For ordinary theatrical use the scenes separated by rows of asterisks are to be omitted.

In the dialogue an e upside down indicates the indefinite vowel, sometimes called obscure or neutral, for which, though it is one of the commonest sounds in English speech, our wretched alphabet has no letter.

ACT I

London at 11.15 p.m. Torrents of heavy summer rain. Cab whistles blowing frantically in all directions. Pedestrians running for shelter into the portico of St Paul's church (not Wren's cathedral but Inigo Jones's church in Covent Garden vegetable market), among them a lady and her daughter in evening dress. All are peering out gloomily at the rain, except one man with his back turned to the rest, wholly preoccupied with a notebook in which he is writing.

The church clock strikes the first quarter.

The Daughter (in the space between the central pillars, close to the one on her left). I'm getting chilled to the bone. What can Freddy be doing all this time? He's been gone twenty minutes.

The Mother (on her daughter's right). Not so long. But he ought to have got us a cab by this.

A Bystander (on the lady's right). He wont get no cab not until half-past eleven, missus, when they come back after dropping their theatre fares.

The Mother. But we must have a cab. We cant stand here until half-past eleven. It's too bad.

The Bystander. Well, it aint my fault, missus.

The Daughter. If Freddy had a bit of gumption, he would have got one at the theatre door.

The Mother. What could he have done, poor boy?

The Daughter. Other people got cabs. Why couldnt he?

Freddy rushes in out of the rain from the Southampton Street side, and comes between them closing a dripping umbrella. He is a young man of twenty, in evening dress, very wet round the ankles.

The Daughter. Well, havnt you got a cab?

Freddy. Theres not one to be had for love or money.

The Mother. Oh, Freddy, there must be one. You cant have tried.

The Daughter. It's too tiresome. Do you expect us to go and get one ourselves?

Freddy. I tell you theyre all engaged. The rain was so sudden: nobody was prepared; and everybody had to take a cab. Ive been to

Charing Cross one way and nearly to Ludgate Circus the other; and they were all engaged.

The Mother. Did you try Trafalgar Square?

Freddy. There wasnt one at Trafalgar Square.

The Daughter. Did you try?

Freddy. I tried as far as Charing Cross Station. Did you expect me to walk to Hammersmith?

The Daughter. You havnt tried at all.

The Mother. You really are very helpless, Freddy. Go again; and dont come back until you have found a cab.

Freddy. I shall simply get soaked for nothing.

The Daughter. And what about us? Are we to stay here all night in this draught, with next to nothing on? You selfish pig —

Freddy. Oh, very well: I'll go. *(He opens his umbrella and dashes off Strandwards, but comes into collision with a flower girl who is hurrying in for shelter, knocking her basket out of her hands. A blinding flash of lightning, followed instantly by a rattling peal of thunder, orchestrates the incident.)*

The Flower Girl. Nah then, Freddy: look wh' y' gowin, deah.

Freddy. Sorry. *(He rushes off.)*

The Flower Girl (picking up her scattered flowers and replacing them in the basket). Theres menners f'yer! Tə-oo banches o voylets trod into the mad. *(She sits down on the plinth of the column, sorting her flowers, on the lady's right. She is not at all a romantic figure. She is perhaps eighteen, perhaps twenty, hardly older. She wears a little sailor hat of black straw that has long been exposed to the dust and soot of London and has seldom if ever been brushed. Her hair needs washing rather badly: its mousy color can hardly be natural. She wears a shoddy black coat that reaches nearly to her knees and is shaped to her waist. She has a brown skirt with a coarse apron. Her boots are much the worse for wear. She is no doubt as clean as she can afford to be; but compared to the ladies she is very dirty. Her features are no worse than theirs; but their condition leaves something to be desired; and she needs the services of a dentist.)*

The Mother. How do you know that my son's name is Freddy, pray?

The Flower Girl. Ow, eez yə-ooa san, is e? Wal, fewd dan y' də-ooty bawmz a mather should, eed now bettern to spawl a pore gel's flahrzn than ran awy athaht pyin. Will ye-oo py me f'them? *(Here, with apologies, this desperate attempt to represent her dialect without a phonetic alphabet must be abandoned as unintelligible outside London.)*

The Daughter. Do nothing of the sort, mother. The idea!

The Mother. Please allow me, Clara. Have you any pennies?

The Daughter. No. Ive nothing smaller than sixpence.

The Flower Girl (hopefully). I can give you change for a tanner, kind lady.

The Mother (to Clara). Give it to me. *(Clara parts reluctantly.)* Now *(to the girl).* This is for your flowers.

The Flower Girl. Thank you kindly, lady.

The Daughter. Make her give you the change. These things are only a penny a bunch.

The Mother. Do hold your tongue, Clara. *(To the girl.)* You can keep the change.

The Flower Girl. Oh, thank you, lady.

The Mother. Now tell how you know that young gentleman's name.

The Flower Girl. I didnt.

The Mother. I heard you call him by it. Dont try to deceive me.

The Flower Girl (protesting). Who's trying to deceive you? I called him Freddy or Charlie same as you might yourself if you was talking to a stranger and wished to be pleasant.

The Daughter. Sixpence thrown away! Really, mamma, you might have spared Freddy that. *(She retreats in disgust behind the pillar.)*

An elderly gentleman of the amiable military type rushes into the shelter, and closes a dripping umbrella. He is in the same plight as Freddy, very wet about the ankles. He is in evening dress, with a light overcoat. He takes the place left vacant by the daughter.

The Gentleman. Phew!

The Mother (to gentleman). Oh sir, is there any sign of its stopping?

The Gentleman. I'm afraid not. It started worse than ever about two minutes ago. *(He goes to the plinth beside the flower girl; puts up his foot on it; and stoops to turn down his trouser ends.)*

The Mother. Oh dear! *(She retires sadly and joins her daughter.)*

The Flower Girl (taking advantage of the military gentleman's proximity to establish friendly relations with him). If it's worse, it's a sign it's nearly over. So cheer up, Captain; and buy a flower off a poor girl.

The Gentleman. I'm sorry. I havnt any change.

The Flower Girl. I can give you change, Captain.

The Gentleman. For a sovereign? Ive nothing less.

The Flower Girl. Garn! Oh do buy a flower off me, Captain. I can change half-a-crown. Take this for tuppence.

The Gentleman. Now dont be troublesome: theres a good girl. *(Trying his pockets.)* I really havnt any change — Stop: heres three hapence, if thats any use to you. *(He retreats to the other pillar.)*

The Flower Girl (disappointed, but thinking three halfpence better than nothing). Thank you, sir.

The Bystander (to the girl). You be careful: give him a flower for it. Theres a bloke here behind taking down every blessed word youre saying. *(All turn to the man who is taking notes.)*

The Flower Girl (springing up terrified). I aint done nothing wrong by speaking to the gentleman. Ive a right to sell flowers if I keep off the kerb. *(Hysterically.)* I'm a respectable girl: so help me, I never spoke to him except to ask him to buy a flower off me.

General hubbub, mostly sympathetic to the flower girl, but deprecating her excessive sensibility. Cries of Dont start hollerin. Who's hurting you? Nobody's going to touch you. Whats the good of fussing? Steady on. Easy easy, etc., *come from the elderly staid spectators, who pat her comfortingly. Less patient ones bid her shut her head, or ask her roughly what is wrong with her. A remoter group, not knowing what the matter is, crowd in and increase the noise with question and answer:* Whats the row? What-she-do? Where is he? A tec taking her down. What! him? Yes: him over there: Took money off the gentleman, etc.

The Flower Girl (breaking through them to the gentleman, crying wildly). Oh, sir, dont let him charge me. You dunno what it means to me. Theyll take away my character and drive me on the streets for speaking to gentlemen. They —

The Note Taker (coming forward on her right, the rest crowding after him). There! there! there! there! who's hurting you, you silly girl? What do you take me for?

The Bystander. It's aw rawt: e's a genleman: look at his bɔ-oots. *(Explaining to the note taker.)* She thought you was a copper's nark, sir.

The Note Taker (with quick interest). Whats a copper's nark?

The Bystander (inapt at definition). It's a — well, it's a copper's nark, as you might say. What else would you call it? A sort of informer.

The Flower Girl (still hysterical). I take my Bible oath I never said a word —

The Note Taker (overbearing but good-humored). Oh, shut up, shut up. Do I look like a policeman?

The Flower Girl (far from reassured). Then what did you take down my words for? How do I know whether you took me down right? You just shew me what youve wrote about me. *(The note taker opens his book and holds it steadily under her nose, though the pressure of the mob trying to read it over his shoulders would upset a weaker man.)* Whats that? That aint proper writing. I cant read that.

The Note Taker. I can. *(Reads, reproducing her pronunciation exactly.)* "Cheer ap, Keptin; n' baw ya flahr orf a pore gel."

The Flower Girl (much distressed). It's because I called him Captain. I meant no harm. *(To the gentleman.)* Oh, sir, dont let him lay a charge agen me for a word like that. You —

The Gentleman. Charge! I make no charge. *(To the note taker.)* Really, sir, if you are a detective, you need not begin protecting me against molestation by young women until I ask you. Anybody could see that the girl meant no harm.

The Bystanders Generally (demonstrating against police espionage). Course they could. What business is it of yours? You mind your own affairs. He wants promotion, he does. Taking down people's words! Girl never said a word to him. What harm if she did? Nice thing a girl cant shelter from the rain without being insulted, etc., etc., etc. *(She is conducted by the more sympathetic demonstrators back to her plinth, where she resumes her seat and struggles with her emotion.)*

The Bystander. He aint a tec. He's a blooming busybody: thats what he is. I tell you, look at his bə-oots.

The Note Taker (turning on him genially). And how are all your people down at Selsey?

The Bystander (suspiciously). Who told you my people come from Selsey?

The Note Taker. Never you mind. They did. *(To the girl.)* How do you come to be up so far east? You were born in Lisson Grove.

The Flower Girl (appalled). Oh, what harm is there in my leaving Lisson Grove? It wasnt fit for a pig to live in; and I had to pay four-and-six a week. *(In tears.)* Oh, boo — hoo — oo —

The Note Taker. Live where you like; but stop that noise.

The Gentleman (to the girl). Come, come! he cant touch you: you have a right to live where you please.

A Sarcastic Bystander (thrusting himself between the note taker and the gentleman). Park Lane, for instance. I'd like to go into the Housing Question with you, I would.

The Flower Girl (subsiding into a brooding melancholy over her basket, and talking very low-spiritedly to herself). I'm a good girl, I am.

The Sarcastic Bystander (not attending to her). Do you know where I come from?

The Note Taker (promptly). Hoxton.

Titterings. Popular interest in the note taker's performance increases.

The Sarcastic One (amazed). Well, who said I didn't? Bly me! you know everything, you do.

The Flower Girl (still nursing her sense of injury). Aint no call to meddle with me, he aint.

The Bystander (to her). Of course he aint. Dont you stand it from him. *(To the note taker.)* See here: what call have you to know about people what never offered to meddle with you?

The Flower Girl. Let him say what he likes. I dont want to have no truck with him.

The Bystander. You take us for dirt under your feet, dont you? Catch you taking liberties with a gentleman!

The Sarcastic Bystander. Yes: tell him where he come from if you want to go fortune-telling.

The Note Taker. Cheltenham, Harrow, Cambridge, and India.

The Gentleman. Quite right.

Great laughter. Reaction in the note taker's favor. Exclamations of He knows all about it. Told him proper. Hear him tell the toff where he come from? etc.

The Gentleman. May I ask, sir, do you do this for your living at a music hall?

The Note Taker. I've thought of that. Perhaps I shall some day.

The rain has stopped; and the persons on the outside of the crowd begin to drop off.

The Flower Girl (resenting the reaction). He's no gentleman, he aint, to interfere with a poor girl.

The Daughter (out of patience, pushing her way rudely to the front and displacing the gentleman, who politely retires to the other side of the pillar). What on earth is Freddy doing? I shall get pneumownia if I stay in this draught any longer.

The Note Taker (to himself, hastily making a note of her pronunciation of "monia") Earlscourt.

The Daughter (violently) Will you please keep your impertinent remarks to yourself.

The Note Taker. Did I say that out loud? I didnt mean to. I beg your pardon. Your mother's Epsom, unmistakeably.

The Mother (advancing between her daughter and the note taker). How very curious! I was brought up in Largelady Park, near Epsom.

The Note Taker (uproariously amused). Ha! ha! What a devil of a name! Excuse me. *(To the daughter.)* You want a cab, do you?

The Daughter. Dont dare speak to me.

The Mother. Oh please, please, Clara. *(Her daughter repudiates her with an angry shrug and retires haughtily.)* We should be so grateful to you, sir, if you found us a cab. *(The note taker produces a whistle.)* Oh, thank you. *(She joins her daughter.)*

The note taker blows a piercing blast.

The Sarcastic Bystander. There! I knowed he was a plainclothes copper.

The Bystander. That aint a police whistle: thats a sporting whistle.

The Flower Girl (still preoccupied with her wounded feelings). He's no right to take away my character. My character is the same to me as any lady's.

The Note Taker. I dont know whether youve noticed it; but the rain stopped about two minutes ago.

The Bystander. So it has. Why didnt you say so before? and us losing our time listening to your silliness! *(He walks off towards the Strand.)*

The Sarcastic Bystander. I can tell where you come from. You come from Anwell. Go back there.

The Note Taker (helpfully). Hanwell.

The Sarcastic Bystander (affecting great distinction of speech). Thenk you, teacher, Haw haw! So long. *(He touches his hat with mock respect and strolls off.)*

The Flower Girl. Frightening people like that! How would he like it himself?

The Mother. It's quite fine now, Clara. We can walk to a motor bus. Come. *(She gathers her skirts above her ankles and hurries off towards the Strand.)*

The Daughter. But the cab — *(Her mother is out of hearing.)* Oh, how tiresome! *(She follows angrily.)*

All the rest have gone except the note taker, the gentleman, and the flower girl, who sits arranging her basket, and still pitying herself in murmurs.

The Flower Girl. Poor girl! Hard enough for her to live without being worried and chivied.

The Gentleman (returning to his former place on the note taker's left). How do you do it, if I may ask?

The Note Taker. Simply phonetics. The science of speech. Thats my profession: also my hobby. Happy is the man who can make a living by his hobby! You can spot an Irishman or a Yorkshireman by his brogue. *I* can place any man within six miles. I can place him within two miles in London. Sometimes within two streets.

The Flower Girl. Ought to be ashamed of himself, unmanly coward!

The Gentleman. But is there a living in that?

The Note Taker. Oh yes. Quite a fat one. This is an age of upstarts. Men begin in Kentish Town with £80 a year, and end in Park Lane with a hundred thousand. They want to drop Kentish Town; but they give themselves away every time they open their mouths. Now I can teach them —

The Flower Girl. Let him mind his own business and leave a poor girl —

The Note Taker (explosively). Woman: cease this detestable boo-hooing instantly; or else seek the shelter of some other place of worship.

The Flower Girl (with feeble defiance). Ive a right to be here if I like, same as you.

The Note Taker. A woman who utters such depressing and disgusting sounds has no right to be anywhere — no right to live. Remember that you are a human being with a soul and the divine gift of articulate speech: that your native language is the language of Shakespear and Milton and The Bible; and dont sit there crooning like a bilious pigeon.

The Flower Girl (quite overwhelmed, looking up at him in mingled wonder and deprecation without daring to raise her head). Ah-ah-ah-ow-ow-ow-oo!

The Note Taker (whipping out his book). Heavens! what a sound! *(He writes; then holds out the book and reads, reproducing her vowels exactly.)* Ah-ah-ah-ow-ow-ow-oo!

The Flower Girl (tickled by the performance, and laughing in spite of herself). Garn!

The Note Taker. You see this creature with her kerbstone English: the English that will keep her in the gutter to the end of her days. Well, sir, in three months I could pass that girl off as a duchess at an ambassador's garden party. I could even get her a place as lady's maid or shop assistant, which requires better English.

The Flower Girl. What's that you say?

The Note Taker. Yes, you squashed cabbage leaf, you disgrace to the noble architecture of these columns, you incarnate insult to the English language: I could pass you off as the Queen of Sheba. *(To the Gentleman.)* Can you believe that?

The Gentleman. Of course I can. I am myself a student of Indian dialects; and —

The Note Taker (eagerly). Are you? Do you know Colonel Pickering, the author of Spoken Sanscrit?

The Gentleman. I am Colonel Pickering. Who are you?

The Note Taker. Henry Higgins, author of Higgins's Universal Alphabet.

Pickering (with enthusiasm). I came from India to meet you.

Higgins. I was going to India to meet you.

Pickering. Where do you live?

Higgins. 27A Wimpole Street. Come and see me tomorrow.

Pickering. I'm at the Carlton. Come with me now and lets have a jaw over some supper.

Higgins. Right you are.

The Flower Girl (to Pickering, as he passes her). Buy a flower, kind gentleman. I'm short for my lodging.

Pickering. I really havnt any change. I'm sorry. *(He goes away.)*

Higgins (shocked at the girl's mendacity). Liar. You said you could change half-a-crown.

The Flower Girl (rising in desperation). You ought to be stuffed with nails, you ought. *(Flinging the basket at his feet.)* Take the whole blooming basket for sixpence.

The church clock strikes the second quarter.

Higgins (hearing in it the voice of God, rebuking him for his Pharisaic want of charity to the poor girl). A reminder. *(He raises his hat solemnly; then throws a handful of money into the basket and follows Pickering.)*

The Flower Girl (picking up a half-crown). Ah-ow-ooh! *(Picking up a couple of florins.)* Aaah-ow-ooh! *(Picking up several coins.)* Aaaaaah-ow-ooh! *(Picking up a half-soverign.)* Aaaaaaaaaaaa-ow-ooh!!!

Freddy (springing out of a taxicab). Got one at last. Hallo! *(To the girl.)* Where are the two ladies that were here?

The Flower Girl. They walked to the bus when the rain stopped.

Freddy. And left me with a cab on my hands! Damnation!

The Flower Girl (with grandeur). Never mind, young man. I'm going home in a taxi. *(She sails off to the cab. The driver puts his hand behind him and holds the door firmly shut against her. Quite understanding his mistrust, she shews him her handful of money.)* A taxi fare aint no object to me, Charlie. *(He grins and opens the door.)* Here. What about the basket?

The Taximan. Give it here. Tuppence extra.

Liza. No: I dont want nobody to see it. *(She crushes it into the cab and gets in, continuing the conversation through the window.)* Goodbye, Freddy.

Freddy (dazedly raising his hat). Goodbye.

Taximan. Where to?

Liza. Bucknam Pellis (Buckingham Palace).

Taximan. What d'ye mean — Bucknam Pellis?

Liza. Dont you know where it is? In the Green Park, where the King live. Goodbye, Freddy. Dont let me keep you standing there. Goodbye.

Freddy. Goodbye. *(He goes.)*

Taximan. Here? Whats this about Bucknam Pellis? What business have you at Bucknam Pellis?

Liza. Of course I havnt none. But I wasnt going to let him know that. You drive me home.

Taximan. And wheres home?

Liza. Angel Court, Drury Lane, next Meiklejohn's oil shop.

Taximan. That sounds more like it, Judy. *(He drives off.)*

• • •

(Let us follow the taxi to the entrance to Angel Court, a narrow little archway between two shops, one of them Meiklejohn's oil shop. When it stops there, Eliza gets out, dragging her basket with her.)

Liza. How much?

Taximan (indicating the taximeter). Cant you read? A shilling.

Liza. A shilling for two minutes!!

Taximan. Two minutes or ten: it's all the same.

Liza. Well, I dont call it right.

Taximan. Ever been in a taxi before?

Liza (with dignity). Hundreds and thousands of times, young man.

Taximan (laughing at her). Good for you, Judy. Keep the shilling, darling, with best love from all at home. Good luck! *(He drives off.)*

Liza (humiliated). Impidence!

She picks up the basket and trudges up the alley with it to her lodging: a small room with very old wall paper hanging loose in the damp places. A broken pane in the window is mended with paper. A portrait of a popular actor and a fashion plate of ladies' dresses, all wildly beyond poor Eliza's means, both torn from newpapers, are pinned up on the wall. A birdcage hangs in the window; but its tenant died long ago: it remains as a memorial only.

These are the only visible luxuries: the rest is the irreducible minimum of poverty's needs: a wretched bed heaped with all sorts of coverings that have any warmth in them, a draped packing case with a basin and jug on it and a little looking glass over it, a chair and table, the refuse of some suburban kitchen, and an American alarum clock on the shelf above the unused fireplace: the whole lighted with a gas lamp with a penny in the slot meter. Rent: four shillings a week.

(Here Eliza, chronically weary, but too excited to go to bed, sits, counting her new riches and dreaming and planning what to do with them, until the gas goes out, when she enjoys for the first time the sensation of being able to put in another penny without grudging it. This prodigal mood does not extinguish her gnawing sense of the need for economy sufficiently to prevent her from calculating that she can dream and plan in bed more cheaply and warmly than sitting up without a fire. So she takes off her shawl and skirt and adds them to the miscellaneous bedclothes. Then she kicks off her shoes and gets into bed without any further change.)

ACT II

Next day at 11 a.m. Higgins's laboratory in Wimpole Street. It is a room on the first floor, looking on the street, and was meant for the drawing room. The double doors are in the middle of the back wall; and persons entering find in the corner to their right two tall file cabinets at right angles to one another against the walls. In this corner stands a flat writing-table, on which are a phono-graph, a laryngoscope, a row of tiny organ pipes with a bellows, a set of lamp chimneys for singing flames with burners attached to a gas plug in the wall by an indiarubber tube, several tuning-forks of different sizes, a life-size image of half a human head, shewing in section the vocal organs, and a box containing a sup-ply of wax cylinders for the phonograph.

Further down the room, on the same side, is a fireplace, with a comfortable leather-covered easy-chair at the side of the hearth nearest the door, and a coal-scuttle. There is a clock on the man-tel-piece. Between the fireplace and the phonograph table is a stand for newspapers.

On the other side of the central door, to the left of the visitor, is a cabinet of shallow drawers. On it is a telephone and the telephone directory. The corner beyond, and most of the side wall, is occupied by a grand piano, with the keyboard at the end furthest from the door, and a bench for the player extending the full length of the keyboard. On the piano is a dessert dish heaped with fruit and sweets, mostly chocolates.

The middle of the room is clear. Besides the easy-chair, the piano bench, and two chairs at the phonograph table, there is

one stray chair. It stands near the fireplace. On the walls, engrav-
ings: mostly Piranesis and mezzotint portraits. No paintings.
   Pickering is seated at the table, putting down some cards and
a tuning-fork which he has been using. Higgins is standing up
near him, closing two or three file drawers which are hanging out.
He appears in the morning light as a robust, vital, appetizing sort
of man of forty or thereabouts, dressed in a professional-looking
black frock-coat with a white linen collar and black silk tie. He is
of the energetic, scientific type, heartily, even violently interested
in everything that can be studied as a scientific subject, and care-
less about himself and other people, including their feelings. He
is, in fact, but for his years and size, rather like a very impetuous
baby "taking notice" eagerly and loudly, and requiring almost as
much watching to keep him out of unintended mischief. His man-
ner varies from genial bullying when he is in a good humor to
stormy petulance when anything goes wrong; but he is so entirely
frank and void of malice that he remains likeable even in his least
reasonable moments.

Higgins (as he shuts the last drawer). Well, I think thats the whole
   show.
Pickering. It's really amazing. I havnt taken half of it in, you know.
Higgins. Would you like to go over any of it again?
Pickering (rising and coming to the fireplace, where he plants him-
   self with his back to the fire). No, thank you: not now. I'm quite
   done up for this morning.
Higgins (following him, and standing beside him on his left). Tired
   of listening to sounds?
Pickering. Yes. It's a fearful strain. I rather fancied myself because I
   can pronounce twenty-four distinct vowel sounds; but your hundred and thirty beat me. I cant hear a bit of difference between
   most of them.
Higgins (chuckling, and going over to the piano to eat sweets). Oh,
   that comes with practice. You hear no difference at first; but you
   keep on listening, and presently you find theyre all as different as
   A from B. *(Mrs Pearce looks in: she is Higgins's housekeeper.)*
   Whats the matter?
Mrs. Pearce (hesitating, evidently perplexed). A young woman asks
   to see you, sir.
Higgins. A young woman! What does she want?
Mrs Pearce. Well, sir, she says youll be glad to see her when you
   know what she's come about. She's quite a common girl, sir. Very
   common indeed. I should have sent her away, only I thought
   perhaps you wanted her to talk into your machines. I hope Ive not

done wrong; but really you see such queer people sometimes —
youll excuse me, I'm sure, sir —

Higgins. Oh, thats all right, Mrs Pearce. Has she an interesting
accent?

Mrs Pearce. Oh, something dreadful, sir, really. I dont know how
you can take an interest in it.

Higgins (to Pickering). Lets have her up. Shew her up, Mrs Pearce.
*(He rushes across to his working table and picks out a cylinder to
use on the phonograph.)*

Mrs Pearce (only half resigned to it). Very well, sir. It's for you to
say. *(She goes downstairs.)*

Higgins. This is rather a bit of luck. I'll shew you how I make records. We'll set her talking; and I'll take it down first in Bell's
Visible Speech; then in broad Romic; and then we'll get her on the
phonograph so that you can turn her on as often as you like with
the written transcript before you.

Mrs Pearce (returning). This is the young woman, sir.

*The flower girl enters in state. She has a hat with three ostrich
feathers, orange, sky-blue, and red. She has a nearly clean apron,
and the shoddy coat has been tidied a little. The pathos of this
deplorable figure, with its innocent vanity and consequential air,
touches Pickering, who has already straightened himself in the
presence of Mrs Pearce. But as to Higgins, the only distinction he
makes between men and women is that when he is neither bullying nor exclaiming to the heavens against some feather-weight
cross, he coaxes women as a child coaxes its nurse when it wants
to get anything out of her.*

*Higgins (brusquely, recognizing her with unconcealed disappoint-
ment, and at once, babylike, making an intolerable grievance of
it).* Why, this is the girl I jotted down last night. She's no use: Ive
got all the records I want of the Lisson Grove lingo; and I'm not
going to waste another cylinder on it. *(To the girl.)* Be off with
you: I dont want you.

The Flower Girl. Dont you be so saucy. You ain't heard what I come
for yet. *(To Mrs Pearce, who is waiting at the door for further
instructions.)* Did you tell him I come in a taxi?

Mrs Pearce. Nonsense, girl! what do you think a gentleman like Mr
Higgins cares what you came in?

The Flower Girl. Oh, we are proud! He aint above giving lessons,
not him: I heard him say so. Well, I aint come here to ask for any
compliment; and if my money's not good enough I can go elsewhere.

Higgins. Good enough for what?

The Flower Girl. Good enough for yə-oo. Now you know, dont you? I'm come to have lessons, I am. And to pay for em tə-oo: make no mistake.

Higgins (stupent). Well!!! *(Recovering his breath with a gasp.)* What do you expect me to say to you?

The Flower Girl. Well, if you was a gentleman, you might ask me to sit down, I think. Dont I tell you I'm bringing you business?

Higgins. Pickering: shall we ask this baggage to sit down, or shall we throw her out of the window?

The Flower Girl (running away in terror to the piano, where she turns at bay). Ah-ah-oh-ow-ow-ow-oo! *(Wounded and whimpering.)* I wont be called a baggage when Ive offered to pay like any lady.

Motionless, the two men stare at her from the other side of the room, amazed.

Pickering (gently). But what is it you want?

The Flower Girl. I want to be a lady in a flower shop stead of sellin at the corner of Tottenham Court Road. But they wont take me unless I can talk more genteel. He said he could teach me. Well, here I am ready to pay him — not asking any favor — and he treats me zif I was dirt.

Mrs Pearce. How can you be such a foolish ignorant girl as to think you could afford to pay Mr Higgins?

The Flower Girl. Why shouldnt I? I know what lessons cost as well as you do; and I'm ready to pay.

Higgins. How much?

The Flower Girl (coming back to him, triumphant). Now youre talking! I thought youd come off it when you saw a chance of getting back a bit of whay you chucked at me last night. *(Confidentially.)* Youd had a drop in, hadnt you?

Higgins (peremptorily). Sit down.

The Flower Girl. Oh, if youre going to make a compliment of it —

Higgins (thundering at her). Sit down.

Mrs Pearce (severely). Sit down, girl. Do as youre told.

The Flower Girl. Ah-ah-ah-ow-ow-oo! *(She stands, half rebellious, half bewildered.)*

Pickering (very courteous). Wont you sit down? *(He places the stray chair near the hearthrug between himself and Higgins.)*

Liza (coyly). Dont mind if I do. *(She sits down. Pickering returns to the hearthrug.)*

Higgins. Whats your name?

The Flower Girl. Liza Doolittle.

Higgins (declaiming gravely).
> Eliza, Elizabeth, Betsy and Bess,
> They went to the woods to get a bird's nes':
Pickering.   They found a nest with four eggs in it:
Higgins.   They took one apiece, and left three in it.

They laugh heartily at their own fun.

Liza. Oh, dont be silly.

Mrs Pearce (placing herself behind Eliza's chair). You mustnt speak to the gentleman like that.

Liza. Well, why wont he speak sensible to me?

Higgins. Come back to business. How much do you propose to pay me for the lessons?

Liza. Oh, I know whats right. A lady friend of mine gets French lessons for eighteenpence an hour from a real French gentleman. Well, you wouldnt have the face to ask me the same for teaching me my own language as you would for French; so I wont give more than a shilling. Take it or leave it.

Higgins (walking up and down the room, rattling his keys and his cash in his pockets). You know, Pickering, if you consider a shilling, not as a simple shilling, but as a percentage of this girl's income, it works out as fully equivalent to sixty or seventy guineas from a millionaire.

Pickering. How so?

Higgins. Figure it out. A millionaire has about £150 a day. She earns about half-a-crown.

Liza (haughtily). Who told you I only —

Higgins (continuing). She offers me two-fifths of her day's income for a lesson. Two-fifths of a millionaire's income for a day would be somewhere about £60. It's handsome. By George, it's enormous! it's the biggest offer I ever had.

Liza (rising, terrified). Sixty pounds! What are you talking about? I never offered you sixty pounds. Where would I get —

Higgins. Hold your tongue.

Liza (weeping). But I aint got sixty pounds. Oh —

Mrs Pearce. Dont cry, you silly girl. Sit Down. Nobody is going to touch your money.

Higgins. Somebody is going to touch you, with a broomstick, if you dont stop snivelling. Sit down.

Liza (obeying slowly). Ah-ah-ah-ow-oo-o! One would think you was my father.

Higgins. If I decide to teach you, I'll be worse than two fathers to you. Here! *(He offers her his silk handkerchief.)*

Liza. What this for?

Higgins. To wipe your eyes. To wipe any part of your face that feels moist. Remember: thats your handkerchief; and thats your sleeve. Dont mistake the one for the other if you wish to become a lady in a shop.

Liza, utterly bewildered, stares helplessly at him.

Mrs Pearce. It's no use talking to her like that, Mr Higgins: she doesnt understand you. Besides, youre quite wrong: she doesnt do it that way at all *(she takes the handkerchief.)*

Liza (snatching it). Here! You give me that handkerchief. He gev it to me, not to you.

Pickering (laughing). He did. I think it must be regarded as her property, Mrs Pearce.

Mrs. Pearce (resigning herself). Serve you right, Mr Higgins.

Pickering. Higgins: I'm interested. What about the ambassador's garden party? I'll say youre the greatest teacher alive if you make that good. I'll bet you all the expenses of the experiment you cant do it. And I'll pay for the lessons.

Liza. Oh, you are real good. Thank you, Captain.

Higgins (tempted, looking at her). It's almost irresistible. She's so deliciously low — so horribly dirty —

Liza (protesting extremely). Ah-ah-ah-ah-ow-ow-oo-oo!!! I aint dirty: I washed my face and hands afore I come, I did.

Pickering. Youre certainly not going to turn her head with flattery, Higgins.

Mrs Pearce (uneasy). Oh, dont say that, sir: theres more ways than one of turning a girl's head; and nobody can do it better than Mr Higgins, though he may not always mean it. I do hope sir, you wont encourage him to do anything foolish.

Higgins (becoming excited as the idea grows on him). What is life but a series of inspired follies? The difficulty is to find them to do. Never lose a chance: it doesnt come every day. I shall make a duchess of this draggletailed guttersnipe.

Liza (strongly deprecating this view of her). Ah-ah-ah-ow-ow-oo!

Higgins (carried away). Yes: in six months — in three if she has a good ear and a quick tongue — I'll take her anywhere and pass her off as anything. We'll start today: now! this moment! Take her away and clean her, Mrs Pearce. Monkey Brand, if it wont come off any other way. Is there a good fire in the kitchen?

Mrs Pearce (protesting). Yes; but —

Higgins (storming on). Take all her clothes off and burn them. Ring up Whiteley or somebody for new ones. Wrap her up in brown paper til they come.

Liza. Youre no gentleman, youre not, to talk of such things. I'm a
good girl, I am; and I know what the like of you are, I do.

Higgins. We want none of your Lisson Grove prudery here, young
woman. Youve got to learn to behave like a duchess. Take her
away, Mrs Pearce. If she gives you any trouble, wallop her.

*Liza (springing up and running between Pickering and Mrs Pearce
for protection).* No! I'll call the police, I will.

Mrs Pearce. But Ive no place to put her.

Higgins. Put her in the dustbin.

Liza. Ah-ah-ah-ow-ow-oo!

Pickering. Oh come, Higgins! be reasonable.

Mrs Pearce (resolutely). You must be reasonable, Mr Higgins: really
you must. You cant walk over everybody like this.

*Higgins, thus scolded, subsides. The hurricane is succeeded by a
zephyr of amiable surprise.*

Higgins (with professional exquisiteness of modulation). I walk over
everybody! My dear Mrs Pearce, my dear Pickering, I never had
the slightest intention of walking over anyone. All I propose is that
we should be kind to this poor girl. We must help her to prepare
and fit herself for her new station in life. If I did not express myself
clearly it was because I did not wish to hurt her delicacy, or yours.

Liza, reassured, steals back to her chair.

Mrs Pearce (to Pickering). Well, did you ever hear anything like that,
sir?

Pickering (laughing heartily). Never, Mrs Pearce: never.

Higgins (patiently). Whats the matter?

Mrs Pearce. Well, the matter is, sir, that you cant take a girl up like
that as if you were picking up a pebble on the beach.

Higgins. Why not?

Mrs Pearce. Why not! But you dont know anything about her. What
about her parents? She may be married.

Liza. Garn!

Higgins. There! As the girl very properly says, Garn! Married indeed! Dont you know that a woman of that class looks a worn out
drudge of fifty a year after she's married?

Liza. Whood marry me?

*Higgins (suddenly resorting to the most thrillingly beautiful low
tones in his best elocutionary style).* By George, Eliza, the streets
will be strewn with the bodies of men shooting themselves for
your sake before Ive done with you.

Mrs Pearce. Nonsense, sir. You mustnt talk like that to her.

Liza (rising and squaring herself determinedly). I'm going away.
He's off his chump, he is. I dont want no balmies teaching me.

*Higgins (wounded in his tenderest point by her insensibility to his
elocution).* Oh, indeed! I'm mad, am I? Very well, Mrs Pearce:
you neednt order the new clothes for her. Throw her out.

Liza (whimpering). Nah-ow. You got no right to touch me.

Mrs Pearce. You see now what comes of being saucy. *(Indicating the
door.)* This way, please.

Liza (almost in tears). I didnt want no clothes. I wouldnt have taken
them. *(She throws away the handkerchief.)* I can buy my own
clothes.

*Higgins (deftly retrieving the handkerchief and intercepting her on
her reluctant way to the door).* Youre an ungrateful wicked girl.
This is my return for offering to take you out of the gutter and dress
you beautifully and make a lady of you.

Mrs Pearce. Stop, Mr Higgins. I wont allow it. It's you that are
wicked. Go home to your parents, girl; and tell them to take better
care of you.

Liza. I aint got no parents. They told me I was big enough to earn my
own living and turned me out.

Mrs Pearce. Wheres your mother?

Liza. I aint got no mother. Her that turned me out was my sixth
stepmother. But I done without them. And I'm a good girl, I am.

Higgins. Very well, then, what on earth is all this fuss about? The
girl doesnt belong to anybody — is no use to anybody but me. *(He
goes to Mrs Pearce and begins coaxing.)* You can adopt her, Mrs
Pearce: I'm sure a daughter would be a great amusement to you.
Now dont make any more fuss. Take her downstairs; and —

Mrs Pearce. But whats to become of her? Is she to be paid anything?
Do be sensible, sir.

Higgins. Oh, pay her whatever is necessary: put it down in the housekeeping book. *(Impatiently.)* What on earth will she want with
money? She'll have her food and her clothes. She'll only drink if
you give her money.

Liza (turning on him). Oh you are a brute. It's a lie: nobody ever
saw the sign of liquor on me. *(To Pickering.)* Oh, sir: youre a
gentleman: dont let him speak to me like that.

Pickering (in good-humored remonstrance). Does it occur to you,
Higgins, that the girl has some feelings?

Higgins (looking critically at her). Oh no, I dont think so. Not any
feelings that we need bother about. *(Cheerily.)* Have you, Eliza?

Liza. I got my feelings same as anyone else.

Higgins (to Pickering, reflectively). You see the difficulty?

Pickering. Eh? What difficulty?

Higgins. To get her to talk grammar. The mere pronunciation is easy enough.

Liza. I dont want to talk grammar. I want to talk like a lady in a flower-shop.

Mrs Pearce. Will you please keep to the point, Mr Higgins. I want to know on what terms the girl is to be here. Is she to have any wages? And what is to become of her when youve finished your teaching? You must look ahead a little.

Higgins (impatiently). Whats to become of her if I leave her in the gutter? Tell me that, Mrs Pearce.

Mrs Pearce. Thats her own business, not yours, Mr Higgins.

Higgins. Well, when Ive done with her, we can throw her back into the gutter; and then it will be her own business again; so thats all right.

Liza. Oh, youve no feeling heart in you: you dont care for nothing but yourself. *(She rises and takes the floor resolutely.)* Here! Ive had enough of this. I'm going. *(Making for the door.)* You ought to be ashamed of yourself, you ought.

Higgins (snatching a chocolate cream from the piano, his eyes suddenly beginning to twinkle with mischief). Have some chocolates, Eliza.

Liza (halting, tempted). How do I know what might be in them? Ive heard of girls being drugged by the like of you.

Higgins whips out his penknife; cuts a chocolate in two; puts one half into his mouth and bolts it; and offers her the other half.

Higgins. Pledge of good faith, Eliza. I eat one half: you eat the other. *(Liza opens her mouth to retort: he pops the half chocolate into it.)* You shall have boxes of them, barrels of them, every day. You shall live on them. Eh?

Liza (who has disposed of the chocolate after being nearly choked by it). I wouldnt have ate it, only I'm too ladylike to take it out of my mouth.

Higgins. Listen, Eliza. I think you said you came in a taxi.

Liza. Well, what if I did? Ive as good a right to take a taxi as anyone else.

Higgins. You have, Eliza; and in future you shall have as many taxis as you want. You shall go up and down and round the town in a taxi every day. Think of that, Eliza.

Mrs Pearce. Mr Higgins: youre tempting the girl. It's not right. She should think of the future.

Higgins. At her age! Nonsense! Time enough to think of the future when you havnt any future to think of. No Eliza: do as this lady does: think of other people's futures; but never think of your own. Think of chocolates, and taxis, and gold, and diamonds.

Liza. No: I dont want no gold and no diamonds, I'm a good girl, I am. *(She sits down again, with an attempt at dignity.)*

Higgins. You shall remain so, Eliza, under the care of Mrs Pearce. And you shall marry an officer in the Guards, with a beautiful moustache: the son of a marquis, who will disinherit him for marrying you, but will relent when he sees your beauty and goodness —

Pickering. Excuse me, Higgins; but I really must interfere. Mrs Pearce is quite right. If this girl is to put herself in your hands for six months for an experiment in teaching, she must understand thoroughly what she's doing.

Higgins. How can she? She's incapable of understanding anything. Besides, do any of us understand what we are doing? If we did, would we ever do it?

Pickering. Very clever, Higgins; but not to the present point. *(To Eliza.)* Miss Doolittle —

Liza (overwhelmed). Ah-ah-ow-oo!

Higgins. There! Thats all youll get out of Eliza. Ah-ah-ow-oo! No use explaining. As a military man you ought to know that. Give her her orders: thats enough for her. Eliza: you are to live here for the next six months, learning how to speak beautifully, like a lady in a florist's shop. If youre good and do whatever youre told, you shall sleep in a proper bedroom, and have lots to eat, and money to buy chocolates and take rides in taxis. If your naughty and idle you will sleep in the back kitchen among the black beetles, and be walloped by Mrs Pearce with a broomstick. At the end of six months you shall go to Buckingham Palace in a carriage, beautifully dressed. If the King finds out youre not a lady, you will be taken by the police to the Tower of London, where your head will be cut off as a warning to other presumptuous flower girls. If you are not found out, you shall have a present of seven-and-sixpence to start life with as a lady in a shop. If you refuse this offer you will be a most ungrateful wicked girl; and the angels will weep for you. *(To Pickering.)* Now are you satisfied, Pickering? *(To Mrs Pearce.)* Can I put it more plainly and fairly, Mrs Pearce?

Mrs Pearce (patiently). I think youd better let me speak to the girl properly in private. I dont know that I can take charge of her or consent to the arrangement at all. Of course I know you dont mean her any harm; but when you get what you call interested in people's accents, you never think or care what may happen to them or you. Come with me, Eliza.

Higgins. Thats all right. Thank you, Mrs Pearce. Bundle her off to the bath-room.

Liza (rising ruluctantly and suspiciously). Youre a great bully, you are. I wont stay here if I dont like. I wont let nobody wallop me. I never asked to go to Bucknam Palace, I didnt. I was never in trouble with the police, not me. I'm a good girl —

Mrs Pearce. Dont answer back, girl. You dont understand the gentleman. Come with me. *(She leads the way to the door, and holds it open for Eliza.)*

Liza (as she goes out). Well, what I say is right. I wont go near the King, not if I'm going to have my head cut off. If I'd known what I was letting myself in for, I wouldnt have come here. I always been a good girl; and I never offered to say a word to him; and I dont owe him nothing; and I dont care; and I wont be put upon; and I have my feelings the same as anyone else —

Mrs Pearce shuts the door; and Eliza's plaints are no longer audible.

. . .

(Eliza is taken upstairs to the third floor greatly to her surprise; for she expected to be taken down to the scullery. There Mrs Pearce opens a door and takes her into a spare bedroom.)

Mrs Pearce. I will have to put you here. This will be your bedroom.

Liza. O-h, I couldnt sleep here, missus. It's too good for the likes of me. I should be afraid to touch anything. I aint a duchess yet, you know.

Mrs Pearce. You have got to make yourself as clean as the room: then you wont be afraid of it. And you must call me Mrs Pearce, not missus. *(She throws open the door of the dressingroom, now modernized as a bathroom.)*

Liza. Gawd! whats this? Is this where you wash clothes? Funny sort of copper I call it.

Mrs Pearce. It is not a copper. This is where we wash ourselves, Eliza, and where I am going to wash you.

Liza. You expect me to get into that and wet myself all over! Not me. I should catch my death. I knew a woman did it every Saturday night; and she died of it.

Mrs Pearce. Mr Higgins has the gentlemen's bathroom downstairs; and he has a bath every morning, in cold water.

Liza. Ugh! He's made of iron, that man.

Mrs Pearce. If you are to sit with him and the Colonel and be taught you will have to do the same. They wont like the smell of you if you dont. But you can have the water as hot as you like. There are two taps: hot and cold.

Liza (weeping). I couldnt. I dursnt. Its not natural: it would kill me. Ive never had a bath in my life: not what youd call a proper one.

Mrs Pearce. Well, dont you want to be clean and sweet and decent, like a lady? You know you cant be a nice girl inside if youre a dirty slut outside.

Liza. Boohoo!!!!

Mrs Pearce. Now stop crying and go back into your room and take off all your clothes. Then wrap yourself in this *(Taking down a gown from its peg and handing it to her)* and come back to me. I will get the bath ready.

Liza (all tears). I cant. I wont. I'm not used to it. Ive never took off all my clothes before. It's not right: it's not decent.

Mrs Pearce. Nonsense, child. Dont you take off all your clothes every night when you go to bed?

Liza (amazed). No. Why should I? I should catch my death. Of course I take off my skirt.

Mrs Pearce. Do you mean that you sleep in the underclothes you wear in the daytime?

Liza. What else have I to sleep in?

Mr Pearce. You will never do that again as long as you live here. I will get you a proper nightdress.

Liza. Do you mean change into cold things and lie awake shivering half the night? You want to kill me, you do.

Mrs Pearce. I want to change you from a frowzy slut to a clean respectable girl fit to sit with the gentlemen in the study. Are you going to trust me and do what I tell you or be thrown out and sent back to the flower basket?

Liza. But you dont know what the cold is to me. You dont know how I dread it.

Mrs Pearce. Your bed wont be cold here: I will put a hot water bottle in it. *(Pushing her into the bedroom.)* Off with you and undress.

Liza. Oh, if only I'd a known what a dreadful thing it is to be clean I'd never have come. I didnt know when I was well off. I — *(Mrs Pearce pushes her through the door, but leaves it partly open lest her prisoner should take to flight.)*

Mrs Pearce puts on a pair of white rubber sleeves, and fills the bath, mixing hot and cold, and testing the result with the bath thermometer. She perfumes it with a handful of bath salts and adds a palmful of mustard. She then takes a formidable looking long handled scrubbing brush and soaps it profusely with a ball of scented soap.

Eliza comes back with nothing on but the bath gown huddled tightly round her, a piteous spectacle of abject terror.

Mrs Pearce. Now come along. Take that thing off.

Liza. Oh I couldnt, Mrs Pearce: I reely couldnt. I never done such a thing.

Mrs Pearce. Nonsense. Here: step in and tell me whether its hot enough for you.

Liza. Ah-oo! Ah-oo! It's too hot.

Mrs Pearce (*deftly snatching the gown away and throwing Eliza down on her back*). It wont hurt you. (*She sets to work with the scrubbing brush.*)

Eliza's screams are heartrending.

• • •

(Meanwhile the Colonel has been having it out with Higgins about Eliza. Pickering has come from the hearth to the chair and seated himself astride of it with his arms on the back to cross-examine him.)

Pickering. Excuse the straight question, Higgins. Are you a man of good character where women are concerned?

Higgins (*moodily*). Have you ever met a man of good character where women are concerned?

Pickering. Yes: very frequently.

Higgins (*dogmatically, lifting himself on his hands to the level of the piano, and sitting on it with a bounce*). Well, I havnt. I find that the moment I let a woman make friends with me, she becomes jealous, exacting, suspicious, and a damned nuisance. I find that the moment I let myself make friends with a woman, I become selfish and tyrannical. Women upset everything. When you let them into your life, you find that the woman is driving at one thing and youre driving at another.

Pickering. At what, for example?

Higgins (*coming off the piano restlessly*). Oh, Lord knows! I suppose the woman wants to live her own life; and the man wants to live his; and each tries to drag the other on to the wrong track. One wants to go north and the other south; and the result is that both have to go east, though they both hate the east wind. (*He sits down on the bench at the keyboard.*) So here I am, a confirmed old bachelor, and likely to remain so.

Pickering (*rising and standing over him gravely*). Come, Higgins! You know what I mean. If I'm to be in this business I shall feel responsible for that girl. I hope it's understood that no advantage is to be taken of her position.

Higgins. What! That thing! Sacred, I assure you. *(Rising to explain.)* You see, she'll be a pupil; and teaching would be impossible unless pupils were sacred. Ive taught scores of American million-airesses how to speak English: the best looking women in the world. I'm seasoned. They might as well be blocks of wood. *I* might as well be a block of wood. It's —

Mrs Pearce opens the door. She has Eliza's hat in her hand. Picker-ing retires to the easy-chair at the hearth and sits down.

Higgins (eagerly). Well, Mrs Pearce: is it all right?
Mrs Pearce (at the door). I just wish to trouble you with a word, if I may, Mr Higgins.
Higgins. Yes, certainly. Come in. *(She comes forward.)* Dont burn that, Mrs Pearce. I'll keep it as a curiosity. *(He takes the hat.)*
Mrs Pearce. Handle it carefully, sir, please. I had to promise her not to burn it; but I had better put it in the oven for a while.
Higgins (putting it down hastily on the piano). Oh! thank you. Well, what have you to say to me?
Pickering. Am I in the way?
Mrs Pearce. Not at all, sir. Mr Higgins: will you please be very par-ticular what you say before the girl?
Higgins (sternly). Of course. I'm always particular about what I say. Why do you say this to me?
Mrs Pearce (unmoved). No, sir: youre not at all particular when youve mislaid anything or when you get a little impatient. Now it doesnt matter before me: I'm used to it. But you really must not swear before the girl.
Higgins (indignantly). I swear! *(Most emphatically.)* I never swear. I detest the habit. What the devil do you mean?
Mrs Pearce (stolidly). Thats what I mean, sir. You swear a great deal too much. I dont mind your damning and blasting, and what the devil and where the devil and who the devil —
Higgins. Mrs Pearce: this language from your lips! Really!
Mrs Pearce (not to be put off). — but there is a certain word I must ask you not to use. The girl used it herself when she began to enjoy the bath. It begins with the same letter as bath. She knows no better: she learnt it at her mother's knee. But she must not hear it from your lips.
Higgins (loftily). I cannot charge myself with having ever uttered it, Mrs Pearce. *(She looks at him steadfastly. He adds, hiding an uneasy conscience with a judicial air.)* Except perhaps in a mo-ment of extreme and justifiable excitement.

Mrs Pearce. Only this morning, sir, you applied it to your boots, to the butter, and to the brown bread.

Higgins. Oh, that! Mere alliteration, Mrs Pearce, natural to a poet.

Mrs Pearce. Well, sir, whatever you choose to call it, I beg you not to let the girl hear you repeat it.

Higgins. Oh, very well, very well. Is that all?

Mrs Pearce. No, sir. We shall have to be very particular with this girl as to personal cleanliness.

Higgins. Certainly. Quite right. Most important.

Mrs Pearce. I mean not to be slovenly about her dress or untidy in leaving things about.

Higgins (going to her solemnly). Just so. I intended to call your attention to that. *(He passes on to Pickering, who is enjoying the conversation immensely.)* It is these little things that matter, Pickering. Take care of the pence and the pounds will take care of themselves is as true of personal habits as of money. *(He comes to anchor on the hearthrug, with the air of a man in an unassailable position.)*

Mrs Pearce. Yes, sir. Then might I ask you not to come down to breakfast in your dressing-gown, or at any rate not to use it as a napkin to the extent you do, sir. And if you would be so good as not to eat everything off the same plate, and to remember not to put the porridge saucepan out of your hand on the clean tablecloth, it would be a better example to the girl. You know you nearly choked yourself with a fishbone in the jam only last week.

Higgins (routed from the hearthrug and drifting back to the piano). I may do these things sometimes in absence of mind; but surely I dont do them habitually. *(Angrily.)* By the way: my dressing-gown smells most damnably of benzine.

Mrs Pearce. No doubt it does, Mr Higgins. But if you will wipe your fingers —

Higgins (yelling). Oh very well, very well: I'll wipe them in my hair in future.

Mrs Pearce. I hope youre not offended, Mr Higgins.

Higgins (shocked at finding himself thought capable of an unamiable sentiment). Not at all, not at all. Youre quite right, Mrs Pearce: I shall be particularly careful before the girl. Is that all?

Mrs Pearce. No, sir. Might she use some of those Japanese dresses you brought from abroad? I really cant put her back into her old things.

Higgins. Certainly. Anything you like. Is that all?

Mrs Pearce. Thank you, sir. Thats all. *(She goes out.)*

Higgins. You know, Pickering, that woman has the most extraordinary ideas about me. Here I am, a shy, diffident sort of man. Ive never been able to feel really grown-up and tremendous, like other chaps. And yet she's firmly persuaded that I'm an arbitrary overbearing bossing kind of person. I cant account for it.

Mrs Pearce returns.

Mrs Pearce. If you please, sir, the trouble's beginning already. Theres a dustman° downstairs, Alfred Doolittle, wants to see you. He says you have his daughter here.

Pickering (rising). Phew! I say!

Higgins (promptly). Send the blackguard up.

Mrs Pearce. Oh, very well, sir. *(She goes out).*

Pickering. He may not be a blackguard, Higgins.

Higgins. Nonsense. Of course he's a blackguard.

Pickering. Whether he is or not, I'm afraid we shall have some trouble with him.

Higgins (confidently). Oh no: I think not. If theres any trouble he shall have it with me, not I with him. And we are sure to get something interesting out of him.

Pickering. About the girl?

Higgins. No. I mean his dialect.

Pickering. Oh!

Mrs Pearce (at the door). Doolittle, sir. *(She admits Doolittle and retires.)*

Alfred Doolittle is an elderly but vigorous dustman, clad in the costume of his profession, including a hat with a back brim covering his neck and shoulders. He has well marked and rather interesting features, and seems equally free from fear and conscience. He has a remarkably expressive voice, the result of a habit of giving vent to his feelings without reserve. His present pose is that of wounded honor and stern resolution.

Doolittle (at the door, uncertain which of the two gentlemen is his man). Professor Iggins?

Higgins. Here. Good morning. Sit down.

Doolittle. Morning, Governor. *(He sits down magisterially.)* I come about a very serious matter, Governor.

Higgins (to Pickering). Brought up in Hounslow. Mother Welsh, I should think. *(Doolittle opens his mouth, amazed. Higgins continues.)* What do you want, Doolittle?

Doolittle (menacingly). I want my daughter: thats what I want. See?

Higgins. Of course you do. Youre her father, arnt you? You dont

dustman garbage man

suppose anyone else wants her, do you? I'm glad to see you have some spark of family feeling left. She's upstairs. Take her away at once.

Doolittle (rising, fearfully taken aback). What!

Higgins. Take her away. Do you suppose I'm going to keep your daughter for you?

Doolittle (remonstrating). Now, now, look here, Governor. Is this reasonable? Is it fairity to take advantage of a man like this? The girl belongs to me. You got her. Where do I come in? *(He sits down again.)*

Higgins. Your daughter had the audacity to come to my house and ask me to teach her how to speak properly so that she could get a place in a flower-shop. This gentleman and my housekeeper have been here all the time. *(Bullying him.)* How dare you come here and attempt to blackmail me? You sent her here on purpose.

Doolittle (protesting). No, Governor.

Higgins. You must have. How else could you possibly know that she is here?

Doolittle. Dont take a man up like that, Governor.

Higgins. The police shall take you up. This is a plant — a plot to extort money by threats. I shall telephone for the police. *(He goes resolutely to the telephone and opens the directory.)*

Doolittle. Have I asked you for a brass farthing? I leave it to the gentleman here: have I said a word about money?

Higgins (throwing the book aside and marching down on Doolittle with a poser). What else did you come for?

Doolittle (sweetly). Well, what would a man come for? Be human, Governor.

Higgins (disarmed). Alfred: did you put her up to it?

Doolittle. So help me, Governor, I never did. I take my Bible oath I aint seen the girl these two months past.

Higgins. Then how did you know she was here?

Doolittle ("most musical, most melancholy"). I'll tell you, Governor, if youll only let me get a word in. I'm willing to tell you. I'm wanting to tell you. I'm waiting to tell you.

Higgins. Pickering: this chap has a certain natural gift of rhetoric. Observe the rhythm of his native woodnotes wild. "I'm willing to tell you: I'm wanting to tell you: I'm waiting to tell you." Sentimental rhetoric! thats the Welsh strain in him. It also accounts for his mendacity and dishonesty.

Pickering. Oh, please, Higgins: I'm west country myself. *(To Doolittle.)* How did you know the girl was here if you didnt send her?

Doolittle. It was like this, Governor. The girl took a boy in the taxi to give him a jaunt. Son of her landlady, he is. He hung about on the chance of her giving him another ride home. Well, she sent him back for her luggage when she heard you was willing for her to stop here. I met the boy at the corner of Long Acre and Endell Street.

Higgins. Public house. Yes?

Doolittle. The poor man's club, Governor: why shouldnt I?

Pickering. Do let him tell his story, Higgins.

Doolittle. He told me what was up. And I ask you, what was my feelings and my duty as a father? I says to the boy, "You bring me the luggage," I says —

Pickering. Why didnt you go for it yourself?

Doolittle. Landlady wouldnt have trusted me with it, Governor. She's that kind of woman: you know. I had to give the boy a penny afore he trusted me with it, the little swine. I brought it to her just to oblige you like, and make myself agreeable. Thats all.

Higgins. How much luggage?

Doolittle. Musical instrument, Governor. A few pictures, a trifle of jewlery, and a bird-cage. She said she didnt want no clothes. What was I to think from that, Governor? I ask you as a parent what was I to think?

Higgins. So you came to rescue her from worse than death, eh?

Doolittle (appreciatively: relieved at being so well understood). Just so, Governor. Thats right.

Pickering. But why did you bring her luggage if you intended to take her away?

Doolittle. Have I said a word about taking her away? Have I now?

Higgins (determinedly). Youre going to take her away, double quick. *(He crosses to the hearth and rings the bell.)*

Doolittle (rising). No, Governor. Dont say that. I'm not the man to stand in my girl's light. Heres a career opening for her, as you might say; and —

Mrs. Pearce opens the door and awaits orders.

Higgins. Mrs Pearce: this is Eliza's father. He has come to take her away. Give her to him. *(He goes back to the piano, with an air of washing his hands of the whole affair.)*

Doolittle. No. This is a misunderstanding. Listen here —

Mrs Pearce. He cant take her away, Mr Higgins: how can he? You told me to burn her clothes.

Doolittle. Thats right. I cant carry the girl through the streets like a blooming monkey, can I? I put it to you.

Higgins. You have put it to me that you want your daughter. Take your daughter. If she has no clothes go out and buy her some.

Doolittle (desperate). Wheres the clothes she come in? Did I burn
them or did your missus here?

Mrs Pearce. I am the housekeeper, if you please. I have sent for
some clothes for your girl. When they come you can take her away.
You can wait in the kitchen. This way, please.

*Doolittle, much troubled, accompanies her to the door; then hesi-
tates; finally turns confidentially to Higgins.*

Doolittle. Listen here, Governor. You and me is men of the world
aint we?

Higgins. Oh! Men of the world, are we? Youd better go, Mrs Pearce.

Mrs Pearce. I think so, indeed, sir. *(She goes, with dignity.)*

Pickering. The floor is yours, Mr Doolittle.

Doolittle (to Pickering). I thank you, Governor. *(To Higgins, who
takes refuge on the piano bench, a little overwhelmed by the
proximity of his visitor; for Doolittle has a professional flavour of
dust about him.)* Well, the truth is, Ive taken a sort of fancy to you,
Governor; and if you want the girl, I'm not so set on having her
back home again but what I might be open to an arrangement.
Regarded in the light of a young woman, she's a fine handsome
girl. As a daughter she's not worth her keep; and so I tell you
straight. All I ask is my rights as a father; and youre the last man
alive to expect me to let her go for nothing; for I can see youre
one of the straight sort, Governor. Well, whats a five-pound note
to you? and whats Eliza to me? *(He turns to his chair and sits
down judicially.)*

Pickering. I think you ought to know, Doolittle, that Mr Higgins's
intentions are entirely honorable.

Doolittle. Course they are, Governor. If I thought they wasn't, I'd
ask fifty.

Higgins (revolted). Do you mean to say that you would sell your
daughter for £ 50?

Doolittle. Not in a general way I wouldnt; but to oblige a gentleman
like you I'd do a good deal, I do assure you.

Pickering. Have you no morals, man?

Doolittle (unabashed). Cant afford them, Governor. Neither could
you if you was as poor as me. Not that I mean any harm, you know.
But if Liza is going to have a bit out of this, why not me too?

Higgins (troubled). I dont know what to do, Pickering. There can be
no question that as a matter of morals it's a positive crime to give
this chap a farthing. And yet I feel a sort of rough justice in his
claim.

Doolittle. Thats it, Governor. Thats all I say. A father's heart, as it were.

Pickering. Well, I know the feeling; but really it seems hardly right —

Doolittle. Dont say that, Governor. Dont look at it that way. What am I, Governors both? I ask you, what am I? I'm one of the undeserving poor: thats what I am. Think of what that means to a man. It means that he's up agen middle class morality all the time. If theres anything going, and I put in for a bit of it, it's always the same story: "Youre undeserving; so you cant have it." But my needs is as great as the most deserving widow's that ever got money out of six different charities in one week for the death of the same husband. I dont need less than a deserving man: I need more. I dont eat less hearty than him; and I drink a lot more. I want a bit of amusement, cause I'm a thinking man. I want cheerfulness and a song and a band when I feel low. Well, they charge me just the same for everything as they charge the deserving. What is middle class morality? Just an excuse for never giving me anything. Therefore, I ask you, as two gentlemen, not to play that game on me. I'm playing straight with you. I aint pretending to be deserving. I'm undeserving; and I mean to go on being undeserving. I like it; and thats the truth. Will you take advantage of a man's nature to do him out of the price of his own daughter what he's brought up and fed and clothed by the sweat of his brow until she's growed big enough to be interesting to you two gentlemen? Is five pounds unreasonable? I put it to you; and I leave it to you.

Higgins (rising, and going over to Pickering). Pickering: if we were to take this man in hand for three months, he could choose between a seat in the Cabinet and a popular pulpit in Wales.

Pickering. What do you say to that, Doolittle?

Doolittle. Not me, Governor, thank you kindly. Ive heard all the preachers and all the prime ministers — for I'm a thinking man and game for politics or religion or social reform same as all the other amusements — and I tell you it's a dog's life any way you look at it. Undeserving poverty is my line. Taking one station in society with another, it's — it's — well, it's the only one that has any ginger in it, to my taste.

Higgins. I suppose we must give him a fiver.

Pickering. He'll make a bad use of it, I'm afraid.

Doolittle. Not me, Governor, so help me I wont. Dont you be afraid that I'll save it and spare it and live idle on it. There wont be a penny of it left by Monday: I'll have to go to work same as if I'd never had it. It wont pauperize me, you bet. Just one good spree for myself and the missus, giving pleasure to ourselves and em-

ployment to others, and satisfaction to you to think it's not been
throwed away. You couldnt spend it better.

*Higgins (taking out his pocket book and coming between Doolittle
and the piano).* This is irresistible. Lets give him ten. *(He offers
two notes to the dustman.)*

Doolittle. No, Governor. She wouldnt have the heart to spend ten;
and perhaps I shouldnt neither. Ten pounds is a lot of money: it
makes a man feel prudent like; and then goodbye to happiness.
You give me what I ask you, Governor: not a penny more, and not
a penny less.

Pickering. Why dont you marry that missus of yours? I rather draw
the line at encouraging that sort of immorality.

Doolittle. Tell her so, Governor: tell her so. I'm willing. It's me that
suffers by it. Ive no hold on her. I got to be agreeable to her. I got
to give her presents. I got to buy her clothes something sinful. I'm
a slave to that woman, Governor, just because I'm not her lawful
husband. And she knows it too. Catch her marrying me! Take my
advice, Governor: marry Eliza while she's young and dont know
no better. If you dont youll be sorry for it after. If you do, she'll be
sorry for it after; but better her than you, because youre a man, and
she's only a woman and dont know how to be happy anyhow.

Higgins. Pickering: if we listen to this man another minute, we shall
have no convictions left. *(To Doolittle.)* Five pounds I think you
said.

Doolittle. Thank you kindly, Governor.

Higgins. Youre sure you wont take ten?

Doolittle. Not now. Another time, Governor.

Higgins (handing him a five-pound note). Here you are.

Doolittle. Thank you, Governor. Good morning. *(He hurries to the
door, anxious to get away with his booty. When he opens it he is
confronted with a dainty and exquisitely clean young Japanese
lady in a simple blue cotton kimono printed cunningly with small
white jasmine blossoms. Mrs Pearce is with her. He gets out of her
way deferentially and apologizes.)* Beg pardon, miss.

The Japanese Lady. Garn! Dont you know your own daughter?

Doolittle			
Higgins	*exclaiming*		Bly me! it's Eliza!
Pickering	*simultaneously*		Whats that? This!
			By Jove!

Liza. Dont I look silly?

Higgins. Silly?

Mrs Pearce (at the door). Now, Mr Higgins, please dont say anything to make the girl conceited about herself.

Higgins (conscientiously). Oh! Quite right, Mrs Pearce. *(To Eliza.)*
Yes: damned silly.

Mrs Pearce. Please, sir.

Higgins (correcting himself). I mean extremely silly.

Liza. I should look all right with my hat on. *(She takes up her hat; puts it on; and walks across the room to the fireplace with a fashionable air.)*

Higgins. A new fashion, by George! And it ought to look horrible!

Doolittle (with fatherly pride). Well, I never thought she'd clean up as good looking as that, Governor. She's a credit to me, aint she?

Liza. I tell you, it's easy to clean up here. Hot and cold water on tap, just as much as you like, there is. Woolly towels, there is; and a towel horse so hot, it burns your fingers. Soft brushes to scrub yourself, and a wooden bowl of soap smelling like primroses. Now I know why ladies is so clean. Washing's a treat for them. Wish they could see what it is for the like of me!

Higgins. I'm glad the bathroom met with your approval.

Liza. It didnt: not all of it; and I dont care who hears me say it. Mrs Pearce knows.

Higgins. What was wrong, Mrs Pearce?

Mrs Pearce (blandly). Oh, nothing, sir. It doesnt matter.

Liza. I had a good mind to break it. I didnt know which way to look. But I hung a towel over it, I did.

Higgins. Over what?

Mrs. Pearce. Over the looking-glass, sir.

Higgins. Doolittle: you have brought your daughter up too strictly.

Doolittle. Me! I never brought her up at all, except to give her a lick of a strap now and again. Dont put it on me, Governor. She aint accustomed to it, you see: thats all. But she'll soon pick up your free-and-easy ways.

Liza. I'm a good girl, I am; and I wont pick up no free-and-easy ways.

Higgins. Eliza: if you say again that youre a good girl, your father shall take you home.

Liza. Not him. You dont know my father. All he come here for was to touch you for some money to get drunk on.

Doolittle. Well, what else would I want money for? To put into the plate in church, I suppose. *(She puts out her tongue at him. He is so incensed by this that Pickering presently finds it necessary to step between them.)* Dont you give me none of your lip; and dont let me hear you giving this gentleman any of it neither, or youll hear from me about it. See?

Higgins. Have you any further advice to give her before you go, Doolittle? Your blessing, for instance.

Doolittle. No, Governor: I aint such a mug as to put up my children to all I know myself. Hard enough to hold them in without that. If you want Eliza's mind improved, Governor, you do it yourself with a strap. So long, gentlemen. *(He turns to go.)*

Higgins (impressively). Stop. Youll come regularly to see your daughter. It's your duty, you know. My brother is a clergyman; and he could help you in your talks with her.

Doolittle (evasively). Certainly, I'll come, Governor. Not just this week, because I have a job at a distance. But later on you may depend on me. Afternoon, gentlemen. Afternoon, maam. *(He touches his hat to Mrs Pearce, who disdains the salutation and goes out. He winks at Higgins, thinking him probably a fellow sufferer from Mrs Pearce's difficult disposition, and follows her.)*

Liza. Dont you believe the old liar. He'd as soon you set a bulldog on him as a clergyman. You wont see him again in a hurry.

Higgins. I dont want to, Eliza. Do you?

Liza. Not me. I dont want never to see him again, I dont. He's a disgrace to me, he is, collecting dust, instead of working at his trade.

Pickering. What is his trade, Eliza?

Liza. Talking money out of other people's pockets into his own. His proper trade's a navvy; and he works at it sometimes too — for exercise — and earns good money at it. Aint you going to call me Miss Doolittle any more?

Pickering. I beg your pardon, Miss Doolittle. It was a slip of the tongue.

Liza. Oh, I dont mind; only it sounded so genteel. I should just like to take a taxi to the corner of Tottenham Court Road and get out there and tell it to wait for me, just to put the girls in their place a bit. I wouldnt speak to them, you know.

Pickering. Better wait til we get you something really fashionable.

Higgins. Besides, you shouldnt cut your old friends now that you have risen in the world. Thats what we call snobbery.

Liza. You dont call the like of them my friends now, I should hope. Theyve took it out of me often enough with their ridicule when they had the chance; and now I mean to get a bit of my own back. But if I'm to have fashionable clothes, I'll wait. I should like to have some. Mrs Pearce says youre going to give me some to wear in bed at night different to what I wear in the daytime; but it do seem a waste of money when you could get something to shew. Besides, I never could fancy changing into cold things on a winter night.

Mrs. Pearce (coming back). Now, Eliza. The new things have come for you to try on.

Liza. Ah-ow-oo-ooh! *(She rushes out.)*

Mrs Pearce (following her). Oh, dont rush about like that, girl. *(She shuts the door behind her.)*

Higgins. Pickering: we have taken on a stiff job.

Pickering (with conviction). Higgins: we have.

• • •

(There seems to be some curiosity as to what Higgins's lessons to Eliza were like. Well, here is a sample: the first one.

Picture Eliza, in her new clothes, and feeling her inside put out of step by a lunch, dinner, and breakfast of a kind to which it is unaccustomed, seated with Higgins and the Colonel in the study, feeling like a hospital out-patient at a first encounter with the doctors.

Higgins, constitutionally unable to sit still, discomposes her still more by striding restlessly about. But for the reassuring presence and quietude of her friend the Colonel she would run for her life, even back to Drury Lane.)

Higgins. Say your alphabet.

Liza. I know my alphabet. Do you think I know nothing? I dont need to be taught like a child.

Higgins (thundering). Say your alphabet.

Pickering. Say it, Miss Doolittle. You will understand presently. Do what he tells you; and let him teach you in his own way.

Liza. Oh well, if you put it like that — Ahyee, bəyee, cəyee, dɜee —

Higgins (with the roar of a wounded lion). Stop. Listen to this, Pickering. This is what we pay for as elementary education. This unfortunate animal has been locked up for nine years in school at our expense to teach her to speak and read the language of Shakespear and Milton. And the result is Ahyee, Bə-yee, Cə-yee, Də-yee. *(To Eliza.)* Say A, B, C, D.

Liza (almost in tears). But I'm sayin it. Ahyee, Bəyee, Cə-yee —

Higgins. Stop. Say a cup of tea.

Liza. A cappə tə-ee.

Higgins. Put your tongue forward until it squeezes against the top of your lower teeth. Now say cup.

Liza. C-c-c—I cant. C-Cup.

Pickering. Good. Splendid, Miss Doolittle.

Higgins. By Jupiter, she's done it at the first shot. Pickering: we shall make a duchess of her. *(To Eliza.)* Now do you think you could possibly say tea? Not tə-yee, mind: if you ever say bə-yee cə-yee də-yee again you shall be dragged round the room three times by the hair of your head. *(Fortissimo.)* T, T, T, T.

Liza (weeping). I cant hear no difference cep that it sounds more genteel-like when you say it.

Higgins. Well, if you can hear that difference, what the devil are you crying for? Pickering: give her a chocolate.

Pickering. No, no. Never mind crying a little, Miss Doolittle: you are doing very well; and the lessons wont hurt. I promise you I wont let him drag you round the room by your hair.

Higgins. Be off with you to Mrs Pearce and tell her about it. Think about it. Try to do it by yourself: and keep your tongue well forward in your mouth instead of trying to roll it up and swallow it. Another lesson at half-past four this afternoon. Away with you.

Eliza, still sobbing, rushes from the room.

(And that is the sort of ordeal poor Eliza has to go through for months before we meet her again on her first appearance in London society of the professional class.)

ACT III

It is Mrs Higgins's at-home day. Nobody has yet arrived. Her drawing room, in a flat on Chelsea Embankment, has three windows looking on the river; and the ceiling is not so lofty as it would be in an older house of the same pretension. The windows are open, giving access to a balcony with flowers in pots. If you stand with your face to the windows, you have the fireplace on your left and the door in the right-hand wall close to the corner nearest the windows.

Mrs Higgins was brought up on Morris and Burne-Jones;° and her room, which is very unlike her son's room in Wimpole Street, is not crowded with furniture and little tables and nicknacks. In the middle of the room there is a big ottoman; and this, with the carpet, the Morris wall-papers, and the Morris chintz window curtains and brocade covers of the ottoman and its cushions, supply all the ornament, and are much too handsome to be hidden by odds and ends of useless things. A few good oil-paintings from the exhibitions in the Grosvenor Gallery thirty years ago (the Burne-Jones, not the Whistler side of them) are on the walls. The only landscape is a Cecil Lawson on the scale of a Rubens. There is a portrait of Mrs Higgins as she was when she defied fashion in her youth in one of the beautiful Rosettian costumes which, when

Morris and Burne-Jones William Morris was a designer of furniture and interiors; Edward Burne-Jones was a painter much influenced by the work of Dante Gabriel Rossetti. Shaw's allusion (later in the paragraph) to "Rossettian costumes" alludes to the long flowing gowns his beautiful women wore.

caricatured by people who did not understand, led to the absur-
dities of popular estheticism in the eighteen-seventies.

In the corner diagonally opposite the door Mrs Higgins, now
over sixty and long past taking the trouble to dress out of the
fashion, sits writing at an elegantly simple writing-table with a
bell button within reach of her hand. There is a Chippendale
chair further back in the room between her and the window near-
est her side. At the other side of the room, further forward, is an
Elizabethan chair roughly carved in the taste of Inigo Jones. On
the same side a piano in a decorated case. The corner between the
fireplace and the window is occupied by a divan cushioned in
Morris chintz.

It is between four and five in the afternoon.

The door is opened violently; and Higgins enters with his
hat on.

Mrs Higgins (dismayed). Henry! *(Scolding him:)* What are you doing
here today? It is my at-home day: you promised not to come. *(As
he bends to kiss her, she takes his hat off, and presents it to him.)*

Higgins. Oh bother! *(He throws the hat down on the table.)*

Mrs Higgins. Go home at once.

Higgins (kissing her). I know, mother. I came on purpose.

Mrs Higgins. But you mustnt. I'm serious, Henry. You offend all my
friends: they stop coming whenever they meet you.

Higgins. Nonsense! I know I have no small talk; but people dont
mind. *(He sits on the settee.)*

Mrs Higgins. Oh! dont they? Small talk indeed! What about your
large talk? Really, dear, you mustnt stay.

Higgins. I must. Ive a job for you. A phonetic job.

Mrs Higgins. No use, dear. I'm sorry; but I cant get round your
vowels; and though I like to get pretty postcards in your patent
shorthand, I always have to read the copies in ordinary writing you
so thoughtfully send me.

Higgins. Well, this isnt a phonetic job.

Mrs Higgins. You said it was.

Higgins. Not your part of it. Ive picked up a girl.

Mrs Higgins. Does that mean that some girl has picked you up?

Higgins. Not at all. I dont mean a love affair.

Mrs Higgins. What a pity!

Higgins. Why?

Mrs Higgins. Well, you never fall in love with anyone under forty-
five. When will you discover that there are some rather nice-look-
ing young women about?

Higgins. Oh, I cant be bothered with young women. My idea of a lovable woman is somebody as like you as possible. I shall never get into the way of seriously liking young women: some habits lie too deep to be changed. *(Rising abruptly and walking about, jingling his money and his keys in his trouser pockets.)* Besides, theyre all idiots.

Mrs Higgins. Do you know what you would do if you really loved me, Henry?

Higgins. Oh bother! What? Marry, I suppose.

Mrs Higgins. No. Stop fidgeting and take your hands out of your pockets. *(With a gesture of despair, he obeys and sits down again.)* Thats a good boy. Now tell me about the girl.

Higgins. She's coming to see you.

Mrs Higgins. I dont remember asking her.

Higgins. You didnt. *I* asked her. If youd known her you wouldnt have asked her.

Mrs Higgins. Indeed! Why?

Higgins. Well, it's like this. She's a common flower girl. I picked her off the kerbstone.

Mrs Higgins. And invited her to my at-home!

Higgins (rising and coming to her to coax her). Oh, thatll be all right. Ive taught her to speak properly; and she has strict orders as to her behavior. She's to keep to two subjects: the weather and everybody's health — Fine day and How do you do, you know — and not to let herself go on things in general. That will be safe.

Mrs Higgins. Safe! To talk about our health! about our insides! perhaps about our outsides! How could you be so silly, Henry?

Higgins (impatiently). Well, she must talk about something. *(He controls himself and sits down again.)* Oh, she'll be all right: dont you fuss. Pickering is in it with me. Ive a sort of bet on that I'll pass her off as a duchess in six months. I started on her some months ago; and she's getting on like a house on fire. I shall win my bet. She has a quick ear; and she's been easier to teach than my middle-class pupils because she's had to learn a complete new language. She talks English almost as you talk French.

Mrs Higgins. Thats satisfactory, at all events.

Higgins. Well, it is and it isnt.

Mrs Higgins. What does that mean?

Higgins. You see, Ive got her pronunciation all right; but you have to consider not only how a girl pronounces, but what she pronounces; and that's where —

They are interrupted by the parlormaid, announcing guests.

The Parlormaid. Mrs and Miss Eynsford Hill. *(She withdraws.)*

Higgins. Oh Lord! *(He rises; snatches his hat from the table; and makes for the door; but before he reaches it his mother introduces him.)*

Mrs and Miss Eynsford Hill are the mother and daughter who sheltered from the rain in Covent Garden. The mother is well bred, quiet, and has the habitual anxiety of straitened means. The daughter has acquired a gay air of being very much at home in society: the bravado of genteel poverty.

Mrs Eynsford Hill (to Mrs Higgins). How do you do? *(They shake hands.)*

Miss Eynsford Hill. How d'you do? *(She shakes.)*

Mrs Higgins (introducing). My son Henry.

Mrs Eynsford Hill. Your celebrated son! I have so longed to meet you, Professor Higgins.

Higgins (glumly, making no movement in her direction). Delighted. *(He backs against the piano and bows brusquely.)*

Miss Eynsford Hill (going to him with confident familiarity). How do you do?

Higgins (staring at her). Ive seen you before somewhere. I havnt the ghost of a notion where; but Ive heard your voice. *(Drearily.)* It doesnt matter. Youd better sit down.

Mrs Higgins. I'm sorry to say that my celebrated son has no manners. You mustnt mind him.

Miss Eynsford Hill (gaily). I dont. *(She sits in the Elizabethan chair.)*

Mrs Eynsford Hill (a little bewildered). Not at all. *(She sits on the ottoman between her daughter and Mrs Higgins, who has turned her chair away from the writing-table.)*

Higgins. Oh, have I been rude? I didnt mean to be.

He goes to the central window, through which, with his back to the company, he contemplates the river and the flowers in Battersea Park on the opposite bank as if they were a frozen desert.
The parlormaid returns, ushering in Pickering.

The Parlormaid. Colonel Pickering. *(She withdraws).*

Pickering. How do you do, Mrs Higgins?

Mrs Higgins. So glad youve come. Do you know Mrs Eynsford Hill — Miss Eynsford Hill? *(Exchange of bows. The Colonel brings the Chippendale chair a little forward between Mrs Hill and Mrs Higgins, and sits down.)*

Pickering. Has Henry told you what weve come for?

Higgins (over his shoulder). We were interrupted: damn it!

Mrs Higgins. Oh Henry, Henry, really!

Mrs Eynsford Hill (half rising). Are we in the way?

Mrs Higgins (rising and making her sit down again). No, no. You couldnt have come more fortunately: we want you to meet a friend of ours.

Higgins (turning hopefully). Yes, by George! We want two or three people. Youll do as well as anybody else.

The parlormaid returns, ushering Freddy.

The Parlormaid. Mr Eynsford Hill.

Higgins (almost audibly, past endurance). God of Heaven! another of them.

Freddy (shaking hands with Mrs Higgins). Ahdedo?

Mrs Higgins. Very good of you to come. *(Introducing.)* Colonel Pickering.

Freddy (bowing). Ahdedo?

Mrs Higgins. I dont think you know my son, Professor Higgins.

Freddy (going to Higgins). Ahdedo?

Higgins (looking at him much as if he were a pickpocket). I'll take my oath Ive met you before somewhere. Where was it?

Freddy. I dont think so.

Higgins (resignedly). It dont matter, anyhow. Sit down.

He shakes Freddy's hand, and almost slings him on to the ottoman with his face to the windows; then comes round to the other side of it.

Higgins. Well, here we are, anyhow! *(He sits down on the ottoman next Mrs Eynsford Hill on her left).* And now what the devil are we going to talk about until Eliza comes?

Mrs Higgins. Henry: you are the life and soul of the Royal Society's soirées; but really youre rather trying on more commonplace occasions.

Higgins. Am I? Very sorry. *(Beaming suddenly.)* I suppose I am, you know. *(Uproariously)* Ha, ha!.

Miss Eynsford Hill (who considers Higgins quite eligible matrimonially). I sympathize. I havnt any small talk. If people would only be frank and say what they really think!

Higgins (relapsing into gloom). Lord forbid!

Mrs Eynsford Hill (taking up her daughter's cue). But why?

Higgins. What they think they ought to think is bad enough, Lord knows; but what they really think would break up the whole show. Do you suppose it would be really agreeable if I were to come out now with what I really think?

Miss Eynsford Hill (gaily). Is it so very cynical?

Higgins. Cynical! Who the dickens said it was cynical? I mean it wouldnt be decent.

Mrs Eynsford Hill (seriously). Oh! I'm sure you dont mean that, Mr Higgins.

Higgins. You see, we're all savages, more or less. We're supposed to be civilized and cultured — to know all about poetry and philosophy and art and science, and so on; but how many of us know even the meanings of these names? *(To Miss Hill.)* What do you know of poetry! *(To Mrs Hill.)* What do you know of science? *(Indicating Freddy.)* What does he know of art or science or anything else? What the devil do you imagine I know of philosophy?

Mrs Higgins (warningly). Or of manners, Henry?

The Parlormaid (opening the door). Miss Doolittle. *(She withdraws.)*

Higgins (rising hastily and running to Mrs Higgins). Here she is, mother. *(He stands on tiptoe and makes signs over his mother's head to Eliza to indicate to her which lady is her hostess.)*

Eliza, who is exquisitely dressed, produces an impression of such remarkable distinction and beauty as she enters that they all rise, quite fluttered. Guided by Higgins's signals, she comes to Mrs Higgins with studied grace.

Liza (speaking with pedantic correctness of pronunciation and great beauty of tone). How do you do, Mrs Higgins? *(She gasps slightly in making sure of the H in Higgins, but is quite successful.)* Mr Higgins told me I might come.

Mrs Higgins (cordially). Quite right: I'm very glad indeed to see you.

Pickering. How do you do, Miss Doolittle?

Liza (shaking hands with him). Colonel Pickering, is it not?

Mrs Eynsford Hill. I feel sure we have met before, Miss Doolittle. I remember your eyes.

Liza. How do you do? *(She sits down on the ottoman gracefully in the place just left vacant by Higgins.)*

Mrs Eynsford Hill (introducing). My daughter Clara.

Liza. How do you do?

Clara (impulsively). How do you do? *(She sits down on the ottoman beside Eliza, devouring her with her eyes.)*

Freddy (coming to their side of the ottoman). Ive certainly had the pleasure.

Mrs Eynsford Hill (introducing). My son Freddy.

Liza. How do you do?

Freddy bows and sits down in the Elizabethan chair, infatuated.

Higgins (suddenly). By George, yes: it all comes back to me! *(They stare at him.)* Covent Garden! *(Lamentably.)* What a damned thing!

Mrs Higgins. Henry, please! *(He is about to sit on the edge of the table.)* Dont sit on my writing-table: youll break it.
Higgins (sulkily). Sorry.

He goes to the divan, stumbling into the fender and over the fire-irons on his way; extricating himself with muttered imprecations; and finishing his disastrous journey by throwing himself so impatiently on the divan that he almost breaks it. Mrs Higgins looks at him, but controls herself and says nothing.
A long and painful pause ensues.

Mrs Higgins (at last, conversationally). Will it rain, do you think?
Liza. The shallow depression in the west of these islands is likely to move slowly in an easterly direction. There are no indications of any great change in the barometrical situation.
Freddy. Ha! ha! how awfully funny!
Liza. What is wrong with that, young man? I bet I got it right.
Freddy. Killing!
Mrs Eynsford Hill. I'm sure I hope it wont turn cold. Theres so much influenza about. It runs right through our whole family regularly every spring.
Liza (darkly). My aunt died of influenza: so they said.
Mrs Eynsford Hill (clicks her tongue sympathetically)!!!
Liza (in the same tragic tone). But it's my belief they done the old woman in.
Mrs Higgins (puzzled). Done her in?
Liza. Y-e-e-e-es, Lord love you! Why should she die of influenza? She come through diphtheria right enough the year before. I saw her with my own eyes. Fairly blue with it, she was. They all thought she was dead; but my father he kept ladling gin down her throat til she came to so sudden that she bit the bowl off the spoon.
Mrs Eynsford Hill (startled). Dear me!
Liza (piling up the indictment). What call would a woman with that strength in her have to die of influenza? What become of her new straw hat that should have come to me? Somebody pinched it; and what I say is, them as pinched it done her in.
Mrs Eynsford Hill. What does doing her in mean?
Higgins (hastily). Oh, thats the new small talk. To do a person in means to kill them.
Mrs Eynsford Hill (to Eliza, horrified). You surely dont believe that your aunt was killed?
Liza. Do I not? Them she lived with would have killed her for a hat-pin, let alone a hat.
Mrs Eynsford Hill. But it cant have been right for your father to pour spirits down her throat like that. It might have killed her.

Liza. Not her. Gin was mother's milk to her. Besides, he'd poured so much down his own throat that he knew the good of it.

Mrs Eynsford Hill. Do you mean that he drank?

Liza. Drank! My word! Something chronic.

Mrs Eynsford Hill. How dreadful for you!

Liza. Not a bit. It never did him no harm what I could see. But then he did not keep it up regular. *(Cheerfully.)* On the burst, as you might say, from time to time. And always more agreeable when he had a drop in. When he was out of work, my mother used to give him fourpence and tell him to go out and not come back until he'd drunk himself cheerful and loving-like. Theres lots of women has to make their husbands drunk to make them fit to live with. *(Now quite at her ease.)* You see, it's like this. If a man has a bit of a conscience, it always takes him when he's sober; and then it makes him low-spirited. A drop of booze just takes that off and makes him happy. *(To Freddy, who is in convulsions of suppressed laughter.)* Here! what are you sniggering at?

Freddy. The new small talk. You do it so awfully well.

Liza. If I was doing it proper, what was you laughing at? *(To Higgins)* Have I said anything I oughtnt?

Mrs Higgins (interposing). Not at all, Miss Doolittle.

Liza. Well, thats a mercy, anyhow. *(Expansively)* What I always say is —

Higgins (rising and looking at his watch). Ahem!

Liza (looking round at him; taking the hint; and rising). Well: I must go. *(They all rise. Freddy goes to the door.)* So pleased to have met you. Goodbye. *(She shakes hands with Mrs Higgins.)*

Mrs Higgins. Goodbye.

Liza. Goodbye, Colonel Pickering.

Pickering. Goodbye, Miss Doolittle. *(They shake hands.)*

Liza (nodding to the others). Goodbye, all.

Freddy (opening the door for her). Are you walking across the Park, Miss Doolittle? If so —

Liza (with perfectly elegant diction). Walk! Not bloody likely. *(Sensation.)* I am going in a taxi. *(She goes out.)*

Pickering gasps and sits down. Freddy goes out on the balcony to catch another glimpse of Eliza.

Mrs Eynsford Hill (suffering from shock). Well, I really cant get used to the new ways.

Clara (throwing herself discontentedly into the Elizabethan chair). Oh, it's all right, mamma, quite right. People will think we never go anywhere or see anybody if you are so old-fashioned.

Mrs Eynsford Hill. I daresay I am very old-fashioned; but I do hope you wont begin using that expression, Clara. I have got accus-

tomed to hear you talking about men as rotters, and calling everything filthy and beastly; though I do think it horrible and
unladylike. But this last is really too much. Dont you think so,
Colonel Pickering?

Pickering. Dont ask me. Ive been away in India for several years;
and manners have changed so much that I sometimes dont know
whether I'm at a respectable dinner-table or in a ship's forecastle.

Clara. It's all a matter of habit. Theres no right or wrong in it. Nobody means anything by it. And it's so quaint, and gives such a
smart emphasis to things that are not in themselves very witty. I
find the new small talk delightful and quite innocent.

Mrs Eynsford Hill (rising). Well, after that, I think it's time for us to
go.

Pickering and Higgins rise.

Clara (rising). Oh yes: we have three-at-homes to go to still. Goodbye, Mrs Higgins. Goodbye, Colonel Pickering. Goodbye, Professor Higgins.

*Higgins (coming grimly at her from the divan, and accompanying
her to the door).* Goodbye. Be sure you try on that small talk at the
three-at-homes. Dont be nervous about it. Pitch it in strong.

Clara (all smiles). I will. Goodbye. Such nonsense, all this early
Victorian prudery!

Higgins (tempting her). Such damned nonsense!

Clara. Such bloody nonsense!

Mrs Eynsford Hill (convulsively). Clara!

Clara. Ha! ha! *(She goes out radiant, conscious of being thoroughly
up to date, and is heard descending the stairs in a stream of
silvery laughter.)*

Freddy (to the heavens at large). Well, I ask you — *(He gives it up,
and comes to Mrs Higgins.)* Goodbye.

Mrs Higgins (shaking hands). Goodbye. Would you like to meet
Miss Doolittle again?

Freddy (eagerly). Yes, I should, most awfully.

Mrs Higgins. Well, you know my days.

Freddy. Yes, Thanks awfully. Goodbye. *(He goes out.)*

Mrs Eynsford Hill. Goodbye, Mr Higgins.

Higgins. Goodbye. Goodbye.

Mrs Eynsford Hill (to Pickering). It's no use. I shall never be able to
bring myself to use that word.

Pickering. Dont. It's not compulsory, you know. Youll get on quite
well without it.

Mrs Eynsford Hill. Only, Clara is so down on me if I am not
positively reeking with the latest slang. Goodbye.

Pickering. Goodbye *(They shake hands.)*

Mrs Eynsford Hill (to Mrs Higgins). You mustnt mind Clara. *(Picker-ing, catching from her lowered tone that this is not meant for him to hear, discreetly joins Higgins at the window.)* We're so poor! and she gets so few parties, poor child! She doesnt quite know. *(Mrs Higgins, seeing that her eyes are moist, takes her hand sym-pathetically and goes with her to the door.)* But the boy is nice. Dont you think so?

Mrs Higgins. Oh, quite nice. I shall always be delighted to see him.

Mrs Eynsford Hill. Thank you, dear. Goodbye. *(She goes out.)*

Higgins (eagerly). Well? Is Eliza presentable? *(He swoops on his mother and drags her to the ottoman, where she sits down in Eliza's place with her son on her left.)*

Pickering returns to his chair on her right.

Mrs Higgins. You silly boy, of course she's not presentable. She's a triumph of your art and of her dressmaker's; but if you suppose for a moment that she doesnt give herself away in every sentence she utters, you must be perfectly cracked about her.

Pickering. But dont you think something might be done? I mean something to eliminate the sanguinary element from her conver-sation.

Mrs Higgins. Not as long as she is in Henry's hands.

Higgins (aggrieved). Do you mean that my language is improper?

Mrs Higgins. No, dearest: it would be quite proper — say on a canal barge; but it would not be proper for her at a garden party.

Higgins (deeply injured). Well I must say —

Pickering (interrupting him). Come, Higgins: you must learn to know yourself. I havnt heard such language as yours since we used to review the volunteers in Hyde Park twenty years ago.

Higgins (sulkily). Oh, well, if you say so, I suppose I dont always talk like a bishop.

Mrs Higgins (quieting Henry with a touch). Colonel Pickering: will you tell me what is the exact state of things in Wimpole Street?

Pickering (cheerfully: as if this completely changed the subject). Well, I have come to live there with Henry. We work together at my Indian Dialects; and we think it more convenient —

Mrs Higgins. Quite so. I know all about that: it's an excellent arrange-ment. But where does this girl live?

Higgins. With us, of course. Where should she live?

Mrs Higgins. But on what terms? Is she a servant? If not, what is she?

Pickering (slowly). I think I know what you mean, Mrs Higgins.

Higgins. Well, dash me if *I* do! Ive had to work at the girl every day for months to get her to her present pitch. Besides, she's useful.

She knows where my things are, and remembers my appointments and so forth.

Mrs Higgins. How does your housekeeper get on with her?

Higgins. Mrs Pearce? Oh, she's jolly glad to get so much taken off her hands; for before Eliza came, she used to have to find things and remind me of my appointments. But she's got some silly bee in her bonnet about Eliza. She keeps saying "You dont think, sir": doesnt she, Pick?

Pickering. Yes: thats the formula. "You dont think, sir." Thats the end of every conversation about Eliza.

Higgins. As if I ever stop thinking about the girl and her confounded vowels and consonants. I'm worn out, thinking about her, and watching her lips and her teeth and her tongue, not to mention her soul, which is the quaintest of the lot.

Mrs Higgins. You certainly are a pretty pair of babies, playing with your live doll.

Higgins. Playing! The hardest job I ever tackled: make no mistake about that, mother. But you have no idea how frightfully interesting it is to take a human being and change her into a quite different human being by creating a new speech for her. It's filling up the deepest gulf that separates class from class and soul from soul.

Pickering (drawing his chair closer to Mrs Higgins and bending over to her eagerly). Yes: it's enormously interesting. I assure you, Mrs Higgins, we take Eliza very seriously. Every week — every day almost — there is some new change. *(Closer again.)* We keep records of every stage — dozens of gramophone disks and photographs —

Higgins (assailing her at the other ear). Yes, by George: it's the most absorbing experiment I ever tackled. She regularly fills our lives up: doesnt she, Pick?

Pickering. We're always talking Eliza.

Higgins. Teaching Eliza.

Pickering. Dressing Eliza.

Mrs Higgins. What!

Higgins. Inventing new Elizas.

Higgins.	*(speaking together)*	You know, she has the most extraordinary quickness of ear:
Pickering.		I assure you, my dear Mrs Higgins, that girl
Higgins.		just like a parrot. Ive tried her with every
Pickering.		is a genius. She can play the piano quite beautifully.

Higgins. ⎱ *(speaking* ⎰ possible sort of sound that a human being can make

Pickering. ⎰ *together)* ⎱ We have taken her to classical concerts and to music

Higgins. — Continental dialects, African dialects, Hottentot

Pickering. — halls; and it's all the same to her: she plays everything

Higgins. — clicks, things it took me years to get hold of; and

Pickering. — she hears right off when she comes home, whether it's

Higgins. — she picks them up like a shot, right away, as if she had

Pickering. — Beethoven and Brahms or Lehar and Lionel Monckton;

Higgins. — been at it all her life.

Pickering. — though six months ago, she'd never as much as touched a piano —

Mrs Higgins (putting her fingers in her ears, as they are by this time shouting one another down with an intolerable noise). Sh-sh-sh — sh! *(They stop.)*

Pickering. I beg your pardon. *(He draws his chair back apologetically.)*

Higgins. Sorry. When Pickering starts shouting nobody can get a word in edgeways.

Mrs Higgins. Be quiet, Henry. Colonel Pickering: dont you realize that when Eliza walked into Wimpole Street, something walked in with her?

Pickering. Her father did. But Henry soon got rid of him.

Mrs Higgins. It would have been more to the point if her mother had. But as her mother didnt something else did.

Pickering. But what?

Mrs Higgins (unconsciously dating herself by the word). A problem.

Pickering. Oh, I see. The problem of how to pass her off as a lady.

Higgins. I'll solve that problem. Ive half solved it already.

Mrs Higgins. No, you two infinitely stupid male creatures: the problem of what is to be done with her afterwards.

Higgins. I dont see anything in that. She can go her own way, with all the advantages I have given her.

Mrs Higgins. The advantages of that poor woman who was here just now! The manners and habits that disqualify a fine lady from earning her own living without giving her a fine lady's income! Is that what you mean?

Pickering (indulgently, being rather bored). Oh, that will be all right, Mrs Higgins. *(He rises to go.)*

Higgins (rising also). We'll find her some light employment.

Pickering. She's happy enough. Dont you worry about her. Goodbye. *(He shakes hands as if he were consoling a frightened child, and makes for the door.)*

Higgins. Anyhow, theres no good bothering now. The thing's done. Goodbye, mother. *(He kisses her, and follows Pickering.)*

Pickering (turning for a final consolation). There are plenty of openings. We'll do whats right. Goodbye.

Higgins (to Pickering as they go out together). Lets take her to the Shakespear exhibition at Earls Court.

Pickering. Yes: lets. Her remarks will be delicious.

Higgins. She'll mimic all the people for us when we get home.

Pickering. Ripping. *(Both are heard laughing as they go downstairs.)*

Mrs. Higgins (rises with an impatient bounce, and returns to her work at the writing-table. She sweeps a litter of disarranged papers out of her way; snatches a sheet of paper from her stationery case; and tries resolutely to write. At the third line she gives it up; flings down her pen; grips the table angrily and exclaims). Oh, men! men!! men!!!

. . .

(Clearly Eliza will not pass as a duchess yet; and Higgins's bet remains unwon. But the six months are not yet exhausted; and just in time Eliza does actually pass as a princess. For a glimpse of how she did it imagine an Embassy in London one summer evening after dark. The hall door has an awning and a carpet across the sidewalk to the kerb, because a grand reception is in progress. A small crowd is lined up to see the guests arrive.

A Rolls-Royce car drives up. Pickering in evening dress, with medals and orders, alights, and hands out Eliza, in opera cloak, evening dress, diamonds, fan, flowers and all accessories. Higgins follows. The car drives off; and the three go up the steps and into the house, the door opening for them as they approach.

Inside the house they find themselves in a spacious hall from which the grand staircase rises. On the left are the arrangements for the gentlemen's cloaks. The male guests are depositing their hats and wraps there.

On the right is a door leading to the ladies' cloakroom. Ladies are going in cloaked and coming out in splendor. Pickering whispers to Eliza and points out the ladies' room. She goes into it. Higgins and Pickering take off their overcoats and take tickets for them from the attendant.

One of the guests, occupied in the same way, has his back turned.

Having taken his ticket, he turns round and reveals himself as an important looking young man with an astonishingly hairy face. He has an enormous moustache, flowing out into luxuriant whiskers. Waves of hair cluster on his brow. His hair is cropped closely at the back, and glows with oil. Otherwise he is very smart. He wears several worthless orders. He is evidently a foreigner, guessable as a whiskered Pandour from Hungary; but in spite of the ferocity of his moustache he is amiable and genially voluble.)

Recognizing Higgins, he flings his arms wide apart and approaches him enthusiastically.)

Whiskers. Maestro, maestro. *(He embraces Higgins and kisses him on both cheeks.)* You remember me?

Higgins. No I dont. Who the devil are you?

Whiskers. I am your pupil: your first pupil, your best and greatest pupil. I am little Nepommuck, the marvellous boy. I have made your name famous throughout Europe. You teach me phonetic. You cannot forget ME.

Higgins. Why dont you shave?

Nepommuck. I have not your imposing appearance, your chin, your brow. Nobody notice me when I shave. Now I am famous: they call me Hairy Faced Dick.

Higgins. And what are you doing here among all these swells?

Nepommuck. I am interpreter. I speak 32 languages. I am indispensable at these international parties. You are great cockney specialist: you place a man anywhere in London the moment he open his mouth. I place any man in Europe.

A footman hurries down the grand staircase and comes to Nepommuck.

Footman. You are wanted upstairs. Her Excellency cannot understand the Greek gentleman.

Nepommuck. Thank you, yes, immediately.

The footman goes and is lost in the crowd.

Nepommuck (to Higgins). This Greek diplomatist pretends he cannot speak nor understand English. He cannot deceive me. He is the son of a Clerkenwell watchmaker. He speaks English so villainously that he dare not utter a word of it without betraying his origin. I help him to pretend; but I make him pay through the nose. I make them all pay. Ha Ha! *(He hurries upstairs.)*

Pickering. Is this fellow really an expert? Can he find out Eliza and blackmail her?

Higgins. We shall see. If he finds her out I lose my bet.

Eliza comes from the cloakroom and joins them.

Pickering. Well, Eliza, now for it. Are you ready?

Liza. Are you nervous, Colonel?

Pickering. Frightfully. I feel exactly as I felt before my first battle. It's the first time that frightens.

Liza. It is not the first time for me, Colonel. I have done this fifty times — hundreds of times — in my little piggery in Angel Court in my day-dreams. I am in a dream now. Promise me not to let Professor Higgins wake me; for if he does I shall forget everything and talk as I used to in Drury Lane.

Pickering. Not a word, Higgins. *(To Eliza.)* Now, ready?

Liza. Ready.

Pickering. Go.

They mount the stairs, Higgins last. Pickering whispers to the footman on the first landing.

First Landing Footman. Miss Doolittle, Colonel Pickering, Professor Higgins.

Second Landing Footman. Miss Doolittle, Colonel Pickering, Professor Higgins.

At the top of the staircase the Ambassador and his wife, with Nepommuck at her elbow, are receiving.

Hostess (taking Eliza's hand). How d'ye do?

Host (same play). How d'ye do? How d'ye do, Pickering?

Liza (with a beautiful gravity that awes her hostess). How do you do? *(She passes on to the drawingroom).*

Hostess. Is that your adopted daughter, Colonel Pickering? She will make a sensation.

Pickering. Most kind of you to invite her for me. *(He passes on.)*

Hostess (to Nepommuck). Find out all about her.

Nepommuck (bowing). Excellency — *(He goes into the crowd.)*

Host. How d'ye do, Higgins? You have a rival here tonight. He introduced himself as your pupil. Is he any good?

Higgins. He can learn a language in a fortnight — knows dozens of them. A sure mark of a fool. As a phonetician, no good whatever.

Hostess. How d'ye do, Professor?

Higgins. How do you do? Fearful bore for you this sort of thing. Forgive my part in it. *(He passes on.)*

(In the drawingroom and its suite of salons the reception is in full swing. Eliza passes through. She is so intent on her ordeal that she walks like a somnambulist in a desert instead of a débutante in a fashionable crowd. They stop talking to look at her, admiring her dress, her jewels, and her strangely attractive self. Some of the younger ones at the back stand on their chairs to see.

The Host and Hostess come in from the staircase and mingle with their guests. Higgins, gloomy and contemptuous of the whole business, comes into the group where they are chatting.)

Hostess. Ah, here is Professor Higgins: he will tell us. Tell us all about the wonderful young lady, Professor.

Higgins (almost morosely). What wonderful young lady?

Hostess. You know very well. They tell me there has been nothing like her in London since people stood on their chairs to look at Mrs Langtry.

Nepommuck joins the group, full of news.

Hostess. Ah, here you are at last, Nepommuck. Have you found out all about the Doolittle lady?

Nepommuck. I have found out all about her. She is a fraud.

Hostess. A fraud! Oh no.

Nepommuck. YES, yes. She cannot deceive me. Her name cannot be Doolittle.

Higgins. Why?

Nepommuck. Because Doolittle is an English name. And she is not English.

Hostess. Oh, nonsense! She speaks English perfectly.

Nepommuck. Too perfectly. Can you shew me any English woman who speaks English as it should be spoken? Only foreigners who have been taught to speak it speak it well.

Hostess. Certainly she terrified me by the way she said How d'ye do. I had a schoolmistress who talked like that; and I was mortally afraid of her. But if she is not English what is she?

Nepommuck. Hungarian.

All the Rest. Hungarian!

Nepommuck. Hungarian. And of royal blood. I am Hungarian. My blood is royal.

Higgins. Did you speak to her in Hungarian?

Nepommuck. I did. She was very clever. She said "Please speak to me in English: I do not understand French." French! She pretends not to know the difference between Hungarian and French. Impossible: she knows both.

Higgins. And the blood royal? How did you find that out?

Nepommuck. Instinct, maestro, instinct. Only the Magyar races can produce that air of the divine right, those resolute eyes. She is a princess.

Host. What do you say, Professor?

Higgins. I say an ordinary London girl out of the gutter and taught to speak by an expert. I place her in Drury Lane.

Nepommuck. Ha ha ha! Oh, maestro, maestro, you are mad on the subject of cockney dialects. The London gutter is the whole world for you.

Higgins (to the Hostess). What does your Excellency say?

Hostess. Oh, of course I agree with Nepommuck. She must be a princess at least.

Host. Not necessarily legitimate, of course. Morganatic perhaps. But that is undoubtedly her class.

Higgins. I stick to my opinion.

Hostess. Oh, you are incorrigible.

The group breaks up, leaving Higgins isolated. Pickering joins him.

Pickering. Where is Eliza? We must keep an eye on her.

Eliza joins them.

Liza. I dont think I can bear much more. The people all stare so at me. An old lady has just told me that I speak exactly like Queen Victoria. I am sorry if I have lost your bet. I have done my best; but nothing can make me the same as these people.

Pickering. You have not lost it, my dear. You have won it ten times over.

Higgins. Let us get out of this. I have had enough of chattering to these fools.

Pickering. Eliza is tired; and I am hungry. Let us clear out and have supper somewhere.

ACT IV

The Wimpole Street laboratory. Midnight. Nobody in the room. The clock on the mantelpiece strikes twelve. The fire is not alight: it is a summer night.

Presently Higgins and Pickering are heard on the stairs.

Higgins (calling down to Pickering). I say, Pick: lock up, will you? I shant be going out again.

Pickering. Right. Can Mrs Pearce go to bed? We dont want anything more, do we?

Higgins. Lord, no!

Eliza opens the door and is seen on the lighted landing in all the finery in which she has just won Higgins's bet for him. She comes to the hearth, and switches on the electric lights there. She is tired: her pallor contrasts strongly with her dark eyes and hair;

and her expression is almost tragic. She takes off her cloak; puts her fan and gloves on the piano; and sits down on the bench, brooding and silent. Higgins, in evening dress, with overcoat and hat, comes in, carrying a smoking jacket which he has picked up downstairs. He takes off the hat and overcoat; throws them carelessly on the newspaper stand; disposes of his coat in the same way; puts on the smoking jacket; and throws himself wearily into the easy-chair at the hearth. Pickering, similarly attired, comes in. He also takes off his hat and overcoat, and is about to throw them on Higgins's when he hesitates.

Pickering. I say: Mrs Pearce will row if we leave these things lying about in the drawing room.

Higgins. Oh, chuck them over the bannisters into the hall. She'll find them there in the morning and put them away all right. She'll think we were drunk.

Pickering. We are, slightly. Are there any letters?

Higgins. I didnt look. *(Pickering takes the overcoats and hats and goes downstairs. Higgins begins half singing half yawning an air from La Fanciulla del Golden West. Suddenly he stops and exclaims.)* I wonder where the devil my slippers are!

Eliza looks at him darkly; then rises suddenly and leaves the room.

Higgins yawns again, and resumes his song.

Pickering returns, with the contents of the letter-box in his hand.

Pickering. Only circulars, and this coroneted billet-doux for you. *(He throws the circulars into the fender, and posts himself on the hearthrug, with his back to the grate.)*

Higgins (glancing at the billet-doux). Money-lender. *(He throws the letter after the circulars.)*

Eliza returns with a pair of large down-at-heel slippers. She places them on the carpet before Higgins, and sits as before without a word.

Higgins (yawning again). Oh Lord! What an evening! What a crew! What a silly tomfoolery! *(He raises his shoe to unlace it, and catches sight of the slippers. He stops unlacing and looks at them as if they had appeared there of their own accord.)* Oh! theyre there, are they?

Pickering (stretching himself). Well, I feel a bit tired. It's been a long day. The garden party, a dinner party, and the reception!

Rather too much of a good thing. But youve won your bet, Higgins. Eliza did the trick, and something to spare, eh?

Higgins (fervently). Thank God it's over!

Eliza flinches violently; but they take no notice of her; and she recovers herself and sits stonily as before.

Pickering. Were you nervous at the garden party? *I* was. Eliza didnt seem a bit nervous.

Higgins. Oh, she wasnt nervous. I knew she'd be all right. No: it's the strain of putting the job through all these months that has told on me. It was interesting enough at first, while we were at the phonetics; but after that I got deadly sick of it. If I hadnt backed myself to do it I should have chucked the whole thing up two months ago. It was a silly notion: the whole thing has been a bore.

Pickering. Oh come! the garden party was frightfully exciting. My heart began beating like anything.

Higgins. Yes, for the first three minutes. But when I saw we were going to win hands down, I felt like a bear in a cage, hanging about doing nothing. The dinner was worse: sitting gorging there for over an hour, with nobody but a damned fool of a fashionable woman to talk to! I tell you, Pickering, never again for me. No more artificial duchesses. The whole thing has been simple purgatory.

Pickering. Youve never been broken in properly to the social routine. *(Strolling over to the piano.)* I rather enjoy dipping into it occasionally myself: it makes me feel young again. Anyhow, it was a great success: an immense success. I was quite frightened once or twice because Eliza was doing it so well. You see, lots of the real people cant do it at all: theyre such fools that they think style comes by nature to people in their position; and so they never learn. Theres always something professional about doing a thing superlatively well.

Higgins. Yes: thats what drives me mad: the silly people dont know their own silly business. *(Rising.)* However, it's over and done with; and now I can go to bed at last without dreading tomorrow.

Eliza's beauty becomes murderous.

Pickering. I think I shall turn in too. Still, it's been a great occasion: a triumph for you. Goodnight. *(He goes.)*

Higgins (following him). Goodnight. *(Over his shoulder, at the door.)* Put out the lights, Eliza; and tell Mrs Pearce not to make coffee for me in the morning: I'll take tea. *(He goes out.)*

Eliza tries to control herself and feel indifferent as she rises and walks across to the hearth to switch off the lights. By the time she gets there she is on the point of screaming. She sits down in Higgins's chair and holds on hard to the arms. Finally she gives way and flings herself furiously on the floor, raging.

Higgins (in despairing wrath outside). What the devil have I done with my slippers? *(He appears at the door.)*

Liza (snatching up the slippers, and hurling them at him one after the other with all her force). There are your slippers. And there. Take your slippers; and may you never have a day's luck with them!

Higgins (astounded). What on earth — ! *(He comes to her.)* Whats the matter? Get up. *(He pulls her up.)* Anything wrong?

Liza (breathless). Nothing wrong — with you. Ive won your bet for you, havnt I? Thats enough for you. *I* dont matter, I suppose.

Higgins. You won my bet! You! Presumptuous insect! *I* won it. What did you throw those slippers at me for?

Liza. Because I wanted to smash your face. I'd like to kill you, you selfish brute. Why didnt you leave me where you picked me out of — in the gutter? You thank God it's all over, and that now you can throw me back again there, do you? *(She crisps her fingers frantically.)*

Higgins (looking at her in cool wonder). The creature is nervous, after all.

Liza (gives a suffocated scream of fury, and instinctively darts her nails at his face)!!

Higgins (catching her wrists). Ah! would you? Claws in, you cat. How dare you shew your temper to me? Sit down and be quiet. *(He throws her roughly into the easy-chair.)*

Liza (crushed by superior strength and weight). Whats to become of me? Whats to become of me?

Higgins. How the devil do I know whats to become of you? What does it matter what becomes of you?

Liza. You dont care. I know you dont care. You wouldnt care if I was dead. I'm nothing to you — not so much as them slippers.

Higgins (thundering). Those slippers.

Liza (with bitter submission). Those slippers. I didnt think it made any difference now.

A pause. Eliza hopeless and crushed. Higgins a little uneasy.

Higgins (in his loftiest manner). Why have you begun going on like this? May I ask whether you complain of your treatment here?

Liza. No.

Higgins. Has anybody behaved badly to you? Colonel Pickering? Mrs Pearce? Any of the servants?

Liza. No.

Higgins. I presume you dont pretend that *I* have treated you badly?

Liza. No.

Higgins. I am glad to hear it. *(He moderates his tone.)* Perhaps youre tired after the strain of the day. Will you have a glass of champagne? *(He moves towards the door.)*

Liza. No. *(Recollecting her manners.)* Thank you.

Higgins (good-humored again). This has been coming on you for some days. I suppose it was natural for you to be anxious about the garden party. But thats all over now. *(He pats her kindly on the shoulder. She writhes.)* Theres nothing more to worry about.

Liza. No. Nothing more for you to worry about. *(She suddenly rises and gets away from him by going to the piano bench, where she sits and hides her face.)* Oh God! I wish I was dead.

Higgins (staring after her in sincere surprise). Why? In heaven's name, why? *(Reasonably, going to her.)* Listen to me, Eliza. All this irritation is purely subjective.

Liza. I dont understand. I'm too ignorant.

Higgins. It's only imagination. Low spirits and nothing else. Nobody's hurting you. Nothing's wrong. You go to bed like a good girl and sleep it off. Have a little cry and say your prayers: that will make you comfortable.

Liza. I heard y o u r prayers. "Thank God it's all over!"

Higgins (impatiently). Well, dont you thank God it's all over? Now you are free and can do what you like.

Liza (pulling herself together in desperation). What am I fit for? What have you left me fit for? Where am I to go? What am I to do? Whats to become of me?

Higgins (enlightened, but not at all impressed). Oh, thats whats worrying you, is it? *(He thrusts his hands into his pockets, and walks about in his usual manner, rattling the contents of his pockets, as if condescending to a trivial subject out of pure kindness.)* I shouldnt bother about it if I were you. I should imagine you wont have much difficulty in settling yourself somewhere or other, though I hadnt quite realized that you were going away. *(She looks quickly at him: he does not look at her, but examines the dessert stand on the piano and decides that he will eat an apple.)* You might marry, you know. *(He bites a large piece out of the apple and munches it noisily.)* You see, Eliza, all men are not confirmed old bachelors like me and the Colonel. Most men are the marrying sort (poor devils!); and youre not bad-looking: it's quite a pleasure to look at you sometimes — not now, of course, because youre crying and looking as ugly as the very devil; but when youre all right and quite yourself, youre what I should call attractive. That is, to the people in the marrying line, you understand. You go to bed and have a good nice rest; and then get up and look at yourself in the glass; and you wont feel so cheap.

Eliza again looks at him, speechless, and does not stir.

The look is quite lost on him: he eats his apple with a dreamy expression of happiness, as it is quite a good one.

Higgins *(a genial afterthought occurring to him).* I daresay my mother could find some chap or other who would do very well.

Liza. We were above that at the corner of Tottenham Court Road.

Higgins *(waking up).* What do you mean?

Liza. I sold flowers. I didnt sell myself. Now youve made a lady of me I'm not fit to sell anything else. I wish youd left me where you found me.

Higgins *(slinging the core of the apple decisively into the grate).* Tosh, Eliza. Dont you insult human relations by dragging all this cant about buying and selling into it. You neednt marry the fellow if you dont like him.

Liza. What else am I to do?

Higgins. Oh, lots of things. What about your old idea of a florist's shop? Pickering could set you up in one: he has lots of money. *(Chuckling.)* He'll have to pay for all those togs you have been wearing today; and that, with the hire of the jewellery, will make a big hole in two hundred pounds. Why, six months ago you would have thought it the millennium to have a flower shop of your own. Come! youll be all right. I must clear off to bed: I'm devilish sleepy. By the way, I came down for something: I forget what it was.

Liza. Your slippers.

Higgins. Oh yes, of course. You shied them at me. *(He picks them up, and is going out when she rises and speaks to him.)*

Liza. Before you go, sir —

Higgins *(dropping the slippers in his surprise at her calling him Sir).* Eh?

Liza. Do my clothes belong to me or to Colonel Pickering?

Higgins *(coming back into the room as if her question were the very climax of unreason).* What the devil use would they be to Pickering?

Liza. He might want them for the next girl you pick up to experiment on.

Higgins *(shocked and hurt).* Is that the way you feel towards us?

Liza. I dont want to hear anything more about that. All I want to know is whether anything belongs to me. My own clothes were burnt.

Higgins. But what does it matter? Why need you start bothering about that in the middle of the night?

Liza. I want to know what I may take away with me. I dont want to be accused of stealing.

Higgins (now deeply wounded). Stealing! You shouldnt have said that, Eliza. That shews a want of feeling.

Liza. I'm sorry. I'm only a common ignorant girl; and in my station I have to be careful. There cant be any feelings between the like of you and the like of me. Please will you tell me what belongs to me and what doesnt?

Higgins (very sulky). you may take the whole damned household if you like. Except the jewels. Theyre hired. Will that satisfy you? *(He turns on his heel and is about to go in extreme dudgeon.)*

Liza (drinking in his emotion like nectar, and nagging him to provoke a further supply). Stop, please. *(She takes off her jewels.)* Will you take these to your room and keep them safe? I dont want to run the risk of their being missing.

Higgins (furious). Hand them over. *(She puts them into his hands.)* If these belonged to me instead of to the jeweller, I'd ram them down your ungrateful throat. *(He perfunctorily thrusts them into his pockets, unconsciously decorating himself with the protruding ends of the chains.)*

Liza (taking a ring off). This ring isnt the jeweller's: it's the one you bought me in Brighton. I dont want it now. *(Higgins dashes the ring violently into the fireplace, and turns on her so threateningly that she crouches over the piano with her hands over her face, and exclaims.)* Dont you hit me.

Higgins. Hit you! You infamous creature, how dare you accuse me of such a thing? It is you who have hit me. You have wounded me to the heart.

Liza (thrilling with hidden joy). I'm glad. Ive got a little of my own back, anyhow.

Higgins (with dignity, in his finest professional style). You have caused me to lose my temper: a thing that has hardly ever happened to me before. I prefer to say nothing more tonight. I am going to bed.

Liza (pertly). Youd better leave a note for Mrs Pearce about the coffee; for she wont be told by me.

Higgins (formally). Damn Mrs Pearce; and damn the coffee; and damn you; and *(wildly)* damn my own folly in having lavished my

hard-earned knowledge and the treasure of my regard and intimacy on a heartless guttersnipe. *(He goes out with impressive
decorum, and spoils it by slamming the door savagely.)*

*Eliza goes down on her knees on the hearthrug to look for the
ring. When she finds it she considers for a moment what to do
with it. Finally she flings it down on the dessert stand and goes
upstairs in a tearing rage.*

• • •

(The furniture of Eliza's room has been increased by a big wardrobe
and a sumptuous dressing-table. She comes in and switches on the
electric light. She goes to the wardrobe; opens it; and pulls out a
walking dress, a hat, and a pair of shoes, which she throws on the bed.
She takes off her evening dress and shoes; then takes a padded
hanger from the wardrobe; adjusts it carefully in the evening dress;
and hangs it in the wardrobe, which she shuts with a slam. She puts
on her walking shoes, her walking dress, and hat. She takes her wrist
watch from the dressing-table and fastens it on. She pulls on her
gloves; takes her vanity bag; and looks into it to see that her purse is
there before hanging it on her wrist. She makes for the door. Every
movement expresses her furious resolution.

She takes a last look at herself in the glass.

She suddenly puts out her tongue at herself; then leaves the room,
switching off the electric light at the door.

Meanwhile, in the street outside, Freddy Eynsford Hill, lovelorn,
is gazing up at the second floor, in which one of the windows is still
lighted.

The light goes out.)

Freddy. Goodnight, darling, darling, darling.

Eliza comes out, giving the door a considerable bang behind her.

Liza. Whatever are you doing here?
Freddy. Nothing. I spend most of my nights here. It's the only place
where I'm happy. Dont laugh at me, Miss Doolittle.
Liza. Dont you call me Miss Doolittle, do you hear? Liza's good
enough for me. *(She breaks down and grabs him by the shoulders.)* Freddy: you dont think I'm a heartless guttersnipe, do you?
Freddy. Oh no, no, darling: how can you imagine such a thing? You
are the loveliest, dearest —

*He loses all self-control and smothers her with kisses. She, hungry
for comfort, responds. They stand there in one another's arms.
An elderly police constable arrives.*

Constable (scandalized). Now then! Now then!! Now then!!!

They release one another hastily.

Freddy. Sorry, constable. Weve only just become engaged.

They run away.

(The constable shakes his head, reflecting on his own courtship and on the vanity of human hopes. He moves off in the opposite direction with slow professional steps.

The flight of the lovers takes them to Cavendish Square. There they halt to consider their next move.)

Liza (out of breath). He didnt half give me a fright, that copper. But you answered him proper.

Freddy. I hope I havent taken you out of your way. Where were you going?

Liza. To the river.

Freddy. What for?

Liza. To make a hole in it.

Freddy (horrified). Eliza, darling. What do you mean? What's the matter?

Liza. Never mind. It doesnt matter now. There's nobody in the world now but you and me, is there?

Freddy. Not a soul.

They indulge in another embrace, and are again surprised by a much younger constable.

Second Constable. Now then, you two! What's this? Where do you think you are? Move along here, double quick.

Freddy. As you say, sir, double quick.

(They run away again, and are in Hanover Square before they stop for another conference.)

Freddy. I had no idea the police were so devilishly prudish.

Liza. It's their business to hunt girls off the streets.

Freddy. We must go somewhere. We cant wander about the streets all night.

Liza. Cant we? I think it'd be lovely to wander about for ever.

Freddy. Oh, darling.

They embrace again, oblivious of the arrival of a crawling taxi. It stops.

Taximan. Can I drive you and the lady anywhere, sir?

They start asunder.

Liza. Oh, Freddy, a taxi. The very thing.

Freddy. But, damn it, I've no money.

Liza. I have plenty. The Colonel thinks you should never go out without ten pounds in your pocket. Listen. We'll drive about all night; and in the morning I'll call on old Mrs Higgins and ask her what I ought to do. I'll tell you all about it in the cab. And the police wont touch us there.

Freddy. Righto! Ripping. *(To the Taximan.)* Wimbledon Common. *(They drive off.)*

ACT V

Mrs Higgins's drawing room. She is at her writing-table as before. The parlormaid comes in.

The Parlormaid (at the door). Mr Henry, maam, is downstairs with Colonel Pickering.

Mrs Higgins. Well, shew them up.

The Parlormaid. Theyre using the telephone, maam. Telephoning to the police, I think.

Mrs Higgins. What!

The Parlormaid (coming further in and lowering her voice). Mr Henry is in a state, maam. I thought I'd better tell you.

Mrs Higgins. If you had told me that Mr Henry was not in a state it would have been more surprising. Tell them to come up when theyve finished with the police. I suppose he's lost something.

The Parlormaid. Yes, maam. *(Going.)*

Mrs Higgins. Go upstairs and tell Miss Doolittle that Mr Henry and the Colonel are here. Ask her not to come down til I send for her.

The Parlormaid. Yes, maam.

Higgins bursts in. He is, as the parlormaid has said, in a state.

Higgins. Look here, mother: heres a confounded thing!

Mrs Higgins. Yes, dear. Good morning. *(He checks his impatience and kisses her, whilst the parlormaid goes out.)* What is it?

Higgins. Eliza's bolted.

Mrs Higgins (calmly continuing her writing). You must have frightened her.

Higgins. Frightened her! nonsense! She was left last night, as usual, to turn out the lights and all that; and instead of going to bed she changed her clothes and went right off: her bed wasnt slept in. She came in a cab for her things before seven this morning; and that fool Mrs Pearce let her have them without telling me a word about it. What am I to do?

Mrs Higgins. Do without, I'm afraid, Henry. The girl has a perfect right to leave if she chooses.

Higgins (wandering distractedly across the room). But I cant find anything. I dont know what appointments Ive got. I'm — *(Pickering comes in. Mrs Higgins puts down her pen and turns away from the writing-table.)*

Pickering (shaking hands). Good morning, Mrs Higgins. Has Henry told you? *(He sits down on the ottoman.)*

Higgins. What does that ass of an inspector say? Have you offered a reward?

Mrs Higgins (rising in indignant amazement). You dont mean to say you have set the police after Eliza.

Higgins. Of course. What are the police for? What else could we do? *(He sits in the Elizabethan chair.)*

Pickering. The inspector made a lot of difficulties. I really think he suspected us of some improper purpose.

Mrs Higgins. Well, of course he did. What right have you to go to the police and give the girl's name as if she were a thief, or a lost umbrella, or something? Really! *(She sits down again, deeply vexed.)*

Higgins. But we want to find her.

Pickering. We cant let her go like this, you know, Mrs Higgins. What were we to do?

Mrs Higgins. You have no more sense, either of you, than two children. Why —

The parlormaid comes in and breaks off the conversation.

The Parlormaid. Mr Henry: a gentleman wants to see you very particular. He's been sent on from Wimpole Street.

Higgins. Oh, bother! I cant see anyone now. Who is it?

The Parlormaid. A Mr Doolittle, sir.

Pickering. Doolittle! Do you mean the dustman?

The Parlormaid. Dustman! Oh no, sir: a gentleman.

Higgins (springing up excitedly). By George, Pick, it's some relative of hers that she's gone to. Somebody we know nothing about. *(To the parlormaid.)* Send him up, quick.

The Parlormaid. Yes, sir. *(She goes.)*

Higgins (eagerly, going to his mother). Genteel relatives! now we shall hear something. *(He sits down in the Chippendale chair.)*

Mrs Higgins. Do you know any of her people?

Pickering. Only her father: the fellow we told you about.

The Parlormaid (announcing). Mr Doolittle. *(She withdraws.)*

Doolittle enters. He is resplendently dressed as for a fashionable wedding, and might, in fact, be the bridegroom. A flower in his buttonhole, a dazzling silk hat, and patent leather shoes complete

*the effect. He is too concerned with the business he has come on
to notice Mrs Higgins. He walks straight to Higgins, and accosts
him with vehement reproach.*

Doolittle (indicating his own person). See here! Do you see this?
You done this.

Higgins. Done what, man?

Doolittle. This, I tell you. Look at it. Look at this hat. Look at this
coat.

Pickering. Has Eliza been buying you clothes?

Doolittle. Eliza! not she. Why would she buy me clothes?

Mrs Higgins. Good morning, Mr Doolittle. Wont you sit down?

*Doolittle (taken aback as he becomes conscious that he has forgotten
his hostess).* Asking your pardon, maam. *(He approaches her and
shakes her proffered hand.)* Thank you. *(He sits down on the
ottoman, on Pickering's right.)* I am that full of what has happened
to me that I cant think of anything else.

Higgins. What the dickens has happened to you?

Doolittle. I shouldnt mind if it had only happened to me: anything
might happen to anybody and nobody to blame but Providence, as
you might say. But this is something that you done to me: Yes,
you, Enry Higgins.

Higgins. Have you found Eliza?

Doolittle. Have you lost her?

Higgins. Yes.

Doolittle. You have all the luck, you have. I aint found her; but she'll
find me quick enough now after what you done to me.

Mrs Higgins. But what has my son done to you, Mr Doolittle?

Doolittle. Done to me! Ruined me. Destroyed my happiness. Tied
me up and delivered me into the hands of middle class morality.

Higgins (rising intolerantly and standing over Doolittle). Youre raving. Youre drunk. Youre mad. I gave you five pounds. After that I
had two conversations with you, at half-a-crown an hour. Ive never
seen you since.

Doolittle. Oh! Drunk am I? Mad am I? Tell me this. Did you or did
you not write a letter to an old blighter in America that was giving
five millions to found Moral Reform Societies all over the world,
and that wanted you to invent a universal language for him?

Higgins. What! Ezra D. Wannafeller! He's dead. *(He sits down again
carelessly.)*

Doolittle. Yes: he's dead; and I'm done for. Now did you or did you
not write a letter to him to say that the most original moralist at
present in England, to the best of your knowledge, was Alfred
Doolittle, a common dustman?

Higgins. Oh, after your first visit I remember making some silly joke of the kind.

Doolittle. Ah! you may well call it a silly joke. It put the lid on me right enough. Just give him the chance he wanted to shew that Americans is not like us: that they reckonize and respect merit in every class of life, however humble. Them words is in his bloom- ing will, in which, Henry Higgins, thanks to your silly joking, he leaves me a share in his Predigested Cheese Trust worth three thousand a year on condition that I lecture for his Wannafeller Moral Reform World League as often as they ask me up to six times a year.

Higgins. The devil he does! Whew! *(Brightening suddenly.)* What a lark!

Pickering. A safe thing for you, Doolittle. They wont ask you twice.

Doolittle. It aint the lecturing I mind. I'll lecture them blue in the face, I will, and not turn a hair. It's making a gentleman of me that I object to. Who asked him to make a gentleman of me? I was happy. I was free. I touched pretty nigh everybody for money when I wanted it, same as I touched you, Enry Higgins. Now I am worrited; tied neck and heels; and everybody touches me for money. It's a fine thing for you, says my solicitor. Is it? says I. You mean it's a good thing for you, I says. When I was a poor man and had a solicitor once when they found a pram in the dust cart, he got me off, and got shut of me and got me shut of him as quick as he could. Same with the doctors: used to shove me out of the hospital before I could hardly stand on my legs, and nothing to pay. Now they finds out that I'm not a healthy man and cant live unless they looks after me twice a day. In the house I'm not let do a hand's turn for myself: somebody else must do it and touch me for it. A year ago I hadnt a relative in the world except two or three that wouldnt speak to me. Now Ive fifty, and not a decent week's wages among the lot of them. I have to live for others and not for myself: thats middle class morality. You talk of losing Eliza. Dont you be anx- ious: I bet she's on my doorstep by this: she that could support herself easy by selling flowers if I wasnt respectable. And the next one to touch me will be you, Enry Iggins. I'll have to learn to speak middle class language from you, instead of speaking proper English. Thats where youll come in; and I daresay that what you done it for.

Mrs Higgins. But, my dear Mr Doolittle, you need not suffer all this if you are really in earnest. Nobody can force you to accept this bequest. You can repudiate it. Isnt that so, Colonel Pickering?

Pickering. I believe so.

Doolittle (softening his manner in deference to her sex). Thats the

tragedy of it, maam. It's easy to say chuck it; but I havnt the nerve.
Which of us has? We're all intimidated. Intimidated, maam: thats
what we are. What is there for me if I chuck it but the workhouse
in my old age? I have to dye my hair already to keep my job as a
dustman. If I was one of the deserving poor, and had put by a bit,
I could chuck it; but then why should I, acause the deserving poor
might as well be millionaires for all the happiness they ever has.
They dont know what happiness is. But I, as one of the undeserving poor, have nothing between me and the pauper's uniform but this here blasted three thousand a year that shoves me
into the middle class. (Excuse the expression, maam; youd use it
yourself if you had my provocation.) Theyve got you every way
you turn: it's a choice between the Skilly of the workhouse and the
Char Bydis of the middle class; and I havnt the nerve for the
workhouse. Intimidated: thats what I am. Broke. Bought up. Happier men than me will call for my dust, and touch me for their tip;
and I'll look on helpless, and envy them. And thats what your son
has brought me to. *(He is overcome by emotion.)*

Mrs Higgins. Well, I'm very glad youre not going to do anything
foolish, Mr Doolittle. For this solves the problem of Eliza's future.
You can provide for her now.

Doolittle (with melancholy resignation). Yes, maam: I'm expected to
provide for everyone now, out of three thousand a year.

Higgins (jumping up). Nonsense! he cant provide for her. He shant
provide for her. She doesnt belong to him. I paid him five pounds
for her. Doolittle: either youre an honest man or a rogue.

Doolittle (tolerantly). A little of both, Henry, like the rest of us: a
little of both.

Higgins. Well, you took that money for the girl; and you have no
right to take her as well.

Mrs Higgins. Henry: dont be absurd. If you want to know where
Eliza is, she is upstairs.

Higgins (amazed). Upstairs!!! Then I shall jolly soon fetch her downstairs. *(He makes resolutely for the door.)*

Mrs Higgins (rising and following him). Be quiet, Henry. Sit down.

Higgins. I —

Mrs Higgins. Sit down, dear; and listen to me.

Higgins. Oh very well, very well, very well. *(He throws himself
ungraciously on the ottoman, with his face towards the windows.)*
But I think you might have told us this half an hour ago.

Mrs Higgins. Eliza came to me this morning. She told me of the
brutal way you two treated her.

Higgins (bounding up again). What!

Pickering (rising also). My dear Mrs Higgins, she's been telling you stories. We didnt treat her brutally. We hardly said a word to her; and we parted on particularly good terms. *(Turning on Higgins.)* Higgins: did you bully her after I went to bed?

Higgins. Just the other way about. She threw my slippers in my face. She behaved in the most outrageous way. I never gave her the slightest provocation. The slippers came bang into my face the moment I entered the room — before I had uttered a word. And used perfectly awful language.

Pickering (astonished). But why? What did we do to her?

Mrs Higgins. I think I know pretty well what you did. The girl is naturally rather affectionate, I think. Isnt she, Mr Doolittle?

Doolittle. Very tender-hearted, maam. Takes after me.

Mrs Higgins. Just so. She had become attached to you both. She worked very hard for you, Henry. I dont think you quite realize what anything in the nature of brain work means to a girl of her class. Well, it seems that when the great day of trial came, and she did this wonderful thing for you without making a single mistake, you two sat there and never said a word to her, but talked together of how glad you were that it was all over and how you had been bored with the whole thing. And then you were surprised because she threw your slippers at you! *I* should have thrown the fire-irons at you.

Higgins. We said nothing except that we were tired and wanted to go to bed. Did we, Pick?

Pickering (shrugging his shoulders). That was all.

Mrs Higgins (ironically). Quite sure?

Pickering. Absolutely. Really, that was all.

Mrs Higgins. You didnt thank her, or pet her, or admire her, or tell her how splendid she'd been.

Higgins (impatiently). But she knew all about that. We didnt make speeches to her, if thats what you mean.

Pickering (conscience stricken). Perhaps we were a little inconsiderate. Is she very angry?

Mrs Higgins (returning to her place at the writing-table). Well, I'm afraid she wont go back to Wimpole Street, especially now that Mr Doolittle is able to keep up the position you have thrust on her; but she says she is quite willing to meet you on friendly terms and to let bygones be bygones.

Higgins (furious). Is she, by George? Ho!

Mrs Higgins. If you promise to behave yourself, Henry, I'll ask her to come down. If not, go home; for you have taken up quite enough of my time.

Higgins. Oh, all right. very well. Pick: you behave yourself. Let us put on our best Sunday manners for this creature that we picked out of the mud. *(He flings himself sulkily into the Elizabethan chair.)*

Doolittle (remonstrating). Now, now, Enry Iggins! Have some consideration for my feelings as a middle class man.

Mrs Higgins. Remember your promise, Henry. *(She presses the bell-button on the writing-table).* Mr Doolittle: will you be so good as to step out on the balcony for a moment. I dont want Eliza to have the shock of your news until she has made it up with these two gentlemen. Would you mind?

Doolittle. As you wish, lady. Anything to help Henry to keep her off my hands. *(He disappears through the window.)*

The parlormaid answers the bell. Pickering sits down in Doolittle's place.

Mrs Higgins. Ask Miss Doolittle to come down, please.

The Parlormaid. Yes, maam. *(She goes out.)*

Mrs Higgins. Now, Henry: be good.

Higgins. I am behaving myself perfectly.

Pickering. He is doing his best, Mrs Higgins.

A pause. Higgins throws back his head; stretches out his legs; and begins to whistle.

Mrs Higgins. Henry, dearest, you dont look at all nice in that attitude.

Higgins (pulling himself together). I was not trying to look nice, mother.

Mrs Higgins. It doesnt matter, dear. I only wanted to make you speak.

Higgins. Why?

Mrs Higgins. Because you cant speak and whistle at the same time.

Higgins groans. Another very trying pause.

Higgins (springing up, out of patience). Where the devil is that girl? Are we to wait here all day?

Eliza enters, sunny, self-possessed, and giving a staggeringly convincing exhibition of ease of manner. She carries a little work-basket, and is very much at home. Pickering is too much taken aback to rise.

Liza. How do you do, Professor Higgins? Are you quite well?

Higgins (choking). Am I —*(He can say no more.)*

Liza. But of course you are: you are never ill. So glad to see you again, Colonel Pickering. *(He rises hastily; and they shake hands.)* Quite chilly this morning, isnt it? *(She sits down on his left. He sits beside her.)*

Higgins. Dont you dare try this game on me. I taught it to you; and it doesnt take me in. Get up and come home; and dont be a fool.

Eliza takes a piece of needlework from her basket, and begins to stitch at it, without taking the least notice of this outburst.

Mrs Higgins. Very nicely put, indeed, Henry. No woman could resist such an invitation.

Higgins. You let her alone, mother. Let her speak for herself. You will jolly soon see whether she has an idea that I havnt put into her head or a word that I havnt put into her mouth. I tell you I have created this thing out of the squashed cabbage leaves of Covent Garden; and now she pretends to play the fine lady with me.

Mrs Higgins (placidly). Yes, dear; but youll sit down, wont you?

Higgins sits down again, savagely.

Liza (to Pickering, taking no apparent notice of Higgins, and working away deftly). Will you drop me altogether now that the experiment is over, Colonel Pickering?

Pickering. Oh dont. You mustnt think of it as an experiment. It shocks me, somehow.

Liza. Oh, I'm only a squashed cabbage leaf —

Pickering (impulsively). No.

Liza (continuing quietly). — but I owe so much to you that I should be very unhappy if you forgot me.

Pickering. It's very kind of you to say so, Miss Doolittle.

Liza. It's not because you paid for my dresses. I know you are generous to everybody with money. But it was from you that I learnt really nice manners; and that is what makes one a lady, isnt it? You see it was so very difficult for me with the example of Professor Higgins always before me. I was brought up to be just like him, unable to control myself, and using bad language on the slightest provocation. And I should never have known that ladies and gentlemen didnt behave like that if you hadnt been there.

Higgins. Well!!

Pickering. Oh, thats only his way, you know. He doesnt mean it.

Liza. Oh, *I* didnt mean it either, when I was a flower girl. It was only my way. But you see I did it; and thats what makes the difference after all.

Pickering. No doubt. Still, he taught you to speak; and I couldnt have done that, you know.

Liza (trivially). Of course: that is his profession.

Higgins. Damnation!

Liza (continuing). It was just like learning to dance in the fashionable way: there was nothing more than that in it. But do you know what began my real education?

Pickering. What?

Liza (stopping her work for a moment). Your calling me Miss Doolittle that day when I first came to Wimpole Street. That was the beginning of self-respect for me. *(She resumes her stitching.)* And there were a hundred little things you never noticed, because they came naturally to you. Things about standing up and taking off your hat and opening doors —

Pickering. Oh, that was nothing.

Liza. Yes: things that shewed you thought and felt about me as if I were something better than a scullery-maid; though of course I know you would have been just the same to a scullery-maid if she had been let into the drawing room. You never took off your boots in the dining room when I was there.

Pickering. You mustnt mind that. Higgins takes off his boots all over the place.

Liza. I know. I am not blaming him. It is his way, isnt it? But it made such a difference to me that you didnt do it. You see, really and truly, apart from the things anyone can pick up (the dressing and the proper way of speaking, and so on), the difference between a lady and a flower girl is not how she behaves, but how she's treated. I shall always be a flower girl to Professor Higgins, because he always treats me as a flower girl, and always will; but I know I can be a lady to you, because you always treat me as a lady, and always will.

Mrs Higgins. Please dont grind your teeth, Henry.

Pickering. Well, this is really very nice of you, Miss Doolittle.

Liza. I should like you to call me Eliza, now, if you would.

Pickering. Thank you. Eliza, of course.

Liza. And I should like Professor Higgins to call me Miss Doolittle.

Higgins. I'll see you damned first.

Mrs Higgins. Henry! Henry!

Pickering (laughing). Why dont you slang back at him? Dont stand it. It would do him a lot of good.

Liza. I cant. I could have done it once; but now I cant go back to it. You told me, you know, that when a child is brought to a foreign country, it picks up the language in a few weeks, and forgets its own. Well, I am a child in your country. I have forgotten my own language, and can speak nothing but yours. Thats the real break-

off with the corner of Tottenham Court Road. Leaving Wimpole
Street finishes it.

Pickering (much alarmed). Oh! but youre coming back to Wimpole
Street, arnt you? Youll forgive Higgins?

Higgins (rising). Forgive! Will she, by George! Let her go. Let her
find out how she can get on without us. She will relapse into the
gutter in three weeks without me at her elbow.

*Doolittle appears at the centre window. With a look of dignified
reproach at Higgins, he comes slowly and silently to his daughter,
who, with her back to the window, is unconscious of his approach.*

Pickering. He's incorrigible, Eliza. You wont relapse, will you?

Liza. No: not now. Never again. I have learnt my lesson. I dont
believe I could utter one of the old sounds if I tried. *(Doolittle
touches her on her left shoulder. She drops her work, losing her
self-possession utterly at the spectacle of her father's splendor.)*
A-a-a-a-ah-ow-ooh!

Higgins (with a crow of triumph). Aha! Just so. A-a-a-a-ahowooh! A-
a-a-a-ahowooh! A-a-a-a-ahowooh! Victory! Victory! *(He throws
himself on the divan, folding his arms, and spraddling arro-
gantly.)*

Doolittle. Can you blame the girl? Dont look at me like that, Eliza. It
aint my fault. Ive come into some money.

Liza. You must have touched a millionaire this time, dad.

Doolittle. I have. But I'm dressed something special today. I'm
going to St George's, Hanover Square. Your stepmother is going to
marry me.

Liza (angrily). Youre going to let yourself down to marry that low
common woman!

Pickering (quietly). He ought to, Eliza. *(To Doolittle.)* Why has she
changed her mind?

Doolittle (sadly). Intimidated, Governor. Intimidated. Middle class
morality claims its victim. Wont you put on your hat, Liza, and
come and see me turned off?

Liza. If the Colonel says I must, I — I'll *(almost sobbing)* I'll demean myself. And get insulted for my pains, like enough.

Doolittle. Don't be afraid: she never comes to words with anyone
now, poor woman! respectability has broke all the spirit out of her.

Pickering (squeezing Eliza's elbow gently). Be kind to them, Eliza.
Make the best of it.

Liza (forcing a little smile for him through her vexation). Oh well, just to shew theres no ill feeling. I'll be back in a moment. *(She goes out.)*

Doolittle (sitting down beside Pickering). I feel uncommon nervous about the ceremony, Colonel. I wish youd come and see me through it.

Pickering. But youve been through it before, man. You were married to Eliza's mother.

Doolittle. Who told you that, Colonel?

Pickering. Well, nobody told me. But I concluded — naturally —

Doolittle. No: that aint the natural way, Colonel: it's only the middle class way. My way was always the undeserving way. But dont say nothing to Eliza. She dont know: I always had a delicacy about telling her.

Pickering. Quite right. We'll leave it so, if you dont mind.

Doolittle. And youll come to the church, Colonel, and put me through straight?

Pickering. With pleasure. As far as a bachelor can.

Mrs Higgins. May I come, Mr Doolittle? I should be very sorry to miss your wedding.

Doolittle. I should indeed be honored by your condescension, maam; and my poor old woman would take it as a tremenjous compliment. She's been very low, thinking of the happy days that are no more.

Mrs Higgins (rising). I'll order the carriage and get ready. *(The men rise, except Higgins.)* I shant be more than fifteen minutes. *(As she goes to the door Eliza comes in, hatted and buttoning her gloves.)* I'm going to the church to see your father married, Eliza. You had better come in the brougham with me. Colonel Pickering can go on with the bridegroom.

Mrs Higgins goes out. Eliza comes to the middle of the room between the centre window and the ottoman. Pickering joins her.

Doolittle. Bridegroom! What a word! It makes a man realize his position, somehow. *(He takes up his hat and goes towards the door.)*

Pickering. Before I go, Eliza, do forgive Higgins and come back to us.

Liza. I dont think dad would allow me. Would you, dad?

Doolittle (sad but magnanimous). They played you off very cunning, Eliza, them two sportsmen. If it had been only one of them, you could have nailed him. But you see, there was two; and one of them chaperoned the other, as you might say. *(To Pickering.)* It was artful of you, Colonel; but I bear no malice: I should have done the same myself. I been the victim of one woman after an-

other all my life; and I dont grudge you two getting the better of
Eliza. I shant interfere. It's time for us to go, Colonel. So long,
Henry. See you in St George's, Eliza. *(He goes out.)*
Pickering *(coaxing).* Do stay with us, Eliza. *(He follows Doolittle.)*

Eliza goes out on the balcony to avoid being alone with Higgins.
He rises and joins her there. She immediately comes back into the
room and makes for the door; but he goes along the balcony
quickly and gets his back to the door before she reaches it.

Higgins. Well, Eliza, youve had a bit of your own back, as you call it.
Have you had enough? and are you going to be reasonable? Or do
you want any more?

Liza. You want me back only to pick up your slippers and put up
with your tempers and fetch and carry for you.

Higgins. I havnt said I wanted you back at all.

Liza. Oh, indeed. Then what are we talking about?

Higgins. About you, not about me. If you come back I shall treat you
just as I have always treated you. I cant change my nature; and I
dont intend to change my manners. My manners are exactly the
same as Colonel Pickering's.

Liza. Thats not true. He treats a flower girl as if she was a duchess.

Higgins. And I treat a duchess as if she was a flower girl.

Liza. I see. *(She turns away composedly, and sits on the ottoman,*
facing the window.) The same to everybody.

Higgins. Just so.

Liza. Like father.

Higgins *(grinning, a little taken down).* Without accepting the comparison at all points, Eliza, it's quite true that your father is not a
snob, and that he will be quite at home in any station of life to
which his eccentric destiny may call him. *(Seriously.)* The great
secret, Eliza, is not having bad manners or good manners or any
other particular sort of manners, but having the same manner for
all human souls: in short, behaving as if you were in Heaven,
where there are no third-class carriages, and one soul is as good as
another.

Liza. Amen. You are a born preacher.

Higgins *(irritated).* The question is not whether I treat you rudely,
but whether you ever heard me treat anyone else better.

Liza *(with sudden sincerity).* I dont care how you treat me. I dont
mind your swearing at me. I shouldnt mind a black eye: Ive had
one before this. But *(standing up and facing him)* I wont be
passed over.

Higgins. Then get out of my way; for I wont stop for you. You talk
about me as if I were a motor bus.

Liza. So you are a motor bus: all bounce and go, and no consideration for anyone. But I can do without you: dont think I cant.

Higgins. I know you can. I told you you could.

Liza (wounded, getting away from him to the other side of the ottoman with her face to the hearth). I know you did, you brute. You wanted to get rid of me.

Higgins. Liar.

Liza. Thank you. *(She sits down with dignity.)*

Higgins. You never asked yourself, I suppose, whether *I* could do without you.

Liza (earnestly). Dont try to get round me. Youll have to do without me.

Higgins (arrogant). I can do without anybody. I have my own soul: my own spark of divine fire. But *(with sudden humility)* I shall miss you, Eliza. *(He sits down near her on the ottoman.)* I have learnt something from your idiotic notions: I confess that humbly and gratefully. And I have grown accustomed to your voice and appearance. I like them, rather.

Liza. Well, you have both of them on your gramophone and in your book of photographs. When you feel lonely without me, you can turn the machine on. It's got no feelings to hurt.

Higgins. I cant turn your soul on. Leave me those feelings; and you can take away the voice and the face. They are not you.

Liza. Oh, you are a devil. You can twist the heart in a girl as easy as some could twist her arms to hurt her. Mrs Pearce warned me. Time and again she has wanted to leave you; and you always got round her at the last minute. And you dont care a bit for her. And you dont care a bit for me.

Higgins. I care for life, for humanity; and you are a part of it that has come my way and been built into my house. What more can you or anyone ask?

Liza. I wont care for anybody that doesnt care for me.

Higgins. Commercial principles, Eliza. Like *(reproducing her Covent Garden pronunciation with professional exactness)* s'yollin voylets (selling violets), isnt it?

Liza. Dont sneer at me. It's mean to sneer at me.

Higgins. I have never sneered in my life. Sneering doesnt become either the human face or the human soul. I am expressing my righteous contempt for Commercialism. I dont and wont trade in affection. You call me a brute because you couldnt buy a claim on me by fetching my slippers and finding my spectacles. You were a fool: I think a woman fetching a man's slippers is a disgusting sight: did I ever fetch your slippers? I think a good deal more of you for throwing them in my face. No use slaving for me and then saying you want to be cared for: who cares for a slave? If you come back, come back for the sake of good fellowship; for youll get nothing else. Youve had a thousand times as much out of me as I have out of you; and if you dare to set up your little dog's tricks of fetching and carrying slippers against my creation of a Duchess Eliza, I'll slam the door in your silly face.

Liza. What did you do it for if you didnt care for me?

Higgins (heartily). Why, because it was my job.

Liza. You never thought of the trouble it would make for me.

Higgins. Would the world ever have been made if its maker had been afraid of making trouble? Making life means making trouble. Theres only one way of escaping trouble; and thats killing things. Cowards, you notice, are always shrieking to have troublesome people killed.

Liza. I'm no preacher: I dont notice things like that. I notice that you dont notice me.

Higgins (jumping up and walking about intolerantly). Eliza: youre an idiot. I waste the treasures of my Miltonic mind by spreading them before you. Once for all, understand that I go my way and do my work without caring twopence what happens to either of us. I am not intimidated, like your father and your stepmother. So you can come back or go to the devil: which you please.

Liza. What am I to come back for?

Higgins (bouncing up on his knees on the ottoman and leaning over it to her). For the fun of it. Thats why I took you on.

Liza (with averted face). And you may throw me out tomorrow if I dont do everything you want me to?

Higgins. Yes; and you may walk out tomorrow if I dont do everything you want me to.

Liza. And live with my stepmother?

Higgins. Yes, or sell flowers.

Liza. Oh! if I only could go back to my flower basket! I should be independent of both of you and father and all the world! Why did you take my independence from me? Why did I give it up? I'm a slave now, for all my fine clothes.

Higgins. Not a bit. I'll adopt you as my daughter and settle money on you if you like. Or would you rather marry Pickering?

Liza (looking fiercely round at him). I wouldnt marry you if you asked me; and youre nearer my age than what he is.

Higgins (gently). Than he is: not "than what he is."

Liza (losing her temper and rising). I'll talk as I like. Youre not my teacher now.

Higgins (reflectively). I dont suppose Pickering would, though. He's as confirmed an old bachelor as I am.

Liza. Thats not what I want; and dont you think it. Ive always had chaps enough wanting me that way. Freddy Hill writes to me twice and three times a day, sheets and sheets.

Higgins (disagreeably surprised). Damn his impudence! *(He recoils and finds himself sitting on his heels.)*

Liza. He has a right to if he likes, poor lad. And he does love me.

Higgins (getting off the ottoman). You have no right to encourage him.

Liza. Every girl has a right to be loved.

Higgins. What! By fools like that?

Liza. Freddy's not a fool. And if he's weak and poor and wants me, may be he'd make me happier than my betters that bully me and dont want me.

Higgins. Can he make anything of you? Thats the point.

Liza. Perhaps I could make something of him. But I never thought of us making anything of one another; and you never think of anything else. I only want to be natural.

Higgins. In short, you want me to be as infatuated about you as Freddy? Is that it?

Liza. No I dont. Thats not the sort of feeling I want from you. And dont you be too sure of yourself or of me. I could have been a bad girl if I'd liked. Ive seen more of some things than you, for all your learning. Girls like me can drag gentlemen down to make love to them easy enough. And they wish each other dead the next minute.

Higgins. Of course they do. Then what in thunder are we quarrelling about?

Liza (much troubled). I want a little kindness. I know I'm a common ignorant girl, and you a book-learned gentleman; but I'm not dirt under your feet. What I done *(correcting herself)* what I did was not for the dresses and the taxis: I did it because we were pleasant together and I come — came — to care for you; not to want you to make love to me, and not forgetting the difference between us, but more friendly like.

Higgins. Well, of course. Thats just how I feel. And how Pickering feels. Eliza: youre a fool.

Liza. Thats not a proper answer to give me. *(She sinks on the chair at the writing-table in tears.)*

Higgins. It's all youll get until you stop being a common idiot. If youre going to be a lady, youll have to give up feeling neglected if the men you know dont spend half their time snivelling over you and the other half giving you black eyes. If you cant stand the coldness of my sort of life, and the strain of it, go back to the gutter. Work til youre more a brute than a human being; and then cuddle and squabble and drink til you fall asleep. Oh, it's a fine life, the life of the gutter. It's real: it's warm: it's violent: you can feel it through the thickest skin: you can taste it and smell it without any training or any work. Not like Science and Literature and Classical Music and Philosophy and Art. You find me cold, unfeeling, selfish, dont you? Very well: be off with you to the sort of people you like. Marry some sentimental hog or other with lots of money, and a thick pair of lips to kiss you with and a thick pair of boots to kick you with. If you cant appreciate what youve got, youd better get what you can appreciate.

Liza (desperate). Oh, you are a cruel tyrant. I cant talk to you: you turn everything against me: I'm always in the wrong. But you know very well all the time that youre nothing but a bully. You know I cant go back to the gutter, as you call it, and that I have no real friends in the world but you and the Colonel. You know well I couldnt bear to live with a low common man after you two; and it's wicked and cruel of you to insult me by pretending I could. You think I must go back to Wimpole Street because I have nowhere else to go but father's. But dont you be too sure that you have me under your feet to be trampled on and talked down. I'll marry Freddy, I will, as soon as I'm able to support him.

Higgins (thunderstruck). Freddy!!! that young fool! That poor devil who couldnt get a job as an errand boy even if he had the guts to try for it! Woman: do you not understand that I have made you a consort for a king?

Liza. Freddy loves me: that makes him king enough for me. I dont want him to work: he wasnt brought up to it as I was. I'll go and be a teacher.

Higgins. Whatll you teach, in heaven's name?

Liza. What you taught me. I'll teach phonetics.

Higgins. Ha! ha! ha!

Liza. I'll offer myself as an assistant to that hairy-faced Hungarian.

Higgins (rising in a fury). What! That impostor! that humbug! that toadying ignoramus! Teach him my methods! my discoveries! You take one step in his direction and I'll wring your neck. *(He lays hands on her).* Do you hear?

Liza (defiantly nonresistant). Wring away. What do I care? I knew youd strike me some day. *(He lets her go, stamping with rage at having forgotten himself, and recoils so hastily that he stumbles back into his seat on the ottoman.)* Aha! Now I know how to deal with you. What a fool I was not to think of it before! You cant take away the knowledge you gave me. You said I had a finer ear than you. And I can be civil and kind to people, which is more than you can. Aha! *(Purposely dropping her aitches to annoy him.)* Thats done you, Enry Iggins, it az. Now I dont care that *(snapping her fingers)* for your bullying and your big talk. I'll advertize it in the papers that your duchess is only a flower girl that you taught, and that she'll teach anybody to be a duchess just the same in six months for a thousand guineas. Oh, when I think of myself crawling under your feet and being trampled on and called names, when all the time I had only to lift up my finger to be as good as you, I could just kick myself.

Higgins (wondering at her). You damned impudent slut, you! But it's better than snivelling; better than fetching slippers and finding spectacles, isnt it? *(Rising)* By George, Eliza, I said I'd make a woman of you; and I have. I like you like this.

Liza. Yes: you turn round and make up to me now that I'm not afraid of you, and can do without you.

Higgins. Of course I do, you little fool. Five minutes ago you were like a millstone round my neck. Now youre a tower of strength; a consort battleship. You and I and Pickering will be three old bachelors together instead of only two men and a silly girl.

Mrs Higgins returns, dressed for the wedding. Eliza instantly becomes cool and elegant.

Mrs Higgins. The carriage is waiting, Eliza. Are you ready?

Liza. Quite. Is the Professor coming?

Mrs Higgins. Certainly not. He cant behave himself in church. He makes remarks out loud all the time on the clergyman's pronunciation.

Liza. Then I shall not see you again, Professor. Goodbye. *(She goes to the door.)*

Mrs Higgins (coming to Higgins). Goodbye, dear.

Higgins. Goodbye, mother. *(He is about to kiss her, when he recollects something.)* Oh, by the way, Eliza, order a ham and a Stilton cheese, will you? And buy me a pair of reindeer gloves, number eights, and a tie to match that new suit of mine. You can choose the color. *(His cheerful, careless, vigorous voice shews that he is incorrigible.)*

Liza (disdainfully). Number eights are too small for you if you want them lined with lamb's wool. You have three new ties that you have forgotten in the drawer of your washstand. Colonel Pickering prefers double Gloucester to Stilton; and you dont notice the difference. I telephoned Mrs Pearce this morning not to forget the ham. What you are to do without me I cannot imagine. *(She sweeps out.)*

Mrs Higgins. I'm afraid youve spoilt that girl, Henry. I should

be uneasy about you and her if she were less fond of Colonel
Pickering.

Higgins. Pickering! Nonsense: she's going to marry Freddy. Ha ha!
Freddy! Freddy!! Ha ha ha ha ha!!!!! *(He roars with laughter as
the play ends.)*

. . .

(The rest of the story need not be shewn in action, and indeed, would
hardly need telling if our imaginations were not so enfeebled by their
lazy dependence on the ready-mades and reach-me-downs of the
ragshop in which Romance keeps its stock of "happy endings" to
misfit all stories. Now, the history of Eliza Doolittle, though called a
romance because the transfiguration it records seems exceedingly
improbable, is common enough. Such transfigurations have been
achieved by hundreds of resolutely ambitious young women since
Nell Gwynne set them the example by playing queens and fascinating kings in the theatre in which she began by selling oranges. Nevertheless, people in all directions have assumed, for no other reason
than that she became the heroine of a romance, that she must have
married the hero of it. This is unbearable, not only because her little
drama, if acted on such a thoughtless assumption, must be spoiled,
but because the true sequel is patent to anyone with a sense of
human nature in general, and of feminine instinct in particular.

Eliza, in telling Higgins she would not marry him if he asked her,
was not coquetting: she was announcing a well-considered decision.
When a bachelor interests, and dominates, and teaches, and becomes
important to a spinster, as Higgins with Eliza, she always, if she has
character enough to be capable of it, considers very seriously indeed
whether she will play for becoming that bachelor's wife, especially if
he is so little interested in marriage that a determined and devoted
woman might capture him if she set herself resolutely to do it. Her
decision will depend a good deal on whether she is really free to
choose; and that, again, will depend on her age and income. If she is
at the end of her youth, and has no security for her livelihood, she
will marry him because she must marry anybody who will provide for
her. But at Eliza's age a good-looking girl does not feel that pressure:
she feels free to pick and choose. She is therefore guided by her
instinct in the matter. Eliza's instinct tells her not to marry Higgins. It
does not tell her to give him up. It is not in the slightest doubt as to
his remaining one of the strongest personal interests in her life. It
would be very sorely strained if there was another woman likely to
supplant her with him. But as she feels sure of him on that last point,
she has no doubt at all as to her course, and would not have any, even
if the difference of twenty years in age, which seems so great to
youth, did not exist between them.

As our own instincts are not appealed to by her conclusion, let us
see whether we cannot discover some reason in it. When Higgins

excused his indifference to young women on the ground that they had an irresistible rival in his mother, he gave the clue to his inveterate old-bachelordom. The case is uncommon only to the extent that remarkable mothers are uncommon. If an imaginative boy has a sufficiently rich mother who has intelligence, personal grace, dignity of character without harshness, and a cultivated sense of the best art of her time to enable her to make her house beautiful, she sets a standard for him against which very few women can struggle, besides effecting for him a disengagement of his affections, his sense of beauty, and his idealism from his specifically sexual impulses. This makes him a standing puzzle to the huge number of uncultivated people who have been brought up in tasteless homes by commonplace or disagreeable parents, and to whom, consequently, literature, painting, sculpture, music, and affectionate personal relations come as modes of sex if they come at all. The word passion means nothing else to them; and that Higgins could have a passion for phonetics and idealize his mother instead of Eliza, would seem to them absurd and unnatural. Nevertheless, when we look round and see that hardly anyone is too ugly or disagreeable to find a wife or a husband if he or she wants one, whilst many old maids and bachelors are above the average in quality and culture, we cannot help suspecting that the disentanglement of sex from the associations with which it is so commonly confused, a disentanglement which persons of genius achieve by sheer intellectual analysis, is sometimes produced or aided by parental fascination.

Now, though Eliza was incapable of thus explaining to herself Higgins's formidable powers of resistance to the charm that prostrated Freddy at the first glance, she was instinctively aware that she could never obtain a complete grip of him, or come between him and his mother (the first necessity of the married woman). To put it shortly, she knew that for some mysterious reason he had not the makings of a married man in him, according to her conception of a husband as one to whom she would be his nearest and fondest and warmest interest. Even had there been no mother-rival, she would still have refused to accept an interest in herself that was secondary to philosophic interests. Had Mrs Higgins died, there would still have been Milton and the Universal Alphabet. Landor's remark that to those who have the greatest power of loving, love is a secondary affair, would not have recommended Landor to Eliza. Put that along with her resentment of Higgins's domineering superiority, and her mistrust of his coaxing cleverness in getting round her and evading her wrath when he had gone too far with his impetuous bullying, and you will see that Eliza's instinct had good grounds for warning her not to marry her Pygmalion.

And now, whom did Eliza marry? For if Higgins was a predestinate old bachelor, she was most certainly not a predestinate old maid. Well, that can be told very shortly to those who have not guessed it from the indications she has herself given them.

Almost immediately after Eliza is stung into proclaiming her considered determination not to marry Higgins, she mentions the fact that young Mr Frederick Eynsford Hill is pouring out his love for her daily through the post. Now Freddy is young, practically twenty years younger than Higgins: he is a gentleman (or, as Eliza would qualify him, a toff), and speaks like one. He is nicely dressed, is treated by the Colonel as an equal, loves her unaffectedly, and is not her master, nor ever likely to dominate her in spite of his advantage of social standing. Eliza has no use for the foolish romantic tradition that all women love to be mastered, if not actually bullied and beaten. "When you go to women" says Nietzsche "take your whip with you." Sensible despots have never confined that precaution to women: they have taken their whips with them when they have dealt with men, and been slavishly idealized by the men over whom they have flourished the whip much more than by women. No doubt there are slavish women as well as slavish men; and women, like men, admire those that are stronger than themselves. But to admire a strong person and to live under that strong person's thumb are two different things. The weak may not be admired and hero-worshiped; but they are by no means disliked or shunned; and they never seem to have the least difficulty in marrying people who are too good for them. They may fail in emergencies; but life is not one long emergency: it is mostly a string of situations for which no exceptional strength is needed, and with which even rather weak people can cope if they have a stronger partner to help them out. Accordingly, it is a truth everywhere in evidence that strong people, masculine or feminine, not only do not marry stronger people, but do not shew any preference for them in selecting their friends. When a lion meets another with a louder roar "the first lion thinks the last a bore." The man or woman who feels strong enough for two, seeks for every other quality in a partner than strength.

The converse is also true. Weak people want to marry strong people who do not frighten them too much; and this often leads them to make the mistake we describe metaphorically as "biting off more than they can chew." They want too much for too little; and when the bargain is unreasonable beyond all bearing, the union becomes impossible: it ends in the weaker party being either discarded or borne as a cross, which is worse. People who are not only weak, but silly or obtuse as well, are often in these difficulties.

This being the state of human affairs, what is Eliza fairly sure to do when she is placed between Freddy and Higgins? Will she look forward to a lifetime of fetching Higgins's slippers or to a lifetime of Freddy fetching hers? There can be no doubt about the answer. Unless Freddy is biologically repulsive to her, and Higgins biologically attractive to a degree that overwhelms all her other instincts, she will, if she marries either of them, marry Freddy.

And that is just what Eliza did.

Complications ensued; but they were economic, not romantic.

Freddy had no money and no occupation. His mother's jointure, a last relic of the opulence of Largelady Park, had enabled her to struggle along in Earlscourt with an air of gentility, but not to procure any serious secondary education for her children, much less give the boy a profession. A clerkship at thirty shillings a week was beneath Freddy's dignity, and extremely distasteful to him besides. His prospects consisted of a hope that if he kept up appearances somebody would do something for him. The something appeared vaguely to his imagination as a private secretaryship or a sinecure of some sort. To his mother it perhaps appeared as a marriage to some lady of means who could not resist her boy's niceness. Fancy her feelings when he married a flower girl who had become disclassed under extraordinary circumstances which were now notorious!

It is true that Eliza's situation did not seem wholly ineligible. Her father, though formerly a dustman, and now fantastically disclassed, had become extremely popular in the smartest society by a social talent which triumphed over every prejudice and every disadvantage. Rejected by the middle class, which he loathed, he had shot up at once into the highest circles by his wit, his dustmanship (which he carried like a banner), and his Nietzschean transcendence of good and evil. At intimate ducal dinners he sat on the right hand of the Duchess; and in country houses he smoked in the pantry and was made much of by the butler when he was not feeding in the dining room and being consulted by cabinet ministers. But he found it almost as hard to do all this on four thousand a year as Mrs Eynsford Hill to live in Earlscourt on an income so pitiably smaller that I have not the heart to disclose its exact figure. He absolutely refused to add the last straw to his burden by contributing to Eliza's support.

Thus Freddy and Eliza, now Mr and Mrs Eynsford Hill, would have spent a penniless honeymoon but for a wedding present of 500 pounds from the Colonel to Eliza. It lasted a long time because Freddy did not know how to spend money, never having had any to spend, and Eliza, socially trained by a pair of old bachelors, wore her clothes as long as they held together and looked pretty, without the least regard to their being many months out of fashion. Still, 500 pounds will not last two young people for ever; and they both knew, and Eliza felt as well, that they must shift for themselves in the end. She could quarter herself on Wimpole Street because it had come to be her home; but she was quite aware that she ought not to quarter Freddy there, and that it would not be good for his character if she did.

Not that the Wimpole Street bachelors objected. When she consulted them, Higgins declined to be bothered about her housing problem when that solution was so simple. Eliza's desire to have Freddy in the house with her seemed of no more importance than if she had wanted an extra piece of bedroom furniture. Pleas as to Freddy's character, and the moral obligation on him to earn his own living, were lost on Higgins. He denied that Freddy had any character, and declared that if he tried to do any useful work some competent person would have the trouble of undoing it: a procedure involving a net loss to the community, and great unhappiness to Freddy himself, who was obviously intended by Nature for such light work as amusing Eliza, which, Higgins declared, was a much more useful and honorable occupation than working in the city. When Eliza referred again to her project of teaching phonetics, Higgins abated not a jot of his violent opposition to it. He said she was not within ten years of being qualified to meddle with his pet subject; and as it was evident that the Colonel agreed with him, she felt she could not go against them in this grave matter, and that she had no right, without Higgins's consent, to exploit the knowledge he had given her; for his knowledge seemed to her as much his private property as his watch: Eliza was no communist. Besides, she was superstitiously devoted to them both, more entirely and frankly after her marriage than before it.

It was the Colonel who finally solved the problem, which had cost him much perplexed cogitation. He one day asked Eliza, rather shyly, whether she had quite given up her notion of keeping a flower shop. She replied that she had thought of it, but had put it out of her head, because the Colonel had said, that day at Mrs Higgins's, that it would never do. The Colonel confessed that when he said that, he had not quite recovered from the dazzling impression of the day before. They broke the matter to Higgins that evening. The sole comment vouchsafed by him very nearly led to a serious quarrel with Eliza. It was to the effect that she would have in Freddy an ideal errand boy.

Freddy himself was next sounded on the subject. He said he had been thinking of a shop himself; though it had presented itself to his pennilessness as a small place in which Eliza should sell tobacco at one counter whilst he sold newspapers at the opposite one. But he agreed that it would be extraordinarily jolly to go early every morning with Eliza to Covent Garden and buy flowers on the scene of their first meeting: a sentiment which earned him many kisses from his wife. He added that he had always been afraid to propose anything of the sort, because Clara would make an awful row about a step that must damage her matrimonial chances, and his mother could not be expected to like it after clinging for so many years to that step of the social ladder on which retail trade is impossible.

This difficulty was removed by an event highly unexpected by Freddy's mother. Clara, in the course of her incursions into those artistic circles which were the highest within her reach, discovered that her conversational qualifications were expected to include a grounding in the novels of Mr H. G. Wells. She borrowed them in various directions so energetically that she swallowed them all within two months. The result was a conversion of a kind quite common today. A modern Acts of the Apostles would fill fifty whole Bibles if anyone were capable of writing it.

Poor Clara, who appeared to Higgins and his mother as a disagreeable and ridiculous person, and to her own mother as in some inexplicable way a social failure, had never seen herself in either light; for, though to some extent ridiculed and mimicked in West Kensington like everyone else there, she was accepted as a rational and normal — or shall we say inevitable? — sort of human being. At worst they called her The Pusher; but to them no more than to herself had it ever occurred that she was pushing the air, and pushing it in a wrong direction. Still, she was not happy. She was growing desperate. Her one asset, the fact that her mother was what the Epsom greengrocer called a carriage lady, had no exchange value, apparently. It had prevented her from getting educated, because the only education she could have afforded was education with the Earlscourt greengrocer's daughter. It had led her to seek the society of her mother's class; and that class simply would not have her, because she was much poorer than the greengrocer, and, far from being able to afford a maid, could not afford even a housemaid, and had to scrape along at home with an illiberally treated general servant. Under such circumstances nothing could give her an air of being a genuine product of Largelady Park. And yet its tradition made her regard a marriage with anyone within her reach as an unbearable humiliation. Commercial people and professional people in a small way were odious to her. She ran after painters and novelists; but she did not charm them; and her bold attempts to pick up and practise artistic and literary talk irritated them. She was, in short, an utter failure, an ignorant, incompetent, pretentious, unwelcome, penniless, useless little snob; and though she did not admit these disqualifications (for nobody ever faces unpleasant truths of this kind until the possibility of a way out dawns on them) she felt their effects too keenly to be satisfied with her position.

Clara had a startling eyeopener when, on being suddenly wakened to enthusiasm by a girl of her own age who dazzled her and produced in her a gushing desire to take her for a model, and gain her friendship, she discovered that this exquisite apparition had graduated from the gutter in a few months time. It shook her so violently, that when Mr H. G. Wells lifted her on the point of his puissant pen, and placed her at the angle of view from which the life she was leading and the society to which she clung appeared in its true relation to real human needs and worthy social structure, he effected a conversion and a conviction of sin comparable to the most sensational feats of General Booth or Gypsy Smith. Clara's snobbery went bang. Life suddenly began to move with her. Without knowing how or why, she began to make friends and enemies. Some of the acquaintances to whom she had been a tedious or indifferent or ridiculous affliction, dropped her; others became cordial. To her amazement she found that some "quite nice" people were saturated with Wells, and that this accessibility to ideas was the secret of their niceness. People she had thought deeply religious, and had tried to conciliate on that tack with disastrous results, suddenly took an interest in her, and revealed a hostility to conventional religion which she had never conceived possible except among the most desperate characters. They made her read Galsworthy; and Galsworthy exposed the vanity of Largelady Park and finished her. It exasperated her to think that the dungeon in which she had languished for so many unhappy years had been unlocked all the time, and that the impulses she had so carefully struggled with and stifled for the sake of keeping well with society, were precisely those by which alone she could have come into any sort of sincere human contact. In the radiance of these discoveries, and the tumult of their reaction, she made a fool of herself as freely and conspicuously as when she so rashly adopted Eliza's expletive in Mrs Higgins's drawing room; for the new-born Wellsian had to find her bearings almost as ridiculously as a baby; but nobody hates a baby for its ineptitudes, or thinks the worse of it for tying to eat the matches; and Clara lost no friends by her follies. They laughed at her to her face this time; and she had to defend herself and fight it out as best she could.

When Freddy paid a visit to Earlscourt (which he never did when he could possibly help it) to make the desolating announcement that he and his Eliza were thinking of blackening the Largelady scutcheon by opening a shop, he found the little household already convulsed by a prior announcement from Clara that she also was going to work in an old furniture shop in Dover Street, which had been started by a fellow Wellsian. This appointment Clara owed, after all, to her old social accomplishment of Push. She had made up her mind that, cost what it might, she would see Mr Wells in the flesh; and she had achieved her end at a garden party. She had better luck than so rash an enterprise deserved. Mr Wells came up to her expectations. Age had not withered him, nor could custom stale his infinite variety in half an hour. His pleasant neatness and compactness, his small hands and feet, his teeming ready brain, his unaffected accessibility, and a certain fine apprehensiveness which stamped him as susceptible from his topmost hair to his tipmost toe, proved irresistible. Clara talked of nothing else for weeks and weeks afterwards. And as she happened to talk to the lady of the furniture shop, and that lady also desired above all things to know Mr Wells and sell pretty things to him, she offered Clara a job on the chance of achieving that end through her.

And so it came about that Eliza's luck held, and the expected opposition to the flower shop melted away. The shop is in the arcade of a railway station not very far from the Victoria and Albert Museum; and if you live in that neighborhood you may go there any day and buy a buttonhole from Eliza.

Now here is a last opportunity for romance. Would you not like to be assured that the shop was an immense success, thanks to Eliza's charms and her early business experience in Covent Garden? Alas! the truth is the truth: the shop did not pay for a long time, simply because Eliza and her Freddy did not know how to keep it. True, Eliza had not to begin at the very beginning: she knew the names and prices of the cheaper flowers; and her elation was unbounded when she found that Freddy, like all youths educated at cheap, pretentious, and thoroughly inefficient schools, knew a little Latin. It was very little, but enough to make him appear to her a Porson or Bentley, and to put him at his ease with botanical nomenclature. Unfortunately he knew nothing else; and Eliza, though she could count money up to eighteen shillings or so, and had acquired a certain familiarity with the language of Milton from her struggles to qualify herself for winning Higgins's bet, could not write out a bill without utterly disgracing the establishment. Freddy's power of stating in Latin that Balbus built a wall and that Gaul was divided into three parts did not carry with it the slightest knowledge of accounts or business: Colonel Pickering had to explain to him what a cheque book and a bank account meant. And the pair were by no means easily teachable. Freddy backed up Eliza in her obstinate refusal to believe that they could save money by engaging a bookkeeper with some knowledge of the business. How, they argued, could you possibly save money by going to extra expense when you already could not make both ends meet? But the Colonel, after making the ends meet over and over again, at last gently insisted; and Eliza, humbled to the dust by having to beg from him so often, and stung by the uproarious derision of Higgins, to whom the notion of Freddy succeeding at anything was a joke that never palled, grasped the fact that business, like phonetics, has to be learned.

On the piteous spectacle of the pair spending their evenings in shorthand schools and polytechnic classes, learning bookkeeping and typewriting with incipient junior clerks, male and female, from the elementary schools, let me not dwell. There were even classes at the London School of Economics, and a humble personal appeal to the director of that institution to recommend a course bearing on the flower business. He, being a humorist, explained to them the method of the celebrated Dickensian essay on Chinese Metaphysics by the gentleman who read an article on China and an article on Metaphysics and combined the information. He suggested that they should combine the London School with Kew Gardens. Eliza, to whom the procedure of the Dickensian gentleman seemed perfectly correct (as in fact it was) and not in the least funny (which was only her ignorance), took the advice with entire gravity. But the effort that cost her the deepest humiliation was a request to Higgins, whose pet artistic fancy, next to Milton's verse, was caligraphy, and who himself wrote a most beautiful Italian hand, that he would teach her to write. He declared that she was congenitally incapable of forming a single letter worthy of the least of Milton's words; but she persisted; and again he suddenly threw himself into the task of teaching her with a combination of stormy intensity, concentrated patience, and occasional bursts of interesting disquisition on the beauty and nobility, the august mission and destiny, of human handwriting. Eliza ended by acquiring an extremely uncommercial script which was a positive extension of her personal beauty, and spending three times as much on stationery as anyone else because certain qualities and shapes of paper became indispensable to her. She could not even address an envelope in the usual way because it made the margins all wrong.

Their commercial schooldays were a period of disgrace and despair for the young couple. They seemed to be learning nothing about flower shops. At last they gave it up as hopeless, and shook the dust of the shorthand schools, and the polytechnics, and the London School of Economics from their feet for ever. Besides, the business was in some mysterious way beginning to take care of itself. They had somehow forgotten their objections to employing other people. They came to the conclusion that their own way was the best, and that they had really a remarkable talent for business. The Colonel, who had been compelled for some years to keep a sufficient sum on current account at his bankers to make up their deficits, found that the provision was unnecessary: the young people were prospering. It is true that there was not quite fair play between them and their competitors in trade. Their week-ends in the country cost them nothing, and saved them the price of their Sunday dinners; for the motor car was the Colonel's; and he and Higgins paid the hotel bills. Mr F. Hill, florist and greengrocer (they soon discovered that there was money in asparagus; and asparagus led to other vegetables), had an air which stamped the business as classy; and in private life he was still Frederick Eynsford Hill, Esquire. Not that there was any swank about him: nobody but Eliza knew that he had been christened Frederick Challoner. Eliza herself swanked like anything.

That is all. That is how it has turned out. It is astonishing how much Eliza still manages to meddle in the housekeeping at Wimpole Street in spite of the shop and her own family. And it is notable that though she never nags her husband, and frankly loves the Colonel as if she were his favorite daughter, she has never got out of the habit of nagging Higgins that was established on the fatal night when she won his bet for him. She snaps his head off on the faintest provocation, or on none. He no longer dares to tease her by assuming an abysmal inferiority of Freddy's mind to his own. He storms and bullies and derides; but she stands up to him so ruthlessly that the Colonel has to ask her from time to time to be kinder to Higgins; and it is the only request of his that brings a mulish expression into her face. Nothing but some emergency or calamity great enough to break down all likes and dislikes, and throw them both back on their common humanity — and may they be spared any such trial! — will ever alter this. She knows that Higgins does not need her, just as her father did not need her. The very scrupulousness with which he told her that day that he had become used to having her there, and dependent on her for all sorts of little services, and that he should miss her if she went away (it would never have occurred to Freddy or the Colonel to say anything of the sort) deepens her inner certainty that she is "no more to him than them slippers"; yet she has a sense, too, that his indifference is deeper than the infatuation of commoner souls. She is immensely interested in him. She has even secret mischievous moments in which she wishes she could get him alone, on a desert island, away from all ties and with nobody else in the world to consider, and just drag him off his pedestal and see him making love like any common man. We all have private imaginations of that sort. But when it comes to business, to the life that she really leads as distinguished from the life of dreams and fancies, she likes Freddy and she likes the Colonel; and she does not like Higgins and Mr Doolittle. Galatea never does quite like Pygmalion: his relation to her is too godlike to be altogether agreeable.)

Questions

1. Characterize Clara and Freddy in Act I. In view of the entire play, explain why it is significant that Liza goes home in a taxi. And how does the change in the weather in Act I foreshadow the overall action of the play?

2. Characterize Higgins in Act II. Is he unthinking? Selfish? Deliberately cruel? Playful?

3. Alfred Doolittle would be quite willing to allow his daughter to have a "career" as Higgins's mistress. Is Doolittle a monster? Do you find him amusing?

4. In Act III, how far do Liza's ideals advance over those of Act II?

5. What is your attitude toward Clara when she says she finds "the new small talk delightful and quite innocent" (page 639) and when, tempted by Higgins, she uses "bloody"? ("Bloody" was unacceptable in polite company at the time of *Pygmalion*, as Mrs. Pearce indicates in Act II when she cautions Higgins against using a word that "begins with the same letter as bath." In the American musical adaptation, *My Fair Lady*, an equivalent shocker had to be found, and the authors came up with "Move your bloomin' arse.")

6. How does Shaw, near the end of Act III, prepare us for Act IV?

7. Is Liza being melodramatic or realistic (or a little of both) when she says (page 652), "I sold flowers. I didn't sell myself. Now you've made a lady of me I'm not fit to sell anything else"?

8. In Act V is Shaw implying, through the newly prosperous Alfred Doolittle, that philanthropy is a waste? Or are we to believe that although Doolittle is now less happy he is a more socially useful human being?

9. Does the play imply that any flower girl can be turned into a duchess? Or is Liza exceptionally talented and diligent? Could Higgins have succeeded equally well with Clara?

10. At the end of the play, Higgins is confident that Liza will do his errands and return to him. Shaw tells us in the epilogue that she will marry Freddy, partly because she is "instinctively 'aware that she could never obtain a complete grip" on Higgins. Do you believe Shaw, or — when you read the last lines of the play itself — do you believe that Higgins is right in his assumption that Liza will return?

20 Six Plays for Further Study

Sophocles (496? –406 B.C.)

Oedipus Rex

An English Version by Dudley Fitts and Robert Fitzgerald

List of Characters

Oedipus
A Priest
Creon
Teiresias
Iocastê
Messenger
Shepherd of Laïos
Second Messenger
Chorus of Theban Elders

Scene. *Before the palace of Oedipus, King of Thebes. A central door and two lateral doors open onto a platform which runs the length of the façade. On the platform, right and left, are altars; and three steps lead down into the "orchestra," or chorus-ground. At the beginning of the action these steps are crowded by Suppliants who have brought branches and chaplets of olive leaves and who lie in various attitudes of despair. Oedipus enters.*

PROLOGUE

Oedipus.   My children, generations of the living
    In the line of Kadmos,° nursed at his ancient hearth:
    Why have you strewn yourselves before these altars
    In supplication, with your boughs and garlands?
    The breath of incense rises from the city   5
    With a sound of prayer and lamentation.
                                    Children,
    I would not have you speak through messengers,
    And therefore I have come myself to hear you —
    I, Oedipus, who bear the famous name.
    (To a Priest.) You, there, since you are eldest in the company,   10
    Speak for them all, tell me what preys upon you,
    Whether you come in dread, or crave some blessing:
    Tell me, and never doubt that I will help you
    In every way I can; I should be heartless
    Were I not moved to find you suppliant here.   15
Priest.   Great Oedipus, O powerful King of Thebes!
    You see how all the ages of our people
    Cling to your altar steps: here are boys
    Who can barely stand alone, and here are priests
    By weight of age, as I am a priest of God,   20
    And young men chosen from those yet unmarried;
    As for the others, all that multitude,
    They wait with olive chaplets in the squares,
    At the two shrines of Pallas,° and where Apollo °
    Speaks in the glowing embers.
                                    Your own eyes   25
    Must tell you: Thebes is in her extremity
    And cannot lift her head from the surge of death.
    A rust consumes the buds and fruits of the earth;
    The herds are sick; children die unborn,
    And labor is vain. The god of plague and pyre   30
    Raids like detestable lightning through the city,
    And all the house of Kadmos is laid waste,
    All emptied, and all darkened: Death alone
    Battens upon the misery of Thebes.

    You are not one of the immortal gods, we know;   35
    Yet we have come to you to make our prayer
    As to the man of all men best in adversity

Prologue. [2] *Kadmos* mythical founder of Thebes   [24] *Pallas* Athena, goddess
of wisdom, protectress of Athens   [24] *Apollo* god of light and healing

And wisest in the ways of God. You saved us
From the Sphinx,° that flinty singer, and the tribute
We paid to her so long; yet you were never   40
Better informed than we, nor could we teach you:
It was some god breathed in you to set us free.

Therefore, O mighty King, we turn to you:
Find us our safety, find us a remedy,
Whether by counsel of the gods or the men.   45
A king of wisdom tested in the past
Can act in a time of troubles, and act well.
Noblest of men, restore
Life to your city! Think how all men call you
Liberator for your triumph long ago;   50
Ah, when your years of kingship are remembered,
Let them not say *We rose, but later fell* —
Keep the State from going down in the storm!
Once, years ago, with happy augury,
You brought us fortune; be the same again!   55
No man questions your power to rule the land:
But rule over men, not over a dead city!
Ships are only hulls, citadels are nothing,
When no life moves in the empty passageways.
Oedipus. Poor children! You may be sure I know   60
All that you longed for in your coming here.
I know that you are deathly sick; and yet,
Sick as you are, not one is as sick as I.
Each of you suffers in himself alone
His anguish, not another's; but my spirit   65
Groans for the city, for myself, for you.

I was not sleeping, you are not waking me.
No, I have been in tears for a long while
And in my restless thought walked many ways.
In all my search, I found one helpful course,   70
And that I have taken: I have sent Creon,
Son of Menoikeus, brother of the Queen,
To Delphi, Apollo's place of revelation,
To learn there, if he can,
What act or pledge of mine may save the city.   75

---

³⁹ **Sphinx** a monster (body of a lion, wings of a bird, face of a woman) who
asked the riddle, "What goes on four legs in the morning, two at noon, and
three in the evening?" and who killed those who could not answer. When
Oedipus responded correctly that man crawls on all fours in infancy, walks
upright in maturity, and uses a staff in old age, the Sphinx destroyed herself

I have counted the days, and now, this very day,
I am troubled, for he has overstayed his time.
What is he doing? He has been gone too long.
Yet whenever he comes back, I should do ill
To scant whatever hint the god may give.   80
Priest. It is a timely promise. At this instant
They tell me Creon is here.
Oedipus.   O Lord Apollo!
May his news be fair as his face is radiant!
Priest. It could not be otherwise: he is crowned with bay,
The chaplet is thick with berries.
Oedipus.   We shall soon know;   85
He is near enough to hear us now.

Enter Creon.

                    O Prince:
Brother: son of Menoikeus:
What answer do you bring us from the god?
Creon. It is favorable. I can tell you, great afflictions
Will turn out well, if they are taken well.   90
Oedipus. What was the oracle? These vague words
Leave me still hanging between hope and fear.
Creon. Is it your pleasure to hear me with all these
Gathered around us? I am prepared to speak,
But should we not go in?
Oedipus.   Let them all hear it.   95
It is for them I suffer, more than for myself.
Creon. Then I will tell you what I heard at Delphi.

In plain words
The god commands us to expel from the land of Thebes
An old defilement that it seems we shelter.   100
It is a deathly thing, beyond expiation.
We must not let it feed upon us longer.
Oedipus. What defilement? How shall we rid ourselves of it?
Creon. By exile or death, blood for blood. It was
Murder that brought the plague-wind on the city.   105
Oedipus. Murder of whom? Surely the god has named him?
Creon. My lord: long ago Laïos was our king,
Before you came to govern us.
Oedipus.   I know;
I learned of him from others; I never saw him.
Creon. He was murdered; and Apollo commands us now   110
To take revenge upon whoever killed him.

Oedipus. Upon whom? Where are they? Where shall we find a clue
   To solve that crime, after so many years?
Creon. Here in this land, he said.
                              If we make enquiry,
   We may touch things that otherwise escape us.   115
Oedipus. Tell me: Was Laïos murdered in his house,
   Or in the fields, or in some foreign country?
Creon. He said he planned to make a pilgrimage.
   He did not come home again.
Oedipus.   And was there no one,
   No witness, no companion, to tell what happened?   120
Creon. They were all killed but one, and he got away
   So frightened that he could remember one thing only.
Oedipus. What was that one thing? One may be the key
   To everything, if we resolve to use it.
Creon. He said that a band of highwaymen attacked them,   125
   Outnumbered them, and overwhelmed the King.
Oedipus. Strange, that a highwayman should be so daring —
   Unless some faction here bribed him to do it.
Creon. We thought of that. But after Laïos' death
   New troubles arose and we had no avenger.   130
Oedipus. What troubles could prevent your hunting
   down the killers?
Creon. The riddling Sphinx's song
   Made us deaf to all mysteries but her own.
Oedipus. Then once more I must bring what is dark to light.
   It is most fitting that Apollo shows,   135
   As you do, this compunction for the dead.
   You shall see how I stand by you, as I should,
   To avenge the city and the city's god,
   And not as though it were for some distant friend,
   But for my own sake, to be rid of evil.   140
   Whoever killed King Laïos might — who knows? —
   Decide at any moment to kill me as well.
   By avenging the murdered king I protect myself.
   Come, then, my children: leave the altar steps,
   Lift up your olive boughs!
                              One of you go   145
   And summon the people of Kadmos to gather here.
   I will do all that I can; you may tell them that.   *(Exit a Page.)*
   So, with the help of God,
   We shall be saved — or else indeed we are lost.
Priest. Let us rise, children. It was for this we came,   150
   And now the King has promised it himself.

Phoibos° has sent us an oracle; may he descend
Himself to save us and drive out the plague.

Exeunt Oedipus and Creon into the palace by the central door.
The Priest and the Suppliants disperse right and left. After a short
pause the Chorus enters the orchestra.

PÁRODOS

Chorus. What is God singing in his profound   *Strophe 1*
   Delphi of gold and shadow?
What oracle for Thebes, the sunwhipped city?
Fear unjoints me, the roots of my heart tremble.
Now I remember, O Healer, your power, and wonder;   5
Will you send doom like a sudden cloud, or weave it
Like nightfall of the past?
Speak, speak ot us, issue of holy sound:
Dearest to our expectancy: be tender!

Let me pray to Athenê, the immortal daughter
      of Zeus,   *Antistrophe 1*   10
And to Artemis her sister
Who keeps her famous throne in the market ring,
And to Apollo, bowman at the far butts of heaven —

O gods, descend! Like three streams leap against
The fires of our grief, the fires of darkness;   15
Be swift to bring us rest!

As in the old time from the brilliant house
Of air you stepped to save us, come again!

Now our afflictions have no end,   *Strophe 2*
Now all our stricken host lies down   20
And no man fights off death with his mind;

The noble plowland bears no grain,
And groaning mothers cannot bear —

See, how our lives like birds take wing,
Like sparks that fly when a fire soars,   25
To the shore of the god of evening.

The plague burns on, it is pitiless,   *Antistrophe 2*
Though pallid children laden with death
Lie unwept in the stony ways,

¹⁵² ***Phoibos*** Phoebus Apollo, the sun god

And old gray women by every path   30
Flock to the strand about the altars

There to strike their breasts and cry
Worship of Phoibos in wailing prayers:
Be kind, God's golden child!

There are no swords in this attack by fire,   *Strophe 3*   35
No shields, but we are ringed with cries.
Send the besieger plunging from our homes
Into the vast sea-room of the Atlantic
Or into the waves that foam eastward of Thrace —
For the day ravages what the night spares —   40

Destroy our enemy, lord of the thunder!
Let him be riven by lightning from heaven!

Phoibos Apollo, stretch the sun's bowstring,   *Antistrophe 3*
That golden cord, until it sing for us,
Flashing arrows in heaven!
                              Artemis, Huntress,   45
Race with flaring lights upon our mountains!
O scarlet god, O golden-banded brow,
O Theban Bacchos° in a storm of Maenads,°

Enter Oedipus, center.

Whirl upon Death, that all the Undying hate!
Come with blinding cressets, come in joy!   50

SCENE I

Oedipus. Is this your prayer? It may be answered. Come,
    Listen to me, act as the crisis demands,
    And you shall have relief from all these evils.

    Until now I was a stranger to this tale,
    As I had been a stranger to the crime.   5
    Could I track down the murderer without a clue?
    But now, friends,
    As one who became a citizen after the murder,

Párodos. ⁴⁸ ***Bacchos*** Dionysos, god of wine, thus scarlet-faced   ⁴⁸ ***Maenads***
Dionysos's female attendants

I make this proclamation to all Thebans:
If any man knows by whose hand Laïos, son of Labdakos,   10
Met his death, I direct that man to tell me everything,
No matter what he fears for having so long withheld it.
Let it stand as promised that no further trouble
Will come to him, but he may leave the land in safety.

Moreover: If anyone knows the murderer to be foreign,   15
Let him not keep silent: he shall have his reward from me.
However, if he does conceal it; if any man
Fearing for his friend or for himself disobeys this edict,
Hear what I propose to do:

I solemnly forbid the people of this country,   20
Where power and throne are mine, ever to receive that man
Or speak to him, no matter who he is, or let him
Join in sacrifice, lustration, or in prayer.
I decree that he be driven from every house,

Being, as he is, corruption itself to us: the Delphic   25
Voice of Zeus has pronounced this revelation.
Thus I associate myself with the oracle
And take the side of the murdered king.

As for the criminal, I pray to God —
Whether it be a lurking thief, or one of a number —   30
I pray that that man's life be consumed in evil and wretchedness.
And as for me, this curse applies no less
If it should turn out that the culprit is my guest here,
Sharing my hearth.
                    You have heard the penalty.
I lay it on you now to attend to this   35
For my sake, for Apollo's, for the sick
Sterile city that heaven has abandoned.
Suppose the oracle had given you no command:
Should this defilement go uncleansed for ever?
You should have found the murderer: your king,   40
A noble king, had been destroyed!
                    Now I,
Having the power that he held before me,
Having his bed, begetting children there
Upon his wife, as he would have, had he lived —
Their son would have been my children's brother,   45
If Laïos had had luck in fatherhood!
(But surely ill luck rushed upon his reign) —
I say I take the son's part, just as though

I were his son, to press the fight for him
And see it won! I'll find the hand that brought   50
Death to Labdakos' and Polydoros' child,
Heir of Kadmos' and Agenor's line.
And as for those who fail me,
May the gods deny them the fruit of the earth,
Fruit of the womb, and may they rot utterly!   55
Let them be wretched as we are wretched, and worse!

For you, for loyal Thebans, and for all
Who find my actions right, I pray the favor
Of justice, and of all the immortal gods.
Choragos. Since I am under oath, my lord, I swear   60
I did not do the murder, I cannot name
The murderer. Might not the oracle
That has ordained the search tell where to find him?
Oedipus. An honest question. But no man in the world
Can make the gods do more than the gods will.   65
Choragos. There is one last expedient —
Oedipus.   Tell me what it is.
Though it seem slight, you must not hold it back.
Choragos. A lord clairvoyant to the lord Apollo,
As we all know, is the skilled Teiresias.
One might learn much about this from him, Oedipus.   70
Oedipus. I am not wasting time:
Creon spoke of this, and I have sent for him —
Twice, in fact; it is strange that he is not here.
Choragos. The other matter — that old report — seems useless.
Oedipus. Tell me. I am interested in all reports.   75
Choragos. The King was said to have been killed by highwaymen.
Oedipus. I know. But we have no witnesses to that.
Choragos. If the killer can feel a particle of dread,
Your curse will bring him out of hiding!
Oedipus.   No.
The man who dared that act will fear no curse.   80

Enter the blind seer Teiresias, led by a Page.

Choragos. But there is one man who may detect the criminal.
This is Teiresias, this is the holy prophet
In whom, alone of all men, truth was born.
Oedipus. Teiresias: seer: student of mysteries,
Of all that's taught and all that no man tells,   85
Secrets of Heaven and secrets of the earth:
Blind though you are, you know the city lies

Sick with plague; and from this plague, my lord,
We find that you alone can guard or save us.

Possibly you did not hear the messengers?   90
Apollo, when we sent to him,
Sent us back word that this great pestilence
Would lift, but only if we established clearly
The identity of those who murdered Laïos.
They must be killed or exiled.

                          Can you use   95
Birdflight or any art of divination
To purify yourself, and Thebes, and me
From this contagion? We are in your hands.
There is no fairer duty
Than that of helping others in distress.   100
Teiresias. How dreadful knowledge of the truth can be
  When there's no help in truth! I knew this well,
  But did not act on it: else I should not have come.
Oedipus. What is troubling you? Why are your eyes so cold?
Teiresias. Let me go home. Bear your own fate, and I'll   105
  Bear mine. It is better so: trust what I say.
Oedipus. What you say is ungracious and unhelpful
  To your native country. Do not refuse to speak.
Teiresias. When it comes to speech, your own is neither temperate
  Nor opportune. I wish to be more prudent   110
Oedipus. In God's name, we all beg you —
Teiresias.   You are all ignorant.
  No; I will never tell you what I know.
  Now it is my misery; then, it would be yours.
Oedipus. What! You do know something, and will not tell us?
  You would betray us all and wreck the State?   115
Teiresias. I do not intend to torture myself, or you.
  Why persist in asking? You will not persuade me.
Oedipus. What a wicked old man you are! You'd try a stone's
  Patience! Out with it! Have you no feeling at all?
Teiresias. You call me unfeeling. If you could only see   120
  The nature of your own feelings . . .
Oedipus.   Why,
  Who would not feel as I do? Who could endure
  Your arrogance toward the city?
Teiresias.   What does it matter!
  Whether I speak or not, it is bound to come.
Oedipus. Then, if "it" is bound to come, you are bound to tell me. 125
Teiresias. No, I will not go on. Rage as you please.

Oedipus. Rage? Why not!

                And I'll tell you what I think:

  You planned it, you had it done, you all but

  Killed him with your own hands: if you had eyes,

  I'd say the crime was yours, and yours alone.   130

Teiresias. So? I charge you, then,

  Abide by the proclamation you have made:

  From this day forth

  Never speak again to these men or to me;

  You yourself are the pollution of this country.   135

Oedipus. You dare say that! Can you possibly think you have

  Some way of going free, after such insolence?

Teiresias. I have gone free. It is the truth sustains me.

Oedipus. Who taught you shamelessness? It was not your craft.

Teiresias. You did. You made me speak. I did not want to.   140

Oedipus. Speak what? Let me hear it again more clearly.

Teiresias. Was it not clear before? Are you tempting me?

Oedipus. I did not understand it. Say it again.

Teiresias. I say that you are the murderer whom you seek.

Oedipus. Now twice you have spat out infamy. You'll pay for it!   145

Teiresias. Would you care for more? Do you wish to be really

  angry?

Oedipus. Say what you will. Whatever you say is worthless.

Teiresias. I say you live in hideous shame with those

  Most dear to you. You cannot see the evil.

Oedipus. It seems you can go on mouthing like this for ever.   150

Teiresias. I can, if there is power in truth.

Oedipus.   There is:

  But not for you, not for you,

  You sightless, witless, senseless, mad old man!

Teiresias. You are the madman. There is no one here

  Who will not curse you soon, as you curse me.   155

Oedipus. You child of endless night! You cannot hurt me

  Or any other man who sees the sun.

Teiresias. True: it is not from me your fate will come.

  That lies within Appollo's competence,

  As it is his concern.

Oedipus.   Tell me: 160

  Are you speaking for Creon, or for yourself?

Teiresias. Creon is no threat. You weave your own doom.

Oedipus. Wealth, power, craft of statesmanship!

  Kingly position, everywhere admired!

  What savage envy is stored up against these,   165

  If Creon, whom I trusted, Creon my friend,

For this great office which the city once
Put in my hands unsought — if for this power
Creon desires in secret to destroy me!

He has bought this decrepit fortune-teller, this   170
Collector of dirty pennies, this prophet fraud —
Why, he is no more clairvoyant than I am!
                                        Tell us:
Has your mystic mummery ever approached the truth?
When that hellcat the Sphinx was performing here,
What help were you to these people?   175
Her magic was not for the first man who came along:
It demanded a real exorcist. Your birds —
What good were they? or the gods, for the matter of that?
But I came by,
Oedipus, the simple man, who knows nothing —   180
I thought it out for myself, no birds helped me!
And this is the man you think you can destroy,
That you may be close to Creon when he's king!
Well, you and your friend Creon, it seems to me,
Will suffer most. If you were not an old man,   185
You would have paid already for your plot.
Choragos. We cannot see that his words or yours
    Have been spoken except in anger, Oedipus,
    And of anger we have no need. How can God's will
    Be accomplished best? That is what most concerns us.   190
Teiresias. You are a king. But where argument's concerned
    I am your man, as much a king as you.
    I am not your servant, but Apollo's.
    I have no need of Creon to speak for me.

    Listen to me. You mock my blindness, do you?   195
    But I say that you, with both your eyes, are blind:
    You cannot see the wretchedness of your life,
    Nor in whose house you live, no, nor with whom.
    Who are your father and mother? Can you tell me?
    You do not even know the blind wrongs   200
    That you have done them, on earth and in the world below.
    But the double lash of your parents' curse will whip you
    Out of this land some day, with only night
    Upon your precious eyes.
    Your cries then — where will they not be heard?   205
    What fastness of Kithairon° will not echo them?

Scene I. ²⁰⁶*fastness of Kithairon* stronghold in a mountain near Thebes

And that bridal-descant of yours — you'll know it then,
The song they sang when you came here to Thebes
And found your misguided berthing.
All this, and more, that you cannot guess at now,   210
Will bring you to yourself among your children.

Be angry, then. Curse Creon. Curse my words.
I tell you, no man that walks upon the earth
Shall be rooted out more horribly than you.
Oedipus. Am I to bear this from him? — Damnation   215
Take you! Out of this place! Out of my sight!
Teiresias. I would not have come at all if you had not asked me.
Oedipus. Could I have told that you'd talk nonsense, that
You'd come here to make a fool of yourself, and of me?
Teiresias. A fool? Your parents thought me sane enough.   220
Oedipus. My parents again! — Wait: who were my parents?
Teiresias. This day will give you a father, and break your heart.
Oedipus. Your infantile riddles! Your damned abracadabra!
Teiresias. You were a great man once at solving riddles.
Oedipus. Mock me with that if you like; you will find it true.   225
Teiresias. It was true enough. It brought about your ruin.
Oedipus. But if it saved this town?
Teiresias (to the Page). Boy, give me your hand.
Oedipus. Yes, boy; lead him away.
                              — While you are here
We can do nothing. Go; leave us in peace.
Teiresias. I will go when I have said what I have to say.   230
How can you hurt me? And I tell you again:
The man you have been looking for all this time,
The damned man, the murderer of Laïos,
That man is in Thebes. To your mind he is foreignborn,
But it will soon be shown that he is a Theban,   235
A revelation that will fail to please.
                              A blind man,
Who has his eyes now; a penniless man, who is rich now;
And he will go tapping the strange earth with his staff;
To the children with whom he lives now he will be
Brother and father — the very same; to her   240
Who bore him, son and husband — the very same
Who came to his father's bed, wet with his father's blood.

Enough. Go think that over.
If later you find error in what I have said,
You may say that I have no skill in prophecy.   245

Exit Teiresias, led by his Page. Oedipus goes into the palace.

ODE I

Chorus. The Delphic stone of prophecies   *Strophe 1*
  Remembers ancient regicide
  And a still bloody hand.
  That killer's hour of flight has come.
  He must be stronger than riderless   5
  Coursers of untiring wind,
  For the son of Zeus° armed with his father's thunder
  Leaps in lightning after him;
  And the Furies° follow him, the sad Furies.

  Holy Parnassos' peak of snow   *Antistrophe 1*   10
  Flashes and blinds that secret man,
  That all shall hunt him down:
  Though he may roam the forest shade
  Like a bull gone wild from pasture
  To rage through glooms of stone.   15
  Doom comes down on him; flight will not avail him;
  For the world's heart calls him desolate,
  And the immortal Furies follow, for ever follow.

  But now a wilder thing is heard   *Strophe 2*
  From the old man skilled at hearing Fate in the
      wingbeat of a bird.   20
  Bewildered as a blown bird, my soul hovers and cannot find
  Foothold in this debate, or any reason or rest of mind.
  But no man ever brought — none can bring
  Proof of strife between Thebes' royal house,
  Labdakos' line,° and the son of Polybos;°   25
  And never until now has any man brought word
  Of Laïos' dark death staining Oedipus the King.

  Divine Zeus and Apollo hold   *Antistrophe 2*
  Perfect intelligence alone of all tales ever told;
  And well though this diviner works, he works in his own night;   30
  No man can judge that rough unknown or trust in second sight,
  For wisdom changes hands among the wise.
  Shall I believe my great lord criminal
  At a raging word that a blind old man let fall?
  I saw him, when the carrion woman faced him of old,   35
  Prove his heroic mind! These evil words are lies.

Ode I.   ⁷ ***Son of Zeus*** Apollo   ⁹ ***Furies*** avenging deities   ²⁵ ***Labdakos' line***
family of Laïos   ²⁵ ***son of Polybos*** Oedipus (so the Chorus believes)

SCENE II

Creon. Men of Thebes:
I am told that heavy accusations
Have been brought against me by King Oedipus.
I am not the kind of man to bear this tamely.

If in these present difficulties   5
He holds me accountable for any harm to him
Through anything I have said or done — why, then,
I do not value life in this dishonor.
It is not as though this rumor touched upon
Some private indiscretion. The matter is grave.   10
The fact is that I am being called disloyal
To the State, to my fellow citizens, to my friends.
Choragos. He may have spoken in anger, not from his mind.
Creon. But did you not hear him say I was the one
Who seduced the old prophet into lying?   15
Choragos. The thing was said; I do not know how seriously.
Creon. But you were watching him! Were his eyes steady?
Did he look like a man in his right mind?
Choragos.   I do not know.
I cannot judge the behavior of great men.
But here is the King himself.

Enter Oedipus.

Oedipus.   So you dared come back.   20
Why? How brazen of you to come to my house,
You murderer!
                          Do you think I do not know
That you plotted to kill me, plotted to steal my throne?
Tell me, in God's name: am I coward, a fool,
That you should dream you could accomplish this?   25
A fool who could not see your slippery game?
A coward, not to fight back when I saw it?
You are the fool, Creon, are you not? hoping
Without support or friends to get a throne?
Thrones may be won or bought: you could do neither.   30
Creon. Now listen to me. You have talked; let me talk, too.
You cannot judge unless you know the facts.
Oedipus. You speak well: there is one fact; but I find it hard
To learn from the deadliest enemy I have.
Creon. That above all I must dispute with you.   35

Oedipus. That above all I will not hear you deny.
Creon. If you think there is anything good in being stubborn
　　Against all reason, then I say you are wrong.
Oedipus. If you think a man can sin against his own kind
　　And not be punished for it, I say you are mad.   40
Creon. I agree. But tell me: what have I done to you?
Oedipus. You advised me to send for that wizard, did you not?
Creon. I did. I should do it again.
Oedipus.　　　　　　　　　　Very well. Now tell me:
　　How long has it been since Laïos —
Creon.　　　　　　　　　　What of Laïos?
Oedipus. Since he vanished in that onset by the road?   45
Creon. It was long ago, a long time.
Oedipus.　　　　　　　　　　And this prophet,
　　Was he practicing here then?
Creon.　　　　　　　　　　He was; and with honor, as now.
Oedipus. Did he speak of me at that time?
Creon.　　　　　　　　　　He never did;
　　At least, not when I was present.
Oedipus.　　　　　　　　　　But . . . the enquiry?
　　I suppose you held one?
Creon.　　　　　　　　　　We did, but we learned nothing.   50
Oedipus. Why did the prophet not speak against me then?
Creon. I do not know; and I am the kind of man
　　Who holds his tongue when he has no facts to go on.
Oedipus. There's one fact that you know, and you could tell it.
Creon. What fact is that? If I know it, you shall have it.   55
Oedipus. If he were not involved with you, he could not say
　　That it was I who murdered Laïos.
Creon. If he says that, you are the one that knows it! —
　　But now it is my turn to question you.
Oedipus. Put your questions. I am no murderer.   60
Creon. First, then: You married my sister?
Oedipus.　　　　　　　　　　I married your sister.
Creon. And you rule the kingdom equally with her?
Oedipus. Everything that she wants she has from me.
Creon. And I am the third, equal to both of you?
Oedipus. That is why I call you a bad friend.   65
Creon. No. Reason it out, as I have done.
　　Think of this first. Would any sane man prefer
　　Power, with all a king's anxieties,
　　To that same power and the grace of sleep?
　　Certainly not I.   70

I have never longed for the king's power — only his rights.
Would any wise man differ from me in this?
As matters stand, I have my way in everything
With your consent, and no responsibilities.
If I were king, I should be a slave to policy.   75
How could I desire a scepter more
Than what is now mine — untroubled influence?
No, I have not gone mad; I need no honors,
Except those with the perquisites I have now.
I am welcome everywhere; every man salutes me,   80
And those who want your favor seek my ear,
Since I know how to manage what they ask.
Should I exchange this ease for that anxiety?
Besides, no sober mind is treasonable.
I hate anarchy   85
And never would deal with any man who likes it.

Test what I have said. Go to the priestess
At Delphi, ask if I quoted her correctly.
And as for this other thing: if I am found
Guilty of treason with Teiresias,   90
Then sentence me to death! You have my word
It is a sentence I should cast my vote for —
But not without evidence!
                            You do wrong
When you take good men for bad, bad men for good.
A true friend thrown aside — why, life itself   95
Is not more precious!
                            In time you will know this well:
For time, and time alone, will show the just man,
Though scoundrels are discovered in a day.
Choragos. This is well said, and a prudent man would ponder it.
    Judgments too quickly formed are dangerous.   100
Oedipus. But is he not quick in his duplicity?
    And shall I not be quick to parry him?
    Would you have me stand still, hold my peace, and let
    This man win everything, through my inaction?
Creon. And you want — what is it, then? To banish me?   105
Oedipus. No, not exile. It is your death I want,
    So that all the world may see what treason means.
Creon. You will persist, then? You will not believe me?
Oedipus. How can I believe you?
Creon.   Then you are a fool.

Oedipus. To save myself?
Creon.   In justice, think of me.   110
Oedipus. You are evil incarnate.
Creon.   But suppose that you are wrong?
Oedipus. Still I must rule.
Creon.   But not if you rule badly.
Oedipus. O city, city!
Creon.   It is my city, too!
Choragos. Now, my lords, be still. I see the Queen,
    Iocastê, coming from her palace chambers;   115
    And it is time she came, for the sake of you both.
    This dreadful quarrel can be resolved through her.

    Enter Iocastê.

Iocastê. Poor foolish men, what wicked din is this?
    With Thebes sick to death, is it not shameful
    That you should rake some private quarrel up?   120
    (To Oedipus.) Come into the house.
                       — And you, Creon, go now:
    Let us have no more of this tumult over nothing.
Creon. Nothing? No, sister: what your husband plans for me
    Is one of two great evils: exile or death.
Oedipus. He is right.
              Why, woman, I have caught him squarely   125
    Plotting against my life.
Creon.   No! Let me die
    Accurst if ever I have wished you harm!
Iocastê. Ah, believe it, Oedipus!
    In the name of the gods, respect this oath of his
    For my sake, for the sake of these people here!   130

Choragos. Open your mind to her, my lord. Be ruled by her,
    I beg you!   *Strophe 1*
Oedipus. What would you have me do?
Choragos. Respect Creon's word. He has never spoken like a fool,
    And now he has sworn an oath.
Oedipus. You know what you ask?
Choragos.   I do.
Oedipus.   Speak on, then.
Choragos. A friend so sworn should not be baited so,   135
    In blind malice, and without final proof.
Oedipus. You are aware, I hope, that what you say
    Means death for me, or exile at the least.

Choragos. No, I swear by Helios,° first in Heaven!   *Strophe 2*
  May I die friendless and accurst,   140
  The worst of deaths, if ever I meant that!
    It is the withering fields
      That hurt my sick heart:
    Must we bear all these ills,
      And now your bad blood as well?   145
Oedipus. Then let him go. And let me die, if I must,
  Or be driven by him in shame from the land of Thebes.
  It is your unhappiness, and not his talk,
  That touches me.
           As for him —
  Wherever he is, I will hate him as long as I live.   150
Creon. Ugly in yielding, as you were ugly in rage!
  Natures like yours chiefly torment themselves.
Oedipus. Can you not go? Can you not leave me?
Creon.   I can.
  You do not know me; but the city knows me,
  And in its eyes I am just, if not in yours.   *Exit Creon.*   155

Choragos. Lady Iocastê, did you not ask the King to go
    to his chambers?   *Antistrophe 1*
Iocastê. First tell me what has happened.
Choragos. There was suspicion without evidence; yet it rankled
  As even false charges will.
Iocastê.   On both sides?
Choragos.   On both.
Iocastê.   But what was said?
Choragos. Oh let it rest, let it be done with!   160
  Have we not suffered enough?
Oedipus. You see to what your decency has brought you:
  You have made difficulties where my heart saw none.
Choragos. Oedipus, it is not once only I have
      told you —   *Antistrophe 2*
  You must know I should count myself unwise   165
  To the point of madness, should I now forsake you —
    You, under whose hand,
      In the storm of another time,
    Our dear land sailed out free.
      But now stand fast at the helm!   170
Iocastê. In God's name, Oedipus, inform your wife as well:
  Why are you so set in this hard anger?
Oedipus. I will tell you, for none of these men deserves

---

[139] *Helios* sun god

My confidence as you do. It is Creon's work,
His treachery, his plotting against me. 175
Iocastê. Go on, if you can make this clear to me.
Oedipus. He charges me with the murder of Laïos.
Iocastê. Has he some knowledge? Or does he speak from
    hearsay?
Oedipus. He would not commit himself to such a charge,
But he has brought in that damnable soothsayer 180
To tell his story.
Iocastê.   Set your mind at rest.
If it is a question of soothsayers, I tell you
That you will find no man whose craft gives knowledge
Of the unknowable.
              Here is my proof:

An oracle was reported to Laïos once 185
(I will not say from Phoibos himself, but from
His appointed ministers, at any rate)
That his doom would be death at the hands of his own son —
His son, born of his flesh and of mine!

Now, you remember the story: Laïos was killed 190
By marauding strangers where three highways meet;
But his child had not been three days in this world
Before the King had pierced the baby's ankles
And left him to die on a lonely mountainside.

Thus, Apollo never caused that child 195
To kill his father, and it was not Laïos' fate
To die at the hands of his son, as he had feared.
This is what prophets and prophecies are worth!
Have no dread of them.
           It is God himself
Who can show us what he wills, in his own way. 200
Oedipus. How strange a shadowy memory crossed my mind,
Just now while you were speaking; it chilled my heart.
Iocastê. What do you mean? What memory do you speak of?
Oedipus. If I understand you, Laïos was killed
At a place where three roads meet.
Iocastê.   So it was said; 205
We have no later story.
Oedipus.   Where did it happen?
Iocastê. Phokis, it is called: at a place where the Theban Way
Divides into the roads towards Delphi and Daulia.
Oedipus. When?

Iocastê.   We had the news not long before you came
And proved the right to your succession here.   210
Oedipus.   Ah, what net has God been weaving for me?
Iocastê. Oedipus! Why does this trouble you?
Oedipus.   Do not ask me yet.
First, tell me how Laïos looked, and tell me
How old he was.
Iocastê.   He was tall, his hair just touched
With white; his form was not unlike your own.   215
Oedipus. I think that I myself may be accurst
By my own ignorant edict.
Iocastê.   You speak strangely.
It makes me tremble to look at you, my King.
Oedipus. I am not sure that the blind man cannot see.
But I should know better if you were to tell me —   220
Iocastê. Anything — though I dread to hear you ask it.
Oedipus. Was the King lightly escorted, or did he ride
With a large company, as a ruler should?
Iocastê. There were five men with him in all: one was a herald;
And a single chariot, which he was driving.   225
Oedipus. Alas, that makes it plain enough!
                              But who —
Who told you how it happened?
Iocastê.   A household servant,
The only one to escape.
Oedipus.   And is he still
A servant of ours?
Iocastê.   No; for when he came back at last
And found you enthroned in the place of the dead king,   230
He came to me, touched my hand with his, and begged
That I would send him away to the frontier district
Where only the shepherds go —
As far away from the city as I could send him.
I granted his prayer; for although the man was a slave,   235
He had earned more than this favor at my hands.
Oedipus. Can he be called back quickly?
Iocastê.   Easily.
But why?
Oedipus.   I have taken too much upon myself
Without enquiry; therefore I wish to consult him.
Iocastê. Then he shall come.
                        But am I not one also   240
To whom you might confide these fears of yours!

Oedipus. That is your right; it will not be denied you,
　Now least of all; for I have reached a pitch
　Of wild foreboding. Is there anyone
　To whom I should sooner speak? 245
　Polybos of Corinth is my father.
　My mother is a Dorian: Meropê.
　I grew up chief among the men of Corinth
　Until a strange thing happened —
　Not worth my passion, it may be, but strange. 250

　At a feast, a drunken man maundering in his cups
　Cries out that I am not my father's son!

　I contained myself that night, though I felt anger
　And a sinking heart. The next day I visited
　My father and mother, and questioned them. They
　　　stormed, 255
　Calling it all the slanderous rant of a fool;
　And this relieved me. Yet the suspicion
　Remained always aching in my mind;
　I knew there was talk; I could not rest;
　And finally, saying nothing to my parents, 260
　I went to the shrine at Delphi.
　The god dismissed my question without reply;
　He spoke of other things.
　　　　　　　Some were clear,
　Full of wretchedness, dreadful, unbearable:
　As, that I should lie with my own mother, breed 265
　Children from whom all men would turn their eyes;
　And that I should be my father's murderer.

　I heard all this, and fled. And from that day
　Corinth to me was only in the stars
　Descending in that quarter of the sky, 270
　As I wandered farther and farther on my way
　To a land where I should never see the evil
　Sung by the oracle. And I came to this country
　Where, so you say, King Laïos was killed.

　I will tell you all that happened there, my lady. 275

　There were three highways
　Coming together at a place I passed;
　And there a herald came towards me, and a chariot
　Drawn by horses, with a man such as you describe

Seated in it. The groom leading the horses   280
Forced me off the road at his lord's command;
But as this charioteer lurched over towards me
I struck him in my rage. The old man saw me
And brought his double goad down upon my head
As I came abreast.
                    He was paid back, and more!   285
Swinging my club in this right hand I knocked him
Out of his car, and he rolled on the ground.
                              I killed him.

I killed them all.
Now if that stranger and Laïos were — kin,
Where is a man more miserable than I?   290
More hated by the gods? Citizen and alien alike
Must never shelter me or speak to me —
I must be shunned by all.
                    And I myself
Pronounced this malediction upon myself!

Think of it: I have touched you with these hands,   295
These hands that killed your husband. What defilement!

Am I all evil, then? It must be so,
Since I must flee from Thebes, yet never again
See my own countrymen, my own country,
For fear of joining my mother in marriage   300
And killing Polybos, my father.
                    Ah,
If I was created so, born to this fate,
Who could deny the savagery of God?

O holy majesty of heavenly powers!
May I never see that day! Never!   305
Rather let me vanish from the race of men
Than know the abomination destined me!
Choragos. We too, my lord, have felt dismay at this.
       But there is hope: you have yet to hear the shepherd.
Oedipus. Indeed, I fear no other hope is left me.   310
Iocastê. What do you hope from him when he comes?
Oedipus.   This much:
       If his account of the murder tallies with yours,
       Then I am cleared.
Iocastê.   What was it that I said
       Of such importance?
Oedipus.   Why, "marauders," you said,

Killed the King, according to this man's story.   315
If he maintains that still, if there were several,
Clearly the guilt is not mine: I was alone.
But if he says one man, singlehanded, did it,
Then the evidence all points to me.
Iocastê. You may be sure that he said there were several;   320
And can he call back that story now? He cannot.
The whole city heard it as plainly as I.
But suppose he alters some detail of it:
He cannot ever show that Laïos' death
Fulfilled the oracle: for Apollo said   325
My child was doomed to kill him; and my child —
Poor baby! — it was my child that died first.

No. From now on, where oracles are concerned,
I would not waste a second thought on any.
Oedipus. You may be right.
                But come: let someone go   330
For the shepherd at once. This matter must be settled.
Iocastê. I will send for him.
I would not wish to cross you in anything,
And surely not in this. — Let us go in.

                     Exeunt into the palace.

ODE II

Chorus. Let me be reverent in the ways of right,   *Strophe 1*
Lowly the paths I journey on;
Let all my words and actions keep
The laws of the pure universe
From highest Heaven handed down.   5
For Heaven is their bright nurse,
Those generations of the realms of light;
Ah, never of mortal kind were they begot,
Nor are they slaves of memory, lost in sleep:
Their Father is greater than Time, and ages not.   10

The tyrant is a child of Pride   *Antistrophe 1*
Who drinks from his great sickening cup
Recklessness and vanity,
Until from his high crest headlong
He plummets to the dust of hope.   15
That strong man is not strong.

But let no fair ambition be denied;
May God protect the wrestler for the State
In government, in comely policy,
Who will fear God, and on His ordinance wait.   20

Haughtiness and the high hand of disdain   *Strophe 2*
Tempt and outrage God's holy law;
And any mortal who dares hold
No immortal Power in awe
Will be caught up in a net of pain: 25
The price for which his levity is sold.
Let each man take due earnings, then,
And keep his hands from holy things,
And from blasphemy stand apart —
Else the crackling blast of heaven   30
Blows on his head, and on his desperate heart;
Though fools will honor impious men,
In their cities no tragic poet sings.

Shall we lose faith in Delphi's obscurities,   *Antistrophe 2*
We who have heard the world's core   35
Discredited, and the sacred wood
Of Zeus at Elis praised no more?
The deeds and the strange prophecies
Must make a pattern yet to be understood.
Zeus, if indeed you are lord of all,   40
Throned in light over night and day,
Mirror this in your endless mind:
Our masters call the oracle
Words on the wind, and the Delphic vision blind!
Their hearts no longer know Apollo,   45
And reverence for the gods has died away.

SCENE III

Enter Iocastê.

Iocastê.   Princes of Thebes, it has occurred to me
    To visit the altars of the gods, bearing
    These branches as a suppliant, and this incense.
    Our King is not himself: his noble soul
    Is overwrought with fantasies of dread,   5
    Else he would consider
    The new prophecies in the light of the old.

He will listen to any voice that speaks disaster,
And my advice goes for nothing.

She approaches the altar, right.

                                    To you, then, Apollo,
Lycean lord, since you are nearest, I turn in prayer.   10
Receive these offerings, and grant us deliverance
From defilement. Our hearts are heavy with fear
When we see our leader distracted, as helpless sailors
Are terrified by the confusion of their helmsman.

Enter Messenger.

Messenger. Friends, no doubt you can direct me: 15
    Where shall I find the house of Oedipus,
    Or, better still, where is the King himself?
Choragos. It is this very place, stranger; he is inside.
    This is his wife and mother of his children.
Messenger. I wish her happiness in a happy house,   20
    Blest in all the fulfillment of her marriage.
Iocastê. I wish as much for you: your courtesy
    Deserves a like good fortune. But now, tell me:
    Why have you come? What have you to say to us?
Messenger. Good news, my lady, for your house and your
        husband.   25
Iocastê. What news? Who sent you here?
Messenger.   I am from Corinth.
    The news I bring ought to mean joy for you,
    Though it may be you will find some grief in it.
Iocastê. What is it? How can it touch us in both ways?
Messenger. The people of Corinth, they say,   30
    Intend to call Oedipus to be their king.
Iocastê. But old Polybos — is he not reigning still?
Messenger. No. Death holds him in his sepulchre.
Iocastê. What are you saying? Polybos is dead?
Messenger. If I am not telling the truth, may I die myself.   35
Iocastê (to a Maidservant). Go in, go quickly; tell this to your
        master.

    O riddlers of God's will, where are you now!
    This was the man whom Oedipus, long ago,
    Feared so, fled so, in dread of destroying him —
    But it was another fate by which he died.   40

Enter Oedipus, center.

Oedipus. Dearest Iocastê, why have you sent for me?

Iocastê. Listen to what this man says, and then tell me
  What has become of the solemn prophecies.

Oedipus. Who is this man? What is his news for me?

Iocastê. He has come from Corinth to announce your
      father's death!   45

Oedipus. Is it true, stranger? Tell me in your own words.

Messenger. I cannot say it more clearly: the King is dead.

Oedipus. Was it by treason? Or by an attack of illness?

Messenger. A little thing brings old men to their rest.

Oedipus. It was sickness, then?

Messenger.   Yes, and his many years.   50

Oedipus. Ah!
  Why should a man respect the Pythian hearth,° or
  Give heed to the birds that jangle above his head?
  They prophesied that I should kill Polybos,
  Kill my own father; but he is dead and buried,   55
  And I am here — I never touched him, never,
  Unless he died in grief for my departure,
  And thus, in a sense, through me. No. Polybos
  Has packed the oracles off with him underground.
  They are empty words.

Iocastê.   Had I not told you so?   60

Oedipus. You had; it was my faint heart that betrayed me.

Iocastê. From now on never think of those things again.

Oedipus. And yet — must I not fear my mother's bed?

Iocastê. Why should anyone in this world be afraid,
  Since Fate rules us and nothing can be foreseen?   65
  A man should live only for the present day.
  Have no more fear of sleeping with your mother:
  How many men, in dreams, have lain with their mothers!
  No reasonable man is troubled by such things.

Oedipus. That is true; only —   70
  If only my mother were not still alive!
  But she is alive. I cannot help my dread.

Iocastê. Yet this news of your father's death is wonderful.

Oedipus. Wonderful. But I fear the living woman.

Messenger. Tell me, who is this woman that you fear?   75

Oedipus. It is Meropê, man; the wife of King Polybos.

Messenger. Meropê? Why should you be afraid of her?

Oedipus. An oracle of the gods, a dreadful saying.

Scene III, [52] *Pythian hearth* Delphi (also called Pytho because a great
snake had lived there), where Apollo spoke through a priestess

Messenger. Can you tell me about it or are you sworn to silence?
Oedipus. I can tell you, and I will.   80
   Apollo said through his prophet that I was the man
   Who should marry his own mother, shed his father's blood
   With his own hands. And so, for all these years
   I have kept clear of Corinth, and no harm has come —
   Though it would have been sweet to see my parents again.   85
Messenger. And is this the fear that drove you out of Corinth?
Oedipus. Would you have me kill my father?
Messenger.   As for that
   You must be reassured by the news I gave you.
Oedipus. If you could reassure me, I would reward you.
Messenger. I had that in mind, I will confess: I thought   90
   I could count on you when you returned to Corinth.
Oedipus. No: I will never go near my parents again.
Messenger. Ah, son, you still do not know what you are doing —
Oedipus. What do you mean? In the name of God tell me!
Messenger. — If these are your reasons for not going home.   95
Oedipus. I tell you, I fear the oracle may come true.
Messenger. And guilt may come upon you through your parents?
Oedipus. That is the dread that is always in my heart.
Messenger. Can you not see that all your fears are groundless?
Oedipus. How can you say that? They are my parents, surely?   100
Messenger. Polybos was not your father.
Oedipus.   Not my father?
Messenger. No more your father than the man speaking to you.
Oedipus. But you are nothing to me!
Messenger.   Neither was he.
Oedipus. Then why did he call me son?
Messenger.   I will tell you:
   Long ago he had you from my hands, as a gift.   105
Oedipus. Then how could he love me so, if I was not his?
Messenger. He had no children, and his heart turned to you.
Oedipus. What of you? Did you buy me? Did you find
     me by chance?
Messenger. I came upon you in the crooked pass of Kithairon.
Oedipus. And what were you doing there?
Messenger.   Tending my flocks.   110
Oedipus. A wandering shepherd?
Messenger.   But your savior, son, that day.
Oedipus. From what did you save me?
Messenger.   Your ankles should tell you that.
Oedipus. Ah, stranger, why do you speak of that childhood pain?
Messenger. I cut the bonds that tied your ankles together.

Oedipus. I have had the mark as long as I can remember.   115
Messenger. That was why you were given the name you bear.°
Oedipus. God! Was it my father or my mother who did it?
   Tell me!
Messenger. I do not know. The man who gave you to me
   Can tell you better than I.   120
Oedipus. It was not you that found me, but another?
Messenger. It was another shepherd gave you to me.
Oedipus. Who was he? Can you tell me who he was?
Messenger. I think he was said to be one of Laïos' people.
Oedipus. You mean the Laïos who was king here years ago?   125
Messenger. Yes; King Laïos; and the man was one of
      his herdsmen.
Oedipus. Is he still alive? Can I see him?
Messenger.   These men here
   Know best about such things.
Oedipus.   Does anyone here
   Know this shepherd that he is talking about?
   Have you seen him in the fields, or in the town?   130
   If you have, tell me. It is time things were made plain.
Choragos. I think the man he means is that same shepherd
   You have already asked to see. Iocastê perhaps
   Could tell you something.
Oedipus.   Do you know anything
   About him, Lady? Is he the man we have summoned?   135
   Is that the man this shepherd means?
Iocastê.   Why think of him?
   Forget this herdsman. Forget it all.
   This talk is a waste of time.
Oedipus.   How can you say that,
   When the clues to my true birth are in my hands?
Iocastê. For God's love, let us have no more questioning!   140
   Is your life nothing to you?
   My own is pain enough for me to bear.
Oedipus. You need not worry. Suppose my mother a slave,
   And born of slaves: no baseness can touch you.
Iocastê. Listen to me, I beg you: do not do this thing!   145
Oedipus. I will not listen; the truth must be made known.
Iocastê. Everything that I say is for your own good!
Oedipus.   My own good
   Snaps my patience, then: I want none of it.
Iocastê. You are fatally wrong! May you never learn who you are!

116 *name you bear* "Oedipus" means "swollen-foot"

Oedipus. Go, one of you, and bring the shepherd here.   150
    Let us leave this woman to brag of her royal name.
Iocastê. Ah, miserable!
    That is the only word I have for you now.
    That is the only word I can ever have.

                                    Exit into the palace.

Choragos. Why has she left us, Oedipus? Why has she gone   155
    In such a passion of sorrow? I fear this silence:
    Something dreadful may come of it.
Oedipus.   Let it come!
    However base my birth, I must know about it.
    The Queen, like a woman, is perhaps ashamed
    To think of my low origin. But I   160
    Am a child of luck; I cannot be dishonored.
    Luck is my mother; the passing months, my brothers,
    Have seen me rich and poor.
                        If this is so,
    How could I wish that I were someone else?
    How could I not be glad to know my birth?   165

ODE III

Chorus. If ever the coming time were known   *Strophe*
    To my heart's pondering,
    Kithairon, now by Heaven I see the torches
    At the festival of the next full moon,
    And see the dance, and hear the choir sing   5
    A grace to your gentle shade:
    Mountain where Oedipus was found,
    O mountain guard of a noble race!
    May the god who heals us lend his aid,
    And let that glory come to pass   10
    For our king's cradling-ground.

Of the nymphs that flower beyond the years,   *Antistrophe*
    Who bore you, royal child,
    To Pan of the hills or the timberline Apollo,
    Cold in delight where the upland clears,   15
    Or Hermês for whom Kyllenê's° heights are piled?
    Or flushed as evening cloud,

Ode III.   [16] *Hermês . . . Kyllenê's* Hermês, messenger of the gods, was said
to have been born on Mt. Kyllenê

Great Dionysos, roamer of mountains,
He — was it he who found you there,
And caught you up in his own proud   20
Arms from the sweet god-ravisher
Who laughed by the Muses' fountains?

SCENE IV

Oedipus. Sirs: though I do not know the man,
  I think I see him coming, this shepherd we want:
  He is old, like our friend here, and the men
  Bringing him seem to be servants of my house.
  But you can tell, if you have ever seen him.   5

  Enter Shepherd escorted by servants.

Choragos. I know him, he was Laïos' man. You can trust him.
Oedipus. Tell me first, you from Corinth: is this the shepherd
  We were discussing?
Messenger.   This is the very man.
Oedipus (to Shepherd). Come here. No, look at me. You must
    answer
  Everything I ask. — You belonged to Laïos?   10
Shepherd. Yes: born his slave, brought up in his house.
Oedipus. Tell me: what kind of work did you do for him?
Shepherd. I was a shepherd of his, most of my life.
Oedipus. Where mainly did you go for pasturage?
Shepherd. Sometimes Kithairon, sometimes the hills near-by.   15
Oedipus. Do you remember ever seeing this man out there?
Shepherd. What would he be doing there? This man?
Oedipus. This man standing here. Have you ever seen
    him before?
Shepherd. No. At least, not to my recollection.
Messenger. And that is not strange, my lord. But I'll refresh   20
  His memory: he must remember when we two
  Spent three whole seasons together, March to September,
  On Kithairon or thereabouts. He had two flocks;
  I had one. Each autumn I'd drive mine home
  And he would go back with his to Laïos' sheepfold.—   25
  Is this not true, just as I have described it?
Shepherd. True, yes; but it was all so long ago.
Messenger. Well, then: do you remember, back in those days
  That you gave me a baby boy to bring up as my own?
Shepherd. What if I did? What are you trying to say?   30

Messenger. King Oedipus was once that little child.
Shepherd. Damn you, hold your tongue!
Oedipus.   No more of that!
    It is your tongue needs watching, not this man's.
Shepherd. My King, my Master, what is it I have done wrong?
Oedipus. You have not answered his question about the boy.   35
Shepherd. He does not know . . . He is only making trouble . . .
Oedipus. Come, speak plainly, or it will go hard with you.
Shepherd. In God's name, do not torture an old man!
Oedipus. Come here, one of you; bind his arms behind him.
Shepherd. Unhappy king! What more do you wish to learn?   40
Oedipus. Did you give this man the child he speaks of?
Shepherd.   I did.
    And I would to God I had died that very day.
Oedipus. You will die now unless you speak the truth.
Shepherd. Yet if I speak the truth, I am worse than dead.
Oedipus. Very well; since you insist upon delaying —   45
Shepherd. No! I have told you already that I gave him the boy.
Oedipus. Where did you get him? From your house?
        From somewhere else?
Shepherd. Not from mine, no. A man gave him to me.
Oedipus. Is that man here? Do you know whose slave he was?
Shepherd. For God's love, my King, do not ask me any more!   50
Oedipus. You are a dead man if I have to ask you again.
Shepherd. Then . . . Then the child was from the palace of Laïos.
Oedipus. A slave child? or a child of his own line?
Shepherd. Ah, I am on the brink of dreadful speech!
Oedipus. And I of dreadful hearing. Yet I must hear.   55
Shepherd. If you must be told, then . . .
                              They said it was Laïos' child,
    But it is your wife who can tell you about that.
Oedipus. My wife! — Did she give it to you?
Shepherd.   My lord, she did
Oedipus. Do you know why?
Shepherd.   I was told to get rid of it.
Oedipus. An unspeakable mother!
Shepherd.   There had been prophecies . . .   60
Oedipus. Tell me.
Shepherd.   It was said that the boy would kill his own father.
Oedipus. Then why did you give him over to this old man?
Shepherd. I pitied the baby, my King,
    And I thought that this man would take him far away
    To his own country.
                              He saved him — but for what a fate!   65

For if you are what this man says you are,
No man living is more wretched than Oedipus.
Oedipus. Ah God!
    It was true!
            All the prophecies!
                        — Now,
O Light, may I look on you for the last time!   70
I, Oedipus,
Oedipus, damned in his birth, in his marriage damned,
Damned in the blood he shed with his own hand!

He rushes into the palace.

ODE IV

Chorus. Alas for the seed of men.   *Strophe 1*

What measure shall I give these generations
That breathe on the void and are void
And exist and do not exist?

Who bears more weight of joy   5
Than mass of sunlight shifting in images,
Or who shall make his thought stay on
That down time drifts away?

Your splendor is all fallen.

O naked brow of wrath and tears,   10
O change of Oedipus!
I who saw your days call no man blest —
Your great days like ghósts góne.

That mind was a strong bow.   *Antistrophe 1*
Deep, how deep you drew it then, hard archer,   15
At a dim fearful range,
And brought dear glory down!

You overcame the stranger —
The virgin with her hooking lion claws —
And though death sang, stood like a tower   20
To make pale Thebes take heart.

Fortress against our sorrow!

Divine king, giver of laws,
Majestic Oedipus!

No prince in Thebes had ever such renown,   25
No prince won such grace of power.

And now of all men ever known   *Strophe 2*
Most pitiful is this man's story:
His fortunes are most changed, his state
Fallen to a low slave's   30
Ground under bitter fate.

O Oedipus, most royal one!
The great door that expelled you to the light
Gave at night — ah, gave night to your glory:
As to the father, to the fathering son.   35

All understood too late.

How could that queen whom Laïos won,
The garden that he harrowed at his height,
Be silent when that act was done?

But all eyes fail before time's eye,   *Antistrophe 2* 40
All actions come to justice there.
Though never willed, though far down the deep past,
Your bed, your dread sirings,
Are brought to book at last.
Child by Laïos doomed to die,   45
Then doomed to lose that fortunate little death,
Would God you never took breath in this air
That with my wailing lips I take to cry:

For I weep the world's outcast.

I was blind, and now I can tell why: 50
Asleep, for you had given ease of breath
To Thebes, while the false years went by.

EXODOS

Enter, from the palace, Second Messenger.

Second Messenger. Elders of Thebes, most honored in this land,
    What horrors are yours to see and hear, what weight
    Of sorrow to be endured, if, true to your birth,
    You venerate the line of Labdakos!
    I think neither Istros nor Phasis, those great rivers,   5
    Could purify this place of the corruption

It shelters now, or soon must bring to light —
Evil not done unconsciously, but willed.

The greatest griefs are those we cause ourselves.
Choragos. Surely, friend, we have grief enough already;   10
What new sorrow do you mean?
Second Messenger.   The Queen is dead.
Choragos. Iocastê? Dead? But at whose hand?
Second Messenger.   Her own.
The full horror of what happened you cannot know,
For you did not see it; but I, who did, will tell you
As clearly as I can how she met her death.   15

When she had left us,
In passionate silence, passing through the court,
She ran to her apartment in the house,
Her hair clutched by the fingers of both hands.
She closed the doors behind her; then, by that bed   20
Where long ago the fatal son was conceived —
That son who should bring about his father's death —
We heard her call upon Laïos, dead so many years,
And heard her wail for the double fruit of her marriage,
A husband by her husband, children by her child.   25

Exactly how she died I do not know:
For Oedipus burst in moaning and would not let us
Keep vigil to the end: it was by him
As he stormed about the room that our eyes were caught.
From one to another of us he went, begging a sword,   30
Cursing the wife who was not his wife, the mother
Whose womb had carried his own children and himself.
I do not know: it was none of us aided him,
But surely one of the gods was in control!
For with a dreadful cry   35
He hurled his weight, as though wrenched out of himself,
At the twin doors: the bolts gave, and he rushed in.
And there we saw her hanging, her body swaying
From the cruel cord she had noosed about her neck.
A great sob broke from him heartbreaking to hear,
As he loosed the rope and lowered her to the ground.

I would blot out from my mind what happened next!
For the King ripped from her gown the golden brooches
That were her ornament, and raised them, and
    plunged them down

Straight into his own eyeballs, crying, "No more,   45
No more shall you look on the misery about me,
The horrors of my own doing! Too long you have known
The faces of those whom I should never have seen,
Too long been blind to those for whom I was searching!
From this hour, go in darkness!" And as he spoke,   50
He struck at his eyes — not once, but many times;
And the blood spattered his beard,
Bursting from his ruined sockets like red hail.

So from the unhappiness of two this evil has sprung,
A curse on the man and woman alike. The old   55
Happiness of the house of Labdakos
Was happiness enough: where is it today?
It is all wailing and ruin, disgrace, death — all
The misery of mankind that has a name —
And it is wholly and for ever theirs.   60
Choragos. Is he in agony still? Is there no rest for him?
Second Messenger. He is calling for someone to lead him to
      the gates
So that all the children of Kadmos may look upon
His father's murderer, his mother's — no,
I cannot say it!
                And then he will leave Thebes,   65
Self-exiled, in order that the curse
Which he himself pronounced may depart from the house.
He is weak, and there is none to lead him,
So terrible is his suffering.
                        But you will see:
Look, the doors are opening; in a moment   70
You will see a thing that would crush a heart of stone.

The central door is opened; Oedipus, blinded, is led in.

Choragos. Dreadful indeed for men to see.
      Never have my own eyes
      Looked on a sight so full of fear.

      Oedipus!   75
      What madness came upon you, what daemon°
      Leaped on your life with heavier
      Punishment than a mortal man can bear?
      No: I cannot even
      Look at you, poor ruined one.   80

Exodos. ⁷⁶ *daemon* a spirit, not necessarily evil

And I would speak, question, ponder,
If I were able. No.
You make me shudder.
Oedipus. God. God.
   Is there a sorrow greater?   85
   Where shall I find harbor in this world?
   My voice is hurled far on a dark wind.
   What has God done to me?
Choragos. Too terrible to think of, or to see.

Oedipus. O cloud of night,   *Strophe 1* 90
   Never to be turned away: night coming on,
   I cannot tell how: night like a shroud!
   My fair winds brought me here.
                         Oh God. Again
   The pain of the spikes where I had sight,
   The flooding pain   95
   Of memory, never to be gouged out.
Choragos. This is not strange.
   You suffer it all twice over, remorse in pain,
   Pain in remorse.

Oedipus. Ah dear friend   *Antistrophe 1* 100
   Are you faithful even yet, you alone?
   Are you still standing near me, will you stay here,
   Patient, to care for the blind?
                        The blind man!
   Yet even blind I know who it is attends me,
   By the voice's tone —   105
   Though my new darkness hide the comforter.
Choragos. Oh fearful act!
   What god was it drove you to rake black
   Night across your eyes?

Oedipus. Apollo. Apollo. Dear   *Strophe 2* 110
   Children, the god was Apollo.
   He brought my sick, sick fate upon me.
   But the blinding hand was my own!
   How could I bear to see
   When all my sight was horror everywhere?   115
Choragos. Everywhere; that is true.
Oedipus. And now what is left?
   Images? Love? A greeting even,
   Sweet to the senses? Is there anything?
   Ah, no, friends: lead me away.   120

        Lead me away from Thebes.
                              Lead the great wreck
        And hell of Oedipus, whom the gods hate.
Choragos.   Your fate is clear, you are not blind to that.
        Would God you had never found it out!

Oedipus.   Death take the man who unbound   *Antistrophe 2*   125
        My feet on that hillside
        And delivered me from death to life! What life?
        If only I had died,
        This weight of monstrous doom
        Could not have dragged me and my darlings down.   130
Choragos.   I would have wished the same.
Oedipus.   Oh never to have come here
        With my father's blood upon me! Never
        To have been the man they call his mother's husband!
        Oh accurst! Oh child of evil,   135
        To have entered that wretched bed —
                              the selfsame one!
        More primal than sin itself, this fell to me.
Choragos.   I do not know how I can answer you.
        You were better dead than alive and blind.
Oedipus.   Do not counsel me any more. This punishment   140
        That I have laid upon myself is just.
        If I had eyes,
        I do not know how I could bear the sight
        Of my father, when I came to the house of Death,
        Or my mother: for I have sinned against them both   145
        So vilely that I could not make my peace
        By strangling my own life.
                              Or do you think my children,
        Born as they were born, would be sweet to my eyes?
        Ah never, never! Nor this town with its high walls,
        Nor the holy images of the gods.
                              For I,   150
        Thrice miserable — Oedipus, noblest of all the line
        Of Kadmos, have condemned myself to enjoy
        These things no more, by my own malediction
        Expelling that man whom the gods declared
        To be a defilement in the house of Laïos.   155
        After exposing the rankness of my own guilt,
        How could I look men frankly in the eyes?
        No, I swear it,
        If I could have stifled my hearing at its source,

I would have done it and made all this body   160
A tight cell of misery, blank to light and sound:
So I should have been safe in a dark agony
Beyond all recollection.
                          Ah Kithairon!
Why did you shelter me? When I was cast upon you,
Why did I not die? Then I should never   165
Have shown the world my execrable birth.

Ah Polybos! Corinth, city that I believed
The ancient seat of my ancestors: how fair
I seemed, your child! And all the while this evil
Was cancerous within me!
                          For I am sick   170
In my daily life, sick in my origin.

O three roads, dark ravine, woodland and way
Where three roads met: you, drinking my father's blood,
My own blood, spilled by my own hand: can you remember
The unspeakable things I did there, and the things   175
I went on from there to do?
                          O marriage, marriage!
The act that engendered me, and again the act
Performed by the son in the same bed —
                                   Ah, the net
Of incest, mingling fathers, brothers, sons,
With brides, wives, mothers: the last evil   180
That can be known by men: no tongue can say
How evil!
              No. For the love of God, conceal me
Somewhere far from Thebes; or kill me; or hurl me
Into the sea, away from men's eyes for ever.

Come, lead me. You need not fear to touch me.   185
Of all men, I alone can bear this guilt.

Enter Creon.

Choragos.   We are not the ones to decide; but Creon here
    May fitly judge of what you ask. He only
    Is left to protect the city in your place.
Oedipus.   Alas, how can I speak to him? What right have I   190
    To beg his courtesy whom I have deeply wronged?
Creon.   I have not come to mock you, Oedipus,
    Or to reproach you, either.
    (To Attendants.)   — You, standing there:

If you have lost all respect for man's dignity,
At least respect the flame of Lord Helios: 195
Do not allow this pollution to show itself
Openly here, an affront to the earth
And Heaven's rain and the light of day. No, take him
Into the house as quickly as you can.
For it is proper   200
That only the close kindred see his grief.
Oedipus. I pray you in God's name, since your courtesy
Ignores my dark expectation, visiting
With mercy this man of all men most execrable:
Give me what I ask — for your good, not for mine.   205
Creon. And what is it that you would have me do?
Oedipus. Drive me out of this country as quickly as may be
To a place where no human voice can ever greet me.
Creon. I should have done that before now — only,
God's will had not been wholly revealed to me.   210
Oedipus. But his command is plain: the parricide
Must be destroyed. I am that evil man.
Creon. That is the sense of it, yes; but as things are,
We had best discover clearly what is to be done.
Oedipus. You would learn more about a man like me?   215
Creon. You are ready now to listen to the god.
Oedipus. I will listen. But it is to you
That I must turn for help. I beg you, hear me.

The woman in there —
Give her whatever funeral you think proper: 220
She is your sister.
            — But let me go, Creon!
Let me purge my father's Thebes of the pollution
Of my living here, and go out to the wild hills,
To Kithairon, that has won such fame with me,
The tomb my mother and father appointed for me,   225
And let me die there, as they willed I should.
And yet I know
Death will not ever come to me through sickness
Or in any natural way: I have been preserved
For some unthinkable fate. But let that be.   230
As for my sons, you need not care for them.
They are men, they will find some way to live.
But my poor daughters, who have shared my table,
Who never before have been parted from their father —
Take care of them, Creon; do this for me.   235
And will you let me touch them with my hands

A last time, and let us weep together?
Be kind, my lord,
Great prince, be kind!
                    Could I but touch them,
They would be mine again, as when I had my eyes.   240

Enter Antigonê and Ismenê, attended.

Ah, God!
Is it my dearest children I hear weeping?
Has Creon pitied me and sent my daughters?
Creon. Yes, Oedipus: I knew that they were dear to you
In the old days, and know you must love them still.   245
Oedipus. May God bless you for this — and be a friendlier
Guardian to you than he has been to me!

Children, where are you?
Come quickly to my hands: they are your brother's —
Hands that have brought your father's once clear eyes   250
To this way of seeing —
                    Ah dearest ones,
I had neither sight nor knowledge then, your father
By the woman who was the source of his own life!
And I weep for you — having no strength to see you — ,
I weep for you when I think of the bitterness   255
That men will visit upon you all your lives.
What homes, what festivals can you attend
Without being forced to depart again in tears?
And when you come to marriageable age,
Where is the man, my daughters, who would dare   260
Risk the bane that lies on all my children?
Is there any evil wanting? Your father killed
His father; sowed the womb of her who bore him;
Engendered you at the fount of his own existence!
That is what they will say of you.
                            Then, whom   265
Can you ever marry? There are no bridegrooms for you,
And your lives must wither away in sterile dreaming.
O Creon, son of Menoikeus!
You are the only father my daughters have,
Since we, their parents, are both of us gone for ever.   270
They are your own blood: you will not let them
Fall into beggary and loneliness;
You will keep them from the miseries that are mine!
Take pity on them; see, they are only children,

Friendless except for you. Promise me this,   275
Great Prince, and give me your hand in token of it.

Creon clasps his right hand.

Children:
I could say much, if you could understand me,
But as it is, I have only this prayer for you:
Live where you can, be as happy as you can —   280
Happier, please God, than God has made your father!
Creon. Enough. You have wept enough. Now go within.
Oedipus. I must; but it is hard.
Creon.   Time eases all things.
Oedipus. But you must promise —
Creon.   Say what you desire.
Oedipus. Send me from Thebes!
Creon.   God grant that I may!
Oedipus. But since God hates me . . .
Creon.   No, he will grant your wish.
Oedipus. You promise?
Creon.   I cannot speak beyond my knowledge.
Oedipus. Then lead me in.
Creon.   Come now, and leave your children.
Oedipus. No! Do not take them from me!
Creon.   Think no longer
That you are in command here, but rather think   290
How, when you were, you served your own destruction.

*Exeunt into the house all but the Chorus; the Choragos chants
directly to the audience.*

Choragos. Men of Thebes: look upon Oedipus.

This is the king who solved the famous riddle
And towered up, most powerful of men.
No mortal eyes but looked on him with envy,   295
Yet in the end ruin swept over him.
Let every man in mankind's frailty
Consider his last day; and let none
Presume on his good fortune until he find
Life, at his death, a memory without pain.   300

Questions

1. On the basis of the Prologue, characterize Oedipus. What additional traits are revealed in Scene I and Ode I?

2. How fair is it to say that Oedipus is morally guilty? Does he argue that he is morally innocent because he did not intend to do immoral deeds? Can it be said that he is guilty of *hybris* but that *hybris* has nothing to do with his fall?

3. Oedipus says that he blinds himself in order not to look upon people he should not. What further reasons can be given? Why does he not (like his mother) commit suicide?

4. How fair is it to say that the play shows the contemptibleness of man's efforts to act intelligently?

5. How fair is it to say that in *Oedipus* the gods are evil?

6. Are the choral odes lyrical interludes that serve to separate the scenes, or do they advance the dramatic action?

7. Matthew Arnold said that Sophocles saw life steadily and saw it whole. But in this play is Sophocles facing the facts of life, or, on the contrary, is he avoiding life as it usually is and presenting a series of unnatural and outrageous coincidences?

8. Can you describe your emotions at the end of the play? Do they include pity for Oedipus? Pity for all human beings, including yourself? Fear that you might be punished for some unintended transgression? Awe, engendered by a perception of the interrelatedness of things? Relief that the story is only a story? Exhilaration?

A NOTE ON THE ELIZABETHAN THEATER

Shakespeare's theater was wooden, round or polygonal (the Chorus in *Henry V* calls it a "wooden O"). About eight hundred spectators could stand in the yard in front of — and perhaps along the two sides of — the stage that jutted from the rear wall, and another fifteen hundred or so spectators could sit in the three roofed galleries that ringed the stage. That portion of the galleries that was above the rear of the stage was sometimes used by actors. Entry to the stage was normally gained by doors at the rear but some use was made of a curtained alcove — or perhaps a booth — between the doors that allowed characters to be "discovered" (revealed) as in the modern proscenium theater, which normally employs a curtain. A performance was probably uninterrupted by intermissions or by long pauses for the changing of scenery; a group of characters leaves the stage, another enters, and if the locale has changed, the new characters somehow tell us. (Modern editors customarily add indications of locales to help a reader, but it should be understood that the action of the Elizabethan stage was continuous.)

Othello was first printed in 1621 in a small book of a kind called a quarto; it was printed again in 1623 in a large volume (a folio) containing 36 of Shakespeare's plays. There are numerous differences between the two texts of *Othello,* and scholars are divided about which text represents Shakespeare's final version of the play. The text we give is that prepared by Alvin Kernan for the Signet Shakespeare; it is based on the folio but it includes some readings from the quarto. Material added by the editor, such as indication of locale and some stage directions, is enclosed in square brackets, thus[   ].

William Shakespeare (1564–1616)

The Tragedy of Othello

The Moor of Venice

List of Characters

Othello, the Moor
Brabantio, father to Desdemona
Cassio, an honorable lieutenant
Iago, a villain
Roderigo, a gulled gentleman
Duke of Venice
Senators
Montano, Governor of Cyprus
Gentlemen of Cyprus
Lodovico and Gratiano, two noble Venetians
Sailors
Clown
Desdemona, wife to Othello
Emilia, wife to Iago
Bianca, a courtesan
[*Messenger, Herald, Officers, Gentlemen, Musicians, Attendants*]

[**Scene.**   *Venice and Cyprus.*]

ACT I

Scene I   [*Venice. A street.*]

Enter Roderigo and Iago.

Roderigo.   Tush! Never tell me? I take it much unkindly
    That thou, Iago, who hast had my purse
    As if the strings were thine, shoudst know of this.

Iago. 'Sblood,° but you'll not hear me! If ever I did dream
   Of such a matter, abhor me.
Roderigo.   Thou told'st me   5
   Thou didst hold him in thy hate.
Iago.   Despise me
   If I do not. Three great ones of the city,
   In personal suit to make me his lieutenant,
   Off-capped° to him; and, by the faith of man,
   I know my price; I am worth no worse a place.   10
   But he, as loving his own pride and purposes,
   Evades them with a bombast circumstance,°
   Horribly stuffed with epithets of war;
   Nonsuits° my mediators. For, "Certes," says he,
   "I have already chose my officer." And what was he?   15
   Forsooth, a great arithmetician,°
   One Michael Cassio, a Florentine,
   (A fellow almost damned in a fair wife)°
   That never set a squadron in the field,
   Nor the division of a battle knows
   More than a spinster; unless the bookish theoric,
   Wherein the tongued° consuls can propose.
   As masterly as he. Mere prattle without practice
   Is all his soldiership. But he, sir, had th' election;
   And I, of whom his eyes had seen the proof   25
   At Rhodes, at Cyprus, and on other grounds
   Christian and heathen, must be belee'd and calmed
   By debitor and creditor. This counter-caster,°
   He, in good time, must his lieutenant be,
   And I — God bless the mark! — his Moorship's ancient.°   30
Roderigo. By heaven, I rather would have been his hangman.
Iago. Why, there's no remedy. 'Tis the curse of service:
   Preferment goes by letter and affection,°
   And not by old gradation,° where each second
   Stood heir to th' first. Now, sir, be judge yourself,   35

I.i.   **⁴ blood** by God's blood   **⁹ Off-capped** doffed their caps — as a mark of
respect   **¹² bombast circumstance** stuffed, roundabout speech   **¹⁴ Nonsuits**
rejects   **¹⁶ arithmetician** theorist (rather than practical)   **¹⁸ A . . . wife**
(a much-disputed passage, probably best taken as a general sneer at Cassio as
a dandy and a ladies' man. But in the story from which Shakespeare took his
plot the counterpart of Cassio is married, and it may be that at the beginning
of the play Shakespeare had decided to keep him married but later changed
his mind)   **²² tongued** eloquent   **²⁸ counter-caster** i.e., a bookkeeper who
casts (reckons up) figures on a *counter* (abacus)   **³⁰ ancient** standard-bearer;
an under-officer   **³³ letter and affection** recommendations (from men of
power) and personal preference   **³⁴ old gradation** seniority

Whether I in any just term am affined°
    To love the Moor.
Roderigo.   I would not follow him then.
Iago. O, sir, content you.
    I follow him to serve my turn upon him.
    We cannot all be masters, nor all masters   40
    Cannot be truly followed. You shall mark
    Many a duteous and knee-crooking° knave
    That, doting on his own obsequious bondage,
    Wears out his time, much like his master's ass,
    For naught but provender; and when he's old, cashiered.   45
    Whip me such honest knaves! Others there are
    Who, trimmed in forms and visages of duty,
    Keep yet their hearts attending on themselves,
    And, throwing but shows of service on their lords,
    Do well thrive by them, and when they have lined their coats,   50
    Do themselves homage. These fellows have some soul;
    And such a one do I profess myself. For, sir,
    It is as sure as you are Roderigo,
    Were I the Moor, I would not be Iago.
    In following him, I follow but myself.   55
    Heaven is my judge, not I for love and duty,
    But seeming so, for my peculiar° end;
    For when my outward action doth demonstrate
    The native° act and figure of my heart
    In complement extern,° tis not long after   60
    But I will wear my heart upon my sleeve
    For daws to peck at; I am not what I am.
Roderigo. What a full fortune does the thick-lips owe°
    If he can carry't thus!
Iago.   Call up her father,
    Rouse him. Make after him, poison his delight,   65
    Proclaim him in the streets, incense her kinsmen,
    And though he in a fertile climate dwell,
    Plague him with flies; though that his joy be joy,
    Yet throw such chances of vexation on't
    As it may lose some color.   70
Roderigo. Here is her father's house. I'll call aloud.
Iago. Do, with like timorous° accent and dire yell
    As when, by night and negligence, the fire
    Is spied in populous cities.

---

³⁶ *affined* bound   ⁴² *knee-crooking* bowing   ⁵⁷ *peculiar* personal   ⁵⁹ *native* natural, innate   ⁶⁰ *complement extern* outward appearance   ⁶³ *owe* own   ⁷² *timorous* frightening

Roderigo. What, ho, Brabantio! Signior Brabantio, ho!   75
Iago. Awake! What, ho, Brabantio! Thieves! Thieves!
　　Look to your house, your daughter, and your bags!
　　Thieves! Thieves!

　　Brabantio above° [*at a window*].

Brabantio. What is the reason of this terrible summons?
　　What is the matter there?   80
Roderigo. Signior, is all your family within?
Iago. Are your doors locked?
Brabantio.   Why, wherefore ask you this?
Iago. Zounds, sir, y'are robbed. For shame. Put on your gown!
　　Your heart is burst, you have lost half your soul.
　　Even now, now, very now, an old black ram   85
　　Is tupping your white ewe. Arise, arise!
　　Awake the snorting citizens with the bell,
　　Or else the devil will make a grandsire of you.
　　Arise, I say!
Brabantio.   What, have you lost your wits?
Roderigo. Most reverend signior, do you know my voice?   90
Brabantio. Not I. What are you?
Roderigo. My name is Roderigo.
Brabantio.   The worser welcome!
　　I have charged thee not to haunt about my doors.
　　In honest plainness thou hast heard me say
　　My daughter is not for thee; and now, in madness,   95
　　Being full of supper and distemp'ring draughts,°
　　Upon malicious knavery dost thou come
　　To start° my quiet.
Roderigo. Sir, sir, sir ——
Brabantio.   But thou must needs be sure
　　My spirits and my place° have in their power   100
　　To make this bitter to thee.
Roderigo.   Patience, good sir.
Brabantio. What tell'st thou me of robbing? This is Venice:
　　My house is not a grange.°
Roderigo.   Most grave Brabantio,
　　In simple and pure soul I come to you.
Iago. Zounds, sir, you are one of those that will not serve God   105

---

⁷⁸ s.d. ***above*** (i.e., on the small upper stage above and to the rear of the main platform stage, which resembled the projecting upper story of an Elizabethan house) ⁹⁶ ***distemp'ring draughts*** unsettling drinks ⁹⁸ ***start*** disrupt ¹⁰⁰ ***place*** rank, i.e., of senator ¹⁰³ ***grange*** isolated house

if the devil bid you. Because we come to do you service
and you think we are ruffians, you'll have your daughter
covered with a Barbary° horse, you'll have your nephews°
neigh to you, you'll have coursers for cousins,° and gennets
for germans.°   110
Brabantio. What profane wretch art thou?
Iago. I am one, sir, that comes to tell you your daughter and the
Moor are making the beast with two backs.
Brabantio. Thou art a villain.
Iago.   You are — a senator.
Brabantio. This thou shalt answer. I know thee, Roderigo.   115
Roderigo. Sir, I will answer anything. But I beseech you,
If't be your pleasure and most wise consent,
As partly I find it is, that your fair daughter,
At this odd-even° and dull watch o' th' night,
Transported, with no worse nor better guard   120
But with a knave of common hire, a gondolier,
To the gross clasps of a lascivious Moor —
If this be known to you, and your allowance,
We then have done you bold and saucy wrongs;
But if you know not this, my manners tell me   125
We have your wrong rebuke. Do not believe
That from the sense of all civility°
I thus would play and trifle with your reverence.
Your daughter, if you have not given her leave,
I say again, hath made a gross revolt,   130
Tying her duty, beauty, wit, and fortunes
In an extravagant° and wheeling stranger
Of here and everywhere. Straight satisfy yourself.
If she be in her chamber, or your house,
Let loose on me the justice of the state   135
For thus deluding you.
Brabantio.   Strike on the tinder, ho!
Give me a taper! Call up all my people!
This accident° is not unlike my dream.
Belief of it oppresses me already.
Light, I say! Light!   *Exit [above].*

---

[108] *Barbary* Arabian, i.e., Moorish [108] *nephews* i.e., grandsons [109] *cousins*
relations   [110] *gennets for germans* Spanish horses for blood relatives
[119] *odd-even* between night and morning   [127] *sense of all civility* feeling of
what is proper   [132] *extravagant* vagrant, wandering (Othello is not Venetian
and thus may be considered a wandering soldier of fortune)   [138] *accident*
happening

Iago.   Farewell, for I must leave you.   140
    it seems not meet, nor wholesome to my place,
    To be produced — as, if I stay, I shall —
    Against the Moor. For I do know the State.
    However this may gall him with some check,°
    Cannot with safety cast° him; for he's embarked   145
    With such loud reason to the Cyprus wars,
    Which even now stands in act,° that for their souls
    Another of his fathom° they have none
    To lead their business; in which regard,
    Though I do hate him as I do hell-pains,   150
    Yet, for necessity of present life,
    I must show out a flag and sign of love,
    Which is indeed but sign. That you shall surely find him,
    Lead to the Sagittary° the raisèd search:
    And there will I be with him. So farewell.   *(Exit.)* 155

Enter Brabantio [in his nightgown], with Servants and torches.

Brabantio. It is too true an evil. Gone she is;
    And what's to come of my despised time
    Is naught but bitterness. Now, Roderigo,
    Where didst thou see her? — O unhappy girl! —
    With the Moor, say'st thou? — Who would be a father? —   160
    How didst thou know 'twas she? — O, she deceives me
    Past thought! — What said she to you? Get moe° tapers!
    Raise all my kindred! — Are they married, think you?
Roderigo. Truly I think they are.
Brabantio. O heaven! How got she out? O treason of the blood!
    Fathers, from hence trust not your daughters' minds   165
    By what you see them act.° Is there not charms
    By which the property° of youth and maidhood
    May be abused? Have you not read, Roderigo,
    Of some such thing?
Roderigo.   Yes, sir, I have indeed.
Brabantio. Call up my brother. — O, would you had had her! —   170
    Some one way, some another. — Do you know
    Where we may apprehend her and the Moor?
Roderigo. I think I can discover him, if you please
    To get good guard and go along with me.
Brabantio. Pray you lead on. At every house I'll call;   175
    I may command at most. — Get weapons, ho!

[144] *check* restraint   [145] *cast* dismiss   [147] *stands in act* takes place   [148] *fathom* ability   [154] *Sagittary* (probably the name of an inn)   [162] *moe* more   [166] *act* do   [167] *property* ture nature

And raise some special officers of might. —
On, good Roderigo; I will deserve your pains.°   *(Exeunt.)*

Scene II   [*A street.*]

Enter Othello, Iago, Attendants with torches.

Iago. Though in the trade of war I have slain men,
    Yet do I hold it very stuff° o' th' conscience
    To do no contrived murder. I lack iniquity
    Sometime to do me service. Nine or ten times
    I had thought t' have yerked° him here, under the ribs.   5
Othello. 'Tis better as it is.
Iago.   Nay, but he prated,
    And spoke such scurvy and provoking terms
    Against your honor, that with the little godliness I have
    I did full hard forbear him. But I pray you, sir,
    Are you fast married? Be assured of this,   10
    That the magnifico° is much beloved,
    And hath in his effect a voice potential
    As double as the Duke's.° He will divorce you,
    Or put upon you what restraint or grievance
    The law, with all his might to enforce it on,   15
    Will give him cable.°
Othello.   Let him do his spite.
    My services which I have done the Signiory°
    Shall out-tongue his complaints. 'Tis yet to know° —
    Which when I know that boasting is an honor
    I shall promulgate — I fetch my life and being   20
    From men of royal siege;° and my demerits°
    May speak unbonneted to as proud a fortune
    As this that I have reached.° For know, Iago,
    But that I love the gentle Desdemona,
    I would not my unhoused° free condition   25
    Put into circumscription and confine
    For the seas' worth. But look, what lights come yond?

Enter Cassio, with [Officers and] torches.

Iago. Those are the raised father and his friends.
    You were best go in.
Othello.   Not I. I must be found.
    My parts, my title, and my perfect soul°   30
    Shall manifest me rightly. Is it they?
Iago. By Janus, I think no.
Othello. The servants of the Duke? And my lieutenant?
    The goodness of the night upon you, friends.
    What is the news?
Cassio.   The Duke does greet you, general;   35
    And he requires your haste-posthaste appearance
    Even on the instant.
Othello.   What is the matter, think you?
Cassio. Something from Cyprus, as I may divine.
    It is a business of some heat. The galleys
    Have sent a dozen sequent° messengers   40
    This very night at one another's heels,
    And many of the consuls, raised and met,
    Are at the Duke's already. You have been hotly called for.
    When, being not at your lodging to be found,
    The Senate hath sent about three several° quests   45
    To search you out.
Othello.   'Tis well I am found by you.
    I will but spend a word here in the house,
    And go with you.   [*Exit.*]
Cassio.   Ancient, what makes he here?
Iago. Faith, he tonight hath boarded a land carack.°
    If it prove lawful prize, he's made forever.   50
Cassio. I do not understand.
Iago.   He's married.
Cassio.   To who?

[*Enter Othello.*]

Iago. Marry,° to — Come captain, will you go?
Othello.   Have with you.
Cassio. Here comes another troop to seek for you.

Enter Brabantio, Roderigo, with Officers and torches.

Iago. It is Brabantio. General, be advised.
    He comes to bad intent.
Othello.   Holla! Stand there!   55

°**perfect soul** clear, unflawed conscience °**sequent** successive °**several** separate °**carack** treasure ship °**Marry** By Mary (an interjection)

Roderigo. Signior, it is the Moor.
Brabantio.   Down with him, thief!

> [*They draw swords.*]

Iago. You, Roderigo? Come, sir, I am for you.
Othello. Keep up your bright swords, for the dew will rust them.
Good signior, you shall more command with years
Than with your weapons.   60
Brabantio. O thou foul thief, where hast thou stowed my daughter?
Damned as thou art, thou hast enchanted her!
For I'll refer me to all things of sense,°
If she in chains of magic were not bound,
Whether a maid so tender, fair, and happy,   65
So opposite to marriage that she shunned
The wealthy, curlèd darlings of our nation,
Would ever have, t'incur a general mock,°
Run from her guardage to the sooty bosom
Of such a thing as thou — to fear, not to delight   70
Judge me the world if 'tis not gross in sense°
That thou has practiced° on her with foul charms,
Abused her delicate youth with drugs or minerals
That weaken motion.° I'll have't disputed on;
'Tis probable, and palpable to thinking.   75
I therefore apprehend and do attach° thee
For an abuser of the world, a practicer
Of arts inhibited and out of warrant.°
Lay hold upon him. If he do resist,
Subdue him at his peril.
Othello.   Hold your hands,   80
Both you of my inclining and the rest.
Were it my cue to fight, I should have known it
Without a prompter. Whither will you that I go
To answer this your charge?
Brabantio.   To prison, till fit time
Of law and course of direct session   85
Call thee to answer.
Othello.   What if I do obey?
How may the Duke be therewith satisfied,
Whose messengers are here about my side

---

63 *refer . . . sense* i.e., base (my argument) on all ordinary understanding of
nature **68** *general mock* public shame **71** *gross in sense* obvious **72** *practiced* used tricks **74** *motion* thought, i.e., reason **76** *attach* arrest **78** *inhibited . . . warrant* prohibited and illegal (black magic)

Upon some present° business of the state
To bring me to him?
Officer.   'Tis true, most worthy signior.   90
   The Duke's in council, and your noble self
   I am sure is sent for.
Brabantio.   How? The Duke in council?
   In this time of the night? Bring him away.
   Mine's not an idle cause. The Duke himself,
   Or any of my brothers° of the state,   95
   Cannot but feel this wrong as 'twere their own;
   For if such actions may have passage free,
   Bondslaves and pagans shall our statesmen be.   *Exeunt.*

Scene III   [*A council chamber.*]

Enter Duke, Senators, and Officers [*set at a table, with lights and Attendants*].

Duke.   There's no composition° in this news
   That gives them credit.°
First Senator.   Indeed, they are disproportioned.
   My letters say a hundred and seven galleys.
Duke.   And mine a hundred forty.
Second Senator.   And mine two hundred.
   But though they jump° not on a just accompt° —   5
   As in these cases where the aim° reports
   'Tis oft with difference — yet do they all confirm
   A Turkish fleet, and bearing up to Cyprus.
Duke.   Nay, it is possible enough to judgment.°
   I do not so secure me in the error,   10
   But the main article I do approve
   In fearful sense.°
Sailor (Within).   What, ho! What, ho! What, ho!

Enter Sailor.

Officer.   A messenger from the galleys.
Duke.   Now? What's the business?
Sailor.   The Turkish preparation makes for Rhodes.

---

[89] *present* immediate   [95] *brothers* i.e., the other senators   I.iii.   [1] *composition* agreement   [2] *gives them credit* makes them believable   [5] *jump* agree   [5] *just accompt* exact counting   [6] *aim* approximation   [9] *to judgment* when carefully considered   [10-12] *I do . . . sense* i.e., just because the numbers disagree in the reports, I do not doubt that the principal information (that the Turkish fleet is out) is fearfully true

So was I bid report here to the State   15
   By Signior Angelo.
Duke. How say you by this change?
First Senator.   This cannot be
   By no assay of reason. 'Tis a pageant°
   To keep us in false gaze.° When we consider
   Th' importancy of Cyprus to the Turk,   20
   And let ourselves again but understand
   That, as it more concerns the Turk than Rhodes,
   So may he with more facile question° bear it,
   For that it stands not in such warlike brace,°
   But altogether lacks th' abilities   25
   That Rhodes is dressed in. If we make thought of this,
   We must not think the Turk is so unskillful
   To leave that latest which concerns him first,
   Neglecting an attempt of ease and gain
   To wake and wage a danger profitless.   30
Duke. Nay, in all confidence he's not for Rhodes.
Officer. Here is more news.

   Enter a Messenger.

Messenger. The Ottomites, reverend and gracious,
   Steering with due course toward the isle of Rhodes,
   Have there injointed them with an after° fleet.   35
First Senator. Ay, so I thought. How many, as you guess?
Messenger. Of thirty sail; and now they do restem
   Their backward course, bearing with frank appearance
   Their purposes toward Cyprus. Signior Montano,
   Your trusty and most valiant servitor,   40
   With his free duty° recommends° you thus,
   And prays you to believe him.
Duke. 'Tis certain then for Cyprus.
   Marcus Luccicos, is not he in town?
First Senator. He's now in Florence.   45
Duke. Write from us to him; post-posthaste dispatch.
First Senator. Here comes Brabantio and the valiant Moor.

   Enter Brabantio, Othello, Cassio, Iago, Roderigo, and Officers.

Duke. Valiant Othello we must straight° employ you
   Against the general° enemy Ottoman.

¹⁸ *pageant* show, pretense   ¹⁹ *in false gaze* looking the wrong way   ²³ *facile
question* easy struggle   ²⁴ *warlike brace* "military posture"   ³⁵ *after* following   ⁴¹ *free duty* unlimited respect   ⁴¹ *recommends* informs   ⁴⁸ *straight* at
once   ⁴⁹ *general* universal

[*To Brabantio*] I did not see you. Welcome, gentle signior.   50
We lacked your counsel and your help tonight.
Brabantio. So did I yours. Good your grace, pardon me.
Neither my place, nor aught I heard of business,
Hath raised me from my bed; nor doth the general care
Take hold on me; for my particular grief   55
Is of so floodgate and o'erbearing nature
That it engluts and swallows other sorrows,
And it is still itself.
Duke.   Why, what's the matter?
Brabantio. My daughter! O, my daughter!
Senators.   Dead?
Brabantio.   Ay, to me.
She is abused, stol'n from me, and corrupted   60
By spells and medicines bought of mountebanks;
For nature so prepost'rously to err,
Being not deficient, blind, or lame of sense,
Sans° witchcraft could not.
Duke. Whoe'er he be that in this foul proceeding   65
Hath thus beguiled your daughter of herself,
And you of her, the bloody book of law
You shall yourself read in the bitter letter
After your own sense; yea, through our proper° son
Stood in your action.°
Brabantio.   Humbly I thank your Grace.   70
Here is the man — this Moor, whom now, it seems,
Your special mandate for the state affairs
Hath hither brought.
All.   We are very sorry for't.
Duke [*To Othello*]. What in your own part can you say to this?
Brabantio. Nothing, but this is so.   75
Othello. Most potent, grave, and reverend signiors,
My very noble and approved° good masters,
That I have ta'en away this old man's daughter,
It is most true; true I have married her.
The very head and front° of my offending   80
Hath this extent, no more. Rude am I in my speech,
And little blessed with the soft phrase of peace.
For since these arms of mine had seven years' pith°
Till now some nine moons wasted,° they have used

---

⁶⁴ *Sans* without   ⁶⁹ *proper* own   ⁷⁰ *Stood in your action* were the accused
in your suit   ⁷⁷ *approved* tested, proven by past performance   ⁸⁰ *head and
front* extreme form (*front* = forehead)   ⁸³ *pith* strength   ⁸⁴ *wasted* past

Their dearest° action in the tented field;   85
And little of this great world can I speak
More than pertains to feats of broils and battle;
And therefore little shall I grace my cause
In speaking for myself. Yet, by your gracious patience,
I will a round° unvarnished tale deliver   90
Of my whole course of love — what drugs, what charms,
What conjuration, and what mighty magic,
For such proceeding I am charged withal,
I won his daughter —
Brabantio.   A maiden never bold,
Of spirit so still and quiet that her motion   95
Blushed at herself;° and she, in spite of nature,
Of years, of country, credit, everything,
To fall in love with what she feared to look on!
It is judgment maimed and most imperfect
That will confess perfection so could err   100
Against all rules of nature, and must be driven
To find out practices of cunning hell
Why this should be. I therefore vouch again
That with some mixtures pow'rful o'er the blood,
Or with some dram, conjured to this effect,   105
He wrought upon her.
Duke.   To vouch this is no proof,
Without more wider and more overt test
Than these thin habits° and poor likelihoods
Of modern° seeming do prefer against him.
First Senator. But, Othello, speak.   110
Did you by indirect and forcèd courses
Subdue and poison this young maid's affections?
Or came it by request, and such fair question°
As soul to soul affordeth?
Othello.   I do beseech you,
Send for the lady to the Sagittary   115
And let her speak of me before her father.
If you do find me foul in her report,
The trust, the office, I do hold of you
Not only take away, but let your sentence
Even fall upon my life.
Duke.   Fetch Desdemona hither.   120

---

85 *dearest* most important   90 *round* blunt   95-96 *her motion/Blushed at herself* i.e., she was so modest that she blushed at every thought (and movement)   108 *habits* clothing   109 *modern* trivial   113 *question* discussion

Othello. Ancient, conduct them; you best know the place.

[*Exit Iago, with two or three Attendants.*]

And till she come, as truly as to heaven
I do confess the vices of my blood,
So justly to your grave ears I'll present
How I did thrive in this fair lady's love,   125
And she in mine.
Duke. Say it, Othello.
Othello. Her father loved me; oft invited me;
Still ° questioned me the story of my life
From year to year, the battle, sieges, fortune
That I have passed.   130
I ran it through, even from my boyish days
To th' very moment that he bade me tell it.
Wherein I spoke of most disastrous chances,
Of moving accidents by flood and field,
Of hairbreadth scapes i' th' imminent° deadly breach,   135
Of being taken by the insolent foe
And sold to slavery, of my redemption thence
And portance° in my travel's history,
Wherein of anters ° vast and deserts idle,°
Rough quarries, rocks, and hills whose heads touch heaven,   140
It was my hint to speak. Such was my process.
And of the Cannibals that each other eat,
The Anthropophagi,° and men whose heads
Grew beneath their shoulders. These things to hear
Would Desdemona seriously incline;   145
But still the house affairs would draw her thence;
Which ever as she could with haste dispatch,
She'd come again, and with a greedy ear
Devour up my discourse. Which I observing,
Took once a pliant hour, and found good means   150
To draw from her a prayer of earnest heart
That I would all my pilgrimage dilate,°
Whereof by parcels she had something heard,
But not intentively.° I did consent,
And often did beguile her of her tears   155
When I did speak of some distressful stroke
That my youth suffered. My story being done,

---

128 *Still* regularly   135 *imminent* threatening   138 *portance* manner of acting 139 *anters* caves   139 *idle* empty, sterile   143 *Anthropophagi* man-
eaters   152 *dilate* relate in full   154 *intentively* at length and in sequence

She gave me for my pains a world of kisses.
She swore in faith 'twas strange, 'twas passing° strange;
'Twas pitiful, 'twas wondrous pitiful.   160
She wished she had not heard it; yet she wished
That heaven had made her such a man. She thanked me,
And bade me, if I had a friend that loved her,
I should but teach him how to tell my story,
And that would woo her. Upon this hint I spake.   165
She loved me for the dangers I had passed,
And I loved her that she did pity them.
This only is the witchcraft I have used.
Here comes the lady. Let her witness it.

Enter Desdemona, Iago, Attendants.

Duke. I think this tale would win my daughter too.   170
   Good Brabantio, take up this mangled matter at the best.°
   Men do their broken weapons rather use
   Than their bare hands.
Branbantio.   I pray you hear her speak.
   If she confess that she was half the wooer,
   Destruction on my head if my bad blame   175
   Light on the man. Come hither, gentle mistress.
   Do you perceive in all this noble company
   Where most you owe obedience?
Desdemona.   My noble father,
   I do perceive here a divided duty.
   To you I am bound for life and education;   180
   My life and education both do learn me
   How to respect you. You are the lord of duty,
   I am hitherto your daughter. But here's my husband,
   And so much duty as my mother showed
   To you, preferring you before her father,   185
   So much I challenge° that I may profess
   Due to the Moor my lord.
Brabantio.   God be with you. I have done.
   Please it your Grace, on to the state affairs.
   I had rather to adopt a child than get° it.
   Come hither, Moor.   190
   I here do give thee that with all my heart
   Which, but thou hast already, with all my heart
   I would keep from thee. For your sake,° jewel,
   I am glad at soul I have no other child,

---

¹⁵⁹ *passing* surpassing   ¹⁷¹ *take . . . best* i.e., make the best of this disaster
¹⁸⁶ *challenge* claim as right   ¹⁸⁹ *get* beget   ¹⁹³ *For your sake* because of you

For thy escape would teach me tyranny,   195
To hang clogs on them. I have done, my lord.
Duke.   Let me speak like yourself and lay a sentence°
Which, as a grise° or step, may help these lovers.
When remedies are past, the griefs are ended
By seeing the worst, which late on hopes depended.°   200
To mourn a mischief that is past and gone
Is the next° way to draw new mischief on.
What cannot be preserved when fortune takes,
Patience her injury a mock'ry makes.
The robbed that smiles, steals something from the thief;   205
He robs himself that spends a bootless ° grief.
Brabantio.   So let the Turk of Cyprus us beguile:
We lose it not so long as we can smile.
He bears the sentence well that nothing bears
But the free comfort which from thence he hears;   210
But he bears both the sentence and the sorrow
That to pay grief must of poor patience borrow.
These sentences, to sugar, or to gall,
Being strong on both sides, are equivocal.
But words are words. I never yet did hear   215
That the bruisèd heart was piercèd° through the ear.
I humbly beseech you, proceed to th' affairs of state.
Duke.   The Turk with a most mighty preparation makes for
Cyprus. Othello, the fortitude° of the place is best known to
you; and though we have there a substitute° of most allowed   220
sufficiency,° yet opinion, a more sovereign mistress of ef-
fects, throws a more safer voice on you.° You must therefore
be content to slubber° the gloss of your new fortunes with
this more stubborn and boisterous° expedition.
Othello.   The tyrant Custom, most grave senators,   225
Hath made the flinty and steel couch of war

---

[197] *lay a sentence* provide a maxim   [198] *grise* step   [200] *late on hopes depended* was supported by hope (of a better outcome) until lately   [202] *next*
closest, surest   [206] *bootless* valueless   [216] *pierced* (some editors emend to
pieced, i.e., "healed." But *pierced* makes good sense: Brabantio is saying in
effect that his heart cannot be further hurt [pierced] by the indignity of the
useless, conventional advice the Duke offers him. *Pierced* can also mean,
however, "lanced" in the medical sense, and would then mean "treated")
[219] *fortitude* fortification   [220] *substitute* viceroy   [220-21] *most allowed sufficiency* generally acknowledged capability   [221-22] *opinion . . . you* i.e., the
general opinion, which finally controls affairs, is that you would be the best
man in this situation   [223] *slubber* besmear   [224] *stubborn* and *boisterous*
rough and violent

My thrice-driven° bed of down. I do agnize°
A natural and prompt alacrity
I find in hardness and do undertake
This present wars against the Ottomites.   230
Most humbly, therefore, bending to your state,
I crave fit disposition for my wife,
Due reference of place, and exhibition,°
With such accommodation and besort
As levels with° her breeding.

Duke.   Why, at her father's.   235
Brabantio. I will not have it so.
Othello.   Nor I.
Desdemona. Nor would I there reside,
    To put my father in impatient thoughts
    By being in his eye. Most gracious Duke,
    To my unfolding° lend your prosperous° ear,   240
    And let me find a charter° in your voice,
    T' assist my simpleness.
Duke.   What would you, Desdemona?
Desdemona. That I love the Moor to live with him,
    My downright violence, and storm of fortunes,
    May trumpet to the world. My heart's subdued   245
    Even to the very quality of my lord.°
    I saw Othello's visage in his mind,
    And to his honors and his valiant parts
    Did I my soul and fortunes consecrate.
    So that, dear lords, if I be left behind,   250
    A moth of peace, and he go to the war,
    The rites° for why I love him are bereft me,
    And I a heavy interim shall support
    By his dear absence. Let me go with him.
Othello. Let her have your voice.°   255
    Vouch with me, heaven, I therefore beg it not
    To please the palate of my appetite,
    Nor to comply with heat° — the young affects°
    In me defunct — and proper satisfaction;°

---

²²⁷ *thrice-driven* i.e., softest   ²²⁷ *agnize* know in myself   ²³³ *exhibition* grant of funds   ²³⁵ *levels with* is suitable to   ²⁴⁰ *unfolding* explanation   ²⁴⁰ *prosperous* favoring   ²⁴¹ *charter* permission   ²⁴⁵⁻⁴⁶ *My . . . lord* i.e., I have become one in nature and being with the man I married (therefore, I too would go to the wars like a soldier)   ²⁵² *rites* (may refer either to the marriage rites or to the rites, formalities, of war)   ²⁵⁵ *voice* consent   ²⁵⁸ *heat* lust   ²⁵⁸ *affects* passions   ²⁵⁹ *proper satisfaction* i.e., consummation of the marriage

But to be free and bounteous to her mind;   260
And heaven defend° your good souls that you think
I will your serious and great business scant
When she is with me. No, when light-winged toys
Of feathered Cupid seel° with wanton° dullness
My speculative and offices instrument,°   ⁄   265
That my disports corrupt and taint my business,
Let housewives make a skillet of my helm,
And all indign° and base adversities
Make head° against my estimation!° —
Duke. Be it as you shall privately determine,   270
Either for her stay or going. Th' affair cries haste,
And speed must answer it.
First Senator.   ˙ You must away tonight.
Othello. With all my heart.
Duke. At nine i' th' morning here we'll meet again.
Othello, leave some officer behind,   275
And he shall our commission bring to you,
And such things else of quality and respect
As doth import you.
Othello.   So please your grace, my ancient;
A man he is of honesty and trust.
To his conveyance I assign my wife.   280
With what else needful your good grace shall think
To be sent after me.
Duke.   Let it be so.
Good night to every one. [*To Brabantio*] And, noble signior,
If virtue no delighted° beauty lack,
Your son-in-law is far more fair than black.   285
First Senator. Adieu, brave Moor. Use Desdemona well.
Brabantio. Look to her, Moor, if thou hast eyes to see:
She has deceived her father, and may thee.

[*Exeunt Duke, Senators, Officers, & c.*]

Othello. My life upon her faith! Honest Iago,
My Desdmona must I leave to thee.   290
I prithee let thy wife attend on her,
And bring them after in the best advantage.°
Come, Desdemona. I have but an hour

---

²⁶¹ *defend* forbid   ²⁶⁴ *seel* sew   up   ²⁶⁴ *wanton* lascivious   ²⁶⁵ *speculative
. . . instrument* i.e., sight (and, by extension, the mind   ²⁶⁸ *indign* unworthy
²⁶⁹ *Make head* form an army, i.e., attack   ²⁶⁹ *estimation* reputation   ²⁸⁴ *delighted* delightful   ²⁹² *advantage* opportunity

Of love, of worldly matter, and direction
To spend with thee. We must obey the time.   295

Exit [Moor with Desdemona].

Roderigo. Iago?

Iago. What say'st thou, noble heart?

Roderigo. What will I do, think'st thou?

Iago. Why, go to bed and sleep.

Roderigo. I will incontinently° drown myself.   300

Iago. If thou dost, I shall never love thee after. Why, thou silly
gentleman?

Roderigo. It is silliness to live when to live is torment; and then
have we a prescription to die when death is our physician.

Iago. O villainous! I have looked upon the world for four   305
times seven years, and since I could distinguish betwixt a
benefit and an injury, I never found man that knew how to
love himself. Ere I would say I would drown myself for the
love of a guinea hen, I would change my humanity with a
baboon.   310

Roderigo. What should I do? I confess it is my shame to be so
fond, but it is not in my virtue° to amend it.

Iago. Virtue? A fig! 'Tis in ourselves that we are thus, or
thus. Our bodies are our gardens, to the which our wills are
gardeners; so that if we will plant nettles or sow lettuce, set   315
hyssop and weed up thyme, supply it with one gender of
herbs or distract° it with many — either to have it sterile
with idleness or manured with industry — why, the power
and corrigible° authority of this lies in our wills. If the balance of our lives had not one scale of reason to poise another   320
of sensuality, the blood and baseness of our natures would
conduct us to most prepost'rous conclusions.° But we have
reason to cool our raging motions, our carnal sting or un-
bitted° lusts, whereof I take this that you call love to be a
sect or scion.°   325

Roderigo. It cannot be.

Iago. It is merely a lust of the blood and a permission of the
will. Come, be a man! Drown thyself? Drown cats and blind
puppies! I have professed me thy friend, and I confess me
knit to thy deserving with cables of perdurable toughness. I   330
could never better stead° thee than now. Put money in thy

---

[300] *incontinently* at once   [312] *virtue* strength (Roderigo is saying that his
nature controls him)   [317] *distract* vary   [319] *corrigible* corrective   [322] *conclusions* ends   [324] *unbitted* i.e., uncontrolled   [325] *sect or scion* off-shoot
[331] *stead* serve

purse. Follow thou the wars; defeat thy favor° with an
usurped° beard. I say, put money in thy purse. It cannot be
long that Desdemona should continue her love to the Moor.
Put money in thy purse. Nor he his to her. It was a violent   335
commencement in her and thou shalt see an answerable°
sequestration — put but money in thy purse. These Moors
are changeable in their wills — fill thy purse with money.
The food that to him now is as luscious as locusts° shall be to
him shortly as bitter as coloquintida.° She must change for   340
youth; when she is sated with his body, she will find the
errors of her choice. Therefore, put money in thy purse. If
thou wilt needs damn thyself, do it a more delicate way
than drowning. Make all the money thou canst. If sanc-
timony° and a frail vow betwixt an erring° barbarian and   345
supersubtle Venetian be not too hard for my wits, and all the
tribe of hell, thou shalt enjoy her. Therefore, make money. A
pox of drowning thyself, it is clean out of the way. Seek thou
rather to be hanged in compassing° thy joy than to be
drowned and go without her.   350

Roderigo. Wilt thou be fast to my hopes, if I depend on the
issue?

Iago. Thou art sure of me. Go, make money. I have told thee
often, and I retell thee again and again, I hate the Moor. My
cause is hearted;° thine hath no less reason. Let us be con-   355
junctive° in our revenge against him. If thou canst cuckold
him, thou dost thyself a pleasure, me a sport. There are many
events in the womb of time, which will be delivered. Tra-
verse, go, provide thy money! We will have more of this
tomorrow. Adieu.   360

Roderigo. Where shall we meet i' th' morning?

Iago. At my lodging.

Roderigo. I'll be with thee betimes.

Iago. Go to, farewell. Do you hear, Roderigo?

Roderigo. I'll sell all my land.   *Exit.*   365

Iago. Thus do I ever make my fool my purse;
  For I mine own gained knowledge° should profane
  If I would time expend with such snipe
  But for my sport and profit. I hate the Moor,

---

³³² *defeat thy favor* disguise your face   ³³³ *unsurped* assumed   ³³⁶ *answer-
able* similar   ³³⁹ *locusts* (a sweet fruit)   ³⁴⁰ *coloquintida* a purgative derived from a bitter apple   ³⁴⁵ *sanctimony* sacred bond (of marriage)   ³⁴⁵ *erring* wandering   ³⁴⁹ *compassing* encompassing, achieving   ³⁵⁵ *hearted*
deepseated in the heart   ³⁵⁶ *conjunctive* joined   ³⁶⁷ *gained knowledge* i.e.,
practical, worldly wisdom

And it is thought abroad that 'twixt my sheets   370
H'as done my office. I know not if't be true,
But I, for mere suspicion in that kind,
Will do, as if for surety.° He holds me well;
The better shall my purpose work on him.
Cassio's a proper° man. Let me see now: 375
To get his place, and to plume up my will°
In double knavery. How? How? Let's see.
After some time, to abuse Othello's ears
That he is too familiar with his wife.
He hath a person and a smooth dispose°   380
To be suspected — framed° to make women false.
The Moor is of a free and open nature
That thinks men honest that but seem to be so;
And will as tenderly be led by th' nose
As asses are.   385
I have't! It is engendered! Hell and night
Must bring this monstrous birth to the world's light.

                                                            [*Exit.*]

ACT II

Scene I   [*Cyprus.*]

Enter Montano and two Gentlemen, [one above].°

Montano. What from the cape can you discern at sea?
First Gentleman. Nothing at all, it is a high-wrought flood.
     I cannot 'twixt the heaven and the main
     Descry a sail.
Montano. Methinks the wind spoke aloud at land;   5
     A fuller blast ne'er shook our battlements.
     If it hath ruffianed so upon the sea,
     What ribs of oak, when mountains melt on them,
     Can hold the mortise? What shall we hear of this?
Second Gentleman. A segregation° of the Turkish fleet   10

---

³⁷³ *surety* certainty   ³⁷⁵ *proper* handsome   ³⁷⁶ *plume up my will* (many explanations have been offered for this crucial line, which in Q₁ reads "make up my will." The general sense is something like "to make more proud and gratify my ego")   ³⁸⁰ *dispose* manner   ³⁸¹ *framed* designed II.i. s.d. (the Folio arrangement of this scene requires that the First Gentleman stand above — on the upper stage — and act as a lookout reporting sights which cannot be seen by Montano standing below on the main stage)   ¹⁰ *segregation* separation

For do but stand upon the foaming shore,
The chidden billow seems to pelt the clouds:
The wind-shaked surge, with high and monstrous main,°
Seems to cast water on the burning Bear
And quench the guards of th' ever-fixèd pole.°   15
I never did like molestation view
On the enchafèd flood.
Montano.   If that the Turkish fleet
Be not ensheltered and embayed, they are drowned;
It is impossible to bear it out.

 Enter a [third] Gentleman.

Third Gentleman. News, lads! Our wars are done.   20
The desperate tempest hath so banged the Turks
That their designment halts. A noble ship of Venice
Hath seen a grievous wrack and sufferance°
On most part of their fleet.
Montano. How? Is this true?
Third Gentleman.   The ship is here put in,   25
A Veronesa; Michael Cassio,
Lieutenant to the warlike Moor Othello,
Is come on shore; the Moor himself at sea,
And is in full commission here for Cyprus.
Montano. I am glad on't. 'Tis a worthy governor.   30
Third Gentleman. But this same Cassio, through he speak of
  comfort
Touching the Turkish loss, yet he looks sadly
And prays the Moor be safe, for they were parted
With foul and violent tempest.
Montano.   Pray heavens he be;
For I have served him, and the man commands   35
Like a full soldier. Let's to the seaside, ho!
As well to see the vessel that's come in
As to throw out our eyes for brave Othello,
Even till we make the main and th' aerial blue
And indistinct regard.°
Third Gentleman.   Come, let's do so;   40
For every minute is expectancy
Of more arrivancie.°

 Enter Cassio.

---

[13] *main* (both "ocean" and "strength")   [14-15] *Seems . . . pole* (the constellation Ursa Minor contains two stars which are the *guards*, or companions, of the *pole*, or North Star)   [23] *sufferance* damage   [39-40] *the main . . . regard* i.e., the sea and sky become indistinguishable   [42] *arrivancie* arrivals

Cassio. Thanks, you the valiant of the warlike isle,
That so approve° the Moor. O, let the heavens
Give him defense against the elements,   45
For I have lost him on a dangerous sea.
Montano. Is he well shipped?
Cassio. His bark is stoutly timbered, and his pilot
Of very expert and approved allowance;°
Therefore my hopes, not surfeited to death,°   50
Stand in bold cure.° *(Within)* A sail, a sail, a sail!
Cassio. What noise?
First Gentleman. The town is empty; on the brow o' th' sea
Stand tanks of people, and they cry, "A sail!"
Cassio. My hopes do shape him for the governor.   55

                                                        [*A shot.*]

Second Gentleman. They do discharge their shot of courtesy:
Our friends at least.
Cassio.   I pray you, sir, go forth
And give us truth who 'tis that is arrived.
Second Gentleman. I shall.   [*Exit.*]
Montano. But, good lieutenant, is your general wived?   60
Cassio. Most fortunately. He hath achieved a maid
That paragons° description and wild fame;°
One that excels the quirks of blazoning pens,°
And in th' essential vesture of creation°
Does tire the ingener.°

     Enter [*Second*] *Gentleman.*

                    How now? Who has put in?   65
Second Gentleman. 'Tis one Iago, ancient to the general.
Cassio. H'as had most favorable and happy speed:
Tempests themselves, high seas, and howling winds,
The guttered° rocks and congregated° sands,
Traitors ensteeped° to enclog the guiltless keel,   70
As having sense° of beauty, do omit

---

⁴⁴ *approve* ("honor" or, perhaps, "are as warlike and valiant as your governor")   ⁴⁹ *approved allowance* known and tested   ⁵⁰ *not surfeited to death* i.e., not so great as to be in danger   ⁵¹ *Stand in bold cure* i.e., are likely to be restored   ⁶² *paragons* exceeds   ⁶² *wild fame* extravagant report   ⁶³ *quirks of blazoning pens* ingenuities of praising pens   ⁶⁴ *essential vesture of creation* i.e., essential human nature as given by the Creator   ⁶⁵ *tire the ingener* a difficult line that probably means something like "outdoes the human ability to imagine and picture"   ⁶⁹ *guttered* jagged   ⁶⁹ *congregated* gathered   ⁷⁰ *ensteeped* submerged   ⁷¹ *sense* awareness.

Their mortal° natures, letting go safely by
The divine Desdemona.
Montano.   What is she?
Cassio.   She that I spake of, our great captain's captain,
Left in the conduct of the bold Iago,   75
Whose footing° here anticipates our thoughts
A se'nnight's° speed. Great Jove, Othello guard,
And swell his sail with thine own pow'rful breath,
That he may bless this bay with his tall° ship,
Make love's quick pants in Desdemona's arms,   80
Give renewed fire to our extincted spirits.

Enter Desdemona, Iago, Roderigo, and Emilia.

O, behold! The riches of the ship is come on shore!
You men of Cyprus, let her have your knees.   [*Kneeling.*]
Hail to thee, lady! and the grace of heaven,
Before, behind thee, and on every hand,   85
Enwheel thee round.
Desdemona.   I thank you valiant Cassio.
What tidings can you tell of my lord?
Cassio. He is not yet arrived, nor know I aught
But that he's well and will be shortly here.
Desdemona. O but I fear. How lost you company?   90
Cassio. The great contention of sea and skies
Parted our fellowship. *(Within)* "A sail, a sail!"   [*A shot.*]
But hark. A sail!
Second Gentleman. They give this greeting to the citadel;
This likewise is a friend.
Cassio.   See for the news.   95

[*Exit Gentleman.*]

Good ancient, you are welcome. [*To Emilia*] Welcome, mistress.
Let it not gall your patience, good Iago,
That I extend° my manners. 'Tis my breeding°
That gives me this bold show of courtesy.   [*Kisses Emilia.*]
Iago. Sir, would she give you so much of her lips   100
As of her tongue she oft bestows on me,
You would have enough.
Desdemona.   Alas, she has no speech.
Iago. In faith, too much.

---

⁷² *mortal* deadly   ⁷⁶ *footing* landing   ⁷⁷ *se'n night's* week's   ⁷⁹ *tall* brave
⁹⁸ *extend* stretch   ⁹⁸ *breeding* careful training in manners (Cassio is considerably more the polished gentleman than Iago, and aware of it)

I find it still when I have leave to sleep.°
Marry, before your ladyship,° I grant,   105
She puts her tongue a little in her heart
And chides with thinking.
Emilia.   You have little cause to say so.
Iago. Come on, come on! You are pictures° out of door,
Bells in your parlors, wildcats in your kitchens,
Saints in your injuries,° devils being offended,   110
Players in your housewifery,° and housewives in your beds.
Desdemona. O, fie upon thee, slanderer!
Iago. Nay, it is true, or else I am a Turk:
You rise to play, and go to bed to work.
Emilia. You shall not write my praise.
Iago.   No, let me not.   115
Desdemona. What wouldst write of me, if thou shouldst praise me?
Iago. O gentle lady, do not put me to't.
For I am nothing if not critical.
Desdemona. Come on, assay. There's one gone to the harbor?
Iago. Ay, madam.
Desdemona [*Aside*]. I am not merry; but I do beguile   120
The thing I am by seeming otherwise. —
Come, how wouldst thou praise me?
Iago. I am about it; but indeed my invention
Comes from my pate as birdlime° does from frieze° —
It plucks out brains and all. But my Muse labors,   125
And thus she is delivered:
If she be fair° and wise: fairness and wit,
The one's for use, the other useth it.
Desdemona. Well praised. How if she be black° and witty?
Iago. If she be black, and thereto have a wit,   130
She'll find a white that shall her blackness fit.
Desdemona. Worse and worse!
Emilia. How if fair and foolish?
Iago. She never yet was foolish that was fair,
For even her folly helped her to an heir.   135
Desdemona. These are old fond° paradoxes to make fools

[104] *still . . . sleep* i.e., even when she allows me to sleep she continues to scold
[105] *before your ladyship* in your presence   [108] *pictures* models (of virtue)
[110] *in your injuries* when you injure others   [111] *housewifery* this word can
mean "careful, economical household management," and Iago would then be
accusing women of only pretending to be good housekeepers, while in bed
are either [1] economical of their favors, or more likely [2] serious and
dedicated workers   [124] *birdlime* a sticky substance put on branches to catch
birds   [124] *frieze* rough cloth   [127] *fair* light-complexioned   [129] *black* bru-
nette   [136] *fond* foolish

laugh i' th' alehouse. What miserable praise hast thou for her
that's foul and foolish?

Iago.   There's none so foul, and foolish thereunto,
But does foul pranks which fair and wise ones do.   140

Desdemona.   O heavy ignorance. Thou praisest the worst best.
But what praise couldst thou bestow on a deserving woman
indeed — one that in the authority of her merit did justly put
on the vouch of very malice itself?°

Iago.   She that was ever fair, and never proud;   145
Had tongue at will, and yet was never loud;
Never lacked gold, and yet went never gay;
Fled from her wish, and yet said "Now I may";
She that being angered, her revenge being nigh,
Bade her wrong stay, and her displeasure fly;   150
She that in wisdom never was so frail
To change the cod's head for the salmon's tail;°
She that could think, and nev'r disclose her mind;
See suitors following, and not look behind:
She was a wight° (if ever such wights were) —   155

Desdemona.   To do what?

Iago.   To suckle fools and chronicle small beer.°

Desdemona.   O most lame and impotent conclusion. Do not
learn of him, Emilia, though he be thy husband. How say   160
you, Cassio? Is he not a most profane and liberal° counselor?

Cassio.   He speaks home,° madam. You may relish him more
in° the soldier than in the scholar. [*Takes Desdemona's
hand.*]

Iago [*Aside*].   He takes her by the palm. Ay well said, whisper!   165
With as little a web as this will I ensnare as great a fly as
Cassio. Ay, smile upon her, do! I will gyve° thee in thine
own courtship. — You say true; 'tis so, indeed! — If such
tricks as these strip you out of your lieutenantry, it had been
better you had not kissed your three fingers so oft — which   170
now again you are most apt to play the sir° in. Very good!
Well kissed! An excellent curtsy!° 'Tis so, indeed. Yet again

---

[143-44] *one . . . itself* i.e., a woman so honest and deserving that even malice
would be forced to approve of her   [152] *To . . . tail* i.e., to exchange something
valuable for something useless   [155] *wight* person   [157] *chronicle small
beer* i.e., keep household accounts (the most trivial of occupations in Iago's
opinion)   [161] *liberal* licentious   [163] *speaks home* thrusts deeply with his
speech   [163-64] *relish him more in* enjoy him more as   [167] *gyve* bind   [171] *the
sir* the fashionable gentleman   [172] *curtsy* courtesy, i.e., bow

your fingers to your lips? Would they were clyster pipes°
for your sake! [*Trumpets within.*] The Moor! I know his
trumpet.° 175
Cassio. 'Tis truly so.
Desdemona. Let's meet him and receive him.
Cassio. Lo, where he comes.

Enter Othello and Attendants.

Othello. O my fair warrior!
Desdemona.   My dear Othello.
Othello. It gives me wonder great as my content 180
To see you here before me. O my soul's joy!
If after every tempest come such calms,
May the winds blow till they have wakened death.
And let the laboring bark climb hills of seas
Olympus-high, and duck again as low 185
As hell's from heaven. If it were now to die,
'Twere now to be most happy; for I fear
My soul hath her content so absolute
That not another comfort like to this
Succeeds in unknown fate.
Desdemona.   The heavens forbid 190
But that our loves and comforts should increase
Even as our days do grow.
Othello.   Amen to that, sweet powers!
I cannot speak enough of this content:
It stops me here [*touches his heart*]; it is too much of joy.
And this, and this, the greatest discords be   [*They kiss.*] 195
That e'er our hearts shall make!
Iago. [*Aside*]   O, you are well tuned now!
But I'll set down the pegs° that make this music,
As honest as I am.
Othello.   Come, let us to the castle.
New, friends! Our wars are done; the Turks are drowned.
How does my old acquaintance of this isle? 200
Honey, you shall be well desired in Cyprus;
I have found great love amongst them. O my sweet,
I prattle out of fashion, and I dote
In mine own comforts. I prithee, good Iago,
Go to the bay and disembark my coffers. 205
Bring thou the master to the citadel;

---

173 *clyster pipes* enema tubes   175 *his trumpet* (great men had their own
distinctive calls)   197 *set down the pegs* loosen the strings (to produce dis-
cord)

> He is a good one and his worthiness
> Does challenge° much respect. Come, Desdemona,
> Once more well met at Cyprus.

Exit Othello and Desdemona [and all but Iago and Roderigo].

Iago [*To an Attendant*]. Do thou meet me presently at the   210
harbor. [*To Roderigo*] Come hither. If thou be'st valiant (as
they say base men being in love have then a nobility in their
natures more than is native to them), list me. The lieutenant
tonight watches on the court of guard.° First, I must tell thee
this: Desdemona is directly in love with him.   215
Roderigo. With him? Why, 'tis not possible.
Iago. Lay thy finger thus [*puts his finger to his lips.*], and let
thy soul be instructed. Mark me with what violence she first
loved the Moor but for bragging and telling her fantastical
lies. To love him still for prating? Let not thy discreet heart   220
think it. Her eye must be fed. And what delight shall she
have to look on the devil? When the blood is made dull with
the act of sport, there should be a game° to inflame it and to
give satiety a fresh appetite, loveliness in favor,° sympathy
in years,° manners, and beauties; all which the Moor is defec-   225
tive in. Now for want of these required conveniences,° her
delicate tenderness will find itself abused, begin to heave
the gorge,° disrelish and abhor the Moor. Very nature will
instruct her in it and compel her to some second choice.
Now sir, this granted — as it is a most pregnant° and un-   230
forced position — who stands so eminent in the degree of
this fortune as Cassio does? A knave very voluble; no further
conscionable° than in putting on the mere form of civil and
humane° seeming for the better compass of his salt° and most
hidden loose° affection. Why, none! Why, none! A slipper°   235
and subtle knave, a finder of occasion, that has an eye can
stamp and counterfeit advantages, though true advantage
never present itself. A devilish knave. Besides, the knave is
handsome, young, and hath all those requisites in him that
folly and green minds look after. A pestilent complete knave,   240
and the woman hath found him already.

---

²⁰⁸ *challenge* require, exact   ²¹⁴ *court of guard* guardhouse   ²²³ *game* sport
(with the added sense of "gamey," "rank,")   ²²⁴ *favor* countenance, appearance   ²²⁴⁻²⁵ *sympathy in years* sameness of age   ²²⁶ *conveniences* advantages
²²⁷⁻²⁸ *heave the gorge* vomit   ²³⁰ *pregnant* likely   ²³²⁻³³ *no further con-*
scionable having no more conscience   ²³⁴ *humane* polite   ²³⁴ *salt* lecher-
ous   ²³⁵ *loose* immoral   ²³⁵ *slipper* slippery

Roderigo. I cannot believe that in her; she's full of most blessed condition.

Iago. Blessed fig's-end! The wine she drinks is made of grapes. If she had been blessed, she would never have loved the Moor. Blessed pudding! Didst thou not see her paddle with the palm of his hand? Didst not mark that?   245

Roderigo. Yes, that I did; but that was but courtesy.

Iago. Lechery, by this hand! [*Extends his index finger.*] An index° and obscure prologue to the history of lust and foul thoughts. They met so near with their lips that their breaths embraced together. Villainous thoughts, Roderigo. When these mutualities so marshal the way, hard at hand comes the master and main exercise, th' incorporate° conclusion: Pish! But, sir, be you ruled by me. I have brought you from Venice. Watch you tonight; for the command, I'll lay't upon you. Cassio knows you not. I'll not be far from you. Do you find some occasion to anger Cassio, either by speaking too loud, or tainting° his discipline, or from what other course you please which the time shall more favorably minister.   250 255 260

Roderigo. Well.

Iago. Sir, he's rash and very sudden in choler,° and haply may strike at you. Provoke him that he may; for even out of that will I cause these of Cyprus to mutiny, whose qualification shall come into no true taste° again but by the displanting of Cassio. So shall you have a shorter journey to your desires by the means I shall then have to prefer them; and the impediment most profitably removed without the which there were no expectation of our prosperity.   265

Roderigo. I will do this if you can bring it to any opportunity.   270

Iago. I warrant thee. Meet me by and by at the citadel. I must fetch his necessaries ashore. Farewell.

Roderigo. Adieu.   *Exit.*

Iago. That Cassio loves her, I do well believe't;
That she loves him, 'tis apt and of great credit.   275
The Moor, howbeit that I endure him not,
Is of a constant, loving, noble nature,
And I dare think he'll prove to Desdemona
A most dear° husband. Now I do love her too;
Not out of absolute° lust, though peradventure°   280
I stand accountant for as great a sin,

---

²⁵⁰ *index* pointer   ²⁵⁴ *incorporate* carnal   ²⁵⁹ *tainting* discrediting   ²⁶² *choler* anger   ²⁶⁵ *qualification . . . taste* i.e., appeasement will not be brought about (wine was "qualified" by adding water)   ²⁷⁹ *dear* expensive   ²⁸⁰ *out of absolute* absolutely out of   ²⁸⁰ *peradventure* perchance

But partly led to diet° my revenge,
· For that I do suspect the lusty Moor
Hath leaped into my seat; the thought whereof
Doth, like a poisonous mineral, gnaw my inwards;   285
And nothing can or shall content my soul
Till I am evened with him, wife for wife.
Or failing so, yet that I put the Moor
At least into a jealousy so strong
That judgment cannot cure. Which thing to do,   290
If this poor trash of Venice, whom I trace°
For his quick hunting, stand the putting on,
I'll have our Michael Cassio on the hip,
Abuse him to the Moor in the right garb°
(For I fear Cassio with my nightcap too),   295
Make the Moor thank me, love me, and reward me
For making him egregiously an ass
And practicing upon°his peace and quiet,
Even to madness. 'Tis here, but yet confused:
Knavery's plain face is never seen till used.   *Exit.*   300

Scene II   [*A street.*]

Enter Othello's Herald, with a proclamation.

Herald. It is Othello's pleasure, our noble and valiant general, that upon certain tidings now arrived importing the
mere perdition° of the Turkish fleet, every man put himself
into triumph. Some to dance, some to make bonfires, each
man to what sport and revels his addition° leads him. For,   5
besides these beneficial news, it is the celebration of his
nuptial. So much was his pleasure should be proclaimed. All
offices° are open, and there is full liberty of feasting from
this present hour of five till the bell have told eleven. Bless
the isle of Cyprus and our noble general Othello!   *Exit.*   10

Scene III   [*The citadel of Cyprus.*]

Enter Othello, Desdemona, Cassio, and Attendants.

Othello. Good Michael, look you to the guard tonight.
Let's teach ourselves that honorable stop,
Not to outsport discretion.

²⁸²*diet* feed   ²⁹¹*trace* (most editors emend to "trash," meaning to hang
weights on a dog to slow his hunting: but "trace" clearly means something
like "put on the trace" or "set on the track")   ²⁹⁴*right garb* i.e., "proper
fashion"   ²⁹⁸*practicing upon* scheming to destroy   II.ii.   ³*mere perdition*
absolute destruction   ⁵*addition* rank   ⁸*offices* kitchens and storerooms of
food.

Cassio. Iago hath discretion what to do;
　　But notwithstanding, with my personal eye　　　　　　5
　　Will I look to't.
Othello.　　　　　Iago is most honest.
　　Michael, good night. Tomorrow with your earliest
　　Let me have speech with you. [*To Desdemona*] Come, my'
　　　　dear love,
　　The purchase made, the fruits are to ensue,
　　That profit's yet to come 'tween me and you.　　　　　10
　　Good night.

　　　　　　Exit [*Othello with Desdemona and Attendants*].

　　Enter Iago.

Cassio. Welcome, Iago. We must to the watch.
Iago. Not this hour, lieutenant; 'tis not yet ten o' th' clock.
　　Our general cast° us thus early for the love of his Desde-
　　mona; who let us not therefore blame. He hath not yet made　　15
　　wanton the night with her, and she is sport for Jove.
Cassio. She's a most exquisite lady.
Iago. And, I'll warrant her, full of game.
Cassio. Indeed, she's a most fresh and delicate creature.
Iago. What an eye she has! Methinks it sounds a parley to　　20
　　provocation.
Cassio. An inviting eye; and yet methinks right modest.
Iago. And when she speaks, is it not an alarum° to love?
Cassio. She is indeed perfection.
Iago. Well, happiness to their sheets! Come, lieutenant, I have　　25
　　a stoup° of wine, and here without are a brace of Cyprus
　　gallants that would fain have a measure to the health of black
　　Othello.
Cassio. Not tonight, good Iago. I have very poor and unhappy
　　brains for drinking; I could well wish courtesy would invent　　30
　　some other custom of entertainment.
Iago. O, they are our friends. But one cup! I'll drink for you.
Cassio. I have drunk but one cup tonight, and that was craftily
　　qualified° too; and behold what innovation it makes here. I
　　am unfortunate in the infirmity and dare not task my weak-　　35
　　ness with any more.
Iago. What, man! 'Tis a night of revels, the gallants desire it.
Cassio. Where are they?
Iago. Here, at the door. I pray you call them in.

II.iii.　　¹⁴ *cast* dismissed　²³ *alarum* the call to action, "general quarters"
²⁶ *stoup* two-quart tankard　³⁴ *qualified* diluted

Cassio. I'll do't, but it dislikes me.   *Exit.*   40
Iago. If I can fasten but one cup upon him
   With that which he hath drunk tonight already,
   He'll be as full of quarrel and offense
   As my young mistress' dog. Now, my sick fool Roderigo,
   Whom love hath turned almost the wrong side out,   45
   To Desdemona hath tonight caroused
   Potations pottle-deep;° and he's to watch.
   Three else° of Cyprus, noble swelling spirits,
   That hold their honors in a wary distance,°
   The very elements of this warlike isle,   50
   Have I tonight flustered with flowing cups,
   And they watch too. Now, 'mongst this flock of drunkards
   Am I to put our Cassio in some action
   That may offend the isle. But here they come.

   Enter Cassio, Montano, and Gentlemen.

   If consequence do but approve my dream,   55
   My boat sails freely, both with wind and stream.
Cassio. 'Fore God, they have given me a rouse° already.
Montano. Good faith, a little one; not past a pint, as I am a
   soldier.
Iago. Some wine, ho!   60
   [*Sings*] And let me the canakin clink, clink;
        And let me the canakin clink.
           A soldier's a man;
           O man's life's but a span.
           Why then, let a soldier drink.   65
   Some wine, boys!
Cassio. 'Fore God, an excellent song!
Iago. I learned it in England, where indeed they are most
   potent in potting. Your Dane, your German, and your swag-
   bellied° Hollander — Drink, ho! — are nothing to your En-   70
   glish.
Cassio. Is your Englishman so exquisite° in his drinking?
Iago. Why, he drinks you with facility your Dane dead drunk;
   he sweats not to overthrow your Almain; he gives your Hol-
   lander a vomit ere the next pottle can be filled.   75
Cassio. To the health of our general!
Montano. I am for it, lieutenant, and I'll do you justice.

---

[47] *pottle-deep* to the bottom of the cup   [48] *else* others   [49] *hold . . . distance*
are scrupulous in maintaining their honor   [57] *rouse* drink   [69-70] *swag-bellied*
pendulous-bellied   [72] *exquisite* superb

Iago. O sweet England!
      [*Sings*] King Stephen was and a worthy peer;
          His breeches cost him but a crown;   80
          He held them sixpence all too dear,
          With that he called the tailor lown.°
          He was a wight of high renown,
          And thou art but of low degree:
          'Tis pride that pulls the country down;   85
          And take thine auld cloak about thee.
      Some wine, ho!
Cassio. 'Fore God, this is a more exquisite song than the other.
Iago. Will you hear't again?
Cassio. No, for I hold him to be unworthy of his place that does   90
    those things. Well, God's above all; and there be souls must
    be saved, and there be souls must not be saved.
Iago. It's true, good lieutenant.
Cassio. For mine own part — no offense to the general, nor any
    man of quality — I hope to be saved.   95
Iago. And so do I too, lieutenant.
Cassio. Ay, but, by your leave, not before me. The lieutenant is
    to be saved before the ancient. Let's have no more of this;
    let's to our affairs. — God forgive us our sins! — Gentlemen,
    let's look to our business. Do not think, gentlemen, I am   100
    drunk. This is my ancient; this is my right hand, and this is
    my left. I am not drunk now. I can stand well enough, and I
    speak well enough.
Gentlemen. Excellent well!
Cassio. Why, very well then. You must not think then that I am   105
    drunk.   *Exit.*
Montano. To th' platform, masters. Come, let's set the watch.
Iago. You see this fellow that is gone before.
    He's a soldier fit to stand by Caesar
    And give direction; and do but see his vice.   110
    'Tis to his virtue a just equinox,°
    The one as long as th' other. 'Tis pity of him.
    I fear the trust Othello puts him in,
    On some odd time of his infirmity,
    Will shake this island.
Montano.   But is he often thus?   115
Iago. 'Tis evermore his prologue to his sleep:
    He'll watch the horologe a double set°
    If drink rock not his cradle.

---

⁸² **lown** lout ¹¹¹ **just equinox** exact balance (of dark and light) ¹¹⁷ **watch
. . . set** stay awake twice around the clock

Monatano.   It were well
    The general were put in mind of it.
    Perhaps he sees it not, or his good nature   120
    Prizes the virtue that appears in Cassio
    And looks not on his evils. Is not this true?

    Enter Roderigo.

Iago [*Aside*]. How now, Roderigo?
    I pray you after the lieutenant, go!   [*Exit Roderigo.*]
Montano. And 'tis great pity that the noble Moor   125
    Should hazard such a place as his own second
    With one of an ingraft° infirmity.
    It were an honest action to say so
    To the Moor.
Iago.   Not I, for this fair island!
    I do love Cassio well and would do much   130
    To cure him of this evil.   ("Help! Help!" *Within*.)
    But hark! What noise?

    Enter Cassio, pursuing Roderigo.

Cassio. Zounds, you rogue! You rascal!
Montano. What's the matter, lieutenant?
Cassio. A knave teach me my duty? I'll beat the knave into a   135
    twiggen° bottle.
Roderigo. Beat me?
Cassio. Dost thou prate, rogue?   [*Strikes him.*]
Montano. Nay, good lieutenant! I pray you, sir, hold your hand.

                                                        [*Stays him.*]

Cassio. Let me go, sir, or I'll knock you o'er the mazzard.°   140
Montano. Come, come, you're drunk!
Cassio. Drunk?   [*They fight.*]
Iago [*Aside to Roderigo*]. Away, I say! Go out and cry a mutiny!

                                                        [*Exit Roderigo.*]

    Nay, good lieutenant. God's will, gentlemen!
    Help, ho! Lieutenant. Sir. Montano.   145
    Help, masters! Here's a goodly watch indeed!

                                                        [*A bell rung.*]

---

¹²⁷ **ingraft** ingrained   ¹³⁶ **twiggen** wicker-covered   ¹⁴⁰ **mazzard** head

Who's that which rings the bell? Diablo, ho!
The town will rise. God's will, lieutenant,
You'll be ashamed forever.

Enter Othello and Attendants.

Othello.   What is the matter here?
Montano. Zounds, I bleed still. I am hurt to the death.   150
    He dies.   [*He and Cassio fight again.*]
Othello. Hold for your lives!
Iago. Hold, ho! Lieutenant. Sir. Montano. Gentlemen!
    Have you forgot all place of sense and duty?
    Hold! The general speaks to you. Hold, for shame!   155
Othello. Why, how now, ho? From whence ariseth this?
    Are we turned Turks, and to ourselves do that
    Which heaven hath forbid the Ottomites?°
    For Christian shame put by this barbarous brawl!
    He that stirs next to carve for his own rage   160
    Holds his soul light;° he dies upon his motion.
    Silence that dreadful bell! It frights the isle
    From her propriety.° What is the matter, masters?
    Honest Iago, that looks dead with grieving,
    Speak. Who began this? On thy love, I charge thee.   165
Iago. I do not know. Friends all, but now, even now,
    In quarter° and in terms like bride and groom
    Devesting them for bed; and then, but now —
    As if some planet had unwitted men —
    Swords out, and tilting one at other's breasts   170
    In opposition bloody. I cannot speak
    Any beginning to this peevish odds,°
    And would in action glorious I had lost
    Those legs that brought me to a part of it!
Othello. How comes it, Michael, you are thus forgot?   175
Cassio. I pray you pardon me; I cannot speak.
Othello. Worthy Montano, you were wont to be civil;
    The gravity and stillness of your youth
    The world hath noted, and your name is great
    In mouths of wisest censure.° What's the matter   180
    That you unlace° your reputation thus

---

158 *heaven . . . Ottomites* i.e., by sending the storm which dispersed the Turks
161 *Holds his soul light* values his soul lightly   163 *propriety* proper order
167 *In quarter* on duty   172 *odds* quarrel   180 *censure* judgment   181 *unlace*
undo (the term refers specifically to the dressing of a wild boar killed in
the hunt)

And spend your rich opinion° for the name
Of a night-brawler? Give me answer to it.
Montano. Worthy Othello, I am hurt to danger.
    Your officer, Iago, can inform you.   185
    While I spare speech, which something now offends° me,
    Of all that I do know; nor know I aught
    By me that's said or done amiss this night,
    Unless self-charity be sometimes a vice,
    And to defend ourselves it be a sin   190
    When violence assails us.
Othello.   Now, by heaven,
    My blood begins my safer guides to rule,
    And passion, having my best judgment collied,°
    Assays to lead the way. If I once stir
    Or do but lift this arm, the best of you   195
    Shall sink in my rebuke. Give me to know
    How this foul rout began, who set it on;
    And he that is approved in this offense.
    Though he had twinned with me, both at a birth,
    Shall lose me. What? In a town of war   200
    Yet wild, the people's hearts brimful of fear,
    To manage° private and domestic quarrel?
    In night, and on the court and guard of safety?
    'Tis monstrous. Iago, who began't?
Montano. If partially affined, or leagued in office,°
    Thou dost deliver more or less than truth,   205
    Thou art no soldier.
Iago.   Touch me not so near.
    I had rather have this tongue cut from my mouth
    Than it should do offense to Michael Cassio.
    Yet I persuade myself to speak the truth   210
    Shall nothing wrong him. This it is, general.
    Montano and myself being in speech,
    There comes a fellow crying out for help,
    And Cassio following him with determined sword
    To execute upon him. Sir, this gentleman   215
    Steps in to Cassio and entreats his pause.
    Myself the crying fellow did pursue,
    Lest by his clamor — as it so fell out —
    The town might fall in fright. He, swift of foot,

---

[182] *opinion* reputation   [186] *offends* harms, hurts   [193] *collied* darkened
[202] *manage* conduct   [205] *If . . . office* if you are partial because you are related ("affined") or the brother officer (of Cassio)

Outran my purpose; and I returned then rather 220
For that I heard the clink and fall of swords,
And Cassio high in oath; which till tonight
I ne'er might say before. When I came back —
For this was brief — I found them close together
At blow and thrust, even as again they were 225
When you yourself did part them.
More of this matter cannot I report;
But men are men; the best sometimes forget.
Though Cassio did some little wrong to him,
As men in rage strike those that wish them best, 230
Yet surely Cassio I believe received
From him that fled some strange indignity,
Which patience could not pass.°
Othello. I know, Iago,
Thy honesty and love doth mince° this matter,
Making it light to Cassio. Cassio, I love thee; 235
But never more be officer of mine.

Enter Desdemona, attended.

Look if my gentle love be not raised up.
I'll make thee an example.
Desdemona. What is the matter, dear?
Othello. All's well, sweeting; come away to bed.
[*To Montano*] Sir, for your hurts, myself will be your surgeon. 240
Lead him off. [*Montano led off.*]
Iago, look with care about the town
And silence those whom this vile brawl distracted.
Come, Desdemona: 'tis the soldiers' life
To have their balmy slumbers waked with strife. 245
Exit [*with all but Iago and Cassio*].
Iago. What, are you hurt, lieutenant?
Cassio. Ay, past all surgery.
Iago. Marry, God forbid!
Cassio. Reputation, reputation, reputation! O, I have lost
my reputation! I have lost the immortal part of myself, and 250
what remains is bestial. My reputation, Iago, my reputation.
Iago. As I am an honest man, I had thought you had received
some bodily wound. There is more sense° in that than in
reputation. Reputation is an idle and most false imposition,°
oft got without merit and lost without deserving. You have 255

---

233 *pass* allow to pass   234 *mince* cut up (i.e., tell only part of)   253 *sense*
physical feeling   254 *imposition* external thing

lost no reputation at all unless you repute yourself such a
loser. What, man, there are more ways to recover the general
again. You are but now cast in his mood° — a punishment
more in policy° than in malice — even so as one would beat
his offenseless dog to affright an imperious lion. Sue to him   260
again, and he's yours.

Cassio. I will rather sue to be despised than to deceive so good
a commander with so slight, so drunken, and so indiscreet an
officer. Drunk! And speak parrot!° And squabble! Swagger!
Swear! and discourse fustian° with one's own shadow! O   265
thou invisible spirit of wine, if thou hast no name to be
known by, let us call thee devil!

Iago. What was he that you followed with your sword?
What had he done to you?

Cassio. I know not.   270

Iago. Is't possible?

Cassio. I remember a mass of things, but nothing distinctly: a
quarrel, but nothing wherefore. O God, that men should put
an enemy in their mouths to steal away their brains! that we
should with joy, pleasance, revel, and applause transform   275
ourselves into beasts!

Iago. Why, but you are now well enough. How came you thus
recovered?

Cassio. It hath pleased the devil drunkenness to give place to
the devil wrath. One unperfectness shows me another, to   280
make me frankly despise myself.

Iago. Come, you are too severe a moraler. As the time, the
place, and the condition of this country stands, I could heartily wish this had not befall'n; but since it is as it is, mend it
for your own good.   285

Cassio. I will ask him for my place again: he shall tell me I am
a drunkard. Had I as many mouths as Hydra, such an answer
would stop them all. To be now a sensible man, by and by a
fool, and presently a beast! O strange! Every inordinate cup
is unblest, and the ingredient is a devil.   290

Iago. Come, come, good wine is a good familiar creature if it be
well used. Exclaim no more against it. And, good lieutenant,
I think you think I love you.

Cassio. I have well approved it, sir. I drunk?

Iago. You or any man living may be drunk at a time, man. I   295

---

[258] ***cast in his mood*** dismissed because of his anger   [259] ***in policy*** politically
necessary   [264] ***speak parrot*** gabble without sense   [265] ***discourse fustian***
speak nonsense ("fustian" was a coarse cotton cloth used for stuffing)

tell you what you shall do. Our general's wife is now the
general. I may say so in this respect for all he hath devoted
and given up himself to the contemplation, mark, and devotement of her parts° and graces. Confess yourself freely to her;
importune her help to put you in your place again. She is of   300
so free, so kind, so apt, so blessed a disposition she holds it a
vice in her goodness not to do more than she is requested.
This broken joint between you and her husband entreat her
to splinter;° and my fortunes against any lay° worth naming,
this crack of your love shall grow stronger than it was before.   305

Cassio. You advise me well.

Iago. I protest, in the sincerity of love and honest kindness.

Cassio. I think it freely; and betimes in the morning I will
beseech the virtuous Desdemona to undertake for me. I am
desperate of my fortunes if they check° me.   310

Iago. You are in the right. Good night, lieutenant; I must to the
watch.

Cassio. Good night, honest Iago.   *Exit Cassio.*

Iago. And what's he then that says I play the villain,
When this advice is free° I give, and honest,   315
Probal to° thinking, and indeed the course
To win the Moor again? For 'tis most easy
Th' inclining° Desdemona to subdue
In any honest suit; she's framed as fruitful°
As the free elements.° And then for her   320
To win the Moor — were't to renounce his baptism,
All seals and symbols of redeemèd sin —
His soul is so enfettered to her love
That she may make unmake, do what she list,
Even as her appetite° shall play the god   325
With his weak function.° How am I then a villain
To counsel Cassio to this parallel course,
Directly to his good? Divinity of hell!
When devils will the blackest sins put on,°
They do suggest at first with heavenly shows,°   330
As I do now. For whiles this honest fool
Plies Desdemona to repair his fortune,
And she for him pleads strongly to the Moor,
I'll pour this pestilence into his ear:

298-99 *devotement of her parts* devotion to her qualities   304 *splinter* splint
304 *lay* wager   310 *check* repulse   315 *free* generous and open   316 *Probal
to* provable by   318 *inclining* inclined (to be helpful)   319 *framed as fruitful*
made as generous   320 *elements* i.e., basic nature   325 *appetite* liking
326 *function* thought   329 *put on* advance, further   330 *shows* appearances

That she repeals him° for her body's lust;   335
And by how much she strives to do him good,
She shall undo her credit with the Moor.
So will I turn her virtue into pitch,
And out of her own goodness make the net
That shall enmesh them all. How now, Roderigo?   340

Enter Roderigo.

Roderigo. I do not follow here in the chase, not like a hound
that hunts, but one that fills up the cry.° My money is almost
spent; I have been tonight exceedingly well cudgeled; and I
think the issue will be, I shall have so much experience for
my pains; and so, with no money at all, and a little more wit,   345
return again to Venice.
Iago. How poor are they that have not patience!
What wound did ever heal but by degrees?
Thou know'st we work by wit, and not by witchcraft;
And wit depends on dilatory time.   350
Does't not go well? Cassio hath beaten thee,
And thou by that small hurt hath cashiered Cassio.
Though other things grow fair against the sun,
Yet fruits that blossom first will first be ripe.
Content thyself awhile. By the mass, 'tis morning!   355
Pleasure and action make the hours seem short.
Retire thee; go where thou art billeted.
Away, I say! Thou shalt know more hereafter.
Nay, get thee gone!   *Exit Roderigo.*
Two things are to be done: 360
My wife must move° for Cassio to her mistress;
I'll set her on;
Myself awhile ° to draw the Moor apart
And bring him jump° when he may Cassio find
Soliciting his wife. Ay, that's the way!   365
Dull not device by coldness and delay.   *Exit.*

---

³³⁵ *repeals him* asks for (Cassio's reinstatement)   ³⁴² *fills up the cry* makes
up one of the hunting pack, adding to the noise but not actually tracking
³⁶¹ *move* petition   ³⁶³ *awhile* at the same time   ³⁶⁴ *jump* at the precise
moment and place

ACT III

Scene I   [*A street.*]

Enter Cassio [and] Musicians.

Cassio. Masters, play here. I will content your pains.°
Something that's brief; and bid "Good morrow, general."

                                                [*They play.*]
[*Enter Clown.*°]

Clown. Why, masters, have your instruments been in Naples°
that they speak i' th' nose thus?
Musician. How, sir, how?   5
Clown. Are these, I pray you, wind instruments?
Musician. Ay, marry, are they, sir.
Clown. O, thereby hangs a tale.
Musician. Whereby hangs a tale, sir?
Clown. Marry, sir, by many a wind instrument that I know. But,   10
masters, here's money for you; and the general so likes your
music that he desires you, for love's sake, to make no more
noise with it.
Musician. Well, sir, we will not.
Clown. If you have any music that may not be heard, to't again. 15
But, as they say, to hear music the general does not greatly
care.
Musician. We have none such, sir.
Clown. Then put up your pipes in your bag, for I'll away. Go,
vanish into air, away!   *Exit Musicians.* 20
Cassio. Dost thou hear me, mine honest friend?
Clown. No. I hear not your honest friend. I hear you.
Cassio. Prithee keep up thy quillets.° There's a poor piece of
gold for thee. If the gentlewoman that attends the general's
wife be stirring, tell her there's one Cassio entreats her a   25
little favor of speech. Wilt thou do this?
Clown. She is stirring, sir. If she will stir hither, I shall seem to
notify unto her.°   *Exit Clown.*

Enter Iago.

III.i. **¹** *content your pains* reward your efforts s.d. **Clown** fool **³ Naples**
this may refer either to the Neapolitan nasal tone, or to syphilis — rife in
Naples — which breaks down the nose **²³** *quillets* puns **²⁷⁻²⁸** *seem . . . her*
(the Clown is mocking Cassio's overly elegant manner of speaking)

Cassio. In happy time, Iago.
Iago.   You have not been abed then?
Cassio. Why no, the day had broke before we parted.   30
  I have made bold, Iago, to send in to your wife;
  My suit to her is that she will to virtuous Desdemona
  Procure me some access.
Iago.   I'll send her to you presently,
  And I'll devise a mean to draw the Moor
  Out of the way, that your converse and business   35
  May be more free.
Cassio. I humbly thank you for't.   *Exit* [*Iago*].
  I never knew
  A Florentine° more kind and honest.

  Enter Emilia.

Emilia. Good morrow, good lieutenant. I am sorry   40
  For your displeasure;° but all will sure be well.
  The general and his wife are talking of it,
  And she speaks for you stoutly. The Moor replies
  That he you hurt is of great fame in Cyprus
  And great affinity,° and that in wholesome wisdom   45
  He might not but refuse you. But he protests he loves you.
  And needs no other suitor but his likings
  To bring you in again.
Cassio.   Yet I beseech you,
  If you think fit, or that it may be done,
  Give me advantage of some brief discourse   50
  With Desdemona alone.
Emilia.   Pray you come in.
  I will bestow you where you shall have time
  To speak your bosom° freely.
Cassio. I am much bound to you.   [*Exeunt.*]

Scene II [*The citadel.*]

  Enter Othello, Iago, and Gentlemen.

Othello. These letters give, Iago, to the pilot
  And by him do my duties to the Senate.
  That done, I will be walking on the works;
  Repair° there to me.

---

[39] *Florentine* i.e., Iago is as kind as if he were from Cassio's home town, Florence   [41] *displeasure* discomforting   [45] *affinity* family   [53] *bosom* inmost thoughts   III.ii.   [4] *Repair* go

Iago.   Well, my good lord, I'll do't.
Othello. This fortification, gentlemen, shall we see't?   5
Gentlemen. We'll wait upon your lordship.   *Exeunt.*

Scene III   [*The citadel.*]

Enter Desdemona, Cassio, and Emilia.

Desdemona. Be thou assured, good Cassio, I will do
All my abilities in thy behalf.
Emilia. Good madam, do. I warrant it grieves my husband
As if the cause were his.
Desdemona. O, that's an honest fellow. Do not doubt, Cassio,   5
But I will have my lord and you again
As friendly as you were.
Cassio.   Bounteous madam,
Whatever shall become of Michael Cassio,
He's never anything but your true servant.
Desdemona. I know't; I thank you. You do love my lord.   10
You have known him long, and be you well assured
He shall in strangeness stand no farther off
Than in a politic distance.°
Cassio.   Ay, but, lady,
That policy may either last so long,
Or feed upon such nice° and waterish diet,   15
Or breed itself so out of circumstances,°
That, I being absent, and my place supplied,°
My general will forget my love and service.
Desdemona. Do not doubt° that; before Emilia here
I give thee warrant of thy place. Assure thee,   20
If I do vow a friendship, I'll perform it
To the last article. My lord shall never rest;
I'll watch him tame° and talk him out of patience;
His bed shall seem a school, his board a shrift;°
I'll intermingle everything he does   25
With Cassio's suit. Therefore be merry, Cassio,
For thy solicitor shall rather die
Than give thy cause away.

Enter Othello and Iago [at a distance].

III.iii   ¹²⁻¹³ *He . . . distance* i.e., he shall act no more distant to you than
is necessary for political reasons   ¹⁵ *nice* trivial   ¹⁶ *Or . . . circumstances*
i.e., or grow so on the basis of accidental happenings and political needs
¹⁷ *supplied* filled   ¹⁹ *doubt* imagine   ²³ *watch him tame* (animals were
tamed by being kept awake)   ²⁴ *board a shrift* table (seem) a confessional

Emilia. Madam, here comes my lord.
Cassio. Madam, I'll take my leave.   30
Desdemona. Why, stay, and hear me speak.
Cassio. Madam, not now. I am very ill at ease,
   Unfit for mine own purposes.
Desdemona. Well, do your discretion.   *Exit Cassio.*
Iago. Ha! I like not that.
Othello.   What dost thou say?   35
Iago. Nothing, my lord; or if — I know not what.
Othello. Was not that Cassio parted from my wife?
Iago. Cassio, my lord? No, sure, I cannot think it
   That he would steal away so guilty-like,
   Seeing you coming.
Othello.   I do believe 'twas he.   40
Desdemona [*Coming to them*]. How now, my lord?
   I have been talking with a suitor here,
   A man that languishes in your displeasure.
Othello. Who is't you mean?
Desdemona. Why, your lieutenant, Cassio. Good my lord,   45
   If I have any grace or power to move you,
   His present° reconciliation take.
   For if he be not one that truly loves you,
   That errs in ignorance, and not in cunning,
   I have no judgment in an honest face.   50
   I prithee call him back.
Othello.   Went he hence now?
Desdemona. I' sooth so humbled
   That he hath left part of his grief with me
   To suffer with him. Good love, call him back.
Othello. Not now, sweet Desdemon; some other time.   55
Desdemona. But shall't be shortly?
Othello.   The sooner, sweet, for you.
Desdemona. Shall't be tonight at supper?
Othello.   No, not tonight.
Desdemona. Tomorrow dinner then?
Othello.   I shall not dine at home;
   I meet the captains at the citadel.
Desdemona. Why then, tomorrow night, on Tuesday morn,   60
   On Tuesday noon, or night, on Wednesday morn.
   I prithee name the time, but let it not
   Exceed three days. In faith, he's penitent;
   And yet his trespass, in our common reason

---

[47] ***present*** immediate

(Save that, they say, the wars must make example   65
Out of her best), is not almost a fault
T' incur a private check.° When shall he come?
Tell me, Othello. I wonder in my soul
What you would ask me that I should deny
Or stand so mamm'ring° on. What? Michael Cassio,   70
That came awooing with you, and so many a time,
When I have spoke of you dispraisingly,
Hath ta'en your part — to have so much to do
To bring him in? By'r Lady, I could do much —
Othello.   Prithee no more. Let him come when he will!   75
I will deny thee nothing.
Desdemona.   Why, this is not a boon;
'Tis as I should entreat you wear your gloves,
Or feed on nourishing dishes, or keep you warm,
Or sue to you do a peculiar profit°
To your own person. Nay, when I have a suit   80
Wherein I mean to touch your love indeed,
It shall be full of poise° and difficult weight,
And fearful to be granted.
Othello.   I will deny thee nothing!
Whereon I do beseech thee grant me this,
To leave me but a little to myself.   85
Desdemona.   Shall I deny you? No. Farewell, my lord.
Othello.   Farewell, my Desdemona: I'll come to thee straight.°
Desdemona.   Emilia, come. Be as your fancies teach you;
    Whate'er you be, I am obedient.   *Exit [with Emilia].*
Othello.   Excellent wretch! Perdition catch my soul   90
    But I do love thee! And when I love thee not,
    Chaos is come again.
Iago.   My noble lord —
Othello.   What dost thou say, Iago?
Iago.   Did Michael Cassio, when you wooed my lady,
    Know of your love?   95
Othello.   He did, from first to last. Why dost thou ask?
Iago.   But for a satisfaction of my thought,
    No further harm.
Othello.   Why of thy thought, Iago?
Iago.   I did not think he had been acquainted with her.
Othello.   O, yes, and went between us° very oft.   100

66-67 *is . . . check* is almost not serious enough for a private rebuke (let alone a
public disgrace)   70 *mamm'ring* hesitating   79 *peculiar profit* particularly
personal good   82 *poise* weight   87 *straight* at once   100 *between us* i.e., as
messenger

Iago. Indeed?
Othello. Indeed? Ay, indeed! Discern'st thou aught in that?
     Is he not honest?
Iago.   Honest, my lord?
Othello.   Honest? Ay, honest.
Iago. My lord, for aught I know.
Othello. What dost thou think?
Iago.   Think, my lord?
Othello.   Think, my lord?   105
     By heaven, thou echoest me,
     As if there were some monster in thy thought
     Too hideous to be shown. Thou dost mean something.
     I heard thee say even now, thou lik'st not that,
     When Cassio left my wife. What didst not like?   110
     And when I told thee he was of my counsel°
     Of my whole course of wooing, thou cried'st "Indeed?"
     And didst contract and purse thy brow together,
     As if thou then hadst shut up in thy brain
     Some horrible conceit.° If thou dost love me,   115
     Show me thy thought.
Iago. My lord, you know I love you.
Othello.   I think thou dost;
     And, for I know thou'rt full of love and honesty
     And weigh'st thy words before thou giv'st them breath,
     Therefore these stops° of thine fright me the more;   120
     For such things in a false disloyal knave
     Are tricks of custom;° but in a man that's just
     They're close dilations,° working from the heart
     That passion cannot rule.
Iago.   For Michael Cassio,
     I dare be sworn, I think that he is honest.   125
Othello. I think so too.
Iago.   Men should be what they seem;
     Or those that be not, would they might seem none!
Othello. Certain, men should be what they seem.
Iago. Why then, I think Cassio's an honest man.
Othello. Nay, yet there's more in this?   130
     I prithee speak to me as to thy thinkings,
     As thou dost ruminate, and give thy worst of thoughts
     The worst of words.

---

[111] *of my counsel* in my confidence   [115] *conceit* thought   [120] *stops* interruptions   [122] *of custom* customary   [123] *close dilations* expressions of hidden thoughts

Iago.   Good my lord, pardon me:
    Though I am bound to every act of duty,
    I am not bound to that all slaves are free to.   135
    Utter my thoughts? Why, say they are vile and false,
    As where's that palace whereinto foul things
    Sometimes intrude not? Who has that breast so pure
    But some uncleanly apprehensions
    Keep leets and law days,° and in sessions sit   140
    With meditations lawful?
Othello. Thou dost conspire against thy friend, Iago,
    If thou but think'st him wronged, and mak'st his ear
    A stranger to thy thoughts.
Iago.   I do beseech you —
    Though I perchance am vicious in my guess   145
    (As I confess it is my nature's plague
    To spy into abuses, and of my jealousy
    Shape faults that are not), that your wisdom
    From one that so imperfectly conceits
    Would take no notice, nor build yourself a trouble   150
    Out of his scattering and unsure observance.
    It were not for your quiet nor your good,
    Nor for my manhood, honesty, and wisdom,
    To let you know my thoughts.
Othello.   What dost thou mean?
Iago. Good name in man and woman, dear my lord,   155
    Is the immediate jewel of their souls.
    Who steals my purse steals trash; 'tis something, nothing;
    'Twas mine, 'tis his, and has been slave to thousands;
    But he that filches from me my good name
    Robs me of that which not enriches him   160
    And makes me poor indeed.
Othello. By heaven, I'll know thy thoughts!
Iago. You cannot, if my heart were in your hand;
    Nor shall not whilst 'tis in my custody.
Othello. Ha!
Iago.   O, beware, my lord, of jealousy!   165
    It is the green-eyed monster, which doth mock
    The meat it feeds on. That cuckold lives in bliss
    Who, certain of his fate, loves not his wronger;
    But O, what damned minutes tells° he o'er
    Who dotes, yet doubts — suspects, yet fondly° loves!   170

---

[140] ***leets and law days*** meetings of local courts   [169] ***tells*** counts   [170] ***fondly*** foolishly

Othello. O misery.
Iago. Poor and content is rich, and rich enough;
 But riches fineless° is a poor as winter
 To him that ever fears he shall be poor.
 Good God the souls of all my tribe defend   175
 From jealousy!
Othello.   Why? Why is this?
 Think'st thou I'd make a life of jealousy,
 To follow still° the changes of the moon
 With fresh suspicions? No! To be once in doubt
 Is to be resolved. Exchange me for a goat   180
 When I shall turn the business of my soul
 To such exsufflicate and blown° surmises,
 Matching thy inference. 'Tis not to make me jealous
 To say my wife is fair, feeds well, loves company,
 Is free of speech, sings, plays, and dances;   185
 Where virtue is, these are more virtuous.
 Nor from mine own weak merits will I draw
 The smallest fear or doubt of her revolt,
 For she had eyes, and chose me. No, Iago;
 I'll see before I doubt; when I doubt, prove;   190
 And on the proof there is no more but this:
 Away at once with love or jealousy!
Iago. I am glad of this; for now I shall have reason
 To show the love and duty that I bear you
 With franker spirit. Therefore, as I am bound,   195
 Receive it from me. I speak not yet of proof.
 Look to your wife; observe her well with Cassio;
 Wear your eyes thus: not jealous nor secure.
 I would not have your free and noble nature
 Out of self-bounty° be abused. Look to't.   200
 I know our country disposition well:
 In Venice they do let heaven see the pranks
 They dare not show their husbands; their best conscience
 Is not to leave't undone, but kept unknown.°
Othello. Dost thou say so?   205
Iago. She did deceive her father, marrying you;
 And when she seemed to shake and fear your looks,
 She loved them most.

---

[173] *fineless* infinite [178] *To follow still* to change always (as the phases of the moon) [128] *exsufflicate and blown* inflated and flyblown [200] *self-bounty* innate kindness (which attributes his own motives to others) [203-4] *their . . . unknown* i.e., their morality does not forbid adultery, but it does forbid being found out

Othello.   And so she did.
Iago.   Why, go to then!
　She that so young could give out such a seeming
　To seel° her father's eyes up close as oak° —   210
　He thought 'twas witchcraft. But I am much to blame.
　I humbly do beseech you of your pardon
　For too much loving you.
Othello.   I am bound to thee forever.
Iago. I see this faith hath a little dashed your spirits.
Othello. Not a jot, not a jot.
Iago.   Trust me, I fear it has.   215
　I hope you will consider what is spoke
　Comes from my love. but I do see y' are moved.
　I am to pray you not to strain° my speech
　To grosser issues nor to larger reach°
　Than to suspicion.   220
Othello. I will not.
Iago.   Should you do so, my lord,
　My speech should fall into such vile success
　Which my thoughts aimed not. Cassio's my worthy friend —
　My lord, I see y' are moved.
Othello.   No, not much moved.
　I do not think but Desdemona's honest.   225
Iago. Long live she so. And long live you to think so.
Othello. And yet, how nature erring from itself ——
Iago. Ay there's the point, as (to be bold with you)
　Not to affect many proposèd matches
　Of her own clime, complexion, and degree,°   230
　Whereto we see in all things nature tends° —
　Foh! one may smell in such a will most rank,
　Foul disproportions, thoughts unnatural.
　But, pardon me, I do not in position°
　Distinctly° speak of her; though I may fear   235
　Her will, recoiling to her better judgment,
　May fall to match° you with her country forms,°
　And happily° repent.
Othello.   Farewell, farewell!

---

210 *seel* hoodwink   210 *oak* (a close-grained wood)   218 *strain* enlarge the meaning   230 *degree* social station   231 *in . . . tends* i.e., all things in nature seek out their own kind   234 *position* general argument   235 *Distinctly* specifically   237 *fall to match* happen to compare   237 *country forms* i.e., the familiar appearance of her countrymen   238 *happily* by chance

If more thou dost perceive, let me know more.
Set on thy wife to observe. Leave me, Iago.   240
Iago. My lord, I take my leave.   [*Going.*]
Othello. Why did I marry? This honest creature doubtless
  Sees and knows more, much more, than he unfolds.
Iago [*Returns*]. My lord, I would I might entreat your honor
  To scan this thing no further. Leave it to time.   245
  Although 'tis fit that Cassio have his place,
  For sure he fills it up with great ability,
  Yet, if you please to hold him off awhile,
  You shall by that perceive him and his means,
  Note if your lady strains his entertainment°   250
  With any strong or vehement importunity;
  Much will be seen in that. In the meantime
  Let me be thought too busy in my fears
  (As worthy cause I have to fear I am)
  And hold her free, I do beseech your honor.   255
Othello. Fear not my government.°
Iago.   I once more take my leave.

                                                        Exit.

Othello. This fellow's of exceeding honesty,
  And knows all qualities,° with a learnèd spirit
  Of human dealings. If I do prove her haggard,°
  Though that her jesses° were my dear heartstrings,   260
  I'd whistle her off and let her down the wind°
  To prey at fortune. Haply for° I am black
  And have not those soft parts° of conversation
  That chamberers° have, or for I am declined
  Into the vale of years — yet that's not much —   265
  She's gone. I am abused, and my relief
  Must be to loathe her. O curse of marriage,
  That we can call these delicate creatures ours,
  And not their appetites! I had rather be a toad
  And live upon the vapor of a dungeon   270
  Than keep a corner in the thing I love
  For others' uses. Yet 'tis the plague to great ones;
  Prerogatived are they less than the base.

---

²⁵⁰ *strains his entertainment* urge strongly that he be reinstated   ²⁵⁶ *government* self-control   ²⁵⁸ *qualities* natures, types of people   ²⁵⁹ *haggard* a partly trained hawk which has gone wild again   ²⁶⁰ *jesses* straps which held the hawk's legs to the trainer's wrist   ²⁶¹ *I'd . . . wind* I would release her (like an untamable hawk) and let her fly free   ²⁶² *Haply for* it may be because   ²⁶³ *soft parts* gentle qualities and manners   ²⁶⁴ *chamberers* courtiers — or, perhaps, accomplished seducers

'Tis destiny unshunnable, like death.
Even then this forked° plague is fated to us   275
When we do quicken.° Look where she comes.

Enter Desdemona and Emilia.

If she be false, heaven mocked itself!
I'll not believe't.
Desdemona.   How now, my dear Othello?
Your dinner, and the generous islanders
By you invited, do attend° your presence.   280
Othello.   I am to blame.
Desdemona.   Why do you speak so faintly?
Are you not well?
Othello.   I have a pain upon my forehead, here.°
Desdemona. Why that's with watching; 'twill away again,
Let me but bind it hard, within this hour   285
It will be well.
Othello.   Your napkin° is too little;

[*He pushes the handkerchief away, and it falls.*]

Let it° alone. Come, I'll go in with you.
Desdemona.   I am very sorry that you are not well.

Exit [with Othello].

Emilia.   I am glad I have found this napkin;
This was her first remembrance from the Moor.   290
My wayward husband hath a hundred times
Wooed me to steal it; but she so loves the token
(For he conjured her she should ever keep it)
That she reserves it evermore about her
To kiss and talk to. I'll have the work ta'en out°   295
And give't Iago. What he will do with it,
Heaven knows, not I; I nothing° but to please his fantasy.°

Enter Iago.

Iago.   How now? What do you here alone?
Emilia.   Do not you chide; I have a thing for you.

---

²⁷⁵ *forked* horned (the sign of the cuckold was horns)   ²⁷⁶ *do quicken* are
born   ²⁸⁰ *attend* wait   ²⁸³ *here* (he points to his imaginary horns)   ²⁸⁶ *napkin* elaborately worked handkerchief   ²⁸⁷ *it* (it makes a considerable difference in the interpretation of later events whether this "it" refers to
Othello's forehead or to the handkerchief; nothing in the text makes the
reference clear)   ²⁹⁵ *work ta'en out* needlework copied   ²⁹⁷ *I nothing* I
wish nothing   ²⁹⁷ *fantasy* fancy, whim

Iago. You have a thing for me? It is a common thing —— 300
Emilia. Ha?
Iago. To have a foolish wife.
Emilia. O, is that all? What will you give me now
    For that same handkerchief?
Iago.   What handkerchief?
Emilia. What handkerchief! 305
    Why, that the Moor first gave to Desdemona,
    That which so often you did bid me steal.
Iago. Hast stol'n it from her?
Emilia. No, but she let it drop by negligence,
    And to th' advantage,° I, being here, took't up. 310
    Look, here 't is.
Iago.   A good wench. Give it me.
Emilia. What will you do with't, that you have been so earnest
    To have me filch it?
Iago.   Why, what is that to you?

                                            [Takes it.]

Emilia. If it be not for some purpose of import,°
    Give't me again. Poor lady, she'll run mad 315
    When she shall lack° it.
Iago.   Be not acknown on't°
    I have use for it. Go, leave me.   *Exit Emilia.*
    I will in Cassio's lodging lose this napkin
    And let him find it. Trifles light as air
    Are to the jealous confirmations strong 320
    As proofs of Holy Writ. This may do something.
    The Moor already changes with my poison:
    Dangerous conceits are in their natures poisons,
    Which at the first are scare found to distaste,°
    But with a little,° act upon the blood, 325
    Burn like the mines of sulfur. I did say so.

    Enter Othello.

    Look where he comes! Not poppy nor mandragora,°
    Nor all the drowsy syrups of the world,
    Shall ever medicine thee to that sweet sleep
    Which thou owedst° yesterday.
Othello.   Ha! ha! False to me? 330

---

³¹⁰ *to th' advantage* being lucky   ³¹⁴ *import* importance   ³¹⁶ *lack* miss
³¹⁶ *Be not acknown on't* forget you ever saw it   ³²⁴ *are scarce found to distaste* scarcely can be tasted   ³²⁵ *with a little* in a short time   ³²⁷ *poppy nor mandragora* (soporifics)   ³³⁰ *owedst* possessed

Iago. Why, how now, general? No more of that.
Othello. Avaunt! be gone! Thou hast set me on the rack.
    I swear 'tis better to be much abused
    Than but to know 't a little.
Iago.   How now, my lord?
Othello. What sense had I of her stol'n hours of lust?   335
    I saw 't not, thought it not, it harmed not me;
    I slept the next night well, fed well, was free and merry;
    I found not Cassio's kisses on her lips.
    He that is robbed, not wanting° what is stol'n,
    Let him not know 't, and he's not robbed at all.   340
Iago. I am sorry to hear this.
Othello.   I had been happy if the general camp,
    Pioners° and all, had tasted her sweet body,
    So I had nothing known. O now, forever
    Farewell the tranquil mind! Farewell content!   345
    Farewell the plumèd troops, and the big wars
    That make ambition virtue! O, farewell!
    Farewell the neighing steed and the shrill trump,
    The spirit-stirring drum, th' ear-piercing fife,
    The royal banner, and all quality,   350
    Pride, pomp, and circumstance° of glorious war!
    And O you mortal engines° whose rude throats
    Th' immortal Jove's dread clamors° counterfeit,
    Farewell! Othello's occupation's gone!
Iago. Is 't possible, my lord?   355
Othello. Villain, be sure thou prove my love a whore!
    Be sure of it; give me the ocular proof;
    Or, by the worth of mine eternal soul,
    Thou hadst been better have been born a dog
    Than answer my waked wrath!
Iago.   Is 't come to this?   360
Othello. Make me to see 't; or at the least so prove it
    That the probation° bear no hinge nor loop
    To hang a doubt on — or woe upon thy life!
Iago. My noble lord ——
Othello. If thou dost slander her and torture me,   365
    Never pray more; abandon all remorse;
    On horror's head horrors accumulate;
    Do deeds to make heaven weep, all earth amazed;

---

³³⁹ *wanting* missing   ³⁴³ *Pioners* (the basest manual laborers in the army, who dug trenches and mines)   ³⁵¹ *circumstance* pageantry   ³⁵² *mortal engines* lethal weapons, i.e., cannon   ³⁵³ *clamors* i.e., thunder   ³⁶² *probation* proof

For nothing canst thou to damnation add
Greater than that.
Iago.   O grace! O heaven forgive me!   370
Are you a man? Have you a soul or sense?
God b' wi' you! Take mine office. O wretched fool,
That lov'st to make thine honesty a vice!
O monstrous world! Take note, take note, O world,
To be direct and honest is not safe.   375
I thank you for this profit, and from hence
I'll love no friend, sith° love breeds such offense.
Othello. Nay, stay. Thou shouldst be honest.
Iago. I should be wise; for honesty's a fool
And loses that it works for.
Othello.   By the world,   380
I think my wife be honest, and think she is not;
I think that thou art just, and think thou are not.
I'll have some proof. My name, that was as fresh
As Dian's° visage, is now begrimed and black
As mine own face. If there be cords, or knives,   385
Poison, or fire, or suffocating streams,
I'll not endure it. Would I were satisfied!
Iago. I see you are eaten up with passion.
I do repent me that I put it to you.
You would be satisfied?
Othello.   Would? Nay, and I will.   390
Iago. And may; but how? How satisfied, my lord?
Would you, the supervisor,° grossly gape on?
Behold her topped?
Othello.   Death and damnation! O!
Iago. It were a tedious° difficulty, I think,
To bring them to that prospect.° Damn them then,   395
If ever mortal eyes do see them bolster°
More than their own! What then? How then?
What shall I say? Where's satisfaction?
It is impossible you should see this,
Were they as prime° as goats, as hot as monkeys,   400
As salt° as wolves in pride,° and fools as gross
As ignorance made drunk. But yet, I say,
If imputation and strong circumstances

---

³⁷⁷ *sith* since   ³⁸⁴ *Dian's* Diana's (goddess of the moon and of chastity)
³⁹² *supervisor* onlooker   ³⁹⁴ *tedious* hard to arrange   ³⁹⁵ *prospect* sight
(where they can be seen)   ³⁹⁶ *bolster* go to bed with   ⁴⁰⁰⁻⁰¹ *prime, salt*
lustful   ⁴⁰¹ *pride* heat

Which lead directly to the door of truth
Will give you satisfaction, you might hav't.   405
Othello. Give me a living reason she's disloyal.
Iago. I do not like the office.°
    But sith I am entered in this cause so far,
    Pricked° to't by foolish honesty and love,
    I will go on. I lay with Cassio lately,   410
    And being troubled with a raging tooth,
    I could not sleep.
    There are a kind of men so loose of soul
    That in their sleeps will mutter their affairs.
    One of this kind is Cassio.   415
    In sleep I heard him say, "Sweet Desdemona,
    Let us be wary, let us hide our loves!"
    And then, sir, would he gripe° and wring my hand,
    Cry "O sweet creature!" Then kiss me hard,
    As if he plucked up kisses by the roots   420
    That grew upon my lips; laid his leg o'er my thigh,
    And sigh, and kiss, and then cry, "Cursèd fate
    That gave thee to the Moor!"
Othello. O monstrous! monstrous!
Iago.   Nay, this was but his dream.
Othello. But this denoted a foregone conclusion,°   425
    'Tis a shrewd doubt,° though it be but a dream.
Iago. And this may help to thicken other proofs
    That do demonstrate° thinly.
Othello.   I'll tear her all to pieces!
Iago. Nay, yet be wise. Yet we see nothing done;
    She may be honest yet. Tell me but this: 430
    Have you not sometimes seen a handkerchief
    Spotted with strawberries in your wife's hand?
Othello. I gave her such a one; 'twas my first gift.
Iago. I know not that; but such a handkerchief —
    I am sure it was your wife's — did I today   435
    See Cassio wipe his beard with.
Othello.   If it be that ——
Iago. If it be that or any that was hers,
    It speaks against her with the other proofs.
Othello. O, that the slave had forty thousand lives!
    One is too poor, too weak for my revenge.   440
    Now do I see 'tis true. Look here, Iago:

---

[407] *office* duty   [409] *Pricked* spurred   [418] *gripe* seize   [425] *foregone conclusion* consummated fact   [426] *shrewd doubt* penetrating guess   [428] *demonstrate* show, appear

All my fond love thus do I blow to heaven.
'Tis gone.
Arise, black vengeance, from the hollow hell!
Yield up, O love, thy crown and hearted° throne   445
To tyrannous hate! Swell, bosom, with thy fraught,°
For 'tis of aspics'° tongues.
Iago.   Yet be content.°
Othello. O, blood, blood, blood!
Iago. Patience, I say. Your mind may change.
Othello. Never, Iago. Like to the Pontic Sea,°   450
Whose icy current and compulsive course
Nev'r keeps retiring ebb, but keeps due on
To the Propontic and the Hellespont,
Even so my bloody thoughts, with violent pace,
Shall nev'r look back, nev'r ebb to humble love,   455
Till that a capable and wide° revenge
Swallow them up. [*He kneels.*] Now, by yond marble heaven,
In the due reverence of a sacred vow
I here engage my words.
Iago.   Do not rise yet.

                                              [*Iago kneels.*]

Witness, you ever-burning lights above,   460
You elements that clip° us round about,
Witness that here Iago doth give up
The execution° of his wit, hands, heart
To wronged Othello's service! Let him command,
And to obey shall be in me remorse,°   465
What bloody business ever.°   [*They rise.*]
Othello.   I greet thy love,
Not with vain thanks but with acceptance bounteous,°
And will upon the instant put thee to 't.°
Within these three days let me hear thee say
That Cassio's not alive.   470
Iago. My friend is dead. 'Tis done at your request.
But let her live.

---

⁴⁴⁵ *hearted* seated in the heart   ⁴⁴⁶ *fraught* burden   ⁴⁴⁷ *aspics'* asps'
⁴⁴⁷ *content* patient, quiet   ⁴⁵⁰ *Pontic Sea* the Black Sea (famous for the strong
and constant current with which it flows through the Bosporous into the
Mediterranean, where the water level is lower)   ⁴⁵⁶ *capable and wide* sufficient and far-reaching   ⁴⁶¹ *clip* enfold   ⁴⁶³ *execution* workings, action
⁴⁶⁵ *remorse* pity   ⁴⁶⁶ *ever* soever   ⁴⁶⁷ *bounteous* absolute   ⁴⁶⁸ *to't* i.e., to
the work you have said you are prepared to do

Othello. Damn her, lewd minx! O, damn her! Damn her!
Come, go with me apart. I will withdraw
To furnish me with swift means of death
For the fair devil. Now art thou my lieutenant.   475
Iago. I am your own forever.   *Exeunt.*

Scene IV [*A street.*]

Enter Desdemona, Emilia, and Clown.

Desdemona. Do you know, sirrah, where Lieutenant Cassio lies?°
Clown. I dare not say he lies anywhere.
Desdemona. Why, man?
Clown. He's a soldier, and for me to say a soldier lies, 'tis stabbing.
Desdemona. Go to. Where lodges he?   5
Clown. To tell you where he lodges is to tell you where I lie.
Desdemona. Can anything be made of this?
Clown. I know not where he lodges, and for me to devise a
    lodging, and say he lies here or he lies there, were to lie in
    mine own throat.°   10
Desdemona. Can you enquire him out, and be edified° by re-
    port?
Clown. I will catechize the world for him; that is, make ques-
    tions, and by them answer.
Desdemona. Seek him, bid him come hither. Tell him I have   15
    moved° my lord on his behalf and hope all will be well.
Clown. To do this is within the compass° of man's wit, and
    therefore I will attempt the doing it.   *Exit Clown.*
Desdemona. Where should° I lose the handkerchief, Emilia?
Emilia. I know not, madam.   20
Desdemona. Believe me, I had rather have lost my purse
    Full of crusadoes.° And but my noble Moor
    Is true of mind, and made of no such baseness
    As jealous creatures are, it were enough
    To put him to ill thinking.
Emilia.   Is he not jealous?   25
Desdemona. Who? He? I think the sun where he was born
    Drew all such humors° from him.

III.iv ¹ *lies* lodges   ⁹⁻¹⁰ *lie in mine own throat* (to lie in the throat is to
lie absolutely and completely)   ¹¹ *edified* enlightened (Desdemona mocks
the Clown's overly elaborate diction)   ¹⁶ *moved* pleaded with   ¹⁷ *compass*
reach   ¹⁹ *should* might   ²² *crusadoes* Portuguese gold coins   ²⁷ *humors*
characteristics

Emilia.   Look where he comes.

   Enter Othello.

Desdemona. I will not leave him now till Cassio
   Be called to him. How is't with you, my lord?
Othello. Well, my good lady. [*Aside*] O, hardness to
   dissemble!° —   30
   How do you, Desdemona?
Desdemona.   Well, my good lord.
Othello. Give me your hand. This hand is moist,° my lady.
Desdemona. It hath felt no age nor known no sorrow.
Othello. This argues° fruitfulness and liberal° heart.
   Hot, hot, and moist. This hand of yours requires   35
   A sequester° from liberty; fasting and prayer;
   Much castigation; exercise devout;
   For here's a young and sweating devil here
   That commonly rebels. 'Tis a good hand,
   A frank one.   40
Desdemona.   You may, indeed, say so;
   For 'twas that hand that gave away my heart.
Othello. A liberal hand! The hearts of old gave hands,
   But our new heraldry° is hands, not hearts.
Desdemona. I have sent to bid Cassio come speak with you.   45
Othello. I have a salt and sorry rheum° offends me.
   Lend me thy handkerchief.
Desdemona.   Here, my lord.
Othello. That which I gave you.
Desdemona.   I have it not about me.
Othello. Not?
Desdemona. No, indeed, my lord.
Othello.   That's a fault.   50
   That handkerchief
   Did an Egyptian to my mother give.
   She was a charmer,° and could almost read
   The thoughts of people. She told her, while she kept it
   'Twould make her amiable° and subdue my father   55

---

³⁰ *hardness to dissemble* (Othello may refer here either to the difficulty he
has in maintaining his appearance of composure, or to what he believes to be
Desdemona's hardened hypocrisy)   ³² *moist* (a moist, hot hand was taken as
a sign of a lustful nature)   ³⁴ *argues* suggests   ³⁴ *liberal* free, open (but also
with a suggestion of "licentious"; from here on in this scene Othello's words
bear a double meaning, seeming to be normal but accusing Desdemona of
being unfaithful)   ³⁶ *sequester* separation   ⁴⁴ *heraldry* heraldic symbolism
⁴⁶ *a salt and sorry rheum* a heavy, running head cold   ⁵³ *charmer* magician
⁵⁵ *amiable* desirable

Entirely to her love; but if she lost it
Or made a gift of it, my father's eye
Should hold her loathèd, and his spirits should hunt
After new fancies. She, dying, gave it me,
And bid me, when my fate would have me wived,   60
To give it her. I did so; and take heed on't;
Make it a darling like your precious eye.
To lose't or give't away were such perdition
As nothing else could match.
Desdemona.   Is't possible?
Othello. 'Tis true. There's magic in the web° of it.   65
A sibyl that had numbered in the world
The sun to course two hundred compasses,
In her prophetic fury° sewed the work;
The worms were hallowed that did breed the silk,
And it was dyed in mummy° which the skillful   70
Conserved of maidens' hearts.
Desdemona.   Indeed? Is't true?
Othello. Most veritable. Therefore look to't well.
Desdemona. Then would to God that I had never seen't!
Othello. Ha! Wherefore?
Desdemona. Why do you speak so startingly and rash?   75
Othello. Is't lost? Is't gone? Speak, is it out o' th' way?
Desdemona. Heaven bless us!
Othello. Say you?
Desdemona. It is not lost. But what an if it were?
Othello. How?   80
Desdemona. I say it is not lost.
Othello. Fetch't, let me see't!
Desdemona. Why, so I can; but I will not now.
This is a trick to put me from my suit:
Pray you let Cassio be received again.   85
Othello. Fetch me the handkerchief! My mind misgives.
Desdemona. Come, come!
You'll never meet a more sufficient ° man ——
Othello. The handkerchief!
Desdemona.   A man that all his time
Hath founded his good fortunes on your love,   90
Shared dangers with you ——
Othello. The handkerchief!

---

[65] *web* weaving   [68] *prophetic fury* seized by the spirit and able to prophesy
[70] *mummy* liquid drained from embalmed bodies   [88] *sufficient* complete,
with all proper qualities

Desdemona. I'faith, you are to blame.
Othello. Away!   *Exit Othello.*
Emilia. Is not this man jealous?   95
Desdemona. I nev'r saw this before.
    Sure there's some wonder in this handkerchief;
    I am most unhappy in the loss of it.
Emilia. 'Tis not a year or two shows us a man.
    They are all but stomachs, and we all but food;   100
    They eat us hungerly, and when they are full,
    They belch us.

    Enter Iago and Cassio.

              Look you, Cassio and my husband.
Iago. There is no other way; 'tis she must do't.
    And lo the happiness! Go and importune her.
Desdemona. How now, good Cassio? What's the news with you?   105
Cassio. Madam, my former suit. I do beseech you
    That by your virtuous means I may again
    Exist, and be a member of his love
    Whom I with all the office° of my heart
    Entirely honor. I would not be delayed.   110
    If my offense be of such mortal kind
    That nor my service past, nor present sorrows,
    Nor purposed merit in futurity,
    Can ransom me into his love again,
    But to know so must be my benefit.°   115
    So shall I clothe me in a forced content,
    And shut myself up in some other course
    To fortune's alms.
Desdemona.   Alas, thrice-gentle Cassio,
    My advocation° is not now in tune.
    My lord is not my lord; nor should I know him   120
    Were he in favor° as in humor altered
    So help me every spirit sanctified
    As I have spoken for you all my best
    And stood within the blank° of his displeasure
    For my free speech. You must awhile be patient.   125
    What I can do I will; and more I will
    Than for myself I dare. Let that suffice you.
Iago. Is my lord angry?
Emilia.   He went hence but now,
    And certainly in strange unquietness.

---

109 *office* duty   115 *benefit* good   119 *advocation* advocacy   121 *favor* countenance   124 *blank* bull's-eye of a target

Iago. Can he be angry? I have seen the cannon   130
   When it hath blown his ranks into the air
   And, like the devil, from his very arm
   Puffed his own brother. And is he angry?
   Something of moment° then. I will go meet him.
   There's matter in't indeed if he be angry.   135
Desdemona. I prithee do so.   *Exit* [*Iago*].
                    Something sure of state,°
   Either from Venice or some unhatched practice°
   Made demonstrable here in Cyprus to him,
   Hath puddled° his clear spirit; and in such cases
   Men's natures wrangle with inferior things,   140
   Though great ones are their object. 'Tis even so.
   For let our finger ache, and it endues°
   Our other, healthful members even to a sense
   Of pain. Nay, we must think men are not gods,
   Nor of them look for such observancy   145
   As fits the bridal. Beshrew me much, Emilia,
   I was, unhandsome warrior as I am,
   Arraigning his unkindness with my soul;
   But now I find I had suborned the witness,
   And he's indicted falsely.
Emilia.   Pray heaven it be   150
   State matters, as you think, and no conception
   Nor no jealous toy° concerning you.
Desdemona. Alas the day! I never gave him cause.
Emilia. But jealous souls will not be answered so;
   They are not ever jealous for the cause,   155
   But jealous for they're jealous. It is a monster
   Begot upon itself, born on itself.
Desdemona. Heaven keep the monster from Othello's mind!
Emilia. Lady, amen.
Desdemona. I will go seek him. Cassio, walk here about.   160
   If I do find him fit,° I'll move your suit
   And seek to effect it to my uttermost.
Cassio. I humbly thank your ladyship.

                    Exit [*Desdemona with Emilia*].
   Enter Bianca.

Bianca. Save you, friend Cassio!

---

[134] *moment* importance   [136] *of state* state affairs   [137] *unhatched practice*
undisclosed plot   [139] *puddled* muddied   [142] *endues* leads   [152] *toy* trifle
[161] *fit* receptive

Cassio.   What make you from home?
   How is't with you, my most fair Bianca?   165
   I' faith, sweet love, I was coming to your house.
Bianca. And I was going to your lodging, Cassio.
   What, keep a week away? Seven days and nights?
   Eightscore eight hours? And lovers' absent hours
   More tedious than the dial eightscore times?   170
   O weary reck'ning.°
Cassio.   Pardon me, Bianca.
   I have this while with leaden thoughts been pressed,
   But I shall in a more continuate° time
   Strike off this score° of absence. Sweet Bianca,

                [Gives her Desdemona's handkerchief.]

   Take me this work out.
Bianca.   O Cassio, whence came this?   175
   This is some token from a newer friend.
   To the felt absence now I feel a cause.
   Is't come to this? Well, well.
Cassio.   Go to, woman!
   Throw your vile guesses in the devil's teeth,
   From whence you have them. You are jealous now   180
   That this is from some mistress, some remembrance.
   No, by my faith, Bianca.
Bianca.   Why, whose is it?
Cassio. I know not neither; I found it in my chamber.
   I like the work well; ere it be demanded,°
   As like enough it will, I would have it copied.   185
   Take it and do't, and leave me for this time.
Bianca. Leave you? Wherefore?
Cassio. I do attend here on the general
   And think it no addition, nor my wish,
   To have him see me womaned.
Bianca.   Why, I pray you?   190
Cassio. Not that I love you not.
Bianca.   But that you do not love me!
   I pray you bring° me on the way a little,
   And say if I shall see you soon at night.
Cassio. 'Tis but a little way that I can bring you,

---

¹⁷¹ *reck'ning* addition   ¹⁷³ *continuate* uninterrupted   ¹⁷⁴ *Strike off this score*
i.e., pay this bill (the *score* being the account of drinks kept in a tavern)
¹⁸⁴ *demanded* asked for (by the person who lost it)   ¹⁹² *bring* accompany

For I attend here; but I'll see you soon.   195
Bianca. 'Tis very good. I must be circumstanced.°

                      Exeunt omnes.

ACT IV

Scene I   [*A street.*]

Enter Othello and Iago.

Iago. Will you think so?
Othello.   Think so, Iago?
Iago.   What,
    To kiss in private?
Othello.   . An unauthorized° kiss?
Iago. Or to be naked with her friend in bed
    An hour or more, not meaning any harm?
Othello. Naked in bed, Iago, and not mean harm?   5
    It is hypocrisy against the devil.
    They that mean virtuously, and yet do so,
    The devil their virtue tempts, and they tempt heaven.
Iago. If they do nothing, 'tis a venial slip.
    But if I give my wife a handkerchief ——   10
Othello. What then?
Iago. Why, then 'tis hers, my lord; and being hers,
    She may, I think, bestow't on any man.
Othello. She is protectress of her honor too.
    May she give that?   15
Iago. Her honor is an essence that's not seen;
   They have it very oft that have it not.
   But for the handkerchief ——
Othello. By heaven, I would most gladly have forgot it!
    Thou said'st — O, it comes o'er my memory   20
    As doth the raven° o'er the infected house,
    Boding to all — he had my handkerchief.
Iago. Ay, what of that?
Othello.   That's not so good now.
Iago. What if I had said I had seen him do you wrong?
    Or heard him say — as knaves be such abroad°   25
    Who having, by their own importunate suit,
    Or voluntary dotage° of some mistress,

---

[196] *be circumstanced* accept things as they are   IV.i.   [2] *unauthorized* illicit
[21] *raven* (a harbinger of death)   [25] *abroad* i.e., in the world   [27] *voluntary*
dotage weakness of the will

Convincèd or supplied° them, cannot choose
But they must blab ——
Othello.   Hath he said anything?
Iago. He hath, my lord; but be you well assured,   30
No more than he'll unswear.
Othello.   What hath he said?
Iago. Why, that he did — I know not what he did.
Othello. What? what?
Iago. Lie ——
Othello. With her?
Iago.   With her, on her; what you will.   35
Othello. Lie with her? Lie on her? — We say lie on her when
   they belie her. — Lie with her! Zounds, that's fulsome.°
   — Handkerchief — confessions — handkerchief! — To con-
   fess, and be hanged for his labor — first to be hanged, and
   then to confess! I tremble at it. Nature would not invest   40
   herself in such shadowing passion without some instruction.° It is not words that shakes me thus. — Pish! Noses,
   ears, and lips? Is't possible? — Confess? — Handkerchief?
   — O devil!

                                          Falls in a trance.

Iago. Work on.   45
   My med'cine works! Thus credulous fools are caught,
   And many worthy and chaste dames even thus,
   All guiltless, meet reproach.° What, ho! My lord!
   My lord, I say! Othello!

   Enter Cassio.

                     How now, Cassio?
Cassio. What's the matter?   50
Iago. My lord is fall'n into an epilepsy.
   This is his second fit; he had one yesterday.
Cassio. Rub him about the temples.
Iago. The lethargy° must have his quiet course.
   If not, he foams at mouth, and by and by   55
   Breaks out to savage madness. Look, he stirs.
   Do you withdraw yourself a little while.

---

²⁸ *Convincèd or supplied* persuaded or gratified (the mistress)   ³⁷ *fulsome*
foul, repulsive   ⁴⁰⁻⁴² *Nature . . . instruction* i.e., my mind would not become so darkened (with anger) unless there were something in this (accusation); (it should be remembered that Othello believes in the workings of
magic and supernatural forces)   ⁴⁸ *reproach* shame   ⁵⁴ *lethargy* coma

He will recover straight. When he is gone,
I would on great occasion° speak with you.

[*Exit Cassio.*]

How is it, general? Have you not hurt your head?   60
Othello. Dost thou mock° me?
Iago.   I mock you not, by heaven.
Would you would bear your fortune like a man.
Othello. A hornèd man's a monster and a beast.
Iago. There's many a beast then in a populous city,
And many a civil° monster.   65
Othello. Did he confess it?
Iago.   Good, sir, be a man.
Think every bearded fellow that's but yoked
May draw° with you. There's millions now alive
That nightly lie in those unproper° beds
Which they dare swear peculiar.° Your case is better.   70
O, 'tis the spite of hell, the fiend's arch-mock,
To lip a wanton in a secure couch,
And to suppose her chaste. No, let me know;
And knowing what I am, I know what she shall be.
Othello. O, thou art wise! 'Tis certain.
Iago.   Stand you awhile apart;   75
Confine yourself but in a patient list.°
Whilst you were here, o'erwhelmèd with your grief —
A passion most unsuiting such a man —
Cassio came hither. I shifted him away°
And laid good 'scuses upon your ecstasy,°   80
Bade him anon return, and here speak with me;
The which he promised. Do but encave° yourself
And mark the fleers,° the gibes, and notable° scorns
That dwell in every region of his face.
For I will make him tell the tale anew: 85
Where, how, how oft, how long ago, and when
He hath, and is again to cope your wife.
I say, but mark his gesture. Marry patience,

---

⁵⁹ **great occasion** very important matter   ⁶¹ **mock** (Othello takes Iago's comment as a reference to his horns — which it is)   ⁶⁵ **civil** city-dwelling
⁶⁸ **draw** i.e., like the horned ox   ⁶⁹ **unproper** i.e., not exclusively the husband's   ⁷⁰ **peculiar** their own alone   ⁷⁶ **a patient list** the bounds of patience
⁷⁹ **shifted him away** got rid of him by a stratagem   ⁸⁰ **ecstasy** trance (the literal meaning, "outside oneself." bears on the meaning of the change Othello is undergoing)   ⁸² **encave** hide   ⁸³ **fleers** mocking looks or speeches
⁸³ **notable** obvious

Or I shall say you're all in all in spleen,°
And nothing of a man.
Othello.   Dost thou hear, Iago?   90
    I will be found most cunning in my patience;
    But — dost thou hear? — most bloody.
Iago.   That's not amiss;
    But yet keep time in all. Will you withdraw?

[*Othello moves to one side, where his remarks are not audible to
Cassio and Iago.*]

    Now will I question Cassio of Bianca,
    A huswife° that by selling her desires   95
    Buys herself bread and cloth. It is a creature
    That dotes on Cassio, as 'tis the strumpet's plague
    To beguile many and be beguiled by one.
    He, when he hears of her, cannot restrain
    From the excess of laughter. Here he comes.   100

Enter Cassio.

    As he shall smile, Othello shall go mad:
    And his unbookish° jealousy must conster°
    Poor Cassio's smiles, gestures, and light behaviors
    Quite in the wrong. How do you, lieutenant?
Cassio. The worser that you give me the addition°   105
    Whose want even kills me.
Iago. Ply Desdemona well, and you are sure on't.
    Now, if this suit lay in Bianca's power,
    How quickly should you speed!
Cassio.   Alas, poor caitiff!°
Othello. Look how he laughs already!   110
Iago. I never knew woman love man so.
Cassio. Alas, poor rogue! I think, i' faith, she loves me.
Othello. Now he denies it faintly, and laughs it out.
Iago. Do you hear, Cassio?
Othello.   Now he importunes him
    To tell it o'er. Go to! Well said, well said!   115
Iago. She gives it out that you shall marry her.
    Do you intend it?
Cassio. Ha, ha, ha!
Othello. Do ye triumph, Roman? Do you triumph?

---

⁸⁹ *spleen* passion, particularly anger   ⁹⁵ *huswife* housewife (but with the
special meaning here of "prostitute")   ¹⁰² *unbookish* ignorant   ¹⁰² *conster*
construe   ¹⁰⁵ *addition* title   ¹⁰⁹ *caitiff* wretch

Cassio. I marry? What, a customer?° Prithee bear some charity   120
  to my wit; do not think it so unwholesome. Ha, ha, ha!

Othello. So, so, so, so. They laugh that win.

Iago. Why, the cry goes that you marry her.

Cassio. Prithee, say true.

Iago. I am a very villain else.   125

Othello. Have you scored° me? Well.

Cassio. This is the monkey's own giving out. She is persuaded
  I will marry her out of her own love and flattery, not out of
  my promise.

Othello. Iago beckons me; now he begins the story.   130

  [*Othello moves close enough to hear.*]

Cassio. She was here even now; she haunts me in every place.
  I was the other day talking on the sea bank with certain
  Venetians, and thither comes the bauble,° and falls me thus
  about my neck ——

Othello. Crying "O dear Cassio!" as it were. His gesture im-   135
  ports it.

Cassio. So hangs, and lolls, and weeps upon me; so shakes and
  pulls me! Ha, ha, ha!

Othello. Now he tells how she plucked him to my chamber. O,
  I see that nose of yours, but not that dog I shall throw it to.

Cassio. Well, I must leave her company.   140

Iago. Before me!° Look where she comes.

  Enter Bianca.

Cassio. 'Tis such another fitchew!° Marry a perfumed one?
  What do you mean by this haunting of me?

Bianca. Let the devil and his dam haunt you! What did you
  mean by that same handkerchief you gave me even now? I   145
  was a fine fool to take it. I must take out the work? A likely
  piece of work that you should find it in your chamber and
  know not who left it there! This is some minx's token, and I
  must take out the work? There! [*She throws down the handkerchief.*] Give it your hobbyhorse.° Wheresoever you had   150
  it, I'll take out no work on't.

Cassio. How now, my sweet Bianca? How now? how now?

Othello. By heaven, that should be my handkerchief!

---

¹²⁰ *customer* one who sells, a merchant (here, a prostitute)   ¹²⁶ *scored*
marked, defaced   ¹³³ *bauble* plaything   ¹⁴¹ *Before me!* (an exclamation of
surprise)   ¹⁴² *fitchew* polecat, i.e., strong-smelling creature   ¹⁵⁰ *hobbyhorse*
prostitute

Bianca. If you'll come to supper tonight, you may; if you will
not, come when you are next prepared for.°   *Exit.*   155
Iago. After her, after her!
Cassio. Faith, I must; she'll rail in the streets else.
Iago. Will you sup there?
Cassio. Yes, I intend so.
Iago. Well, I may chance to see you, for I would very fain   160
speak with you.
Cassio. Prithee come. Will you?
Iago. Go to, say no more.   [*Exit Cassio.*]
Othello [*Comes forward*]. How shall I murder him, Iago?
Iago. Did you perceive how he laughed at his vice?   165
Othello. O Iago!
Iago. And did you see the handkerchief?
Othello. Was that mine?
Iago. Yours, by this hand! And to see how he prizes the foolish
woman your wife! She gave it him, and he hath giv'n it his   170
whore.
Othello. I would have him nine years a-killing! — A fine
woman, a fair woman, a sweet woman?
Iago. Nay, you must forget that.
Othello. Ay, let her rot, and perish, and be damned tonight; for 175
she shall not live. No, my heart is turned to stone; I strike it,
and it hurts my hand. O, the world hath not a sweeter creature! She might lie by an emperor's side and command him
tasks.
Iago. Nay, that's not your way.°   180
Othello. Hang her! I do but say what she is. So delicate with
her needle. An admirable musician. O, she will sing the
savageness out of a bear! Of so high and plenteous wit and
invention° ——
Iago. She's the worse for all this.   185
Othello. O, a thousand, a thousand times. And then, of so
gentle a condition?°
Iago. Ay, too gentle.
Othello. Nay, that's certain. But yet the pity of it, Iago. O Iago,
the pity of it, Iago.   190
Iago. If you are so fond over her iniquity, give her patent to
offend; for if it touch° not you, it comes near nobody.
Othello. I will chop her into messes!° Cuckold me!

Iago. O, 'tis foul in her.

Othello. With mine officer!   195

Iago. That's fouler.

Othello. Get me some poison, Iago, this night I'll not expostu-
    late with her, lest her body and beauty unprovide my mind°
    again. This night, Iago!

Iago. Do it not with poison. Strangle her in her bed, even the   200
    bed she hath contaminated.

Othello. Good, good! The justice of it pleases. Very good!

Iago. And for Cassio, let me be his undertaker.° You shall hear
    more by midnight.

Othello. Excellent good!   [*A trumpet.*]

                What trumpet is that same?   205

Iago. I warrant something from Venice.

        Enter Lodovico, Desdemona, and Attendants.

                        'Tis Lodovico.
    This comes from the Duke. See, your wife's with him.

Lodovico. God save you, worthy general.

Othello.   With° all my heart, sir.

Lodovico. The Duke and the senators of Venice greet you.

                                [*Gives him a letter.*]

Othello. I kiss the instrument of their pleasures.   210

                        [*Opens the letter and reads.*]

Desdemona. And what's the news, good cousin Lodovico?

Iago. I am very glad to see you, signior.
    Welcome to Cyprus.

Lodovico. I thank you. How does Lieutenant Cassio?

Iago.   Lives, sir.

Desdemona. Cousin, there's fall'n between him and my lord   215
    An unkind° breach; but you shall make all well.

Othello. Are you sure of that?

Desdemona. My lord?

Othello [*Reads*]. "This fail you not to do, as you will —— "

Lodovico. He did not call; he's busy in the paper.   220
    Is there division 'twixt my lord and Cassio?

Desdemona. A most unhappy one. I would do much
    T' atone° them, for the love I bear to Cassio.

---

[198] *unprovide my mind* undo my resolution   [203] *undertaker* (not "burier"
but "one who undertakes to do something")   [208] *With* i.e., I greet you with
[216] *unkind* unnatural   [223] *atone* reconcile

Othello. Fire and brimstone!
Desdemona.   My lord?
Othello.   Are you wise?
Desdemona. What, is he angry?
Lodovico.   May be th' letter moved him;   225
    For, as I think, they do command him home,
    Deputing Cassio in his government.°
Desdemona. Trust me, I am glad on't.
Othello.   Indeed?
Desdemona.   My lord?
Othello. I am glad to see you mad.
Desdemona.   Why, sweet Othello ——
Othello. Devil!   [*Strikes her.*]   230
Desdemona. I have not deserved this.
Lodovico. My lord, this would not be believed in Venice,
    Though I should swear I saw't. 'Tis very much.
    Make her amends; she weeps.
Othello.   O devil, devil!
    If that the earth could teem° with woman's tears,   235
    Each drop she falls° would prove a crocodile.°
    Out of my sight!
Desdemona.   I will not stay to offend you.   [*Going.*]
Lodovico. Truly, an obedient lady.
    I do beseech your lordship call her back.
Othello. Mistress!
Desdemona.   My lord?
Othello.   What would you with her, sir?   240
Lodovico. Who? I, my lord?
Othello. Ay! You did wish that I would make her turn.
    Sir, she can turn, and turn, and yet go on
    And turn again; and she can weep, sir, weep;
    And she's obedient; as you say, obedient.   245
    Concerning this, sir — O well-painted passion!
    I am commanded home. — Get you away;
    I'll send for you anon. — Sir, I obey the mandate
    And will return to Venice. — Hence, avaunt!

                 [*Exit Desdemona.*]

    Cassio shall have my place. And, sir, tonight   250
    I do entreat that we may sup together.
    You are welcome, sir, to Cyprus. — Goats and monkeys!   *Exit.*

---

[227] *government* office [235] *teem* conceive [236] *falls* drops [236] *crocodile* (the crocodile was supposed to shed false tears to lure its victims)

Lodovico. Is this the noble Moor whom our full Senate
　　Call all in all sufficient? Is this the nature
　　Whom passion could not shake? whose solid virtue   255
　　The shot of accident nor dart of chance
　　Could neither graze nor pierce?
Iago.　　　　　　　　　　　He is much changed.
Lodovico. Are his wits safe? Is he not light of brain?
Iago. He's that he is; I may not breathe my censure.
　　What he might be (if, what he might, he is not)   260
　　I would to heaven he were!
Lodovico.　　　　　　　　What, strike his wife?
Iago. Faith, that was not so well; yet would I knew
　　That stroke would prove the worst.
Lodovico.　　　　　　　　　　Is it his use?°
　　Or did the letters work upon his blood°
　　And new-create his fault?
Iago.　　　　　　　Alas, alas!   265
　　It is not honesty in me to speak
　　What I have seen and known. You shall observe him,
　　And his own courses° will denote him so
　　That I may save my speech. Do but go after
　　And mark how he continues.   270
Lodovico. I am sorry that I am deceived in him.　　　　　*Exeunt.*

　　Scene II　[*The citadel.*]

　　Enter Othello and Emilia.

Othello. You have seen nothing then?
Emilia. Nor ever heard, nor ever did suspect.
Othello. Yes, you have seen Cassio and she together.
Emilia. But then I saw no harm, and then I heard
　　Each syllable that breath made up° between them.   5
Othello. What, did they never whisper?
Emilia.　　　　　　　　　　Never, my lord.
Othello. Nor send you out o' th' way?
Emilia. Never.
Othello. To fetch her fan, her gloves, her mask, nor nothing?
Emilia. Never, my lord.   10
Othello. That's strange.
Emilia. I durst, my lord, to wager she is honest,

---

²⁶³ *use* habit　　²⁶⁴ *blood* passion　　²⁶⁸ *courses* actions　　IV.ii.　　⁵ *that breath
made up* spoken

Lay down my soul at stake.° If you think other,
Remove your thought. It doth abuse your bosom.
If any wretch have put this in your head,   15
Let heaven requite it with the serpent's curse,°
For if she be not honest,° chaste, and true,
There's no man happy. The purest of their wives
Is foul as slander.
Othello.   Bid her come hither, Go.   *Exit Emilia.*
She says enough; yet she's a simple bawd°   20
That cannot say as much. This is a subtle whore,
A close lock and key of villainous secrets,
And yet she'll kneel and pray; I have seen her do't.

Enter Desdemona and Emilia.

Desdemona. My lord, what is your will?
Othello.   Pray you, chuck, come hither.
Desdemona. What is your pleasure?
Othello.   Let me see your eyes.   25
Look in my face.
Desdemona.   What horrible fancy's this?
Othello [To Emilia]. Some of your function,° mistress:
Leave procreants alone and shut the door;
Cough or cry hem if anybody come.
Your mystery,° your mystery! Nay, dispatch!   30

Exit Emilia.

Desdemona. Upon my knee, what doth your speech import?
I understand a fury in your words.°
Othello. Why, what art thou?
Desdemona.   Your wife, my lord; your true
And loyal wife.
Othello.   Come, swear it, damn thyself;
Lest, being like one of heaven, the devils themselves   35
Should fear to seize thee. Therefore be doubledamned:
Swear thou art honest.
Desdemona.   Heaven doth truly know it.
Othello. Heaven truly knows that thou art false as hell.
Desdemona. To whom, my lord? With whom? How am I false?
Othello. Ah, Desdemon! Away! Away! Away!   40

---

¹³ *at stake* as the wager   ¹⁶ *serpent's curse* (God's curse on the serpent after the fall in Eden   ¹⁷ *honest* chaste   ²⁰ *bawd* procuress   ²⁷ *Some of your function* do your proper work (as the operator of a brothel)   ³⁰ *mystery* trade   ³² *words* (Q1 adds to this line, "But not the words")

Desdemona. Alas the heavy day! Why do you weep?
   Am I the motive° of these tears, my lord?
   If haply° you my father do suspect
   An instrument of this your calling back,
   Lay not your blame on me. If you have lost him,   45
   I have lost him too.
Othello.   Had it pleased heaven
   To try with affliction, had they rained
   All kinds of sores and shames on my bare head,
   Steeped° me in poverty to the very lips,
   Given to captivity me and my utmost hopes,   50
   I should have found in some place of my soul
   A drop of patience. But alas, to make me
   The fixèd figure for the time of scorn°
   To point his slow and moving finger at.
   Yet could I bear that too, well, very well.   55
   But there where I have garnered up my heart,
   Where either I must live or bear no life,
   The fountain from the which my current runs
   Or else dries up — to be discarded thence,
   Or keep it as a cistern for foul toads   60
   To knot and gender° in — turn thy complexion there,
   Patience, thou young and rose-lipped cherubin!
   I here look grim as hell!°
Desdemona. I hope my noble lord esteems me honest.
Othello. O, ay, as summer flies are in the shambles,°   65
   That quicken even with blowing.° O thou weed,
   Who art so lovely fair, and smell'st so sweet,
   That the sense aches at thee, would thou hadst never
      been born!
Desdemona. Alas, what ignorant° sin have I committed?
Othello. Was this fair paper, this most goodly book,   70
   Made to write "whore" upon? What committed?
   Committed? O thou public commoner,°
   I should make very forges of my cheeks
   That would to cinders burn up modesty,
   Did I but speak thy deeds. What committed?   75

---

[42] *motive* cause   [43] *haply* by chance   [49] *Steeped* submerged   [53] *The . . . scorn* the very image of scorn in our time   [61] *knot and gender* twist in bunches and procreate   [61-63] *turn . . . hell* (the rough sense would seem to be "even Patience would grow pale, turn complexion, at Desdemona's perfidy, but that Othello looks grimly on")   [65] *shambles* abattoirs   [66] *quicken even with blowing* become impregnated as soon as they lay their eggs   [69] *ignorant* unknowing   [72] *commoner* prostitute

Heaven stops the nose at it, and the moon winks;°
The bawdy wind that kisses all it meets
Is hushed within the hollow mine of earth
And will not hear't. What committed?
Desdemona. By heaven, you do me wrong!   80
Othello. Are not you a strumpet?
Desdemona.   No, as I am a Christian!
If to preserve this vessel for my lord
From any other foul unlawful touch
Be not to be a strumpet, I am none.
Othello. What, not a whore?
Desdemona.   No, as I shall be saved!   85
Othello. Is't possible?
Desdemona. O, heaven forgive us!
Othello.   I cry you mercy° then.
I took you for that cunning whore of Venice
That married with Othello. [*Calling*] You, mistress,

Enter Emilia.

That have the office opposite to Saint Peter   90
And keep the gate of hell! You, you, ay, you!
We have done our course; there's money for your pains.

                    [*Throws her some coins.*]

I pray you turn the key and keep our counsel.

                                        Exit.

Emilia. Alas, what does this gentleman conceive?
How do you, madam? How do you, my good lady?   95
Desdemona. Faith, half asleep.
Emilia. Good madam, what's the matter with my lord?
Desdemona. With who?
Emilia. Why, with my lord, madam.
Desdemona. Who is thy lord?
Emilia.   He that is yours, sweet lady.   100
Desdemona. I have none. Do not talk to me, Emilia.
I cannot weep, nor answers have I none
But what should go by water.° Prithee tonight
Lay on my bed my wedding sheets, remember;
And call thy husband hither.
Emilia.   Here's a change indeed!   105

                                        Exit.

[76] ***winks*** closes its eyes (the moon was the symbol of chastity)   [87] ***cry you mercy*** ask your pardon   [103] ***water*** tears

Desdemona. 'Tis meet I should be use'd so, very meet.
   How have I been behaved, that he might stick
   The small'st opinion on my least misuse?°

   Enter Iago and Emilia.

Iago. What is your pleasure, madam? How is't with you?
Desdemona. I cannot tell. Those that do teach young babes   110
   Do it with gentle means and easy tasks.
   He might have chid me so; for, in good faith,
   I am a child to chiding.
Iago.   What is the matter, lady?
Emilia. Alas, Iago, my lord hath so bewhored her,
   Thrown such despite° and heavy terms upon her   115
   That true hearts cannot bear it.
Desdemona. Am I that name, Iago?
Iago.   What name, fair lady?
Desdemona. Such as she said my lord did say I was.
Emilia. He called her whore. A beggar in his drink
   Could not have laid such terms upon his callet.°   120
Iago. Why did he so?
Desdemona. I do not know; I am sure I am none such.
Iago. Do not weep, do not weep. Alas the day.
Emilia. Hath she forsook so many noble matches,
   Her father and her country, and her friends,   125
   To be called whore? Would it not make one weep?
Desdemona. It is my wretched fortune.
Iago.   Beshrew° him for 't!
   How comes this trick upon him?
Desdemona.   Nay, heaven doth know.
Emilia. I will be hanged if some eternal villain,
   Some busy and insinuating rogue,   130
   Some cogging,° cozening slave, to get some office,
   Have not devised this slander. I will be hanged else.
Iago. Fie, there is no such man! It is impossible.
Desdemona. If any such there be, heaven pardon him.
Emilia. A halter pardon him! And hell gnaw his bones!   135
   Why should he call her whore? Who keeps her company?
   What place? What time? What form? What likelihood?
   The Moor's abused by some most villainous knave,
   Some base notorious knave, some scurvy fellow.

---

¹⁰⁷⁻⁰⁸ *stick . . . misuse* base any doubt on my smallest fault   ¹¹⁵ *despite* abuse
¹²⁰ *callet* slut   ¹²⁷ *Beshrew* curse   ¹³¹ *cogging* cheating

O heavens, that such companions° thou'dst unfold,°   140
And put in every honest hand a whip
To lash the rascals naked through the world
Even from the east to th' west!
Iago.   Speak within door.°
Emilia. O, fie upon them! Some such squire° he was
That turned your wit the seamy side without   145
And made you to suspect me with the Moor.
Iago.   You are a fool. Go to.
Desdemona.   .   Alas, Iago,
What shall I do to win my lord again?
Good friend, go to him, for, by this light of heaven,
I know not how I lost him. Here I kneel: 150
If e'er my will did trespass 'gainst his love
Either in discourse of thought° or actual deed,
Or that mine eyes, mine ears, or any sense
Delighted them in any other form;
Or that I do not yet, and ever did,   155
And ever will (though he do shake me off
To beggarly divorcement) love him dearly,
Comfort forswear me. Unkindness may do much,
And his unkindness may defeat° my life,
But never taint my love. I cannot say "whore."   160
It does abhor me now I speak the word;
To do the act that might the addition earn
Not the world's mass of vanity could make me.
Iago.   I pray you be content. 'Tis but his humor.°
The business of the state does him offense.   165
Desdemona.   If 'twere no other.
Iago.   It is but so, I warrant.

                                        [*Trumpets within.*]

Hark how these instruments summon to supper.
The messengers of Venice stay the meat.°
Go in, and weep not. All things shall be well.

                          [*Exeunt Desdemona and Emilia.*]

Enter Roderigo.

How now, Roderigo?   170
Roderigo.   I do not find that thou deal'st justly with me.

¹⁴⁰ *companions* fellows, rogues   ¹⁴⁰ *unfold* disclose   ¹⁴³ *within door* more quietly and moderately   ¹⁴⁴ *squire* (a term of contempt)   ¹⁵² *discourse of thought* thinking   ¹⁵⁹ *defeat* destroy   ¹⁶⁴ *humor* mood   ¹⁶⁸ *stay the meat* await the meal

Iago. What in the contrary?

Roderigo. Every day thou daff'st° me with some device° Iago,
and rather, as it seems to me now, keep'st from me all con-
veniency° than suppliest me with the least advantage of   175
hope. I will indeed no longer endure it; nor am I yet persuaded to put up° in peace what already I have foolishly
suffered.

Iago. Will you hear me, Roderigo?

Roderigo. I have heard too much, and your words and perform-   180
ances are no kin together.

Iago. You charge me most unjustly.

Roderigo. With naught but truth. I have wasted myself out of
my means. The jewels you have had from me to deliver
Desdemona would half have corrupted a votarist.° You have   185
told me she hath received them, and returned me expectations and comforts of sudden respect° and acquaintance; but
I find none.

Iago. Well, go to; very well.

Roderigo. Very well? Go to? I cannot go to, man; nor 'tis not   190
very well. Nay, I think it is scurvy, and begin to find myself
fopped° in it.

Iago. Very well.

Roderigo. I tell you 'tis not very well. I will make myself
known to Desdemona. If she will return me my jewels, I   195
will give over my suit and repent my unlawful solicitation. If
not, assure yourself I will seek satisfaction of you.

Iago. You have said now?

Roderigo. Ay, and said nothing but what I protest° intendment
of doing.   200

Iago. Why, now I see there's mettle° in thee, and even from
this instant do build on thee a better opinion than ever before. Give me thy hand, Roderigo. Thou hast taken against
me a most just exception;° but yet I protest I have dealt most
directly° in thy affair.   205

Roderigo. It hath not appeared.

Iago. I grant indeed it hath not appeared, and your suspicion
is not without wit and judgment. But, Roderigo, if thou hast
that in thee indeed which I have greater reason to believe
now than ever — I mean purpose, courage, and valor — this   210

---

173 *daff'st* put off   173 *device* scheme   174-75 *conveniency* what is needful
177 *put up* accept   185 *votarist* nun   187 *sudden respect* immediate consideration   192 *fopped* duped   199 *protest* aver   201 *mettle* spirit   204 *exception*
objection   205 *directly* straightforwardly

might show it. If thou the next night following enjoy not
Desdemona, take me from this world with treachery and
devise engines for° my life.
Roderigo. Well, what is it? Is it within reason and compass?°
Iago. Sir, there is especial commission come from Venice to   215
depute Cassio in Othello's place.
Roderigo. Is that true? Why, then Othello and Desdemona re-
turn again to Venice.
Iago. O, no; he goes into Mauritania and taketh away with him
the fair Desdemona, unless his abode be lingered here by   220
some accident; wherein none can be so determinate° as the
removing of Cassio.
Roderigo. How do you mean, removing him?
Iago. Why, by making him uncapable of Othello's place —
knocking out his brains.   225
Roderigo. And that you would have me to do?
Iago. Ay, if you dare do yourself a profit and a right. He sups
tonight with a harlotry,° and thither will I go to him. He
knows not yet of his honorable fortune. If you will watch his
going thence, which I will fashion to fall out° between   230
twelve and one, you may take him at your pleasure. I will be
near to second° your attempt, and he shall fall between us.
Come, stand not amazed at it, but go along with me. I will
show you such a necessity in his death that you shall think
yourself bound to put it on him. It is now high supper time,   235
and the night grows to waste. About it.
Roderigo. I will hear further reason for this.
Iago. And you shall be satisfied.   *Exeunt.*

Scene III   [*The citadel.*]

Enter Othello, Lodovico, Desdemona, Emilia, and Attendants.

Lodovico. I do beseech you, sir, trouble yourself no further.
Othello. O, pardon me; 'twill do me good to walk.
Lodovico. Madam, good night. I humbly thank your ladyship.
Desdemona. Your honor is most welcome.
Othello. Will you walk, sir? O, Desdemona.   5
Desdemona. My lord?

---

²¹³ *engines for* schemes against   ²¹⁴ *compass* possibility   ²²¹ *determinate*
effective   ²²⁸ *harlotry* female   ²³⁰ *fall out* occur   ²³² *second* support

Othello. Get you to bed on th' instant; I will be returned
     forthwith.
     Dismiss your attendant there. Look't be done.
Desdemona. I will, my lord.

                    Exit [*Othello, with Lodovico and Attendants*].

Emilia. How goes it now? He looks gentler than he did.   10
Desdemona. He says he will return incontinent,°
     And hath commanded me to go to bed.
     And bade me to dismiss you.
Emilia.   Dismiss me?
Desdemona. It was his bidding; therefore, good Emilia,
     Give me my nightly wearing, and adieu.   15
     We must not now displease him.
Emilia. I would you had never seen him!
Desdemona. So would not I. My love doth so approve him
     That even his stubborness, his checks,° his frowns —
     Prithee unpin me — have grace and favor.   20
Emilia. I have laid these sheets you bade me on the bed.
Desdemona. All's one.° Good Father, how foolish are our
     minds!
     If I do die before, prithee shroud me
     In one of these same sheets.
Emilia.   Come, come! You talk.   25
Desdemona. My mother had a maid called Barbary,
     She was in love; and he she loved proved mad
     And did forsake her. She had a song of "Willow";
     An old thing 'twas, but it expressed her fortune,
     And she died singing it. That song tonight   30
     Will not go from my mind; I have much to do
     But to go hang my head all at one side
     And sing it like poor Barbary. Prithee dispatch.
Emilia. Shall I go fetch your nightgown?
Desdemona. No, unpin me here.   35
     This Lodovico is a proper man.
Emilia. A very handsome man.
Desdemona. He speaks well.
Emilia. I know a lady in Venice would have walked barefoot to
     Palestine for a touch of his nether lip.   40
Desdemona [*Sings*].
          "The poor soul sat singing by a sycamore tree,
             Sing all a green willow;

IV.iii.   ¹¹ *incontinent* at once   ¹⁹ *checks* rebukes   ²² *All's one* no matter

Her hand on her bosom, her head on her knee,
   Sing willow, willow, willow.
The fresh streams ran by her and murmured her moans;   45
   Sing willow, willow, willow;
Her salt tears fell from her, and soft'ned the stones —
   Sing willow, willow, willow — "
Lay by these.   [*Gives Emilia her clothes.*]
   "Willow, Willow" ——   50
Prithee hie° thee; he'll come anon.°
   "Sing all a green willow must be my garland.
   Let nobody blame him; his scorn I approve" ——
Nay, that's not next. Hark! Who is't that knocks?
Emilia. It is the wind.   55
Desdemona [*Sings*].
   "I called my love false love; but what said he then?
   Sing willow, willow, willow:
   If I court moe° women, you'll couch with moe men."
So, get thee gone; good night. Mine eyes do itch.
Doth that bode weeping?
Emilia.   'Tis neither here nor there.   60
Desdemona. I have heard it said so. O, these men, these men.
Dost thou in conscience think, tell me, Emilia,
That there be women do abuse their husbands
In such gross kind?
Emilia.   There be some such, no question.
Desdemona. Wouldst thou do such a deed for all the world?   65
Emilia. Why, would not you?
Desdemona.   No, by this heavenly light!
Emilia. Nor I neither by this heavenly light.
I might do't as well i' th' dark.
Desdemona. Wouldst thou do such a deed for all the world?
Emilia. The world's a huge thing; it is a great price for a small   70
vice.
Desdemona. In troth, I think thou wouldst not.
Emilia. In troth, I think I should; and undo't when I had done.
Marry, I would not do such a thing for a joint-ring,° nor for
measures of lawn,° nor for gowns, petticoats, nor caps, nor   75
any petty exhibition,° but for all the whole world? Why, who
would not make her husband a cuckold to make him a
monarch? I should venture purgatory for't.

---

⁵¹ *hie* hurry ⁵¹ *anon* at once ⁵⁸ *moe* more ⁷⁴ *joint-ring* (a ring with two
interlocking halves) ⁷⁵ *lawn* fine linen ⁷⁶ *exhibition* payment

Desdemona. Beshrew me if I would do such a wrong for the
    whole world.   80
Emilia. Why, the wrong is but a wrong i' th' world; and having
    the world for your labor, 'tis a wrong in your own world, and
    you might quickly make it right.
Desdemona. I do not think there is any such woman.
Emilia. Yes, a dozen; and as many to th' vantage as would   85
    store° the world they played for.
    But I do think it is their husbands' faults
    If wives do fall. Say that they slack their duties
    And pour our treasures into foreign° laps;
    Or else break out in peevish jealousies,   90
    Throwing restraint upon us; or say they strike us,
    Or scant our former having in despite° —
    Why, we have galls; and though we have some grace,
    Yet have we some revenge. Let husbands know
    Their wives have sense like them. They see, and smell,   95
    And have their palates both for sweet and sour,
    As husbands have. What is it that they do
    When they change° us for others? Is it sport?
    I think it is. And doth affection° breed it?
    I think it doth. Is't frailty that thus errs?   100
    It is so too. And have not we affections?
    Desires for sport? and frailty? as men have?
    Then let them use us well; else let them know,
    The ills we do, their ills instruct us so.°
Desdemona. Good night, good night. Heaven me such uses°   105
    send,
    Not to pick bad from bad, but by bad mend.   *Exeunt.*

ACT V

Scene I [*A street.*]

Enter Iago and Roderigo.

Iago. Here, stand behind this bulk;° straight will he come.
    Wear thy good rapier bare, and put it home.

85-86 *to . . . store* in addition as would fill   89 *foreign* alien, i.e., other than the
wife   92 *scant . . . despite* reduce, in spite, our household allowance (?)
98 *change* exchange   99 *affection* strong feeling, desire   104 *instruct us so*
teach us to do likewise   105 *uses* practices   V.i.   1 *bulk* projecting stall of a
shop

Quick, quick! Fear nothing; I'll be at thy elbow.
It makes us, or it mars us, think on that,
And fix most firm thy resolution.   5
Roderigo. Be near at hand; I may miscarry in't.
Iago. Here, at thy hand. Be bold, and take thy stand.

> [*Moves to one side.*]

Roderigo. I have no great devotion to the deed,
  And yet he hath given me satisfying reasons.
  'Tis but a man gone. Forth my sword! He dies!   10
Iago. I have rubbed this young quat° almost to the sense,°
  And he grows angry. Now, whether he kill Cassio,
  Or Cassio him, or each do kill the other,
  Every way makes my gain. Live Roderigo,
  He calls me to a restitution large   15
  Of gold and jewels that I bobbed° from him
  As gifts to Desdemona.
  It must not be. If Cassio do remain,
  He hath a daily beauty in his life
  That makes me ugly; and besides, the Moor   20
  May unfold me to him; there stand I in much peril.
  No, he must die. But so, I hear him coming.

Enter Cassio.

Roderigo. I know his gait. 'Tis he. Villain, thou diest!

> [*Thrusts at Cassio.*]

Cassio. That thrust had been mine enemy indeed
  But that my coat° is better than thou know'st.   25
  I will make proof of thine.   [*Fights with Roderigo.*]
Roderigo.   O, I am slain!°
Cassio. I am maimed forever. Help, ho! Murder! Murder!

Enter Othello [*to one side*].

Othello. The voice of Cassio. Iago keeps his word.
Roderigo. O, villain that I am!
Othello.   It is even so.

---

¹¹ *quat* pimple   ¹¹ *to the sense* raw   ¹⁶ *bobbed* swindled   ²⁵ *coat* i.e., a
mail shirt or bulletproof vest   ²⁶ *slain* most editors add here a stage direction
that has Iago wounding Cassio in the leg from behind, but remaining unseen.
However, nothing in the text requires this, and Cassio's wound can be given
him in the fight with Roderigo, for presumably when Cassio attacks Roderigo
the latter would not simply accept the thrust but would parry. Since Iago
enters again at line 46, he must exit at some point after line 22

Cassio. O help, ho! Light! A surgeon!   30
Othello. 'Tis he. O brave Iago, honest and just,
    That hast such noble sense o'f thy friend's wrong!
    Thou teachest me. Minion,° your dear lies dead,
    And your unblest° fate hies.° Strumpet, I come.
    Forth of my heart those charms, thine eyes, are blotted.   35
    Thy bed, lust-stained, shall with lust's blood be spotted.
                                                        Exit Othello.

        Enter Lodovico and Gratiano.

Cassio. What, ho? No watch? No passage?° Murder! Murder!
Gratiano. 'Tis some mischance. The voice is very direful.
Cassio. O, help!
Lodovico. Hark!   40
Roderigo. O wretched villain!
Lodovico. Two or three groan. 'Tis heavy night.
    These may be counterfeits. Let's think't unsafe
    To come into the cry without more help.
Roderigo. Nobody come? Then shall I bleed to death.   45
Lodovico. Hark!

        Enter Iago [with a light].

Gratiano. Here's one comes in his shirt, with light and weapons.
Iago. Who's there? Whose noise is this that cries on murder?
Lodovico. We do not know.
Iago.   Do not you hear a cry?
Cassio. Here, here! For heaven's sake, help me!
Iago.   What's the matter?   50
Gratiano. This is Othello's ancient, as I take it.
Lodovico. The same indeed, a very valiant fellow.
Iago. What are you here that cry so grievously?
Cassio. Iago? O, I am spoiled, undone by villians.
    Give me some help.   55
Iago. O me, lieutenant! What villains have done this?
Cassio. I think that one of them is hereabout
    And cannot make away.
Iago.   O treacherous villains!
    [*To Lodovico and Gratiano*] What are you there?
    Come in, and give some help.
Roderigo. O, help me there!   60
Cassio. That's one of them.

---

³³ *Minion* hussy, i.e., Desdemona   ³⁴ *unblest* unsanctified   ³⁴ *hies* approaches swiftly   ³⁷ *passage* passers-by

Iago.   O murd'rous slave! O villain!

[*Stabs Roderigo.*]

Roderigo. O damned Iago! O inhuman dog!
Iago. Kill men i' th' dark? — Where be these bloody thieves? —
How silent is this town! — Ho! Murder! Murder! —
What may you be? Are you of good or evil?   65
Lodovico. As you shall prove us, praise us.
Iago. Signior Lodovico?
Lodovico. He, sir.
Iago. I cry you mercy. Here's Cassio hurt by villains.
Gratiano. Cassio?   70
Iago. How is't, brother?
Cassio. My leg is cut in two.
Iago.   Marry, heaven forbid!
Light, gentlemen. I'll bind it with my shirt.

Enter Bianca.

Bianca. What is the matter, ho? Who is't that cried?
Iago. Who is't that cried?   75
Bianca. O my dear Cassio! My sweet Cassio!
O Cassio, Cassio, Cassio!
Iago. O notable strumpet! — Cassio, may you suspect
Who they should be that have thus mangled you?
Cassio. No.   80
Gratiano. I am sorry to find you thus. I have been to seek you.
Iago. Lend me a garter. So. O for a chair
To bear him easily hence.
Bianca. Alas, he faints! O Cassio, Cassio, Cassio!
Iago. Gentlemen all, I do suspect this trash   85
To be a party in this injury. —
Patience awhile, good Cassio. — Come, come.
Lend me a light. Know we this face or no?
Alas, my friend and my dear countryman
Roderigo? No. — Yes, sure. — Yes, 'tis Roderigo!   90
Gratiano. What, of Venice?
Iago. Even he, sir. Did you know him?
Gratiano.   Know him? Ay.
Iago. Signior Gratiano? I cry your gentle pardon.
These bloody accidents must excuse my manners
That so neglected you.
Gratiano.   I am glad to see you.   95
Iago. How do you, Cassio? — O, a chair, a chair!
Gratiano. Roderigo?

Iago. He, he, 'tis he! [*A chair brought in.*] O, that's well
    said;° the chair.
    Some good man bear him carefully from hence.
    I'll fetch the general's surgeon. [*To Bianca*] For you,
        mistress,   100
    Save you your labor. [*To Cassio*] He that lies slain
        here, Cassio,
    Was my dear friend. What malice was between you?
Cassio. None in the world; nor do I know the man.
Iago. What, look you pale? — O, bear him out o' th' air.

                                  [*Cassio is carried off.*]

    Stay you, good gentlemen. — Look you pale, mistress?   105
    Do you perceive the gastness° of her eye?
    Nay, if you stare, we shall hear more anon.
    Behold her well; I pray you look upon her.
    Do you see, gentlemen? Nay, guiltiness will speak,
    Though tongues were out of use.°   110

    [*Enter Emilia.*]

Emilia. Alas, what is the matter? What is the matter, husband?
Iago. Cassio hath here been set on in the dark
    By Roderigo and fellows that are scaped.
    He's almost slain, and Roderigo quite dead.
Emilia. Alas, good gentleman! Alas good Cassio!   115
Iago. This is the fruits of whoring. Prithee, Emilia,
    Go know of Cassio where he supped tonight.
    [*To Bianca*] What, do you shake at that?
Bianca. He supped at my house; but I therefore shake not.
Iago. O, did he so? I charge° you go with me.   120
Emilia. Oh fie upon thee, strumpet!
Bianca. I am no strumpet, but of life as honest
    As you that thus abuse me.
Emilia.   As I ? Fie upon thee!
Iago. Kind gentlemen, let's go see poor Cassio dressed.°
    [*To Bianca*] Come, mistress, you must tell's another tale.   125
    Emilia, run you to the citadel
    And tell my lord and lady what hath happed.

                                    [*Exit Emilia.*]

---

⁹⁸ *well said* well done   ¹⁰⁶ *gastness* terror   ¹¹⁰ *tongues were out of use* men
no longer spoke   ¹²⁰ *charge* command   ¹²⁴ *dressed* bandaged

Will you go on afore?   *Exeunt [all but Iago].*
   This is the night
That either makes me or fordoes me quite.°   [*Exit.*]

Scene II.   [*Desdemona's chamber.*]

Enter Othello [with a light]; and Desdemona in her bed.

Othello. It is the cause, it is the cause, my soul.
Let me not name it to you, you chaste stars.
It is the cause. Yet I'll not shed her blood,
Nor scar that whiter skin of hers than snow
And smooth as monumental alabaster.   5
Yet she must die, else she'll betray more men.
Put out the light, and then put out the light.
If I quench thee, thou flaming minister,°
I can again thy former light restore,
Should I repent me; but once put out thy light,   10
Thou cunning'st° pattern of excelling nature,
I know not where is that Promethean heat°
That can thy light relume.° When I have plucked the rose,
I cannot give it vital° growth again;
It needs must wither. I'll smell thee on the tree.   15

       [*He kisses her.*]

O balmy breath, that dost almost persuade
Justice to break her sword. One more, one more!
Be thus when thou art dead, and I will kill thee,
And love thee after. One more, and that's the last!
So sweet was ne'er so fatal. I must weep,   20
But they are cruel tears. This sorrow's heavenly;
It strikes where it doth love. She wakes.
Desdemona. Who's there? Othello?
Othello.   Ay, Desdemona.
Desdemona. Will you come to bed, my lord?
Othello. Have you prayed tonight, Desdemon?
Desdemona.   Ay, my lord.   25
Othello. If you bethink yourself of any crime

---

¹²⁹ *fordoes me quite* completely ruins me V.ii ⁸ *minister* worker, servant
¹¹ *cunning'st* most intricate and skillfully wrought (by nature excelling itself)
¹² *Promethean heat* divine fire (Prometheus is the Titan who stole fire from
heaven and gave it to man) ¹³ *relume* relight ¹⁴ *vital* living

Unreconciled as yet to heaven and grace,
    Solicit for it straight.
Desdemona. Alack, my lord, what may you mean by that?
Othello. Well, do it, and be brief; I will walk by.°   30
    I would not kill thy unprepared spirit.
    No, heavens forfend! I would not kill thy soul.
Desdemona. Talk you of killing?
Othello.   Ay, I do.
Desdemona.   Then heaven
    Have mercy on me!
Othello.   Amen, with all my heart.
Desdemona. If you say so, I hope you will not kill me.   35
Othello. Humh.
Desdemona. And yet I fear you; for you're fatal then
    When your eyes roll so. Why I should fear I know not,
    Since guiltiness I know not; but yet I feel I fear.
Othello. Think on thy sins.
Desdemona.   They are loves I bear to you.   40
Othello. Ay, and for that thou diest.
Desdemona. That death's unnatural that kills for loving.
    Alas, why gnaw you so your nether lip?
    Some bloody passion shakes your very frame.
    These are portents; but yet I hope, I hope,   45
    They do not point on me.
Othello.   Peace and be still.
Desdemona. I will so. What's the matter?
Othello. That handkerchief which I so loved and gave thee
    Thou gav'st to Cassio.
Desdemona.   No, by my life and soul!
    Send for the man and ask him.
Othello.   Sweet soul, take heed,   50
    Take heed of perjury; thou art on thy deathbed.
Desdemona. Ay, but not yet to die.
Othello.   Presently,°
    Therefore confess thee freely of thy sin,
    For to deny each article° with oath
    Cannot remove nor choke the strong conception   55
    That I do groan withal. Thou art to die.
Desdemona. Then Lord have mercy on me.
Othello.   I say, amen.
Desdemona. And have you mercy too. I never did

---

[30] *by* nearby   [52] ***Presently*** immediately   [54] ***article*** item (of the charge of adultery. Othello makes heavy use of legal terms in this scene)

Offend you in my life; never loved Cassio
But with such general warranty° of heaven   60
As I might love. I never gave him token.
Othello. By heaven, I saw my handkerchief in's hand!
    O perjured woman! thou dost stone° my heart,
    And mak'st me call what I intend to do
    A murder, which I thought a sacrifice.   65
    I saw the handkerchief.
Desdemona.   He found it then.
    I never gave it him. Send for him hither.
    Let him confess a truth.
Othello.   He hath confessed.
Desdemona. What, my lord?
Othello. That he hath used thee.
Desdemona.   How? Unlawfully?
Othello.   Ay.   70
Desdemona. He will not say so.
Othello.   No, his mouth is stopped.
    Honest Iago hath ta'en order for't.°
Desdemona. O, my fear interprets. What, is he dead?
Othello. Had all his hairs been lives, my great revenge
    Had stomach° for them all.   75
Desdemona. Alas, he is betrayed, and I undone!
Othello. Out, strumpet! Weep'st thou for him to my face?
Desdemona. O, banish me, my lord, but kill me not!
Othello. Down, strumpet!
Desdemona. Kill me tomorrow; let me live tonight!   80
Othello. Nay, if you strive ——
Desdemona. But half an hour!
Othello.   Being done, there is no pause.
Desdemona. But while I say one prayer!
Othello.   It is too late.

                                          Smothers her.

Emilia at the door.

Emilia [*Calls within*]. My lord, my lord! What, ho, my lord,
    my lord!
Othello. What noise is this? Not dead? Not yet quite dead? 85
    I that am cruel am yet merciful;
    I would not have thee linger in thy pain.
Emilia. [*Within*]. What, ho! My lord, my lord!

---

⁶⁰ *warranty* allowance   ⁶³ *stone* turn to stone   ⁷² *ta'en order for't* made sure
of it   ⁷⁵ *stomach* appetite

Othello.   So, so. Who's there?

Emilia [Within]. O, good my lord, I would speak a word with you.

Othello. Yes, 'tis Emilia. — By and by. — She's dead. —   90
　'Tis like she comes to speak of Cassio's death.
　The noise was high.° Ha! No more moving?
　Still as the grave. — Shall she come in? Were't good? —
　I think she stirs again. No. — What's best to do?
　If she come in, she'll sure speak to my wife.   95
　My wife! My wife! What wife? I have no wife.
　O, insupportable! O heavy hour!
　Methinks it should be now a huge eclipse
　Of sun and moon, and that th' affrighted globe
　Should yawn° at alteration.°

Emilia. [*Within*]   I do beseech you   100
　That I may speak with you, O good my lord!

Othello. I had forgot thee. O, come in, Emilia.
　Soft, by and by. — Let me the curtains draw. —

　　　　　　[*Draws the bed hangings and then opens the door.*]

　Where art thou?

　Enter Emilia.

　　　　　　What's the matter with thee now?

Emilia. O my good lord, yonder's foul murders done!   105

Othello. What? Now?

Emilia. But now, my lord.

Othello. It is the very error° of the moon.
　She comes more nearer earth than she was wont
　And makes men mad.   110

Emilia. Cassio, my lord, hath killed a young Venetian
　Called Roderigo.

Othello.   Roderigo killed?
　And Cassio killed?

Emilia.   No, Cassio is not killed.

Othello. Not Cassio killed? Then murder's out of tune,
　And sweet revenge grows harsh.   115

Desdemona. O, falsely, falsely murdered!

Emilia.   O Lord! What cry is that?

Othello. That? What?

---

⁹²*high* loud (Q₁ reads "here")   ⁹⁸⁻¹⁰⁰*Methinks . . . alteration* (the Elizabethans believed that great changes in human affairs were reflected by disorders in nature)   ¹⁰⁰*yawn* gape open (as in an earthquake)   ¹⁰⁸*error* wandering out of regular course (disorders in the heavens were believed by some to cause disorders on earth, as well as vice versa)

Emilia. Out and alas! that was my lady's voice.
  Help! Help, ho! Help! O lady, speak again!
  Sweet Desdemona! O sweet mistress, speak!   120
Desdemona. A guiltless death I die.
Emilia. O, who hath done this deed?
Desdemona. Nobody — I myself. Farewell.
  Commend me to my kind lord. O, farewell!

                                                        [*She dies.*]

Othello. Why, how should she be murd'red?
Emilia.   Alas, who knows?   125
Othello. You heard her say herself, it was not I.
Emilia. She said so. I must needs report the truth.
Othello. She's like a liar gone to burning hell!
  'Twas I that killed her.
Emilia.   O, the more angel she,
  And you the blacker devil!   130
Othello. She turned to folly, and she was a whore.
Emilia. Thou dost belie her, and thou art a devil.
Othello. She was false as water.
Emilia.   Thou art rash as fire to say
  That she was false. O, she was heavenly true!
Othello. Cassio did top her. Ask thy husband else.   135
  O, I were damned beneath all depth in hell
  But that I did proceed upon just grounds
  To this extremity. Thy husband knew it all.
Emilia. My husband?
Othello.   Thy husband.
Emilia.   That she was false to wedlock?
Othello. Ay, with Cassio. Had she been true,   140
  If heaven would make me such another world
  Of one entire and perfect chrysolite,°
  I'd not have sold her for it.
Emilia.   My husband?
Othello. Ay, 'twas he that told me on her first.
  An honest man he is, and hates the slime   145
  That sticks on filthy deeds.
Emilia.   My husband?
Othello. What needs this iterance? Woman, I say
      thy husband.
Emilia. O mistress, villainy hath made mocks with love!
  My husband say she was false?

---

142 **chrysolite** topaz

Othello.   He, woman.
    I say, thy husband. Dost understand the word?   150
    My friend, thy husband; honest, honest Iago.
Emilia. If he say so, may his pernicious soul
    Rot half a grain a day! He lies to th' heart.
    She was too fond of her most filthy bargain.
Othello. Hah?   155
Emilia. Do thy worst.
    This deed of thine is no more worthy heaven
    Than thou wast worthy her.
Othello.   Peace, you were best.°
Emilia. Thou hast not half that pow'r to do me harm
    As I have to be hurt. O gull! O dolt!   160
    As ignorant as dirt! Thou has done a deed —

                 [*Othello moves to draw his sword.*]

    I care not for thy sword; I'll make thee known,
    Though I lost twenty lives. Help! Help! Ho! Help!
    The Moor hath killed my mistress! Murder! murder!

    Enter Montano, Gratiano, and Iago [and Others].

Montano. What is the matter? How now, general?   165
Emilia. O, are you come, Iago? You have done well,
    That men must lay their murders on your neck.
Gratiano. What is the matter?
Emilia. Disprove this villain, if thou be'st a man.
    He says thou told'st him that his wife was false   170
    I know thou didst not; thou'rt not such a villain.
    Speak, for my heart is full.
Iago. I told him what I thought, and told no more
    Than what he found himself was apt and true.
Emilia. But did you ever tell him she was false?   175
Iago. I did.
Emilia. You told a lie, an odious damnèd lie!
    Upon my soul, a lie! A wicked lie!
    She false with Cassio? Did you say with Cassio?
Iago. With Cassio, mistress. Go to, charm° your tongue.   180
Emilia. I will not charm my tongue; I am bound to speak:
    My mistress here lies murdered in her bed.
All. O heavens forfend!
Emilia. And your reports have set the murder on.
Othello. Nay, stare not, masters. It is true indeed.   185

---

[158] ***Peace, you were best*** i.e., you had better be silent   [180] ***charm*** control

Gratiano. 'Tis a strange truth.
Montano. O monstrous act!
Emilia.   Villainy, villainy, villainy!
 I think upon't — I think I smell't! — O villainy!
 I thought so then. — I'll kill myself for grief. —
 O villainy, villainy!   190
Iago. What, are you mad? I charge you get you home.
Emilia. Good gentlemen, let me have leave to speak.
 'Tis proper I obey him, but not now.
 Perchance, Iago, I will ne'er go home.
Othello. O! O! O!   [*Falls on the bed.*]
Emilia.   Nay, lay thee down and roar,   195
 For thou hast killed the sweetest innocent
 That e'er did lift up eye.
Othello.   O, she was foul!   [*Rises.*]
 I scarce did know you, uncle. There lies your niece,
 Whose breath, indeed, these hands have newly stopped.
 I know this act shows horrible and grim.   200
Gratiano. Poor Desdemon! I am glad thy father's dead.
 Thy match was mortal to him, and pure grief
 Shore his old thread in twain. Did he live now,
 This sight would make him do a desperate turn;
 Yea, curse his better angel from his side,   205
 And fall to reprobation.°
Othello. 'Tis pitiful; but yet Iago knows
 That she with Cassio hath the act of shame
 A thousand times committed. Cassio confessed it;
 And she did gratify his amorous works   210
 With that recognizance and pledge of love,
 Which I first gave her. I saw it in his hand.
 It was a handkerchief, an antique token
 My father gave my mother.
Emilia. O God! O heavenly God!   215
Iago. Zounds, hold your peace!
Emilia.   'Twill out, 'twill out! I peace?
 No, I will speak as liberal as the north.°
 Let heaven and men and devils, let them all,
 All, all, cry shame against me, yet I'll speak.
Iago. Be wise, and get you home.
Emilia.   I will not.   220

[*Iago draws and threatens Emilia.*]

---

²⁰⁶ ***reprobation*** damnation   ²¹⁷ ***liberal as the north*** freely (and bitingly) as
the north wind blows

Gratiano. Fie! Your sword upon a woman?
Emilia. O thou dull Moor, that handkerchief thou speak'st of
    I found by fortune, and did give my husband;
    For often with a solemn earnestness —
    More than indeed belonged to such a trifle —   225
    He begged of me to steal't.
Iago.   Villainous whore!
Emilia. She give it Cassio? No, alas, I found it,
    And I did give't my husband.
Iago.   Filth, thou liest!
Emilia. By heaven, I do not, I do not, gentlemen.
    O murd'rous coxcomb! What should such a fool   230
    Do with so good a wife?
Othello.   Are there no stones° in heaven
    But what serves for the thunder? Precious villain!

    [*The Moor runs at Iago, but is disarmed by Montano. Iago kills
      his wife.*]
Gratiano. The woman falls. Sure he hath killed his wife.
Emilia. Ay, ay. O, lay me by my mistress' side.
                                   [*Exit Iago.*]
Gratiano. He's gone, but his wife's killed.   235
Montano. 'Tis a notorious° villain. Take you this weapon,
    Which I have recovered from the Moor.
    Come, guard the door without. Let him not pass,
    But kill him rather. I'll after that same villain,
    For 'tis a damnèd slave.

              Exit [*with all but Othello and Emilia*].

Othello.   I am not valiant neither;   240
    But every puny whipster° gets my sword.
    But why should honor outlive honesty?
    Let it go all.
Emilia.   What did thy song bode, lady?
    Hark, canst thou hear me? I will play the swan,
    And die in music. [*Sings*] "Willow, willow, willow."   245
    Moor, she was chaste. She loved thee, cruel Moor,
    So come my soul to bliss as I speak true.
    So speaking as I think, alas, I die.   [*She dies.*]
Othello. I have another weapon in this chamber;
    It was a sword of Spain, the ice-brook's temper.   250
    O, here it is. — Uncle, I must come forth.

---

231 *stones* thunderbolts   236 *notorious* out-and-out   241 *puny whipster* small
top-whipping boy (?)

Gratiano. [Within] If thou attempt it, it will cost thee dear.
   Thou hast no weapon, and perforce must suffer.
Othello. Look in upon me then and speak with me,
   Or, naked as I am, I will assault thee.   255

   [*Enter Gratiano.*]

Gratiano. What is the matter?
Othello.   Behold, I have a weapon;
   A better never did itself sustain
   Upon a soldier's thigh. I have seen the day
   That with this little arm and this good sword
   I have made my way through more impediments   260
   Than twenty times your stop. But O vain boast!
   Who can control his fate? 'Tis not so now.
   Be not afraid, though you do see me weaponed.
   Here is my journey's end, here is my butt,°
   And very seamark of my utmost sail.°   265
   Do you go back dismayed? 'Tis a lost fear.
   Man but a rush° against Othello's breast.
   And he retires. Where should Othello go?
   Now, how dost thou look now? O ill-starred wench!
   Pale as thy smock! When we shall meet at compt,°   270
   This look of thine will hurl my soul from heaven,
   And fiends will snatch at it. Cold, cold, my girl?
   Even like thy chastity.
   O cursèd, cursèd slave! Whip me, ye devils,
   From the possession of° this heavenly sight!   275
   Blow me about in winds! roast me in sulfur!
   Wash me in steep-down gulfs of liquid fire!
   O Desdemon! Dead Desdemon; dead. O! O!

   *Enter Lodovico, Cassio, Montano, and Iago [as prisoner,] with
   Officers.*

Lodovico. Where is this rash and most unfortunate man?
Othello. That's he that was Othello? Here I am.   280
Lodovico. Where is that viper? Bring the villain forth.
Othello. I look down towards his feet° — but that's a fable.
   If that thou be'st a devil, I cannot kill thee.

                                          [*Wounds Iago.*]

---

²⁶⁴ *butt* target, stopping place   ²⁶⁵ *seamark of my utmost sail* maker of my
furthest journey   ²⁶⁷ *Man but a rush* attack with only a reed   ²⁷⁰ *compt*
Judgement Day   ²⁷⁵ *the possession of* being possessed by   ²⁸² *towards his feet*
i.e., for his cloven hoofs

Lodovico. Wrench his sword from him.

[*Othello is disarmed.*]

Iago.   I bleed, sir, but not killed.

Othello. I am not sorry neither. I'd have thee live;   285
   For in my sense, 'tis happiness to die.

Lodovico. O thou Othello that was once so good,
   Fall'n in the practice° of a cursèd slave,
   What shall be said to thee?

Othello.   Why, anything:
   An honorable murderer, if you will;   290
   For naught I did in hate, but all in honor.

Lodovico. This wretch hath part confessed his villainy.
   Did you and he consent in Cassio's death?

Othello. Ay.

Cassio. Dear general, I never gave you cause.   295

Othello. I do believe it, and I ask your pardon.
   Will you, I pray, demand that demi-devil
   Why he hath thus ensnared my soul and body?

Iago. Demand me nothing. What you know, you know.
   From this time forth I never will speak word.   300

Lodovico. What, not to pray?

Gratiano.   Torments will ope your lips.

Othello. Well, thou dost best.

Lodovico. Sir, you shall understand what hath befall'n,
   Which, as I think, you know not. Here is a letter
   Found in the pocket of the slain Roderigo;   305
   And here another. The one of them imports
   The death of Cassio to be undertook
   By Roderigo.

Othello. O villain!

Cassio.   Most heathenish and most gross!

Lodovico. Now here's another discontented paper   310
   Found in his pocket too; and this, it seems,
   Roderigo meant t' have sent this damnèd villain;
   But that, belike, Iago in the interim
   Came in and satisfied him.

Othello.   O thou pernicious caitiff!
   How came you, Cassio, by that handkerchief   315
   That was my wife's?

Cassio.   I found it in my chamber;
   And he himself confessed it but even now

---

[288] *practice* plotting

That there he dropped it for a special purpose
Which wrought to his desire.
Othello.   O fool! Fool! Fool!
Cassio. There is besides in Roderigo's letter,   320
How he upbraids Iago that he made him
Brave me upon the watch; whereon it came
That I was cast; and even but now he spake,
After long seeming dead — Iago hurt him,
Iago set him on.   325
Lodovico. You must forsake this room and go with us.
Your power and your command is taken off,
And Cassio rules in Cyprus. For this slave,
If there be any cunning cruelty
That can torment him much and hold him long,   330
It shall be his. You shall close prisoner rest
Till that the nature of your fault be known
To the Venetian state. Come, bring away.
Othello. Soft you, a word or two before you go.
I have done the state some service and they know't.   335
No more of that. I pray you, in your letters,
When you shall these unlucky deeds relate,
Speak of me as I am. Nothing extenuate,
Nor set down aught in malice. Then must you speak
Of one that loved not wisely, but too well;   340
Of one not easily jealous, but, being wrought,
Perplexed in the extreme; of one whose hand,
Like the base Judean,° threw a pearl away
Richer than all his tribe; of one whose subdued eyes,
Albeit unusèd to the melting mood.   345
Drops tears as fast as the Arabian trees
Their med'cinable gum. Set you down this.
And say besides that in Aleppo once,
Where a malignant and a turbaned Turk
Beat a Venetian and traduced the state,   350
I took by th' throat the circumcised dog
And smote him — thus.   [*He stabs himself.*]
Lodovico. O bloody period!°
Gratiano.   All that is spoke is marred.
Othello. I kissed thee ere I killed thee. No way but this,
Killing myself, to die upon a kiss.   355

[*He falls over Desdemona and dies.*]

---

[343] *Judean* (most editors use the Q1 reading, "Indian," here, but F is clear:
both readings point toward the infidel, the unbeliever   [353] *period* end

Cassio. This did I fear, but thought he had no weapon;
 For he was great of heart.
Lodovico. [*To Iago*]   O Spartan dog,
 More fell° than anguish, hunger, or the sea!
 Look on the tragic loading of this bed.
 This is thy work. The object poisons sight;   360
 Let it be hid.   [*Bed curtains drawn.*]
        Gratiano, keep° the house,
 And seize upon the fortunes of the Moor,
 For they succeed on you. To you, lord governor,
 Remains the censure of this hellish villain,
 The time, the place, the torture. O, enforce it!   365
 Myself will straight aboard, and to the state
 This heavy act with heavy heart relate.   *Exeunt.*

Questions

Act I

1. Iago, contemptuous of dutiful servants, compares them in I.i.44 to asses. What other animal images does he use in the first scene? What does the use of such images tell us about Iago?

2. Is there any need to do more than knock loudly at Brabantio's door? What does I.1.72–74 tell us about Iago?

3. In I.i.105 ff., and in his next speech, Iago uses prose instead of blank verse. What effect is gained?

4. What is Iago trying to do to Othello in the first speech of I.ii? In I.ii.29 why does Iago urge Othello to "go in"? When Othello first speaks (I.ii.6) does he speak as we might have expected him to, given Iago's earlier comments about Othello? In Othello's second speech is there anything that resembles Iago's earlier description of him?

5. Is it incredible that a girl who has rejected "the wealthy, curlèd darlings" (I.ii.67) of Venice should choose a Moor?

6. Iago had said (I.i.12) that Othello uses "bombast circumstance." Is I.iii.127 ff. an example? Why?

7. Is the love of Othello and Desdemona impetuous and irrational? What is its basis?

8. The last speech in I.iii. is in verse, though previous speeches are in prose. What is the effect of the change?

9. Is it a fault that Othello "thinks men honest that but seem to be so" (I.iii.383)?

---

358 *fell* cruel   361 *keep* remain in

Act II

1. In II.i.1–19, why does Shakespeare introduce a description of a storm? What symbolic overtones, if any, may it have?

2. In Iago's last speech in this act he gives several reasons why he hates Othello. List them, and add to the list any reasons he gave earlier. How convincing are they?

3. Again (II.i.274 ff.) Shakespeare gives Iago verse, when alone, after prose dialogue. Why?

4. In II.iii.13–24, what sort of thing is Iago trying to get Cassio to say?

5. How does II.iii.190–203 prepare us for Othello's later tragic deed of killing Desdemona?

Act III

1. What is the point of the repetition (III.iii.97–129) of "thought," "think," "know," and "honest"?

2. Is it surprising that Othello speaks (III.iii.180) of a goat? In later scenes keep an eye out for his use of animal imagery.

3. Emilia gets possession of the handkerchief by accident (III.iii.287–90). Is it fair, then, to say that the tragic outcome is based on mere accident?

Act IV

1. In IV.i.36 ff. Othello uses prose. What does this shift suggest about Othello's state of mind?

2. Othello says (IV.193) "I will chop her into messes! Cuckold me!" Do we feel that in this scene Othello's ferocity toward Desdemona is chiefly motivated by a sense of personal injury? What does Shakespeare do here to prevent us from merely loathing Othello?

3. What is Othello's emotional state in the first nineteen lines of IV.ii?

4. In IV.ii. Othello's baseness, very evident in the previous scene, continues here. But what lines in this scene tend to work against the view that he is merely base, and give him the stature of a tragic hero?

5. Why is it that Othello "looks gentler than he did" (IV.iii.10)?

Act V

1. What does V.ii.16–17 tell us about the spirit with which Othello is about to kill Desdemona? Is he acting from a sense of wounded pride?

2. Emilia calls Othello "gull," "dolt," "ignorant as dirt" (V.ii.160–61). Has she a point? Do these words prevent Othello from being a tragic hero?

3. T. S. Eliot, in "Shakespeare and the Stoicism of Seneca," *Selected Essays,* says of V.ii.334–52: "Othello . . . is *cheering himself up.* He is endeavoring to escape reality, he has ceased to think about Desdemona, and is thinking about himself." Evaluate this view. To what does Othello in effect compare himself in the last line of this speech?

4. In Christian thought suicide is a sin. Do we judge it sinful here?

General Questions

1. W. H. Auden, in *The Dyer's Hand,* says that "in most tragedies the fall of the hero from glory to misery and death is the work, either of the gods, or of his own freely chosen acts, or, more commonly, a mixture of both. But the fall of Othello is the work of another human being; nothing he says or does originates with himself. In consequence we feel pity for him but no respect; our esthetic respect is reserved for Iago." Evaluate.

2. Harley Granville-Barker, in *Prefaces to Shakespeare,* says: "The mere sight of such beauty and nobility and happiness, all wickedly destroyed, must be a harrowing one. Yet the pity and terror of it come short of serving for the purgation of our souls, since Othello's own soul stays unpurged. . . . It is a tragedy without meaning, and that is the ultimate horror of it." Evaluate.

Henrik Ibsen (1828–1906)

A Doll's House

A New Translation by Otto Reinert

List of Characters

Torvald Helmer, a lawyer
Nora, his wife
Dr. Rank
Mrs. Linde
Krogstad
The Helmers' three small children
Anne-Marie, the children's nurse
A housemaid
A porter

Scene. *The Helmers' living room*

Act I

A pleasant, tastefully but not expensively furnished, living room. A door on the rear wall, right, leads to the front hall, another door, left, to Helmer's study. Between the two doors a piano. A third door in the middle of the left wall; further front a window. Near the window a round table and a small couch. Towards the rear of the right wall a fourth door; further front a tile stove with a rocking chair and a couple of armchairs in front of it. Between the stove and the door a small table. Copperplate etchings on the walls. A whatnot with porcelain figurines and other small objects. A small bookcase with de luxe editions. A rug on the floor; fire in the stove. Winter day.

The doorbell rings, then the sound of the front door opening. Nora, dressed for outdoors, enters, humming cheerfully. She carries several packages, which she puts down on the table, right. She leaves the door to the front hall open; there a Porter is seen holding a Christmas tree and a basket. He gives them to the Maid, who has let them in.

Nora. Be sure to hide the Christmas tree, Helene. The children mustn't see it before tonight when we've trimmed it. *(Opens her purse; to the Porter.)* How much?
Porter. Fifty øre.

Nora. Here's a crown. No, keep the change. *(The Porter thanks her, leaves. Nora closes the door. She keeps laughing quietly to herself as she takes off her coat, etc. She takes a bag of macaroons from her pocket and eats a couple. She walks cautiously over to the door to the study and listens.)* Yes, he's home. *(Resumes her humming, walks over to the table, right.)*

Helmer (in his study). Is that my little lark twittering out there?

Nora (opening some of the packages). That's right.

Helmer. My squirrel bustling about?

Nora. Yes.

Helmer. When did squirrel come home?

Nora. Just now. *(Puts the bag of macaroons back in her pocket, wipes her mouth.)* Come out here, Torvald. I want to show you what I've bought.

Helmer. I'm busy! *(After a little while he opens the door and looks in, pen in hand.)* Bought, eh? All that? So little wastrel has been throwing money around again?

Nora. Oh but Torvald, this Christmas we can be a little extravagant, can't we? It's the first Christmas we don't have to scrimp.

Helmer. I don't know about that. We certainly don't have money to waste.

Nora. Yes, Torvald, we do. A little, anyway. Just a tiny little bit? Now that you're going to get that big salary and make lots and lots of money.

Helmer. Starting at New Year's, yes. But payday isn't till the end of the quarter.

Nora. That doesn't matter. We can always borrow.

Helmer. Nora! *(Goes over to her and playfully pulls her ear.)* There you go being irresponsible again. Suppose I borrowed a thousand crowns today and you spent it all for Christmas and on New Year's Eve a tile hit me in the head and laid me out cold.

Nora (putting her hand over his mouth). I won't have you say such horrid things.

Helmer. But suppose it happened. Then what?

Nora. If it did, I wouldn't care whether we owed money or not.

Helmer. But what about the people I had borrowed from?

Nora. Who cares about them! They are strangers.

Helmer. Nora, Nora, you *are* a woman. No, really! You know how I feel about that. No debts! A home in debt isn't a free home, and if it isn't free it isn't beautiful. We've managed nicely so far, you and I, and that's the way we'll go on. It won't be for much longer.

Nora (walks over toward the stove). All right, Torvald. Whatever you say.

Helmer (follows her). Come, come, my little songbird mustn't droop her wings. What's this? Can't have a pouty squirrel in the house, you know. *(Takes out his wallet.)* Nora, what do you think I have here?

Nora (turns around quickly). Money!

Helmer. Here. *(Gives her some bills.)* Don't you think I know Christmas is expensive?

Nora (counting). Ten — twenty — thirty — forty. Thank you, thank you, Torvald. This helps a lot.

Helmer. I certainly hope so.

Nora. It does, it does. But I want to show you what I got. It was cheap, too. Look. New clothes for Ivar. And a sword. And a horse and trumpet for Bob. And a doll and a little bed for Emmy. It isn't any good, but it wouldn't last, anyway. And here's some dress material and scarves for the maids. I feel bad about old Anne-Marie, though. She really should be getting much more.

Helmer. And what's in here?

Nora (cries). Not till tonight!

Helmer. I see. But now what does my little prodigal have in mind for herself?

Nora. Oh, nothing. I really don't care.

Helmer. Of course you do. Tell me what you'd like. Within reason.

Nora. Oh, I don't know. Really, I don't. The only thing —

Helmer. Well?

Nora (fiddling with his buttons, without looking at him). If you really want to give me something, you might — you could —

Helmer. All right, let's have it.

Nora (quickly). Some money, Torvald. Just as much as you think you can spare. Then I'll buy myself something one of these days.

Helmer. No, really Nora —

Nora. Oh yes, please, Torvald. Please? I'll wrap the money in pretty gold paper and hang it on the tree. Won't that be nice?

Helmer. What's the name for little birds that are always spending money?

Nora. Wastrels, I know. But please let's do it my way, Torvald. Then I'll have time to decide what I need most. Now that's sensible, isn't it?

Helmer (smiling). Oh, very sensible. That is, if you really bought yourself something you could use. But it all disappears in the household expenses or you buy things you don't need. And then you come back to me for more.

Nora. Oh, but Torvald —

Helmer. That's the truth, dear little Nora, and you know it. *(Puts his arm around her.)* My wastrel is a little sweetheart, but she *does* go through an awful lot of money awfully fast. You've no idea how expensive it is for a man to keep a wastrel.

Nora. That's not fair, Torvald. I really save all I can.

Helmer (laughs). Oh, I believe that. All you can. Meaning, exactly nothing!

Nora (hums, smiles mysteriously). You don't know all the things we songbirds and squirrels need money for, Torvald.

Helmer. You know, you're funny. Just like your father. You're always looking for ways to get money, but as soon as you do it runs through your fingers and you can never say what you spent it for. Well, I guess I'll just have to take you the way you are. It's in your blood. Yes, that sort of thing is hereditary, Nora.

Nora. In that case, I wish I had inherited many of Daddy's qualities.

Helmer. And I don't want you any different from just what you are — my own sweet little songbird. Hey! — I think I just noticed something. Aren't you looking — what's the word? — a little — sly — ?

Nora. I am?

Helmer. You definitely are. Look at me.

Nora (looks at him). Well?

Helmer (wagging a finger). Little sweet-tooth hasn't by any chance been on a rampage today, has she?

Nora. Of course not. Whatever makes you think that?

Helmer. A little detour by the pastryshop maybe?

Nora. No, I assure you, Torvald —

Helmer. Nibbled a little jam?

Nora. Certainly not!

Helmer. Munched a macaroon or two?

Nora. No, really, Torvald, I honestly —

Helmer. All right. Of course I was only joking.

Nora (walks toward the table, right). You know I wouldn't do anything to displease you.

Helmer. I know. And I have your promise. *(Over to her.)* All right, keep your little Christmas secrets to yourself, Nora darling. They'll all come out tonight, I suppose, when we light the tree.

Nora. Did you remember to invite Rank?

Helmer. No, but there's no need to. He knows he'll have dinner with us. Anyway, I'll see him later this morning. I'll ask him then. I did order some good wine. Oh Nora, you've no idea how much I'm looking forward to tonight!

Nora. Me too. And the children, Torvald! They'll have such a good time!

Helmer. You know, it *is* nice to have a good, safe job and a comfortable income. Feels good just thinking about it. Don't you agree?

Nora. Oh, it's wonderful!

Helmer. Remember last Christmas? For three whole weeks you shut yourself up every evening till long after midnight, making ornaments for the Christmas tree and I don't know what else. Some big surprise for all of us, anyway. I'll be damned if I've ever been so bored in my whole life!

Nora. I wasn't bored at all.

Helmer (smiling). But you've got to admit you didn't have much to show for it in the end.

Nora. Oh, don't tease me again about that! Could I help it that the cat got in and tore up everything?

Helmer. Of course you couldn't, my poor little Nora. You just wanted to please the rest of us, and that's the important thing. But I *am* glad the hard times are behind us. Aren't you?

Nora. Oh yes. I think it's just wonderful.

Helmer. This year I won't be bored and lonely. And you won't have to strain your dear eyes and your delicate little hands —

Nora (claps her hands). No I won't, will I, Torvald? Oh, how wonderful, how lovely, to hear you say that! *(Puts her arm under his.)* Let me tell you how I think we should arrange things, Torvald. Soon as Christmas is over — *(The doorbell rings.)* Someone's at the door. *(Straightens things up a bit.)* A caller, I suppose. Bother!

Helmer. Remember, I'm not home for visitors.

The Maid (in the door to the front hall). Ma'am, there's a lady here —

Nora. All right. Ask her to come in.

The Maid (to Helmer). And the Doctor just arrived.

Helmer. Is he in the study?

The Maid. Yes, sir.

Helmer exits into his study. The Maid shows Mrs. Linde in and closes the door behind her as she leaves. Mrs. Linde is in travel dress.

Mrs. Linde (timid and a little hesitant). Good morning, Nora.

Nora (uncertainly). Good morning.

Mrs. Linde. I don't believe you know who I am.

Nora. No — I'm not sure — Though I know I should — Of course! Kristine! It's you!

Mrs. Linde. Yes, it's me.

Nora. And I didn't even recognize you! I had no idea! *(In a lower voice.)* You've changed, Kristine.

Mrs. Linde. I'm sure I have. It's been nine or ten long years.

Nora. Has it really been that long? Yes, you're right. I've been so happy these last eight years. And now you're here. Such a long trip in the middle of winter. How brave!

Mrs. Linde. I got in on the steamer this morning.

Nora. To have some fun over the holidays, of course. That's lovely. For we *are* going to have fun. But take off your coat! You aren't cold, are you? *(Helps her.)* There, now! Let's sit down here by the fire and just relax and talk. No, you sit there. I want the rocking chair. *(Takes her hands.)* And now you've got your old face back. It was just for a minute, right at first — Though you are a little more pale, Kristine. And maybe a little thinner.

Mrs. Linde. And much, much older, Nora.

Nora. Maybe a little older. Just a teeny-weeny bit, not much. *(Interrupts herself, serious.)* Oh, but how thoughtless of me, chatting away like this! Sweet, good Kristine, can you forgive me?

Mrs. Linde. Forgive you what, Nora?

Nora (in a low voice). You poor dear, you lost your husband, didn't you?

Mrs. Linde. Three years ago, yes.

Nora. I know. I saw it in the paper. Oh please believe me, Kristine. I really meant to write you, but I never got around to it. Something was always coming up.

Mrs. Linde. Of course, Nora. I understand.

Nora. No, that wasn't very nice of me. You poor thing, all you must have been through. And he didn't leave you much, either, did he?

Mrs. Linde. No.

Nora. And no children?

Mrs. Linde. No.

Nora. Nothing at all, in other words?

Mrs. Linde. Not so much as a sense of loss — a grief to live on —

Nora (incredulous). But Kristine, how can that *be?*

Mrs. Linde (with a sad smile, strokes Nora's hair). That's the way it sometimes is, Nora.

Nora. All alone. How awful for you. I have three darling children. You can't see them right now, though; they're out with their nurse. But now you must tell me everything —

Mrs. Linde. No, no; I'd rather listen to you.

Nora. No, you begin. Today I won't be selfish. Today I'll think only of you. Except there's one thing I've just got to tell you first. Something marvelous that's happened to us just these last few days. You haven't heard, have you?

Mrs. Linde. No; tell me.

Nora. Just think. My husband's been made manager of the Mutual Bank.

Mrs. Linde. Your husband — ! Oh, I'm so glad!

Nora. Yes, isn't that great? You see, private law practice is so uncertain, especially when you won't have anything to do with cases that aren't — you know — quite nice. And of course Torvald won't do that, and I quite agree with him. Oh, you've no idea how delighted we are! He takes over at New Year's, and he'll be getting a big salary and all sorts of extras. From now on we'll be able to live in quite a different way — exactly as we like. Oh, Kristine! I feel so carefree and happy! It's lovely to have lots and lots of money and not have to worry about a thing! Don't you agree?

Mrs. Linde. It would be nice to have enough, at any rate.

Nora. No, I don't mean just enough. I mean lots and lots!

Mrs. Linde (smiles). Nora, Nora, when are you going to be sensible? In school you spent a great deal of money.

Nora (quietly laughing). Yes, and Torvald says I still do. *(Raises her finger at Mrs. Linde.)* But "Nora, Nora" isn't so crazy as you all think. Believe me, we've had nothing to be extravagant with. We've both had to work.

Mrs. Linde. You too?

Nora. Yes. Oh, it's been little things mostly — sewing, crocheting, embroidery — that sort of thing. *(Casually.)* And other things too. You know, of course, that Torvald left government service when we got married? There was no chance of promotion in his department, and of course he had to make more money than he had been making. So for the first few years he worked altogether too hard. He had to take jobs on the side and work night and day. It turned out to be too much for him. He became seriously ill. The doctors told him he needed to go south.

Mrs. Linde. That's right; you spent a year in Italy, didn't you?

Nora. Yes, we did. But you won't believe how hard it was to get away. Ivar had just been born. But of course we had to go. Oh, it was a wonderful trip. And it saved Torvald's life. But it took a lot of money, Kristine.

Mrs. Linde. I'm sure it did.

Nora. Twelve hundred specie dollars. Four thousand eight hundred crowns. That's a lot of money.

Mrs. Linde. Yes. So it's lucky you have it when something like that happens.

Nora. Well, actually we got the money from Daddy.

Mrs. Linde. I see. That was about the time your father died, I believe.

Nora. Yes, just about then. And I couldn't even go and take care of him. I was expecting little Ivar any day. And I had poor Torvald to look after, desperately sick and all. My dear, good Daddy! I never saw him again, Kristine. That's the saddest thing that's happened to me since I got married.

Mrs. Linde. I know you were very fond of him. But then you went
to Italy?

Nora. Yes, for now we had the money, and the doctors urged us to go.
So we left about a month later.

Mrs. Linde. And when you came back your husband was well again?

Nora. Healthy as a horse!

Mrs. Linde. But — the doctor?

Nora. What do you mean?

Mrs. Linde. I thought the maid said it was the doctor, that gentleman
who came the same time I did.

Nora. Oh, that's Dr. Rank. He doesn't come as a doctor. He's our
closest friend. He looks in at least once every day. No, Torvald
hasn't been sick once since then. And the children are strong and
healthy, too, and so am I. (*Jumps up and claps her hands.*) Oh
God, Kristine! Isn't it wonderful to be alive and happy! Isn't it just
lovely! — But now I'm being mean again, talking only about myself and my things. (*Sits down on a footstool close to Mrs. Linde
and puts her arms on her lap.*) Please, don't be angry with me!
Tell me, is it really true that you didn't care for your husband?
Then why did you marry him?

Mrs. Linde. Mother was still alive then, but she was bedridden and
helpless. And I had my two younger brothers to look after. I didn't
think I had the right to turn him down.

Nora. No, I suppose not. So he had money then?

Mrs. Linde. He was quite well off, I think. But it was an uncertain
business, Nora. When he died, the whole thing collapsed and
there was nothing left.

Nora. And then — ?

Mrs. Linde. Well, I had to manage as best I could. With a little store
and a little school and anything else I could think of. The last three
years have been one long work day for me, Nora, without any rest.
But now it's over. My poor mother doesn't need me any more. She
passed away. And the boys are on their own too. They've both got
jobs and support themselves.

Nora. What a relief for you —

Mrs. Linde. No, not relief. Just a great emptiness. Nobody to live for
any more. (*Gets up, restlessly.*) That's why I couldn't stand it any
longer in that little hole. Here in town it has to be easier to find
something to keep me busy and occupy my thoughts. With a little
luck I should be able to find a permanent job, something in an
office —

Nora. Oh but Kristine, that's exhausting work, and you look worn out
already. It would be much better for you to go to a resort.

Mrs. Linde (walks over to the window). I don't have a Daddy who
can give me the money, Nora.

Nora (getting up). Oh, don't be angry with me.

Mrs. Linde (over to her). Dear Nora, don't *you* be angry with *me*. That's the worst thing about my kind of situation: you become so bitter. You've nobody to work for, and yet you have to look out for yourself, somehow. You've got to keep on living, and so you become selfish. Do you know — when you told me about your husband's new position I was delighted not so much for your sake as for my own.

Nora. Why was that? Oh, I see. You think maybe Torvald can give you a job?

Mrs. Linde. That's what I had in mind.

Nora. And he will too, Kristine. Just leave it to me. I'll be ever so subtle about it. I'll think of something nice to tell him, something he'll like. Oh I so much want to help you.

Mrs. Linde. That's very good of you, Nora — making an effort like that for me. Especially since you've known so little trouble and hardship in your own life.

Nora. I — ? — have known so little — ?

Mrs. Linde (smiling). Oh well, a little sewing or whatever it was. You're still a child, Nora.

Nora (with a toss of her head, walks away). You shouldn't sound so superior.

Mrs. Linde. I shouldn't?

Nora. You're just like all the others. None of you think I'm good for anything really serious.

Mrs. Linde. Well, now —

Nora. That I've never been through anything difficult.

Mrs. Linde. But Nora! You just told me all your troubles!

Nora. That's nothing *(Lowers her voice.)* I haven't told you about *it.*

Mrs. Linde. It? What's that? What do you mean?

Nora. You patronize me, Kristine, and that's not fair. You're proud that you worked so long and so hard for your mother.

Mrs. Linde. I don't think I patronize anyone. But it *is* true that I'm both proud and happy that I could make mother's last years comparatively easy.

Nora. And you're proud of all you did for your brothers.

Mrs. Linde. I think I have the right to be.

Nora. And so do I. But now I want to tell you something, Kristine. I have something to be proud and happy about too.

Mrs. Linde. I don't doubt that for a moment. But what exactly do you mean?

Nora. Not so loud! Torvald mustn't hear — not for anything in the world. Nobody must know about this, Kristine. Nobody but you.

Mrs. Linde. But what is it?

Nora. Come here. *(Pulls her down on the couch beside her.)* You see,
I *do* have something to be proud and happy about. I've saved
Torvald's life.

Mrs. Linde. Saved — ? How do you mean — "saved"?

Nora. I told you about our trip to Italy. Torvald would have died if he
hadn't gone.

Mrs. Linde. I understand that. And so your father gave you the
money you needed.

Nora (smiles). Yes, that's what Torvald and all the others think.
But —

Mrs. Linde. But what?

Nora. Daddy didn't give us a penny. *I* raised that money.

Mrs. Linde. You did? That whole big amount?

Nora. Twelve hundred specie dollars. Four thousand eight hundred
crowns. *Now* what do you say?

Mrs. Linde. But Nora, how could you? Did you win in the state
lottery?

Nora (contemptuously). State lottery! *(Snorts.)* What is so great
about that?

Mrs. Linde. Where did it come from then?

Nora (humming and smiling, enjoying her secret). Hmmm. Tra-la-la-
la-la!

Mrs. Linde. You certainly couldn't have borrowed it.

Nora. Oh? And why not?

Mrs. Linde. A wife can't borrow money without her husband's consent.

Nora (with a toss of her head). Oh, I don't know — take a wife with a
little bit of a head for business — a wife who knows how to manage things —

Mrs. Linde. But Nora, I don't understand at all —

Nora. You don't have to. I didn't say I borrowed the money, did I? I
could have gotten it some other way. *(Leans back.)* An admirer
may have given it to me. When you're as tolerably goodlooking as
I am —

Mrs. Linde. Oh, you're crazy.

Nora. I think you're dying from curiosity, Kristine.

Mrs. Linde. I'm beginning to think you've done something very foolish, Nora.

Nora (sits up). Is it foolish to save your husband's life?

Mrs. Linde: I say it's foolish to act behind his back.

Nora. But don't you see: he couldn't be told! You're missing the
whole point, Kristine. We couldn't even let him know how seriously ill he was. The doctors came to *me* and told me his life was
in danger, that nothing could save him but a stay in the south.

Don't you think I tried to work on him? I told him how lovely it would be if I could go abroad like other young wives. I cried and begged. I said he'd better remember what condition I was in, that he had to be nice to me and do what I wanted. I even hinted he could borrow the money. But that almost made him angry with me. He told me I was being irresponsible and that it was his duty as my husband not to give in to my moods and whims — I think that's what he called it. All right, I said to myself, you've got to be saved somehow, and so I found a way —

Mrs. Linde. And your husband never learned from your father that the money didn't come from him?

Nora. Never. Daddy died that same week. I thought of telling him all about it and ask him not to say anything. But since he was so sick — It turned out I didn't have to —

Mrs. Linde. And you've never told your husband?

Nora. Of course not! Good heavens, how could I? He, with his strict principles! Besides, you know how men are. Torvald would find it embarrassing and humiliating to learn that he owed me anything. It would upset our whole relationship. Our happy, beautiful home would no longer be what it is.

Mrs. Linde. Aren't you ever going to tell him?

Nora (reflectively, half smiling). Yes — one day, maybe. Many, many years from now, when I'm no longer young and pretty. Don't laugh! I mean when Torvald no longer feels about me the way he does now, when he no longer thinks it's fun when I dance for him and put on costumes and recite for him. Then it will be good to have something in reserve — *(Interrupts herself.)* Oh, I'm just being silly! That day will never come. — Well, now, Kristine, what do you think of my great secret? Don't you think I'm good for something too? — By the way, you wouldn't believe all the worry I've had because of it. It's been very hard to meet my obligations on schedule. You see, in business there's something called quarterly interest and something called installments on the principal, and those are terribly hard to come up with. I've had to save a little here and a little there, whenever I could. I couldn't use much of the housekeeping money, for Torvald has to eat well. And I couldn't use what I got for clothes for the children. They have to look nice, and I didn't think it would be right to spend less than I got — the sweet little things!

Mrs. Linde. Poor Nora! So you had to take it from your own allowance?

Nora. Yes, of course. After all, it was my affair. Every time Torvald gave me money for a new dress and things like that, I never used more than half of it. I always bought the cheapest, simplest things for myself. Thank God, everything looks good on me, so Torvald never noticed. But it was hard many times, Kristine, for it's fun to have pretty clothes. Don't you think?

Mrs. Linde. Certainly.

Nora. Anyway, I had other ways of making money too. Last winter I was lucky enough to get some copying work. So I locked the door and sat up writing every night till quite late. God! I often got so tired — ! But it was great fun, too, working and making money. It was almost like being a man.

Mrs. Linde. But how much have you been able to pay off this way?

Nora. I couldn't tell you exactly. You see, it's very difficult to keep track of business like that. All I know is I have been paying off as much as I've been able to scrape together. Many times I just didn't know what to do. *(Smiles.)* Then I used to imagine a rich old gentleman had fallen in love with me —

Mrs. Linde. What! What old gentleman?

Nora. Phooey! And now he was dead and they were reading his will, and there it said in big letters, "All my money is to be paid in cash immediately to the charming Mrs. Nora Helmer."

Mrs. Linde. But dearest Nora — who *was* this old gentleman?

Nora. For heaven's sake, Kristine, don't you see! There *was* no old gentleman. He was just somebody I made up when I couldn't think of any way to raise the money. But never mind him. The old bore can be anyone he likes to for all I care. I have no use for him or his last will, for now I don't have a single worry in the world. *(Jumps up.)* Dear God, what a lovely thought that is! To be able to play and have fun with the children, to have everything nice and pretty in the house, just the way Torvald likes it! Not a care! And soon spring will be here, and the air will be blue and high. Maybe we can travel again. Maybe I'll see the ocean again! Oh, yes, yes! — it's wonderful to be alive and happy!

The doorbell rings.

Mrs. Linde (getting up). There's the doorbell. Maybe I better be going.

Nora. No, please stay. I'm sure it's just someone for Torvald —

The Maid (in the hall door). Excuse me, ma'am. There's a gentleman here who'd like to see Mr. Helmer.

Nora. You mean the bank manager.

The Maid. Sorry, ma'am; the bank manager. But I didn't know — since the Doctor is with him —

Nora. Who is the gentleman?

Krogstad (appearing in the door). It's just me, Mrs. Helmer.

Mrs. Linde starts, looks, turns away toward the window.

Nora (takes a step toward him, tense, in a low voice). You? What do you want? What do you want with my husband?

Krogstad. Bank business — in a way. I have a small job in the Mutual, and I understand your husband is going to be our new boss —

Nora. So it's just —

Krogstad. Just routine business, ma'am. Nothing else.

Nora. All right. In that case, why don't you go through the door to the office.

Dismisses him casually as she closes the door. Walks over to the stove and tends the fire.

Mrs. Linde. Nora — who was that man?

Nora. His name's Krogstad. He's a lawyer.

Mrs. Linde. So it *was* him.

Nora. Do you know him?

Mrs. Linde. I used to — many years ago. For a while he clerked in our part of the country.

Nora. Right. He did.

Mrs. Linde. He has changed a great deal.

Nora. I believe he had a very unhappy marriage.

Mrs. Linde. And now he's a widower, isn't he?

Nora. With many children. There now; it's burning nicely again. *(Closes the stove and moves the rocking chair a little to the side.)*

Mrs. Linde. They say he's into all sorts of business.

Nora. Really? Maybe so. I wouldn't know. But let's not think about business. It's such a bore.

Dr. Rank (appears in the door to Helmer's study). No, I don't want to be in the way. I'd rather talk to your wife a bit. *(Closes the door and notices Mrs. Linde.)* Oh, I beg your pardon. I believe I'm in the way here too.

Nora. No, not at all. *(Introduces them.)* Dr. Rank. Mrs. Linde.

Rank. Aha. A name often heard in this house. I believe I passed you on the stairs coming up.

Mrs. Linde. Yes. I'm afraid I climb stairs very slowly. They aren't good for me.

Rank. I see. A slight case of inner decay, perhaps?

Mrs. Linde. Overwork, rather.

Rank. Oh, is that all? And now you've come to town to relax at all the parties?

Mrs. Linde. I have come to look for a job.

Rank. A proven cure for overwork, I take it?

Mrs. Linde. One has to live, Doctor.

Rank. Yes, that seems to be the common opinion.

Nora. Come on, Dr. Rank — you want to live just as much as the rest of us.

Rank. Of course I do. Miserable as I am, I prefer to go on being tortured as long as possible. All my patients feel the same way. And that's true of the moral invalids too. Helmer is talking with a specimen right this minute.

Mrs. Linde (in a low voice). Ah!

Nora. What do you mean?

Rank. Oh, this lawyer, Krogstad. You don't know him. The roots of his character are decayed. But even he began by saying something about having *to live* — as if it were a matter of the highest importance.

Nora. Oh? What did he want with Torvald?

Rank. I don't really know. All I heard was something about the bank.

Nora. I didn't know that Krog — that this Krogstad had anything to do with the Mutual Bank.

Rank. Yes, he seems to have some kind of job there. *(To Mrs. Linde.)* I don't know if you are familiar in your part of the country with the kind of person who is always running around trying to sniff out cases of moral decrepitude and as soon as he finds one puts the individual under observation in some excellent position or other. All the healthy ones are left out in the cold.

Mrs. Linde. I should think it's the sick who need looking after the most.

Rank (shrugs his shoulders). There we are. That's the attitude that turns society into a hospital.

Nora, absorbed in her own thoughts, suddenly starts giggling and clapping her hands.

Rank. What's so funny about that? Do you even know what society is?

Nora. What do I care about your stupid society! I laughed at something entirely different — something terribly amusing. Tell me, Dr. Rank — all the employees in the Mutual Bank, from now on they'll all be dependent on Torvald, right?

Rank. Is that what you find so enormously amusing?

Nora (smiles and hums). That's my business, that's my business! *(Walks around.)* Yes, I do think it's fun that we — that Torvald is going to have so much influence on so many people's lives. *(Brings out the bag of macaroons.)* Have a macaroon, Dr. Rank.

Rank. Well, well — macaroons. I thought they were banned around here.

Nora. Yes, but these were some that Kristine gave me.

Mrs. Linde. What! I?

Nora. That's all right. Don't look so scared. You couldn't know that Torvald won't let me have them. He's afraid they'll ruin my teeth. But who cares! Just once in a while — ! Right, Dr. Rank? Have one! *(Puts a macaroon into his mouth.)* You too, Kristine. And one for me. A very small one. Or at most two. *(Walks around again.)* Yes, I really feel very, very happy. Now there's just one thing I'm dying to do.

Rank. Oh? And what's that?

Nora. Something I'm dying to say so Torvald could hear.

Rank. And why can't you?

Nora. I don't dare to, for it's not nice.

Mrs. Linde. Not nice?

Rank. In that case, I guess you'd better not. But surely to the two of us — ? What is it you'd like to say for Helmer to hear?

Nora. I want to say, "Goddammit!"

Rank. Are you out of your mind!

Mrs. Linde. For heaven's sake, Nora!

Rank. Say it. Here he comes.

Nora (hiding the macaroons). Shhh!

Helmer enters from his study, carrying his hat and overcoat.

Nora (going to him). Well, dear, did you get rid of him?

Helmer. Yes, he just left.

Nora. Torvald, I want you to meet Kristine. She's just come to town.

Helmer. Kristine — ? I'm sorry; I don't think —

Nora. Mrs. Linde, Torvald dear. Mrs. Kristine Linde.

Helmer. Ah, yes. A childhood friend of my wife's, I suppose.

Mrs. Linde. Yes, we've known each other for a long time.

Nora. Just think; she has come all this way just to see you.

Helmer. I'm not sure I understand —

Mrs. Linde. Well, not really —

Nora. You see, Kristine is an absolutely fantastic secretary, and she would so much like to work for a competent executive and learn more than she knows already —

Helmer. Very sensible, I'm sure, Mrs. Linde.

Nora. So when she heard about your appointment — there was a wire — she came here as fast as she could. How about it, Torvald? Couldn't you do something for Kristine? For my sake. Please?

Helmer. Quite possibly. I take it you're a widow, Mrs. Linde?

Mrs. Linde. Yes.

Helmer. And you've had office experience?

Mrs. Linde. Some — yes.

Helmer. In that case I think it's quite likely that I'll be able to find you a position.

Nora (claps her hands). I knew it! I knew it!

Helmer. You've arrived at a most opportune time, Mrs. Linde.

Mrs. Linde. Oh, how can I ever thank you —

Helmer. Not at all, not at all. *(Puts his coat on.)* But today you'll have to excuse me —

Rank. Wait a minute; I'll come with you. *(Gets his fur coat from the front hall, warms it by the stove.)*

Nora. Don't be long, Torvald.

Helmer. An hour or so; no more.

Nora. Are you leaving, too, Kristine?

Mrs. Linde (putting on her things). Yes, I'd better go and find a place to stay.

Helmer. Good. Then we'll be going the same way.

Nora (helping her). I'm sorry this place is so small, but I don't think we very well could —

Mrs. Linde. Of course! Don't be silly, Nora. Goodbye, and thank you for everything.

Nora. Goodbye. We'll see you soon. You'll be back this evening, of course. And you too, Dr. Rank; right? If you feel well enough? Of course you will. Just wrap yourself up.

General small talk as all exit into the hall. Children's voices are heard on the stairs.

Nora. There they are! There they are! *(She runs and opens the door. The nurse Anne-Marie enters with the children.)*

Nora. Come in! Come in! *(Bends over and kisses them.)* Oh, you sweet, sweet darlings! Look at them, Kristine! Aren't they beautiful?

Rank. No standing around in the draft!

Helmer. Come along, Mrs. Linde. This place isn't fit for anyone but mothers right now.

Dr. Rank, Helmer, and Mrs. Linde go down the stairs. The Nurse enters the living room with the children. Nora follows, closing the door behind her.

Nora. My, how nice you all look! Such red cheeks! Like apples and roses. *(The children all talk at the same time.)* You've had so much fun? I bet you have. Oh, isn't that nice! You pulled both Emmy and Bob on your sleigh? Both at the same time? That's very good, Ivar. Oh, let me hold her for a minute, Anne-Marie. My sweet little doll baby! *(Takes the smallest of the children from the Nurse and dances with her.)* Yes, yes, of course; Mama'll dance with you too,

Bob. What? You threw snowballs? Oh, I wish I'd been there! No, no; *I* want to take their clothes off, Anne-Marie. Please let me; I think it's so much fun. You go on in. You look frozen. There's hot coffee on the stove.

The Nurse exits into the room to the left. Nora takes the children's wraps off and throws them all around. They all keep telling her things at the same time.

Nora. Oh, really? A big dog ran after you? But it didn't bite you. Of course not. Dogs don't bite sweet little doll babies. Don't peek at the packages, Ivar! What's in them? Wouldn't you like to know! No, no; that's something terrible! Play? You want to play? What do you want to play? Okay, let's play hide-and-seek. Bob hides first. You want *me* to? All right. I'll go first.

Laughing and shouting, Nora and the children play in the living room and in the adjacent room, right. Finally, Nora hides herself under the table; the children rush in, look for her, can't find her. They hear her low giggle, run to the table, lift the rug that covers it, see her. General hilarity. She crawls out, pretends to scare them. New delight. In the meantime there has been a knock on the door between the living room and the front hall, but nobody has noticed. Now the door is opened halfway; Krogstad appears. He waits a little. The play goes on.

Krogstad. Pardon me, Mrs. Helmer —

Nora (with a muted cry turns around, jumps up). Ah! What do you want?

Krogstad. I'm sorry. The front door was open. Somebody must have forgotten to close it —

Nora (standing up). My husband isn't here, Mr. Krogstad.

Krogstad. I know.

Nora. So what do you want?

Krogstad. I'd like a word with you.

Nora. With — ? *(To the children.)* Go in to Anne-Marie. What? No, the strange man won't do anything bad to Mama. When he's gone we'll play some more.

She takes the children into the room to the left and closes the door.

Nora (tense, troubled). You want to speak with me?

Krogstad. Yes I do.

Nora. Today — ? It isn't the first of the month yet.

Krogstad. No, it's Christmas Eve. It's up to you what kind of holiday you'll have.

Nora. What do you want? I can't possibly —

Krogstad. Let's not talk about that just yet. There's something else. You do have a few minutes, don't you?

Nora. Yes. Yes, of course. That is, —

Krogstad. Good. I was sitting in Olsen's restaurant when I saw your husband go by.

Nora. Yes — ?

Krogstad. — with a lady.

Nora. What of it?

Krogstad. May I be so free as to ask: wasn't that lady Mrs. Linde?

Nora. Yes.

Krogstad. Just arrived in town?

Nora. Yes, today.

Krogstad. She's a good friend of yours, I understand?

Nora. Yes, she is. But I fail to see —

Krogstad. I used to know her myself.

Nora. I know that.

Krogstad. So you know about that. I thought as much. In that case, let me ask you a simple question. Is Mrs. Linde going to be employed in the bank?

Nora. What makes you think you have the right to cross-examine me like this, Mr. Krogstad — you, one of my husband's employees? But since you ask, I'll tell you. Yes, Mrs. Linde is going to be working in the bank. And it was I who recommended her, Mr. Krogstad. Now you know.

Krogstad. So I was right.

Nora (walks up and down). After all, one does have a little influence, you know. Just because you're a woman, it doesn't mean that — Really, Mr. Krogstad, people in a subordinate position should be careful not to offend someone who — oh well —

Krogstad. — has influence?

Nora. Exactly.

Krogstad (changing his tone). Mrs. Helmer, I must ask you to be good enough to use your influence on my behalf.

Nora. What do you mean?

Krogstad. I want you to make sure that I am going to keep my subordinate position in the bank.

Nora. I don't understand. Who is going to take your position away from you?

Krogstad. There's no point in playing ignorant with me, Mrs. Helmer. I can very well appreciate that your friend would find it unpleasant to run into me. So now I know who I can thank for my dismissal.

Nora. But I assure you —

Krogstad. Never mind. Just want to say you still have time. I advise you to use your influence to prevent it.

Nora. But Mr. Krogstad, I don't have any influence — none at all.

Krogstad. No? I thought you just said —

Nora. Of course I didn't mean it that way. I! Whatever makes you think that I have any influence of that kind on my husband?

Krogstad. I went to law school with your husband. I have no reason to think that the bank manager is less susceptible than other husbands.

Nora. If you're going to insult my husband, I'll ask you to leave.

Krogstad. You're brave, Mrs. Helmer.

Nora. I'm not afraid of you any more. After New Year's I'll be out of this thing with you.

Krogstad (more controlled). Listen, Mrs. Helmer. If necessary, I'll fight as for my life to keep my little job in the bank.

Nora. So it seems.

Krogstad. It isn't just the money; that's really the smallest part of it. There is something else — Well, I guess I might as well tell you. It's like this. I'm sure you know, like everybody else, that some years ago I committed — an impropriety.

Nora. I believe I've heard it mentioned.

Krogstad. The case never came to court, but from that moment all doors were closed to me. So I took up the kind of business you know about. I had to do something, and I think I can say about myself that I have not been among the worst. But now I want to get out of all that. My sons are growing up. For their sake I must get back as much of my good name as I can. This job in the bank was like the first rung on the ladder. And now your husband wants to kick me down and leave me back in the mud again.

Nora. But I swear to you, Mr. Krogstad; it's not at all in my power to help you.

Krogstad. That's because you don't want to. But I have the means to force you.

Nora. You don't mean you're going to tell my husband I owe you money?

Krogstad. And if I did?

Nora. That would be a mean thing to do. *(Almost crying.)* That secret, which is my joy and my pride — for him to learn about it in such a coarse and ugly manner — to learn it from *you* — ! It would be terribly unpleasant for me.

Krogstad. Just unpleasant?

Nora (heatedly). But go ahead! Do it! It will be worse for you than for me. When my husband realizes what a bad person you are, you'll be sure to lose your job.

Krogstad. I asked you if it was just domestic unpleasantness you were afraid of?

Nora. When my husband finds out, of course he'll pay off the loan, and then we won't have anything more to do with you.

Krogstad (stepping closer). Listen, Mrs. Helmer — either you have a very bad memory, or you don't know much about business. I think I had better straighten you out on a few things.

Nora. What do you mean?

Krogstad. When your husband was ill, you came to me to borrow twelve hundred dollars.

Nora. I knew nobody else.

Krogstad. I promised to get you the money —

Nora. And you did.

Krogstad. I promised to get you the money on certain conditions. At the time you were so anxious about your husband's health and so set on getting him away that I doubt very much that you paid much attention to the details of our transaction. That's why I remind you of them now. Anyway, I promised to get you the money if you would sign an I.O.U., which I drafted.

Nora. And which I signed.

Krogstad. Good. But below your signature I added a few lines, making your father security for the loan. Your father was supposed to put his signature to those lines.

Nora. Supposed to — ? He did.

Krogstad. I had left the date blank. That is, your father was to date his own signature. You recall that, don't you, Mrs. Helmer?

Nora. I guess so —

Krogstad. I gave the note to you. You were to mail it to your father. Am I correct?

Nora. Yes.

Krogstad. And of course you did so right away, for no more than five or six days later you brought the paper back to me, signed by your father. Then I paid you the money.

Nora. Well? And haven't I been keeping up with the payments?

Krogstad. Fairly well, yes. But to get back to what we were talking about — those were difficult days for you, weren't they, Mrs. Helmer?

Nora. Yes, they were.

Krogstad. Your father was quite ill, I believe.

Nora. He was dying.

Krogstad. And died shortly afterwards?

Nora. That's right.

Krogstad. Tell me, Mrs. Helmer; do you happen to remember the date of your father's death? I mean the exact day of the month?

Nora. Daddy died on September 29.

Krogstad. Quite correct. I have ascertained that fact. That's why there is something peculiar about this *(takes out a piece of paper)*, which I can't account for.

Nora. Peculiar? How? I don't understand —

Krogstad. It seems very peculiar, Mrs. Helmer, that your father signed this promissory note three days after his death.

Nora. How so? I don't see what —

Krogstad. Your father died on September 29. Now look. He has dated his signature October 2. Isn't that odd?

Nora remains silent.

Krogstad. Can you explain it?

Nora is still silent.

Krogstad. I also find it striking that the date and the month and the year are not in your father's handwriting but in a hand I think I recognize. Well, that might be explained. Your father may have forgotten to date his signature and somebody else may have done it here, guessing at the date before he had learned of your father's death. That's all right. It's only the signature itself that matters. And that is genuine, isn't it, Mrs. Helmer? Your father *did* put his name to this note?

Nora (after a brief silence tosses her head back and looks defiantly at him). No, he didn't. *I* wrote Daddy's name.

Krogstad. Mrs. Helmer — do you realize what a dangerous admission you just made?

Nora. Why? You'll get your money soon.

Krogstad. Let me ask you something. Why didn't you mail this note to your father?

Nora. Because it was impossible. Daddy was sick — you know that. If I had asked him to sign it, I would have had to tell him what the money was for. But I couldn't tell him, as sick as he was, that my husband's life was in danger. That was impossible. Surely you can see that.

Krogstad. Then it would have been better for you if you had given up your trip abroad.

Nora. No, that was impossible! That trip was to save my husband's life. I couldn't give it up.

Krogstad. But didn't you realize that what you did amounted to fraud against me?

Nora. I couldn't let that make any difference. I didn't care about you at all. I hated the way you made all those difficulties for me, even though you knew the danger my husband was in. I thought you were cold and unfeeling.

Krogstad. Mrs. Helmer, obviously you have no clear idea of what you have done. Let me tell you that what I did that time was no more and no worse. And it ruined my name and reputation.

Nora. You! Are you trying to tell me that you did something brave once in order to save your wife's life?

Krogstad. The law doesn't ask about motives.

Nora. Then it's a bad law.

Krogstad. Bad or not — if I produce this note in court you'll be judged according to the law.

Nora. I refuse to believe you. A daughter shouldn't have the right to spare her dying old father worry and anxiety? A wife shouldn't have the right to save her husband's life? I don't know the laws very well, but I'm sure that somewhere they make allowance for cases like that. And you, a lawyer, don't know that? I think you must be a bad lawyer, Mr. Krogstad.

Krogstad. That may be. But business — the kind of business you and I have with one another — don't you think I know something about that? Very well. Do what you like. But let me tell you this: if I'm going to be kicked out again, you'll keep me company. *(He bows and exits through the front hall.)*

Nora (pauses thoughtfully; then, with a defiant toss of her head). Oh, nonsense! Trying to scare me like that! I'm not all that silly. *(Starts picking up the children's clothes; soon stops.)* But — ? No! That's impossible! I did it for love!

The Children (in the door to the left). Mama, the strange man just left. We saw him.

Nora. Yes, yes; I know. But don't tell anybody about the strange man. Do you hear? Not even Daddy.

The Children. We won't. But now you'll play with us again, won't you, Mama?

Nora. No, not right now.

The Children. But Mama — you promised.

Nora. I know, but I can't just now. Go to your own room. I've so much to do. Be nice now, my little darlings. Do as I say. *(She nudges them gently into the other room and closes the door. She sits down on the couch, picks up a piece of embroidery, makes a few stitches, then stops.)* No! *(Throws the embroidery down, goes to the hall door and calls out.)* Helene! Bring the Christmas tree in here, please! *(Goes to the table, left, opens the drawer, halts.)* No — that's impossible!

The Maid (with the Christmas tree). Where do you want it, ma'am?

Nora. There. The middle of the floor.

The Maid. You want anything else?

Nora. No, thanks. I have everything I need. *(The Maid goes out. Nora starts trimming the tree.)* I want candles — and flowers — That awful man! Oh, nonsense! There's nothing wrong. This will be a lovely tree. I'll do everything you want me to, Torvald. I'll sing for you — dance for you —

Helmer, a bundle of papers under his arm, enters from outside.

Nora. Ah — you're back already?

Helmer. Yes. Has anybody been here?

Nora. Here? No.

Helmer. That's funny. I saw Krogstad leaving just now.

Nora. Oh? Oh yes, that's right. Krogstad was here for just a moment.

Helmer. I can tell from your face that he came to ask you to put in a word for him.

Nora. Yes.

Helmer. And it was supposed to be your own idea, wasn't it? You were not to tell me he'd been here. He asked you that too, didn't he?

Nora. Yes, Torvald, but —

Helmer. Nora, Nora, how could you! Talk to a man like that and make him promises! And lying to me about it afterwards — !

Nora. Lying — ?

Helmer. Didn't you say nobody had been here? *(Shakes his finger at her.)* My little songbird must never do that again. Songbirds are supposed to have clean beaks to chirp with — no false notes. *(Puts his arm around her waist.)* Isn't that so? Of course it is. *(Lets her go.)* And that's enough about that. *(Sits down in front of the fireplace.)* Ah, it's nice and warm in here. *(Begins to leaf through his papers.)*

Nora (busy with the tree; after a brief pause). Torvald.

Helmer. Yes.

Nora. I'm looking forward so much to the Stenborgs' costume party day after tomorrow.

Helmer. And I can't wait to find out what you're going to surprise me with.

Nora. Oh, that silly idea!

Helmer. Oh?

Nora. I can't think of anything. It all seems so foolish and pointless.

Helmer. Ah, my little Nora admits that?

Nora (behind his chair, her arms on the back of the chair). Are you very busy, Torvald?

Helmer. Well —

Nora. What are all those papers?

Helmer. Bank business.

Nora. Already?

Helmer. I've asked the board to give me the authority to make certain changes in organization and personnel. That's what I'll be doing over the holidays. I want it all settled before New Year's.

Nora. So that's why this poor Krogstad —

Helmer. Hm.

Nora (leisurely playing with the hair on his neck). If you weren't so busy, Torvald, I'd ask you for a great big favor.

Helmer. Let's hear it, anyway.

Nora. I don't know anyone with better taste than you, and I want so much to look nice at the party. Couldn't you sort of take charge of me, Torvald, and decide what I'll wear — Help me with my costume?

Helmer. Aha! Little Lady Obstinate is looking for someone to rescue her?

Nora. Yes, Torvald. I won't get anywhere without your help.

Helmer. All right. I'll think about it. We'll come up with something.

Nora. Oh, you *are* nice! *(Goes back to the Christmas tree. A pause.)* Those red flowers look so pretty. — Tell me, was it really all that bad what this Krogstad fellow did?

Helmer. He forged signatures. Do you have any idea what that means?

Nora. Couldn't it have been because he felt he had to?

Helmer. Yes, or like so many others he may simply have been thoughtless. I'm not so heartless as to condemn a man absolutely because of a single imprudent act.

Nora. Of course not, Torvald!

Helmer. People like him can redeem themselves morally by openly confessing their crime and taking their punishment.

Nora. Punishment — ?

Helmer. But that was not the way Krogstad chose. He got out of it with tricks and evasions. That's what has corrupted him.

Nora. So you think that if — ?

Helmer. Can't you imagine how a guilty person like that has to lie and fake and dissemble wherever he goes — putting on a mask before everybody he's close to, even his own wife and children. It's this thing with the children that's the worst part of it, Nora.

Nora. Why is that?

Helmer. Because when a man lives inside such a circle of stinking lies he brings infection into his own home and contaminates his whole family. With every breath of air his children inhale the germs of something ugly.

Nora (moving closer behind him). Are you so sure of that?

Helmer. Of course I am. I have seen enough examples of that in my
  work. Nearly all young criminals have had mothers who lied.

Nora. Why mothers — particularly?

Helmer. Most often mothers. But of course fathers tend to have the
  same influence. Every lawyer knows that. And yet, for years this
  Krogstad has been poisoning his own children in an atmosphere of
  lies and deceit. That's why I call him a lost soul morally. *(Reaches
  out for her hands.)* And that's why my sweet little Nora must
  promise me never to take his side again. Let's shake on that. —
  What? What's this? Give me your hand. There! Now that's settled.
  I assure you, I would find it impossible to work in the same room
  with that man. I feel literally sick when I'm around people like
  that.

*Nora (withdraws her hand and goes to the other side of the Christ-
  mas tree).* It's so hot in here. And I have so much to do.

Helmer (gets up and collects his papers). Yes, and I really should try
  to get some of this reading done before dinner. I must think about
  your costume too. And maybe just possibly I'll have something to
  wrap in gilt paper and hang on the Christmas tree. *(Puts his hand
  on her head.)* Oh my adorable little songbird! *(Enters his study
  and closes the door.)*

Nora (after a pause, in a low voice). It's all a lot of nonsense. It's not
  that way at all. It's impossible. It has to be impossible.

The Nurse (in the door, left). The little ones are asking ever so nicely
  if they can't come in and be with their mama.

Nora. No, no, no! Don't let them in here! You stay with them, Anne-
  Marie.

The Nurse. If you say so, ma'am. *(Closes the door.)*

Nora (pale with terror). Corrupt my little children — ! Poison my
  home — ? *(Brief pause; she lifts her head.)* That's not true. Never.
  Never in a million years.

ACT II

*The same room. The Christmas tree is in the corner by the piano,
stripped shabby-looking, with burnt-down candles. Nora's outside clothes are on the couch. Nora is alone. She walks around
restlessly. She stops by the couch and picks up her coat.*

Nora (drops the coat again). There's somebody now! *(Goes to the
  door, listens.)* No. Nobody. Of course not — not on Christmas. And

not tomorrow either.° — But perhaps — *(Opens the door and looks.)* No, nothing in the mailbox. All empty. *(Comes forward.)* How silly I am! Of course he isn't serious. Nothing like that could happen. After all, I have three small children.

The Nurse enters from the room, left, carrying a big carton.

The Nurse. Well, at last I found it — the box with your costume.

Nora. Thanks. Just put it on the table.

Nurse (does so). But it's all a big mess, I'm afraid.

Nora. Oh, I wish I could tear the whole thing to little pieces!

Nurse. Heavens! It's not as bad as all that. It can be fixed all right. All it takes is a little patience.

Nora. I'll go over and get Mrs. Linde to help me.

Nurse. Going out again? In this awful weather? You'll catch a cold.

Nora. That might not be such a bad thing. How are the children?

Nurse. The poor little dears are playing with their presents, but —

Nora. Do they keep asking for me?

Nurse. Well, you know, they're used to being with their mamma.

Nora. I know. But Anne-Marie, from now on I can't be with them as much as before.

Nurse. Oh well. Little children get used to everything.

Nora. You think so? Do you think they'll forget their mamma if I were gone altogether?

Nurse. Goodness me — gone altogether?

Nora. Listen, Anne-Marie — something I've wondered about. How could you bring yourself to leave your child with strangers?

Nurse. But I had to, if I were to nurse you.

Nora. Yes, but how could you *want* to?

Nurse. When I could get such a nice place? When something like that happens to a poor young girl, she'd better be grateful for whatever she gets. For *he* didn't do a thing for me — the louse!

Nora. But your daughter has forgotten all about you, hasn't she?

Nurse. Oh no! Not at all! She wrote to me both when she was confirmed and when she got married.

Nora (putting her arms around her neck). You dear old thing — you were a good mother to me when I was little.

Nurse. Poor little Nora had no one else, you know.

Nora. And if my little ones didn't, I know you'd — oh, I'm being silly! *(Opens the carton.)* Go in to them, please. I really should — . Tomorrow you'll see how pretty I'll be.

And not tomorrow either In Norway both December 25 and 26 are legal holidays

Nurse. I know. There won't be anybody at that party half as pretty as you, ma'am. *(Goes out, left.)*

Nora (begins to take clothes out of the carton; in a moment she throws it all down). If only I dared to go out. If only I knew nobody would come. That nothing would happen while I was gone. — How silly! Nobody'll come. Just don't think about it. Brush the muff. Beautiful gloves. Beautiful gloves. Forget it. Forget it. One, two, three, four, five, six — *(Cries out.)* There they are! *(Moves toward the door, stops irresolutely.)*

Mrs. Linde enters from the hall. She has already taken off her coat.

Nora. Oh, it's you, Kristine. There's no one else out there, is there? I'm so glad you're here.

Mrs. Linde. They told me you'd asked for me.

Nora. I just happened to walk by. I need your help with something — badly. Let's sit here on the couch. Look. Torvald and I are going to a costume party tomorrow night — at Consul Stenborg's upstairs — and Torvald wants me to go as a Neapolitan fisher girl and dance the tarantella. I learned it when we were on Capri.

Mrs. Linde. Well, well! So you'll be putting on a whole show?

Nora. Yes. Torvald thinks I should. Look, here's the costume. Torvald had it made for me while we were there. But it's all so torn and everything. I just don't know —

Mrs. Linde. Oh, that can be fixed. It's not that much. The trimmings have come loose in a few places. Do you have needle and thread? Ah, here we are. All set.

Nora. I really appreciate it, Kristine.

Mrs. Linde (sewing). So you'll be in disguise tomorrow night, eh? You know — I may come by for just a moment, just to look at you. — Oh dear. I haven't even thanked you for the nice evening last night.

Nora (gets up, moves around). Oh, I don't know. I don't think last night was as nice as it usually is. — You should have come to town a little earlier, Kristine. — Yes, Torvald knows how to make it nice and pretty around here.

Mrs. Linde. You too, I should think. After all, you're your father's daughter. By the way, is Dr. Rank always as depressed as he was last night?

Nora. No, last night was unusual. He's a very sick man, you know — very sick. Poor Rank, his spine is rotting away. Tuberculosis, I think. You see, his father was a nasty old man with mistresses and all that sort of thing. Rank has been sickly ever since he was a little boy.

Mrs. Linde (dropping her sewing to her lap). But dearest Nora, where have you learned about things like that?

Nora (still walking about). Oh, you know — with three children you sometimes get to talk with — other wives. Some of them know quite a bit about medicine. So you pick up a few things.

Mrs. Linde (resumes her sewing; after a brief pause). Does Dr. Rank come here every day?

Nora. Every single day. He's Torvald's oldest and best friend, after all. And my friend too, for that matter. He's part of the family, almost.

Mrs. Linde. But tell me, is he quite sincere? I mean, isn't he the kind of man who likes to say nice things to people?

Nora. No, not at all. Rather the opposite, in fact. What makes you say that?

Mrs. Linde. When you introduced us yesterday, he told me he'd often heard my name mentioned in this house. But later on it was quite obvious that your husband really had no idea who I was. So how could Dr. Rank — ?

Nora. You're right, Kristine, but I can explain that. You see, Torvald loves me so very much that he wants me all to himself. That's what he says. When we were first married he got almost jealous when I as much as mentioned anybody from back home that I was fond of. So of course I soon stopped doing that. But with Dr. Rank I often talk about home. You see, he likes to listen to me.

Mrs. Linde. Look here, Nora. In many ways you're still a child. After all, I'm quite a bit older than you and have had more experience. I want to give you a piece of advice. I think you should get out of this thing with Dr. Rank.

Nora. Get out of what thing?

Mrs. Linde. Several things in fact, if you want my opinion. Yesterday you said something about a rich admirer who was going to give you money —

Nora. One who doesn't exist, unfortunately. What of it?

Mrs. Linde. Does Dr. Rank have money?

Nora. Yes, he does.

Mrs. Linde. And no dependents?

Nora. No. But — ?

Mrs. Linde. And he comes here every day?

Nora. Yes, I told you that already.

Mrs. Linde. But how can that sensitive man be so tactless?

Nora. I haven't the slightest idea what you're talking about.

Mrs. Linde. Don't play games with me, Nora. Don't you think I know who you borrowed the twelve hundred dollars from?

Nora. Are you out of your mind! The very idea — ! A friend of both of us who sees us every day — ! What a dreadfully uncomfortable position that would be!

Mrs. Linde. So it really isn't Dr. Rank?

Nora. Most certainly not! I would never have dreamed of asking him — not for a moment. Anyway, he didn't have any money then. He inherited it afterwards.

Mrs. Linde. Well, I still think it may have been lucky for you, Nora dear.

Nora. The idea! It would never have occurred to me to ask Dr. Rank — . Though I'm sure that if I *did* ask him —

Mrs. Linde. But of course you wouldn't.

Nora. Of course not. I can't imagine that that would ever be necessary. But I am quite sure that if I told Dr. Rank —

Mrs. Linde. Behind your husband's back?

Nora. I must get out of — this other thing. That's also behind his back. I *must* get out of it.

Mrs. Linde. That's what I told you yesterday. But —

Nora (walking up and down). A man manages these things so much better than a woman —

Mrs. Linde. One's husband, yes.

Nora. Silly, silly! *(Stops.)* When you've paid off all you owe, you get your I.O.U. back; right?

Mrs. Linde. Yes, of course.

Nora. And you can tear it into a hundred thousand little pieces and burn it — that dirty, filthy, paper!

Mrs. Linde (looks hard at her, puts down her sewing, rises slowly). Nora — you're hiding something from me.

Nora. Can you tell?

Mrs. Linde. Something's happened to you, Nora, since yesterday morning. What is it?

Nora (going to her). Kristine! *(Listens.)* Shhh. Torvald just came back. Listen. Why don't you go in to the children for a while. Torvald can't stand having sewing around. Get Anne-Marie to help you.

Mrs. Linde (gathers some of the sewing things together). All right, but I'm not leaving here till you and I have talked.

She goes out left, just as Helmer enters from the front hall.

Nora (towards him). I have been waiting and waiting for you, Torvald.

Helmer. Was that the dressmaker?

Nora. No, it was Kristine. She's helping me with my costume. Oh Torvald, just wait till you see how nice I'll look!

Helmer. I told you. Pretty good idea I had, wasn't it?

Nora. Lovely! And wasn't it nice of me to go along with it?

Helmer (his hand under her chin). Nice? To do what your husband tells you? All right, you little rascal; I know you didn't mean it that way. But don't let me interrupt you. I suppose you want to try it on.

Nora. And you'll be working?

Helmer. Yes. *(Shows her a pile of papers.)* Look. I've been down to the bank. *(Is about to enter his study.)*

Nora. Torvald.

Helmer (halts). Yes?

Nora. What if your little squirrel asked you ever so nicely —

Helmer. For what?

Nora. Would you do it?

Helmer. Depends on what it is.

Nora. Squirrel would run around and do all sorts of fun tricks if you'd be nice and agreeable.

Helmer. All right. What is it?

Nora. Lark would chirp and twitter in all the rooms, up and down —

Helmer. So what? Lark does that anyway.

Nora. I'll be your elfmaid and dance for you in the moonlight, Torvald.

Helmer. Nora. don't tell me it's the same thing you mentioned this morning?

Nora (closer to him). Yes, Torvald. I beg you!

Helmer. You really have the nerve to bring that up again?

Nora. Yes. You've just got to do as I say. You *must* let Krogstad keep his job.

Helmer. My dear Nora. It's his job I intend to give to Mrs. Linde.

Nora. I know. And that's ever so nice of you. But can't you just fire somebody else?

Helmer. This is incredible! You just don't give up, do you? Because you make some foolish promise, *I* am supposed to — !

Nora. That's not the reason, Torvald. It's for your own sake. That man writes for the worst newspapers. You've said so yourself. There's no telling what he may do to you. I'm scared to death of him.

Helmer. Ah, I understand. You're afraid because of what happened before.

Nora. What do you mean?

Helmer. You're thinking of your father, of course.

Nora. Yes. Yes, you're right. Remember the awful things they wrote about Daddy in the newspapers. I really think they might have forced him to resign if the ministry hadn't sent you to look into the charges and if you hadn't been so helpful and understanding.

Helmer. My dear little Nora, there is a world of difference between your father and me. Your father's official conduct was not above reproach. Mine is, and I intend for it to remain that way as long as I hold my position.

Nora. Oh, but you don't know what vicious people like that may think of. Oh, Torvald! Now all of us could be so happy together here in our own home, peaceful and carefree. Such a good life, Torvald, for you and me and the children! That's why I implore you —

Helmer. And it's exactly because you plead for him that you make it impossible for me to keep him. It's already common knowledge in the bank that I intend to let Krogstad go. If it gets out that the new manager has changed his mind because of his wife —

Nora. Yes? What then?

Helmer. No, of course, that wouldn't matter at all as long as little Mrs. Pighead here got her way! Do you want me to make myself look ridiculous before my whole staff — make people think I can be swayed by just anybody — by outsiders? Believe me, I would soon enough find out what the consequences would be! Besides, there's another thing that makes it absolutely impossible for Krogstad to stay on in the bank now that I'm in charge.

Nora. What's that?

Helmer. I suppose in a pinch I could overlook his moral shortcomings —

Nora. Yes, you could; couldn't you, Torvald?

Helmer. And I understand he's quite a good worker, too. But we've known each other for a long time. It's one of those imprudent relationships you get into when you're young that embarrass you for the rest of your life. I guess I might as well be frank with you: he and I are on a first name basis. And that tactless fellow never hides the fact even when other people are around. Rather, he seems to think it entitles him to be familiar with me. Every chance he gets he comes out with his damn "Torvald, Torvald." I'm telling you, I find it most awkward. He would make my position in the bank intolerable.

Nora. You don't really mean any of this, Torvald.

Helmer. Oh? I don't? And why not?

Nora. No, for it's all so petty.

Helmer. What! Petty? You think I'm being petty!

Nora. No, I *don't* think you are petty, Torvald dear. That's exactly why I —

Helmer. Never mind. You think my reasons are petty, so it follows that I must be petty too. Petty! Indeed! By God, I'll put an end to

this right now! *(Opens the door to the front hall and calls out.)*
Helene!

Nora. What are you doing?

Helmer (searching among his papers). Making a decision. *(The Maid enters.)* Here. Take this letter. Go out with it right away. Find somebody to deliver it. But quick. The address is on the envelope. Wait. Here's money.

The Maid. Very good, sir. *(She takes the letter and goes out.)*

Helmer (collecting his papers). There now, little Mrs. Obstinate!

Nora (breathless). Torvald — what was that letter?

Helmer. Krogstad's dismissal.

Nora. Call it back, Torvald! There's still time! Oh Torvald, please — call it back! For my sake, for your own sake, for the sake of the children! Listen to me, Torvald! Do it! You don't know what you're doing to all of us!

Helmer. Too late.

Nora. Yes. Too late.

Helmer. Dear Nora, I forgive you this fear you're in, although it really is an insult to me. Yes, it is! It's an insult to think that I am scared of a shabby scrivener's revenge. But I forgive you, for it's such a beautiful proof how much you love me. *(Takes her in his arms.)* And that's the way it should be, my sweet darling. Whatever happens, you'll see that when things get really rough I have both strength and courage. You'll find out that I am man enough to shoulder the whole burden.

Nora (terrified). What do you mean by that?

Helmer. All of it, I tell you —

Nora (composed). You'll never have to do that.

Helmer. Good. Then we'll share the burden, Nora — like husband and wife, the way it ought to be. *(Caresses her.)* Now are you satisfied? There, there, there. Not that look in your eyes — like a frightened dove. It's all your own foolish imagination. — Why don't you practice the tarantella — and your tambourine, too. I'll be in the inner office and close both doors, so I won't hear you. You can make as much noise as you like. *(Turning in the doorway.)* And when Rank comes, tell him where to find me. *(He nods to her, enters his study carrying his papers, and closes the door.)*

Nora (transfixed by terror, whispers). He would do it. He'll do it. He'll do it in spite of the whole world. — No, this mustn't happen. Anything rather than that! There must be a way — ! *(The doorbell rings.)* Dr. Rank! Anything rather than that! Anything — anything at all!

She passes her hand over her face, pulls herself together, and opens the door to the hall. Dr. Rank is out there, hanging up his coat. Darkness begins to fall during the following scene.

Nora. Hello there, Dr. Rank. I recognized your ringing. Don't go in to Torvald yet. I think he's busy.

Rank. And you?

Nora *(as he enters and she closes the door behind him).* You know I always have time for you.

Rank. Thanks. I'll make use of that as long as I can.

Nora. What do you mean by that — As long as you can?

Rank. Does that frighten you?

Nora. Well, it's a funny expression. As if something was going to happen.

Rank. Something is going to happen that I've long been expecting. But I admit I hadn't thought it would come quite so soon.

Nora *(seizes his arm).* What is it you've found out? Dr. Rank — tell me!

Rank *(sits down by the stove).* I'm going downhill fast. There's nothing to do about that.

Nora *(with audible relief).* So it's you —

Rank. Who else? No point in lying to myself. I'm in worse shape than any of my other patients, Mrs. Helmer. These last few days I've been making up my inner status. Bankrupt. Chances are that within a month I'll be rotting up in the cemetery.

Nora. Shame on you! Talking that horrid way!

Rank. The thing itself is horrid — damn horrid. The worst of it, though, is all that other horror that comes first. There is only one more test I need to make. After that I'll have a pretty good idea when I'll start coming apart. There is something I want to say to you. Helmer's refined nature can't stand anything hideous. I don't want him in my sick room.

Nora. Oh, but Dr. Rank —

Rank. I don't want him there. Under no circumstance. I'll close my door to him. As soon as I have full certainty that the worst is about to begin I'll give you my card with a black cross on it. Then you'll know the last horror of destruction has started.

Nora. Today you're really quite impossible. And I had hoped you'd be in a particularly good mood.

Rank. With death on my hands? Paying for someone else's sins? Is there justice in that? And yet there isn't a single family that isn't ruled by that same law of ruthless retribution, in one way or another.

Nora *(puts her hands over her ears).* Poppycock! Be fun! Be fun!

Rank. Well, yes. You may just as well laugh at the whole thing. My poor, innocent spine is suffering for my father's frolics as a young lieutenant.

Nora (over by the table, left). Right. He was addicted to asparagus and goose liver paté, wasn't he?

Rank. And truffles.

Nora. Of course. Truffles. And oysters too, I think.

Rank. And oysters. Obviously.

Nora. And all the port and champagne that go with it. It's really too bad that goodies like that ruin your backbone.

Rank. Particularly an unfortunate backbone that never enjoyed any of it.

Nora. Ah yes, that's the saddest part of it all.

Rank (looks searchingly at her). Hm —

Nora (after a brief pause). Why did you smile just then?

Rank. No, it was you that laughed.

Nora. No, it was you that smiled, Dr. Rank!

Rank (gets up). You're more of a mischief-maker than I thought.

Nora. I feel in the mood for mischief today.

Rank. So it seems.

Nora (with both her hands on his shoulders). Dear, dear Dr. Rank, don't you go and die and leave Torvald and me.

Rank. Oh, you won't miss me for very long. Those who go away are soon forgotten.

Nora (with an anxious look). Do you believe that?

Rank. You'll make new friends, and then —

Nora. Who'll make new friends?

Rank. Both you and Helmer, once I'm gone. You yourself seem to have made a good start already. What was this Mrs. Linde doing here last night?

Nora. Aha — Don't tell me you're jealous of poor Kristine?

Rank. Yes, I am. She'll be my successor in this house. As soon as I have made my excuses, that woman is likely to —

Nora. Shh — not so loud. She's in there.

Rank. Today too? There you are!

Nora. She's mending my costume. My God, you really *are* unreasonable. *(Sits down on the couch.)* Now be nice, Dr. Rank. Tomorrow you'll see how beautifully I'll dance, and then you are to pretend I'm dancing just for you — and for Torvald too, of course. *(Takes several items out of the carton.)* Sit down, Dr. Rank; I want to show you something.

Rank (sitting down). What?

Nora. Look.

Rank. Silk stockings.

Nora. Flesh-colored. Aren't they lovely? Now it's getting dark in here, but tomorrow — No, no. You only get to see the foot. Oh well, you might as well see all of it.

Rank. Hmm.

Nora. Why do you look so critical? Don't you think they'll fit?

Rank. That's something I can't possibly have a reasoned opinion about.

Nora (looks at him for a moment). Shame on you. *(Slaps his ear lightly with the stocking.)* That's what you get. *(Puts the things back in the carton.)*

Rank. And what other treasures are you going to show me?

Nora. Nothing at all, because you're naughty. *(She hums a little and rummages in the carton.)*

Rank (after a brief silence). When I sit here like this, talking confidently with you, I can't imagine — I can't possibly imagine what would have become of me if I hadn't had you and Helmer.

Nora (smiles). Well, yes — I do believe you like being with us.

Rank (in a lower voice, lost in thought). And then to have to go away from it all —

Nora. Nonsense. You are not going anywhere.

Rank (as before).   — and not to leave behind as much as a poor little token of gratitude, hardly a brief memory of someone missed, nothing but a vacant place that anyone can fill.

Nora. And what if I were to ask you — ? No —

Rank. Ask me what?

Nora. For a great proof of your friendship —

Rank. Yes, yes — ?

Nora. No, I mean — for an enormous favor —

Rank. Would you really for once make me as happy as all that?

Nora. But you don't even know what it is.

Rank. Well, then; tell me.

Nora. Oh, but I can't, Dr. Rank. It's altogether too much to ask — It's advice and help and a favor —

Rank. So much the better. I can't even begin to guess what it is you have in mind. So for heaven's sake tell me! Don't you trust me?

Nora. Yes, I trust you more than anyone else I know. You are my best and most faithful friend. I know that. So I will tell you. All right, Dr. Rank. There is something you can help me prevent. You know how much Torvald loves me — beyond all words. Never for a moment would he hesitate to give his life for me.

Rank (leaning over to her). Nora — do you really think he's the only one — ?

Nora (with a slight start). Who — ?

Rank.   — would gladly give his life for you.

Nora (heavily). I see.

Rank. I have sworn an oath to myself to tell you before I go. I'll never find a better occasion. — All right, Nora; now you know. And now you also know that you can confide in me more than in anyone else.

Nora (gets up; in a calm, steady voice). Let me get by.

Rank (makes room for her but remains seated). Nora —

Nora (in the door to the front hall). Helene, bring the lamp in here, please. *(Walks over to the stove.)* Oh, dear Dr. Rank. That really wasn't very nice of you.

Rank (gets up). That I have loved you as much as anybody — was that not nice?

Nora. No, not that. But that you told me. There was no need for that.

Rank. What do you mean? Have you known — ?

The Maid enters with the lamp, puts it on the table, and goes out.

Rank. Nora — Mrs. Helmer — I'm asking you: did you know?

Nora. Oh, how can I tell what I knew and didn't know! I really can't say — But that you could be so awkward, Dr. Rank! Just when everything was so comfortable.

Rank. Well, anyway, now you know that I'm at your service with my life and soul. And now you must speak.

Nora (looks at him). After what just happened?

Rank. I beg of you — let me know what it is.

Nora. There is nothing I can tell you now.

Rank. Yes, yes. You mustn't punish me this way. Please let me do for you whatever anyone *can* do.

Nora. Now there is nothing you can do. Besides, I don't think I really need any help, anyway. It's probably just my imagination. Of course that's all it is. I'm sure of it! *(Sits down in the rocking chair, looks at him, smiles.)* Well, well, well, Dr. Rank! What a fine gentleman you turned out to be! Aren't you ashamed of yourself, now that we have light?

Rank. No, not really. But perhaps I ought to leave — and not come back?

Nora. Don't be silly; of course not! You'll come here exactly as you have been doing. You know perfectly well that Torvald can't do without you.

Rank. Yes, but what about you?

Nora. Oh, I always think it's perfectly delightful when you come.

Rank. That's the very thing that misled me. You are a riddle to me. It has often seemed to me that you'd just as soon be with me as with Helmer.

Nora. Well, you see, there are people you love, and then there are other people you'd almost rather be with.

Rank. Yes, there is something in that.

Nora. When I lived at home with Daddy, of course I loved him most. But I always thought it was so much fun to sneak off down to the maids' room, for they never gave me good advice and they always talked about such fun things.

Rank. Aha! So it's *their* place I have taken.

Nora (jumps up and goes over to him). Oh dear, kind Dr. Rank, you know very well I didn't mean it that way. Can't you see that with Torvald it is the way it used to be with Daddy?

The Maid enters from the front hall.

The Maid. Ma'am! *(Whispers to her and gives her a caller's card.)*

Nora (glances at the card). Ah! *(Puts it in her pocket.)*

Rank. Anything wrong?

Nora. No, no; not at all. It's nothing — just my new costume —

Rank. But your costume is lying right there!

Nora. Oh yes, that one. But this is another one. I ordered it. Torvald mustn't know —

Rank. Aha. So that's the great secret.

Nora. That's it. Why don't you go in to him, please. He's in the inner office. And keep him there for a while —

Rank. Don't worry. He won't get away. *(Enters Helmer's study.)*

Nora (to The Maid). You say he's waiting in the kitchen?

The Maid. Yes. He came up the back stairs.

Nora. But didn't you tell him there was somebody with me?

The Maid. Yes, but he wouldn't listen.

Nora. He won't leave?

The Maid. No, not till he's had a word with you, ma'am.

Nora. All right. But try not to make any noise. And, Helene — don't tell anyone he's here. It's supposed to be a surprise for my husband.

The Maid. I understand, ma'am — *(She leaves.)*

Nora. The terrible is happening. It's happening, after all. No, no, no. It can't happen. It won't happen. *(She bolts the study door.)*

The Maid opens the front hall door for Krogstad and closes the door behind him. He wears a fur coat for traveling, boots, and a fur hat.

Nora (toward him). Keep your voice down. My husband's home.

Krogstad. That's all right.

Nora. What do you want?

Krogstad. To find out something.

Nora. Be quick, then. What is it?

Krogstad. I expect you know I've been fired.

Nora. I couldn't prevent it, Mr. Krogstad. I fought for you as long and as hard as I could, but it didn't do any good.

Krogstad. Your husband doesn't love you any more than that? He knows what I can do to you, and yet he runs the risk —

Nora. Surely you didn't think I'd tell him?

Krogstad. No, I really didn't. It wouldn't be like Torvald Helmer to show that kind of guts —

Nora. Mr. Krogstad, I insist that you show respect for my husband.

Krogstad. By all means. All due respect. But since you're so anxious to keep this a secret, may I assume that you are a little better informed than yesterday about exactly what you have done?

Nora. Better than *you* could ever teach me.

Krogstad. Of course. Such a bad lawyer as I am —

Nora. What do you want of me?

Krogstad. I just wanted to find out how you are, Mrs. Helmer. I've been thinking about you all day. You see, even a bill collector, a pen pusher, a — anyway, someone like me — even he has a little of what they call a heart.

Nora. Then show it. Think of my little children.

Krogstad. Have you and your husband thought of mine? Never mind. All I want to tell you is that you don't need to take this business too seriously. I have no intention of bringing charges right away.

Nora. Oh no, you wouldn't; would you? I knew you wouldn't.

Krogstad. The whole thing can be settled quite amiably. Nobody else needs to know anything. It will be between the three of us.

Nora. My husband must never find out about this.

Krogstad. How are you going to prevent that? Maybe you can pay me the balance on the loan?

Nora. No, not right now.

Krogstad. Or do you have a way of raising the money one of these next few days?

Nora. None I intend to make use of.

Krogstad. It wouldn't do you any good, anyway. Even if you had the cash in your hand right this minute, I wouldn't give you your note back. It wouldn't make any difference *how* much money you offered me.

Nora. Then you'll have to tell me what you plan to use the note *for*.

Krogstad. Just keep it; that's all. Have it on hand, so to speak. I won't say a word to anybody else. So if you've been thinking about doing something desperate —

Nora. I have.

Krogstad. — like leaving house and home —

Nora. I have!

Krogstad. — or even something worse —

Nora. How did you know?

Krogstad. — then: don't.

Nora: How did you know I was thinking of *that?*

Krogstad. Most of us do, right at first. I did, too, but when it came down to it I didn't have the courage —

Nora (tonelessly). Nor do I.

Krogstad (relieved). See what I mean? I thought so. You don't either.

Nora. I don't. I don't.

Krogstad. Besides, it would be very silly of you. Once that first domestic blow-up is behind you — . Here in my pocket is a letter for your husband.

Nora. Telling him everything?

Krogstad. As delicately as possible.

Nora (quickly). He mustn't get that letter. Tear it up. I'll get you the money somehow.

Krogstad. Excuse me, Mrs. Helmer. I thought I just told you —

Nora. I'm not talking about the money I owe you. Just let me know how much money you want from my husband, and I'll get it for you.

Krogstad. I want no money from your husband.

Nora. Then, what *do* you want?

Krogstad. I'll tell you, Mrs. Helmer. I want to rehabilitate myself; I want to get up in the world; and your husband is going to help me. For a year and a half I haven't done anything disreputable. All that time I have been struggling with the most miserable circumstances. I was content to work my way up step by step. Now I've been kicked out, and I'm no longer satisfied just getting my old job back. I want more than that; I want to get to the top. I'm being quite serious. I want the bank to take me back but in a higher position. I want your husband to create a new job for me —

Nora. He'll never do that!

Krogstad. He will. I know him. He won't dare not to. And once I'm back inside and he and I are working together, you'll see! Within a year I'll be the manager's right hand. It will be Nils Krogstad and not Torvald Helmer who'll be running the Mutual Bank!

Nora. You'll never see that happen!

Krogstad. Are you thinking of — ?

Nora. Now I *do* have the courage.

Krogstad. You can't scare me. A fine, spoiled lady like you —

Nora. You'll see, you'll see!

Krogstad. Under the ice, perhaps? Down into that cold, black water?

Then spring comes, and you float up again — hideous, can't be identified, hair all gone —

Nora. You don't frighten me.

Krogstad. Nor you me. One doesn't do that sort of thing, Mrs. Helmer. Besides, what good would it do? He'd still be in my power.

Nora. Afterwards? When I'm no longer — ?

Krogstad. Aren't you forgetting that your reputation would be in my hands?

Nora stares at him, speechless.

Krogstad. All right; now I've told you what to expect. So don't do anything foolish. When Helmer gets my letter I expect to hear from him. And don't you forget that it's your husband himself who forces me to use such means again. That I'll never forgive him. Goodbye, Mrs. Helmer. *(Goes out through the hall.)*

Nora (at the door, opens it a little, listens). He's going. And no letter. Of course not! That would be impossible! *(Opens the door more.)* What's he doing? He's still there. Doesn't go down. Having second thoughts — ? Will he — ?

The sound of a letter dropping into the mailbox. Then Krogstad's steps are heard going down the stairs, gradually dying away.

Nora (with a muted cry runs forward to the table by the couch; brief pause). In the mailbox. *(Tiptoes back to the door to the front hall.)* There it is. Torvald, Torvald — now we're lost!

Mrs. Linde (enters from the left, carrying Nora's Capri costume). There now. I think it's all fixed. Why don't we try it on you —

Nora (in a low, hoarse voice). Kristine, come here.

Mrs. Linde. What's wrong with you? You look quite beside yourself.

Nora. Come over here. Do you see that letter? There, look — through the glass in the mailbox.

Mrs. Linde. Yes, yes; I see it.

Nora. That letter is from Krogstad.

Mrs. Linde. Nora — it was Krogstad who lent you the money!

Nora. Yes, and now Torvald will find out about it.

Mrs. Linde. Oh believe me, Nora. That's the best thing for both of you.

Nora. There's more to it than you know. I forged a signature —

Mrs. Linde. Oh my God — !

Nora. I just want to tell you this, Kristine, that you must be my witness.

Mrs. Linde. Witness? How? Witness to what?

Nora. If I lose my mind — and that could very well happen —

Mrs. Linde. Nora!

Nora. — or if something were to happen to me — something that made it impossible for me to be here —

Mrs. Linde. Nora, Nora! You're not yourself!

Nora. — and if someone were to take all the blame, assume the whole responsibility — Do you understand — ?

Mrs. Linde. Yes, yes; but how can you think — !

Nora. — then you are to witness that that's not so, Kristine. I am not beside myself. I am perfectly rational, and what I'm telling you is that nobody else has known about this. I've done it all by myself, the whole thing. Just remember that.

Mrs. Linde. I will. But I don't understand any of it.

Nora. Oh, how could you! For it's the wonderful that's about to happen.

Mrs. Linde. The wonderful?

Nora. Yes, the wonderful. But it's so terrible, Kristine. It mustn't happen for anything in the whole world!

Mrs. Linde. I'm going over to talk to Krogstad right now.

Nora. No, don't. Don't go to him. He'll do something bad to you.

Mrs. Linde. There was a time when he would have done anything for me.

Nora. He!

Mrs. Linde. Where does he live?

Nora. Oh, I don't know — Yes, wait a minute — *(Reaches into her pocket.)* here's his card. — But the letter, the letter — !

Helmer (in his study, knocks on the door). Nora!

Nora (cries out in fear). Oh, what is it? What do you want?

Helmer. That's all right. Nothing to be scared about. We're not coming in. For one thing, you've bolted the door, you know. Are you modeling your costume?

Nora. Yes, yes; I am. I'm going to be so pretty, Torvald.

Mrs. Linde (having looked at the card). He lives just around the corner.

Nora. Yes, but it's no use. Nothing can save us now. The letter is in the mailbox.

Mrs. Linde. And your husband has the key?

Nora. Yes. He always keeps it with him.

Mrs. Linde. Krogstad must ask for his letter back, unread. He's got to think up some pretext or other —

Nora. But this is just the time of day when Torvald —

Mrs. Linde. Delay him. Go in to him. I'll be back as soon as I can. *(She hurries out through the hall door.)*

Nora (walks over to Helmer's door, opens it, and peeks in). Torvald!

Helmer (still offstage). Well, well! So now one's allowed in one's own living room again. Come on, Rank. Now we'll see — *(In the doorway.)* But what's this?

Nora. What, Torvald dear?

Helmer. Rank prepared me for a splendid metamorphosis.

Rank (in the doorway). That's how I understood it. Evidently I was mistaken.

Nora. Nobody gets to admire me in my costume before tomorrow.

Helmer. But, dearest Nora — you look all done in. Have you been practicing too hard?

Nora. No, I haven't practiced at all.

Helmer. But you'll have to, you know.

Nora. I know it, Torvald. I simply must. But I can't do a thing unless you help me. I have forgotten everything.

Helmer. Oh it will all come back. We'll work on it.

Nora. Oh yes, please, Torvald. You just have to help me. Promise? I am so nervous. That big party — . You mustn't do anything else tonight. Not a bit of business. Don't even touch a pen. Will you promise, Torvald?

Helmer. I promise. Tonight I'll be entirely at your service — you helpless little thing. — Just a moment, though. First I want to — *(Goes to the door to the front hall.)*

Nora. What are you doing out there?

Helmer. Just looking to see if there's any mail.

Nora. No, no! Don't, Torvald!

Helmer. Why not?

Nora. Torvald, I beg you. There is no mail.

Helmer. Let me just look, anyway. *(Is about to go out.)*

Nora by the piano, plays the first bars of the tarantella dance.

Helmer (halts at the door). Aha!

Nora. I won't be able to dance tomorrow if I don't get to practice with you.

Helmer (goes to her). Are you really all that scared, Nora dear?

Nora. Yes, so terribly scared. Let's try it right now. There's still time before we eat. Oh please, sit down and play for me, Torvald. Teach me, coach me, the way you always do.

Helmer. Of course I will, my darling, if that's what you want. *(Sits down at the piano.)*

Nora takes the tambourine out of the carton, as well as a long, many-colored shawl. She quickly drapes the shawl around herself, then leaps into the middle of the floor.

Nora. Play for me! I want to dance!

> *Helmer plays and Nora dances. Dr. Rank stands by the piano behind Helmer and watches.*

Helmer (playing). Slow down, slow down!
Nora. Can't!
Helmer. Not so violent, Nora!
Nora. It has to be this way.
Helmer (stops playing). No, no. This won't do at all.
Nora (laughing, swinging her tambourine). What did I tell you?
Rank. Why don't you let me play?
Helmer (getting up). Good idea. Then I can direct her better.

> *Rank sits down at the piano and starts playing. Nora dances more and more wildly. Helmer stands over by the stove, repeatedly correcting her. She doesn't seem to hear. Her hair comes loose and falls down over her shoulders. She doesn't notice but keeps on dancing. Mrs. Linde enters.*

Mrs. Linde (stops by the door, dumbfounded). Ah — !
Nora (dancing). We're having such fun, Kristine!
Helmer. My dearest Nora, you're dancing as if it were a matter of life and death!
Nora. It is! It is!
Helmer. Rank, stop. This is sheer madness. Stop, I say!

> *Rank stops playing; Nora suddenly stops dancing.*

Helmer (goes over to her). If I hadn't seen it I wouldn't have believed it. You've forgotten every single thing I ever taught you.
Nora (tosses away the tambourine). See? I told you.
Helmer. Well! You certainly need coaching.
Nora. Didn't I tell you I did? Now you've seen for yourself. I'll need your help till the very minute we're leaving for the party. Will you promise, Torvald?
Helmer. You can count on it.
Nora. You're not to think of anything except me — not tonight and not tomorrow. You're not to read any letters — not to look in the mailbox —
Helmer. Ah, I see. You're still afraid of that man.
Nora. Yes — yes, that too.
Helmer. Nora, I can tell from looking at you. There's a letter from him out there.
Nora. I don't know. I think so. But you're not to read it now. I don't want anything ugly to come between us before it's all over.

Rank (to Helmer in a low voice). Better not argue with her.

Helmer (throws his arm around her). The child shall have her way. But tomorrow night, when you've done your dance —

Nora. Then you'll be free.

The Maid (in the door, right). Dinner can be served any time, ma'am.

Nora. We want champagne, Helene.

The Maid. Very good, ma'am. *(Goes out.)*

Helmer. Aha! Having a party, eh?

Nora. Champagne from now till sunrise! *(Calls out.)* And some macaroons, Helene. Lots! — just this once.

Helmer (taking her hands). There, there — I don't like this wild — frenzy — Be my own sweet little lark again, the way you always are.

Nora. Oh, I will. But you go on in. You too, Dr. Rank. Kristine, please help me put up my hair.

Rank (in a low voice to Helmer as they go out). You don't think she is — you know — expecting — ?

Helmer. Oh no. Nothing like that. It's just this childish fear I was telling you about. *(They go out, right.)*

Nora. Well?

Mrs. Linde. Left town.

Nora. I saw it in your face.

Mrs. Linde. He'll be back tomorrow night. I left him a note.

Nora. You shouldn't have. I don't want you to try to stop anything. You see, it's a kind of ecstasy, too, this waiting for the wonderful.

Mrs. Linde. But what is it you're waiting *for?*

Nora. You wouldn't understand. Why don't you go in to the others. I'll be there in a minute.

Mrs. Linde enters the dining room, right.

Nora (stands still for a little while, as if collecting herself; she looks at her watch). Five o'clock. Seven hours till midnight. Twenty-four more hours till next midnight. Then the tarantella is over. Twenty-four plus seven — thirty-one more hours to live.

Helmer (in the door, right). What's happening to my little lark?

Nora (to him, with open arms). Here's your lark!

ACT III

The same room. The table by the couch and the chairs around it have been moved to the middle of the floor. A lighted lamp is on

*the table. The door to the front hall is open. Dance music is heard
from upstairs.*

*Mrs. Linde is seated by the table, idly leafing through the pages
of a book. She tries to read but seems unable to concentrate. Once
or twice she turns her head in the direction of the door, anxiously listening.*

Mrs. Linde. (looks at her watch). Not yet. It's almost too late. If only
he hasn't — *(Listens again.)* Ah! There he is. *(She goes to the hall
and opens the front door carefully. Quiet footsteps on the stairs.
She whispers.)* Come in. There's nobody here.

Krogstad (in the door). I found your note when I got home. What's
this all about

Mrs. Linde. I've got to talk to you.

Krogstad. Oh? And it has to be here?

Mrs. Linde. It couldn't be at my place. My room doesn't have a
separate entrance. Come in. We're quite alone. The maid is asleep
and the Helmers are at a party upstairs.

Krogstad (entering). Really? The Helmers are dancing tonight, are
they?

Mrs. Linde. And why not?

Krogstad. You're right. Why not, indeed.

Mrs. Linde. All right, Krogstad. Let's talk, you and I.

Krogstad. I didn't know we had anything to talk about.

Mrs. Linde. We have much to talk about.

Krogstad. I didn't think so.

Mrs. Linde. No, because you've never really understood me.

Krogstad. What was there to understand? What happened was perfectly commonplace. A heartless woman jilts a man when she gets
a more attractive offer.

Mrs. Linde. Do you think I'm all that heartless? And do you think it
was easy for me to break with you?

Krogstad. No?

Mrs. Linde. You really thought it was?

Krogstad. If it wasn't, why did you write the way you did that time?

Mrs. Linde. What else could I do? If I had to make a break, I also had
the duty to destroy whatever feelings you had for me.

Krogstad (clenching his hands). So that's the way it was. And you
did — *that* — just for money!

Mrs. Linde. Don't forget I had a helpless mother and two small
brothers. We couldn't wait for you, Krogstad. You know yourself
how uncertain your prospects were then.

Krogstad. All right. But you still didn't have the right to throw me
over for somebody else.

Mrs. Linde. I don't know. I have asked myself that question many times. Did I have that right?

Krogstad (in a lower voice). When I lost you I lost my footing. Look at me now. A shipwrecked man on a raft.

Mrs. Linde. Rescue may be near.

Krogstad. It *was* near. Then you came between.

Mrs. Linde. I didn't know that, Krogstad. Only today did I find out it's your job I'm taking over in the bank.

Krogstad. I believe you when you say so. But now that you *do* know, aren't you going to step aside?

Mrs. Linde. No, for it wouldn't do you any good.

Krogstad. Whether it would or not — *I* would do it.

Mrs. Linde. I have learned common sense. Life and hard necessity have taught me that.

Krogstad. And life has taught me not to believe in pretty speeches.

Mrs. Linde. Then life has taught you a very sensible thing. But you do believe in actions, don't you?

Krogstad. How do you mean?

Mrs. Linde. You referred to yourself just now as a shipwrecked man.

Krogstad. It seems to me I had every reason to do so.

Mrs. Linde. And I am a shipwrecked woman. No one to grieve for, no one to care for.

Krogstad. You made your choice.

Mrs. Linde. I had no other choice that time.

Krogstad. Let's say you didn't. What then?

Mrs. Linde. Krogstad, how would it be if we two shipwrecked people got together?

Krogstad. What's this!

Mrs. Linde. Two on one wreck are better off than each on his own.

Krogstad. Kristine!

Mrs. Linde. Why do you think I came to town?

Krogstad. Surely not because of me?

Mrs. Linde. If I'm going to live at all I must work. All my life, for as long as I can remember, I have worked. That's been my one and only pleasure. But now that I'm all alone in the world I feel nothing but this terrible emptiness and desolation. There is no joy in working just for yourself. Krogstad — give me someone and something to work for.

Krogstad. I don't believe this. Only hysterical females go in for that kind of high-minded self-sacrifice.

Mrs. Linde. Did you ever know me to be hysterical?

Krogstad. You really could do this? Listen — do you know about my past? All of it?

Mrs. Linde. Yes, I do.

Krogstad. Do you also know what people think of me around here?

Mrs. Linde. A little while ago you sounded as if you thought that together with me you might have become a different person.

Krogstad. I'm sure of it.

Mrs. Linde. Couldn't that still be?

Krogstad. Kristine — do you know what you are doing? Yes, I see you do. And you think you have the courage — ?

Mrs. Linde. I need someone to be a mother to, and your children need a mother. You and I need one another. Nils, I believe in you — in the real you. Together with you I dare to do anything.

Krogstad (seizes her hands). Thanks, thanks, Kristine — now I know I'll raise myself in the eyes of others. — Ah, but I forget — !

Mrs. Linde (listening). Shh! — There's the tarantella. You must go; hurry!

Krogstad. Why? What is it?

Mrs. Linde. Do you hear what they're playing up there? When that dance is over they'll be down.

Krogstad. All right. I'm leaving. The whole thing is pointless, anyway. Of course you don't know what I'm doing to the Helmers.

Mrs. Linde. Yes, Krogstad; I do know.

Krogstad. Still, you're brave enough — ?

Mrs. Linde. I very well understand to what extremes despair can drive a man like you.

Krogstad. If only it could be undone!

Mrs. Linde. It could, for your letter is still out there in the mailbox.

Krogstad. Are you sure?

Mrs. Linde. Quite sure. But —

Krogstad (looks searchingly at her). Maybe I'm beginning to understand. You want to save your friend at any cost. Be honest with me. That's it, isn't it?

Mrs. Linde. Krogstad, you may sell yourself once for somebody else's sake, but you don't do it twice.

Krogstad. I'll demand my letter back.

Mrs. Linde. No, no.

Krogstad. Yes, of course. I'll wait here till Helmer comes down. Then I'll ask him for my letter. I'll tell him it's just about my dismissal — that he shouldn't read it.

Mrs. Linde. No, Krogstad. You are not to ask for that letter back.

Krogstad. But tell me — wasn't that the real reason you wanted to meet me here?

Mrs. Linde. At first it was, because I was so frightened. But that was yesterday. Since then I have seen the most incredible things going on in this house. Helmer must learn the whole truth. This miserable secret must come out in the open; those two must come to a full understanding. They simply can't continue with all this concealment and evasion.

Krogstad. All right; if you want to take that chance. But there is one thing I *can* do, and I'll do that right now.

Mrs. Linde (listening). But hurry! Go! The dance is over. We aren't safe another minute.

Krogstad. I'll be waiting for you downstairs.

Mrs. Linde. Yes, do. You must see me home.

Krogstad. I've never been so happy in my whole life. *(He leaves through the front door. The door between the living room and the front hall remains open.)*

Mrs. Linde (straightens up the room a little and gets her things ready). What a change! Oh yes! — what a change! People to work for — to live for — a home to bring happiness to. I can't wait to get to work — ! If only they'd come soon — *(Listens.)* Ah, there they are. Get my coat on — *(Puts on her coat and hat.)*

Helmer's and Nora's voices are heard outside. A key is turned in the lock, and Helmer almost forces Nora into the hall. She is dressed in her Italian costume, with a big black shawl over her shoulders. He is in evening dress under an open black cloak.

Nora (in the door, still resisting). No, no, no! I don't want to! I want to go back upstairs. I don't want to leave so early.

Helmer. But dearest Nora —

Nora. Oh please, Torvald — please! I'm asking you as nicely as I can — just another hour!

Helmer. Not another minute, sweet. You know we agreed. There now. Get inside. You'll catch a cold out here. *(She still resists, but he guides her gently into the room.)*

Mrs. Linde. Good evening.

Nora. Kristine!

Helmer. Ah, Mrs. Linde. Still here?

Mrs. Linde. I know. I really should apologize, but I so much wanted to see Nora in her costume.

Nora. You've been waiting up for me?

Mrs. Linde. Yes, unfortunately I didn't get here in time. You were already upstairs, but I just didn't feel like leaving till I had seen you.

Helmer (removing Nora's shawl). Yes, do take a good look at her, Mrs. Linde. I think I may say she's worth looking at. Isn't she lovely?

Mrs. Linde. She certainly is —

Helmer. Isn't she a miracle of loveliness, though? That was the general opinion at the party, too. But dreadfully obstinate — that she

is, the sweet little thing. What can we do about that? Will you
believe it — I practically had to use force to get her away.

Nora. Oh Torvald, you're going to be sorry you didn't give me even
half an hour more.

Helmer. See what I mean, Mrs. Linde? She dances the tarantella —
she is a tremendous success — quite deservedly so, though perhaps her performance was a little too natural — I mean, more than
could be reconciled with the rules of art. But all right! The point
is: she's a success, a tremendous success. So should I let her stay
after that? Weaken the effect? Of course not. So I take my lovely
little Capri girl — I might say, my capricious little Capri girl —
under my arm — a quick turn around the room — a graceful bow
in all directions, and — as they say in the novels — the beautiful
apparition is gone. A finale should always be done for effect, Mrs.
Linde, but there doesn't seem to be any way of getting that into
Nora's head. Poooh — ! It's hot in here. *(Throws his cloak down
on a chair and opens the door to his room.)* Why, it's dark in here!
Of course. Excuse me — *(Goes inside and lights a couple of candles.)*

Nora (in a hurried, breathless whisper). Well?

Mrs. Linde (in a low voice). I have talked to him.

Nora. And — ?

Mrs. Linde. Nora — you've got to tell your husband everything.

Nora (no expression in her voice). I knew it.

Mrs. Linde. You have nothing to fear from Krogstad. But you must
speak.

Nora. I'll say nothing.

Mrs. Linde. Then the letter will.

Nora. Thank you, Kristine. Now I know what I have to do. Shh!

Helmer (returning). Well, Mrs. Linde, have you looked your fill?

Mrs. Linde. Yes. And now I'll say goodnight.

Helmer. So soon? Is that your knitting?

Mrs. Linde (takes it). Yes, thank you. I almost forgot.

Helmer. So you knit, do you?

Mrs. Linde. Oh yes.

Helmer. You know — you ought to take up embroidery instead.

Mrs. Linde. Oh? Why?

Helmer. Because it's so much more beautiful. Look. You hold the
embroidery so — in your left hand. Then with your right you move
the needle — like this — in an easy, elongated arc — you see?

Mrs. Linde. Maybe you're right —

Helmer. Knitting, on the other hand, can never be anything but ugly.
Look here: arms pressed close to the sides — the needles going up

and down — there's something Chinese about it somehow — . That really was an excellent champagne they served us tonight.

Mrs. Linde. Well, goodnight, Nora. And don't be obstinate any more.

Helmer. Well said, Mrs. Linde!

Mrs. Linde. Goodnight, sir.

Helmer (sees her to the front door). Goodnight, goodnight. I hope you'll get home all right? I'd be very glad to — but of course you don't have far to walk, do you? Goodnight, goodnight. *(She leaves. He closes the door behind her and returns to the living room.)* There! At last we got rid of her. She really is an incredible bore, that woman.

Nora. Aren't you very tired, Torvald?

Helmer. No, not in the least.

Nora. Not sleepy either?

Helmer. Not at all. Quite the opposite. I feel enormously — animated. How about you? Yes, you do look tired and sleepy.

Nora. Yes, I am very tired. Soon I'll be asleep.

Helmer. What did I tell you? I was right, wasn't I? Good thing I didn't let you stay any longer.

Nora. Everything you do is right.

Helmer (kissing her forehead). Now my little lark is talking like a human being. But did you notice what splendid spirits Rank was in tonight?

Nora. Was he? I didn't notice. I didn't get to talk with him.

Helmer. Nor did I — hardly. But I haven't seen him in such a good mood for a long time. *(Looks at her, comes closer to her.)* Ah! It does feel good to be back in our own home again, to be quite alone with you — my young, lovely, ravishing woman!

Nora. Don't look at me like that, Torvald!

Helmer. Am I not to look at my most precious possession? All that loveliness that is mine, nobody's but mine, all of it mine.

Nora (walks to the other side of the table). I won't have you talk to me like that tonight.

Helmer (follows her). The tarantella is still in your blood. I can tell. That only makes you all the more alluring. Listen! The guests are beginning to leave. *(Softly.)* Nora — soon the whole house will be quiet.

Nora. Yes, I hope so.

Helmer. Yes, don't you, my darling? Do you know — when I'm at a party with you, like tonight — do you know why I hardly ever talk to you, why I keep away from you, only look at you once in a while — a few stolen glances — do you know why I do that? It's because I pretend that you are my secret love, my young, secret bride-to-be, and nobody has the slightest suspicion that there is anything between us.

Nora. Yes, I know. All your thoughts are with me.

Helmer. Then when we're leaving and I lay your shawl around your delicate young shoulders — around that wonderful curve of your neck — then I imagine you're my young bride, that we're coming away from the wedding, that I am taking you to my home for the first time — that I am alone with you for the first time — quite alone with you, you young, trembling beauty! I have desired you all evening — there hasn't been a longing in me that hasn't been for you. When you were dancing the tarantella, chasing, inviting — my blood was on fire; I couldn't stand it any longer — that's why I brought you down so early —

Nora. Leave me now, Torvald. Please! I don't want all this.

Helmer. What do you mean? You're only playing your little teasing bird game with me; aren't you, Nora? Don't want to? I'm your husband, aren't I?

There is a knock on the front door.

Nora (with a start). Did you hear that —?

Helmer (on his way to the hall). Who is it?

Rank (outside). It's me. May I come in for a moment?

Helmer (in a low voice, annoyed). Oh, what does he want now? *(Aloud.)* Just a minute. *(Opens the door.)* Well! How good of you not to pass by our door.

Rank. I thought I heard your voice, so I felt like saying hello. *(Looks around.)* Ah yes — this dear, familiar room. What a cozy, comfortable place you have here, you two.

Helmer. Looked to me as if you were quite comfortable upstairs too.

Rank. I certainly was. Why not? Why not enjoy all you can in this world? As much as you can for as long as you can, anyway. Excellent wine.

Helmer. The champagne, particularly.

Rank. You noticed that too? Incredible how much I managed to put away.

Nora. Torvald drank a lot of champagne tonight, too.

Rank. Did he?

Nora. Yes, he did, and then he's always so much fun afterwards.

Rank. Well, why not have some fun in the evening after a well spent day?

Helmer. Well spent? I'm afraid I can't claim that.

Rank (slapping him lightly on the shoulder). But you see, I can!

Nora. Dr. Rank, I believe you must have been conducting a scientific test today.

Rank. Exactly.

Helmer. What do you know — little Nora talking about scientific tests!

Nora. May I congratulate you on the result?

Rank. You may indeed.

Nora. It was a good one?

Rank. The best possible for both doctor and patient — certainty.

Nora (a quick query). Certainty?

Rank. Absolute certainty. So why shouldn't I have myself an enjoyable evening afterwards?

Nora. I quite agree with you, Dr. Rank. You should.

Helmer. And so do I. If only you don't pay for it tomorrow.

Rank. Oh well — you get nothing for nothing in this world.

Nora. Dr. Rank — you are fond of costume parties, aren't you?

Rank. Yes, particularly when there is a reasonable number of amusing disguises.

Nora. Listen — what are the two of us going to be the next time?

Helmer. You frivolous little thing! Already thinking about the next party!

Rank. You and I? That's easy. You'll be Fortune's Child.

Helmer. Yes, but what is a fitting costume for that?

Rank. Let your wife appear just the way she always is.

Helmer. Beautiful. Very good indeed. But how about yourself? Don't you know what you'll go as?

Rank. Yes, my friend. I know precisely what I'll be.

Helmer. Yes?

Rank. At the next masquerade I'll be invisible.

Helmer. That's a funny idea.

Rank. There's a certain black hat — you've heard about the hat that makes you invisible, haven't you? You put that on, and nobody can see you.

Helmer (suppressing a smile). I guess that's right.

Rank. But I'm forgetting what I came for. Helmer, give me a cigar — one of your dark Havanas.

Helmer. With the greatest pleasure. *(Offers him his case.)*

Rank (takes one and cuts off the tip). Thanks.

Nora (striking a match). Let me give you a light.

Rank. Thanks. *(She holds the match; he lights his cigar.)* And now goodbye!

Helmer. Goodbye, goodbye, my friend.

Nora. Sleep well, Dr. Rank.

Rank. I thank you.

Nora. Wish me the same.

Rank. You? Well, if you really want me to — . Sleep well. And thanks for the light. *(He nods to both of them and goes out.)*

Helmer (in a low voice). He had had quite a bit to drink.

Nora (absently). Maybe so.

Helmer takes out his keys and goes out into the hall.

Nora. Torvald — what are you doing out there?

Helmer. Emptying the mailbox. It is quite full. There wouldn't be room for the newspapers in the morning —

Nora. Are you going to work tonight?

Helmer. You know very well I won't. — Say! What's this? Somebody's been at the lock.

Nora. The lock — ?

Helmer. Yes. Why, I wonder. I hate to think that any of the maids — . Here's a broken hairpin. It's one of yours. Nora.

Nora (quickly). Then it must be one of the children.

Helmer. You better make damn sure they stop that. Hm, hm. — There! I got it open, finally. *(Gathers up the mail, calls out to the kitchen.)* Helene? — Oh Helene — turn out the light here in the hall, will you? *(He comes back into the living room and closes the door.)* Look how it's been piling up. *(Shows her the bundle of letters. Starts leafing through it.)* What's this?

Nora (by the window). The letter! Oh no, no, Torvald!

Helmer. Two calling cards — from Rank.

Nora. From Dr. Rank?

Helmer (looking at them). "Doctor medicinae Rank." They were on top. He must have put them there when he left just now.

Nora. Anything written on them?

Helmer. A black cross above the name. What a macabre idea. Like announcing his own death.

Nora. That's what it is.

Helmer. Hm? You know about this? Has he said anything to you?

Nora. That card means he has said goodbye to us. He'll lock himself up to die.

Helmer. My poor friend. I knew of course he wouldn't be with me very long. But so soon — . And hiding himself away like a wounded animal —

Nora. When it has to be, it's better it happens without words. Don't you think so, Torvald?

Helmer (walking up and down). He'd grown so close to us. I find it hard to think of him as gone. With his suffering and loneliness he was like a clouded background for our happy sunshine. Well, it

may be better this way. For him, at any rate. *(Stops.)* And perhaps
for us, too, Nora. For now we have nobody but each other. *(Embraces her.)* Oh you — my beloved wife! I feel I just can't hold you
close enough. Do you know, Nora — many times I have wished
some great danger threatened you, so I could risk my life and
blood and everything — everything, for your sake.

Nora (frees herself and says in a strong and firm voice). I think you
should go and read your letters now, Torvald.

Helmer. No, no — not tonight. I want to be with you, my darling.

Nora. With the thought of your dying friend — ?

Helmer. You are right. This has shaken both of us. Something not
beautiful has come between us. Thoughts of death and dissolution. We must try to get over it — out of it. Till then — we'll
each go to our own room.

Nora (her arms around his neck). Torvald — goodnight! Goodnight!

Helmer (kisses her forehead). Goodnight, my little songbird. Sleep
well, Nora. Now I'll read my letters. *(He goes into his room, carrying the mail. Closes the door.)*

*Nora (her eyes desperate, her hands groping, finds Helmer's black
cloak and throws it around her; she whispers, quickly, brokenly,
hoarsely).* Never see him again. Never. Never. Never. *(Puts her
shawl over her head.)* And never see the children again, either.
Never; never. — The black, icy water — fathomless — this — ! If
only it was all over. — Now he has it. Now he's reading it. No, no;
not yet. Torvald — goodbye — you — the children —

She is about to hurry through the hall, when Helmer flings open
the door to his room and stands there with an open letter in his
hand.

Helmer. Nora!

Nora (cries out). Ah — !

Helmer. What is it? You know what's in this letter?

Nora. Yes, I do! Let me go! Let me out!

Helmer (holds her back). Where do you think you're going?

Nora (trying to tear herself loose from him). I won't let you save me,
Torvald!

Helmer (tumbles back). True! Is it true what he writes? Oh my God!
No, no — this can't possibly be true.

Nora. It is true. I have loved you more than anything else in the
whole world.

Helmer. Oh, don't give me any silly excuses.

Nora (taking a step towards him). Torvald — !

Helmer. You wretch! What have you done!

Nora. Let me go. You are not to sacrifice yourself for me. You are not to take the blame.

Helmer. No more playacting. *(Locks the door to the front hall.)* You'll stay here and answer me. Do you understand what you have done? Answer me! Do you understand?

Nora (gazes steadily at him with an increasingly frozen expression). Yes. Now I'm beginning to understand.

Helmer (walking up and down). What a dreadful awakening. All these years — all these eight years — she, my pride and my joy — a hypocrite, a liar — oh worse! worse! — a criminal! Oh, the bottomless ugliness in all this! Damn! Damn! Damn!

Nora, silent, keeps gazing at him.

Helmer (stops in front of her). I ought to have guessed that something like this would happen. I should have expected it. All your father's loose principles — Silence! You have inherited every one of your father's loose principles. No religion, no morals, no sense of duty — . Now I am being punished for my leniency with him. I did it for your sake, and this is how you pay me back.

Nora. Yes. This is how.

Helmer. You have ruined all my happiness. My whole future — that's what you have destroyed. Oh, it's terrible to think about. I am at the mercy of an unscrupulous man. He can do with me whatever he likes, demand anything of me, command me and dispose of me just as he pleases — I dare not say a word! To go down so miserably, to be destroyed — all because of an irresponsible woman!

Nora. When I am gone from the world, you'll be free.

Helmer. No noble gestures, please. Your father was always full of such phrases too. What good would it do me if you were gone from the world, as you put it? Not the slightest good at all. He could still make the whole thing public, and if he did, people would be likely to think I had been your accomplice. They might even think it was my idea — that it was I who urged you to do it! And for all this I have you to thank — you, whom I've borne on my hands through all the years of our marriage. *Now* do you understand what you've done to me?

Nora (with cold calm). Yes.

Helmer. I just can't get it into my head that this is happening; it's all so incredible. But we have to come to terms with it somehow. Take your shawl off. Take it off, I say! I have to satisfy him one way or another. The whole affair must be kept quiet at whatever cost. — And as far as you and I are concerned, nothing must seem to have changed. I'm talking about appearances, of course. You'll go on living here; that goes without saying. But I won't let you bring up the children; I dare not trust you with them. — Oh! Having to say this to one I have loved so much, and whom I still — ! But all that is past. It's not a question of happiness any more but of hanging on to what can be salvaged — pieces, appearances — *(The doorbell rings.)*

Helmer (jumps.) What's that? So late. Is the worst — ? Has he — ! Hide, Nora! Say you're sick.

Nora doesn't move. Helmer opens the door to the hall.

The Maid (half dressed, out in the hall). A letter for your wife, sir.

Helmer. Give it to me. *(Takes the letter and closes the door.)* Yes, it's from him. But I won't let you have it. I'll read it myself.

Nora. Yes — you read it.

Helmer (by the lamp). I hardly dare. Perhaps we're lost, both you and I. No; I've got to know. *(Tears the letter open, glances through it, looks at an enclosure; a cry of joy.)* Nora!

Nora looks at him with a question in her eyes.

Helmer. Nora! — No, I must read it again. — Yes, yes; it is so! I'm saved! Nora, I'm saved!

Nora. And I?

Helmer. You too, of course; we're both saved, both you and I. Look! He's returning your note. He writes that he's sorry, he regrets, a happy turn in his life — oh, it doesn't matter what he writes. We're saved, Nora! Nobody can do anything to you now. Oh Nora, Nora — . No, I want to get rid of this disgusting thing first. Let me see — *(Looks at the signature.)* No, I don't want to see it. I don't want it to be more than a bad dream, the whole thing. *(Tears up the note and both letters, throws the pieces in the stove, and watches them burn.)* There! Now it's gone. — He wrote that ever since Christmas Eve — . Good God, Nora, these must have been three terrible days for you.

Nora. I have fought a hard fight these last three days.

Helmer. And been in agony and seen no other way out than — . No, we won't think of all that ugliness. We'll just rejoice and tell ourselves it's over, it's all over! Oh, listen to me, Nora. You don't seem to understand. It's over. What *is* it? Why do you look like that — that frozen expression on your face? Oh my poor little Nora, don't you think I know what it is? You can't make yourself believe that I have forgiven you. But I have, Nora; I swear to you, I have forgiven you for everything. Of course I know that what you did was for love of me.

Nora. That is true.

Helmer. You have loved me the way a wife ought to love her husband. You just didn't have the wisdom to judge the means. But do you think I love you any less because you don't know how to act on your own? Of course not. Just lean on me. I'll advise you; I'll guide you. I wouldn't be a man if I didn't find you twice as attractive because of your womanly helplessness. You mustn't pay any attention to the hard words I said to you right at first. It was just that first shock when I thought everything was collapsing all around me. I have forgiven you, Nora. I swear to you — I really have forgiven you.

Nora. I thank you for your forgiveness. (*She goes out through the door, right.*)

Helmer. No, stay — (*Looks into the room she entered.*) What are you doing in there?

Nora (within). Getting out of my costume.

Helmer (by the open door). Good, good. Try to calm down and compose yourself, my poor little frightened songbird. Rest safely; I have broad wings to cover you with. (*Walks around near the door.*) What a nice and cozy home we have, Nora. Here's shelter for you. Here I'll keep you safe like a hunted dove I have rescued from the hawk's talons. Believe me: I'll know how to quiet your beating heart. It will happen by and by, Nora; you'll see. Why, tomorrow you'll look at all this in quite a different light. And soon everything will be just the way it was before. I won't need to keep reassuring you that I have forgiven you; you'll feel it yourself. Did you really think I could have abandoned you, or even reproached you? Oh, you don't know a real man's heart, Nora. There is something unspeakably sweet and satisfactory for a man to know deep in himself that he has forgiven his wife — forgiven her in all the fullness of his honest heart. You see, that way she becomes his very own all over again — in a double sense, you might say. He has, so to speak, given her a second birth; it is as if she had become his wife and his child, both. From now on that's what you'll be to me, you lost and helpless creature. Don't worry about a thing, Nora. Only be frank with me, and I'll be your will and your conscience. — What's this? You're not in bed? You've changed your dress — !

Nora (in an everyday dress). Yes, Torvald. I have changed my dress.

Helmer. But why — now — this late — ?

Nora. I'm not going to sleep tonight.

Helmer. But my dear Nora —

Nora (looks at her watch). It isn't all that late. Sit down here with me, Torvald. You and I have much to talk about. (*Sits down at the table.*)

Helmer. Nora — what is this all about? That rigid face —
Nora. Sit down. This will take a while. I have much to say to you.
Helmer (sits down, facing her across the table). You worry me, Nora.
    I don't understand you.
Nora. No, that's just it. You don't understand me. And I have never
    understood you — not till tonight. No, don't interrupt me. Just
    listen to what I have to say. — This is a settling of accounts, Tor-
    vald.
Helmer. What do you mean by that?
Nora (after a brief silence). Doesn't one thing strike you, now that we
    are sitting together like this?
Helmer. What would that be?
Nora. We have been married for eight years. Doesn't it occur to you
    that this is the first time that you and I, husband and wife, are
    having a serious talk?
Helmer. Well — serious — . What do you mean by that?
Nora. For eight whole years — longer, in fact — ever since we first
    met, we have never talked seriously to each other about a single
    serious thing.
Helmer. You mean I should forever have been telling you about
    worries you couldn't have helped me with anyway?
Nora. I am not talking about worries. I'm saying we have never tried
    seriously to get to the bottom of anything together.
Helmer. But dearest Nora, I hardly think that would have been some-
    thing *you* —
Nora. That's the whole point. You have never understood me. Great
    wrong has been done to me, Torvald. First by Daddy and then by
    you.
Helmer. What! By us two? We who have loved you more deeply than
    anyone else?
Nora (shakes her head). You never loved me — neither Daddy nor
    you. You only thought it was fun to be in love with me.
Helmer. But, Nora — what an expression to use!
Nora. That's the way it has been, Torvald. When I was home with
    Daddy, he told me all his opinions, and so they became my opin-
    ions too. If I disagreed with him I kept it to myself, for he wouldn't
    have liked that. He called me his little doll baby, and he played
    with me the way I played with my dolls. Then I came to your
    house —
Helmer. What a way to talk about our marriage!
Nora (imperturbably). I mean that I passed from Daddy's hands into
    yours. You arranged everything according to your taste, and so I
    came to share it — or I pretended to; I'm not sure which. I think it

was a little of both, now one and now the other. When I look back on it now, it seems to me I've been living here like a pauper — just a hand-to-mouth kind of existence. I have earned my keep by doing tricks for you, Torvald. But that's the way you wanted it. You have great sins against me to answer for, Daddy and you. It's your fault that nothing has become of me.

Helmer. Nora, you're being both unreasonable and ungrateful. Haven't you been happy here?

Nora. No, never. I thought I was, but I wasn't.

Helmer. Not — not happy!

Nora. No; just having fun. And you have always been very good to me. But our home has never been more than a playroom. I have been your doll wife here, just the way I used to be Daddy's doll child. And the children have been my dolls. I thought it was fun when you played with me, just as they thought it was fun when I played with them. That's been our marriage, Torvald.

Helmer. There is something in what you are saying — exaggerated and hysterical though it is. But from now on things will be different. Playtime is over; it's time for growing up.

Nora. Whose growing up — mine or the children's?

Helmer. Both yours and the children's, Nora darling.

Nora. Oh Torvald, you're not the man to bring me up to be the right kind of wife for you.

Helmer. How can you say that?

Nora. And I — ? What qualifications do I have for bringing up the children?

Helmer. Nora!

Nora. You said so yourself a minute ago — that you didn't dare to trust me with them.

Helmer. In the first flush of anger, yes. Surely, you're not going to count that.

Nora. But you were quite right. I am *not* qualified. Something else has to come first. Somehow I have to grow up myself. And you are not the man to help me do that. That's a job I have to do by myself. And that's why I'm leaving you.

Helmer (jumps up). What did you say!

Nora. I have to be by myself if I am to find out about myself and about all the other things too. So I can't stay here with you any longer.

Helmer. Nora, Nora!

Nora. I'm leaving now. I'm sure Kristine will put me up for tonight.

Helmer. You're out of your mind! I won't let you! I forbid you!

Nora. You can't forbid me anything any more; it won't do any good.

I'm taking my own things with me. I won't accept anything from you, either now or later.

Helmer. But this is madness!

Nora. Tomorrow I'm going home — I mean back to my old home town. It will be easier for me to find some kind of job there.

Helmer. Oh, you blind, inexperienced creature — !

Nora. I must see to it that I get experience, Torvald.

Helmer. Leaving your home, your husband, your children! Not a thought of what people will say!

Nora. I can't worry about that. All I know is that I have to leave.

Helmer. Oh, this is shocking! Betraying your most sacred duties like this!

Nora. And what do you consider my most sacred duties?

Helmer. Do I need to tell you that? They are your duties to your husband and your children.

Nora. I have other duties equally sacred.

Helmer. You do not. What duties would they be?

Nora. My duties to myself.

Helmer. You are a wife and a mother before you are anything else.

Nora. I don't believe that any more. I believe I am first of all a human being, just as much as you — or at any rate that I must try to become one. Oh, I know very well that most people agree with you, Torvald, and that it says something like that in all the books. But what people say and what the books say is no longer enough for me. I have to think about these things myself and see if I can't find the answers.

Helmer. You mean to tell me you don't know what your proper place in your own home is? Don't you have a reliable guide in such matters? Don't you have religion?

Nora. Oh but Torvald — I don't really know what religion is.

Helmer. What are you saying!

Nora. All I know is what the Reverend Hansen told me when he prepared me for confirmation. He said that religion was *this* and it was *that.* When I get by myself, away from here, I'll have to look into that, too. I have to decide if what the Reverend Hansen said was right, or anyway if it is right for *me.*

Helmer. Oh, this is unheard of in a young woman! If religion can't guide you, let me appeal to your conscience. For surely you have moral feelings? Or — answer me — maybe you don't?

Nora. Well, you see, Torvald, I don't really know what to say. I just don't know. I am confused about these things. All I know is that my ideas are quite different from yours. I have just found out that the laws are different from what I thought they were, but in no way can I get it into my head that those laws are right. A woman shouldn't have the right to spare her dying old father or save her husband's life! I just can't believe that.

Helmer. You speak like a child. You don't understand the society you live in.

Nora. No, I don't. But I want to find out about it. I have to make up my mind who is right, society or I.

Helmer. You are sick, Nora; you have a fever. I really don't think you are in your right mind.

Nora. I have never felt so clearheaded and sure of myself as I do tonight.

Helmer. And clearheaded and sure of yourself you're leaving your husband and children?

Nora. Yes.

Helmer. Then there is only one possible explanation.

Nora. What?

Helmer. You don't love me any more.

Nora. No, that's just it.

Helmer. Nora! Can you say that?

Nora. I am sorry, Torvald, for you have always been so good to me. But I can't help it. I don't love you any more.

Helmer (with forced composure). And this too is a clear and sure conviction?

Nora. Completely clear and sure. That's why I don't want to stay here any more.

Helmer. And are you ready to explain to me how I came to forfeit your love?

Nora. Certainly I am. It was tonight, when the wonderful didn't happen. That was when I realized you were not the man I thought you were.

Helmer. You have to explain. I don't understand.

Nora. I have waited patiently for eight years, for I wasn't such a fool that I thought the wonderful is something that happens any old day. Then this — thing — came crashing in on me, and then there wasn't a doubt in my mind that now — now comes the wonderful. When Krogstad's letter was in that mailbox, never for a moment did it even occur to me that you would submit to his conditions. I was so absolutely certain that you would say to him: make the whole thing public — tell everybody. And when that had happened —

Helmer. Yes, then what? When I had surrendered my wife to shame and disgrace — !

Nora. When that had happened, I was absolutely certain that you would stand up and take the blame and say, "I'm the guilty one."

Helmer. Nora!

Nora. You mean I never would have accepted such a sacrifice from you? Of course not. But what would my protests have counted against yours? *That* was the wonderful I was hoping for in terror. And to prevent that I was going to kill myself.

Helmer. I'd gladly work nights and days for you, Nora — endure sorrow and want for your sake. But nobody sacrifices his *honor* for his love.

Nora. A hundred thousand women have done so.

Helmer. Oh, you think and talk like a silly child.

Nora. All right. But you don't think and talk like the man I can live with. When you had gotten over your fright — not because of what threatened *me* but because of the risk to *you* — and the whole danger was past, then you acted as if nothing at all had happened. Once again I was your little songbird, your doll, just as before, only now you had to handle her even more carefully, because she was so frail and weak. (*Rises.*) Torvald — that moment I realized that I had been living here for eight years with a stranger and had borne him three children — Oh, I can't stand thinking about it! I feel like tearing myself to pieces!

Helmer (heavily). I see it, I see it. An abyss has opened up between us. — Oh but Nora — surely it can be filled?

Nora. The way I am now I am no wife for you.

Helmer. I have it in me to change.

Nora. Perhaps — if your doll is taken from you.

Helmer. To part — to part from you! No, no, Nora! I can't grasp that thought!

Nora (goes out, right). All the more reason why it has to be. (*She returns with her outdoor clothes and a small bag, which she sets down on the chair by the table.*)

Helmer. Nora, Nora! Not now! Wait till tomorrow.

Nora (putting on her coat). I can't spend the night in a stranger's rooms.

Helmer. But couldn't we live here together like brother and sister—?

Nora (tying on her hat): You know very well that wouldn't last long —. (*Wraps her shawl around her.*) Goodbye, Torvald. I don't want to see the children. I know I leave them in better hands than mine. The way I am now I can't be anything to them.

Helmer. But some day, Nora — some day — ?

Nora. How can I tell? I have no idea what's going to become of me.

Helmer. But you're still my wife, both as you are now and as you will be.

Nora. Listen, Torvald — when a wife leaves her husband's house, the way I am doing now, I have heard he has no more legal responsibilities for her. At any rate, I now release you from all responsibility. You are not to feel yourself obliged to me for anything, and I have no obligations to you. There has to be full freedom on both sides. Here is your ring back. Now give me mine.

Helmer. Even this?

Nora. Even this.

Helmer. Here it is.

Nora. There. So now it's over. I'm putting the keys here. The maids know everything about the house — better than I. Tomorrow, after I'm gone, Kristine will come over and pack my things from home. I want them sent after me.

Helmer. Over! It's all over! Nora, will you never think of me?

Nora. I'm sure I'll often think of you and the children and this house.

Helmer. May I write to you, Nora?

Nora. No — never. I won't have that.

Helmer. But send you things — ? You must let me.

Nora. Nothing, nothing.

Helmer. — help you, when you need help —

Nora. I told you, no; I won't have it. I'll accept nothing from strangers.

Helmer. Nora — can I never again be more to you than a stranger?

Nora (picks up her bag). Oh Torvald — then the most wonderful of all would have to happen —

Helmer. Tell me what that would be — !

Nora. For that to happen, both you and I would have to change so that — Oh Torvald, I no longer believe in the wonderful.

Helmer. But I *will* believe. Tell me! Change, so that — ?

Nora. So that our living together would become a true marriage. Goodbye. *(She goes out through the hall.)*

Helmer (sinks down on a chair near the door and covers his face with his hands). Nora! Nora! *(Looks around him and gets up.)* All empty. She's gone. *(With sudden hope.)* The most wonderful — ?!

From downstairs comes the sound of a heavy door slamming shut.

Questions

1. Near the beginning of the play, how does Mrs. Linde's presence help to define Nora's character? How does Nora's response to Krogstad's entrance tell us something about Nora?

2. What does Dr. Rank contribute to the play? If he were eliminated, what would be lost?

3. Ibsen very reluctantly acceded to a request for an alternate ending for a German production. In the new ending Helmer forces Nora to look at their sleeping children and reminds her that "tomor-

row, when they wake up and call for their mother, they will be
— motherless." Nora "struggles with herself" and concludes by
saying, "Oh, this is a sin against myself, but I cannot leave them." In
view of the fact that the last act several times seems to be moving
toward a "happy ending" (e.g., Krogstad promises to recall his letter),
what is wrong with this alternate ending?

4. Can it be argued that although at the end Nora goes out to
achieve self-realization, her abandonment of her children — especially to Torvald's loathsome conventional morality — is a crime? (By
the way, exactly why does Nora leave the children? She seems to
imply, in some passages, that because she forged a signature she is
unfit to bring them up. But do you agree with her?)

5. Michael Meyer, in his splendid biography *Henrik Ibsen*, says
that the play is not so much about women's rights as about "the need
of every individual to find out the kind of person he or she really is,
and to strive to become that person." What evidence can you offer to
support this interpretation?

6. In *The Quintessence of Ibsenism* Bernard Shaw says that
Ibsen, reacting against a common theatrical preference for strange
situations, "saw that . . . the more familiar the situation, the more
interesting the play. Shakespear had put ourselves on the stage but
not our situations. Our uncles seldom murder our fathers and . . .
marry our mothers. . . . Ibsen . . . gives us not only ourselves, but
ourselves in our own situations. The things that happen to his stage
figures are things that happen to us. One consequence is that his
plays are much more important to us than Shakespear's. Another is
that they are capable both of hurting us cruelly and of filling us with
excited hopes of escape from idealistic tyrannies, and with visions of
intenser life in the future." How much of this do you believe?

Tennessee Williams (b. 1914)

The Glass Menagerie

Nobody, not even the rain, has such small hands.
                                    — *E. E. Cummings*

List of Characters

Amanda Wingfield, the mother. A little woman of great but confused vitality clinging frantically to another time and place. Her
characterization must be carefully created, not copied from type.
She is not paranoiac, but her life is paranoia. There is much to

admire in Amanda, and as much to love and pity as there is to laugh at. Certainly she has endurance and a kind of heroism, and though her foolishness makes her unwittingly cruel at times, there is tenderness in her slight person.

Laura Wingfield, her daughter. Amanda, having failed to establish contact with reality, continues to live vitally in her illusions, but Laura's situation is even graver. A childhood illness has left her crippled, one leg slightly shorter than the other, and held in a brace. This defect need not be more than suggested on the stage. Stemming from this, Laura's separation increases till she is like a piece of her own glass collection, too, exquisitely fragile to move from the shelf.

Tom Wingfield, her son. And the narrator of the play. A poet with a job in a warehouse. His nature is not remorseless, but to escape from a trap he has to act without pity.

Jim O'Connor, the gentleman caller. A nice, ordinary, young man.

Scene. *An alley in St. Louis.*

Part I *Preparation for a Gentleman Caller.*
Part II *The Gentleman Calls.*

Time. *Now and the Past.*

SCENE I

The Wingfield apartment is in the rear of the building, one of those vast hive-like conglomerations of cellular living-units that flower as warty growths in overcrowded urban centers of lower middle-class population and are symptomatic of the impulse of this largest and fundamentally enslaved section of American society to avoid fluidity and differentiation and to exist and function as one interfused mass of automatism.

The apartment faces an alley and is entered by a fire-escape, a structure whose name is a touch of accidental poetic truth, for all of these huge buildings are always burning with the slow and implacable fires of human desperation. The fire-escape is included in the set — that is, the landing of it and steps descending from it.

The scene is memory and is therefore nonrealistic. Memory takes a lot of poetic license. It omits some details; others are exaggerated, according to the emotional value of the articles it

*touches, for memory is seated predominantly in the heart. The
interior is therefore rather dim and poetic.*

*At the rise of the curtain, the audience is faced with the dark,
grim rear wall of the Wingfield tenement. This building, which
runs parallel to the footlights, is flanked on both sides by dark,
narrow alleys which run into murky canyons of tangled clothes-
lines, garbage cans and the sinister latticework of neighboring
fire-escapes. It is up and down these side alleys that exterior entrances and exits are made, during the play. At the end of Tom's
opening commentary, the dark tenement wall slowly reveals (by
means of a transparency) the interior of the ground floor
Wingfield apartment.*

*Downstage is the living room, which also serves as a sleeping
room for Laura, the sofa unfolding to make her bed. Upstage,
center, and divided by a wide arch or second proscenium with
transparent faded portieres (or second curtain), is the dining
room. In an old-fashioned what-not in the living room are seen
scores of transparent glass animals. A blown-up photograph of
the father hangs on the wall of the living room, facing the audience, to the left of the archway. It is the face of a very handsome
young man in a doughboy's First World War cap. He is gallantly
smiling, ineluctably smiling, as if to say, "I will be smiling
forever."*

*The audience hears and sees the opening scene in the dining
room through both the transparent fourth wall of the building
and the transparent gauze portieres of the dining-room arch. It is
during this revealing scene that the fourth wall slowly ascends,
out of sight. This transparent exterior wall is not brought down
again until the very end of the play, during Tom's final speech.*

*The narrator is an undisguised convention of the play. He takes
whatever license with dramatic convention as is convenient to his
purposes.*

*Tom enters dressed as a merchant sailor from alley, stage left,
and strolls across the front of the stage to the fire-escape. There he
stops and lights a cigarette. He addresses the audience.*

Tom. Yes, I have tricks in my pocket, I have things up my sleeve. But
I am the opposite of a stage magician. He gives you illusion that
has the appearance of truth. I give you truth in the pleasant disguise of illusion. To begin with, I turn back time. I reverse it to
that quaint period, the thirties, when the huge middle class of
America was matriculating in a school for the blind. Their eyes
had failed them, or they had failed their eyes, and so they were

having their fingers pressed forcibly down on the fiery Braille alphabet of a dissolving economy. In Spain there was revolution. Here there was only shouting and confusion. In Spain there was Guernica. Here there were disturbances of labor, sometimes pretty violent, in otherwise peaceful cities such as Chicago, Cleveland, Saint Louis. . . . This is the social background of the play.

(Music.)

The play is memory. Being a memory play, it is dimly lighted, it is sentimental, it is not realistic. In memory everything seems to happen to music. That explains the fiddle in the wings. I am the narrator of the play, and also a character in it. The other characters are my mother, Amanda, my sister, Laura, and a gentleman caller who appears in the final scenes. He is the most realistic character in the play, being an emissary from a world of reality that we were somehow set apart from. But since I have a poet's weakness for symbols, I am using this character also as a symbol; he is the long delayed but always expected something that we live for. There is a fifth character in the play who doesn't appear except in this larger-than-life photograph over the mantel. This is our father who left us a long time ago. He was a telephone man who fell in love with long distances; he gave up his job with the telephone company and skipped the light fantastic out of town . . . The last we heard of him was a picture post-card from Mazatlan, on the Pacific coast of Mexico, containing a message of two words — "Hello — Good-bye!" and an address. I think the rest of the play will explain itself. . . .

Amanda's voice becomes audible through the portieres.

(Legend on Screen: "Où Sont Les Neiges.")

He divides the portieres and enters the upstage area.
  Amanda and Laura are seated at a drop-leaf table. Eating is indicated by gestures without food or utensils. Amanda faces the audience. Tom and Laura are seated in profile.
  The interior has lit up softly and through the scrim we see Amanda and Laura seated at the table in the upstage area.

Amanda (calling). Tom?
Tom. Yes, Mother.
Amanda. We can't say grace until you come to the table!
Tom. Coming, Mother. (*He bows slightly and withdraws, reappearing a few moments later in his place at the table.*)

Amanda (to her son). Honey, don't *push* with your *fingers.* If you
have to push with something, the thing to push with is a crust of
bread. And chew — chew! Animals have sections in their stom-
achs which enable them to digest food without mastication, but
human beings are supposed to chew their food before they swallow it down. Eat food leisurely, son, and really enjoy it. A well-
cooked meal has lots of delicate flavors that have to be held in the
mouth for appreciation. So chew your food and give your salivary
glands a chance to function!

*Tom deliberately lays his imaginary fork down and pushes his
chair back from the table.*

Tom. I haven't enjoyed one bite of this dinner because of your constant directions on how to eat it. It's you that makes me rush
through meals with your hawk-like attention to every bite I take.
Sickening — spoils my appetite — all this discussion of animals'
secretion — salivary glands — mastication!
Amanda (lightly). Temperament like a Metropolitan star! *(He rises
and crosses downstage.)* You're not excused from the table.
Tom. I am getting a cigarette.
Amanda. You smoke too much.

Laura rises.

Laura. I'll bring in the blanc mange.

*He remains standing with his cigarette by the portieres during
the following.*

Amanda (rising). No, sister, no, sister — you be the lady this time
and I'll be the darky.
Laura. I'm already up.
Amanda. Resume your seat, little sister — I want you to stay fresh
and pretty — for gentlemen callers!
Laura. I'm not expecting any gentlemen callers.
Amanda (crossing out to kitchenette. Airily). Sometimes they come
when they are least expected! Why, I remember one Sunday after-
noon in Blue Mountain — *(Enters kitchenette.)*
Tom. I know what's coming!
Laura. Yes. But let her tell it.
Tom. Again?
Laura. She loves to tell it.

Amanda returns with bowl of dessert.

Amanda. One Sunday afternoon in Blue Mountain — your mother
received — *seventeen!* — gentlemen callers! Why, sometimes

there weren't chairs enough to accommodate them all. We had to send the nigger over to bring in folding chairs from the parish house.

Tom (remaining at portieres). How did you entertain those gentlemen callers?

Amanda. I understood the art of conversation!

Tom. I bet you could talk.

Amanda. Girls in those days *knew* how to talk, I can tell you.

Tom. Yes?

(Image: Amanda As A Girl On A Porch Greeting Callers.)

Amanda. They knew how to entertain their gentlemen callers. It wasn't enough for a girl to be possessed of a pretty face and a graceful figure — although I wasn't slighted in either respect. She also needed to have a nimble wit and a tongue to meet all occasions.

Tom. What did you talk about?

Amanda. Things of importance going on in the world! Never anything coarse or common or vulgar. (*She addresses Tom as though he were seated in the vacant chair at the table though he remains by portieres. He plays this scene as though he held the book.*) My callers were gentlemen — all! Among my callers were some of the most prominent young planters of the Mississippi Delta — planters and sons of planters!

Tom motions for music and a spot of light on Amanda.
    Her eyes lift, her face glows, her voice becomes rich and elegiac.

(Screen legend: "Où Sont Les Neiges.")

There was young Champ Laughlin who later became vice-president of the Delta Planters Bank. Hadley Stevenson who was drowned in Moon Lake and left his widow one hundred and fifty thousand in Government bonds. There were the Cutrere brothers, Wesley and Bates. Bates was one of my bright particular beaux! He got in a quarrel with that wild Wainright boy. They shot it out on the floor of Moon Lake Casino. Bates was shot through the stomach. Died in the ambulance on his way to Memphis. His widow was also well-provided for, came into eight or ten thousand acres, that's all. She married him on the rebound — never loved her — carried my picture on him the night he died! And there was that boy that every girl in the Delta had set her cap for! That beautiful, brilliant young Fitzhugh boy from Green County!

Tom. What did he leave his widow?

Amanda. He never married! Gracious, you talk as though all of my old admirers had turned up their toes to the daisies!

Tom. Isn't this the first you mentioned that still survives?

Amanda. That Fitzhugh boy went North and made a fortune — came to be known as the Wolf of Wall Street! He had the Midas touch, whatever he touched turned to gold! And I could have been Mrs. Duncan J. Fitzhugh, mind you! But — I picked your *father!*

Laura (rising). Mother, let me clear the table.

Amanda. No dear, you go in front and study your typewriter chart. Or practice your shorthand a little. Stay fresh and pretty! — It's almost time for our gentlemen callers to start arriving. *(She flounces girlishly toward the kitchenette.)* How many do you suppose we're going to entertain this afternoon?

Tom throws down the paper and jumps up with a groan.

Laura (alone in the dining room). I don't believe we're going to receive any, Mother.

Amanda (reappearing, airily). What? No one — not one? You must be joking! *(Laura nervously echoes her laugh. She slips in a fugitive manner through the half-open portieres and draws them gently behind her. A shaft of very clear light is thrown on her face against the faded tapestry of the curtains.)* **(Music: "The Glass Menagerie" Under Faintly.)** *(Lightly.)* Not one gentleman caller? It can't be true! There must be a flood, there must have been a tornado!

Laura. It isn't a flood, it's not a tornado, Mother. I'm just not popular like you were in Blue Mountain. . . . *(Tom utters another groan. Laura glances at him with a faint, apologetic smile. Her voice catching a little.)* Mother's afraid I'm going to be an old maid.

(The Scene Dims Out With "Glass Menagerie" Music.)

SCENE II

"Laura, Haven't You Ever Liked Some Boy?"

On the dark stage the screen is lighted with the image of blue roses.

 Gradually Laura's figure becomes apparent and the screen goes out.

 The music subsides.

 Laura is seated in the delicate ivory chair at the small clawfoot table.

She wears a dress of soft violet material for a kimono — her hair tied back from her forehead with a ribbon.
She is washing and polishing her collection of glass.
Amanda appears on the fire-escape steps. At the sound of her ascent, Laura catches her breath, thrusts the bowl of ornaments away and seats herself stiffly before the diagram of the typewriter keyboard as though it held her spellbound. Something has happened to Amanda. It is written in her face as she climbs to the landing: a look that is grim and hopeless and a little absurd.
She has on one of those cheap or imitation velvety-looking cloth coats with imitation fur collar. Her hat is five or six years old, one of those dreadful cloche hats that were worn in the late twenties, and she is clasping an enormous black patent-leather pocketbook with nickel clasp and initials. This is her full-dress outfit, the one she usually wears to the D.A.R.
Before entering she looks through the door.
She purses her lips, opens her eyes wide, rolls them upward and shakes her head.
Then she slowly lets herself in the door. Seeing her mother's expression Laura touches her lips with a nervous gesture.

Laura. Hello, Mother, I was — (*She makes a nervous gesture toward the chart on the wall. Amanda leans against the shut door and stares at Laura with a martyred look.*)
Amanda. Deception? Deception? (*She slowly removes her hat and gloves, continuing the swift suffering stare. She lets the hat and gloves fall on the floor — a bit of acting.*)
Laura (*shakily*). How was the D.A.R. meeting? (*Amanda slowly opens her purse and removes a dainty white handkerchief which she shakes out delicately and delicately touches to her lips and nostrils.*) Didn't you go the D.A.R. meeting, Mother?
Amanda (*faintly, almost inaudibly*) — No. — No. (*Then more forcibly.*) I did not have the strength — to go the D.A.R. In fact, I did not have the courage! I wanted to find a hole in the ground and hide myself in it forever! (*She crosses slowly to the wall and removes the diagram of the typewriter keyboard. She holds it in front of her for a second, staring at it sweetly and sorrowfully — then bites her lips and tears it in two pieces.*)
Laura (*faintly*). Why did you do that, Mother? (*Amanda repeats the same procedure with the chart of the Gregg Alphabet.*) Why are you —
Amanda. Why? Why? How old are you, Laura?
Laura. Mother, you know my age.
Amanda. I thought that you were an adult; it seems that I was mis-

taken. *(She crosses slowly to the sofa and sinks down and stares at Laura.)*

Laura. Please don't stare at me, Mother.

Amanda closes her eyes and lowers her head. Count ten.

Amanda. What are we going to do, what is going to become of us, what is the future?

Count ten.

Laura. Has something happened, Mother? *(Amanda draws a long breath and takes out the handkerchief again. Dabbing process.)* Mother, has — something happened?

Amanda. I'll be all right in a minute. I'm just bewildered — *(count five)* — by life. . . .

Laura. Mother, I wish that you would tell me what's happened.

Amanda. As you know, I was supposed to be inducted into my office at the D.A.R. this afternoon. **(Image: A Swarm of Typewriters.)** But I stopped off at Rubicam's Business College to speak to your teachers about your having a cold and ask them what progress they thought you were making down there.

Laura. Oh. . . .

Amanda. I went to the typing instructor and introduced myself as your mother. She didn't know who you were. Wingfield, she said. We don't have any such student enrolled at the school! I assured her she did, that you had been going to classes since early in January. "I wonder," she said, "if you could be talking about that terribly shy little girl who dropped out of school after only a few 'days' attendance?" "No," I said, "Laura, my daughter, has been going to school every day for the past six weeks!" "Excuse me," she said. She took the attendance book out and there was your name, unmistakably printed, and all the dates you were absent until they decided that you had dropped out of school. I still said, "No, there must have been some mistake! There must have been some mix-up in the records!" And she said, "No — I remember her perfectly now. Her hand shook so that she couldn't hit the right keys! The first time we gave a speed-test, she broke down completely — was sick at the stomach and almost had to be carried into the wash-room! After that morning she never showed up any more. We phoned the house but never got any answer" — while I was working at Famous and Barr, I suppose, demonstrating those — Oh! I felt so weak I could barely keep on my feet. I had to sit down while they got me a glass of water! Fifty dollars' tuition, all of our plans — my hopes and ambitions for you — just gone up the spout, just gone up the spout like that. *(Laura draws a long breath and gets awkwardly to her feet. She crossed to the victrola and winds it up.)* What are you doing?

Laura. Oh! *(She releases the handle and returns to her seat.)*

Amanda. Laura, where have you been going when you've gone out pretending that you were going to business college?

Laura. I've just been going out walking.

Amanda. That's not true.

Laura. It is. I just went walking.

Amanda. Walking? Walking? In winter? Deliberately courting pneumonia in that light coat? Where did you walk to, Laura?

Laura. It was the lesser of two evils, Mother. (**Image: Winter Scene In Park.**) I couldn't go back up. I — threw up — on the floor!

Amanda. From half past seven till after five every day you mean to tell me you walked around in the park, because you wanted to make me think that you were still going to Rubicam's Business College?

Laura. It wasn't as bad as it sounds. I went inside places to get warmed up.

Amanda. Inside where?

Laura. I went in the art museum and the bird-houses at the Zoo. I visited the penguins every day! Sometimes I did without lunch and went to the movies. Lately I've been spending most of my afternoons in the Jewel-box, that big glass house where they raise the tropical flowers.

Amanda. You did all this to deceive me, just for the deception? *(Laura looks down.)* Why?

Laura. Mother, when you're disappointed, you get that awful suffering look on your face, like the picture of Jesus' mother in the museum!

Amanda. Hush!

Laura. I couldn't face it.

Pause. A whisper of strings.

(**Legend: "The Crust of Humility."**)

Amanda (hopelessly fingering the huge pocketbook). So what are we going to do the rest of our lives? Stay home and watch the parades go by? Amuse ourselves with the glass menagerie, darling? Eternally play those worn-out phonograph records your father left as a painful reminder of him? We won't have a business career — we've given that up because it gave us nervous indigestion! *(Laughs wearily.)* What is there left but dependency all our lives?

I know so well what becomes of unmarried women who aren't prepared to occupy a position. I've seen such pitiful cases in the South — barely tolerated spinsters living upon the grudging patronage of sister's husband or brother's wife! — stuck away in some little mouse-trap of a room — encouraged by one in-law to visit another — little birdlike women without any nest — eating the crust of humility all their life! Is that the future that we've mapped out for ourselves? I swear it's the only alternative I can think of! It isn't a very pleasant alternative, is it? Of course — some girls *do marry. (Laura twists her hands nervously.)* Haven't you ever liked some boy?

Laura. Yes. I liked one once. *(Rises.)* I came across his picture a while ago.

Amanda (with some interest). He gave you his picture?

Laura. No, it's in the year-book.

Amanda (disappointed). Oh — a high-school boy.

(Screen Image: Jim As A High-School Hero Bearing A Silver Cup.)

Laura. Yes. His name was Jim. *(Laura lifts the heavy annual from the clawfoot table.)* Here he is in *The Pirates of Penzance.*

Amanda (absently). The what?

Laura. The operetta the senior class put on. He had a wonderful voice and we sat across the aisle from each other Mondays, Wednesdays and Fridays in the Aud. Here he is with the silver cup for debating! See his grin?

Amanda (absently). He must have had a jolly disposition.

Laura. He used to call me — Blue Roses.

(Image: Blue Roses.)

Amanda. Why did he call you such a name as that?

Laura. When I had that attack of pleurosis — he asked me what was the matter when I came back. I said pleurosis — he thought that I said Blue Roses! So that's what he always called me after that. Whenever he saw me, he'd holler, "Hello, Blue Roses!" I didn't care for the girl that he went out with. Emily Meisenbach. Emily was the best-dressed girl at Soldan. She never struck me, though, as being sincere . . . It says in the Personal Section — they're engaged. That's — six years ago! They must be married by now.

Amanda. Girls that aren't cut out for business careers usually wind up married to some nice man. *(Gets up with a spark of revival.)* Sister, that's what you'll do!

Laura utters a startled, doubtful laugh. She reaches quickly for a piece of glass.

Laura. But, Mother —
Amanda. Yes? *(Crossing to photograph.)*
Laura (in a tone of frightened apology). I'm — crippled!

(Image: Screen.)

Amanda. Nonsense! Laura, I've told you never, never to use that word. Why, you're not crippled, you just have a little defect — hardly noticeable, even! When people have some slight disadvantage like that, they cultivate other things to make up for it — develop charm — and vivacity — and — *charm!* That's all you have to do! *(She turns again to the photograph.)* One thing your father had *plenty of — was charm!*

Tom motions to the fiddle in the wings.

(The Scene Fades Out With Music.)

SCENE III

(Legend On The Screen: "After The Fiasco — ")

Tom speaks from the fire-escape landing.

Tom. After the fiasco at Rubicam's Business College, the idea of getting a gentleman caller for Laura began to play a more important part in Mother's calculations. It became an obsession. Like some archetype of the universal unconscious, the image of the gentleman caller haunted our small apartment. . . . **(Image: Young Man At Door With Flowers.)** An evening at home rarely passed without some allusion to this image, this spectre, this hope. . . . Even when he wasn't mentioned, his presence hung in Mother's preoccupied look and in my sister's frightened, apologetic manner — hung like a sentence passed upon the Wingfields! Mother was a woman of action as well as words. She began to take logical steps in the planned direction. Late that winter and in the early spring — realizing that extra money would be needed to properly feather the nest and plume the bird — she conducted a vigorous campaign on the telephone, roping in subscribers to one of those magazines for matrons called *The Home-maker's Companion,* the type of journal that features the serialized sublimations of ladies of

letters who think in terms of delicate cup-like breasts, slim, taper-
ing waists, rich, creamy thighs, eyes like wood-smoke in autumn,
fingers that soothe and caress like strains of music, bodies as
powerful as Etruscan sculpture.

(**Screen Image: Glamor Magazine Cover.**)

*Amanda enters with phone on long extension cord. She is spotted
in the dim stage.*

Amanda. Ida Scott? This is Amanda Wingfield! We *missed* you at the
D.A.R. last Monday! I said to myself: She's probably suffering
with that sinus condition! How is that sinus condition? Horrors!
Heaven have mercy! — You're a Christian martyr, yes, that's what
you are, a Christian martyr! Well, I just now happened to notice
that your subscription to the *Companion's* about to expire! Yes, it
expires with the next issue, honey! — just when that wonderful
new serial by Bessie Mae Hopper is getting off to such an exciting
start. Oh, honey, it's something that you can't miss! You remember
how *Gone With the Wind* took everybody by storm? You simply
couldn't go out if you hadn't read it. All everybody *talked* was
Scarlett O'Hara. Well, this is a book that critics already compare to
Gone With the Wind. It's the *Gone With the Wind* of the post–
World War generation! — What? — Burning? — Oh, honey, don't
let them burn, go take a look in the oven and I'll hold the wire!
Heavens — I think she's hung up!

(**Dim Out.**)

(**Legend On Screen: "You Think I'm In Love With Continental
Shoemakers?"**)

*Before the stage is lighted, the violent voices of Tom and Amanda
are heard. They are quarreling behind the portieres. In front of
them stands Laura with clenched hands and panicky expression.
A clear pool of light on her figure throughout this scene.*

Tom. What in Christ's name am I —
Amanda (shrilly). Don't you use that —
Tom. Supposed to do!
Amanda. Expression! Not in my —
Tom. Ohhh!
Amanda. Presence! Have you gone out of your senses?
Tom. I have, that's true, *driven* out!

Amanda. What is the matter with you, you — big — big — IDIOT!

Tom. Look — I've got *no thing*, no single thing —

Amanda. Lower your voice!

Tom. In my life here that I can call my OWN! Everything is —

Amanda. Stop that shouting!

Tom. Yesterday you confiscated my books! You had the nerve to —

Amanda. I took that horrible novel back to the library — yes! That hideous book by that insane Mr. Lawrence. *(Tom laughs wildly.)* I cannot control the output of diseased minds or people who cater to them — *(Tom laughs still more wildly.)* BUT I WON'T ALLOW SUCH FILTH BROUGHT INTO MY HOUSE! No, no, no, no, no!

Tom. House, house! Who pays rent on it, who makes a slave of himself to —

Amanda (fairly screeching). Don't you DARE to —

Tom. No, no, *I* mustn't say things! *I've* got to just —

Amanda. Let me tell you —

Tom. I don't want to hear any more! *(He tears the portieres open. The upstage area is lit with a turgid smoky red glow.)*

Amanda's hair is in metal curlers and she wears a very old bathrobe, much too large for her slight figure, a relic of the faithless Mr. Wingfield.

An upright typewriter and a wild disarray of manuscripts are on the drop-leaf table. The quarrel was probably precipitated by Amanda's interruption of his creative labor. A chair lying overthrown on the floor.

Their gesticulating shadows are cast on the ceiling by the fiery glow.

Amanda. You *will* hear more, you —

Tom. No, I won't hear more, I'm going out!

Amanda. You come right back in —

Tom. Out, out out! Because I'm —

Amanda. Come back here, Tom Wingfield! I'm not through talking to you!

Tom. Oh, go —

Laura (desperately). Tom!

Amanda. You're going to listen, and no more insolence from you! I'm at the end of my patience! *(He comes back toward her.)*

Tom. What do you think I'm at? Aren't I supposed to have any patience to reach the end of, Mother? I know, I know. It seems unimportant to you, what I'm *doing* — what I *want* to do — having a little *difference* between them! You don't think that —

Amanda. I think you've been doing things that you're ashamed of. That's why you act like this. I don't believe that you go every night to the movies. Nobody goes to the movies night after night. Nobody in their right minds goes to the movies as often as you pretend to. People don't go to the movies at nearly midnight, and movies don't let out at two A.M. Come in stumbling. Muttering to yourself like a maniac! You get three hours sleep and then go to work. Oh, I can picture the way you're doing down there. Moping, doping, because you're in no condition.

Tom (wildly). No, I'm in no condition!

Amanda. What right have you got to jeopardize your job? Jeopardize the security of us all? How do you think we'd manage if you were —

Tom. Listen! You think I'm crazy *about* the *warehouse? (He bends fiercely toward her slight figure.)* You think I'm in love with the Continental Shoemakers? You think I want to spend fifty-five *years* down there in that — *celotex interior!* with — *fluorescent* — *tubes!* Look! I'd rather somebody picked up a crowbar and battered out my brains — than go back mornings! I *go!* Every time you come in yelling that God damn *"Rise and Shine!" "Rise and Shine!"* I say to myself "How *lucky dead* people are!" But I get up. I *go!* For sixty-five dollars a month I give up all that I dream of doing and being *ever!* And you say self — *self's* all I ever think of. Why, listen, if self is what I thought of, Mother, I'd be where he is — GONE! *(Pointing to father's picture.)* As far as the system of transportation reaches! *(He starts past her. She grabs his arm.)* Don't grab at me, Mother!

Amanda. Where are you going?

Tom. I'm going to the *movies!*

Amanda. I don't believe that lie!

Tom (crouching toward her, overtowering her tiny figure. She backs away, gasping). I'm going to opium dens! Yes, opium dens, dens of vice and criminals' hang-outs, Mother. I've joined the Hogan gang, I'm a hired assassin, I carry a tommy-gun in a violin case! I run a string of cat-houses in the Valley! They call me Killer, Killer Wingfield, I'm leading a double-life, a simple, honest warehouse worker by day, by night a dynamic *czar* of the *underworld,* Mother. I go to gambling casinos, I spin away fortunes on the roulette table! I wear a patch over one eye and a false mustache, sometimes I put on green whiskers. On those occasions they call me — *El Diablo!* Oh, I could tell you things to make you sleepless! My enemies plan to dynamite this place. They're going to blow us all sky-high some night! I'll be glad, very happy, and so

will you! You'll go up, up on a broomstick, over Blue Mountain
with seventeen gentlemen callers! You ugly — babbling old —
witch. . . . *(He goes through a series of violent, clumsy move-*
ments, seizing his overcoat, lunging to the door, pulling it fiercely
open. The women watch him, aghast. His arm catches in the
sleeve of the coat as he struggles to pull it on. For a moment he is
pinioned by the bulky garment. With an outraged groan he tears
the coat off again, splitting the shoulders of it, and hurls it across
the room. It strikes against the shelf of Laura's glass collection,
there is a tinkle of shattering glass. Laura cries out as if
wounded.)

(Music Legend: "The Glass Menagerie.")

Laura (shrilly). My glass! — menagerie. . . . *(She covers her face and*
turns away.)

But Amanda is still stunned and stupefied by the "ugly witch" so
that she barely notices this occurrence. Now she recovers her
speech.

Amanda (in an awful voice). I won't speak to you — until you apologize! *(She crosses through portieres and draws them together*
behind her. Tom is left with Laura. Laura clings weakly to the
mantel with her face averted. Tom stares at her stupidly for a
moment. Then he crosses to shelf. Drops awkwardly to his knees
to collect the fallen glass, glancing at Laura as if he would speak
but couldn't.)

"The Glass Menagerie" steals in as

(The Scene Dims Out.)

SCENE IV

The interior is dark. Faint light in the alley.
    A deep-voiced bell in a church is tolling the hour of five as the
scene commences.
    Tom appears at the top of the alley. After each solemn boom of
the bell in the tower, he shakes a little noise-maker or rattle as if
to express the tiny spasm of man in contrast to the sustained
power and dignity of the Almighty. This and the unsteadiness of
his advance make it evident that he has been drinking.
    As he climbs the few steps to the fire-escape landing light steals

up inside. Laura appears in night-dress, observing Tom's empty bed in the front room.

Tom fishes in his pockets for the door-key, removing a motley assortment of articles in the search, including a perfect shower of movie-ticket stubs and an empty bottle. At last he finds the key, but just as he is about to insert it, it slips from his fingers. He strikes a match and crouches below the door.

Tom (bitterly). One crack — and it falls through!

Laura opens the door.

Laura. Tom! Tom, what are you doing?
Tom. Looking for a door-key.
Laura. Where have you been all this time?
Tom. I have been to the movies.
Laura. All this time at the movies?
Tom. There was a very long program. There was a Garbo picture and a Mickey Mouse and a travelogue and a newsreel and a preview of coming attractions. And there was an organ solo and a collection for the milk-fund — simultaneously — which ended up in a terrible fight between a fat lady and an usher!
Laura (innocently). Did you have to stay through everything?
Tom. Of course! And, oh, I forgot! There was a big stage show! The headliner on this stage show was Malvolio the Magician. He performed wonderful tricks, many of them, such as pouring water back and forth between pitchers. First it turned to wine and then it turned to beer and then it turned to whiskey. I know it was whiskey it finally turned into because he needed somebody to come up out of the audience to help him, and I came up — both shows! It was Kentucky Straight Bourbon. A very generous fellow, he gave souvenirs. *(He pulls from his back pocket a shimmering rainbow-colored scarf.)* He gave me this. This is his magic scarf. You can have it, Laura. You wave it over a canary cage and you get a bowl of gold-fish. You wave it over the gold-fish bowl and they fly away canaries. . . . But the wonderfullest trick of all was the coffin trick. We nailed him into a coffin and he got out of the coffin without removing one nail. *(He has come inside.)* There is a trick that would come in handy for me — get me out of this 2 by 4 situation! *(Flops onto bed and starts removing shoes.)*
Laura. Tom—Shhh!
Tom. What you shushing me for?
Laura. You'll wake up Mother.
Tom. Goody, goody! Pay 'er back for all those "Rise an' Shines."

(Lies down, groaning.) You know it don't take much intelligence to get yourself into a nailed-up coffin, Laura. But who in hell ever got himself out of one without removing one nail?

As if in answer, the father's grinning photograph lights up.

(Scene Dims Out.)

Immediately following: The church bell is heard striking six. At the sixth stroke the alarm clock goes off in Amanda's room, and after a few moments we hear her calling: "Rise and Shine! Rise and Shine! Laura, go tell your brother to rise and shine!"

Tom (sitting up slowly). I'll rise — but I won't shine.

The light increases.

Amanda. Laura, tell your brother his coffee is ready.

Laura slips into front room.

Laura. Tom! it's nearly seven. Don't make Mother nervous. *(He stares at her stupidly. Beseechingly.)* Tom, speak to Mother this morning. Make up with her, apologize, speak to her!
Tom. She won't to me. It's her that started not speaking.
Laura. If you just say you're sorry she'll start speaking.
Tom. Her not speaking — is that such a tragedy?
Laura. Please — please!
Amanda (calling from kitchenette). Laura, are you going to do what I asked you to do, or do I have to get dressed and go out myself?
Laura. Going, going — soon as I get on my coat! *(She pulls on a shapeless felt hat with nervous, jerky movement, pleadingly glancing at Tom. Rushes awkwardly for coat. The coat is one of Amanda's, inaccurately made-over, the sleeves too short for Laura.)* Butter and what else?
Amanda (entering upstage). Just butter. Tell them to charge it.
Laura. Mother, they make such faces when I do that.
Amanda. Sticks and stones may break my bones, but the expression on Mr. Garfinkel's face won't harm us! Tell your brother his coffee is getting cold.
Laura (at door). Do what I asked you, will you, will you, Tom?

He looks sullenly away.

Amanda. Laura, go now or just don't go at all!
Laura (rushing out). Going — going! *(A second later she cries out. Tom springs up and crosses to the door. Amanda rushes anxiously in. Tom opens the door.)*

Tom. Laura?

Laura. I'm all right. I slipped, but I'm all right.

Amanda (peering anxiously after her). If anyone breaks a leg on those fire-escape steps, the landlord ought to be sued for every cent he possesses! *(She shuts door. Remembers she isn't speaking and returns to other room.)*

As Tom enters listlessly for his coffee, she turns her back to him and stands rigidly facing the window on the gloomy gray vault of the areaway. Its light on her face with its aged but childish features is cruelly sharp, satirical as a Daumier print.

(Music Under: "Ave Maria.")

Tom glances sheepishly but sullenly at her averted figure and slumps at the table. The coffee is scalding hot; he sips it and gasps and spits in back in the cup. At his gasp, Amanda catches her breath and half turns. Then catches herself and turns back to window.

Tom blows on his coffee, glancing sidewise at his mother. She clears her throat. Tom clears his. He starts to rise. Sinks back down again, scratches his head, clears his throat again. Amanda coughs. Tom raises his cup in both hands to blow on it, his eyes staring over the rim of it at his mother for several moments. Then he slowly sets the cup down and awkwardly and hesitantly rises from the chair.

Tom (hoarsely). Mother. I — I apologize. Mother. *(Amanda draws a quick, shuddering breath. Her face works grotesquely. She breaks into childlike tears.)* I'm sorry for what I said, for everything that I said, I didn't mean it.

Amanda (sobbingly). My devotion has made me a witch and so I make myself hateful to my children!

Tom. No, you *don't.*

Amanda. I worry so much, don't sleep, it makes me nervous!

Tom (gently). I understand that.

Amanda. I've had to put up a solitary battle all these years. But you're my right-hand bower! Don't fall down, don't fail!

Tom (gently). I try, Mother.

Amanda (with great enthusiasm). Try and you will SUCCEED! *(The notion makes her breathless.)* Why, you — you're just *full* of natural endowments! Both of my children — they're *unusual* children! Don't you think I know it? I'm so — *proud!* Happy and — feel I've — so much to be thankful for but — Promise me one thing, son!

Tom. What, Mother?

Amanda. Promise, son, you'll — never be a drunkard!

Tom (turns to her grinning). I will never be a drunkard, Mother.

Amanda. That's what frightened me so, that you'd be drinking! Eat a bowl of Purina!

Tom. Just coffee, Mother.

Amanda. Shredded wheat biscuit?

Tom. No. No, Mother, just coffee.

Amanda. You can't put in a day's work on an empty stomach. You've got ten minutes — don't gulp! Drinking too-hot liquids makes cancer of the stomach. . . . Put cream in.

Tom. No, thank you.

Amanda. To cool it.

Tom. No! No, thank you, I want it black.

Amanda. I know, but it's not good for you. We have to do all that we can to build ourselves up. In these trying times we live in, all that we have to cling to is — each other. . . . That's why it's so important to — Tom, I — I sent out your sister so I could discuss something with you. If you hadn't spoken I would have spoken to you. *(Sits down.)*

Tom (gently). What is it, Mother, that you want to discuss?

Amanda. Laura!

Tom puts his cup down slowly.

(Legend On Screen: "Laura.")

(Music: "The Glass Menagerie.")

Tom. — Oh. — Laura . . .

Amanda (touching his sleeve). You know how Laura is. So quiet but — still water runs deep! She notices things and I think she — broods about them. *(Tom looks up.)* A few days ago I came in and she was crying.

Tom. What about?

Amanda. You.

Tom. Me?

Amanda. She has an idea that you're not happy here.

Tom. What gave her that idea?

Amanda. What gives her any idea? However, you do act strangely. I — I'm not criticizing, understand *that!* I know your ambitions do not lie in the warehouse, that like everybody in the whole wide world — you've had to — make sacrifices, but — Tom — Tom — life's not easy, it calls for — Spartan endurance! There's so many things in my heart that I cannot describe to you! I've never told you but I — *loved* your father. . . .

Tom (gently). I know that, Mother.

Amanda. And you — when I see you taking after his ways! Staying out late — and — well, you *had* been drinking the night you were in that — terrfying condition! Laura says that you hate the apartment and that you go out nights to get away from it! Is that true, Tom?

Tom. No. You say there's so much in your heart that you can't describe to me. That's true of me, too. There's so much in my heart that I can't describe to *you!* So let's respect each other's —

Amanda. But, why — *why*, Tom — are you always so *restless?* Where do you go to, nights?

Tom. I — go to the movies.

Amanda. Why do you go to the movies so much, Tom?

Tom. I go to the movies because — I like adventure. Adventure is something I don't have much of at work, so I go to the movies.

Amanda. But, Tom, you go to the movies *entirely* too *much!*

Tom. I like a lot of adventure.

Amanda looks baffled, then hurt. As the familiar inquisition resumes he becomes hard and impatient again. Amanda slips back into her querulous attitude toward him.

(Image On Screen: Sailing Vessel With Jolly Roger.)

Amanda. Most young men find adventure in their careers.

Tom. Then most young men are not employed in a warehouse.

Amanda. The world is full of young men employed in warehouses and offices and factories.

Tom. Do all of them find adventure in their careers?

Amanda. They do or they do without it! Not everybody has a craze for adventure.

Tom. Man is by instinct a lover, a hunter, a fighter, and none of those instincts are given much play at the warehouse!

Amanda. Man is by instinct! Don't quote instinct to me! Instinct is something that people have got away from! It belongs to animals! Christian adults don't want it!

Tom. What do Christian adults want, then, Mother?

Amanda. Superior things! Things of the mind and the spirit! Only animals have to satisfy instincts! Surely your aims are somewhat higher than theirs! Than monkeys — pigs —

Tom. I reckon they're not.

Amanda. You're joking. However, that isn't what I wanted to discuss.

Tom (rising). I haven't much time.

Amanda (pushing his shoulders). Sit down.

Tom. You want me to punch in red at the warehouse, Mother?
Amanda. You have five minutes. I want to talk about Laura.

(Legend: "Plans And Provisions.")

Tom. All right! What about Laura?
Amanda. We have to be making plans and provisions for her. She's older than you, two years, and nothing has happened. She just drifts along doing nothing. It frightens me terribly how she just drifts along.
Tom. I guess she's the type that people call home girls.
Amanda. There's no such type, and if there is, it's a pity! That is unless the home is hers, with a husband!
Tom. What?
Amanda. Oh, I can see the handwriting on the wall as plain as I see the nose in front of my face! It's terrifying! More and more you remind me of your father! He was out all hours without explanation — Then *left! Goodbye!* And me with a bag to hold. I saw that letter you got from the Merchant Marine. I know what you're dreaming of. I'm not standing here blindfolded. Very well, then. Then *do* it! But not till there's somebody to take your place.
Tom. What do you mean?
Amanda. I mean that as soon as Laura has got somebody to take care of her, married, a home of her own, independent — why, then you'll be free to go wherever you please, on land, on sea, whichever way the wind blows! But until that time you've got to look out for your sister. I don't say me because I'm old and don't matter! I say for your sister because she's young and dependent. I put her in business college — a dismal failure! Frightened her so it made her sick to her stomach. I took her over to the Young People's League at the church. Another fiasco. She spoke to nobody, nobody spoke to her. Now all she does is fool with those pieces of glass and play those worn-out records. What kind of a life is that for a girl to lead!
Tom. What can I do about it?
Amanda. Overcome selfishness! Self, self, self is all that you ever think of! *(Tom springs up and crosses to get his coat. It is ugly and bulky. He pulls on a cap with earmuffs.)* Where is your muffler? Put your wool muffler on! *(He snatches it angrily from the closet and tosses it around his neck and pulls both ends tight.)* Tom! I haven't said what I had in mind to ask you.
Tom. I'm too late to —
Amanda (catching his arms — very importunately. Then shyly).
Down at the warehouse, aren't there some — nice young men?
Tom. No!

Amanda. There *must* be — *some* . . .
Tom. Mother —

Gesture.

Amanda. Find out one that's clean-living — doesn't drink and — ask him out for sister!
Tom. What?
Amanda. For *sister!* To *meet!* Get *acquainted!*
Tom (stamping to door). Oh, my *go-osh!*
Amanda. Will you? *(He opens door. Imploringly.)* Will you? *(He starts down.)* Will you? *Will* you, dear?
Tom (calling back). YES!

Amanda closes the door hesitantly and with a troubled but faintly hopeful expression.

(Screen Image: Glamor Magazine Cover.)

Spot Amanda at phone.

Amanda. Ella Cartwright? This is Amanda Wingfield! How are you, honey? How is that kidney condition? *(Count five.)* Horrors! *(Count five.)* You're a Christian martyr, yes, honey, that's what you are, a Christian martyr! Well, I just happened to notice in my little red book that your subscription to the *Companion* has just run out! I knew that you wouldn't want to miss out on the wonderful serial starting in this new issue. It's by Bessie Mae Hopper, the first thing she's written since *Honeymoon for Three.* Wasn't that a strange and interesting story? Well, this one is even lovelier, I believe. It has a sophisticated society background. It's all about the horsey set on Long Island!

(Fade Out.)

SCENE V

(Legend On Screen: "Annunciation.") *Fade with music.*

It is early dusk of a spring evening. Supper has just been finished in the Wingfield apartment. Amanda and Laura in light colored dresses are removing dishes from the table, in the upstage area, which is shadowy, their movements formalized almost as a dance or ritual, their moving forms as pale and silent as moths.

Tom, in white shirt and trousers, rises from the table and crosses toward the fire-escape.

Amanda (as he passes her). Son, will you do me a favor?

Tom. What?

Amanda. Comb your hair! You look so pretty when your hair is combed! *(Tom slouches on sofa with evening paper. Enormous caption "Franco Triumphs.")* There is only one respect in which I would like you to emulate your father.

Tom. What respect is that?

Amanda. The care he always took of his appearance. He never allowed himself to look untidy. *(He throws down the paper and crosses to fire-escape.)* Where are you going?

Tom. I'm going out to smoke.

Amanda. You smoke too much. A pack a day at fifteen cents a pack. How much would that amount to in a month? Thirty times fifteen is how much, Tom? Figure it out and you will be astounded at what you could save. Enough to give you a night-school course in accounting at Washington U! Just think what a wonderful thing that would be for you, son!

Tom is unmoved by the thought.

Tom. I'd rather smoke. *(He steps out on landing, letting the screen door slam.)*

Amanda (sharply). I know! That's the tragedy of it. . . . *(Alone, she turns to look at her husband's picture.)*

(Dance Music: "All The World Is Waiting For the Sunrise!")

Tom (to the audience). Across the alley from us was the Paradise Dance Hall. On evenings in spring the windows and doors were open and the music came outdoors. Sometimes the lights were turned out except for a large glass sphere that hung from the ceiling. It would turn slowly about and filter the dusk with delicate rainbow colors. Then the orchestra played a waltz or a tango, something that had a slow and sensuous rhythm. Couples would come outside, to the relative privacy of the alley. You could see them kissing behind ash-pits and telephone poles. This was the compensation for lives that passed like mine, without any change or adventure. Adventure and change were imminent in this year. They were waiting around the corner for all these kids. Suspended in the midst over Berchtesgaden, caught in the folds of Chamberlain's umbrella — In Spain there was Guernica! But here there was only hot swing music and liquor, dance halls, bars, and movies, and sex that hung in the gloom like a chandelier and flooded the world with brief, deceptive rainbows. . . . All the world was waiting for bombardments!

Amanda turns from the picture and comes outside.

Amanda (sighing). A fire-escape landings' a poor excuse for a porch. *(She spreads a newspaper on a step and sits down, gracefully and demurely as if she were settling into a swing on a Mississippi veranda.)* What are you looking at?

Tom. The moon.

Amanda. Is there a moon this evening?

Tom. It's rising over Garfinkel's Delicatessen.

Amanda. So it is! A little silver slipper of a moon. Have you made a wish on it yet?

Tom. Um-hum.

Amanda. What did you wish for?

Tom. That's a secret.

Amanda. A secret, huh? Well, I won't tell mine either. I will be just as mysterious as you.

Tom. I bet I can guess what yours is.

Amanda. Is my head so transparent?

Tom. You're not a sphinx.

Amanda. No, I don't have secrets. I'll tell you what I wished for on the moon. Success and happiness for my precious children! I wish for that whenever there's a moon, and when there isn't a moon, I wish for it, too.

Tom. I thought perhaps you wished for a gentleman caller.

Amanda. Why do you say that?

Tom. Don't you remember asking me to fetch one?

Amanda. I remember suggesting that it would be nice for your sister if you brought home some nice young man from the warehouse. I think I've made that suggestion more than once.

Tom. Yes, you have made it repeatedly.

Amanda. Well?

Tom. We are going to have one.

Amanda. What?

Tom. A gentleman caller!

(The Annunciation Is Celebrated With Music.)

Amanda rises.

(Image on Screen: Caller With Bouquet.)

Amanda. You mean you have asked some nice young man to come over?

Tom. Yep. I've asked him to dinner.

Amanda. You really did?

Tom. I did!

Amanda. You did, and did he — *accept?*

Tom. He did!

Amanda. Well, well — well, well! That's — lovely!

Tom. I thought that you would be pleased.

Amanda. It's definite, then?

Tom. Very definite.

Amanda. Soon?

Tom. Very soon.

Amanda. For heaven's sake, stop putting on and tell me some things, will you?

Tom. What things do you want me to tell you?

Amanda. *Naturally* I would like to know when he's *coming!*

Tom. He's coming tomorrow.

Amanda. *Tomorrow?*

Tom. Yep. Tomorrow.

Amanda. But, Tom!

Tom. Yes, Mother?

Amanda. Tomorrow gives me no time!

Tom. Time for what?

Amanda. Preparations! Why didn't you phone me at once, as soon as you asked him, the minute that he accepted? Then, don't you see, I could have been getting ready!

Tom. You don't have to make any fuss.

Amanda. Oh, Tom, Tom, Tom, of course I have to make a fuss! I want things nice, not sloppy! Not thrown together. I'll certainly have to do some fast thinking, won't I?

Tom. I don't see why you have to think at all.

Amanda. You just don't know. We can't have a gentleman caller in a pig-sty! All my wedding silver has to be polished, the mono-grammed table linen ought to be laundered! The windows have to be washed and fresh curtains put up. And how about clothes? We have to *wear* something, don't we?

Tom. Mother, this boy is no one to make a fuss over!

Amanda. Do you realize he's the first young man we've introduced to your sister? It's terrible, dreadful, disgraceful that poor little sister has never received a single gentleman caller! Tom, come inside! *(She opens the screen door.)*

Tom. What for?

Amanda. I want to ask you some things.

Tom. If you're going to make such a fuss, I'll call it off, I'll tell him not to come.

Amanda. You certainly won't do anything of the kind. Nothing of-fends people worse than broken engagements. It simply means I'll have to work like a Turk! We won't be brilliant, but we'll pass inspection. Come on inside. *(Tom follows, groaning.)* Sit down.

Tom. Any particular place you would like me to sit?

Amanda. Thank heavens I've got that new sofa! I'm also making payments on a floor lamp I'll have sent out! And put the chintz covers on, they'll brighten things up! Of course I'd hoped to have these walls re-papered. . . . What is the young man's name?

Tom. His name is O'Connor.

Amanda. That, of course, means fish — tomorrow is Friday! I'll have that salmon loaf — with Durkee's dressing! What does he do? He works at the warehouse?

Tom. Of course! How else would I —

Amanda. Tom, he — doesn't drink?

Tom. Why do you ask me that?

Amanda. Your father *did!*

Tom. Don't get started on that!

Amanda. He *does* drink, then?

Tom. Not that I know of!

Amanda. Make sure, be certain! The last thing I want for my daughter's a boy who drinks!

Tom. Aren't you being a little premature? Mr. O'Connor has not yet appeared on the scene!

Amanda. But will tomorrow. To meet your sister, and what do I know about his character? Nothing! Old maids are better off than wives of drunkards!

Tom. Oh, my God!

Amanda. Be still!

Tom (leaning forward to whisper). Lots of fellows meet girls whom they don't marry!

Amanda. Oh, talk sensibly, Tom — and don't be sarcastic! *(She has gotten a hairbrush.)*

Tom. What are you doing?

Amanda. I'm brushing that cow-lick down! What is this young man's position at the warehouse?

Tom (submitting grimly to the brush and the interrogation). This young man's position is that of a shipping clerk, Mother,

Amanda. Sounds to me like a fairly responsible job, the sort of a job *you* would be in if you just had more *get-up*. What is his salary? Have you got any idea?

Tom. I would judge it to be approximately eighty-five dollars a month.

Amanda. Well — not princely, but —

Tom. Twenty more than I make.

Amanda. Yes, how well I know! But for a family man, eighty-five dollars a month is not much more than you can just get by on. . . .

Tom. Yes, but Mr. O'Connor is not a family man.

Amanda. He might be, mightn't he? Some time in the future?

Tom. I see. Plans and provisions.

Amanda. You are the only young man that I know of who ignores the fact that the future becomes the present, the present the past, and the past turns into everlasting regret if you don't plan for it!

Tom. I will think that over and see what I can make of it.

Amanda. Don't be supercilious with your mother! Tell me some more about this — what do you call him?

Tom. James D. O'Connor. The D. is for Delaney.

Amanda. Irish on *both* sides! *Gracious!* And doesn't drink?

Tom. Shall I call him up and ask him right this minute?

Amanda. The only way to find out about those things is to make discreet inquiries at the proper moment. When I was a girl in Blue Mountain and it was suspected that a young man drank, the girl whose attentions he had been receiving, if any girl *was,* would sometimes speak to the minister of his church, or rather her father would if her father was living, and sort of feel him out on the young man's character. That is the way such things are discreetly handled to keep a young woman from making a tragic mistake!

Tom. Then how did you happen to make a tragic mistake?

Amanda. That innocent look of your father's had everyone fooled! He *smiled* — the world was *enchanted!* No girl can do worse than put herself at the mercy of a handsome appearance! I hope that Mr. O'Connor is not too good-looking.

Tom. No, he's not too good-looking. He's covered with freckles and hasn't too much of a nose.

Amanda. He's not right-down homely, though?

Tom. Not right-down homely. Just medium homely, I'd say.

Amanda. Character's what to look for in a man.

Tom. That's what I've always said, Mother.

Amanda. You've never said anything of the kind and I suspect you would never give it a thought.

Tom. Don't be suspicious of me.

Amanda. At least I hope he's the type that's up and coming.

Tom. I think he really goes in for self-improvement.

Amanda. What reason have you to think so?

Tom. He goes to night school.

Amanda (beaming). Splendid! What does he do, I mean study?

Tom. Radio engineering and public speaking!

Amanda. Then he has visions of being advanced in the world! Any young man who studies public speaking is aiming to have an executive job some day! And radio engineering? A thing for the future! Both of these facts are very illuminating. Those are the sort of things that a mother should know concerning any young man who comes to call on her daughter. Seriously or — not.

Tom. One little warning. He doesn't know about Laura. I didn't let on that we had dark ulterior motives. I just said, why don't you come have dinner with us? He said okay and that was the whole conversation.

Amanda. I bet it was! You're eloquent as an oyster. However, he'll know about Laura when he gets here. When he sees how lovely and sweet and pretty she is, he'll thank his lucky stars he was asked to dinner.

Tom. Mother, you mustn't expect too much of Laura.

Amanda. What do you mean?

Tom. Laura seems all those things to you and me because she's ours and we love her. We don't even notice she's crippled any more.

Amanda. Don't say crippled! You know that I never allow that word to be used!

Tom. But face facts, Mother. She is and — that's not all —

Amanda. What do you mean "not all"?

Tom. Laura is very different from other girls.

Amanda. I think the difference is all to her advantage.

Tom. Not quite all — in the eyes of others — strangers — she's terribly shy and lives in a world of her own and those things make her seem a little peculiar to people outside the house.

Amanda. Don't say peculiar.

Tom. Face the facts. She is.

(The Dance-hall Music Changes To A Tango That Has A Minor And Somewhat Ominous Tone.)

Amanda. In what way is she peculiar — may I ask?

Tom (gently). She lives in a world of her own — a world of — little glass ornaments, Mother. . . . *(Gets up. Amanda remains holding brush, looking at him, troubled.)* She plays old phonograph records and — that's about all — *(He glances at himself in the mirror and crosses to door.)*

Amanda (sharply). Where are you going?

Tom. I'm going to the movies. *(Out screen door.)*

Amanda. Not to the movies, every night to the movies! *(Follows quickly to screen door.)* I don't believe you always go to the movies! *(He is gone. Amanda looks worriedly after him for a moment. Then vitality and optimism return and she turns from the door. Crossing to portieres.)* Laura! Laura! *(Laura answers from kitchenette.)*

Laura. Yes, Mother.

Amanda. Let those dishes go and come in front! *(Laura appears with dish towel. Gaily.)* Laura, come here and make a wish on the moon!

Laura (entering). Moon — moon?

Amanda. A little silver slipper of a moon. Look over your left shoulder, Laura, and make a wish! *(Laura looks faintly puzzled as if called out of sleep. Amanda seizes her shoulders and turns her at an angle by the door.)* No! Now, darling, *wish!*

Laura. What shall I wish for, Mother?

Amanda (her voice trembling and her eyes suddenly filling with tears). Happiness! Good Fortune!

The violin rises and the stage dims out.

SCENE VI

(Image: High School Hero.)

Tom. And so the following evening I brought Jim home to dinner. I had known Jim slightly in high school. In high school Jim was a hero. He had tremendous Irish good nature and vitality with the scrubbed and polished look of white chinaware. He seemed to move in a continual spotlight. He was a star in basketball, captain of the debating club, president of the senior class and the glee club and he sang the male lead in the annual light operas. He was always running or bounding, never just walking. He seemed always at the point of defeating the law of gravity. He was shooting with such velocity through his adolescence that you would logically expect him to arrive at nothing short of the White House by the time he was thirty. But Jim apparently ran into more interference after his graduation from Soldan. His speed had definitely slowed. Six years after he left high school he was holding a job that wasn't much better than mine.

(Image: Clerk.)

He was the only one at the warehouse with whom I was on friendly terms. I was valuable to him as someone who could remember his former glory, who had seen him win basketball games and the silver cup in debating. He knew of my secret practice of retiring to a cabinet of the washroom to work on poems when business was slack in the warehouse. He called me Shakespeare. And while the other boys in the warehouse regarded me with suspicious hostility, Jim took a humorous attitude toward me. Gradually his attitude affected the others, their hostility wore off and they also began to smile at me as people smile at an oddly fashioned dog who trots across their path at some distance.

I knew that Jim and Laura had known each other at Soldan, and I had heard Laura speak admiringly of his voice. I didn't know if Jim remembered her or not. In high school Laura had been as unobtrusive as Jim had been astonishing. If he did remember Laura, it was not as my sister, for when I asked him to dinner, he grinned and said, "You know, Shakespeare, I never thought of you as having folks!"

He was about to discover that I did. . . .

(Light Up Stage.)

(Legend On Screen: "The Accent Of A Coming Foot.")

Friday evening. It is about five o'clock of a late spring evening which comes "scattering poems in the sky."

A delicate lemony light is in the Wingfield apartment.

Amanda has worked like a Turk in preparation for the gentleman caller. The results are astonishing. The new floor lamp with its rose-silk shade is in place, a colored paper lantern conceals the broken light fixture in the ceiling, new billowing white curtains are at the windows, chintz covers are on chairs and sofa, a pair of new sofa pillows make their initial appearance.

Open boxes and tissue paper are scattered on the floor.

Laura stands in the middle with lifted arms while Amanda crouches before her, adjusting the hem of the new dress, devout and ritualistic. The dress is colored and designed by memory. The arrangement of Laura's hair is changed; it is softer and more becoming. A fragile, unearthly prettiness has come out in Laura: she is like a piece of translucent glass touched by light, given a momentary radiance, not actual, not lasting.

Amanda (impatiently). Why are you trembling?
Laura. Mother, you've made me so nervous!
Amanda. How have I made you nervous?
Laura. By all this fuss! You make it seem so important!
Amanda. I don't understand you, Laura. You couldn't be satisfied with just sitting home, and yet whenever I try to arrange something for you, you seem to resist it. *(She gets up.)* Now take a look at yourself. No, wait! Wait just a moment — I have an idea!
Laura. What is it now?

Amanda produces two powder puffs which she wraps in hand-kerchiefs and stuffs in Laura's bosom.

Laura. Mother, what are you doing?
Amanda. They call them "Gay Deceivers"!
Laura. I won't wear them!
Amanda. You will!
Laura. Why should I?
Amanda. Because, to be painfully honest, your chest is flat.
Laura. You make it seem like we were setting a trap.
Amanda. All pretty girls are a trap, a pretty trap, and men expect them to be. (**Legend: "A Pretty Trap."**) Now look at yourself, young lady. This is the prettiest you will ever be! I've got to fix myself now! You're going to be surprised by your mother's appearance! *(She crosses through portieres, humming gaily.)*

Laura moves slowly to the long mirror and stares solemnly at herself.

A wind blows the white curtains inward in a slow, graceful motion and with a faint, sorrowful sighing.

Amanda (off stage). It isn't dark enough yet. *(She turns slowly before the mirror with a troubled look.)*

(**Legend On Screen: "This Is My Sister: Celebrate Her With Strings!" Music.**)

Amanda (laughing, off). I'm going to show you something. I'm going to make a spectacular appearance!
Laura. What is it, mother?
Amanda. Possess your soul in patience — you will see! Something I've resurrected from that old trunk! Styles haven't changed so terribly much after all. . . . *(She parts the portieres.)* Now just look at your mother! *(She wears a girlish frock of yellowed voile with a blue silk sash. She carries a bunch of jonquils — the legend of her youth is nearly revived. Feverishly.)* This is the dress in which I led the cotillion. Won the cakewalk twice at Sunset Hill, wore one spring to the Governor's ball in Jackson! See how I sashayed around the ballroom, Laura? *(She raises her skirt and does a mincing step around the room.)* I wore it on Sundays for my gentlemen callers! I had it on the day I met your father — I had malaria fever all that spring. The change of climate from East Tennessee to the Delta — weakened resistance — I had a little temperature all the time — not enough to be serious — just enough to make me restless and giddy! Invitations poured in — parties all

over the Delta! — "Stay in bed," said Mother, "you have fever!" — but I just wouldn't. — I took quinine but kept on going, going! — Evenings, dances! — Afternoons, long, long rides! Picnics — lovely! — So lovely, that country in May. — All lacy with dogwood, literally flooded with jonquils! — That was the spring I had the craze for jonquils. Jonquils became an absolute obsession. Mother said, "Honey, there's no more room for jonquils." And still I kept bringing in more jonquils. Whenever, wherever I saw them, I'd say, "Stop! Stop! I see jonquils!" I made the young men help me gather the jonquils! It was a joke, Amanda and her jonquils! Finally there were no more vases to hold them, every available space was filled with jonquils. No vases to hold them? All right, I'll hold them myself! And then I — (*She stops in front of the picture.*) (**Music**) met your father! Malaria fever and jonquils and then — this — boy. . . . (*She switches on the rose-colored lamp.*) I hope they get here before it starts to rain. (*She crosses upstage and places the jonquils in bowl on table.*) I gave your brother a little extra change so he and Mr. O'Connor could take the service car home.

Laura (with altered look). What did you say his name was?

Amanda. O'Connor.

Laura. What is his first name?

Amanda. I don't remember. Oh, yes, I do. It was — Jim!

Laura sways slightly and catches hold of a chair.

(**Legend On Screen: "Not Jim!"**)

Laura (faintly). Not — Jim!

Amanda. Yes, that was it, it was Jim! I've never known a Jim that wasn't nice!

(**Music: Ominous.**)

Laura. Are you sure his name is Jim O'Connor?

Amanda. Yes. Why?

Laura. Is he the one that Tom used to know in high school?

Amanda. He didn't say so. I think he just got to know him at the warehouse.

Laura. There was a Jim O'Connor we both knew in high school — (*Then, with effort.*) If that is the one that Tom is bringing to dinner — you'll have to excuse me, I won't come to the table.

Amanda. What sort of nonsense is this?

Laura. You asked me once if I'd ever liked a boy. Don't you remember I showed you this boy's picture?

Amanda. You mean the boy you showed me in the year book?

Laura. Yes, that boy.

Amanda. Laura, Laura, were you in love with that boy?

Laura. I don't know, Mother. All I know is I couldn't sit at the table if it was him!

Amanda. It won't be him! It isn't the least bit likely. But whether it is or not, you will come to the table. You will not be excused.

Laura. I'll have to be, Mother.

Amanda. I don't intend to humor your silliness, Laura. I've had too much from you and your brother, both! So just sit down and compose yourself till they come. Tom has forgotten his key so you'll have to let them in, when they arrive.

Laura (panicky). Oh, Mother — *you* answer the door!

Amanda (lightly). I'll be in the kitchen — busy!

Laura. Oh, Mother, please answer the door, don't make me do it!

Amanda (crossing into kitchenette). I've got to fix the dressing for the salmon. Fuss, fuss — silliness! — over a gentleman caller!

Door swings shut. Laura is left alone.

(Legend: "Terror!")

She utters a low moan and turns off the lamp — sits stiffly on the edge of the sofa, knotting her fingers together.

(Legend On Screen: "The Opening Of A Door!")

Tom and Jim appear on the fire-escape steps and climb to landing. Hearing their approach, Laura rises with a panicky gesture. She retreats to the portieres.

The doorbell. Laura catches her breath and touches her throat. Low drums.

Amanda (calling). Laura, sweetheart! The door!

Laura stares at it without moving.

Jim. I think we just beat the rain.

Tom. Uh-huh. *(He rings again, nervously. Jim whistles and fishes for a cigarette.)*

Amanda (very, very gaily). Laura, that is your brother and Mr. O'Connor! Will you let them in, darling?

Laura crosses toward kitchenette door.

Laura (breathlessly). Mother — you go to the door!

Amanda steps out of kitchenette and stares furiously at Laura. She points imperiously at the door.

Laura. Please, please!

Amanda (in a fierce whisper). What is the matter with you, you silly thing?

Laura (desperately). Please, you answer it, *please!*

Amanda. I told you I wasn't going to humor you, Laura. Why have you chosen this moment to lose your mind?

Laura. Please, please, please, you go!

Amanda. You'll have to go to the door because I can't!

Laura (despairingly). I can't either!

Amanda. Why?

Laura. I'm *sick!*

Amanda. I'm sick, too — of your nonsense! Why can't you and your brother be normal people? Fantastic whims and behavior! *(Tom gives a long ring.)* Preposterous goings on! Can you give me one reason — *(Calls out lyrically.)* COMING! JUST ONE SECOND! — why should you be afraid to open a door? Now you answer it, Laura!

Laura. Oh, oh, oh . . . *(She returns through the portieres. Darts to the victrola and winds it frantically and turns it on.)*

Amanda. Laura Wingfield, you march right to that door!

Laura. Yes — yes, Mother!

A faraway, scratchy rendition of "Dardanella" softens the air and gives her strength to move through it. She slips to the door and draws it cautiously open.

Tom enters with the caller, Jim O'Connor.

Tom. Laura, this is Jim. Jim this is my sister, Laura.

Jim (stepping inside). I didn't know that Shakespeare had a sister!

Laura (retreating stiff and trembling from the door). How — how do you do?

Jim (heartily extending his hand). Okay!

Laura touches it hesitantly with hers.

Jim. Your hand's *cold,* Laura!

Laura. Yes, well — I've been playing the victrola. . . .

Jim. Must have been playing classical music on it! You ought to play a little hot swing music to warm you up!

Laura. Excuse me — I haven't finished playing the victrola. . . .

She turns awkwardly and hurries into the front room. She pauses a second by the victrola. Then catches her breath and darts through the portieres like a frightened deer.

Jim (grinning). What was the matter?

Tom. Oh — with Laura? Laura is — terribly shy.

Jim. Shy, huh? It's unusual to meet a shy girl nowadays. I don't believe you ever mentioned you had a sister.

Tom. Well, now you know. I have one. Here is the *Post Dispatch.* You want a piece of it?

Jim. Uh-huh.

Tom. What piece? The comics?

Jim. Sports! *(Glances at it.)* Ole Dizzy Dean is on his bad behavior.

Tom (disinterest). Yeah? *(Lights cigarette and crosses back to fire-escape door.)*

Jim. Where are *you* going?

Tom. I'm going out on the terrace.

Jim (goes after him). You know, Shakespeare — I'm going to sell you a bill of goods!

Tom. What goods?

Jim. A course I'm taking.

Tom. Huh?

Jim. In public speaking! You and me, we're not the warehouse type.

Tom. Thanks — that's good news. But what has public speaking got to do with it?

Jim. It fits you for — executive positions!

Tom. Awww.

Jim. I tell you it's done a helluva lot for me.

(Image: Executive At Desk.)

Tom. In what respect?

Jim. In every! Ask yourself what is the difference between you an' me and men in the office down front? Brains? — No! — Ability? — No! Then what? Just one little thing —

Tom. What is that one little thing?

Jim. Primarily it amounts to — social poise! Being able to square up to people and hold your own on any social level!

Amanda (off stage). Tom?

Tom. Yes, Mother?

Amanda. Is that you and Mr. O'Connor?

Tom. Yes, Mother.

Amanda. Well, you just make yourselves comfortable in there.

Tom. Yes, Mother.

Amanda. Ask Mr. O'Connor if he would like to wash his hands.

Jim. Aw — no — no — thank you — I took care of that at the warehouse. Tom —

Tom. Yes?

Jim. Mr. Mendoza was speaking to me about you.

Tom. Favorably?

Jim. What do you think?
Tom. Well —
Jim. You're going to be out of a job if you don't wake up.
Tom. I am waking up —
Jim. You show no signs.
Tom. The signs are interior.

(Image On Screen: The Sailing Vessel With Jolly Roger Again.)

Tom. I'm planning to change. *(He leans over the rail speaking with quiet exhilaration. The incandescent marquees and signs of the first-run movie houses light his face from across the alley. He looks like a voyager.)* I'm right at the point of committing myself to a future that doesn't include the warehouse and Mr. Mendoza or even a night-school course in public speaking.
Jim. What are you gassing about?
Tom. I'm tired of the movies.
Jim. Movies!
Tom. Yes, movies! Look at them —*(A wave toward the marvels of Grand Avenue.)* All of those glamorous people — having adventures — hogging it all, gobbling the whole thing up! You know what happens? People go to the *movies* instead of *moving!* Hollywood characters are supposed to have all the adventures for everybody in America, while everybody in America sits in a dark room and watches them have them! Yes, until there's a war. That's when adventure becomes available to the masses! *Everyone's* dish, not only Gable's! Then the people in the dark room come out of the dark room to have some adventures themselves — Goody, goody — It's our turn now, to go to the South Sea Island — to make a safari — to be exotic, far-off — But I'm not patient. I don't want to wait till then. I'm tired of the *movies* and I am *about* to *move!*
Jim (incredulously). Move?
Tom. Yes.
Jim. When?
Tom. Soon!
Jim. Where? Where?

(Theme Three: Music Seems To Answer The Question, While Tom Thinks It Over. He Searches Among His Pockets.)

Tom. I'm starting to boil inside. I know I seem dreamy, but inside — well, I'm boiling! Whenever I pick up a shoe, I shudder a little

thinking how short life is and what I am doing! — Whatever that
means. I know it doesn't mean shoes — except as something to
wear on a traveler's feet! *(Finds paper.)* Look —
Jim. What?
Tom. I'm a member.
Jim (reading). The Union of Merchant Seamen.
Tom. I paid my dues this month, instead of the light bill.
Jim. You will regret it when they turn the lights off.
Tom. I won't be here.
Jim. How about your mother?
Tom. I'm like my father. The bastard son of a bastard! See how he
grins? And he's been absent going on sixteen years!
Jim. You're just talking, you drip. How does your mother feel about
it?
Tom. Shhh — Here comes Mother! Mother is not acquainted with
my plans!
Amanda (enters portieres). Where are you all?
Tom. On the terrace, Mother.

*They start inside. She advances to them. Tom is distinctly
shocked at her appearance. Even Jim blinks a little. He is making
his first contact with girlish Southern vivacity and in spite of the
night-school course in public speaking is somewhat thrown off
the beam by the unexpected outlay of social charm.*

*Certain responses are attempted by Jim but are swept aside by
Amanda's gay laughter and chatter. Tom is embarrassed but after
the first shock Jim reacts very warmly. Grins and chuckles, is
altogether won over.*

(Image: Amanda As A Girl.)

Amanda (coyly smiling, shaking her girlish ringlets). Well, well,
well, so this is Mr. O'Connor. Introductions entirely unnecessary.
I've heard so much about you from my boy. I finally said to him,
Tom — good gracious! — why don't you bring this paragon to supper? I'd like to meet this nice young man at the warehouse! —
Instead of just hearing him sing your praises so much! I don't
know why my son is so stand-offish — that's not Southern behavior! Let's sit down and — I think we could stand a little more air in
here! Tom, leave the door open. I felt a nice fresh breeze a moment ago. Where has it gone? Mmm, so warm already! And not
quite summer, even. We're going to burn up when summer really
gets started. However, we're having — we're having a very light
supper. I think light things are better fo' this time of year. The

same as light clothes are. Light clothes an' light food are what warm weather calls fo'. You know our blood gets so thick during th' winter — it takes a while fo' us to *adjust* ou'selves! — when the season changes . . . It's come so quick this year. I wasn't prepared. All of a sudden — heavens! Already summer! — I ran to the trunk an' pulled out this light dress — Terribly old! Historical almost! But feels so good — so good an' co-ol, y'know. . . .

Tom. Mother —

Amanda. Yes, honey?

Tom. How about — supper?

Amanda. Honey, you go ask Sister if supper is ready! You know that Sister is in full charge of supper! Tell her you hungry boys are waiting for it. *(To Jim.)* Have you met Laura?

Jim. She —

Amanda. Let you in? Oh, good, you've met already! It's rare for a girl as sweet an' pretty as Laura to be domestic! But Laura is, thank heavens, not only pretty but also very domestic. I'm not at all. I never was a bit. I never could make a thing but angel-food cake. Well, in the South we had so many servants. Gone, gone, gone. All vestiges of gracious living! Gone completely! I wasn't prepared for what the future brought me. All of my gentlemen callers were sons of planters and so of course I assumed that I would be married to one and raise my family on a large piece of land with plenty of servants. But man proposes — and woman accepts the proposal! — To vary that old, old saying a little bit — I married no planter! I married a man who worked for the telephone company! — that gallantly smiling gentleman over there! *(Points to the picture.)* A telephone man who — fell in love with long-distance! — Now he travels and I don't even know where! — But what am I going on for about my — tribulations? Tell me yours — I hope you don't have any! Tom?

Tom (returning). Yes, Mother?

Amanda. Is supper nearly ready?

Tom. It looks to me like supper is on the table.

Amanda. Let me look — *(She rises prettily and looks through portieres.)* Oh, lovely — But where is Sister?

Tom. Laura is not feeling well and she says that she thinks she'd better not come to the table.

Amanda. What? — Nonsense! — Laura? Oh, Laura!

Laura (off stage, faintly). Yes, Mother.

Amanda. You really must come to the table. We won't be seated until you come to the table! Come in, Mr. O'Connor. You sit over there and I'll — Laura? Laura Wingfield! You're keeping us waiting, honey! We can't say grace until you come to the table!

The back door is pushed weakly open and Laura comes in. She is obviously quite faint, her lips trembling, her eyes wide and staring. She moves unsteadily toward the table.

(Legend: "Terror!")

Outside a summer storm is coming abruptly. The white curtains billow inward at the windows and there is a sorrowful murmur and deep blue dusk.
    Laura suddenly stumbles — She catches at a chair with a faint moan.

Tom. Laura!
Amanda. Laura! *(There is a clap of thunder.)* (Legend: "Ah!") *(Despairingly.)* Why, Laura, you *are* sick, darling! Tom, help your sister into the living room, dear! Sit in the living room, Laura — rest on the sofa. Well! *(To the gentleman caller.)* Standing over the hot stove made her ill! — I told her that it was just too warm this evening, but — *(Tom comes back in. Laura is on the sofa.)* Is Laura all right now?
Tom. Yes.
Amanda. What *is* that? Rain? A nice cool rain has come up! *(She gives the gentleman caller a frightened look.)* I think we may — have grace — now . . . *(Tom looks at her stupidly.)* Tom, honey — you say grace!
Tom. Oh . . . "For these and all thy mercies — " *(They bow their heads, Amanda stealing a nervous glance at Jim. In the living room Laura, stretched on the sofa, clenches her hand to her lips, to hold back a shuddering sob.)* God's Holy Name be praised —

(The Scene Dims Out.)

SCENE VII

(A Souvenir.)

Half an hour later. Dinner is just being finished in the upstage area which is concealed by the drawn portieres.
    As the curtain rises Laura is still huddled upon the sofa, her feet drawn under her, her head resting on a pale blue pillow, her eyes wide and mysteriously watchful. The new floor lamp with its shade of rose-colored silk gives a soft, becoming light to her face, bringing out the fragile, unearthly prettiness which usually escapes attention. There is a steady murmur of rain, but it is slack-

ening and stops soon after the scene begins; the air outside be-
comes pale and luminous as the moon breaks out.

A moment after the curtain rises, the lights in both rooms
flicker and go out.

Jim. Hey, there, Mr. Light Bulb!

Amanda laughs nervously.

(Legend: "Suspension Of A Public Service.")

Amanda. Where was Moses when the lights went out? Ha-ha. Do you
know the answer to that one, Mr. O'Connor?

Jim. No, Ma'am, what's the answer?

Amanda. In the dark! (*Jim laughs appreciatively.*) Everybody sit
still. I'll light the candles. Isn't it lucky we have them on the
table? Where's a match? Which of you gentlemen can provide a
match?

Jim. Here.

Amanda. Thank you, sir.

Jim. Not at all, Ma'am!

Amanda. I guess the fuse has burnt out. Mr. O'Connor, can you tell a
burnt-out fuse? I know I can't and Tom is a total loss when it comes
to mechanics. (**Sound: Getting Up: Voices Recede A Little To
Kitchenette.**) Oh, be careful you don't bump into something. We
don't want our gentleman caller to break his neck. Now wouldn't
that be a fine howdy-do?

Jim. Ha-ha! Where is the fuse-box?

Amanda. Right here next to the stove. Can you see anything?

Jim. Just a minute.

Amanda. Isn't electricity a mysterious thing? Wasn't it Benjamin
Franklin who tied a key to a kite? We live in such a mysterious
universe, don't we? Some people say that science clears up all the
mysteries for us. In my opinion it only creates more! Have you
found it yet?

Jim. No, Ma'am. All these fuses look okay to me.

Amanda. Tom!

Tom. Yes, Mother?

Amanda. That light bill I gave you several days ago. The one I told
you we got the notices about?

Tom. Oh. — Yeah.

(Legend: "Ha!")

Amanda. You didn't neglect to pay it by any chance?

Tom. Why, I —

Amanada. Didn't! I might have known it!

Jim. Shakespeare probably wrote a poem on that light bill, Mrs. Wingfield.

Amanda. I might have know better than to trust him with it! There's such a high price for negligence in this world!

Jim. Maybe the poem will win a ten-dollar prize.

Amanda. We'll just have to spend the remainder of the evening in the nineteenth century, before Mr. Edison made the Mazda lamp!

Jim. Candlelight is my favorite kind of light.

Amanda. That shows you're romantic! But that's no excuse for Tom. Well, we got through dinner. Very considerate of them to let us get through dinner before they plunged us into everlasting darkness, wasn't it, Mr. O'Connor?

Jim. Ha-ha!

Amanda. Tom, as a penalty for your carelessness you can help me with the dishes.

Jim. Let me give you a hand.

Amanda. Indeed you will not!

Jim. I ought to be good for something.

Amanda. Good for something? *(Her tone is rhapsodic.) You?* Why, Mr. O'Connor, nobody, *nobody's* given me this much entertainment in years — as you have!

Jim. Aw, now, Mrs. Wingfield!

Amanda. I'm not exaggerating, not one bit! But Sister is all by her lonesome. You go keep her company in the parlor! I'll give you this lovely old candelabrum that used to be on the altar at the church of the Heavenly Rest. It was melted a little out of shape when the church burnt down. Lightning struck it one spring. Gypsy Jones was holding a revival at the time and he intimated that the church was destroyed because the Episcopalians gave card parties.

Jim. Ha-ha.

Amanda. And how about coaxing Sister to drink a little wine? I think it would be good for her! Can you carry both at once?

Jim. Sure. I'm Superman!

Amanda. Now, Thomas, get into this apron!

The door of kitchenette swings closed on Amanda's gay laughter; the flickering light approaches the portieres.

    Laura sits up nervously as he enters. Her speech at first is low and breathless from the almost intolerable strain of being alone with a stranger.

(The Legend: "I Don't Suppose You Remember Me At All!")

*In her first speeches in this scene, before Jim's warmth overcomes
her paralyzing shyness, Laura's voice is thin and breathless as
though she has run up a steep flight of stairs.*
*Jim's attitude is gently humorous. In playing this scene it
should be stressed that while the incident is apparently unimportant, it is to Laura the climax of her secret life.*

Jim. Hello, there, Laura.
Laura *(faintly).* Hello. *(She clears her throat.)*
Jim. How are you feeling now? Better?
Laura. Yes. Yes, thank you.
Jim. This is for you. A little dandelion wine. *(He extends it toward
her with extravagant gallantry.)*
Laura. Thank you.
Jim. Drink it — but don't get drunk! *(He laughs heartily. Laura
takes the glass uncertainly; laughs shyly.)* Where shall I set the
candles?
Laura. Oh — oh, anywhere . . .
Jim. How about here on the floor? Any objections?
Laura. No.
Jim. I'll spread a newspaper under to catch the drippings. I like to sit
on the floor. Mind if I do?
Laura. Oh, no.
Jim. Give me a pillow?
Laura. What?
Jim. A pillow!
Laura. Oh . . . *(Hands him one quickly.)*
Jim. How about you? Don't you like to sit on the floor?
Laura. Oh — yes.
Jim. Why don't you , then?
Laura. I — will.
Jim. Take a pillow! *(Laura does. Sits on the other side of the candela-
brum. Jim crosses his legs and smiles engagingly at her.)* I can't
hardly see you sitting way over there.
Laura. I can — see you.
Jim. I know, but that's not fair, I'm in the limelight. *(Laura moves
her pillow closer.)* Good! Now I can see you! Comfortable?
Laura. Yes.
Jim. So am I. Comfortable as a cow. Will you have some gum?
Laura. No, thank you.
Jim. I think that I will induge, with your permission. *(Musingly un-
wraps it and holds it up.)* Think of the fortune made by the guy
that invented the first piece of chewing gum. Amazing, huh? The
Wrigley Building is one of the sights of Chicago. — I saw it sum-

mer before last when I went up to the Century of Progress. Did
you take in the Century of Progess?
Laura. No, I didn't.
Jim. Well, it was quite a wonderful exposition. What impressed me
most was the Hall of Science. Gives you an idea of what the future
will be in America, even more wonderful than the present time is!
(Pause. Smiling at her.) Your brother tells me you're shy. Is that
right, Laura?
Laura. I — don't know.
Jim. I judge you to be an old-fashioned type of girl. Well, I think
that's a pretty good type to be. Hope you don't think I'm being to
personal — do you?
Laura (hastily, out of embarrassment). I believe I *will* take a piece
of gum, if you — don't mind. *(Clearing her throat.)* Mr.
O'Connor, have you — kept up with your singing?
Jim. Singing? Me?
Laura. Yes. I remember what a beautiful voice you had.
Jim. When did you hear me sing?

(Voice Offstage In The Pause.)

Voice (offstage).
   O blow, ye winds, heigh-ho,
   A-roving I will go!
   I'm off to my love
   With a boxing glove —
   Ten thousand miles away!

Jim. You say you've heard me sing?
Laura. Oh, yes! Yes, very often . . . I — don't suppose you remember
me — at all?
Jim (smiling doubtfully). You know I have an idea I've seen you
before. I had that idea soon as you opened the door. It seemed
almost like I was about to remember your name. But the name that
I started to call you — wasn't a name! And so I stopped myself
before I said it.
Laura. Wasn't it — Blue Roses?
Jim (springs up, grinning). Blue Roses! My gosh, yes — Blue Roses!
That's what I had on my tongue when you opened the door! Isn't it
funny what tricks your memory plays? I didn't connect you with
the high school somehow or other. But that's where it was; it was
high school. I didn't even know you were Shakespeare's sister!
Gosh, I'm sorry.
Laura. I didn't expect you to. You — barely knew me!

Jim. But we did have a speaking acquaintance, huh?

Laura. Yes, we — spoke to each other.

Jim. When did you recognize me?

Laura. Oh, right away!

Jim. Soon as I came in the door?

Laura. When I heard your name I thought it was probably you. I knew that Tom used to know you a little in high school. So when you came in the door — Well, then I was — sure.

Jim. Why didn't you *say* something, then?

Laura (breathlessly). I didn't know what to say, I was — too surprised!

Jim. For goodness' sakes! You know, this sure is funny!

Laura. Yes! Yes, isn't it, though . . .

Jim. Didn't we have a class in something together?

Laura. Yes, we did.

Jim. What class was that?

Laura. It was — singing — Chorus!

Jim. Aw!

Laura. I sat across the aisle from you in the Aud.

Jim. Aw.

Laura. Mondays, Wednesdays and Fridays.

Jim. Now I remember — you always came in late.

Laura. Yes, it was so hard for me, getting upstairs. I had that brace on my leg — it clumped so loud!

Jim. I never heard any clumping.

Laura (wincing at the recollection). To me it sounded like — thunder!

Jim. Well, well, well. I never even noticed.

Laura. And everybody was seated before I came in. I had to walk in front of all those people. My seat was in the back row. I had to go clumping all the way up the aisle with everyone watching!

Jim. You shouldn't have been self-conscious.

Laura. I know, but I was. It was always such a relief when the singing started.

Jim. Aw, yes, I've placed you now! I used to call you Blue Roses. How was it that I got started calling you that?

Laura. I was out of school a little while with pleurosis. When I came back you asked me what was the matter. I said I had pleurosis — you thought I said Blue Roses. That's what you always called me after that!

Jim. I hope you didn't mind.

Laura. Oh, no — I liked it. You see, I wasn't acquainted with many — people. . . .

Jim. As I remember you sort of stuck by yourself.

Laura. I — I — never had much luck at — making friends.

Jim. I don't see why you wouldn't.

Laura. Well, I — started out badly.

Jim. You mean being —

Laura. Yes, it sort of — stood between me —

Jim. You shouldn't have let it!

Laura. I know, but it did, and —

Jim. You were shy with people!

Laura. I tried not to be but never could —

Jim. Overcome it?

Laura. No, I — I never could!

Jim. I guess being shy is something you have to work out of kind of gradually.

Laura (sorrowfully). Yes — I guess it —

Jim. Takes time!

Laura. Yes —

Jim. People are not so dreadful when you know them. That's what you have to remember! And everybody has problems, not just you, but practically everybody has got some problems. You think of yourself as having the only problems, as being the only one who is disappointed. But just look around you and you will see lots of people as disappointed as you are. For instance, I hoped when I was going to high school that I would be further along at this time, six years later, than I am now — You remember that wonderful write-up I had in *The Torch?*

Laura. Yes! *(She rises and crosses to table.)*

Jim. It said I was bound to succeed in anything I went into! *(Laura returns with the annual.)* Holy Jeez! *The Torch!* (*He accepts it reverently. They smile across it with mutual wonder. Laura crouches beside him and they begin to turn through it. Laura's shyness is dissolving in his warmth.*)

Laura. Here you are in *Pirates of Penzance!*

Jim (wistfully). I sang the baritone lead in that operetta.

Laura (rapidly). So — *beautifully!*

Jim (protesting). Aw —

Laura. Yes, yes — beautifully — beautifully!

Jim. You heard me?

Laura. All three times!

Jim. No!

Laura. Yes!

Jim. All three performances?

Laura (looking down). Yes.

Jim. Why?

Laura. I — wanted to ask you to — autograph my program.

Jim. Why didn't you ask me to?

Laura. You were always surrounded by your own friends so much that I never had a chance to.

Jim. You should have just —

Laura. Well, I — thought you might think I was —

Jim. Thought I might think you was — what?

Laura. Oh —

Jim (with reflective relish). I was beleaguered by females in those days.

Laura. You were terribly popular!

Jim. Yeah —

Laura. You had such a — friendly way —

Jim. I was spoiled in high school.

Laura. Everybody — liked you!

Jim. Including you?

Laura. I — yes, I — I did, too —*(She gently closes the book in her lap.)*

Jim. Well, well, well! — Give me that program, Laura. *(She hands it to him. He signs it with a flourish.)* There you are — better late than never!

Laura. Oh, I — what a — surprise!

Jim. My signature isn't worth very much right now. But some day — maybe — it will increase in value! Being disappointed is one thing and being discouraged is something else. I am disappointed but I'm not discouraged. I'm twenty-three years old. How old are you?

Laura. I'll be twenty-four in June.

Jim. That's not old age!

Laura. No, but —

Jim. You finished high school?

Laura (with difficulty). I didn't go back.

Jim. You mean you dropped out?

Laura. I made bad grades in my final examinations. *(She rises and replaces the book and the program. Her voice strained.)* How is — Emily Meisenbach getting along?

Jim. Oh, that kraut-head!

Laura. Why do you call her that?

Jim. That's what she was.

Laura. You're not still — going with her?

Jim. I never see her.

Laura. It said in the Personal Section that you were — engaged!

Jim. I know, but I wasn't impressed by that — propaganda!

Laura. It wasn't — the truth?
Jim. Only in Emily's optimistic opinion!
Laura. Oh —

(Legend: "What Have You Done Since High School?")

Jim lights a cigarette and leans indolently back on his elbows smiling at Laura with a warmth and charm which light her inwardly with altar candles. She remains by the table and turns in her hands a piece of glass to cover her tumult.

Jim (after several reflective puffs on a cigarette). What have you done since high school? *(She seems not to hear him.)* Huh? *(Laura looks up.)* I said what have you done since high school, Laura?
Laura. Nothing much.
Jim. You must have been doing something these six long years.
Laura. Yes.
Jim. Well, then, such as what?
Laura. I took a business course at business college —
Jim. How did that work out?
Laura. Well, not very — well — I had to drop out, it gave me — indigestion —

Jim laughs gently.

Jim. What are you doing now?
Laura. I don't do anything — much. Oh, please don't think I sit around doing nothing! My glass collection takes up a good deal of my time. Glass is something you have to take good care of.
Jim. What did you say — about glass?
Laura. Collection I said — I have one — *(She clears her throat and turns away again, acutely shy).*
Jim (abruptly). You know what I judge to be the trouble with you? Inferiority complex! Know what that is? That's what they call it when someone low-rates himself! I understand it because I had it, too. Although my case was not so aggravated as yours seems to be. I had it until I took up public speaking, developed my voice, and learned that I had an aptitude for science. Before that time I never thought of myself as being outstanding in any way whatsoever! Now I've never made a regular study of it, but I have a friend who says I can analyze people better than doctors that make a profession of it. I don't claim that to be necessarily true, but I can sure guess a person's psychology, Laura! *(Takes out his gum.)* Excuse me, Laura. I always take it out when the flavor is gone. I'll use this scrap of paper to wrap it in. I know how it is to get it stuck on a

shoe. Yep — that's what I judge to be your principal trouble. A lack of confidence in yourself as a person. You don't have the proper amount of faith in yourself. I'm basing that fact on a number of your remarks and also on certain observations I've made. For instance that clumping you thought was so awful in high school. You say that you even dreaded to walk into class. You see what you did? You dropped out of school, you gave up an education because of a clump, which as far as I know was practically non-existent! A little physical defect is what you have. Hardly noticeable even! Magnified thousands of times by imagination! You know what my strong advice to you is? Think of yourself as *superior* in some way!

Laura. In what way would I think?

Jim. Why, man alive, Laura! Just look about you a little. What do you see? A world full of common people! All of 'em born and all of 'em going to die! Which of them has one-tenth of your good points! Or mine! Or anyone else's, as far as that goes — Gosh! Everybody excels in some one thing. Some in many! *(Unconsciously glances at himself in the mirror.)* All you've got to do is discover in *what!* Take me, for instance. *(He adusts his tie at the mirror.)* My interest happens to lie in electro-dynamics. I'm taking a course in radio engineering at night school, Laura, on top of a fairly responsible job at the warehouse. I'm taking that course and studying public speaking.

Laura. Ohhhh.

Jim. Because I believe in the future of television! *(Turning back to her.)* I wish to be ready to go up right along with it. Therefore I'm planning to get in on the ground floor. In fact, I've already made the right connections and all that remains is for the industry itself to get under way! Full steam — *(His eyes are starry.)* Knowledge — Zzzzzp! *Money* — Zzzzzzp! — *Power!* That's the cycle democracy is built on! *(His attitude is convincingly dynamic. Laura stares at him, even her shyness eclipsed in her absolute wonder. He suddenly grins.)* I guess you think I think a lot of myself!

Laura. No — o-o-o, I —

Jim. Now how about you? Isn't there something you take more interest in than anything else?

Laura. Well, I do — as I said — have my — glass collection —

A peal of girlish laughter from the kitchen.

Jim. I'm not right sure I know what you're talking about. What kind of glass is it?

Laura. Little articles of it, they're ornaments mostly! Most of them are little animals made out of glass, the tiniest little animals in the world. Mother calls them a glass menagerie! Here's an example of one, if you'd like to see it! This one is one of the oldest. It's nearly thirteen. *(He stretches out his hand.)* **(Music: "The Glass Menagerie.")** Oh, be careful — if you breathe, it breaks!

Jim. I'd better not take it. I'm pretty clumsy with things.

Laura. Go on, I trust you with him! *(Places it in his palm.)* There now — you're holding him gently! Hold him over the light, he loves the light! You see how the light shines through him?

Jim. It sure does shine!

Laura. I shouldn't be partial, but he is my favorite one.

Jim. What kind of a thing is this one supposed to be?

Laura. Haven't you noticed the single horn on his forehead?

Jim. A unicorn, huh?

Laura. Mmm-hmmm!

Jim. Unicorns, aren't they extinct in the modern world?

Laura. I know!

Jim. Poor little fellow, he must feel sort of lonesome.

Laura (smiling). Well, if he does he doesn't complain about it. He stays on a shelf with some horses that don't have horns and all of them seem to get along nicely together.

Jim. How do you know?

Laura (lightly). I haven't heard any arguments among them!

Jim (grinning). No arguments, huh? Well, that's a pretty good sign! Where shall I set him?

Laura. Put him on the table. They all like a change of scenery once in a while!

Jim (stretching). Well, well, well, well — Look how big my shadow is when I stretch!

Laura. Oh, oh, yes — it stretches across the ceiling!

Jim (crossing to door). I think it's stopped raining. *(Opens fire-escape door.)* Where does the music come from?

Laura. From the Paradise Dance Hall across the alley.

Jim. How about cutting the rug a little, Miss Wingfield?

Laura. Oh, I —

Jim. Or is your program filled up? Let me have a look at it. *(Grasps imaginary card.)* Why, every dance is taken! I'll just have to scratch some out. **(Waltz Music: "La Golondrina.")** Ahhh, a waltz! *(He executes some sweeping turns by himself, then holds his arms toward Laura.)*

Laura (breathlessly). I — can't dance!

Jim. There you go, that inferiority stuff!

Laura. I've never danced in my life!

Jim. Come on, try!

Laura. Oh, but I'd step on you!

Jim. I'm not made out of glass.

Laura. How — how — how do we start?

Jim. Just leave it to me. You hold your arms out a little.

Laura. Like this?

Jim. A little bit higher. Right. Now don't tighten up, that's the main thing about it — relax.

Laura (laughing breathlessly). It's hard not to.

Jim. Okay.

Laura. I'm afraid you can't budge me.

Jim. What do you bet I can't? *(He swings her into motion.)*

Laura. Goodness, yes, you can!

Jim. Let yourself go, now, Laura, just let yourself go.

Laura. I'm —

Jim. Come on!

Laura. Trying!

Jim. Not so stiff — Easy does it!

Laura. I know but I'm —

Jim. Loosen th' backbone! There now, that's a lot better.

Laura. Am I?

Jim. Lots, lots better! *(He moves her about the room in a clumsy waltz.)*

Laura. Oh, my!

Jim. Ha-ha!

Laura. Goodness, yes you can!

Jim. Ha-ha-ha! *(They suddenly bump into the table. Jim stops.)* What did we hit on?

Laura. Table.

Jim. Did something fall off it? I think —

Laura. Yes.

Jim. I hope that it wasn't the little glass horse with the horn!

Laura. Yes.

Jim. Aw, aw, aw. Is it broken?

Laura. Now it is just like all the other horses.

Jim. It's lost its —

Laura. Horn! It doesn't matter. Maybe it's a blessing in disguise.

Jim. You'll never forgive me. I bet that that was your favorite piece of glass.

Laura. I don't have favorites much. It's no tragedy, Freckles. Glass breaks so easily. No matter how careful you are. The traffic jars the shelves and things fall off them.

Jim. Still I'm awfully sorry that I was the cause.

Laura (smiling). I'll just imagine he had an operation. The horn was

removed to make him feel less — freakish! *(They both laugh.)*
Now he will feel more at home with the other horses, the ones that
don't have horns . . .

Jim. Ha-ha, that's very funny! *(Suddenly serious.)* I'm glad to see that
you have a sense of humor. You know — you're — well — very
different! Surprisingly different from anyone else I know! *(His
voice becomes soft and hesitant with a genuine feeling.)* Do you
mind me telling you that? *(Laura is abashed beyond speech.)* You
make me feel sort of — I don't know how to put it! I'm usually
pretty good at expressing things, but — This is something that I
don't know how to say! *(Laura touches her throat and clears it —
turns the broken unicorn in her hands.) (Even softer.)* Has anyone
ever told you that you were pretty? **(Pause: Music.)** *(Laura looks
up slowly, with wonder, and shakes her head.)* Well, you are! In a
very different way from anyone else. And all the nicer because of
the difference, too. *(His voice becomes low and husky. Laura
turns away, nearly faint with the novelty of her emotions.)* I wish
that you were my sister. I'd teach you to have some confidence in
yourself. The different people are not like other people, but being
different is nothing to be ashamed of. Because other people are
not such wonderful people. They're one hundred times one thousand. You're one times one! They walk all over the earth. You
just stay here. They're common as — weeds, but — you — well,
you're — *Blue Roses!*

(Image On Screen: Blue Roses.)

(Music Changes.)

Laura. But blue is wrong for — roses . . .
Jim. It's right for you — You're — pretty!
Laura. In what respect am I pretty?
Jim. In all respects — believe me! Your eyes — your hair — are
pretty! Your hands are pretty! *(He catches hold of her hand.)* You
think I'm making this up because I'm invited to dinner and have to
be nice. Oh, I could do that! I could put on an act for you, Laura,
and say lots of things without being very sincere. But this time I
am. I'm talking to you sincerely. I happened to notice you had this
inferiority complex that keeps you from feeling comfortable with
people. Somebody needs to build your confidence up and make
you proud instead of shy and turning away and — blushing —
Somebody ought to — Ought to — *kiss* you, Laura! *(His hand
slips slowly up her arm to her shoulder.)* **(Music Swells Tumultuously.)** *(He suddenly turns her about and kisses her on the lips.*

When he releases her Laura sinks on the sofa with a bright, dazed look. Jim backs away and fishes in his pocket for a cigarette.) **(Legend On Screen: "Souvenir.")** Stumble-john! *(He lights the cigarette, avoiding her look. There is a peal of girlish laughter from Amanda in the kitchen. Laura slowly raises and opens her hand. It still contains the little broken glass animal. She looks at it with a tender, bewildered expression.)* Stumble-john! I shouldn't have done that — That was way off the beam. You don't smoke, do you? *(She looks up, smiling, not hearing the question. He sits beside her a little gingerly. She looks at him speechlessly — waiting. He coughs decorously and moves a little farther aside as he considers the situation and senses her feelings, dimly, with perturbation. Gently.)* Would you — care for a — mint? *(She doesn't seem to hear him but her look grows brighter even.)* Peppermint — Life Saver? My pocket's a regular drug store — wherever I go . . .*(He pops a mint in his mouth. Then gulps and decides to make a clean breast of it. He speaks slowly and gingerly.)* Laura, you know, if I had a sister like you, I'd do the same thing as Tom. I'd bring out fellows — introduce her to them. The right type of boys of a type to — appreciate her. Only — well — he made a mistake about me. Maybe I've got no call to be saying this. That may not have been the idea in having me over. But what if it was? There's nothing wrong about that. The only trouble is that in my case — I'm not in a situation to — do the right thing. I can't take down your number and say I'll phone. I can't call up next week and — ask for a date. I thought I had better explain the situation in case you misunderstood it and — hurt your feelings. . . .*(Pause. Slowly, very slowly, Laura's look changes, her eyes returning slowly from his to the ornament in her palm.)*

Amanda utters another gay laugh in the kitchen.

Laura (faintly). You — won't — call again?
Jim. No, Laura, I can't. *(He rises from the sofa.)* As I was just explaining, I've — got strings on me, Laura, I've — been going steady! I go out all the time with a girl named Betty. She's a home-girl like you, and Catholic, and Irish, and in a great many ways we — get along fine. I met her last summer on a moonlight boat trip up the river to Alton, on the *Majestic.* Well — right away from the start it was — love! **(Legend: Love!)** *(Laura sways slightly forward and grips the arm of the sofa. He fails to notice, now enrapt in his own comfortable being.)* Being in love has made a new man of me! *(Leaning stiffly forward, clutching the arm of the sofa, Laura struggles visibly with her storm. But Jim is oblivious, she is a long way off.)* The power of love is really pretty tremendous! Love is

something that — changes the whole world, Laura! *(The storm abates a little and Laura leans back. He notices her again.)* It happened that Betty's aunt took sick, she got a wire and had to go to Centralia. So Tom — when he asked me to dinner — I naturally just accepted the invitation, not knowing that you —that he — that I — *(He stops awkwardly.)* Huh — I'm a stumble-john! *(He flops back on the sofa. The holy candles in the altar of Laura's face have been snuffed out! There is a look of almost infinite desolation. Jim glances at her uneasily.)* I wish that you would — say something. *(She bites her lip which was trembling and then bravely smiles. She opens her hand again on the broken glass ornament. Then she gently takes his hand and raises it level with her own. She carefully places the unicorn in the palm of his hand, then pushes his fingers closed upon it.)* What are you — doing that for? You want me to have him? — Laura? *(She nods.)* What for?

Laura. A — souvenir . . .

She rises unsteadily and crouches beside the victrola to wind it up.

(Legend On Screen: "Things Have A Way Of Turning Out So Badly.")

(Or Image: "Gentleman Caller Waving Good-bye! — Gaily.")

At this moment Amanda rushes brightly back in the front room. She bears a pitcher of fruit punch in an old-fashioned cut-glass pitcher and a plate of macaroons. The plate has a gold border and poppies painted on it.

Amanda. Well, well, well! Isn't the air delightful after the shower? I've made you children a little liquid refreshment. *(Turns gaily to the gentleman caller.)* Jim, do you know that song about lemonade?

"Lemonade, lemonade
Made in the shade and stirred with a spade —
Good enough for any old maid!"

Jim (uneasily). Ha-ha! No — I never heard it.
Amanda. Why, Laura! You look so serious!
Jim. We were having a serious conversation.
Amanda. Good! Now you're better acquainted!
Jim (uncertainly). Ha-ha! Yes.
Amanda. You modern young people are much more serious-minded than my generation. I was so gay as a girl!
Jim. You haven't changed, Mrs. Wingfield.

Amanda. Tonight I'm rejuvenated! The gaiety of the occasion, Mr. O'Connor! *(She tosses her head with a peal of laughter. Spills lemonade.)* Oooo! I'm baptizing myself!

Jim. Here — let me —

Amanda (setting the pitcher down). There now. I discovered we had some maraschino cherries. I dumped them in, juice and all!

Jim. You shouldn't have gone to that trouble, Mrs. Wingfield.

Amanda. Trouble, trouble? Why it was loads of fun! Didn't you hear me cutting up in the kitchen? I bet your ears were burning! I told Tom how outdone with him I was for keeping you to himself so long a time! He should have brought you over much, much sooner! Well, now that you've found your way, I want you to be a very frequent caller! Not just occasional but all the time. Oh, we're going to have a lot of gay times together! I see them coming! Mmm, just breathe that air! So fresh, and the moon's so pretty! I'll skip back out — I know where my place is when young folks are having a — serious conversation!

Jim. Oh, don't go out. Mrs. Wingfield. The fact of the matter is I've got to be going.

Amanda. Going, now? You're joking! Why, it's only the shank of the evening, Mr. O'Connor!

Jim. Well, you know how it is.

Amanda. You mean you're a young workingman and have to keep workingmen's hours. We'll let you off early tonight. But only on the condition that next time you stay later. What's the best night for you? Isn't Saturday night the best night for you workingmen?

Jim. I have a couple of time-clocks to punch, Mrs. Wingfield. One at morning, another one at night!

Amanda. My, but you *are* ambitious! You work at night, too?

Jim. No, Ma'am, not work but — Betty! *(He crosses deliberately to pick up his hat. The band at the Paradise Dance Hall goes into a tender waltz.)*

Amanda. Betty? Betty? Who's — Betty! *(There is an ominous cracking sound in the sky.)*

Jim. Oh, just a girl. The girl I go steady with! *(He smiles charmingly. The sky falls.)*

(Legend: "The Sky Falls.")

Amanda (a long-drawn exhalation). Ohhhh . . . Is it a serious romance, Mr. O'Connor?

Jim. We're going to be married the second Sunday in June.

Amanda. Ohhhh — how nice! Tom didn't mention that you were engaged to be married.

Jim. The cat's not out of the bag at the warehouse yet. You know how they are. They call you Romeo and stuff like that. *(He stops at the oval mirror to put on his hat. He carefully shapes the brim and the crown to give a discreetly dashing effect.)* It's been a wonderful evening, Mrs. Winfield. I guess this is what they mean by Southern hospitality.

Amanda. It really wasn't anything at all.

Jim. I hope it don't seem like I'm rushing off. But I promised Betty I'd pick her up at the Wabash depot, an' by the time I get my jalopy down there her train'll be in. Some women are pretty upset if you keep 'em waiting.

Amanda. Yes, I know — The tyranny of women! *(Extends her hand.)* Goodbye, Mr. O'Connor. I wish you luck — and happiness — and success! All three of them, and so does Laura! — Don't you, Laura?

Laura. Yes!

Jim (taking her hand). Goodbye, Laura. I'm certainly going to treasure that souvenir. And don't you forget the good advice I gave you. *(Raises his voice to a cheery shout.)* So long, Shakespeare! Thanks again, ladies — Good night!

He grins and ducks jauntily out.

Still bravely grimacing, Amanda closes the door on the gentleman caller. Then she turns back to the room with a puzzled expression. She and Laura don't dare to face each other. Laura crouches beside the victrola to wind it.

Amanda (faintly). Things have a way of turning out so badly. I don't believe that I would play the victrola. Well, well — well — Our gentleman caller was engaged to be married! Tom!

Tom (from back). Yes, Mother?

Amanda. Come in here a minute. I want to tell you something awfully funny.

Tom (enters with macaroon and a glass of the lemonade). Has the gentleman caller gotten away already?

Amanda. The gentleman caller has made an early departure. What a wonderful joke you played on us!

Tom. How do you mean?

Amanda. You didn't mention that he was engaged to be married.

Tom. Jim? Engaged?

Amanda. That's what he just informed us.

Tom. I'll be jiggered! I didn't know about that.

Amanda. That seems very peculiar.

Tom. What's peculiar about it?

Amanda. Didn't you call him your best friend down at the warehouse?

Tom. He is, but how did I know?

Amanda. It seems extremely peculiar that you wouldn't know your best friend was going to be married!

Tom. The warehouse is where I work, not where I know things about people!

Amanda. You don't know things anywhere! You live in a dream; you manufacture illusions! *(He crosses to door.)* Where are you going?

Tom. I'm going to the movies.

Amanda. That's right, now that you've had us make such fools of ourselves. The effort, the preparations, all the expense! The new floor lamp, the rug, the clothes for Laura! All for what? To entertain some other girl's fiancé! Go to the movies, go! Don't think about us, a mother deserted, an unmarried sister who's crippled and has no job! Don't let anything interfere with your selfish pleasure! Just go, go, go — to the movies!

Tom. All right, I will! The more you shout about my selfishness to me the quicker I'll go, and I won't go to the movies!

Amanda. Go, then! Then go to the moon — you selfish dreamer!

Tom smashes his glass on the floor. He plunges out on the fire-escape, slamming the door, Laura screams — cut by door.

Dance-hall music up. Tom goes to the rail and grips it desperately, lifting his face in the chill white moonlight penetrating the narrow abyss of the alley.

(Legend On Screen: "And So Good-bye . . .")

Tom's closing speech is timed with the interior pantomime. The interior scene is played as though viewed through sound-proof glass. Amanda appears to be making a comforting speech to Laura who is huddled upon the sofa. Now that we cannot hear the mother's speech, her silliness is gone and she has dignity and tragic beauty. Laura's dark hair hides her face until at the end of the speech she lifts it to smile at her mother. Amanda's gestures are slow and graceful, almost dancelike, as she comforts the daughter. At the end of her speech she glances a moment at the father's picture — then withdraws through the portieres. At close of Tom's speech, Laura blows out the candles, ending the play.

Tom. I didn't go to the moon, I went much further — for time is the longest distance between two places — Not long after that I was fired for writing a poem on the lid of a shoe-box. I left Saint Louis.

I descended the steps of this fire-escape for a last time and followed, from then on, in my father's footsteps, attempting to find in motion what was lost in space — I traveled around a great deal. The cities swept about me like dead leaves, leaves that were brightly colored but torn away from the branches. I would have stopped, but I was pursued by something. It always came upon me unawares, taking me altogether by surprise. Perhaps it was a familiar bit of music. Perhaps it was only a piece of transparent glass — Perhaps I am walking along a street at night, in some strange city, before I have found companions. I pass the lighted window of a shop where perfume is sold. The window is filled with pieces of colored glass, tiny transparent bottles in delicate colors, like bits of a shattered rainbow. Then all at once my sister touches my shoulder. I turn around and look into her eyes . . . Oh, Laura, Laura, I tried to leave you behind me, but I am more faithful than I intended to be! I reach for a cigarette, I cross the street, I run into the movies or a bar, I buy a drink, I speak to the nearest stranger — anything that can blow your candles out! *(Laura bends over the candles.)* — for nowadays the world is lit by lightning! Blow out your candles, Laura — and so goodbye . . .

She blows the candles out.

(The Scene Dissolves.)

PRODUCTION NOTES

Being a "memory play," *The Glass Menagerie* can be presented with unusual freedom of convention. Because of its considerably delicate or tenuous material, atmospheric touches and subtleties of direction play a particularly important part. Expressionism and all other unconventional techniques in drama have only one valid aim, and that is a closer approach to truth. When a play employs unconventional techniques, it is not, or certainly shouldn't be, trying to escape its responsibility of dealing with reality, or interpreting experience, but is actually or should be attempting to find a closer approach, a more penetrating and vivid expression of things as they are. The straight realistic play with its genuine frigidaire and authentic ice-cubes, its characters that speak exactly as its audience speaks, corresponds to the academic landscape and has the same virtue of a photographic likeness. Everyone should know nowadays the unimportance of the photographic in art: that truth, life, or reality is an organic thing which the poetic imagination can represent or suggest, in essence, only through transformation, through changing into other forms than those which were merely present in appearance.

These remarks are not meant as comments only on this particular play. They have to do with a conception of a new, plastic theater which must take the place of the exhausted theater of realistic conventions if the theater is to resume vitality as a part of our culture.

The Screen Device

There is *only one important difference between the original and acting version of the play* and that is the *omission* in the latter of the device which I tentatively included in my *original* script. This device was the use of a screen on which were projected magic-lantern slides bearing images or titles. I do not regret the omission of this device from the . . . Broadway production. The extraordinary power of Miss Taylor's performance made it suitable to have the utmost simplicity in the physical production. But I think it may be interesting to some readers to see how this device was conceived. So I am putting it into the published manuscript. These images and legends, projected from behind, were cast on a section of wall between the front-room and dining-room areas, which should be indistinguishable from the rest when not in use.

The purpose of this will probably be apparent. It is to give accent to certain values in each scene. Each scene contains a particular point (or several) which is structurally the most important. In an episodic play, such as this, the basic structure or narrative line may be obscured from the audience; the effect may seem fragmentary rather than architectural. This may not be the fault of the play so much as a lack of attention in the audience. The legend or image upon the screen will strengthen the effect of what is merely allusion in the writing and allow the primary point to be made more simply and lightly than if the entire responsibility were on the spoken lines. Aside from this structural value, I think the screen will have a definite emotional appeal, less definable but just as important. An imaginative producer or director may invent many other uses for this device than those indicated in the present script. In fact the possibilities of the device seem much larger to me than the instance of this play can possibly utilize.

The Music

Another extra-literary accent in this play is provided by the use of music. A single recurring tune, "The Glass Menagerie," is used to give emotional emphasis to suitable passages. This tune is like circus music, not when you are on the grounds or in the immediate vicinity of the parade, but when you are at some distance and very likely thinking of something else. It seems under those circumstances to continue almost interminably and it weaves in and out of your preoccupied consciousness; then it is the lightest, most delicate music in the world and perhaps the saddest. It expresses the surface vivacity of life with the underlying strain of immutable and inexpressible sorrow. When you look at a piece of delicately spun glass you think of two things: how beautiful it is and how easily it can be broken. Both of those ideas should be woven into the recurring tune, which dips in and out of the play as if it were carried on a wind that changes. It serves as a thread of connection and allusion between the narrator with his separate point in time and space and the subject of his story. Between each episode it returns as reference to the emotion, nostalgia, which is the first condition of the play. It is primarily Laura's music and therefore comes out most clearly when the play focuses upon her and the lovely fragility of glass which is her image.

The Lighting

The lighting in the play is not realistic. In keeping with the atmosphere of memory, the stage is dim. Shafts of light are focused on selected areas or actors, sometimes in contradistinction to what is the apparent center. For instance, in the quarrel scene between Tom and Amanda, in which Laura has no active part, the clearest pool of light is on her figure. This is also true of the supper scene. The light upon Laura should be distinct from the others, having a peculiar pristine clarity such as light used in early religious portraits of female saints or madonnas. A certain correspondence to light in religious paintings, such as El Greco's, where the figures are radiant in atmosphere that is relatively dusky, could be effectively used throughout the play. (It will also permit a more effective use of the screen.) A free, imaginative use of light can be of enormous value in giving a mobile, plastic quality to plays of a more or less static nature.

Questions

1. When produced in New York, the magic-lantern slides were omitted. Is the device an extraneous gimmick? Might it even interfere with the play, by oversimplifying and thus in a way belittling the actions?

2. What does the victrola offer to Laura? Why is the typewriter a better symbol (for the purposes of the play) than, say, a piano? After

all, Laura could have been taking piano lessons. Explain the symbolism of the unicorn, and the loss of its horn. What is Laura saying to Jim in the gesture of giving him the unicorn?

3. Laura escapes to her glass menagerie. To what do Amanda and Tom escape? How complete is Tom's escape at the end of the play?

4. What is meant at the end when Laura blows out the candles? Is she blowing out illusions? Or life? Or both?

5. Did Williams make a slip in having Amanda say Laura is "crippled" on page 945?

6. There is an implication that had Jim not been going steady he might have rescued Laura, but Jim also seems to represent (for example in his lines about money and power) the corrupt outside world that no longer values humanity. Is this a slip on Williams's part, or is it an interesting complexity?

7. On page 945 Williams says, in a stage direction, "Now that we cannot hear the mother's speech, her silliness is gone and she has dignity and tragic beauty." Is Williams simply dragging in the word "tragic" because of its prestige, or is it legitimate? "Tragedy" is often distinguished from "pathos": in the tragic, the suffering is experienced by persons who act and are in some measure responsible for their suffering; in the pathetic, the suffering is experienced by the passive and the innocent. For example, in discussing Aeschylus's *The Suppliants* (in *Greek Tragedy*), H. D. F. Kitto says: "The Suppliants are not only pathetic, as the victims of outrage, but also tragic, as the victims of their own misconceptions." Given this distinction, to what extent are Amanda and Laura tragic? Pathetic?

Arthur Miller (b. 1915)

Death of a Salesman

Certain Private Conversations in Two
Acts and a Requiem

List of Characters

Willy Loman
Linda
Biff
Happy
Bernard
The Woman
Charley
Uncle Ben
Howard Wagner
Jenny
Stanley
Miss Forsythe
Letta

Scene. *The action takes place in Willy Loman's house and yard
and in various places he visits in the New York and Boston of
today.*

ACT I

Scene: *A melody is heard, played upon a flute. It is small and
fine, telling of grass and trees and the horizon. The curtain rises.*

*Before us is the Salesman's house. We are aware of towering,
angular shapes behind it, surrounding it on all sides. Only the
blue light of the sky falls upon the house and forestage; the surrounding area shows an angry glow of orange. As more light
appears, we see a solid vault of apartment houses around the
small, fragile-seeming home. An air of the dream clings to the
place a dream rising out of reality. The kitchen at center seems
actual enough, for there is a kitchen table with three chairs, and a
refrigerator. But no other fixtures are seen. At the back of the
kitchen there is a draped entrance, which leads to the living room.
To the right of the kitchen, on a level raised two feet, is a bedroom
furnished only with a brass bedstead and a straight chair. On a*

shelf over the bed a silver athletic trophy stands. A window opens onto the apartment house at the side.

Behind the kitchen, on a level raised six and a half feet, is the boys' bedroom, at present barely visible. Two beds are dimly seen, and at the back of the room a dormer window. (This bedroom is above the unseen living room.) At the left a stairway curves up to it from the kitchen.

The entire setting is wholly or, in some places, partially transparent. The roof-line of the house is one-dimensional; under and over it we see the apartment buildings. Before the house lies an apron, curving beyond the forestage into the orchestra. This forward area serves as the back yard as well as the locale of all Willy's imaginings and of his city scenes. Whenever the action is in the present the actors observe the imaginary wall-lines, entering the house only through its door at the left. But in the scenes of the past these boundaries are broken, and characters enter or leave a room by stepping "through" a wall onto the forestage.

From the right, Willy Loman, the Salesman, enters, carrying two large sample cases. The flute plays on. He hears but is not aware of it. He is past sixty years of age, dressed quietly. Even as he crosses the stage to the doorway of the house, his exhaustion is apparent. He unlocks the door, comes into the kitchen, and thankfully lets his burden down, feeling the soreness of his palms. A word-sigh escapes his lips — it might be "Oh, boy, oh, boy." He closes the door, then carries his cases out into the living room, through the draped kitchen doorway.

Linda, his wife, has stirred in her bed at the right. She gets out and puts on a robe, listening. Most often jovial, she has developed an iron repression of her exceptions to Willy's *behavior — she more than loves him, she admires him, as though his mercurial nature, his temper, his massive dreams and little cruelties, served her only as sharp reminders of the turbulent longings within him, longings which she shares but lacks the temperament to utter and follow to their end.*

Linda (hearing Willy outside the bedroom, calls with some trepidation). Willy!

Willy. It's all right. I came back.

Linda. Why? What happened? *(Slight pause.)* Did something happen, Willy?

Willy. No, nothing happened.

Linda. You didn't smash the car, did you?

Willy (with casual irritation). I said nothing happened. Didn't you hear me?

Linda. Don't you feel well?

Willy. I'm tired to the death. (*The flute has faded away. He sits on the bed beside her, a little numb.*) I couldn't make it. I just couldn't make it, Linda.

Linda (*very carefully, delicately*). Where were you all day? You look terrible.

Willy. I got as far as a little above Yonkers. I stopped for a cup of coffee. Maybe it was the coffee.

Linda. What?

Willy (*after a pause*). I suddenly couldn't drive any more. The car kept going off onto the shoulder, y'know?

Linda (*helpfully*). Oh. Maybe it was the steering again. I don't think Angelo knows the Studebaker.

Willy. No, it's me, it's me. Suddenly I realize I'm goin' sixty miles an hour and I don't remember the last five minutes. I'm — I can't seem to — keep my mind to it.

Linda. Maybe it's your glasses. You never went for your new glasses.

Willy. No, I see everything. I came back ten miles an hour. It took me nearly four hours from Yonkers.

Linda (*resigned*). Well, you'll just have to take a rest, Willy, you can't continue this way.

Willy. I just got back from Florida.

Linda. But you didn't rest your mind. Your mind is overactive, and the mind is what counts, dear.

Willy. I'll start out in the morning. Maybe I'll feel better in the morning. (*She is taking off his shoes.*) These goddam arch supports are killing me.

Linda. Take an aspirin. Should I get you an aspirin? It'll soothe you.

Willy (*with wonder*). I was driving along, you understand? And I was fine. I was even observing the scenery. You can imagine, me looking at scenery, on the road every week of my life. But it's so beautiful up there, Linda, the trees are so thick, and the sun is warm. I opened the windshield and just let the warm air bathe over me. And then all of a sudden I'm goin' off the road! I'm tellin' ya, I absolutely forgot I was driving. If I'd've gone the other way over the white line I might've killed somebody. So I went on again — and five minutes later I'm dreamin' again, and I nearly . . . (*He presses two fingers against his eyes.*) I have such thoughts, I have such strange thoughts.

Linda. Willy, dear. Talk to them again. There's no reason why you can't work in New York.

Willy. They don't need me in New York. I'm the New England man. I'm vital in New England.

Linda. But you're sixty years old. They can't expect you to keep traveling every week.

Willy. I'll have to send a wire to Portland. I'm supposed to see Brown and Morrison tomorrow morning at ten o'clock to show the line. Goddammit, I could sell them! *(He starts putting on his jacket.)*

Linda (taking the jacket from him). Why don't you go down to the place tomorrow and tell Howard you've simply got to work in New York? You're too accommodating, dear.

Willy. If old man Wagner was alive I'd a been in charge of New York now! That man was a prince, he was a masterful man. But that boy of his, that Howard, he don't appreciate. When I went north the first time, the Wagner Company didn't know where New England was!

Linda. Why don't you tell those things to Howard, dear?

Willy (encouraged). I will, I definitely will. Is there any cheese?

Linda. I'll make you a sandwich.

Willy. No, go to sleep. I'll take some milk. I'll be up right away. The boys in?

Linda. They're sleeping. Happy took Biff on a date tonight.

Willy (interested). That so?

Linda. It was so nice to see them shaving together, one behind the other, in the bathroom. And going out together. You notice? The whole house smells of shaving lotion.

Willy. Figure it out. Work a lifetime to pay off a house. You finally own it, and there's nobody to live in it.

Linda. Well, dear, life is a casting off. It's always that way.

Willy. No, no, some people — some people accomplish something. Did Biff say anthing after I went this morning?

Linda. You shouldn't have criticized him, Willy, especially after he just got off the train. You mustn't lose your temper with him.

Willy. When the hell did I lose my temper? I simply asked him if he was making any money. Is that a criticism?

Linda. But, dear, how could he make any money?

Willy (worried and angered). There's such an undercurrent in him. He became a moody man. Did he apologize when I left this morning?

Linda. He was crestfallen, Willy. You know how he admires you. I think if he finds himself, then you'll both be happier and not fight any more.

Willy. How can he find himself on a farm? Is that a life? A farmhand? In the beginning, when he was young, I thought, well, a young man, it's good for him to tramp around, take a lot of different jobs.

But it's more than ten years now and he has yet to make thirty-five dollars a week!

Linda. He's finding himself, Willy.

Willy. Not finding yourself at the age of thirty-four is a disgrace!

Linda. Shh!

Willy. The trouble is he's lazy, goddammit!

Linda. Willy, please!

Willy. Biff is a lazy bum!

Linda. They're sleeping. Get something to eat. Go on down.

Willy. Why did he come home? I would like to know what brought him home.

Linda. I don't know. I think he's still lost, Willy. I think he's very lost.

Willy. Biff Loman is lost. In the greatest country in the world a young man with such — personal attractiveness, gets lost. And such a hard worker. There's one thing about Biff — he's not lazy.

Linda. Never.

Willy (with pity and resolve). I'll see him in the morning; I'll have a nice talk with him. I'll get him a job selling. He could be big in no time. My God! Remember how they used to follow him around in high school? When he smiled at one of them their faces lit up. When he walked down the street . . . *(He loses himself in reminiscences.)*

Linda (trying to bring him out of it). Willy, dear, I got a new kind of American-type cheese today. It's whipped.

Willy. Why do you get American when I like Swiss?

Linda. I just thought you'd like a change . . .

Willy. I don't want a change! I want Swiss cheese. Why am I always being contradicted?

Linda (with a covering laugh). I thought it would be a surprise.

Willy. Why don't you open a window in here, for God's sake?

Linda (with infinite patience). They're all open, dear.

Willy. The way they boxed us in here. Bricks and windows, windows and bricks.

Linda. We should've bought the land next door.

Willy. The street is lined with cars. There's not a breath of fresh air in the neighborhood. The grass don't grow any more, you can't raise a carrot in the back yard. They should've had a law against apartment houses. Remember those two beautiful elm trees out there? When I and Biff hung the swing between them?

Linda. Yeah, like being a million miles from the city.

Willy. They should've arrested the builder for cutting those down. They massacred the neighborhood. *(Lost.)* More and more I think of those days, Linda. This time of year it was lilac and wisteria.

And then the peonies would come out, and the daffodils. What fragrance in this room!

Linda. Well, after all, people had to move somewhere.

Willy. No, there's more people now.

Linda. I don't think there's more people. I think . . .

Willy. There's more people! That's what's ruining this country! Population is getting out of control. The competition is maddening! Smell the stink from that apartment house! And another one on the other side . . . How can they whip cheese?

On Willy's last line, Biff and Happy raise themselves up in their beds, listening.

Linda. Go down, try it. And be quiet.

Willy (turning to Linda, guiltily). You're not worried about me, are you, sweetheart?

Biff. What's the matter?

Happy. Listen!

Linda. You've got too much on the ball to worry about.

Willy. You're my foundation and my support, Linda.

Linda. Just try to relax, dear. You make mountains out of molehills.

Willy. I won't fight with him any more. If he wants to go back to Texas, let him go.

Linda. He'll find his way.

Willy. Sure. Certain men just don't get started till later in life. Like Thomas Edision, I think. Or B. F. Goodrich. One of them was deaf. *(He starts for the bedroom doorway.)* I'll put my money on Biff.

Linda. And Willy — if it's warm Sunday we'll drive in the country. And we'll open the windshield, and take lunch.

Willy. No, the windshields don't open on the new cars.

Linda. But you opened it today.

Willy. Me? I didn't. *(He stops.)* Now isn't that peculiar! Isn't that a remarkable . . . *(He breaks off in amazement and fright as the flute is heard distantly.)*

Linda. What, darling?

Willy. That is the most remarkable thing.

Linda. What, dear?

Willy. I was thinking of the Chevvy. *(Slight pause.)* Nineteen twenty-eight . . . when I had that red Chevvy . . . *(Breaks off.)* That funny? I coulda sworn I was driving that Chevvy today.

Linda. Well, that's nothing. Something must've reminded you.

Willy. Remarkable. Ts. Remember those days? The way Biff used to simonize that car? The dealer refused to believe there was eighty

thousand miles on it. *(He shakes his head.)* Heh! *(To Linda.)* Close
your eyes, I'll be right up. *(He walks out of the bedroom.)*
Happy (to Biff). Jesus, maybe he smashed up the car again!
Linda (calling after Willy). Be careful on the stairs, dear! The cheese
  is on the middle shelf. *(She turns, goes over to the bed, takes his
  jacket, and goes out of the bedroom.)*

*Light has risen on the boys' room. Unseen, Willy is heard talking
to himself, "Eighty thousand miles," and a little laugh. Biff gets
out of bed, comes downstage a bit, and stands attentively. Biff is
two years older than his brother Happy, well built, but in these
days bears a worn air and seems less self-assured. He has succeeded less, and his dreams are stronger and less acceptable than
Happy's. Happy is tall, powerfully made. Sexuality is like a visible
color on him, or a scent that many women have discovered. He,
like his brother, is lost, but in a different way, for he has never
allowed himself to turn his face toward defeat and is thus more
confused and hard-skinned, although seemingly more content.*

Happy (getting out of bed). He's going to get his license taken away
  if he keeps that up. I'm getting nervous about him, y'know, Biff?
Biff. His eyes are going.
Happy. No, I've driven with him. He sees all right. He just doesn't
  keep his mind on it. I drove into the city with him last week. He
  stops at a green light and then it turns red and he goes. *(He
  laughs.)*
Biff. Maybe he's color-blind.
Happy. Pop? Why he's got the finest eye for color in the business.
  You know that.
Biff (sitting down on his bed). I'm going to sleep.
Happy. You're not still sour on Dad, are you, Biff?
Biff. He's all right, I guess.
Willy (underneath them, in the living room). Yes, sir, eighty thou-
  sand miles — eighty-two thousand!
Biff. You smoking?
Happy (holding out a pack of cigarettes). Want one?
Biff (taking a cigarette). I can never sleep when I smell it.
Willy. What a simonizing job, heh!
Happy (with deep sentiment). Funny, Biff, y'know? Us sleeping in
  here again? The old beds. *(He pats his bed affectionately.)* All the
  talk that went across those two beds, huh? Our whole lives.
Biff. Yeah. Lotta dreams and plans.
Happy (with a deep and masculine laugh). About five hundred
  women would like to know what was said in this room. *(They
  share a soft laugh.)*

Biff. Remember that big Betsy something — what the hell was her name — over on Bushwick Avenue?

Happy (combing his hair). With the collie dog!

Biff. That's the one. I got you in there, remember?

Happy. Yeah, that was my first time — I think. Boy, there was a pig. *(They laugh, almost crudely.)* You taught me everything I know about women. Don't forget that.

Biff. I bet you forgot how bashful you used to be. Especially with girls.

Happy. Oh, I still am, Biff.

Biff. Oh, go on.

Happy. I just control it, that's all. I think I got less bashful and you got more so. What happened, Biff? Where's the old humor, the old confidence? *(He shakes Biff's knee. Biff gets up and moves restlessly about the room.)* What's the matter?

Biff. Why does Dad mock me all the time?

Happy. He's not mocking you, he . . .

Biff. Everything I say there's a twist of mockery on his face. I can't get near him.

Happy. He just wants you to make good, that's all. I wanted to talk to you about Dad for a long time, Biff. Something's — happening to him. He — talks to himself.

Biff. I noticed that this morning. But he always mumbled.

Happy. But not so noticeable. It got so embarrassing I sent him to Florida. And you know something? Most of the time he's talking to you.

Biff. What's he say about me?

Happy. I can't make it out.

Biff. What's he say about me?

Happy. I think the fact that you're not settled, that you're still kind of up in the air . . .

Biff. There's one or two other things depressing him, Happy.

Happy. What do you mean?

Biff. Never mind. Just don't lay it all to me.

Happy. But I think if you just got started — I mean — is there any future for you out there?

Biff. I tell ya, Hap, I don't know what the future is. I don't know — what I'm supposed to want.

Happy. What do you mean?

Biff. Well, I spent six or seven years after high school trying to work myself up. Shipping clerk, salesman, business of one kind or another. And it's a measly manner of existence. To get on that subway on the hot mornings in summer. To devote your whole life to keeping stock, or making phone calls, or selling or buying. To suffer fifty weeks of the year for the sake of a two-week vacation, when all you really desire is to be outdoors, with your shirt off. And always to have to get ahead of the next fella. And still — that's how you build a future.

Happy. Well, you really enjoy it on a farm? Are you content out there?

Biff (with rising agitation). Hap, I've had twenty or thirty different kinds of jobs since I left home before the war, and it always turns out the same. I just realized it lately. In Nebraska when I herded cattle, and the Dakotas, and Arizona, and now in Texas. It's why I came home now, I guess, because I realized it. This farm I work on, it's spring there now, see? And they've got about fifteen new colts. There's nothing more inspiring or — beautiful than the sight of a mare and a new colt. And it's cool there now, see? Texas is cool now, and it's spring. And whenever spring comes to where I am, I suddenly get the feeling, my God, I'm not gettin' anywhere! What the hell am I doing, playing around with horses, twenty-eight dollars a week! I'm thirty-four years old, I oughta be makin' my future. That's when I come running home. And now, I get here, and I don't know what to do with myself. *(After a pause.)* I've always made a point of not wasting my life, and everytime I come back here I know that all I've done is to waste my life.

Happy. You're a poet, you know that, Biff? You're a — you're an idealist!

Biff. No, I'm mixed up very bad. Maybe I oughta get married. Maybe I oughta get stuck into something. Maybe that's my trouble. I'm like a boy. I'm not married, I'm not in business, I just — I'm like a boy. Are you content, Hap? You're a success, aren't you? Are you content?

Happy. Hell, no!

Biff. Why? You're making money, aren't you?

Happy (moving about with energy, expressiveness). All I can do now is wait for the merchandise manager to die. And suppose I get to be merchandise manager? He's a good friend of mine, and he just built a terrific estate on Long Island. And he lived there about two months and sold it, and now he's building another one. He can't enjoy it once it's finished. And I know that's just what I would do. I don't know what the hell I'm workin' for. Sometimes I sit in my apartment — all alone. And I think of the rent I'm paying. And it's crazy. But then, it's what I always wanted. My own apartment, a car, and plenty of women. And still, goddammit, I'm lonely.

Biff (with enthusiasm). Listen, why don't you come out West with me?

Happy. You and I, heh?

Biff. Sure, maybe we could buy a ranch. Raise cattle, use our muscles. Men built like we are should be working out in the open.

Happy (avidly). The Loman Brothers, heh?

Biff (with vast affection). Sure, we'd be known all over the counties!

Happy (enthralled). That's what I dream about, Biff. Sometimes I want to just rip my clothes off in the middle of the store and outbox that goddam merchandise manager. I mean I can outbox, outrun, and outlift anybody in that store, and I have to take orders from those common, petty sons-of-bitches till I can't stand it any more.

Biff. I'm tellin' you, kid, if you were with me I'd be happy out there.

Happy (enthused). See, Biff, everybody around me is so false that I'm constantly lowering my ideals . . .

Biff. Baby, together we'd stand up for one another, we'd have someone to trust.

Happy. If I were around you . . .

Biff. Hap, the trouble is we weren't brought up to grub for money. I don't know how to do it.

Happy. Neither can I!

Biff. Then let's go!

Happy. The only thing is — what can you make out there?

Biff. But look at your friend. Builds an estate and then hasn't the peace of mind to live in it.

Happy. Yeah, but when he walks into the store the waves part in front of him. That's fifty-two thousand dollars a year coming through the revolving door, and I got more in my pinky finger than he's got in his head.

Biff. Yeah, but you just said . . .

Happy. I gotta show some of those pompous, self-important executives over there that Hap Loman can make the grade. I want to walk into the store the way he walks in. Then I'll go with you, Biff. We'll be together yet, I swear. But take those two we had tonight. Now weren't they gorgeous creatures?

Biff. Yeah, yeah, most gorgeous I've had in years.

Happy. I get that any time I want, Biff. Whenever I feel disgusted. The only trouble is, it gets like bowling or something. I just keep knockin' them over and it doesn't mean anything. You still run around a lot?

Biff. Naa. I'd like to find a girl — steady, somebody with substance.

Happy. That's what I long for.

Biff. Go on! You'd never come home.

Happy. I would! Somebody with character, with resistance! Like Mom, y'know? You're gonna call me a bastard when I tell you this.

That girl Charlotte I was with tonight is engaged to be married in five weeks. *(He tries on his new hat.)*

Biff. No kiddin'!

Happy. Sure, the guy's in line for the vice-presidency of the store. I don't know what gets into me, maybe I just have an overdeveloped sense of competition or something, but I went and ruined her, and furthermore I can't get rid of her. And he's the third executive I've done that to. Isn't that a crummy characteristic? And to top it all, I go to their weddings! *(Indignantly, but laughing.)* Like I'm not supposed to take bribes. Manufacturers offer me a hundred-dollar bill now and then to throw an order their way. You know how honest I am, but it's like this girl, see. I hate myself for it. Because I don't want the girl, and, still, I take it and — I love it!

Biff. Let's go to sleep.

Happy. I guess we didn't settle anything, heh?

Biff. I just got one idea that I think I'm going to try.

Happy. What's that?

Biff. Remember Bill Oliver?

Happy. Sure, Oliver is very big now. You want to work for him again?

Biff. No, but when I quit he said something to me. He put his arm on my shoulder, and he said, "Biff, if you ever need anything, come to me."

Happy. I remember that. That sounds good.

Biff. I think I'll go to see him. If I could get ten thousand or even seven or eight thousand dollars I could buy a beautiful ranch.

Happy. I bet he'd back you. 'Cause he thought highly of you, Biff. I mean, they all do. You're well liked, Biff. That's why I say to come back here, and we both have the apartment. And I'm tellin' you, Biff, any babe you want . . .

Biff. No, with a ranch I could do the work I like and still be something. I just wonder though. I wonder if Oliver still thinks I stole that carton of basketballs.

Happy. Oh, he probably forgot that long ago. It's almost ten years. You're too sensitive. Anyway, he didn't really fire you.

Biff. Well, I think he was going to. I think that's why I quit. I was never sure whether he knew or not. I know he thought the world of me, though. I was the only one he'd let lock up the place.

Willy (below). You gonna wash the engine, Biff?

Happy. Shh!

Biff looks at Happy, who is gazing down, listening. Willy is mumbling in the parlor.

Happy. You hear that?

They listen. Willy laughs warmly.

Biff (growing angry). Doesn't he know Mom can hear that?

Willy. Don't get your sweater dirty, Biff!

A look of pain crosses Biff's face.

Happy. Isn't that terrible? Don't leave again, will you? You'll find a job here. You gotta stick around. I don't know what to do about him, it's getting embarrassing.

Willy. What a simonizing job!

Biff. Mom's hearing that!

Willy. No kiddin', Biff, you got a date? Wonderful!

Happy. Go on to sleep. But talk to him in the morning, will you?

Biff (reluctantly getting into bed) With her in the house. Brother!

Happy (getting into bed). I wish you'd have a good talk with him.

The light on their room begins to fade.

Biff (to himself in bed). That selfish, stupid . . .

Happy. Sh . . . Sleep, Biff.

Their light is out. Well before they have finished speaking, Willy's form is dimly seen below in the darkened kitchen. He opens the refrigerator, searches in there, and takes out a bottle of milk. The apartment houses are fading out, and the entire house and surroundings become covered with leaves. Music insinuates itself as the leaves appear.

Willy. Just wanna be careful with those girls, Biff, that's all. Don't make any promises. No promises of any kind. Because a girl, y'know, they always believe what you tell 'em, and you're very young, Biff, you're too young to be talking seriously to girls. ·

Light rises on the kitchen. Willy, talking, shuts the refrigerator door and comes downstage to the kitchen table. He pours milk into a glass. He is totally immersed in himself, smiling faintly.

Willy. Too young entirely, Biff. You want to watch your schooling first. Then when you're all set, there'll be plenty of girls for a boy like you. *(He smiles broadly at a kitchen chair.)* That so? The girls pay for you? *(He laughs).* Boy, you must really be makin' a hit.

Willy is gradually addressing — physically — a point offstage, speaking through the wall of the kitchen, and his voice has been rising in volume to that of a normal conversation.

Willy. I been wondering why you polish the car so careful. Ha! Don't leave the hubcaps, boys. Get the chamois to the hubcaps. Happy, use newspaper on the windows, it's the easiest thing. Show him how to do it Biff! You see, Happy? Pad it up, use it like a pad. That's it, that's it, good work. You're doin' all right, Hap. *(He pauses, then nods in approbation for a few seconds, then looks upward.)* Biff, first thing we gotta do when we get time is clip that big branch over the house. Afraid it's gonna fall in a storm and hit the roof. Tell you what. We get a rope and sling her around, and then we climb up there with a couple of saws and take her down. Soon as you finish the car, boys, I wanna see ya. I got a surprise for you, boys.

Biff (offstage). Whatta ya got, Dad?

Willy. No, you finish first. Never leave a job till you're finished — remember that. *(Looking toward the "big trees.")* Biff, up in Albany I saw a beautiful hammock. I think I'll buy it next trip, and we'll hang it right between those two elms. Wouldn't that be something? Just swingin' there under those branches. Boy, that would be . . .

Young Biff and Young Happy appear from the direction Willy was addressing. Happy carries rags and a pail of water. Biff, wearing a sweater with a block "S," carries a football.

Biff (pointing in the direction of the car offstage). How's that, Pop, professional?

Willy. Terrific. Terrific job, boys. Good work, Biff.

Happy. Where's the surprise, Pop?

Willy. In the back seat of the car.

Happy. Boy! *(He runs off.)*

Biff. What is it, Dad? Tell me, what'd you buy?

Willy (laughing, cuffs him). Never mind, something I want you to have.

Biff (turns and starts off). What is it, Hap?

Happy (offstage). It's a punching bag!

Biff. Oh, Pop!

Willy. It's got Gene Tunney's signature on it!

Happy runs onstage with a punching bag.

Biff. Gee, how'd you know we wanted a punching bag?

Willy. Well, it's the finest thing for the timing.

Happy (lies down on his back and pedals with his feet). I'm losing weight, you notice, Pop?

Willy (to Happy). Jumping rope is good too.

Biff. Did you see the new football I got?

Willy (examining the ball). Where'd you get a new ball?

Biff. The coach told me to practice my passing.

Willy. That so? And he gave you the ball, heh?

Biff. Well, I borrowed it from the locker room. *(He laughs confidentially.)*

Willy (laughing with him at the theft). I want you to return that.

Happy. I told you he wouldn't like it!

Biff (angrily). Well, I'm bringing it back!

Willy (stopping the incipient argument, to Happy). Sure, he's gotta practice with a regulation ball, doesn't he? *(To Biff.)* Coach'll probably congratulate you on your initiative!

Biff. Oh, he keeps congratulating my initiative all the time, Pop.

Willy. That's because he likes you. If somebody else took that ball there'd be an uproar. So what's the report, boys, what's the report?

Biff. Where'd you go this time, Dad? Gee we were lonesome for you.

Willy (pleased, puts an arm around each boy and they come down to the apron). Lonesome, heh?

Biff. Missed you every minute.

Willy. Don't say? Tell you a secret, boys. Don't breathe it to a soul. Someday I'll have my own business, and I'll never have to leave home any more.

Happy. Like Uncle Charley, heh?

Willy. Bigger than Uncle Charley! Because Charley is not — liked. He's liked, but he's not — well liked.

Biff. Where'd you go this time, Dad?

Willy. Well, I got on the road, and I went north to Providence. Met the Mayor.

Biff. The Mayor of Providence!

Willy. He was sitting in the hotel lobby.

Biff. What'd he say?

Willy. He said, "Morning!" And I said, "You got a fine city here, Mayor." And then he had coffee with me. And then I went to Waterbury. Waterbury is a fine city. Big clock city, the famous Waterbury clock. Sold a nice bill there. And then Boston — Boston is the cradle of the Revolution. A fine city. And a couple of other towns in Mass., and on to Portland and Bangor and straight home!

Biff. Gee, I'd love to go with you sometime, Dad.

Willy. Soon as summer comes.

Happy. Promise?

Willy. You and Hap and I, and I'll show you all the towns. America is full of beautiful towns and fine, upstanding people. And they know me, boys, they know me up and down New England. The finest people. And when I bring you fellas up, there'll be open sesame for all of us, 'cause one thing, boys: I have friends. I can park my car in any street in New England, and the cops protect it like their own. This summer, heh?

Biff and Happy (together). Yeah! You bet!

Willy. We'll take our bathing suits.

Happy. We'll carry your bags, Pop!

Willy. Oh, won't that be something! Me comin' into the Boston stores with you boys carryin' my bags. What a sensation!

Biff is prancing around, practicing passing the ball.

Willy. You nervous, Biff, about the game?

Biff. Not if you're gonna be there.

Willy. What do they say about you in school, now that they made you captain?

Happy. There's a crowd of girls behind him everytime the classes change.

Biff (taking Willy's hand). This Saturday, Pop, this Saturday — just for you, I'm going to break through for a touchdown.

Happy. You're supposed to pass.

Biff. I'm takin' one play for Pop. You watch me, Pop, and when I take off my helmet, that means I'm breakin' out. Then you watch me crash through that line!

Willy (kisses Biff). Oh, wait'll I tell this in Boston!

Bernard enters in knickers. He is younger than Biff, earnest and loyal, a worried boy.

Bernard. Biff, where are you? You're supposed to study with me today.

Willy. Hey, looka Bernard. What're you lookin' so anemic about, Bernard?

Bernard. He's gotta study, Uncle Willy. He's got Regents next week.

Happy (tauntingly, spinning Bernard around). Let's box, Bernard!

Bernard. Biff! (*He gets away from Happy.*) Listen, Biff, I heard Mr. Birnbaum say that if you don't start studyin' math he's gonna flunk you, and you won't graduate. I heard him!

Willy. You better study with him, Biff. Go ahead now.

Bernard. I heard him!

Biff. Oh, Pop, you didn't see my sneakers! (*He holds up a foot for Willy to look at.*)

Willy. Hey, that's a beautiful job of printing!

Bernard (wiping his glasses). Just because he printed University of Virginia on his sneakers doesn't mean they've got to graduate him, Uncle Willy!

Willy (angrily). What're you talking about? With scholarships to three universities they're gonna flunk him?

Bernard. But I heard Mr. Birnbaum say . . .

Willy. Don't be a pest, Bernard! *(To his boys.)* What an anemic!

Bernard. Okay, I'm waiting for you in my house, Biff.

Bernard goes off. The Lomans laugh.

Willy. Bernard is not well liked, is he?

Biff. He's liked, but he's not well liked.

Happy. That's right, Pop.

Willy. That's just what I mean. Bernard can get the best marks in school, y'understand, but when he gets out in the business world, y'understand, you are going to be five times ahead of him. That's why I thank Almighty God you're both built like Adonises. Because the man who makes an appearance in the business world, the man who creates personal interest, is the man who gets ahead. Be liked and you will never want. You take me, for instance. I never have to wait in line to see a buyer. "Willy Loman is here!" That's all they have to know, and I go right through.

Biff. Did you knock them dead, Pop?

Willy. Knocked 'em cold in Providence, slaughtered 'em in Boston.

Happy (on his back, pedaling again). I'm losing weight, you notice, Pop?

Linda enters as of old, a ribbon in her hair, carrying a basket of washing.

Linda (with youthful energy). Hello, dear!

Willy. Sweetheart!

Linda. How'd the Chevvy run?

Willy. Chevrolet, Linda, is the greatest car ever built. *(To the boys.)* Since when do you let your mother carry wash up the stairs?

Biff. Grab hold there, boy!

Happy. Where to, Mom?

Linda. Hang them up on the line. And you better go down to your friends, Biff. The cellar is full of boys. They don't know what to do with themselves.

Biff. Ah, when Pop comes home they can wait!

Willy (laughs appreciatively). You better go down and tell them what to do, Biff.

Biff. I think I'll have them sweep out the furnace room.

Willy. Good work, Biff.

Biff (goes through wall-line of kitchen to doorway at back and calls down). Fellas! Everybody sweep out the furnace room! I'll be right down!

Voices. All right! Okay, Biff.

Biff. George and Sam and Frank, come out back! We're hangin' up the wash! Come on, Hap, on the double! *(He and Happy carry out the basket.)*

Linda. The way they obey him!

Willy. Well, that's training, the training. I'm tellin' you, I was sellin' thousands and thousands, but I had to come home.

Linda. Oh, the whole block'll be at that game. Did you sell anything?

Willy. I did five hundred gross in Providence and seven hundred gross in Boston.

Linda. No! Wait a minute, I've got a pencil. *(She pulls pencil and paper out of her apron pocket.)* That makes your commission . . . Two hundred — my God! Two hundred and twelve dollars!

Willy. Well, I didn't figure it yet, but . . .

Linda. How much did you do?

Willy. Well, I — I did — about a hundred and eighty gross in Providence. Well, no — it came to — roughly two hundred gross on the whole trip.

Linda (without hesitation). Two hundred gross That's . . . *(She figures.)*

Willy. The trouble was that three of the stores were half-closed for inventory in Boston. Otherwise I woulda broke records.

Linda. Well, it makes seventy dollars and some pennies. That's very good.

Willy. What do we owe?

Linda. Well, on the first there's sixteen dollars on the refrigerator . . .

Willy. Why sixteen?

Linda. Well, the fan belt broke, so it was a dollar eighty.

Willy. But it's brand new.

Linda. Well, the man said that's the way it is. Till they work themselves in, y'know.

They move through the wall-line into the kitchen.

Willy. I hope we didn't get stuck on that machine.

Linda. They got the biggest ads of any of them!

Willy. I know, it's a fine machine. What else?

Linda. Well, there's nine-sixty for the washing machine. And for the vacuum cleaner there's three and a half due on the fifteenth. Then the roof, you got twenty-one dollars remaining.

Willy. It don't leak, does it?

Linda. No, they did a wonderful job. Then you owe Frank for the carburetor.

Willy. I'm not going to pay that man! That goddam Chevrolet, they ought to prohibit the manufacture of that car!

Linda. Well, you owe him three and a half. And odds and ends, comes to around a hundred and twenty dollars by the fifteenth.

Willy. A hundred and twenty dollars! My God, if business don't pick up I don't know what I'm gonna do!

Linda. Well, next week you'll do better.

Willy. Oh, I'll knock 'em dead next week. I'll go to Hartford. I'm very well liked in Hartford. You know, the trouble is, Linda, people don't seem to take to me.

They move onto the forestage.

Linda. Oh, don't be foolish.

Willy. I know it when I walk in. They seem to laugh at me.

Linda. Why? Why would they laugh at you? Don't talk that way, Willy.

Willy moves to the edge of the stage. Linda goes into the kitchen and starts to darn stockings.

Willy. I don't know the reason for it, but they just pass me by. I'm not noticed.

Linda. But you're doing wonderful, dear. You're making seventy to a hundred dollars a week.

Willy. But I gotta be at it ten, twelve hours a day. Other men — I don't know — they do it easier. I don't know why — I can't stop myself — I talk too much. A man oughta come in with a few words. One thing about Charley. He's a man of few words, and they respect him.

Linda. You don't talk too much, you're just lively.

Willy (smiling). Well, I figure, what the hell, life is short, a couple of jokes. *(To himself.)* I joke too much! *(The smile goes.)*

Linda. Why? You're . . .

Willy. I'm fat. I'm very — foolish to look at, Linda. I didn't tell you, but Christmas time I happened to be calling on F. H. Stewarts, and a salesman I know, as I was going in to see the buyer I heard him say something about — walrus. And I — I cracked him right across the face. I won't take that. I simply will not take that. But they do laugh at me. I know that.

Linda. Darling . . .

Willy. I gotta overcome it. I know I gotta overcome it. I'm not dressing to advantage, maybe.

Linda. Willy, darling, you're the handsomest man in the world . . .

Willy. Oh, no, Linda.

Linda. To me you are. *(Slight pause.)* The handsomest.

From the darkness is heard the laughter of a woman. Willy doesn't turn to it, but it continues through Linda's lines.

Linda. And the boys, Willy. Few men are idolized by their children the way you are.

Music is heard as behind a scrim, to the left of the house; The Woman, dimly seen, is dressing.

Willy (with great feeling). You're the best there is, Linda, you're a pal, you know that? On the road — on the road I want to grab you sometimes and just kiss the life outa you.

The laughter is loud now, and he moves into a brightening area at the left, where The Woman has come from behind the scrim and is standing, putting on her hat, looking into a "mirror" and laughing.

Willy. 'Cause I get so lonely — especially when business is bad and there's nobody to talk to. I get the feeling that I'll never sell anything again, that I won't make a living for you, or a business, a business for the boys. *(He talks through The Woman's subsiding laughter; The Woman primps at the "mirror.")* There's so much I want to make for . . .

The Woman. Me? You didn't make me, Willy. I picked you.

Willy (pleased). You picked me?

The Woman (who is quite proper-looking, Willy's age). I did. I've been sitting at that desk watching all the salesmen go by, day in, day out. But you've got such a sense of humor, and we do have such a good time together, don't we?

Willy. Sure, sure. *(He takes her in his arms.)* Why do you have to go now?

The Woman. It's two o'clock . . .

Willy. No, come on in! *(He pulls her.)*

The Woman. . . . my sisters'll be scandalized. When'll you be back?

Willy. Oh, two weeks about. Will you come up again?

The Woman. Sure thing. You do make me laugh. It's good for me. *(She squeezes his arm, kisses him.)* And I think you're a wonderful man.

Willy. You picked me, heh?

The Woman. Sure. Because you're so sweet. And such a kidder.

Willy. Well, I'll see you next time I'm in Boston.

The Woman. I'll put you right through to the buyers.

Willy (slapping her bottom). Right. Well, bottoms up!

The Woman (slaps him gently and laughs). You just kill me.

Willy (He suddenly grabs her and kisses her roughly.) You kill me. And thanks for the stockings. I love a lot of stockings. Well, good night.

Willy. Good night. And keep your pores open!

The Woman. Oh, Willy!

The Woman bursts out laughing, and Linda's laughter blends in. The Woman disappears into the dark. Now the area at the kitchen table brightens. Linda is sitting where she was at the kitchen table, but now is mending a pair of her silk stockings.

Linda. You are, Willy. The handsomest man. You've got no reason to feel that . . .

Willy (coming out of The Woman's dimming area and going over to Linda). I'll make it all up to you, Linda, I'll . . .

Linda. There's nothing to make up, dear. You're doing fine, better than . . .

Willy (noticing her mending). What's that?

Linda. Just mending my stockings. They're so expensive . . .

Willy (angrily, taking them from her). I won't have you mending stockings in this house! Now throw them out!

Linda puts the stockings in her pocket.

Bernard (entering on the run). Where is he? If he doesn't study!

Willy (moving to the forestage, with great agitation). You'll give him the answers!

Bernard. I do, but I can't on a Regents! That's a state exam! They're liable to arrest me!

Willy. Where is he? I'll whip him, I'll whip him!

Linda. And he'd better give back that football, Willy, it's not nice.

Willy. Biff! Where is he? Why is he taking everything?

Linda. He's too rough with the girls, Willy. All the mothers are afraid of him!

Willy. I'll whip him!

Bernard. He's driving the car without a license!

The Woman's laugh is heard.

Willy. Shut up!

Linda. All the mothers . . .

Willy. Shut up!

Bernard (backing quietly away and out). Mr. Birnbaum says he's stuck up.

Willy. Get outa here!

Bernard. If he doesn't buckle down he'll flunk math! *(He goes off.)*

Linda. He's right, Willy, you've gotta . . .

Willy (exploding at her). There's nothing the matter with him! You want him to be a worm like Bernard? He's got spirit, personality . . .

As he speaks, Linda, almost in tears, exits into the living room. Willy is alone in the kitchen, wilting and staring. The leaves are gone. It is night again, and the apartment houses look down from behind.

Willy. Loaded with it. Loaded! What is he stealing? He's giving it back, isn't he? Why is he stealing? What did I tell him? I never in my life told him anything but decent things.

Happy in pajamas has come down the stairs; Willy suddenly becomes aware of Happy's presence.

Happy. Let's go now, come on.

Willy (sitting down at the kitchen table). Huh! Why did she have to wax the floors herself? Everytime she waxes the floors she keels over. She knows that!

Happy. Shh! Take it easy. What brought you back tonight?

Willy. I got an awful scare. Nearly hit a kid in Yonkers. God! Why didn't I go to Alaska with my brother Ben that time! Ben! That man was a genius, that man was success incarnate! What a mistake! He begged me to go.

Happy. Well, there's no use in . . .

Willy. You guys! There was a man started with the clothes on his back and ended up with diamond mines!

Happy. Boy, someday I'd like to know how he did it.

Willy. What's the mystery? The man knew what he wanted and went out and got it! Walked into a jungle, and comes out, the age of twenty-one, and he's rich! The world is an oyster, but you don't crack it open on a mattress!

Happy. Pop, I told you I'm gonna retire you for life.

Willy. You'll retire me for life on seventy goddam dollars a week? And your women and your car and your apartment, and you'll retire me for life! Christ's sake, I couldn't get past Yonkers today! Where are you guys, where are you? The woods are burning! I can't drive a car!

Charley has appeared in the doorway. He is a large man, slow of speech, laconic, immovable. In all he says, despite what he says, there is pity, and, now, trepidation. He has a robe over pajamas, slippers on his feet. He enters the kitchen.

Charley. Everything all right?

Happy. Yeah, Charley, everything's . . .

Willy. What's the matter?

Charley. I heard some noise. I thought something happened. Can't we do something about the walls? You sneeze in here, and in my house hats blow off.

Happy. Let's go to bed, Dad. Come on.

Charley signals to Happy to go.

Willy. You go ahead, I'm not tired at the moment.

Happy (to Willy). Take it easy, huh? *(He exits.)*

Willy. What're you doin' up?

Charley (sitting down at the kitchen table opposite Willy). Couldn't sleep good. I had a heartburn.

Willy. Well, you don't know how to eat.

Charley. I eat with my mouth.

Willy. No, you're ignorant. You gotta know about vitamins and things like that.

Charley. Come on, let's shoot. Tire you out a little.

Willy (hesitantly). All right. You got cards?

Charley (taking a deck from his pocket). Yeah, I got them. Someplace. What is it with those vitamins?

Willy (dealing). They build up your bones. Chemistry.

Charley. Yeah, but there's no bones in a heartburn.

Willy. What are you talkin' about? Do you know the first thing about it?

Charley. Don't get insulted.

Willy. Don't talk about something you don't know anything about.

They are playing. Pause.

Charley. What're you doin' home?

Willy. A little trouble with the car.

Charley. Oh. *(Pause.)* I'd like to take a trip to California.

Willy. Don't say.

Charley. You want a job?

Willy. I got a job, I told you that. *(After a slight pause.)* What the hell are you offering me a job for?

Charley. Don't get insulted.

Willy. Don't insult me.

Charley. I don't see no sense in it. You don't have to go on this way.

Willy. I got a good job. *(Slight pause.)* What do you keep comin' in here for?

Charley. You want me to go?

Willy (after a pause, withering). I can't understand it. He's going
back to Texas again. What the hell is that?

Charley. Let him go.

Willy. I got nothin' to give him, Charley, I'm clean, I'm clean.

Charley. He won't starve. None a them starve. Forget about him.

Willy. Then what have I got to remember?

Charley. You take it too hard. To hell with it. When a deposit bottle
is broken you don't get your nickel back.

Willy. That's easy enough for you to say.

Charley. That ain't easy for me to say.

Willy. Did you see the ceiling I put up in the living room?

Charley. Yeah, that's a piece of work. To put up a ceiling is a mystery
to me. How do you do it?

Willy. What's the difference?

Charley. Well, talk about it.

Willy. You gonna put up a ceiling?

Charley. How could I put up a ceiling?

Willy. Then what the hell are you bothering me for?

Charley. You're insulted again.

Willy. A man who can't handle tools is not a man. You're disgusting.

Charley. Don't call me disgusting, Willy.

*Uncle Ben, carrying a valise and an umbrella, enters the forestage
from around the right corner of the house. He is a stolid man, in
his sixties, with a mustache and an authoritative air. He is utterly
certain of his destiny, and there is an aura of far places about
him. He enters exactly as Willy speaks.*

Willy. I'm getting awfully tired, Ben.

Ben's music is heard. Ben looks around at everything.

Charley. Good, keep playing; you'll sleep better. Did you call me
Ben?

Ben looks at his watch.

Willy. That's funny. For a second there you reminded me of my
brother Ben.

Ben. I only have a few minutes. *(He strolls, inspecting the place.*
Willy and Charley continue playing.)

Charley. You never heard from him again, heh? Since that time?

Willy. Didn't Linda tell you? Couple of weeks ago we got a letter
from his wife in Africa. He died.

Charley. That so.

Ben (chuckling). So this is Brooklyn, eh?

Charley. Maybe you're in for some of his money.

Willy. Naa, he had seven sons. There's just one opportunity I had with that man . . .

Ben. I must make a train, William. There are several properties I'm looking at in Alaska.

Willy. Sure, sure! If I'd gone with him to Alaska that time, everything would've been totally different.

Charley. Go on, you'd froze to death up there.

Willy. What're you talking about?

Ben. Opportunity is tremendous in Alaska, William. Surprised you're not up there.

Willy. Sure, tremendous.

Charley. Heh?

Willy. There was the only man I ever met who knew the answers.

Charley. Who?

Ben. How are you all?

Willy (taking a pot, smiling). Fine, fine.

Charley. Pretty sharp tonight.

Ben. Is Mother living with you?

Willy. No, she died a long time ago.

Charley. Who?

Ben. That's too bad. Fine specimen of a lady, Mother.

Willy (to Charley). Heh?

Ben. I'd hoped to see the old girl.

Charley. Who died?

Ben. Heard anything from Father, have you?

Willy (unnerved). What do you mean, who died?

Charley (taking a pot). What're you talkin' about?

Ben (looking at his watch). William, it's half-past eight!

Willy (as though to dispel his confusion he angrily stops Charley's hand). That's my build!

Charley. I put the ace . . .

Willy. If you don't know how to play the game I'm not gonna throw my money away on you!

Charley (rising). It was my ace, for God's sake!

Willy. I'm through, I'm through!

Ben. When did Mother die?

Willy. Long ago. Since the beginning you never knew how to play cards.

Charley (picks up the cards and goes to the door). All right! Next time I'll bring a deck with five aces.

Willy. I don't play that kind of game!

Charley (turning to him). You ought to be ashamed of yourself!

Willy. Yeah?

Charley. Yeah! *(He goes out.)*

Willy (slamming the door after him). Ignoramus!

Ben (as Willy comes toward him through the wall-line of the kitchen). So you're William.

Willy (shaking Ben's hand). Ben! I've been waiting for you so long! What's the answer? How did you do it?

Ben. Oh, there's a story in that.

Linda enters the forestage, as of old, carrying the wash basket.

Linda. Is this Ben?

Ben (gallantly). How do you do, my dear.

Linda. Where've you been all these years? Willy's always wondered why you . . .

Willy (pulling Ben away from her impatiently). Where is Dad? Didn't you follow him? How did you get started?

Ben. Well, I don't know how much you remember.

Willy. Well, I was just a baby, of course, only three or four years old . . .

Ben. Three years and eleven months.

Willy. What a memory, Ben!

Ben. I have many enterprises, William, and I have never kept books.

Willy. I remember I was sitting under the wagon in — was it Nebraska?

Ben. It was South Dakota, and I gave you a bunch of wild flowers.

Willy. I remember you walking away down some open road.

Ben (laughing). I was going to find Father in Alaska.

Willy. Where is he?

Ben. At that age I had a very faulty view of geography, William. I discovered after a few days that I was heading due south, so instead of Alaska, I ended up in Africa.

Linda. Africa!

Willy. The Gold Coast!

Ben. Principally diamond mines.

Linda. Diamond mines!

Ben. Yes, my dear. But I've only a few minutes . . .

Willy. No! Boys! Boys! (*Young Biff and Happy appear.*) Listen to this. This is your Uncle Ben, a great man! Tell my boys, Ben!

Ben. Why, boys, when I was seventeen I walked into the jungle, and when I was twenty-one I walked out. (*He laughs.*) And by God I was rich.

Willy (to the boys). You see what I been talking about? The greatest things can happen!

Ben (glancing at his watch). I have an appointment in Ketchikan Tuesday week.

Willy. No, Ben! Please tell about Dad. I want my boys to hear. I want them to know the kind of stock they spring from. All I remember is a man with a big beard, and I was in Mamma's lap, sitting around a fire, and some kind of high music.

Ben. His flute. He played the flute.

Willy. Sure, the flute, that's right!

New music is heard, a high, rollicking tune.

Ben. Father was a very great and a very wild-hearted man. We would start in Boston, and he'd toss the whole family into the wagon, and then he'd drive the team right across the country; through Ohio, and Indiana, Michigan, Illinois, and all the Western states. And we'd stop in the towns and sell the flutes that he'd made on the way. Great inventor, Father. With one gadget he made more in a week than a man like you could make in a lifetime.

Willy. That's just the way I'm bringing them up, Ben — rugged, well liked, all-around.

Ben. Yeah? *(To Biff.)* Hit that, boy — hard as you can. *(He pounds his stomach.)*

Biff. Oh, no, sir!

Ben (taking boxing stance). Come on, get to me! *(He laughs.)*

Willy. Go to it, Biff! Go ahead, show him!

Biff. Okay! *(He cocks his fists and starts in.)*

Linda (to Willy). Why must he fight, dear?

Ben (sparring with Biff). Good boy! Good boy!

Willy. How's that, Ben, heh?

Happy. Give him the left, Biff!

Linda. Why are you fighting?

Ben. Good boy! *(Suddenly comes in, trips Biff, and stands over him, the point of his umbrella poised over Biff's eye.)*

Linda. Look out, Biff!

Biff. Gee!

Ben (Patting Biff's knee). Never fight fair with a stranger, boy. You'll never get out of the jungle that way. *(Taking Linda's hand and bowing.)* It was an honor and a pleasure to meet you, Linda.

Linda (withdrawing her hand coldly, frightened). Have a nice — trip.

Ben (to Willy). And good luck with your — what do you do?

Willy. Selling.

Ben. Yes. Well . . . *(He raises his hand in farewell to all.)*

Willy. No, Ben, I don't want you to think . . . *(He takes Ben's arm to show him.)* It's Brooklyn, I know, but we hunt too.

Ben. Really, now.

Willy. Oh, sure, there's snakes and rabbits and — that's why I moved out here. Why, Biff can fell any one of these trees in no time! Boys!

Go right over to where they're building the apartment house and
get some sand. We're gonna rebuild the entire front stoop right
now! Watch this, Ben!

Biff. Yes, sir! On the double, Hap!

Happy (as he and Biff run off). I lost weight, Pop, you notice?

Charley enters in knickers, even before the boys are gone.

Charley. Listen, if they steal any more from that building the watchman'll put the cops on them!

Linda (to Willy). Don't let Biff . . .

Ben laughs lustily.

Willy. You shoulda seen the lumber they brought home last week. At
least a dozen six-by-tens worth all kinds a money.

Charley. Listen, if that watchman . . .

Willy. I gave them hell, understand. But I got a couple of fearless
characters there.

Charley. Willy, the jails are full of fearless characters.

Ben (clapping Willy on the back, with a laugh at Charley). And the
stock exchange, friend!

Willy (joining in Ben's laughter). Where are the rest of your pants?

Charley. My wife bought them.

Willy. Now all you need is a golf club and you can go upstairs and go
to sleep. *(To Ben.)* Great athlete! Between him and his son Bernard they can't hammer a nail!

Bernard (rushing in). The watchman's chasing Biff!

Willy (angrily). Shut up! He's not stealing anything!

Linda (alarmed, hurrying off left). Where is he? Biff, dear! *(She
exits.)*

Willy (moving toward the left, away from Ben). There's nothing
wrong. What's the matter with you?

Ben. Nervy boy. Good!

Willy (laughing). Oh, nerves of iron, that Biff!

Charley. Don't know what it is. My New England man comes back
and he's bleedin', they murdered him up there.

Willy. It's contacts, Charley, I got important contacts!

Charley (sarcastically). Glad to hear it, Willy. Come in later, we'll
shoot a little casino. I'll take some of your Portland money. *(He
laughs at Willy and exits.)*

Willy (turning to Ben). Business is bad, it's murderous. But not for
me, of course.

Ben. I'll stop by on my way back to Africa.

Willy (longingly). Can't you stay a few days? You're just what I need,

Ben, because I — I have a fine position here, but I — well, Dad left when I was such a baby and I never had a chance to talk to him and I still feel — kind of temporary about myself.

Ben. I'll be late for my train.

They are at opposite ends of the stage.

Willy. Ben, my boys — can't we talk? They'd go into the jaws of hell for me, see, but I . . .

Ben. William, you're being first-rate with your boys. Outstanding, manly chaps!

Willy (hanging on to his words). Oh, Ben, that's good to hear! Because sometimes I'm afraid that I'm not teaching them the right kind of — Ben, how should I teach them?

Ben (giving great weight to each word, and with a certain vicious audacity). William, when I walked into the jungle, I was seventeen. When I walked out I was twenty-one. And, by God, I was rich! *(He goes off into darkness around the right corner of the house.)*

Willy. . . . was rich! That's just the spirit I want to imbue them with! To walk into a jungle! I was right! I was right! I was right!

Ben is gone, but Willy is still speaking to him as Linda, in nightgown and robe, enters the kitchen, glances around for Willy, then goes to the door of the house, looks out and sees him. Comes down to his left. He looks at her.

Linda. Willy, dear? Willy?

Willy. I was right!

Linda. Did you have some cheese? *(He can't answer.)* It's very late, darling. Come to bed, heh?

Willy (looking straight up). Gotta break your neck to see a star in this yard.

Linda. You coming in?

Willy. Whatever happened to that diamond watch fob? Remember? When Ben came from Africa that time? Didn't he give me a watch fob with a diamond in it?

Linda. You pawned it, dear. Twelve, thirteen years ago. For Biff's radio correspondence course.

Willy. Gee, that was a beautiful thing. I'll take a walk.

Linda. But you're in your slippers.

Willy (starting to go around the house at the left). I was right! I was! *(Half to Linda, as he goes, shaking his head.)* What a man! There was a man worth talking to. I was right!

Linda (calling after Willy). But in your slippers, Willy!

Willy is almost gone when Biff, in his pajamas, comes down the stairs and enters the kitchen.

Biff. What is he doing out there?

Linda. Sh!

Biff. God Almighty, Mom, how long has he been doing this?

Linda. Don't, he'll hear you.

Biff. What the hell is the matter with him?

Linda. It'll pass by morning.

Biff. Shouldn't we do anything?

Linda. Oh, my dear, you should do a lot of things, but there's nothing to do, so go to sleep.

Happy comes down the stair and sits on the steps.

Happy. I never heard him so loud, Mom.

Linda. Well, come around more often; you'll hear him. *(She sits down at the table and mends the lining of Willy's jacket.)*

Biff. Why didn't you ever write me about this, Mom?

Linda. How would I write to you? For over three months you had no address.

Biff. I was on the move. But you know I thought of you all the time. You know that, don't you, pal?

Linda. I know, dear, I know. But he likes to have a letter. Just to know that there's still a possibility for better things.

Biff. He's not like this all the time, is he?

Linda. It's when you come home he's always the worst.

Biff. When I come home?

Linda. When you write you're coming, he's all smiles, and talks about the future, and — he's just wonderful. And then the closer you seem to come, the more shaky he gets, and then, by the time you get here, he's arguing, and he seems angry at you. I think it's just that maybe he can't bring himself to — to open up to you. Why are you so hateful to each other? Why is that?

Biff (evasively). I'm not hateful, Mom.

Linda. But you no sooner come in the door than you're fighting!

Biff. I don't know why. I mean to change. I'm tryin', Mom, you understand?

Linda. Are you home to stay now?

Biff. I don't know. I want to look around, see what's doin'.

Linda. Biff, you can't look around all your life, can you?

Biff. I just can't take hold, Mom. I can't take hold of some kind of a life.

Linda. Biff, a man is not a bird, to come and go with the springtime.

Biff. Your hair . . . *(He touches her hair.)* Your hair got so gray.

Linda. Oh, it's been gray since you were in high school. I just stopped dyeing it, that's all.

Biff. Dye it again, will ya? I don't want my pal looking old. *(He smiles.)*

Linda. You're such a boy! You think you can go away for a year and . . . You've got to get it into your head now that one day you'll knock on this door and there'll be strange people here . . .

Biff. What are you talking about? You're not even sixty, Mom.

Linda. But what about your father?

Biff (lamely). Well, I meant him too.

Happy. He admires Pop.

Linda. Biff, dear, if you don't have any feeling for him, then you can't have any feeling for me.

Biff. Sure I can, Mom.

Linda. No. You can't just come to see me, because I love him. *(With a threat, but only a threat, of tears.)* He's the dearest man in the world to me, and I won't have anyone making him feel unwanted and low and blue. You've got to make up your mind now, darling, there's no leeway any more. Either he's your father and you pay him that respect, or else you're not to come here. I know he's not easy to get along with — nobody knows that better than me — but . . .

Willy (from the left, with a laugh). Hey, hey, Biffo!

Biff (starting to go out after Willy). What the hell is the matter with him? *(Happy stops him.)*

Linda. Don't — don't go near him!

Biff. Stop making excuses for him! He always, always wiped the floor with you. Never had an ounce of respect for you.

Happy. He's always had respect for . . .

Biff. What the hell do you know about it?

Happy (surlily). Just don't call him crazy!

Biff. He's got no character — Charley wouldn't do this. Not in his own house — spewing out that vomit from his mind.

Happy. Charley never had to cope with what he's got to.

Biff. People are worse off than Willy Loman. Believe me, I've seen them!

Linda. Then make Charley your father, Biff. You can't do that, can you? I don't say he's a great man. Willy Loman never made a lot of money. His name was never in the paper. He's not the finest character that ever lived. But he's a human being, and a terrible thing is happening to him. So attention must be paid. He's not to be allowed to fall into his grave like an old dog. Attention, attention must be finally paid to such a person. You called him crazy . . .

Biff. I didn't mean . . .

Linda. No, a lot of people think he's lost his — balance. But you don't have to be very smart to know what his trouble is. The man is exhausted.

Happy. Sure!

Linda. A small man can be just as exhausted as a great man. He works for a company thirty-six years this March, opens up unheard-of territories to their trademark, and now in his old age they take his salary away.

Happy (indignantly). I didn't know that, Mom.

Linda. You never asked, my dear! Now that you get your spending money someplace else you don't trouble your mind with him.

Happy. But I gave you money last . . .

Linda. Christmas time, fifty dollars! To fix the hot water it cost ninety-seven fifty! For five weeks he's been on straight commission, like a beginner, an unknown!

Biff. Those ungrateful bastards!

Linda. Are they any worse than his sons? When he brought them business, when he was young, they were glad to see him. But now his old friends, the old buyers that loved him so and always found some order to hand him in a pinch — they're all dead, retired. He used to be able to make six, seven calls a day in Boston. Now he takes his valises out of the car and puts them back and takes them out again and he's exhausted. Instead of walking he talks now. He drives seven hundred miles, and when he gets there no one knows him any more, no one welcomes him. And what goes through a man's mind, driving seven hundred miles home without having earned a cent? Why shouldn't he talk to himself? Why? When he has to go to Charley and borrow fifty dollars a week and pretend to me that it's his pay? How long can that go on? How long? You see what I'm sitting here and waiting for? And you tell me he has no character? The man who never worked a day but for your benefit? When does he get the medal for that? Is this his reward — to turn around at the age of sixty-three and find his sons, who he loved better than his life, one a philandering bum . . .

Happy. Mom!

Linda. That's all you are, my baby! *(To Biff.)* And you! What happened to the love you had for him? You were such pals! How you used to talk to him on the phone every night! How lonely he was till he could come home to you!

Biff. All right, Mom. I'll live here in my room, and I'll get a job. I'll keep away from him, that's all.

Linda. No, Biff. You can't stay here and fight all the time.

Biff. He threw me out of this house, remember that.

Linda. Why did he do that? I never knew why.

Biff. Because I know he's a fake and he doesn't like anybody around who knows!

Linda. Why a fake? In what way? What do you mean?

Biff. Just don't lay it all at my feet. It's between me and him — that's all I have to say. I'll chip in from now on. He'll settle for half my pay check. He'll be all right. I'm going to bed. *(He starts for the stairs.)*

Linda. He won't be all right.

Biff (turning on the stairs, furiously). I hate this city and I'll stay here. Now what do you want?

Linda. He's dying, Biff.

Happy turns quickly to her, shocked.

Biff (after a pause). Why is he dying?

Linda. He's been trying to kill himself.

Biff (with great horror). How?

Linda. I live from day to day.

Biff. What're you talking about?

Linda. Remember I wrote you that he smashed up the car again? In February?

Biff. Well?

Linda. The insurance inspector came. He said that they have evidence. That all these accidents in the last year — weren't — weren't — accidents.

Happy. How can they tell that? That's a lie.

Linda. It seems there's a woman . . . *(She takes a breath as:)*

⎰ *Biff (sharply but contained).* What woman?

⎱ *Linda (simultaneously).* . . . and this woman . . .

Linda. What?

Biff. Nothing. Go ahead.

Linda. What did you say?

Biff. Nothing. I just said what woman?

Happy. What about her?

Linda. Well, it seems she was walking down the road and saw his car. She says that he wasn't driving fast at all, and that he didn't skid. She says he came to that little bridge, and then deliberately smashed into the railing, and it was only the shallowness of the water that saved him.

Biff. Oh, no, he probably just fell asleep again.

Linda. I don't think he fell asleep.

Biff. Why not?

Linda. Last month . . . *(With great difficulty.)* Oh, boys, it's so hard to say a thing like this! He's just a big stupid man to you, but I tell you there's more good in him than in many other people. *(She chokes, wipes her eyes.)* I was looking for a fuse. The lights blew out, and I went down the cellar. And behind the fuse box — it happened to fall out — was a length of rubber pipe — just short.

Happy. No kidding!

Linda. There's a little attachment on the end of it. I knew right away. And sure enough, on the bottom of the water heater there's a new little nipple on the gas pipe.

Happy (angrily). That — jerk.

Biff. Did you have it taken off?

Linda. I'm — I'm ashamed to. How can I mention it to him? Every day I go down and take away that little rubber pipe. But, when he comes home, I put it back where it was. How can I insult him that way? I don't know what to do. I live from day to day, boys. I tell you, I know every thought in his mind. It sounds so old-fashioned and silly, but I tell you he put his whole life into you and you've turned your backs on him. *(She is bent over in the chair, weeping, her face in her hands.)* Biff, I swear to God! Biff, his life is in your hands!

Happy (to Biff). How do you like that damned fool!

Biff (kissing her). All right, pal, all right. It's all settled now. I've been remiss. I know that, Mom. But now I'll stay, and I swear to you, I'll apply myself. *(Kneeling in front of her, in a fever of self-reproach.)* It's just — you see, Mom, I don't fit in business. Not that I won't try. I'll try, and I'll make good.

Happy. Sure you will. The trouble with you in business was you never tried to please people.

Biff. I know, I . . .

Happy. Like when you worked for Harrison's. Bob Harrison said you were tops, and then you go and do some damn fool thing like whistling whole songs in the elevator like a comedian.

Biff (against Happy). So what? I like to whistle sometimes.

Happy. You don't raise a guy to a responsible job who whistles in the elevator!

Linda. Well, don't argue about it now.

Happy. Like when you'd go off and swim in the middle of the day instead of taking the line around.

Biff (his resentment rising). Well, don't you run off? You take off sometimes, don't you? On a nice summer day?

Happy. Yeah, but I cover myself!

Linda. Boys!

Happy. If I'm going to take a fade the boss can call any number where I'm supposed to be and they'll swear to him that I just left. I'll tell you something that I hate to say, Biff, but in the business world some of them think you're crazy.

Biff (angered). Screw the business world!

Happy. All right, screw it! Great, but cover yourself!

Linda. Hap, Hap!

Biff. I don't care what they think! They've laughed at Dad for years, and you know why? Because we don't belong in this nuthouse of a city! We should be mixing cement on some open plain or — or carpenters. A carpenter is allowed to whistle!

Willy walks in from the entrance of the house, at left.

Willy. Even your grandfather was better than a carpenter. *(Pause. They watch him.)* You never grew up. Bernard does not whistle in the elevator, I assure you.

Biff (as though to laugh Willy out of it). Yeah, but you do, Pop.

Willy. I never in my life whistled in an elevator! And who in the business world thinks I'm crazy?

Biff. I didn't mean it like that, Pop. Now don't make a whole thing out of it, will ya?

Willy. Go back to the West! Be a carpenter, a cowboy, enjoy yourself!

Linda. Willy, he was just saying . . .

Willy. I heard what he said!

Happy (trying to quiet Willy). Hey, Pop, come on now . . .

Willy (continuing over Happy's line). They laugh at me, heh? Go to Filene's, go to the Hub, go to Slattery's, Boston. Call out the name Willy Loman and see what happens! Big shot!

Biff. All right, Pop.

Willy. Big!

Biff. All right!

Willy. Why do you always insult me?

Biff. I didn't say a word. *(To Linda.)* Did I say a word?

Linda. He didn't say anything, Willy.

Willy (going to the doorway of the living room). All right, good night, good night.

Linda. Willy, dear, he just decided . . .

Willy (to Biff). If you get tired hanging around tomorrow, paint the ceiling I put up in the living room.

Biff. I'm leaving early tomorrow.

Happy. He's going to see Bill Oliver, Pop.

Willy (interestedly). Oliver? For what?

Biff (with reserve, but trying, trying). He always said he'd stake me. I'd like to go into business, so maybe I can take him up on it.

Linda. Isn't that wonderful?

Willy. Don't interrupt. What's wonderful about it? There's fifty men in the City of New York who'd stake him. *(To Biff.)* Sporting goods?

Biff. I guess so. I know something about it and . . .

Willy. He knows something about it! You know sporting goods better than Spalding, for God's sake! How much is he giving you?

Biff. I don't know, I didn't even see him yet, but . . .

Willy. Then what're you talkin' about?

Biff (getting angry). Well, all I said was I'm gonna see him, that's all!

Willy (turning away). Ah, you're counting your chickens again.

Biff (starting left for the stairs). Oh, Jesus, I'm going to sleep!

Willy (calling after him). Don't curse in this house!

Biff (turning). Since when did you get so clean?

Happy (trying to stop them). Wait a . . .

Willy. Don't use that language to me! I won't have it!

Happy (grabbing Biff, shouts). Wait a minute! I got an idea. I got a feasible idea. Come here, Biff, let's talk this over now, let's talk some sense here. When I was down in Florida last time, I thought of a great idea to sell sporting goods. It just came back to me. You and I, Biff — we have a line, the Loman Line. We train a couple of weeks, and put on a couple of exhibitions, see?

Willy. That's an idea!

Happy. Wait! We form two basketball teams, see? Two water-polo teams. We play each other. It's a million dollars' worth of publicity. Two brothers, see? The Loman Brothers. Displays in the Royal Palms — all the hotels. And banners over the ring and the basketball court: "Loman Brothers." Baby, we could sell sporting goods!

Willy. That is a one-million-dollar idea!

Linda. Marvelous!

Biff. I'm in great shape as far as that's concerned.

Happy. And the beauty of it is, Biff, it wouldn't be like a business. We'd be out playin' ball again . . .

Biff (enthused). Yeah, that's . . .

Willy. Million-dollar . . .

Happy. And you wouldn't get fed up with it, Biff. It'd be the family again. There'd be the old honor, and comradeship, and if you wanted to go off for a swim or somethin' — well, you'd do it! Without some smart cooky gettin' up ahead of you!

Willy. Lick the world! You guys together could absolutely lick the civilized world.

Biff. I'll see Oliver tomorrow. Hap, if we could work that out . . .

Linda. Maybe things are beginning to . . .

Willy (wildly enthused, to Linda). Stop interrupting! *(To Biff.)* But don't wear sport jacket and slacks when you see Oliver.

Biff. No, I'll . . .

Willy. A business suit, and talk as little as possible, and don't crack any jokes.

Biff. He did like me. Always liked me.

Linda. He loved you!

Willy (to Linda). Will you stop! *(To Biff.)* Walk in very serious. You are not applying for a boy's job. Money is to pass. Be quiet, fine, and serious. Everybody likes a kidder, but nobody lends him money.

Happy. I'll try to get some myself, Biff. I'm sure I can.

Willy. I see great things for you kids, I think your troubles are over. But remember, start big and you'll end big. Ask for fifteen. How much you gonna ask for?

Biff. Gee, I don't know . . .

Willy. And don't say "Gee." "Gee" is a boy's word. A man walking in for fifteen thousand dollars does not say "Gee!"

Biff. Ten, I think, would be top though.

Willy. Don't be so modest. You always started too low. Walk in with a big laugh. Don't look worried. Start off with a couple of your good stories to lighten things up. It's not what you say, it's how you say it — because personality always wins the day.

Linda. Oliver always thought the highest of him . . .

Willy. Will you let me talk?

Biff. Don't yell at her, Pop, will ya?

Willy (angrily). I was talking, wasn't I?

Biff. I don't like you yelling at her all the time, and I'm tellin' you, that's all.

Willy. What're you, takin' over this house?

Linda. Willy . . .

Willy (turning to her). Don't take his side all the time, goddammit!

Biff (furiously). Stop yelling at her!

Willy (suddenly pulling on his cheek, beaten down, guilt ridden). Give my best to Bill Oliver — he may remember me. *(He exits through the living room doorway.)*

Linda (her voice subdued). What'd you have to start that for? *(Biff turns away.)* You see how sweet he was as soon as you talked hopefully? *(She goes over to Biff.)* Come up and say good night to him. Don't let him go to bed that way.

Happy. Come on, Biff, let's buck him up.

Linda. Please, dear. Just say good night. It takes so little to make him happy. Come. *(She goes through the living room doorway, calling upstairs from within the living room.)* Your pajamas are hanging in the bathroom, Willy!

Happy (looking toward where Linda went out). What a woman! They broke the mold when they made her. You know that, Biff?

Biff. He's off salary. My God, working on commission!

Happy. Well, let's face it: he's no hot-shot selling man. Except that sometimes, you have to admit, he's a sweet personality.

Biff (deciding). Lend me ten bucks, will ya? I want to buy some new ties.

Happy. I'll take you to a place I know. Beautiful stuff. Wear one of my striped shirts tomorrow.

Biff. She got gray. Mom got awful old. Gee, I'm gonna go in to Oliver tomorrow and knock him for a . . .

Happy. Come on up. Tell that to Dad. Let's give him a whirl. Come on.

Biff (steamed up). You know, with ten thousand bucks, boy!

Happy (as they go into the living room). That's the talk, Biff, that's the first time I've heard the old confidence out of you! *(From within the living room, fading off.)* You're gonna live with me, kid, and any babe you want just say the word . . . *(The last lines are hardly heard. They are mounting the stairs to their parents' bedroom.)*

Linda (entering her bedroom and addressing Willy, who is in the bathroom. She is straightening the bed for him). Can you do anything about the shower? It drips.

Willy (from the bathroom). All of a sudden everything falls to pieces. Goddam plumbing, oughta be sued, those people. I hardly finished putting it in and the thing . . . *(His words rumble off.)*

Linda. I'm just wondering if Oliver will remember him. You think he might?

Willy (coming out of the bathroom in his pajamas). Remember him? What's the matter with you, you crazy? If he'd've stayed with Oliver he'd be on top by now! Wait'll Oliver gets a look at him. You don't know the average caliber any more. The average young man today — *(he is getting into bed)* — is got a caliber of zero. Greatest thing in the world for him was to bum around.

Biff and Happy enter the bedroom. Slight pause.

Willy (stops short, looking at Biff). Glad to hear it, boy.

Happy. He wanted to say good night to you, sport.

Willy (to Biff). Yeah. Knock him dead, boy. What'd you want to tell me?

Biff. Just take it easy, Pop. Good night. *(He turns to go.)*

Willy (unable to resist). And if anything falls off the desk while you're talking to him — like a package or something — don't you pick it up. They have office boys for that.

Linda. I'll make a big breakfast . . .

Willy. Will you let me finish? *(To Biff.)* Tell him you were in the business in the West. Not farm work.

Biff. All right, Dad.

Linda. I think everything . . .

Willy (going right through her speech). And don't undersell yourself. No less than fifteen thousand dollars.

Biff (unable to bear him). Okay. Good night, Mom. *(He starts moving.)*

Willy. Because you got a greatness in you, Biff, remember that. You got all kinds a greatness . . . *(He lies back, exhausted. Biff walks out.)*

Linda (calling after Biff). Sleep well, darling!

Happy. I'm gonna get married, Mom. I wanted to tell you.

Linda. Go to sleep, dear.

Happy (going). I just wanted to tell you.

Willy. Keep up the good work. *(Happy exits.)* God . . . remember that Ebbets Field game? The championship of the city?

Linda. Just rest. Should I sing to you?

Willy. Yeah. Sing to me. *(Linda hums a soft lullaby.)* When that team came out — he was the tallest, remember?

Linda. Oh, yes. And in gold.

Biff enters the darkened kitchen, takes a cigarette, and leaves the house. He comes downstage into a golden pool of light. He smokes, staring at the night.

Willy. Like a young god. Hercules — something like that. And the sun, the sun all around him. Remember how he waved to me? Right up from the field, with the representatives of three colleges standing by? And the buyers I brought, and the cheers when he came out — Loman, Loman, Loman! God Almighty, he'll be great yet. A star like that, magnificent, can never really fade away!

The light on Willy is fading. The gas heater begins to glow through the kitchen wall, near the stairs, a blue flame beneath red coils.

Linda (timidly). Willy dear, what has he got against you?

Willy. I'm so tired. Don't talk any more.

Biff slowly returns to the kitchen. He stops, stares toward the heater.

Linda. Will you ask Howard to let you work in New York?

Willy. First thing in the morning. Everything'll be all right.

Biff reaches behind the heater and draws out a length of rubber tubing. He is horrified and turns his head toward Willy's room, still dimly lit, from which the strains of Linda's desperate but monotonous humming rise.

Willy (staring through the window into the moonlight). Gee, look at the moon moving between the buildings!

Biff wraps the tubing around his hand and quickly goes up the stairs.

ACT II

Scene: *Music is heard, gay and bright. The curtain rises as the music fades away. Willy, in shirt sleeves, is sitting at the kitchen table, sipping coffee, his hat in his lap. Linda is filling his cup when she can.*

Willy. Wonderful coffee. Meal in itself.

Linda. Can I make you some eggs?

Willy. No. Take a breath.

Linda. You look so rested, dear.

Willy. I slept like a dead one. First time in months. Imagine, sleeping till ten on a Tuesday morning. Boys left nice and early, heh?

Linda. They were out of here by eight o'clock.

Willy. Good work!

Linda. It was so thrilling to see them leaving together. I can't get over the shaving lotion in this house!

Willy (smiling). Mmm . . .

Linda. Biff was very changed this morning. His whole attitude seemed to be hopeful. He couldn't wait to get downtown to see Oliver.

Willy. He's heading for a change. There's no question, there simply are certain men that take longer to get — solidified. How did he dress?

Linda. His blue suit. He's so handsome in that suit. He could be a — anything in that suit!

Willy gets up from the table. Linda holds his jacket for him.

Willy. There's no question, no question at all. Gee, on the way home tonight I'd like to buy some seeds.

Linda (laughing). That'd be wonderful. But not enough sun gets back there. Nothing'll grow any more.

Willy. You wait, kid, before it's all over we're gonna get a little place out in the country, and I'll raise some vegetables, a couple of chickens . . .

Linda. You'll do it yet, dear.

Willy walks out of his jacket. Linda follows him.

Willy. And they'll get married, and come for a weekend. I'd build a little guest house. 'Cause I got so many fine tools, all I'd need would be a little lumber and some peace of mind.

Linda (joyfully). I sewed the lining . . .

Willy. I could build two guest houses, so they'd both come. Did he decide how much he's going to ask Oliver for?

Linda (getting him into the jacket). He didn't mention it, but I imagine ten or fifteen thousand. You going to talk to Howard today?

Willy. Yeah. I'll put it to him straight and simple. He'll just have to take me off the road.

Linda. And Willy, don't forget to ask for a little advance, because we've got the insurance premium. It's the grace period now.

Willy. That's a hundred . . . ?

Linda. A hundred and eight, sixty-eight. Because we're a little short again.

Willy. Why are we short?

Linda. Well, you had the motor job on the car . . .

Willy. That goddam Studebaker!

Linda. And you got one more payment on the refrigerator . . .

Willy. But it just broke again!

Linda. Well, it's old, dear.

Willy. I told you we should've bought a well-advertised machine. Charley bought a General Electric and it's twenty years old and it's still good, that son-of-a-bitch.

Linda. But, Willy . . .

Willy. Whoever heard of a Hastings refrigerator? Once in my life I would like to own something outright before it's broken! I'm always in a race with the junkyard! I just finished paying for the car and it's on its last legs. The refrigerator consumes belts like a goddam maniac. They time those things. They time them so when you finally paid for them, they're used up.

Linda (buttoning up his jacket as he unbuttons it). All told, about two hundred dollars would carry us, dear. But that includes the last payment on the mortgage. After this payment, Willy, the house belongs to us.

Willy. It's twenty-five years!

Linda. Biff was nine years old when we bought it.

Willy. Well, that's a great thing. To weather a twenty-five year mortgage is . . .

Linda. It's an accomplishment.

Willy. All the cement, the lumber, the reconstruction I put in this house! There ain't a crack to be found in it any more.

Linda. Well, it served its purpose.

Willy. What purpose? Some stranger'll come along, move in, and that's that. If only Biff would take this house, and raise a family . . . *(He starts to go.)* Good-by, I'm late.

Linda (suddenly remembering). Oh, I forgot! You're supposed to meet them for dinner.

Willy. Me?

Linda. At Frank's Chop House on Forty-eighth near Sixth Avenue.

Willy. Is that so! How about you?

Linda. No, just the three of you. They're gonna blow you to a big meal!

Willy. Don't say! Who thought of that?

Linda. Biff came to me this morning, Willy, and he said, "Tell Dad, we want to blow him to a big meal." Be there six o'clock. You and your two boys are going to have dinner.

Willy. Gee whiz! That's really somethin'. I'm gonna knock Howard for a loop, kid. I'll get an advance, and I'll come home with a New York job. Goddammit, now I'm gonna do it!

Linda. Oh, that's the spirit, Willy!

Willy. I will never get behind a wheel the rest of my life!

Linda. It's changing, Willy, I can feel it changing!

Willy. Beyond a question. G'by, I'm late. *(He starts to go again.)*

Linda (calling after him as she runs to the kitchen table for a hand-kerchief). You got your glasses?

Willy (feels for them, then comes back in). Yeah, yeah, got my glasses.

Linda (giving him the handkerchief). And a handkerchief.

Willy. Yeah, handkerchief.

Linda. And your saccharine?

Willy. Yeah, my saccharine.

Linda. Be careful on the subway stairs.

She kisses him, and a silk stocking is seen hanging from her hand. Willy notices it.

Willy. Will you stop mending stockings? At least while I'm in the house. It gets me nervous. I can't tell you. Please.

Linda hides the stocking in her hand as she follows Willy across the forestage in front of the house.

Linda. Remember, Frank's Chop House.

Willy (passing the apron). Maybe beets would grow out there.

Linda (laughing). But you tried so many times.

Willy. Yeah. Well, don't work hard today. *(He disappears around the right corner of the house.)*

Linda. Be careful!

> As Willy vanishes, Linda waves to him. Suddenly the phone rings. She runs across the stage and into the kitchen and lifts it.

Linda. Hello? Oh, Biff! I'm so glad you called, I just . . . Yes, sure, I just told him. Yes, he'll be there for dinner at six o'clock, I didn't forget. Listen, I was just dying to tell you. You know that little rubber pipe I told you about? That he connected to the gas heater? I finally decided to go down the cellar this morning and take it away and destroy it. But it's gone! Imagine? He took it away himself, it isn't there! *(She listens.)* When? Oh, then you took it. Oh — nothing, it's just that I'd hoped he'd taken it away himself. Oh, I'm not worried, darling, because this morning he left in such high spirits, it was like the old days! I'm not afraid any more. Did Mr. Oliver see you? . . . Well, you wait there then. And make a nice impression on him, darling. Just don't perspire too much before you see him. And have a nice time with Dad. He may have big news too! . . . That's right, a New York job. And be sweet to him tonight, dear. Be loving to him. Because he's only a little boat looking for a harbor. *(She is trembling with sorrow and joy.)* Oh, that's wonderful, Biff, you'll save his life. Thanks, darling. Just put your arm around him when he comes into the restaurant. Give him a smile. That's the boy . . . Good-by, dear. . . . You got your comb? . . . That's fine. Good-by, Biff dear.

> In the middle of her speech, Howard Wagner, thirty-six, wheels on a small typewriter table on which is a wire-recording machine and proceeds to plug it in. This is on the left forestage. Light slowly fades on Linda as it rises on Howard. Howard is intent on threading the machine and only glances over his shoulder as Willy appears.

Willy. Pst! Pst!

Howard. Hello, Willy, come in.

Willy. Like to have a little talk with you, Howard.

Howard. Sorry to keep you waiting. I'll be with you in a minute.

Willy. What's that, Howard?

Howard. Didn't you ever see one of these? Wire recorder.

Willy. Oh. Can we talk a minute?

Howard. Records things. Just got delivery yesterday. Been driving me crazy, the most terrific machine I ever saw in my life. I was up all night with it.

Willy. What do you do with it?

Howard. I bought it for dictation, but you can do anything with it. Listen to this. I had it home last night. Listen to what I picked up. The first one is my daughter. Get this. *(He flicks the switch and "Roll out the Barrel" is heard being whistled.)* Listen to that kid whistle.

Willy. That is lifelike, isn't it?

Howard. Seven years old. Get that tone.

Willy. Ts, ts. Like to ask a little favor if you . . .

The whistling breaks off, and the voice of Howard's daughter is heard.

His Daughter. "Now you, Daddy."

Howard. She's crazy for me! *(Again the same song is whistled.)* That's me! Ha! *(He winks.)*

Willy. You're very good!

The whistling breaks off again. The machine runs silent for a moment.

Howard. Sh! Get this now, this is my son.

His Son. "The capital of Alabama is Montgomery; the capital of Arizona is Phoenix; the capital of Arkansas is Little Rock; the capital of California is Sacramento . . ." *(and on, and on.)*

Howard (holding up five fingers). Five years old, Willy!

Willy. He'll make an announcer some day!

His Son (continuing). "The capital . . ."

Howard. Get that — alphabetical order! *(The machine breaks off suddenly.)* Wait a minute. The maid kicked the plug out.

Willy. It certainly is a . . .

Howard. Sh, for God's sake!

His Son. "It's nine o'clock, Bulova watch time. So I have to go to sleep."

Willy. That really is . . .

Howard. Wait a minute! The next is my wife.

They wait.

Howard's Voice. "Go on, say something." *(Pause.)* "Well, you gonna talk?"

His Wife. "I can't think of anything."

Howard's Voice. "Well, talk — it's turning."

His Wife (shyly, beaten) "Hello." *(Silence.)* "Oh, Howard, I can't talk into this . . ."

Howard (snapping the machine off). That was my wife.

Willy. That is a wonderful machine. Can we . . .

Howard. I tell you, Willy, I'm gonna take my camera, and my band-saw, and all my hobbies, and out they go. This is the most fascinating relaxation I ever found.

Willy. I think I'll get one myself.

Howard. Sure, they're only a hundred and a half. You can't do without it. Supposing you wanna hear Jack Benny, see? But you can't be at home at that hour. So you tell the maid to turn the radio on when Jack Benny comes on, and this automatically goes on with the radio . . .

Willy. And when you come home you . . .

Howard. You can come home twelve o'clock, one o'clock, any time you like, and you get yourself a Coke and sit yourself down, throw the switch, and there's Jack Benny's program in the middle of the night!

Willy. I'm definitely going to get one. Because lots of times I'm on the road, and I think to myself, what I must be missing on the radio!

Howard. Don't you have a radio in the car?

Willy. Well, yeah, but who ever thinks of turning it on?

Howard. Say, aren't you supposed to be in Boston?

Willy. That's what I want to talk to you about, Howard. You got a minute? *(He draws a chair in from the wing.)*

Howard. What happened? What're you doing here?

Willy. Well . . .

Howard. You didn't crack up again, did you?

Willy. Oh, no. No . . .

Howard. Geez, you had me worried there for a minute. What's the trouble?

Willy. Well, tell you the truth, Howard. I've come to the decision that I'd rather not travel any more.

Howard. Not travel! Well, what'll you do?

Willy. Remember, Christmas time, when you had the party here? You said you'd try to think of some spot for me here in town.

Howard. With us?

Willy. Well, sure.

Howard. Oh, yeah, yeah. I remember. Well, I couldn't think of anything for you, Willy.

Willy. I tell ya, Howard. The kids are all grown up, y'know. I don't need much any more. If I could take home — well, sixty-five dollars a week, I could swing it.

Howard. Yeah, but Willy, see I . . .

Willy. I tell ya why, Howard. Speaking frankly and between the two of us, y'know — I'm just a little tired.

Howard. Oh, I could understand that, Willy. But you're a road man,

Willy, and we do a road business. We've only got a half-dozen salesmen on the floor here.

Willy. God knows, Howard. I never asked a favor of any man. But I was with the firm when your father used to carry you in here in his arms.

Howard. I know that, Willy, but . . .

Willy. Your father came to me the day you were born and asked me what I thought of the name of Howard, may he rest in peace.

Howard. I appreciate that, Willy, but there just is no spot here for you. If I had a spot I'd slam you right in, but I just don't have a single solitary spot.

He looks for his lighter. Willy has picked it up and gives it to him. Pause.

Willy (with increasing anger). Howard, all I need to set my table is fifty dollars a week.

Howard. But where am I going to put you, kid?

Willy. Look, it isn't a question of whether I can sell merchandise, is it?

Howard. No, but it's a business, kid, and everybody's gotta pull his own weight.

Willy (desperately). Just let me tell you a story, Howard . . .

Howard. 'Cause you gotta admit, business is business.

Willy (angrily). Business is definitely business, but just listen for a minute. You don't understand this. When I was a boy — eighteen, nineteen — I was already on the road. And there was a question in my mind as to whether selling had a future for me. Because in those days I had a yearning to go to Alaska. See, there were three gold strikes in one month in Alaska, and I felt like going out. Just - for the ride, you might say.

Howard (barely interested). Don't say.

Willy. Oh, yeah, my father lived many years in Alaska. He was an adventurous man. We've got quite a little streak of self-reliance in our family. I thought I'd go out with my older brother and try to locate him, and maybe settle in the North with the old man. And I was almost decided to go, when I met a salesman in the Parker House. His name was Dave Singleman. And he was eighty-four years old, and he'd drummed merchandise in thirty-one states. And old Dave, he'd go up to his room, y'understand, put on his green velvet slippers — I'll never forget — and pick up his phone and call the buyers, and without ever leaving his room, at the age of eighty-four, he made his living. And when I saw that, I realized that selling was the greatest career a man could want. 'Cause what could be more satisfying than to be able to go, at the age of eighty-four, into twenty or thirty different cities, and pick up a phone, and be remembered and loved and helped by so many different people? Do you know? when he died — and by the way he died the death of a salesman, in his green velvet slippers in the smoker of the New York, New Haven and Hartford, going into Boston — when he died, hundreds of salesmen and buyers were at his funeral. Things were sad on a lotta trains for months after that. *(He stands up. Howard has not looked at him.)* In those days there was personality in it, Howard. There was respect, and comradeship, and gratitude in it. Today, it's all cut and dried, and there's no chance for bringing friendship to bear — or personality. You see what I mean? They don't know me any more.

Howard (moving away, to the right). That's just the thing, Willy.

Willy. If I had forty dollars a week — that's all I'd need. Forty dollars, Howard.

Howard. Kid, I can't take blood from a stone, I . . .

Willy (desperation is on him now). Howard, the year Al Smith was nominated, your father came to me and . . .

Howard (starting to go off). I've got to see some people, kid.

Willy (stopping him). I'm talking about your father! There were promises made across this desk! You mustn't tell me you've got people to see — I put thirty-four years into this firm, Howard, and now I can't pay my insurance! You can't eat the orange and throw the peel away — a man is not a piece of fruit! *(After a pause.)* Now pay attention. Your father — in 1928 I had a big year. I averaged a hundred and seventy dollars a week in commissions.

Howard (impatiently). Now, Willy, you never averaged . . .

Willy (banging his hand on the desk). I averaged a hundred and seventy dollars a week in the year of 1928! And your father came to me — or rather, I was in the office here — it was right over this desk — and he put his hand on my shoulder . . .

Howard (getting up). You'll have to excuse me, Willy, I gotta see some people. Pull yourself together. *(Going out.)* I'll be back in a little while.

On Howard's exit, the light on his chair grows very bright and strange.

Willy. Pull myself together! What the hell did I say to him? My God, I was yelling at him! How could I? *(Willy breaks off, staring at the light, which occupies the chair, animating it. He approaches this chair, standing across the desk from it.)* Frank, Frank, don't you remember what you told me that time? How you put your hand on my shoulder, and Frank . . . *(He leans on the desk and as he speaks the dead man's name he accidentally switches on the recorder, and instantly)*

Howard's Son. " . . . of New York is Albany. The capital of Ohio is Cincinnati, the capital of Rhode Island is . . . " *(The recitation continues.)*

Willy (leaping away with fright, shouting). Ha! Howard! Howard! Howard!

Howard (rushing in). What happened?

Willy (pointing at the machine, which continues nasally, childishly, with the capital cities). Shut it off! Shut it off!

Howard (pulling the plug out). Look, Willy . . .

Willy (pressing his hands to his eyes). I gotta get myself some coffee. I'll get some coffee . . .

Willy starts to walk out. Howard stops him.

Howard (rolling up the cord). Willy, look . . .

Willy. I'll go to Boston.

Howard. Willy, you can't go to Boston for us.

Willy. Why can't I go?

Howard. I don't want you to represent us. I've been meaning to tell you for a long time now.

Willy. Howard, are you firing me?

Howard. I think you need a good long rest, Willy.

Willy. Howard . . .

Howard. And when you feel better, come back, and we'll see if we can work something out.

Willy. But I gotta earn money, Howard. I'm in no position to . . .

Howard. Where are your sons? Why don't your sons give you a hand?

Willy. They're working on a very big deal.

Howard. This is no time for false pride, Willy. You go to your sons and you tell them that you're tired. You've got two great boys, haven't you?

Willy. Oh, no question, no question, but in the meantime . . .

Howard. Then that's that, heh?

Willy. All right, I'll go to Boston tomorrow.

Howard. No, no.

Willy. I can't throw myself on my sons. I'm not a cripple!

Howard. Look, kid, I'm busy this morning.

Willy (grasping Howard's arm). Howard, you've got to let me go to Boston!

Howard (hard, keeping himself under control). I've got a line of people to see this morning. Sit down, take five minutes, and pull yourself together, and then go home, will ya? I need the office, Willy. *(He starts to go, turns, remembering the recorder, starts to push off the table holding the recorder.)* Oh, yeah. Whenever you can this week, stop by and drop off the samples. You'll feel better, Willy, and then come back and we'll talk. Pull yourself together, kid, there's people outside.

Howard exits, pushing the table off left. Willy stares into space, exhausted. Now the music is heard — Ben's music — first distantly, then closer, closer. As Willy speaks, Ben enters from the right. He carries valise and umbrella.

Willy. Oh, Ben, how did you do it? What is the answer? Did you wind up the Alaska deal already?

Ben. Doesn't take much time if you know what you're doing. Just a short business trip. Boarding ship in an hour. Wanted to say goodby.

Willy. Ben, I've got to talk to you.

Ben (glancing at his watch). Haven't the time, William.

Willy (crossing the apron to Ben). Ben, nothing's working out. I don't know what to do.

Ben. Now, look here, William. I've bought timberland in Alaska and I need a man to look after things for me.

Willy. God, timberland! Me and my boys in those grand outdoors!

Ben. You've a new continent at your doorstep, William. Get out of these cities, they're full of talk and time payments and courts of law. Screw on your fists and you can fight for a fortune up there.

Willy. Yes, yes! Linda, Linda!

Linda enters as of old, with the wash.

Linda. Oh, you're back?

Ben. I haven't much time.

Willy. No, wait! Linda, he's got a proposition for me in Alaska.

Linda. But you've got . . . *(To Ben.)* He's got a beautiful job here.

Willy. But in Alaska, kid, I could . . .

Linda. You're doing well enough, Willy!

Ben (to Linda). Enough for what, my dear?

Linda (frightened of Ben and angry at him). Don't say those things to him! Enough to be happy right here, right now. *(To Willy, while Ben laughs.)* Why must everybody conquer the world? You're well liked, and the boys love you, and someday — *(To Ben)* — why, old man Wagner told him just the other day that if he keeps it up he'll be a member of the firm, didn't he, Willy?

Willy. Sure, sure. I am building something with this firm, Ben, and if a man is building something he must be on the right track, mustn't he?

Ben. What are you building? Lay your hand on it. Where is it?

Willy (hesitantly). That's true, Linda, there's nothing.

Linda. Why? *(To Ben.)* There's a man eighty-four years old . . .

Willy. That's right, Ben, that's right. When I look at that man I say, what is there to worry about?

Ben. Bah!

Willy. It's true, Ben. All he has to do is go into any city, pick up the phone, and he's making his living and you know why?

Ben (picking up his valise). I've got to go.

Willy (holding Ben back). Look at this boy!

Biff, in his high school sweater, enters carrying suitcase. Happy carries Biff's shoulder guards, gold helmet, and football pants.

Willy. Without a penny to his name, three great universities are begging for him, and from there the sky's the limit, because it's not what you do, Ben. It's who you know and the smile on your face! It's contacts, Ben, contacts! The whole wealth of Alaska passes over the lunch table at the Commodore Hotel, and that's the wonder, the wonder of this country, that a man can end with diamonds here on the basis of being liked! *(He turns to Biff.)* And that's why when you get out on that field today it's important. Because thousands of people will be rooting for you and loving you. *(To Ben, who has again begun to leave.)* And Ben! when he walks into a business office his name will sound out like a bell and all the doors will open to him! I've seen it, Ben, I've seen it a thousand times! You can't feel it with your hand like timber, but it's there!

Ben. Good-by, William.

Willy. Ben, am I right? Don't you think I'm right? I value your advice.

Ben. There's a new continent at your doorstep, William. You could walk out rich. Rich! *(He is gone.)*

Willy. We'll do it here, Ben! You hear me? We're gonna do it here!

Young Bernard rushes in. The gay music of the Boys is heard.

Bernard. Oh, gee, I was afraid you left already!

Willy. Why? What time is it?

Bernard. It's half-past one!

Willy. Well, come on, everybody! Ebbets Field next stop! Where's the pennants? *(He rushes through the wall-line of the kitchen and out into the living room.)*

Linda (to Biff). Did you pack fresh underwear?

Biff (who has been limbering up). I want to go!

Bernard. Biff, I'm carrying your helmet, ain't I?
Happy. No, I'm carrying the helmet.
Bernard. Oh, Biff, you promised me.
Happy. I'm carrying the helmet.
Bernard. How am I going to get in the locker room?
Linda. Let him carry the shoulder guards. (*She puts her coat and hat on in the kitchen.*)
Bernard. Can I, Biff? 'Cause I told everybody I'm going to be in the locker room.
Happy. In Ebbets Field it's the clubhouse.
Bernard. I meant the clubhouse. Biff!
Happy. Biff!
Biff (*grandly, after a slight pause*). Let him carry the shoulder guards.
Happy (*as he gives Bernard the shoulder guards*). Stay close to us now.

Willy rushes in with the pennants.

Willy (*handing them out*). Everybody wave when Biff comes out on the field. (*Happy and Bernard run off.*) You set now, boy?

The music has died away.

Biff. Ready to go, Pop. Every muscle is ready.
Willy (*at the edge of the apron*). You realize what this means?
Biff. That's right, Pop.
Willy (*feeling Biff's muscles*). You're comin' home this afternoon captain of the All-Scholastic Championship Team of the City of New York.
Biff. I got it, Pop. And remember, pal, when I take off my helmet, that touchdown is for you.
Willy. Let's go! (*He is starting out, with his arm around Biff, when Charley enters, as of old, in knickers.*) I got no room for you, Charley.
Charley. Room? For what?
Willy. In the car.
Charley. You goin' for a ride? I wanted to shoot some casino.
Willy (*furiously*). Casino! (*Incredulously.*) Don't you realize what today is?
Linda. Oh, he knows, Willy. He's just kidding you.
Willy. That's nothing to kid about!
Charley. No, Linda, what's goin on?
Linda. He's playing in Ebbets Field.
Charley. Baseball in this weather?

Willy. Don't talk to him. Come on, come on! *(He is pushing them out.)*

Charley. Wait a minute, didn't you hear the news?

Willy. What?

Charley. Don'y you listen to the radio? Ebbets Field just blew up.

Willy. You go to hell! *(Charley laughs. Pushing them out.)* Come on, come on! We're late.

Charley (as they go). Knock a homer, Biff, knock a homer!

Willy (the last to leave, turning to Charley). I don't think that was funny, Charley. This is the greatest day of his life.

Charley. Willy, when are you going to grow up?

Willy. Yeah, heh? When this game is over, Charley, you'll be laughing out of the other side of your face. They'll be calling him another Red Grange. Twenty-five thousand a year.

Charley (kidding). Is that so?

Willy. Yeah, that's so.

Charley. Well, then, I'm sorry, Willy. But tell me something.

Willy. What?

Charley. Who is Red Grange?

Willy. Put up your hands. Goddam you, put up your hands!

Charley, chuckling, shakes his head and walks away, around the left corner of the stage. Willy follows him. The music rises to a mocking frenzy.

Willy. Who the hell do you think you are, better than everybody else? You don't know everything, you big, ignorant, stupid . . . Put up your hands!

Light rises, on the right side of the forestage, on a small table in the reception room of Charley's office. Traffic sounds are heard. Bernard, now mature, sits whistling to himself. A pair of tennis rackets and an overnight bag are on the floor beside him.

Willy (offstage). What are you walking away for? Don't walk away! If you're going to say something say it to my face! I know you laugh at me behind my back. You'll laugh out of the other side of your goddam face after this game. Touchdown! Touchdown! Eighty thousand people! Touchdown! Right between the goal posts.

Bernard is a quiet, earnest, but self-assured young man. Willy's voice is coming from right upstage now. Bernard lowers his feet off the table and listens. Jenny, his father's secretary, enters.

Jenny (distressed). Say, Bernard, will you go out in the hall?

Bernard. What is that noise? Who is it?

Jenny. Mr. Loman. He just got off the elevator.

Bernard (getting up). Who's he arguing with?

Jenny. Nobody. There's nobody with him. I can't deal with him any more, and your father gets all upset everytime he comes. I've got a lot of typing to do, and your father's waiting to sign it. Will you see him?

Willy (entering). Touchdown! Touch — *(He sees Jenny.)* Jenny, Jenny, good to see you. How're ya? Workin'? Or still honest?

Jenny. Fine. How've you been feeling?

Willy. Not much any more, Jenny. Ha, ha! *(He is surprised to see the rackets.)*

Bernard. Hello, Uncle Willy.

Willy (almost shocked). Bernard! Well, look who's here! *(He comes quickly, guiltily, to Bernard and warmly shakes his hand.)*

Bernard. How are you? Good to see you.

Willy. What are you doing here?

Bernard. Oh, just stopped by to see Pop. Get off my feet till my train leaves. I'm going to Washington in a few minutes.

Willy. Is he in?

Bernard. Yes, he's in his office with the accountant. Sit down.

Willy (sitting down). What're you going to do in Washington?

Bernard. Oh, just a case I've got there, Willy.

Willy. That so? *(Indicating the rackets.)* You going to play tennis there?

Bernard. I'm staying with a friend who's got a court.

Willy. Don't say. His own tennis court. Must be fine people, I bet.

Bernard. They are, very nice. Dad tells me Biff's in town.

Willy (with a big smile). Yeah, Biff's in. Working on a very big deal, Bernard.

Bernard. What's Biff doing?

Willy. Well, he's been doing very big things in the West. But he decided to establish himself here. Very big. We're having dinner. Did I hear your wife had a boy?

Bernard. That's right. Our second.

Willy. Two boys! What do you know!

Bernard. What kind of a deal has Biff got?

Willy. Well, Bill Oliver — very big sporting-goods man — he wants Biff very badly. Called him in from the West. Long distance, carte blanche, special deliveries. Your friends have their own private tennis court?

Bernard. You still with the old firm, Willy?

Willy (after a pause). I'm — I'm overjoyed to see how you made the grade, Bernard, overjoyed. It's an encouraging thing to see a young man really — really . . . Looks very good for Biff — very . . . *(He breaks off, then.)* Bernard . . . *(He is so full of emotion, he breaks off again.)*

Bernard. What is it, Willy?

Willy (small and alone). What — what's the secret?

Bernard. What secret?

Willy. How — how did you? Why didn't he ever catch on?

Bernard. I wouldn't know that, Willy.

Willy (confidentially, desperately). You were his friend, his boyhood friend. There's something I don't understand about it. His life ended after that Ebbets Field game. From the age of seventeen nothing good ever happened to him.

Bernard. He never trained himself for anything.

Willy. But he did, he did. After high school he took so many correspondence courses. Radio mechanics; television; God knows what, and never made the slightest mark.

Bernard (taking off his glasses). Willy, do you want to talk candidly?

Willy (rising, faces Bernard). I regard you as a very brilliant man, Bernard. I value your advice.

Bernard. Oh, the hell with the advice, Willy. I couldn't advise you. There's just one thing I've always wanted to ask you. When he was supposed to graduate, and the math teacher flunked him . . .

Willy. Oh, that son-of-a-bitch ruined his life.

Bernard. Yeah, but, Willy, all he had to do was go to summer school and make up that subject.

Willy. That's right, that's right.

Bernard. Did you tell him not to go to summer school?

Willy. Me? I begged him to go. I ordered him to go!

Bernard. Then why wouldn't he go?

Willy. Why? Why! Bernard, that question has been trailing me like a ghost for the last fifteen years. He flunked the subject, and laid down and died like a hammer hit him!

Bernard. Take it easy, kid.

Willy. Let me talk to you — I got nobody to talk to. Bernard, Bernard, was it my fault? Y'see? It keeps going around in my mind, maybe I did something to him. I got nothing to give him.

Bernard. Don't take it so hard.

Willy. Why did he lay down? What is the story there? You were his friend!

Bernard. Willy, I remember, it was June, and our grades came out. And he'd flunked math.

Willy. That son-of-a-bitch!

Bernard. No, it wasn't right then. Biff just got very angry, I remember, and he was ready to enroll in summer school.

Willy (surprised). He was?

Bernard. He wasn't beaten by it at all. But then, Willy, he dis-appeared from the block for almost a month. And I got the idea that he'd gone up to New England to see you. Did he have a talk with you then?

Willy stares in silence.

Bernard. Willy?

Willy (with a strong edge of resentment in his voice). Yeah, he came to Boston. What about it?

Bernard. Well, just that when he came back — I'll never forget this, it always mystifies me. Because I'd thought so well of Biff, even though he'd always taken advantage of me. I loved him, Willy, y'know? And he came back after that month and took his sneakers — remember those sneakers with "University of Virginia" printed on them? He was so proud of those, wore them every day. And he took them down in the cellar, and burned them up in the furnace. We had a fist fight. It lasted at least half an hour. Just the two of us, punching each other down the cellar, and crying right through it. I've often thought of how strange it was that I knew he'd given up his life. What happened in Boston, Willy?

Willy looks at him as at an intruder.

Bernard. I just bring it up because you asked me.

Willy (angrily). Nothing. What do you mean, "What happened?" What's that got to do with anything?

Bernard. Well, don't get sore.

Willy. What are you trying to do, blame it on me? If a boy lays down is that my fault?

Bernard. Now, Willy, don't get . . .

Willy. Well, don't — don't talk to me that way! What does that mean, "What happened?"

Charley enters. He is in his vest, and he carries a bottle of bour-bon.

Charley. Hey, you're going to miss that train. (He waves the bottle.)

Bernard. Yeah, I'm going. (He takes the bottle.) Thanks, Pop. (He picks up his rackets and bag.) Good-by, Willy, and don't worry about it. You know, "If at first you don't succeed . . ."

Willy. Yes, I believe in that.

Bernard. But sometimes, Willy, it's better for a man just to walk away.

Willy. Walk away?

Bernard. That's right.

Willy. But if you can't walk away?

Bernard (after a slight pause). I guess that's when it's tough. *(Extending his hand.)* Good-by, Willy.

Willy (shaking Bernard's hand). Good-by, boy.

Charley (an arm on Bernard's shoulder). How do you like this kid? Gonna argue a case in front of the Supreme Court.

Bernard (protesting). Pop!

Willy (genuinely shocked, pained, and happy). No! The Supreme Court!

Bernard. I gotta run. 'By, Dad!

Charley. Knock 'em dead, Bernard!

Bernard goes off.

Willy (as Charley takes out his wallet). The Supreme Court! And he didn't even mention it!

Charley (counting out money on the desk). He don't have to — he's gonna do it.

Willy. And you never told him what to do, did you? You never took any interest in him.

Charley. My salvation is that I never took any interest in anything. There's some money — fifty dollars. I got an accountant inside.

Willy. Charley, look . . . *(With difficulty.)* I got my insurance to pay. If you can manage it — I need a hundred and ten dollars.

Charley doesn't reply for a moment; merely stops moving.

Willy. I'd draw it from my bank but Linda would know, and I . . .

Charley. Sit down, Willy.

Willy (moving toward the chair). I'm keeping an account of everything, remember. I'll pay every penny back. *(He sits.)*

Charley. Now listen to me, Willy.

Willy. I want you to know I appreciate . . .

Charley (sitting down on the table). Willy, what're you doin'? What the hell is going on in your head?

Willy. Why? I'm simply . . .

Charley. I offered you a job. You make fifty dollars a week. and I won't send you on the road.

Willy. I've got a job.

Charley. Without pay? What kind of a job is a job without pay? *(He rises.).* Now, look, kid, enough is enough. I'm no genius but I know when I'm being insulted.

Willy. Insulted!

Charley. Why don't you want to work for me?

Willy. What's the matter with you? I've got a job.

Charley. Then what're you walkin' in here every week for?

Willy (getting up). Well, if you don't want me to walk in here . . .

Charley. I'm offering you a job.

Willy. I don't want your goddam job!

Charley. When the hell are you going to grow up?

Willy (furiously). You big ignoramus, if you say that to me again I'll
    rap you one! I don't care how big you are! *(He's ready to fight.)*

    Pause.

Charley (kindly, going to him). How much do you need, Willy?

Willy. Charley, I'm strapped. I'm strapped. I don't know what to do.
    I was just fired.

Charley. Howard fired you?

Willy. That snotnose. Imagine that? I named him. I named him How-
    ard.

Charley. Willy, when're you gonna realize that them things don't
    mean anything? You named him Howard, but you can't sell that.
    The only thing you got in this world is what you can sell. And the
    funny thing is that you're a salesman, and you don't know that.

Willy. I've always tried to think otherwise, I guess. I always felt that
    if a man was impressive, and well liked, that nothing . . .

Charley. Why must everybody like you? Who liked J. P. Morgan?
    Was he impressive? In a Turkish bath he'd look like a butcher. But
    with his pockets on he was very well liked. Now listen, Willy, I
    know you don't like me, and nobody can say I'm in love with you,
    but I'll give you a job because — just for the hell of it, put it that
    way. Now what do you say?

Willy. I — I just can't work for you, Charley.

Charley. What're you, jealous of me?

Willy. I can't work for you, that's all, don't ask me why.

Charley (angered, takes out more bills). You been jealous of me all
    your life, you dammed fool! Here, pay your insurance. *(He puts the
    money in Willy's hand.)*

Willy. I'm keeping strict accounts.

Charley. I've got some work to do. Take care of yourself. And pay
    your insurance.

Willy (moving to the right). Funny, y'know? After all the highways,
    and the trains, and the appointments, and the years, you end up
    worth more dead than alive.

Charley. Willy, nobody's worth nothin' dead. *(After a slight pause.)*
    Did you hear what I said?

    Willy stands still, dreaming.

Charley. Willy!

Willy. Apologize to Bernard for me when you see him. I didn't mean
    to argue with him. He's a fine boy. They're all fine boys, and

they'll end up big — all of them. Someday they'll all play tennis together. Wish me luck, Charley. He saw Bill Oliver today.

Charley. Good luck.

Willy (on the verge of tears). Charley, you're the only friend I got. Isn't that a remarkable thing? *(He goes out.)*

Charley. Jesus!

Charley stares after him a moment and follows. All light blacks out. Suddenly raucous music is heard, and a red glow rises behind the screen at right. Stanley, a young waiter, appears, carrying a table, followed by Happy, who is carrying two chairs.

Stanley (putting the table down). That's all right, Mr. Loman, I can handle it myself. *(He turns and takes the chairs from Happy and places them at the table.)*

Happy (glancing around). Oh, this is better.

Stanley. Sure, in the front there you're in the middle of all kinds of noise. Whenever you got a party, Mr. Loman, you just tell me and I'll put you back here. Y'know, there's a lotta people they don't like it private, because when they go out they like to see a lotta action around them because they're sick and tired to stay in the house by theirself. But I know you, you ain't from Hackensack. You know what I mean?

Happy (sitting down). So how's it coming, Stanley?

Stanley. Ah, it's a dog's life. I only wish during the war they'd a took me in the Army. I coulda been dead by now.

Happy. My brother's back, Stanley.

Stanley. Oh, he come back, heh? From the Far West.

Happy. Yeah, big cattle man, my brother, so treat him right. And my father's coming too.

Stanley. Oh, your father too!

Happy. You got a couple of nice lobsters?

Stanley. Hundred per cent, big.

Happy. I want them with the claws.

Stanley. Don't worry, I don't give you no mice. *(Happy laughs.)* How about some wine? It'll put a head on the meal.

Happy. No. You remember, Stanley, that recipe I brought you from overseas? With the champagne in it?

Stanley. Oh, yeah, sure. I still got it tacked up yet in the kitchen. But that'll have to cost a buck apiece anyways.

Happy. That's all right.

Stanley. What'd you, hit a number or somethin'?

Happy. No, it's a little celebration. My brother is — I think he pulled off a big deal today. I think we're going into business together.

Stanley. Great! That's the best for you. Because a family business, you know what I mean? — that's the best.

Happy. That's what I think.

Stanley. 'Cause what's the difference? Somebody steals? It's in the family. Know what I mean? *(Sotto voce.)* Like this bartender here. The boss is goin' crazy what kinda leak he's got in the cash register. You put it in but it don't come out.

Happy (raising his head). Sh!

Stanley. What?

Happy. You notice I wasn't lookin' right or left, was I?

Stanley. No.

Happy. And my eyes are closed.

Stanley. So what's the ... ?

Happy. Strudel's comin'.

Stanley (catching on, looks around). Ah, no, there's no ...

He breaks off as a furred, lavishly dressed girl enters and sits at the next table. Both follow her with their eyes.

Stanley. Geez, how'd ya know?

Happy. I got radar or something. *(Staring directly at her profile.)* Ooooooo ... Stanley.

Stanley. I think that's for you, Mr. Loman.

Happy. Look at that mouth. Oh, God. And the binoculars.

Stanley. Geez, you got a life, Mr. Loman.

Happy. Wait on her.

Stanley (going to the Girl's table). Would you like a menu, ma'am?

Girl. I'm expecting someone, but I'd like a ...

Happy. Why don't you bring her — excuse me, miss, do you mind? I sell champagne, and I'd like you to try my brand. Bring her a champagne, Stanley.

Girl. That's awfully nice of you.

Happy. Don't mention it. It's all company money. *(He laughs.)*

Girl. That's a charming product to be selling, isn't it?

Happy. Oh, gets to be like everything else. Selling is selling, y'know.

Girl. I suppose.

Happy. You don't happen to sell, do you?

Girl. No, I don't sell.

Happy. Would you object to a compliment from a stranger? You ought to be on a magazine cover.

Girl (looking at him a little archly). I have been.

Stanley comes in with a glass of champagne.

Happy. What'd I say before, Stanley? You see? She's a cover girl.
Stanley. Oh, I could see, I could see.
Happy (to the Girl). What magazine?
Girl. Oh, a lot of them. *(She takes the drink.)* Thank you.
Happy. You know what they say in France, don't you? "Champagne is the drink of the complexion" — Hya, Biff!

Biff has entered and sits with Happy.

Biff. Hello, kid. Sorry I'm late.
Happy. I just got here. Uh, Miss . . . ?
Girl. Forsythe.
Happy. Miss Forsythe, this is my brother.
Biff. Is Dad here?
Happy. His name is Biff. You might've heard of him. Great football player.
Girl. Really? What team?
Happy. Are you familiar with football?
Girl. No, I'm afraid I'm not.
Happy. Biff is quarterback with the New York Giants.
Girl. Well, that is nice, isn't it? *(She drinks.)*
Happy. Good health.
Girl. I'm happy to meet you.
Happy. That's my name. Hap. It's really Harold, but at West Point they called me Happy.
Girl (now really impressed). Oh, I see. How do you do? *(She turns her profile.)*
Biff. Isn't Dad coming?
Happy. You want her?
Biff. Oh, I could never make that.
Happy. I remember the time that idea would never come into your head. Where's the old confidence, Biff?
Biff. I just saw Oliver . . .
Happy. Wait a minute. I've got to see that old confidence again. Do you want her? She's on call.
Biff. Oh, no. *(He turns to look at the Girl.)*
Happy. I'm telling you. Watch this. *(Turning to the Girl.)* Honey? *(She turns to him.)* Are you busy?
Girl. Well, I am . . . but I could make a phone call.
Happy. Do that, will you, honey? And see if you can get a friend. We'll be here for a while. Biff is one of the greatest football players in the country.
Girl (standing up). Well, I'm certainly happy to meet you.
Happy. Come back soon.
Girl. I'll try.

Happy. Don't try, honey, try hard.

The Girl exits. Stanley follows, shaking his head in bewildered admiration.

Happy. Isn't that a shame now? A beautiful girl like that? That's why I can't get married. There's not a good woman in a thousand. New York is loaded with them, kid!

Biff. Hap, look...

Happy. I told you she was on call!

Biff (strangely unnerved). Cut it out, will ya? I want to say something to you.

Happy. Did you see Oliver?

Biff. I saw him all right. Now look, I want to tell Dad a couple of things and I want you to help me.

Happy. What? Is he going to back you?

Biff. Are you crazy? You're out of your goddam head, you know that?

Happy. Why? What happened?

Biff (breathlessly). I did a terrible thing today, Hap. It's been the strangest day I ever went through. I'm all numb, I swear.

Happy. You mean he wouldn't see you?

Biff. Well, I waited six hours for him, see? All day. Kept sending my name in. Even tried to date his secretary so she'd get me to him, but no soap.

Happy. Because you're not showin' the old confidence, Biff. He remembered you, didn't he?

Biff (stopping Happy with a gesture). Finally, about five o'clock, he comes out. Didn't remember who I was or anything. I felt like such an idiot, Hap.

Happy. Did you tell him my Florida idea?

Biff. He walked away. I saw him for one minute. I got so mad I could've torn the walls down! How the hell did I ever get the idea I was a salesman there? I even believed myself that I'd been a salesman for him! And then he gave me one look and — I realized what a ridiculous lie my whole life has been! We've been talking in a dream for fifteen years. I was a shipping clerk.

Happy. What'd you do?

Biff (with great tension and wonder). Well, he left, see. And the secretary went out. I was all alone in the waiting room. I don't know what came over me, Hap. The next thing I know I'm in his office — paneled walls, everything. I can't explain it. I — Hap, I took his fountain pen.

Happy. Geez, did he catch you?

Biff. I ran out. I ran down all eleven flights. I ran and ran and ran.

Happy. That was an awful dumb — what'd you do that for?

Biff (agonized). I don't know, I just — wanted to take something, I don't know. You gotta help me, Hap, I'm gonna tell Pop.

Happy. You crazy? What for?

Biff. Hap, he's got to understand that I'm not the man somebody lends that kind of money to. He thinks I've been spiting him all these years and it's eating him up.

Happy. That's just it. You tell him something nice.

Biff. I can't.

Happy. Say you got a lunch date with Oliver tomorrow.

Biff. So what do I do tomorrow?

Happy. You leave the house tomorrow and come back at night and say Oliver is thinking it over. And he thinks it over for a couple of weeks, and gradually it fades away and nobody's the worse.

Biff. But it'll go on forever!

Happy. Dad is never so happy as when he's looking forward to something!

Willy enters.

Happy. Hello, scout!

Willy. Gee, I haven't been here in years!

Stanley has followed Willy in and sets a chair for him. Stanley starts off but Happy stops him.

Happy. Stanley!

Stanley stands by, waiting for an order.

Biff (going to Willy with guilt, as to an invalid). Sit down, Pop. You want a drink?

Willy. Sure, I don't mind.

Biff. Let's get a load on.

Willy. You look worried.

Biff. N-no. *(To Stanley.)* Scotch all around. Make it doubles.

Stanley. Doubles, right. *(He goes.)*

Willy. You had a couple already, didn't you?

Biff. Just a couple, yeah.

Willy. Well, what happened, boy? *(Nodding affirmatively, with a smile.)* Everything go all right?

Biff (takes a breath, then reaches out and grasps Willy's hand). Pal . . . *(He is smiling bravely, and Willy is smiling too.)* I had an experience today.

Happy. Terrific, Pop.

Willy. That so? What happened?

Biff (high, slightly alcoholic, above the earth). I'm going to tell you everything from first to last. It's been a strange day. *(Silence. He looks around, composes himself as best he can, but his breath keeps breaking the rhythm of his voice.)* I had to wait quite a while for him, and . . .

Willy. Oliver?

Biff. Yeah, Oliver. All day, as a matter of cold fact. And a lot of — instances — facts, Pop, facts about my life came back to me. Who was it, Pop? Who ever said I was a salesman with Oliver?

Willy. Well, you were.

Biff. No, Dad, I was shipping clerk.

Willy. But you were practically . . .

Biff (with determination). Dad, I don't know who said it first, but I was never a salesman for Bill Oliver.

Willy. What're you talking about?

Biff. Let's hold on to the facts tonight, Pop. We're not going to get anywhere bullin' around. I was a shipping clerk.

Willy (angrily). All right, now listen to me . . .

Biff. Why don't you let me finish?

Willy. I'm not interested in stories about the past or any crap of that kind because the woods are burning, boys, you understand? There's a big blaze going on all around. I was fired today.

Biff (shocked). How could you be?

Willy. I was fired, and I'm looking for a little good news to tell your mother, because the woman has waited and the woman has suffered. The gist of it is that I haven't got a story left in my head, Biff. So don't give me a lecture about facts and aspects. I am not interested. Now what've you got to say to me?

Stanley enters with three drinks. They wait until he leaves.

Willy. Did you see Oliver?

Biff. Jesus, Dad!

Willy. You mean you didn't go up there?

Happy. Sure he went up there.

Biff. I did. I — saw him. How could they fire you?

Willy (on the edge of his chair). What kind of a welcome did he give you?

Biff. He won't even let you work on commission?

Willy. I'm out! *(Driving.)* So tell me, he gave you a warm welcome?

Happy. Sure, Pop, sure!

Biff (driven). Well, it was kind of . . .

Willy. I was wondering if he'd remember you. *(To Happy.)* Imagine, man doesn't see him for ten, twelve years and gives him that kind of a welcome!

Happy. Damn right!

Biff (trying to return to the offensive). Pop, look . . .

Willy. You know why he remembered you, don't you? Because you impressed him in those days.

Biff. Let's talk quietly and get this down to the facts, huh?

Willy (as though Biff had been interrupting). Well, what happened? It's great news, Biff. Did he take you into his office or'd you talk in the waiting room?

Biff. Well, he came in, see, and . . .

Willy (with a big smile). What'd he say? Betcha he threw his arm around you.

Biff. Well, he kinda . . .

Willy. He's a fine man. *(To Happy.)* Very hard man to see, y'know.

Happy (agreeing). Oh, I know.

Willy (to Biff). Is that where you had the drinks?

Biff. Yeah, he gave me a couple of — no, no!

Happy (cutting in). He told him my Florida idea.

Willy. Don't interrupt. *(To Biff.)* How'd he react to the Florida idea?

Biff. Dad, will you give me a minute to explain?

Willy. I've been waiting for you to explain since I sat down here! What happened? He took you into his office and what?

Biff. Well — I talked. And — and he listened, see.

Willy. Famous for the way he listens, y'know. What was his answer?

Biff. His answer was — *(He breaks off, suddenly angry.)* Dad, you're not letting me tell you what I want to tell you!

Willy (accusing, angered). You didn't see him, did you?

Biff. I did see him!

Willy. What'd you insult him or something? You insulted him, didn't you?

Biff. Listen, will you let me out of it, will you just let me out of it!

Happy. What the hell!

Willy. Tell me what happened!

Biff (to Happy). I can't talk to him!

A single trumpet note jars the ear. The light of green leaves stains the house, which holds the air of night and a dream. Young Bernard enters and knocks on the door of the house.

Young Bernard (frantically). Mrs. Loman, Mrs. Loman!

Happy. Tell him what happened!

Biff (to Happy). Shut up and leave me alone!

Willy. No, no! You had to go and flunk math!

Biff. What math? What're you talking about?

Young Bernard. Mrs. Loman, Mrs. Loman!

Linda appears in the house, as of old.

Willy (wildly). Math, math, math!

Biff. Take it easy, Pop!

Young Bernard. Mrs. Loman!

Willy (furiously). If you hadn't flunked you'd've been set by now!

Biff. Now, look, I'm gonna tell you what happened, and you're going
to listen to me.

Young Bernard. Mrs. Loman!

Biff. I waited six hours . . .

Happy. What the hell are you saying?

Biff. I kept sending in my name but he wouldn't see me. So finally
he . . . *(He continues unheard as light fades low on the restaurant.)*

Young Bernard. Biff flunked math!

Linda. No!

Young Bernard. Birnbaum flunked him! They won't graduate him!

Linda. But they have to. He's gotta go to the university. Where is he?
Biff! Biff!

Young Bernard. No, he left. He went to Grand Central.

Linda. Grand — You mean he went to Boston!

Young Bernard. Is Uncle Willy in Boston?

Linda. Oh, maybe Willy can talk to the teacher. Oh, the poor, poor
boy!

Light on house area snaps out.

Biff (at the table, now audible, holding up a gold fountain pen). . . .
so I'm washed up with Oliver, you understand? Are you listening
to me?

Willy (at a loss). Yeah, sure. If you hadn't flunked . . .

Biff. Flunked what? What're you talking about?

Willy. Don't blame everything on me! I didn't flunk math — you did!
What pen?

Happy. That was awful dumb, Biff, a pen like that is worth —

Willy (seeing the pen for the first time). You took Oliver's pen?

Biff (weakening). Dad, I just explained it to you.

Willy. You stole Bill Oliver's fountain pen!

Biff. I didn't exactly steal it! That's just what I've been explaining to
you!

Happy. He had it in his hand and just then Oliver walked in, so he
got nervous and stuck it in his pocket!

Willy. My God, Biff!

Biff. I never intended to do it, Dad!

Operator's Voice. Standish Arms, good evening!

Willy (shouting). I'm not in my room!

Biff (frightened). Dad, what's the matter? *(He and Happy stand up.)*
Operator. Ringing Mr. Loman for you!
Willy. I'm not there, stop it!
Biff (horrified, gets down on one knee before Willy). Dad, I'll make
good, I'll make good. *(Willy tries to get to his feet. Biff holds him
down.)* Sit down now.
Willy. No, you're no good, you're no good for anything.
Biff. I am, Dad, I'll find something else, you understand? Now don't
worry about anything. *(He holds up Willy's face.)* Talk to me, Dad.
Operator. Mr. Loman does not answer. Shall I page him?
*Willy (attempting to stand, as though to rush and silence the Oper-
ator).* No, no, no!
Happy. He'll strike something, Pop.
Willy. No, no . . .
Biff (desperately, standing over Willy). Pop, listen! Listen to me!
I'm telling you something good. Oliver talked to his partner about
the Florida idea. You listening? He — he talked to his partner, and
he came to me . . . I'm going to be all right, you hear? Dad, listen to
me, he said it was just a question of the amount!
Willy. Then you . . . got it?
Happy. He's gonna be terrific, Pop!
Willy (trying to stand). Then you got it, haven't you? You got it! You
got it!
Biff (agonized, holds Willy down). No, no. Look, Pop. I'm supposed
to have lunch with them tomorrow. I'm just telling you this so
you'll know that I can still make an impression, Pop. And I'll make
good somewhere, but I can't go tomorrow, see?
Willy. Why not? You simply . . .
Biff. But the pen, Pop!
Willy. You give it to him and tell him it was an oversight!
Happy. Sure, have lunch tomorrow!
Biff. I can't say that . . .
Willy. You were doing a crossword puzzle and accidentally used his
pen!
Biff. Listen, kid, I took those balls years ago, now I walk in with his
fountain pen? That clinches it, don't you see? I can't face him like
that! I'll try elsewhere.
Page's Voice. Paging Mr. Loman!
Willy. Don't you want to be anything?
Biff. Pop, how can I go back?
Willy. You don't want to be anything, is that what's behind it?
Biff (now angry at Willy for not crediting his sympathy). Don't take
it that way! You think it was easy walking into that office after

what I'd done to him? A team of horses couldn't have dragged me back to Bill Oliver!

Willy. Then why'd you go?

Biff. Why did I go? Why did I go! Look at you! Look at what's become of you!

Off left, The Woman laughs.

Willy. Biff, you're going to go to that lunch tomorrow, or . . .

Biff. I can't go. I've got no appointment!

Happy. Biff, for . . . !

Willy. Are you spiting me?

Biff. Don't take it that way! Goddammit!

Willy (strikes Biff and falters away from the table). You rotten little louse! Are you spiting me?

The Woman. Someone's at the door, Willy!

Biff. I'm no good, can't you see what I am?

Happy (separating them). Hey, you're in a restaurant! Now cut it out, both of you! *(The girls enter.)* Hello, girls, sit down.

The Woman laughs, off left.

Miss Forsythe. I guess we might as well. This is Letta.

The Woman. Willy, are you going to wake up?

Biff (ignoring Willy). How're ya, miss, sit down. What do you drink?

Miss Forsythe. Letta might not be able to stay long.

Letta. I gotta get up very early tomorrow. I got jury duty. I'm so excited! Were you fellows ever on a jury?

Biff. No, but I been in front of them! *(The girls laugh.)* This is my father.

Letta. Isn't he cute? Sit down with us, Pop.

Happy. Sit him down, Biff!

Biff (going to him). Come on, slugger, drink us under the table. To hell with it! Come on, sit down, pal.

On Biff's last insistence, Willy is about to sit.

The Woman (now urgently). Willy, are you going to answer the door!

The Woman's call pulls Willy back. He starts right, befuddled.

Biff. Hey, where are you going?

Willy. Open the door.

Biff. The door?

Willy. The washroom . . . the door . . . where's the door?

Biff (leading Willy to the left). Just go straight down.

Willy moves left.

The Woman. Willy, Willy, are you going to get up, get up, get up, get up?

Willy exits left.

Letta. I think it's sweet you bring your daddy along.

Miss Forsythe. Oh, he isn't really your father!

Biff (at left, turning to her resentfully). Miss Forsythe, you've just seen a prince walk by. A fine, troubled prince. A hard-working, unappreciated prince. A pal, you understand? A good companion. Always for his boys.

Letta. That's so sweet.

Happy. Well, girls, what's the program? We're wasting time. Come on, Biff. Gather round. Where would you like to go?

Biff. Why don't you do something for him?

Happy. Me!

Biff. Don't you give a damn for him, Hap?

Happy. What're you talking about? I'm the one who . . .

Biff. I sense it, you don't give a good goddam about him. *(He takes the rolled-up hose from his pocket and puts it on the table in front of Happy.)* Look what I found in the cellar, for Christ's sake. How can you bear to let it go on?

Happy. Me? Who goes away? Who runs off and . . .

Biff. Yeah, but he doesn't mean anything to you. You could help him — I can't! Don't you understand what I'm talking about? He's going to kill himself, don't you know that?

Happy. Don't I know it! Me!

Biff. Hap, help him! Jesus . . . help him . . . Help me, help me, I can't bear to look at his face! *(Ready to weep, he hurries out, up right.)*

Happy (starting after him). Where are you going?

Miss Forsythe. What's he so mad about?

Happy. Come on, girls, we'll catch up with him.

Miss Forsythe (as Happy pushes her out). Say, I don't like that temper of his!

Happy. He's just a little overstrung, he'll be all right!

Willy (off left, as The Woman laughs). Don't answer! Don't answer!

Letta. Don't you want to tell your father . . .

Happy. No, that's not my father. He's just a guy. Come on, we'll catch Biff, and, honey, we're going to paint this town! Stanley, where's the check! Hey, Stanley!

They exit. Stanley looks toward left.

Stanley (calling to Happy indignantly). Mr. Loman! Mr. Loman!

Stanley picks up a chair and follows them off. Knocking is heard off left. The Woman enters, laughing. Willy follows her. She is in a black slip; he is buttoning his shirt. Raw, sensuous music accompanies their speech:

Willy. Will you stop laughing? Will you stop?

The Woman. Aren't you going to answer the door? He'll wake the whole hotel.

Willy. I'm not expecting anybody.

The Woman. Whyn't you have another drink, honey, and stop being so damn self-centered?

Willy. I'm so lonely.

The Woman. You know you ruined me, Willy? From now on, whenever you come to the office, I'll see that you go right through to the buyers. No waiting at my desk anymore, Willy. You ruined me.

Willy. That's nice of you to say that.

The Woman. Gee, you are self-centered! Why so sad? You are the saddest, self-centeredest soul I ever did see-saw. *(She laughs. He kisses her.)* Come on inside, drummer boy. It's silly to be dressing in the middle of the night. *(As knocking is heard.)* Aren't you going to answer the door?

Willy. They're knocking on the wrong door.

The Woman. But I felt the knocking. And he heard us talking in here. Maybe the hotel's on fire!

Willy (his terror rising). It's a mistake.

The Woman. Then tell him to go away!

Willy. There's nobody there.

The Woman. It's getting on my nerves, Willy. There's somebody standing out there and it's getting on my nerves!

Willy (pushing her away from him). All right, stay in the bathroom here, and don't come out. I think there's a law in Massachusetts about it, so don't come out. It may be that new room clerk. He looked very mean. So don't come out. It's a mistake, there's no fire.

The knocking is heard again. He takes a few steps away from her, and she vanishes into the wing. The light follows him, and now he is facing Young Biff, who carries a suitcase. Biff steps toward him. The music is gone.

Biff. Why didn't you answer?

Willy. Biff! What are you doing in Boston?

Biff. Why didn't you answer? I've been knocking for five minutes, I called you on the phone . . .

Willy. I just heard you. I was in the bathroom and had the door shut. Did anything happen home?

Biff. Dad — I let you down.

Willy. What do you mean?

Biff. Dad . . .

Willy. Biffo, what's this about? *(Putting his arm around Biff.)* Come on, let's go downstairs and get you a malted.

Biff. Dad, I flunked math.

Willy. Not for the term?

Biff. The term. I haven't got enough credits to graduate.

Willy. You mean to say Bernard wouldn't give you the answers?

Biff. He did, he tried, but I only got a sixty-one.

Willy. And they wouldn't give you four points?

Biff. Birnbaum refused absolutely. I begged him, Pop, but he won't give me those points. You gotta talk to him before they close the school. Because if he saw the kind of man you are, and you just talked to him in your way, I'm sure he'd come through for me. The class came right before practice, see, and I didn't go enough. Would you talk to him? He'd like you, Pop. You know the way you could talk.

Willy. You're on. We'll drive right back.

Biff. Oh, Dad, good work! I'm sure he'll change it for you!

Willy. Go downstairs and tell the clerk I'm checkin' out. Go right down.

Biff. Yes, sir! See, the reason he hates me, Pop — one day he was late for class so I got up at the blackboard and imitated him. I crossed my eyes and talked with a lithp.

Willy (laughing). You did? The kids like it?

Biff. They nearly died laughing!

Willy. Yeah? What'd you do?

Biff. The thquare root of thixthy twee is . . . *(Willy bursts out laughing; Biff joins.)* And in the middle of it he walked in!

Willy laughs and The Woman joins in offstage.

Willy (without hesitation). Hurry downstairs and . . .

Biff. Somebody in there?

Willy. No, that was next door.

The Woman laughs offstage.

Biff. Somebody got in your bathroom!

Willy. No, it's the next room, there's a party . . .

The Woman (enters, laughing; she lisps this). Can I come in? There's something in the bathtub, Willy, and it's moving!

Willy looks at Biff, who is staring open-mouthed and horrified at The Woman.

Willy. Ah — you better go back to your room. They must be finished painting by now. They're painting her room so I let her take a shower here. Go back, go back . . . *(He pushes her.)*

The Woman (resisting). But I've got to get dressed, Willy, I can't . . .

Willy. Get out of here! Go back, go back . . . *(Suddenly striving for the ordinary.)* This is Miss Francis, Biff, she's a buyer. They're painting her room. Go back, Miss Francis, go back . . .

The Woman. But my clothes, I can't go out naked in the hall!

Willy (pushing her offstage). Get outa here! Go back, go back!

Biff slowly sits down on his suitcase as the argument continues offstage.

The Woman. Where's my stockings? You promised me stockings, Willy!

Willy. I have no stockings here!

The Woman. You had two boxes of size nine sheers for me, and I want them!

Willy. Here, for God's sake, will you get outa here!

The Woman (enters holding a box of stockings). I just hope there's nobody in the hall. That's all I hope. *(To Biff.)* Are you football or baseball?

Biff. Football.

The Woman (angry, humiliated). That's me too. G'night. *(She snatches her clothes from Willy, and walks out.)*

Willy (after a pause). Well, better get going. I want to get to the school first thing in the morning. Get my suits out of the closet. I'll get my valise. *(Biff doesn't move.)* What's the matter! *(Biff remains motionless, tears falling.)* She's a buyer. Buys for J. H. Simmons. She lives down the hall — they're painting. You don't imagine — *(He breaks off. After a pause.)* Now listen, pal, she's just a buyer. She sees merchandise in her room and they have to keep it looking just so . . . *(Pause. Assuming command.)* All right, get my suits. *(Biff doesn't move.)* Now stop crying and do as I say. I gave you an order. Biff, I gave you an order! Is that what you do when I give you an order? How dare you cry! *(Putting his arm around Biff.)* Now look, Biff, when you grow up you'll understand about these things. You mustn't — you mustn't overemphasize a thing like this. I'll see Birnbaum first thing in the morning.

Biff. Never mind.

Willy (getting down beside Biff). Never mind! He's going to give you those points. I'll see to it.

Biff. He wouldn't listen to you.

Willy. He certainly will listen to me. You need those points for the U. of Virginia.

Biff. I'm not going there.

Willy. Heh? If I can't get him to change that mark you'll make it up in summer school. You've got all summer to . . .

Biff (his weeping breaking from him). Dad . . .

Willy (infected by it). Oh, my boy . . .

Biff. Dad . . .

Willy. She's nothing to me, Biff. I was lonely, I was terribly lonely.

Biff. You — you gave her Mama's stockings! *(His tears break through and he rises to go.)*

Willy (grabbing for Biff). I gave you an order!

Biff. Don't touch me, you — liar!

Willy. Apologize for that!

Biff. You fake! You phony little fake! You fake! *(Overcome, he turns quickly and weeping fully goes out with his suitcase. Willy is left on the floor on his knees.)*

Willy. I gave you an order! Biff, come back here or I'll beat you! Come back here! I'll whip you!

Stanley comes quickly in from the right and stands in front of Willy.

Willy (shouts at Stanley). I gave you an order . . .

Stanley. Hey, let's pick it up, pick it up, Mr. Loman. *(He helps Willy to his feet.)* Your boys left with the chippies. They said they'll see you home.

A second waiter watches some distance away.

Willy. But we were supposed to have dinner together.

Music is heard, Willy's theme.

Stanley. Can you make it?

Willy. I'll — sure, I can make it. *(Suddenly concerned about his clothes.)* Do I — I look all right?

Stanley. Sure, you look all right. *(He flicks a speck off Willy's lapel.)*

Willy. Here — here's a dollar.

Stanley. Oh, your son paid me. It's all right.

Willy (putting it in Stanley's hand). No, take it. You're a good boy.

Stanley. Oh, no, you don't have to . . .

Willy. Here — here's some more, I don't need it any more *(After a slight pause)* Tell me — is there a seed store in the neighborhood?

Stanley. Seeds? You mean like to plant?

As Willy turns, Stanley slips the money back into his jacket pocket.

Willy. Yes. Carrots, peas . . .

Stanley. Well, there's hardware stores on Sixth Avenue, but it may be too late now.

Willy (anxiously). Oh, I'd better hurry. I've got to get some seeds.

(He starts off to the right.) I've got to get some seeds, right away. Nothing's planted. I don't have a thing in the ground.

Willy hurries out as the light goes down. Stanley moves over to the right after him, watches him off. The other waiter has been staring at Willy.

Stanley (to the waiter). Well, whatta you looking at?

The waiter picks up the chairs and moves off right. Stanley takes the table and follows him. The light fades on this area. There is a long pause, the sound of the flute coming over. The light gradually rises on the kitchen, which is empty. Happy appears at the door of the house, followed by Biff. Happy is carrying a large bunch of long-stemmed roses. He enters the kitchen, looks around for Linda. Not seeing her, he turns to Biff, who is just outside the house door, and makes a gesture with his hands, indicating "Not here, I guess." He looks into the living room and freezes. Inside, Linda, unseen is seated, Willy's coat on her lap. She rises ominously and quietly and moves toward Happy, who backs up into the kitchen, afraid.

Happy. Hey, what're you doing up? *(Linda says nothing but moves toward him implacably.)* Where's Pop? *(He keeps backing to the right, and now Linda is in full view in the doorway to the living room.)* Is he sleeping?

Linda. Where were you?

Happy (trying to laugh it off). We met two girls, Mom, very fine types. Here, we brought you some flowers. *(Offering them to her.)* Put them in your room, Ma.

She knocks them to the floor at Biff's feet. He has now come inside and closed the door behind him. She stares at Biff, silent.

Happy. Now what'd you do that for? Mom, I want you to have some flowers . . .

Linda (cutting Happy off, violently to Biff). Don't you care whether he lives or dies?

Happy (going to the stairs). Come upstairs, Biff.

Biff (with a flare of disgust, to Happy). Go away from me! *(To Linda.)* What do you mean, lives or dies? Nobody's dying around here, pal.

Linda. Get out of my sight! Get out of here!

Biff. I wanna see the boss.

Linda. You're not going near him!

Biff. Where is he? *(He moves into the living room and Linda follows.)*

Linda (shouting after Biff). You invite him for dinner. He looks forward to it all day — *(Biff appears in his parents' bedroom, looks around, and exits)* — and then you desert him there. There's no stranger you'd do that to!

Happy. Why? He had a swell time with us. Listen, when I — *(Linda comes back into the kitchen)* — desert him I hope I don't outlive the day!

Linda. Get out of here!

Happy. Now look, Mom . . .

Linda. Did you have to go to women tonight? You and your lousy rotten whores!

    Biff re-enters the kitchen.

Happy. Mom, all we did was follow Biff around trying to cheer him up! *(To Biff.)* Boy, what a night you gave me!

Linda. Get out of here, both of you, and don't come back! I don't want you tormenting him any more. Go on now, get your things together! *(To Biff.)* You can sleep in his apartment. *(She starts to pick up the flowers and stops herself.)* Pick up this stuff, I'm not your maid any more. Pick it up, you bum, you!

    Happy turns his back to her in refusal. Biff slowly moves over and gets down on his knees, picking up the flowers.

Linda. You're a pair of animals! Not one, not another living soul would have had the cruelty to walk out on that man in a restaurant!

Biff (not looking at her). Is that what he said?

Linda. He didn't have to say anything. He was so humiliated he nearly limped when he came in.

Happy. But, Mom, he had a great time with us . . .

Biff (cutting him off violently). Shut up!

    Without another word, Happy goes upstairs.

Linda. You! You didn't even go in to see if he was all right!

Biff (still on the floor in front of Linda, the flowers in his hand; with self-loathing.). No. Didn't. Didn't do a damned thing. How do you like that, heh? Left him babbling in a toilet.

Linda. You louse. You . . .

Biff. Now you hit it on the nose! *(He gets up, throws the flowers in the wastebasket.)* The scum of the earth, and you're looking at him!

Linda. Get out of here!

Biff. I gotta talk to the boss, Mom. Where is he?

Linda. You're not going near him. Get out of this house!

Biff (with absolute assurance, determination). No. We're gonna have an abrupt conversation, him and me.
Linda. You're not talking to him.

Hammering is heard from outside the house, off right. Biff turns toward the noise.

Linda (suddenly pleading). Will you please leave him alone?
Biff. What's he doing out there?
Linda. He's planting the garden!
Biff (quietly). Now? Oh, my God!

Biff moves outside, Linda following. The light dies down on them and comes up on the center of the apron as Willy walks into it. He is carrying a flashlight, a hoe, and a handful of seed packets. He raps the top of the hoe sharply to fix it firmly, and then moves to the left, measuring off the distance with his foot. He holds the flashlight to look at the seed packets, reading off the instructions. He is in the blue of night.

Willy. Carrots . . . quarter-inch apart. Rows . . . one-foot rows. *(He measures it off.)* One foot. *(He puts down a package and measures off.)* Beets. *(He puts down another package and measures again.)* Lettuce. *(He reads the package, puts it down.)* One foot — *(He breaks off as Ben appears at the right and moves slowly down to him.)* What a proposition, ts,ts. Terrific, terrific. 'Cause she's suffered, Ben, the woman has suffered. You understand me? A man can't go out the way, he came in, Ben, a man has got to add up to something. You can't, you can't — *(Ben moves toward him as though to interrupt.)* You gotta consider, now. Don't answer so quick. Remember, it's a guaranteed twenty-thousand-dollar proposition. Now look, Ben, I want you to go through the ins and outs of this thing with me. I've got nobody to talk to, Ben, and the woman has suffered, you hear me?
Ben (standing still, considering). What's the proposition?
Willy. It's twenty thousand dollars on the barrelhead. Guaranteed, gilt-edged, you understand?
Ben. You don't want to make a fool of yourself. They might not honor the policy.
Willy. How can they dare refuse? Didn't I work like a coolie to meet every premium on the nose? And now they don't pay off? Impossible!
Ben. It's called a cowardly thing, William.
Willy. Why? Does it take more guts to stand here the rest of my life ringing up a zero?

Ben (yielding). That's a point, William. *(He moves, thinking, turns.)* And twenty thousand — that *is* something one can feel with the hand, it is there.

Willy (now assured, with rising power). Oh, Ben, that's the whole beauty of it! I see it like a diamond, shining in the dark, hard and rough, that I can pick up and touch in my hand. Not like — like an appointment! This would not be another damned-fool appointment, Ben, and it changes all the aspects. Because he thinks I'm nothing, see, and so he spites me. But the funeral . . . *(Straightening up.)* Ben, that funeral will be massive! They'll come from Maine, Massachusetts, Vermont, New Hampshire! All the old-timers with the strange license plates — that boy will be thunderstruck, Ben, because he never realized — I am known! Rhode Island, New York, New Jersey — I am known, Ben, and he'll see it with his eyes once and for all. He'll see what I am, Ben! He's in for a shock, that boy!

Ben (coming down to the edge of the garden). He'll call you a coward.

Willy (suddenly fearful). No, that would be terrible.

Ben. Yes. And a damned fool.

Willy. No, no, he mustn't, I won't have that! *(He is broken and desperate.)*

Ben. He'll hate you, William.

The gay music of the Boys is heard.

Willy. Oh, Ben, how do we get back to all the great times? Used to be so full of light, and comradeship, the sleigh-riding in winter, and the ruddiness on his cheeks. And always some kind of good news coming up, always something nice coming up ahead. And never even let me carry the valises in the house, and simonizing, simonizing that little red car! Why, why can't I give him something and not have him hate me?

Ben. Let me think about it. *(He glances at his watch.)* I still have a little time. Remarkable proposition, but you've got to be sure you're not making a fool of yourself.

Ben drifts off upstage and goes out of sight. Biff comes down from the left.

Willy (suddenly conscious of Biff, turns and looks up at him, then begins picking up the packages of seeds in confusion.) Where the hell is that seed? *(Indignantly.)* You can't see nothing out here! They boxed in the whole goddam neighborhood!

Biff. There are people all around here. Don't you realize that?

Willy. I'm busy. Don't bother me.

Biff (taking the hoe from Willy). I'm saying good-by to you, Pop. *(Willy looks at him, silent, unable to move.)* I'm not coming back any more.

Willy. You're not going to see Oliver tomorrow?

Biff. I've got no appointment, Dad.

Willy. He put his arm around you, and you've got no appointment?

Biff. Pop, get this now, will you? Everytime I've left it's been a fight that sent me out of here. Today I realized something about myself and I tried to explain it to you and I — I think I'm just not smart enough to make any sense out of it for you. To hell with whose fault it is or anything like that. *(He takes Willy's arm.)* Let's just wrap it up, heh? Come on in, we'll tell Mom. *(He gently tries to pull Willy to left.)*

Willy (frozen, immobile, with guilt in his voice). No, I don't want to see her.

Biff. Come on! *(He pulls again, and Willy tries to pull away.)*

Willy (highly nervous). No, no, I don't want to see her.

Biff (tries to look into Willy's face, as if to find the answer there). Why don't you want to see her?

Willy (more harshly now). Don't bother me, will you?

Biff. What do you mean, you don't want to see her? You don't want them calling you yellow, do you? This isn't your fault; it's me, I'm a bum. Now come inside! *(Willy strains to get away.)* Did you hear what I said to you?

Willy pulls away and quickly goes by himself into the house. Biff follows.   •

Linda (to Willy). Did you plant, dear?

Biff (at the door, to Linda). All right, we had it out. I'm going and I'm not writing any more.

Linda (going to Willy in the kitchen). I think that's the best way, dear. 'Cause there's no use drawing it out, you'll just never get along.

Willy doesn't respond.

Biff. People ask where I am and what I'm doing, you don't know, and you don't care. That way it'll be off your mind and you can start brightening up again. All right? That clears it, doesn't it? *(Willy is silent, and Biff goes to him.)* You gonna wish me luck, scout? *(He extends his hand.)* What do you say?

Linda. Shake his hand, Willy.

Willy (turning to her, seething with hurt). There's no necessity to mention the pen at all, y'know.

Biff (gently). I've got no appointment, Dad.

Willy (erupting fiercely). He put his arm around . . . ?

Biff. Dad, you're never going to see what I am, so what's the use of arguing? If I strike oil I'll send you a check. Meantime forget I'm alive.

Willy (to Linda). Spite, see?

Biff. Shake hands, Dad.

Willy. Not my hand.

Biff. I was hoping not to go this way.

Willy. Well, this is the way you're going. Good-by.

Biff looks at him a moment, then turns sharply and goes to the stairs.

Willy (stops him with). May you rot in hell if you leave this house!

Biff (turning). Exactly what is it that you want from me?

Willy. I want you to know, on the train, in the mountains, in the valleys, wherever you go, that you cut down your life for spite!

Biff. No, no.

Willy. Spite, spite, is the word of your undoing! And when you're down and out, remember what did it. When you're rotting somewhere beside the railroad tracks, remember, and don't you dare blame it on me!

Biff. I'm not blaming it on you!

Willy. I won't take the rap for this, you hear?

Happy comes down the stairs and stands on the bottom step, watching.

Biff. That's just what I'm telling you!

Willy (sinking into a chair at a table, with full accusation). You're trying to put a knife in me — don't think I don't know what you're doing!

Biff. All right, phony! Then let's lay it on the line. *(He whips the rubber tube out of his pocket and puts it on the table.)*

Happy. You crazy . . .

Linda. Biff! *(She moves to grab the hose, but Biff holds it down with his hand.)*

Biff. Leave it there! Don't move it!

Willy (not looking at it). What is that?

Biff. You know goddam well what that is.

Willy (caged, wanting to escape). I never saw that.

Biff. You saw it. The mice didn't bring it into the cellar! What is this supposed to do, make a hero out of you? This supposed to make me sorry for you?

Willy. Never heard of it.

Biff. There'll be no pity for you, you hear it? No pity!

Willy (to Linda). You hear the spite!

Biff. No, you're going to hear the truth — what you are and what I am!

Linda. Stop it!

Willy. Spite!

Happy (coming down toward Biff). You cut it now!

Biff (to Happy). The man don't know who we are! The man is gonna know! *(To Willy.)* We never told the truth for ten minutes in this house!

Happy. We always told the truth!

Biff (turning on him). You big blow, are you the assistant buyer? You're one of the two assistants to the assistant, aren't you?

Happy. Well, I'm practically . . .

Biff. You're practically full of it! We all are! And I'm through with it *(to Willy.)* Now hear this, Willy, this is me.

Willy. I know you!

Biff. You know why I had no address for three months? I stole a suit in Kansas City and I was in jail. *(To Linda, who is sobbing.)* Stop crying. I'm through with it.

Linda turns away from them, her hands covering her face.

Willy. I suppose that's my fault!

Biff. I stole myself out of every good job since high school!

Willy. And whose fault is that?

Biff. And I never got anywhere because you blew me so full of hot air I could never stand taking orders from anybody! That's whose fault it is!

Willy. I hear that!

Linda. Don't, Biff!

Biff. It's goddam time you heard that! I had to be boss big shot in two weeks, and I'm through with it!

Willy. Then hang yourself! For spite, hang yourself!

Biff. No! Nobody's hanging himself, Willy! I ran down eleven flights with a pen in my hand today. And suddenly I stopped, you hear me? And in the middle of that office building, do you hear this? I stopped in the middle of that building and I saw — the sky. I saw the things that I love in this world. The work and the food and time to sit and smoke. And I looked at the pen and said to myself, what the hell am I grabbing this for? Why am I trying to become what I don't want to be? What am I doing in an office, making a contemptuous, begging fool of myself, when all I want is out there, waiting for me the minute I say I know who I am! Why can't I say that, Willy? *(He tries to make Willy face him, but Willy pulls away and moves to the left.)*

Willy (with hatred, threateningly). The door of your life is wide open!

Biff. Pop! I'm a dime a dozen, and so are you!

Willy (turning on him now in an uncontrolled outburst). I am not a dime a dozen! I am Willy Loman, and you are Biff Loman!

Biff starts for Willy, but is blocked by Happy. In his fury, Biff seems on the verge of attacking his father.

Biff. I am not a leader of men, Willy, and neither are you. You were never anything but a hard-working drummer who landed in the ash can like all the rest of them! I'm one dollar an hour, Willy! I tried seven states and couldn't raise it. A buck an hour! Do you gather my meaning? I'm not bringing home any prizes any more, and you're going to stop waiting for me to bring them home!

Willy (directly to Biff). You vengeful, spiteful mut!

Biff breaks from Happy. Willy, in fright, starts up the stairs. Biff grabs him.

Biff (at the peak of his fury). Pop, I'm nothing! I'm nothing, Pop. Can't you understand that? There's no spite in it any more. I'm just what I am, that's all.

Biff's fury has spent itself, and he breaks down, sobbing, holding on to Willy, who dumbly fumbles for Biff's face.

Willy (astonished). What're you doing? What're you doing? *(To Linda.)* Why is he crying?

Biff (crying, broken). Will you let me go, for Christ's sake? Will you take that phony dream and burn it before something happens? *(Struggling to contain himself, he pulls away and moves to the stairs.)* I'll go in the morning. Put him — put him to bed. *(Exhausted, Biff moves up the stairs to his room.)*

Willy (after a long pause, astonished, elevated). Isn't that — isn't that remarkable? Biff — he likes me!

Linda. He loves you, Willy!

Happy (deeply moved). Always did, Pop.

Willy. Oh, Biff! *(staring wildly.)* He cried! Cried to me. *(He is choking with his love, and now cries out his promise.)* That boy — that boy is going to be magnificent!

Ben appears in the light just outside the kitchen.

Ben. Yes, outstanding, with twenty thousand behind him.

Linda (sensing the racing of his mind, fearfully, carefully). Now come to bed, Willy. It's all settled now.

Willy (finding it difficult not to rush out of the house). Yes, we'll
sleep. Come on. Go to sleep, Hap.

Ben. And it does take a great kind of a man to crack the jungle.

In accents of dread, Ben's idyllic music starts up.

Happy (his arm around Linda). I'm getting married, Pop, don't forget it. I'm changing everything. I'm gonna run that department
before the year is up. You'll see, Mom. *(He kisses her.)*

Ben. The jungle is dark but full of diamonds, Willy.

Willy turns, moves, listening to Ben.

Linda. Be good. You're both good boys, just act that way, that's all.

Happy. 'Night, Pop. *(He goes upstairs.)*

Linda (to Willy). Come, dear.

Ben (with greater force). One must go in to fetch a diamond out.

*Willy (to Linda, as he moves slowly along the edge of kitchen, toward
the door).* I just want to get settled down, Linda. Let me sit alone
for a little.

Linda (almost uttering her fear). I want you upstairs.

Willy (taking her in his arms). In a few minutes, Linda. I couldn't
sleep right now. Go on, you look awful tired. *(He kisses her.)*

Ben. Not like an appointment at all. A diamond is rough and hard to
the touch.

Willy. Go on now. I'll be right up.

Linda. I think this is the only way, Willy.

Willy. Sure, it's the best thing.

Ben. Best thing!

Willy. The only way. Everything is gonna be — go on, kid, get to
bed. You look so tired.

Linda. Come right up.

Willy. Two minutes.

*Linda goes into the living room, then reappears in her bedroom.
Willy moves just outside the kitchen door.*

Willy. Loves me. *(Wonderingly.)* Always loved me. Isn't that a remarkable thing? Ben, he'll worship me for it!

Ben (with promise). It's dark there, but full of diamonds.

Willy. Can you imagine that magnificence with twenty thousand dollars in his pocket?

Linda (calling from her room). Willy! Come up!

Willy (calling into the kitchen). Yes! yes. Coming! It's very smart,
you realize that, don't you, sweetheart? Even Ben sees it. I gotta
go, baby. 'By! 'By! *(Going over to Ben, almost dancing.)* Imagine?
When the mail comes he'll be ahead of Bernard again!

Ben. A perfect proposition all around.

Willy. Did you see how he cried to me? Oh, if I could kiss him, Ben!

Ben. Time, William, time!

Willy. Oh, Ben, I always knew one way or another we were gonna make it, Biff and I!

Ben (looking at his watch). The boat. We'll be late. *(He moves slowly off into the darkness.)*

Willy (elegiacally, turning to the house). Now when you kick off, boy, I want a seventy-yard boot, and get right down the field under the ball, and when you hit, hit low and hit hard, because it's important, boy. *(He swings around and faces the audience.)* There's all kinds of important people in the stands, and the first thing you know . . . *(Suddenly realizing he is alone.)* Ben! Ben, where do I . . . ? *(He makes a sudden movement of search.)* Ben, how do I . . . ?

Linda (calling). Willy, you coming up?

Willy (uttering a gasp of fear, whirling about as if to quiet her). Sh! *(He turns around as if to find his way; sounds, faces, voices, seem to be swarming in upon him and he flicks at them, crying.)* Sh! Sh! *(Suddenly music, faint and high, stops him. It rises in intensity, almost to an unbearable scream. He goes up and down on his toes, and rushes off around the house.)* Shhh!

Linda. Willy?

There is no answer. Linda waits. Biff gets up off his bed. He is still in his clothes. Happy sits up. Biff stands listening.

Linda (with real fear). Willy, answer me! Willy!

There is the sound of a car starting and moving away at full speed.

Linda. No!

Biff (rushing down the stairs). Pop!

As the car speeds off, the music crashes down in a frenzy of sound, which becomes the soft pulsation of a single cello string. Biff slowly returns to his bedroom. He and Happy gravely don their jackets. Linda slowly walks out of her room. The music has developed into a dead march. The leaves of day are appearing over everything. Charley and Bernard, somberly dressed, appear and knock on the kitchen door. Biff and Happy slowly descend the stairs to the kitchen as Charley and Bernard enter. All stop a moment when Linda, in clothes of mourning, bearing a little bunch of roses, comes through the draped doorway into the kitchen. She goes to Charley and takes his arm. Now all move toward the audience, through the wall-line of the kitchen. At the limit of the apron, Linda lays down the flowers, kneels, and sits back on her heels. All stare down at the grave.

REQUIEM

Charley. It's getting dark, Linda.

Linda doesn't react. She stares at the grave.

Biff. How about it, Mom? Better get some rest, heh? They'll be closing the gate soon.

Linda makes no move. Pause.

Happy (deeply angered). He had no right to do that. There was no necessity for it. We would've helped him.

Charley (grunting). Hmmm.

Biff. Come along, Mom.

Linda. Why didn't anybody come?

Charley. It was a very nice funeral.

Linda. But where are all the people he knew? Maybe they blame him.

Charley. Naa. It's a rough world, Linda. They wouldn't blame him.

Linda. I can't understand it. At this time especially. First time in thirty-five years we were just about free and clear. He only needed a little salary. He was even finished with the dentist.

Charley. No man only needs a little salary.

Linda. I can't understand it.

Biff. There were a lot of nice days. When he'd come home from a trip; or on Sundays, making the stoop; finishing the cellar; putting on the new porch; when he built the extra bathroom; and put up the garage. You know something, Charley, there's more of him in that front stoop than in all the sales he ever made.

Charley. Yeah. He was a happy man with a batch of cement.

Linda. He was so wonderful with his hands.

Biff. He had the wrong dreams. All, all, wrong.

Happy (almost ready to fight Biff). Don't say that!

Biff. He never knew who he was.

Charley (stopping Happy's movement and reply; to Biff). Nobody dast blame this man. You don't understand: Willy was a salesman. And for a salesman, there is no rock bottom to the life. He don't put a bolt to a nut, he don't tell you the law or give you medicine. He's a man way out there in the blue, riding on a smile and a shoeshine. And when they start not smiling back — that's an earthquake. And then you get yourself a couple of spots on your hat, and you're finished. Nobody dast blame this man. A salesman is got to dream, boy. It comes with the territory.

Biff. Charley, the man didn't know who he was.

Happy (infuriated). Don't say that!

Biff. Why don't you come with me, Happy?

Happy. I'm not licked that easily. I'm staying right in this city, and I'm gonna beat this racket! *(He looks at Biff, his chin set.)* The Loman Brothers!

Biff. I know who I am, kid.

Happy. All right, boy. I'm gonna show you and everybody else that Willy Loman did not die in vain. He had a good dream. It's the only dream you can have — to come out number-one man. He fought it out here, and this is where I'm gonna win it for him.

Biff (with a hopeless glance at Happy, bends toward his mother). Let's go, Mom.

Linda. I'll be with you in a minute. Go on, Charley. *(He hesitates.)* I want to, just for a minute. I never had a chance to say good-by.

Charley moves away, followed by Happy. Biff remains a slight distance up and left of Linda. She sits there, summoning herself. The flute begins, not far away, playing behind her speech.

Linda. Forgive me, dear. I can't cry. I don't know what it is, but I can't cry. I don't understand it. Why did you ever do that? Help me, Willy, I can't cry. It seems to me that you're just on another trip. I keep expecting you. Willy, dear, I can't cry. Why did you do it? I search and search and I search, and I can't understand it, Willy. I made the last payment on the house today. Today, dear. And there'll be nobody home. *(A sob rises in her throat.)* We're free and clear. *(Sobbing more fully, released.)* We're free. *(Biff comes slowly toward her.)* We're free . . . We're free . . .

Biff lifts her to her feet and moves out up right with her in his arms. Linda sobs quietly. Bernard and Charley come together and follow them, followed by Happy. Only the music of the flute is left on the darkening stage as over the house the hard towers of the apartment buildings rise into sharp focus, and the curtain falls.

Questions

1. Miller said in the *New York Times*, 27 February 1949, Sec. II, p.1, that tragedy shows man's struggle to secure "his sense of personal dignity," and that "his destruction in the attempt posits a wrong or an evil in his environment." Does this make sense when applied to some earlier tragedy (for example, *Oedipus Rex* or *Othello),* and does

it apply convincingly to *Death of a Salesman?* Is this the tragedy of
an individual's own making? Or is society at fault for corrupting and
exploiting Willy? Or both?

2. Is Willy pathetic rather than tragic? If pathetic, does this imply
that the play is less worthy than if he is tragic?

3. Do you feel that Miller is straining too hard to turn a play about
a little man into a big, impressive play? For example, do the musical
themes, the unrealistic setting, the appearances of Ben, and the
speech at the grave seem out of keeping in a play about the death of a
salesman?

4. We don't know what Willy sells, and we don't know whether or
not the insurance will be paid after his death. Do you consider these
uncertainties to be faults in the play?

Eugène Ionesco (b. 1912)

The Gap

Translated by Rosette Lamont

List of Characters

The Friend
The Academician
The Academician's Wife
The Maid

Set. *A rich bourgeois living room with artistic pretensions. One
or two sofas, a number of armchairs, among which, a green,
Régence style one, right in the middle of the room. The walls are
covered with framed diplomas. One can make out, written in
heavy script at the top of a particularly large one, "Doctor Honoris causa." This is followed by an almost illegible Latin inscrip-
tion. Another equally impressive diploma states: "Doctorat honoris causa," again followed by a long, illegible text. There is an
abundance of smaller diplomas, each of which bears a clearly
written "doctorate."*

A door to the right of the audience.

*As the curtain rises, one can see The Academician's Wife
dressed in a rather crumpled robe. She has obviously just gotten
out of bed, and has not had time to dress. The Friend faces her. He*

is well dressed: hat, umbrella in hand, stiff collar, black jacket and striped trousers, shiny black shoes.

The Wife. Dear friend, tell me all.

The Friend. I don't know what to say.

The Wife. I know.

The Friend. I heard the news last night. I did not want to call you. At the same time I couldn't wait any longer. Please forgive me for coming so early with such terrible news.

The Wife. He didn't make it! How terrible! We were still hoping. . . .

The Friend. It's hard, I know. He still had a chance. Not much of one. We had to expect it.

The Wife. I didn't expect it. He was always so successful. He could always manage somehow, at the last moment.

The Friend. In that state of exhaustion. You shouldn't have let him!

The Wife. What can we do, what can we do! . . . How awful!

The Friend. Come on, dear friend, be brave. That's life.

The Wife. I feel faint: I'm going to faint. *(She falls in one of the armchairs.)*

The Friend (holding her, gently slapping her cheeks and hands). I shouldn't have blurted it out like that. I'm sorry.

The Wife. No, you were right to do so. I had to find out somehow or other.

The Friend. I should have prepared you, carefully.

The Wife. I've got to be strong. I can't help thinking of him, the wretched man. I hope they won't put it in the papers. Can we count on the journalists' discretion?

The Friend. Close your door. Don't answer the telephone. It will still get around. You could go to the country. In a couple of months, when you are better, you'll come back, you'll go on with your life. People forget such things.

The Wife. People won't forget so fast. That's all they were waiting for. Some friends will feel sorry, but the others, the others. . . . *) The Academician comes in, fully dressed: uniform, chest covered with decorations, his sword on his side.)*

The Academician. Up so early, my dear? *(To The Friend.)* You've come early too. What's happening? Do you have the final results?

The Wife. What a disgrace!

The Friend. You mustn't crush him like this, dear friend. *(To The Academician.)* You have failed.

The Academician. Are you quite sure?

The Friend. You should never have tried to pass the baccalaureate examination.

The Academician. They failed me. The rats! How dare they do this to me!

The Friend. The marks were posted late in the evening.

The Academician. Perhaps it was difficult to make them out in the dark. How could you read them?

The Friend. They had set up spotlights.

The Academician. They're doing everything to ruin me.

The Friend. I passed by in the morning; the marks were still up.

The Academician. You could have bribed the concierge into pulling them down.

The Friend. That's exactly what I did. Unfortunately the police were there. Your name heads the list of those who failed. Everyone's standing in line to get a look. There's an awful crush.

The Academician. Who's there? The parents of the candidates?

The Friend. Not only they.

The Wife. All your rivals, all your colleagues must be there. All those you attacked in the press for ignorance: your undergraduates, your graduate students, all those you failed when you were chairman of the board of examiners.

The Academician. I am discredited! But I won't let them. There must be some mistake.

The Friend. I saw the examiners. I spoke with them. They gave me your marks. Zero in mathematics.

The Academician. I had no scientific training.

The Friend. Zero in Greek, zero in Latin.

The Wife (to her husband). You, a humanist, the spokesman for humanism, the author of that famous treatise "The Defense of Poesy and Humanism."

The Academician. I beg your pardon, but my book concerns itself with twentieth century humanism. *(To The Friend.)* What about composition? What grade did I get in composition?

The Friend. Nine hundred. You have nine hundred points.

The Academician. That's perfect. My average must be all the way up.

The Friend. Unfortunately not. They're marking on the basis of two thousand. The passing grade is one thousand.

The Academician. They must have changed the regulations.

The Wife. They didn't change them just for you. You have a frightful persecution complex.

The Academician. I tell you they changed them.

The Friend. They went back to the old ones, back to the time of Napoleon.

The Academician. Utterly outmoded. Besides, when did they make those changes? It isn't legal. I'm chairman of the Baccalaureate Commission of the Ministry of Public Education. They didn't consult me, and they cannot make any changes without my approval. I'm going to expose them. I'm going to bring government charges against them.

The Wife. Darling, you don't know what you're doing. You're in your dotage. Don't you recall handing in your resignation just before taking the examination so that no one could doubt the complete objectivity of the board of examiners?

The Academician. I'll take it back.

The Wife. You should never have taken that test. I warned you. After all, it's not as if you needed it. But you have to collect all the honors, don't you? You're never satisfied. What did you need this diploma for? Now all is lost. You have your Doctorate, your Master's, your high school diploma, your elementary school certificate, and even the first part of the baccalaureate.

The Academician. There was a gap.

The Wife. No one suspected it.

The Academician. But *I* knew it. Others might have found out. I went to the office of the Registrar and asked for a transcript of my record. They said to me: "Certainly Professor, Mr. President, Your Excellency. . . . " Then they looked up my file, and the Chief Registrar came back looking embarrassed, most embarrassed indeed. He said: "There's something peculiar, very peculiar. You have your Master's, certainly, but it's no longer valid." I asked him why, of course. He answered: "There's a gap behind your Master's. I don't know how it happened. You must have registered and been accepted at the University without having passed the second part of the baccalaureate examination."

The Friend. And then?

The Wife. Your Master's degree is no longer valid?

The Academician. No, not quite. It's suspended. "The duplicate you are asking for will be delivered to you upon completion of the baccalaureate. Of course you will pass the examination with no trouble." That's what I was told, so you see now that I had to take it.

The Friend. Your husband, dear friend, wanted to fill the gap. He's a conscientious person.

The Wife. It's clear you don't know him as I do. That's not it at all. He wants fame, honors. He never had enough. What does one diploma more or less matter? No one notices them anyway, but he sneaks in at night, on tiptoe, into the living room, just to look at them, and count them.

The Academician. What else can I do when I have insomnia?

The Friend. The questions asked at the baccalaureate are usually known in advance. You were admirably situated to get this particular information. You could also have sent in a replacement to take the test for you. One of your students, perhaps. Or if you wanted to take the test without people realizing that you already knew the questions, you could have sent your maid to the black market, where one can buy them.

The Academician. I don't understand how I could have failed in my composition. I filled three sheets of paper, I treated the subject fully, taking into account the historical background. I interpreted the situation accurately . . . at least plausibly. I didn't deserve a bad grade.

The Friend. Do you recall the subject?

The Academician. Hum . . . let's see. . . .

The Friend. He doesn't even remember what he discussed.

The Academician. I do . . . wait . . . hum.

The Friend. The subject to be treated was the following: "Discuss the influence of Renaissance painters on novelists of the Third Republic." I have here a photostatic copy of your examination paper, Here is what you wrote.

The Academician (grabbing the photostat and reading). "The trial of Benjamin: After Benjamin was tried and acquitted, the assessors holding a different opinion from that of the President murdered him, and condemned Benjamin to the suspension of his civic rights, imposing on him a fine of nine hundred francs. . . . "

The Friend. That's where the nine hundred points come from.

The Academician. "Benjamin appealed his case . . . Benjamin appealed his case. . . ." I can't make out the rest. I've always had bad handwriting. I ought to have taken a typewriter along with me.

The Wife. Horrible handwriting, scribbling and crossing out; ink spots didn't help you much.

The Academician (goes on with his reading after having retrieved the text his wife had pulled out of his hand). "Benjamin appealed his case. Flanked by policemen dressed in zouave uniforms . . . in zouave uniforms. . . . " It's getting dark. I can't see the rest. . . . I don't have my glasses.

The Wife. What you've written has nothing to do with the subject.

The Friend. Your wife's quite right, friend. It has nothing to do with the subject.

The Academician. Yes, it has. Indirectly.

The Friend. Not even indirectly.

The Academician. Perhaps I chose the second question.

The Friend. There was only one.

The Academician. Even if there was only that one, I treated another quite adequately. I went to the end of the story. I stressed the important points, explaining the motivations of the characters, highlighting their behavior. I explained the mystery, making it plain and clear. There was even a conclusion at the end. I can't make out the rest. *(To The Friend.)* Can you read it?

The Friend. It's illegible. I don't have my glasses either.

The Wife (taking the text). It's illegible and I have excellent eyes. You pretended to write. Mere scribbling.

The Academician. That's not true. I've even provided a conclusion. It's clearly marked here in heavy print: "Conclusion or sanction . . . Conclusion or sanction. . . . " They can't get away with it. I'll have this examination rendered null and void.

The Wife. Since you treated the wrong subject, and treated it badly, setting down only titles, and writing nothing in between, the mark you received is justified. You'd lose your case.

The Friend. You'd most certainly lose. Drop it. Take a vacation.

The Academician. You're always on the side of the Others.

The Wife. After all, these professors know what they're doing. They haven't been granted their rank for nothing. They passed examinations, received serious training. They know the rules of composition.

The Academician. Who was on the board of examiners?

The Friend. For Mathematics, a movie star. For Greek, one of the Beatles. For Latin, the champion of the automobile race, and many others.

The Academician. But these people aren't any more qualified than I am. And for composition?

The Friend. A woman, a secretary in the editorial division of the review *Yesterday, the Day Before Yesterday, and Today.*

The Academician. Now I know. This wretch gave me a poor grade out of spite because I never joined her political party. It's an act of vengeance. But I have ways and means of rendering the examination null and void. I'm going to call the President.

The Wife. Don't. You'll make yourself look even more ridiculous. *(To The Friend.)* Please try to restrain him. He listens to you more than to me. *(The Friend shrugs his shoulders, unable to cope with the situation. The Wife turns to her husband, who has just lifted the receiver off the hook.)* Don't call!

The Academician (on the telephone). Hello, John? It is I . . . What? . . . What did you say? . . . But, listen, my dear friend . . . but, listen to me . . . Hello! Hello! *(Puts down the receiver.)*

The Friend. What did he say?

The Academician. He said . . . He said . . . , "I don't want to talk to you. My mummy won't let me make friends with boys at the bottom of the class." Then he hung up on me.

The Wife. You should have expected it. All is lost. How could you do this to me? How could you do this to me?

The Academician. Think of it! I lectured at the Sorbonne, at Oxford, at American universities. Ten thousand theses have been written on my work; hundreds of critics have analyzed it. I hold an *honoris causa* doctorate from Amsterdam as well as a secret university Chair with the Duchy of Luxembourg. I received the Nobel Prize three times. The King of Sweden himself was amazed by my erudition. A doctorate *honoris causa, honoris causa* . . . and I failed the baccalaureate examination!

The Wife. Everyone will laugh at us!

The Academician takes off his sword and breaks it on his knee.

The Friend (picking up the two pieces). I wish to preserve these in memory of our ancient glory.

The Academician meanwhile in a fit of rage is tearing down his decorations, throwing them on the floor, and stepping on them.

The Wife (trying to salvage the remains). Don't do this! Don't! That's all we've got left.

Curtain

Questions

1. Why is the Academician so distressed by the gap in his education?

2. Ionesco has said, "'The authentic nature of things, the truth, can only be revealed to us through fantasy." How much sense does this make? How might the idea be relevant to *The Gap?*

3. Bernard Shaw once wrote, "It is the business of a writer of comedy to wound the susceptibilities of his audience. The classic definition of his function is 'the chastening of morals by ridicule.'" Does *The Gap* wound susceptibilities? If so, to any purpose?

4. What is funny in the play? Is the play also frightening? If you think it is funny *and* frightening, do you find these qualities in separate parts of the play or are they mingled together? For example, is the Academician's desperation one or the other or both?

21 Some Observations on Film

A film is rather like a play: a story is presented by means of actors. The film, of course, regularly uses some techniques not possible in the playhouse, such as close-ups and rapid changes of scene, but even these techniques can usually be approximated in the playhouse, for example by means of lighting. It may seem, then, that one can experience a film as though it were a photographic record of a play. And indeed some films are nothing more than film records of plays.

There are, however, crucial distinctions between film and drama. First, though drama uses such visual matters as gestures, tableaux effects, and scenery, the plays that we value most highly are *literature:* the word dominates, the visual component is subordinate. One need not be one of those film fanatics who believe that the invention of the sound track was an impediment to film to believe that a film is more a matter of pictures than of words. The camera usually roves, giving us crowded streets, empty skies, rainy nights, or close-ups of filled ashtrays and chipped coffee cups. A critic has aptly said that in Ingmar Bergman's *Smiles of a Summer Night* "the almost unbearably ornate crystal goblets, by their aspect and their positioning in the image, convey the oppressive luxuriousness of the diners' lives in purely and uniquely filmic terms." In the words of the Swiss director Eric Rohmer, "the cinema is the description of man and his surroundings." Some of the greatest sequences in cinema, such as the battle scene in Orson Welles's *Falstaff* (also titled *Chimes at Midnight*), or parts of the search for Anna in Michelangelo Antonioni's *L'Avventura,* have no dialogue but concentrate on purely visual matters. In *L'Avventura* a group of rich and bored Italians go on a yachting excursion and visit a volcanic island off the coast of Sicily, where one member of the party — Anna — disappears. Anna's fiancé, Sandro, and Anna's best friend, Claudia, search for her but during the search they find that they are attracted to each other and they become lovers; Claudia later discovers that Sandro is unfaithful to her — but she and Sandro both were unfaithful to Anna, and the implication is that Claudia and Sandro will (in their way) remain weary partners. During the film's two hours there are long sequences when, in a conventional sense, little "happens" — for example, there are shots of the sea, or of a character, far from the camera, walking on the island during bad weather. But of course in this film the setting itself is an important part of the story, the barren and crumbling island being symbolic of the decadent people who walk on it and symbolic also of the vast inhospitable universe in which these figures — rendered small by their distance from the camera — aimlessly move. The long silences (there are episodes without dialogue or background music) are as important as what is said, and what is seen is more important than what is said.

In short, the speaker in a film does not usually dominate. In a play the speaker normally holds the spectator's attention, but in a film when a character speaks, the camera often gives us a **reaction shot,** focusing not on the speaker but on the face or gestures of a character who is affected by the speech, thus giving the spectator a visual interpretation of the words. In Truffaut's *The 400 Blows,* for example, we hear a reform school official verbally assault a boy, but we see the uncomfortable boy, not the official. Even when the camera does focus on the speaker it is likely to offer an interpretation. An extreme example is a scene from *Brief Encounter:* a gossip is talking, and the camera gives us a close-up of her jabbering mouth, which monstrously fills the screen. This distance between film and drama can be put in another way: a film is more like a novel than a play, the action being presented not directly by actors but by a camera that, like a novelist's point of view, comments on the story while telling it. A novelist may, like a dramatist, convey information about a character through dialogue and gesture, but he may also simply tell us about the character's state of mind. Similarly, a film-maker may use his camera to inform us about unspoken thought. In Murnau's *The Last Laugh,* when the hotel doorman reads a note firing him, the camera blurs; when he gets drunk, the camera spins so that the room seems to revolve. Somewhat similarly, Antonioni's *Red Desert* occasionally uses out-of-focus shots to convey Giuliana's view of the world; when she is more at ease, for example with her husband, the shots are in proper focus. Even the choice of the kind of emulsion-coated celluloid is part of the comment. A highly sensitive or "fast" film requires less light to catch an image than a "slow" film does, but it is usually grainier. Perhaps because newsreels commonly use fast film a grainy quality is often associated with realism. Moreover, because fast film shows less subtle gradations from black to white than slow film does, its harsh contrasts make it especially suitable for the harsh, unromantic *The Battle of Algiers*. Different film stocks may be used within a single motion picture. In *Wild Strawberries*, for instance, Bergman uses high contrast stock for the nightmare sequence, though elsewhere in the film the contrasts are subtle. The medium, as everyone knows, is part of the message; Laurence Olivier made Shakespeare's *Henry V* in color but *Hamlet* in black and white because these media say different things. Peter Brook's film of *King Lear* is also in black and white, with an emphasis on an icy whiteness that catches the play's spirit of old age and desolation; a *Lear* in color probably would have an opulence that would work against the lovelessness and desolation of much of the play. John Houseman said that he produced *Julius Caesar* in black and white because he wanted "intensity" rather than "grandeur," and because black and white evoked newsreels of Hitler and thus helped to establish the connection between Shakespeare's play and relatively recent politics. Peter Ustinov said that he made *Billy Budd* in black and white because he wanted it to seem real; Richard Brooks's *In Cold Blood* was done in black and white to look like a documentary.

The kind of lens used also helps to determine what the viewer sees. In *The Graduate* Benjamin runs toward the camera (he is trying to reach a church before his girl marries another man) but he seems to make no progress because a telephoto lens was used and thus his size does not increase as it normally would. The lens, that is, helps to communicate his desperate sense of frustration. Conversely, a wide angle lens makes a character approach the camera with menacing rapidity; he quickly looms into the foreground. But of course a filmmaker, though he resembles a novelist in offering pervasive indirect comment, is not a novelist any more than he is a playwright or director of a play; his medium has its own techniques, and he works with them, not with the novel's or the drama's. The wife who came out of the movie theater saying to her husband "What a disappointment; it was exactly like the book" knew what a film ought to be.

TECHNIQUES OF FILM-MAKING

Here is a brief grammar and dictionary of film, naming and explaining the cinematic devices that help film-makers embody their vision in a work of art.

A **shot** (very rarely a fraction of a second, and usually not more than fifteen or so seconds) is what is recorded between the time a camera starts and the time it stops, i.e., between the director's call for "action" and his call to "cut." Perhaps the average shot is about ten seconds; the average film is about an hour and a half, with about 600 shots, but Hitchcock's *The Birds* uses 1360 shots. Three common shots are: (1) a **long shot** or **establishing shot,** showing the main object at a considerable distance from the camera and thus presenting it in relation to its general surroundings (for example, captured soldiers, seen across a prison yard, entering the yard); (2) a **medium shot,** showing the object in relation to its immediate surroundings (a couple of soldiers, from the knees up, with the yard's wall behind them); (3) a **close-up,** showing only the main object, or, more often, only a part of it (a soldier's face, or his bleeding feet).

In the outside world we can narrow our vision to the detail that interests us by moving our head and by focusing our eyes, ignoring what is not of immediate interest. The close-up is the movie director's chief way of directing our vision and of emphasizing a detail. (Another way is to focus sharply on the significant image, leaving the rest of the image in soft focus.) The close-up, a way of getting emphasis, has been heavily used in recent years, not always successfully. As Dwight Macdonald said of *Midnight Cowboy* and *Getting Straight,* "a movie told in close-up is like a comic book, or like a novel composed in punchy one-sentence paragraphs and set throughout in large caps. How refreshing is a long or middle shot, a glimpse of the real world, so lovely and so *far away,* in the midst of those interminable processions of [a] hairy ogre face."

While taking a shot, the camera can move: it can swing to the right or left while its base remains fixed (a **pan shot**), up or down while fixed on its axis (a **tilt shot**), forward or backward (a **traveling shot**), or in and out and up and down fastened to a crane (a **crane shot**). The fairly recent invention of the **zoom** lens enables the camera to change its focus fluidly, so it can approach a detail — as a traveling shot does — while remaining fixed in place. Much will depend on the angle (high or low) from which the shots are made. If the camera is high (a **high angle shot**), looking down on a group of people it will dwarf them, perhaps even reduce them to crawling insects, making them pitiful or contemptible; if the camera is low (a **low angle shot**), close to the ground and looking up toward the people, thereby showing them against the sky, it probably will give them added dignity. But these are not invariable principles. A shot in *Citizen Kane,* for example, shows Kane from above but it does not dwarf him; rather, it shows him dominating his wife and then in effect obliterating her by casting a shadow over her. Similarly, a low angle shot does not always add dignity: films in which children play important parts often have lots of low angle shots showing adults as menacing giants, and in *Dr. Strangelove* Stanley Kubrick regularly photographed Colonel Jack D. Ripper from low angles, thus emphasizing the colonel's power. In *Citizen Kane*, Kane is often photographed from floor level, similarly emphasizing his power, but some low angle shots late in the film, showing him in his cavernous mansion, help to convey his loneliness. In short, by its distance from the subject, its height from the ground, and its angle of elevation, the camera comments on or interprets what happens. It seems to record reality, but it offers its own version. It is only a slight exaggeration to say that the camera always lies, i.e., gives a personal vision of reality.

A group of related scenes — such as the three scenes of soldiers mentioned earlier — is a **sequence,** though a sequence is more likely to have thirty scenes than three. A sequence corresponds roughly to a chapter in a novel, the shots being sentences, and the scenes being paragraphs. Within a sequence there may be an **intercut,** a switch to another action that, for example, provides an ironic comment on the main action of the sequence. If intercuts are so abundant in a sequence that, in effect, two or more sequences are going at once (e.g., shots of the villain about to ravish the heroine alternating with shots of the hero riding to her rescue), we have a **cross-cut.** In the example just given, probably the tempo would increase, the shots being progressively shorter as we get to the rescue. Though often a sequence will early have an establishing shot, it need not. Sometimes an establishing shot is especially effective if delayed, as in Dreyer's *Day of Wrath*, where scenes of a witch tied to the top rungs of a ladder lead to a long shot of the context: the witch has been tied to the top of a tall ladder near a great heap of burning faggots. Still at a distance, the next shot shows the soldiers tilting the ladder up into the air and onto the pyre.

Within a sequence the transitions normally are made by **straight cuts** — a strip of film is spliced to another, resulting in an instantaneous transfer from one scene to the next. Usually an audience is scarcely if at all conscious of transitions from, say, a long shot of a character to a medium shot of him, or from a close-up of a speaker to a close-up of his auditor. But sometimes the director wants the audience to be fully aware of the change, as an author may emphasize a change by beginning a new paragraph or, even more sharply, by beginning a new chapter. Two older and now rather unfashionable relatively conspicuous transitions are sometimes still used, usually between sequences rather than within a sequence. These are the **dissolve** (the scene dissolves while a new scene appears to emerge from beneath it, there being a moment when we get a blur of both scenes), and the **fade** (in the **fade-out** the screen grows darker until black, in the **fade-in** the screen grows lighter until the new scene is fully visible). In effect the camera is saying "Let us now leave X and turn to Y," or "Two weeks later." In *2001* a prehistoric ape-like creature discovers that he can use a bone as a tool, and he destroys a skeleton with it. Then he throws the bone triumphantly into the air, where it dissolves into a spaceship of the year 2001. The point is that the spaceship is the latest of man's weapons and progress is linked with destructiveness. Two other methods, even less in favor today than the dissolve and the fade but used in many excellent old films and in some modern films that seek an archaic effect, are the **wipe** (a sort of windshield wiper crosses the screen, wiping off the first scene and revealing the next), and the **iris** (in an **iris-in**, the new scene first appears in the center of the previous scene and then this circle expands until it fills the screen; an **iris-out** shows the new scene first appearing along the perimeter and then the circle closes in on the previous scene). Chaplin more than once ended a scene with an iris-out of the tramp walking jauntily toward the horizon. In Kurosawa's *High and Low* a wipe is used with no archaic effect: an industrialist, trying to decide whether to pay an enormous ransom to free a child, has been told to toss the money from a train; the scene showing him arriving at his decision in his luxurious home is wiped off by a train that rushes across the screen. He has decided to pay.

A film, no less than a poem or a play or a picture or a palace, is something made, and it is not made by simply exposing some footage. Shots — often taken at widely separated times and places — must be appropriately joined. For example, we see a man look off to the right, then we get a shot of what he is looking at, and then a shot of his reaction. Until the shots are assembled, we don't have a film, we merely have footage. V. I. Pudovkin put it this way: "The film is not *shot*, but built, built up from the separate strips of celluloid that are its raw material." This building-up is the process of **editing**. In *Film Technique* Pudovkin gives some examples of editing. (1) In the simplest kind of editing, the film tells a story from the best viewpoints, i.e., sometimes from long shots, sometimes from medium shots, sometimes from close-ups. (2) Simultaneous actions, occurring in different places, can be narrated by cutting back and forth from one to the other. (3) Relationships can be conveyed by contrast (shots of starvation cut in with shots of gluttony), by symbolism (in Pudovkin's *Mother*, shots of an ice floc melting are cut into shots of a procession of workers, thereby suggesting that the workers' movement is a natural force coming to new life), and by *leitmotif* (i.e., repetition of the same shot to emphasize a recurring theme). More than a story can be told, of course; something of the appropriate emotion can be communicated by juxtaposing against, say, a medium-long shot of a group of impassively advancing soldiers a close-up of a single terrified victim. Similarly, emotion can be communicated by the duration of the shots (quick shots suggest haste, prolonged shots suggest slowness) and by the lighting (progressively darker shots can suggest melancholy, progressively lighter shots can suggest hope or joy). The Russian theorists of film called this process of building by quick cuts **montage**. The theory held that shots, when placed together, add up to more than the sum of the parts. Montage, for them, was what made a film a work of art and not a mere replica of reality. American writers commonly use the term merely to denote quick cutting, and French writers use it merely in the sense of cutting.

All this talk about ingenious shots and their arrangement, then, assumes that the camera is a sort of pen, carefully setting forth images and thus at every point guiding the perceiver. The director (through his actors, camera crew, cutters, and a host of others) makes an artifact, rather as a novelist makes a book or a sculptor makes a statue, and this artifact is a sort of elaborate contraption that manipulates the spectator by telling him at every second exactly how he ought to feel. But recently there has been a reaction against such artistry, a feeling that although the elaborate editing of, say, Eisenstein and the other Russians is an esthetic triumph, it is also a moral failure because by its insistent tricky commentary it seems to deny the inherent worth of the event in itself as it happens. Moreover, just as the nineteenth-century narrator in the novel, who continually guided the reader ("Do not fear, gentle reader, for even at this moment plans were being laid . . . ") was in the twentieth-century novel sloughed off, forcing the reader in large measure to deduce the story for himself, so too some contemporary film-makers emphasize improvisation, fully aware that the film thus made will not at every point guide or dominate the viewer. Rather, the viewer of such a film becomes something of a creator himself, making the work of art by sorting out the relevant from the irrelevant images. Norman Mailer, in an essay on his film *Maidstone,* calls attention to the fact that in making this sort of film the camera, expecting an interesting bit of acting, may zoom in on what later turns out to be dull, but the scene is not deleted or shot again. The dull parts, the mistakes, are kept, and what was missed is not reenacted. In *Maidstone,* Mailer says, "when significant movement was captured, it was now doubly significant because one could not take it for granted. Watching film became an act of interpretation and restoration for what was missed."

WHAT MAKES A GOOD FILM?

Mastery of technique, though necessary to good film-making, will not in itself make a good film. A good film is not a bag of cinematic devices, but the embodiment, through cinematic devices, of a vision. What is this vision? Well, it is a film-maker's perception of some aspect of existence that he thinks is worthy of our interest. Normally this perception involves characters and a plot. Though recent American films, relying heavily on color, rock music in stereophonic sound, quick cutting, and the wide screen, have tended to emphasize the emotional experience and have tended to deemphasize narrative, still most of the best cinema is concerned with what people do — that is, with character and plot. Character is what people are and plot is what happens, but the line between character and plot fades, for what people are is in large measure what they do, and what is done is in large measure the result of what people are. Character and plot, then, finally are inseparable; in a good film, everything hangs together. Harold Lloyd said that he had idea men who suggested numerous bits of comic business, and then he chose "the ones that [he] thought would be most appropriate to the particular film we were doing." The operative words are "most appropriate." A very funny bit of business might not be appropriate — might somehow not seem to fit — in a particular film because it was not in harmony with the underlying vision or idea, the "clothes rack" (Lloyd's term) on which the funny bits (the clothes) were hung. In *The Freshman,* Lloyd said, the underlying idea or theme was the student's enormous desire for popularity, and everything in the film had to further this theme. Or, to take the comments of a more recent film-maker, we can listen to Truffaut on the themes of *The 400 Blows* and *Jules and Jim,* and on the disastrous lack of a theme in *Shoot the Piano Player:*

> *In 400 Blows,* I was guided by the desire to portray a child as honestly as possible, and to invest his actions with a moral significance. Similarly, with *Jules and Jim,* my desire to keep the film from seeming either pornographic, indelicate, or conventional guided me. The trouble with *Shoot the Piano Player* was that I was able to do anything — that the subject itself didn't impose its own form. . . . As it stands, there are some nice bits in the film, but it can't be said: this is the best work on this particular theme. There isn't any theme.

(It does not follow, of course, that the artist is fully aware of his theme from the start. Antonioni mentions that "it often happens that I experience fragmentary feelings before the experiences themselves take hold." But if they do not finally take hold, the film will probably arouse the sort of response that Truffaut mentions in his comments on *Shoot the Piano Player.*)

And so we come back to the idea of a vision, or, in a less exalted word, a theme. Some critics have argued that the concept of theme is meaningless: a film is only a detailed presentation of certain imaginary people in imaginary situations, not a statement about an aspect of life. But such a view is reductive. If we read in a newspaper about a marriage or a business failure or a baseball game, we take it only as a particular happening of some interest, and we do not assume that it implies much if anything at all beyond itself. It tells of something that has happened, but it does not tell what ought to happen or what usually happens; that is, it does not imply anything about the ways of people in general. When, however, we read a novel, or see on the stage or screen a happening, we inevitably feel — if only because we are asked to give the event an hour or more of our attention — that it is offered to us as noteworthy, an example not of what *happened* (it didn't happen, it's fictional) but an example of what *happens*. The characters in the fictional work are (like the characters in newspaper items) individuals, not mere abstractions, but (unlike those in newspaper items) they are significant individuals, in some measure revealing to us a whole class of people or a way of life. An artist gives us a representation that can be thought about. Sometimes we sense that a film has an arguable thesis. Stanley Kubrick, for example, has said that *A Clockwork Orange* "warns against the new psychedelic fascism — the eye-popping, multimedia, quadrasonic, drug-oriented conditioning of human beings by other human beings — which many believe will usher in the forfeiture of human citizenship and the beginning of zombiedom." A film-maker, however, need not argue a thesis that is subject to verification (e.g., the older generation seeks to repress the younger generation); it is enough if he sees in the human experience something worth our contemplation (e.g., the conflict between generations) and embodies it on film. A theme can usually be named by an abstract noun or phrase (the quest for happiness, the difficulty of achieving self-knowledge, the fragility of love) and though we recognize that any such formula is not the whole of life, it is nonetheless important. Adequately embodied in a film (or in any other kind of art) this exploration of experience alters our experience of life, including our experience of ourselves. Let Truffaut have the last word:

> I also believe that every film must contain some degree of "planned violence" upon its audience. In a good film, people must be made to see something that they don't want to see: they must be made to approve of someone of whom they had disapproved, they must be forced to look where they had refused to look.

APPENDIX
Writing Essays about Literature

WHY WRITE?

People write about literature to clarify and account for their responses to works that interest or excite or frustrate them. In putting words on paper you will have to take a second and a third look at what is in front of you and what is within you. And so writing is a way of learning. The last word about complex thoughts and feelings is never said, but when we write we hope to make at least a little progress in the difficult but rewarding job of talking about our responses. We learn, and then we hope to interest our reader because we are communicating to him our responses to something that for one reason or another is worth talking about.

This communication is, in effect, teaching. You may think that you are writing for the teacher, but that is a misconception; when you write, *you* are the teacher. An essay on literature is an attempt to help someone see the work as you see it. If this chapter had to be boiled down to a single sentence, that sentence would be: Because you are teaching, your essay should embody those qualities that you value in teachers — probably intelligence, open-mindedness, and effort; and certainly a desire to offer what help one can.

TWO COMMON APPROACHES

Explication

A line-by-line commentary on what is going on in a text — usually a short poem — is an **explication** (literally, unfolding or spreading out). It takes some skill to work one's way along without saying, "In line one . . . , in the second line . . . , in the third line. . . ." One must sometimes boldly say something like "The next stanza begins with . . . and then introduces. . . ." And, of course, one can discuss the second line before the first if that seems the best way of handling the passage.

An explication is not concerned with the writer's life or times, and it is not a paraphrase (a rewording) — though it may include paraphrase. It is a study — almost word by word — that reveals the meaning of a work. It may seem to "read into" the work, but if it is done well it really "reads out" what is within the work. To this end it calls attention, as it proceeds, to the implications of words, the function of rhymes, the shifts in point of view, the development of contrasts, and any other contributions to the meaning. (Try to avoid saying, "What the author is trying to say. . . . " If the work is any good, presumably the author succeeded in saying what he or she had to say. *You* are trying to show how the author embodied a meaning in the words.)

Because the language of a literary work is denser (richer in associations or connotations (than the language of such prose as this paragraph, explication is much concerned with bringing to the surface the meanings in the words that may not be immediately apparent. Explication, in short, seeks to make explicit what is *implicit* (literally, folded or entangled) in the text.

Below we print an explication by a student.

A Sample Explication

Robert Frost

Acquainted with the Night

I have been one acquainted with the night.
I have walked out in rain — and back in rain.
I have outwalked the furthest city light.   3

I have looked down the saddest city lane.
I have passed by the watchman on his beat
And dropped my eyes, unwilling to explain.   6

I have stood still and stopped the sound of feet
When far away an interrupted cry
Came over houses from another street,   9

But not to call me back or say good-bye;
And further still at an unearthly height
One luminary clock against the sky   12

Proclaimed the time was neither wrong nor right.
I have been one acquainted with the night.

The words in Robert Frost's "Acquainted with the Night,"
except "luminary" in line 12, are all common ones, but if we
look closely at these words we see some unusual implications.
Take the title: "Acquainted with the Night." We are usually
acquainted with a person or with a fact, not with the night.
And so "night" must have some special suggestion that is not
yet clear. And to be "acquainted" with someone or something
usually implies familiarity (as in "I am acquainted with John
Jones") but not thorough knowledge. "I have been one acquainted
with the night," then, is an unusual and cautious statement.

The first stanza is matter-of-fact. It consists of three
sentences, each beginning "I have," and each sentence fills
exactly one line. It almost sounds flat, but it is not flat
because, as I have said, "acquainted with the night" is an
unusual expression. Also, the repetition of words and grammatical structure makes for special emphasis. Furthermore,
when "I have walked out" turns into "I have outwalked the
furthest city light," we realize that we are being told about
a special journey, not just a literal walk. We don't yet
know what this journey was, but even if this walk beyond "the
furthest city light" was a literal walk, Frost also means for

us to take it as a walk beyond manmade illumination, civilization, order. It must have been meant as an experience with
something dark in the way that grief, ignorance, loss of faith,
or loneliness are dark.

The second stanza resembles the previous stanza but it is
more expansive. It continues the use of "I have," but now only
in the first two of its three lines, and only the first line is
a complete sentence. And it introduces people other than the
speaker, first in "the saddest city lane" (line 4), and next in
the watchman (line 5). The lane cannot literally be sad;
"saddest" implies that sad people live in the lane, or that the
speaker feels sad when he thinks of the people who live in the
lane. The watchman perhaps is one of these, and the speaker
avoids his glance, explaining only that he is "unwilling to
explain" (line 6). The speaker, then, not only is walking
alone but also isolates himself from his fellows. That is,
he feels isolated and therefore shuns contact.

The third stanza begins with "I have," as five of the
previous six lines have begun, but it is even less closely
patterned on the first stanza than the second was; that is,
the poem becomes looser. In fact, the thought overflows the
stanza; the first stanza of three lines was three sentences,
and their tone was assertive, almost confident: "I have been
one acquainted. . . . I have walked out . . . and back"
(there is a survivor's note of understated triumph in that
"and back"), and I have "outwalked" (again a note of triumph).
But the quiet yet firm self-assertion then begins to dissolve.

The second stanza was two sentences, and now the third

stanza cannot contain even one complete sentence--the sen-

tence flows into the next two stanzas, running almost to the

end of the poem. To put it slightly differently, all but the

last line of the octave (final eight lines) of this sonnet is

a single sentence.

In the second stanza the speaker ignores human society,

suggested by the watchman; in the third and fourth stanzas

human society ignores the speaker, for the "cry" (line 8) is

not directed to the speaker: it is "not to call me back or say

good-bye" (line 10). In addition to this suggestion of man-

kind's indifference to the speaker, there is a suggestion that

the speaker almost doesn't exist--even in his own perceptions:

"I have stood still and stopped the sound of feet" (line 7).

A paraphrase of the last six words might be, "and stopped

producing the noise of footsteps." Thus, by standing still

the speaker became inaudible not only to the city-dwellers

but also to himself.

The "interrupted cry" of line 8 is sorrowful, for it is

a "cry" and not a "call" or "shout" or "laugh." And the cry

is mysterious because we do not know its cause, its source, its

message, or why it is "interrupted." The fourth stanza con-

tinues to deepen the sense of mystery by referring to a clock

"at an unearthly height." Maybe this is a real clock, perhaps

with an illuminated face, high on a church or town hall, but

it seems more likely that this "luminary" clock is something

beyond "the furthest city light"; probably it is a metaphor

describing the full moon, which is literally "unearthly." Its
unearthliness is emphasized by the unusual use of the unusual
word "luminary," for "luminary" is usually a noun meaning "a
source of illumination," but here it is used as an adjective.
In any case, a real clock can be right or wrong, and it can
tell us that the time is right or wrong for eating, sleeping,
attending class, or whatever. But this "luminary clock," at an
"unearthly height," offers no heavenly guidance and it cannot
be either corrected or obeyed. The speaker can only look at
the clock (whether a real clock or the moon) and increasingly
sense that he has nothing to communicate with.

The last line of the poem, a complete sentence in itself,
repeats the first line exactly, and it restores the tone of
assurance. Now we have a sharper idea of what the speaker
means when he says he has been "one acquainted with the
night," but we still cannot say that the "night" equals or
symbolizes this or that. "Loneliness," for example, is too
simple a translation, because loneliness implies isolation
from people, and in the poem we sense that the speaker's
isolation may be not only from other people but also from
himself (from a sense of any individual purpose) and also
from a meaningless universe. Moreover, we must also say--
and the poem is as much about this as it is about "the
night"--that the speaker is not crushed by the experience.
The poem is not a lament, and not a descent into self-pity.
The speaker does not sadly say "I _am_ one acquainted with the
night"; rather, the experience is put at a distance by being

set in the past: "I <u>have</u> <u>been</u> one acquainted with the night."

And though the memory of the experience is still sharp, the

speaker keeps his response under control. The closest he comes

to telling us explicitly of his feelings is in the terse first

and last lines. For the most part he shows us the situation

rather than tells us his feelings, and thus he conveys a sense

of control--a sense, we might say, of being able to deal with

the experience, to survive it (since the last line repeats the

first line we can say that he literally comes out where he

went in), and even to get it down on paper.

Analysis

If one has world enough and time, one can set out to explicate all of *Moby-Dick* or *Othello*. More likely, one will explicate a page in *Moby-Dick* or a speech in *Othello;* in writing about works longer than a page or two, a more common approach than explicating is analyzing (literally, separating into parts in order to understand). An analysis commonly considers one part and the relation of this part to the whole. For example, it may consider only the functions of the setting in *The Adventures of Huckleberry Finn* or the comedy in *Othello* or the allusions in T. S. Eliot's "The Love Song of J. Alfred Prufrock."

Analysis, of course, is not a process used only in talking about literature. It is commonly applied in thinking about almost any complex matter. Jimmy Connors plays a deadly game of tennis: What makes it so good? How does his backhand contribute? What does his serve do to the opponent? In short, given the whole, how do the parts fit together?

If a work is fairly long, and you are writing only a few pages and you are not explicating a short passage from the work, almost surely you will write an analysis of some part. Unless you have an enormous amount of time for reflection and revision you cannot write a meaningful essay of five hundred words or even a thousand words on "Shakespeare's *Othello*" or "Melville's *Moby-Dick*." You cannot even write on "Character in *Othello*" or "Symbolism in *Moby-Dick*." And probably you won't really want to write on such topics anyway. Probably *one* character or *one* symbol has caught your interest. Trust your feelings; you are probably onto something interesting, and it will be best to think about this smaller topic for the relatively few hours that you have. A "smaller" topic need not be a dull or trivial topic; treated properly, it may illuminate the entire work or, to change the metaphor, it may serve as a mine shaft that gives entry to the work. "Othello's Relationship to Cassio," carefully thought about, will in five hundred or a thousand words tell a reader more (and will have taught its author more) than will "*Othello* as a Tragedy." Similarly, "Huck Finn's Imagination" is a better topic than "The Character of Huck Finn," and "The Meanings of 'Economy' in *Walden*" a better topic than "The Meaning of *Walden*."

How do you find a topic and how do you turn it into a **thesis** (an argument or proposition)? An idea may hit you suddenly; as you are reading you find yourself jotting in the margin, "contrast with Joyce's treatment of disillusionment," "too heavy irony," or "ugh." Or an idea may come slowly upon rereading. Perhaps you gradually become aware of the frequency of the word "really" in *The Catcher in the Rye,* and you notice that Holden Caulfield, who is regularly given to saying things such as "if you really want to know" and "I really mean it," at one point explicitly comments on the nature of reality. You work on this and begin to relate it to his abundant discussions of phoneys, and you emerge, perhaps, with the thesis, or argument, that in Holden's mouth "really" is not merely the filler it seems to be but is a clue to his quest for the real in a world of appearances and phoneys. If you have thought about the topic, converted it into a thesis, and stripped it of irrelevancies, you should be able to formulate it in a few words. (This formula, or something like it, can be your title. There is nothing wrong with a title as direct as "Holden Caulfield's Use of the Word 'Really' "; although it is scarcely exciting, it is informative. Beware of cute titles, especially those that do not give the reader a good idea of what will follow, such as "Really!" or "A Boy's Word." "The Real Holden and Reality" is about as far as one should go.)

Let's dwell a moment longer on the distinction between a topic and a thesis. It may be useful to think of it this way: a topic is a subject (for example, Othello's relation to Cassio); to arrive at a thesis you have to add a predicate (for example, Othello's relation to Cassio helps to reveal Othello's character). Of course, some theses are more promising than others. For example, "Othello's relationship to Cassio is interesting" is a thesis, but it is vague and provides little direction, little help in shaping your essay. "Othello's relation to Cassio is one of army general to lower officer" is better, but not much. It provides a focus, but it is not likely to help you see anything beyond the obvious. Let's try again. "Othello's relation to Cassio helps to reveal

Othello's ability to sternly subordinate a close personal relationship to a high ethical code." When you get to a thesis like this you have something that will greatly aid you in organizing your essay. Probably such an essay will announce the thesis, will then go on to give examples of Othello's firm devotion to his code, and will draw conclusions about the relevance of this stern attitude to the play as a whole: his ability to reject Cassio foreshadows and helps to make understandable his violent rejection of his wife, Desdemona.

Every literary work affords its own topics for analysis, and every essayist must set forth his own thesis, but a few useful generalizations may be made. You can often find a thesis by asking one of two questions:

1. *What purpose does this serve?* That is, why is this scene in the novel or play? Why is Beckett's *Waiting for Godot* in two acts, rather than one or three? Why the biblical allusions in *Waiting for Godot?* Why is there a clown in *Othello?* Why are these lines unrhymed? Why is this stanza form employed? What is the significance of the parts of the work? (Titles are often highly significant parts of the work: Ibsen's *A Doll's House,* Kesey's *One Flew Over the Cuckoo's Nest,* and Roth's *The Great American Novel* would be slightly different if they had other titles.)

2. *Why do I have this response?* Why do I find this poem clever or moving or puzzling? How did the author make this character funny or dignified or pathetic? How did he communicate the idea that this character is a bore without boring me?

The first of these questions, "What purpose does this serve?" requires that you identify yourself with the author, wondering, for example, whether this opening scene is the best possible for this story. The second question, "Why do I have this response?" requires that you trust your feelings. If you are amused or bored or puzzled or annoyed, assume that these responses are appropriate and follow them up, at least until a rereading of the work provides other responses.

A Sample Analysis

Let's look at an analysis of one aspect of a literary work, the structure of Tennessee Williams's *The Glass Menagerie.* After thinking about the play and consulting the jottings made while thinking and reading, one finds that the essay's underlying thesis — that the play *has* a coherent structure — breaks down into, say, six parts or paragraphs. (Of course it takes a good deal of thinking before one develops a thesis and sees that the notes can be reasonably arranged into these groups.) The topic ideas — stated in sentences that will be developed in a series of paragraphs — might be these:

1. The play has several scenes, but they fit together, or balance.
2. The first scene is a sort of prologue, and the last scene is a sort of epilogue, so there is a pattern.
3. The first three scenes show things going downhill.
4. The next three scenes show things getting better.
5. The seventh scene, the longest, seems at first to show things getting better, but it ends by leaving things at their worst.
6. The scenes, then, are carefully arranged to build up hope and then shatter it.

With proper amplification — *not* padding, but convincing detail — the student's essay turned out as follows.

The Solid Structure of The Glass Menagerie

In the "Production Notes" Tennessee Williams calls The

Glass Menagerie a "memory play," a term that the narrator in

the play also uses. Memories often consist of fragments of

episodes so loosely connected that they seem chaotic, and

therefore we might think that The Glass Menagerie will con-

sist of very loosely related episodes. However, the play

covers only one episode, and though it gives the illusion of

random talk it really has a firm structure and moves steadily

toward a foregone conclusion.

Tennessee Williams divides the play into seven scenes.

The first scene begins with a sort of prologue and the last

scene concludes with a sort of epilogue that is related to

the prologue. In the prologue Tom addresses the audience and

comments on the 1930s as a time when America was "blind" and

a place of "shouting and confusion." Tom also mentions that

our lives consist of expectations, and though he does not say
that our expectations are unfulfilled, near the end of the
prologue he quotes a postcard that his father wrote to the
family he deserted: "Hello--Good-bye." In the epilogue Tom
tells us that he followed his "father's footsteps," deserting
the family. And just before the epilogue, near the end of
Scene VII, we see what can be considered another desertion:
Jim explains to Tom's sister Laura that he is engaged and
therefore cannot visit Laura again. Thus the end is closely
related to the beginning, and the play is the steady development of the initial implications.

The first three scenes show things going from bad to
worse. Amanda is a nagging mother who finds her only relief
in talking about the past to her crippled daughter Laura and
her frustrated son Tom. When she was young she was beautiful
and was eagerly courted by rich young men, but now the family
is poor and this harping on the past can only bore or infuriate
Tom and embarrass or depress Laura. These two have no happy
past to look back to, see no happy future, and can only be
upset by Amanda's insistence that they should behave as she
behaved long ago. The second scene deepens the despair:
Amanda learns that the timorous Laura has not been attending
a business school but has retreated in terror from this confrontation with the contemporary world. Laura's helplessness
is made clear to the audience, and so is Amanda's lack of
understanding. Near the end of the second scene, however,
Jim's name is introduced; he is a boy Laura had a crush on in

high school, and so the audience gets a glimpse of a happier
Laura and a sense that possibly Laura's world is wider than the
stifling tenement in which she and her mother and brother live.
But in the third scene things get worse, when Tom and Amanda
have so violent an argument that they are no longer on speaking
terms. Tom is so angry with his mother that he almost by
accident destroys his sister's treasured collection of glass
animals, the fragile lifeless world that is her refuge. The
apartment is literally full of the "shouting and confusion"
that Tom spoke of in his prologue.

The first three scenes have revealed a progressive
worsening of relations; the next three scenes reveal a progressive improvement in relations. In Scene IV Tom and his
mother are reconciled and Tom reluctantly--apparently in an
effort to make up with his mother--agrees to try to get a
friend to come to dinner so that Laura will have "a gentleman caller." In Scene V Tom tells his mother that Jim will
come to dinner on the next night, and Amanda brightens because
she sees a possibility of security for Laura at last. In
Scene VI Jim arrives, and despite Laura's initial terror,
there seems, at least in Amanda's mind, to be the possibility
that things will go well.

The seventh scene, by far the longest, at first seems to
be fulfilling Amanda's hopes. Despite the ominous fact that
the lights go out because Tom has not paid the electric bill,
Jim is at ease. He is an insensitive oaf, but that doesn't
seem to bother Amanda, and almost miraculously he manages to

draw Laura somewhat out of her sheltered world. Even when Jim
in his clumsiness breaks the horn off Laura's treasured glass
unicorn she is not upset. In fact, she is almost relieved
because the loss of the horn makes the animal less "freakish"
and he "will feel more at home with the other horses." In a
way, of course, the unicorn symbolizes the crippled Laura, who
at least for the moment feels less freakish and isolated now
that she is somewhat reunited with society through Jim. But
this is a play about life in a blind and confused world, and
though in a previous age the father escaped, there can be no
escape now. Jim reveals that he is engaged, Laura relapses
into "desolation," Amanda relapses into rage and bitterness,
and Tom relapses into dreams of escape. In a limited sense
Tom does escape. He leaves the family and joins the merchant
marine, but his last speech, the "epilogue," tells us that he
cannot escape the memory of his sister: "Oh, Laura, Laura, I
tried to leave you behind me, but I am more faithful than I
intended to be!" And so the end of the last scene brings us
back again to the beginning of the first scene: we are still
in a world of "the blind" and of "confusion." But now at the
end the darkness is deeper and the characters are lost forever
in their unhappiness as Laura "blows the candles out," the
darkness being literal but also symbolic of their extin-
guished hopes.

Numerous devices, such as repeated references to the
absent father, Amanda's youth, Laura's victrola, and of
course Laura's glass menagerie help to tie the scenes together

into a unified play. But beneath these threads of imagery and recurring motifs is a fundamental pattern that involves the movement from nagging (Scenes I and II) to open hostilities (Scene III) to temporary reconciliation (Scene IV) to false hopes (Scenes V and VI) to an impossible heightening of false hopes and then, in a swift descent, to an inevitable collapse (Scene VII). Tennessee Williams has constructed his play carefully. G. B. Tennyson says that a "playwright must 'build' his speeches, as the theatrical expression has it."[1] But a playwright must do more--he must also build his play out of scenes. Like Ibsen, if Williams were introduced to an architect he might say, "Architecture is my business too."

_____

[1] An Introduction to Drama (New York: Holt, 1967), p. 13.

Let us look at several principles illustrated by this essay.

1. The title is informative.

2. The introductory paragraph, especially at its end, gives us a good idea of the writer's thesis.

3. The next five paragraphs, the body of the essay, fulfill the commitment made by the title and the introductory paragraph. The first of these paragraphs discusses scenes that can be considered the prologue and the epilogue, and thus gives a sense of the overall shape of the play. The next paragraph discusses the first three scenes, which form a block. Then the next paragraph discusses the next three scenes, which form a contrasting block. The last of these paragraphs discusses the last scene (except the epilogue). Because this scene is the longest and the point toward which everything has been moving, it gets a paragraph to itself.

4. Some brief and relevant quotations are used. They give the reader the necessary details but they do not interrupt the flow of the argument as long quotations are likely to do.

5. The writer assumes that the reader has read the work being discussed; therefore he does not fill his essay with a tedious synopsis. But aware that the reader has not memorized the work, he gives

helpful reminders, as in "The seventh scene, by far the longest. . . . "

6. The writer has opinions, but he talks more about the work than about himself.

7. The present tense is used in narrating the action of a play or a piece of fiction, as in "Tom addresses the audience" and "In Scene VI Jim arrives." Of course, earlier actions normally require the present perfect ("Tom has already let us know that . . . ") and later actions the future. ("Tom will later say . . . "), but in narrating what *is* happening, use the present.

8. The concluding paragraph does not simply restate what has been stated, nor does it introduce a wholly new topic. It summarizes, but in such a way that the material is set in a slightly new light.

Only points 3 and 5 can be thought of as embodying rules: an essay must be organized and must not synopsize unnecessarily. The other points illustrate not rules but time-tested procedures that may be of help.

COMPARISON AND CONTRAST

Something should be said about an essay organized around a **comparison** or a **contrast,** say, of the settings in two short stories, of two characters in a novel, or of the symbolism in two poems. (A comparison emphasizes resemblances and a contrast emphasizes differences, but we can use the word "comparison" to cover both kinds of writing.) Probably the student's first thought, after making some jottings, is to discuss one-half of the comparison and then go on to the second half. Instructors and textbooks usually condemn such an organization, arguing that the essay breaks into two parts and that the second part involves a good deal of repetition of categories set up in the first part. Usually they recommend that the student organize his thoughts differently, somewhat along these lines:

1. First similarity
   a. first work (or character, or characteristic)
   b. second work
2. Second similarity
   a. first work
   b. second work
3. First difference
   a. first work
   b. second work
4. Second difference
   a. first work
   b. second work

and so on, for as many additional differences as seem relevant. For example, if one wishes to compare *Huckleberry Finn* with *The Catcher in the Rye*, one may organize the material thus:

1. First similarity: the narrator and his quest
   a. Huck
   b. Holden
2. Second similarity: the corrupt world surrounding the narrator
   a. society in *Huckleberry Finn*
   b. society in *Catcher*
3. First difference: degree to which the narrator fulfills his quest and escapes from society
   a. Huck's plan to "light out" to the frontier
   b. Holden's breakdown

Here is another way of organizing a comparison and contrast:

1. First point: the narrator and his quest
   a. similarities between Huck and Holden
   b. differences between Huck and Holden
2. Second point: the corrupt world
   a. similarities between the worlds in *Huck* and *Catcher*
   b. differences between the worlds in *Huck* and *Catcher*
3. Third point: degree of success
   a. similarities between Huck and Holden
   b. differences between Huck and Holden

But a comparison need not employ either of these structures. There is even the danger that an essay employing either of them may not come into focus until the essayist stands back from his seven-layer cake and announces, in his concluding paragraph, that the odd layers taste better. In one's preparatory thinking, one may want to make comparisons in pairs (Good-natured humor: the clown in *Othello*, the clownish grave-digger in *Hamlet*; Social satire: the clown in *Othello*, the grave-digger in *Hamlet*; Relevance to main theme: . . . ; Length of role: . . . ; Comments by other characters: . . .), but one must come to some conclusions about what these add up to before writing the final version. This final version should not duplicate the thought processes; rather, it should be organized to make the point clearly and effectively. After reflection, one may believe that although there are superficial similarities between the clown in *Othello* and the clownish grave-digger in *Hamlet*, there are essential differences; then in the finished essay one probably will not wish to obscure the main point by jumping back and forth from play to play, working through a series of similarities and differences. It may be better to discuss the clown in *Othello* and then to point out that, although the grave-digger in *Hamlet* resembles him in A, B, and C, the grave-digger also has other functions (D, E, and F) and is of greater consequence to *Hamlet* than the clown is to *Othello.* Some repetition in the second half of the essay (for example, "The grave-digger's puns come even faster than the clown's. . . . ") will serve to bind the two halves into a meaningful whole, making clear the degree of similarity or difference. The point of the essay presumably is not to list pairs of similarities or differences, but to illuminate a work or works by making thoughtful comparisons. Although in a long essay one cannot postpone until page 30 a discussion of the second half of the comparison, in an essay of, say, fewer than ten pages nothing is wrong with setting forth one-half of the comparison and then, in light of it, the second half. The essay will break into two unrelated parts if the second half makes no use of the first or if it fails to modify the first half, but not if the second half looks back to the first half and calls attention to differences that the new material reveals. One ought to learn how to write an essay with interwoven comparisons, but one ought also to know that there is another, simpler and clearer way to write a comparison.

COMMUNICATING JUDGMENTS

Because a critical essay is a judicious attempt to help a reader see what is going on in a work or in a part of a work, the voice of the critic sounds, on first hearing, impartial; but good criticism includes — at least implicitly — evaluation. You may say not only that the setting changes (a neutral expression) but also that "the novelist aptly shifts the setting" or "unconvincingly describes . . . " or "effectively juxtaposes. . . . " These evaluations you support with evidence. You have feelings about the work under discussion and you reveal them, not by continually saying "I feel" and "this moves me," but by calling attention to the degree of success or failure you perceive. Nothing is wrong with occasionally using "I," and the noticeable avoidances of it — "this writer," "we," and the like — suggest an offensive sham modesty; on the other hand, too much talk of "I" makes a writer sound like an egomaniac.

One final remark on communicating judgments: write sincerely. Any attempt to neglect your own thoughtful responses and replace them with fabrications designed to please an instructor will surely fail. It is hard enough to find the words that clearly communicate your responses; it is almost impossible to find the words that express your hunch about what your instructor expects your responses to be. George Orwell shrewdly commented on the obvious signs of insincere writing: "When there is a gap between one's real and one's declared aims, one turns as it were instinctively to long words and exhausted idioms, like a cuttlefish squirting out ink."

TOPICS IN FICTION, POETRY, DRAMA, AND FILM

The editorial apparatus throughout this book is intended to help you read, enjoy, and discuss literature as fully as possible. When you are sitting down to write about literature you may want to reread some parts of this apparatus for guidance on your topic. The following brief notes summarize only a few of the earlier discussions, but they also add a few suggestions. They may help you to find a topic and thesis, and they may remind you to reread some of the earlier material in the book.

Fiction

Here are some questions that may trigger ideas for essays on fiction.

Plot: Does the plot grow out of the characters or does it depend on chance or coincidence? Are there irrelevant episodes or do episodes that at first seem irrelevant have a function? Does surprise play an important role or does foreshadowing? Is the title a good one? How is the gist of the story embodied in the structure? For example, are certain episodes told out of chronological order? If so, why? And are certain juxtapositions of happenings especially suggestive? Are certain situations repeated? Is the story about a change in a situation or a change in personality — or a change in our understanding of a situation or personality? If there is a change, what forces work for it and what forces work against it?

Character: Are there characters who by their similarities and differences define each other? How else is a particular character defined (words, actions — including thoughts and emotions — dress, setting, narrative point of view)? To what extent does a character change, and what causes the change? Or do we change our attitude because we come to know the character better? If the characters change, why and how do they change? Do certain characters act differently in the same, or in a similar, situation? Are the characters highly realistic, or are they stereotypes? Do they suggest people or abstractions?

Point of view: How does the point of view (see pages 32–36) help shape the theme? After all, the basic story of "Little Red Riding Hood" remains unchanged whether told from the wolf's point of view or the girl's, but (to simplify grossly) if we hear the story from the wolf's point of view we may feel that the story is about terrifying yet pathetic compulsive behavior; if from the girl's point of view, about terrified innocence. Does the language of the narrator help us understand his attitude and his strengths and limitations? (Notice especially any figurative language, patterns of imagery.) How far can we trust the narrator? Why?

Setting: What is the relation of the setting to the plot and the characters? What would be lost if the setting were changed?

Style: What role is played by the author's style? Is the style simple, understated, figurative, or what, and why?

Theme: Is the title of the story significant? Does it help us to perceive the theme? Do certain passages — dialogue or description — especially point us to the theme? Are certain repetitions or juxtapositions highly suggestive? Do certain episodes or characters seem irrelevant? If so, pay special attention to them, for they may not really be irrelevant; they may help to establish the theme of the work.

Poetry

A good essay is based on a genuine response to a poem; a response may in part be stimulated by considering the following questions:

1. Exactly what sort of person is the speaker? Is he fully aware of himself? Is he sentimental? Ironic? Does he joke in earnest?

2. To whom is the speaker speaking; that is, what is the situation?

3. Does the poem proceed in a straightforward way, or at some points does the poet or speaker reverse his course, altering his tone or perception?

4. Is the interest chiefly in a story? In a character's state of mind? In the philosophic content? If descriptive, is the description offered for its own sake or for what it reveals about the speaker's state of mind?

5. Do certain words have rich and relevant associations that relate to other words to help define the theme? What is the role of the figurative language, if any? Does it help to define the speaker or the theme? What is to be taken symbolically, and what literally?

6. What is the role of sound effects, including repetitions of sounds and of entire words, and shifts in versification?

Writing about poetry may seem easier than writing about fiction or drama because most poems that the student encounters are fairly short. He can usually keep the entire work before his eyes, and he need not be endowed with an exceptional memory. But the brevity may be deceptive. Because most of us are not used to reading poetry we overlook a good deal of its complexity. Prose runs straight on, but poetry is always turning back on itself, complicating its pattern of sound and meaning.

Of course the prose of fiction is not the prose of a newspaper or a history book; it is not used merely as a vehicle to give information about something outside itself; rather, word by word it builds its own world. (Another way of putting it: The words of newspapers and textbooks aim, or should aim, at being inconspicuous. They are a sort of window, or telescope, through which we see things, but generally we do not value them for themselves. They are road signs, telling us where Boston is, or how to get to the expressway. But the words of a piece of literature, especially of a poem, are among the things we are looking at and looking for.) Still, fiction tells a story, and the story is a major part of its interest. We are not expected to dwell on each word in a story; the narrative line carries us forward. But in poetry we tend to delight in the words themselves or, better, in their combinations, as well as in the experience they point to. A poet exploits more fully than does the writer of fiction such devices as alliteration and rhythm; a substantial part of the meaning of his work resides in them. Frost touched on this matter when he defined poetry as "what gets lost in translation." Auden touched on it when he said that his ideal reader notices misprints.

Drama

First, a word about mechanics. In citing references to a play whose lines have been numbered, the usual practice is to give the act in capital roman numerals, the scene in small roman numerals, and the line in arabic numerals. Periods follow the act and the scene, thus: II.ii.2–4.

Some of the following questions may help you to find topics:

Plot: Are certain happenings or situations recurrent? If so, what significance do you attach to them? If there is a subplot, how is it related? What is the function of a particular scene? Why do certain scenes occur when and where they do? Are there irrelevant scenes? Does the plot depend on chance? Is the resolution satisfactory?

Character: What sort of person is So-and-so? (Of course a dramatic character is not likely to be thoroughly realistic in the sense of being a copy of someone we might know, but is the character coherent, perhaps representative of some human type?) How is the character defined? (Consider what the character says and does, what others say about him and do to him, and also consider other characters who more or less resemble the character in question, because the similarities — and the differences — may be significant.) If a character is tragic, does the tragedy proceed from a moral flaw, from an intellectual error, from the malice of others, from sheer chance, or from some combination of these? If comic, do we laugh with him or at him? Are the characters adequately motivated? Do the characters change as the play goes on, or do we simply know them better at the end? Is the character so meditative that we feel he is engaged less in a dialogue with others than in a dialogue with his own mind? If so, do we feel that this character is in large degree a spokesman for the author, commenting on the world not only of the play but on the outside world too?

In a typical college course paper you need not and probably should not take on all aspects of a character. With a play of great complexity — for example, one of Shakespeare's major plays — a short essay may do well to take an even smaller topic, such as Iago's use of prose (Why does he sometimes speak in prose, sometimes in verse, and what does it tell us about him?) or Othello's sexual innuendoes (Why does this noble man sometimes make foul remarks?). Even here we will not be able merely to hunt through the play looking at Iago's prose or Othello's bawdry; we will have to pay some attention to other uses of prose in *Othello*, or to other jesting, if we are to see the exact nature of the problem we have chosen to isolate.

Nonverbal language: Words are not, as has been suggested in our discussion of drama (see especially page 548), the only language of drama, and a student will sometimes want to explore matters of staging. What is especially difficult for most of us confronted with only a printed page is to catch the full dramatic quality of a play — to read the words and also to have a sense of how they sound in the context of gestures and a setting. We tend to read drama as literature rather than as dramatic literature — that is, theater. (When the author is Shakespeare or Shaw we can sometimes justly examine his works as literature, although even here we may find that things that seem flat on the page come alive in the theater.) Consider the setting, for example. Is it functional? Are changes of scenes symbolic? How is Shaw's use of darkness and light in *Pygmalion* significant? If you set out to write an essay on gestures in *Othello* you may come to see how rich the play is in such symbolic gestures as bowing, kneeling, displaying swords, and kissing. And it is similarly rich in sound effects, such as the clinking of drinking vessels, the sounds of musical instruments, and the ringing of an alarm bell.

Film

These questions may help to bring impressions out into the open and may with some reworking provide topics for essays.

1. If the film is adapted from fiction or drama, does it slavishly follow its original and neglect the potentialities of the camera? Or does it so revel in cinematic devices that it distorts the original work? If visual symbols are used, are they used effectively?

2. If the film is adapted from fiction or drama, does it do violence to the theme of the original? Is the film better than its source? Are the additions or omissions due to the medium or to a crude or faulty interpretation of the original?

3. Can film deal as effectively with inner action — mental processes — as with external, physical action? In a given film, how is the inner action conveyed?

4. Are shots and sequences adequately developed or do they seem jerky? (Sometimes, of course, jerkiness may be desirable.)

5. Are the characters believable?

6. Are the actors appropriately cast? (Was it a mistake to cast Robert Redford as Gatsby? Audrey Hepburn as Liza Doolittle?

7. Is the music appropriate and functional? (Among other things, music may imitate natural sounds, give a sense of locale, suggest states of mind, provide ironic commentary, or — by repeated melodies — help to establish connections.)

8. All works of art are contrivances, of course, but (as a Roman saying puts it) the art is to conceal art. Does the film seem arty, a mere *tour de force*, or does it have the effect of inevitability, the effect of rightness, conveying a sense that a vision has been honestly expressed? Are characters or scenes clumsily dragged in? Are unusual effects significant? Does the whole add up to something? Do we get scenes or characters or techniques that at first hold us by their novelty but then have nothing further to offer?

9. Is the title significant? Are the newspaper or television advertisements appropriate?

Some final advice: Early in the essay it is usually desirable to sketch enough of the plot to give the reader an idea of what happens. But do not try to recount everything that happens: it can't be done, and the attempt will frustrate you and bore your reader. Once you introduce the main characters and devote a few sentences to the plot, thus giving the reader a comfortable seat, get down to the job of convincing him that you have something interesting to say about the film — that the plot is trivial, or that the hero is not really cool but cruel, or that the plot and the characters are fine achievements but the camera work is sometimes needlessly tricky, or that all is well.

Incidentally, a convenient way to give an actor's name in your essay is to put it in parentheses after the character's name or role, thus: "The detective, Sam Spade (Humphrey Bogart), finds a clue. . . ." Then, as you go on to talk about the film, use the names of the characters or the roles, not the names of the actors, except of course when you are talking about the actors themselves, as in "Bogart is exactly right for the part."

REMARKS ABOUT MANUSCRIPT FORM

Basic Manuscript Form

Much of what follows is nothing more than common sense.

1. Use 8½″ x 11″ paper of good weight. Keep as lightweight a carbon copy as you wish or make a photocopy, but hand in a sturdy original.

2. If you typewrite, use a reasonably fresh ribbon, double-space, and type on one side of the page only. If you submit a handwritten copy, use lined paper and write on one side of the page only, in ink, on every other line. Most instructors do *not* want papers to be enclosed in any sort of binder. And most instructors want papers to be clipped together in the upper left corner; do not crimp or crease corners and expect them to hold together.

3. Leave an adequate margin — an inch or an inch and a half — at top, bottom, and sides.

4. Number the pages consecutively, using arabic numerals in the upper right-hand corner.

5. Put your name and class or course number in the upper right-hand corner of the first page. It is a good idea to put your name in the upper right corner of each page so that if a page gets separated it can easily be restored to the proper essay.

6. Create your own title — one that reflects your topic or thesis. For example, a paper on Shirley Jackson's "The Lottery" should *not* be called "The Lottery," but might be called "Suspense in 'The Lottery.'" (On titles, see also page 1056.)

7. Center the title of your essay below the top margin of the first page. Begin the first word of the title with a capital, and capitalize each subsequent word except articles, conjunctions, and prepositions, thus:

```
The Diabolic and Celestial Images in The Scarlet Letter.
```

8. Begin the essay an inch or two below the title.

9. Your extensive revisions should have been made in your drafts, but minor last-minute revisions may be made — neatly — on the

finished copy. Proofreading may catch some typographical errors, and you may notice some small weakness. You can make corrections with the following proofreader's symbols:

Changes in wording may be made by crossing through words and rewriting them:

> The influence of Yeats and Eliot ~~have~~ *has* greatly diminished.

Additions should be made above the line, with a caret below the line at the appropriate place:

> The influence of Yeats and Eliot has *greatly* diminished.

Transpositions of letters may be made thus:

> The influence of Yeats and Eliot has greatly diminished.

Deletions are indicated by a horizontal line through the word or words to be deleted. Delete a single letter by drawing a vertical or diagonal line through it:

> The influence of Yeats and ~~and~~ Eliot has greatly diminished.

Separation of words accidentally run together is indicated by a vertical line, *closure* by a curved line connecting the letters to be closed up:

> The influence of Yeats and Eliot has greatly diminished.

Paragraphing may be indicated by the symbol ¶ before the word that is to begin the new paragraph:

> The influence of Yeats and Eliot has greatly diminished. ¶The influence of William Carlos Williams has greatly increased.

Quotations and Quotation Marks

Excerpts from the literature you are writing about are indispensable. Such quotations not only let the reader know what you are talking about but also present him the material you are responding to, thus letting the reader share your responses.

Here are some mechanical matters:

1. Identify the speaker or writer of the quotation, so that the reader is not left with a sense of uncertainty. Usually this identifica-

tion precedes the quoted material ("Iago says . . . ") in accordance with the principle of letting the reader know where he is going, but occasionally it may follow the quotation, especially if it will provide something of a pleasant surprise. For instance, in a discussion of T. S. Eliot's poetry you might quote a hostile comment on one of the poems and then reveal that Eliot himself was the speaker.

2. The quotation must fit grammatically into your sentence. Suppose you want to use Othello's line, "I have done the state some service." It would be ungrammatical to write:

> Near the end of the play Othello says that he "have done the state some service."

Say instead:

> Near the end of the play Othello says that he has "done the state some service."

Or, of course, you can say:

> Near the end of the play Othello says, "I have done the state some service."

3. The quotation must be exact. Any material that you add — even one or two words — must be in square brackets, thus:

> When Pope says that Belinda is "the rival of his [that is, the sun's] beams," he uses comic hyperbole.

> Stephen Dedalus sees the ball as a "greasy leather orb [that] flew like a heavy bird through the grey light."

If you wish to omit material from within a quotation, indicate the ellipsis by three spaced periods. If your sentence ends in an omission, add a closed-up period and then three spaced periods to indicate the omission. The following example is based on a quotation from the sentences immediately above this one:

> The instructions say that "if you . . . omit material from within a quotation, [you must] indicate the ellipsis. . . . If your sentence ends in an omission, add a closed-up period and then three spaced periods. . . ."

Notice that although material preceded "If you," periods are not needed to indicate the omission because "If you" began a sentence in the original. Customarily, initial and terminal omissions are indicated only when they are part of the sentence you are quoting. Even such omissions need not be indicated when the quoted material is

obviously incomplete — when, for instance, it is a word or phrase.
(See the first example in this section, which quotes Pope's phrase
"the rival of his beams.") Notice, too, that although quotations must
be given word for word, the initial capitalization can be adapted, as
here where "If" is reduced to "if."

When a line or more of verse is omitted from a passage that is set
off, the three spaced periods are printed on a separate line:

> Nothing in Heaven functions as it ought:
> Peter's bifocals, blindly sat on, crack;
> . . .
> But Hell, sleek Hell hath no freewheeling part:
> None takes his own sweet time, none quickens pace.

4. Distinguish between short and long quotations, and treat each
appropriately. Short quotations (usually defined as less than three
lines of poetry or five lines of prose) are enclosed within quotation
marks and run into the text (rather than set off, without quotation
marks). For example:

> LeRoi Jones's poem ends with a glimpse of the speaker's daughter
> peeking into her "clasped hands," either playfully or madly.

> Pope's *Essay on Criticism* begins informally with a contraction, but the
> couplets nevertheless have an authoritative ring: " 'Tis hard to say, if
> greater want of skill / Appear in writing or in judging ill."

Notice in the first passage that although only two words are being
quoted, quotation marks are used, indicating that these are LeRoi
Jones's words, not the essayist's. Notice also that in the second example a slash (diagonal line, virgule) is used to indicate the end of a
line of verse other than the last line quoted. The slash is, of course,
not used if the poetry is set off, indented, and printed as verse, thus:

> Pope's *Essay on Criticism* begins informally with a contraction, but
> the couplets nevertheless have an authoritative ring:
>
> > 'Tis hard to say, if greater want of skill
> > Appear in writing or in judging ill;
> > But of the two less dangerous is the offense
> > To tire our patience than mislead our sense.

To set off, triple-space before and after the quotation and single-space
the quotation. Poetry should be centered; prose quotations should
not be indented. Some style manuals, however, do call for indenting
prose quotations (ten spaces on both right and left margins) and for

double-spacing; whichever procedure you adopt, be consistent. Be sparing in your use of long quotations. Use quotations as evidence, not as padding. Do not bore the reader with material that can be effectively reduced by cutting. If you cut, indicate ellipses as explained above under 3.

5. Commas and periods go inside the quotation marks. (Exception: if the quotation is immediately followed by material in parentheses or in square brackets, close the quotation, then give the parenthetic or bracketed material, and then — after the closing parenthesis or bracket — put the comma or period.) Marks of punctuation other than periods and commas (semicolons, colons, and dashes) go outside. Question marks and exclamation points go inside if they are part of the quotation, outside if they are your own.

> Amanda ironically says to her daughter, "How old are you, Laura?" Is it possible to fail to hear Laura's weariness in her reply, "Mother, you know my age"?

6. Use *single* quotation marks for material contained within a quotation that itself is within quotation marks, thus:

> T. S. Eliot says, "Mr. Richards observes that 'poetry is capable of saving us.'"

7. Use quotation marks around titles of short works — that is, for titles of chapters in books and for stories, essays, and poems that might not be published by themselves. Use italics (indicated by underlining) for titles of books, periodicals, collections of essays, plays, and long poems such as *The Rime of the Ancient Mariner* and *Paradise Lost*.

A Note on Footnotes

You may wish to use a footnote, telling the reader of your paper that the literary work you are discussing is found in this book on such-and-such a page. Let us assume that you have already mentioned the author and the title of the story, poem, or play, and have just quoted a passage. After the period at the end of the sentence that includes the quotation, or at the end of the quotation if you are offering it as an independent sentence, type or write the number 1, elevating it slightly above the line. Do not put a period after the digit. Near the bottom of the paper, indent a few spaces and type or write the number 1, elevated and without a period. Then write your footnote in this form (giving the appropriate page number):

[1] Reprinted in Sylvan Barnet, Morton Berman, and William Burto, *An Introduction to Literature*, 6th ed. (Boston: Little, Brown, 1977), p. 236.

Notice that the abbreviation for *page* is *p.*, not *pg.*; the abbreviation for *pages* is *pp.*, thus: pp. 236–237.

If you have not mentioned the author and title of the work quoted, you must give that information in the note, thus:

[1] William Faulkner, "The Bear," reprinted in [and so on].

In short, you need not give information in the note that is already given in the main body of the essay.

In order to eliminate writing many footnotes, each one merely citing the page of a quotation, you can explain in the first footnote, after the bibliographical information, that further references will be given in the main body of the essay:

[1] Reprinted in Sylvan Barnet, Morton Berman, and William Burto, *An Introduction to Literature*, 6th ed. (Boston: Little, Brown, 1977), p. 236. All further references to this work will be cited parenthetically, within the text of the essay.

Thus, when you quote the next passage from the story, you do not need another footnote; you need only insert parentheses enclosing the page number immediately after closing the quotation. Here is an example:

At this point Faulkner tells us that the boy "could find the crooked print now almost whenever he liked" (p. 55).

Notice that the closing quotation mark *precedes* the parenthesis and that the period *follows* the parenthesis.

If you are writing about a poem, it will probably be useful in the first footnote to cite the page, but subsequent references probably ought to be not to page numbers but to line numbers, again indicated in parentheses in the main body of your essay. If your quotation from the poem is brief and is worked into your sentence, give this reference immediately after the quotation, thus:

Browning's Duke calls attention to "Neptune . . . / Taming a sea-horse" (ll. 54–55) as he descends the stairs.

But if the quotation is long enough to set off, put a period at the end of the quotation (assuming that it is grammatically appropriate to put a period there) and give the citation for lines in parentheses immediately below the quotation, at the right. The abbreviation for *line* is *l.*, for *lines* is *ll.* Here is an example:

> I repeat,
> The Count your master's known munificence
> Is ample warrant that no just pretense
> Of mine for dowry will be disallowed;
> Though his fair daughter's self, as I avowed
> At starting, is my object.
>
>   (ll. 48–53)

If you are writing about a play, especially one whose lines as well as acts and scenes are numbered, it may be better to refer to act, scene, and line than to page. Give the act in capital roman numerals, the scene in small roman numerals, and the line in arabic numerals, thus:

Othello says that he is "one that loved not wisely, but too-well" (V.ii.340).

REVIEW: HOW TO WRITE AN EFFECTIVE ESSAY

Everyone must work out his own procedures and rituals (John C. Calhoun liked to plough his farm before writing), but the following suggestions may provide some help.

1. Read the work carefully.
2. Choose a worthwhile and compassable subject, something that interests you and is not so big that your handling of it must be superficial. As you work, shape and narrow your topic — for example, from "The Character of Hester Prynne" to "The Effects of Alienation on Hester Prynne."
3. Reread the work, jotting down notes of all relevant matters. As you read, reflect on your reading and record your reflections. If you have a feeling or an idea, jot it down; don't assume that you will remember it when you get around to writing your essay. The margins of the book are a good place for initial jottings, but many people find that in the long run it is easiest to transfer these notes to 3 x 5 cards, writing on one side only.
4. Sort out your cards into some kind of reasonable divisions, and reject cards irrelevant to your topic. As you work you may discover a better way to group your notes. If so, start reorganizing. If you are

writing an explication, the order probably is essentially the order of the lines or of the episodes, but if you are writing an analysis you may wish to organize your essay from the lesser material to the greater (to avoid anticlimax) or from the simple to the complex (to insure intelligibility). If, for example, you are discussing the roles of three characters in a story, it may be best to build up to the one of the three that you think the most important. If you are comparing two characters it may be best to move from the most obvious contrasts to the least obvious. When you have arranged your notes into a meaningful sequence of packets, you have approximately divided your material into paragraphs.

5. Get it down on paper. Most essayists find it useful to jot down some sort of outline, indicating the main idea of each paragraph and, under each main idea, supporting details that give it substance. An outline — not necessarily anything highly formal with capital and lowercase letters and roman and arabic numerals but merely key phrases in some sort of order — will help you to overcome the paralysis called "writer's block" that commonly afflicts professionals as well as students. A page of paper with ideas in some sort of sequence, however rough, ought to encourage you to realize that you do have something to say. And so, despite the temptation to sharpen another pencil or put a new ribbon into the typewriter, the best thing to do at this point is to sit down and start writing. If you don't feel that you can work from note cards and a rough outline, try another method: get something down on paper, writing freely, sloppily, automatically, or whatever, but allowing your ideas about what the work means to you and how it conveys its meaning — rough as your ideas may be — to begin to take visible form. If you are like most people, you can't do much precise thinking until you have committed to paper at least a rough sketch of your initial ideas. Later you can push and polish your ideas into shape, perhaps even deleting all of them and starting over, but it's a lot easier to improve your ideas once you see them in front of you than it is to do the job in your head. On paper one word leads to another; in your head one word often blocks another.

Just keep going; you may realize, as you near the end of a sentence, that you no longer believe it. O.K., be glad that your first idea led you to a better one, and pick up your better one and keep going with it. What you are doing is, in a sense, by trial and error pushing your way not only toward clear expression but also toward sharper ideas and richer responses.

6. If there is time, reread the work, looking for additional material that strengthens or weakens your main point; take account of it in your outline or draft.

7. With your outline or draft in front of you, write a more lucid

version, checking your notes for fuller details, such as supporting quotations. If, as you work, you find that some of the points in your earlier jottings are no longer relevant, eliminate them, but make sure that the argument flows from one point to the next. As you write, your ideas will doubtless become clearer; some may prove to be poor ideas. (We rarely know exactly what our ideas are until we have them set down on paper. As the little girl said, replying to the suggestion that she should think before she spoke, "How do I know what I think until I say it?") Not until you have written a draft do you really have a strong sense of how good your essay may be.

8. After a suitable interval, preferably a few days, read the draft with a view toward revising it, not with a view toward congratulating yourself. A revision, after all, is a re-vision, a second (and presumably sharper) view. When you revise, you will be in the company of Picasso, who said that in painting he advanced by a series of destructions. A revision — say, the substitution of a precise word for an imprecise one — is not a matter of prettifying but of thinking. As you read, correct things that disturb you (for example, awkward repetitions that bore, inflated utterances that grate), add supporting detail where the argument is undeveloped (a paragraph of only one or two sentences is usually an undeveloped paragraph), and ruthlessly delete irrelevancies however well written they may be. But remember that a deletion probably requires some adjustment in the preceding and subsequent material. Make sure that the argument, aided by transitions, runs smoothly. The details should be relevant, the organization reasonable, the argument clear. Check all quotations for accuracy. Quotations are evidence, usually intended to support your assertions, and it is not nice to alter the evidence, even unintentionally. If there is time (there almost never is), put the revision aside, reread it in a day or two, and revise it again, especially with a view toward shortening it.

9. Type or write a clean copy, following the principles concerning margins, pagination, footnotes, and so on set forth on pages 1071–1077. If you have borrowed any ideas, be sure to give credit, usually in footnotes, to your sources. Remember that plagiarism is not limited to the unacknowledged borrowing of words; a borrowed idea, even when put into your own words, requires acknowledgment.

10. Proofread and make corrections as explained on pages 1071–1072.

INDEX
Critical Terms

INDEX
Authors, Titles, First Lines of Poems

(The number in *italic* indicates the page on which the selection appears.)

To the Student

As educational publishers, we realize it is part of our job to continually try to improve the textbooks we publish. When we revise our textbooks we take into account the experiences of instructors and students alike with the previous edition. At some time, your instructor will be asked to comment extensively on *An Introduction to Literature*, 6th edition. We want to hear from you, too; after all, although instructors assign texts, students are the ones who buy them.

Please complete this questionnaire and return it to **College English Developmental Group, Little, Brown and Company, 34 Beacon St., Boston, Massachusetts 02106.**

School: _____

Course title: _____

Other texts required: _____

Instructor's full name: _____

1. Did you like the book overall? Why or why not? _____

   _____

2. **Fiction**
   Approximately how many stories were assigned? _____

   Which stories did you like most? _____

   Which stories did you like least? _____

   Which stories had you read previously? _____

   Are there any authors or stories not included you would like to

   see added? _____

   Did you read "Some Observations on the Novel" and did you

   find it useful? _____

3. **Poetry**
   Approximately how many poems were assigned? _____

   Which poems did you like most? _____

Which poems did you like least? _____

Which poems had you read previously? _____

Are there any poets or poems not included you would like to see added? _____

4. **Drama**
   Approximately how many plays were assigned? _____

   Which plays did you like most? _____

   Which plays did you like least? _____

   Which plays had you read previously? _____

   Are there any plays or playwrights not included you would like to see added? _____

   Did you read "Some Observations on Film" and did you find it useful? _____

5. Did you read "Writing Essays about Literature" and did you find it useful? _____

   How might that section be improved? _____

6. Did you like the looks of the book? _____

7. Was the type easy to read? _____

8. Do you feel your instructor should assign this book again next year? _____

9. Will you keep your copy for your library? _____

10. Please add any other comments and suggestions _____

    May we quote you in our promotion efforts for this book?
    _____Yes _____No

    Date _____ Name _____

    Home Address _____